COMPARATIVE POLITICS

COMPARATIVE POLITICS

A Global Introduction

Michael J. Sodaro

The George Washington University

With contributions by:

Nathan J. Brown
The George Washington University

Dean W. Collinwood
University of Utah

Bruce J. Dickson
The George Washington University

Joseph L. Klesner
Kenyon College

Timothy D. Sisk
University of Denver

Boston   Burr Ridge, IL   Dubuque, IA   Madison, WI   New York   San Francisco   St. Louis
Bangkok   Bogotá   Caracas   Kuala Lumpur   Lisbon   London   Madrid   Mexico City
Milan   Montreal   New Delhi   Santiago   Seoul   Singapore   Sydney   Taipei   Toronto

McGraw-Hill Higher Education

A Division of The **McGraw-Hill** Companies

COMPARATIVE POLITICS: A GLOBAL INTRODUCTION

Published by McGraw-Hill, an imprint of The McGraw-Hill Companies, Inc., 1221 Avenue of the Americas, New York, NY 10020. Copyright © 2001 by The McGraw-Hill Companies, Inc. All rights reserved. No part of this publication may be reproduced or distributed in any form or by any means, or stored in a database or retrieval system, without the prior written consent of The McGraw-Hill Companies, Inc., including, but not limited to, in any network or other electronic storage or transmission, or broadcast for distance learning.

Some ancillaries, including electronic and print components, may not be available to customers outside the United States.

 This book is printed on recycled, acid-free paper containing 10% postconsumer waste.

3 4 5 6 7 8 9 0 QPD/QPD 0 9 8 7 6 5 4 3 2

ISBN 0–697–30809–X

Vice president and editor-in-chief: *Thalia Dorwick*
Editorial director: *Jane E. Vaicunas*
Sponsoring editor: *Monica Eckman*
Marketing manager: *Janise A. Fry*
Project manager: *Mary Lee Harms*
Media technology senior producer: *Sean Crowley*
Production supervisor: *Laura Fuller*
Coordinator of freelance design: *Michelle D. Whitaker*
Cover designer: *Kristy Goddard*
Cover image: *Stock Illustration Source, Inc.*
Senior photo research coordinator: *Lori Hancock*
Photo research: *Pam Carley/Sound Reach*
Supplement producer: *Sandra M. Schnee*
Compositor: *Shepherd, Inc.*
Typeface: *10/12 Palatino*
Printer: *Quebecor World Dubuque Inc.*

The credits section for this book begins on page 847 and is considered an extension of the copyright page.

Library of Congress Cataloging-in-Publication Data

Sodaro, Michael J.
     Comparative politics : a global introduction / Michael J. Sodaro. — 1st ed.
        p.   cm.
     Includes bibliographical references and index.
     ISBN 0–697–30809–X
     1. Comparative government.   I. Title.

JF51 .S548   2001
320.3—dc21   00–063811
                                                         CIP

www.mhhe.com

ABOUT THE AUTHORS

MICHAEL JOSEPH SODARO (chapters 1–18 and 21) is the principal author and editor of *Comparative Politics: A Global Introduction*. As Professor of Political Science and International Affairs at the George Washington University, he is a member of the Institute for European, Russian and Eurasian Studies at George Washington's Elliott School of International Affairs. He has a BA from Fordham University, an MA from the School of Advanced International Studies of the Johns Hopkins University, and a Ph.D. from Columbia University. He earned a Certificate at the Institut d'Etudes Politiques in Paris and studied in Berlin in 1974–76. He has conducted research in France, Germany, Italy, and Russia. He is the recipient of the Marshall Shulman prize for his book, *Moscow, Germany, and the West from Khrushchev to Gorbachev* (Cornell, 1990), and the Oscar and Shoshana Trachtenberg prize for excellence in teaching at George Washington.

NATHAN J. BROWN (chapter 20, "Israel") is Professor of Political Science and International Affairs at the George Washington University. He has a BA from the University of Chicago and an MA and Ph.D. from Princeton University. The recipient of Fulbright grants to conduct research and teach in Egypt, Israel, and the Arabian peninsula, he is the author of three books: *Peasant Politics in Modern Egypt* (Yale, 1990), *The Rule of Law in the Arab World* (Cambridge, 1997), and *Constitutions in a Nonconstitutional World: Arab Basic Laws and the Prospects for Accountable Government* (Suny, 2001). He is currently writing a book on Palestinian politics.

DEAN W. COLLINWOOD (chapter 19, "Japan") is Research Professor of Management and Director of the Global Business Program and of the U.S.-Japan and China Centers at the University of Utah in Salt Lake City. He has a BA from Brigham Young University, an MA from the University of London, and a Ph.D. from the University of Chicago. He was a Fulbright scholar at the University of Tokyo in 1986–87 and is a past president of the Western Conference of the Association for Asian Studies. The author of several books on Japan and Korea, he is the editor of the Annual Edition of *Japan and the Pacific Rim,* published by Dushkin/McGraw-Hill.

BRUCE J. DICKSON (chapter 22, "China") is Associate Professor of Political Science and International Affairs at the George Washington University and the Director of the Sigur Center for Asian Studies at George Washington's Elliot School of International Affairs. He obtained his BA, MA, and Ph.D. from the University of Michigan. In 1997 he published *Democratization in China and Taiwan* (Oxford). He is currently conducting research on relations between the Chinese Communist Party and the private sector.

JOSEPH L. KLESNER (chapter 23, "Mexico and Brazil") is Professor of Political Science and Director of the International Studies Program at Kenyon College. He received his BA at Central College and his MA and Ph.D. at the Massachusetts Institute of Technology. The author of articles appearing in *Comparative Politics, Mexican Studies,* and the *Latin American Research Review,* in addition to many book chapters, he has worked on politics in Mexico and on public opinion and political culture in Latin America. His research has been supported by Fulbright grants and by funding from the National Science Foundation and the National Endowment for the Humanities.

TIMOTHY D. SISK (chapter 24, "Nigeria and South Africa") is a Senior Research Associate at the Graduate School of International Studies and a faculty member in the Conflict Resolution Program at the University of Denver. He obtained his BA and MA from Baylor University and his Ph.D. from the George Washington University. After experience as a journalist in South Africa and a legislative assistant in the U.S. Senate, he served as a program officer and research scholar at the federally chartered United States Institute of Peace in Washington, D.C. His books include *Democratization in South Africa* (Princeton, 1995), *Power Sharing and International Mediation in Ethnic Conflicts* (Carnegie Commission, 1995), and, with Andrew Reynolds, *Elections and Conflict Management in South Africa* (U.S. Institute of Peace, 1998).

BRIEF CONTENTS

CONTENTS

PREFACE

The time appears ripe for a new introduction to comparative politics. Three motivations have inspired this fresh approach to the way we learn and teach the important subject of political life around the world.

Concepts   The first motivating factor is a quest for *conceptual richness:* our aim is to provide greater coverage of the core concepts of comparative politics than students and instructors are likely to find in most other introductory textbooks. Rather than confining itself to just one particular approach (such as structural functionalism) or to just a few topics (such as state institutions), this book surveys a wide expanse of political concepts and terminology, drawing on seminal works of academic political science and traditional political philosophy. These ideas come to life through numerous illustrative examples taken from recent events around the world.

The first fifteen chapters of this book address such basic topics of comparative politics as democracy and democratization; authoritarianism; power; state institutions; electoral systems; voting behavior; parties and interest groups; class, ethnicity, gender, and other aspects of political sociology; nationalism; political culture; ideology (including Marxism, fascism, and Islam); dissent and revolution; political economy; and political development, among others. It is perhaps unusual for an introductory-level textbook on comparative politics to devote so many pages to concepts. It is often assumed that undergraduates cannot handle much conceptual material. The teaching experiences of this volume's authors, however, confirm precisely the opposite point of view. We are certain that students can learn the value of concepts and theories, *as long as they are clearly presented* and *as long as the students are shown how the conceptual tools of comparative politics relate to real-world situations.* Throughout this volume the authors have persistently strived for clarity and ease of expression. We want this book to be interesting and fun to read. We also want students to appreciate the relevance of concepts and ideas to the events they read about in newspapers and see on television.

Terms such as "human rights," "national identity," "coalition government," "liberalism," "civil society," "social democracy," "voter dealignment," "corporatism," "clientelism," "privatization," "debt servicing," "welfare state," "newly industrializing countries," "postmodern values," "zero-sum game," "free rider," and a seemingly endless stream of others are the everyday stuff of political discourse around the world. What do they mean? More than ever before, students in today's close-knit global environment need a firm grasp of the world's political lexicon.

Critical Thinking   The second motive underlying this textbook's creation is even more overtly pedagogical in nature. One of the book's unique features is that it systematically seeks to enhance the *critical-thinking skills* of its readers by introducing them to some of the ways scientific logic applies to the study of politics. At a rudimentary level and in a clearly written fashion, it explains the application of such elementary scientific devices as theories, hypotheses, variables, correlations, models, paradigms, and the like to the study of political phenomena. It also walks students through the logic of qualitative hypothesis testing in political science and provides numerous examples of how it is done. To drive home the step-by-step logic of this analytical technique, *virtually every chapter in the book contains a hypothesis-testing exercise.* (As the classical masters insisted, *"Repetitio est mater studiorum"*—"Repetition is the mother of studies.") Like the conceptual definitions introduced in part I, these exercises are taken from real-world political phenomena and from influential works by scholars and political thinkers.

A central aim in this analytically oriented endeavor is to impart to our readers a clearer sense of what political science is all about than they may derive from many other introductory texts. We address head-on that nagging classroom question, "But, professor, is political science *really* a science?" Hypothesis testing and related techniques of scientific method are defining elements of the discipline and form the reigning paradigm for scholarly research. And yet few—if any—introductory textbooks on comparative politics (or, for that matter, on American politics or international relations) actually employ these methods or teach students how they can be used. The "scientific" side of the field tends to be confined to textbooks on the "scope and methods" of political science or handbooks on research methodology, publications typically aimed at fairly advanced political science majors or graduate students. We believe that students can, and should, be exposed to the methodological foundations of the discipline right from their very first courses. And we believe that students will especially appreciate their value if they can see how scientific logic *helps them understand the real world of politics.*

While trying to deepen our students' understanding of political science, we are also motivated by the widely perceived need in contemporary academia to engage students as directly and creatively as possible in sharpening their ability to think logically and coherently. As educators, we have an obligation to inculcate critical-thinking skills in our students as vital elements of their general education. Political science courses—even introductory ones—can be ideally suited to this heuristic purpose if the discipline's analytical premises and methods are spelled out plainly and explained precisely. Students need to realize that the analytical methods they learn in political science classes can be applied without too much tweaking in other fields as well, above all in cognate social sciences, though not exclusively. And they need to know that, wherever their career paths may lead them, a variety of professions will require well-honed analytical abilities, from the law and government service to a host of other careers less immediately associated with political science. Helping students learn *how to think for themselves* is one of the most important tasks this book undertakes as it exposes them to the rudiments of social scientific logic.

Meanwhile, our scientific forays do not misdirect us into ignoring the non-scientific sides of political reality. Values, ideals, norms, and preferences invariably play a central role in critical thinking about politics. How we address the normative questions of politics ("What *should* we do to make this a better world?") is just as important as how we investigate the factual realities of politics ("What *is* political reality?"). For many professional students of the subject, politics is as much an art as it is a science, as much an exercise in normative (value-centered) philosophy as it is an exercise in empirical (fact-based) analysis, and as much an attempt to craft real-world policies as it is an attempt simply to understand political reality. This book seeks to clarify the differences—and the dynamic interactions—between facts and values, between empirical science and normative political thought, and between policy analysis and policy prescription. Not only do we want our students to improve their analytical skills, we also challenge them to think through their own political orientations and to figure out *what they would do* in addressing some practical issues of political life.

Part I of this book, encompassing the first fifteen chapters, addresses these conceptual and analytical concerns in a crystal-clear style that is specifically aimed at students taking their first course in comparative politics.

Countries and Leaders   The third factor that prompted the writing of this book is a desire to provide as much breadth and depth as possible in covering an assortment of *countries* around the world, integrating their treatment with the conceptual and analytical frameworks developed in part I. To this end, we devote the nine chapters of part II to eleven major nations: the United Kingdom, France, Germany, Japan, Israel, Russia, China, Mexico, Brazil, Nigeria, and South Africa. Each chapter highlights key historical events in the development of the country under investigation and explores its political system in detail.

To enliven these accounts and to illustrate how personalities interact with institutions, all of these chapters contain vivid biographical profiles of important *leaders.* The personages singled out for special attention have either made a decisive impact on present-day politics through their actions in the recent past or they are currently serving in a leadership capacity. These capsule biographies provide substantial grist for courses focused on the theory and practice of leadership. The country studies also treat some of the most salient political issues animating debate in these countries, such as economic policy, gun control, ethnic conflict, campaign financing, and the like, and they invite students to make comparisons with the ways roughly similar issues are dealt with in their own country.

All eleven of these nations have experienced important changes over the past ten years; in some cases these transformations have been truly revolutionary in nature. In Britain, France, and Germany, social democratic parties under the leadership of Tony Blair, Lionel Jospin, and Gerhard Schroeder, respectively, replaced conservative governments in 1997 and 1998. Japan's political system witnessed the collapse of the Liberal Democratic Party's grip on power in 1993 after nearly forty years of dominance, along with the collapse of its high-flying economy. Israel has undergone prolonged political instability in connection with the tortuous Middle East peace process.

Russia experienced perhaps the most profound upheavals of all the countries surveyed in part II. The collapse of the Soviet Union at the end of 1991—one of the most momentous political events of the twentieth century—was followed by a shaky start on the path to democracy under President Boris Yeltsin and his successor, Vladimir Putin. Among the many challenges Putin faces is the one he set for himself when he pledged to reassert the central government's authority over a country in the throes of disintegration, while simultaneously promising to bolster democratic freedoms. China's communist leadership appeared momentarily shaken by spontaneous pro-democracy demonstrations in 1989. Although the ruling elite smashed the protests, the growth of private enterprise under the party's auspices and the country's widening trade relationships with the outside world have raised the question of whether real political change may be part of China's imminent future.

In the developing world, Mexico experienced a revolution of its own as Vicente Fox won an unexpectedly solid victory in the presidential election of July 2000, ousting the ruling Institutional Revolutionary Party from its stranglehold on the presidency after seventy-one years in power. Brazil in the 1990s was immersed in the process of consolidating the new democratic regime it had established in the previous decade, following more than twenty years of military rule. Under the presidency of Fernando Henrique Cardoso, a former Marxist turned champion of market reforms, Brazil by decade's end confronted serious economic challenges, both domestic and international in nature, as well as enormous environmental hazards and a political system marked by a highly divided multiparty parliament. Across the ocean, strikingly similar challenges connected with the transition to full-scale democracy face two of Africa's largest countries. Nigeria, the continent's most populous nation, elected Olusegun Obasanjo as its new president in 1999. A former general who once headed the government in the 1970s, Obasanjo promised to restore democracy to a country that had been governed by corrupt military dictators for most of its history as an independent state. South Africa, dominated for decades by a white minority representing less than one-fifth of the population, effected a clean break with whites-only rule, holding its first multiracial elections in 1994. Nelson Mandela, a democracy advocate who endured twenty-seven years of imprisonment for challenging white supremacy, was elected South Africa's first black president. His successor, Thabo Mbeki, took over in 1999, inheriting a country characterized by glaring economic inequalities and racial tensions that have not entirely died out.

Our in-depth explorations of these countries are grounded in the canons of comparative analysis. In addition to relating each country to various conceptual criteria for comparison generated in part I—such as conditions for democracy—the nine chapters of part II also make explicit comparisons to the United States and other relevant countries. Cross-references to pertinent portions of other chapters help readers make these connections. Our time line follows late events through the summer of 2000, when this book went to press. (A selection of important subsequent developments can be accessed via McGraw-Hill's comparative politics website, <www.mhhe.com/comparative>)

Along with the eleven countries explored in part II, this book examines a broad sampling of additional countries in part I. These briefer country studies are intended primarily to illustrate concepts introduced in the first fifteen chapters. For example, various aspects of political power, such as class rule, autocracy, and theocratic authoritarianism, are illustrated with reference to countries like Haiti, Iraq, and Iran, respectively; the disintegration of nation-states is exemplified by the fate of Yugoslavia; and various conditions for democracy are applied to countries like Poland, Romania, South Korea, and India. There are numerous references to other countries as well, including the United States. The premise underlying these focused analyses of individual countries is that concepts and political realities are analytically inseparable: students cannot fully appreciate what is going on in individual nations without a clear understanding of concepts, and they cannot fully understand conceptual abstractions without a close look at how they apply in the real world.

A Global Approach   Taken together, the three motivating purposes of this book—conceptual richness, critical thinking, and wide country coverage—have resulted in what we believe to be an unusually comprehensive one-volume introduction to comparative politics, an approach that is truly global in scope. We have also sought to unite high scholarly standards with an engaging style. This is not a dumbed-down textbook, nor is it excessively advanced for introductory-level students. All of its contributors—accomplished scholars with a commitment to educating students—have labored mightily to translate sophisticated scholarship into a format readily accessible to today's undergraduates, a daunting scholarly task in its own right! We hope that students and teachers alike will find *Comparative Politics: A Global Introduction* a useful—and readable—guide to the complexities of our highly globalized new millennium.

ACKNOWLEDGMENTS

A book of this size is inevitably the product of many hands. Both collectively and individually, my fellow authors and I are deeply grateful to a number of people whose help proved invaluable, whether in the form of intellectual inspiration, editorial support, research assistance, or that ever-important morale-boosting encouragement that scholars and scriveners tend to require in unlimited amounts.

Starting with the latter category, all of us owe a spirited round of applause to our families and loved ones, above all for making our efforts worthwhile, and no less for enduring our absences and for nudging us along as we gaped into our computers and struggled with our thoughts. I would like to express my personal gratitude to my mother, Ellen DeVincentiis Sodaro, and to Gloria, Paul, Alexandra, and Marshall Wilson, for their unstinting love and support during the many years I devoted to this book. It could not have come about without them.

It is a particular pleasure for me to thank my five collaborators: Nathan Brown, Dean Collinwood, Bruce Dickson, Joseph Klesner, and Tim Sisk. I cannot imagine a more talented and cooperative group of contributors. Successful scholars in their own right, all five rightly regarded their contributions from the outset as serious works of scholarship. Their substantive expertise and writing skills have immeasurably enhanced the quality of this book, helping to make it what we intended it to be: a scholarly contribution to the discipline of political science and a creative approach to the education of our readers.

Each of us assumes final responsibility for our respective contributions. As the author of chapters 1–18 and 21, I am solely responsible for their content, including any errors or shortcomings they contain. I am also responsible for the book's overall concept and structure, which I tried to impose on my co-authors as gently as possible. While

I provided certain basic parameters and requirements—such as the list of conditions for democracy and the need to include a biographical profile and a hypothesis-testing exercise in each chapter—I gave the contributors free rein to employ their knowledge and analytical talents to the full. The quality of their chapters, in my view, thoroughly reflects the high standards we all set for ourselves.

Putting out a textbook of this length is a huge team effort. The authors are all indebted to the superb people at McGraw-Hill who kept our project on track year after year and then—dazzlingly!—put it all together in a few brief months. It was a pleasure to work with such competent professionals and delightful personalities as primary editor Monica Eckman, project manager Mary Lee Harms, and editorial coordinators Hannah Glover and Shannon Morrow. Our thanks also go to Michelle D. Whitaker and Kristie Goddard, who designed the cover; Pamela Carley, who tracked down the photos; and Beth Kundert and Carrie Braun, who arranged for my students at the George Washington University to read pre-publication versions of the manuscript. Behind them stands a small legion of people who made important contributions of their own to this volume's publication. I also want to thank Irv Rockwood, my editor at Dushkin Publishers, who got me started on this book and encouraged me to forge ahead.

A long list of research assistants over the years helped me assemble the vast quantity of books, clippings, and other sources of information that went into this volume. For their vital contribution I wish to thank Priscilla Cavalca, Michele Christ, Melissa Dodge, Vanessa Frigan, Jacqueline McLaren, Kimberly Penland, and Ioiana Voiculescu. In this connection I also wish to thank the Institute for European, Russian, and Eurasian Studies at George Washington, and particularly its director, James R. Millar, and acting director James Goldgeier, for providing my assistants with generous financial support and for providing me with a congenial research base. The Institute's administrative assistant, Suzanne Stephenson, supervised these efforts with her unfailing efficiency.

I am also indebted to a number of friends and colleagues who provided important research material, especially Dieter Dettke, Shoshana Foster, Julius Friend, Ann Phillips, Marco Rimanelli and Ann Rogers. My location in the Washington, D.C. area, with its immense human and institutional resources, proved especially fortunate. I was able to count on the courteous assistance of more than a dozen embassies and to take advantage of research facilities like the American Institute for Contemporary German Studies and the International Foundation for Election Systems. My thanks also go to several anonymous reviewers whose critiques resulted in a significantly improved final product.

Finally I wish to thank my colleagues and students at the George Washington University for providing such a supportive and stimulating environment for research and teaching over the course of my career. I am especially grateful to the Department of Political Science and the Elliott School of International Affairs, my principal academic homes (along with the Institute) since 1977. The students in my "Introduction to Comparative Politics" class in the spring 2000 deserve special thanks for giving the pre-publication version of the text a trial run. Shannon Hobbs, Helen Hubbard-Davis, Rajesh Parekh, and other members of the class provided timely criticisms and useful suggestions for improvements.

My co-authors and I would like to dedicate this book to our students. As an eternally youthful source of information, insight, amusement, joy, and—occasionally—bewilderment, it is the students at our colleges and universities who inspire us to write such tomes as this one, and with whom we wish to share our love of the world.

Michael J. Sodaro
October 2000

CONCEPTS AND CRITICAL THINKING

CHAPTER 1

COMPARATIVE POLITICS

What Is It? Why Study It?

As the world enters the new millennium, a survey of front-page headlines reveals two starkly contrasting tendencies. On the one hand there is no shortage of serious problems. International conflicts and civil wars, the proliferation of weapons of mass destruction, widespread human rights abuses, festering poverty, and accelerating environmental degradation all continue to spread misery and fear throughout the world.

- In 1999, the nineteen countries comprising the NATO alliance went to war with Yugoslavia over Kosovo. Kosovo is a Yugoslav province whose largely Albanian population was subjected to harsh reprisals, mass murder, forced deportations, and other atrocities by the government of Yugoslav President Slobodan Milosevic. More than eight hundred thousand Albanian Kosovars fled the province before Milosevic agreed to peace terms and a NATO-led peacekeeping force entered Kosovo. Fearing reprisals, some one hundred thousand Serbs fled the province soon after the completion of NATO's eleven-week bombing campaign. The Kosovo conflict was one of more than a dozen inter-state wars and civil wars occurring in the 1990s. These conflicts, inflaming parts of Europe, the Middle East, Africa, Asia, and Latin America, claimed more than 6 million lives and created an even larger number of refugees.

- Nuclear devices and other agents of mass destruction, such as chemical and biological weapons, pose a continuing threat. The United States and Russia, despite agreements requiring sizable cutbacks in their nuclear arsenals, together have more than 14,500 nuclear bombs capable of being delivered at long range. Though they have been on amicable terms since the final stages of the Cold War, the danger of an accident or the theft of nuclear material from Russian storage areas constitutes a deadly hazard. Eight countries are known to possess nuclear weapons, with the total estimated to exceed forty thousand. At least four other countries, all of them dictatorships hostile to the United States and its democratic allies, are thought to be developing their own nuclear weapons programs.[1]

- Human rights abuses are flagrant in many parts of the world. They include violations of fundamental democratic freedoms, such as the freedom of speech and the right to vote, the arrest and torture of political dissidents, mass atrocities committed in times of civil war or unrest, religious and ethnic persecution, the abuse and repression of women, and the exploitation of some 250 million child laborers between the ages of five and fourteen, among other offenses. Political corruption is also endemic, even in established democracies.[2]

- Abject poverty is a widespread phenomenon, especially in the developing countries of Asia, Africa, and Latin America. Though some of these countries have increased their economic growth in the past decade or two, the number of people subsisting on less than one dollar per day actually rose in the 1990s, reaching 1.5 billion by the end of the decade. Of some 4.4 billion people in the developing world, about 60 percent lack basic sanitation; one out of three lacks access to clean water; one-fourth do not have adequate housing; and one-fifth do not have access to modern health facilities. Twenty percent of children do not receive minimal amounts of protein and calories in their diets; a similar percentage fail to complete five years of schooling. Eighty-two countries dependent on subsistence farming cannot adequately feed their populations or afford food imports. Despite gains in public health, infectious diseases—some of them preventable—claim millions of lives every year because of lack of treatment. The maldistribution of the world's wealth is also striking: the net worth of the richest 225 people in the world equals one year's income for the poorest 2.5 billion.[3]
- Threats to the global environment and life systems stemming from emissions of chlorofluorocarbons (CFCs), greenhouse gases, and other pollutants, together with deforestation and harmful agricultural and fishing practices, result in a variety of perils, including illnesses, the disruption of global climactic patterns, the deterioration of the Earth's ozone layer, and the depletion of its food and medicinal supplies.

On a more encouraging note, there are some unmistakably positive trends. The end of the Cold War, the unprecedented spread of democracy, the advancement of international trade and economic cooperation, the extraordinary achievements of science and technology, and the development of widening cultural connections among the peoples of the world have created opportunities for peace, prosperity, and social well-being that are literally unparalleled in human history.

- In 1987 there were approximately sixty-nine countries with procedures for democratic elections. By the late 1990s there were 117, including a number of former communist countries involved in nearly fifty years of Cold War confrontation with the United States and its allies.
- International trade and other forms of economic exchange have risen exponentially in the past two decades, embracing virtually every corner of the globe. Exports of merchandise around the world rose from $1.8 trillion in 1983 to $5.4 trillion in 1998; exports of services (such as banking services, insurance, and the like) went from $357 billion to $1.3 trillion in roughly the same time span. Private and government investment in foreign countries also rose dramatically. The value of the world's stock markets appreciated from $9 trillion to $23 trillion between 1990 and 1998 alone. The creation of the World Trade Organization (WTO) in 1995 was designed to promote these global economic links. By 1999 the WTO consisted of 135 member countries, with China expected to join their ranks. The global economic marketplace has surely taken a toll on many people, shifting jobs and investment capital around the world with few restraints. Still, the overall growth in employment opportunities and economic development, though unevenly distributed, has been unmistakable.[4]
- The creation of the Internet and the World Wide Web has had an impact of gargantuan proportions on the growth of international economic, cultural, and political linkages. Internet hosts grew from virtually zero at the start of the 1990s to more than 40 million worldwide by 1999. Though computer literacy and access to the web are most prevalent in the wealthier countries, their global proliferation is expected to widen appreciably in the coming years.
- International travel for business, tourism, and other purposes has increased significantly, contributing to closer connections among the peoples of the world. The number of travelers arriving in destinations beyond their own borders skyrocketed from 69.3 million in 1960 to more than 625 million in 1998.[5]

In one way or another, governments are central to these and many other developments that shape the world we live in. Governments make war and negotiate peace, promote scientific research and take responsibility for the environment. Governments set the ground rules for international trade, while managing public expenditures and influencing private enterprise at home. And governments decide to what extent the people under their jurisdiction will be granted basic human rights, such as the right to elect their leaders and enjoy freedom of expression and religious worship, the right to travel abroad, and other civil liberties. It is no exaggeration to say that the fate of all humanity depends to a considerable degree on the governments of the world. How governments are organized, how they relate to their own populations, and how they deal with the rest of humankind are realities that directly determine such life-and-death matters as war, civil strife, and public health, while materially influencing the quality of life for more than 6 billion people who now inhabit our planet.[6]

Any clear understanding of the contemporary world therefore requires a concentrated focus on governments and politics. This task is especially necessary in view of the unprecedented scope of governmental activity around the globe and the expanding web of relationships that link the nations of the world far more closely than ever before. Scarcely more than a hundred years ago, the governments of most countries were considerably smaller than they are now. In democracies like the United States and Great Britain, officials tended to maintain a hands-off policy toward the economy, leaving private businesses and individuals to fend largely for themselves in the free marketplace. State investment in scientific research, education, public health, and general human welfare was minimal. Most other countries were not democracies at all. China, Japan, Germany, and Russia, to name just a few, were governed by emperors whose regimes exercised dictatorial supremacy over their populations. Although they maintained sizable bureaucracies and military establishments, these and similar dictatorships devoted minuscule sums to citizen welfare. Meanwhile, much of Asia, Africa, and the Middle East in 1900 was ruled by colonial powers whose governments in London, Paris, or elsewhere paid scant regard to the rights or welfare of the millions under their sway.

As the twentieth century began, international transactions were also considerably less intense than they are at the start of the new millennium. World trade was feeble by today's standards. Communications links were confined to print media and the telegraph. International travel was a privilege enjoyed by a few. Most people lived in veritable isolation from the rest of the world.

The extraordinary developments of the twentieth century—in politics, economics, science, and a multiplicity of other fields—decisively changed all that. The world of 2000 is a world where politics touches almost everything and isolation is not a viable option. It is a world where events in the country next door or on the other side of the globe sooner or later have an impact on one's own life at home. And it is a world where the age-old question of how we should govern ourselves—whether as democracies that respect human rights or as dictatorships that severely limit them or deny them altogether—retains an enduring immediacy. The world of the new millennium, in short, is a world where the study of comparative politics matters more than ever.

Comparative politics *examines political realities in countries all over the world. It looks at the many ways governments operate and the ways people behave in political life.*

More specifically, comparative politics examines such things as the following:

- How governments are structured and how they function, including different forms of democracy and various forms of non-democratic government. This area of inquiry focuses mainly on *governmental institutions.*
- The processes through which governments interact with their populations in pursuing community goals (such as improving health care, reducing unemployment, and so on) and in dealing with conflicts that arise over a variety of political, economic, and social issues. Here the emphasis is on *public policy,* such as health policy, economic policy, and the like.
- How political leaders and the population behave in politics, including the ideas they have about politics and the ways they participate in politics through such mechanisms as elections, political parties, interest groups, and other modes of political activity. The focus here is on *elite and mass political behavior* and includes such things as *political ideologies* and *political participation.*

- How political leaders and the mass public think and feel about politics, and how these attitudes affect their behavior. This topic is known as *political culture.*

In this book we'll look at politics in a wide range of countries in Europe, the former Soviet Union, Asia, Latin America, Africa, and the Middle East. We'll also make quite a few references to political life in the United States.

A GLOBAL INTRODUCTION

True to its title, this book is introductory in nature. It assumes you have little or no background in studying the politics of different countries on a systematic basis. Of course, no single volume, not even one as lengthy as this one, can substitute for extensive reading across a wide range of sources. Nor can this book make you an expert on any particular country or region. Its principal aims are simply to widen your horizons by introducing you to political life in a variety of countries and to provide you with some concepts and analytical methods so that you can think for yourself more coherently about politics and the world in which we live.

Our approach is "global" in three senses of the term: (1) *global coverage of the nations of the world,* (2) *conceptual comprehensiveness,* and (3) *critical thinking.*

Global Coverage of the Nations of the World

In the most literal sense, this book is global in its coverage of a representative selection of countries spread across all the world's geographic regions. Chapters 16 through 24 are devoted to specific countries. In addition, chapters 1 through 15 present a considerable amount of information about other countries not covered in subsequent chapters—Canada, India, Iraq, Poland, Haiti, and South Korea, among others—for the purpose of illustrating various concepts in comparative politics. Though there is no chapter devoted specifically to the United States, there are numerous references to the United States throughout the book for comparative purposes.

We also provide biographical *profiles of world leaders* in various countries. They include past leaders who have decisively influenced the contemporary world—Margaret Thatcher, Charles de Gaulle, Mikhail Gorbachev, and Nelson Mandela, among others—as well as leaders who were in power as the new millennium began, like Saddam Hussein, Slobodan Milosevic, Tony Blair, Gerhard Schroeder, Ehud Barak, and Fernando Henrique Cardoso. Portraits of these and a host of additional leaders can tell us a great deal not only about political developments in their respective countries but also about the nature of political leadership more generally.

Conceptual Comprehensiveness

In another sense, this book is global in its comprehensive *conceptual* treatment of the field of comparative politics. In order to understand political life in the United States, Japan, or any other country, we must not only examine relevant facts concerning the country's history, political institutions, public opinion, and other essential features of its political system; we must also pay close attention to the ways *general political processes and concepts* apply to them. For example, in order to understand the way democracy works in countries like Israel, France, or South Africa, we need to know something about democracy in general. What is it? How does it come about? Why is it that some countries have managed to develop and sustain democratic institutions for long periods of time (such as the United States, Canada, and Britain), while others have experienced the collapse of democracy (like Germany, Argentina, and Brazil) or have never really had democracy at all (China, for example)? Why do some countries build their democracy around a strong president and a weak legislature, while others favor powerful legislatures? In other words, to understand democracy in any specific country we need to understand the *concept* of democracy in more general terms. *Comparative politics almost always involves the interaction of the general and the specific.*

There are numerous additional concepts and categories of political phenomena that must also be examined if we are to get a good grasp of political reality around the world. Accordingly, chapters 5 through 15 are specifically designed to introduce you to some of the main concepts in comparative politics. A brief look at the titles of these chapters will give you an indication of what some of these concepts are. They include such things as *power,* the *state, nationalism, ideology, political culture,* and *political economy.* In order to help you see how these and other conceptual notions and analytical categories pertain to the real world, these chapters provide a considerable amount of material drawn from a vast array of countries as well as from a broad sampling of scholarly literature produced by some of the top specialists in comparative politics. They also present some of the core ideas of prominent political thinkers whose theories have helped shape political history and the ways we think about politics: Aristotle, John Locke, James Madison, and Karl Marx, to name just a few. In sum, our approach to comparative politics is not confined to giving you just "a bunch of facts" about individual countries. It seeks to deepen your understanding of political life in today's world by broadening your understanding of politics in general.

Critical Thinking

The third sense in which this text is global relates to another form of comprehensiveness. Relevant facts and key concepts are necessary, but by themselves they are still not enough to round out a truly comprehensive introduction to comparative politics. To appreciate the complexities of political reality more fully, we need to know *how to think* about politics and *how to analyze* it in a logical and systematic manner.

Comparative politics is a subfield of political science. Students often ask, "Is political science *really* a science?" The answer to this question obviously requires an understanding of what science is. While the term may conjure up images of people in lab coats measuring chemicals or observing mice, in fact science is primarily a system of logic. *Science is a set of rules and methods for investigating reality logically and systematically.* Political science is therefore a science to the extent that it observes the cardinal rules of scientific logic. To be more specific, political science is "scientific" when it engages in the following operations: **definition, description, explanation, prediction,** and **prescription.**

Definition Any science must define its terms as precisely as possible, and political science is no different. Just as biologists must refine their definitions of life and physicists wrestle with the meanings of space and time, political scientists must clarify political terminology in order to make sense out of the world of politics. Definitional clarity is especially necessary in politics because terms like "democracy," "socialism," "liberalism," and other commonly used political concepts often have more than one meaning and are frequently misused. Without clear definitions of the words we habitually employ, we may completely misunderstand one another when we talk about politics, and we run the potentially damaging risk of failing to appreciate what politicians actually mean when they speak to us about political issues. To avoid these pitfalls, we need precise and consistent definitions of political terms and concepts as well as a subtle appreciation of their variations and shades of meaning in particular contexts.

Description The systematic observation of things and their accurate description is another essential component of comprehending reality scientifically. Physicists must describe the atom in meticulous detail in order to unlock its secrets, and doctors must have a clear description of their patients' symptoms in order to make an appropriate diagnosis. Similarly, political scientists need to describe the phenomena they are examining as accurately as possible in order to understand them. How, for example, does the U.S. system of checks and balances among the three branches of government actually work? How does the British parliamentary system work? How does the Russian variant of a strong president and a weak legislature work? How can we categorize various types of government, such as the several existing variants of democracy and the numerous different forms of non-democratic regimes (monarchies, military dictatorships, and the like)? These and a plethora of other political phenomena need to be carefully described if we are to make any sense out of them.

Explanation *Why* do things happen the way they do? Just as physicists ask why atoms work the way they do and biologists ask why diseases occur, political scientists are curious about why political phenomena occur. Why, for example, does democracy succeed in some countries but not in others? Why do some countries have large voter turnouts while others attract smaller proportions of eligible voters to the polls? Why did the communist party dictatorship collapse in the Soviet Union but not in China? The list of political phenomena begging for explanation is practically endless.

In an effort to explain the realities that intrigue them, scientists of all kinds frequently make **generalizations** about the phenomena they seek to understand. Very often these generalizations are expressed as **theories** or **hypotheses** that posit a **cause-and-effect relationship** between things. Sir Isaac Newton hypothesized that gravity causes physical objects to conform to certain general laws of motion. Charles Darwin theorized that evolutionary processes linking all animal life forms provide the causative explanation of how the human species developed. Using similar logic, political scientists formulate generalizations that seek to address the causes of such things as democracy, war, voter turnout, fascism, and other political realities. And like natural scientists, political scientists are frequently engaged in **testing** their generalizations against the hard facts of reality to determine whether they are true or false, or whether perhaps they are true under some conditions but not in others.

> **Hypothesis testing is a central activity of political science.** *One of the main aims of this book is to teach you to think about politics in terms of hypotheses that can be tested against relevant evidence.*

Prediction In some cases the physical sciences have predictive capabilities. Astronomers are able to calculate the future positions of the planets hundreds of years into the future, and biologists can trace out the likely course of a disease if it is not medically treated. Even the physical sciences, however, must acknowledge limits to their predictive abilities. Astronomers cannot predict when the next asteroid will hit planet Earth until it is well in view, and biologists may not be able to predict how an individual patient will react to medication. To be sure, political scientists cannot predict future events. The realities of human be-

havior and political life are so variegated that we have no ability to foretell with any accuracy what will happen in any particular country over the near term, let alone the long term. Nevertheless, we can observe **trends** and **patterns** in various aspects of political life. As a consequence, we can sometimes extrapolate from these observable trends and suggest, however tentatively, what broad tendencies are *possible,* or even *probable,* assuming that certain conditions hold.

While we cannot say with certainty that democracy is bound to succeed or doomed to fail in Brazil or Russia or somewhere else, we can at least specify the factors that may make democracy's success or failure more probable. While we may not wish to make any bets on the outcome of next year's elections, we may be willing to hazard a prediction after seeing the last public opinion polls taken a few days before the vote. In other words, prediction in political science is **probabilistic** in nature. It can sketch out alternative possibilities and probabilities, while modestly desisting from claims to foolproof reliability.

Prescription The theories of Albert Einstein, Enrico Fermi, and other physicists led to formulas for building the atomic and hydrogen bombs. Doctors can prescribe medicines on the basis of the findings of research biologists and pharmacologists. Can political science prescribe remedies to the political problems besetting the nations of the world?

Yes and no. In some instances we can provide recommendations that, if followed, may increase the probability that a desirable outcome will ensue at some indeterminate point in time. We can prescribe, for example, a set of actions that need to be taken in order to establish a democracy and enhance its prospects for success. Thus we can urge the adoption of a body of laws ensuring fair elections, civil rights, an independent judiciary, and so forth. No political advisor can compel any country to take her advice, however, and no one can guarantee that, even if all the prescribed steps are followed, democracy will inevitably succeed. The particularities of each individual country and the unforeseeability of future events may dash even the most scrupulously observed efforts to make democracy triumph. Still, our prescriptions for democracy can at least increase the *chances* that democracy will succeed.

Another obstacle to the prescription of desirable political actions is that people often differ over what is desirable. If our calculations reliably demonstrate that the economy will be better off if we avoid budget deficits and maintain prudent surpluses, should we achieve these goals by raising taxes or by slashing government spending? If we agree to raise taxes, should we increase them equally for everybody or raise them disproportionately on the rich? If budget surpluses permit us to reduce taxes, how should we do so? And if we agree to reduce spending, how should we apportion the budget cuts among such claimants to public money as the poor, the disabled, the elderly, the military, and advocates for government expenditures on highways, education, the environment, the space program, and so on? Although science can show us with statistical objectivity that the country as a whole will benefit from deficit reduction and rising surpluses, it cannot demonstrate the objective correctness of *individual preferences or values.* If you do not wish to pay more taxes or see your government-subsidized education loan eliminated, science cannot prove that you are right or wrong. If I place a higher value on military spending than on welfare benefits for the poor, or vice versa, science cannot prove that my values are either correct or incorrect.

In actual practice, much of what occurs in politics is about how we deal with competing individual preferences and values. Science can help us figure out the costs and consequences of our preferred choices, but it cannot always prescribe with objective certainty what is "right" or "good" for you or me. A great deal of what goes on in political life, therefore, is beyond the reach of science and scientific logic. **Political discussion and debate are thus only partially "scientific"; in addition to scientific logic, they also involve values and preferences.** When we study political science as an academic discipline, we must be constantly attentive to both its scientific, factual side and its "non-scientific," value-centered side.

The two frequently go together. The scientific aspect of political science helps us understand political reality in a coherent, systematic fashion. In the process, it provides important knowledge and insights that may help us think through our own political preferences and values. Many readers of this book may be drawn to the study of politics out of a desire to make some impact on the real world. Whether one seeks to embark on a political career, to be an activist in a political cause, or simply to become a better informed citizen, a scientific approach to politics can assist us in devising policy prescriptions or in assessing the recommendations offered by politicians, government officials, and others engaged in political action and debate. *Sound government policies rest on sound analysis.* To the extent that a scientific approach to politics contributes to intelligent analyses of political reality, it also contributes to intelligent policy prescription.

Thus the third global aspect of this book is designed to teach you how political scientists think when they study comparative politics in accordance with scientific rules and methods. In the process, this book explicitly seeks to *improve your own critical-thinking skills.* The value of taking a scientific approach to the study of politics thus extends well beyond the field of political science. The ability to think logically and coherently is a vitally necessary skill in a large number of academic disciplines and non-academic careers. Its cultivation deserves the highest priority in your education. The analytical techniques employed in this volume, while rudimentary, can be applied across a wide spectrum of intellectual and professional endeavors. In helping you understand the world of politics, therefore, this book contributes to your general education by helping you learn how to think more sharply and effectively.

The scientific approach to comparative politics is spelled out in chapters 3 and 4. To get the most out of these chapters, and out of the rest of the book, you are advised to read them with great care. In addition, every subsequent chapter contains at least one *hypothesis-testing exercise* designed to bolster your comprehension of how scientific analysis can be applied to the study of politics. A considerable number of additional references to the application of hypotheses, models, and other aspects of scientific reasoning are also sprinkled throughout the book.

GETTING STARTED

In sum, the global approach to comparative politics presented in this volume provides an all-encompassing, conceptually integrated introduction to the study of political life around the contemporary world. Of course, a book is not a newspaper. Inevitably, this volume is only as current as the day it was signed to press in the summer of 2000. Many important events will surely have occurred since then. It is up to you to stay on top of world developments as you read this book and pursue your future explorations. (You can take advantage of the McGraw-Hill Supersite on comparative politics to stay abreast of some recent occurrences related to this book's themes.) As we've already indicated, our chief goals are to introduce you to political realities in a wide variety of settings and to improve your ability to think for yourself about politics. With those aims in mind, *let's get started!*

COMPARATIVE POLITICS AND INTERNATIONAL POLITICS: WHAT'S THE DIFFERENCE? HOW ARE THEY CONNECTED?

Political scientists make a basic distinction between two areas of inquiry: *comparative politics* and *international politics.*

Comparative politics examines political activities *within* individual countries. It looks at politics inside, say, the United States, Russia, Japan, Mexico, or South Africa. It then compares the domestic experiences of particular countries with the domestic experiences of others. The focus is on each country's *internal* politics, with a view to making generalizations about politics in a variety of domestic settings. For example, we can compare various democracies with one another to learn more about the process of democracy. We can also compare various non-democratic governments to learn more about how they work, such as communist countries or military dictatorships.

International politics, by contrast, concerns relations *between* countries. Here the focus is on the *external* relationships of individual countries. Diplomacy, international law, international economic relations, war, and peacemaking are among the chief topics studied by political scientists concerned with international affairs. Their task is to look at relationships between, say, the United States and Russia, Israel and Egypt, Western Europe and Eastern Europe, the countries of the Northern Hemisphere and those of the Southern

Hemisphere, and so on. These investigations aim at explaining how these relationships work and seek to provide us with a more general theoretical understanding of the processes of international politics as such.

If you wish to combine your study of comparative politics with a study of international politics in theory and practice, or if you want to concentrate primarily on the international relations of the countries examined here, you will need to read other books and articles and perhaps take other courses devoted principally to international relations.

The dividing line between comparative and international politics is razor thin, however, and it's getting thinner all the time. Domestic and international politics are increasingly intertwined within virtually every country in the world today. We cannot really understand the domestic politics of most nations without some reference to their international relationships. What goes on internally is often affected by events occurring externally, beyond the country's borders. Conversely, we cannot fully comprehend international affairs without a good look inside the domestic political systems of individual countries. The actions of individual governments frequently have a powerful impact on other countries or on the world as a whole. Somewhat like biology and chemistry, comparative politics and international politics are complementary: though they are separate fields of analysis, they are intimately interrelated.

GLOBAL INTERDEPENDENCE

This ever-tightening linkage between domestic and international politics is one of the chief manifestations of global **interdependence.** As we noted at the start of this chapter, the nations of today's world are increasingly enmeshed in a web of interactions, with their governments playing a pivotal role in many of them.

Interdependence *refers to the fact that the countries of the world do not live in isolation from one another but are linked through a variety of political, economic, environmental, and other relationships.*

One of the most prominent types of global interdependence is economic **globalization.** (By it-

FIGURE 1.1   Growth in World Trade and Output, 1950–1990s
With the total volume of world trade and the world's output of goods and services assigned a value of 100 in 1950, the graph shows that trade was thirteen times greater by the 1990s while output had grown more than fivefold. Part of the rise in output was due to the steep rise in trade. (*Source:* General Agreement on Tariffs and Trade.)

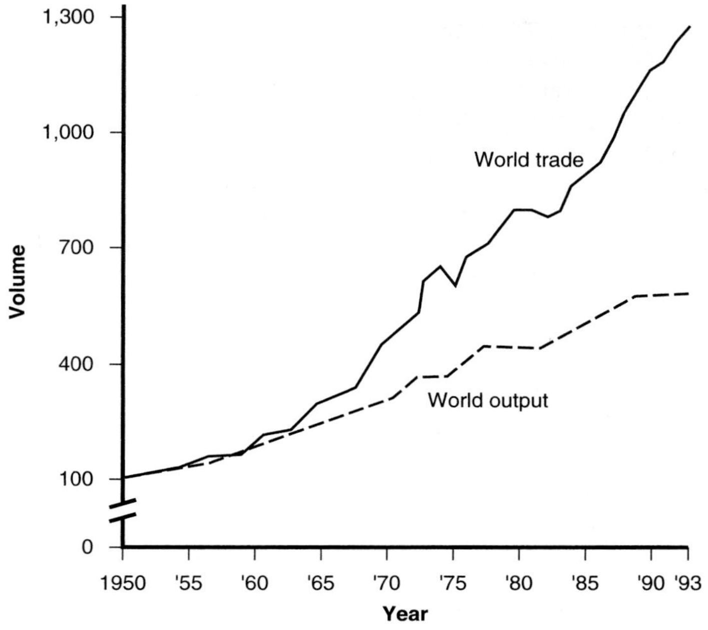

self, the term "globalization" as it is commonly used in the press and academic literature usually refers to *economic* relationships.) Former U.S. Secretary of Labor Robert Reich has observed that it no longer makes sense to speak of the "national economy" of any individual country, such as "the American economy" or "the Chinese economy," as though it can be separated from the economies of other countries. We are now living in a truly global economy. International trade is intensifying, as figure 1.1 shows. Businesses are not only selling their goods in a rapidly expanding and highly competitive global marketplace; they are setting up factories and offices outside the borders of their home countries to an extent unimaginable even a few decades ago, moving jobs and money around the world at a dizzying pace.

Some people are hurt by these developments. When companies close down their plants in one locality and relocate in countries that offer cheaper wages, lower taxes, or other advantages, those who are left behind must often cope with unemployment or other harsh consequences of economic change. But for others, the forces of globalization are creating unprecedented possibilities. As Reich points out, the fastest-growing career opportunities are precisely in areas that are tightly plugged into the world economy. Globalization holds out rich rewards to those who possess the intellectual skills these careers require (especially analytical skills) along with a keen sensitivity to the economic, political, and cultural factors at work in the international arena.[7]

The forces of economic globalization are by no means limited to private companies. Governments around the world are also caught up in the globalization process, whether as active promoters of international trade or as sources of jobs, unemployment compensation, retraining, and other forms of assistance to those whose livelihood is jeopardized by the maelstrom of global economic activity. *It therefore matters who governs.* Some political leaders may deal with the effects of economic globalization differently from others. Studying comparative politics helps us understand these differences and why they occur. The global financial crises of 1997–99 are a superb example of globalization.

THE GLOBAL FINANCIAL CRISES OF 1997–99:
Asia, Russia, and Brazil

It all started on July 2, 1997, when domestic economic difficulties forced the government of Thailand to announce that it could no longer support the value of its currency, the baht.

The currencies of the world—U.S. dollars, Japanese yen, the euro and so on—are like stocks and bonds: they are traded on world markets every business day. As a consequence, the value of individual currencies relative to other currencies is constantly shifting. If the dollar is strong and the yen is growing weaker, for example, people involved in currency exchanges, whether they are Japanese tourists visiting the United States or professional currency traders, will have to pay out more yen for each dollar they wish to buy. On a typical day the value of most currencies against other currencies does not change very much, usually by a small fraction of 1 percent. But if a country's economy is in severe crisis, the value of its currency may plummet very quickly as the world's currency speculators rapidly sell their holdings of that currency. When that happens, the government must usually come to its own currency's rescue by buying it in world currency markets. But when the government cannot afford to take such remedial action, as in Thailand's case, its currency may go into a tailspin. Immediately after the Thai government made its announcement, the value of the baht fell a whopping 20 percent against the dollar.

Sell-Offs Rock Wall Street, World Markets

Although Thailand is a small country, the effects of its currency crisis had global repercussions. Because the economies of Southeast Asia are closely linked, Thailand's neighbors Malaysia, Singapore, and Indonesia immediately experienced currency troubles of their own. A ripple of currency devaluations and stock market slides spread to Hong Kong, Taiwan, and South Korea over the following weeks and months. Even more ominously, the Asian currency crisis coincided with other economic problems that had been brewing throughout the region for quite some time. Japan and South Korea, for example, witnessed the collapse of several of its largest banks in late 1997.

The deterioration of East Asia's previously dynamic economies sent shock waves throughout the global economy. Because private companies and governments around the world, from the United States and Canada to Latin America and Europe, were heavily involved in trade and other economic transactions with Asia, it was not long before their economies felt the effects of the Asian crisis. On October 27, 1997, the New York Stock exchange fell 554 points, until then its biggest one-day loss in history. The sudden plunge reflected the fears of investors that Asia would no longer be able to purchase American-made goods as actively as in the past, thereby reducing the profits of U.S. corporations. Wall Street quickly recovered from this drop, but other countries were not so fortunate. Some were affected by a substantial loss of revenue from trade with Asian partners. A number of countries were also affected by a decline of foreign investments as the Asian crisis made many international investors squeamish about placing their funds in risky economies known in the investment world as "emerging markets." India and South Africa, among others, experienced severe economic problems before too long.

While the consequences of the Asian crisis were still reverberating around the world, Russia and Brazil suffered financial shocks of their own. In August 1998, the Russian government declared its inability to prop up the ruble. Within a week the currency lost about a third of its value against the dollar and plunged considerably lower by year's end.

Brazil's woes were precipitated in 1998 by the decision of one of the country's governors to withhold his region's tax payment to the federal government. That decision made it very unlikely that Brazil's government would be able to balance the national budget, a prospect that severely jeopardized President Fernando Henrique Cardoso's carefully constructed economic reform program. For several years, Cardoso had sought to stimulate Brazil's chronically underperforming economy by cutting excess government spending, smothering inflation, and encouraging private investment. The 1999 financial pinch occurred just as these efforts were bearing fruit. Nervous investors, still reeling from the Asian and Russian crises, began pulling money out of Brazil, and Cardoso's government could no longer support the country's currency, the real. The real's value dipped 20 percent against the dollar in early 1999. Brazil's stature as the eighth largest economy in the world and the largest in Latin America inevitably meant that its financial troubles would have international consequences. On Wall Street, for example, U.S. companies whose business was tied to the Brazilian market suffered losses. And by mid-1999, much of Latin America was in a deep economic slump.

The ramifications of these multiple financial crises were by no means limited to economics. Political changes also ensued in a number of places. Indonesia's financial crunch precipitated riots and student demonstrations that ultimately brought about the resignation of President Suharto, who had ruled the country as its unchallenged dictator since 1965. South Korea's economic woes paved the way for the election of a new government under President Kim Dae Jung, a courageous advocate of democracy and an outspoken opponent of his country's previous military governments. In elections held in July 1998, Japan's ruling party received a rude jolt from an electorate worried about continuing stagnation in the world's second largest economy. The prime minister resigned and a new government under Keizo Obuchi came to power. Russian President Boris Yeltsin fired his prime minister as the ruble disintegrated but got into a dispute with the Russian parliament over his replacement. In Brazil, Cardoso managed to gain parliamentary approval for the main elements of his reform program, but only after protracted negotiations. In other countries affected by the global financial turmoil, a number of political leaders found themselves under intense pressure to deal with the economic hardships the crises had created or exacerbated. For governments and their populations around the world, the crises provided indisputable evidence that economic globalization is a daily reality, and that it has profound *political* consequences.

A key player in the Asian financial crisis, and in many other global economic transactions, is the **International Monetary Fund (IMF).** The IMF is an international organization that provides financial assistance to governments that have currency problems or difficulty repaying loans borrowed from other governments or commercial banks. Before providing any assistance, however, IMF officials may impose fairly stringent conditions on the recipient government. They may require it to cut its budget deficit, for example, compelling it to raise taxes or eliminate unaffordable government spending programs. Such measures may have unwelcome domestic political implications for the government in need of IMF aid. Raising taxes invariably sparks protests, and slashing government spending may terminate jobs for bureaucrats and funding for students, private businesses, social welfare recipients, and others. Problems of this nature are now being experienced by numerous countries around the world. As the 1997–99 financial crises unfolded, the IMF pledged a $17 billion rescue package for Thailand, $23 billion for Indonesia, $57 billion for South Korea, $22.6 billion for Russia, and $41.5 billion for Brazil. All these loans were to be doled out in periodic allotments stretched out over a period of one year or more. The payment of each disbursement typically depends on the country's fulfillment of the IMF's demands for economic restructuring, providing vivid examples of *how international forces can affect a country's domestic political framework.*[8]

International security constitutes a particularly vital aspect of global interdependence. With the disintegration of the Soviet Union (the USSR) at the end of 1991, the Cold War that dominated international political life from the end of World War II came to an abrupt end. The tensions that kept the United States and the USSR, together with their allies, on the brink of nuclear annihilation for more than forty years suddenly dissolved as the Soviet Union's largest constituent element— Russia—embarked on the path to democracy. Cooperation between the two largest military powers in the world replaced confrontation. Landmark arms reduction agreements, several of which were actually concluded before the collapse of Communist Party rule in the USSR, led to the destruction of thousands of nuclear weapons and deadly guided missiles on both sides, together with the demobilization of hundreds of thousands of troops. The late 1980s and early 1990s truly marked one of the most important political turning points in world history.

Despite these auspicious developments, the world remains a dangerous place, as the Kosovo conflict amply demonstrated. In 2000 Russia still possessed well over twenty thousand nuclear bombs. There is considerable concern that some of those bombs may not always be kept under effective safeguards against theft by terrorists or others who might sell them to countries abroad. Just as important, the long-term stability of Russia's nascent democracy is by no means a sure thing. Communists and other political groups who have confrontational attitudes toward the United States pose the continuing possibility of a return to a conflictual relationship with the West should they come to power. *It therefore matters who governs Russia.* As was the case during the Cold War, global security still hinges in large measure on political developments *inside* the two largest nuclear powers.

In addition to the United States and Russia, several other countries are known to possess nuclear weapons as well. Britain, France, and Israel are firm U.S. allies. But China, India, and Pakistan are pursuing their nuclear weapons programs in ways that at times conflict with U.S. interests. China's Communist Party dictatorship is building nuclear bombs and missiles capable of striking several neighboring countries, including Russia and Japan. In 1998 India and Pakistan, arch rivals that share a disputed border, engaged in a series of nuclear tests that were patently aimed at mutual intimidation. How these countries manage their nuclear weapons programs obviously depends on who governs them.

The security of hundreds of millions of people is also affected by a host of potential sources of military conflagration or international terrorism spread across the globe. Here are just a few examples:

- **Iraq** under the dictatorship of Saddam Hussein invaded Kuwait in 1990, sparking the Persian Gulf War of the following year. Saddam's transparent efforts to build a large chemical weapons capability and obtain nuclear weapons have mobilized an international campaign to stop him. In 1998 the United States bombed alleged Iraqi weapons facilities.
- **Iran** has been identified as a source of terrorist activity aimed against the United States and Israel ever since its government was taken over by fundamentalist Islamic clerics in 1979.
- **North Korea,** which has been governed by a repressive communist dictatorship since the end of World War II, has posed a continuing mili-

tary danger to South Korea's pro–U.S. government, threatening a reprise of the Korean War of 1950–53.

These and other flashpoints of potential conflagration make it abundantly evident that security *among* the nations of the world depends in the first instance on who holds governmental power *within* them.

Another form of global interdependence is **environmental interdependence.** Ecological developments occurring inside one country can have immediate and long-term repercussions in neighboring areas as well as in countries clear across the planet. The unabated rise in industrial emissions, the degradation of the rain forests, and other environmental perils of recent decades have compellingly underscored the fragile unity of the global ecological system.

- Since the mid-1960s, ozone in the globe's stratosphere has been decreasing over North America, Europe, and Australia at rates of about 10 percent in winter and 5 percent in summer. An especially large ozone hole opens up over Antarctica every year, at times amounting to 60 percent of the region's total protective layer. By the mid-1990s, the Earth's ozone hole was as large as Africa. Alarming increases in skin cancer and eye problems have resulted. More than three-fourths of ozone depletion is caused by human emissions of chlorofluorocarbons such as chlorine and bromine. Various agreements concluded under United Nations auspices have brought about significant reductions in CFC emissions, but the continuing cooperation of the signatory governments will be necessary to restore the ozone layer to acceptable levels by the middle of the twenty-first century.
- A hundred years ago, rain forests covered 14 percent of the Earth's land surface. Deforestation in recent decades has destroyed half of it. Some 500,000 trees are cut down every *hour* in tropical rain forests, resulting in the annual destruction of an area as large as Florida. At these rates, the rain forests will disappear completely by 2040. Rain forest depletion destabilizes global climactic patterns and contributes to the loss of between twenty thousand and one hundred thousand plant and animal

species a year, depriving humanity of potential cures for cancer and other pharmaceuticals. By 2000, approximately one million species had already disappeared before they were even identified.[9]

- The emission of greenhouse gases such as carbon dioxide and methane has quadrupled since the 1960s. These gases promote global warming, which has a major impact on ocean temperatures, the melting of polar icecaps, and other climactic phenomena.[10]

These problems present obvious challenges to the international scientific community. But they also provoke reactions from governments and from those who seek to influence governmental policy, as the cases of Chernobyl and Brazil indicate.

THE POLITICS OF THE ENVIRONMENT

CHERNOBYL

In April 1986, Swedish monitors detected unusual amounts of radiation in the immediate atmosphere. Their projections traced the source of the emissions to the Soviet Union. After first denying any problem, Soviet officials admitted that a nuclear reactor used to generate electricity had exploded in Chernobyl (cher-NO-bil), in Soviet Ukraine. For ten days the burning reactor released deadly atomic debris into the air, contaminating the atmosphere with more than ten times the amount of radiation emitted by the atomic bomb

Chernobyl nuclear reactor shown after explosion and prior to its encasement.

that exploded over Hiroshima in 1945. The area around Chernobyl was evacuated, but more than 3.5 million people in Ukraine were affected by the radiation, along with more than 2 million in neighboring Belarus and over 3 million in Russia. Farmland within a wide radius of the blast suffered nuclear contamination whose effects could last thousands of years. Carried by wind and rain, the effects of the disaster were felt not only in Scandinavia but in Eastern Europe, Germany, and other countries far from the explosion. A United Nations report released in 2000 stated that 1,800 children who had been exposed to radiation had developed thyroid cancer, while another study predicted that about 3,500 cancer deaths attributable to the blast would probably occur in the future. People continued to consume contaminated milk and food from the region, however, and no one knows how many people will be affected over the coming years and generations.

The incident had immediate political implications. Mikhail Gorbachev, the head of the Soviet Communist Party, had been in office for little more than a year. Although he was a lifelong communist, Gorbachev knew that the Soviet economy was in serious trouble and that the political system needed major changes. Accordingly, he used the Chernobyl catastrophe to improve Moscow's relations with the outside world as well as to loosen up some of the more rigid aspects of the party's dictatorial rule. Soviet requests for medical and scientific assistance brought an immediate response from the United States and other countries, thereby reducing Cold War confrontation. Recognizing the enormous fears of nuclear devastation that the accident had provoked, the Soviet leader joined with President Ronald Reagan in signing an unprecedented nuclear weapons agreement in December 1987. For the first time ever, the two superpowers agreed to destroy large quantities of missiles and nuclear warheads, something Gorbachev's predecessors had steadfastly resisted. Domestically, Gorbachev responded to the Chernobyl accident by calling for more "openness" in the way Soviet leaders dealt with their population. No longer would natural disasters and other problems confronting the country be kept secret by the Communist Party leadership, as they had been in the past. The quest for greater openness ultimately increased popular pressures for political democracy in the USSR, leading to the dissolution of the communist dictatorship several years later.

With the Soviet Union's collapse at the end of 1991, Ukraine became an independent country and ultimately assumed responsibility for Chernobyl. After several years of negotiations, forty countries agreed to provide Ukraine with more than $700 million to close down

Chernobyl's remaining reactors and re-encase the damaged one. The Ukrainian government promised to shut down Chernobyl by the end of 2000.

THE BRAZILIAN RAIN FORESTS

The Amazon region of Brazil, an area about half the size of the United States, contains the world's largest rain forest. This vast ecosystem encompasses about a third of all surviving tropical forests on Earth and nurtures hundreds of animal and plant species. Like other rain forests around the globe, it makes a vital contribution to the global atmospheric balance and is a significant source of medicinal plants. It is also home to some of the last remaining Stone Age people on Earth.

Until the 1960s, Amazonia was largely undeveloped. Brazilian leaders were acutely aware of the region's potential for economic development, however, especially its untapped mineral resources and its vast expanses of cultivable land. They also hoped that a flourishing Amazon would encourage migration from the country's increasingly overcrowded cities. The military, in particular, was determined to secure the region against possible foreign incursions and to exploit Amazonia's hidden wealth with the aim of catapulting Brazil into the ranks of the world's great powers.

In 1964 a military coup put an end to a succession of ineffective elected governments that had failed to stabilize the economy. The military governed Brazil until democracy returned in 1985. During that period the government launched a series of ambitious programs designed to fulfill its dreams of Amazonian development. Highways, dams, and earthmoving projects attracted large-scale agricultural, mining and industrial interests to take advantage of Amazonia's natural riches. Many of these undertakings were financed with funds the government borrowed from foreign banks and other international lenders. By the early 1980s Brazil had run up a debt of approximately $90 billion to foreign creditors.

Meanwhile, the accelerated pace of Amazonian development wreaked havoc on the environment. The clearing of wide tracts of forest for agricultural purposes, much of it carried out with slash-and-burn methods, resulted in persistent brush fires and the release of carbon dioxide and other noxious greenhouse gases into the atmosphere. Indiscriminate deforestation also threatened the world's climactic patterns and the survival of indigenous species and plant life. The harnessing of lakes and rivers for hydroelectric power severely jeopardized the region's delicate ecology. These government-sponsored programs also took a harsh toll on local populations as small farmers were pushed off their lands by powerful agrobusinesses while rubber workers, miners, and other laborers were exploited by industrial companies. The Yanomami Indians and other native tribes were subjected to the rude intrusion of outsiders who upset their traditional way of life.

In the 1970s and 1980s a global coalition of environmental groups, governments, and international organizations exerted mounting pressure on the Brazilian government to change its policies. In 1985 the military, cognizant of its failure to solve Brazil's economic problems, gave up power and permitted free elections. When the new president died after only a few weeks in office, power passed to Jose Sarney, a former colleague of the military rulers. Although he governed in accordance with a new constitution passed by a democratically elected assembly, Sarney was powerfully influenced by the leading members of Brazil's political elite, above all by large business interests and the military. Accordingly, his government resisted international pressures for a shift in Brazil's Amazonian development policy. Sarney and his supporters were particularly resentful of efforts by the United States and West European countries, which had environmental problems of their own, to interfere in Brazil's internal affairs and to "keep Brazil down." But the world's focus on Brazil's problems only intensified in 1988 when Chico Mendes, a Brazilian environmentalist who led a rubber workers' union in Amazonia, was murdered. The following year, President Sarney refused to attend a global environmental conference.

Following his victory in the election of 1989, Fernando Collor de Mello assumed the presidency. The new president quickly acted to reverse the tone and substance of his predecessor's environmental policy. He appointed one of Brazil's most widely respected environmentalists as secretary of the environment, launched efforts to halt the illegal burning of forests, saw to it that Mendes's murderers were arrested and convicted, and initiated a variety of programs to improve environmental conditions in Amazonia. He also took measures to protect the region's Indians. Most important, Collor replaced Sarney's antagonistic attitude toward international concern about Brazil's environment with a more cooperative stance. By the end of 1990 Brazil reported a significant decline in the rate of deforestation.

The change in Brazil's government thus resulted in a marked change in its environmental policies. Nevertheless, the nature of the Brazilian political system imposed noticeable limits on these policy shifts. Today Brazil's political affairs remain in the hands of a small elite. Large corporations and the military high command exert an ever-present influence on elected officials and the government bureaucracy. The powers of the president are circumscribed by the national legislature and the competing political parties represented in it. These and other factors resulted in severe neglect of the rain forest in the 1990s. In 1995 more than eleven thousand square miles of forest were lost, a single-year high. Environmentalists around the world criticized the Brazilian government for failing to keep its promises. In all likelihood, the future of the Brazilian rain forests will continue to depend on fluctuating relationships between the international community and Brazil's complicated domestic political processes.

The Chernobyl and Brazilian rain forest cases amply demonstrate that, when it comes to the environment, *it matters who governs*. Soviet leaders before Gorbachev would probably have handled the Chernobyl situation very differently, in all likelihood refusing to level with the population about the severity of the country's environmental problems. Successive governments in Brazil dealt with the rain forest in different ways. Clearly, anyone interested in the global environment needs to be a keen student of comparative politics.

Meanwhile, the international spillover effects of events occurring in countries wracked by civil conflict or ineffective government continue to manifest themselves in **migration and refugee flows.** For example:

- Collapsing governments and bloody civil wars in Liberia, Somalia, and a number of other African countries produced more than 5 million refugees throughout the continent by the mid-1990s. One of the deadliest of these tragedies was the bitter tribal clash between Tutsis and Hutus in Burundi and Rwanda. In 1993 at least ten thousand people were killed in Burundi and some five hundred thousand were slaughtered the following year in Rwanda. As panic spread, more than a million refugees streamed into neighboring Uganda, Zaire (now called the Congo), and Tanzania. Lacking the means to support the new arrivals, these governments relied on the United Nations and other international relief organizations to provide the refugees with shelter, food, and medical treatment. Continuing political turmoil in Africa over the following years only exacerbated the plight of the burgeoning refugee populations.

- As Yugoslavia broke up into five separate countries in the early 1990s, long-simmering ethnic hatreds erupted into brutal warfare. The most severe initial confrontations, occurring in and around Bosnia, involved clashes between Bosnian Muslims and Serbs, and resulted in massacres and forced evacuations from native villages, a process that Serb leaders called "ethnic cleansing." Fighting between Serbs and Croats, and between Croats and Bosnians, also took place. Before the Bosnian fighting stopped in 1995 more than 250,000 people were killed and some 1.8 million were left homeless. Over a million of these uprooted people emigrated to Germany, Sweden, and other countries willing to take them. The Kosovo conflict of 1999 produced an additional eight hundred thousand refugees or more prior to the end of the war. Most of them returned home after peace was restored, but new refugees, mostly Serbs, have left Kosovo since then.

The United Nations estimated that there were 22 million refugees scattered throughout the world by the end of the 1990s. Here, again, it is evident that political events occurring in one country can have profound consequences for other countries around the world, requiring us to pay serious attention to what is going on within individual states.[11]

Additional examples of global interdependence abound. In **public health,** the scourge of AIDS, the world's most infectious disease with more than 2 million deaths annually, requires intense international cooperation among scientists and governments to contain and eventually eliminate the epidemic. In **communications,** the global expansion of the Internet opens up unprecedented possibilities while at the same time creating problems regarding intellectual property rights and other legal issues that governments must resolve. In **law enforcement,** international drug trafficking and organized crime present daily challenges to societies and governments around the world. In these and other fields, the distinction between what is "domestic" and what is "international" is increasingly blurred. So, too, is the distinction between what is "political" and what is not.

Not even the United States is immune to the all-embracing forces of interdependence. As the country with the world's largest economy and most powerful military arsenal, the United States is strategically positioned at the hub of the world's political, economic, and security interconnections. Inevitably, the United States cannot help but have a tangible impact on virtually every country in the world. At the same time, the accelerating forces of global interdependence cannot help but expose the United States to far more external influences on its domestic life than ever before.

THE INTERNATIONALIZATION OF THE U.S. DOMESTIC AGENDA

JOB MARKET

In the 1950s and 1960s, the United States had relatively low levels of imports and foreign competition. In 1960 the United States imported only 4 percent of its autos and steel and 6 percent of its consumer electronics. Employment remained high in domestic companies manufacturing steel, cars, and various consumer goods. Auto and other imports began to rise in the 1970s, and by the following decade the United States was importing 28 percent of its cars, 25 percent of its steel, 25 percent of its computers, 66 percent of its radios and TVs, and 100 percent of its VCRs. In addition, a growing number of U.S. firms relocated abroad. As a result, the United States lost well over a million jobs in the auto, steel, and textile industries in the 1980s.

ENERGY

Until the 1960s, the United States did not import any oil. Inflation (i.e., price increases) remained low. During the 1970s U.S. oil imports rose from one-third to about one-half of its domestic consumption. A watershed occurred in October 1973, when the leading Middle East oil producers suddenly quadrupled world petroleum prices, causing a significant economic slowdown and double-digit inflation (known as *stagflation*) in the United States and other countries around the world. Subsequent oil price hikes aggravated these conditions until well into the 1980s. Chastened by this experience, the United States reacted quickly when Iraq invaded Kuwait, a major oil producer, in 1990. Fearing Iraq's intention of continuing its aggression and significantly raising world oil prices, the United States organized a forty-nation alliance that evicted Iraqi forces from Kuwait in the Persian Gulf War of February 1991.

ENVIRONMENT

Early efforts focused on the cleanup of domestic air and water. The Clean Air Act of 1970 required, among other things, the installation of tall smokestacks to disperse industrial pollution. Later in the decade it was discovered that these smokestacks were responsible for creating acid rain in the northeastern United States and Canada, creating frictions with that country. In addition, the United States, along with most other countries, was materially affected by ozone depletion, tropical deforestation, global warming, and other worldwide phenomena.

IMMIGRATION

In 1960, there were 9.7 million foreign-born people in the United States, 5.4 percent of its total population. By 1990 the figure was 19.8 million, 7.9 percent of the total. Though most immigrants came from Europe until 1970, by 1990 43 percent of foreign-born Americans were from Latin America and 25 percent were from Asia. An estimated two hundred thousand immigrants enter the United States illegally every year.

HEALTH

Health policies in the 1950s and 1960s focused on combating cancer and heart disease and initiating anti-smoking campaigns in the United States. The emergence of AIDS in the 1980s necessitated international cooperation and resulted in a ban on HIV-infected individuals seeking immigration.

CRIME

Until the 1980s, most violent crime was linked with urban poverty and some imported drugs (mostly heroin). Most murders were due to disputes among family members or personal acquaintances. In the 1980s, violent crime (especially murders) rose significantly, much of it linked with criminal activity involving imported narcotics (e.g., crack cocaine) and foreign drug gangs. Accordingly, the United States increased international drug enforcement efforts in Asia, Latin America, and the Caribbean.

ETHNIC STRIFE

In the 1950s, most ethnic conflict centered on black-white tensions. By the 1980s there was a rise in conflicts involving immigrants from Latin America, Asia, and elsewhere.

One of the chief implications of global interdependence is that the sovereignty of individual countries is weaker than it used to be. **Sovereignty** *means the exclusive legal authority of a government over its population and territory, indepen-*

dent of external authorities. While virtually all governments still subscribe to the principle of sovereignty, which remains enshrined in international law, in actual practice most of them find it increasingly difficult to maintain full control over the various economic, environmental, and other influences that penetrate their borders. Countries today are considerably more porous than in the past. In addition to the examples we've just considered, the Internet alone makes it practically impossible for dictatorships to shield their citizens from the outside world. Many countries, moreover, have voluntarily surrendered large portions of their sovereignty in exchange for the rewards of closer international cooperation. The fifteen nations of the European Union (EU), for example, have ceded many of their sovereign rights to EU institutions in hopes of promoting prosperity. Most of them have even abandoned their national currency in favor of a multinational denomination, the euro. (For a fuller description of the European Union, see chapter 7.) Whether voluntarily or involuntarily, governments will probably continue to see sovereignty slip away as global interdependence intensifies.[12]

DEMOCRATIZATION

Another major example of the relationship between domestic politics and international politics in the contemporary world is the spread of democracy. A global process of **democratization—***the transition from non-democratic to democratic forms of government*—is unfolding before our very eyes.

THE DEMOCRATIC REVOLUTIONS OF OUR TIMES

WESTERN EUROPE
The latest trend toward democracy began as the last remaining dictatorships of Western Europe fell apart in the 1970s.

- **Greece,** the "cradle of democracy," where democratic ideas and practices first blossomed more than two thousand years ago, experienced a military coup in 1967. A group of senior officers seized control of the government and established dictatorial rule, abolishing democratic rights and freedoms. But in 1974 the Greek military gave up power and democratic procedures were restored.
- **Portugal,** which had been governed by dictators since the 1920s, held free, competitive elections in 1975. It has maintained democratic procedures ever since.
- **Spain** had been ruled by a dictatorship ever since the victory of Generalissimo Francisco Franco in the Spanish Civil War of 1936–39. Franco's death in 1975 led to the creation of a new democratic system of government that enjoyed the solid support of King Juan Carlos. A majority of Spanish voters expressed their approval of democratic reforms in a referendum held the following year. A freely elected assembly then drafted a democratic constitution, which won the electorate's approval in 1978.

LATIN AMERICA
In the late 1970s and 1980s democratic tendencies spread through Latin America, a continent where democracies have come and gone ever since Spain and Portugal gave up their colonies there in the nineteenth century.

- In **Peru,** the military clique (or *junta*) that ruled the country permitted elections to a constitutional assembly in 1978; elections to the presidency under the new democratic constitution followed in 1980. Authoritarian rule returned in 1992, however, as President Alberto Fujimori suspended the constitution and assumed virtually dictatorial powers. His reelection in 2000 was denounced as fraudulent by the Organization of American States, Latin America's leading international organization.
- **Ecuador**'s military government stepped down and permitted free elections in 1979.
- Military rule gave way to the democratic process and civilian government in **Bolivia** in 1982, **Argentina** in 1983, **Uruguay** in 1984, and **Brazil** in 1985.
- **Chile,** whose forty-six-year-old democracy was extinguished in a bloody military coup in 1973, returned to the democratic fold as elections were held for a civilian government in 1989.
- Central American countries like **Honduras, Guatemala,** and **El Salvador** also underwent transitions from military juntas to democratically elected civilian governments in the first half of the 1980s. **Nicaragua,** which had come under the domination of a communist-oriented dictatorship in 1979, held elections in 1990 that swept pro-democracy forces into power.
- And **Mexico** took a giant step toward genuine multiparty democracy in 2000 as Vicente Fox won the presidency, ousting the party that had dominated the country's political life since 1929.

EAST-CENTRAL EUROPE

Communist governments that were installed by the Soviet Union in the aftermath of World War II fell like a row of dominos in the final frenetic months of 1989.

- **Poland**'s communist authorities were pressured into holding competitive elections in September, the first free elections held in that country since the 1920s. The communist candidates were roundly defeated by their pro-democracy rivals, a result that accelerated the adoption of more formal democratic procedures and institutions in the 1990s.
- On November 9, the communist authorities who ruled **East Germany,** pressured by mounting public demonstrations against communist rule, opened the Berlin Wall—the infamous barrier that divided West Berliners, who lived under democracy, from East Berliners, who lived under communism. This unanticipated event astounded the world and had immediate repercussions throughout the region.
- Several weeks later in **Czechoslovakia,** people came out into the streets of Prague by the hundreds of thousands to demand an end to more than forty years of communist domination. Finding no visible support from Soviet leaders, who were no longer willing to save communism in Eastern Europe by armed force, the Czechoslovak communists simply gave up. In a nonviolent "velvet revolution," they conferred power on Vaclav Havel, a playwright internationally respected for his decades of brave opposition to communist dictatorship. Over the following months and years, Havel presided over the installation of democratic institutions. In 1993, Czechoslovakia split up into two countries, the Czech Republic and Slovakia.
- As 1989 came to a breathtaking close, the repressive communist dictators of **Romania** and **Bulgaria** were also compelled to give up power. Finally, elections held in 1990 led to the ouster of communist rule in **Hungary** and the institution of a democratic government.

AFRICA

This vast continent, where democracy has traditionally enjoyed little success, witnessed numerous democratic developments in the 1980s and 1990s.

- Elections were held, in some cases for the first time, in such countries as **Angola, Ethiopia, Ghana, Kenya, Mozambique, Niger, and Nigeria,** among others.
- **South Africa,** governed for decades by a white minority that refused to grant political rights to blacks and other non-whites, experienced a particularly promising transformation. In April 1994, blacks were allowed to vote for the first time. Nelson Mandela, a black leader who had spent twenty-seven years in prison for his opposition to white supremacy, was elected to the presidency of the country's first multiracial government.

ASIA

Several countries spread across Asia also experienced democratic changes.

- **Turkey,** an Islamic country with both European and Asiatic roots, returned to electoral democracy in 1983 after years of military rule.
- **India,** whose democratic institutions were abruptly suspended by Prime Minister Indira Gandhi in 1975, restored democracy two years later.
- Neighboring **Pakistan** also returned to democracy in 1988 following eleven years of military rule. The military reclaimed power in a coup in October 1999, however.
- Farther to the east, **South Korea,** governed for decades by a succession of strong military rulers, moved progressively closer to democracy in the late 1980s. In 1992 a proponent of democratic government, Kim Young Sam, was elected to the presidency, followed by a veteran pro-democracy activist, Kim Dae Jung, in 1997.
- Pressures to restore democratic freedoms to the **Philippines** succeeded in 1986 as Corazón Aquino, the wife of an assassinated political leader, replaced Ferdinand Marcos as president. Marcos had ruled the Philippines as a veritable dictator since declaring martial law in 1972.
- In **Indonesia,** President Suharto's resignation in the midst of his country's financial crisis in 1998 led to parliamentary elections the following year, the first since the 1950s. Opponents of the regime won the upper hand, resulting in the assembly's election later in the year of Abdurrahman Wahid, a pro-democracy Muslim cleric, as president. Another proponent of democracy, Megawati Sukarnoputri (the daughter of a former dictator, Gen. Sukarno), was elected vice president.
- And in the **Republic of China** (better known as **Taiwan**), democratic tendencies by the 1990s were exercising a growing impact on a government monopolized by one party for more than forty years. That party was finally defeated in elections held in 2000.

THE CARIBBEAN

Free elections held in **Haiti** in December 1991 resulted in the victory of Jean-Baptiste Aristide, a champion of the island's impoverished masses. After being ousted by a military coup the following year, Aristide was returned to power through U.S. political and military intervention in the fall of 1994.

Perhaps the most stunning example of this development was the collapse of the Soviet Union. In one of the most extraordinary political events that has ever occurred, the Soviet Union's communist government, which had been in power since 1917, simply gave up control over a country with more than 260 million inhabitants. The various subdivisions that constituted the USSR—Russia, Ukraine, and other areas—split up into fifteen separate countries. Many of them are now engaged in the arduous task of replacing decades of repressive communist dictatorship with democratic modes of government.

The USSR's collapse, and the current process of building democracies in its place, are truly revolutionary events. But they are not the only democratic transformations to have taken place in recent years, as we have just seen. In places as far apart as Latin America, Europe, Africa, and East Asia, quite a few countries have been switching their form of government from dictatorship of one kind or another to democracy. The dominance of powerful ruling cliques who permit little or no political freedom to the people has been giving way to such democratic practices as the free expression of political views, competitive elections to political offices, and other liberties and procedures typically associated with democracies. Between the early 1970s and the late 1990s, the number of democratic governments in the world increased from just over forty to 117.

Will the new democracies last? Or will they collapse in failure, as numerous democracies have failed in the past? What factors account for the success or failure of democracy? What can the experiences of some democratizing countries tell us about the possible fate of others? And what can established democracies like the United States do to help these fledgling democracies survive? One of the principal purposes of studying comparative politics is to address questions such as these.

These democratization tendencies provide another example of the connections linking comparative politics and international politics. Perhaps the most important of these connections centers on the relationship between democracy (a typical concern of comparative politics) and peace (a typical concern of international politics).

Are democracies inherently more peaceful than non-democracies?

DEMOCRACY AND PEACE

President Woodrow Wilson was a firm believer in the hypothesis that democracies are inherently more peaceful than non-democracies. "A steadfast concert of peace can never be maintained," he said, "except by a partnership of democratic nations." For that reason, Wilson justified American involvement in World War I on the grounds that American troops in Europe would be fighting to "make the world safe for democracy." If democracies could be set up throughout Europe after the war, replacing such non-democratic regimes as the kaiser's government in Germany and the Austro-Hungarian monarchy, Wilson believed that World War I would turn out to be the "war to end all wars."

Was Wilson right? If we look at the historical evidence, we find that democracies can sometimes be just as aggressive as non-democracies are. To begin with, democratically elected governments often defend themselves quite vigorously if they or their allies have been attacked. Britain and France, which had democratically elected governments in 1914, both responded rapidly to the aggressive actions of Germany and Austria-Hungary at the start of World War I. The United States entered World War II after the Japanese bombed Pearl Harbor in December 1941. These and other historical examples provide ample evidence that democracies can—and do—undertake massive military commitments for *defensive* purposes.

Woodrow Wilson

Surely, a nation can defend itself against attack and still be fundamentally peace loving. The real test of whether democracies are peaceful by nature centers on the question of whether they refrain from launching unprovoked attacks on others. In fact, democratic governments have at times taken the initiative in starting military conflicts. When the French Revolution replaced the monarchy in the 1790s with a government that was more representative of popular sentiments, France attacked its neighbors on the European continent with the aim of bringing the blessings of "liberty, equality, fraternity" to the Germans, the Austrians, and other people who still lived under monarchies of one form or another. One of the guiding principles of the revolutionaries was the notion that, in a democracy, every male citizen has the duty to fight for his country. As a consequence, democratic ideals led to the introduction of mass conscription in France, a novelty in late eighteenth-century Europe.

British and French imperialism provide additional examples of unprovoked aggression by democracies. Both countries had democratically elected governments in the latter decades of the nineteenth century when they sent troops to Africa and other parts of the world to impose their imperial rule on the peoples they conquered. These and other historical examples suggest that democracies can sometimes be just as aggressive as non-democracies in *starting* military conflicts, even when they are not militarily threatened.

But the historical record also indicates that *democracies generally do not fight one another*. The world's leading democracies, such as the United States, Britain, and France, have tended to be allies rather than enemies. Why haven't these democracies gone to war against one another? One reason is that a fundamental principle of democracy asserts that conflicts should be settled peacefully, through negotiation and compromise, rather than by force. Another reason is that democratic governments require popular consent in order to govern. If a majority of the people are opposed to war, a democratically elected government may find it difficult to engage military forces abroad. President Franklin D. Roosevelt, who opposed Germany's aggression in Europe and Japan's aggression in Asia, could not take military action against those countries as long as most Americans opposed it. Only when public sentiment turned around after Pearl Harbor was Roosevelt able to get Congress to declare war. In later years, the U.S. government sought negotiated settlements to end American military involvement in the Korean War (1950–53) and the Vietnam War (1961–73) once a majority of Americans turned against armed intervention.

Still, there are exceptions to the rule that democracies do not fight one another. The United States and Britain clashed in the War of 1812, for example, and the American Civil War pitted the North against the South in a four-year conflict that left over six hundred thousand dead. Both the northern Republic and the southern Confederacy were governed by democratically elected officials (though the right to vote was restricted to white males).

We must therefore conclude that President Wilson's hypothesis is only partially correct. Democracies are not always peaceful by nature; they have at times launched unprovoked attacks against non-democracies, and they have even gone to war against one another. War can be a popular choice; it can be supported by a majority of the people, at times with considerable patriotic passion. Nevertheless, the record also shows that democracies *usually* do not go to war against one another. Certainly in the twentieth century, democracies tended to stick together against authoritarian regimes like Nazi Germany and the Soviet Union while resolving their own disputes through peaceful negotiation. Hence we may accept *as a general tendency* Wilson's idealistic proposition that "a partnership of democratic nations" will promote world peace.

As in virtually all human affairs, nothing can be guaranteed. Nevertheless, it appears that *democracy increases the probability of peace, at least among democratic nations*. Hence it may be no exaggeration to state that peace *among* the nations of the world may ultimately depend on the fate of democracy *within* the nations of the world.[13]

The apparent connection between democracy and peace is crucially important today because it bears directly on the issue of how much the United States and other established democracies should do to help democracy succeed in a country like Russia. When Russia was under communist rule during the days of the Soviet Union, Cold War tensions between the democracies and the communist world drove both sides to divert hundreds of billions of dollars to military expenditures. With thousands of deadly nuclear weapons targeted at each other and their allies, and with confrontations occurring at one time or another in virtually every corner of the globe, the USSR and the United States held out the grim threat of mutual—indeed global—extinction for more than four decades. Will Russia become a peaceful partner of the established democracies if it succeeds in stabilizing its own democracy over the long term?

THE PURPOSES OF COMPARISON

What exactly is "comparative" about comparative politics? What are we comparing, and for what aims?

As we indicated at the start of this chapter, *comparative politics examines the ways governments operate and the ways people behave in political life in a variety of countries.* In order to understand political life comprehensively, we must compare. If humanity's political experience can be summed up in any single word, it is *diversity.* Whether we look back into history and survey the plethora of governments and political relationships that have existed over thousands of years, or confine our view just to the contemporary world, it is abundantly evident that there is—and always has been—an extraordinary variety of governments, political organizations, ideologies, behaviors, and attitudes.

Thus we cannot possibly understand democracy by simply concentrating on one example of a democratic government, such as the United States or Britain. Democracies organize their executive, legislative, and judicial institutions in different ways. Some have encouraged free enterprise while others have favored greater government interference in the economy. Some democracies have succeeded while others have failed. Democracy is not a single phenomenon; it has many manifestations. The same is true of non-democratic regimes. To deepen our appreciation of politics, therefore, we need to look at political life in a wide variety of cases.

Another reason for making systematic comparisons between different countries and political systems is that we can learn a great deal more about any one particular case (country X) by comparing it with other relevant cases (countries A, B, and C). If you are interested in South Africa, China, Russia, or any other country, you will acquire a deeper appreciation of its history and politics by holding it up against the experiences of other nations. This simple idea is central to the logic of comparative analysis. And it strikes very close to home: we can learn a lot more about politics in our *own* country by comparing it with other countries. Specialists in comparative politics are fond of quoting Rudyard Kipling in this regard. "And what should they know of England," the poet inquired, "who only England know?" Presumably,

not much. At least, not as much as they would know if they ventured outside their homeland and savored life's possibilities in other places.

To a considerable extent, studying comparative politics is like traveling abroad. It awakens us to the varieties of human experience and shows us that there are different ways of doing things than what we are used to in our own country. In the end we come home with a greater sensitivity to both the positive and negative features of our homeland as well as an enhanced appreciation of why other people do things differently.

Thus for people in the United States, a comparative analysis of Britain, Japan, Israel, or other established democracies can shed an illuminating light on how the American political system actually works. Both the similarities the United States shares with these countries and the peculiarities that set America apart from them will stand out in sharp relief. Here are some examples:

- The U.S. system of government is based on *a separation of powers* and *checks and balances.* But how does this system compare with the British system? Or the Brazilian, French, or South African? In fact, these and other democracies are organized quite differently. The U.S. system is unique in many of its most essential features. What are the advantages and disadvantages of the U.S. system as compared with other democratic systems of government? How do other democracies differ from the United States in their procedures for removing their top leaders should they become highly unpopular or are accused of wrongdoing while in office?

- One of the most frequent criticisms Americans level at their own system of government is that it is prone to *gridlock:* between Congress and the president, major decisions often do not get made effectively. Is gridlock a peculiarly American phenomenon, or do other governments have it, too? Can the United States reduce or eliminate gridlock by adopting constitutional procedures used in other democracies?

- Americans complain that their elected officials are not always very effective when it comes to keeping their campaign pledges once they are in office. How effective are governments around the world when it comes to pursuing their declared goals or fulfilling their election campaign promises? To what extent are government leaders in various countries compelled by domestic or international pressures to take actions contrary to what they would prefer to do?

- Some of the most controversial political issues in the United States center on such topics as campaign financing, health care, and gun control. How do other democracies handle these problems? Can the United States learn anything from these countries, or vice versa?

The principal purposes of studying comparative politics may therefore be summarized as follows:

- *to widen our understanding of politics in other countries*
- *to increase our appreciation of the advantages and disadvantages of our own political system and to enable us to learn from other countries*
- *to develop a more sophisticated understanding of politics in general, including the nature of democracy and non-democratic governments, the relationships between governments and people, the interdependencies connecting individual countries with the rest of the world, and other concepts and processes*
- *to help us see the relationship between politics around the world and such fields as science and technology, the environment, public health, law, business, religion, ethnicity, culture, and the like*
- *to enable us to become more informed citizens, so that we can more effectively develop our own political opinions, participate in political life, evaluate the actions and proposals of political leaders, and make our own political decisions and electoral choices*
- *to sharpen our critical thinking skills by applying scientific logic and coherent argumentation to our understanding of political phenomena*

Of course, you may have your own special reasons for studying comparative politics. Whatever your main field of study may be and whatever your personal goals, we hope this introductory text is sufficiently comprehensive to appeal to your interests and stimulate your curiosity about the world in which we live. By studying comparative politics, you will not only gain greater insight into the dangers afflicting the modern world as well as the extraordinary possibilities that lie before us; far more important, you will have a better understanding of how you fit into the global web of human interdependencies. By studying comparative politics, you will truly be studying *yourself* in relation to the rest of humankind.

KEY TERMS
(Underlined in the text)

Comparative politics
International politics
Interdependence
Globalization
International Monetary Fund (IMF)
Sovereignty

NOTES

1. The countries known to possess nuclear weapons are the United States (with 8,420 operational warheads—that is, bombs—and 3,650 in reserve or awaiting dismantlement in 1998); Russia (10,240 operational warheads and about 18,000 in reserve or awaiting dismantlement); Britain (200 operational warheads and 200 awaiting retirement or dismantlement); France (460 operational warheads and 50 awaiting dismantlement); China (425 operational warheads); Israel (70 to 125 nuclear weapons); India (60 to 80); and Pakistan (10 to 15). The four countries seeking to acquire nuclear weapons are North Korea, Iran, Iraq, and Libya. See The Arms Control Association's website, <www.armscontrol.org>.
2. The figure on child laborers is in the World Bank's *World Development Report 1999/2000* (New York: Oxford University Press, 1999), 62.
3. Ibid., 24–27. See also <www.populationinstitute.org>. Another source of information on economic development issues is the United Nations Development Program, which publishes an annual *Human Development Report* and other studies. Its website is <www.undp.org>. On global population issues, contact the website of the United Nations Population Fund at <www.unpfa.org>.
4. The WTO's website is <www.wto.org>.
5. *Compendium of Tourism Statistics, 1993–1997* (Madrid: World Tourism Organization, 1999).
6. The United Nations designated October 12, 1999, as the official birthday of the planet's 6 billionth person.

7. Robert B. Reich, *The Work of Nations* (New York: Alfred A. Knopf, 1991).

8. The IMF consists of 182 member countries; all contribute to its funds. The United States contributes $35 billion to the IMF's assets, 18 percent of the total. The United States is therefore entitled to 18 percent of the vote in IMF deliberations. The Fund's major decisions are taken by its executive committee, usually by consensus. For further information, contact <www.imf.org>.

9. Norman Myers and Nancy J. Myers, *The Primary Source: Tropical Forests and Our Future* (New York: W. W. Norton, 1992). Also, consult <www.rainforest.org>.

10. See the report by the United Nations Environment Program, *Global Environment Outlook 2000,* available online at <www.unep.org/geo2000>.

11. See the 1999 Global Appeal issued by the United Nations High Commissioner for Refugees, <www.unhcr.ch>.

12. Stephen D. Krasner, *Sovereignty: Organized Hypocrisy* (Princeton: Princeton University Press, 1999).

13. For arguments supporting the proposition that democracies are peaceful, see Immanuel Kant, *Perpetual Peace,* published in 1795; Bruce Russett, *Grasping the Democratic Peace* (Princeton: Princeton University Press, 1993); Michael W. Doyle, "Liberalism and World Politics," *American Political Science Review* 80, no. 4 (December 1986): 1151–69. For counterarguments, see Christopher Layne, "Kant or Cant: The Myth of the Democratic Peace," *International Security* 19, no. 2 (fall 1994): 5–49; and David E. Spiro, "The Insignificance of the Liberal Peace," ibid., 50–86.

CHAPTER 2

MAJOR TOPICS OF COMPARATIVE POLITICS

As we noted in chapter 1, science requires us to define our terms as accurately as possible. It is therefore only fitting that we begin this overview of major topics of comparative politics by defining politics itself. Though most people probably have a general idea of what politics is all about and though you can find any number of valid definitions of the term in dictionaries and textbooks, we present our own working definition here for the sake of clarity and consistency.

WHAT IS POLITICS?

Politics *is the process by which communities pursue collective goals and deal with their conflicts authoritatively by means of government.*

When we say that politics is a *process,* we mean that it is a continuing sequence of events and interactions among various actors, such as individuals, organizations, and governments. The concept of process also implies that these political interactions generally take place within a structure of rules, procedures, and institutions rather than haphazardly.

More than anything else, politics is about how people organize their communities for the purpose of collectively tackling the problems they face. A *community* can be any interacting collectivity of individuals, from the tiniest village to the world as a whole. In this book our main focus is on national communities, that is, entire countries and their national governments. We'll devote less attention to subnational administrative units (such as counties or cities) or to international organizations (such as the United Nations).

Whichever size the community may be, human beings from time immemorial have found ways to organize their interactions in order to promote various *goals* or endeavors. Perhaps the most basic goals sought by just about every country in the world are physical security and material well-being. Virtually all nations want to secure the safety of their population and territory against outside aggression, and most would want to improve their living standards. Beyond these basic goals, communities can choose from a long list of potential ones, from maximizing individual freedom to improving social welfare, from cleaning up the environment to building powerful military establishments.

In the best of circumstances, the members of a community are able to define and accomplish their goals on the basis of cooperation. But few communities are so fortunate as to be without conflict. Even if there is wide consensus on what the community's goals should be, conflicts frequently arise over how to go about achieving them. Indeed, many political observers would assert that conflict is the driving force of politics. At times these conflicts are fairly mild and can be dealt with in a peaceful manner through negotiation, bargaining, and compromise. But under less propitious circumstances political conflict may turn violent, exploding into bloody demonstrations, terrorism, or outright warfare.

Note that our definition says that politics involves "dealing with" conflict; it does not say "resolving" conflict. In some cases communities manage to resolve certain conflicts fairly decisively: government authorities impose a strike settlement, racial segregation is outlawed, a contentious tax bill becomes law. But in many cases the conflicts are not resolved or are settled only partially or temporarily: labor disputes keep flaring up, racial tensions persist, tax codes are made to be rewritten. Some conflicts are so intractable that they must be "dealt with" on a continuing basis over years or even decades. It may even happen that a society is so internally divided that *no* enduring settlement can be achieved. The result may be stalemate, civil war, or a one-sided dictatorship that imposes its will on the population.

The most important part of our definition refers to the manner in which communities pursue their goals and deal with their conflicts: they do so *authoritatively by means of government*. Actually, this phrase is a bit redundant: "authoritative action" in politics *means* "action taken by government." *Governments are "authoritative" to the extent that they make laws and enforce them.* In effect they have the final say in political matters and do not allow citizens to take the law into their own hands. We indulged in the redundancy in order to emphasize the central importance of government in political life. The term *politics*, after all, has all sorts of everyday usages, such as campus politics, office politics, and the like. But *politics as we study it in political science ultimately involves government in one way or another.*

It is government that makes authoritative decisions on the community's goals, whatever those goals may be. And it is to governments that people turn for authoritative decisions in dealing with their conflicts (for or against abortion, for or against handguns, and so on). Even people who want the government to stay out of a particular matter and leave the citizens free to deal with it on their own are still engaged in a political process

insofar as they seek to define the scope and limits of government authority. Whatever their nature, conflicts are "political" to the extent that governments are somehow involved, whether directly or indirectly, immediately or potentially, extensively or minimally.

How governments are organized, how they work, how people interact with them, and, in some cases, how they break down are topics of critical significance in comparative politics. So let's take a look at the two main forms of government in the modern world: **democracy** and **authoritarianism.**

DEMOCRACY AND AUTHORITARIANISM

A fundamental distinction must be made between two broad types of governmental system: *democracies* and *authoritarian governments*. Much of humankind's political history has been dominated by these two regimes. (The term **regime** means, among other things, **a form of government.**)

The essential idea of <u>democracy</u> *is that the people have the right to determine who governs them. In most cases they elect the principal governing officials and hold them accountable for their actions. Democracies also impose legal limits on the government's authority by guaranteeing certain rights and freedoms to their citizens.*

<u>Authoritarianism</u> *is the opposite of democracy.* Whereas democracy places the people above the government, *authoritarianism (or dictatorship) places the governing authorities above the people.* The people have little, if any, say in who governs them or how they are governed. Authoritarian regimes thus tend to be the principal violators of what advocates of democracy would regard as fundamental human rights, such as the right to free speech, the right to form political associations, religious freedom, and various other rights and liberties.

There are several different types of authoritarian government. Perhaps the oldest is the traditional monarchy, in which a king, queen, or emperor, often flanked by a small entourage of privileged nobles, wields exclusive power. A modern type of authoritarianism is a dictatorship run by a single political party with a virtually all-powerful leader. Hitler's Nazi regime in Germany or the communist governments of the Soviet Union and China are particularly virulent strains

FIGURE 2.1   Freedom Map of the World, 1999

Source: Freedom in the World 1998–1999. (New York: Freedom House, 1999) © 1999 Freedom House.

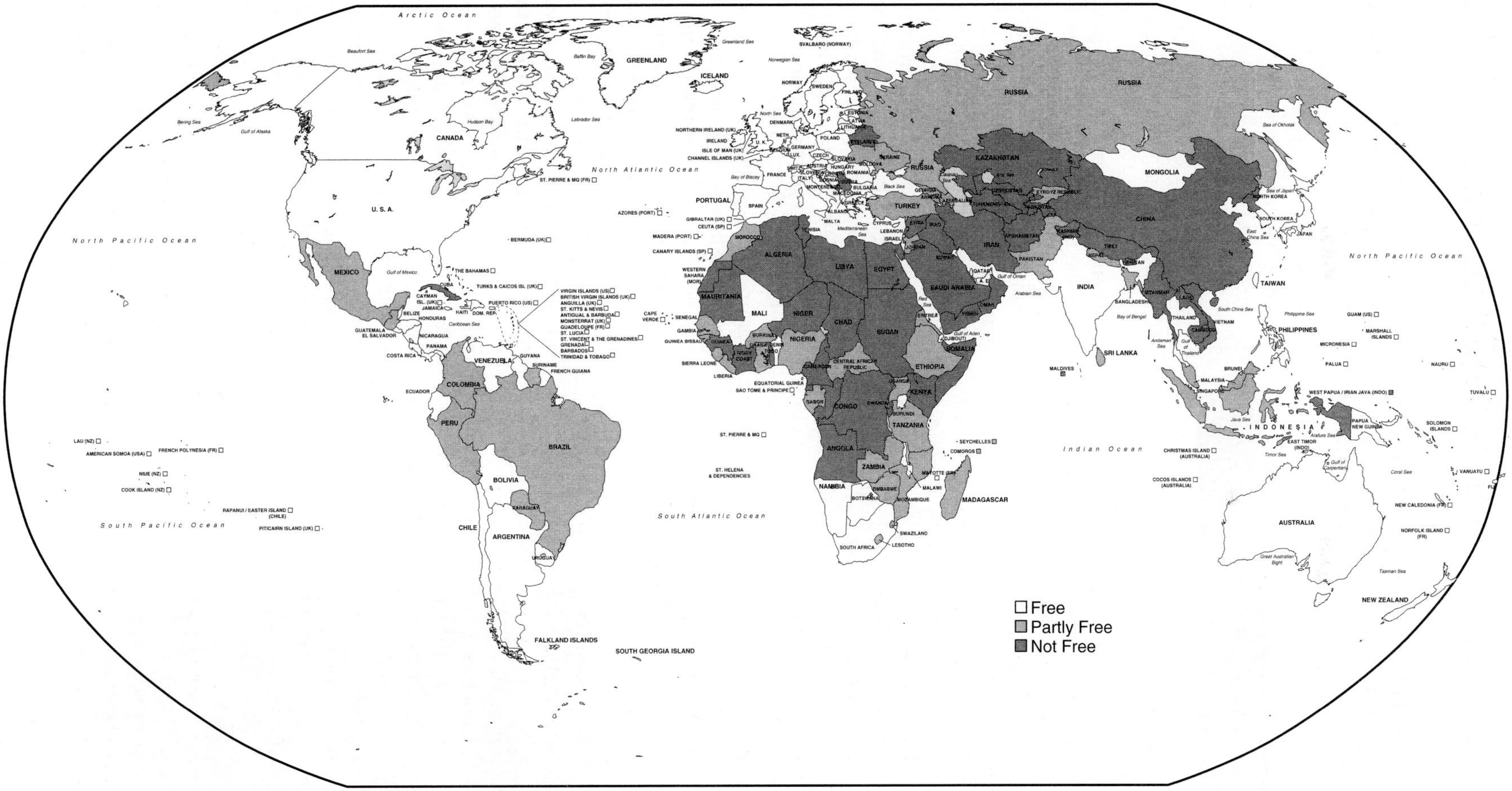

☐ Free
▨ Partly Free
▩ Not Free

of this kind of authoritarianism. Governments run by the military high command constitute yet another variant of authoritarianism. Myanmar is an example.

POLITICAL RIGHTS IN MYANMAR

A chill went through the hushed courtroom as the sentences were pronounced. Five American students, along with thirteen other human rights activists, had just been ordered to spend five years at hard labor in Burmese prisons. All had been found guilty of distributing leaflets in Rangoon on August 8, 1998 to commemorate the tenth anniversary of a pro-democracy uprising by Burmese students and workers against the country's military dictatorship.

Burma, officially known as Myanmar, has been governed by the military since 1962. Throughout its rule, the regime has been denounced by democratic governments and defenders of civil liberties as one of the world's most egregious violators of basic human rights. Aung San Suu Kyi, a Burmese pro-democracy activist, won the Nobel Peace Prize in 1991 for her courageous efforts to publicize the regime's oppressive activities, a crusade that also earned her several years of imprisonment and house arrest. The sentences just imposed on the eighteen activists who were drawn to her cause from neighboring countries and U.S. campuses prom-

ised to be brutally severe. Luckily, a Myanmar official immediately announced that the sentences would be suspended and the defendants allowed to return home as long as they agreed never to violate Burmese law again. Stark terror gave way to cheers of relief among the convicted activists, who were quickly deported. But the prospects for replacing decades of military authoritarianism with democracy in Myanmar had suffered a new setback.

Aung San Suu Kyi

Myanmar is one of many governments around the globe that are regularly condemned for fundamental human rights violations. Virtually all are authoritarian regimes, though even established democracies can be criticized for violating their own laws or for other transgressions, such as the mistreatment of prisoners. Democratic governments as well as non-governmental organizations such as Amnesty International and Human Rights Watch keep a vigilant eye on these violations, publicizing them through annual reports and other publications and mobilizing activists around the world through the Internet and other modes of communication. Anyone interested in getting involved in the global campaign for human rights should contact these organizations.[1]

The idea of authoritarianism is particularly attractive to rulers who believe that the vast majority of people are too ignorant, too selfish, or otherwise too incompetent to govern themselves wisely. People therefore need strong dictators to tell them what to do. Authoritarianism also attracts people who believe that any society that tolerates too much individual freedom is at the mercy of its richest or most ambitious members and is bound to suffer intolerable economic and social inequalities as a result. An all-powerful government, such people would argue, can distribute the goods of society to the population far more equitably. Still others have argued that democracy encourages too much conflict between social groups, political parties, and other competitors in the democratic process. Freedom, they insist, undermines national unity and promotes a level of disorder that borders on chaos. Dictatorial rule is therefore necessary to maintain domestic order and discourage potential aggressors. These arguments have been advanced by a rogues' gallery of dictators, from fascists like Germany's Adolph Hitler to military strongmen in numerous countries. But in the end, many, if not most, authoritarian regimes are designed mainly to assert the power of the ruler over the ruled. In these cases, power is an end in itself.

Although democracy and authoritarianism are fundamentally different, both are consistent with our definition of politics: they are authoritative institutions that make decisions on the community's goals and in dealing with its conflicts. Let us now make some explicit comparisons between democratic and authoritarian regimes with respect to the ways they approach these basic tasks of political life. In the process, we'll also identify some of the main topics of comparative politics.

POLITICAL PROCESSES

As we've indicated, politics is a process that takes place within a structure of rules and procedures. Viewed in the broadest of terms, the political process typically consists of *bargaining* or *coercion* or some combination of the two.

> **Bargaining** *is a process in which individuals and groups pursue their goals and deal with their conflicts through direct negotiation or indirect forms of exchange.*

Bargaining typically involves compromise, deal-making, or other forms of give-and-take. It can also involve efforts by one party to exert pressure on other parties. In most instances bargaining is a relatively peaceful process.

Coercion, by contrast, *means the use of force or the threat to use it.* In a coercive political process, A *forces* B to do something, often against B's will.

Democracies and authoritarian regimes employ both bargaining as well as coercion in their political processes. Democracies tend to favor bargaining. Voting, for example, is essentially a bargaining process in which candidates for office make various promises to the voters in exchange for their votes. Voters and candidates in effect bargain with one another over what the voters want and what the politicians believe they can deliver if they are elected. Once in office, government officials in democracies routinely bargain with one another at various levels—in the legislature, in the executive branch, or between the two—to work out laws and policies.

Bargaining is not the only process democracies employ, however; they also engage in coercion. All democracies are based on law and its effective enforcement. In its most extreme application, the enforcement of the law ultimately depends on force, even in a democracy. The police, the courts, and the penal system are all coercive institutions. It should not surprise us that the word *politics* derives from the same Latin and Greek roots as the word *police.*

Authoritarian regimes, for their part, are strongly oriented toward coercion. Many rule through outright force, using intimidation and terror to stay in power. The military, the secret police, and other forms of coercive power may be displayed quite demonstratively to keep the population and potential opposition groups in line. Still, even authoritarian regimes sometimes engage in bargaining. The mightiest dictators may seek to gain the people's acquiescence by providing economic and social benefits, in effect exchanging such goods for the population's tacit acceptance of the regime. Within the councils of government, meanwhile, the individuals who rule authoritarian regimes may bargain with one another over how to share power at the top or how to govern the country.

The two regime types also tend to differ in their use of certain institutional mechanisms that are typically involved in the political process. In addition to governmental institutions, various **non-governmental organizations (NGOs)** also play a major role in contemporary political life in most countries. **Political parties** and **interest groups,** for instance, frequently assume the important function of facilitating communication between the government and the population. They are known as "intermediate organizations" because they are located between the government and the people.

In democracies, the main role of parties is to field candidates for elective office, thereby providing voters with a choice among potential government officials. Interest groups are free to speak up for various segments of the population who want the government to do something for them. Labor unions, business associations, women's groups, and ethnic organizations are typically among the most well-organized interest groups, but democracy provides fertile ground for the proliferation of thousands of other groups and social movements, most of which take full advantage of their right to seek authoritative governmental action in their behalf.

In authoritarian regimes, by contrast, political parties and interest groups tend be instruments of the government's domination over the populace. The Nazi party of Hitler's Germany and the Communist Party of the former Soviet Union, for example, had the express aim of keeping the population under the strict control of the governing authorities while endeavoring to cultivate the public's support for their dictatorial rule. Other organizations set up by these governments served as instruments for maintaining control over the labor force, youth, journalists, and other segments of society. These organizations were known as "transmission belts" of party rule. In today's world the Chinese Communist Party maintains a stern monopoly on political power in the People's Republic of China.

In general, parties and interest groups facilitate the process of **political participation.** They play an important role in structuring the ways political leaders (or **elites**) as well as ordinary citizens (the **masses**) take part in the political process. Elite and mass political participation, in both democracies and non-democracies, are forms of **political behavior,** another important topic in the study of comparative politics.

When examining **elite behavior** in democracies, comparative politics looks for patterns among people who seek political leadership. What types of people run for office or become ardent political activists? It also looks at the various ways public officials behave when carrying out their roles as government officials. How responsive are they to the public? How do they go about making decisions? Are they corrupt?

When examining **mass behavior** in democracies, comparative politics investigates such things as the ways people vote. (What types of people vote regularly and what types tend to stay home on election day or turn their backs on any kind of political activity? What types of people tend to support liberal candidates, conservative candidates, socialists, communists, or others?)

In addition to addressing questions concerning participation and other forms of political behavior, students of comparative politics also investigate elite and mass **attitudes** about politics. How do people think about politics? What factors tend to motivate the ways they behave in political life? Are most people essentially driven by the quest for personal gain, or do altruistic considerations about the good of society as a whole affect political behavior? Specialists on democracy are particularly interested in the basic attitudes people have about government and political life, such as the extent to which they trust their government, tolerate others, or favor compromise. These attitudes can usually be ascertained through systematic public opinion surveys. *Widely shared attitudes toward politics form the basis of what is known as a country's* **political culture,** which constitutes another important topic in comparative politics.

Authoritarian regimes do not have competitive elections and rarely provide information about public opinion. Consequently, political behavior and attitudes are more difficult to study in authoritarian regimes than in democracies. Despite these limitations, it is still sometimes possible to make systematic observations about political behavior and political culture in such regimes. For example, some dictatorships have had to deal with unruly populations that are not afraid to demonstrate their discontent in spite of the government's coercive power. Poland under communist rule is a good example. From the earliest stages of Soviet-imposed communism at the end of World War II until the ultimate collapse of communism in 1989–90, millions of Poles dared to defy the governing authorities by openly supporting the Catholic Church, staging demonstrations and strikes, and organizing an independent trade union ("Solidarity") that proved instrumental in bringing down the communist regime. In stark contrast, other populations have put up with oppressive dictatorships with apparent resignation or even apparent approval. Until the late 1980s, most of the Soviet population fell into those categories, exhibiting few open signs of discontent.

In sum, political processes in both democracies and non-democracies offer much to consider. In addition to studying governments and intermediate organizations, students of comparative politics also look directly at *people,* focusing on the ways they behave in political life and how they think about politics.

GOALS

"To govern is to choose," runs an old adage. While democracies and authoritarian regimes may both pursue such things as national security and economic prosperity, and while both may find themselves unable to afford all their desired goals at once, the two regimes differ fundamentally in the ways they go about choosing their goals.

In keeping with democratic principles, democracies are guided by the free expression of public opinion and the free play of organized political parties and interest groups in determining what their goals shall be. Should the government lower taxes and reduce public expenditures, or instead increase welfare benefits to the population even if it means higher taxes? People are free to differ on these and other issues, and government officials responsible for making decisions on these issues will be held accountable for their actions on election day.

Authoritarian leaders also make decisions concerning the goals of the communities they govern, but they are less bound by public opinion or the views of organized opposition groups. Nevertheless, many a dictator has learned the hard way that a population seething with discontent may be very difficult to govern. Consequently, some authoritarian leaders have sought to cultivate the support of certain groups in society, such as the aristocracy, the business community, the working class, a favored religious or ethnic group, or some other segment of the population. Dictators may also seek to convince the population as a whole that the government's policies are good for them, and sometimes they succeed. Even so, dictators are nowhere near as formally accountable to their people as elected officials are.

SOURCES OF POLITICAL CONFLICT

What kinds of conflicts do communities and their governments typically face in political life, and how do democracies and authoritarian regimes tend to deal with them?

If we think about it, we can probably come up with a long list of real or potential issues that spark political controversy. In this book, we focus on *five main sources of political conflict:* **power, resources, social identity, ideas,** and **values.**

Power

Power centers on **domination** and **influence.** Throughout history, some people have dominated others. Masters have dominated slaves, aristocrats have dominated commoners, the rich have dominated the poor. If the government sides with any of these or other groups or plays some role in mediating between them, the question of who has power in society then becomes a question of who has **political power.**

If a particular group in society manages to gain control of the governmental apparatus, including the courts, the police, and the military, it can use that power to get its way all or most of the time, sometimes extending its domination over virtually the entire population. At various stages in history and in various countries, such groups as the upper class, the religious hierarchy, or a political party have exercised political dominance through their pervasive control of the government.

By contrast, if the government plays a mediating role between the various social and political groups in society, a certain balance of power may exist. In that case, no group may be able to exercise exclusive dominance over everyone else. Rather, society's main groups (such as business, labor, the middle class, religious groups, ethnic groups, and so forth) may try to *influence* the government to help them out or favor them in one way or another. These groups may use a wide variety of methods in seeking to exercise their influence: personal persuasion, public demonstrations, campaign contributions, votes on election day, bribery, and so forth. Typically, some of these groups will have more influence over government decision makers than others.

In most democracies, the predominant mode of exercising political power is *influence.* In accordance with the law, numerous participants in the political process compete with one another to gain political office or to induce the government to make favorable decisions in their behalf. In most authoritarian regimes, the predominant mode of political power is *domination.* In these regimes, a ruling clique typically monopolizes governmental authority and imposes its will on the population. However, as we shall see in chapter 5, patterns of domination as well as influence can be found in democracies and authoritarian governments alike. The point stressed here is that, regardless of the nature of the regime, politics is frequently a conflict over power itself.

Resources

Resources are another source of political contention. Land is a resource over which much blood has flowed in history. Many disputes both within and between countries have centered over the simple control of territory. Natural resources, such as oil, are also capable of stimulating intense political contention. Whether the issue concerns drilling rights in Alaska or the more explosive matter of who controls the Middle East's abundant petroleum reserves, oil has provoked conflicts ranging in severity from legislative wrangling to mortal combat.

Money itself is also a resource around which political controversy often swirls. How will next year's national budget be divvied up? How much will the government spend on the military, the elderly, students, big business, the sick, the poor, the middle class? How much will the government let individuals and businesses keep for themselves? Which policies will the government adopt to stimulate economic growth, reduce prices, or alleviate poverty?

Conflicts of these kinds are typically *economic* conflicts. **Political economy** *refers broadly to the relationship between politics and economics.* It constitutes yet another major topic in comparative politics. Students of political economy look at a wide variety of questions in which various resources are dealt with through the political process. Labor-management relations; class conflicts involving the rich, the poor, and those in between; governmental policies on economic growth, taxes, inflation, interest rates, the minimum wage, and a host of other issues related to the economy—such bread-and-butter issues are the raw stuff of political controversy on a day-to-day basis in virtually every country in the world.

How these conflicts work their way through the political process and how governments deal with economic issues can vary—at times considerably—from one country to the next. In some countries the government plays a relatively small or indirect role in the economy, leaving the better part of economic activity in the hands of private businesses and workers. Democracies tend to grant considerable latitude to private enterprise. Some theorists maintain that private enterprise is essential to democracy on the grounds that economic freedoms promote political freedoms. Although private businesses indeed abound in most democracies, democratic governments in today's world also play a major role in the national economy, raising taxes, regulating private businesses, and in some cases actually owning corporations.

Authoritarian regimes, for their part, are generally prone to restrict the freedoms of private enterprises. Control over the country's population requires control over its economy. A comparison of the economic policies of various authoritarian regimes, however, reveals considerable variability. In the most extreme cases, the government may own and operate virtually the entire economy, as was the case in the former USSR. Such a system is called a *centrally planned economy*. But even dictatorships sometimes allow private enterprise, though the government usually keeps a watchful eye on the private sector and may impose stringent regulations to make sure that its activities conform to the government's general policy objectives. Hitler's dictatorship in Nazi Germany, communist China since the 1980s, and various military dictatorships around the world have permitted private enterprise but have usually taken measures to ensure that the business sector complies with the government's economic and political goals.

The private sector and its activities—including the production of goods and services by businesses and their sale to consumers—are broadly referred to as the **market economy,** *or simply as* **the marketplace** *or* **markets.** *Government in general is frequently referred to as* **the state.**

One of the most important questions in comparative politics centers on the relationship between states and markets. How much economic activity should be controlled or regulated by the state, and how much should be left to the free play of market forces? This question is one of the most controversial in modern politics, in democracies as well as non-democracies, and it continues to spark vigorous debate and authoritative decisions in just about every country in today's world.[2]

Social Identity

Social identity constitutes a third source of political conflict. **Social identity** *refers to the ways in which individuals and groups are defined in society.* (Here we define society in simple terms as a country's population.) Every individual consists of a multiplicity of identities. Biologically, every person has a *gender identity,* a *racial* or *ethnic identity,* and a *generational* identity. Many people also identify themselves with some form of *religion,* whether it is an organized religion or a set of religious beliefs. (A non-religious attitude may also define religious identity.) Most people, as they enter school or the work force, acquire an *occupational identity:* as a student, for example, or a factory worker, a lawyer, or an unemployed parent. Educational attainments establish a person's *educational identity* as poorly educated, highly educated, or some intermediate category. Many people also belong to a particular socioeconomic *class,* such as the upper class, the middle class, or the poor. Some people may strongly identify themselves with the area or region in which they live. Southerners, country folk, suburbanites, and city dwellers exemplify various types of *regional identity.* Some people may identify themselves with a particular language group (or *ethno-linguistic* group), such as English-speaking Canadians and French-speaking Canadians. And most people share a *national identity* with their compatriots or their "people" (Americans, Japanese, Swiss, and so on).

The branch of comparative politics that focuses on how these various social identities and the groups associated with them behave in the political process is known as **political sociology.**

> **Political sociology** *is the study of the relationship between social identity and political behavior, and of how political power is distributed among social groups.*

All too often, conflict is the central behavior that arises from these different group identities. Conflicts over opportunities for women and homosexuals, racial or ethnic antagonisms, the clash of generations, religious strife or intolerance, class struggles, or regional rivalries can be found in almost every country in the world.

Whenever governments get involved in taking sides or mediating among conflicting identity groups, these conflicts become politicized. Sometimes social identity conflicts are closely associated with issues of power or resources. Christians may insist on dominating Muslims living in the same country, for example. Or the poor want access to financial resources to alleviate their poverty, resources that may have to come out of the pockets of the rich or middle classes. To the extent that governments intervene with the force of law to support the demands of Christians or Muslims, the poor or other classes, these identity conflicts become political conflicts over who has power or how the economy operates.

At a deeper and more personal level, however, social identity conflicts can be far more intense than issues involving just power or resources. They can be a matter of fundamental dignity and respect, qualities to which all human beings feel rightfully entitled. When our basic human worth is at stake, when the essence of who we are and how we live is bound up with profound emotional attachments to our ethnic group, our religion, our native region, or some other identity group, we can become fiercely determined to defend ourselves whenever our group is discriminated against or threatened by antagonistic forces. For this reason, identity conflicts are often extremely difficult to resolve.

Democracies and authoritarian regimes tend to deal with social identity conflicts, as with most other matters, in different ways. Democracies approach social conflicts through the ground rules of the democratic process: electoral competition, political bargaining, and the right to organize interest groups. In the most successful cases, democratic governments manage to reduce social antagonisms by helping the contending parties compromise their differences and cooperate on the basis of tolerance and non-discrimination. If cooperation proves impossible, governments may at least manage to keep the opposing groups from harming each other. Unfortunately, these ground rules are not always observed with scrupulous fairness. Democracies are not immune to social discrimination. Electoral majorities can find ways to subjugate minorities by supporting discriminatory laws or by refusing to support laws aimed at eliminating discriminatory practices. For much of its history, the United States has wrestled with the question of how—and at times even whether—to

TABLE 2.1

Socioeconomic Classes in the United States, 1996

Annual Income in Dollars	All Families (%)	White Families (%)	Black Families (%)	Hispanic Families (%)
Low income:				
Under $10,000	7.6	5.9	18.9	14.6
$10,000–14,999	6.1	5.4	10.7	11.6
Middle:				
$15,000–24,999	13.5	13.0	17.6	21.5
25,000–34,999	13.5	13.5	14.3	15.5
35,000–49,999	17.7	18.3	15.1	15.2
50,000–74,999	21.3	22.3	14.4	13.0
Upper:				
$75,000 and above	20.3	21.7	9.0	8.5

Source: U.S. Bureau of the Census, *Statistical Abstract of the United States 1998.*

integrate African Americans into the democratic process on an equal basis with whites. Until multiracial elections were held in 1994, South Africa's government represented the white minority, which comprised only 18 percent of the population, against the country's massive non-white majority. Other democracies have had their own difficulties implementing the ideals of democratic non-discrimination with respect to various social groups.

Still, for all their problems, democracies are usually better disposed than authoritarian regimes to dealing with social conflicts with relative fairness. Fairness is a democratic ideal that many authoritarian regimes cynically spurn. Quite a few dictatorships have rested on privileged social groups such as the upper class or a dominant ethnic or religious grouping. Most communist governments paid lip service to social equality but were actually ruled by a privileged communist party elite. At times these ruling elites have oppressed various subjugated groups with cold-blooded ruthlessness, taking full advantage of the government's ability to use its coercive powers without any legal restraint or accountability. Under more chaotic conditions, civil tranquillity may break down altogether if the government cannot prevent rival social groups from assailing one another. In recent decades such violent turmoil has plagued both democracies and authoritarian regimes alike, especially in countries torn apart by intractable ethnic or religious divisions.

In order to get a better understanding of how comparative politics addresses social identity, let's take a brief look at some issues connected with **class, ethnicity, religion, gender,** and **generational** identities. We'll be looking at these and other forms of identity conflict in greater detail at various points in this volume.

Class   The concept of class usually refers to the economic position of an individual or group in society. Class thus refers to a person's *socioeconomic identity.* The division of a country's population into socioeconomic classes is called *social stratification.*

Traditionally, there have been two main ways of determining the socioeconomic class to which people belong. One way, the objective approach, is to divide the population in accordance with specified levels of annual income or accumulated wealth. Those people falling within the designated brackets are automatically categorized within a specified class. Table 2.1 shows annual income levels in U.S. families in 1996 and arbitrarily draws the line between the middle and upper-income classes at $75,000.

Another way of assigning class status is more subjective: we simply ask people to which class they think they belong. The results of this self-assignment can at times be quite similar to the objective categories indicated in table 2.1, but by no means always. In contemporary Britain, for example, nearly two out of three adults identify themselves as "working class," even though many of them would be considered middle class by more objective measures. Most Americans tend to regard themselves as middle class, even if some have traditional working-class jobs. As a general

TABLE 2.2

Gini Coefficients and Income Distribution in Selected Countries

Country	Year	Gini Coefficient	Lowest 20%	Second 20%	Third 20%	Fourth 20%	Highest 20%
Slovakia	1992	19.5	11.9	15.8	18.8	22.2	31.4
Denmark	1992	24.7	9.6	14.9	18.3	22.7	34.5
Norway	1991	25.2	10.0	14.3	17.9	22.4	35.3
Sweden	1992	25.0	9.6	14.5	18.1	23.2	34.5
Finland	1991	25.6	10.0	14.2	17.6	22.3	35.8
Czech Republic	1993	26.6	10.5	13.9	16.9	21.3	37.4
Republic of China (Taiwan)	1995	27.7	(not available)				
Poland	1992	27.2	9.3	13.8	17.7	22.6	36.6
India	1994	29.7	9.2	13.0	16.8	21.7	39.3
Germany	1994	30.0	(not available)				
Italy	1991	31.2	7.6	12.9	17.3	23.2	38.9
Netherlands	1991	31.5	8.0	13.0	16.7	22.5	39.9
Canada	1991	31.5	7.5	12.9	17.2	23.0	39.3
United Kingdom	1995	34.6	7.1	12.8	17.2	23.1	39.8
France	1989	32.7	7.2	12.7	17.1	22.8	40.1
Israel	1992	35.5	6.9	11.4	16.3	22.9	42.5
United States	1994	40.1	4.8	10.5	16.0	23.5	45.2
People's Republic of China	1995	41.5	5.5	9.8	14.9	22.3	47.5
Nigeria	1992–93	45.0	4.0	8.9	14.4	23.4	49.3
Russia	1996	48.0	4.2	8.8	13.6	20.7	52.8
Mexico	1995	53.7	3.6	7.2	11.8	19.2	58.2
South Africa	1993–94	59.3	2.9	5.5	9.2	17.7	64.8
Brazil	1995	60.1	2.5	5.7	9.9	17.7	64.2

Sources: World Bank, *World Development Report 1999/2000;* Luxembourg Income Study.

rule, people act on their *perceptions* of reality: if they perceive themselves as middle class or working class, they are likely to behave accordingly, such as voting for politicians who represent their perceived class interests.

One approach to examining class identity is to analyze the distribution of wealth in society. There are several different methods of calculating the ratio of rich people to poor people quantitatively. One widely used measure is the **Gini coefficient** (or **Gini index**). This figure *measures the relative degree of socioeconomic inequality* within a particular country. *Perfect equality equals zero:* all individuals (or households) receive the same annual income; there is zero inequality. *Maximum inequality equals 100:* only one individual (or household) monopolizes all (100 percent) of society's income while everybody else gets nothing. Any number between 0 and 100 represents the degree to which society's income distribution pattern deviates from perfect equality.

The significance of the Gini index figures is largely relative: they show that some countries have a more equal sharing of wealth than others do. *The lower the Gini index, the greater the degree of socioeconomic equality; the higher the number, the greater the degree of inequality.* As table 2.2 shows, no country comes even close to perfect equality (zero); but among the countries selected here, real differences are evident. Note, for instance, that the United States has a higher Gini coefficient (hence more inequality) than the other economically advanced democracies listed here.

Another method of measuring class distinctions is to look at the percentage of national income of successive percentiles or quintiles of the population. Next to the Gini coefficient column, table 2.2 displays World Bank figures showing the percentage of annual national income that each succeeding fifth of the population earns. At the bottom of the table, for example, the figures show that in Brazil in 1995, the poorest 20 percent of the population collectively shared 2.5 percent of the nation's income; the second poorest 20 percent shared 5.7 percent; the next quintile shared 9.9 percent; and the next quintile got 17.7 percent of the country's income for that year. At the upper end of the income ladder, the wealthiest 20 percent of the Brazilian population earned 64.2 percent of all income in 1995. The richest fifth of the population thus collectively earned almost two-thirds of the nation's income. World Bank data also show that, in the same year, the richest 10 percent in Brazil kept 47.9 percent of the nation's income, while the bottom 10 percent divided up a mere 0.8 percent among themselves. The richest 10 percent were thus about 48 times richer than the poorest 10 percent. Brazil has the greatest income inequality of all the countries on the World Bank's list.

The other countries show a greater spread of annual income across their respective populations, but the extent of the spread varies measurably. Countries with the most evened out income distributions are at the top of the table. Note that the United States has the highest incidence of inegalitarian income distribution across the quintiles than the other economically advanced democracies shown in the table (such as Canada and the West European countries). In 1994, the bottom 10 percent of the U.S. population shared 1.5 percent of the national income, while the top 10 percent got 28.5 percent.

These and other World Bank figures point out that *all* countries are socially stratified, with the richest 20 percent possessing roughly 30 percent to 65 percent of society's wealth and the poorest 20 percent sharing about 12 percent or less. In some countries, however, a fairly sizable middle class located between these extremes holds the bulk of the nation's wealth (e.g., Britain, France, the United States). In other countries the middle class is decidedly smaller (e.g., Brazil, South Africa, Mexico).

In democracies and non-democracies alike, class distinctions are a powerful influence on political behavior and government policies. In democracies, class is one of the main factors affecting the way people vote. The commonly held notion that "people vote their wallet" captures this phenomenon. Though the actual impact of class identity on voting varies from country to country

as well as from election to election, the game of politics in most democracies revolves to a considerable degree around conflicts between the rich, the poor, and the middle classes over the national budget. These conflicts, in turn, affect such government policies as tax rates, education expenditures, and welfare benefits. Class distinctions also help explain why some people tend to vote or engage in other forms of political participation more regularly than other people do. Especially in the United States, wealthier citizens vote more often than the less wealthy.[3]

Indeed, social class often goes a long way to explaining how democracy itself comes about and endures over the long run. As many observers have pointed out, democracies tend to flourish when there is a vibrant middle class. Countries that are sharply polarized between a small number of extremely rich people and masses of impoverished laborers and peasants, with few middle-class professionals or private business people in between, are more likely to succumb to authoritarianism. Class issues are connected with authoritarianism in other ways as well. Karl Marx, the founder of modern socialist ideology, regarded class conflict as the single most important factor in political life. His ideas led to the formation of socialist and communist parties throughout the world.

In sum, class as a source of social identity is intimately bound up with how a society's economic resources are distributed among the population. Class conflicts, as a result, frequently overlap with conflicts over resources.[4]

Ethnicity   **Ethnicity** *is a form of group identification or distinctiveness based in many instances on a* **common biological ancestry** *in the distant past. More accurately, it is typically based on the* **belief** *in such a common biological ancestry*, because the fact itself cannot normally be proven with scientific accuracy.

The terms *ethnicity* and *ethnic group* sometimes refer to *race*. Traditionally, anthropologists and other scientists have applied the term *race* to only a few large groupings of human beings who are assumed to have various biological commonalities. Caucasians (whites), Negroids (blacks), Mongoloids (East Asians), and three or four other such groupings have often been characterized as the main racial categories. Despite certain noticeable physical differences, there is no such thing as a completely distinct race that is biologically separate from all other races. Each of these groups contains a mixture of biological characteristics, including blood types and DNA.

The same can be said for the many subgroups that fall within these larger racial categories. Caucasians, for example, include Indo-Europeans, a category that is further subdivided into such groupings as Scandinavians, Anglo-Saxons, Slavs, and others. These latter groups in turn can be further divided into smaller groupings. Slavs, for example, would include Russians, Poles, Czechs, Slovaks, Ukrainians, Serbs, Croats, and still others. Although each of these groups is typically defined as an ethnic group, none is biologically distinct. Any racial or ethnic group that is defined in biological terms is bound to consist of a mixture of biological influences—the result of mass migrations, invasions, and other forms of intergroup contact—stretching far back in unrecorded time. The notion that individual races or other biologically defined groupings are fundamentally distinct is symptomatic of *racism*, which falsely exalts some ethnic groups as genetically superior while demeaning others as fundamentally inferior.

To say that no ethnic group is biologically homogeneous, however, is not to deny the reality of kinship patterns within identifiable groups. Centuries of living together within relatively circumscribed geographical boundaries and intramarriage among members of the same group can create real biological bonds among its members. These bonds explain why so many ethnic groups define themselves on the basis of blood ties. Japanese, Germans, Koreans, Russians, and hundreds of other collectivities regard themselves as distinctive ethnic groups largely on the basis of kinship ties, forged in the course of a long history of living together. It is therefore perfectly acceptable to acknowledge that ethnicity often has a genuine biological basis, at least to some extent, as long as we also recognize that no ethnic group can certify an unbroken lineage from a unique set of identifiable common ancestors. As Donald Horowitz, a noted scholar of ethno-politics, puts it, ethnicity is frequently based on the "myth of collective ances-

try." Myths can be powerful integrative forces in ethnic identity, however.[5]

Kinship ties are not the only defining features of ethnicity. Ethnographers and other students of ethnicity also point to such non-biological phenomena as language, social customs, cuisine, clothing, art, and other cultural phenomena as factors that may distinguish one ethnic group from another. In some cases the concept of ethnicity may even include the group's predominant religious beliefs. More typically, however, ethnicity and religion are separate identities.

Despite the complexities of defining ethnicity, most people in today's world identify themselves with an ethnic group. It also happens that some people *are defined by others* as belonging to a particular ethnic group. In some countries, persons of mixed race, for example black and white, may be considered black (or, in some countries, colored) by others in society, irrespective of how such people might prefer to define themselves. Ethnic self-definitions, along with the definitions imposed on people by others, can have a profound effect on political behavior. Tragically, they can also lead to intractable political conflicts, at times with violent results. Here are just a few recent examples:

- **Yugoslavia** - The disintegration of communist Yugoslavia in the 1990s was accompanied by fierce fratricidal conflict among Serbs, Croats, and Bosnians. Many Serbs engaged in what they called "ethnic cleansing": the uprooting of non-Serbs from their towns and farms. All three of these groups are Slavs, and their main distinctions are religious in origin. Another round of ethnic cleansing occurred in Kosovo as Yugoslav forces depopulated the area of ethnic Albanians. After the 1999 war over Kosovo, ethnic antagonisms between Kosovar Albanians and Serbs continued in spite of the presence of a 50,000-strong international peacekeeping force.
- **Sudan** - Approximately 1.5 million people in Sudan have perished in a civil war that has raged since 1983 between the largely Arab majority, who reside mostly in the northern part of the country and dominate its government, and black groups located mostly in the south.
- **Sri Lanka** - This island nation, once known as Ceylon, has been ravaged by a civil war since

1983 between the largest ethnic group, the Sinhalese, and their main ethnic rivals, the Tamils, who comprise about 18 percent of the population. Some 57,000 people have lost their lives.

Religion Religion is another social identity that can have a demonstrable impact on the way people behave in politics. Whether people are devout adherents of a particular faith or outspoken atheists, attitudes toward religion often influence how they vote, how they view the relationship between church and state, and how tolerant they are of those who profess a different faith. In the United States and other democracies, for example, religious affiliation influences the way at least some voters cast their ballots on election day. When a Catholic voter supports pro-life candidates because the church opposes abortion, or when an advocate of the strict separation of church and state opposes prayers in public schools, religion takes on a political character. In Israel, many voters cast their ballots on the basis of one of several alternative interpretations of Judaism, while many Israeli citizens vote as Muslims or on the basis of non-religious attitudes.

In the most tranquil of circumstances, societies divided along religious lines find a way to permit adherents of different religions to live peacefully side by side, at times minimizing the role of the state in religious affairs. The United States is a premier example. Some countries have an official church. In Britain, for example, the Church of England is the *established church,* which mainly means that the monarch is its formal head. And some countries are **theocracies**, *which are governments run by the clergy.* Iran is a current example.

In some cases religious identity gives rise to sharp political conflict. (Religious conflict is often called *sectarian,* from the word *sect.*) Sectarian strife at times takes a violent turn because of the passion and certitude with which many people profess their creed. The Yugoslav crisis, for example, has religious dimensions, inasmuch as Serbs are mostly Orthodox, Croats and Slovenes are mostly Roman Catholics, and Bosnians and Kosovar Albanians are largely Muslims (see chapter 7). Ethnic divisions in Sudan are reinforced by religious divisions: the Arabs are predominantly Muslim whereas blacks are mostly animist or Christian. Sectarian violence in Northern Ireland between

Protestants and Catholics claimed more than 3,200 lives from 1969 to 1999. Lebanon, a country with no fewer than seventeen officially recognized religious groups, was shattered from 1975 to 1991 by a civil war that involved contending Christian and Muslim factions and resulted in more than 150,000 deaths.

Religious differences intensified a conflict centered on East Timor in 1999. The island was colonized by Portugal starting around 1520, and most of its inhabitants became Catholics. After the Portuguese left, Indonesia under President Suharto invaded the island in 1975 and annexed it. The Indonesians are predominantly Muslim. Sporadic violence and starvation claimed 200,000 lives over the ensuing decades. After Suharto's departure, 78.5 percent of East Timorese voted for full independence in a 1999 referendum. The vote sparked a rampage by Indonesian troops, who drove some 800,000 people from their homes before United Nations troops stepped in to restore order.

Gender Ever since the 1960s and 1970s, feminist movements around the world have been quite vocal in promoting general public awareness of the subaltern status of women in various spheres of social and political life. In some cases, governments have responded. Legislation has been passed in a number of countries to address such issues as job discrimination and sexual harassment. In other cases, governmental action has not been as effective as many women would wish, even in democ-

Corazón Aquino

racies. In most non-democracies, women have few or no opportunities to speak up for a more equitable status in society. Afghanistan for example, is governed by a group of Islamic fundamentalists known as the Taliban. Their strict religious codes forbid women from attending school or taking jobs and subject them to various additional forms of oppression. These measures have provoked an international outcry. In India, Bangladesh, and other countries, killings and suicides over dowries are common, as are indignities imposed by centuries-old customs. Various African groups practice the ritual genital mutilation of women. Rape and domestic violence are common around the world, and in many countries such acts routinely go unpunished. An international women's rights conference sponsored by the United Nations in 1996 addressed some of these issues.

Despite the fact that politics is a male-dominated enterprise in virtually every country in the world, women have registered some important gains in recent decades, at least in democratically governed countries. Since the 1970s, the number of women who have succeeded in gaining positions in the executive, legislative, or judicial branches of government has risen appreciably in most economically advanced democracies. In a few cases women have risen to the apex of the political pyramid. Women who have occupied the post of elected head of state or government in recent years include the following:

Corazón Aquino, president of the Philippines, 1986–92

Sirimavo Bandaranaike, prime minister of Sri Lanka, 1960–65, 1970–77, and 1994 to present

Benazir Bhutto, prime minister of Pakistan, 1988–90 and 1993–96

Gro Harlem Brundtland, prime minister of Norway, 1981 and 1986–89

Kim Campbell, prime minister of Canada, 1993

Violeta Chamorro, president of Nicaragua, 1990–97

Mary Eugenia Charles, prime minister of Dominica, 1980–95

Tansu Ciller, prime minister of Turkey, 1993–96

Edith Cresson, prime minister of France, 1991–92

Vigdis Finnbogadottir, president of Iceland, 1980–96

Indira Gandhi, prime minister of India, 1966–1977 and 1980–84

Tarja Halonen, president of Finland, 2000 to present

Sheik Hasina, prime minister of Bangladesh, 1996 to present

Violeta Chamorro

Indira Gandhi

TABLE 2.3

Percentage of Female Members of Lower House or Unicameral Legislature in Selected Democracies (April 2000)					
Country	%	Country	%	Country	%
Sweden	42.7	Mexico	18.2	Slovenia	10.0
Denmark	37.4	Estonia	17.8	Nicaragua	9.7
Finland	36.5	Lithuania	17.5	Bangladesh	9.1
Norway	36.4	Botswana	17.0	India	9.0
Netherlands	36.0	Latvia	17.0	Hungary	8.3
Iceland	34.9	Czech Republic	15.0	Indonesia	8.0
Germany	30.9	Burundi	14.4	Ukraine	7.8
Mozambique	30.0	Slovakia	14.0	Russia	7.7
South Africa	29.8	Jamaica	13.3	Romania	7.3
New Zealand	29.2	Poland	13.0	Greece	6.3
Bosnia & Herzegovina	28.6	United States*	12.9	Brazil	5.7
Venezuela	28.6	Israel	12.5	Japan	5.0
Spain	28.3	Philippines	12.4	Turkey	4.2
Argentina	26.5	Mali	12.2	South Korea	3.7
Switzerland	23.0	Ireland	12.0	Algeria	3.4
Australia	22.4	Bolivia	11.5	Nigeria	3.4
Croatia	20.5	Italy	11.1		
Canada	19.9	France	10.9		
Costa Rica	19.3	Chile	10.8		
United Kingdom	18.4	Bulgaria	10.8		

*The 100-member U.S. Senate had 9 women.
Source: International Parliamentary Union, <www.ipu.org>.

Chandrika Bandanraike Kumaratunga, prime minister of Sri Lanka, 1994; president, 1994 to present

Mary McAleese, president of Ireland, 1997 to present

Golda Meir, prime minister of Israel, 1969–74

Isabel Perón, president of Argentina, 1974–76

Mary Robinson, president of Ireland, 1990–99

Hanna Suchocka, prime minister of Poland, 1992–93

Margaret Thatcher, prime minister of the United Kingdom, 1979–90

Khaleda Zia, prime minister of Bangladesh, 1991–96

Despite these high achievements, women are still under-represented in the governmental structures of most democracies today; that is, their share of governmental positions is less than their share of the population, which is usually 50 percent or slightly more. By the spring of 2000, women held only 13.8 percent of the seats in 177 national parliaments. As table 2.3 illustrates, they do better in some countries than in others.[6]

When political scientists look at the role that gender plays in shaping political behavior, one of the essential questions they ask is, to what extent is the political activity of women determined *mainly* by their identity as women? In other words, do women vote primarily *as women* for candidates who favorably address women's issues? Are the political opinions and attitudes of women shaped fundamentally by their gender? Or do women behave essentially the same as men?

In most democracies the answers are mixed. Some women place gender above all other considerations in their political activity, but by no means do all women within a given society do so. Opinion surveys show that large numbers of women think and vote differently from men on a host of political issues, but many other women agree with men on the same topics and vote accordingly.[7] In virtually every country in the world, gender is a social identity that frequently has important political implications, even in those countries where women's voices are largely silenced.

Age "Never trust anyone over 30!" was the cynical warning echoed by millions of young Americans who came of political age in the 1960s, the decade in which the term *generation gap* captured the clash of attitudes between the young and their elders on a spectrum of issues ranging from the Vietnam war to sex.[8] Although this tumultuous period has receded into history, generational factors have in fact always played a prominent role in the political life of most countries. According to one hypothesis, every generation tends to be stamped by the political and social events of its youth. The attitudes that most people take through life, in this view, are substantially molded by the political experiences they encounter in their teens and twenties. In the United States, for example, successive generations of youth came of age during the Great Depression of the 1930s; World War II; the Cold War; Vietnam; the decades of rising prosperity and budget deficits of the 1970s and 1980s; and the post–Cold War decade of the 1990s. Each succeeding age cohort could not help but be affected by the defining events of their early adult years.

As a general rule, different generations are likely to have different political outlooks. In contemporary Russia, for example, those citizens who favor a revolutionary transition from an authoritarian state to a democratic one and from a state-controlled economy to a more liberal one tend to be less than forty years old; older people are more likely to be resistant to these changes. Dramatic demands for radical change on the part of Chinese students occurred in 1989 when young pro-democracy demonstrators occupied Tiananmen Square in the heart of Beijing for several weeks before being crushed by troops called into action by the aging communist party leadership. With many leading officials in their eighties, China at the time was a true **gerontocracy:** a government of old people. Throughout history, young people—especially students—have frequently been in the forefront of movements for political transformation in numerous countries around the world, waving the banners of such contradictory causes as democracy and fascism, global harmony and national assertiveness, peaceful reform and violent

TABLE 2.4

Generational Trends in Selected Countries

	Population over 65 (%)			
	1950	**1975**	**2000**	**2025**
United States	8	10	12	16
United Kingdom	10	14	15	17
Sweden	10	15	16	20
Japan	5	7	15	23
China	5	5	6	11

	Workers per Retiree	
	1995	**2025**
United States*	4.7	3.3
Canada	5.2	2.7
Japan	2.8	2.1
France	2.8	1.7
Germany	3.1	2.3
Italy	2.4	1.8

*In the 1930s, the ratio of workers per retiree in the United States was 42:1.
Sources: United Nations; *Washington Post,* 31 October 1995 and 20 December 1995.

revolution. In recent years courageous young activists, boldly risking incarceration or death, have pressed their demands for democracy against entrenched dictatorships in Indonesia, Iran, Nigeria, Mexico, Myanmar, and elsewhere.

On a somewhat more mundane economic level, demographic trends in recent years have set the stage for what may turn out to be significant generational conflicts in a number of countries. As the elderly come to constitute a rising percentage of the population, younger people may have to pay higher taxes and make other sacrifices in order to satisfy the needs of older generations for adequate pensions, health care, and other necessities. Table 2.4 shows some of these trends.[9]

Cross-Cutting and Polarizing Cleavages As we examine these and other social identity conflicts in the ensuing chapters, we should keep in mind the distinction between **cross-cutting cleavages** and **polarizing cleavages.** Social divisions (or cleavages) are said to be **cross-cutting** *when the various factors that make up an individual's social identity tend to pull that person in* **different** *political directions.* Take, for example, a twenty-year-old

FIGURE 2.2   Cross-Cutting and Polarizing Social Cleavages

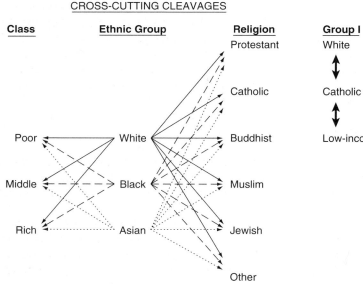

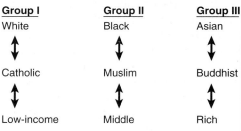

African-American female student in New York City who is a devout Catholic opposed to abortion, whose parents together earn $100,000 a year, and who hopes to pursue a career in the military. Public opinion polls and voting studies demonstrate that most African Americans, most females, most college students, and most New Yorkers in the 1990s tended to vote for Democrats in presidential and Congressional elections, whereas most opponents of abortion, most upper-income families, and most military officers tended to vote Republican. In the jargon of political sociology, this individual's ethnic, gender, generational, and regional identities are said to *cut across* her class, religious, and career identities, leading her to support Democrats on some issues and Republicans on others.

Social cleavages are **polarizing** *when the factors composing one's social identity tend to pull in the* **same** *political direction.* Consider a forty-five-year-old white male corporate executive who earns $250,000 a year and who is a born-again evangelical Protestant residing in Charleston, South Carolina. Every one of his separate social identities reinforces the others in a cumulative fashion to pull him toward the Republicans and away from Democratic candidates. By contrast, a twenty-five-year-old Hispanic female agnostic earning $20,000 a year as a

clerk in New York City has all the attributes of a typical Democratic voter. In terms of their various social identities, these two people are polar opposites. Of course, they are both free individuals and may vote any way they please. There is nothing to prevent the former from voting for Democrats or the latter from voting solely for Republicans. All we can do as political scientists is *hypothesize* how these individuals *may* vote, given the general voting patterns of the population. Once these two people have voted, however, and all the votes are counted, real voting patterns invariably emerge.

Now let's move from individual cases to entire countries. Suppose Country X has a highly complex society with a diversity of ethnic groups (white, black, Asian, etc.). *Each one* of these ethnic groups has members at different socioeconomic levels (low-income, middle class, rich) and *each one* has members who profess different religions (Catholic, Muslim, Buddhist, Protestant, etc.). This society as a whole is characterized by *cross-cutting cleavages*: ethnicity cuts across class and religion in a multiplicity of ways (see figure 2.2).

Country Z, by contrast, consists of three *completely unique* groups, each with a distinctive combination of social identities. For example, all the whites are impoverished Catholics, all the blacks are middle-class Muslims, and all the Asians are rich Buddhists. There are no other combinations of ethnicity, class, and religion. Within each group, the key factors of social identity combine in such a way as to create three polarized groups with virtually nothing in common.

Which of these two hypothetical countries is more likely to be characterized by cooperation and compromise, and which is more likely to be divided into hostile social camps unable to find common ground on anything? Most political scientists would hypothesize that the society of Country X, characterized by cross-cutting cleavages, is better suited for democracy and cooperative interaction than deeply polarized societies. In view of its extreme polarization, Country Z is a prime candidate for prolonged social confrontation, political stalemate, and, in the worst of scenarios, a civil war that might only be terminated by the dictatorial domination of one group over the other two. As a general rule, whenever two or more identities reinforce each other, social conflicts are likely to be all the more intense.

Ideas

Ideas also spark political controversy. Some of the oldest and most contentious conflicts in world history have centered on political ideas. In some cases these conflicts have revolved around what may be called the "grand questions" of politics: What is the best form of government? What is the optimal way of resolving conflicts in society? What should the community's most important goals be? freedom? equality? social welfare? military strength?

Not surprisingly, such grand questions have provoked a variety of grand answers. The most far-reaching and intellectually ambitious of these political grand designs are called **ideologies.**

> An **ideology** *is a coherent set of ideas and guidelines that defines what the nature and role of government should be and prescribes the main goals the community should pursue through political action.*

Democracy, socialism, and *fascism* are among the most influential political ideologies that have emerged over the course of humankind's political development. Other political ideologies have derived from various religions, such as *Christian*

Democracy, Zionism (which derives from Judaism), and various ideological orientations that stem from Islam. Each of these ideologies spells out certain ideas about the proper role of government and the relationship between the ruling authorities and the population. Whereas some ideologies and their variants favor democracy, others espouse authoritarianism. Each one of these broad ideologies, moreover, has variations.

Democracy as an ideology has at least two main tendencies:

- **Liberal democracy** tends to emphasize the freedom of the individual. Intellectual and religious freedom, freedom of speech, freedom to participate in political life, and the freedom to own and operate one's own private business are among the chief liberties celebrated in the liberal-democratic tradition. As a rule, liberal democracy favors serious limitations on the powers of government so as to maximize personal liberty.
- **Social democracy** tends to emphasize the collective welfare of society as a whole. Although it also favors freedom of thought, speech, religious worship, and political activity and although it may favor a certain amount of private economic enterprise, social democracy seeks to ensure a certain minimum level of economic welfare for all members of society while striving to expand general welfare as much as possible. To this end, social-democratic ideology favors expanding the powers of government and limiting the liberties of private enterprise so as to provide the population with such benefits as education, adequate health care, unemployment insurance, and retirement pensions.

In reality, most modern democracies, such as the United States, Canada, and the countries of Western Europe, seek to strike a balance between the freedoms of liberal democracy and the benefits of social democracy. Still, some of these countries tend to lean more heavily in one of these two ideological directions. The United States usually leans toward liberal democracy (though it also provides numerous social welfare benefits), whereas most West European countries typically lean toward social democracy (though they also provide basic political and economic liberties). The tension between liberty and welfare is one of the central characteristics of politics in most democracies today.

Socialism is an ideology whose central premise is that an economy based on private enterprise (also known as *capitalism*) places excessive economic and political power in the hands of a small band of private entrepreneurs. Socialists contend that this capitalist elite, driven exclusively by greed for profits, invariably uses its powers to exploit the working masses who constitute the vast majority of the population. Socialist ideology maintains that humanity would be better off if the free-enterprise system were abolished altogether. In its place, a socialist economy would put control over factories, farms, banks, stores, and other economic enterprises in the hands of the people as a whole. Once the majority of the population controls the economy, it can reorganize economic life so as to promote the welfare of all rather than the privileges of a few.

While generally agreeing on these basic axioms, socialists have historically disagreed over *how* the ideals of socialism should be put into practice.

Karl Marx (1818–1883), the most influential theorist of socialist ideology, believed that a socialist society would not require any government at all. In his view, governments are always agents of social domination: they permit the most powerful groups in society (such as the capitalists) to exercise control over the weaker ones (the workers). Socialism, in his view, would put a definitive end to all forms of social domination, thereby obviating the need for all-powerful governmental authority. Everyone would belong to one large class of humanity working harmoniously for the common good. Marx did not view socialism in authoritarian terms; he saw it as a liberating force that would free the masses from economic exploitation.

Soviet-style communists, by contrast, believed in an all-powerful government operated by a well-organized communist party claiming to represent the workers. Under such leaders as **V. I. Lenin** (1870–1924) and **Joseph Stalin** (1879–1953) in Russia, and **Mao Zedong** (1893–1976) in China, communists of this type set up oppressive authoritarian regimes that placed exclusive political and economic power in the hands of a small party elite. Although they considered themselves Marxists because they opposed private enterprise, they deviated significantly from Marx's design for an unregimented socialist paradise by erecting ruthless dictatorships that dominated the populations they ruled, often through intimidation and mass violence.

Additional variants of socialist ideology have been advanced by other theoreticians and political activists.

Fascism is an ideology that emerged in various parts of Europe in the 1920s and 1930s. Its most malignant manifestation was **Adolph Hitler's** Nazi movement, which ruled Germany from 1933 to 1945. Hitler and his Nazi cohorts opposed democracy on the grounds that it undermined the unity of the German people. In their view, the solidarity and strength of the German nation were the supreme political values. The German nation, moreover, was defined in strictly racial terms: Jews and other so-called non-Aryans were stigmatized as subhumans and ultimately targeted for extermination. Proponents of social democracy and communism were similarly vilified as traitors.

As Germany's first experiment with democracy (1919–1933) degenerated into squabbling factions and a deteriorating economy over the course of the 1920s and early 1930s, the Nazis promised order, prosperity, and a resurgence of national pride. Once in power, they abolished all democratic rights and freedoms and set Germany on a headlong path toward war, which culminated in the ultimate destruction of Hitler's fascist rule.

Fascists also succeeded in taking power in Italy. Under the leadership of **Benito Mussolini** (1883–1945), the Italian fascist party took control of the government in 1922. Like its German counterpart, Italian fascist ideology stressed the importance of national solidarity and pride, opposing democracy and glorifying military strength.

Although ideologies may constitute the grand ideas of politics, they are not the only examples of how ideas can stir up political conflict. On a more routine level, ideas are constantly at the heart of political dialogues and controversies in both democracies and authoritarian regimes. In democracies, people are constantly debating such issues

FIGURE 2.3   The Left-Right Spectrum

Radical left	Communism	Democracy	Conservative authoritarian regimes (monarchies, military governments, etc.)	Fascism

as what the proper role of government should be and which policies the government should adopt in addressing the community's problems. Even authoritarian regimes must decide from a menu of alternative ways of pursuing the ruling elite's chosen goals. Here, too, contending ideas may come into play as the governing authorities, even with little or no input from the populations they rule, go about making day-to-day decisions about domestic and foreign affairs. Regardless of the political system, political ideas and ideologies are major topics of comparative politics.

Political ideologies can be placed along a **left-right spectrum.** The terms <u>left</u> and <u>right</u> in politics derive from the French Revolution. When the French legislature known as the Convention convened in 1792, revolutionaries who favored replacing the monarchy with a fundamentally different political system took their seats to the left of the presiding officer, and conservatives who wished to preserve the monarchy were seated to his right. Moderates who sought some kind of compromise gathered in the center. These seating arrangements endured and so did the political alignments associated with them. Accordingly, proponents of political change became known as *leftists* (or the *left wing*), conservative advocates of the status quo became known as *rightists* (or *right-wingers*), and those in the middle became identified, quite appropriately, as *centrists*. Over time these generic meanings caught on in other countries as well.

Radicals are people at the extreme ends of either the left or right. Leftwing radicals favor the most thorough-going changes, such as all-out revolution. The most extreme right-wing radicals are often called *reactionaries* because they want to turn the clock back to some previously existing (or idealized) governmental system or concept of government. The term *radical* derives from the Latin *radix*, meaning "root." Radicals are not content with superficial measures; they want to change things at their roots.

Over the course of the nineteenth and twentieth centuries certain political ideologies became identified as leftist or rightist. Socialism in its many shadings became permanently identified as a leftist orientation. Conservatism, whether authoritarian or democratic in nature, became identified with the political right. Fascism is typically regarded as an extreme right-wing ideology. In most contemporary democracies the distinctions between the main left and right orientations are not very extreme. In the United States, most Democrats are slightly left of center and most Republicans are slightly right of center. Roughly similar distinctions between a moderate left and a moderate right can be found among mainstream parties in Western Europe, Japan, and other contemporary democracies. To be sure, more extreme leftist or rightist movements can also be found in some of these countries, but politics tends to be dominated by parties that gravitate toward the center of the left-right spectrum. In football terms, the game of politics in these countries is played mostly in midfield, between the forty-yardlines.

Values

<u>Values</u> *may be defined as spiritual or moral principles, ideals, or qualities of life that people favor for their own sake.*

Among the most important values to be found in political life are *freedom, justice, equality, security, order,* and *community.* People often cherish these principles and ideals because of their intrinsic merit in promoting human dignity and civilized relationships, not simply because they may confer wealth or power. In addition, people may also attach a special value to certain qualities of life. A healthy environment, for example, or "family values" may be prized for their own sake as a desirable or necessary condition of civilized existence.

What makes these values *political* is that people often call on their governments to provide or guarantee them. Freedom to express political or religious views or to operate a private business may be secured by specified constitutional rights. Justice in the application of the law requires a fair judicial system. A healthy environment may necessitate legislation against pollution or government funding of cleanup activities, and so on.

Political conflicts may arise over values for a variety of reasons. Sometimes the multiple values that a society favors may clash with one another, making it difficult or impossible to fulfill one value without limiting another. Freedom and equality are frequently in conflict, for example. The freedom to operate a business without any governmental interference, despite the attendant risks of failure and bankruptcy, may clash with employees' demands for a just wage and social welfare benefits or for the non-discriminatory treatment of females or ethnic minorities in the workplace. To ensure the rights of the labor force and a measure of social fairness, governments may infringe on the freedoms of the private entrepreneur. Similarly, peoples' freedom to keep as much of their earnings as possible may clash with the desire of other people for greater egalitarianism through social welfare benefits, which may require higher taxes. The clash over abortion rights is fundamentally a clash over values: pro-life groups place their primary value on the rights of the unborn child; pro-choice groups place their primary value on the rights of parents to determine how many children they will bring into the world.

Some political values tend to promote democracy, while others are often invoked to justify authoritarian rule. Freedom is one of the most hallowed democratic values, one that is seldom, if ever, embraced by dictators. People who support authoritarian regimes attach a higher value to order than to freedom and justify the use of dictatorial rule and unrestrained force as necessary to ensure domestic tranquillity. Indeed, democracy ultimately rests on certain core values that include not only freedom but also the notion that human dignity and equality are impossible under dictatorial oppression and require the state's full accountability to the people. The clash between democracy and dictatorship is thus in large measure a clash over values, not simply a conflict over power or resources.

On a global scale, some of the most contentious issues in today's world center around values. Whereas proponents of liberal democracy and private enterprise cherish freedom and individualism, some people reject these ideals as "Western values" that they regard as incompatible with the prevailing cultural norms and value systems of their own societies. For example, some East Asians, (though by no means all) regard the West's exaltation of individual freedom as dangerously excessive and argue that it leads to decadent egoism and social breakdown. They prefer what they call "Asian values," which stress the individual's responsibilities to the collective community, deference to established authority, hard work, frugality, and intense family loyalty. Although these values are rooted in Confucianism, a philosophy with centuries-old roots in China, they are by no means confined to East Asia. Other schools of thought embrace a roughly similar set of values, including various tendencies associated with Islam, the Eastern Orthodox churches, and other religious and philosophical traditions. At times their proponents can be harshly critical of the West, insisting that Western concepts of accountability and human rights are ill-suited to their own countries and cannot be applied there.[10]

While there is no doubt that societies differ in the priorities they attach to core values and that the West's value system is by no means universally copied or admired, many advocates of democracy insist that its basic procedures are universally applicable and can be adapted to local cultures and value systems. Not coincidentally, they point out, some people who place a higher value on deference to authority are authoritarian rulers and their apologists. According to this argument, Asian values and other non-Western value systems are not incompatible with democratic modes of government, despite the fact that the idea of liberal democracy originated in the West and is practiced mainly in the West. The question of whether the values of liberal democracy can be universally adapted has sparked one of the central political conflicts of our time.

In sum, all governments have to deal with conflicts of one kind or another. One of the chief differences between democratic governments and authoritarian ones is that democracies deal with their conflicts out in the open, through procedures that guarantee the government's accountability to the public, whereas authoritarian regimes typically deal with their conflicts behind closed doors and with little or no accountability. *Democracy is not a recipe for eliminating conflict; rather, it is a mechanism for dealing with it in accordance with generally accepted rules.* As we shall see in greater detail in the coming chapters, the many ways that governments and their populations deal with these conflicts and the ways they cooperate in achieving their goals provide the essence—and the fascination—of comparative politics.

KEY TERMS
(Underlined in the text)

Politics
Democracy
Authoritarianism
Non-governmental organizations (NGOs)
Political culture
Political economy
Market economy
Social identity
Political sociology
Gini coefficient
Ethnicity
Theocracy
Cross-cutting cleavages
Polarizing cleavages
Ideology
Liberal democracy
Social democracy
Socialism
Fascism
Left
Right
Values

NOTES

1. The website of Amnesty International is <www.amnesty.org>. The website of Human Rights Watch is <www.hrw.org>. The U.S. State Department also publishes an annual human rights report, available on its website at <www.state.gov>. On the rise in international human rights activism, see Margaret E. Keck and Kathryn Sikkink, *Activists Beyond Borders* (Ithaca, N.Y.: Cornell University Press, 1998).

2. Daniel Yergin and Joseph Stanislaw, *The Commanding Heights: The Battle Between Government and the Marketplace That Is Remaking the Modern World* (New York: Simon and Schuster, 1998).

3. Sidney Verba, Norman H. Nie, and Jae-on Kim, *Participation and Political Equality: A Seven-Nation Comparison* (Cambridge: Cambridge University Press, 1978).

4. For an overview, see Patrick Joyce, ed., *Class* (Oxford: Oxford University Press, 1995).

5. Donald L. Horowitz, *Ethnic Groups in Conflict* (Berkeley: University of California Press, 1985), 52.

6. For comparative studies, see Michael A. Genovese, *Women as National Leaders: The Political Performance of Women as Heads of Government* (Newbury Park, Calif.: Sage, 1993), and Barbara J. Nelson and Najma Chowdhury, *Women and Politics Worldwide* (New Haven: Yale University Press, 1994).

7. By the mid-1990s, gender differentiation was becoming increasingly visible with respect to party loyalties and political opinions in the United States, particularly among whites. In 1994, 53 percent of white males identified themselves as Republicans, 37 percent as Democrats, and 10 percent as independents. Among women, 42 percent identified themselves with the GOP, 48 percent as Democrats, and 10 percent as independents. Some 75 percent of black males identified themselves as Democrats versus 88 percent of black females. There were even detectable gender differences among married and single voters. A higher percentage (55 percent) of married males expressed support for Republican policies in Congress than did single white males (44 percent), married women (36 percent), and unmarried women (27 percent) (*Washington Post*, 15 August 1995).

8. Seymour Martin Lipset and Philip G. Altbach, *Students in Revolt* (Boston: Houghton Mifflin, 1969).

9. One estimate by the U.S. Health Care Financing Agency, which administers Medicare, predicted that there will be 3.9 million new Medicare enrollees in 2020, with lifetime Medicare expenses likely to reach $210 billion. In 1990 there were only 2.1 million new Medicare enrollees, whose total Medicare expenses were expected to be $112 billion (*Washington Post*, 13 April 1995). It is estimated that in 2025 there will be two persons in the United States over age 65 for every one teenager.

10. On Asian values as conceived in Singapore, see Kishore Mahbubani, "The United States: 'Go East, Young Man'," *The Washington Quarterly* 17, no. 2 (spring 1994): 5–23. On the views of Malaysia's leader Mohamad Mahathir, see Khoo Boo Teik, *Paradoxes of Mahathirism* (Oxford: Oxford University Press, 1995). See also Lijun Goo, "The 'Analects' and the Political Philosophy of Confucius" (Ph.D. diss., George Washington University, 1995).

CRITICAL THINKING ABOUT POLITICS

(I) Analytical Techniques of Political Science

As we pointed out in chapter 1, comparative politics is a subfield of **political science.** Political science, in turn, is a science to the extent that its practitioners engage in the following tasks:

- *Definition:* **as political scientists, we** *define* **terms and concepts as precisely as possible;**
- *Description:* **we** *observe, collect* **and** *describe* **facts systematically, make relevant descriptive comparisons, and build descriptive models;**
- *Explanation:* **we** *explain* **the phenomena being studied, often by making** *generalizations* **about them in the form of** *hypotheses* **and** *theories* **and** *testing* **these generalizations against reality;**
- *Probabilistic prediction:* **without predicting future events precisely, we seek to project future trends and tendencies in a** *probabilistic* **manner, often by specifying various** *conditions* **for future development; and**
- *Prescription:* **depending on the issue, we can sometimes** *prescribe* **policies or actions that address the real-world problems of political life.**

Ought-**questions and** *Is*-**questions** As a general rule, political science asks two broad types of questions: *is*–questions (What *is* political reality?) and *ought*-questions (What *ought* to be done about political reality?). The two sets of questions are intimately related: we cannot adequately determine what ought to be done through practical political activity without a thorough comprehension of the realities we are facing. Good policy prescription requires good analysis. We must always keep in mind, however, that is-questions and ought-questions are fundamentally different. Is-questions concentrate on *facts* and *explanations* of facts, whereas ought-questions frequently deal with *personal preferences* and *values.* The systematic analysis of facts is called *empirical analysis.* This chapter and the next one are mainly concerned with the logic of empirical analysis. Before turning our attention to that subject, however, we need to clarify the relationship between is-questions and ought-questions a bit further.

Ought-**questions and Policy Prescription** Because one of the purposes of studying comparative politics is to decide what we ought to do about the world we live in through political action, comparative politics is, at least in part, a *policy science:* it helps us devise and select governmental policies aimed at improving things. In this sense, comparative politics can be used to serve *prescriptive* and *meliorative* purposes, helping us choose the right policy prescriptions with a view to making the world a better place. (The Latin word *melior* means "better.") One of the problems with determining what ought to be done in politics, however, is that people often disagree over personal preferences and values. Although we can use the analytical

TABLE 3.1

Values and Facts in Selected Issues		
Issue Areas	Value Judgments	Facts
Abortion	Abortion is/is not morally wrong	In the United States and some other countries, abortion is legal in the first trimester
Government	In principle, big government is/is not a bad thing	The U.S. government budget in 2000 was nearly $400 billion
Socialism	Socialism is/is not morally superior to capitalism	The U.S. economy produced greater national wealth than the Soviet economy
War and peace	The use of nuclear weapons is/is not immoral	Japan surrendered after the United States destroyed two cities with atomic bombs

tools of science to dig up facts and explain how they fit together, science cannot determine the rightness or wrongness of *value judgments*.

Value judgments *are evaluations that we make on the basis of values, standards, or ideals.* They are based on such things as ethical principles, aesthetic standards, or personal tastes. Value judgments thus reflect **personal preferences** about what is moral or immoral, beautiful or ugly, good or bad. Value judgments are not simply statements of fact, nor are they explanations of how various facts come about or interact. When we say, "Democracy is morally superior to authoritarianism," we are making a value judgment. When we say, "In today's world there is a trend toward more democracies," we are making a statement of fact, not a value judgment. Table 3.1 provides some additional examples.

In principle, facts and explanations can be proved or disproved as true or false with reference to the facts themselves. We can look at reality and see if there is—or is not—a trend toward democracy, for example. Facts are independent of the individual observer and are therefore considered *objective* (that is, they are the *object* of the individual's observations). But value judgments cannot be proved or disproved as true or false. They represent the *preferences* or *ideals* of the individual and are therefore considered *subjective* (that is, they are rooted in the mind of the individual *subject*). We can study the origins and development of democracies objectively by examining the relevant facts. But whether you or I prefer democracy to dictatorship, or the Republicans to the Democrats, may involve a considerable amount of subjective preference.

As we noted, is-questions and ought-questions, though different, are frequently related. Political

arguments resting on value judgments cannot be completely oblivious to knowable facts. If we want to argue that democracies are morally superior to dictatorships *because* they maximize political participation, freedom, and human dignity, we had better be sure that democracies in fact really do these things. If someone can point out that democracies have at times permitted the majority of the people to dominate and exploit a minority (as occurred in the United States when slavery was permitted), we may have to modify our position to take account of this factually verifiable reality. The facts may force us to admit that democracy does not necessarily maximize freedom and dignity in all cases. It may do so only when specific measures are taken to prevent the majority from subjugating the minority.

By the same token, apologists for authoritarianism who argue that an enlightened dictator may know better than the masses what is best for the country must acknowledge that dictators are not always "enlightened" rulers, motivated solely by benevolent purposes. As the realities of Nazi Germany, the Soviet Union, and numerous other dictatorial regimes testify, dictatorships are often characterized by brutality, corruption, and economic stagnation.

Within the academic traditions of political science, ought-questions are the special province of two fields of the discipline: *political philosophy* and *public policy analysis.*

Political philosophy, which is also called *political thought,* is perhaps the oldest form of systematic thinking about politics. Its roots in the Western tradition go back to ancient Greece and such seminal thinkers as **Plato** (427–347 B.C.) and **Aristotle**

(384–322 B.C.). Non-Western philosophers and religious visionaries like **Confucius** (557?–479 B.C.) and **Muhammad** (570–632) have also propounded ideas about life and society that have had a profound impact on political developments around the world down to the present day. For most political philosophers, the central question of political philosophy has traditionally been, "What is the best form of politics?" This broad question has inspired a chorus of related ones: "What is the best form of government?" "What ought to be the main goals of political action: freedom? order? equality? justice?" "How do we define these goals in practical circumstances?" These and similar questions are characterized above all by their concern with political *values* and with optimal *standards* of political organization and behavior. Such values and standards are called **norms.** Consequently, the field of political philosophy is also called **normative political theory.** Its principle purpose is to get us to think coherently about the ultimate aims of politics and to think through the possible consequences of alternative courses of political action. In the process, it often asks us to make value judgments.[1]

Public policy analysis is the other subfield of political science that is primarily concerned with ought-questions, but it also employs a lot of empirical analysis to assess the impact of policy decisions. *Public* policy essentially means *governmental* policy. Public policy analysis is concerned with the decisions that governments make (or should make) in order to reach certain specified community goals. It defines particular goals that governments may wish to achieve (such as balancing the budget or improving health care), it proposes various methods for carrying out those goals, and it frequently seeks to predict the possible outcomes of alternative courses of action. Once the government has reached its decisions and has begun implementing them, public policy analysts often monitor governmental programs as they operate and may recommend pertinent adjustments and corrections. The emphasis throughout this process is usually on concrete, narrowly defined policy issues.[2]

This textbook concentrates on comparative politics, not on political philosophy or public policy analysis per se. Nevertheless, we believe that modern comparative politics cannot be properly understood in isolation from some of the leading traditions of political thought. We cannot gain sufficient insight into such prominent features of the contemporary world as democratization or political culture unless we examine their normative foundations in the thought of various political philosophers, even though some of them may have lived hundreds or even thousands of years ago. (As Mark Twain put it, "The ancients stole our best ideas!") We are also interested in various public policy issues confronting the governments of the world, such as economic policies, health policies, and environmental policies. By studying public policy in a comparative manner, we can gain a better understanding of what our own government ought to be doing in grappling with similar problems.

"WHAT IS?": A GUIDE TO EMPIRICAL POLITICAL ANALYSIS

In addition to being interested in what people ought to do in the realm of politics, political science is concerned with *describing* and *explaining* political realities. To this end it takes a close look at the facts of political life and searches for patterns or relationships that help explain those facts. What is democracy and how does it work? What are the various connections between politics and the economy? How do people behave in politics? What is a military dictatorship? How does it differ from other forms of authoritarianism? Why does it tend to occur in some countries but not in others? Questions such as these probe the *what*, the *how*, and the *why* of political reality.

> **Empirical analysis** *is centered on facts. It seeks to discover, describe, and explain facts and factual relationships, to the extent that the facts are knowable.*

The term *empirical* derives from the ancient Greek word for experience. Empirical analysis is based strictly on what we can experience or perceive through our senses: namely, *facts*. Empirical analysis is not concerned with our values, ideals, or preferences. It does not make value judgments. And it cannot probe spiritual phenomena, such as God or the human soul. We cannot empirically prove or disprove God's existence or demonstrate the intentions or actions of any deity.

At least in principle, when we study politics empirically we are supposed to put aside our personal preferences and religious faith and just stick to the observable facts. As a consequence, empirical political science is sometimes called *value-free* political science: it requires us to keep our investigations of political reality free from our own particular values and biases, no matter how well-intentioned or well-reasoned our convictions may be. If we favor democracy, for example, we must not allow this preference to intrude into our efforts to understand how democracies work in actual fact. Otherwise, we may blind ourselves to certain realities about democracies that we may find unpalatable. The same admonition applies to adherents of all political persuasions. In practice, however, it can be quite difficult to keep our subjective inclinations completely separate from our fact-centered analyses. Personal values and preferences sometimes creep into the way we select the topics we are interested in and the ways we look at them. The canons of science require us to acknowledge our biases and make sure that they do not get in the way of our quest for objective truth when conducting empirical investigations.

The principal approach of this book is empirical. Its main purpose is to present and explain facts about politics and to teach you various ways of viewing and analyzing political reality from an empirical perspective. At the same time, the authors freely acknowledge that we are not unbiased. To put our cards on the table, we unabashedly proclaim that we favor democracy over any known form of authoritarianism. Though we may differ among ourselves about how democracies can be run or should be run in actual practice, we favor democracy as a general principle because it provides far more opportunities for human dignity and self-expression than authoritarian regimes, which either limit these opportunities substantially or deny them altogether. Beyond this normative commitment to the principle of democracy, we agree and disagree on a wide range of political issues. Nevertheless, we make a sincere effort in this volume to be as objective as possible in presenting comparative politics as an empirical political science.

Definition

All sciences must strive for definitional clarity with respect to the phenomena they study and the terms and concepts they employ. Unless we are clear about the meanings of the terms we use, we may end up in a conceptual muddle. The same terms may mean different things to different people, or they may have several different meanings that depend on the context in which they are used. The meanings we attach to key terms and concepts may also change over time. Biologists, for example, must be as precise as they can about the meaning of such concepts as cellular metabolism, evolution, and even life itself. These basic concepts do not lend themselves to simple definitions that are valid for all time and circumstances. Biologists may have to revise their definitions from time to time, and they may even disagree among themselves about what these and other biological concepts actually mean. A considerable part of the work of natural science thus involves a continuing quest for conceptual clarification.

As political scientists, we too must define our concepts and refine our definitions so that they accurately apply to reality and clearly reflect our ideas and preferences about political reality. ***A concept is a word, a term, or a label that applies to a whole class or category of phenomena or ideas.*** In political science, such terms as *freedom, power, democracy, liberalism, conservatism, socialism, and interdependence* are concepts whose meanings need to be carefully spelled out if we are to be able to talk about them intelligibly and consistently. Like many political concepts, each of them can be defined in more than one way. For James Madison and the framers of the U.S. constitution, for example, freedom meant above all freedom from the tyranny of an excessively powerful state. For Karl Marx, however, it meant freedom from economic exploitation by private industrialists. In early twentieth-century Germany, a conservative was a staunch opponent of democracy who favored a militarily powerful authoritarian state. Conservatives in contemporary Germany, by contrast, favor both democracy and civilian control over the military. Conceptual clarity is imperative whether we are discussing political values (e.g., freedom) or describing political facts (e.g., German conservatism). Achieving such clarity is one of the principal aims of political science.

Description: Observing, Collecting, Comparing

Natural scientists must be keen observers of nature. They must look very closely at natural phenomena, record their observations, and gather them together in some systematic fashion. Political scientists must be equally acute observers of politics. To understand how the facts of political life fit together, they must record and gather the facts at hand as systematically as they can.

To study things *systematically* means *to employ a particular method.* One of the oldest ways of studying the natural world has involved the **comparative method.** Biologists, for example, compare various forms of animal and plant life and group them into categories, such as kingdom, genus, and species. In a roughly similar manner, political scientists can examine systems of government, describe their similarities and differences, and classify them in various categories. Starting with democracy and authoritarianism as the two broadest categories, we can group different types of democracy under the first rubric and different forms of authoritarian government under the second. Gabriel Almond, a pioneering figure in the study of comparative politics, once suggested that it is especially interesting to look for *dissimilarities* between *similar* forms of government (such as democracies) and *similarities* between *dissimilar* forms of government (such as democracies and non-democracies). By employing these descriptive and comparative techniques, we can get a better understanding of how governments work. In the process, we might also gain some insight into how we can improve the way governments work, employing scientific description in the cause of policy prescription. We can use these same techniques to understand other political phenomena as well, such as power, political behavior, political economy, and so forth.

The precise methods we use to carry out our observations and comparisons will vary from case to case, usually depending on the specific topic we are interested in exploring. If we are interested in the way people vote, we will want to gather election returns as well as relevant information about the voters, such as their social class, religion, ethnicity and the like. If we want to understand how political elites view politics, it may be helpful to conduct interviews with relevant officials, such as parliamentarians or bureaucrats, to see how they perceive politics and their own role in political affairs. To increase the breadth and depth of these observations on a comparative basis, we may wish

to examine voting patterns or elite attitudes in a variety of countries over extended periods of time. The more information we observe, the more likely it is that patterns will emerge that will permit us to go beyond merely describing reality. It will then be possible to *make generalizations* about reality with the aim of *explaining* it.

Explanation and Generalization

Are American voters becoming less loyal to political parties over time? Are similar tendencies occurring in other democracies? If so, then why?

Do political elites in democratizing countries share similar conceptions of democracy, or do they differ? What accounts for these similarities or differences? Are these attitudes conducive to stabilizing democracy or might they tend to undermine it?

Questions such as these take us beyond merely isolated facts about politics in this or that country, however intriguing they may be. They prompt us to *generalize* from those facts in order to gain a broader perspective on political reality. One of the central purposes of studying politics systematically is to make sense out of the bewildering array of political facts that constantly barrage us in newspapers and on television screens. By themselves, facts are not especially meaningful. (As one wag put it, "History is just one damned thing after another!") The facts of political life, whether historical or contemporary in nature, assume meaning only when we visualize them as general patterns, tendencies, or relationships. The same is true of the natural world. We may gaze in fascination at the antics of a chimp, the trajectory of the moon, or the melting of an icicle. But these incidental phenomena become scientifically meaningful only when we see them as part of more general patterns in nature, such as the processes of biological evolution, the laws of gravity, or the molecular structure of solids and liquids.

Similarly, if we want to comprehend the significance of discrete facts or events in political life, we must integrate them into larger processes or frameworks. Today's headlines, for example, may announce that the prime minister of a major democratic country has resigned, that the government's central bank in a leading trading nation has just raised interest rates, or that the military in a country struggling to establish democracy has seized power in a coup d'état. Governments, private businesses, journalists and other interested parties around the world must pay instant attention to these occurrences and assess their implications for decision makers or average citizens. As political scientists, we too may be interested in the immediate practical effects of these events. But we will also be interested in what they tell us about *politics* more generally.

What does the prime minister's resignation tell us about how democracies work? What does the central bank's actions tell us about the relationship between politics and economics? What does the latest coup tell us about military intervention in politics? Our aim in this more conceptual endeavor is to deepen our understanding of democracy *in general,* political economy *in general,* and military authoritarianism *in general.* **Generalization is a central purpose of science.** At the same time, we can apply our understanding of these general processes and tendencies to sharpen our understanding of the specific events at hand. As we noted in chapter 1, *comparative politics is constantly concerned with the relationship between the general and the specific:* between general concepts and explanations (like democracy and theories about democracy) and their manifestations in specific countries and historical periods.

In order to construct meaningful generalizations from a welter of political events and information and in order to determine how accurate these generalizations are, we must use **scientific methods of analyzing facts and testing general propositions.** Many students of science maintain that *the essence of science lies in its methods of analysis.*[3]

Analysis *is simply the quest for understanding through close observation and broad generalization.* In pursuit of this objective, scientific analysis makes use of a number of concepts and procedural operations. **Variables, correlations, laws, theories, hypotheses, models, and paradigms** are some of the most important ones, and they are particularly important in political science. They sharpen our critical-thinking skills and enable us to understand the real world of politics by applying scientific logic. What follows is a brief explanation of each of these terms, coupled with some elementary examples of how they can be employed in political science.

Variables

A **variable** *is something that can vary or change. That is, it can take* **different forms** *or be a* **changeable characteristic** *of a phenomenon.*

Suppose we want to understand democracy. Democracy has many different characteristics that can vary or come in different forms. For example, there are *stable* democracies that endure over long periods of time with few major alterations (such as the United States); there are *unstable* democracies that experience frequent changes of government (e.g., Italy) or that alternate over time with non-democratic modes of government (e.g., Argentina). *Stability* is thus a characteristic of democracy that can vary. We can focus on stability as one among several variables about democracy that can be analyzed systematically. We can define exactly what we mean by stability and instability, we can collect information on stable and unstable democracies, compare different cases of each variant, and look for possible *explanations* of why some democracies are stable and others are not. The explanatory factors that account for stability or instability are also variables. For example, we may find that, of all the possible characteristics of a given country, national wealth is the variable that best explains democratic stability: rich democracies may turn out to be the most stable, poor ones the most unstable.

Suppose we want to figure out why people vote the way they do. The choices voters make can vary. People can vote for different parties or candidates, or they can stay home and not vote at all. The voters themselves also have variable characteristics. The electorate consists of different social classes, ethnic groups, religions, and other social categories. We can systematically gather information on all these variables and analyze the extent to which the various characteristics of the electorate account for the population's electoral choices.

Suppose we want to learn more about political elites in a newly democratizing country such as South Africa. Members of the South African political elite can vary in a number of ways: they come from different racial or tribal groups, they have different levels of education, they may have different attitudes on political and social issues, and so forth. By conducting attitude surveys, we can gather information on various attitudes held by these elites on such issues as democracy or race relations in South Africa. We can then categorize different types of attitudes among various members of South Africa's political elite. Some may be categorized as "hostile to other racial groups," others as "open to cooperation with other racial groups," and so on. Further study may reveal that a cooperative racial attitude on the part of a large number of white and non-white South African elites is an *explanatory variable* that accounts for the relative stability of the country's fledgling multiracial democracy in the 1990s. We could conduct similar studies of elite attitudes in other newly democratizing countries such as South Korea or Russia in order to assess the prospects for democracy in those countries. And by comparing elite attitudes in several newly democratizing countries, we may be able to make some broad generalizations that apply across the board to democratization processes in general.

Just about any general topic in political science has characteristics that can vary, such as types of government (e.g., democracy, authoritarianism), governmental institutions (e.g., unicameral and bicameral legislatures), or the political behavior of people (e.g., mass voting behavior, elite decision-making behavior). When we engage in the scientific study of politics, it is these variables that occupy our most direct analytical attention. In some cases we may wish simply to *observe* these phenomena, collecting information about them and perhaps classifying them in some way. Things get especially interesting, however, when we find *relationships* between two or more observed variables.

Is there perhaps a relationship between *democratic stability* and a country's *level of economic development*? (Are stable democracies predominantly rich countries? Are poor countries doomed to authoritarianism?) Is there a relationship between *voting for conservative candidates* and the voters' *income level* or *religion* or *ethnic group* or *gender*? (Do upper-income voters, whether in the United States or other countries, tend to vote mainly for conservatives?) Is there a relationship between peoples' *willingness to compromise* in a newly democratizing country and their *educational level*? (Are better educated people more willing to compromise than

less well educated ones?) One of the first ways of generalizing about politics is to look for relationships of these kinds.

Dependent and Independent Variables   Whenever we are looking for patterns or connections between two variables: one variable is the *dependent variable* and the other is the *independent variable*.

> *The* <u>**dependent variable**</u> *is the variable we are most interested in examining or explaining; it is the main object of our study. It is the* <u>effect or outcome</u> *that is influenced or caused by another variable or variables. It is the variable whose value changes in response to changes in the value of other variables (viz., independent variables).*

Let's say that we are interested in understanding voting behavior in the United States and other democracies. One variable characteristic of voting behavior is *turnout,* in other words, the number of people who turn out to vote. Some voters go the polls but others stay home. Electoral statistics over the past fifty years show that Americans tend to vote at consistently lower rates than West Europeans or the Japanese. What explains these differences? Are there any patterns we can find that might be associated with the level of voter turnout? Put another way, on what factors is turnout *dependent*? Turnout is thus our *dependent* variable. It is the variable we seek to explain; we want to see what it *depends* on.

> *The* <u>**independent variable**</u> *is the factor or characteristic that influences or causes the dependent variable. In cause-and-effect relationships, it is the* causal *or* explanatory *variable. Changes in the value of the independent variable may produce changes in the value of the dependent variable.*

In our hypothetical study of voting behavior, the independent variables are various characteristics of the electorate that may help account for variations in voter turnout. These characteristics would include income level, age, education level, ideological proclivities, and other pertinent factors. For example, low-income voters may be less inclined to vote than upper-income voters; younger voters may be less inclined to turn out than older ones; and so on. Independent variables could also include different attitudes about politics, as evidenced in public opinion surveys. Some

FIGURE 3.1 Independent and Dependent Variables

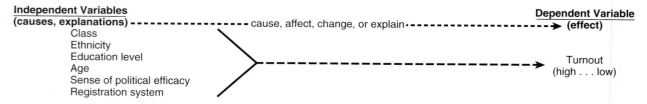

Independent Variables
(causes, explanations) - - - - - - - - - - - - - cause, affect, change, or explain - - - - - - - - - - - - - - ➤ **Dependent Variable**
        Class   **(effect)**
        Ethnicity
        Education level
        Age   Turnout
        Sense of political efficacy   (high . . . low)
        Registration system

people may not vote because they believe their vote doesn't really matter and that voters can't change anything for the better; they therefore have a low sense of *political efficacy* and feel alienated from the political system. By contrast, others may have a high sense of political efficacy: they believe that "every vote counts" and that voters can in fact influence politicians to make desirable decisions while in office. Turnout might also hinge on registration procedures: it may be higher in countries where registering to vote is easy and lower where it is more inconvenient (as in the United States). Just about anything that might affect turnout can be an independent variable in our investigation. Figure 3.1 illustrates these variables.

We can try out our independent variables individually to see to what extent each one is associated with our dependent variable, or we can try different combinations of independent variables. For example, we can focus first on the relationship between ethnicity and turnout in the United States, examining turnout levels for whites, blacks, Asians, Hispanics, and so on. We can do the same for the income-level variable, the religious variable, and so on. In these instances we are engaging in *single-variable analysis*. We can also examine two or more independent variables in combination against the dependent variable (e.g., rich whites, poor blacks; Protestants who attend church regularly and Protestants who do not attend church regularly, and so on). Such analyses are *multi-variable analyses*.

Our aim in this study is to determine whether, or to what extent, there are any connections between the independent variables and our dependent variable, voter turnout. Such connections between variables are called **correlations,** or **associations.**

Correlations

A **correlation** (*or* **association**) *is a relationship in which two or more variables change together.*

Variables are positively correlated when they vary in the same direction. Two variables are positively correlated when they go up or down together (i.e., they *increase together* or *decrease together*).

If our variables are quantifiable, we can plot them on a graph. Usually we plot the dependent variable along the y-axis (vertical axis), and the independent variable along the x-axis (horizontal axis). Let's measure the relationship between turnout and the electorate's income levels in a hypothetical country. Figure 3.2 illustrates a *positive correlation* between the voters' income levels (the independent variable) and the percentage of people who turn out to vote (the dependent variable). The higher the income level, the higher the turnout; the lower the income level, the lower the turnout. Ninety percent of people in the highest income bracket turn out to vote, but only 5 percent of the people in the lowest income level show up at the polls. Note that when the correlation is positive, the plotted line goes from bottom left to top right.

Variables are inversely correlated when they vary in opposite or reverse directions. In quantitative terms, an inverse correlation occurs when one variable *increases* and the other variable *decreases*, or vice versa. We can illustrate an inverse correlation rather easily by looking at the relationship between turnout (the dependent variable) and the voters' sense of *alienation* from the political system (the independent variable). (Alienation means a low sense of political efficacy and a basic distrust of politicians and government officials.) As figure 3.3 illustrates, voters with the lowest sense of alienation

FIGURE 3.2 Positive Correlation Between Income Levels and Turnout

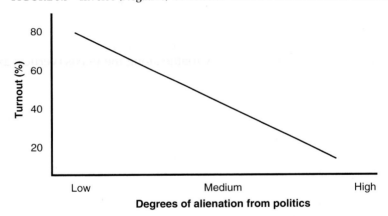

FIGURE 3.3 Inverse (Negative) Correlation Between Alienation and Turnout

have the highest turnout rates; voters with the highest sense of alienation have the lowest turnout rates. Thus there is an *inverse correlation* between alienation and turnout. Inverse correlations are also called **negative correlations.** Note that when the correlation is negative, the plotted line goes from top left to bottom right.

In some cases we cannot chart quantifiable degrees of variation on a graph, but we can display different examples of the variable on a **histogram.** Figure 3.4 shows the relationship between turnout and voter registration in the United States. Because we cannot distinguish among different magnitudes of "registered-ness," we cannot plot variations in turnout rates *within* these two groups. The

histogram compares the percentage of registered voters who have turned out to vote in elections to the House of Representatives with the percentage of total eligible voters who have turned out.

Conceivably, we could undertake a different research project by taking one of the independent variables just listed and making it our dependent variable. Suppose, for example, we are primarily interested in focusing on the phenomenon of political alienation: what factors might affect or cause it? In this study, political alienation becomes the dependent variable, and we then try out various independent variables to see if they are correlated with it. To what extent (if any) is political alienation dependent on race or ethnicity? on religious

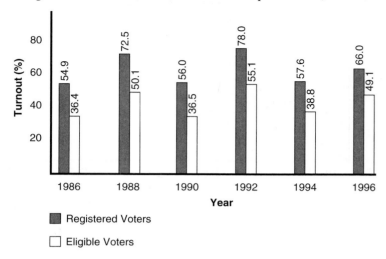

FIGURE 3.4   Histogram Comparing Turnout Rates of Registered and Unregistered U.S. Voters (Elections to House of Representatives, 1986–96)

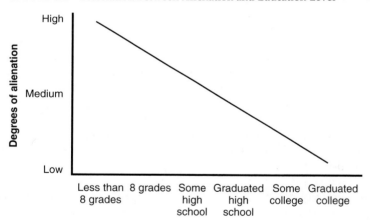

FIGURE 3.5   Correlation Between Alienation and Education Level

orientation? on income level? on education level? on psychological factors? on other variables? on some combination of variables? Figure 3.5 shows a negative (inverse) correlation between alienation (the dependent variable) and education level (the independent variable). The less educated people are, the higher their sense of alienation; the more educated people are, the lower their sense of alienation. Our point here is that, depending on the main focus of our analysis—that is, the main effect

we wish to understand or explain—alienation can be either an independent variable or a dependent variable. Many other variables can also be used either way.

Keep in mind that *correlations are not explanations.* Even though our data may show a clear correlation, positive or negative, between the dependent and independent variables, they do not explain *why* the variables are related. Let's take another look at figure 3.2, which shows a positive

FIGURE 3.6   Intervening Variables

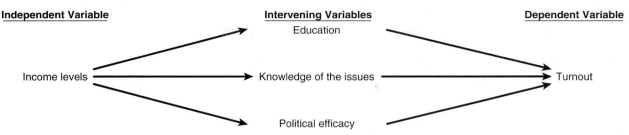

correlation between voter turnout and income levels. *Why* do higher-income people vote at higher rates than less well-off citizens? We cannot get answers to this question just by looking at the graph depicting the correlation.

To find out why higher-income voters come out on election day at higher rates than the less well-to-do voters do, we will have to extend our investigations by conducting surveys of voter attributes and attitudes. These surveys may reveal that wealthier citizens tend to be better educated than poorer ones and thus more knowledgeable about political issues. They may also have a higher sense of their own political efficacy, that is, their ability to have a real impact on government policies. The surveys may further reveal that poor citizens tend to be poorly educated, display less knowledge of the issues of the day, and have a markedly lower sense of political efficacy. These results suggest that income levels (the independent variable) affect election day turnout (the dependent variable) by working through such intermediary factors as education, knowledge of the issues, and a citizen's sense of political efficacy. These intermediary factors are called **intervening variables.** As figure 3.6 shows, intervening variables *are located in between the independent and dependent variables.*

As a general rule, *correlations do not prove that one variable* (i.e., income level) *actually **causes** the other variable* (i.e., voter turnout). In other words, **correlations do not conclusively demonstrate causality**. All a correlation does is to *suggest* or *imply* that there *may be* a cause-and-effect relationship between the variables under observation. Of course, in order to show that a causal relationship does in fact exist, it is first necessary to demon-

strate that a correlation exists. Correlations are *necessary* to demonstrate causality, but by themselves they are not *sufficient* to do so.

Sometimes variables may be positively or negatively correlated but it turns out on further investigation that there is *no direct* cause-and-effect relationship between them. We then have a **spurious correlation.**

One type of spurious correlation occurs when there *appears* to be a correlation between the variables but in fact no real relationship of any kind exists. One of the most famous examples concerns the fairy tale that babies are delivered by storks. The story comes from actual statistical data from northern Europe in the past showing an increase in human births whenever stork births increased. When stork births declined, so did human births. No one ever came up with any verifiable explanations as to why human and stork birthrates were positively correlated. Obviously, the one event could not have caused the other, but neither was there any evidence that some other variable (climactic patterns? lunar cycles?) caused the two birthrates to rise and fall together. Until someone brings forward convincing evidence of a causative variable, we can assume that the correlation between human births and stork births is entirely fortuitous. Thus a spurious correlation can at times be a matter of pure coincidence, with *no* causal factors at work.

In other circumstances, a spurious correlation can be said to exist when two apparently correlated variables (let's say A and B) are not *directly* linked in a cause-and-effect relationship (A does not cause B, and B does not cause A); rather, they are *indirectly* linked because some other variable is causing one or the other, or both (C causes both A and B, or

FIGURE 3.7   Spurious Correlations

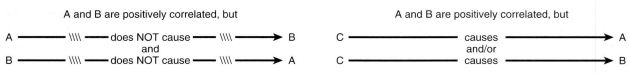

just one of them). In other words, the stork-and-baby correlation would still be considered spurious even if it could be shown that some third factor (like climactic patterns) caused the two infant populations to increase and decrease together.

> **In sum, a <u>spurious correlation</u>** *occurs when two variables* **appear** *to be directly linked in a cause-and-effect relationship but in fact (a) there is no causal linkage whatsoever, or (b) they are linked indirectly by some other causative variable or variables.* Figure 3.7 depicts these spurious correlations.

As political scientists we must constantly be on guard against spurious correlations when conducting or examining scientific research. We should be similarly vigilant as citizens. In the rough-and-tumble world of politics, it is common-place for politicians seeking to oust their opponents from office in the next elections to blame the incumbents for virtually everything that has gone wrong in the country, and perhaps even in the rest of the world, during the government's term in office. In some cases, the elected officials may indeed be responsible for the problems they are accused of creating. But not always. It could happen, for example, that a downturn in the national economy that occurs when the Freedom Party is in power actually had its causative roots in policies pursued several years earlier when the Independence Party was in office. The correlation between the Freedom Party's incumbency and the deterioration of the economy is spurious because a third variable, the Independence Party, actually caused the economic tailspin.

Alternatively, it could happen that the actions of neither party were responsible for the economic decline. Other factors over which the two rival parties had little or no control while in office may have been at fault, such as unfavorable international economic conditions or the effects of disas-

trous weather on the national economy. Examples of spurious correlations in the real world of politics are rarely in short supply.

Laws

> *In science, a <u>law</u> is a regularly occurring association (or correlation) between two or more variables.*

A *deterministic law* means that whenever X occurs, Y *always* occurs. The laws of gravity are an example. Starting with the simple observation that what goes up must come down (at least within the Earth's atmosphere), Sir Isaac Newton showed with mathematical precision that physical bodies have a general tendency to be pulled toward one another in patterns determined by their mass and distance. Albert Einstein's famous equation, $E = mc^2$, is a law specifying that energy always occurs as the product of mass times the square of the speed of light. The physical world has a number of deterministic laws, many of them translatable into timeless mathematical equations. As Einstein put it, "God does not play dice with the universe!"

A less stringent type of scientific law is a *probabilistic law*. In this case, whenever A occurs, B *sometimes* occurs. Occasionally we can calculate the *degree of probability* with which B is likely to occur. In the natural world, weather predictions are frequently based on probabilistic laws. Given certain temperatures, humidity levels, and other atmospheric conditions, we can predict when snow will probably fall. Depending on the accuracy of our weather data and the sophistication of our computer models, we may be able to make accurate forecasts with a very high degree of probability. Nevertheless, so many variables are at work that we cannot be absolutely certain when it will snow, or if it does, we cannot be completely sure how much will fall on which spots.

Human behavior is not as law-bound as inanimate nature. Unlike the planets or atomic particles, human beings are capable of conscious volitional behavior as well as completely erratic irrational behavior. We can make decisions about how we wish to behave by choosing from a menu of alternative courses of action. We can change our minds. We can act singly or in all sorts of groups; we can act cooperatively or at cross-purposes. Moreover, our social or political behavior can be affected by a multitude of variables (ethnic group, religion, economic interests, parents, peers, etc.). Sometimes we miscalculate, acting on the basis of false assumptions, inadequate information, or faulty logic. Sometimes we may not even be consciously aware of the factors that induce us to behave in certain ways, as when our biases, emotions, or subconscious impulses intrude on our actions.

As a consequence, human behavior is extremely variable and unpredictable. Hence the social sciences, which focus on human behavior (especially in large social groups), cannot predict the future with unfailing accuracy. Whereas the planets and other celestial bodies obligingly conform to the laws of gravitational motion, making it possible to pinpoint with mathematical precision the position of the moon or Halley's comet hundreds or even thousands of years from now, human behavior is so variegated that no one can foretell what political, social, or economic realities will look like ten years from now or even ten months from now. Perhaps for this reason Einstein also declared, "Politics is more difficult than physics."

Hence there are no *deterministic* laws in political science. Nevertheless, in political science as in other social sciences (such as sociology, economics, and social psychology), researchers can frequently discern real patterns and tendencies in human social activity. And even though we cannot foretell with any degree of certainty exactly what the future will bring, social scientists can sometimes suggest which future developments are more probable or less probable, at least in the near term.

Prediction *of the future in the social sciences is* **thus** *suggestive or* **probabilistic** *in nature.* If we can identify regularities in a population's voting patterns, for example, we can *suggest* how people *may* vote in the next elections. The closer we get to election day, the greater the confidence we may

have in our estimation of *probable* outcomes. Even the most sophisticated statistical analyses of the most comprehensive polling data we can obtain, however, may not be sufficient to predict the way people actually will vote the very next day. Many pollsters were as surprised as virtually everyone else by Harry Truman's upset victory over Thomas Dewey in 1948 and by the magnitude of the Republicans' sweeping takeover of the U.S. Senate and House of Representatives in 1994. Similarly, experts on the Soviet Union were shocked at the USSR's complete collapse in 1991; veteran China-watchers did not foresee the eruption of pro-democracy student demonstrations in Beijing in 1989; and specialists on South Africa could scarcely have predicted in the early 1980s that the white minority would finally allow multiracial elections to take place there in the early 1990s, bringing Nelson Mandela, a black man, to the presidency.

Only in a suggestive and probabilistic sense, therefore, can we speak of *laws* in social science. Actually, social scientists rarely use the term at all. In a few cases, they apply the term to certain patterns of social behavior that occur with considerable frequency and in a relatively regularized manner. Even these cases, however, are probabilistic rather than deterministic laws.

In economics, for example, the **law of supply and demand** states that, as a general rule, prices in a market economy will rise whenever the supply of goods is low or the demand for goods rises. Conversely, prices tend to fall whenever supply increases or demand declines. Thus, prices are positively correlated with demand and negatively correlated with supply.

In political science, **Duverger's law,** named after a French political scientist, stipulates that an electoral system in which the voters choose competing candidates by a simple majority (i.e., the highest number of votes) in a single ballot tends to produce a two-party system. Examples would include elections to the U.S. House of Representatives and the British House of Commons.

Virtually every scientific law has its exceptions, as even natural scientists acknowledge with respect to nature. This reality is especially true in the social sciences. Economists therefore recognize that the law of supply and demand, although a general tendency, does not always operate perfectly. Even in a market economy, factors such as monopolies or fluctuating consumer demands may interfere with it. Similarly, Duverger's law may not apply in all circumstances, as Duverger himself acknowledged.[4] (Britain, for example, has more than two parties represented in the House of Commons.) Any so-called law in the social sciences must be constantly put to the test against the evidence of reality to determine whether, or to what extent, it holds true. In social science as in the physical sciences, laws are occasionally broken.

Moreover, laws—like correlations—are not *explanations*. They simply point out that two or more variables generally go together, but they do not explain why. To find out why these patterns exist, social scientists must conduct other exploratory investigations. The principal ways of explaining political realities scientifically are by formulating *theories* and *hypotheses.*

Theories

The term <u>theory</u> can have several different meanings in political science.

1. In its broadest sense, theory simply refers to *thinking about politics as opposed to practicing it.* As such, it is an *abstract intellectual exercise.* Theorizing can mean nothing more than *making generalizations* about politics, whether in accordance with strict scientific rules or far more informally, as in late-night political discussions with friends.

    In this elementary definition of the term, theory also refers to *general principles or abstract ideas* that may not necessarily be true in actual fact. For example, when we say, "In theory, democracy is government by the people," we are referring to some general principle or idea of democracy; we are not explaining how democracy actually works in practice.

2. More restrictively, theory can mean *normative theory:* that is, value-centered political philosophy (or political thought), as we defined these terms earlier in this chapter.

3. In the natural and social sciences, theory most frequently means *a generalization, or set of generalizations, that seeks to* explain, *and perhaps* predict, *relationships among variables. This is* explanatory theory.

Explanation is the main aim of theory in empirical political science. The word *because* is stated or implied in just about every explanatory theory.

Parsimonious and Middle-range Theories   Scientists use the term **parsimonious theory** to refer to a *theory that explains a vast range of phenomena in very succinct terms.* Charles Darwin's theory of evolution is an example of parsimonious theory. His theory states that all animal life evolved from lower animal forms through a process of natural selection. In just one brief sentence, Darwin's theory purports to account for all animal species. Parsimonious theories are said to have a high level of *explanatory power.*

Political science has few parsimonious theories. (Some political scientists maintain that it has none.) Instead of enunciating bold generalizations capable of explaining all or even most political phenomena in a sentence or two, political science largely confines itself to so-called **middle-range theories.** These are theories that explain specific categories, or segments, of political reality. Typically, middle-range theories in political science are sets of statements and hypotheses that are strung together to explain a particular subfield of political reality. Here are some examples:

Democratic theory consists of descriptions of how democracies are supposed to work in principle and how they work in practice, along with various explanations of how democracies emerge or endure. It also specifies certain conditions that may be necessary for democratic government.

Elite theory describes the roles that political elites play and makes a variety of explanatory generalizations about their social backgrounds, their political perceptions, their relationships with the masses, and so on.

Rational choice theory explains political behavior by regarding virtually all individuals as "rational actors" who seek to maximize their personal gains and minimize their losses or risks. Some proponents of rational choice theory assert that it is a parsimonious theory that can explain a vast array of political phenomena. Others, however, insist that it is just another middle-range theory that has its limits.

Middle-range theories also exist on a host of other political phenomena, such as *electoral behavior, the state, revolution, and war.* Subsequent chapters in this book examine a number of these theories.

As a general rule, explanations that merit the term theory have usually gained wide acceptance over long periods of time because their ability to explain the facts has been confirmed in repeated scientific investigations. Theories thus tend to be more solidly grounded in empirical reality than hypotheses, which are typically assumptions that have yet to be sufficiently tested. Nevertheless, even the most widely respected theories are not unchallengeable truths. They are meant to be constantly challenged against the hard facts of reality. In political science as in the natural sciences, *explanatory theories are not abstractions that are divorced from reality; on the contrary, they seek to explain* reality. Theories are valid only as long as they are consistent with the facts they endeavor to explain. If new evidence comes to light that contradicts the theory, then the theory is probably either partially or entirely wrong. It must then be modified or discarded and replaced by a better theory that fits the facts. All explanatory theories must therefore be regarded as tentatively valid explanations of empirical reality. They need to be repeatedly subjected to verification against the hard data of reality. The main way of accomplishing this task is by breaking theories down into hypotheses and testing them against the available evidence.

Hypotheses

A hypothesis *is an assumption or supposition that needs to be tested against relevant evidence.*

In some cases hypotheses can be purely *descriptive* in nature. For example, we can hypothesize that democracy has broad popular support in Russia. We can then test this hypothesis by surveying a large number of Russians and asking them whether they support democracy, and if so, how strongly. After we've collected and analyzed our research data we will end up with a description, a picture, of mass attitudes toward Russian democracy. The data will permit us to describe the Russian electorate as mostly supportive of democracy or mostly unsupportive of it by providing statistical readings of the proportion of the voters who support it strongly, the percentage of those who support it with less conviction, and the percentage of those who don't support it very much or not at all.

This descriptive hypothesis simply proposes certain facts about the Russian electorate, and the hypothesis-testing survey seeks to determine whether and to what extent those facts are really occurring. The descriptive hypothesis does not suggest an *explanation* as to *why* the proposed phenomena might be occurring, however. It is not an *explanatory* hypothesis that explains *why* Russians feel as thay do about democracy. But in political science as in the physical sciences, *explanation is the ultimate goal.*

> **Explanatory hypotheses** *posit a cause-and-effect relationship between dependent and independent variables that can be tested empirically (i.e., against factual evidence).*

By formulating explanatory hypotheses about politics, we force ourselves to specify our dependent and independent variables and to be clear about the sharp difference between cause and effect. By *testing* hypotheses empirically, we submit them to a reality check: we take a close look at all the available facts to see if they substantiate or contradict the relationships we propose in our hypotheses. For example, we might find that, contrary to our hypothesis, popular support for democracy in Russia is in fact much weaker than we had originally surmised. We must then formulate explanatory hypotheses that might suggest possible reasons for this phenomenon. We could hypothesize that public dissatisfaction with the economy is causing people to turn against democracy; or we could hypothesize that disgust at political corruption may be the main explanatory variable accounting for Russian attitudes; or we could assume that public ignorance about democracy may be the explanation; or we could develop a host of other possible explanations, whether singly or in combination.

We could then test these various explanatory hypotheses by going back to Russia and resurveying the electorate, asking them more specific questions about their attitudes on the economy, corruption, and so forth. After analyzing our survey data, we

FIGURE 3.8   Independent Variables Affecting Negative Attitudes Toward Democracy

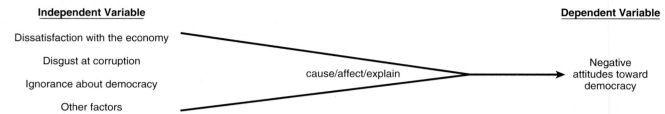

can then come to some conclusions about which of these explanatory variables explain why many Russians are suspicious of democracy. We may find, for example, that *all* of them play a role, albeit to varying degrees, among the voters. In these explanatory hypotheses, *"negative attitudes toward democracy"* is the *dependent variable*. The *possible explanations* to be tested are the *independent variables.* (See figure 3.8.)

Chapter 4 is devoted to an extended exercise in testing the proposition that *"national wealth promotes democracy."* Is this hypothesis correct? Is it only partially correct? Or is it perhaps just plain wrong? Reading the next chapter attentively will give you a more comprehensive idea of how the logic of hypothesis testing applies to the study of politics.

Scientific Generalization and Practical Politics

Explanatory theories and hypotheses in political science greatly enhance our understanding of the real world of politics. They can also help us figure out our own positions on the political problems of our times. Indeed, many of the practical policy choices facing governmental decision makers and average citizens are rooted in some overarching theory. Debates over welfare reform and crime are connected with theories about the ability of governments to change the population's behavioral patterns. Debates on tax policy are connected with theories about how or whether governments can stimulate economic growth while cutting budget deficits and keeping inflation low. Debates on foreign aid to struggling democracies are connected with theories about democracy. The list of theory-related policy issues could be extended indefinitely.

Although some people dismiss theory as completely detached from the real world, in fact most individuals act in political life on the basis of certain assumptions and understandings about politics that are the equivalent of theoretical generalizations,

even if they do not always realize it. As the British economist John Maynard Keynes once observed, "Practical men, who believe themselves to be exempt from any intellectual influences, are usually the slaves of some defunct economist." By the same token, politicians and the people they govern can be the slaves of political ideas they accept uncritically. An intelligent approach to politics requires a keen understanding of the relevance of explanatory theory and hypothesis testing to the real world of political action. To put it succinctly, *the scientific approach to politics requires us to support our political generalizations with relevant evidence and systematic logic.*

Models

In political science, **a model** *is a simplified representation of reality in descriptive or abstract form.*

A desktop scale model of a Stealth bomber can neither fly nor drop bombs. Its sleek proportions, however, provide some understanding of how the real aircraft is able to avoid radar detection. An auto designer's computer model of next year's dream car indicates how all its components will mesh together in perfect harmony once the vehicle hits the road. Environmental scientists have built a large model of the Chesapeake Bay designed to replicate the bay's complex ecological system. Economists construct graphical and mathematical models of various dynamic economic processes, such as a perfectly competitive market economy or a global free trade system.

Though the composition of these models is different, they all serve the same function: they enable us to understand some aspect of reality, whether aerodynamics or the economy, by *representing* some of its essential features in a simplified or idealized form. Obviously, these scaled-down physical or mathematical models cannot be perfect copies of the realities they represent. The car designer does not plan for the car to malfunction, but at some point it probably will. Economists know that purely free market systems, which are devoid of any governmental interference or monopolies, exist nowhere in today's world.

The purpose of a model is not to represent reality perfectly but to enable us to understand reality by allowing us to compare it against some standard or pattern. If the car has stalling problems, the computer design can help us find the source. If world trade is declining, the mathematical model of how a free trade system works in theory may help us understand how to deal with existing trade barriers in the global economy. When viewed against the model, the complexities of the real world stand out all the more prominently by comparison with the simplified version. As one economist put it, "Models are to be used, not believed." They are to be used, more specifically, as guides to further understanding. As learning devices, models serve a *heuristic* purpose, a term that derives from the Greek word meaning "to find out."

In roughly similar fashion, political scientists use models of various kinds to help us understand political realities. Sometimes these models are purely descriptive. For example, we can construct a model of democracy just by listing its characteristic features: a competitive electoral system, legal guarantees of certain freedoms and rights, and so forth. Although many democracies of today's world may actually diverge from this model of an "ideal" democracy in one way or another, these divergences will tend to stand out when compared with the model, prompting us to investigate how and why they occur.

A descriptive model of this sort is known as an *ideal type*. An **ideal type** *is a model of a political or social phenomenon that describes its main characteristic features.* The term was coined by the German sociologist **Max Weber** (1864–1920), one of the founders of modern sociology. Weber was among the first students of modern bureaucracy. Based on his observations of European bureaucracies in the early twentieth century, Weber devised an ideal type of a modern bureaucracy that specified the features most commonly found in them. He described this standard (or ideal-typical) bureaucracy as a highly impersonal organization run in accordance with strict rules and legal procedures. Not all bureaucracies in Europe conformed exactly to this standard type in every respect, however. For Weber, an ideal type is not just a carbon copy of one or two real-world examples of the phenomenon it represents. Rather, it is an abstract conception constructed from a variety of observations and trends. Weber used it as a conceptual standard against which social scientists could study and compare the world's bureaucracies and come to a better understanding of the phenomenon of bureaucracy itself. The concept of the ideal type is very useful in describing all sorts of political phenomena.

In addition to ideal types, political science makes use of several other types of models. *Static models* simply define the fundamental attributes of a phenomenon (like ideal types), but they do not describe how those attributes change or develop over time. By contrast, *dynamic models* describe processes of change. For example, the *modernization model* describes how so-called "traditional societies" develop into "modern societies" through the process of industrialization. As a nation's economy becomes more industrialized, people tend to move from the countryside into the cities, communications networks expand, educational opportunities improve, and traditional religious practices and superstitions give way to more secularized lifestyles and beliefs. Modernization theorists base this model on the historical development of Europe and the United States, and they believe that most countries of the world sooner or later will move in much the same directions. The modernization model of political development has provoked considerable controversy. Its critics contend that it is too narrowly based on European and American experiences and that it pays inadequate attention to the special experiences and cultures of Asia, Africa, the Middle East, and other regions of the developing world. Some of these critics propose alternative models of political development that combine elements of both modern and traditional societies. We shall return to this issue in chapters 12 and 15.

Some models are *analogies*. In these cases, political scientists clarify political phenomena by comparing them to something else. For example, one scholar likens democracy to a market economy, with voters choosing candidates in the political "marketplace" on the basis of considerations very similar to those motivating consumers shopping for a good buy.[5] Another political scientist compares the ways governments work to cybernetic processes, complete with feedback mechanisms, communications loops, and other features of computer technology.[6] Some analysts regard many forms of political behavior as analogous to games. *Game theory* is a widely used method of modeling political interactions as though they were games involving elements of both cooperation and conflict. We'll take a look at one of the most famous of these games, Prisoners' Dilemma, in chapter 12.

Some models are simply *diagrams,* or schematic depictions of processes and relationships. Figures 3.9 and 3.10 diagram two alternative forms of democracy: *direct democracy* and *representative democracy.* Under direct democracy, the citizens themselves assemble and make authoritative decisions for their community. Under representative democracy, as the term implies, the citizens elect their representatives to the legislative and executive branches of government and entrust the elected officials and their appointees to make governmental decisions on their behalf. Once some of these decisions take effect, the citizens have the opportunity to evaluate their impact and to hold their elected representatives acountable in the next elections by voting them out of office or reelecting them.

Finally, like economists and natural scientists, political scientists sometimes construct complex mathematical models in an effort to represent various political phenomena as precisely as possible. This book will not examine such statistically advanced modeling techniques.

Strictly speaking, a model is not an explanatory theory. Whereas explanatory theory *explains* reality, models *represent* and *describe* reality. However simplified or sophisticated its form may be, a model is just a picture, not an explanation. Very frequently, however, we use the term *theoretical model* (or *conceptual model*). This term can have two meanings.

In one meaning, a model is said to be theoretical if it is an intellectual abstraction as opposed to a physical representation of something. Computer models, mathematical models, diagrams, and even ideal types are theoretical models in this sense of the term. They are *intellectual* or *abstract* representations of reality, not physical objects.

In the second meaning of the term, a theoretical model *represents* explanatory theories. A theory that states, for example, that national wealth *causes* democracies to come about by promoting education and communication can be depicted in a diagram. Figure 3.11 is a *causal model* that graphically represents this theory. Causal models can be a useful of way of specifying causal relationships and clarifying our thinking about how different variables interact.

Moreover, models can stimulate explanatory theory. Just as environmental scientists use their model of the Chesapeake Bay to develop theories about how marine life develops or why so much of it is dying prematurely, political scientists can use their models to come up with explanatory theories about how and why various political phe-

FIGURE 3.9   Model of Direct Democracy

Decisions

↑

Citizens

FIGURE 3.10   Model of Representative Democracy

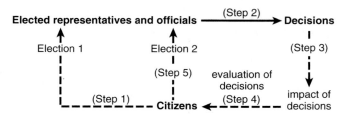

nomena occur as they do. Models, in short, are yet another useful method for generalizing systematically about politics.

Paradigms

The term paradigm has two meanings in political science:

> **In one sense, *a paradigm is a prime example of a particular phenomenon or pattern.***

For example, the British system of government is a *paradigm* of parliamentary democracy. This is not to say that all parliamentary governments are exactly like Britain's in every respect. Italy, Israel, and other parliamentary political systems differ from the British version (and from one another) in various ways. Still, they are all close to the British example in certain fundamental respects. We can understand how these various governments work more clearly by comparing them to the British paradigm.

Paradigms are quite useful in comparative politics because they help us observe and analyze variations on a theme (such as parliamentary democracy). In this respect they serve the same purpose as models. The difference is that whereas models tend to be abstract or intellectually idealized representations of reality, paradigms are usually real-world phenomena (like Britain's governmental system).

> **In another sense, *a paradigm is a particular way of looking at phenomena, formulating questions and generalizations, and conducting research.***

This second definition of paradigm construes it as a particular form of intellectual inquiry or a specific approach to scientific investigation. This meaning of the term was popularized by Thomas Kuhn, a philosopher interested in the nature of scientific thought. Kuhn argued that over the centuries Western science developed several radically different paradigms of scientific thinking, based on very different assumptions about the natural world and about how to study it. Ptolemaic astronomy, for example, held that the sun and planets revolve around the Earth. Only in the sixteenth century did Ptolemy's ancient paradigm give way to the heliocentric astronomy of Copernicus, based on more precise methods of observing the solar system. Similarly, Aristotle's views on physics were eventually supplanted by Newton's laws of mechanics; Newton's paradigm gave way to twentieth-century relativity theory and quantum mechanics; and so on.[7]

This meaning of paradigm also applies to political science. The paradigm of political science presented in this chapter conforms in its essential features to the rules of scientific logic that emerged from the empirical approach to scientific inquiry pioneered by Copernicus, Newton, and other seminal contributors to modern science. This scientific approach to studying politics is a fairly recent development, however. It emerged slowly in the United States in the 1930s and 1940s and increasingly shaped the way American political scientists were trained to think about politics in the 1950s and subsequently. Earlier, the dominant paradigm of political science research was largely descriptive and tended to concentrate on governmental institutions and constitutional law. It was less concerned with studying how people behave in political life, and it did not employ such concepts as variables, hypotheses, correlations, and other nuts and bolts of modern scientific thinking. It was also considerably less quantitative. Even today, many

FIGURE 3.11 Model Depicting Causes of Democracy

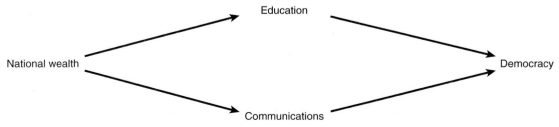

important books and articles are written about politics that employ the more traditional descriptive approach. But the scientific paradigm presented in this book is currently the leading one in most American universities.

QUANTITATIVE AND QUALITATIVE POLITICAL SCIENCE

Political science offers two basic approaches to investigating relationships among variables: *quantitative* approaches and *qualitative* approaches.

Quantitative political science is "by the numbers." It looks mainly at phenomena that can vary in measurable degrees or quantities, such as the number of votes cast in an election or in legislative balloting, or the percentages of people who express various opinions in a public opinion survey. Statisticians have developed a variety of sophisticated techniques and software programs for performing different types of measurements involving quantifiable dependent and independent variables, and many of these tools can be adapted to research on politics.[8]

We will not use any of these sophisticated statistical techniques in this book, but they can be quite useful in the study of political science at more advanced levels, depending on the nature of the problem being investigated.

Statistical rigor is not always possible in the study of politics, however. Sometimes we would like to have relevant statistical information but it is not available, or if available, it is unreliable. Authoritarian regimes, for example, rarely permit contested elections or release public opinion poll information, and the statistics they do publish (such as economic data) may be untrustworthy. At other times we may have statistical information available that can be quite useful in helping us understand a situation, but all we need do is report this information in tables or graphs without getting into highly sophisticated calculations. Economic statistics, election returns, and other relevant quantitative data are often used in this uncomplicated but vitally important way in political science, and we shall employ such raw data quite extensively in subsequent chapters. Finally, in some cases statistical analysis is only partially helpful in enabling us to understand political reality and must be combined with other factual information that is not readily quan-

tifiable, such as historical accounts or other descriptions of political events, processes, or ideas.

Research and analysis in political science that is not primarily quantitative in nature is called *qualitative* political science. Political scientists who are engaged in qualitative research rely largely on descriptive accounts of the political realities they study. In seeking to explain political processes and interactions, analysts frequently use qualitative research to provide detailed descriptions of such things as how governmental institutions work, or how parties and interest groups are organized, or how political ideas and ideologies define the issues facing the country. These and similar political phenomena cannot be fully understood if we confine ourselves strictly to statistical analysis; descriptive detail may also be necessary.

Many qualitatively oriented analysts are especially sensitive to the broader historical and contemporary *contexts* within which political life takes place in any given country. In order to understand current events in, say, contemporary China or India, qualitative analysts often remind us that the specific details of politics—such as a recent leadership change or the latest elections—do not occur in a vacuum. These events have historical roots, and they may also be related to complex social, cultural, economic, or other conditions in ways that cannot be adequately explained just by referring to numerical data or by performing statistical operations. Statistics, such analysts would argue, can't explain everything. We need to immerse ourselves in the history, culture, and languages of individual countries if we want to understand their political systems.

Advocates of quantitative and qualitative approaches to political science have engaged in sharp debates about which mode of analysis is superior. Quantitatively oriented analysts cherish the precision and neatness of statistical rigor; they often accuse qualitatively oriented researchers of being vague or mushy. Qualitatively inclined political scientists, for their part, tend to accuse their number-crunching colleagues of ignoring everything about politics that cannot be reduced to mere statistics. As a consequence, they contend, the quantifiers fail to appreciate the full scope of political reality in all its complexity.

A substantial number of political scientists today would admit that quantitative and qualitative approaches are complementary and that the approach an analyst chooses depends on the nature of the problem being studied. Some problems especially lend themselves to quantitative analysis (such as electoral behavior or public opinion); others are less amenable to statistical methods. In many cases the two can go together. Most important, both quantitative and qualitative approaches utilize scientific analysis, and both must observe the ground rules of scientific logic.[9]

LOGICAL FALLACIES

To round out this chapter's introduction to critical thinking about politics, we must warn against certain logical fallacies that are commonly committed in political argumentation. Our list can be only a partial one, given space limitations, and it cannot substitute for a book on logic. Nevertheless, the fallacies presented here are common enough to warrant special attention.

Fallacy of composition We commit this fallacy when we assume that the whole is exactly the same as its parts. Beware of ascribing attributes (such as attitudes, behaviors, etc.) to an entire class or group when those attributes may apply only to a portion of that group. For example, do not say, "The Germans are highly disciplined" or "Americans are well off," when in fact only *some* Germans may be highly disciplined and *not all* Americans are well off. This fallacy is the basis of **stereotyping,** that is, regarding all individuals of a particular group as similar while overlooking their differences.

Tautology (circular reasoning) ascribes causation to the very phenomenon whose causes we are trying to explain. (To put it another way, beware of using your dependent variable as an independent variable that accounts for it.) The term comes from the ancient Greek word for "the same." Here's an example: "Armed conflict among Yugoslavia's contending groups produced a bitter civil war." The statement is tautological because civil war *is* armed conflict among a country's contending groups. The two points are essentially the same thing; hence, the one cannot cause the other. To ascertain the

causes of the civil war, we must look at real explanatory variables such as ethnic and religious hatreds. One of the most famous tautologies ever attributed to a politician was the remark allegedly uttered by President Calvin Coolidge, "When a great many people are unable to find work, unemployment results."

Post hoc ergo propter hoc ("After it, therefore because of it") is the fallacy of concluding that A *caused* B just because A *preceded* B. For example, "The U.S.–led victory over Iraq in the Persian Gulf War at the start of 1991 precipitated the collapse of the Soviet Union later that same year." The statement does not explain *why* the war was a cause of the USSR's demise but simply assumes that it was. In fact, the war had no demonstrable effect on the Soviet collapse.

A fortiori ("All the more") assumes that what is true of a phenomenon at one level or degree is automatically true of the same phenomenon at larger levels or degrees. The statement, "The more private enterprise there is in the economy, the more democracy will flourish," assumes without empirical evidence that, just because a certain amount of private enterprise may be good for democracy, then a totally private economy, with no government involvement in economic affairs whatsoever, will be even better for democracy. It overlooks the possibility that a completely private economy, with no government-sponsored safety net to help the poor and the middle class, could create great disparities in wealth and perhaps lead to intense social conflicts capable of destroying democracy.

False analogy is the fallacy of making inappropriate or inexact analogies or comparisons between one phenomenon or situation and another. One example is the statement "Political systems are like organisms: they are born, they grow, and they inevitably decay and die." This "organic" analogy does not stand up to the facts. Historical analogies are also frequently misused. Here's an example: "The Persian Gulf War was exactly like World War II: Saddam Hussein was another Hitler, and Hitler showed that we must not appease dictators." Despite some evident similarities, the two cases are not exactly similar. (For one thing, Hitler's army was far more militarily prepared for a long war than Saddam's.) Prior to the successful U.S.–led attack against Iraqi troops occupying Kuwait in 1991, some people warned that such an invasion would result in a protracted military standoff similar to the Vietnam War. Once again, the analogy was incorrect: the Persian Gulf War lasted only a few weeks. In fact, no two historical cases are ever *exactly* alike in all respects, and one must pay as much attention to dissimilarities as to similarities when comparing them.[10]

Non–falsifiable hypothesis The only kind of hypothesis that can be tested empirically is one that is capable of being *contradicted* by factual evidence. An example of a non–falsifiable hypothesis is,"Our country's fate is in God's hands." Since we cannot physically see or hear God, we have no empirical evidence enabling us to *disprove* the hypothesis; everything that happens to our country, good or bad, can be interpreted as consistent with it. Another example: "The laws of history make the collapse of capitalism inevitable in the long run, though it may succeed in the short run." Because we cannot have empirical evidence on the future, we have no basis for proving that the hypothesis is wrong (or right). Both hypotheses are articles of faith and cannot be empirically tested against hard evidence.

False inference is the fallacy of making unwarranted inferences from statistical data or other facts, especially when trying to establish causation. (See chapter 4.)

Reductivism is the fallacy of explaining something in terms of one sole cause when other causes could also be at work. (See chapter 4.)

KEY TERMS
(Underlined in the text)

Political science
Value judgment
Empirical analysis
Dependent variable
Independent variable
Correlation (association)

Intervening variable
Spurious correlation
Law
Probabilistic prediction
Theory
Hypothesis
Model
Ideal type
Paradigm
Fallacy of composition
Tautology

NOTES

1. For an introduction to some of the timeless themes of political philosophy, see Glenn Tinder, *Political Thinking: The Perennial Questions,* 6th ed. (New York: HarperCollins, 1995).

2. For an overview of the field, see Stuart S. Nagel, *Public Policy: Goals, Means, and Methods* (Lanham, Md.: University Press of America, 1991). Some universities have a department or school of *public administration,* where analytical techniques of public policy analysis are taught. See also Wolfgang H. Reinicke, *Global Public Policy* (Washington: Brookings Institution, 1998).

3. In *The Grammar of Science,* written in 1892, the scientist and philosopher Karl Pearson wrote, "The unity of all science consists alone in its method, not its material."

4. Maurice Duverger, *Political Parties,* rev. ed., translated by Barbara and Robert North (London: Methuen, 1959), 217. Duverger asserted that the correlation between single-ballot plurality electoral procedures and two-party systems "approaches the most nearly perhaps to a true sociological law." He observed, however, that this electoral system "does not necessarily and absolutely lead to bipartism in all cases." It was with this caveat in mind that he called the correlation a "brazen law" (228). For a description of the electoral system, see chapter 9; for further discussion of Duverger's law, see chapter 11.

5. Anthony Downs, *An Economic Theory of Democracy* (New York: Harper & Row, 1957).

6. Karl W. Deutsch, *The Nerves of Government* (New York: Free Press, 1966).

7. Thomas Kuhn, *The Structure of Scientific Revolutions,* 2d ed. (Chicago: University of Chicago Press, 1970).

8. For example, there exist rigorous tests for determining the *statistical significance* of particular statistical results. In addition, the relative *strength* of a correlation between dependent and independent variables can be calculated and specified in numerical terms.

The resulting *correlation coefficient* is a very useful tool in political analysis. Another statistical technique that is widely used in political science is *regression analysis*, which permits analysts to measure the probable effect of a change (or *variance*) in one or more independent variables on a dependent variable. It is very useful in analyzing voting patterns and other quantifiable relationships.

9. For a concise outline of the scientific approach, see Stephen Van Evera, *Guide to Methods for Students of Political Science* (Ithaca, N.Y.: Cornell University Press, 1997). A more advanced text is Gary King, Robert O. Keohane, and Sidney Verba, *Designing Social Inquiry* (Princeton. N.J.: Princeton University Press, 1994).

10. For a study of the dangers of false historical analogies, see Richard E. Neustadt and Ernest R. May, *Thinking in Time: The Uses of History for Decision-Makers* (New York: Free Press, 1986).

CRITICAL THINKING ABOUT POLITICS

(II) *The Logic of Hypothesis Testing*

Hypothesis testing is a central activity of political science. It is one of the things that makes it a science in the formal meaning of the word. By learning how to formulate and test hypotheses we can learn a lot about both political science and, not incidentally, political reality itself.

Furthermore, by learning some of the main rules of hypothesis testing, we can also learn a great deal about how to think logically and coherently. One of our most important tasks in this regard is to learn some of the cardinal **rules of causation.** Just what do we really know about politics for sure, and what are we less sure about? To what extent can we really "prove" that one thing actually causes another? How valid are our generalizations? Questions like these lie at the heart of *epistemology,* the field of inquiry that seeks to clarify the scope and limits of our ability to know. Epistemological issues are of fundamental importance in all the sciences, including political science, and they are vital to the development of critical reasoning skills more generally.

Definitions . . . again! It might be useful to begin this chapter by recalling some key definitions that we presented in chapter 3.

- *A* **hypothesis** *is an assumption or supposition that needs to be tested against relevant evidence.* **Explanatory hypotheses** *posit a cause-and-effect relationship between dependent and independent variables that can be tested empirically (that is, against factual evidence).*
- *The* **dependent variable** *is the variable to be explained.*
- *An* **independent variable** *is an explanatory variable, or a possible explanatory variable, whose relationship to the dependent variable must be tested.*
- *A* **correlation (or association)** *is a demonstrated relationship between dependent and independent variables. The relationship may be causative in nature (i.e., the independent variable is causing something to happen in the dependent variable), but not necessarily. The observed relationship could be* **spurious,** *with no causal connection.*

SOURCES OF HYPOTHESES

Hypotheses about politics can spring from a variety of sources. In some instances they may derive from questions that pop into our minds from our observations of reality. Just from reading the newspaper, for example, we may notice the rather obvious fact that some countries have democratic systems of government and others do not. How come? From a superficial survey of these news accounts, a few possible answers may come to mind. One possible explanation centers on economics: the world's most successful and enduring democracies, we observe, are among the richest countries

FIGURE 4.1   Diagram of Inductive Reasoning

Generalization: "National wealth promotes democracy"

Specific facts or observations:
Countries like the United States, Canada, Britain, and Germany are wealthy and democratic;
Countries like Vietnam, Egypt, the Congo, and Cuba are poor and are not democracies

of the world. We notice, in particular, that such well-to-do countries as the United States, Canada, Britain, France, Germany, and Japan are successful democracies. Countries that lack democracy and countries that are currently engaged in the process of building democracy following the collapse of an authoritarian regime appear for the most part to be less economically developed. Many countries in Latin America and Africa fall into these latter categories, along with China and Russia.

A cursory glance at these facts prompts us to formulate the following hypothesis: *"National wealth promotes democracy."* This hypothesis implies a cause-and-effect relationship: national wealth somehow *causes* democracy to come about and endure, whereas national poverty precludes or undermines democracy.

The technique we have just used to formulate our hypothesis is called *induction*. **Induction** *is a reasoning process that goes from the specific to the general.* We begin with some *specific facts or observations,* and on the basis of these specifics we devise an overarching *generalization* that applies to the phenomena we have observed as well as to related phenomena that we have not as yet observed, as depicted in figure 4.1. ("Induction" derives from the Latin word for "lead into"; in essence, specific facts lead into a generalization.) Thus our observation of a few specific wealthy democracies and a few specific poor non-democracies leads us to suspect that national wealth is perhaps associated with *all* democracies and national poverty is perhaps associated with *all* non-democracies. We say "perhaps" because at this point these broad generalizations are only suspicions or guesses that we have made on the basis of a small number of observations. That is precisely what hypotheses frequently are: suspicions, educated guesses, or hunches. We don't know yet if our hunch is true or false in actual reality. Only when we

have tested our hypothesis by looking at a far wider number of democracies and non-democracies will we have a better idea of whether, or to what extent, our proposed generalization is valid.

Another source of hypotheses consists of generalizations that have already been formulated. In the course of our newspaper gleanings we may have come across an editorial arguing in favor of major international efforts to promote the economic development of nascent democracies like Russia and South Africa. The editorialist justifies this policy recommendation on the basis of a broad generalization: *"National wealth,"* she writes, *"promotes democracy."*

The editorialist then sets forth a number of reasons explaining why national wealth promotes democracy. One reason is that democracy requires an educated populace that understands political issues and actively participates in the electoral process and other opportunities for political involvement. Educated people, she argues, are more likely than the uneducated to take part in political affairs. But an educated electorate requires a good mass education system, and that costs money. Wealthy countries are in a better position than poor ones to provide their citizens with a good education. Democracy, we are told, also requires a well-developed mass communications system so that people can keep themselves informed about political developments. That too costs money.

Furthermore, the writer maintains, democracy requires a fairly sizable middle class that is eager to have a say in the way the country is governed. The middle class, she believes, is a prime source of pro-democracy activism. By contrast, the rich may be perfectly content with an authoritarian regime that allows them to retain their wealth, while the poor may be insufficiently educated or too unorganized to push for democratic reforms. Wealthy countries are more likely than impoverished ones to have a sizable middle class.

In addition, the writer notes, wealthy countries are better equipped than poor ones to meet their citizens' demands for government services. Democracy gives the mass public an opportunity to demand such benefits as education, decent housing, health care, job training, and pensions. Poor countries are less able to meet these popular demands, and their rulers therefore deny their populations a chance to articulate them in an open democratic process. A repressive authoritarian government is the likely result. Thus if we want democracy to succeed around the world, the writer concludes, the wealthy democracies must do whatever they can to assist the less developed nations of the world in overcoming their poverty.

In this particular case, the editorialist did not look at specific democratic and non-democratic countries, as we did in our perusal of newspaper articles. Rather, she derived her hypothesis from *generalizations* about what causes democracies to come about. Her supposition that national wealth promotes democracy is based on a general explanation of various factors needed to build a democratic regime, all of which ultimately depend on national wealth. Thus *generalizations themselves*, not just specific facts, can also be a source of hypotheses.

STEPS OF HYPOTHESIS TESTING

Are the editorialist's sweeping generalizations correct? In order to find out, we need to break them down into testable propositions and test them against hard evidence. Let's concentrate on her central hypothesis, "National wealth promotes democracy." How do we go about testing this proposition?

We can choose from a variety of methods, depending on whether we are relying mainly on quantitative or qualitative analysis (or some combination of the two) and on whether we want to examine a large number of countries or confine ourselves to a few particularly illustrative ones. In most cases, however, the logic of hypothesis testing will involve the following five steps:

1. Defining key terms
2. Identifying the variables
3. Specifying the expectations of the hypothesis
4. Collecting and examining the evidence
5. Drawing conclusions from the evidence

Defining Key Terms

Because our hypothesis is about democracy, we must define the term. "Democracy" is capable of several different definitions, as we shall see in greater detail in chapter 8. How we choose to define democracy in our hypothesis-testing exercise will have a tremendous impact on the way we conduct our study and the results we get from it. For the purposes of our study we'll define democracy in fairly simple terms as *a system of government in which the main governing officials are elected in competitive elections involving two or more parties and in which all citizens over the age of twenty-one have the right to vote.*

This definition allows us to include a large number of countries throughout the contemporary world. But it would exclude other putative "democracies" during those periods of their history when the vote was denied to women. By the terms of this definition, the United States, Britain, France, Italy, and other countries were not democracies until after World War I. Women throughout the United States were not guaranteed the constitutional right to vote until the Nineteenth Amendment was ratified in 1920. British women did not gain voting privileges until 1918. French women did not have the right to vote until 1944, Italian women not until 1948, and Swiss women could not vote in national elections until 1971.

If we want to extend our study to include American, British, French, Italian, and other "democracies" before these years, we would have to redefine democracy, perhaps by applying the term to political systems in which a majority of *males* have the right to vote. Even then, the date at which individual countries actually met this qualification typically came after the introduction of the *principle* of government by election, a principle that is certainly essential to most definitions of democracy. African-American males, for example, were not guaranteed the constitutional right to vote until 1870, more than eighty years after the election of George Washington as president. Most white males did not have the vote in the United States until 1828. When the United States Constitution took effect in 1789, only about one in thirty adults had the right to vote, most of them white males who met specified property-owning requirements.[1]

Quite clearly, any attempt to define democracy in fairly simple terms by linking it just to the principle or actual practice of elections runs into thorny problems. But as we shall see in chapter 8, democracy involves far more than just elections. It also requires the government to make sure that the elections are scrupulously fair and that people have the right to organize opposition parties and other organizations that may oppose those who wield governmental power. The mere fact of elections is not enough. Some governments rig elections in their favor or find ways to suppress opposition parties so that they do not really have a fair chance to unseat the ruling authorities in a truly competitive electoral contest.

Democracies must also must observe the basic principle of the *rule of law;* that is, they must make sure that all government officials, no matter how powerful, observe certain laws that define or limit the scope of their power. No one may be exempted from the laws of the land. To this end, democracies must provide continuing opportunities for the people to have a say in how the laws are made and implemented. Accordingly, they must permit elected legislatures to have an input into the law-making process. They must also require the governing officials to conduct the government's business out in the open, enabling the public and the press to have adequate information about what the government is actually doing. In addition, democracies must also guarantee certain rights and freedoms to their citizens, such as the right to free speech, political opinion, and religious belief. And they must guarantee minorities the same legal rights and freedoms as the majority.

In short, democracy is a very complicated phenomenon, with numerous interacting components. Any conception of what democracy entails must take these multiple factors into consideration if our hypothesis-testing exercise is to be meaningful. We cannot adequately test hypotheses about democracy unless we have an explicit and realistic definition that we use consistently in our testing operation.

One way of defining democracy in its multifaceted complexity has been suggested by the authors of *Freedom in the World,* which is an annual survey of the world's governments published by Freedom House, an organization devoted to the study of democratic rights and freedoms around the globe. Using basic criteria of political rights and civil liberties such as the ones just indicated, the Freedom House experts rate the nations of the world on a numerical scale. In the 1998–99 edition of *Freedom in the World,* countries that provided the greatest democratic rights and liberties were given a top rating of 1, while countries that provided the least amount of democracy were given a bottom score of 7. On the basis of the Freedom House rating system, we'll categorize countries with an average score of 1 to 2.5 as "democratic"; those whose average scores go from 3 to 5 as "partly democratic"; and those whose ratings go from 5.5 to 7 as "authoritarian."[2]

We can narrow our conception of democracy even further by singling out *successful* democracies, the ones that endure over fairly lengthy periods of time. For the purposes of this exercise, we'll define a *long-term democracy* as one that has existed for at least forty years in succession.

Since we are looking for a relationship between democracy and national wealth, we must also specify what we mean by "wealth" and "poverty." One way of defining these terms is to categorize countries on the basis of their annual gross national product (GNP) per capita. The GNP is a measure of how much a country's economy produces; per capita GNP is the GNP divided by the country's population. The World Bank and other international agencies publish annual GNP statistics for most nations of the world. These figures allow us to stratify countries into *high-income* economies (defined by the World Bank as countries whose per capita GNP in 1998 was $9,361 or more); *upper-middle-income* countries (those whose 1998 per capita GNP went from $3,031 to $9,360); *lower-middle-income* countries (whose per capita GNP in 1998 went from $761 to $3,030); and *low-income* economies ($760 or less).[3]

To be sure, these income categories present definitional problems of their own. At what level of per capita GNP is a country "wealthy" or "poor"? Why is the dividing line between lower-middle-income countries and upper-middle-income countries fixed at $3,030 and not, say, $2,900 or $1,500? Obviously, the placement of the dividing lines is a bit arbitrary. We are dealing here with *relative* levels of wealth and poverty, not absolute ones. These and other potential problems make it very clear that, in the social sciences, finding a perfect definition for our variables may be difficult and at times impossible. Despite these problems, definitional clarity is essential. We'll therefore regard those countries classified in the upper-income category as "wealthy"; those in the upper-middle-income category as "relatively wealthy"; those in the lower-middle-income group as "relatively poor"; and those in the low-income group as "poor."

Finally, what do we mean when we hypothesize that national wealth *"promotes"* democracy? Here we need to specify that national wealth somehow "causes" democracy. More specifically, we mean that (a) wealth causes democracy to come into existence, replacing authoritarian modes of government, and (b) it causes democracies already in existence to succeed over protracted periods of time.

Identifying Our Variables

The next step we must take is to identify our dependent and independent variables. Since the *existence of democracy* is the effect we wish to explain, it is our **dependent variable**.

Our **independent variable** is the *level of national wealth*. We want to see how varying levels of national wealth, as specified in the per capita GNP categories listed earlier, relate to democratic and non-democratic systems of government. This independent variable is our presumed *explanatory* variable. We can *manipulate* it by observing how different gradations of national wealth are related to democracy.

Specifying the Expectations of the Hypothesis

Hypotheses are usually stated as declarative propositions. Thus far we have stated our hypothesis as a declarative sentence, that is, *"National wealth promotes democracy."* In order to test a hypothesis systematically, we must restate it in terms that will indicate *what we should look for as we hunt*

for evidence that might confirm or contradict its validity: *if* the hypothesis is valid, *then* what would we *expect* to find as we sift through the available facts? In other words, what are the **expectations** of our hypothesis? To guide our research, therefore, *it is helpful to restate our hypothesis in "if . . . then" form:*

> *If* national wealth promotes democracy, *then* we would expect to find that (a) relatively wealthy states are democracies and (b) relatively poor states are not.

Logically, we would also expect to find that (c) democracies will be relatively wealthy, and (d) authoritarian regimes will be relatively poor. It would also be reasonable to expect middle-income countries to fall between the rich democratic countries and the poor authoritarian ones. Specifically, we'd expect the upper-middle-income countries to be either democratic or partly democratic and the lower-middle-income countries to be either partly democratic or authoritarian, with the political and civil rights ratings of these countries reflecting their respective levels of national wealth. The more wealth a country has, the greater is the likelihood that it will be democratic; a country with poor economic fortunes has a poor prospect for democracy and a greater likelihood for authoritarianism.

The process of translating our hypothesis into "if . . . then" form is an example of *deduction*. **Deduction** *is a reasoning process that proceeds from the general to the specific.* It begins with a generalization that covers a wide range or class of phenomena and then applies that generalization to specific cases (see figure 4.2). In our example, we start with our hypothesis, which proposes that national wealth promotes democracy *in general*, and we apply that generalization to specific countries. In deductive logic, the applications of the generalization to specific cases **must follow with logical necessity**. In other words, *if* A is true, *then* B *must* be true; if B is true, it follows that C is true; and so on. ("Deduction" comes from the Latin term for "lead from": each conclusion leads from the preceding one with logical necessity.) As we've already suggested, *if* national wealth promotes democracy, *then* it is only logical that specific countries that are relatively wealthy should be democracies, while specific countries that are

FIGURE 4.2   Diagram of Deductive Reasoning

Generalization: "National wealth promotes democracy"

Logical deductions: "If national wealth promotes democracy, then it logically follows that . . ."

Specific cases: specific wealthy countries   specific poor countries
                        will be democracies   will be non-democracies

relatively poor should be non-democracies. When phrased in "if . . . then" terms, a hypothesis *predicts* a certain research result as a logically specified outcome.

The deductions we have just drawn from our hypothesis tell us what we should *expect* to find in reality. But whether we actually *will* find these results is another matter. If the facts that we gather in our hypothesis-testing research are consistent with these predicted results, then the hypothesis itself may be factually correct. But if the facts deviate from the expected results, the hypothesis may be wrong. We must now look at the facts to see if the predicted outcomes occur.

Collecting and Examining the Evidence

Empirical analysis, as we've already pointed out, is based on facts. Unless there is a sufficient body of factual evidence bearing on our hypothesis, we cannot properly test it. Suppose, for example, that there is only one democracy in the world, and it happens to be quite rich. All the other governments of the world are non-democracies, and all are economically undeveloped. On the basis of this evidence, we can conclude that the available evidence is *consistent* with our hypothesis linking democracy with a relatively high level of national wealth. But one case is scarcely enough to warrant high confidence in the generality of this conclusion. It does not convince us that national wealth is really necessary to *promote* democracies elsewhere. Other factors may be more important (such as the degree of social harmony, the nature of religious beliefs, and so on). The fact that our lone democracy is wealthy may be purely coincidental and have nothing whatsoever to do with causing or promoting democracy. Our confidence in the

validity of a generalization tends to rise with the number of cases we have in its support.

As it happens, quite a few democracies in the world meet our definition of the term. We must now identify them and see if they meet our criteria of national wealth. The countries listed in table 4.1 meet these criteria: they are among the richest countries of the world, and all are bona fide democracies with political and civil rights ratings of 1 to 2.5. All but a few are also long-term democracies that have sustained democratic institutions for at least forty years.

There is also a large number of upper-middle-income countries that can be classified as either democracies or partial democracies, once again in conformity with our expectations (table 4.2 on page 82). Unlike the majority of high-income countries, however, none of these countries qualifies as a long-term democracy that has maintained democratic institutions and practices for at least forty years without interruption.

While there seems to be abundant evidence confirming our expectation that wealthy and upper-middle-income countries tend to be democracies, there is also evidence in support of our assumption that, conversely, poor countries tend to be authoritarian regimes. Take a look at table 4.3 on page 83.

Our expectation that lower-middle-income countries will tend to be either partial democracies or authoritarian regimes also has evidence in its support, as table 4.4 on page 84 demonstrates. Note how many of the partial democracies listed in this table have a political and civil rights index of 4 or worse, an indication that the country has serious problems meeting some of the principal criteria for democracy. These data support the expectations of our hypothesis that the poorer a country is, the less democratic it is likely to be.

TABLE 4.1

High-Income Democracies

(Political/Civil Rights Index of 1 to 2.5; 1998 Per Capita GNP of $9,361 or More)

Country	1998 Per Capita GNP	Political/Civil Rights Index	Long-Term Democracy
Luxembourg	$43,570	1	X
Switzerland	40,080	1	X
Norway	34,330	1	X
Denmark	33,260	1	X
Japan	32,380	1.5	X
United States	29,340	1	X
Iceland	28,010	1	X
Austria	26,850	1	X
Germany	25,850	1.5	X
Sweden	25,620	1	X
Belgium	25,380	1.5	X
France	24,940	1.5	X
Netherlands	24,760	1	X
Finland	24,110	1	X
United Kingdom	21,400	1.5	X
Australia	20,300	1	X
Italy	20,250	1.5	X
Canada	20,020	1	X
Ireland	18,340	1	X
Israel	15,940	2	X
New Zealand	14,700	1	X
Spain	14,080	1.5	
Greece	11,650	2	
Portugal	10,690	1	
Slovenia	9,760	1.5	
Malta	9,440	1	
Andorra	estimated high income	1	
Bahamas	estimated high income	1.5	
Liechtenstein	estimated high income	1	
Monaco	estimated high income	1.5	
Taiwan (Republic of China)	estimated high income	2	

We have now found quite a few contemporary democracies classified as wealthy or relatively wealthy (the latter having upper-middle-level incomes) and a large number of non-democracies classified as poor or relatively poor (the latter having lower-middle-level incomes). Countries with the highest score on the political rights index are predominantly in the wealthy category, as are all the long-term democracies. These data are *consistent* with what our hypothesis predicted we would find.

Our collection of evidence bearing on the hypothesis is by no means finished, however.

In scientific hypothesis testing, it is never sufficient just to look for evidence that *confirms* the hypothesis or to terminate our research after finding such
evidence. We must also look for evidence that might *contradict* the hypothesis.

The quest for information contrary to our prevailing assumptions is vital to all forms of logical argumentation. Some scientists would go even further and say that science itself consists above all in the formulation and testing of generalizations that are capable of being empirically *falsified.*[4]

We must therefore try to find evidence of (a) democracies that are *not* wealthy or relatively wealthy, and (b) non-democracies that *are* wealthy or relatively wealthy.

As it happens, quite a few democracies (with a political and civil rights index of 1 to 2.5) are categorized as lower-middle-income or low-income

TABLE 4.2

Upper-Middle-Income Democracies and Partial Democracies

(Political/Civil Rights Index of 1 to 2.5 for Democracies, 3 to 5 for Partial Democracies;
1998 Per Capita GNP of $3,031 to $9,360)

Democratic			Partly Democratic		
Country	1998 Per Capita GNP	Political/Civil Rights Index	Country	1998 Per Capita GNP	Political/Civil Rights Index
South Korea	$7,970	2	Argentina	$8,970	3
Barbados	7,890	1	Antigua and Barbuda	7,970	3.5
Uruguay	6,180	1.5	Seychelles	6,450	3
St. Kitts and Nevis	6,130	1.5	Brazil	4,570	3.5
Czech Republic	5,040	1.5	Croatia	4,520	4
Chile	4,810	2.5	Mexico	3,970	3.5
Hungary	4,510	1.5	Gabon	3,950	4.5
Trinidad and Tobago	4,430	1.5	Slovakia	3,700	3
Poland	3,900	1.5	Malaysia	3,600	5
Mauritius	3,700	1.5	Turkey	3,160	4.5
Botswana	3,600	2			
Venezuela	3,500	2.5			
St. Lucia	3,410	1.5			
Estonia	3,390	1.5			
Grenada	3,170	1.5			
Panama	3,080	2.5			
Palau	estimated upper-middle income	1.5			

economies, as indicated in table 4.5 on page 85. Only one of these countries—Costa Rica—is a long-term democracy; it has maintained democratic institutions continuously since 1949. However, one of the poorest (and largest) countries in the world—India—is a democracy today and has sustained democratic procedures for most of its existence as an independent country since 1947. (Democracy in India was briefly suspended in the 1970s. See chapter 15 for an outline of India's political development.)

The existence of so many democracies in the lower-middle-income category and of a smaller but not insignificant number of low-income democracies runs counter to our expectations. This mundane analytical detail contains a powerful real-world lesson: the countries listed in table 4.5 provide incontrovertible evidence that *poverty does not constitute an insurmountable barrier to democracy.* Whereas a relatively low-income economy may indeed make it more difficult for a country to build and sustain democratic institutions and practices, by no means does it doom its chances irreparably.

Table 4.6 on page 85 provides some reinforcement for this conclusion. It lists low-income countries whose political systems may be considered at least partly democratic. The implications of these figures are actually rather mixed. On the one hand, the table makes it clear that poor countries are less likely than wealthier ones to be viable, full-fledged democracies that guarantee a wide range of political and civil rights. (Note that the countries listed in table 4.6 have Freedom House ratings from 3 to 5.) This observation is *consistent* with our assumption that national wealth and democracy are positively correlated. On the other hand, while the countries listed in table 4.6 are not as well developed economically as the democracies listed in table 4.5, they nonetheless *contradict* our expectation that very poor countries are not likely to have much democracy at all. At the very least, these countries provide some hope that severe levels of national poverty may not preclude future improvements on the path to democratic rights and freedoms.

TABLE 4.3

Low-Income Authoritarian Regimes

(Political/Civil Rights Index of 5.5 to 7; 1998 Per Capita GNP of $760 or Less)

Country	1998 Per Capita GNP	Political/Civil Rights Index
People's Republic of China	$750	6.5
Ivory Coast	700	5*
Republic of Congo	690	6.5
Cameroon	610	6
Guinea	540	5.5
Mauritania	410	5.5
Tajikistan	350	6
The Gambia	340	6
Angola	340	6
Vietnam	330	7
Laos	330	6.5
Kenya	330	5.5
Togo	330	5.5
Yemen	300	5.5
Sudan	290	7
Kampuchea (Cambodia)	280	6
Rwanda	230	6.5
Chad	230	5*
Niger	190	6
Burundi	140	7
Democratic Rep. of the Congo (formerly Zaire)	110	6
Afghanistan	estimated low income	7
Bhutan	estimated low income	7
Cuba	estimated low income	7
Djibouti	estimated low income	5.5
Myanmar	estimated low income	7
Somalia	estimated low income	7
Turkmenistan	estimated low income	7

*This country was rated "not free" (i.e., authoritarian) by Freedom House, even though its score is 5.

An equally important political lesson emerges from table 4.7 on page 86. It lists high-income and upper-middle-income countries that are *not* full-fledged democracies. The information presented in this table contradicts our expectation that wealthy countries are likely to be democracies that guarantee a high level of political and civil rights. Of the five high-income countries listed, three are authoritarian regimes. The other two—Singapore and Kuwait—are each partial democracies with an unenviable political and civil rights index of 5 despite their status as two of the richest countries in the world as measured by per capita GNP. The data also contradict our expectation that upper-middle-income countries are likely to be democratic or at least partly democratic. The five upper-middle-income countries shown in table 4.7 are all

authoritarian regimes. The obvious lesson to be gleaned from these figures is that *national wealth provides no guarantee of democracy*. It doesn't even provide a guarantee against highly repressive authoritarianism and flagrant abuses of fundamental political and civil rights.

We now have conflicting evidence bearing on our hypothesis. Most of the high-income countries of the world are democracies; indeed, this income category has by far the highest concentration of long-term democracies. Moreover, there is a large number of lower-middle-income and poor countries that are authoritarian. These facts are *consistent* with our hypothesis.

But some high-income countries are not democracies. There are also quite a few upper-middle-income countries that are not democracies. In

TABLE 4.4

Lower-Middle-Income Partly Democratic and Authoritarian Regimes

(Political/Civil Rights Index of 3 to 5 for Partly Democratic and 5.5 to 7 for Authoritarian Regimes;
1998 Per Capita GNP of $761 to $3,030)

	Partly Democratic			Authoritarian	
Country	1998 Per Capita GNP	Political/Civil Rights Index	Country	1998 Per Capita GNP	Political/Civil Rights Index
Colombia	$2,600	3.5	Belarus	$2,200	6
Peru	2,460	4.5	Tunisia	2,050	5.5
Russia	2,300	4	Iran	1,770	6
Fiji	2,110	3.5	Algeria	1,550	5.5
Paraguay	1,760	3.5	Equatorial Guinea	1,500	7
Tonga	1,690	4	Swaziland	1,400	5*
Suriname	1,660	3	Kazakhstan	1,310	5.5
Guatemala	1,640	3.5	Egypt	1,290	6
Jordan	1,520	4.5	Maldives	1,230	5.5
Macedonia	1,290	3	Syria	1,020	7
Morocco	1,250	4.5	Uzbekistan	870	7
Georgia	930	3.5	Iraq	estimated lower-middle income	7
Ukraine	850	3.5			
Sri Lanka	810	3.5	North Korea	estimated lower-middle income	7
Albania	810	4.5			
Guyana	770	4.5	Yugoslavia	estimated lower-middle income	6
Bosnia-Herzegovina	estimated lower-middle income	5			

*Although this score is 5, this country was rated "not free" (i.e., authoritarian) by Freedom House.

addition, a substantial list of lower-middle-income and even poor countries *are* democracies (though only one has been successful over the long term). These data are *inconsistent* with our hypothesis: they contradict our expectations. Our next step is to determine what conclusions we can draw from this conflicting evidence.

Drawing Conclusions from the Evidence

The first question we are tempted to ask when drawing conclusions from the available evidence is whether we have "proved" that our hypothesis is correct. The term "proof" implies absolute certitude, however, and most scientists doubt that we can ever prove anything with complete certainty. For one thing, the evidence we collect, no matter how exhaustive our search, may not be enough to permit a final verdict on the *universal* validity of our conclusions. (A proposition is *universally* valid if it applies to *all* relevant cases.) Even if all the evidence at our disposal confirms our hypothesis,

there may still exist contrary evidence of which we are unaware. Instead of boasting that the evidence conclusively "proves" that a hypothesis is correct, therefore, we'll have to settle for the more modest conclusion that the evidence is **consistent** with the hypothesis. Any conclusion that a hypothesized relationship is "true" can only be tentative.

It is easier to *disprove* the universal validity of a hypothesis than to prove it. If we can find any evidence at all that is contrary to the results predicted by the hypothesis, we can demonstrate that the hypothesized relationship is not *universally* valid. The relationship may be valid sometimes, but not always. In some instances we can show that the hypothesis is *never* valid. In any event, evidence that is contrary to the results predicted by the hypothesis is designated simply as **inconsistent** with the hypothesis.

In short, when drawing conclusions from our evidence, we have to distinguish between evidence that is *consistent* with our hypothesis and evidence that is *inconsistent* with it.

TABLE 4.5

Lower-Middle-Income and Low-Income Democracies

(Political/Civil Rights Index of 1 to 2.5; 1998 Per Capita GNP of $761 to $3,030 for Lower-Middle-Income Countries and $760 or Less for Low-Income Countries)

Lower-Middle Income

Country	1998 Per Capita GNP	Political/Civil Rights Index
Dominica	$3,010	1
South Africa	2,880	1.5
Costa Rica*	2,780	1.5
Belize	2,610	1
Lithuania	2,440	1.5
Latvia	2,430	1.5
St. Vincent and Grenadines	2,420	1.5
Namibia	1,940	2.5
El Salvador	1,850	2.5
Micronesia	1,800	1.5
Dominican Republic	1,770	2.5
Jamaica	1,680	2
Marshall Islands	1,540	1
Ecuador	1,530	2.5
Romania	1,390	2
Vanuatu	1,270	2
Bulgaria	1,230	2.5
Kiribati	1,180	1
Cape Verde	1,060	1.5
Philippines	1,050	2.5
Samoa	1,020	2.5
Bolivia	1,000	2
Papua-New Guinea	890	2.5
Nicaragua	estimated lower-middle income	2.5

*Long-term democracy

Low Income

Country	1998 Per Capita GNP	Political/Civil Rights Index
Honduras	$750	2.5
Solomon Islands	750	1.5
India	430	2.5
Mongolia	400	2.5
Benin	380	2
Malawi	200	2
Sao Tome and Principe	180	1.5

TABLE 4.6

Partly Democratic, Low-Income Countries

(Political/Civil Rights Index of 3.5 to 5; 1998 Per Capita GNP of $760 or Less)

Country	1998 Per Capita GNP	Political/Civil Rights Index
Indonesia	$680	5
Zimbabwe	610	5
Lesotho	570	4
Senegal	530	4
Nigeria	500	5
Azerbaijan	490	5
Armenia	480	5
Pakistan	480	4.5
Haiti	410	4.5
Moldova	410	3
Ghana	390	3
Comoros	370	3.5
Bangladesh	350	3
Kyrgyzia	350	5
Zambia	330	4.5
Uganda	320	4.5
Central African Republic	300	3.5
Madagascar	260	3
Mali	250	3
Burkina Faso	240	4.5
Nepal	210	3
Mozambique	210	3.5
Tanzania	210	4.5
Eritrea	200	5
Niger	190	4
Guinea-Bissau	160	4
Sierra Leone	140	4
Ethiopia	100	4
Liberia	estimated low income	4.5

In some cases our evidence will be entirely one or the other. But in many cases it will cut both ways: some of it will be consistent with the hypothesis, some inconsistent. In these cases the results of our research are *mixed* and lead us to conclude that the hypothesis appears to be partly true and partly false. (At times the evidence may be *mostly* true or *mostly* false.) If possible, we then need to specify the conditions under which the hypothesis is correct and those under which it is not.

In yet another set of cases, the evidence may be so evenly mixed, confusing, or simply inadequate as to be *inconclusive:* we cannot really be sure whether our hypothesis is true or false, or to what extent it is

TABLE 4.7

High-Income and Upper-Middle-Income Non-Democracies

High-Income Countries			Upper-Middle-Income Countries		
Country	1998 Per Capita GNP	Political/Civil Rights Index	Country	1998 Per Capita GNP	Political/Civil Rights Index
Singapore	$30,030	5	Bahrain	$7,660	6.5
United Arab Emirates	18,220	5.5	Lebanon	3,560	5.5
Kuwait	estimated high income	5	Saudi Arabia	estimated upper-middle income	7
Qatar	estimated high income	6.5	Oman	estimated upper-middle income	6
Brunei	estimated high income	6	Libya	estimated upper-middle income	7

the one or the other. In these cases, our final conclusion must be "we don't know." Frustrating though it may be, "we don't know" is sometimes the right answer in science. *Science is characterized not by the conclusiveness of its results but by the logic of its methods.* Its value is just as great when it shows us what we do *not* know as when it points out what we do know with considerable confidence.

Taking these general observations into account, let's now draw some conclusions from the evidence we've garnered on democracies and national wealth. To begin with, we have evidence that is both consistent and inconsistent with the hypothesized relationship between democracy and national wealth. There are relatively wealthy democracies as well as non-democracies; there are relatively poor democracies as well as non-democracies. Taken in its entirety, therefore, the evidence we have examined is *mixed:* some of it supports the hypothesis, some contradicts it. The evidence we have seen does not consistently and exclusively link relative wealth with democracy, nor does it conclusively rule out a relationship between these two variables.

Nevertheless, we can still discern some broad patterns. The overwhelming majority of the highest-scoring long-term democracies are clustered in the high-income category. Very low-scoring authoritarian regimes (with a rating of 6 or 7) tend to be clustered in the low-income category. These data suggest an observable association between democracy and national wealth. Although the correlation between democracy and national wealth may not be universally applicable, as tables 4.5, 4.6, and 4.7 make clear, it is still an observable tendency.

Establishing a correlation between variables is a vital first step in the direction of demonstrating a causal relationship between them. If there is no evident relationship of any kind, obviously there can be no causal one. Keep in mind, however, that a correlation does not by itself establish causality. To what extent does our evidence demonstrate that national wealth "promotes" democracy in the sense that it actually *causes* democracy to come about or endure? At this point we need to consider a few basic principles of causal inference and the process of reasoning by induction.

Induction As we noted earlier, *induction proceeds from the specific to the general. It is the process of drawing conclusions or generalizations from specific information or evidence.* The inductive process is also characterized by the fact that, unlike deduction, *the evidence does not lead to logically determined conclusions.* Rather, the facts may be consistent with two or more possible conclusions, some perhaps closer to the actual truth than others. Our specific information on democracy and national wealth, for example, does not logically compel us to conclude that national wealth always promotes democracy. It merely suggests that wealth *may* promote democracy, but only in certain cases, if then. Drawing conclusions from empirical tests of hypotheses in political science is often an inductive process. In these cases, whatever conclusions we are able to draw from our evidence can only be tentative and uncertain; the laws of logic provide no ironclad guarantee of their validity.

Indirect Hypothesis Testing   Notice that we did not test our hypothesis, "National wealth promotes democracy," directly. We did not directly observe a single case in which national wealth clearly caused a democracy to come about when none existed before or caused an existing democracy to remain in existence over a protracted period of time. All we did was to categorize the countries of the contemporary world by income group and type of government to see if any patterns emerged. We did not undertake in-depth investigations of these countries individually to see if wealth really does account for the presence or absence of democracy in each case, and if it does, *how* it does so. We never directly looked for evidence demonstrating the editorialist's contention that wealth promotes democracy by promoting education, mass communications, a middle class, or a government responsive to its citizens' demands.

Although the data we presented on nearly 200 countries displays a *general pattern* linking wealth and highly successful, long-term democracies, they do not permit us to conclude that wealth *always* promotes democracy. They don't even permit us to conclude that wealth is definitely responsible for creating or sustaining democracy in any of the wealthiest democracies listed in table 4.1. The data simply tell us that wealth is *associated* (or *correlated*) with the most successful democracies as a general rule. Although this correlation is consistent with the hypothesis that national wealth *promotes* (i.e., *causes*) democracy, the evidence we presented in this chapter does not *definitively* demonstrate that the hypothesis is in fact true.

Most of the hypotheses we test in political science are tested indirectly, not directly. Especially when we look at aggregate data for a variety of countries, the best we can do is draw tentative inferences from whichever general patterns we can discern. Case studies of individual countries would give us deeper, more detailed information about whether, and how, national wealth actually promotes democracy in practice. In other words, we would have to undertake in-depth examinations of the relationship between national wealth and democracy in, say, the United States, Japan, or other democracies to see if (and how) wealth actually *promotes* democracy. But individual case studies are usually too narrowly focused to enable us

to draw grand conclusions about the relationship between wealth and democracy *in general.* Such studies typically cannot show us how this relationship might apply to all or most of the nations of the world in different historical periods. Once again, we are forced to be very modest about the scope and certitude of our knowledge.

Multicausality   Sometimes a phenomenon has only one cause. Heat alone, for example, causes ice to melt. But far more often, even in the natural world, events occur because of a multiplicity of causes. These multiple causes can work simultaneously or in different sequences; they can work in a variety of combinations and quantities. Political and social phenomena, in particular, rarely have only one cause; in human affairs, **multicausality** is far more likely than monocausality. Whether we are trying to explain democracy, dictatorship, voter turnout, economic growth, or why nations go to war, two or more independent variables typically account for the dependent variable we are trying to explain. Thus the level of national wealth *by itself* may not account for democracy or its absence in any of the countries listed in our tables.

Conceivably, national wealth may promote democracy by working through other variables that may play a more direct role in stimulating the birth of a democracy or in undergirding a successful democracy over time. As our editorialist suggested, such variables as an educated public, mass communications, and a politically active middle class may ultimately depend on the size of a nation's wealth, but it is these so-called *intervening variables,* not wealth per se, that may have a more immediate impact on the fate of democracy. These variables intervene between national wealth and democracy, enabling the one to exert a causative effect on the other, as illustrated in figure 4.3.

As noted earlier, however, our data that show a general tendency to relate successful democracy to national wealth do not tell us anything about these or other intervening variables. To find out whether, or to what extent, such variables affect democracy, we would have to look for specific data on these phenomena in the countries on our lists, or we must undertake more direct studies of these factors within individual countries.[5]

FIGURE 4.3   Intervening Variables Between National Wealth and Democracy

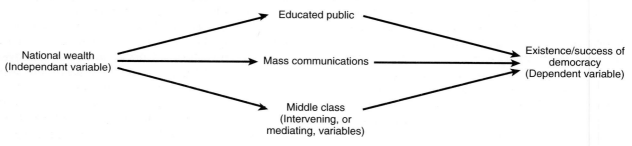

These tasks can get pretty complicated. The many variables that have a demonstrable causative impact on democracy or some other political phenomenon may be so intertwined that it may be very difficult to disentangle them. Statistical analysis can sometimes measure the relative impact of different independent variables on a dependent variable, but not always. The recipe for a successful democracy, for example, has so many ingredients that it is virtually impossible to specify statistically or in some rigorous manner which ones are more important than others. In addition to national wealth and the intervening variables it can buy, democracies may need such things as a general respect for the law, a tradition of cooperation and compromise among social groups, a political elite that respects the rights and liberties of the population, and quite possibly a host of additional factors as well. The precise mixture of these ingredients may vary from democracy to democracy. Rarely, if ever, is democracy simply the product of one sole causal variable.

Although the analysis we have just conducted shows a strong association between national wealth and successful democracy, it by no means rules out the possibility that *additional* independent variables (other than those connected with wealth) may also be of crucial significance in accounting for the existence or long-term success of democracies.

In trying to understand political reality, we must always be sensitive to the possibility (indeed the likelihood) of multicausality. Reducing complex realities to just one explanatory variable while paying insufficient attention to other contributing explanations is a logical fallacy called **reductivism**. Reductivism is just as fallacious in everyday political discourse as it is in political science. When we make such statements as, "In U.S.

politics, race determines everything," or "Big business runs the country," we may be just as reductivist in our reasoning as is someone who would suggest that national wealth alone explains the existence or success of democracy. Before we single out one particular variable as the sole explanation of the phenomenon at hand, therefore, we had better make certain that we have systematically ruled out all other potential explanatory variables. *A scientific approach to politics requires us to be on the lookout at all times for multiple sources of explanation and causation in political life and to pay close attention to the ways they interact.* To do otherwise is to engage in illogical argumentation and oversimplification.

Necessary and Sufficient Conditions   One of the most basic distinctions in the logic of causation is the distinction between *necessary* and *sufficient* conditions.

A **necessary condition** is one that *must* be present in order for some phenomenon or event to occur; without it, the event cannot occur. A certain amount of sunlight is a necessary condition for most plant growth. By itself, however, sunlight may not be sufficient to ensure the steady growth of a plant to maturity. Anyone who raises tomatoes or houseplants knows that regular watering may also be necessary.

A **sufficient condition** is one that *by itself* suffices for the phenomenon to occur. When a sufficient condition is present, the phenomenon *must* occur. It is not necessary, for example, to focus sunlight on paper through a magnifying glass in order to ignite a fire. Striking a match or spontaneous combustion is just as incendiary. Any one of these methods, however, is *sufficient* to start a fire.

Some causative agents are both necessary *and* sufficient conditions simultaneously. The gravitational attraction of the Earth and the moon are both necessary and sufficient to cause the tides to change.

Other agents may exert a discernible causative effect on phenomena, but are neither necessary nor sufficient to cause the observed outcomes. Numerous studies show that smokers contract lung cancer at significantly higher rates than non-smokers. Yet smoking is not a necessary condition for lung cancer, since non-smokers also contract the disease. Nor is smoking a sufficient cause for lung cancer, since smoking does not always result in cancer; many life-long smokers remain cancer-free all their lives.[6]

Is a high level of national wealth a necessary or sufficient condition for democracy? The data presented in the tables show that it is neither. Costa Rica, a lower-middle-income country, has been relatively successful in maintaining democratic electoral procedures since 1949. This country provides evidence that a relatively high level of wealth is not absolutely *necessary* to build and sustain electoral democracy. By implication, factors other than those that depend on national wealth may be very important in creating a democracy and even sustaining it over many decades. We'll have to look specifically at fairly poor democracies like India to find out exactly what these democracy-sustaining forces are.

At the same time, our data show that wealth is not *sufficient* to establish or maintain democracy. Fairly rich countries like Saudi Arabia, Singapore, Kuwait, and the United Arab Emirates are not democracies, nor are several countries in the upper-middle-income category, as indicated in table 4.7. The Soviet Union in its heyday had the world's second largest GNP after the United States, yet it was never a democracy. Again, by implication, factors in addition to those that depend on national wealth may be necessary to build and sustain democracy. Once more, we'll have to undertake more intensive country-by-country investigations to identify these variables.

To what extent, then, does the information presented here permit us to conclude that national wealth "promotes" (or "causes") democracy? The best answer we can give is that *national wealth is strongly correlated with democracy and therefore increases the likelihood of democracy.* The wealthier a country is, the *more likely* it will be democratic. Conversely, the poorer a country is, the *less likely* it will

have democracy. The correlation is not perfect, however; as we have seen, there are exceptions to it.

Furthermore, the data do not tell us exactly when a new democracy will come into existence, replacing some form of authoritarianism. Still, it is evident that such transitions to democracy are more likely to occur in middle-income countries than in lower-income countries. The data also show that national wealth promotes the success of democracy over prolonged periods of time, at least among the wealthiest democratic nations.

In sum, the evidence at hand tells us that national wealth *tends* to promote and sustain democracy and increases the *chances* for democracy. But it does not *determine* that democracy will actually come about, or even necessarily succeed, over the long run.

PARADOXES OF CAUSATIVE LOGIC

As the preceding hypothesis-testing exercise has shown, demonstrating causation is not easy. We now come to a great paradox of scientific logic: *although one of the most important aims of science is to discover the causes of things, causation is one of the most difficult of all phenomena to demonstrate conclusively.* This paradox is especially evident in political science, where we are dealing with so many interacting variables. Only rarely in political life do we come upon an instance in which A demonstrably causes B, necessarily and sufficiently. It is far more likely that B is caused by more than one factor.

To make things even more complicated, we may be confronted with the conundrum of the chicken and the egg. Evidence indicating a strong correlation between A and B does not necessarily mean that A is a cause of B; it could mean that B is a cause of A. Thus the data presented in this chapter may not be telling us that national wealth tends to promote democracy; rather, it may be indicating that democracy promotes national wealth. Alternatively, A and B could be related in a mutually reinforcing *interactive* process known as **reciprocal causation**. In that case, national wealth promotes democracy, and democracy in turn raises national wealth (see figure 4.4). To learn exactly which is causing which and *how* these processes work, we have to look more deeply into specific cases and observe the relationship between national wealth

FIGURE 4.4   Reciprocal Causation

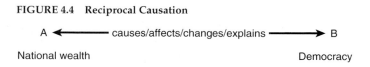

A ◄———————— causes/affects/changes/explains ————————► B

National wealth   Democracy

and democracy in individual countries, and then compare the results. The systematic comparison of such individual cases is one of the main activities of comparative politics.

Political science must also contend with another problem: *it is rarely able to test its hypotheses under controlled laboratory conditions.* Whereas natural scientists can frequently test their hypotheses in scrupulously controlled experiments by manipulating their lab rats, chemicals, and atom-smashing devices as they wish, political scientists are seldom so fortunate. In some cases, to be sure, we can exercise a modicum of control over our variables. We can conduct focus group surveys or elite interviews with a manageable number of individuals, for example, and derive some generalizations about politics from their responses to our questionnaires. Even these kinds of studies have problems, however. Our respondents may misinterpret our questions, or their responses may be ambiguous and hard to interpret. Still more problematically, we must often test our hypotheses against whatever factual information we can dig up from the rough terrain of historical and contemporary reality. The information we may need in order to come to reliable conclusions may be insufficient or unreliable. The generalizations we make from this patchy evidence are all the more uncertain as a result.

And so we come to another paradox: *political science seeks to generalize about politics, but most of our generalizations are at best tentative or only partially valid.* The logic of causal inference and the complexities of political reality impose definable limits on our ability to make universally valid statements about political life. Some of our generalizations apply only under certain conditions; there are exceptions to most every rule. Nevertheless, it is vitally important to specify what these conditions are and why the exceptions occur. Paradoxically yet again, *defining the limits of our generalizations is a major purpose of scientific generalization itself.*

Thus the scientific approach to politics cautions us to be modest in our claims to political certitude.

Political science teaches us that, when it comes to making explanatory generalizations about politics, *uncertainty is more likely than certainty.* This lesson is an important one. In every science, recognizing the limits of our knowledge is the start of wisdom.

THE PRACTICAL IMPORTANCE OF HYPOTHESIS TESTING

In spite of the difficulties of causative logic, hypothesis testing is still a powerful analytical mechanism for understanding politics. It compels us to be explicit in our use of political terminology. It makes us check our generalizations against available evidence. It forces us to consider evidence *against* our prevailing assumptions and biases, not just evidence supporting them. It requires us to be systematic and logical in analyzing the evidence and drawing conclusions from it. It clarifies what we know, and what we don't know, about political life.

The logic of hypothesis testing is therefore essential to political science. But the benefits of hypothesis testing are by no means confined to the ivory-tower world of academic abstractions. They have an immense practical value as well. In the real world of political action and debate, politicians, pundits, and ordinary people hold all sorts of opinions on all sorts of political issues. Not uncommonly, people cling to their most cherished political beliefs with unshakable obstinacy, regarding their certainty as beyond question. In actuality, however, a great deal of what people know (or think they know) about politics really amounts to *hypotheses*: assumptions, impressions, or hunches that in many instances are only vaguely articulated or insufficiently examined. Many of us, for example, have heard such platitudes as "The longer politicians stay in office, the more they are out of touch with public opinion," or "Governments just waste money," or "Foreign aid does not work," or countless other generalizations about politics that animate everyday political discussion. Political scientists are not the only ones who like to generalize about politics! Politicians and average citizens do, too. Such generalizations frequently provide the underlying rationale for important decisions political leaders make and for the way people behave within their respective political systems. But are those generalizations true? Only a systematic analysis of the evidence can tell us.

Consider as an example the editorialist's recommendation that wealthy democracies should provide economic assistance to newly democratizing countries. How do our findings about the relationship between national wealth and democracy help us formulate our own opinion on this practical policy issue? As we saw, national wealth is strongly—but not perfectly—correlated with democracy. It would seem, therefore, that the promotion of economic development in these countries would increase their chances of stabilizing a democratic government. But we also saw that most of the stable, long-term democracies have a per capita GNP that exceeds $9,000 per year. Countries below that threshold are less likely to sustain democratic rule over the long run. In addition, we saw that national wealth per se does not necessarily promote democracy; only when it is funneled into such intervening variables as education, an open communications system, or a middle class is wealth more likely to strengthen the conditions for democratic rule. And we also concluded that factors *other than* wealth may also be necessary to build and maintain democratic modes of government.

Thus our empirical analysis compels the conclusion that economic assistance aimed at raising the national wealth of democratizing countries may indeed be very helpful in supporting democracy, but it provides no guarantee that democracy will actually succeed. A great deal depends on how the money is spent. Will it be used to expand education or encourage the growth of a pro-democracy middle class? Or will it be spent on things that do not necessarily increase the chances for democracy, such as higher salaries for bureaucrats or graft for corrupt politicians? Even then, such factors as attitudes toward democracy on the part of elites and masses may exert an effect of their own on the chances for democracy, independently of national wealth and outside economic assistance. If key elites or broad segments of the population simply do not want democracy or do not try to make it work, wealth alone may not save the democratic cause.

Unfortunately, not everybody subjects their generalizations to a systematic reality check as we've just done. As a consequence, the generalizations people commonly make about politics often tend to oversimplify matters. But testing our political assumptions against reality is precisely what a scientific approach to politics demands. *Applying scientific logic to the study of politics helps us avoid oversimplification and enables us to appreciate the complexities of the real world.*

Accordingly, one of the most important "scientific" questions we can ask about any political generalization is, *"What is the evidence to support it?"* Another is, *"What is the evidence against it?"* We must then be very cautious and scrupulously logical in interpreting the results of these inquiries.

COUNTERINTUITIVE RESULTS

Systematic hypothesis testing is especially interesting when its results are *counterintuitive.* **Counterintuitive** results *are those that run counter to what we expect.* Not infrequently, they contradict widely held preconceptions or what "everybody knows" on the basis of "common sense." For centuries, "everybody knew" that the Earth is flat. Evidence to the contrary was counterintuitive. Though perhaps less dramatic, hypothesis testing in political science can also yield counterintuitive outcomes. Quite a few generalizations people make about politics on the basis of "common sense" or personal experience turn out, on examination, either to be completely false or true only in certain instances. Here are a few examples:

- Democracy, it is widely assumed, is government "by the people," not by elites. Comparative studies of democracies show, however, that elites may be even more important than the people are in creating and sustaining democratic modes of government. In some cases, elites are more respectful of democratic values—such as tolerance and freedom of speech—than the general public is.
- Another widely held assumption about democracy is that people will take full advantage of the opportunities it offers to stand up for their rights and actively promote their interests through the political process. In fact, however, most people

in democracies do *not* engage in such "collective action," even when their own economic interests or other concerns are at stake. Ironically, they are far more likely to believe that their personal interests are best served by doing nothing.

- It is often assumed that revolutions and mass uprisings against unpopular governments are most likely to take place when the population hits bottom, that is, when poverty and political subjugation reach intolerable extremes. In reality, however, revolutions and mass unrest are more likely to take place *after* a noticeable improvement has taken place in living conditions. It is not the extremely poor who most often rebel, but people who are experiencing "rising expectations" of still more improvements. Their anger may reach the boiling point when these expectations are then frustrated.

These and other illustrations of counterintuitive research findings will be discussed in greater detail in subsequent chapters. For a discussion of elites and democracy, see chapter 10. The reluctance of most people in democracies to get involved in "collective action" is addressed in chapter 11, as is the topic of revolutions and "rising expectations."

Scientific hypothesis testing is also important for another practical reason: *it can help you examine your own political assumptions in a rational and coherent manner.* One of the main objectives of your political science education should be to learn how to spell out your own political ideas in terms of propositions that can be put to a systematic test against the facts. Critical-thinking skills of this kind are invaluable in dealing not only with empirical (i.e., factual) questions about politics but with normative issues as well. As we noted earlier in this chapter, even our political values and ideals need to be addressed with reference to the realities of political life. The rules of hypothesis testing provide a method for determining what those realities are and for clarifying how well we know them.

SOME CONCLUDING THOUGHTS

Now that you have examined some key scientific terminology in political science and walked through a hypothesis-testing exercise, you should have a better idea of what political science is. Of course, you won't get a deeper feel for it until you've studied it more thoroughly, but you should at least be in a position to appreciate some generalizations about what political science tries to do.

Let's emphasize what political science is *not*. First, it is not "just opinion." Although the study of politics usually provides ample opportunities to formulate and express one's personal political views, political science makes a basic distinction between subjective value judgments and objective facts. To the extent that an opinion is in any way based on assumptions or assertions about facts, political science *as an empirical science* insists on the observance of strict rules of collecting, analyzing, and interpreting the facts. It requires us to support our opinions with relevant evidence and to modify our opinions (or perhaps discard them entirely) in the light of contrary information. Thus political science does not regard all political opinions as equally valid. Those opinions that can meet the acid test of empirical "reality checks" based on the rigors of scientific logic are generally more valid than are those based on insufficient evidence or faulty logic.

Of course, sometimes we just do not have the evidence we need to draw a reasoned, "scientific" conclusion. At times the information we need does not exist; at times it may not be readily available. In these cases, it is incumbent on us to *acknowledge* that the evidence we need to substantiate our case is lacking.

Even though the canons of empirical science are demanding, there is still plenty of room for rational debate and disagreement over controversial political issues. Subjective value judgments and preferences invariably play—indeed *must* play—a major role in political thinking. Just as important, the rules of scientific logic, as we have seen in this chapter, open up a vast realm of empirical uncertainty with respect to many political questions. By itself, empirical political science cannot compel you to be a liberal or a conservative, a moderate or a radical. It simply tells you that, whatever your personal political predilections, you must take the rules of scientific logic into account when shaping and defending your political views.

Second, political science is not "just current events," nor is it "just facts" or "just stories." As we indicated in chapter 1, political science is an effort to understand current events as well as the past (and, to some extent, the future) by generalizing about humanity's political experience. Political science *uses* facts to formulate and test these generalizations. Political scientists may be just as fascinated or amused as anyone else by stories and anecdotes about politics, but as social scientists we are mainly concerned with connecting particular incidents to broader trends and processes. In telling stories about politics, we are especially interested in what the stories tell us about politics. Moreover, random facts or *anecdotal evidence* may not be enough to sustain a political generalization. We may need to analyze a vast array of available evidence before we can come to any reliable conclusions. And if the evidence available is incomplete or merely anecdotal, we must say so.

More than anything else, political science is a *mode of thinking* about politics. It is an academic "discipline" in that it disciplines our minds to think in certain ways, in accordance with a specified logic and systematic methods of analysis.

Developing Critical-Thinking Skills   Depending on the career path you take, you may need more advanced analytical skills than we can provide in this book. This volume is purely introductory. In the pages that follow, we do not engage in formal statistical hypothesis testing, nor do we teach you how to design a research project of your own. Rather, we present numerous examples of hypotheses that have been advanced by political scientists who have written on the topics and countries covered in this volume. Along the way we introduce you to key concepts in political science, and to prominent theories and models as they apply to the study of comparative politics. We shall also expose you to some of the most imaginative and influential scholarship in the field. Throughout this enterprise, we are guided by one overriding pedagogical aim: to accustom you to *think for yourself* about politics in terms of the scientific terminology and logic presented in this and the preceding chapter.

Accordingly, this book provides numerous synopses of scholarly arguments that use the five-step hypothesis-testing logic presented here:

1. **Statement of the hypothesis and definition of key terms**
2. **Identification of the variables**

3. **Expectations of the hypothesis in "if . . . then" form**
4. **Collection and examination of the evidence**
5. **Conclusions (*consistent* with the hypothesis, *inconsistent, mixed,* or *inconclusive*)**

*Every chapter that follows contains a **hypothesis-testing exercise** that employs this format.* We hope that by learning how these logical steps are used in comparative politics, you will learn not only how to think like a political scientist but also how to apply these steps yourself to analytical tasks in various areas of inquiry.

KEY TERMS
(Underlined in the text)

Induction
Expectation
Deduction
Multicausality
Reductivism
Necessary condition
Sufficient condition
Reciprocal causation
Counterintuitive results

NOTES

1. Hugh A. Bone and Austin Ranney, *Politics and Voters,* 4th ed. (New York: McGraw-Hill, 1976), 4.
2. *Freedom in the World 1998–1999* (New York: Freedom House, 1999). Freedom House bases its ratings on two checklists of criteria. The *political rights checklist* addresses the following questions: (1) Is the head of state and/or government or other chief authority elected through free and fair elections? (2) Are the legislative representatives elected through free and fair elections? (3) Are there fair electoral laws, equal campaigning opportunities, fair polling, and honest tabulation of ballots? (4) Are the voters able to endow their freely elected representatives with real power? (5) Do the people have the right to organize in different political parties or other competitive groupings of their choice, and is the system open to the rise and fall of these competing parties or groupings? (6) Is there a significant opposition vote and a realistic possibility for the opposition to increase its support or gain power through elections? (7) Are the people free from domination by the military, foreign powers, totalitarian parties, religious hierarchies, economic oligarchies, or any

other powerful group? (8) Do cultural, ethnic, religious, and other minority groups have reasonable self-determination, self-government, autonomy, or participation through informal consensus in the decision-making process? The *civil liberties checklist* addresses a series of questions dealing with freedom of expression and beliefs; association and organizational rights; the rule of law; human rights and personal autonomy; and economic rights. Freedom House considers countries with an average combined rating of political and civil rights to be "free" if they score 1 to 2.5; "partly free" if they score 3 to 5 (with the exception of Chad, the Ivory Coast, and Swaziland, which were considered "not free" in 1998–99 even though each had a score of 5), and "not free" if they score 5.5 or above. We substitute the terms "democratic," "partly democratic," and "authoritarian" for the respective Freedom House designations.

3. World Bank, *World Development Report 1999/2000* (New York: Oxford University Press, 1999).

4. An epidemiologist studying the possible effects of smoking on lung cancer must not only look for signs that smoking causes lung cancer but also for signs that it does not. She will therefore examine the lung cancer rates of a *test group* of people who smoke and of a *control group* of non-smokers. A debater preparing for a verbal sparring match must not only gather evidence in support of the proposition he is defending; he must also anticipate his opponent's potential counterarguments by thoroughly looking for contrary evidence. The philosopher Karl Popper popularized the notion that the essence of the scientific method is empirical falsifiability. See *The Logic of Scientific Discovery* (New York: Harper and Row, 1968).

5. For a famous study relating some of these and other variables to democracy, see Seymour Martin Lipset, "Economic Development and Democracy," in *Political Man* (New York: Doubleday, 1960), chap. 2. Lipset concluded, "The more well-to-do a nation, the greater the chances that it will sustain democracy."

6. As a consequence, many scientists prefer to call smoking a "risk factor" that is "strongly associated" or "strongly correlated" with cancer.

CHAPTER 5

POWER

POWER IN HAITI

In October 1994, **Jean-Baptiste Aristide** returned to Haiti on the wings of a U.S. government plane. Thanks to American diplomatic and military intervention, Aristide was restored to power as Haiti's president, the post to which he had been elected by a wide majority in 1990. He had been ousted in a military coup d'état in September 1991 after serving less than eight months in office. Fearing for his life, he fled the country, eventually landing in the United States, where he spent the next three years in exile. Five thousand of his supporters were killed in the interval.

Aristide's triumphant return was only the first step in his effort to solidify democratic practices in a nation that, for much of its history, has been ruled by dictators of one kind or another. One of his main tasks in reestablishing his authority was to rein in the political ambitions of the Haitian military. He moved quickly to reduce the 7,500-man force to just the few dozen needed for the army band. Another organization to be brought under control was the dreaded secret police, which had spread terror throughout the country under the dictatorships of "Papa Doc" Duvalier, who ruled Haiti from 1957 to 1971, and his son, "Baby Doc," who held power from 1971 to 1986. Bringing these agencies of coercion under effective control was vital to Aristide's effort to replace the rule of force with the rule of law.

In addition, Aristide had to deal with the dominance of the leading class in Haitian society: a privileged group comprising about 10 percent of the population and spear-

President Aristide (left), shown next to the new chief of the Haitian armed Forces.

headed by twelve prominent families. For decades, this small elite controlled the country's economy while backing the two Duvalier regimes and the military government that ran Haiti prior to Aristide's return. While the vast majority of Haiti's population, numbering more than 6.5 million, lives in abject poverty, this social minority enjoys spectacular wealth. It is accustomed to wielding enormous political influence, having won all sorts of special favors from friends in previous governments. Many functionaries in Haiti's dictatorial regimes and the military officer corps came from this select group.

In addition to constituting a privileged economic and political elite, the dominant class also shares ethnic characteristics that set it apart from the bulk of the population. While the majority of Haiti's people are blacks, most of these influential families are mulattoes, consisting of mixed African and French stock. (Aristide is black, and his main base of support is the country's poverty-stricken black majority.) One of the most urgent questions facing Haiti is whether its traditionally powerful social elite can be won over to the cause of democracy. If not, it can pose a constant danger to Haiti's fragile democratic system. In addition, the abuse of governmental power remains a problem in spite of democracy's return. Both Aristide and his successor as president, René Préval, were accused of vote fraud. Parliamentary elections set for 1998 were postponed until 2000 while Préval ruled by decree. As the new millennium dawned and the last U.S. troops prepared to leave by 2001, political corruption flourished and the Haitian government still had not managed to assert its authority over former soldiers, criminals, private security forces, and others engaged in political violence. Aristide, meanwhile, declared his intention to run for the presidency again in elections scheduled for December 2000.[1]

Power, authority, control, coercion, influence, force, dominance: these and similar terms are the stuff of everyday newspaper fare and political contention. What do they mean? In addressing the meanings of power and its attributes, we are addressing not only one of the most basic conceptual problems in political science but one of the most contentious issues in the real world of politics as well.

POWER AND POLITICAL POWER

The concept of power goes straight to the question of who is strong and who is weak in political life. Power is as central in the world of politics as money is in economics. Some political scientists have even likened it to money. Much like a currency, power can be accumulated and "spent" in exchange for other things, such as one group's domination over other groups (through its "ownership" of the government) or a country's domination over other countries (through its "expenditure" of military power, for example).[2] Although such analogies can be useful in clarifying what power is, they cannot substitute for a clear definition of the term. So let's begin by defining power and political power, and then move on to discuss some kindred concepts.

In its most general sense, **power** *is the capacity to effect outcomes.*

To *effect* means to *cause* or *bring about.* Outcomes are *actions* or *results.* Power is thus **the capacity to cause or bring about actions or results.**

Power is above all a *capability* or a *potential.* The words "power" and "potent" derive from the Latin *potere,* "to be able." Power is not any specific thing (such as a law, a fist, or an atomic bomb), nor is it any specific action (a veto, a punch, an explosion). Rather, it is an *ability* that someone possesses or that inheres in something. Depending on its specific form, this ability can be held by inanimate objects (the sun, the atom), animals (as in horsepower), individuals (a strong leader), groups (a dominant class), or institutions (the U.S. presidency). Moreover, power does not have to be exercised. It is a potential that can exist without being used.

In chapter 2, you will recall, we defined *politics* as *the process by which communities pursue collective goals and deal with their conflicts authoritatively by means of government.* In keeping with this definition,

political power *is the capacity to effect outcomes by controlling or influencing the state. The* **state** *means government* at any level.

To put it in somewhat more precise terms, **political power** means *the ability to* **determine or influence** *the decisions, actions, or behavior of government officials.* In comparative politics we focus on the various ways power can be used *within* countries to affect the actions of domestic government authorities. Students of international politics tend to focus on the ways power is used in relations *between* countries.[3]

Who Has Political Power? Political power is above all wielded by people who hold official positions in government. To begin with, government officials possess *legal powers,* or *legal authority,* to take certain actions and make certain decisions. The extent of this official legal power differs from one governmental system to another. The president of the United States possesses more decision-making power than the president of Germany but less than the president of France. Members of the U.S. Congress have more legal authority than the members of the French legislature but less than British parliamentarians. Authoritarian leaders typically possess more power to take official action than the leaders of most democracies. The legal powers of individual leaders and the members of various governmental institutions can be compared from one country to the next, and in this and subsequent chapters we'll provide some illustrative examples.

The capacity to determine or influence governmental actions is by no means confined to office-holders. In some cases political parties, social classes, or other groups that are formally separate from the state may have an extraordinary amount of control or influence over what government officials do. The Nazi party of Hitler's Germany and the Communist Party of the former Soviet Union are examples of political parties that completely dominated the governments of those countries. Haiti's most prominent families exemplify the political dominance of a social class.

So when we ask ourselves, "Who possesses political power?" we generally focus on two distinct sets of people: (1) *government officials,* and (2) *individuals and groups who are outside the government (or distinct from the government) but who have some capacity to determine or influence what the government does.* People in these two categories have political power to the extent that they can *cause* governments to make decisions or engage in other actions or behaviors.

Now, what do we mean by "determine" and "influence"? These terms reflect real, if subtle, differences.

TWO DIMENSIONS OF POWER: DOMINANCE AND INFLUENCE

One way of refining our conception of power is to distinguish between two *dimensions* of power:

dominance and **influence.** Both are forms of power in that they are ways of causing outcomes. Their difference is mainly one of degree: *dominance* implies a larger scope of power than *influence,* though the precise extent of this difference may at times be difficult to specify with precision.

Power as Dominance

The ability to *determine* or *control* political outcomes—especially when it exists on a regular or continuing basis rather than just occasionally—is the ability to exercise *dominance* in political life. **Dominance** *is the maximum degree of political power.* Those who possess power-as-dominance can usually get whatever they want from the government. This type of political power can be exercised either by government officials who enjoy an exceptionally large measure of legal authority (such as powerful dictators) or by non-governmental groups or individuals who possess a large capacity to determine how the government operates or what its main policy orientations must be. South Africa's white minority was such a dominant social group prior to the historic elections of 1994. Until then, the whites completely dominated the non-white majority, denying them voting rights and enforcing strict racial segregation laws.

Power as Influence

The term "influence," like many terms in political science, is itself a source of considerable controversy. Some scholars have used "power" and "influence" interchangeably while others have stressed their differences. As the eminent political scientist Robert Dahl rightly acknowledged, "One writer's 'influence' is another's 'power'."[4]

As defined here, political influence is a *form* of power, not something different from it. More specifically, it is a degree or dimension of power, one that is less all-encompassing than domination. But the distinction between influence and dominance is not always clear-cut: sometimes it's hard to specify what the difference is between a "dominant" person or group and a "highly influential" one. Alas, our quest for definitional precision is not always crowned with success.

We define __influence__ *as the capacity to effect outcomes indirectly or partially.* Accordingly, **political influence** *means the capacity to* **affect** *government decisions, actions, or behavior without fully controlling them.* Depending on the particular circumstances, the ability to influence the outcomes of state activity is usually less direct, or less decisive or definitive, than the capacity to determine them. To have power-as-influence over a particular governmental decision means to have some say in the matter without necessarily being able to dictate the ultimate outcome. It frequently means that one has some access to state decision makers but not complete control over their decisions.

As in the case of the capacity to determine political outcomes, the capacity to influence them can be held by either government officials or non-governmental individuals or groups. The president of the United States provides a good example of a government official who has more influence than dominance when it comes to exercising official power. The U.S. Constitution confers upon the president the legal power to veto acts of Congress. The president does not "influence" the decision whether or not to impose a veto; he has the sole power to determine it. But although he has the legal capacity to make this and other decisions on his own, in many other instances the president cannot take definitive action by himself but must share power with the Congress or other institutions. In order to get a voting majority of the House and Senate to enact the laws and programs he wants, he will usually have to negotiate with key members of Congress and make compromises with them. In such situations the president does not "control" Congress or "determine" the final outcome of the legislation; he can only *influence* those outcomes by bargaining with Congressional leaders. To different degrees, governing executives in most democracies must bargain with legislators and other officials (not to mention the voters) in order to get their way. For even the most powerful executives in democratic countries, power is exercised largely as influence rather than as dominance.

By contrast, authoritarian rulers tend to exert dominance over the population, but their degree of power within the state tends to differ. Some individual dictators are able to impose virtually complete dominance over other government officials (Hitler, for example), while others must share power with other officials and bargain with them over state decisions.

Similarly, groups or individuals outside government may also have the capacity to influence the outcomes of governmental activities without being able to determine or dictate whatever they want or to exercise a pervasive dominance over the state's activities. Typically they try to affect outcomes indirectly, often by working through intermediaries. Such people possess political influence to the extent that they are able to persuade or pressure authoritative state officials or agencies to do favors for them or meet their demands, if only partially or in specific, discrete instances. Business leaders, labor union officials, editorialists, "policy wonks," and countless others utilize whatever sources of influence they may have at their disposal—votes, campaign contributions, bribes, moral suasion, or a sensible argument—to bring about favorable outcomes from governmental decision makers. Invariably, some people are more politically influential than others. But even these highly influential people do not necessarily control the government or win every time. Meanwhile, the right to vote gives the citizens of a democracy varying amounts of influence over the officials they elect.

As we've suggested, the distinction between *dominance* and *influence* is not always clear-cut. Difficulties frequently arise when we try to differentiate "dominant" government officials and non-government groups from "influential" or "highly influential" ones. As various political scientists have pointed out, it is very difficult to measure influence accurately.[5] Did the twelve families comprising the Haitian social elite truly "dominate" Haitian dictatorships, in the sense of determining what the dictators did, or were they merely "influential," having a major affect on the dictators without necessarily controlling them? Sometimes it is hard to answer these kinds of questions with precision. The long-running debate over whether the United States is dominated by a "power elite" reflects these ambiguities.

IS THE UNITED STATES DOMINATED BY A "POWER ELITE"?

An especially sharp controversy over relative degrees of dominance and influence has long divided analysts of political power in the United States. In the 1950s, the sociologist C. Wright Mills set off a lively debate when he argued that the U.S. political system was dominated by a **power elite.** These "higher circles" of powerful politicians, corporate executives, and military leaders, in his view, formed a unified and organized network of "interlocking directorates" that dominated the decision-making levers of American political and economic life. They consisted almost exclusively of white males, mostly Protestant. Beneath them, the middle layers of American society were considerably less influential, while the overwhelming majority of the population constituted a fragmented "mass society" with virtually no power of any kind. Roughly similar views have been expressed by more recent critics of American politics and society. Others have applied variations of the power-elite concept to other democracies or to democracy in general.

These provocative arguments have ignited counterattacks by scholars who maintain that, while various elite groups may indeed enjoy considerable political power in the United States, they do not form as cohesive and well-organized a clique as the power-elite theorists contend. Sometimes these politically powerful people disagree among themselves on matters of government policy. Moreover, the counterargument goes, they do not leave the rest of the population utterly powerless; public opinion and election results *do* have an impact on what the government does. Most critics of the power-elite hypothesis maintain, in effect, that while some individuals and groups may indeed be exceptionally *influential* in American political life, they do not necessarily *dominate* it to the exclusion of everyone else. Furthermore, their influence over government actions tends to vary with the issue: corporate executives of firms that manufacture military equipment may influence the government's military expenditures, but they may not have much influence over environmental or health care policy.

Many of these critics of the power-elite concept are known as *pluralists.* The concept of **pluralism** contends that political power in the United States and other democracies is shared by a plurality of social classes, political parties, interest groups, voters, and other participants in the political process and is not dominated by a single, all-powerful elite.[6]

Power Is Relational

As the distinctions we've made between dominance and influence suggest, power can be conceptualized in various ways. Scholars have proposed all sorts of conceptualizations of the term, including the following:

- A has power over B if A can influence B's behavior.
- A has power over B to the extent that A can cause B to do something that B would not otherwise do.
- A exercises power over B when A affects B in a manner contrary to B's interests.
- A has power over B to the extent that B *believes* that A is more powerful.

All these proposed conceptions have one assumption in common: power is *relational.* That is, power consists in a relationship between a power holder (A) and someone else (B) over whom A has some kind of power. In all these hypothetical relationships, A is able to get B to do something. (Even in the last example, which has a psychological element, B may simply *believe* that A can make him do something, and acts accordingly.) The relationships differ over the issue of precisely *what* it is that A gets B to do.

In some cases the state gets the population to do certain things that the leading government officials want people to do (such as pay taxes or fight wars). Conversely, in other instances the population, or relatively powerful elements of the population, gets the state to do certain things they want it to do (such as provide them with benefits or penalize polluters). Depending on the specific circumstances, A may get B to do something B would not otherwise do. The government, for example, may use its legal powers to compel people to pay taxes or join the military, actions many people might decline to undertake voluntarily. Nevertheless, in quite a few instances the citizenry may be perfectly willing to pay taxes if they believe they get some benefit out of them (such as better schools or roads) and they may favor being drafted into the military and fighting abroad in order to defend the country. In these cases, the state still possesses the legal power to compel people to do these things, even though they may wish to do them anyway and believe that it is in their best interest to do so.

As we noted in chapter 2, the political process often involves either *bargaining* or *coercion.* Both processes are at work in power relationships, at times to exert influence and at times to impose dominance. Sometimes A exercises power over B by using bargaining techniques. *Persuasion* is a frequently used bargaining device that can take many forms in politics. Politicians constantly strive to persuade people to follow them, whether by appealing to their individual self-interest, to their concern for community welfare, or to their basest fears and prejudices. *Propaganda* is an especially well-orchestrated form of political persuasion. Nazi Germany, the Soviet Union, and other dictatorial regimes have used their control of the media and the educational system with the determined aim of manipulating public attitudes and behaviors. Some critics of modern democracies have argued that democratic systems propagandize their citizens as well, with the most prominent elites (such as big business or a dominant ethnic group) imposing their "dominant ideology" on the masses.[7]

Another bargaining technique involves offering rewards in return for favorable behavior. Political figures in democracies and dictatorships alike often hold out the promise of material rewards (jobs, tax cuts, welfare benefits) or psychological rewards (national greatness, spiritual upliftment) in an effort to induce people to follow them. **Co-optation** is a particular way of providing rewards in exchange for political support. The term typically applies when *political figures offer benefits to hostile or indifferent individuals or groups in order to elicit their neutrality or cooperation.* For example, Hitler co-opted, or "bought off," the support of leading German industrialists by allowing them to keep their companies and reap substantial profits by producing military equipment and other goods for the Nazi state.

The capacity to *punish,* or to threaten someone with a potential punishment, can also be used as a bargaining technique. In some cases the threat does not carry the potential use of physical force but it can still be effective. In democracies, for example, voters can influence elected officials by threatening to punish them at the polls in the next elections. In other instances, however, the power to punish assumes harsher proportions, involving the capacity to employ force.

With considerable frequency in political life, physical force can be threatened in an effort to influence the behavior of others or it can be applied directly in an effort to dominate them. Slaveowners did not subject people to slavery by trying to "influence" them; they enslaved them by physical force, which was often supported and implemented by pro-slavery governments. Nazis, Communists, and other authoritarians have seldom flinched from using force in order to stamp out opposition at home or carry out unprovoked aggression outside their borders. As we noted in chapter 2, however, authoritarian regimes have no monopoly on the use of force. Even in democracies, governments routinely arrest people and throw them into jail for violating the law. In all countries, the legal authority of the state ultimately rests on force. Of course, unlike authoritarian regimes, democracies permit their populations to hold the governing officials accountable at election time and they set legal limits to the powers of the state.

Coercion is closely related to force. Coercion *is the act of compelling people to do something,* usually by threatening them with some kind of punishment if they fail to comply. Obviously, force is the ultimate sanction. The *coercive power of the state* refers to the government's ability to enforce its laws with all the means of force at its command. In most cases, governments do not actually have to use force very often to coerce their citizens to comply with the law. In democracies the population's acceptance of the state's legal authority is largely voluntary because opportunities are available to change laws that people don't like. Repressive regimes, by contrast, tend to rely to a greater degree than democracies do on the threat or use of force in governing their populations. However, if an authoritarian state has to use its physical power constantly to enforce its hold over the population and to repress opposition, chances are that it is rather weak and is so perceived by elements of the populace.

Who Gets What?

In the vast majority of instances, governments and the people who interact with them use whatever power they have in order to effect outcomes that they somehow regard as favorable, whether favorable to themselves or favorable for the community as a whole. In other words, power in political relationships very often amounts to *the capacity to get what you want through authoritative action.*

The prospect of "getting something" out of government is one of the most compelling reasons why many people get involved in political life to begin with, whether as dedicated activists or as occasional voters. To be sure, the things people want from politics are exceedingly varied. Some may enter the political fray out of the purest of motives, seeking authoritative governmental action to redress legitimate grievances, ensure basic rights, or promote the general welfare of the community at large. Others may act out of pure selfishness, demanding privileges and powers that can only be obtained at the expense of other citizens. In short, politics is often a game of *competing demands on government.*

Realities being what they are, the means available to meet these demands are usually limited. We live in a world of scarce resources. There is only so much wealth that can be distributed to the members of any given society. Even in the richest countries, discernible limits exist to the amount of natural resources, manufactured goods, money, and jobs that can be shared by the population. In poor countries there may be far more drastic limits in the supply of food, medicine, and other basic necessities of life. In a number of instances, rights and privileges themselves may be limited. Certain rights cannot be granted to some people without limiting—or even eliminating—the rights of others. My proclaimed right to preferential hiring in order to make up for past discrimination against my ethnic group may limit your right to get the same job I want. Your right to sell handguns may limit my right to a safe neighborhood. Finally, power itself is a limited commodity. For one thing, government offices are strictly limited. In the United States there can be only one president and a hundred senators. In many authoritarian regimes there is room for only one supreme leader. There are also realistic limits to the number of individuals or groups in society who may be considered politically influential. Most political scientists would agree that the number of people who have direct influence over government decisions and decision makers, even in a democracy, is confined to little more than 1 percent or 2 percent of the population. Government officials are typically able (or willing) to pay attention to the demands of only a select number of supplicants.

More often than not, politics therefore involves a continuing competition over limited resources and rights. It also involves a competition over power itself, that is, over the very *ability* to make governmental decisions or to influence those who do. It is this competitive aspect of political reality that we sought to capture in our definition of politics when referring to conflict. Conflicts are inevitable when the demands people make cannot all be fulfilled at once, if ever. And as our definition of politics specifies, it is governments that must ultimately deal with many of these conflicts in trying to meet these competing needs and demands.

Typically they do so by *distributing* (or *allocating*) resources they may have at their disposal: budgetary funds, food stockpiles, civil service jobs, public health services, and so on. Governments also make decisions regarding the allocation of various rights and privileges. They decide, for example, which groups (if any) are entitled to preferential treatment in hiring or education, which types of guns (if any) may be manufactured and sold on the open market, and so on. And governments ultimately decide on the allocation of power itself, whether by determining the legal powers of governmental decision makers or by distributing the degree of influence that various elements of the population will be permitted to exercise over state officials.

The decisions governments make on these and many other issues are authoritative in the sense that they are binding on the population with the force of law. One of the main tasks of any government, therefore, is *the authoritative allocation of resources, rights, privileges, and power itself.*[8] Stated somewhat more starkly, governments make authoritative decisions about "who gets what." A considerable amount of political activity in practically every country in the world concerns "who gets what" through governmental action. Not surprisingly, one of the most well-known books ever written in political science is appropriately entitled *Politics: Who Gets What, When, and How.*[9]

Presumably, those with more political power succeed in getting more of what they want from government than those with less. Power is rarely, if ever, distributed evenly in society. Even in the most open democracies, where the people are supposed to have power based on the egalitarian principle of "one person, one vote," some persons or groups will invariably end up with more usable political power, or clout, than others. As students of comparative politics, we must be acutely sensitive to the various ways political power is distributed and utilized in different countries and in different political systems.

AUTHORITY

Authority is a term we've already used several times without properly defining it. Like most words in the world's political dictionary, authority can take on several meanings that vary with the context in which it is used. We'll focus on two of these meanings here because they are often used as synonyms for power. They are (1) *legal authority* and (2) *personal authority*. We'll discuss a third one—authority as *legitimacy*—in chapter 6.

Power as Legal Authority

When the term "power" is used with reference to governmental institutions, it usually means **the legal authority of the state.** This type of authority refers to **the state's capacity to make, implement, and enforce the law.** In other words, it means the *legal competence* or *jurisdiction* of the government as a whole, or of some particular governmental office or institution (such as the presidency or the legislature, the courts or the police). While this definition of authority applies to democracies and authoritarian regimes alike, there are major differences in the ways these two types of government exercise their authority.

Democracies are based on the principle of *the rule of law.* **The rule of law** *means that the legal authority of the state and its officials is limited by law, and that no one is above the law.* Even the most powerful government officials must observe the laws that define and limit their decision-making authority. In the United States, for example, the Constitution prescribes that the legal powers of the president, the Congress, and the Supreme Court are to be balanced roughly evenly. Under a system of *checks and balances,* the legal authority of each of these branches of the national government is more or less equal. Britain, by contrast, does not have the American system of checks and balances. The British system is based on *parliamentary supremacy,* a concept first in-

stituted in the late seventeenth century. Parliament has predominant legal authority over all other governmental institutions, including the crown, the prime minister, and the courts. Other democracies distribute legal powers among their respective governmental institutions in a variety of ways, but as a general rule these powers are limited by law.

Authoritarian regimes are rarely based on the rule of law. In most authoritarian regimes, the leading government officials place themselves *above* the law, and they do not always observe legal limits on their capacity to make authoritative decisions. They themselves define the extent of the state's authority, without granting the people the right to have any say in the matter. Hitler's Germany is one obvious example, but there are many others, ranging in nature from other one-party dictatorships (like the Soviet Union and Communist China) to military regimes, traditional monarchies, and various other forms of authoritarianism. Consider, for example, **Saddam Hussein** of Iraq.

PROFILE: Saddam Hussein

Saddam Hussein, the president of Iraq, was conducting a cabinet meeting during a crucial period in his country's fierce war with Iran. As the talk turned to a discussion of how the war might be brought to an end, the minister of health suggested that Saddam should temporarily step down from the presidency and allow another prominent Iraqi political figure, former President Ahmad Hasan al-Bakr, to assume the office in an effort to persuade Iran to start negotiations. "Let us go to the other room and discuss the matter further," Saddam told his minister. The two men adjourned to the next room, and several moments later, a shot rang out. Saddam Hussein returned to the cabinet meeting alone. His government subsequently announced that the minister of health had been executed for "corruption." The minister's dismembered remains were brought to his wife the next day.

This story was not the only one to be circulated in the Western press about Saddam Hussein's personal use of violence on suspected political opponents. Although some of them may be apocryphal, there is no doubt that Saddam Hussein built his entire political career on brutality and mass fear. Born in the centuries-old town of Tikrit in 1937, Saddam had a troubled childhood. His father died before he was born and his stepfather took pleasure in humiliating and beating him. Saddam was raised by his uncle, a

Saddam Hussein

With a firm grip on Iraq's main security organs, Saddam solidified his own power base and extended his reign of terror to elements of the Iraqi population. Under his direction some of the highest officials in the government, the military, and the Ba'ath Party were subjected to arrests, torture, and murder. During the 1970s, while maintaining a low profile behind the president, Saddam took charge of key elements of Iraq's economic policies and foreign relations, earning an international reputation as "the strong man of Baghdad." By the end of the decade he had expanded the party militia, the army, and the police into a security empire comprising an estimated 677,000 members, a total that accounted for 20 percent of Iraq's labor force. The Ba'ath Party grew apace, with twenty-five thousand fanatical members and 1.5 million followers. Meanwhile, Saddam surrounded himself with a small following of loyalists that included relatives and other associates from Tikrit.

In 1979 Saddam decided to take full political power for himself. He prevailed upon President al-Bakr to resign and immediately assumed the presidency. Within weeks he saw to it that as many as five hundred high-ranking Ba'ath Party officials were executed. With his potential rivals either eliminated or cowed, Saddam launched a propaganda campaign exalting himself as the country's supreme ruler. He frequently compared himself to Nebuchadnezzar, the Mesopotamian king who attacked Jerusalem in 587 B.C., and expressed admiration for Adolph Hitler and Joseph Stalin.

In 1980, concerned that neighboring Iran's new rulers were trying to destabilize his government, Saddam declared war on that country. The conflict dragged on for eight years, consuming hundreds of thousands of lives. In addition to fighting the Iranians, Saddam also wreaked havoc on Iraqis suspected of disloyalty. The Kurds, an ethnic minority that comprised 20 percent of Iraq's population, were subjected to aerial gas attacks. Saddam had been fighting Kurdish separatists for years; some 250,000 of them now fled to Iran and Turkey in hopes of escaping the bombardments. Another targeted group was Iraq's Shi'ite Muslim community. The Shi'ites hold beliefs that differ from the Sunni Muslims, their rivals in a dispute that dates back to the seventh century. Iran's leaders were Shi'ites. Although Shi'ites formed the religious majority in Iraq, with 60 percent of the population, Saddam and his cohorts were Sunnis. They lost no time ordering executions of Shi'ite clergymen and expelling as many as one hundred thousand Shi'ites from Iraq. Saddam also ordered the executions of hundreds of Iraqi officers for poor performance on the battlefield.

In 1988, their populations exhausted, Iran and Iraq made peace. Neither side had gained any territorial advantage. With Iraq's economy now in shambles, Saddam

politically impassioned man who spelled out his hatreds in a book entitled *Three Whom God Should Not Have Created: Persians, Jews, and Flies.* After failing the entrance exam for Iraq's leading military academy, Saddam turned to politics. At the age of twenty he joined the Ba'ath (Renaissance) Party, an organization dedicated to uniting Arabs throughout the Middle East on a program of anti-Western assertiveness and economic regeneration.

Two years later, Saddam participated in an assassination attempt on the general who then ruled Iraq. The plot failed and Saddam fled the country. Within a few years he was back, gradually gaining control over the Ba'ath Party's private militia. Over the next several years Saddam emerged as a central figure while the Ba'ath Party seized power and then split into rival factions. Through a succession of coups, assassination plots, and other ruthless intrigues, Saddam schemed his way into the highest reaches of power. By 1968 he was the second most powerful man in the country behind his close political ally, President al-Bakr, a relative from Tikrit.

pressured the oil-rich Arab sheikdoms of the Persian Gulf to boost world oil prices and provide Iraq with cash. Iraq's oil exports were earning only about $13 billion a year, but the country needed over $300 billion to rebuild its economy and pay back foreign loans. When the Gulf states showed reluctance to comply with Saddam's demands, he invaded neighboring Kuwait in July 1990, incorporating it into Iraq. The United States and other Western countries, fearful that Saddam would next attack Saudi Arabia and perhaps other states in the region, responded with a devastating missile and aerial bombardment of Iraq starting in January 1991. In February a massive ground assault evicted the Iraqi occupation force from Kuwait and pushed it back into Iraq, crumbling its ability to resist, within forty-eight hours. Saddam's vaunted army suffered one hundred thousand casualties, and its Soviet-built tank armada was largely destroyed.

Saddam Hussein managed to hang on to power nevertheless. In recent years he has survived several assassination attempts, most of them organized by senior military officers. His transparent efforts to acquire nuclear weapons technology, along with chemical and biological weapons, have galvanized the international community into taking preventive action, including a wave of bombing by U.S. aircraft in 1998. But Saddam's personal authority as Iraq's supreme leader endures. In 1995 he had himself "reelected" in a carefully controlled "election" in which he was the only candidate. The following year he had his sons-in-law executed after they attempted to flee the country. He has thrived in a political system where the legal authority of the rulers is unrestrained by higher laws. As long as he remains in power, Saddam Hussein *is* the law.[10]

Although authoritarian rulers generally rule above the law rather than under it, sometimes they recognize certain legal limits to their governmental power. For instance, when Britain was ruled by monarchs prior to the advent of parliamentary supremacy, the crown's legal authority was progressively subjected to limitations over the course of several centuries. One of the landmarks in this development was the **Magna Carta** (the Great Charter), signed in 1215 by King John and a group of powerful barons and churchmen anxious to protect their privileges against excessive monarchical power. Faced with a veritable rebellion, the king agreed to respect certain baronial rights and to observe various limits on the crown's powers in such matters as taxation, property ownership, and judicial appointments. The Charter also stated that the barons could seize the crown's "castles, lands and possessions" if the agreements were not observed.

Although King John and subsequent monarchs strove to evade Magna Carta's terms, the document became a legal weapon in the hands of all those who sought to limit the powers of the crown in British politics. It plainly implied that the monarchy itself was not above the law, but was bound by it. Eventually this principle triumphed in Britain. Other authoritarian regimes have also observed certain legal limitations on their power, but only rarely.

Power as Personal Authority

Another meaning of authority that is commonly associated with power is what may be called *personal authority*. **Personal authority *essentially means leadership ability. It is the capacity to effect outcomes by getting others to acknowledge and follow one's leadership.*** To a large extent, personal authority is the ability to inspire trust and confidence in one's leadership or to command the respect of those one wishes to lead. When we speak of a "strong leader" or a "powerful president," we often refer not just to their legal powers but also to their personal authority. These individuals have personal authority to the extent that they are able to convince others to follow their lead.

The methods they use to evoke such "followership" are multiple. In some cases successful leaders are able to elicit the voluntary support of their followers through their powers of persuasion, or through their exemplary moral or intellectual character, or perhaps through their proven success as "winners." Franklin D. Roosevelt was able to convince a majority of American voters to cast their ballots for him in four presidential elections, winning the loyal support of Democratic Party politicians in the process. In the 1930s and 1940s, India's Mahatma Gandhi inspired millions of his compatriots with his principled opposition to British colonial rule and his deep commitment to nonviolence and religious tolerance. Especially magnetic leaders are said to have **charisma,** the Greek word for "divine gift."

In other cases, leaders establish their personal authority by compelling others to submit to their rule. Such leaders are more interested in cultivating the respect and fear of those they rule than in eliciting their love or trust. A famous exponent of this leadership style was the Italian statesman and philosopher **Niccolò Machiavelli** (1469–1527). In *The Prince*

(1513), Machiavelli asserted that a leader must not be bound by moral scruples, but must be willing to use violence against the population and ruthlessly employ deceit if necessary to ensure the preservation and prosperity of the state. Saddam Hussein exemplifies an extreme form of Machiavellianism, often placing his own personal power ahead of his country's security and well-being. Even in authoritarian regimes, however, the forms of exercising personal authority are varied. Some authoritarians are more powerful than others, even within the same country or governmental system. The former Soviet Union provides examples.

POWER IN THE SOVIET UNION

In 1917, the Communist Party took over Russia and quickly eliminated other contenders for power. The founder of the party, **V. I. Lenin,** was the new regime's first top leader. Lenin had accumulated considerable personal authority among Russia's communists over the previous decades, in large part because of the force of his intellect and his superior organizational skills. Lenin was also acutely sensitive to the importance of power. Politics, he believed, essentially revolves around the central question, "Who—whom?," by which he meant, "Who *dominates* whom?" Lenin was determined to ensure the dominance of the Communist Party over Russia; his success in achieving this goal only enhanced his luster among communists as the party's venerated number one.

Although his personal charisma undergirded his authority, Lenin failed to establish constitutional procedures for choosing his successor. In a regime that had no respect for the rule of law, the absence of scrupulously observed rules for succession led to a *struggle for power* among the top leaders once Lenin became ill and died. Over the course of the 1920s and 1930s, **Joseph Stalin** managed to secure his personal authority by using methods Lenin probably would have repudiated. Stalin initially outmaneuvered a number of rivals in the Communist Party hierarchy in the 1920s and subsequently consolidated his supreme power by killing off dozens of party leaders, hundreds of thousands of party members, and millions of citizens who did not belong to the party. Stalin also built up his personal authority by expanding jobs and other benefits for party functionaries and millions of industrial workers and by leading the USSR to victory over Germany in World War II.

After Stalin died in 1953, another power struggle broke out in the Soviet party leadership among the principal contenders for the top job. The ultimate winner, **Nikita S. Khrushchev,** never ruled with Stalin's bloody

supremacy. Khrushchev renounced Stalin's technique of mass murder and his actual governing power remained limited by the power of other Soviet Communist Party leaders in the highest echelons of the leadership. Through a series of actions that rankled party leaders, Khrushchev progressively lost his personal authority among the ruling elite. In 1964 a small group of conspirators in the party hierarchy quietly removed him from power, forcing him into retirement. Khrushchev's successor, **Leonid Brezhnev,** remained the top Soviet leader until his death in 1982. But Brezhnev's real power—his capacity to make decisions—was, like Khrushchev's, no match for Stalin's. Brezhnev ruled by building a consensus among the top party leaders, scarcely more than a dozen or two in all.

Following the brief rule of Brezhnev's two immediate successors, both of whom died in office, **Mikhail Gorbachev** was selected by the top party leadership in 1985 to lead the Soviet Union. Gorbachev recognized that reforms were needed to rescue the deteriorating Soviet economy and that cooperation with the West was preferable to Cold War confrontation. These views won him plaudits throughout the world, but Gorbachev's failure to come up with a coherent plan to revive the economy resulted in a steep loss of personal authority both within the Communist Party and among the Soviet population. Reformers criticized him for not changing the old system fast enough while hardline authoritarians condemned him for changing things too much. In the summer of 1991 a group of archcommunist conspirators tried to oust him from power in a coup d'état. The plot was foiled, but Gorbachev was forced to resign. With his personal political demise, the Soviet Union itself disintegrated at the end of the year. Power in Russia passed to President Boris Yeltsin, who was the first Russian leader ever elected to office by the people.

These examples indicate that, though the Communist Party itself never observed any legal limits on its governmental power in the Soviet Union, *the personal authority of the top leader varied, depending on his relationship with the other highest party officials.*

In contemporary Iran, meanwhile, power is concentrated in the hands of a religious elite in spite of popular elections for the country's president and parliament.

POWER IN IRAN

Iran has been an authoritarian state for most of its history. From 1953 to 1979, its leader, or **Shah,** was **Mohammed Reza Pahlavi.** With the support of a succession of U.S. presidents, who valued his efforts to protect the oil-rich

Iranian demonstrators with portrait of Khomeini and anti-U.S. placard, 1979.

Persian Gulf against potential Soviet encroachments, the Shah had virtually no limits on his power. Opposition mounted, however, and in 1979 he was toppled in a revolution. His successor was the **Ayatollah Khomeini,** an Islamic cleric. Khomeini created a theocracy, imposing an austere version of Islamic law on the population. (A **theocracy** is a government by religious leaders.) The new regime scathingly condemned Western culture and compelled women to veil their heads. Khomeini had the firm backing of Iran's Islamic clergy, but he also enjoyed considerable popularity among the country's destitute masses as well as among segments of the middle class. In the eyes of millions of his followers, Khomeini radiated charismatic personal authority. It was under his rule that Islamic militants stormed the U.S. embassy in Tehran in 1979 and held its personnel hostage for more than a year.

After Khomeini's death in 1989, governing authority remained in the hands of the Islamic clerics. Iran's most powerful political figure today is **Ayatollah Ali Khamenei,** who succeeded Khomeini as the country's supreme religious leader. Only those candidates formally approved by the religious authorities are permitted to run for the presidency and the 270-member parliament, the *Majlis.* Nevertheless, in recent years a large segment of the public has managed to express its opposition to the dictatorship of the clerical hardliners, and real change may be on its way.

In 1997, 90 percent of the eligible voters turned out for a hotly contested presidential election that pitted several government-backed candidates against a more liberal cleric, **Mohammed Khatami.** Though Khatami was officially nominated by the Council of Guardians, the twelve-member religious body that dominates the political system, he was regarded as an opponent of the ruling clique and an advocate of greater tolerance for women's rights, expanded educational opportunities for students, economic liberalization, and a possible resumption of friendly ties with the United States, a country long vilified by the regime as "the great satan." Unexpectedly, Khatami captured 70 percent of the vote. The new president assumed office with little decision-making power, however. President Khatami's legal authority is narrowly circumscribed by Ayatollah Khamenei, the Council of Guardians, and a parliament that, at least until 2000, generally did their bidding. A number of Khatami's followers have been harassed, tortured, and even murdered by the ruling authorities. One of them, the former mayor of Tehran, was convicted of graft in a summary trial and sentenced to sixty lashes and five years in prison. Other reformers, many of them advocates of democracy, were hauled before kangeroo courts. Hundreds were subjected to summary executions, while others have been gunned down by officially sanctioned murder squads.

Discontent has been rising in Iranian society due to a stagnant economy, religious severity, and prolonged international isolation. As a result, President Khatami's popularity has held steady, enabling him to wring a few concessions from the ruling authorities. Women have increasingly been allowed to violate the official Islamic dress code with impunity, and press freedoms have been widened. In 1999, Khatami intervened in behalf of university students who were attacked by military forces after staging public demonstrations against the regime.

Progress toward potentially radical reform took a giant step forward in early 2000, as the Iran Participation Front, under the leadership of the president's brother, won a resounding victory in parliamentary elections. Reformist candidates in other parties also won seats, giving the forces for change in Iran a decisive majority in the Majlis. Whether they would prove successful in moving the political system closer to democracy remained an open question. The Council of Guardians, still dominated by Islamic hardliners, has the authority to veto legislation passed by the parliament. If the Majlis challenges a veto, the ultimate decision is taken by the Expediency Council, a body appointed by Iran's supreme religious authority. These institutional arrangements, together with the sharpening conflict between reformers and conservatives, portend a serious struggle for power in Iran in the years ahead.

Autocracies and Oligarchies

Some authoritarian regimes are *autocracies*. **Autocracy** *means one-person rule.* In these cases, one individual exercises supreme governing authority and is acknowledged as the maximum leader by the country's dominant cliques or groups. While an autocrat may listen to advice or may feel it necessary or desirable to accommodate the wishes of certain key figures in his government, ultimately he has considerable latitude to make final decisions. Hitler and Stalin are examples of autocrats. Another term for certain types of autocrats is *sultanistic* rulers, a term coined by Max Weber in reference to the sultans of the Ottoman empire. Sultanistic leaders exercise highly concentrated personal power, often appointing trusted family members and cronies to positions of political responsibility. Saddam Hussein is an example.

Other authoritarian regimes are *oligarchies*. **Oligarchy** *means rule by a few.* In an oligarchy, a small number of individuals at the top of the ruling group share power among themselves. Usually these arrangements involve compromises and understandings on the part of extremely powerful officials who believe that it is in their own best interest to share power rather than tolerate an autocrat. The Soviet Union was governed by oligarchies under Khrushchev and Brezhnev. About two dozen key figures shared power, all of them probably fearing the emergence of another murderous tyrant like Stalin. Contemporary China is governed by a Communist Party oligarchy.

Authoritarianism and Totalitarianism

As several of the previously discussed cases suggest, authoritarian political systems come in different varieties. Some have provided a certain degree of freedom or legal rights to their populations, such as Britain during the centuries after Magna Carta. But others have been considerably more domineering, allowing the population virtually no rights or freedoms. In these more severe regimes, the government controls or regulates almost every aspect

of social life, including the economy, religion, education, the media, art and culture, leisure activities, and so on. Such systems are called *totalitarian.*

> **Totalitarianism** *is a form of authoritarianism in which the government's domination of social life is virtually total. Individuals have few, if any, rights or freedoms; the government controls or regulates nearly every aspect of human life. Typically such political systems are ruled by an autocracy or oligarchy that relies on the use of brute force to keep the population under control.*

Nazi Germany, the Soviet Union (especially under Stalin), and Saddam Hussein's Iraq are examples of totalitarian regimes.

Totalitarian regimes penetrate society far more thoroughly and ruthlessly than other authoritarian regimes, such as traditional monarchies. Whereas some authoritarian regimes may permit the individual a certain sphere of privacy in areas regarded as essentially nonpolitical, totalitarian regimes regard virtually everything as political and almost nothing as private. Under both Hitler and Stalin, the educational system, the media, religion, art, scientific research, and a considerable amount of economic activity all came under the oversight, or outright control, of the ruling authorities.

Although the distinction between a totalitarian government and one that is merely "authoritarian" can sometimes be fairly easy to make, in other cases the distinction is less clear. Was the Soviet Union totalitarian under Khrushchev or Brezhnev? Neither of these leaders resorted to terror against the population as massively as Stalin had, yet the Communist Party oligarchy still dominated every major aspect of social life in the USSR. A similar question could be raised about Communist China. Prior to the mid-1970s, the Chinese Communist rulers controlled just about the entire economy, permitting little, if any, private enterprise. Since that period, however, the leadership has permitted considerable private enterprise but no political freedoms. Is China now simply "authoritarian" rather than "totalitarian"? Some scholars would say yes but others would disagree.[11]

HYPOTHESES ON POWER

Economics and Power

Does economic strength automatically lead to political power? Does individual wealth, or control over large corporations, inevitably confer a correspondingly large amount of influence over government decision makers? Numerous political thinkers and writers have proposed or tested the hypothesis that economic power brings about political power.

Karl Marx believed that in societies with private enterprise, the capitalist class always maintains its dominance over the rest of the population by virtue of its control over the economy. For Marx, economics is the main factor influencing politics. By abolishing the capitalist system in a revolution, he maintained, the exploited working class would eventually establish an economy without private economic power. Once private enterprise was destroyed, there would no longer be an economic basis for the domination of one class by another. A socialist economy, rooted in common ownership of productive assets by the whole population, would create a truly classless society. Marx further believed that the truth of these propositions was determined by certain iron laws of history that he claimed to have discovered. Inevitably, he argued, these laws would soon be verified as capitalism collapsed from its own internal "contradictions" in the leading industrialized countries and as socialist societies emerged in its place.

In fact, history did not bear out Marx's predictions. The leading capitalist countries of the nineteenth and twentieth centuries—Britain, Germany, the United States, and France—never experienced the revolutionary upheavals he foresaw. The countries that experienced socialist revolutions, such as Russia, China, and Cuba, were nowhere nearly as industrialized as Marx would have expected them to be when their revolutions occurred. Moreover, the type of socialism that triumphed in these countries, engineered by powerful communist party dictatorships, was very different from the benign socialist utopia Marx had anticipated.

Still, Marx and his followers illuminated a widespread phenomenon: economic power can indeed bring a considerable amount of political power. But does this reality *always* lead to the simple equation, *economic power = political power?* Political scientists who have studied the question have found a variety of real-world relationships

between economic and political power, some with expected results and some not so expected. A prominent example is Robert Dahl's classic study of power in New Haven, Connecticut.

HYPOTHESIS-TESTING EXERCISE: Power in New Haven

HYPOTHESIS AND VARIABLES

In his widely read book *Who Governs?*, Robert Dahl of Yale University tested the hypothesis that economic power confers political power on the wealthiest segments of society. In this hypothesis, *economic power* is the **independent variable** and *political power* is the **dependent variable.** In the 1950s Dahl decided to see if this hypothesis applied in New Haven, Connecticut.[12]

EXPECTATIONS

Dahl's initial expectation was that, if economics determines politics, then the richest families of New Haven and the city's most successful businesspeople should always get their way any time they needed the local government to make a decision in their behalf. Another expectation was that their dominance of the local economy would provide them with a general control over the city's governmental affairs. If that were true, then New Haven's mayor and other elected officials would be expected to pay more attention to the needs and demands of the city's economic elite than to the voters who elected them to office. Indeed, the hypothesis plainly implies that electoral democracy is a sham: in the end, the wealthy minority always enjoys considerably more political power than the voting majority.

EVIDENCE

Dahl focused his research on key decisions taken by local politicians in three issue areas: public education, urban redevelopment, and nominations for public office by the Democratic and Republican parties. He found that New Haven's most well-established wealthy families in fact possessed very little political influence on these issues. Many of them were not even interested in politics at all. He further found that the most prominent local business leaders—the so-called "economic notables"—had no real influence on any of these issues, either. Although they occasionally succeeded in getting what they wanted through the political process, economic power did not confer on this small group a general control over the city. Even on issues of vital importance to the business community, New Haven's elected officials were able to make major decisions without undue interference by business leaders. Moreover, less powerful groups, such as factory workers and the lower middle class, also had significant political resources that they could utilize to influence governmental policy on a host of questions. By electing city officials sympathetic to their views, they could often succeed in getting the local government to decide certain questions in their favor.

CONCLUSIONS

Dahl therefore concluded that the evidence was *inconsistent* with the hypothesis: New Haven was not ruled by "the hidden hand of an economic elite," he wrote, but was governed by a *plurality* of social classes, political parties, and public and private institutions. These conclusions contradicted the assertions of C. Wright Mills and other proponents of the power-elite hypothesis and supported the concept of *pluralism* in American political life.[13]

James Madison

Dahl's book and the debates it provoked prompted a number of political scientists to undertake their own studies of the relationship between economic and political power in various communities. In most cases it has been found that economic power definitely provides political influence, though rarely does it confer complete domination over political life.[14] Various scholars have noted that, at least in some situations, the power of money can be offset by other forms of power. *Organization*, in particular, can often provide a method for enabling less well-off groups to compensate for their economic weakness by getting what they want through such mechanisms as trade unions, civil rights groups, homeless advocacy organizations, and similar associations. The political economist John Kenneth Galbraith once characterized the U.S. political economy in terms of "countervailing powers," with the power of big business counterbalanced by the power of organized labor. Galbraith's study, written in the 1950s, would surely have to be revised today, however, as most trade unions in the United States are weaker now than they were back then.[15]

The Abuse of Power

Another topic under the heading of power concerns the *abuse of power:* how can it be prevented? This age-old question was of vital importance to the founding fathers of the American revolution. **James Madison** (1751–1836) was especially interested in creating a system of government that protected individual liberties from the encroachments of an ob-

trusive and all-powerful state. "If men were angels," he wrote in *The Federalist*, "neither external nor internal controls on government would be necessary. In framing a government to be administered by men over men, the great difficulty lies in this: You must first enable the government to control the governed; and in the next place, oblige it to control itself." Accordingly, "to control the abuses of government," Madison reasoned that a carefully constructed constitutional system in which the various branches of the state—the legislature, the executive, and the judiciary—checked and balanced one another's legal authority would prevent the abuse of power by any one of these branches. Madison's design, of course, became the basis of the U.S. Constitution that took effect in 1789.[16]

The abuse of governmental power by political leaders is only one form of the abuse of power to be found in political life. Madison and other political theorists have also cautioned against another potential tyranny, the **tyranny of the majority**. Even in a democracy with a narrowly circumscribed governmental system, it is possible that a large majority of voters, exercising their constitutional rights, may find ways to restrict the rights and opportunities of minority groups in society. In the same passage from *The Federalist* just cited, Madison wrote that it was important not only to guard society against the oppression of its rulers, but also "to guard one part of the society against the injustice of the other part."

To this end, Madison favored a large, "extended" American republic whose laws would cover all the various states of the union. Such a system, in his view, was preferable to a more fractionated system in which individual states (say, Rhode Island) would be so independent of the national government that they could pass whatever laws they wanted, even those that violated minority rights. Madison argued that large societies are likely to be divided into a wide variety of social groups and interests that provide minorities with an opportunity to forge effective coalitions in defense of their rights. By contrast, smaller societies provide fewer opportunities for such coalitions and are thus more susceptible to the domination of a well-organized majority over the minority. Madison thus hypothesized that "the larger the society, . . . the more duly capable it will be of self government."

Evidence from a much later period in American history proved quite consistent with Madison's propositions. Efforts by the elected officials of certain southern states to deny voting rights, equal educational opportunities, and other civil rights to African Americans were overturned largely through the actions of the federal government. In 1954, the U.S. Supreme Court—a federal institution—declared that legally protected racial segregation in local public school systems violated the Constitution. In the 1960s the U.S. Congress, propelled into action by President Lyndon B. Johnson, passed landmark legislation ensuring that the right to vote and other basic constitutional guarantees were not abridged by state governments. The congressional majority that passed these laws exemplified the type of broad-based national coalition in defense of minority rights that Madison had envisioned.

One astute observer of the United States in its formative decades singled out the tyranny of the majority as a particularly grave threat to America's fledgling democracy. **Alexis de Tocqueville** (1805–1859) was a brilliantly perceptive Frenchman who traveled around the United States at the age of 26 in 1831. De Tocqueville heaped praise on the young republic but warned against tendencies to intellectual conformity and mediocrity in American life as a result of the majority's vulgarizing influences. His prediction that slavery would one day threaten the United States with civil war proved particularly prophetic. "If ever freedom is

lost in America," he wrote, "that will be due to the omnipotence of the majority driving the minorities to desperation and forcing them to appeal to physical force." De Tocqueville's magisterial work, *Democracy in America,* still stands as one of the most insightful examinations ever undertaken of American politics and, more broadly, of democracy itself.

Corruption and Power

"Power corrupts; absolute power corrupts absolutely." This oft-quoted phrase of the British historian Robert Acton appears to have a timeless validity. Corruption is one of the most widespread examples of the abuse of power; scarcely any country in the world is immune to it. Construed in the most general terms, corruption signifies the moral degradation of the individual. As countless cases from the ancient world down to the present day have confirmed, power tempts those in authority to exploit the opportunities at their disposal for personal advantage. Absolute power, unchecked by any practical or legal limitations, can take this process to its most perverse extremes, culminating in tyranny and megalomania. Even in democracies, where it is tempered by the rule of law, political power holds out temptations to self-enrichment or other ill-gotten gains that some public officials find impossible to resist.

We define **political corruption** *as the illegal or unethical use of a political position to provide special advantages for individuals or groups.* Though the present age is probably no more or less corrupt than prior eras, recent years have witnessed a rash of sensational cases of corrupt practices by political figures in authoritarian regimes and democracies alike. Here are just two examples:

- In the 1990s the entire Italian political system was rocked by political scandals that devastated the country's political elites and reshaped its political parties and electoral system. More than eight thousand political figures, including some of the most respected leaders of the post–World War II decades, were indicted for accepting bribes and other favors from the Mafia, private businesses, and various other sources. The scandals led to the collapse of established political parties and to major electoral reforms.

- Mobutu Sese Seko was the dictator of Zaire from 1965 to 1997. During his long reign he was regarded as one of the world's most corrupt political leaders. Though the overwhelming majority of Zaire's population of approximately 43 million were mired in poverty, the country's profitable copper, cobalt, and diamond exports provided a rich source of income for Mobutu and his cronies. The national bank printed money at the dictator's whims. As a consequence, Zaire had the highest inflation rate in the world in 1994: 12,500 percent. Under Mobutu's direction, Zaire had become a veritable *kleptocracy:* a state ruled by thieves. Mobutu fled the country in 1997 as rebel forces won a bloody civil war. The new government, which changed the country's name to the Democratic Republic of the Congo, claimed that Mobutu still had $8 billion in Swiss banks.

In subsequent chapters we'll look at outbreaks of corruption in a variety of countries.

What causes political corruption? If we assume that its root cause lies in the acquisitive appetites of those who demand wealth and power, then we had better turn to psychologists rather than political scientists for an explanation of the phenomenon. But even if we concede that corruption springs from the human personality, are there any *political* variables that may help explain *how* corruption manifests itself and perhaps shed some light on how it might be reduced or discouraged?

These questions are far too large to permit an adequate response within the confines of this book. The most we can do is mention a few hypotheses that seek to explain the politics of corruption. Although some of these hypotheses have been put to empirical tests by the authors cited, others still await a systematic investigation.

Among the many independent variables that might account for political corruption, one of the more obvious ones is *the absence of the rule of law.* Quite clearly, authoritarian regimes in which the leaders are unrestrained by any higher law are especially susceptible to the ravages of personal greed and the lust for power. Even when the rule of law prevails as a general principle, as it does in democracies, corruption may still exist if it is not adequately detected and the law is not properly enforced. Effective detection and enforcement

TABLE 5.1

Rank Ordering of Corrupt Countries

An organization known as Transparency International compiles a rank ordering of countries based on the perceptions of businesspeople of the corruption they encounter in their dealings with government and non-government personnel around the world. The *Corruption Perceptions Index* (CPI) gives a rating of 10 to a corruption-free country; the lower the number, the greater the perceived corruption. The eighty-five countries ranked in the 1998 Corruption Perceptions Index include the following:

Country	Rank	CPI score
Denmark	1	10.0
Finland	2	9.6
Sweden	3	9.5
New Zealand	4	9.4
Iceland	5	9.3
Canada	6	9.2
Singapore	7	9.1
Netherlands	8	9.0
Norway	8	9.0
Switzerland	10	8.9
United Kingdom	11	8.7
Germany	15	7.9
United States	17	7.5
Israel	19	7.1
France	21	6.7
Japan	25	5.8
South Africa	32	5.2
Italy	39	4.6
Poland	39	4.6
South Korea	43	4.2
Brazil	46	4.0
People's Rep. of China	52	3.5
Turkey	54	3.4
Mexico	55	3.3
Yugoslavia	61	3.0
Egypt	66	2.9
India	66	2.9
Ukraine	69	2.8
Russia	76	2.4
Indonesia	80	2.0
Nigeria	81	1.9
Cameroon	85	1.4

Source: Transparency International, <www.transparency.de>.

mechanisms are therefore essential to discourage corrupt practices in democratic states.

A considerably more vexatious problem arises in democracies when the law permits activities that, in the minds of some people, should be regarded as corrupt. The weakness of campaign financing laws is regarded by many observers as the Achilles' heel of democracy. Most of the world's democracies permit private political contributions to the election campaign war chests of individual candidates or political parties. Although some countries place limits on these allowable contributions, ample opportunities still remain for private campaign funding. Unquestionably, the purpose of many of these contributions is to extract political favors from the recipients should they get elected. And though this money is usually supposed to be used to finance election campaigns, sometimes a certain amount of it ends up in the personal bank accounts of politicians. In addition to cash, the law sometimes permits legislators or other officials to accept additional kinds of benefits: golf-club weekends sponsored by lobbyists, invitations to speak aboard privately sponsored cruises, and so on.

Should such favors be allowed, even if there is no guarantee that the politicians will give their benefactors what they want? While some people consider such practices as a perfectly acceptable aspect of modern democracy, others regard them as pure corruption.[17] The controversy illustrates the difficulty of defining "corruption" in a manner that suits everybody, even in a democracy. Practices that are currently *legal* may be regarded by some people as *unethical* and should, in their view, be outlawed.

A second independent variable impinging on corruption is the *lack of alternation in power.* If the highest government officials are not rotated by the electorate on a periodic basis and if they have good reason to believe that they will not be removed from their positions in the foreseeable future, the likelihood rises that they will engage in corrupt activities. Authoritarian rulers are particularly well-armed against removal from power; they suppress their opponents by force. Hence they feel free to engage in extreme forms of corruption that most people in democracies would surely regard as unethical, even though such actions are "legal" under the authoritarians' arbitrary codes.

But democracies can also experience inadequate alternation in power. Italy and Japan provide telling examples. Prior to the elections of 1994, Italy had been governed by coalition cabinets consisting of the same four or five parties for over thirty years.

Because these governing parties could be quite certain that they would not be voted out of office by opposition parties, they felt relatively free to enjoy the spoils of political corruption without fearing the wrath of an angry electorate large enough to vote them out of office. (The chief opposition party was the Italian Communist Party, which was never sufficiently popular to unseat the ruling coalitions.) In Japan, the Liberal Democratic Party (LDP) ruled uninterruptedly for almost forty years. Throughout that stretch it trounced its opponents in every election. This relative guarantee of prolonged incumbency convinced a number of LDP leaders that they could get away with corruption indefinitely. That calculation proved correct until 1993, when the party lost its majority because of a massive corruption scandal. The evidence from Italy and Japan is thus quite consistent with our hypothesis that *the likelihood of corruption varies inversely with the likelihood of alternation in power:* the less likely it is that a government will be removed from office, the more likely it is that it will engage in illegal corruption.

Some students of political corruption have explored other independent variables that impinge on the frequency, extent, or form of corruption. In one comparative study of the topic, James C. Scott hypothesized that political corruption is a "normal," routine part of governing in most political systems. Such practices as vote-buying, embezzlement, and nepotism (i.e., favoritism shown to the family members of public officials) can be found in both democracies and non-democracies. In some cases certain types of corruption, such as providing favors to one's political friends while in office, may even be necessary for the survival of society's basic arrangements for dealing with the demands of its social groups. Scott also points out that the definition of corruption varies with time and place. Practices that are legal at one point in a country's history may be outlawed in another one. In Britain, it was once legal for the state to sell public offices; that custom is now illegal. Practices that may be condemned as unethical in some cultures may be viewed as perfectly acceptable, even desirable, in other ones. Giving money or gifts to officials in exchange for favors is considered bribery in some places, but courteous gift giving in others.[18]

Two especially important aspects of political corruption that can be examined comparatively are the extent of its impact on the political system and the extent to which it can be eliminated. A significant difference exists between political systems in which corruption is occasional or confined to specific individuals, on the one hand, and those in which it is pervasive and symptomatic of the way politics generally operates, on the other. There are various gradations between these two extremes. There is also a significant difference between systems in which corruption is exposed to the glare of public scrutiny and to legal procedures that can punish the miscreants, and systems in which nothing can be done about it, no matter how widely known the corrupt practices may be.

As a general rule, authoritarian regimes are especially susceptible to pervasive corruption that is virtually ineradicable. Democracies, while by no means faultless, at least possess mechanisms like a free press and the rule of law that are capable of publicizing acts of corruption and subjecting the perpetrators to public condemnation or legal sanctions. Italy and Japan have been trying to deal with their corruption problems through the democratic process. The Soviet Union and the former communist states of East-Central Europe, by contrast, gave their citizens no effective political or legal opportunities to combat political corruption. Extensive corruption weakened these regimes considerably in the 1970s and 1980s, reducing even further what little popular support or acceptance they may have had. Communist China, where official corruption festers, may be heading in the same direction.[19]

Powerlessness

Thus far we have looked almost exclusively at those who wield power. But what of the powerless? Are the weak who must endure the hegemony of all-powerful governments or dominant social groups doomed to pure submission? The weak may have subtle weapons of their own.

WEAPONS OF THE WEAK

History provides striking evidence that subjugated peoples can sometimes find effective ways to turn the tables on their masters. Although successful revolutions are rel-

atively rare, it was as recently as 1989 and 1990 that the people of East Germany, Poland, Czechoslovakia, and other countries of East-Central Europe managed to cast off decades of Communist Party rule. In other places, groups that do not accept their subservient status have found attention-grabbing ways to express their dissatisfaction: car-bombings, skyjackings, insurrections, and other acts of violence are often sufficiently explosive to capture world headlines.

But do there exist instances of discontent that are too quiet or hidden to stir public notice? Can subjugated groups find ways to express their resentments in countries that appear to be under the complete mastery of the dominant classes and authorities?

James C. Scott has addressed these questions quite perceptively. In *Weapons of the Weak*, Scott observed the subtle dynamics of class relationships between Malaysian peasants and the landowners and officials who controlled their world. When the landlords began imposing new rice production techniques that worked to the peasants' disadvantage, the peasants did not openly rebel. On the contrary, they appeared at first glance to be quietly resigned to the new procedures, presumably because they saw no chance of overturning them. Closer scrutiny revealed, however, that many peasants were not as complacent as they seemed. Although they appeared outwardly deferential when speaking publicly with their social superiors, they could be highly critical of their overlords when speaking about them in private.

In addition to noticing this sharp distinction between the peasants' public demeanor and their private discourse, Scott also discovered a third realm of peasant behavior located in between these public and private domains. Some peasants engaged in clandestine acts of poaching or minor property destruction aimed directly at the landlords. Some spread malicious gossip about landlords or their family members in a manifest attempt at character assassination, or they discreetly shunned individuals from the dominant class. These and similar actions, while occurring in public, remained surreptitious and anonymous; the peasants were careful not to provoke their masters into violent retaliation. Even so, Scott concluded, these behaviors constituted deliberate *political* acts of defiance that expressed the peasants' opposition to the prevailing power structures in Malaysia.

In a subsequent work, *Domination and the Arts of Resistance*, Scott widened his analysis into a comparative study of low-level political defiance in a variety of countries and historical eras. Drawing on accounts of slavery in the United States, serfdom in nineteenth-century Russia, British colonialism in Burma, castes in India, communist rule in the Soviet Union and Eastern Europe, and numerous other instances of relations between dominant and powerless groups, Scott probed the hypothesis that "relations of dominance are, at the same time, relations of resistance." Even when resistance is not overt or violently confrontational, he suggested, it is present nonetheless.

Both the powerful and the weak, Scott observed, engage in certain routinized behaviors when dealing with each other directly. The weak are respectful. The strong present themselves as worthy of being in authority. Beneath the surface of these "public transcripts," however, both groups employ "hidden transcripts" that express their deepest attitudes. Subjugated groups vent their rage when talking among themselves; dominant elites violate their image of probity by indulging in secret privileges and corruption. But the oppressed groups, in addition to expressing their resentments privately, invariably engage in low-profile forms of public resistance: pilfering, foot-dragging, sabotaging crops or machinery, squatting, withholding taxes or food deliveries, shoddy workmanship, arson, and the like. In addition, dominated peoples in a variety of settings have found relatively "safe" ways of articulating their hidden transcripts openly. Through gossip, rumors, jokes, folk tales, and other modes of coded or symbolic public discourse, they cleverly employ elliptical modes of mocking or vilifying the ruling groups that oppress them.

Such insubordinate activities, in Scott's view, constitute the "infrapolitics" of the powerless. "Every subordinate group," he writes, "creates, out of its ordeal, a 'hidden transcript' that represents a critique of power spoken behind the back of the dominant." Far from being a *substitute* for resistance, these hidden transcripts are themselves a *form* of resistance. Moreover, the cumulative effects of seemingly petty acts of defiance can exact a heavy toll in economic and other costs to the dominant classes. In some cases, they can also pave the way to a more explosive mass uprising. If we want to understand the realities of power relations, therefore, we must penetrate the veneer of outward appearances and explore the many ways the weak "speak truth to power."[20]

As this chapter has shown, power permeates political life. In one way or another, it plays a role in all the other "grand themes" of politics that we shall consider in subsequent chapters.

KEY TERMS AND NAMES
(Underlined in the text)

Power
Political power
Dominance

Influence
Power elite
Pluralism
Co-optation
Coercion
Authority
Rule of law
Saddam Hussein
Charisma
Niccolò Machiavelli
Autocracy
Oligarchy
Totalitarianism
James Madison
Tyranny of the majority
Alexis de Tocqueville
Political corruption

NOTES

1. Brian Weinstein and Aaron Segal, *Haiti: The Failure of Politics* (New York: Praeger, 1992); Michel S. Laguerre, *The Military and Society in Haiti* (Knoxville: The University of Tennessee Press, 1993); Jean-Bertrand Aristide (with Christophe Hargny), *Aristide: An Autobiography* (Maryknoll, N.Y.: Orbis Books, 1993).

2. For a comparison of power and money, see Karl W. Deutsch, *The Nerves of Government* (New York: Free Press, 1966), 120–22; and Robert E. Lane, "Experiencing Money and Experiencing Power," in *Power, Inequality, and Democratic Politics*, ed. Ian Shapiro and Grant Reeher (Boulder, Colo.: Westview Press, 1988), 80–105.

3. For books that deal with power in international relations, see the classic study by Hans J. Morgenthau, *Politics among Nations,* 6th ed. (New York: Knopf, 1985); and Michael P. Sullivan, *Power in Contemporary International Politics* (Columbia: University of South Carolina Press, 1990).

4. Robert A. Dahl, *Modern Political Analysis,* 5th ed. (Englewood Cliffs, N.J.: 1991), 12. Dahl stresses the similarities between power and influence. See his discussion in chapters 2–4. For a contrary view emphasizing the distinctions between power and influence, see Peter Morriss, *Power: A Philosophical Analysis* (New York: St. Martin's Press, 1987), 8–13 and 23–24. Edward C. Banfield defines influence as "the ability to get others to act, think, or feel as one intends" and power as "the ability to exercise control over another." He regards influence as "a generic term in-

cluding authority, control, and power." See his *Political Influence* (New York: Free Press, 1961), 3, 348 n.

5. See Dahl, 32–34. For a sophisticated attempt to measure power in quantitative terms, see Jack H. Nagel, *The Descriptive Analysis of Power* (New Haven, Conn.: Yale University Press, 1975).

6. C. Wright Mills, *The Power Elite* (London: Oxford University Press, 1956); and G. William Domhoff, *Who Rules America? A View for the '80s* (Englewood Cliffs, N.J.: Prentice Hall, 1983) and *The Power Elite and the State* (New York: Aldine de Gruyter, 1990). See also Albrecht Rothacher, *The Japanese Power Elite* (New York: St. Martin's Press, 1993). For more generalized critiques of power elites in democracies, see Steven Lukes, *Power: A Radical View* (London: Macmillan, 1974); and Thomas E. Wartenberg, ed., *Rethinking Power* (Albany: State University of New York Press, 1992). For some opposing views, see Nelson Polsby, *Community Power and Political Theory* (New Haven, Conn.: Yale University Press, 1963); Jack E. Walker, "A Critique of the Elitist Theory of Democracy," *American Political Science Review* 60 (1966): 285–95; and Andrew M. Greeley, *Building Coalitions* (Chicago: Franklin Watts, 1974).

7. Nicholas Abercrombie, Stephen Hill, and Bryan S. Turner, *The Dominant Ideology Thesis* (London: Allen and Unwin, 1980); and id., eds., *Dominant Ideologies* (London: Unwin Hyman, 1990).

8. For a definition of politics as the "authoritative allocation of values," see David Easton, *A Framework for Political Analysis* (Englewood Cliffs, N.J.: Prentice Hall, 1965), 50.

9. Harold Lasswell, *Politics: Who Gets What, When, and How* (New York: McGraw-Hill, 1936). See also Lasswell and Abraham Kaplan, *Power in Society: A Framework for Political Inquiry* (New Haven, Conn: Yale University Press, 1950).

10. Samir al-Khalil, *Republic of Fear: The Politics of Modern Iraq* (Berkeley: University of California Press, 1989); Efraim Karsh and Inari Rautsi, *Saddam Hussein: A Political Biography* (New York: Free Press, 1991).

11. On the concept of totalitarianism, see Abbott Gleason, *Totalitarianism: The Inner History of the Cold War* (New York: Oxford University Press, 1995); Hannah Arendt, *The Origins of Totalitarianism* (New York: Harcourt, Brace, and World, 1968); and Carl J. Friedrich and Zbigniew K. Brzezinski, *Totalitarian Dictatorship and Autocracy* (New York: Praeger, 1961).

12. Robert Dahl, *Who Governs?* (New Haven, Conn.: Yale University Press, 1961).

13. Dahl's findings did not go unchallenged. Peter Bachrach and Morton S. Baratz argued that Dahl had failed to consider decisions that the New Haven government did *not* make because the local business elite would have disapproved of them. Such behind-the-scenes influence, they argued, constitutes a real form of power that can result in "non-decisions" by government officials. See Peter Bachrach and Morton S. Baratz, "Two Faces of Power," *American Political Science Review* 56, no. 4 (December 1962): 947–52. See also, by the same authors, "Decisions and Nondecisions: An Analytical Framework," *American Political Science Review* 57, no. 3 (September 1963): 632–42, and *Power and Poverty: Theory and Practice* (New York: Oxford University Press, 1970). See also Geoffrey Debnam, "Nondecisions and Power: The Two Faces of Bachrach and Baratz," *American Political Science Review* 69, no. 3 (September 1975): 889–904, followed by replies.

14. In the 1980s, for example, two political scientists tested the relationship between economic power and political power in an American city by examining the role of General Motors in the Detroit area. They concluded that GM's prodigious economic strength gave it a decisive edge in limiting what the local governments could do in various aspects of economic policy. If the auto magnates wanted to close down a plant, throwing thousands of people out of work, there was little the local government could do to stop them. Nevertheless, some municipal officials possessed bargaining skills that, when utilized creatively, were able to get General Motors to alter its actions to accommodate the local population, including auto workers eager to retain their jobs. Despite its economic power, GM did not *always* control political outcomes. See Bryan D. Jones and Lynn W. Bachelor, *The Sustaining Hand* (Lawrence: University of Kansas Press, 1986).

15. John Kenneth Galbraith, *American Capitalism: The Concept of Countervailing Power* (Boston: Houghton Mifflin, 1952). For a more recent analysis of the U.S. labor movement, see Michael Goldfield, *The Decline of Organized Labor in the United States* (Chicago: University of Chicago Press, 1989).

16. The passage quoted here is from *The Federalist*, Number 51. *The Federalist* was a series of newspaper articles by James Madison, Alexander Hamilton, and John Jay. Writing in the late 1780s, the authors opposed the loosely structured government established under the Articles of Confederation and argued in favor of a new constitution that would establish a somewhat stronger central U.S. government.

17. A study by Herbert E. Alexander and Anthony Corrado estimated that the total cost of the 1992 elections in the United States was $3.2 billion (compared with $1.2 billion in 1980). Of the former amount, the

presidential candidates spent $550 million, Congressional candidates spent $678 million, and candidates for state and local offices spent the rest. About $1 billion of this sum was spent by political parties and organizations. Most of this money was raised from private sources. The $3.2 billion figure represented only about .06 percent of U.S. gross domestic product in 1992. Cited in Robert J. Samuelson, "The Price of Politics," *Washington Post*, August 23, 1995.

18. James C. Scott, *Comparative Political Corruption* (Englewood Cliffs, N.J.: Prentice Hall, 1972). Also Susan Rose-Ackerman, *Corruption and Government* (Cambridge: Cambridge University Press, 1999).

19. For an analysis of corruption in the USSR, communist Eastern Europe, and China, see Leslie Holmes, *The End of Communist Power: Anti-Corruption Campaigns and Legitimation Crisis* (New York: Oxford University Press, 1993).

20. James C. Scott, *Weapons of the Weak: Everyday Forms of Peasant Resistance* (New Haven, Conn.: Yale University Press, 1985), and *Domination and the Arts of Resistance: Hidden Transcripts* (New Haven, Conn.: Yale University Press, 1990). See also John Gaventa, *Power and Powerlessness: Quiescence and Rebellion in an Appalachian Valley* (Urbana: University of Illinois Press, 1980).

CHAPTER 6

THE STATE
AND ITS INSTITUTIONS

DEFINING THE STATE

Thus far we have been using the term "government" as a synonym for the state. When discussing government in general, political scientists tend to prefer "the state" as a generic term encompassing all the governmental institutions within an individual country. Note that this particular usage has a *domestic* focus. In this sense of the term,

> the **state** *means the totality of a country's governmental institutions and officials.*

This definition is all-inclusive. It incorporates *all* government officials and agencies at all levels of a country's governmental system, from the highest officials of the national government to the local cop on the beat.

The most important function of the state is its *exercise of legal authority*.

> *The state possesses the legal authority to make, and coercively enforce, laws that are binding on the population.*

It is these law-making and law-enforcing powers that distinguish the state from non-state institutions, groups, and individuals within a given country. These powers differentiate the state from society, the public sector from the private sector, the official from the unofficial. In most instances the state jealously guards these powers, maintaining a *monopoly* of legal authority. Above all it monopolizes the principal mechanisms of coercive power—the courts, the police, and the military—to make sure that the laws of the land are observed by the population. If the state cannot employ its coercive power effectively and is challenged by elements of society capable of taking arms against official authorities, then it can lose its very ability to govern.

Although governmental institutions form the core of this definition of the state, some political scientists argue for a more expansive conception of the term that would include as part of the state certain non-governmental organizations or groups that have a particularly strong impact on governmental authorities. As we observed in the preceding chapter, dominant political parties or especially influential social groups can at times be so politically powerful and so tightly linked with the government as to be virtually indistinguishable from it. In Nazi Germany, Hitler's Nazi Party was not, strictly speaking, a governmental institution; it was a political party. Once Hitler became head of government in 1933, the Nazis completely took over Germany's state institutions and certain party organs were given official powers. In Nazi Germany the state and the party interpenetrated each other so thoroughly that it was impossible to draw a clear line of demarcation between the two. The same may be said of Soviet-style communist countries like contemporary China.

Marxists traditionally contend that, in capitalist countries, the big-business elite so completely dominates government decision makers that the state is essentially "the guardian and protector" of this economically powerful social class. Accordingly, at least some Marxists contend that the capitalist "ruling class" is part of the "state system."[1] Many non-Marxists would dispute this co-identification of the state and the capitalist class. Nevertheless, as all the preceding cases demonstrate, the dividing line between "state" and "non-state" may sometimes be blurry. Though the state, in the strictest sense, means government, it may occasionally be advisable to adopt a more flexible conception of the term that takes account of certain non-state organizations and groups.[2]

THREE MEANINGS OF "STATE"

The definition of the "state" as the totality of a country's governmental institutions and officials represents only one way in which the term "state" is used in political science.

As we pointed out in chapter 1, "state" is also used as a synonym for an entire country. This usage is especially common in international affairs. In this sense, the United States, Japan, Mexico, and South Africa are all "states"; relations between their respective governments are "inter-state relations."

In a third usage, "state" is sometimes used to designate an administrative subdivision within certain countries. The United States of America consists of fifty states. Germany consists of sixteen *Laender*, a term translated into English as "states."

CATEGORIZING GOVERNMENTS

Aristotle (384–322 B.C.) was one of the great categorizers in western thought. His passion for identifying and classifying things extended from plant and animal life to different forms of government. In his treatise *The Politics*, Aristotle compared the constitutions of several Greek states and systematically described such alternative governmental forms as kingships, tyrannies, democracies, and others. This seminal work in Western political thought established Aristotle's enduring reputation as the founder of the study of comparative government.

Ever since, the task of identifying, describing, and comparing different governmental systems has been a major preoccupation of political science. As the classificatory scheme (or *typology*) that is shown in table 6.1 plainly indicates, the countries that exist today can be grouped under several different headings. The most obvious distinction differentiates democracies from authoritarian forms of rule. Variations exist within each of these two broad categories.

Democracies, for example, can be divided in accordance with their constitutional structure. Most democracies in today's world are *parliamentary democracies.* In the parliamentary form of democracy, the people elect the national legislature, and the legislature elects or approves the head of government and the cabinet. Alternatively, there are several forms of non-parliamentary democracies. The United States, for example, has a *separation-of-powers system* consisting of three roughly coequal branches of national government. France has a system that combines a powerful presidency with a parliamentary form of government, the so-called *presidential-parliamentary system.* Just about every democracy in today's world is a variant of one of these three systems. We'll describe and compare them more fully in chapter 9. In addition, some democracies have a *federal* structure, which confers various powers on regional or local governments, while others concentrate power in the central government. We'll elaborate on this distinction later in this chapter.

Our typology separately lists those countries that are currently in the process of building or rebuilding democracy after prolonged periods of authoritarian rule. Some of them are making reasonable progress toward democracy while others are moving haltingly or hardly at all. By the time you read this book, one or more of these transitional states may have already relapsed into authoritarianism of one type or another. Of these transitional regimes, some have adopted a parliamentary form of democracy, others are trying out the U.S. separation of powers system, and still others the presidential-parliamentary system. Another group of transitional states are leaning more heavily toward authoritarianism rather than democracy.

Similarly, there are various types of authoritarian regimes. A few are still communist countries whose governments are more or less firmly in the

TABLE 6.1

Typology of Governmental Systems, 1999

DEMOCRACIES
(F indicates federal system)

Variants of U.S. System

Argentina (F)	Costa Rica	El Salvador	Panama	South Africa
Bolivia	Cyprus	Guatemala	Paraguay	Taiwan
Brazil (F)	Dominican	Honduras	Philippines	USA
Chile	Republic	Mozambique	Seychelles	Uruguay
Colombia (insurgency)	Ecuador	Namibia	Sierra Leone (insurgency)	

Parliamentary Democracies

Andorra	Dominica	Japan	Norway	Sweden
Australia (F)	Germany (F)	Kiribati	Palau	Switzerland (F)
Austria (F)	Greece	Luxembourg	Papua–	Thailand
Bahamas	Grenada	Macedonia	New Guinea	(military influence)
Bangladesh	Guyana	Malta	St. Kitts and Nevis	Trinidad and Tobago
Barbados	Hungary	Marshall Island	St. Lucia	Tuvalu
Belgium	Iceland	Mauritius	St. Vincent and	United Kingdom
Belize	India	Micronesia (F)	the Grenadines	Vanuatu
Bulgaria	Ireland	Nauru	San Marino	
Canada (F)	Israel	Nepal	Slovakia	
Czech Rep.	Italy	Netherlands	Solomon Island	
Denmark	Jamaica	New Zealand	Spain	

Presidential-Parliamentary Democracies

Albania	France	Liberia	Kyrgyzia	Sri Lanka (insurgency)
Benin	Georgia	Lithuania	Portugal	Mongolia
Bosnia-Herzegovina	Ghana	Madagascar	Romania	Suriname
Cape Verde	Guinea-Bissau	Malawi	Russia	Poland
Central African Republic	(military influence)	Mali	Sao Tome	Turkey
Croatia	Haiti	Moldova	and Principe	(military influence)
Estonia	Latvia	South Korea	Slovenia	Ukraine
Finland				

Transitional and Other Regimes

Algeria (transition to elected president)	Indonesia (transition to president elected by parliament)	Niger (transition to democracy)
Botswana (parliamentary plus traditional chiefs)	Lesotho (transition to elections in 2000)	Nigeria (transition to presidential-parliamentary democracy)
Eritrea (wartime transition to democracy)	Liechtenstein (principality plus parliamentary democracy)	Samoa (parliamentary democracy plus family heads)
Ethiopia (wartime transition to democracy)	Mexico (1-party dominance plus elected opposition and insurgency)	Venezuela (transition to new presidential system)
Fiji (parliamentary plus native chieftains)	Monaco (principality plus parliamentary democracy)	

continued

TABLE 6.1 (CONTINUED)

AUTHORITARIAN REGIMES

Traditional Regimes
(monarchies, unless otherwise indicated)

Afghanistan (warlords, traditional rulers, local councils)	Kuwait (monarchy plus limited parliament)	Saudi Arabia
Bahrain	Maldives (elite and clan dominance)	Swaziland
Bhutan	Morocco (monarchy plus limited parliament)	Tonga (monarchy plus partly elected parliament)
Brunei	Oman	United Arab Emirates
Iran (theocracy)	Qatar	
Jordan (monarchy plus elected parliament)		

Military and Mixed Military-Civilian Regimes

Burundi	The Gambia	Pakistan	Sudan
Cameroon	Libya	Rwanda (plus dominant party)	Syria
Chad	Myanmar (Burma)		

Dominant-Party Regimes
(CP indicates communist party)

Antigua and Barbuda	Egypt (military influence)	Senegal
Azerbaijan	Equatorial Guinea (military influence)	Singapore
Burkina Faso	Gabon	Tanzania
China (CP)	Guinea (military influence)	Togo
Comoros	Ivory Coast	Tunisia
Democratic Republic of Congo (insurgency)	Kenya	Uganda
Republic of Congo	North Korea (CP)	Vietnam (CP)
Cuba (CP)	Laos (CP)	Yugoslavia
Djibouti	Malaysia	Zambia
	Mauritania	Zimbabwe

Other Authoritarian Regimes

Belarus (presidential dictatorship)	Tajikistan (presidential dominance)
Iraq (autocracy; dominant party plus military)	Turkmenistan (presidential dominance)
Kazakhstan (presidential dominance plus dominant party)	Uzbekistan (presidential dominance)
Peru (presidential dominance)	Yemen (dominant coalition plus military influence)

Civil War, Insurgency, and so on

Angola	Lebanon (partly foreign occupied)	Sierra Leone
Kampuchea (Cambodia)		Somalia

hands of the communist party. Others are military dictatorships. Another group consists of what may be called "traditional" authoritarian states: monarchies, sheikdoms, and the like. Other authoritarian regimes tend to be dominated by a single political party other than a communist party. In the latter cases, competing parties are basically forbidden, and state power is monopolized by a ruling party.

Finally there exist a number of countries that are embroiled in a civil war or some other conflict that makes it difficult to tell who, if anyone, is in charge of the government. In some of these countries there is virtually no functioning central government at all; in others, there is an identifiable government but its authority is under direct challenge from a rival group or groups seeking to take power through organized violence.

As with just about any attempt to fit complex phenomena into neat categories, this typology cannot help but oversimplify things a bit. For example, some countries categorized as one-party authoritarian regimes could just as easily be considered military dictatorships in view of the commanding political role played by military figures in the government. Egypt is an example. Some countries have elections and other democratic institutions but nonetheless retain strong elements of authoritarianism. In Mexico, for example, a single party, the Institutional Revolutionary Party, ruled the country from 1929 until it lost the presidency, the centerpiece of its power, in 2000. Prior to that historic defeat, the party permitted elections but resorted to non-democratic measures (such as fraudulent vote-counting) to maintain its paramountcy. In 1999 it was still classified as a "transitional" democracy, but the 2000 elections results warranted its reclassification as a democracy roughly patterned on the U.S. model. In addition, one can find significant differences among the countries within each of our categories in terms of their economic conditions and the ways their governments deal with economic issues. One also finds variations among democracies in terms of the number of parties that effectively compete for power. The two-party system of the United States is a rarity; most other democracies have more than two parties represented in their national legislatures.

In other words, we could have found other ways to categorize the states of the world. The typology offered here is simply a handy, but by no means definitive, guide. It is also a snapshot taken in 1999, not long before this book went to press. In the rush of political events, some of the countries on our list may have moved from one category to another since then, Mexico constituting just one example.

LEGITIMACY

Legitimacy *means the right to rule.* By what right do some human beings rule over others? This question is as old as organized civilization and as current as today's headlines.

The term "legitimacy" is usually attached to an entire governmental system rather than just to an individual ruler or ruling coalition. People may become disenchanted with this president or that military dictator and may rejoice if the president loses the next election or the dictator is overthrown. When that happens, people sometimes say that the leader in question has lost his or her legitimacy. Generally, however, "legitimacy" has a

much wider application, extending beyond individual leaders. What matters most for the concept of legitimacy is whether democracy itself, or military dictatorship itself (or any other governmental system, for that matter) is regarded as a proper or acceptable form of government.

"Legitimacy" is often used interchangeably with *authority*. As we saw in the last chapter, authority can have several different meanings. The chief distinction we need to make here is between *legal authority* and *legitimate authority* (i.e., *legitimacy*). **Legal authority is the *ability* to rule; legitimacy is the *right* to rule.** No one doubted that Hitler and the Nazi Party had the *ability* to make and enforce the law while they held power in Germany. Although Hitler was appointed head of government in 1933 in accordance with Germany's democratic constitution, he ruled the country for the next dozen years on the basis of brute force, without the slightest pretense of democracy. Did the Nazis have the *right* to rule Germany? The answer to this question depends on how one views the *source* of legitimacy: *who* determines whether or not a government is legitimate, and *how* is this determination made?

Many theorists regard democracy as the only truly legitimate form of government on the grounds that it is explicitly based on the consent of the governed. *In democracies, the people are the source of the state's legitimacy.* Because the people, either directly or through their elected representatives, can adopt the constitution and laws they want and because they have the opportunity to change these laws as well as their leaders through periodic elections and related procedures, democracies provide observable evidence of popular approval or disapproval of the political system itself. Freely conducted and openly published public opinion surveys also constitute a barometer of public attitudes in democratic polities. Presumably, if enough people no longer accept the way their democracy works, they can always vote to alter it. If they wish to abolish democracy itself, they can do that too, even by utilizing the very methods of democracy. In 1932, more than half of Germany's voters cast their ballots for political parties that were avowedly hostile to democracy, such as the Nazis and the Communists. Democracies, in other words, place their legitimacy on the line on a continuing basis.

Not all political theorists or practitioners have regarded the people as the chief source of governmental legitimacy. Throughout most of the Middle Ages in Europe, monarchs ruled on the basis of the "divine right of kings," the notion that God—not human beings—conferred legitimacy on the reigning kings, queens, and emperors. A roughly similar view held sway in China, where for nearly two thousand years a succession of dynasties claimed that their right to govern derived from the "mandate of heaven." This notion was endorsed by the philosopher **Confucius,** who upheld the legitimacy of established authority while insisting on virtuous behavior on the part of the ruling hierarchy. Japan's emperors also traced their legitimacy to divine sources. Following Japan's capitulation at the end of World War II, Emperor Hirohito issued a statement announcing that he was not a descendant of the deity. This admission came as a shock to millions of Japanese, who had been brought up to believe that the royal family descended directly from the Sun Goddess.

For his part, Karl Marx believed that the laws of history determined legitimacy. Although he did not tend to use the terms "legitimacy" or "illegitimacy" explicitly, in effect he maintained that the laws of historical development, which he claimed to have discovered, determined the illegitimacy of capitalism and the legitimacy of communism as social and economic systems.

Even among those theorists of legitimacy who identify the people as the primary source of the state's legitimacy there have been some interesting differences of opinion. Although most students of contemporary democracy in places like the United States and Western Europe would probably say that the people confer legitimacy on their governmental systems through their constitutions, electoral procedures, and other explicitly formulated legal mechanisms, a number of democratic theorists in earlier centuries justified democracy on slightly different grounds. In their view, the people exercised their right to rule on the basis of *natural law* and an unwritten *social contract*. At a time when mass democracies as we know them today, with their elaborate legal structures and mass electorates, did not exist anywhere in the world, the social contract theorists took the view that we human beings have a natural right to choose whichever

form of government we want. That right springs naturally from the very fact of our humanity. (Many natural law theorists maintained that God conferred this right on humanity. In Thomas Jefferson's famous words, the people are "endowed by their Creator with certain inalienable rights.") They further argued that, before there could be any explicit legal system defining how these natural rights were to be implemented in practice, people exercised their natural right to choose the form of government they wanted on the basis of an implicit agreement called the **social contract.**

Although quite a few theorists of democracy subscribed to the doctrines of natural law and the social contract, these ideas had several variants. Some of those who accepted natural law as the source of the people's right to rule argued that the unwritten social contract had to be reinforced with carefully spelled out *written* laws. James Madison and other authors of the U.S. Constitution are good examples. And some who accepted the notion of the social contract took very divergent positions on the question of *how* the people should exercise their natural right to choose their preferred form of government.

Three of the most famous social contract theorists were **Thomas Hobbes, John Locke,** and **Jean-Jacques Rousseau.** While agreeing that human beings have the right to determine their own political destiny, these thinkers differed radically on the type of government the people ought to choose. Their profound influence on the development of political thought reverberates to the present day and still fuels current debates about the nature of politics and government.

THOMAS HOBBES
(1588–1679)

Thomas Hobbes lived in an epoch of political and scientific tumult. Within months of his birth, the English navy defeated the Spanish armada, a feat that would solidify Britain's mastery of the seas for more than three centuries. In a few decades, however, the English monarchy's mastery over its own realm would be shaken to the core. Two civil wars in the 1640s brought about the dissolution of the monarchical system of government that had endured for more than a thousand years. In 1649 King Charles I was beheaded and a com-

Thomas Hobbes

moner, Oliver Cromwell, eventually assumed power. Two years after Cromwell's death in 1658, the monarchy was restored under Charles II, but the basis of the crown's rule would never be the same. Britain's parliament was determined to assert its own rights against the king's traditional prerogatives. Meanwhile, a scientific revolution was in progress. Astronomers like Kepler and Galileo, building on the earlier work of Copernicus, demolished the assumptions of ancient and medieval cosmology by providing factual evidence that the Earth revolves around the sun, not vice versa.

Hobbes was profoundly affected by these events. After graduating from Oxford, which he had entered at the age of fourteen, he worked as a private tutor and avidly pursued his interests in science, philosophy, and the translation of classical Greek texts. He was personally acquainted with some of Europe's leading philosophers and scientists. His fascination with the latest discoveries of natural science, combined with a deep-seated respect for the logical certitudes of Euclidean geometry, inspired him to build a theory of politics that would be as timeless and certain as mathematics and the new physics. "Knowledge," Hobbes proclaimed, "is power."

Hobbes's political predilections leaned heavily in favor of order and strong monarchical rule. Hobbes abhorred the English civil wars as a time of "slaughter" and "solitude." Rather than live in strife-torn England, he fled to France in 1640. He did not return until 1651, the year in which he published his most renowned work, *Leviathan.*

The book's ominous tone reflected the horrors of the civil war that had just ended. Civil war is humanity's natural condition, Hobbes warns us. In trying to imagine what society must have been like in a so-called "state of nature," before there were any governments, Hobbes conjured up the image of permanent warfare, "and such a war, as is of every man against every man." As long as there is no strong government, everyone must be constantly on guard against everyone else.

> In such condition, there is no place for industry; because the fruit thereof is uncertain: and consequently no culture of the earth; no navigation, nor use of the commodities that may be imported by sea; no commodious building; no instruments of moving and removing, such things as require much force; no knowledge of the face of the earth; no account of time; no arts; no letters; no society; and which is worst of all, continual fear, and danger of violent death; and the life of man, solitary, poor, nasty, brutish, and short.

This chilling image of humanity as naturally predatory and insecure provides the premise upon which Hobbes built his theory of government. The fundamental purpose of the state, he maintained, is to impose order on people and prevent them from killing one another, whether through invasion from abroad or civil war at home. Human beings need an all-powerful state to protect them from themselves.

It is at this point that Hobbes made an interesting departure from the theory of government that had predominated in his own country and throughout Europe for centuries. In Hobbes's time, most European governments were monarchies of one kind or another, and virtually all of them based their legitimacy on the divine right of kings: the notion that God, not man, determines who shall have the right to rule. In *Leviathan*, Hobbes ignored the concept of divine right and instead placed the source of governmental legitimacy squarely in humanity's hands. The people, in his view, have a natural right to choose their own form of government.

In an ironic twist, however, Hobbes proposed that the ideal form of government is not a democracy but a state so powerful that its subjects will have little control over it once they have installed it. In other words, Hobbes proposed a kind of **dictatorship on the basis of the consent of the governed:**

> The only way to erect such a common power, as may be able to defend them from the invasion of foreigners, and the injuries of one another, is . . . to confer all their power and strength upon one man, or upon one assembly of men, . . . and therein to submit their wills every one to his will, and their judgments,

to his judgment. This is more than consent, or concord; it is a real unity of them all . . . made by covenant of every man with every man, in such manner, as if every man should say to every man, *I authorize and give up my right of governing myself, to this man, or to this assembly of men, on this condition, that thou give up thy right to him, and authorize all his actions in like manner . . . to the end he may use the strength and means of them all, as he shall think expedient, for their peace and common defense.*

Hobbes's notion of a "covenant" is precisely what is meant by a *social contract:* people freely agreeing with one another to be governed in a certain way. For Hobbes, that way is anything but a democracy. It is "Leviathan," a giant of a state to which everyone should voluntarily submit for their own good. As his other writings make clear, Hobbes favored an absolute monarchy as the best form of government. But in all probability he would have been appalled by the brutality of twentieth-century dictatorships. In his view, the purpose of the all-powerful state was to reduce fear and violence, not perpetrate it. Nevertheless, in his decidedly pessimistic reading of human nature, Hobbes provides powerful philosophical support for all those who believe that liberty breeds chaos and civil tranquility requires repression.[3]

Within a generation another Oxford scholar, John Locke, would offer a strikingly different concept of social contract theory.

JOHN LOCKE
(1632–1704)

John Locke studied medicine and taught philosophy at Oxford University for fourteen years. Soon after leaving Oxford he became embroiled in political intrigues aimed at enhancing parliamentary power at the expense of the crown. Although Locke was a student and teacher at the time Hobbes's *Leviathan* appeared, his own political tendencies were quite different. Though both men believed in the concepts of natural law and the social contract, their interpretations of these ideas were worlds apart. And though both witnessed the continuing disintegration of monarchical power in England, they drew diametrically opposite conclusions from this transformation.

Like Hobbes, Locke believed that when humankind lived in a "state of nature," before the establishment of governments, insecurity and uncertainty prevailed. So-

John Locke

ciety without government was "full of fears and continual dangers," exacerbated by the "corruption and viciousness of degenerate men," along with a host of other "inconveniences." While Locke did not go as far as Hobbes in predicating a state of continual warfare, he still regarded life without government as "very unsafe."

Nevertheless, Locke contended, humans were born free. People owned their own lives and their own labor. As a result, everybody had a right to own whatever they could "appropriate" or "take advantage of" with their own labor, as long as they did not harm anyone else in the process. There were no limits placed on the amount of goods one could acquire. These were natural laws, Locke declared, discernable through reason. Before there were governments, in short, all men were created equal: all enjoyed a natural right to their lives and liberties as well as to the tangible goods (or "estates") they acquired through their own efforts. In Locke's terms, these three possessions—life, liberty, and estate—together comprised each individual's "property."

For Locke, a "commonwealth" is a form of government that is created precisely to preserve these natural rights and possessions. **The great and *chief end*, therefore, of men's uniting into commonwealths, and putting themselves under government, *is the preservation of their property.*** The fundamental source of the commonwealth's legitimacy is common consent. People voluntarily establish a government of this sort by mutual agreement; in other words, on the basis of a social contract. They further agree to maintain such a government only so long as it manages to "secure everyone's property" and preserve the basic freedoms to be found in the state of nature. Locke implicitly argued that any government that pursues these basic purposes is legitimate, because it springs from natural laws. Conversely, he would regard as illegitimate all forms of government—such as monarchies or tyrannies—that violate these laws by abridging humanity's natural rights to life, liberty, and estate. The powers of the state, in Locke's view, must be strictly limited and always subordinate to popular control.

A passage in one of Locke's most celebrated works, *Second Treatise of Government,* succinctly captures the essence of his thought:

> The *natural liberty* of man is to be free from any power on earth, and not to be under the will or legislative authority of man, but to have only the law of nature for his rule. The *liberty of man,* is to be under no other legislative power, but that established, by common consent, in the commonwealth; nor under the dominion of any will, or restraint of any law, but what that legislative shall enact . . . *Freedom of men under government* is . . . not to be subject to the inconstant, unknown, arbitrary will of another man: as *freedom of nature* is, to be under no other restraint but the law of nature.
>
> This *freedom* from absolute, arbitrary power, is so necessary to, and closely joined with a man's preservation, that he cannot part with it.

At the same time, however, Locke made it clear that these natural rights and freedoms did not apply to slaves. Slaves were "captives taken in a just war," who, through their own fault, had forfeited their right to life, liberty, and estate. These rights applied only to free men in "civil society," and slaves were outside civil society. As a consequence, Locke contended, slaves were "by the right of nature subjected to the absolute dominion and arbitrary power of their masters." Locke himself made a fortune through investments in the Royal Africa Company, which was heavily involved in the slave trade.

Notwithstanding his views on slavery, Locke's general concepts of liberty and popular sovereignty were truly revolutionary. Their publication in 1689 could not have come at a more timely moment, because the English Parliament was in open revolt against the king, James II. The king's insistence on ruling on the basis of divine right met a sharp rebuff in Parliament's decision to establish its own supremacy over the crown. In a series of actions taken in 1688 and 1689, Parliament deposed James and replaced him with a new king of its own choosing. These extraordinary events, in which Locke was personally involved, became known as Britain's "Glorious Revolution."

Locke's notion that the fundamental purpose of government was to preserve "property" (i.e., life, liberty, and estate) had a tremendous impact on many of the

founding fathers of the United States a century later. The American revolutionaries' battle cry, "No taxation without representation," was a restatement of Locke's notion that government should not impose taxes without popular consent. Indeed, Locke may rightfully be considered the intellectual founding father of the doctrine of limited government, a doctrine that above all defines the principal aim of the state as that of protecting the rights of the individual, including the right to private property.

The notion that the principal purpose of government is the preservation of political and economic liberty is the core idea of the ideology of **liberalism.**[4]

Whereas Locke's impact was especially strong in the English-speaking world, many continental Europeans looked to another social contract theorist, Jean-Jacques Rousseau.

JEAN-JACQUES ROUSSEAU
(1712–1778)

"Man was born free, but everywhere he is in chains." So begins one of the most profoundly influential works in the history of political thought, *The Social Contract,* published in 1762. In this and a host of other writings, such as his *Discourse on the Origins of Inequality* (1755), Rousseau expounded on human nature and directly addressed the question of political legitimacy.

Like Hobbes and Locke, Rousseau imagined what humanity must have been like before the establishment of government. Contrary to the unflattering image of vile and insecure creatures depicted by the two English writers, Rousseau in the *Discourse* painted a portrait of essentially gentle and timid beings living harmoniously in a tranquil, if primitive, state of nature. Humans in this condition were neither inherently good nor evil, Rousseau believed, but were guided by such benign "natural" tendencies as nonviolence and pity for one's fellow man. The primitive human was thus a "noble savage," peaceful and uncorrupted, "free, healthy, honest and happy." As long as there was no organized social life, however, humanity could not improve its material welfare or educate itself about the universe in which it dwelt. The noble savage was a child, barely above the level of animals.

It was precisely by developing a more complicated economy that humankind built the basis of "civil society," that is, organized group relationships. In Rousseau's view, this process began with the advent of

Jean-Jacques Rousseau

private property. "The first man who, after enclosing a piece of ground, took it into his head to say, *this is mine* and found people simple enough to believe him, was the real founder of civil society." With the development of wider social interactions and an explicit division of labor came all the evils of advanced social life: greed, vanity, social inequality, and aggression. It is society that corrupts human beings and encourages evil tendencies (though we also retain some tendencies to do good).

Nevertheless, society—and some form of government—are necessary for humankind's preservation and prosperity. How, then, should we govern ourselves? Rousseau's main answer, as provided in *The Social Contract,* was that government must be based on popular consent. In order for a government to be truly legitimate, "the people in each generation should have the option of accepting or rejecting it." Legitimacy is therefore based on a tacit social contract among free people who collectively constitute what Rousseau calls "the sovereign." It is the collective sovereign that is the ultimate source of law. The people are capable of conferring legitimacy on whatever form of government they approve.

In one of his most controversial doctrines, Rousseau maintained that the people are united in an organic "body politic" on the basis of a "general will." The general will is the common good; it represents what is best for the community as a whole rather than what may be in the interest of a single individual or a segment of the community at any given moment. For Rousseau, freedom ultimately depends upon conformity with the general will: the liberty of each depends upon the liberty of all. If the general will were to break

down into a plethora of competing individual wills, humanity would lose its freedom to govern itself on the basis of common consent. Life would become insecure for everyone and tyrants would impose their own wills on the rest of society; no one would be free. To avoid such a breakdown of popular sovereignty, everyone must ultimately subordinate his or her private will to the community's collective interest. Consequently, "whoever refuses to obey the general will shall be constrained to do so by the whole body; which means nothing else than that he shall be forced to be free." Even the right to private property, while guaranteed, "is always subordinate to the right which the community has over all." In a commonwealth based on these principles, people agree to limit their *individual* freedom in order to share in the blessings of *collective* freedom.

How can the general will be ascertained? On very important matters, Rousseau indicated that community opinion should approach unanimity. On less important issues, a simple majority would suffice. Rousseau admitted, however, that a majority can vote to violate the common good of the entire community. In that case, the general will is shattered "and there is no longer any liberty." If a nation likes to injure itself, Rousseau asked, who has a right to prevent it from doing so?

Rousseau defined a "republic" as any form of government that is based on general consent. Only republican governments, in his view, are truly legitimate. But a republic, he contended, does not have to be a democracy. A state run by an aristocratic elite can also be considered a legitimate republic as long as the people, exercising their sovereign will, periodically meet in a free assembly to confirm or withdraw their approval of the government and those who manage it. In fact, Rousseau believed that an "elective aristocracy" was the best of all forms of government. "The wisest should govern the multitude," he declared, provided that they governed for the common good and not for their own personal advantage. Popular sovereignty was most effective when it was confined to preventing the abuse of governmental power by the ruling elite. This goal could be accomplished in popular assemblies that might meet only a few days each year. Otherwise, the day-to-day business of government was best left in the hands of an enlightened elite, aristocrats who would probably have a better understanding of the common good than would the masses themselves.

Rousseau opposed representative democracy, in which the people elect their representatives to govern them. He maintained that the sovereign authority of the people resided in the community as a whole: it was indivisible and could not be delegated to elected representatives. The people could exercise their sovereignty only in free assemblies open to all qualified citizens, where every man could represent himself. (In Rousseau's time, "citizens" usually meant males who owned a specified amount of property.) Assemblies of this kind, however, also presupposed relatively small communities; large states, he believed, were unsuited to democracy. "If there were a nation of gods," Rousseau wrote, "it would be governed democratically. So perfect a government is unsuited to men."

What Rousseau sought was a balance between popular sovereignty—the consent of the governed—and effective executive leadership. While insistent upon the people's natural right to choose their form of government, he was ambivalent about their ability to govern themselves on a day-to-day basis. Ultimately, Rousseau's political philosophy can be located in between the all-out authoritarianism of Hobbes and the individualistic parliamentarism of Locke.[5]

Despite its considerable impact on political thought and action over the centuries, the influence of social contract theory waned. Today most theorists of democracy maintain that democracy is the most legitimate form of government, not because it rests on a social contract, but because it rests on the rule of law and on specified constitutional procedures that permit the population on a continuing basis to change those in authority through peaceful legal mechanisms.

But what about legitimacy in countries that do not have regularized democratic procedures? Is it possible for non-democratic regimes to be considered legitimate? One answer to this question was provided by a seminal contributor to modern social science, the German sociologist **Max Weber** (1864–1920).

WEBER'S THREE TYPES OF LEGITIMATE AUTHORITY

Max Weber argued that, even when democratic procedures for legally removing governments from office do not exist, some political regimes are still regarded as legitimate by their populations. In his view there have been essentially three ways in which political leaders throughout history have convinced their populations to accept their rule as legitimate.

The first is *traditional authority*. This type of legitimacy rests on "an established belief in the sanctity of immemorial traditions." Over vast stretches of time, people come to accept the existing political realities simply because they have been there for prolonged periods. Centuries-old monarchies, such as those that once held sway in Britain, China, Japan, and elsewhere, are examples of this kind of tradition-based legitimacy.

The second type of legitimacy is *legal-rational authority*. This type is rooted in "the belief in the legality of rules and in the right of those who occupy positions by virtue of those rules to issue commands." This type of legitimacy is most prominent in democracies, which establish very rigorous rules for determining who has the right to issue governmental commands. Conceivably, some non-democracies may also be based on at least an element of legal-rational authority. As we noted in the previous chapter, Britain's monarchs gradually came to accept the notion that they too were subject to certain laws.

The third type of legitimate authority was what Weber called *charismatic authority*. This type of legitimacy attaches itself to a certain uniquely magnetic or inspiring leader and "rests upon the devotion" of his followers to his "extraordinary sanctity, heroism or exemplary character" as well as to the "patterns of order revealed or ordained by him." In these rare cases, the charismatic leader is perceived by others as "set apart from ordinary men" and as "endowed with supernatural, superhuman, or at least specifically exceptional powers or qualities." Religious figures like Moses, Jesus, Mohammed, and Buddha clearly fit this description. So, too, do certain political figures. For good or ill, such riveting personalities as Napoleon, Hitler, Stalin, Franklin D. Roosevelt, Gandhi, de Gaulle, and a few other notable leaders were able to exert a charismatic effect on their followers. In most of these cases, the loyalties they inspired were not confined merely to their personalities, but also to the programs and political ideas they espoused.

Charismatic authority, in Weber's view, is the most unstable form of legitimacy. Once such leaders die, their ideas and following can die with them. It is therefore incumbent upon the charismatic leader and successive generations of followers to institutionalize (or "routinize") the leader's charisma by building institutions that will survive him or her, such as an organized religion, a political party, or a state. These efforts are not always successful, however.

Ultimately Weber argued that political legitimacy is grounded in the *beliefs* of those who are governed. If the masses believe that their rulers are legitimate, for whatever reason, then those rulers *are* legitimate. And if the masses believe in their leaders' legitimacy, they are more likely to comply with the laws of the land voluntarily rather than because they are forced to do so. Government based on legitimacy is therefore likely to be more stable and enduring than one based on sheer coercion.[6]

What about such highly authoritarian regimes as Nazi Germany or the Soviet Union? Is there any way that we can determine if their populations regarded them as legitimate? In the absence of public opinion polls that might have answered these questions, we can only speculate about the extent of these regimes' legitimacy. For example, we can at least hypothesize that the population in Nazi Germany and the Soviet Union (and, quite possibly, in other authoritarian countries as well) can be crudely divided into three groups. One group fully supports the governmental system. Its members are the devotees of whatever ruling clique happens to control the state, such as die-hard Nazis or communists. Let's label these people the *adherents* (or *true believers*). Another group is at the opposite extreme. These people completely oppose the existing system of government and can never be convinced that it is proper. We'll call this camp the *rejectionists.* In the middle stands a third group of people who are largely ambivalent about the regime. They dislike some aspects of it (such as the absence of the right to travel abroad) but they may like other aspects (such as improved living conditions). Or they may just be politically indifferent. Such people may "accept" the existing governmental system without ever fully condoning it. This in-between group may accordingly be designated the *ambivalents.* We should think of them as spread out along a spectrum reflecting varying shades of intensity in their attitudes for or against the regime. It is quite possible that the ambivalents in such regimes constitute a large segment of the population, in some cases perhaps the majority. Without hard evidence gleaned from public opinion surveys, however, it is practically impossible to test this hypothetical description of the populace.

Though authoritarian states can have very serious legitimacy problems, democracies are by no means immune from legitimacy problems of their own. Large segments of a democracy's population, for example, may favor democracy in principle but object to the way it works in actual practice in their own country. Italy and Japan, which have ex-perienced major corruption scandals in recent years, are vivid examples.

ANARCHISM

Who needs government? Throughout history and down to the present day, some people have argued that *no* state can ever be truly legitimate: all are sources of intolerable power over the people and must therefore be repudiated. This idea, known as **anarchism,** asserts that the people can get along better without an institutionalized state.

Anarchy comes from the Greek for "without a leader." Prominent anarchist theorists have included such diverse thinkers and activists as the impassioned Russian revolutionaries Mikhail Bakunin (1814–1876) and Peter Kropotkin (1842–1921), both of whom were aristocrats; the pacifistic Russian writer Leo Tolstoy (1828–1910); the Russian-born American feminist Emma Goldman (1869–1940), who returned to Russia to participate in the revolution of 1917; and the American political philosopher Robert Paul Wolff.[7]

Recognizing that some kind of organized structure may be necessary in order to enable people to interact with one another socially and to manage the economy, some anarchists have proposed various substitutes for a full-blown state. One of the most popular alternatives advanced in the nineteenth century and the first half of the twentieth century was the *workers council.* In place of an organized state and privately owned factories, the workers themselves would organize the tasks of economic production. In most variants of this blueprint for a new society, workers at each enterprise would elect a delegation from among their own ranks to manage the firm. In various towns and other locales, larger councils would be elected to coordinate economic cooperation among producers, consumers, and farmers as well. One of the most grandiose schemes of this kind was designed by the French political philosopher **Pierre-Joseph Proudhon** (1809–1865). Proudhon called his councils *syndicates,* and his political program became known as **anarcho-syndicalism.**

Can anarchism work? Would "politics" as we know it cease to exist in the absence of a state? These questions are difficult to answer in large part because anarchism has never been tried on a large scale. Though anarchist movements have attracted devoted adherents in such diverse countries as the United States, Russia, and Spain, they were overshadowed by more powerful political movements: liberal democracy, communism, military rule, or some other orientation. Today's world is a world of states. For all its problems and occasional horrors, the state appears to be the most feasible mechanism for ordering political interactions. When mass anarchy occurs, it is usually the result of a complete breakdown of governmental authority rather than the product of an alternative design that enjoys widespread support. Anarchist movements in today's world, few as they are, consist of small and largely isolated political groups, such as the fiercely anti-government militias operating in sparsely populated areas of Montana and other U.S. states.

STATE INSTITUTIONS

Ultimately the topic of the state centers on governmental institutions. It focuses, for one thing, on *the way legal authority is distributed* among these institutions in accordance with constitutional principles and other statutory provisions. What are the powers of the president of the United States vis-à-vis the Congress? What is the legal authority of the British House of Commons and House of Lords? What are the express legal powers of the presidents of France, Germany, Russia, Mexico, and South Africa? And above all, *why* do states distribute legal authority the way they do?

In most countries the legal competence of the leading governmental institutions is spelled out in a national constitution, usually a single written document. The United States was the first country to establish itself from the beginning on the basis of a written constitution and, in this sense, has been called "the first new nation."[8] The U.S. Constitution, which has been amended twenty-six times, is the oldest constitution in the world in the form of a single document. The constitutions of most other states are much more recent. Germany, Italy, and Japan, for instance, adopted new constitutional arrangements after World War II. France's present constitution took effect in 1958. Most of the countries that abandoned communism after 1989 have written new constitutions and some are still in the process of revising them. South Africa, Brazil, and

a host of other states are also engaged in inaugurating relatively new constitutional orders.

Not all constitutions are single documents. Britain has one of the oldest continuous constitutional traditions in the world, but its constitution consists of hundreds of laws and practices that have been developed over the course of centuries of parliamentary interactions with the crown and courts. Israel, established in 1948, also has no formal constitution but a set of Basic Laws and other legislation that substitute for one. The same is true of Germany.

In addition to looking at the constitutionally determined ground rules of governmental authority, political scientists also like to investigate the ways state institutions operate in real life. Quite often a constitution provides only the skeletal structure of a governmental system. It doesn't necessarily indicate how the system's institutional parts really work or how effectively the laws of the land are implemented. Constitutions can also be vague or silent on certain aspects of governmental authority or can be subject to conflicting interpretations. They can even be ignored altogether. In 1935, for example, the USSR under Joseph Stalin's dictatorial rule issued a new constitution that guaranteed all sorts of rights and freedoms. But in fact Stalin and his communist partners had no intention whatsoever of implementing them. Yugoslavia's Slobodan Milosevic in the 1990s completely ignored his country's constitutional guarantees of autonomy for national minorities like the Albanians of Kosovo. Many Latin American constitutions in past decades were modeled on the U.S. system of separation of powers. In practice, however, these provisions were largely ignored, and state authority tilted heavily in the direction of highly personalized presidential power.

Which governmental institutions should we look at in our attempts to get a better understanding of how politics works in a variety of settings?

The Executive

The executive branch is obviously of primary importance in all political systems. Presidents, prime ministers, dictators, governing monarchs, and other officials at the apex of the governmental pyramid inevitably command considerable analytical attention, and with good reason. In most cases, it is they who decide government policy and who are ultimately responsible for the state's successes and failures.

As we look at the role of political executives in the chapters that follow, it is important to keep in mind a basic distinction between two distinct executive functions: *head of state* and *head of government*. In most countries, these are two separate offices occupied by two different people who are selected through separate procedures. Although there are some notable exceptions, usually the **head of state** is a *ceremonial* position that carries with it little or no real decision-making power. In these cases the head of state is often an individual who stands above the country's ongoing political battles and personifies the nation's unity or the continuity of its history. In some instances the person occupying this symbolically prestigious but politically neutral post is an unelected figure (such as a hereditary monarch in a democracy) or a personage who enjoys the respect of the country's population and political elites, including those from opposing parties. The head of state's main duties in such cases are generally limited to making speeches on ceremonial occasions, representing the state at non-political functions, and greeting foreign dignitaries. In some countries the head of state has limited powers of intervention in the political process, in other countries none.

By contrast, the **head of government** is usually the country's chief political officer and is responsible for presenting and conducting its principal policies. Unlike a ceremonial head of state, the head of government has real decision-making authority. He or she normally supervises the entire executive branch of the state, including its senior ministers (who collectively comprise the cabinet) and their respective ministries, as well as a host of executive-level agencies designed to propose and execute government policies. In many countries, the term "government," in addition to being a synonym for the state as we defined it earlier, also refers more specifically to just the head of government and the cabinet. In this context it is used much the way the term "administration" is used in the United States to refer to a particular president and his executive-level colleagues: "Tony Blair's government" in Britain and "the Clinton administration" are analogous designations.

In Britain, the head of state is the monarch; the head of government is the prime minister. In Japan, the head of state is the emperor; the head of government is the prime minister. In Germany, the head of state is the president; the head of government is the chancellor. The list could be extended considerably, as many countries make roughly similar distinctions.

As noted, there are exceptions. In the United States, the president is both head of state *and* head of government. That is why U.S. presidents, in addition to having major decision-making responsibilities, must invariably devote considerable time to duties that would ordinarily be carried out by a ceremonial head of state in other countries (such as greeting Boy Scouts, signing commemorative proclamations, and the like). Another exception to the pattern just described is France, which has an unusual "dual executive." In the French system, the president, who is the head of state, often has even greater decision-making authority than the prime minister, who is the head of government. Post-communist Russia and Poland also combine a politically powerful head of state (the president) with an active head of government (the prime minister). Not all heads of state, in other words, are purely ceremonial; some have real power. Other variants also exist, and we shall look at some of them later in this volume.[9]

The Legislature

Legislatures (or *parliaments* with a small *p*) are also important state institutions. Their chief functions, especially in democracies, are to make laws (sometimes in conjunction with the executive branch) and to represent the people in the law-making process. In some cases legislatures also keep a check on the executive branch and its bureaucratic departments by holding inquiries and investigations into their activities. This latter function is known as *legislative oversight*.

Some democracies have a *parliamentary system* of government. In these countries the national legislature actually elects (or approves) the head of government and holds that person, along with the entire cabinet, continuously accountable for their actions. Canada, Britain, Germany, Italy, Japan, Israel, India—these and a host of other states all have one form or another of parliamentary government.

The United States has a different system entirely, one in which the constitutional powers of Congress and the president are balanced more or less evenly. Even authoritarian regimes often have legislative bodies that play a certain role in the political system, though their real law-making powers may be negligible or non-existent.

Like the executive branch of government, legislatures around the world display considerable variation. Some countries have a *unicameral* national legislature, consisting of only one house (or *chamber*) of parliament. Others have a *bicameral* legislature, consisting of two houses. Typically one of these chambers is considered the *lower house* (e.g., the U.S. House of Representatives) and the second is regarded as the *upper house* (e.g., the U.S. Senate). The advantage of a unicameral legislature is that it does not have to share authority with a second legislative chamber in making laws. At least in principle, this arrangement is supposed to reduce the possibility of excessive legislative wrangling, delay, and gridlock. The main advantages of a bicameral legislature, again in principle, are that it provides greater representation for the population and requires greater deliberation in the law-making process. In actual practice, however, bicameral legislatures vary in terms of their representative function and their actual role. Subsequent chapters will discuss national legislatures in various countries around the world.[10]

The Judiciary

The judiciary represents a third institution whose significance, while usually considerable, varies from place to place. All states have some form of legal structure, and the role of the judiciary is rarely limited to such routine tasks as adjudicating civil and criminal cases. Inevitably the system of justice is intimately bound up with the state's fundamental political essence.

In some states the judiciary is relatively independent of the political authorities in the executive and legislative branches. It may even possess the legal competence to impose restrictions on what these political leaders may do. In others (especially authoritarian ones), the legal system is often

highly politicized and remains tightly controlled by the ruling clique, which manipulates the courts in an effort to keep the population in line. And in yet another category of cases, the judiciary may play a critical role in defining and even widening the scope of civil rights and liberties for the population when these rights are limited or violated by other branches of government. The courts have played this quasi-independent role (or have at least attempted to play it) in such countries as Egypt, where the central executives have used heavy-handed methods of repression against political opponents, and in post-communist Russia and other countries in transition to democracy, where the formal definition of the executive's authority and the population's rights are still being worked out.[11]

Some countries, like the United States, have constitutional courts with fairly wide latitude to interpret the highest laws of the land; in some cases they can invalidate laws passed by the legislative and executive bodies as unconstitutional, a power known as **judicial review**.[12] Others have different patterns. In Britain, for instance, the House of Lords—the upper house of the legislature—functions as the country's highest constitutional court.

Justice is not always blind; it is often keenly political. In our comparative exploration of political systems around the world, we'll have to pay attention to judicial processes if we want to gain a better appreciation of political processes.[13]

Beyond the familiar tripartite division of the executive, legislative, and judicial branches of government, two more state institutions deserve special consideration in view of their vital importance to the political process. They are the *bureaucracy* and the *military*.

The Bureaucracy

The bureaucracy, or **civil service,** is indispensable to the functioning of government in virtually every country in the world. Without a well-developed network of state organs charged with advising political decision makers about different policy options and implementing policies once they have been decided upon, governments could not govern. The modern state invariably includes a vast

TABLE 6.2

Government Employment as a Percentage of Total Civilian Employment in Selected Countries (1990)	
Country	Percentage
Canada	19.7
Denmark	30.5
France	22.6
Germany	15.1
Japan	6.0
Netherlands	14.7
Norway	27.7
Sweden	31.7
United Kingdom	19.2
United States	14.4

Source: Jan-Erik Lane et al., *Political Data Handbook OECD Countries* (Oxford: Oxford University Press, 1997).

array of ministries, departments, agencies, bureaus, and other officiously titled institutions whose purview may range from the domestic economy to such diverse policy areas as education, health, the environment, international trade, foreign relations, and so on. The growth of bureaucracies, and of government employment more generally, has been a long-term political phenomenon in most countries. Table 6.2 provides some comparative figures on the relative size of the civilian work force on the central government's payroll in various countries.

Although just about all large states are endowed with imposing bureaucratic structures, they differ significantly with respect to the roles their bureaucracies play. In some cases the bureaucracy's functions are largely limited to providing policy guidance to executive or legislative officials in need of professional expertise, and to making sure that the policies selected by these officials are expeditiously carried out. The ability of civil servants to issue regulations on their own authority in these cases is kept within fairly narrow limits. Legislative bodies, and in some cases the courts, exercise oversight functions in an effort to rein in the decision-making independence of these fairly restricted bureaucracies. The United States is an example.

In other instances bureaucrats enjoy wider discretionary powers when it comes to specifying how the government's policy aims, which may be

simply sketched out in broad guidelines, are to be interpreted and implemented. Such broad rule-making authority can be found in democracies like Japan and France, as well as in non-democracies like the former Soviet Union and certain military dictatorships in Latin America.

Some bureaucracies consist of a fairly stable core of career civil servants who take pride in their technical professionalism and political neutrality. Britain and France are renowned for having such a highly professionalized civil service, which accordingly attracts some of the best educated individuals in the country and confers considerable social prestige on those who work their way up the bureaucratic ranks. These **technocrats** provide government decision makers with indispensable information and policy analysis in their respective areas of expertise, such as economics, defense, technology, social welfare, and the like. The agencies of the federal bureaucracy in the United States are also populated with well-trained and dedicated careerists. In contrast to countries like Britain, France, and Japan, however, the United States has reserved a growing number of bureaucratic positions for political appointees. One of the chief spoils of political power in Washington is the opportunity given each new presidential administration to appoint faithful supporters to choice government jobs. As the president-elect prepares for inauguration, the government prints the famous "plum book," a compilation of federal positions available for appointment by the incoming administration. The United States usually provides more politically appointed bureaucratic plums than Britain, France, or most other democracies. Meanwhile, the United States, Britain, Italy, and other countries have been engaged in a significant process of downsizing their bureaucracies since the 1980s and 1990s.

Some political scientists hypothesize that a bureaucracy that is subject to fairly high levels of turnover because of changing governments is not well suited to pursuing policy initiatives in a systematic, coherent manner. A more stable civil service whose administrative personnel remain in place even though the government changes hands is considered preferable, according to this argument, because career civil servants tend to be more knowledgeable about the problems they are dealing with than are political newcomers, and they are less likely to be politically biased. Proponents of political appointments counter that bureaucratic policy formulation in a democracy should reflect the popular majority: if the people elect new political leaders, the bureaucracy should follow the policy inclinations of the current electoral majority. Different countries respond to these competing arguments in different ways.

Bureaucracies can also differ in terms of their operating procedures, the class and educational backgrounds of their personnel, their propensity to corruption, and so on. In subsequent chapters we'll glance at the shape of bureaucratic structures in several countries.[14]

The Military

Military establishments can have a formidable impact of their own on the organization of institutional authority. As a glimpse at table 6.1 demonstrates, quite a few contemporary political systems are run directly by elements of the military command. Others may be influenced indirectly by military officials who lurk in the background, keeping civilian governments dependent on their approval. A considerable number of states listed among those currently in transition to democracy were ruled by military officials, either directly or indirectly, just prior to embarking on the democratic path. These include such disparate countries as Spain, Portugal, Greece, South Korea, and a host of countries in Latin America and Africa. Some of these countries have undergone cyclical oscillations between military rule and democracy through much of their modern history. One of the main tasks these countries face as they seek to stabilize democracy is to ensure civilian control of the military.

Even in countries where the military's dominance is not very conspicuous, the civilian authorities must frequently take the military's interests into account when formulating domestic as well as foreign policy. It was precisely for the purpose of avoiding even the slightest prospect of military intervention in civilian politics that Costa Rica abolished its entire military establishment in 1949. It has been a successful democracy ever since.

Why would a "man on horseback"—an old euphemism for the professional soldier—want to leave

Chile's army commander-in-chief, Gen. Augusto Pinochet (right), commemorating the 1973 coup d'état that toppled President Salvador Allende. Chileans voted to end military rule in a 1988 referendum; a civilian government was elected the following year.

the barracks and intervene in politics? When is a military **coup d'état**—in other words, a forceful takeover of state power—most likely to occur? How is it that some countries are more prone to military coups than others? Political scientists who have studied *praetorianism*—the phenomenon of military intervention in a country's domestic politics—have identified a multiplicity of variables that answer these and related questions. Predictive models have even been developed that specify the circumstances under which military coups are most probable. Studies have shown that the likelihood and frequency of coups can be explained by such independent variables as economic stagnation, poorly developed political institutions and poor governmental performance, low levels of popular support for civilian politicians, a breakdown in law and order, a willingness on the part of key military officers to assert their political interests, and other identifiable factors. The precise mixture of these explanatory variables will vary from country to country and from one period of time to another, but certain patterns are discernible.[15]

How States Are Organized

Thus far our survey of state institutions has focused exclusively on the national government, that is, on the central organs (usually located in the capital city) that have responsibility for the country as a whole. But local governments can also be of fundamental importance in determining how the political system works in this or that country. Just how important these subnational governmental bodies are can vary considerably from one place to the next.

Some countries provide relatively little room for subnational authorities to govern independently of the national government. Decision-making authority and disposition over revenues in such cases tend to be concentrated in the central institutions. These highly centralized governments are called **unitary states.** France and Japan are examples.

Other states, called **federations,** seek to combine a relatively strong central government with real authority for various administrative units below the national level: regions, federal states (e.g., California), counties, municipalities, and so forth. In these federal systems the subnational units usually have their own locally selected officials and, in some cases, the right to raise their own revenue through local taxes of various kinds. At the same time, they are usually dependent on the national government for some of their budgetary funding, and they must conform to certain national laws. Examples of **federalism** include the United States, Germany, the Russian Federation, and India. Until 1999, the United Kingdom of Great Britain and Northen Ireland used to be a classic example of a unitary state, but the establishment of local legislatures in Scotland, Wales, and Northern Ireland signified a historic shift toward a federal system. Switzerland is an especially loose federation. This socially diverse country, with four language groups, consists of twenty cantons and six half-cantons. Some cantons, steeped in a long history of independence, still boast of themselves as "republics" (e.g., the Republic of Geneva). The Swiss central government, which is fairly weak, possesses only those powers explicitly ceded to it by the cantonal governments.[16]

Confederations are even looser arrangements characterized by a weak central government and a group of constituent subnational elements that enjoy significant local autonomy or even independence as sovereign states. In confederal systems the central government's functions are mainly confined to such basic tasks as providing for the national defense, issuing the currency, and delivering the mail. In many issues the central government cannot act at all without the express consent of the subnational governments. The United Arab Emirates, consisting of seven traditional Arab monarchies, is an example of a confederation in today's world.

Sometimes the distinction between a confederation and a very loose federation is hazy. Some consider Switzerland a confederation. Prior to the adoption of the U.S. Constitution in 1789, the thirteen states were organized under the Articles of Confederation of 1777. That system proved to be too decentralized for many Americans, and at the urging of "federalists" like James Madison and Alexander Hamilton, a federal system was established in its place. During the American Civil War, the Confederacy of southern states was so named because it granted more authority to the individual states comprising it than to the central government in Richmond. The realities of the contemporary world, with the enormous demands people place on their governments and the tightness of global interdependencies, make it difficult for confederal political systems to survive however. A relatively well-organized central government is now a virtual necessity in most countries.

HYPOTHESES ON THE STATE

"Why can't the government get it right?" Anyone who has ever asked this question has probably experienced the frustration of watching government officials or agencies fail to respond in an effective or timely manner to some problem affecting the population. Sometimes the state takes too long to legislate or dictate authoritative decisions on pressing issues. At other times government officials make bad decisions that fail to resolve the problem or only make matters worse.

Sometimes laws or regulations are not implemented in accordance with their intended purposes. In some cases local governments may not have the resources needed to carry out decisions imposed on them by the national government. In others, enforcement officials deliberately refuse to carry out laws they do not like, a phenomenon that has occurred in the United States over such issues as civil rights and gun control. Sometimes laws and regulations work at cross-purposes.

(The U.S. government has routinely subsidized tobacco growers while simultaneously conducting anti-smoking campaigns.) And sometimes governmental institutions are unable to make *any* kind of decision in response to well-known problems, especially when the alternative solutions are politically controversial. A prime example of such gridlock occurred in 1994, when the U.S. Congress failed to pass any new health care legislation after a year and a half of intense debate and more than two decades of periodic consideration (see chapter 11). Bureaucratic red tape, wasteful government spending, inefficient managerial practices—the catalog of complaints is often a long one, and the complaints themselves are strikingly common throughout the world.[17]

The list of possible explanations for these phenomena is just as long. Inept or indecisive leaders; corruption; inadequate oversight of politicians and bureaucrats by the legislature or the courts; insufficient governmental accountability to the public; excessive influence on the part of powerful groups or lobbies; too much money at the government's disposal, or not enough—these are just a few of the variables that help account for the inability of governments to do the right thing, or to avoid doing the wrong thing, or to do anything effectively at all. To be sure, sometimes governments do get things right; people often take for granted the positive things that governmental actions actually accomplish. Moreover, it is rarely possible for governments to please everybody. State actions that accommodate your demands or interests may contradict mine: welfare benefits for you may result in higher taxes for me. Nevertheless, governments seldom operate at optimal levels of efficiency or effectiveness.

> **Efficiency** *is the process of making decisions in a smooth and timely fashion.*
>
> **Effectiveness** *means resolving problems successfully.*

While we cannot possibly look into all the possible reasons for these inadequacies here, we can at least briefly examine a few hypotheses concerning the ways governments formulate and implement their policies.

Divided Government Some political analysts maintain that when the executive branch is controlled by one political party and the legislature is controlled by the opposition party or parties, gridlock is virtually a sure thing. The United States is frequently singled out in this regard. When the president is a Republican and the Congressional majority is in the hands of the Democrats—or vice versa—the result is **divided government,** a situation some regard as a recipe for prolonged inaction. In 1995, to cite just one example, most of the U.S. federal government had to be shut down for six days while the Democratic president and the Republican-controlled Congress quarreled over a new budget. In such circumstances other issues may take even longer to resolve or are not resolved at all. Conversely, the hypothesis goes, when the executive branch and the legislative majority represent the same party or parties, it is much easier for the governing majority to get things done. The leading state institutions are then unified and in sync.

Some people use these points to extol the advantages of the parliamentary system of democratic government, such as Britain's, and to highlight the disadvantages of the U.S. system of separation of powers. *In a parliamentary system, the legislature elects or approves the prime minister and the cabinet.* As a consequence, the executive branch and the legislative majority usually represent the same party or parties. Divided government occurs only in rare exceptions to this general rule. For example, Britain's Labor Party won 63 percent of the seats in the House of Commons in the 1997 elections. Labor's leader, Tony Blair, was promptly installed as the country's new prime minister as a result. Blair's government has consequently managed to get virtually all its legislation passed by the Labor majority in the Commons with considerable efficiency.

In the United States, by contrast, the president and the Congress are elected separately, thereby setting up the possibility of divided government. Two years after the election of Bill Clinton, a Democrat, to the presidency, the Republicans won control of both houses of Congress in 1994 and retained those majorities through the end of Clinton's second term. There was considerable legislative conflict between Clinton and the Republicans throughout those years. The normal political rivalry between the two parties became especially intense during the year-long impeachment crisis of 1998–99. Clinton was impeached for "high crimes and misdemeanors," as specified in the Constitution, by the Republican majority in the House of Representatives. In the ensuing trial in the Senate, where Republicans outnumbered Democrats by 55–45, the president was acquitted because his opponents could not muster the two-thirds majority needed for conviction. In an earlier crisis, President Richard Nixon, a Republican, resigned in 1974 shortly before an impeachment vote was to be taken by a Democratic majority in the House of Representatives.

If the British prime minister were to be accused of criminal wrongdoing or lost favor for other reasons, he or she could be voted out of office by a majority of the members of the House of Commons, *but that majority would require a considerable number of votes from members of the prime minister's own party.* Alternatively, the prime minister's party, through its own leadership selection procedures, could vote to remove its leader from power. As a general rule, British prime ministers cannot be voted out of office by the *opposing* parties for the simple reason that these parties, by the very nature of the parliamentary system, do not have a voting majority in the House of Commons (see chapter 16 for details).

Whether the issue is one of removing a head of government from office or more routine matters of legislation, there is considerable evidence that the U.S. system, which permits divided government, experiences more problems under these circumstances than a British-style parliamentary system. Nevertheless, there are exceptions to this general rule. In an incisive study of lawmaking in the United States, David Mayhew concluded that divided control of the presidency and Congress "has probably *not* made a notable difference during the postwar era." From the Truman administration (1945–53) down to the first half of the Bush administration (1989–93), Mayhew found that a large number of major laws were enacted *in spite of the fact* that one party held the presidency and the other party held the Congressional majority. Mayhew attributed these outcomes to a pragmatic, problem-solving ethos that is shared by elected officials in both parties.[18] The ability of President Clinton and the Republican Congressional majority to reach agreement on the federal budget for

2000 with relative ease, in spite of the rancor provoked by the 1998 impeachment crisis, provided additional evidence that the two parties in the United States can find ways to bridge the chasm of divided government when they want to.

Moreover, there is no guarantee that laws will be passed quickly and smoothly when the president and the Congressional majority represent the same party. Democratic presidents like Roosevelt, Carter, and Clinton, to name just a few, did not always get what they wanted out of Democratic-controlled Congresses. (President Clinton, for example, failed to get a Democratic majority to pass his health care legislation in 1994, the single most important piece of legislation on his first-term agenda. See chapter 11 for details.) Democrats in Congress do not always exhibit "party discipline"; that is, they do not always vote together unanimously. The same is largely true of Republicans. Party delegations in the British parliament, by contrast, have tended to stick together more often, thereby allowing the government and its parliamentary majority to work together more effectively in adopting legislation. Much the same can be said of party delegations in the legislatures of most parliamentary democracies around the world.

But sometimes not even a parliamentary-style government can govern efficiently. One of the most graphic examples comes from Britain itself, where the Conservative Party's majority collapsed in the 1990s due to internal squabbles over Britain's relationship with the European Union. The fratricidal dissension tore the Conservatives apart, snapping their party discipline and making it virtually impossible for Prime Minister John Major to govern. These Conservative divisions helped pave the way for Labor's victory in 1997.

The cursory evidence we have just reviewed is therefore *inconclusive* when it comes to determining whether unified government is decisively better than divided government in the lawmaking process. As so often happens in political science, our efforts to make clear-cut, universally valid generalizations run into empirical evidence of considerable complexity.

Rational Decision Making Versus "Satisficing"
The process of transforming ideas into laws through executive-legislative interaction is invari-

ex: no taxes but want welfare

ably a complicated one, especially in democracies. Government decision makers must consider a diversity of competing demands and interests and measure what needs to be done against the resources available to do it. It should hardly be surprising that the lawmaking process does not always result in the "best" laws, if by "best" we mean the most rational solutions to specific problems or the most effective ways of improving the general well-being of the population. In a great number of cases, the laws that emerge from the executive-legislative process reflect such things as the priorities of legislative majorities, the pressures of highly influential lobbies or social groups, and the outcomes of bargaining and compromises among elected officials, most of whom are motivated largely by the desire to get reelected. Instead of "the best" or the most rational laws, the lawmaking process in democracies frequently produces laws that are *the most politically acceptable* to a majority of legislators and to relevant executive branch decision makers.

Decisions that are the most politically acceptable to a fairly large group of lawmakers, however, may not be what is most needed to improve the economy, protect the environment, enhance national security, or solve some other problem facing the community in the most effective manner. Instead of optimal decisions, we get decisions that are considered *good enough* by the lawmakers.

The term that most often describes this process is "satisficing." The term comes from the old English word "satisfice," which meant "to satisfy." In contemporary political science, **satisficing** *means making decisions that are satisfactory, or "good enough," rather than the best of all available alternatives.* In large organizations like governments, satisficing reflects the central reality that decisions must often be reached through a bargaining process involving negotiation and compromise. Decisions reached through a process of satisficing are not necessarily the "best" decisions because those who make them cannot agree on what the best decision is, or because the best decision for the community at large may damage the interests of some specific segment of it.

What is best for the national economy? Economists may tell us that we need to reduce or eliminate budget deficits, and they may supply all sorts of statistical analyses charting the widespread benefits to

be gained from such measures. Analytical studies may also provide convincing evidence that the most efficient and rational way to cut the deficit is to raise taxes *and* curtail government spending simultaneously. But if some people do not want to pay higher taxes and others don't want to give up their government jobs or welfare benefits, how can the elected officials who represent them manage to take the "best" and most appropriate action? All too often, they cannot. As the record of many contemporary democracies indicates, national economic policies are often the result of satisficing. Rather than raising taxes and reducing expenditures in the most economically efficient manner, cabinets and legislatures may decide to raise taxes only slightly (or not at all) and to curtail government spending only slightly (or not at all). Quite often, lawmaking in democracies is characterized less by rationality and optimality than by accommodation and compromise.

Elected legislatures are especially prone to satisficing. Legislators are often divided among themselves for the simple reason that the people who elected them are divided. But what about the executive branch and its bureaucracies? Shouldn't we expect the cabinet, which generally consists of a small number of relatively like-minded individuals chosen by the president or prime minister, to make policy decisions far more efficiently than a fractious legislature? Shouldn't we expect executive-level bureaucracies, such as the Defense Department or the Finance Ministry, to follow executive guidance, providing policy advice and implementing orders in accordance with the cabinet ministers' directives?

One model that focuses mainly on the ways bureaucracies function suggests that the executive branch of government does in fact operate in a relatively efficient and unified manner. The German sociologist Max Weber, whose views on legitimacy were highlighted earlier in this chapter, was one of the first students of modern bureaucracy. Drawing his information largely from Germany's bureaucracy at the start of the twentieth century, Weber developed a hypothetical *ideal type* of bureaucratic structure and behavior emphasizing the following characteristics:

• *Hierarchy.* Bureaucracies, in Weber's model, are structured in a hierarchical fashion from the top down, with a clear chain of command enabling them to respond efficiently to directives.

- *Specialization.* There is a clearly demarcated, stable division of labor among the bureaucracy's organizational components, and the bureaucrats themselves are chosen solely on the basis of their professional competence.
- *Impersonal rules.* Bureaucracies are run in accordance with carefully spelled out rules and regulations, another factor that makes for efficient and predictable operations. In its dealings with other components of the state or with citizens, the modern bureaucracy applies these rules impersonally, without granting special favors to privileged individuals or groups.
- *Rationality.* "Bureaucracy," Weber wrote, "has a 'rational' character: rules, means, ends, and matter-of-factness dominate its bearing." The whole bureaucratic process is highly organized to achieve the state's objectives efficiently and effectively. "Precision, speed, unambiguity, knowledge of the files, continuity, discretion, unity, strict subordination, reduction of friction and of material and personal costs—these are raised to the optimum point in the strictly bureaucratic administration."[19]

Weber's model is known as the **unitary actor** model of decision making. If state bureaucracies functioned accordingly, we would expect the policy making process to be a fairly smooth one, at least in the executive branch. All the elements of a state's bureaucracy would work together as though they were a single actor. Bureaucrats would respond to the requests and commands of their executives quickly and effectively, marshaling all the information needed to come up with the "best" feasible alternatives and implementing policy on the basis of clearly defined rules. But do modern governments actually function this way?

A far different picture of executive-level policy making emerges from more recent studies of organizational behavior. The pioneering work of economists James March and Herbert Simon demonstrated that large organizations, whether private corporations or government bureaucracies, rarely operate as rationally and efficiently as Weber maintained. Hierarchical chains of command are frequently ignored. Critical information may not be available. The "best" alternative solutions are not always carefully considered, let alone chosen. On the contrary, bureaucracies, like legislatures, often indulge in satisficing, with executives and staff personnel engaging in negotiations and compromises that lead to decisions that are good enough to win a large consensus, but not necessarily the most effective ways to resolve the problem under consideration. Moreover, bureaucrats tend to stick to familiar "standard operating procedures": they don't like to take bold initiatives whose results are unpredictable or ambiguous. New approaches to dealing with society's problems therefore tend to differ very little from past approaches, even if they haven't worked very well.

The result is **incrementalism**: change, if it comes at all, is marginal rather than radical. Experimentation is discouraged. If asked by the head of government or cabinet chiefs to come up with innovative solutions to problems or if ordered to implement unfamiliar directives or rules, bureaucracies may misunderstand, ignore, or even sabotage the new commands.[20]

President Harry Truman probably would have recognized this model of bureaucratic unresponsiveness. Sympathizing with the problems Dwight D. Eisenhower would inherit on assuming the presidency, Truman predicted, "He'll sit here, and he'll say, 'Do this! Do that!' And nothing will happen. Poor Ike—it won't be a bit like the Army. He'll find it very frustrating."[21] Political leaders the world over would probably understand Truman's lament from their own experiences in dealing with their state bureaucracies, both in democracies and authoritarian regimes.

A particularly gripping account of how bureaucratic behavior and executive-level decision making can go awry is Graham Allison's analysis of the Cuban missile crisis of 1962.

HYPOTHESIS-TESTING EXERCISE: The Cuban Missile Crisis

In October 1962, American spy planes flying over Fidel Castro's communist Cuba noticed Soviet construction crews building missile sites on the island. The discovery came several weeks after the missile construction program had begun. It did not occur earlier because the U.S. State Department had temporarily suspended aerial surveillance of Cuba after a U.S. spy plane was shot down over China. The delay was further protracted when the U.S. Air

President Kennedy meets with the National Security Council during the Cuban missile crisis.

Force and the Central Intelligence Agency became snarled in a bureaucratic battle over whose pilots would fly a new U-2 reconnaissance aircraft. The dispute took a week to resolve. Had it dragged on longer, the United States might not have uncovered Soviet operations in Cuba until after all the missiles were already in place. This delay was one of many bureaucratic bungles and misunderstandings that complicated President John F. Kennedy's attempts to get the Soviets to remove the missiles while at the same time avoiding a full-scale nuclear war.

HYPOTHESIS AND VARIABLES

In a classic analysis of the crisis, Graham Allison tested the hypothesis that bureaucratic rationality, as characterized by the unitary actor model of decision making, explained U.S. government behavior in the Cuban missile crisis. In this hypothesis, the **dependent variable** is *U.S. government behavior,* and the **independent variable** is *bureaucratic rationality.*

EXPECTATIONS

If the unitary actor model is an accurate representation of how the U.S. government operated during the Cuban missile crisis, then we would expect to find that the president, his key advisors, and the various agencies of the U.S. government involved in making and implementing policy decisions possessed all the information they needed to make well-considered, rational decisions; that they were essentially unified in their analysis of the situation and on the measures that needed to be taken; and that these measures were implemented smoothly and effectively, following the established lines of command.

EVIDENCE

Whereas rational decision making requires relatively complete information about the problem at hand, Allison showed that Kennedy and his advisors did not

have *any* information about Soviet activities in Cuba until it was almost too late. Moreover, they had no clear information about Soviet motives. Were the Soviets putting missiles in Cuba in order to bomb or threaten the United States? Were they trying to set up a bargaining situation in hopes of inducing the United States to remove its missiles from Turkey, a NATO ally located on the USSR's borders, in exchange for withdrawing the new missiles from Cuba? Were they simply trying to defend Castro's regime against a potential U.S. attack? The administration was similarly in the dark about Soviet resolve. Would Kremlin leaders back down if the United States used military force to compel Moscow to remove the missiles, or would they risk mutual nuclear annihilation rather than give in? These questions epitomized a general dilemma in governmental decision making: all too often, the decision makers do not have the information they need to make informed, "rational" choices. Sometimes they just have to guess; reality can be a mysterious black box.

The evidence also showed that the key government agencies involved in the crisis did not act in a unified fashion. The tug-of-war between the Air Force and the CIA over the U-2 flights was one example. In addition, the military chiefs of the Air Force and the Navy had their own ideas about how to implement a possible "surgical" air strike of the missile sites and a naval blockade of Cuba, ideas that differed considerably from the ways the president, the secretary of defense, and other top decision makers understood those policy options. "Established, rather boring organizational routines," Allison concluded, "determined hundreds of additional, seemingly unimportant details—any one of which might have served as a fuse for disaster."

Even the Soviets were not immune from their own organizational problems. Allison noted that the U.S. spy flights were able to detect the missile sites largely because Soviet construction crews had cleared the surrounding forests. Such behavior reflected the standard operating procedures of a missile construction bureaucracy accustomed to building missile sites in the flat, treeless plains of the USSR. By sticking to organizational routine, the missile builders in Cuba failed to take advantage of the natural camouflage provided by the forests.

In looking at the fourteen key individuals involved in the decision-making process, Allison once again saw no evidence of unity. Each of these individuals had his own set of perceptions of what the Soviets were up to and how best to deal with them. Some of these individuals were influenced by the nature of their professional roles. In accordance with the adage, "Where you stand depends on where you sit," the chief military advisors favored military solutions, including bombardment of the missile sites and an invasion of Cuba. Others, like the president and his brother Attorney General Robert Kennedy, feared that this approach might lead to all-out nuclear war. They favored a political solution. Over the course of the two-week-long crisis, this team of decision makers engaged in a continuing process of negotiating, bargaining, and coalition building. Some changed their minds in the process.

Ultimately the president decided on a naval blockade of the island to prevent more missile shipments from coming in. The world breathed a sigh of relief when the Soviet leadership decided to remove the missiles from Cuba. President Kennedy pledged never to invade the island. Decades later it became known that he had also agreed to remove the U.S. missiles from Turkey.

CONCLUSIONS

The evidence Allison uncovered was largely *inconsistent* with the hypothesis of rational decision-making as predicted by the unitary actor model. Allison concluded that two other models offered more accurate depictions of decision making in the Cuban missile crisis. One of them, the *organizational process* model, describes decision making as a more disjointed process involving miscommunication, insufficient information, poor coordination, and other "irrational" phenomena described by analysts like March and Simon. The other one, which Allison called the *bureaucratic politics* (or *governmental politics*) model, emphasizes the different viewpoints that divided President Kennedy and the thirteen other key individuals involved in finding a solution to the crisis. Allison's analysis provides important generalizations about state decision-making processes that have a far wider application than just this particular incident. Variants of the *organizational process* model and the *bureaucratic politics* model have been used by a variety of scholars to study governmental policy processes in a number of countries and settings.[22]

Far from being a smooth, "rational" undertaking, the policy process in most countries is often a disjointed affair. One political scientist referred to governing as "the science of muddling through."[23] Problems such as those we've mentioned can arise at any of six stages in what we may call the *policy process.*

THE POLICY PROCESS

STAGE 1. AGENDA SETTING

In this initial stage, problems and issues that require some kind of governmental action are identified. In democracies the agenda-setting process is usually aired in public: television, radio, newspapers, academia, public opinion polls, and the like. Participants in this process interact in a so-called *policy arena.*

STAGE 2. POLICY FORMULATION

In this stage, relevant state agencies and legislative officials gather information about what the problems are, establish a set of priorities, and consider alternative options to dealing with them. If the process is an open one, government officials will consider alternative solutions that are proposed by people outside the government, such as professional experts or interest-group representatives.

STAGE 3. DECISION MAKING

In this stage, relevant government agencies and legislative decision makers decide on specific responses to the problems being addressed. In some cases the decision makers may decide to take certain actions, but in other cases they may do nothing.

STAGE 4. IMPLEMENTATION

Relevant state agencies, whether at the national level or in subnational units, put the decisions into effect. Policy implementation also includes *policy enforcement*, which above all means enforcing policy decisions against those who violate them.

STAGE 5. EVALUATION

In this stage state officials and agencies evaluate the implementation of the policies that have been undertaken. This is the so-called *feedback* stage.

STAGE 6. POLICY ADJUSTMENT

In some cases policies are changed or adapted in response to negative feedback or the need for improvements. Sometimes the policy adjustment stage triggers an entire new policy process cycle that may go on for years or even decades.[24]

A **policy** *is a governmental approach to dealing with a problem or issue.* It can consist of (a) ideas, goals, and proposals; (b) a decision or set of decisions; or (c) an elaborate program or set of actions. Economic policy, health policy, and foreign policy, to cite some examples, consist at one time or another of any of these notions of "policy."

Strong States and Weak States   Some countries are especially successful at all or most stages of the policy process. They manage to formulate, decide, implement, evaluate, and adjust their policies with considerable skill and effectiveness. Such governmental systems are often called **strong states.** Strong states can be either democracies or authoritarian regimes. Democratic countries like France, Germany, and Japan are often singled out as "strong states"; but so are ruthless but effective dictatorships like Hitler's Germany or the Soviet Union in Stalin's time. As we've suggested, however, even strong states are vulnerable to such problems as satisficing, incrementalism, and various other pitfalls of the governing process.

Authoritarian states are particularly susceptible to feedback problems. If an autocrat or a small clique of oligarchs close themselves off to information they do not wish to hear and if their subordinates are afraid to tell them bad news, they may not be sufficiently aware of problems that are arising under their rule. Sometimes they learn the true dimensions of these problems only when it is too late to fix them. At other times they may not even wish to make necessary adjustments in policies that are manifestly failing. Hitler's refusal to believe that the war was a lost cause; the Soviet leadership's failure to fundamentally alter the USSR's poorly functioning state-managed economic system; and Saddam Hussein's unwillingness to withdraw from Kuwait before the U.S.-led attack are all examples of how obstinacy can spell disaster for even the strongest authoritarian rulers.

Weak states, by contrast, are not especially successful at managing their policy process. They come up short in any or all of the six stages just outlined. Sometimes their leaders lack the skills necessary to devise relevant policies and to see to it that they are effectively carried through. In other cases the problem is institutional. Efforts to get the executive, the legislature, the judiciary, and other relevant elements of the state to cooperate in an effective fashion may result in very cumbersome decision-making procedures, faulty implementation, or other problems. The United States is often called a "weak state" for these reasons. In other instances a country may simply lack effective institutions. Poor countries, for example, often lack the resources or personnel needed to undertake expensive or complicated policy programs.[25] Weak states, like strong ones, can also be either democracies or authoritarian regimes.

In sum, the state—government—is the central reality of political life. How states are organized, how

they operate, and how people interact with them are issues that lie at the heart of comparative politics.

KEY TERMS AND NAMES
(Underlined in the text)

State
Aristotle
Legitimacy
Social contract
Thomas Hobbes
John Locke
Jean-Jacques Rousseau
Max Weber
Anarchism
Head of state
Head of government
Judicial review
Coup d'état
Unitary state
Federation
Confederation
Efficiency
Effectiveness
Divided government
Satisficing
Unitary actor
Incrementalism

NOTES

1. Ralph Miliband, *The State in Capitalist Society* (New York: Basic Books, 1969).
2. For discussions of different conceptions of the state, see James A. Caporaso, ed., *The Elusive State: International and Comparative Perspectives* (Newbury Park, Calif.: Sage, 1989).
3. Thomas Hobbes, *Leviathan* (New York: Cambridge University Press, 1991); Deborah Baumgold, *Hobbes's Political Theory* (New York: Cambridge University Press, 1988); Arnold A. Rogow, *Thomas Hobbes: Radical in the Service of Reaction* (New York: W. W. Norton, 1986).
4. John Locke, *Two Treatises of Government* (New York: Cambridge University Press, 1988); Ruth Grant, *John Locke's Liberalism* (Chicago: University of Chicago Press, 1987); Maurice Cranston, *John Locke: A Biography* (New York: Macmillan, 1967).
5. Jean-Jacques Rousseau, *The Collected Works of Jean-Jacques Rousseau* (Hanover, N.H.: University Press of

New England, 1990); Maurice Cranston, *Jean-Jacques: The Early Life and Work of Jean-Jacques Rousseau* (Chicago: University of Chicago Press, 1983), and *The Noble Savage: Jean-Jacques Rousseau, 1754–1762* (University of Chicago Press, 1991); Hilail Gildin, *Rousseau's "Social Contract": The Design of the Argument* (Chicago: University of Chicago Press, 1983); Richard Fralin, *Rousseau and Representation* (New York: Columbia University Press, 1978); Judith N. Shklar, *Men and Citizens: A Study of Rousseau's Social Theory* (Cambridge: Cambridge University Press, 1969).

6. Max Weber, *On Charisma and Institution Building: Selected Papers,* ed. S. N. Eisenstadt (Chicago: University of Chicago Press, 1968).

7. April Carter, *The Political Theory of Anarchism* (New York: Harper and Row, 1971); Emma Goldman, *Anarchism, and Other Essays* (New York: Dover, 1969) and *Living My Life* (New York: AMS Press, 1970); Marian J. Morton, *Emma Goldman and the American Left: "Nowhere at Home"* (New York: Twayne, 1992); Robert Paul Wolff, *In Defense of Anarchism* (New York: Harper and Row, 1970).

8. See Seymour Martin Lipset, *The First New Nation: The United States in Historical and Comparative Perspective* (New York: Basic Books, 1963).

9. Richard Rose and Ezra Suleiman, eds., *Presidents and Prime Ministers* (Washington, D.C.: American Enterprise Institute, 1980).

10. Jean Blondel, *Comparative Legislatures* (Englewood Cliffs, N.J.: Prentice Hall, 1973); Gerhard Loewenberg and Samuel C. Patterson, *Comparing Legislatures* (Boston: Little, Brown, 1979); Michael L. Mezey, *Comparative Legislatures* (Durham, N.C.: Duke University Press, 1979); Hannah F. Pitkin, *The Concept of Representation* (Berkeley: University of California Press, 1972).

11. Nathan J. Brown, *The Rule of Law in the Arab World* (Cambridge, England: Cambridge University Press, 1997).

12. The U.S. Constitution does not specifically confer on the Supreme Court the authority to declare laws unconstitutional, though the founding fathers may have intended the Court to have this power. In deciding the case of *Marbury vs. Madison* in 1803, the Supreme Court emphatically asserted its right to invalidate laws it considered incompatible with the Constitution, thereby establishing the principle of "judicial review" of the laws of the land. For a classic study of the U.S. judiciary in comparative perspective, see Henry Abraham, *The Judicial Process,* 5th ed. (New York: Oxford University Press, 1986).

13. For some comparative approaches to the judiciary, see Mauro Cappelletti, *The Judicial Process in a Com-*

parative Perspective (New York: Oxford University Press, 1989); Alan M. Katz, ed., *Legal Traditions and Systems: An International Handbook* (Westport, Conn.: Greenwood Press, 1986); Jerold L. Waltman and Kenneth M. Holland, eds., *The Political Role of the Law Courts in Modern Democracies* (New York: St. Martin's Press, 1988).

14. On the U.S. bureaucracy, see James Q. Wilson, *Bureaucracy: What Government Agencies Do and Why They Do It* (New York: Basic Books, 1989); and William T. Gormley, Jr., *Taming the Bureaucracy* (Princeton, N.J.: Princeton University Press, 1989). For comparative studies, see B. Guy Peters, *The Politics of Bureaucracy: A Comparative Perspective,* 3d ed. (White Plains, N.Y.: Longman, 1989); Frank Fischer, *Technocracy and the Politics of Expertise* (Newbury Park, Calif.: Sage, 1990); Jon Pierre, *Bureaucracy in the Modern State: An Introduction to Comparative Public Administration* (Aldershot, England: E. Elgar, 1995); Joel D. Auerbach, Robert A. Putnam, and Bert A. Rockman, *Bureaucrats and Politicians in Western Democracies* (Cambridge: Harvard University Press, 1981).

15. The literature on the military and politics is far too vast to be surveyed here. Three classic studies are Morris Janowitz, *The Professional Soldier: A Social and Political Portrait* (Glencoe, Ill.: Free Press, 1960); Samuel P. Huntington, *The Soldier and the State: The Theory and Politics of Civil-Military Relations* (New York: Vintage, 1964); and Samuel E. Finer, *The Man on Horseback* (Oxford: Pall Mall Press, 1962). For a sweeping comparative analysis, see Eric A. Nordlinger, *Soldiers in Politics: Military Coups and Governments* (Englewood Cliffs, N.J.: Prentice Hall, 1977). For area-specific studies, see Samuel Decalo, *Coups and Army Rule in Africa* (New Haven, Conn.: Yale University Press, 1975); Isaac James Monroe, ed., *The Performance of Soldiers as Governors: African Politics and the African Military* (Washington, D.C.: University Press of America, 1980); Thomas E. Skidmore, *The Politics of Military Rule in Brazil, 1964–85* (New York: Oxford University Press, 1988); Zakaria Haji Ahmad and Harold Crouch, eds., *Military-Civilian Relations in South-East Asia* (Oxford: Oxford University Press, 1985). For an advanced statistical study, see Robert W. Jackman, "The Predictability of Coups d'état: A Model with African Data," *American Political Science Review* 72, no. 4 (December 1978): 1262–75.

16. Wolf Linder, *Swiss Democracy: Possible Solutions to Conflict in Multicultural Societies* (New York: St. Martin's Press, 1994).

17. On policy implementation in the United States, see Jeffrey Pressman and Aaron Wildavsky, *Implementa-*

tion: How Great Expectations in Washington Are Dashed in Oakland, 3d ed. (Berkeley: University of California Press, 1984).

18. David R. Mayhew, *Divided We Govern* (New Haven, Conn.: Yale University Press, 1991). Also David W. Brady, "The Causes and Consequences of Divided Government: Toward a New Theory of American Politics?" *American Political Science Review* 87, no. 1 (March 1993): 189–94.

19. Max Weber, *From Max Weber: Essays in Sociology,* ed. H. H. Gerth and C. Wright Mills (New York: Oxford University Press, 1971), 196–244.

20. James G. March and Herbert A. Simon, *Organizations* (New York: Wiley, 1958); Simon, *Administrative Behavior,* 3d ed. (New York: Free Press, 1975), and *Models of Man: Social and Rational* (New York: Wiley, 1957); March, *Decisions and Organizations* (Oxford: Blackwell, 1989).

21. Cited in Richard Neustadt, *Presidential Power* (New York: Wiley, 1960), 9.

22. Graham T. Allison, *Essence of Decision* (Boston: Little, Brown, 1971). The notion that "where you stand depends upon where you sit" is attributed to Rufus Miles, a former U.S. assistant secretary of Health, Education and Welfare, and is known as "Miles's law."

23. Charles E. Lindblom, "The Science of 'Muddling Through'," *Public Administration Review* 19 (1959): 79–88, and "Still Muddling, Not Yet Through," *Public Administration Review* 39 (1979): 517–26.

24. The policy process has been variously conceptualized. For an eight-phase model, see Brian Hogwood, *From Crisis to Complacency: Shaping Public Policy* (Oxford: Oxford University Press, 1987). See also Charles E. Lindblom and Edward J. Woodhouse, *The Policy-Making Process,* 3d ed. (Englewood Cliffs, N.J.: Prentice Hall, 1993).

25. On these problems see Joel Migdal, *Weak States, Strong Societies: State-Society Relations and State Capabilities in the Third World* (Princeton, N.J.: Princeton University Press, 1988).

CHAPTER 7

NATION-STATES, NATIONALISM, AND SUPRANATIONA

THE NATION-STATE

As we noted in chapter 6, individual countries are frequently referred to as *nation-states.* We also noted that "nation" is sometimes used as a short-hand synonym for the same term. Thus the nations referred to in the *United Nations* are the member countries of that organization. But the term "nation" also has another meaning:

> A **nation** *is a large group whose members believe they belong together on the basis of a shared identity as a people.*

A "state," as spelled out in the previous chapter, is a system of government within a particular country.

> A **nation-state**, *then, is the combination of a "people" and a functioning state within a precisely defined territory.*

On what basis does a large collectivity of individuals, ranging in number from tens of thousands to hundreds of millions, feel they are a "people" who belong together? What, in essence, is the source of a people's sense of *national identity* or *"nationhood"?*

One such source is **ethnicity.** As indicated in chapter 2, ethnicity is a form of group identification or distinctiveness that is usually rooted in a *common biological ancestry* in the distant past or, more accurately, in a people's *belief* in a common biological ancestry. In this sense, Japanese, Germans, Russians, and many other peoples around the world think of themselves as nations because of these ancestral bonds of kinship. These feelings of belonging together as a people have endured over time as the result of living together in the same country or area over centuries and speaking a common language or a related dialect. In many instances this sense of common ethnic identity continues to exert a strong hold on a people's national consciousness in spite of intermarriage with other groups and migration to other lands.

In addition to ethnicity, another source of nationhood is **civic identity.** That is, people feel that they constitute a nation on the basis of certain *shared principles* or *ideals* or *community goals*, however broadly they may be defined. The United States provides a good example. More than 265 million people representing a wide diversity of ethnic groups and backgrounds identify themselves as "Americans" largely because of a shared involvement in an "American way of life" that includes democratic rights and freedoms, private enterprise, and various cultural attitudes and behaviors.

Nationhood is often the result of shared *patterns of social communication.* Over time, according to Karl Deutsch, the members of a large group take part in such a wide range of common experiences that they come to think of themselves as a people who are distinct from other peoples. "The Swiss may speak four diffferent languages and still act people," Deutsch pointed out. Centuries of d habits, preferences, symbols, memories, torical events, and other bonding forces have made it easier for the Swiss to communicate with one another than with others outside their borders.[1] Another scholar has suggested that nations are *imagined political communities.* The nation is imagined, writes Benedict Anderson, "because the members of even the smallest nation will never know most of their fellow-members, meet them, or even hear of them, yet in the minds of each lives the image of their communion."[2]

NATIONALISM

Such concepts as *nation, national identity* and a *people* are usually steeped in emotional and psychological attachments. They reflect a sense of commonness and solidarity forged over generations, resulting in sentiments and understandings that promote a general spirit of togetherness.

The concept of *nationalism* is a bit stronger and more explicitly articulated. Although the term is defined differently by different people and has various connotations,

> **nationalism** *in its broadest meaning is an* **idea,** *a consciously formulated* **concept** *that emphasizes the distinctiveness of one's "nation" and articulates certain "national" interests, purposes or goals for action.*

Whereas the *sentiment* of nationhood proclaims, "We are a people and we belong together," the *idea* of nationalism declares, "We belong together and *we must act together* to fulfill our common political aims." So construed, nationalism has both domestic and international dimensions. On the domestic, "at home" level, nationalism affirms a people's right to determine its own collective political destiny; its chief aim is usually some form of self-government. On the international plane, nationalism generally refers to a national government's resolve to affirm or defend certain "national interests" in its diplomatic, military, and economic dealings with the outside world.

Domestic Nationalism   By domestic nationalism we mean **self-determination:** that is, a people who conceive of themselves as a distinct nation demand the right to come together and *govern them-*

selves with little or no interference by other governments or political forces. Nationalism in this sense of the word refers to a nation's determination to establish its own domestic political order, constituting its own political institutions and a wide measure of self-rule. For example, when Italy was nothing more than a "geographic expression" prior to the late nineteenth century, with its regions variously controlled by France, Austria, Spain, and the papacy, Italian nationalists were determined to unite the Italian people under a self-governing Italian state. Through a combination of diplomatic and military efforts, they succeeded by 1870 in creating a united Italy whose territorial boundaries were roughly similar to those prevailing today. In the same period, German nationalists were determined to put an end to the fragmentation of more than 40 million Germans into a multiplicity of kingdoms, duchies, city-states, principalities, and other mini-states. They demanded a single German nation-state under one political leadership. This national goal was finally achieved in 1871. In contemporary Russia, nationalists in the small region of Chechnya—a territory taken over by Russia in the nineteenth century—have been fighting for independence on the grounds that they are not Russians and do not want to be controlled by the Russian government. They are *separatists* (or *secessionists*): they want full separation from Russia.

In these and virtually all other instances of nationalism in its domestic variant, self-determination tends to be *territorial* in nature: the people seeking self-rule are usually concentrated within an identifiable geographic area. Quite often the boundaries of the territory the nationalists claim as their own are fairly clear; Chechnya is an example. In other cases the precise demarcation of the nation's territory can be more complicated. After 1870, Italian nationalists continued to claim territories held by the Austro-Hungarian empire. The German nationalists who created Germany in 1871 deliberately excluded Austria from their new state, even though many Austrians considered themselves German.

Historically, nationalism as an expression of a people's desire for territorial self-determination has most often taken the form of a demand for a sovereign, independent state. The idea of the nation-state derives mainly from this concept of full governmental independence. Italy, Germany, and a host of countries throughout the world were formed on the basis of this identification of nationalism with statehood.[3]

But another form of territorial self-determination also exists, one that falls short of complete state independence. In some instances, a people sharing a distinctive national identity who happen to live within the confines of a country dominated by another group may be willing to settle for a measure of self-administration within their respective territory, even though they remain a part of the larger country and are formally subordinate to its central government. This form of partial independence is called *autonomy*. **Autonomy** *means territorial self-government within a country.* Local autonomy may include such things as the right to use the locally spoken language in official documents and meetings and on street signs, control over the territory's school system, and the like. People who accept local autonomy may consider themselves just as nationalistic as other members of their nation who insist on a fully independent state.

Nationalism in International Affairs   The terms nationalist and nationalistic as they are used in international affairs generally refer to certain orientations that national governments take in their relations with other states, international organizations, and other actors on the world scene such as transnational corporations. A nationalistic foreign policy is one that affirms, with varying degrees of intensity, that the country is entitled to have its voice heard and its interests and policy positions taken into account. It aims above all at making sure that the country will not be ignored, dominated, or pushed around by external forces. Virtually every government in the world is nationalistic to some degree. In its most benign manifestation, nationalism in the global arena usually amounts to little more than a state's demand to be included as a cooperative partner in world affairs and to have its most vital interests—such as its sovereignty and territorial integrity—respected.

But governments, political leaders, and political movements that are singled out as particularly nationalistic are typically more emphatic, and sometimes frighteningly extreme, in their advocacy of nationalist causes. Arch-nationalists tend to drive a

harder bargain than less assertive leaders in international negotiations, and the most recalcitrant may not want compromise at all. In its most virulent form, nationalism can assume an arrogant stance that regards other countries with contempt, at times unleashing unprovoked aggression. *Extreme nationalism* of this kind is called **hypernationalism.** British, French, and American imperialists of past centuries, Hitler's Nazis, and Serbs bent on establishing "Greater Serbia" on the basis of "ethnic cleansing" are a few examples of hypernationalists. At times hypernationalism in a country's external relations rests on an extreme form of domestic nationalism. The Nazis, for example, had a racially exclusive concept of the German nation that rejected Jews, Slavs, and other ethnic minorities as non-German, even though members of these groups had lived on German soil for long periods of time. Preaching bigotry and hostility, the Nazis evinced an outspoken *chauvinism*, which means distrust and hatred of foreigners.

Nationalism as an Ideology   Because nationalism involves a set of political ideas and goals, and is more than just a people's collective sense of belonging together as a nation, many historians and political scientists regard nationalism as a political ideology. In most cases nationalist ideas are created and propagated by political thinkers and actors. Whereas a *sense of nationhood* comes about through the social interactions of a mass of people over a protracted period of time, the *idea of nationalism* is usually the work of a small number of individuals who take it upon themselves to promote national values, create a national culture (including language, literature, and art), and design programs for political action. Nationalism as a set of ideas, in short, is typically produced by political and intellectual elites. These nationalist elites typically consist of party leaders, governing officials, the leaders of movements for national unification or independence from foreign domination, or others involved in political activity on a grand scale. They also frequently include writers and academics who propagate nationalist ideas in their publications. Whoever they may be, some nationalist elites may favor democracy while others may prefer communism, fascism, or some other political system. Nationalism as an ideology can be combined with any of these or other political ideologies. For some nationalists, however, the nation itself is the supreme political value and outweighs all other political ideals.

Nationalism and Patriotism　Nationalism often carries with it a *normative content:* it places a high premium on national pride, national loyalty, and national solidarity as desirable norms. Accordingly, nationalists often undertake concerted efforts to inculcate these values in their populations, with the express purpose of intensifying the people's sense of sharing a common national identity. Nationalism above all stresses national unity, exalting the nation and the ties that bind it together as more important than the ethnic, religious, political, economic, or other factors that tend to fragment it. To the extent that it encompasses the population of an entire country, nationalism demands love of country and respect for its symbols (such as the flag or, in the case of symbolic leaders, the monarch). It may also demand sacrifices in defense of the country's vital national interests, especially if it is attacked or threatened by other countries.

To some degree then, nationalism has certain values and attitudes in common with patriotism. **Patriotism** *means love of country (or love of one's nation),* a sentiment nationalists would certainly share. But the differences between nationalism and patriotism, while subtle, can be quite significant. Nationalism may demand support for certain types of political action, such as a fight for independence or the assertion of an aggressive foreign policy, whereas patriotism is a more diffuse sentiment that is not necessarily tied to any specific policy or course of action. Especially in its more assertive forms, nationalism can demand attitudes and personal commitments that extend far beyond the limits of patriotic loyalty. When the Nazis ruled Germany, most Germans considered themselves patriots because they loved their country, but not all of them approved of Hitler's brutal racism and aggressive hypernationalism. When called to arms, millions of Germans dutifully trooped into the military out of love for their fatherland, though they did not all necessarily share Hitler's grandiose dreams of conquest. Other Germans, many of them acting out of their own notions of patriotism, fled the country or joined anti-Nazi movements. In view of the Nazis' efforts to link patriotism with hypernationalism, some Germans to this day are still uncomfortable with patriotic displays, such as singing the national anthem or honoring the flag.

In some instances the demands of nationalism and patriotism create competing sets of loyalties that can be very difficult for the average person to sort out. Consider the choices facing the Scottish people. Scotland was repeatedly attacked by England and forced to join Great Britain under the English monarchy in 1707. But Scottish national sentiment has never fully died out. If you are a Scot, you must decide whether you favor an independent Scotland, as the most outspoken Scottish nationalists demand, or the continuation of Scotland's status as part of Britain. If you favor staying in Britain, how much autonomy for Scotland would you demand? Would you consider yourself a Scottish nationalist? a Scottish patriot? a British nationalist? a British patriot? What would these terms mean in practice? Similar dilemmas are faced by French-speaking Quebecers in Canada, as we shall see later in this chapter.

Nationalism in the Developing World

As we observed earlier in this chapter, nationalism has both domestic and international components. As students of comparative politics, we have a special interest in the ways nationalism affects politics *inside* individual countries. While this is a vast topic that cannot possibly be explored in detail in these pages, a glance at a few examples can at least convey some idea of the various forms the relationship between nationalism and domestic political development can take.

In some cases nationalism led to communism. In countries like China, Vietnam, and Cuba, communist parties came to power not so much because of their Marxist ideology, which was largely misplaced in societies that were predominantly agricultural rather than industrialized; rather, they came to power, and held on to it, at least in part by galvanizing latent forces of nationalism, The form that nationalism took in these countries typically involved opposition to political or economic domination exercised by outside powers like Japan, France, or the United States. In other countries once colonized by imperial states like Britain and

France, a generation of leaders maintained their grip on power at home through a combination of firm dictatorial rule, usually backed by the military, and nationalistic appeals to the anti-colonial sentiments of the population. Quite a few African dictators based their rule on these methods, though the strategy has by no means been confined to Africa. Contemporary Iran, under the theocratic leadership of Islamic clerics since the fall of the Shah in 1979, has also witnessed a combination of dictatorial rule and nationalistic anti-Westernism, nurtured by a profound antipathy to foreign dictates on the part of many Iranians.

Issues of nationalism have also been a source of political contestation in the domestic politics of developing countries. Not infrequently, these debates have hinged on attitudes toward outside powers like the United States. Attitudes toward American military bases in the Philippines, U.S. economic penetration of Latin America, or U.S. prescriptions for economic or political reform in a host of developing countries (prescriptions that are often similar to those advanced by the International Monetary Fund and other providers of development assistance) often animate intense nationalistic feelings on the part of political elites and even the mass public. While some leaders in the developing world may wish to come to terms with the global superpower, others may feel too threatened or manipulated to comply with American wishes, a posture often rooted in national pride and an insistence on sovereign independence. In roughly similar ways, various developing countries have faced similar domestic political debates over relations with Western Europe, Japan, or other external actors.

Although comparative politics concentrates on the domestic side of things, it bears repeating that what takes place inside individual countries often affects what transpires outside their borders. Some political leaders may be more nationalistic in their interactions with the outside world than other politicians within their respective states. Remember, *it matters who governs.* Hypernationalism can be a particularly potent force in the developing world, where memories of past domination by imperial powers and opposition to the political, military, and economic dominance of the wealthy countries in today's world often provoke sharp resentments.

Antagonism toward the United States can be especially fierce in view of its commanding presence in every corner of the globe. The notion that the United States is capable of manipulating countries large and small and of getting its way in virtually every situation is widely shared throughout the world. Meanwhile, admiration for its democratic values and economic dynamism is also widespread and appears to have grown in the 1990s.

Nationalism in the developing world by no means takes aim exclusively at the West or at other former colonial powers like Japan. Rivalries and antagonisms between developing countries can be just as sharp. Sometimes these clashes are rooted in the manipulative practices of the imperial powers of a bygone era. Border and ethnic conflicts between neighboring African nations, for example, often trace their origins to the boundaries that were imposed on them by their European overlords. Territorial disputes deriving from the breakup of British India in 1947 into India and Pakistan account for at least some of the hostility between those two countries. While religious animosities between Hindus and Muslims are at the heart of the conflict, in 1999 the two South Asian neighbors exchanged fire over Kashmir, a border area still hotly contested by leaders of both countries. In the previous year India and Pakistan engaged in serious nuclear saber rattling, conducting underground nuclear explosions designed to display their military capabilities. Conflicts attendant upon the breakup of the Soviet Union also reflect deep-seated national rivalries, at times exacerbated by border disputes. Fighting between Armenia and Azerbaijan and civil strife between contending nationality groups in Georgia, Moldova, and other Soviet successor states provide ample proof that nationalism is likely to be a source of acute contention in this part of the world for some time to come.

For the student of comparative politics, it is particularly interesting to explore the conditions under which individual countries in the developing world might alter or vary their approaches to nationalism. Are democratically elected leaders less hostile or mistrustful in their attitudes to the West or to other democracies than authoritarian leaders are? Will the forces of economic globalization, which may raise some boats in the developing world while engulfing others, lead to more hypernationalism among developing countries, or less? Does national poverty itself promote nationalistic antagonisms by giving people an emotional outlet for their frustrations and sense of powerlessness? These and related questions cannot be answered here, but their pertinence to some of the most pressing issues in comparative and international politics is beyond doubt. By converting them into testable hypotheses, we can learn a great deal about how nationalism affects the problems of political and economic development, and vice versa.

THE FORMATION OF NATION-STATES

How are nation-states created? The answer to this question will vary from one country to another, but there are enough similarities across countries to permit some generalizations.

Numerous students of the subject have pointed out that the formation of nation-states in much of the world, and across most periods of history, has been a violent affair. In contrast to the benign notions of the social contract theorists, who stressed the cooperative coming together of enlightened and free individuals, most national-level state governments have in fact been formed through brute force. In many cases the combatants were domestic rivals for control of large swatches of territory and, ultimately, state power itself. Countries like China, Japan, Russia, Britain, and France all developed into powerful nation-states following extended periods of internal turmoil, in some cases lasting for centuries. Rival dynastic claimants to the throne, warring clans, organized combatants in civil wars, warlords staking out their own turf—these and other contenders for territory and ruling authority have been the chief players in the struggle to establish state authority within a host of countries. Once entrenched in power, the winning family or faction would often seek to expand the power of the state through a variety of measures: building large armies, undertaking vast construction projects (such as canals and roads), squeezing tax revenues out of the populace, fighting territorial wars against neighboring states, and so on. Violent contention for control of the national government did not die down until the eighteenth century in Britain, the nineteenth century in Japan, and the twentieth century in Russia and China.[4]

In some instances the effort to construct a single nation-state by a powerful monarchy determined to centralize control over a diverse kingdom was never fully completed. Lingering national sentiments on the part of various minorities are still alive in today's world in a number of nation-states that have been formally unified for centuries. The United Kingdom (UK), for example, has consisted of Great Britain (that is, England, Scotland, and Wales) and all or part of Ireland since 1801. Nevertheless, most of Ireland broke away in 1922, and anti-English sentiments still resound among Catholics in Northern Ireland (which remains part of the UK). Similar sentiments also abound in Scotland, where the Scottish Nationalist Party wants complete independence, and, to a lesser degree, in Wales. All three of these non-English regions of the United Kingdom now have their own local legislatures. Spain was forged into a single country by the fifteenth century, but regions like Catalonia and the Basque country, where languages other than Castillian Spanish are still spoken, are hotbeds of local nationalism. In Mexico, Indians in the Chiapas region—the decendants of the Maya—have taken arms against the government in pressing their claims for greater economic assistance. Other examples of regional self-assertion, at times taking a violent turn, can be pinpointed around the globe.

The result in a number of these countries is **regionalism,** that is, *the expression of a distinct local identity on the part of the inhabitants of particular geographic regions within a country.* This regional identity is sometimes accompanied by demands for greater autonomy for local governing authorities, or even for secession from the country and full-scale independence. But not always: at times regionalism manifests itself simply as a demand for better treatment at the hands of the central government, calling for better roads, more economic development funds, and so on.

In other cases, nation-states were built upon territorial arrangements and state institutions that were forcefully imposed by foreign intervention. From Latin America to the Middle East, from Eastern Europe to Central Asia, and from Africa to Southeast Asia, the boundaries of many countries to be found on today's maps were carved out by imperialist invaders or the victors of wars, with scant regard to the composition or desires of local populations. Nation-states as diverse as Brazil, Iraq, China, and almost all the countries of Africa, are the products of foreign conquerors who ultimately determined the territorial boundaries of the areas they controlled. In a number of cases the countries that emerged consisted of diverse ethnic, tribal, religious, linguistic, or other groupings with little or no sense of common identity as a nation. Even today, the process of "nation building"—of building a common *national* identity—is still a difficult problem for a number of these countries, some of which continue to experience internal unrest or civil wars. Nigeria, to pick a typical example, was a British creation: its boundaries enclosed numerous ethno-linguistic groups with no real sense of belonging to a common Nigerian nation. The clash between Arabs and Kurds in Iraq and the fierce intergroup warfare occurring in a number of African states provide vivid examples of how quite a few nation-states in the contemporary world are still struggling with the legacy of the imperialist past.

WHEN "THE NATION" AND "THE STATE" DON'T FIT

In theory, the "ideal" nation-state would consist of one nation that is governed by one state. But in fact this perfect symmetry is rare. One investigation conducted in 1971 showed that out of 132 countries, only 12 (9.1 percent) met these strict criteria.[5] The situation is not much different today. Our world contains states with more than one nation and nations without their own states. *In most cases the term "nation-state" is thus a misnomer, at least in its most literal sense.* Nevertheless, many people use the term "nation-state" anyway as a synonym for a country. When we use that term in this book, keep in mind that we do not necessarily mean that the country consists of only one completely unified "nation."

In the vast majority of cases, countries today consist of one *dominant* national group and one or more minority groups. At the end of the 1990s there were 114 countries in which at least two-thirds of the population consisted of the dominant ethnic group, with considerable ethnic diversity in quite a few of these countries. Even greater fragmentation characterized seventy-seven countries where no ethnic group comprised as much as two-thirds of the population.[6] In some countries, the largest single national grouping constituted less than half the population and was itself a minority. (In 1971 there were thirty-nine countries in the latter category, comprising 29.5 percent of the total.) In a number of these states certain minority groups may be considered **national minorities** because they seek some form of self-government, independent of the existing national government. Canada provides a vivid example.

CANADA

Today's lingering conflicts between English and French Canadians trace their roots to the colonization of this vast country that began more than five hundred years ago. In 1497 John Cabot, an Italian explorer working for the English monarch, reached Canada's eastern shores and anointed his discovery "New Founde Lande." In 1534 Jacques Cartier landed on Canadian soil and claimed Canada for the King of France. In the following century English and French claimants extended their holdings. In 1604 Samuel de Champlain proclaimed "New France" on Nova Scotia, but after several harsh winters he moved his small colony up the St. Lawrence River, establishing the French settlement of **Quebec** in 1608. In 1670 the Hudson's Bay Company, chartered by King Charles II, gained a solid English foothold in eastern Canada.

Fierce rivalries over the lucrative fur trade led to a succession of skirmishes between French and British forces in the early eighteenth century, with the English taking Newfoundland, Nova Scotia (Acadia), and Hudson Bay in 1713. In 1759 British troops defeated French forces outside Quebec. At the end of the Seven Years' War in 1763, the Treaty of Paris gave full control of Canada to England. Although the country was populated mainly by French speakers at that time, successive waves of new arrivals from Britain and the American colonies tilted the balance in favor of English-speaking Canadians over the ensuing decades. In 1867 the British North America Act created the Dominion of Canada with the right of self-government. Only in 1982, however, did Canada gain full independence from Britain's theoretical right to veto its legislation. To this very day Canada recognizes the British monarch as its ceremonial head of state, with a governor-general serving as the crown's representative.

Ever since 1867, many French Canadians have regarded themselves as second-class citizens. Today Quebec is one of Canada's ten provinces, with a population of

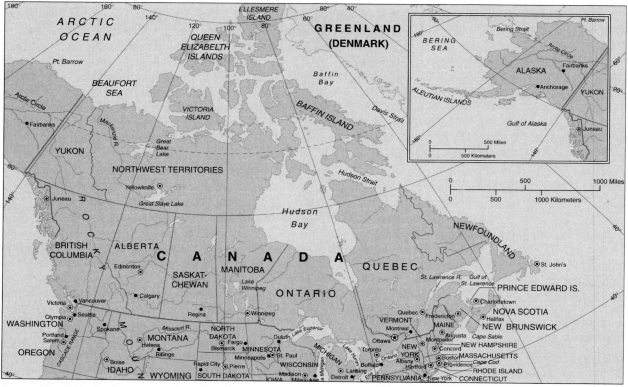

FIGURE 7.1   Canada

more than 7 million, roughly one-fourth of Canada's total. In the 1960s a separatist movement became increasingly vocal in the region, its leaders militating for an independent Quebec nation-state. In 1974 the local legislature passed a law declaring French as the only official language in the province. School instruction became exclusively French; English was demoted throughout the province. The Canadian government under Prime Minister Pierre Elliott Trudeau, a French Canadian, was willing to promote bilingualism and a greater measure of autonomy for Quebec, but it staunchly resisted its outright secession from Canada. In 1979 Canada's Supreme Court struck down as unconstitutional Quebec's proclaimed right to ban English. The following year some 60 percent of Quebecers voted against a proposal giving their leaders the right to negotiate an agreement establishing Quebec's sovereignty; a clear majority of French Canadians, it appeared, opposed the province's secession from Canada. Full independence for Quebec now seemed out of the question. Nevertheless, some two hundred thousand English speakers residing in Quebec left the province in the late 1970s and early 1980s. Today only about 750,000 residents of Quebec are predominantly English speakers.

In 1987 Canada's leaders tried to reach a compromise aimed at satisfying Quebec's demands for greater autonomy while keeping the province in Canada. The accord recognized Quebec as a "distinct society" and granted Canada's provinces the right to veto major constitutional amendments. But the agreement fell apart when key Quebec politicians felt it did not go far enough while their English-speaking opponents in other parts of Canada felt it went too far. Another constitutional reform recognizing Quebec as a "distinct society" was voted down in a national referendum in 1992. Meanwhile, separatist sentiment in Quebec gathered new momentum. In 1990 the provincial government banned English-language signs.

In 1994 the Parti Quebecois emerged as the largest party in the province, and its leader, Jacques Parizeau, became the chief of Quebec's provincial government. An outspoken proponent of an independent Quebec, Parizeau campaigned on the pledge of promoting a nationwide referendum on independence for Quebec. However, the margin of his party's vote (44.7 percent) suggested that most Quebecers did not share his dreams of a separate Quebec state. By the end of the year public opinion polls indicated that only about 40 percent of the province's voters favored independence; the vast majority remained opposed. Some people in Quebec questioned the possible costs of secession, since an independent Quebec would have to assume its share of Canada's national debt, pay for environmental cleanups, duplicate various government services, and run up other expenses. One study estimated the price tag of independence at more than $100 billion. Meanwhile, Canada's French-speaking prime minister, Jean Chrétien, openly opposed independence for Quebec.

On October 30, 1995, the long-awaited referendum was held. In the weeks leading up to the vote, a sudden surge of support for separation was generated by Lucien Bouchard, an impassioned orator who led Quebec's parliamentary bloc in the Canadian legislature. The referendum question asked the residents of Quebec, "Do you agree that Quebec should become sovereign, after having made a formal offer to Canada for a new economic and political partnership . . .?" This time the result was closer than ever: 50.25 percent voted no, barely enough to defeat the proposal. As Canada heads into the twenty-first century, the issue of Quebec's ultimate status remains controversial.[7]

FIGURE 7.2   Kurdish Areas (Shown in Gray)

Just as there are nation-states with more than one nation, there are also nations without a state. Here are some examples.

- The **Kurds** are a nation of some 22 million people occupying more than seventy thousand square miles of territory that sprawls across six countries. Though they were promised a state of their own after World War I, they are still struggling to create an independent Kurdistan (see figure 7.2). Today most Kurds live in Turkey (about 10 million), Iran (5.5 million), and Iraq (3.5 million), with smaller communities in Syria, Armenia, and Azerbaijan. Kurdish fighters have been engaged in virtually continuous conflict for decades, mostly with the governments of Turkey and Iraq. Persistent attacks by Saddam Hussein's government prompted the United States, Britain, and France to provide aerial protection for Kurds in Iraq. Turkey has been repeatedly condemned by western governments for violating the Kurds' rights, but U.S. ties with Turkey, a NATO ally, have precluded official American support for Kurdish independence.
- In the Middle East, **Palestinians** have sought to establish their own national state, but these hopes have been frustrated by the opposition of Israel and Jordan (see chapter 20).
- In South Asia, in the area of Pakistan and Afghanistan, the **Baluchis** have also sought national independence.

THE DISINTEGRATION OF NATION-STATES

Though we may be tempted to think of nation-states, once established, as enduring entities, they are by no means always so. The recent collapse of the Soviet Union and the unification of Germany following more than forty years of Cold War division into two separate states should alert us to the reality that nation-states may fall apart and disappear altogether. The map of Europe, to pick just one part of the globe, has changed kaleidoscopically over time. Like geological formations, nations and states may undergo all sorts of seismic convulsions. They can grow, lose territory, disintegrate, become reconstituted, or get absorbed into larger states.

In some cases, the implosion of severely divided countries can lead to civil war. Nigeria, a country whose boundaries were fixed by Britain, experienced a brutal conflict between 1967 and 1970 when the Igbos, a predominantly Christian group that had been persecuted by the politically dominant Muslims, attempted to secede and form their own country, which they called Biafra. Between five hundred thousand and 1 to 2 million people were killed or died of starvation before the rebellion was suppressed by the Nigerian military government.

One of the most volcanic examples of the disintegration of a state that once consisted of several nations is the former **Yugoslavia.** Its explosive self-destruction, accompanied by the killing of over 250,000 people and the forcible expulsion of more than 2 million from their homes and villages, is one of the great tragedies of post–World War II Europe.

U.S. troops examine a mass grave site in Bosnia, 1998. The victims were thought to be Muslims killed in 1992 by Serb forces.

THE DISINTEGRATION OF YUGOSLAVIA

ORIGINS
The roots of this region's intense conflicts extend more than a thousand years into the past. Starting in the late sixth century, successive waves of Slavic tribes from the eastern steppes, located in what is now Russia and Central Asia, gradually moved into the peninsula whose spine is formed by the Balkan mountains. Though these tribes were biologically related, their subsequent histories took very divergent paths. Religion was one factor accounting for these differences; diverse patterns of interaction with neighboring peoples was another.

- **Slovenes,** who occupied the northernmost part of the area, formed close links with the nearby Germans. In the eighth century the majority of Slovenes were converted to Roman Catholicism. Most of what is now Slovenia was part of the Austrian-led Habsburg empire from 1335 to 1918. Today Slovenia is a democracy. Still predominantly Catholic, it retains close ties with Austria. In 1998 it began negotiations for eventual membership in the European Union.
- **Croats** became Roman Catholics in the tenth century and are still mostly Catholic today. Though parts of Croatia, such as the Dalmatian coast, were variously controlled over the centuries by the Ottoman empire, Venice, and France, most of what is now Croatia gradually came under the control of Austria and Hungary and remained part of the Habsburg empire until the end of World War I.

- **Serbs** initially occupied the valleys where Bosnia, Montenegro, and Kosovo meet. In the ninth century they were converted to the eastern rite of Orthodox Christianity—the basis of the Russian Orthodox church—by two brothers, Saints Cyril and Methodius. Cyril was the founder of what evolved into the Russian (Cyrillic) alphabet. These religious and linguistic developments established a close connection between Serbs and Russians that still endures. The Turks held much of this region from the fourteenth century to the late nineteenth century. Under Russia's patronage, the kingdom of Serbia was established in 1882. Russia's support for Serbia against Austria-Hungary in 1914 was one of the key events that led to World War I.
- **Montenegrins** were originally Serbs. They broke off from the rest of the Serbs in the early fifteenth century in order to escape the advancing Turks, establishing their own monarchy in an inaccessible mountainous region. Montenegro (the Black Mountain) remained an independent state until 1918.
- **Bosnians** were also originally Serbs. They fled Serbia proper in the fourteenth century in advance of the Turks and established their own kingdom in what eventually became known as Bosnia. In 1463 the Turks overran all of Bosnia except a small area around Mostar that was ruled by the duke (*herzeg*) of St. Sava. This area, known as Herzegovina, fell to the Turks twenty years later. Over the course of the next several centuries under Ottoman rule, most Bosnians became Muslims. But others retained their Serbian identity as Orthodox Christians; they became known as "Bosnian Serbs." The Austro-Hungarian empire took over Bosnia from the Turks in 1878. It was a Bosnian Serb who assassinated Austria's Archduke Franz Ferdinand in Sarajevo in 1914, igniting World War I.

FIGURE 7.3   The Balkan States in 1914

- **Macedonians** probably stemmed from Slavic tribes but they also had close ancestral ties with the non-Slavic Bulgars. In the ninth century a Macedo-Bulgarian empire was formed, but the Ottomans took over most of its territory in the following century, ruling it almost uninterruptedly until 1913. Parts of Macedonia were taken by Serbia, Greece, and Bulgaria in the course of two Balkan wars fought in 1912 and 1913.

- **Albanians** are a non-Slavic people who were ruled by the Ottomans for 450 years until 1912, when Albania became an independent country. Most Albanians became Muslims. Though the majority of them live in Albania, many Albanians have lived for centuries in the region of Kosovo, which is part of Serbia.

In the nineteenth century, Slovenes and Croats increasingly voiced demands for greater autonomy within the Austro-Hungarian empire, while Serbian nationalists collaborated with Russia under the banner of "pan-Slavism" to end five hundred years of Turkish domination. Following the collapse of the Habsburg empire in 1918, these diverse peoples gradually formed a new country, which took the name Yugoslavia, "the land of the southern Slavs." (Albania, meanwhile, retained its independence.) Intense rivalries virtually doomed the new Yugoslav state from the start. Efforts to establish a stable democracy foundered on the uncompromising attitudes of the various nationality groups and their leaders. In 1934 Yugoslavia's constitutional monarch, who was a Serb, was murdered by Croatian assassins.

Internal turmoil was exacerbated by external threats. In 1941 Nazi Germany took over Yugoslavia and occupied the country until 1944. While thousands of Yugoslavs took up arms against the Germans in resistance movements, the centuries-old conflicts among the various Yugoslav nationalities erupted into civil war. Fighting between Serbs and Croats was especially intense. Approximately 1.75 million Yugoslavs lost their lives during World War II. About half were killed by the Germans; the other half died at the hands of other Yugoslavs.

The most successful anti-German resistance movement during the war years was organized by Yugoslav communists. Their leader was Josip Broz, known by his pseudonym, Tito. Tito's communists swiftly took control of Yugoslavia following the Germans' withdrawal. Initially, the Yugoslav communists attempted to reorganize the country along the lines of Stalin's harsh Soviet dictatorship. But in 1948 Tito and Stalin got into a feud when the Yugoslav communists expressed their resentment at Soviet interference in their internal affairs. In Tito's conception, Yugoslav nationalism took precedence over communist ideology. "We are good communists," he said, "but we are good Yugoslavs first." Yugoslavia and the Soviet Union broke off their alliance and Tito steered a more neutral course, pursuing economic ties with the West.

As long as Tito remained the country's supreme leader, the ethnic antagonisms simmering just below the surface of Yugoslavia's authoritarian regime did not explode into violence. But they did not disappear entirely. Tito, who was part Croat and part Slovene, occasionally had to take personal action to prevent excessive displays of ethnic nationalism by Serbs, Croats, and other groups. Like the keystone of an arch, it was Tito's towering presence that held the country together. His death in 1980 at the age of 88 compelled Yugoslavia's nationalities to confront their abiding rivalries anew.

Shortly before his death, Tito bequeathed Yugoslavia a new constitution that required the communist leaders of the country's main nationality groups to share power after his departure. This shaky arrangement lasted little more than ten years. As the winds of freedom fanned across the Soviet Union and Eastern Europe in the late 1980s and early 1990s, toppling decades of communist rule, Yugoslavs of every nationality demanded similar liberties. For most Yugoslavs, however, democratic self-expression meant ethnic self-assertion.

Following referendums that showed vast majorities in favor of complete independence, Slovenia and Croatia seceded from Yugoslavia and declared their sovereignty in June 1991. Macedonia followed suit in September of the same year, and the Muslim leaders of

FIGURE 7.4   Yugoslavia Prior to Its Break-up

Bosnia-Herzegovina declared independence in December. Serbia and Montenegro did not declare their independence but together formed what remained of Yugoslavia. Serbia has dominated this partnership under the leadership of **Slobodan Milosevic,** a former communist functionary who initially spoke of uniting all the region's Serbs into a "Greater Serbia."

The Disintegration of Yugoslavia continues on page 158.

PROFILE: Slobodan Milosevic

Born in 1941 of Montenegrin descent, Milosevic (Mee-LOH-sheh-vich) was raised by his mother, an ardent communist, after his father left the family. In later years, both his parents as well as his brother would commit suicide. While in high school he met his future wife and chief political collaborator, Mirjana Markovic, who came from a staunchly communist family. As a young man Milosevic began working as a functionary in Tito's communist party, the League of Communists of Yugoslavia,

Slobodan Milosevic

and also embarked on a successful business career, first as a factory manager and subsequently as a banker whose dealings took him frequently to New York. His

FIGURE 7.5   The Balkans Today

loyalty to Tito was fully evident in the 1970s, when the party leader expelled reform-minded members of the party who favored Western-style democracy and private enterprise. Milosevic backed the purges and rose up the party's ranks with solid anti-liberal credentials. In the following decade he rode the political coattails of a close friend from law school, Ivan Stambolic. When Stambolic became president of Serbia in 1986, he appointed Milosevic chief of the communist party of Serbia. Milosevic quickly buttressed his reputation as a foe of political and economic liberalization and stood out as an early opponent of the reform-oriented communism being initiated in the Soviet Union by Mikhail Gorbachev.

Though he appeared to be a typical communist party burueaucrat with no charismatic flair, Milosevic had a keen eye for power. In 1987 and 1988 he consolidated his position within the party, removing liberal-oriented opponents and promoting hardline loyalists. Most significantly, he departed from the traditional reticence of other Yugoslav communist leaders, including Tito himself, to drum up nationalist sentiments. Milosevic fully understood the fears and hatreds of the country's diverse ethnic groups, and he had a particular apprecia-

tion for the feelings of many Serbs that they were the chief victims of the Yugoslav leadership's policies of ethnic balance. Accordingly, Milosevic sought to solidify his own power base by deliberately stirring up Serbian national passions, a potentially dangerous move that other leaders like Stambolic shunned. Milosevic hit a raw nerve within Serbia, and in 1989 he and his supporters within the communist-dominated legislature prevailed upon Stambolic to resign. Milosevic thereupon replaced his former mentor as president of Serbia, the most populous republic of Yugoslavia.

Shortly after taking office, Milosevic addressed a huge throng of Serbs on the site of Kosovo Pole, the "Field of Blackbirds," where the Serbian army had been defeated by the Turks exactly six hundred years earlier. That defeat still rankled many Serbs as a dark day in their history, and Milosevic's fiery speech promised that Serbia would never again relinquish its control over Kosovo, the province revered as the historic birthplace of the Serbian nation. Hundreds of years of Turkish occupation had left Kosovo with a large ethnic Albanian majority, virtually all of them Muslims. Of the province's 2.2 million residents, 90 percent were

Albanians. Tito had granted the Albanian Kosovars a number of rights and privileges, and between the 1960s and mid-1980s as many as three hundred thousand Serbs left Kosovo because of local Albanian domination. Milosevic was determined to reverse this process. In 1989 he began terminating the rights of the Albanian Kosovars, removing them from their jobs by the hundreds of thousands. In their place came Serbs determined to reclaim control of the province. The antagonisms set off by these actions ultimately culminated in a wholesale Serbian onslaught in Kosovo in 1998 and 1999, followed by the NATO bombing campaign. But Milosevic first had to deal with the secession movements in Slovenia, Croatia, and Bosnia.[8]

The Disintegration of Yugoslavia continued from page 156.

THE BALKAN WARS OF THE 1990s

Fighting broke out in Slovenia, Croatia, and Bosnia shortly after the initial declarations of independence. Milosevic deployed the Yugoslav army, led predominantly by Serb officers, in an effort to halt Yugoslavia's disintegration. Slovenia quickly repulsed these forces and retained its independence. Croatia and Bosnia-Herzegovina, however, became mired in lengthy conflicts. Not only were they attacked by the Serb-controlled Yugoslav army, they were also assaulted by local Serbs, many of whom were armed by Milosevic's Serbian government. Croatian Serbs seized control of the Krajina, a portion of Croatia where Serbs had lived since the eighteenth century.

In what turned out to be a protracted and brutal conflict, Bosnian Serbs fought to take over as much of Bosnia-Herzegovina as they could in an effort to liberate themselves from Bosnia's Muslim-controlled government. By early 1995 Bosnian Serbs, backed by the Yugoslav government, were in control of 70 percent of Bosnia-Herzegovina; mass murders, gang rapes, and house burnings became routine occurrences as the Bosnian Serbs carried out a policy they called "ethnic cleansing": the removal of Bosnian Muslims from areas claimed exclusively by Serbs. Between 1992 and 1995 the Bosnian capital of Sarajevo, once a model of multi-ethnic harmony, was besieged by Serb artillery.

Efforts by the United Nations and the NATO alliance to promote a settlement of these disputes proved ineffective until the summer of 1995. In August the Croatian government launched a massive assault on Krajina, evicting more than 150,000 Serbs. Prodded into action by a new wave of Bosnian Serb atrocities, including the murder of thousands of men and boys and their burial in mass graves, the U.S. government and its NATO allies launched a series of air attacks on Serb positions throughout Bosnia-Herzegovina. Muslim forces took the offensive and regained control of several areas from the Bosnian Serbs. At the same time, fresh diplomatic initiatives succeeded in convincing Serbia's Milosevic to curtail his support for the Bosnian Serbs and come to the peace table.

Peace talks involving the leaders of Croatia, Bosnia-Herzegovina, and Serbia took place under U.S. auspices at the Wright-Patterson Air Force Base outside Dayton, Ohio. After three weeks of intense bargaining, the main parties initialed a comprehensive peace agreement on November 21, 1995. A formal signing ceremony took place in Paris the following month. The Dayton Accords divided Bosnia-Herzegovina into a Muslim-Croat Federation and a Serbian zone known as Republika Srpska. This agreement was initially policed by a NATO force of some sixty thousand troops, of whom twenty thousand were Americans. In 1997 the NATO force, now called SFOR ("Stabilization Force"), was reduced in size and its U.S. contingent cut to 8,500 troops. Under the aegis of NATO security forces and outside monitors from the Organization for Security and Cooperation in Europe (OSCE), several elections have taken place at the federal and local levels. Still, ethnic tensions remain high. Several Serbs and Croats have been arrested as war criminals and sentenced by a special tribunal in the Hague, but the leaders responsible for the most flagrant atrocities have thus far evaded arrest.

After the Dayton Accords, attention turned once more to Kosovo. Starting in 1997, a force of ethnic Albanians known as the Kosovo Liberation Army (KLA) took up arms against Serbian forces in an effort to gain the province's complete independence. Serbian reprisals were intense, and by the summer of 1998 some seven hundred thousand refugees had fled the province. The United States and five other governments forming the Balkan "Contact Group" (United Kingdom, France, Germany, Italy, and Russia) pressured both sides to negotiate a compromise that would grant Kosovo wide autonomy within Serbia but not full independence. In the spring of 1999 the Contact Group sought to impose its plan on the Yugoslav government, but Milosevic rejected it, claiming that his government had the sovereign right to defend itself against KLA secessionists and affirming that he would never accept an international peacekeeping force in Kosovo.

As Serb forces pressed their campaign against the KLA and civilian non-combatants, the NATO alliance began an intensive bombing campaign in April. Swarms of refugees streamed out of Kosovo into neighboring Albania and Macedonia, many bearing tales of summary murders, gang rapes, extortion, and other atrocities committed by Serbian military and special police forces. The ethnic cleansing of Kosovo by some forty thousand Serbian troops and paramilitary fighters was in full swing. After eleven weeks of bombing, which destroyed power plants, bridges, and other facilities in Belgrade and other parts of Serbia and Montenegro, Milosevic suddenly gave up and accepted NATO peace terms. All Yugoslav troops were compelled to leave Kosovo and a fifty-thousand-strong international peacekeeping force led by NATO took their place. Some thirty countries have provided troops for the force, including Russia. By the end of 1999 most of the Kosovar Albanian refugees had returned to Kosovo, often to find their loved ones killed and their property destroyed. Reprisals against the Serbs who remained have been frequent, despite the peacekeepers' efforts to prevent them. About one hundred thousand Serbs have left the province, about half the number who lived there before the bombing campaign.

After giving in to NATO, Milosevic remained in office until a spontaneous revolution forced his resignation. In September 2000 it appeared that he lost the presidential election to Vojislav Kostunica, a constitutional lawyer. When Milosevic tried to suppress the election results, hundreds of thousands of protesters stormed Belgrade, seizing official buildings and media outlets on October 5. Milosevic resigned the next day. He faced an uncertain future as an indicted war criminal wanted for trial by a United Nations tribunal.[9]

SUPRANATIONALISM

In all its many functions and manifestations, the state remains the central form of political organization in today's world. To be sure, the forces of global interdependence—economic interactions, communications links, environmental spillovers, and the like—are driving sovereign governments to cooperate with one another more than at any other time in history. No country in today's world can claim to be fully self-sufficient or capable of living in complete isolation from the rest of humanity, a reality that places the very concept of national sovereignty in doubt.[10] The everyday realities of international relationships have in some cases led to highly structured attempts to promote cooperation across state boundaries. The most far-reaching of these efforts thus far has been the **European Union**.

The European Union (EU) is a prime example of supranationalism at work. **Supranationalism** *refers to efforts on the part of two or more countries to limit their sovereignty by establishing new decision-making structures over and above*

their national governments. In the case of the EU, these supranational bodies have the authority to make laws that are binding on the member states.

THE EUROPEAN UNION

In 1957, six West European countries signed a historic agreement designed to expand their economic cooperation. Those countries were **France, West Germany, Italy,** and the three Benelux countries (**Belgium,** the **Netherlands,** and **Luxembourg**). At the start of the following year the terms of their agreement, known as the Treaty of Rome, took effect. The European Economic Community became a reality.

From the outset, West Europeans have been divided between those who have wanted to widen and accelerate the process of economic—and even political—integration and those who have wished to keep integration within stricter limits in order to preserve greater freedom of action for their own national governments. It took a long time before the community was enlarged to include new members. After arduous negotiations, **Britain, Ireland,** and **Denmark** finally joined in 1973. **Greece** joined in 1981; **Spain** and **Portugal** became members in 1986. In 1995, **Austria, Sweden,** and **Finland** brought the total number of members to fifteen. Several other countries have applied for membership, including Turkey, Malta, and the democratizing nations of Eastern Europe. In the process, the organization that began as the European Economic Community changed its name to the European Community in the 1970s and to the European Union (EU) in 1993.

Efforts to deepen economic integration also took a slow path. Only in 1986 did the organization's members agree in the Single European Act to establish a true *single market* over the course of 1990s. This step went beyond the elimination of tariff barriers to include a host of other measures aimed at eliminating impediments to the free movement of goods, services, money, and labor from one member country to another. The ultimate purpose of the single market is to make it easier for Europeans to do business or find work throughout the EU. Most Europeans realize that Britain, France, and the other EU members are individually too small to compete with the United States or Japan. Only by integrating their economies into one vast European market, with a combined population of more than 370 million people, will they be able to improve their international economic competitiveness and accelerate their own economic growth.

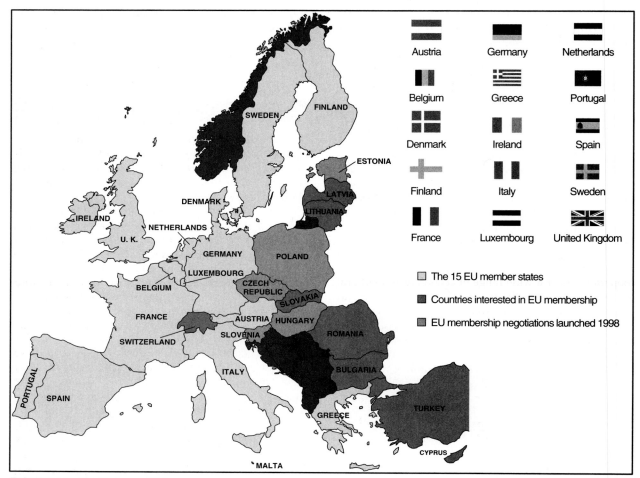

FIGURE 7.6   The European Union

To promote the Community's cooperative purposes, the Treaty of Rome established several supranational institutions, with legal powers over and above the authority of the individual member states. They include:

- The **European Commission.** Its task is to propose and implement common policies for the member countries. Each member state appoints one or more Commission members, who must take an oath to place "the general interest of the Community" ahead of the interests of any member country, including their own. Accordingly, Commission members are not allowed to take instructions from their respective governments. The **President of the Commission** is appointed by agreement of the member governments, but must act independently of them. The Commission now consists of twenty members. Since 1999 the Commission's president has been Romano Prodi of Italy.

- The **Council of Ministers.** This is the EU's main decision-making body. It consists of periodic meetings of cabinet ministers of the member states. If common agricultural matters are being discussed, the Council consists of the agriculture ministers. If environmental issues are being discussed, the Council consists of the member states' environmental ministers, and so on. The purpose of the Council is to ensure that the government of each member country has an input into the making of common EU policies.

- The **European Court of Justice.** This Court, consisting of judges appointed by the member states, is empowered to make rulings in cases involving member governments, private businesses, associations (such as labor unions), and individuals in matters concerning European Union law. In many instances, the laws of the Union take precedence over the national or local laws of the member states.

- The **European Parliament.** Originally set up as an Assembly appointed by the national parliaments of the member states, the European Parliament has been directly elected by the people of the member countries since 1979. It meets in Strasbourg, France, and now has 626 delegates. Its formal powers are still limited, but the EP won new respect in 1999 when it pressured the entire Commission and its president to resign over a corruption scandal.

Other community institutions include **Euratom,** established in 1957 to coordinate certain atomic energy policies, and the **European Council,** which consists of periodic meetings of the heads of government of the member states. Various other committees and agencies also exist. The **Common Agricultural Policy** is a fund that subsidizes farmers throughout the community. A *cohesion fund* provides assistance to the community's poorest members. An *Economic and Social Committee* promotes cooperation over a wide range of economic and cultural matters. In addition, there is a permanent EU bureaucracy consisting of about twenty-five thousand "Eurocrats," most of whom work in Brussels, the European Union's headquarters. The EU budget now exceeds $90 billion annually.

In November 1991, the leaders of the European Community governments met in the Dutch town of Maastricht to consider still higher levels of economic and political integration. On the basis of these discussions, they signed the Treaty on European Union in Maastricht three months later. The Treaty laid out the most ambitious goal ever agreed to by European leaders: the "economic and monetary union" of the member states (EMU). Among other things, it called for the following goals to be reached by the late 1990s:

- A common community currency, the euro, to replace the national currencies of the member states (such as the French franc and the German mark)
- A common European Central Bank, with enormous supranational authority to influence the economic policies of the member states
- Common defense and foreign policies
- A common European citizenship for the people of the member countries

The Maastricht Treaty created a firestorm of controversy throughout Western Europe. Its proponents hailed it as a long overdue leap toward a truly united Europe as well as a vital necessity to promote economic growth. But its detractors warned that the Treaty's provisions would place excessive powers in the hands of supranational institutions in Brussels. They charged that the ability of the separate member states to control their own economic and political destiny would be vastly curtailed. Some Treaty opponents insisted that a "democratic deficit" would ensue: as national governments in Paris, London, Athens, and other European capitals lose control over their own domestic and foreign policy choices to community-wide decision-making bodies, the citizens who vote for these governments will be increasingly deprived of their ability to have a say in the way they are governed in their own country. Furthermore, the stringent conditions set for economic and monetary union called for significant budget cuts by all the EU countries. These cuts proved very painful for many citizens and led to rising opposition to EMU throughout Western Europe.

Despite heated debates over the merits of the Treaty on European Union in virtually every member country, each one ratified the agreement by the end of 1993. In January 1999 the new common currency, the euro, was introduced for most banking transactions. Twelve of the fifteen members—all but Britain, Denmark, and Greece—took part in this initial phase of the new currency. In 2002, euro bills and coins will replace French francs, German marks, Italian lire, and all the other national currencies of those countries using the euro.

Conflict over the goals proclaimed in the Treaty remains intense. As full economic and monetary union comes about, the EU's supranational institutions will have enormous influence over business practices, tax laws, currency regulations, labor policies, social welfare benefits, and a host of other policy areas traditionally the exclusive prerogative of individual sovereign states. Already the EU's supranational bodies determine most of the business legislation of the member countries. It is quite likely that the debates over the implementation of these measures will continue well into the future.

Meanwhile, as the new century opens, the European Union is engaged in painstaking negotiations with a number of potential new members, mostly former communist states in Central and Eastern Europe. In the coming years the EU may consist of as many as twenty-six countries. As it deepens its economic and political integration among its current members, it is widening its membership to embrace almost all of Europe.

As these processes of deepening and widening integration go forward, one thing is certain: **there is a growing connection between the *internal* and *international* politics of every EU member country.** What goes on *inside* Britain, France, Germany, Italy, and the other EU countries cannot possibly be understood unless we take full account of their relations with their EU partners.[11]

Other regions of the world have also embarked on closer attempts at economic cooperation, though none has gone as far in the direction of supranational institutions as the European Union.[12] Meanwhile, even the EU countries have not entirely dispensed with their own national identities, as the following hypothesis-testing exercise shows.

HYPOTHESIS-TESTING EXERCISE: Are Europeans Developing a Common Supranational Identity?

These integrative processes have led some observers to forecast the eventual demise of the nation-state as an independent political entity. Sooner or later, they contend, the imperatives of transnational interdependence will dissolve inter-state borders and merge many of today's countries into multinational super-states, integrated under common governmental institutions and resting on the increasingly supranational consciousness of populations that once identified themselves solely in terms of their own separate nation. Is this happening in the European Union?

HYPOTHESIS

Let's hypothesize that supranational political and economic institutions and practices are creating a common European identity that is superseding national and regional identities among the people of the member states.

VARIABLES

In this hypothesis, the **dependent variable** is a common European identity. The **independent variable** is the EU's supranational institutions and practices.

EXPECTATIONS

If our hypothesis is correct, then we'd expect the evidence to show that, over time, the citizens of the EU countries have exhibited (1) increasingly positive evaluations of the European Union; (2) growing levels of trust of other member states; (3) a noticeable decline in their national and regional attachments; and (4) a correspondingly greater inclination to identify themselves as "European" rather than as French, Italian, Danish, and so on.

EVIDENCE

The evidence bearing on our hypothesis comes mainly from public opinion surveys conducted by the EU over the years and published in *Eurobarometer*. These surveys provide considerable confirmation for the first two expectations. Europeans in virtually all the EU states have expressed positive evaluations of EU membership at increasing rates since the 1970s. Those expressing a positive

attitude toward European integration rose on average from 63 percent in 1973 to 80 percent by 1990. And those who said that their country's membership in the European organization was a good thing rose from 56 percent to 68 percent in the same years. On the whole, people living in the region have also displayed rising levels of trust in other EU countries, though the results differ from one country to the next. (Trust in Britain on the part of people in other countries actually fell in the 1980s, probably due to Prime Minister Margaret Thatcher's hostility to European supranationalism.) Still, these rising levels of trust are remarkable, considering the brutal wars and national hatreds that ravaged Europe in the first half of the twentieth century.

The evidence does not corroborate our third expectation to any significant degree, however. Instead of diminishing their national or local attachments, people living in EU countries have continued to affirm these loyalties. A survey in 1990 revealed that 88 percent felt attached to their country, 87 percent to their region, 85 percent to their town or village, and only 47 percent to 48 percent to the European Community or to Europe as a whole. In 1999, national, regional, and local attachments remained much the same, though attachment to Europe rose somewhat, to an average of 56 percent. There is considerable variation within individual EU countries on the question of attachment to Europe, moreover. In Luxembourg, Sweden, and Denmark, more than 70 percent of the population felt attached to Europe in 1999, but in Greece only 41 percent expressed such attachments and in Britain the figure was the lowest of all at 37 percent. In ten EU countries, 58 percent of the population or more said they felt attached to Europe.

Similarly, the evidence contradicts our fourth expectation, that a common European identity is replacing separate national identities. A series of *Eurobarometer* surveys conducted in the 1990s asked people in the EU countries if they saw themselves in the near future as their "nationality only"; their "nationality and European"; "European and their nationality"; or "European only." The results were precisely the opposite of what our hypothesis would predict. The percentage of people who defined themselves in terms of their "nationality only" actually rose between 1994 and 1997 from 33 percent to 45 percent. The percentage of those who defined themselves in terms of their "nationality and European" fell from 46 percent to 40 percent perhaps indicating a declining willingness on the part of "nationalists" to combine their national loyalties with a European identity. Those who combine national and European identities and *placing Europe first* ("European and nationality") also declined, from 10 percent to 6 percent. Most telling of all, the percentage of people who saw themselves in the near future as "Europeans only" was small to begin with in 1994 (7 percent), and their share of the total fell further, to 5 percent by 1997.

CONCLUSIONS

The data bearing on our hypothesis are mixed. Evidence indicating rising approval ratings for the EU and rising trust of other member countries is largely consistent with our expectations. But the most important evidence, indicating growing levels of national identity and declining levels of European identity, completely contradicts our expected outcome. Although the percentage of people who expressed at least some degree of European identity, either exclusively or in combination with their nationality, stood at 63 percent in 1994, their ranks fell to 51 percent by 1997. We must therefore conclude that, on balance, the preponderance of the evidence is *inconsistent* with our hypothesis that European integration is reducing national identities and substituting for them an overarching European identity. Most people in the EU countries profess multiple identities, with national and local identities coexisting with attachment to Europe. It is noteworthy, however, that abiding national sentiments are sufficiently benign to allow the process of European integration to go forward; they bear no resemblance to the visceral hypernationalism that makes inter-state cooperation impossible.[13]

Thus, as our hypothesis-testing exercise illustrates, even in the European Union, the world's most ambitious attempt at forging supranational institutions among a multiplicity of countries, people in the member states still retain deep attachments to their own and even local national identities. From this reality we may infer that the nation-state (and in, some cases, regional governments) are still in favor as mechanisms for governing large masses of people who share a strong sense of common national or local identity, even as international and supranational integration moves forward.[14]

In the next chapter we'll begin examining what has lately become the most widely used method for the governance of nation-states: *democracy.*

KEY TERMS

(Underlined in the text)

Nation
Nation-state
Nationalism
Self-determination
Autonomy
Hypernationalism
Regionalism
Quebec
Yugoslavia
European Union
Supranationalism

NOTES

1. Karl Deutsch, *Nationalism and Social Communication,* 2d ed. (Cambridge, Mass.: MIT Press, 1966), 96–98.

2. Benedict Anderson, *Imagined Communities,* rev. ed. (London: Verso, 1991), 6, 7.

3. For a variety of scholarly views on nationalism, see John Hutchinson and Anthony D. Smith, eds., *Nationalism* (Oxford: Oxford University Press, 1994). Also, E. J. Hobsbawm, *Nations and Nationalism Since 1870* (New York: Cambridge University Press, 1970); Adrian Hastings, *The Construction of Nationhood* (New York: Cambridge University Press, 1997); Ernest Gellner, *Nationalism* (Washington Square, NY: New York University Press, 1997); and Lowell W. Barrington, "'Nation' and 'Nationalism': The Misuse of Key Concepts in Political Science," *PS: Political Science and Politics,* vol. xxx, no. 4 (December 1997), 712–716. On the development of nationalism in England, France, Russia, Germany, and the United States, see Liah Greenfeld, *Nationalism: Five Roads to Modernity* (Cambridge, Mass.: Harvard University Press, 1992).

4. Some scholars have likened these tactics to the activities of bandits or modern-day mobsters engaged in protection rackets. In exchange for supplying "protection" to the population against foreign invaders or local marauders, those in authority demand obedience, loyalty, and tribute (i.e., taxes) in return. See Charles Tilly, "War Making and State Making as Organized Crime," in Peter B. Evans, Dietrich Rueschemeyer, and Theda Skocpol, eds., *Bringing the State Back In* (Cambridge, England: Cambridge University Press, 1985), 169–91; Mancur Olson, "Dictatorship, Democracy, and Development," *American Political Science Review* 87, no. 3 (September 1993): 567–76; and Charles Tilly, ed., *The Formation of National States in Western Europe* (Princeton, N.J.: Princeton University Press, 1975).

5. Cited by Walker Connor in Hutchinson and Smith, *Nationalism,* 39.

6. *Freedom in the World 1998–1999* (New York: Freedom House, 1999), 11.

7. Desmond Morton, *A Short History of Canada,* 2d rev. ed. (Toronto: McClelland and Stewart, 1994); Robert

Rothwell, *Canada and Quebec: One Country, Two Histories*, rev. ed. (Vancouver, B.C.: UBC Press, 1998); and Ronald G. Landes, *The Canadian Polity: A Comparative Introduction*, 4th ed. (Scarborough, Ontario: Prentice Hall Canada, 1995).

8. Aleksa Djilas, "A Profile of Slobodan Milosevic," *Foreign Affairs* 72, no. 3 (summer 1993): 81–96; Dusko Doder and Louise Branson, *Milosevic: Portrait of a Tyrant* (New York: Simon and Schuster, 1999).

9. On the history of Yugoslavia before its breakup, see Fred Singleton, *Twentieth Century Yugoslavia* (New York: Columbia University Press, 1976); Ivo Banac, *The National Question in Yugoslavia* (Ithaca, N.Y.: Cornell University Press, 1984); Jaspar Ridley, *Tito* (London: Constable, 1994); Richard West, *Tito and the Rise and Fall of Yugoslavia* (New York: Carroll and Graf, 1995). On the dissolution process, see Misha Glenny, *The Fall of Yugoslavia* (New York: Penguin, 1992); Susan L. Woodward, *Balkan Tragedy* (Washington, D.C.: Brookings Institution, 1995); Laura Silber and Allan Little, *The Death of Yugoslavia* (New York: Penguin, 1995); Noel Malcolm, *Bosnia: A Short History* (New York: Knopf, 1996), and *Kosovo: A Short History* (New York: New York University Press, 1998); Richard Holbrooke, *To End a War* (New York: Random House, 1998).

10. Stephen D. Krasner, *Sovereignty: Organized Hypocrisy* (Princeton, NJ: Princeton University Press, 1999).

11. For an overview of the history and structure of the EU, see Desmond Dinan, *Ever Closer Union*, 2d ed. (Boulder, Colo.: Lynne Rienner, 1999); also Neill Nugent, *The Government and Politics of the European Union*, 3d ed. (Durham, N.C.: Duke University Press, 1994); John Van Oudenaren, *Uniting Europe* (Lanham, MD: Rowman and Littlefield 2000).

12. Examples of regional trading groups include the North Atlantic Free Trade Agreement (NAFTA), concluded in 1992 among the United States, Canada, and Mexico; the Common Market of the Southern Cone, or Mercosur, consisting of Argentina, Brazil, Paraguay, and Uruguay (with Chile as an associate member); the Central American Common Market (Costa Rica, El Salvador, Guatemala, Honduras, Nicaragua); the Caribbean Community and Common Market (CARICOM), with fourteen members; the Asia Pacific Economic Cooperation (APEC) organization, with nineteen members; the Association of Southeast Asian Nations (ASEAN), with nine members; the twenty-member Common Market for Eastern and Southern Africa; the sixteen-member Economic Community of West African States; and the twelve-member Southern African Development Community.

13. *Eurobarometer* is published periodically by the European Commission, Brussels. See, in particular, *Trends 1974–1993* (published in May 1994), and numbers 40 (December 1993), 41 (July 1994), 42 (spring 1995), and 51 (spring 1999). See also Mattei Dogan, "The Decline of Nationalism Within Western Europe," *Comparative Politics*, April 1994, 281–303; Richard Eichenberg and Russel J. Dalton, "Europeans and the European Community: the Dynamics of Public Support for European Integration," *International Organization* 47, no. 4 (autumn 1993), 507–34; and Gulnaz Sharafutdinova, "The Evolution of a Common European Identity," unpublished manuscript, 1995.

14. For differing views on the decline of the nation-state, see the special issue of *Daedalus* entitled, "What Future for the State?" 124, no. 2 (spring 1995). Also Kenichi Ohmae, *The End of the Nation State* (New York: Free Press, 1995); Jean-Marie Guehenno, *The End of the Nation-State*, trans. by Victoria Elliott (Minneapolis: University of Minnesota Press, 1995); and "The Nation-State Is Dead. Long Live the Nation-State," *The Economist*, December 23, 1995, 15–16.

CHAPTER 8

DEMOCRACY: WHAT IS IT?

Thus far we have talked about democracy quite a bit without providing more than a rudimentary definition of the term. In chapter 2 we put it this way:

> The essential idea of **democracy** is that the people have the right to determine who governs them. In most cases they elect the principal governing officials and hold them accountable for their actions. Democracies also impose legal limits on the government's authority by guaranteeing certain rights and freedoms to their citizens.

As a brief definition, this conceptualization of democracy captures several of the core notions most often associated with democracy: *legitimacy* based on popular determination; *elected governments; accountability; limited government;* and guaranteed *civil rights* and *freedoms*. Like many dictionary-style definitions, however, this one oversimplifies a highly complex and multifaceted phenomenon. For one thing, it fails to indicate how these various components of democracy actually work or interact. It also fails to tell us whether some of these constituent elements of democracy are more important than others. And some critics would assert that it leaves out certain things they would regard as indispensable to democracy, such as economic equality or fairness.

In actual fact democracy can take a variety of forms. It can mean different things to different people. For some theorists of democracy, representation based on free, fair, competitive elections

is the main defining principle of democratic governance. Most theorists would probably agree that a country with these features at least meets the minimum requirements of an *electoral democracy*. But many students of democratic theory would add that electoral rights, while vitally important, are by no means sufficient to establish a democracy worthy of the name. In their view, democracy requires certain legally protected rights and liberties for the population. Without such things as freedom of speech, freedom of assembly, freedom of religion, and other basic liberties that the government must not infringe, elections are meaningless. Indeed these rights must be secure against the whims of the electorate: *they must not be removable by popular vote.* If a majority of the population should turn against these fundamental rights and liberties or deny them to certain elements of the population, democracy itself is diminished, according to this view.

A particularly controversial bone of contention centers on the proper role of the state. Some people insist that democracy necessitates strictly limited government. The main purpose of democracy, they contend, is to maximize individual freedom. People should therefore be as free as possible from governmental intrusion in their personal lives, social relationships, and economic undertakings. An intrusive state with broad powers of intervention is undemocratic, in this view, because it limits the citizenry's ability to control its own destiny. By contrast, others maintain that democracy necessitates certain fundamental economic equalities and social rights for the entire population, such as equality of opportunity or the right to education and medical care. In this view, any society built on glaring social inequalities is inherently undemocratic, especially if reasonable opportunities to surmount these disparities are not made available to everyone on an equal, or at least equitable, basis. Proponents of these ideas would argue that a strong interventionist state may therefore be necessary to make sure that all citizens have a fair chance to live a decent life, irrespective of their economic or social background.

We could add quite a few more contending arguments about what is, or is not, a democracy. If we want to have a comprehensive and realistic conception of what democracy signifies, therefore, we must begin by acknowledging that *no single definition of democracy suffices.* Several different definitions of democracy are possible, and we must take account of them. Democracy is not a fixed thing that comes in only one size and shape. As we shall see, there are different aspects of democracy and there can be different degrees of democracy.

Consequently, this chapter will not confine itself to just one concept of democracy or insist upon some notion of the "right" definition of the term. Instead we'll expose you to a variety of definitions and let you make up your own mind about what democracy "really" means. The next chapter will examine various institutional forms of democracy, and chapter 10 will present a number of hypotheses about what it takes to build and sustain a democracy.

In addition to provoking you to think for yourself about how democracy ought to be defined, the multidefinitional approach of the present chapter also seeks to enhance your understanding of democracy in empirical terms. As opinion surveys and other data repeatedly reveal, people around the world have different conceptions of what democracy means. When asked to define the term, a typical American may conjure up images of election campaigns and voting booths, but a typical Russian may define democracy mainly in terms of prosperity and relative economic equality. For a

Chinese student, democracy may above all mean freedom of speech or safeguards against arbitrary arrest; for a Japanese, it may mean more power for elected officials and less for the unelected bureaucracy. For a black South African, democracy may mean the absence of white domination; for an Italian, it may mean a system of government that is free of political corruption. To be sure, people in all countries may agree that democracy entails a combination of such things as voting rights, economic opportunity, free speech, parliamentary lawmaking, and the absence of racial discrimination and official corruption. Even so, people will often differ about what democracy *primarily* means to them, depending on the political circumstances under which they live. As students of comparative politics, we must be very sensitive to the various ways people conceive of democracy.

FOUR FACES OF DEMOCRACY

One way of sharpening our appreciation of democracy is to think about it in terms of four aspects or *faces*:

Face I is the concept of **popular sovereignty.** This is the notion that the people have the right to govern themselves. In implementing this right they either exercise control of governmental authority directly or they establish effective mechanisms for holding their government formally accountable to them. Popular sovereignty flatly contradicts the defining feature of authoritarianism, which is that the state rules over the people.

Face II centers on **rights and liberties.** It consists of certain basic rights and freedoms that must be guaranteed by law to the citizenry. They may not be taken away either by the state acting on its own or even by the people exercising their sovereign rights of majority rule.

Face III consists of core **democratic values.** Tolerance, fairness, and compromise are among the most important of these values.

Face IV is the concept of **economic democracy.** It establishes various criteria of fairness or equality as social and economic components of democracy.

Each of these four faces can take a variety of forms. Popular sovereignty can be exercised either directly, through the active exercise of governmental authority by the people themselves, or indirectly, through the people's elected representatives. The list of guaranteed civil rights and liberties can be a short one or a long one. Democratic values can be moral norms that are informally shared by the population or they can be legally binding social obligations. Economic democracy can range from a vague commitment to equity of opportunity to the systematic distribution of a country's wealth among the population on a relatively equal basis. As we might expect, people will differ not only over how to define popular sovereignty or the other three faces, but also over the practical question of how to put these various aspects of democracy into practice most effectively.

In view of these multiple—and conflicting— conceptualizations of democracy, we might legitimately wonder at this point if any definition of the term is possible on the basis of elements that all democracies universally share. Fortunately, there do exist several fundamental principles that most theorists and political activists in today's world would probably agree are absolutely essential for a system of government to be considered democratic. *These three basic principles of democracy are (1) the rule of law, (2) inclusion, and (3) equality.*

The rule of law *is the principle that the power of the state must be limited by law and that no one is above the law.*

Stated simply, the rule of law means that those who govern including the most powerful figures in the government, shall be under the law rather than above the law. It also means that the powers of government to make and enforce laws shall be limited by legal restraints as opposed to being unlimited in the absence of such restraints.

These notions are captured in the famous statement by one of the founding fathers who described the American system as "a government of laws, not of men." The rule of law is the fundamental bedrock upon which democratic government rests. It requires the state to spell out the limitations to its authority in official documents, such as a written constitution, or in some other explicit

form, such as legislation, court rulings, or publicly acknowledged understandings of what the law is. Without the rule of law, power can be wielded indiscriminately by governing officials, unchecked by any limits.

For all its conceptual simplicity, the rule of law has been a scarce commodity in humankind's political history. It emerged gradually in Britain over the course of several centuries, slowly enmeshing successive monarchs in legal limitations imposed by Parliament and ultimately eventuating in a mass electoral democracy in the twentieth century. The rule of law was the foundation stone of the U.S. constitutional system from the earliest days of the Republic. Aside from Britain and the United States, however, until the second half of the twentieth century the rule of law in most countries was conspicuous mainly by its absence.

Prior to World War II only a handful of countries, mainly in Western Europe, managed to establish governments based on the rule of law. Most of them failed to last very long, succumbing to the authoritarian forces of unconstrained state power. Fascism destroyed democracy in Italy and Germany, and Nazi aggression destroyed it in France. Only after the war did these countries succeed in stabilizing democratic governance based on the rule of law. Japan established its first real democratic government based on the rule of law under the guidance of the American Occupation authorities in the years following its surrender in 1945. Even today, a number of countries struggling to establish democratic regimes for the first time in their history (such as Russia) are simultaneously discovering the principle of the rule of law for the very first time. And countries that are seeking to reestablish democracy after having tried it unsuccessfully in the past (such as Argentina, Brazil, and the Philippines) are having to rediscover the rule of law with a view to anchoring their governing institutions and political practices in it more firmly than ever before.

The effort is not an easy one. Political leaders who publicly commit themselves to the rule of law and who fully understand what it entails cannot always be counted on to observe the limitations it imposes. Violations of the civil rights of the population, illegal activities aimed at thwarting political opponents, and all sorts of corrupt practices are perpetrated by elected officials or their appointees with alarming frequency, even in countries where the rule of law has been long established. Unless the rule of law is enshrined as the first principle of government, democracy cannot exist. But unless it is routinely observed by governing officials, democracy may not survive.

> **Inclusion** *means that democratic rights and freedoms must be for everyone. They must not be denied to specifically targeted elements of the population, such as women or minority groups.*

In other words, if a country has such democratic procedures as the right to vote, the right to stand for elective office, the right to free speech, and other explicitly defined political rights, these rights must not be denied or limited on a discriminatory basis to particular segments of the population. *All* must be included; otherwise, the political system can be considered only partially democratic at best. Even then, some people may regard a partial democracy as no democracy at all.

Inclusion also means that all the main social groups that comprise the population—ethnic groups, religious groups, social classes, and so on—should have reason to feel that they are better off under a democracy than under some nondemocratic form of government. Every group should have a realistic chance to gain something from abiding by democratic rules and procedures. None should be systematically excluded from ever acquiring any advantages through the democratic process. If the "rules of the game" in a democracy are rigged against specific social groups or consistently work to some group's disadvantage, it is questionable whether such a system may legitimately be considered a democracy. Such an outcome might occur if democratic election procedures result in the permanent "tyranny of the majority" over minorities, for example.

Actually, just about every country that has ever been considered a democracy has either significantly reduced or completely denied certain political rights to targeted elements of the population. In some cases the reasons for these discriminatory limitations are generally regarded as reasonable or acceptable. No democracy gives children the right to vote, for example, and some deny voting rights or other political rights to felons and resident foreigners. In other circumstances, however, overt political discrimination against singled-out social groups may be so intentionally repressive as to place the country's democratic credentials in doubt. The denial of voting rights or other political rights to women, to non-property-owning classes, or to racial and religious minorities inevitably raises serious questions about how democratic such a political system really is. The definition of citizenship itself may be deliberately manipulated so as to disenfranchise certain segments of the population unfairly, as recent experiences in the Baltic states demonstrate.

WHO IS A CITIZEN?
Voting Rights in the Baltic States

Three countries bordering the Baltic Sea—**Estonia, Latvia,** and **Lithuania**—were independent states between 1918 and 1940. On August 23, 1939, slightly more than a week before the start of World War II in Europe, Nazi Germany concluded a secret pact with the Soviet Union pledging to hand over all three countries to the Soviet regime. Shortly after the German army overran Eastern Europe, the USSR in accordance with the agreement annexed the Baltic states in 1940, immediately imposing harsh communist rule on their populations. Hitler's willingness to permit Soviet domination over the area was purely tactical, however. He needed Moscow's temporary forbearance while he consolidated Nazi control over the rest of continental Europe. By the early summer of 1941 the Nazis were ready to double-cross Stalin and invade the Soviet Union. As German troops surged eastward they quickly wrested the Baltic region back from the Soviets. For the next several years the three Baltic nations were exposed to the successive horrors of the Nazi occupation and fierce Soviet efforts to retake them. In 1944 the Soviets finally succeeded in pushing the German army out of the USSR. In the process they reasserted sovereignty over their recent Baltic acquisitions. The United States never recognized the legality of the Soviet annexations of the Baltic states, but there was little it could do about the situation.

In August 1991, with communist authority in disarray at the highest levels of the Soviet government, Estonia, Latvia, and Lithuania formally declared their independence from the USSR. In all three states the rebirth of national sovereignty was accompanied by democracy. With widespread public support, democratic constitutions were adopted and a multiparty system quickly

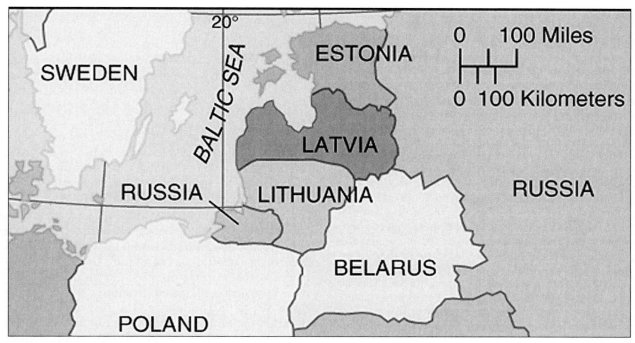

FIGURE 8.1 The Baltic States

supplanted communism's one-party rule. Not everyone who lived in these countries greeted these developments with joy, however. Especially in Estonia and Latvia, the installation of democratic rights and freedoms coincided with blatant attempts by the ethnic majority to exclude minorities from the democratic process.

When the USSR annexed the Baltic states in 1940, ethnic Estonians comprised 88 percent of Estonia's population and ethnic Latvians constituted 77 percent of the population of Latvia. During the subsequent decades of Soviet rule, large numbers of ethnic Russians moved into these republics. Many were drawn there by the lure of the highest living standards in the Soviet Union; others were military personnel assigned to the region by Soviet defense authorities. By 1991, only 61 percent of Estonia's population of 1.6 million consisted of ethnic Estonians. The rest were ethnic minorities, with Russians comprising 30 percent of the total population. Latvia's population of about 2.5 million became even more diverse, with ethnic Latvians constituting a mere 52 percent of the total and Russians comprising 34 percent. In fact, Latvians today constitute a minority in the country's largest cities. Lithuania's population of 3.7 million in the early 1990s was less heterogeneous but still ethnically mixed, with ethnic Lithuanians representing 80 percent of the total, ethnic Russians 9 percent, and other ethnic groups such

as Ukrainians and Belarusans constituting the remainder. In all three of these countries, most Russians could not speak the language of the ethnic majority. Their presence was sharply resented by large segments of the native ethnic majority because it provided a constant reminder of their domination at the hands of the predominantly Russian leadership of the Soviet Union.

In 1992 Estonia instituted a new citizenship law similar to the one that had been in effect in 1938, two years before annexation by the USSR. The new law denied full citizenship to nearly all of the country's 600,000 ethnic Russians, effectively denying them the right to vote and other vital democratic privileges. In 1993 the Estonian parliament passed a Law on Aliens that classified people who had assumed residency in Estonia after 1940 and their descendants as "aliens" rather than as citizens. Persons so designated were required to apply for special status as "permanent residents," but very few of them were allowed under the legislation to apply for citizenship.

Latvia followed a similar path. Regulations instituted by the Latvian parliament in 1991 granted full citizenship only to those who were citizens of Latvia prior to 1940 and their descendants. All others, including the sizable Russian minority, were not allowed to apply for citizenship unless they had lived in Latvia at least sixteen years, could demonstrate conversational ability in the Latvian language, and could meet various additional conditions. These guidelines disenfranchised some 700,000 people, nearly one-third of the country's voting-age population. Another law enacted in 1994 set a strict limit on the number of non-ethnic Latvians who could qualify for citizenship by 2000.

These efforts to deny voting rights and other perquisites of democratic citizenship to ethnic minorities met with sharp criticism by the governments of the United States and the members of the European Union. When confronted with the disapproval of the community of democratic nations, the governing authorities in Estonia and Latvia relaxed their initial restrictions on minority rights somewhat, but by no means entirely. By the end of the 1990s, the vast majority of Russians in Estonia and Latvia still had no citizenship rights and the process of becoming naturalized citizens remained difficult. Lithuania in 1992 extended citizenship to all people born there, including about 90 percent of all non-Lithuanian ethnic minorities. Nevertheless, Russians and other ethnic minority groups living there have repeatedly complained of cultural discrimination and other forms of intolerance on the part of the Lithuanian majority.

Equality *means that democratic rights and freedoms must be accorded to everyone on an equal basis. No group in society should have fewer democratic privileges than other groups.*

Whereas the principle of inclusiveness asserts that democratic rights and freedoms must be for *everyone*, the principle of equality asserts that these same rights and freedoms must be distributed to everyone *equally*. No group or segment of the population should get more rights or freedoms than others. This principle is especially applicable with respect to basic civil rights, such as the right to vote, the right to run for office, the right to free speech, and other rights that are directly related to the political relationship between the citizenry and the state. If the rules and practices of democracy are skewed in such as way as to deny the enjoyment of these civil rights to some segments of society *on an equal basis with everyone else*, democracy itself is diminished accordingly.

Thus if some members of society must meet higher voting qualifications than others, the distribution of civil rights is fundamentally unequal. (Until federal legislation was passed in the 1960s,

for example, African Americans in several states were required to pass much stiffer examinations than whites in order to qualify to vote.) Similarly, if the laws of the land are applied on a discriminatory basis, with some groups getting better treatment than others, the government violates the principle of "equal treatment under the law," a basic civil right in any true democracy.

The concept of equality is a complex one, however. It can take on different meanings in different contexts. To begin with, there is an important distinction to be made between the principles of *equality* and *equity*. **Equity** *means fairness.* It requires only that we accord people a reasonably fair chance to realize their ambitions and improve their well-being under the same laws that apply to everyone else. It does not require us to make sure that everyone starts out or ends up on the same social or economic plane or enjoys the same degree of political influence. The rich usually have greater social and political advantages than the poor, such as access to elite schools, superior medical care, and the "right connections." The principle of equity does not demand that we equalize wealth so that nobody is rich or poor; it simply insists that the poor be given a fair opportunity to improve their economic, social, or political welfare. Society can promote these goals by providing quality public education, medical care, legal assistance, and similar benefits to everyone at no cost, for example.

Equality, by contrast, is a more rigorous concept. It *implies that everyone should ultimately be exactly or approximately equal,* whether in terms of their political rights (e.g., the right to vote) or their economic and social conditions. If everyone were truly equal in socioeconomic terms, everyone would have approximately the same amount of wealth and there would be no class distinctions. Very often when people use the term "equality" they really mean "equity," and we should remain aware of the distinction.

While there is general agreement that democracies must grant their citizens *political* equality, there is continuing controversy over the question of *economic* equality. Some would argue that democracies should grant their citizens maximum freedom to pursue their economic fortunes with minimum government interference. If economic disparities result, creating different levels of wealth in society, so be it. Against this view, others would maintain that the equality of political rights must be accompanied by some form of equal social and economic rights. In this more egalitarian view, equal voting rights and other political rights, while necessary, are meaningless if certain groups are systematically excluded from enjoying various social advantages (such as access to education or decent housing) or economic opportunities (such as access to jobs or professional advancement) on a fair or equal basis with all other groups in society. Democracy, from this perspective, is not confined to equal political inclusion but requires social and economic inclusiveness on a relatively equal—or at least equitable—basis as well. We'll examine some of these controversies later in this chapter.

As we shall see, *all four faces of democracy are predicated on the notions of the rule of law, inclusion, and equality.*

Minimum and Maximum Forms of Democracy

As we have pointed out, all four faces of democracy come in different forms and degrees. In order to grasp these various possibilities we should think of each face as containing a *minimum* as well as a *maximum* variant. The minimum conception prescribes certain rudimentary criteria for defining and implementing each face of democracy. It can be argued that, in order to have a democracy at all, a country must meet certain minimum levels or standards of popular sovereignty, civil rights and liberties, democratic values, and economic democracy. Not everyone will agree with this proposition, to be sure, and there is ample room for debate about which criteria are necessary for democracy to exist. Our discussion of minimal forms of democracy, therefore, is intended mainly to spark your own thinking about democracy and provide you with a framework for organizing your ideas.

By the same token, our discussion of maximum conceptions of democracy is similarly aimed at stimulating your own understanding of what democracy is all about. Maximum conceptions widen the degree or extent of democracy in each face to the greatest feasible extent. In general, maximum forms of democracy may be viewed as desirable but *not absolutely necessary* for democracy to exist. But as our discussion points out, what some people may regard as maximum forms of democracy may be regarded by others as minimal forms of democracy and thus as essential to the very existence of democracy itself. Additional forms and gradations of democracy can also exist in each of the four faces of democracy, situated along a continuum in between these minimum and maximum variants. These distinctions will become clearer as we examine each face of democracy in turn.

Face I. Democracy as Popular Sovereignty

Popular sovereignty *is the idea that the people have the right to determine how they are governed.* The people themselves, in other words, are the source of the state's legitimacy; they are sovereign over their governing institutions and officials. They have the right to determine the type of governmental institutions they want, along with other aspects of their political system. They have the right to determine the actions and policies the government adopts as well as the right to hold their governing officials responsible for their actions. The notion of popular sovereignty is conveyed in such phrases as "government by consent of the governed" and Abraham Lincoln's famous characterization of democracy as "government of the people, by the people, and for the people."

So construed, popular sovereignty is an essential aspect of democracy. Without it, democracy would be impossible. The very word "democracy" derives from the Greek words *demos,* which means "the people," and *kratia,* which means "authority" or "rule." Taken literally, democracy means "rule by the people."

Popular sovereignty implies two key concepts: **participation** and **accountability.** If the people are sovereign, they have the right to participate in politics themselves. They also possess the right to hold those who govern them accountable for their actions. Moreover, the principle of the rule of law requires democracies to make sure that participation and accountability are guaranteed by the laws of the land.

But how do the people participate in political life? How do they exercise accountability? Over more than two thousand years the experiences of numerous democratic political systems and the ideas generated by democratic theorists have produced a number of different responses to these questions. We'll concentrate on two of them here: *representative democracy* and *direct democracy*.

Representative democracy may be regarded as a *minimum* form of popular sovereignty. It realizes the goals of citizen participation and governmental accountability largely through indirect methods, above all through elections. Without any public participation or accountability at all, it is generally agreed that popular sovereignty itself would not exist. For all its shortcomings, representative democracy at least fulfills certain minimal requirements of popular sovereignty.

Direct democracy constitutes the *maximum* form of popular sovereignty. In its most far-reaching variant, it would permit all adult citizens to participate *directly* in making authoritative political decisions for their community. In such a system, the people *are* the government; they govern themselves directly and not through representatives. Consequently they are accountable only to themselves for their own actions.

In between these extremes of representative and direct democracy, other modes of implementing popular sovereignty are also possible, usually involving mixtures of representative procedures and direct self-government.

Representative Democracy   In a representative democracy, *elections* are the principal mechanism by which the people exercise their sovereign rights to participate in politics and hold their chosen representatives in government accountable for their actions. In the modern world representative democracy is largely **electoral democracy.** The single most important form of the accountability of the main state officials in a democracy is their **removability.** Through elections and other procedures (such as impeachment), the chief governmental officials can be removed from power by the people's elected representatives.

In order to fulfill their task of ensuring citizen participation and accountability effectively, electoral procedures must meet certain basic criteria. They must be:

- *Meaningful:* The positions to be filled through the electoral process must be positions of serious gov-

ernmental power and responsibility. The people should have the opportunity to elect those officials most responsible for making laws and for appointing other senior-level state authorities.

- *Competitive:* There must be genuine competition for positions of elective office. At a minimum, there must be no laws or practices that might preclude competition or guarantee that candidates run unopposed. Competition allows the public to choose between alternative political orientations and individuals.

- *Free:* Voters must have the freedom to vote as they see fit. They must not be subjected to any forms of coercion or intimidation by state authorities or by individuals or organizations outside the state.

- *Secret:* To protect the confidentiality of the voters' choices, elections must be held by secret ballot. The secret ballot is known as the *Australian ballot.*[1]

- *Fair:* The processes used for selecting candidates, conducting elections, and counting the votes must be untainted by favoritism, discrimination, fraud, or any other form of unfairness to the participants or to the population as a whole.

- *Frequent:* Elections must be held at regular intervals. The shorter the interval between elections, the greater the voters' opportunity to participate in politics and exercise their rights of accountability.

- *Inclusive:* All adults above a fairly young age (say, eighteen) must have the right to vote, with exceptions kept to a reasonable minimum.

- *Equal:* Voting rights should be distributed equally to individuals in accordance with the principle of "one person, one vote."

Participation in Representative Democracies   In addition to voting in elections, people can take part in electoral politics by taking an active role in a political party or by working for a candidate at election time. Very few people actually avail themselves of these opportunities, however. Aside from these activities, which obviously fall short of direct participation in the government's actual decision-making processes, the other main method by which citizens in representative democracies can take part in the political process is by publicly expressing their opinions on issues facing their community. Most modern democracies provide a number of opportunities for the free and open expression of public opinion, ranging from newspapers and other printed material to radio and TV talk shows, the Internet, and the like. In virtually all democracies, people can write their elected representatives to let them know where they stand on the issues, speak up at community meetings or other forums at which ordinary citizens have a chance to address public officials, and form organizations of like-minded citizens to publicize their cause. And they can respond to public opinion polls and attitude surveys conducted by polling organizations.

These and other mechanisms of public expression are all aimed at transmitting to the people's representatives in government the opinions, attitudes, demands, and complaints of the citizenry. Like the act of voting, their impact on the decisions taken by government officials is indirect: the people can express their will but they cannot make authoritative decisions. Nevertheless, most politicians, especially those who are elected to office, pay close attention to public attitudes and ignore them at their peril. The methods available to the citizens of a representative democracy for voicing their opinions and demands serve, however indirectly, the important function of **agenda setting**. They give the population a chance to participate in formulating the agenda of issues and priorities that government officials will be expected to address when drafting legislation or making official decisions. In the process, they permit the citizenry to have an input into the political decision-making process.[2]

Popular sovereignty thus requires **political openness** and **transparency.** To the greatest possible extent, state officials must share information with the general population regarding the decisions they make. While most advocates of democracy would concede that some decisions must be taken in secret in the interests of public safety or national security, it is generally accepted that the sphere of government secretiveness in a democracy should be kept as narrow as possible while the sphere of *open, transparent government* should be spread as wide as possible. State officials who violate this vitally important requirement by engaging in illegal or unethical acts of secret or deceitful conduct, in contravention of the public's

right to know what their representatives are doing, strike a harsh blow against the rule of law and thus against democracy itself. Democracies must therefore take effective measures to safeguard the principle of transparency and ensure its effective observance. To this end most representative democracies give their parliaments, judicial organs, or other authoritative agencies specific investigatory powers that can be used to keep a watchful eye on all elements of the government and probe allegations of wrongdoing.

By the same token, openness requires the free flow of information. Accordingly, freedom of the press and freedom of access to information bearing on governmental decisions are fundamental elements of popular sovereignty. The availability of *multiple sources of information,* such as newspapers, journals, and broadcast media that permit the diffusion of different political viewpoints and the gathering of all sorts of political information, is one of the distinguishing hallmarks of a democracy. Similarly, private polling organizations must have the right to survey public opinion and publish the results without interference by the state.

Political openness also means that people must have the freedom to express themselves openly and to criticize their government without fear of retribution. Censorship and the deliberate spread of misinformation are typical governing techniques of authoritarian regimes; they have no place in a democracy.

Accountability in Representative Democracies Just as elections are the principal method of political participation in representative democracies, they also provide the chief mechanism for ensuring the government's accountability to the people. The essence of representative democracy lies in the *delegation of governmental power and responsibility* to a small number of people by the citizenry as a whole. In every democracy in the contemporary world, the actual work of government is carried on by an extremely small portion of the country's population. At any given time only a minority of the national population is engaged in full-time government work in democracies like the United States, Canada, Japan, and the nations of Western Europe.[3] A much smaller minority consists of elected officials and high-level unelected bureaucrats with significant decision-making responsibilities. Because they constitute such a tiny portion of the population, the people who occupy positions of governmental authority constitute an *elite.*

Representative democracies, in other words, are governed by political elites. As a practical necessity these governing elites enjoy a considerable amount of discretion when it comes to managing the community's affairs. Elections provide the main mechanism by which the population can hold these powerful governing authorities accountable and influence their decisions, but there are other methods as well. In some cases, as in various states and local jurisdictions in the United States, citizens incensed at elected incumbents have the right to petition for a *recall* vote before the expiration of the politician's term in office. If the individual in question loses this special election, he or she must step down.

Another institution that seeks to protect the public interest against state authority is the position of *ombudsman.* As initially instituted in Scandinavia and New Zealand, the ombudsman is a state official, usually appointed by the legislature, whose job is to investigate citizen complaints against government agencies. In many cases these complaints involve little more than instances of human error or ineptitude by bureaucratic personnel. In others, however, they point to deliberate malfeasance or abuses of power by state officials.[4]

How Democratic Is Representative Democracy? In view of the enormous decision-making power state officials possess in representative democracies, can such a political system really be considered democratic? To what extent can it be regarded as "government of the people, by the people, and for the people"?

One of the most persuasive answers to these questions was provided by **Joseph Schumpeter** (1883–1950), an Austrian-born economist and political theorist who taught at Harvard University. In 1942 he published *Capitalism, Socialism, and Democracy,* a landmark work that took issue with eighteenth- and nineteenth-century notions of representative democracy and redefined the concept in more realistic terms. Whereas classical concepts of representation had emphasized the power of the people over their elected representatives, who

are elected precisely in order to carry out the popular will, Schumpeter's concept reversed this order of primacy by emphasizing the power of political leaders to make authoritative decisions and by downplaying the significance of the popular will. In fact, Schumpeter noted, modern democracies confer enormous decision-making authority on governing elites while limiting the role of the people to participating in periodic elections. In Schumpeter's view, representative democracy as it actually exists is not "government *by* the people" but rather "government *chosen by* the people." The people have the right to elect their leaders, to be sure; but once elected, the leaders have a considerable amount of latitude to formulate, decide, and implement the laws through which the people are governed.[5]

Representative democracy, in short, can be characterized as **democratic elitism.** It involves a complicated mixture of popular sovereignty and government by elites.

Robert Dahl, one of the foremost theorists of modern democracy, devised the term *"polyarchy"* to capture these realities. Whereas democracy means "rule by the people," **polyarchy** *literally means "rule by the many."* Dahl uses the term as a synonym for modern democracy as it emerged in the nineteenth century and developed in the twentieth century. Polyarchies are large-scale democracies, governing entire countries. By contrast, democracy in its literal sense of "rule by the people" is possible only in much smaller political communities, such as small towns or ancient Greek city-states, where the people themselves have an opportunity to operate the government directly or closely oversee the actions of their designated leaders. Dahl's notion of "rule by the many" recognizes that large modern democracies combine elite decision making with mass participation, meaningful competition for power, and the accountability of the governing elites to the governed.[6]

Direct Democracy   In contrast to representative democracy, direct democracy is characterized by the direct exercise of governmental power by the people themselves. It is "government *by* the people" in its most literal sense. Real-world examples of direct democracies are exceedingly rare. In the ancient world a few Greek city-states, most notably Athens, had their own variants of this form of government. During the peak years of Athenian democracy, from roughly 500 to 300 B.C., citizens had the right to participate in public debates on the issues facing the city and to vote on alternative proposals for dealing with them. In effect, the citizens were the legislature. The political executive was largely an administrative body charged with implementing the citizenry's wishes; it had little authority to undertake major policy initiatives on its own, and its officials were usually chosen from among the qualified citizenry by lot for a one-year term.[7] The city-state of Geneva in the eighteenth century provided another version of direct democracy.

Neither of these examples of classical direct democracy met very high standards of inclusion or equality, however. Both ancient Athens and eighteenth-century Geneva denied citizenship rights to women. Certain categories of males were also excluded. Slaves, foreign-born "aliens," and men who did not meet certain property-owning qualifications were not included in the self-governing procedures of Athens. It is estimated that only about two in five adult Athenian males enjoyed the rights of citizenship. Geneva similarly imposed property requirements for citizenship. Moreover, Geneva's democracy conferred considerable decision-making powers on the elites who operated the political executive on a day-to-day basis. The right to participate in direct democratic procedures was only slightly more open in town meetings in the United States, a form of direct democracy prevalent in nineteenth-century New England.[8]

Even with such limited participatory rights, these direct democracies of the past could not have functioned except on a very small scale. The population of Athens probably included between twenty-five thousand and forty thousand adult males who were classified as citizens during the fifth century B.C. On any given occasion, perhaps a few thousand actually took part in the deliberative assemblies that decided the city-state's laws and policies. Geneva in 1760 had a population of approximately twenty-five thousand; only about fifteen hundred males were qualified to take part in the town's general assembly.[9]

Though direct democracies do not exist in today's world, there still exist several possibilities for expanding the immediacy of citizen participation in authoritative decision making in between the extremes of representative democracy and direct democracy. One is **plebiscitary democracy,** a concept that has been in use for about a century. The other is a much newer possibility, one that is evolving before our very eyes thanks to the latest developments in communications technology. Let's call it **techno-democracy.** Both forms of popular participation have advantages as well as problems.

Plebiscitary Democracy The term "plebiscitary" derives from the Latin word *plebs,* which referred to the common people of ancient Rome as opposed to the patrician elite. Over the course of the twentieth century, a number of representative democracies have provided their citizens the opportunity to vote on specific policy questions in a *referendum* (or *plebiscite*). In the United States, referendums are quite common at state and local levels of government, where voters are often asked to approve or reject such things as local tax increases or bond issues for public expenditures on roads, school construction, and the like. Among the more controversial state-level referendums held in the 1990s, Maryland held one on gun control, Oregon had one on gay rights, and California held one on the question of granting benefits to aliens. Referendums have not been employed at the federal level in the United States, however. In Canada, several referendums have been held in Quebec on the issue of that province's possible secession. Several West European countries have held referendums on membership in the European Union and other issues. A number of other democracies have also held nationwide referendums on various questions.

In some cases the results of a referendum are binding on government officials, in which instance the people are engaging in a form of direct democracy. In other cases the results are merely a popular recommendation with no binding force on official decision makers. In either case, referendums and plebiscites constitute an electoral mechanism located in between representative democracy and full-scale direct democracy.

Techno-Democracy   Today's exciting advances in communications technologies provide unprecedented opportunities for enhancing the citizenry's abilities to transmit their wishes to their representatives directly and instantaneously. Telephone call-ins, fax transmissions, websites, e-mail, chat rooms, and similar devices open up the extraordinary possibility of creating a kind of high-tech semi-direct democracy within today's representative polyarchies. Just consider the following scenario.

TECHNO-DEMOCRACY

At 9:00 A.M. you turn your TV set to C-SPAN, the cable channel that broadcasts live from the U.S. Congress. On your screen is a schedule of the bills that are expected to come up for a floor vote today. One of them, concerning government-sponsored student loans, is of particular interest to you. For the last several weeks you've been following the course of this bill, reading newspaper articles on it and occasionally tuning in to C-SPAN's coverage of committee hearings and floor debate in the House and Senate. A final vote is scheduled in the House of Representatives at 4:00 P.M. Since you expect to be tied up all day in class and at your job, you won't be able to watch the final proceedings or the vote itself. But your screen indicates that you have until 12:00 noon to contact the member of Congress who represents your district, Representitive James "Biff" Peopleman, to indicate whether you support or oppose the bill. Every fifteen minutes C-SPAN displays the main points of the bill that will be voted on later in the day. It also displays a web page you can access in order to get the bill's full text, along with all Congressional discussion on it as recorded in the *Congressional Record.*

At frequent intervals, the screen also displays a telephone number you can call to find out your representative's Voter Opinion Number. Every member of Congress has a toll-free telephone number, a fax number, and an e-mail address specifically designed to record incoming popular votes on Congressional bills. As a frequent caller, you know Representative Peopleman's toll-free number by heart. You also know from perusing his home page on the Web that Peopleman does not support the bill in its present form. Just before heading off to class, you dial the toll-free number. A recorded message instructs you to press in your Social Security number. After a few seconds, the voice announces that your right to vote has been confirmed and reminds you that the system will record only one phone-vote per registered voter on any

individual bill. The recorded speaker then presents you with a menu of bills that are due to come up for a House vote over the next several days. "If you would like to vote on HR 23170, the School Loan Bill, press 3 now," the speaker says. After pressing 3, you are instructed to press 1 if you favor the School Loan Bill, 2 if you oppose it. After you've punched in your choice, the ever-cheerful voice confirms your selection, offers you a chance to change it, then thanks you on Biff Peopleman's behalf.

At approximately 12:30 a member of Representative Peopleman's staff scans her computer and learns that 4,675 people in his district have communicated their support for the School Loan Bill, while 1,520 have "voted" against it. Some constituents have voted by phone; others have contacted the Congressman's office by fax or e-mail. (Once again, only one vote per individual is recorded.) "I guess that settles it," the Congressman declares on hearing the news. "While I still have my reservations about the present bill, the people have spoken and Peopleman listens. I'm voting for it."

Far-fetched? As is generally known, the technology to put such a system of direct-dial democracy into operation is already available. Over the course of the 1990s, the number of people who contacted their representatives' offices by telephone, fax, and e-mail in the United States rose dramatically. But no country has yet adopted a citizen vote-in procedure exactly as we've just described it. It is still usually possible, for example, for a single individual to deluge his or her representative's office with an unlimited number of phone calls, letters, faxes, and the like on a single legislative item, a reality that flatly contradicts the principle of "one person, one vote." But assuming that a vote-recording system similar to the one we've described here is technologically feasible, the normative question arises as to whether democracies *should* institute such a system. Should the laws of modern polyarchies be rewritten to *compel* our elected representatives to vote on bills exactly in accordance with the wishes of the majority in their respective districts, as recorded in the citizen-voting procedures we've described? Or should our representatives still be allowed to vote on bills as they see fit, irrespective of what the "electronic majority" wants on any given piece of legislation?

As so often happens in political life, political institutions must adapt themselves to the latest in-

FIGURE 8.2   Continuum of Popular Sovereignty

Representative democracy	Plebiscitary democracy	Techno-democracy	Direct democracy
Minimum			Maximum

novations in science and technology. Opportunities for expanding popular sovereignty that were unimaginable only a few years ago are rapidly becoming a part of our everyday world. Inevitably, they confront us with the exciting but difficult task of defining anew the very meaning of democracy itself.[10]

Face II. Democracy as Rights and Liberties

We hold these truths to be self-evident, that all men are created equal, that they are endowed by their Creator with certain unalienable rights, that among these are life, liberty, and the pursuit of happiness.

—*Declaration of Independence*
July 4, 1776

Thomas Jefferson's memorable words captured the spirit of the American revolution. For the founding fathers of the United States, the single most important purpose of government was to guarantee certain individual rights and liberties, safeguarding the citizenry against potential tyranny through the rule of law. To be sure, the founders honored these lofty ideals more in the breach than in actual practice. Jefferson, George Washington, James Madison, and other architects of the U.S. system of government were slaveowners. They also favored a limited suffrage, reserving the "consent of the governed" to property-owning males. In the view of the founders, a mass democracy based on universal suffrage actually threatened the survival of political liberty because the uneducated majority, acting out of ignorance or greed, might misuse their voting rights by electing a tyrant. Consequently, the word democracy does not appear in the U.S. Constitution. The best way to preserve liberty for all, in their view, was to erect a "republic" that would be governed by a wise and incorruptible elite. The best form of government that the founders could imagine would be a government of strictly limited powers under the direction of men very much like themselves: enlightened, socially respectable, and utterly devoted to the prevention of despotic rule.

It was not until 1791 that the founding fathers codified into law the specific rights and liberties they regarded as sacrosanct. Known as the **Bill of Rights,** these legal guarantees against excessive governmental power were ratified by the end of that year as the first ten amendments of the new U.S. Constitution, which itself had taken effect only two years earlier. Several of these amendments are worth citing here:

- *First Amendment: Freedom of religion, speech, press, assembly, and petition*. Congress shall make no law respecting an establishment of religion, or prohibiting the free exercise thereof; or abridging the freedom of speech, or of the press; or the right of the people peaceably to assemble, and to petition the Government for a redress of grievances.
- *Second Amendment: The right to bear arms*. A well regulated Militia, being necessary to the security of a free State, the right of the people to keep and bear arms, shall not be infringed.
- *Fourth Amendment: The right of security against unreasonable searches and seizures*. The right of the people to be secure in their persons, houses, papers, and effects, against unreasonable searches and seizures, shall not be violated, and no Warrants shall issue, but upon probable cause, supported by Oath or affirmation, and particularly describing the place to be searched and the persons or things to be seized.
- *Fifth Amendment: Legal and property rights*. No person shall be held to answer for a capital, or otherwise infamous crime, unless on presentment or indictment of a Grand Jury, . . . nor shall any person be subject for the same offence to be twice put in jeopardy of life or limb; nor shall be compelled in any criminal case to be a witness against himself, nor be deprived of life, liberty, or property, without due process of law; nor shall private property be taken for public use, without just compensation.

Other amendments contained in the Bill of Rights provide for such things as the right to a "speedy" trial by jury and the assistance of defense counsel (Sixth Amendment) and a guarantee against "cruel and unusual punishments" (Eighth Amendment).

Nowhere in the original U.S. Constitution or in its first ten amendments is there an explicitly specified right to vote. Only after the Civil War, with the ratification of the Fourteenth Amendment in 1868, were males over the age of twenty-one, including former slaves, formally guaranteed voting rights. Even this provision, however, explicitly excluded non-tax-paying American Indians and criminals. Females obtained the right to vote throughout the United States only in 1920, with the ratification of the Nineteenth Amendment. Prior to that year, women could vote only in about a dozen states. In actual practice, African Americans continued to face limitations to their voting rights in a number of states for nearly a hundred years after the passage of the Fourteenth Amendment. The process of including all American citizens equally under the constitutional guarantees of "due process of law" has also been a protracted one.

In addition, the American experience has shown that there can be considerable controversy over how the rights and liberties guaranteed by the Constitution are to be interpreted. The First Amendment's guarantees of freedom of speech and assembly, for example, raise all sorts of problems. Should the free speech guarantee apply to publications or Internet transmissions regarded as pornographic or racially inflammatory? Should the right of free assembly extend to demonstra-tions by hate groups or political organizations opposed to democracy itself? Does the "right to life" begin with conception, as opponents of legalized abortion argue, or subsequently, as its advocates maintain? Does the death penalty constitute "cruel and unusual punishment"? Just about every constitutional provision concerning the rights and liberties of the citizenry raises thorny questions about the scope and limits of its applicability.

The United States is by no means the only democracy that has had to wrestle with the problems of codifying various rights and liberties into law while making sure that their application meets the criteria of inclusion and equality. Virtually every other democracy in today's world, no matter how old or new, must also confront the unceasing tasks of defining what the rights of the citizens are and of implementing them broadly and fairly. In addition to looking at the U.S. Bill of Rights for guidance, civil rights advocates can also draw inspiration from such documents as the Universal Declaration of Human Rights adopted by the United Nations in 1948 and the European Union's Convention for the Protection of Human Rights and Fundamental Freedoms.

Can we draw up a list of basic rights and liberties that might be considered absolutely essential to a modern democracy? The list in table 8.1 would probably be regarded by most theorists and practitioners of democratic politics as containing the fundamental rights and liberties necessary to distinguish a democracy from a non-democracy. It is therefore a list of *minimal* criteria: at a *minimum*, it can be argued, these rights and liberties must be guaranteed by law for a country's political system

---

TABLE 8.1

Democratic Rights and Liberties: A Minimal List

1. The right to life and the security of one's person and property against government interference without probable cause of illegal activity
2. Freedom of conscience, thought, and expression (including freedom of the press)
3. Freedom of religion
4. The right to vote in meaningful, fair, competitive elections and to hold governing officials accountable
5. The right to assemble and organize peacefully for political purposes
6. Freedom of movement, that is, the right to travel freely within and outside the country's borders and to live where one chooses
7. The right to equal treatment under the law and to the due process of law, including the right to a fair trial
8. The right to own and alienate (i.e., buy and sell) private property and to engage in private business activity
9. The right to publicly funded education

to be considered democratic. We should nevertheless keep in mind our initial warning that no definition of democracy is likely to please everybody. Some people may want to extend this list of minimal criteria by including additional rights or liberties they regard as fundamentally necessary. And we should also remind ourselves that there may be serious conflicts about how to interpret and apply these minimal criteria.

Some people may proclaim that the right to bear arms ought to be included among these fundamental democratic rights. The issue of gun ownership for private purposes is a contentious one in the United States but less so in most other democracies.[11] Britain, France, Germany, and Japan, among others, have more stringent gun control laws than the United States does. Other people might object that the right to private property, and particularly the right to profit from private business activity, is not necessarily a fundamental democratic right. It is still possible to have a true democracy without such rights, some people would contend. And still others may wish to broaden this list of political, legal, and property rights to include various social or economic rights, such as the right to employment or health care.[12]

The question of which rights and liberties are absolutely essential for a democracy to exist and which ones are not so indispensable is a matter of enduring political controversy. Ultimately it is up to you to decide for yourself which rights and liberties are necessary for a political system to be considered a democracy and which ones might be included in a longer list of "maximal" rights and liberties that, however good and desirable, may be missing in a country whose governmental system may nonetheless be regarded as a democracy.

Face III. Democracy as a Value System

The first two faces of democracy deal mainly with the citizens' political and legal rights vis-à-vis the state, that is, their **civil rights.** These civil rights guarantee the citizen a say in how the country is governed and provide legal safeguards against arbitrary state power with respect to the individual's person and property. But are these civil rights suf-

ficient to establish a democracy? Consider the following possibility.

DEMOCRACY IN MAJORITANIA

Elections have just been held in the imaginary country of Majoritania. Once again, the People's Majority Party has won a landslide electoral victory against several competing parties, garnering 86 percent of the popular vote. Everyone agrees that the elections were scrupulously fair, including the losing parties. There is also broad agreement that the country's constitution, which guarantees all the rights and freedoms listed in table 8.1, provides a wide array of political and legal rights to all citizens on an equal basis. It also provides some economic rights. All male and female adults are entitled to a job or to unemployment benefits if no jobs are available. They are also entitled to state-funded medical care and retirement pensions on an equal basis.

Having recaptured control of both the national legislature and the presidency for the fiftieth year in a row, the leaders of the People's Majority Party will continue pursuing the same general policies their constituents have expected of them for decades. Since roughly 90 percent of the people of Majoritania are green-eyed, the government will continue to maintain a rigidly segregated education system. Though all citizens have an equal right to free education all the way through graduate study, there are separate schools for the green-eyed majority and the non-green-eyed minorities. There are also separate housing zones, public conveyances, and publicly funded hospitals. Private businesses such as banks, stores, restaurants, and motels are free to serve any customers they wish, and they also enjoy the freedom to deny service to anyone they wish. Green-eyed and non-green-eyed persons have the right to intermarry, but their offspring are legally classified as non-green-eyed.

While acknowledging that they enjoy the same rights listed in table 8.1 as the green-eyed majority, along with the same employment, health, and pension entitlements, most non-green-eyed citizens of Majoritania regard the country's system of legal segregation as an affront to their dignity. They feel like second-class citizens. They know that they are powerless to change things, however, as long as their political parties lack the votes to take control of the government. Both the leaders of the People's Majority Party and the vast majority of the green-eyed population are fundamentally intolerant of non-green-eyed people and remain adamantly opposed to any compromise on Majoritania's system of social segregation.

Is Majoritania a democracy? Or should it be disqualified as a bona fide democratic system of government on the grounds that it represents a blatant example of the "tyranny of the majority"? Should it perhaps be regarded as some kind of "partial democracy"?

Many people would argue that the electoral procedures associated with Face I and the rights and liberties listed under Face II are necessary but not sufficient to establish a real democracy. Democracy, in this view, also requires the observance of certain *core values.* The most important of these values, or *norms,* are

- *Fairness,* which means that all groups in society should be treated equivalently and equitably, and none should have opportunities denied to others on a systematically discriminatory basis
- *Tolerance,* which means respect for those who are different from ourselves and willingness to live in harmony with them
- *Compromise,* which is the effort to reconcile our differences on the basis of cooperation, fair bargaining, and mutual willingness to make concessions
- *Trust,* which requires the members of society, and particularly politicians and government officials, to behave in ways that inspire confidence in their dependability, integrity, and honesty
- A commitment to the *peaceful resolution of international disputes* in the country's dealings with the outside world, with force to be used only as a last resort

These core values may be said to exemplify the "spirit of democracy." In any democracy worthy of the name, not only must these values be publicly embraced by political leaders and others involved in setting the tone of the country's political and social life, but they must also be effectively implemented, if necessary with the full force of state authority. In other words, they must be rooted in the *rule of law.* To the extent that they are widely cherished and rigorously applied, these norms help democracies realize the principles of *inclusion* and *equality.* They promote inclusion by insisting that everyone is entitled to be treated on a fair and non-discriminatory basis, regardless of religion, race, gender, or some other social characteristic. They promote equality by insisting on the

equal dignity and intrinsic worth of every human being, regardless of wealth, talent, or other marks of individual distinction. Internationally, democratic values also promote peace by ruling out naked aggression and reserving the use of force to self-defense or the defense of one's allies.[13]

Like the first two faces of democracy, Face III can have both minimal and maximal variants. *At a minimum,* some people would maintain that democracies must reject systematic discrimination aimed at selected social groups. At the very least democracies must refrain from using the law to perpetrate such forms of social discrimination. When governments make unfair laws that suppress or demean certain target groups, they institutionalize discrimination and violate the spirit of democracy. In this view, when the elected government of Majoritania uses its legal authority and the taxpayers' money to institutionalize a system of rigid social segregation in education, public transportation, and public health, it is acting in a flagrantly undemocratic fashion.

Examples of such undemocratic official behavior are not difficult to find. Until the 1950s and 1960s, certain states in the United States maintained school systems that were racially segregated by law while some local governments required African-American bus passengers to ride in the back of the bus. It took the active intervention of federal authorities to overturn these discriminatory laws as incompatible with the U.S. Constitution. More recent incidences of the institutionalized "tyranny of the majority" can be found in a number of countries that profess to be democracies or that are in transition from authoritarianism to democracy.

Moving toward a more expanded notion of democratic values, some political observers would argue that democracies must do more than simply refrain from imposing discriminatory laws on target groups. They must also use the law to prevent unfair discrimination or acts of bigotry in *private* exchanges. If private bankers or restaurant owners refuse to give service to non-green-eyed customers, for example, the government must step in and prohibit such discriminatory practices. Many proponents of this view would further insist that individuals should not even be legally permitted to engage in unfair discrimination when selling their own house. Obviously, legal re-

FIGURE 8.3 Continuum of Democratic Values: Relations Between the Majority and Minorities

Non-discrimination (political rights, private sector rights)	Tolerance, compromise	Affirmative action
Minimum		Maximum

strictions against such private discrimination would place limits on the right to alienate one's property and engage in private business transactions, rights we included in our list of fundamental democratic rights in table 8.1. Advocates of governmental action against private discrimination would reply that the right to engage in private property transactions should not be an absolute one; it must be limited by law in an effort to prevent the violation of other essential elements of democracy, such as the right to fair and non-discriminatory treatment. Debates on these issues were especially sharp in the United States in the 1960s, when the federal government and many states and local communities confronted the questions of fair housing and equal access to public accommodations. The conflict between private property rights and the right to fair and equal treatment still poses thorny problems today in the United States and other democracies.

An even more expansive understanding of democratic norms asserts that governments should go beyond simply outlawing unfair discrimination: they should take special efforts to assist groups that are, or have been, the targets of discriminatory abuse. State prosecutors, for example, should be empowered to initiate legal action on behalf of citizens who have been the victims of specific acts of unfair discrimination. Preferential hiring laws and educational admissions policies should be mandated by law to enable ill-treated minorities to make up for past discrimination and overcome current unfair barriers to employment or education. In the United States, *affirmative action laws* have been instituted in an effort to help African Americans, Hispanics, and Native Americans achieve such goals. At times these laws have sparked resistance from white Americans who argue that legally mandated preferences for minorities amount to reverse discrimination, resulting in unfair treatment for the white majority.

Realistically, no government can force people to love one another. The most a democratic government can do is require its citizens to deal with their various conflicts peacefully and in accordance with certain broadly agreed-upon rules and procedures. But what happens when the conflicts that divide a society are so deep and contentious that the normal procedures of democracy—competitive elections, free speech, and the like—keep the main competing groups in a state of constant turmoil and uncompromising hostility? What happens if democratic elections result in a legislature or executive so divided into mutually antagonistic parties that the country's governmental institutions threaten to become hopelessly gridlocked, incapable of taking any authoritative action at all? Far from being a panacea for society's ills, the normal institutions of democracy can at times actually aggravate them, just by giving everyone the right to express their hostility to other groups openly and organize for political action against them.

In exceptionally divided societies, special institutions and procedures may sometimes be necessary to prevent the country from plunging into violence or its government from being mired in eternal gridlock. To save democracy itself, deeply divided societies may need the special arrangements of a **consociational democracy**.

HYPOTHESIS-TESTING EXERCISE: Consociational Democracy

HYPOTHESIS

Some theorists hypothesize that a stable, effective democracy requires a relatively homogeneous population. They assume that a society whose people share a common ethnic background, a common religion, compatible economic interests, and fairly similar political outlooks is more likely to sustain democratic institutions and make governmental decisions effectively than heterogeneous societies, which are characterized by a plurality of ethnic groups, religious affiliations, economic interests, or political ideologies. Democracy, after all, rests on cooperation. People who are linked together by common social bonds and political attitudes are presumably more likely to cooperate with one another than populations that are split into widely diverse social groups. Social diversity, in this view, can be expected to produce permanent political animosity rather than a viable democracy.

VARIABLES

Actually, we have two interrelated hypotheses here. In the "homogeneity hypothesis," the **dependent variable** is a *stable and effective democracy;* the **independent variable** is a *homogeneous population.* In the "heterogeneity hypothesis," which is the converse of the first one, the **dependent variable** is an *unstable, ineffective democracy;* the **independent variable** is a *heterogeneous population.*

EXPECTATIONS

The hypotheses suggest that heterogeneous societies are essentially doomed to failure in their attempts to build and maintain a stable and effective democracy. Since the Netherlands has a politically and socially heterogeneous population, we would expect democracy to fail in that country or at least to be highly unstable and ineffective in its lawmaking processes.

EVIDENCE

In a classic study of the Netherlands, the Dutch political scientist Arend Lijphart pointed out that, for much of its modern history, his country has exhibited some of the distinctive hallmarks of a highly fragmented society. Although the Dutch share a common ethnic identity, they have been divided along religious lines into Roman Catholics and Protestants (mostly Calvinists) ever since the sixteenth century. In addition, starting in the nineteenth century a secular element of the population became divided primarily along economic and ideological lines. Middle- and upper-class liberals who favored wide freedoms to pursue their private business activities vied with working-class socialists who preferred restrictions on private enterprise along with policies designed to enhance the bargaining power of labor unions and to provide social welfare benefits to workers and their families. By the twentieth century four well-organized "camps" had formed in Dutch society: Catholics, Protestants, liberals, and socialists. Each camp had its own political party, interest groups, newspapers, and other forms of association. Moreover, the four camps were relatively isolated from one another: their respective members did not cross over into the organizations of the other camps or interact with one another very much. Even intermarriage between camps was rare.

And yet, defying the odds, the Netherlands emerged in the twentieth century as one of the most stable democracies in the world. Competitive elections have taken place on a regular basis; political liberties flourish; the rule of law is not in doubt. A succession of governments has proven quite effective in making decisions that address the country's principal problems.

CONCLUSIONS

Lijphart concluded that the evidence of modern Dutch history was *inconsistent* with the heterogeneity hypothesis. Instead of disintegrating into instability and ineffectiveness, Dutch democracy was a stellar success. What accounted for this seemingly paradoxical combination of social fragmentation and healthy democracy? According to Lijphart's explanation, Holland's success was attributable above all to the value its elites attached to *tolerance* and *accommodation.* Recognizing that democratic institutions and political liberties might well founder if their respective groups did not get along, the leaders of the four camps made special efforts to tolerate their differences and accommodate their conflicting interests and demands. Through patient negotiation they continually worked out bargains and compromises aimed at providing each group with a fair chance at political power and a relatively equitable distribution of state revenues. Such things as educational funding and civil service jobs were divided up in approximate proportion to each group's share of the population. At the same time, the leaders of all four groups maintained an outspoken commitment to democracy and a determination to implement their agreements effectively.

These arrangements were facilitated, Lijphart noted, by pervasive attitudes of deference on the part of Holland's population. Most Dutch citizens deferred to their leaders, granting them considerable latitude to strike bargains with the leaders of the competing camps without pressuring them into adopting rigidly uncompromising positions. What Lijphart calls "the politics of accommodation" in the Netherlands was thus a highly elitist form of democracy. It ultimately depended on the ability of the leading personalities representing the four camps to overcome their differences and reach effective compromises, sometimes in secret, for the good of the general population.

Consociational democracy is the term Lijphart applied to this system of *elite accommodation in a socially heterogeneous society.* In the Netherlands it emerged around 1917 and reached its peak in the 1950s and early 1960s. Since the mid-1960s Dutch society and political processes have undergone a series of changes that have significantly altered the accommodationist practices of previous years. New parties have come into existence, for example, and Dutch citizens are less deferential toward their leaders than in the past, increasingly insisting on having a greater say in affecting the political decisions that touch their lives. Despite these changes, democracy remains secure in Holland, perhaps in large part because of the firm foundation it acquired during the long decades of consociationalism. In any event, Lijphart argues that consociational democracy, either in its pure form as it once existed in Holland or in some modified variant, constitutes a distinct model of democracy that may be highly applicable in deeply divided societies.

The Dutch experience, Lijphart concludes, demonstrates that "deep, mutually reinforcing social cleavages do not form an insuperable barrier to viable democracy." This is a lesson many countries struggling to build democracy in today's world may find encouraging. It is also a lesson in the fundamental importance of democratic values—such as tolerance, compromise, accommodation—in the creation and sustenance of democracy.[14]

Should democratic values that are shared by large segments of the population be regarded as *minimal* criteria for democracy, in the absence of which a country should not be considered a democracy at all? Or should they more properly be viewed as *maximal* criteria, highly desirable in an advanced democracy, perhaps, but not really necessary in the early stages of a democracy's development?

Some highly respected political scientists maintain that such democratic virtues as tolerance, moderation, mutual respect, fair play, and compromise may require generations to take root in the thought and behavior of politically active citizens, not to mention the larger population. Nevertheless, they contend, a democracy can still be said to exist as long as those involved in politics stick to certain rules and procedures, such as fair and frequent elections, open competition for power, and legally guaranteed rights and liberties. These procedures, they point out, can be implemented effectively even when the population is divided into suspicious and mutually antagonistic groups. In other words, this view holds that democracy ultimately is defined by the principles we have outlined in Face I and Face II of democracy. The benevolent values of Face III, in this view, "are better thought of as a *product* and not a producer of democracy."[15]

A contrary view asserts that democratic values are vital to the fundamental concept of democracy. One such argument was advanced more than a century and a half ago by Alexis de Tocqueville, the insightful Frenchman whose book *Democracy in America* is still essential reading for anyone interested in American history or the nature of democracy. Tocqueville attributed the success of America's young republic in the early 1830s primarily to certain values that derived from such sources as religion, higher education, and the experience of interpersonal cooperation in local governments and non-governmental associations. These values, which included the love of liberty and the spirit of cooperation, constituted what Tocqueville called the "mores" of society, "the sum of ideas that shape mental habits." Mores, in his opinion, are even more important than laws in establishing a viable democracy. "Laws are always unsteady when unsupported by mores," he wrote; "mores are the only tough and durable power in a nation." Tocqueville contended that democratic values, far from being the end product of long experience with elections and other institutional aspects of democracy, are part of the very essence of democracy.[16]

A more recent variant of this argument has been advanced by Robert Putnam. In a study that sought to explain why some regions in Italy were more successful than others at maintaining stable local governments and delivering basic services

Alexis de Tocqueville

to the population, Putnam and his associates found that the principal variable accounting for these differences was the extent to which civic values were shared by the local citizenry. Whereas the more successful regions feature fairly high levels of interpersonal trust and cooperativeness, the less successful ones are characterized by a suspicious and socially isolated populace. In some regions these diverging patterns can be traced back hundreds of years. To be sure, Putnam acknowledges that the institutions of democracy, such as fair elections and legally guaranteed liberties (Faces I and II), are integral components of any functioning democracy. But, like Tocqueville, he concludes that democratic values come first. "Effective and responsive institutions depend," Putnam asserts, ". . . on republican virtues and practices."[17]

A recent trend in political theory provides philosophical support for the notion that democracies are defined as much by their values as by their institutions. Advocates of **communitarianism** argue that democracy requires the widespread acceptance of mutual obligations and responsibilities on the part of its members, including such norms as cooperation and community service.[18]

Face IV. Economic Democracy

One of the most controversial issues surrounding the definition of democracy centers on the relationship between the citizenry and the economy. Two questions are especially pertinent to **economic democracy**:

1. What *goals* should a democratically governed country pursue with respect to the socioeconomic status of the population: equality of opportunity, equality of wealth, maximum liberty to pursue one's fortunes, or some other ideal?
2. How much *power* should the people have in determining or influencing economic decisions?

The first of these questions deals with the ways that the resources and opportunities available in a democratic society are distributed to the population. The second deals with the distribution of economic decision-making power. The two questions are interrelated, and the answers we give to one inevitably have an impact on the answers we give to the other.

Democracy and Economic Goals   One of the central problems all societies must face is the question of how its scarce resources and opportunities will be distributed to the population. Who gets to make use of a country's energy resources or farmland? How should food be distributed? How should human resources be distributed, such as access to doctors or lawyers? And how should jobs and educational opportunities be parceled out among the population? These questions ultimately boil down to the fundamentally political issue of "who gets what, when, and how." Depending on the nature of a country's political arrangements, those who enjoy political power may arrogate more economic advantages to themselves than to those with little or no political power. Conceivably, however, a political system can be so organized as to make the distribution of resources and opportunities more balanced, permitting the population to share in the country's economic assets more fairly or equally. Hence economic issues are of immediate relevance to the meaning and practical implementation of democracy.

Can we say that some economic goals are more "democratic" than others? For economic goals to be considered democratic, we would expect them to conform to such concepts and values as inclusion, equality, popular sovereignty, and liberty. Let's begin by assuming that economies that manage to distribute their resources and opportunities to the many in some relatively equal fashion are more democratic than those economies that concentrate them in the hands of a few. By the same token, let's assume that economies that guarantee various economic liberties to the population, such as the freedom to operate a privately owned business or to dispose of one's income as one wishes with minimal governmental interference, may be regarded as more democratic than those that confine economic power and initiative to the state or to a privileged elite. Is it possible to achieve both these goals—equality and liberty—simultaneously, or does the one exclude the other?

Like the first three faces of democracy, Face IV can be viewed in terms of a continuum. Some people would argue that, at a minimum, a democracy must strive to implement the principle of *equitable opportunity* for all. As noted earlier in this chapter, equitable means fair. Under this principle, political leaders as well as the business community and others actively involved in a country's political or economic life would work toward ensuring everyone in society a relatively fair chance at achieving economic security and advancement. Even the very poor, by this standard, should at least have a fair chance at climbing out of poverty, working their way into the middle class, and perhaps even getting rich. To be sure, the concept of fairness is not as precise as that of full equality. Different societies and individuals will measure fairness differently, sometimes quite subjectively. Some people will say it is fair enough if the government provides free education through high school to all its citizens; after that, people should be on their own to get their education and earn their income as best they can. Others will insist that the state has an obligation to provide tuition-free education all the way to the top of the academic ladder. Otherwise, only those who can afford college or medical school will be able to advance their career goals, a condition many people would condemn as unfair. Some would maintain that the state, in fairness to the whole population, has the further obligation of providing job training programs to help prepare people for the real-world job market. And some would insist that the state must use its legal powers to prevent discriminatory practices in education and the job market in order to ensure the fair treatment of women and minorities.

In addition to favoring a fair allocation of opportunities, some people would assert that the government should also provide a fair allocation of economic resources to the population. To this end they would favor various welfare measures designed to guarantee that no one falls below a certain level of poverty and to make sure that the poor have adequate food, housing, and medical care. The list of what may be considered necessary to ensure equitable opportunity for everyone may of course be extended considerably, with heated arguments likely to arise over a number of these proposals.

Meanwhile, the concept of fair opportunity allows ample scope for economic liberty. Under most conceptualizations it would permit individuals and private corporations to run their own businesses and dispose of their private possessions with considerable freedom. The government would have to impose some limitations on these private activities, to be sure. In the interests of fair-

ness it might have to collect taxes to pay for mass education, job training programs, and various other social welfare benefits. It may have to intervene to prevent discrimination. Despite these interventions, however, the economy could still function largely in accordance with rules of the private marketplace and still meet the basic criteria for equitable opportunity.

The next principle of distribution along our continuum is *equality of opportunity.* Equality is a more exacting standard than mere fairness. Fairness implies that inequalities will still exist as people start out in life and pursue their careers. Equality of opportunity, by contrast, requires efforts by the state and the private sector to make sure that everyone in society is relatively or truly equal when it comes to sharing in the opportunities for economic advancement. Under this rigorous guideline, no one should have a significant social advantage over anyone else in enjoying access to opportunities for education or employment. Of course, individuals vary considerably in terms of their talents, ambitions, psychologies, and other purely personal traits. No government can equalize these personality differences. But governments can take measures to equalize the *social* differences among the population, which generally depend on the wealth and social status of individuals, families, and larger social groups (such as ethnic or religious groups).

One way of moving toward greater equality of opportunity is to prohibit, or severely restrict, the right of inheritance. By preventing parents from bequeathing their financial assets to their children or other beneficiaries, the state can prevent the accumulation of vast concentrations of wealth in the hands of particularly successful families and thereby reduce the number of especially privileged children over the long run. In order to prevent the children of well-to-do parents from having an educational advantage over less privileged youth by attending expensive private schools and universities, the state could abolish such institutions and make quality public education available to everyone on an equal-opportunity basis. In an effort to provide greater equality of opportunity in the job market, the government might go beyond the practice of simply punishing discriminatory behavior as it occurs and require businesses to set aside certain jobs on a quota basis for particular segments of the population, such as females and various minority groups. These and other steps would all be undertaken with the express purpose of creating a relatively level playing field for all citizens as they start out in life and move up their academic and career ladders.

Whether they can actually succeed in achieving this aim is another question; even the most ambitious efforts at ensuring truly equal opportunity may fail to achieve this goal. Some people may still enjoy more opportunities than others. Private property and a private-enterprise economy could still exist in a country pursuing the goal of equality of opportunity, creating all sorts of unequal opportunities rooted in economic disparities. Even if equality of opportunity could be significantly enhanced, individuals would still be expected to take responsibility for their own economic advancement. One thing, however, is certain: the scope of government intrusion in the educational system and the private business sector would have to be much larger in the quest for greater *equality* of opportunity than would be the case when the goal is simply *equity* of opportunity. As a general rule, therefore, the range of economic liberty for individuals and businesses declines as the pursuit of equality intensifies.

At the maximum end of our continuum is the goal of *equality of condition*. Whereas the concept of opportunity suggests that, at the end of the day, some individuals will come out ahead of others in

their pursuit of economic well-being, equality of condition means that everyone will ultimately enjoy roughly the same amount of wealth. Obviously the pursuit of such an outcome would require the state to undertake major efforts to redistribute wealth throughout society and perhaps to control incomes as well. Tax policies and other modes of government intervention in the economy would be explicitly aimed at preventing the stratification of society into upper, middle, and lower classes. Their aim would be to ensure that all citizens belong to the same socioeconomic class. Under these conditions the freedom of individuals and private businesses to conduct their economic affairs as they wish would necessarily be severely constricted. Once again, as the scope of economic equality widens, the scope of economic liberty narrows.

Thus we are faced with a real dilemma in our efforts to establish a "democratic" distribution of resources and opportunities. Democracy requires both equality and liberty, but the more equality we want, the less liberty we are likely to get (figure 8.4 shows the inverse correlation betweeen them). One of the most highly charged controversies in virtually every modern democracy is the clash between *two conceptions of economic democracy*. Some people tend to define economic democracy primarily in terms of *equality*. The most radical of those who do so would argue that capitalist countries like the United States are *not* democracies precisely because

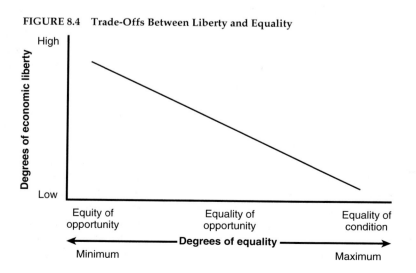

FIGURE 8.4   Trade-Offs Between Liberty and Equality

the private sector creates undemocratic levels of economic inequality. More moderate variants of this argument accept the compatibility of capitalism and democracy but fault private enterpise for failing to provide greater equality or even greater equity. By contrast, other people prefer to define economic democracy primarily in terms of the *liberties* of the marketplace. The goals of equality, equity, and social welfare are typically the priorities of European social democrats or American liberals in the grand tradition of Franklin D. Roosevelt and his political descendants. The goals of private initiative, property rights, and the pursuit of wealth are the preferences of most conservatives. At least some proponents of maximum economic liberty espouse a concept of economic democracy known as "people's capitalism," which aims at promoting small business entrepreneurship, stock acquisition, and home ownership among the broadest possible segments of the population, not just among a superfluously wealthy minority.

Most democracies strive to resolve the conflict between these competing notions of economic democracy by trying to strike a balance between equality and liberty. They may, for example, emphasize the concept of equity rather than full equality while at the same time seeking to harmonize state intervention in the economy with ample freedom for private enterprise. The modern *democratic welfare state* is the product of this balancing act; it is the most widely adopted form of political economy among the world's economically advanced democracies. Variations in the application of the welfare state model abound, however; some countries (like the United States) place greater accents on economic liberty; others (like the Scandinavian countries) stress its egalitarian and welfarist components. Though proponents of both orientations are to be found in most any democratic welfare state, in some countries a majority will lean noticeably in one direction or the other, while in others the population will be more evenly divided. Figure 8.5 shows how the public in various West European democracies views the tradeoff between liberty and equality.

The distributive goals a democracy wishes to achieve cannot be separated from the decision-making mechanisms through which these goals are chosen. *What* we choose depends to a considerable extent on *how* we go about making our choices. To better understand the concept of economic democracy, therefore, we now turn to alternative mechanisms through which the citizenry can influence or control the economy.

Democracy and Economic Decision Making In virtually every democracy that has ever existed, including all the democracies in the contemporary world, privately owned businesses have played a major role in the nation's economic life. Whether in the form of giant corporations or smaller entities like family-owned companies or farms, private enterprises have been the principal motor force of economic activity in most democracies, dominating the production and distribution of resources and job opportunities.

To be sure, governments have always played a role of their own in the economic life of democratic nations. In some cases that role has been quite limited, with the state allowing private owners and managers maximum freedom to run their businesses as they see fit. This type of economic system in its purest form is known as *laissez-faire capitalism*. "Laissez-faire" means "let do" in French. In effect, the state lets private entrepreneurs do what they want in running their business operations with minimal interference. The founding fathers of the United States were firm believers in laissez-faire

In today's world there are no remaining examples of pure laissez-faire capitalism. Just about every democracy in our day and age involves a mixture of private enterprise and fairly active government intervention in the economy. Hence they are known as "mixed economies." (Chapter 14 provides a more detailed discussion of laissez-faire and mixed economies.) To what extent can we apply the term '"economic democracy" to laissez-faire capitalism or to modern mixed economies? Both systems are based on a strict distinction between the *private sector* (privately owned businesses) and the *public sector* (government). And both are based on the legal guarantee of private property, a guarantee many people regard as a fundamental democratic right. Both guarantee various liberties to business owners to operate their enterprises in the marketplace. These economic liberties, too, are widely cherished by many as freedoms that are indispensable to democracy. But how much influence do the citizens

FIGURE 8.5   Breakdown by Country of the Preference for Either Liberty
or Equality
Source: Eurobarometer, Special Issue on Racism and Xenophobia, 1987.

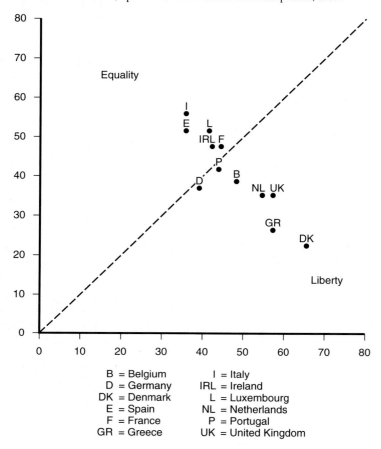

B	= Belgium	I	= Italy
D	= Germany	IRL	= Ireland
DK	= Denmark	L	= Luxembourg
E	= Spain	NL	= Netherlands
F	= France	P	= Portugal
GR	= Greece	UK	= United Kingdom

who live in such systems actually have when it comes to making economic decisions?

Quite clearly, citizen input is minimal in a laissez-faire economy. Laissez-faire capitalism confers virtually all economic decision-making power on the owners and managers of private enterprises. They are largely unrestrained by government, even governments elected by the people, when it comes to operating their businesses.

The impact of the population on economic decisions is somewhat greater in a mixed economy. In just about all of today's democracies, elected officials are expected by various segments of the electorate to impose rules and regulations on private businesses. Workers may want minimum wage

guarantees and collective bargaining rights; women and minorities may want guarantees against job discrimination; advocates of clean air and water may want tighter restrictions on private-sector polluters, and so on. At the same time, citizens who favor greater freedom for private businesses will want their elected officials to keep government interference in the private sector to a reasonable minimum. Whichever side they take, the citizens of modern democracies will most likely have only an indirect effect on the country's economic decisions. If they are stockholders in a private corporation, they may be able to influence company policy to a limited degree through internal voting procedures. But for the vast majority of citizens, the chief means

FIGURE 8.6   Continuum of Economic Decision-Making Regimes

Laissez-faire	Electoral democracy and the welfare state	Councils and participatory democracy
Minimum democracy		Maximum democracy

of influencing the direction of the economy is by electing and pressuring public officials who, in turn, may exercise a certain measure of influence on the private sector through legislative or executive action. In most of today's mixed economies, the main levers of economic decision making remain in the hands of private owners and managers.

Moving toward the maximum level of mass input into economic decisions, we can conceive of several alternative political-economic systems that are very different from laissez-faire and from today's mixed-economy democracies. In nineteenth-century Europe, for example, a number of socialist thinkers proposed that the workers should take control of the factories where they worked, dispossessing the private owners. According to some of these schemes the workers in each factory would elect workers' councils to manage their enterprises. This type of system was typically known as *council democracy* or *socialist democracy*.

Another variant was proposed for adoption in the United States by Robert Dahl. He argued that there has always been a tension in American political thought between political rights and private property rights. In Dahl's opinion, the political rights of the population to exercise its sovereignty through the democratic process should take precedence over the property rights of owners and managers to operate their private companies. While he favored private property as a vital component of liberty, Dahl contended that private corporations should be subject to the democratic process. "*If* democracy is justified in governing the state," he wrote, "then it must *also* be justified in governing economic enterprises." He therefore proposed the reorganization of private companies into "self-governing enterprises" that would be "collectively owned and democratically governed by all the people who work in them." Everyone who works in a firm should have the right to participate in its decision-making process on the basis of the principle of "one person, one vote." Roughly similar ideas were proposed in the 1960s by

politically active students and other proponents of "participatory democracy" who argued that the people have a right to elect those who make decisions that affect their lives in just about every walk of life, including private businesses, universities, and other economic and social institutions.[19]

No major democracy in the contemporary world has adopted the far-reaching systems of economic democracy conceptualized by thinkers like Dahl. Some countries, however, have adopted modified versions of economic democracy by permitting people who work in a private corporation to have at least some say in how owners and managers run their companies. Germany, France, Italy, and other contemporary democracies have in recent decades developed various mechanisms of *co-participation* (or *co-determination*) that enable workers to have an input into certain managerial decisions. Even in these cases, however, most private business decisions are made by corporate executives acting in accordance with the laws of the land, which in turn are enacted by democratically accountable governments.

HOW PEOPLE VIEW DEMOCRACY

As we pointed out earlier, people tend to define democracy in different ways. International surveys conducted in the 1990s revealed that in East-Central Europe, where the construction of democracy was still in its initial phases following the collapse of communism, relatively large segments of the population, usually a substantial majority, tended to define democracy primarily in *economic* terms. When asked to identify the *most* essential or important characteristics of democracy, a majority of East Europeans mentioned an improved economy, greater economic equality, or guarantees of basic needs ahead of such political characteristics as freedom of speech, an independent judiciary, or the right to vote in multiparty elections. Most citizens in West European democracies, by contrast, tended to define democracy *primarily* in political rather than economic terms (see figures 8.7 and 8.8). At the same time, most East Europeans also considered political liberties to be important or essential aspects of democracy, while large numbers of West Europeans regarded economic benefits as important, or even essential. The surveys provide empirical evidence that economic notions of democracy, however crudely they may be conceptualized, can resonate powerfully in the political consciousness of average citizens.

The four faces of democracy, summarized in table 8.2, convey some of the complexities of a

FIGURE 8.7   The Most Important Elements of a Democracy to East Europeans (in %)
Source: U.S. Information Agency, *The People Have Spoken: Global Views of Democracy,* vol. II (1999), pp. 32, 34. (See also the surveys on pp. 33 and 35.)

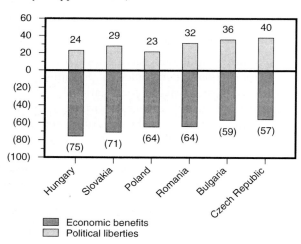

Economic benefits
Political liberties

FIGURE 8.8   The Most Important Elements of a Democracy to West Europeans (in %)

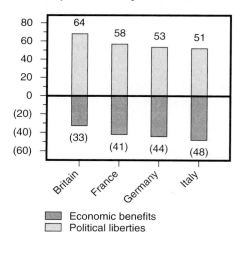

Economic benefits
Political liberties

TABLE 8.2
The Four Faces of Democracy

All Four Faces Rest on the Principles of the Rule of Law, Inclusion, and Equality

	Key Features	Minimum Variant	Intermediary Variants	Maximum Variant
Face I: Popular sovereignty	Participation, accountability	Representative democracy	Plebiscitary democracy; techno-democracy	Direct democracy
Face II: Civil rights and liberties	Enumerated inalienable rights (may not be abridged by majority)	Basic civil rights	Additional rights, as determined through democratic procedures	
Face III: Democratic values	Values and attitudes concerning relations between majority and minorities	Non-discrimination	Tolerance, compromise	Affirmative action
Face IV: Economic democracy	Distribution of wealth and economic decision-making power	Equity of opportunity; laissez-faire	Equality of opportunity; electoral democracy plus welfare state	Equality of condition; council or participatory democracy

multifaceted concept of democracy. The next chapter looks at various ways modern democracies are organized.

KEY TERMS
(Underlined in the text)

Inclusion
Equality
Equity
Popular sovereignty
Accountability
Representative democracy
Direct democracy
Agenda setting
Democratic elitism
Polyarchy
Civil rights
Consociational democracy
Communitarianism
Economic democracy

NOTES

1. Secret voting was first employed in South Australia in 1858. It was adopted for general use in Britain in 1872 and in U.S. presidential elections only after the fraud-tainted contest of 1884. Prior to these dates, various forms of non-secret balloting were the rule, such as a voice vote or show of hands at a public election meeting.

2. See James S. Fishkin, *Democracy and Deliberation: New Directions for Democratic Reform* (New Haven, Conn.: Yale University Press, 1991).

3. In 1990, 14.4 percent of total civilian employment in the United States consisted of central government employees. Corresponding figures included 31.7 percent in Sweden, 27.7 percent in Norway, 22.6 percent in France, 19.7 percent in Canada, 19.2 percent in the United Kingdom, and 6 percent in Japan. See Jan-Erik Lane, David McKay, and Kenneth Newton, eds., *Political Data Handbook OECD Countries*, 2d ed. (Oxford: Oxford University Press, 1997), table 3.9.

4. Walter Gelhorn, *Ombudsmen and Others: Citizens' Protectors in Nine Countries* (Cambridge, Mass.: Harvard University Press, 1967); Frank Stacey, *Ombudsmen Compared* (Oxford: Clarendon, 1978); Gerald E. Caiden, *International Handbook of the Ombudsman* (Westport, Conn.: Greenwood, 1982); and Donald C.

Rowat, *The Ombudsman Plan: Th[e] an Idea* (Lanham, Md.: Universi[ty] 1985).

5. Schumpeter defined represen[tative] "that institutional arrangement for arriving at po[liti]cal decisions in which individuals acquire the power to decide by means of a competitive struggle for the people's vote." *Capitalism, Socialism, and Democracy*, 3d ed. (New York: Harper and Row, 1950).

6. Among Dahl's voluminous writings, see *Polyarchy: Participation and Opposition* (New Haven, Conn.: Yale University Press, 1971); *Dilemmas of Pluralist Democracy* (New Haven, Conn.: Yale University Press, 1982); *Democracy and Its Critics* (New Haven, Conn.: Yale University Press, 1989); and *On Democracy* (New Haven, Conn.: Yale University Press, 1999).

7. On Athenian democracy, see David Stockton, *The Classical Athenian Democracy* (Oxford: Oxford University Press, 1990); M. I. Finley, *Politics in the Ancient World* (Cambridge: Cambridge University Press, 1983); and A. H. M. Jones, *Athenian Democracy* (Oxford: Basil Blackwell, 1969).

8. Joseph F. Zimmerman, *The Massachusetts Town Meeting: A Tenacious Institution* (Albany, N.Y.: Graduate School of Public Affairs, SUNY, 1967).

9. R. R. Palmer, *The Age of the Democratic Revolution*, vol. 1 (Princeton, N.J.: Princeton University Press, 1959), 111, 127–28.

10. On techno-democracy, see Lawrence K. Grossman, *The Electronic Republic: Reshaping Democracy in the Information Age* (New York: Viking, 1995). For arguments in behalf of greater citizen participation in the decision-making process, see Benjamin R. Barber, *Strong Democracy* (Berkeley: University of California Press, 1984) and *A Place for Us* (New York: Hill and Wang, 1998).

11. On the right to bear arms in the United States, see Robert J. Cottrol, ed., *Gun Control and the Constitution: Sources and Explorations on the Second Amendment* (New York: Garland, 1994).

12. See Cass R. Sunstein, *After the Rights Revolution* (Cambridge, Mass.: Harvard University Press, 1990).

13. The historian Gordon S. Wood has pointed out that the concept of "democratic dignity" was a radical notion associated with the American Revolution and the revolt against British conceptions of a society rigidly divided between well-born aristocrats and lowly commoners. "Equality became so potent for Americans because it came to mean that everyone was really the same as everyone else, not just at birth, not in talent or property or wealth, and not

just in some transcendental religious sense of the equality of all souls. Ordinary Americans came to believe that no one in a basic down-to-earth and day-in-day-out manner was really better than anyone else." Wood argues that this notion of equal human worth made the United States "the most egalitarian nation in the history of the world, and it remains so today, regardless of its great disparities of wealth." *The Radicalism of the American Revolution* (New York: A. A. Knopf, 1992), 235–36.

14. Arend Lijphart, *The Politics of Accommodation,* 2d ed. (Berkeley: University of California Press, 1975).

15. Philippe C. Schmitter and Terry Lynn Karl, "What Democracy Is . . . and Is Not," in *The Global Resurgence of Democracy,* 2d ed., ed. Larry Diamond and Marc F. Plattner (Baltimore, MD.: Johns Hopkins University Press, 1996), 57.

16. Alexis de Tocqueville, *Democracy in America,* ed. J. P. Mayer, trans. George Lawrence (New York: Harper and Row, 1966).

17. Robert D. Putnam, with Robert Leonardi and Raffaella Y. Nanetti, *Making Democracy Work* (Princeton, N.J.: Princeton University Press, 1993), 182.

18. Amitai Ezioni, *Spirit of Community: Rights, Responsibilities, and the Communitarian Agenda* (New York: Crown, 1993), *Rights and the Common Good* (New York: St. Martin's Press, 1995), ed., *New Communitarian Thinking* (Charlottesville: University of Virginia Press, 1995), and ed., *The Essential Communitarian Reader* (Lanham, Md.: Rowman and Littlefield, 1998).

19. Robert A. Dahl, *A Preface to Economic Democracy* (Berkeley: University of California Press, 1985). See also the "Port Huron Statement" adopted by the Students for a Democratic Society in 1962, excerpted in Robert A. Goldwin, ed., *How Democratic Is America? Responses to the New Left Challenge* (Chicago: Rand McNally, 1971), 1–15.

CHAPTER 9

DEMOCRACY: HOW DOES IT WORK?

State Institutions and Electoral Systems

How do modern democratic governments work? Obviously this is a huge question with as many answers as there are democracies. In this chapter we address it by focusing on two key aspects of democratic government: *state institutions* and *electoral systems*. First we provide a comparative overview of three of the most prominent methods of organizing national governmental institutions: the U.S. system of *separation of powers* and *checks and balances*; the British-style system of *parliamentary government*; and the French-style mixed *presidential-parliamentary system*. In the second part of the chapter we compare the most widely used methods of electing presidents and national legislatures.

STATE INSTITUTIONS

How are modern, democratically elected governments organized? In the course of history there have emerged three leading models of representative democracy: (1) the **separation-of-powers** and **checks-and-balances system** pioneered in the United States; (2) the **parliamentary system** that initially evolved in Britain, and (3) the **presidential-parliamentary system,** which is currently utilized in France, Russia, and elsewhere. Each model prescribes a set of methods for selecting the three main branches of national government—the executive, the legislative, and judicial—and stipulates how

legal authority is to be distributed among these three branches. All three models have experienced important evolutionary transformations in the countries where they first emerged. In addition, variants of all three have appeared in other countries as political leaders have sought to copy their essential features while adjusting them to the contours of their own national history and specific political conditions. (See table 6.1 for a list of countries currently using these three models.)

What follows in this section is a summary description of these three types of democratic government. Our aim is to help you understand them better by comparing their main characteristics side by side. To keep this chapter within limits, however, we'll concentrate on the essential features of these systems, leaving the details of how they work in specific countries to subsequent chapters.

The U.S. Separation of Powers System

The U.S. system of government was instituted with the Constitution, which was drafted in 1787 and ratified in 1789. The United States has a federal system, with legal authority shared between the national government and the fifty states. At the national level, which is our principal focus here, the three main institutions are the *presidency,* the centerpiece of the executive branch of government; the *Congress*, which is the national legislature; and the *Supreme Court,* which is the highest judicial authority in the land.

The main architects of this system, led by James Madison, did not want any of these three branches to dominate the other two. They therefore endowed each branch with certain powers designed to check, or counterbalance, the legal authority of the others. In constructing this system of **separation of powers** and **checks and balances**, Madison and other founding fathers were profoundly influenced by the writings of Aristotle, who believed that the best constitution required a mixture of elite rule and responsible citizens. While he was vague as to details, Aristotle clearly distrusted mass electoral democracy, fearing it would degenerate into mob rule.[1] Another notable influence was the French philosopher Montesquieu (1689–1755). In *The Spirit of Laws* (1748), Montesquieu argued in favor of a carefully constructed separation of powers between the executive, the legislative, and the judicial branches of government so that the same individuals would not be able to dominate two or more of these branches. He hypothesized that such a system would reduce opportunities for the abuse of power.[2] For Madison and other framers of the constitution, preventing the abuse of state power was the most important priority of the U.S. system of government.

Although certain specific aspects of American government have evolved since the Constitution took effect in 1789, it is based today on these core principles, centering on the following features:

- *The president and the Congress are elected separately.* The president is elected by the electoral college, which is elected by the voters in each state. The two houses of Congress—the Senate and the House of Representatives—are elected by the voters. Congress does not elect the president. Members of Congress may vote to remove the president from office only for "high crimes and misdemeanors," not because they do not like his policies.

- *Law making depends on a balance of Congressional and presidential powers.* Strictly speaking, only members of Congress have the right to propose bills for adoption as law. The president's own legislative proposals are submitted to the Congress by members acting in his behalf. Laws are enacted when both houses of Congress pass bills by majority vote and the president signs the legislation. The president may veto Congressional legislation. Congress may override the president's veto by a two-thirds majority.

- *The Supreme Court may strike down laws as unconstitutional.* Although this right of *judicial review* is not explicitly contained in the Constitution, ever since the case of Marbury vs. Madison in 1803 the Supreme Court has asserted the right to nullify laws on the grounds that they violate the Constitution.

- *The president, the Congress, and the states can together override decisions of the Supreme Court.* The justices of the Supreme Court are selected by the president, with the "advice and consent" of the Senate. If the Court strikes down a law as unconstitutional, the constitution can be amended. Constitutional amendments require a vote of two-thirds of the members of each house of Congress and the approval of three-fourths of the state legislatures.

Much in keeping with the intentions of its creators, the primary advantage of this system is that neither the president, the Congress, nor the Supreme Court

FIGURE 9.1   U.S. System

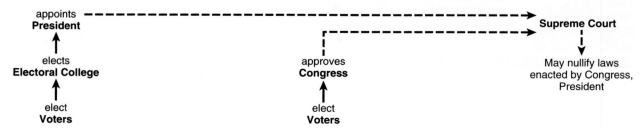

can dominate American government. The checks-and-balances system's primary disadvantage, however, is its potential for gridlock. Separate elections for the president and Congress make it possible for the president to be a Democrat and the Congressional majority to be Republican (or, of course, vice versa), a condition known as **divided government.** If the two sides disagree, it can be very difficult to enact legislation or concur on appointments to the Supreme Court. A more positive view of this situation, however, stresses its potential for compromise. Those who regard compromise as a good thing argue that the possibility of gridlock exerts pressure on both the president and Congress to work out mutually acceptable legislation. Madison himself shared this perspective, arguing that a slow and deliberate process of making laws was preferable to one in which laws are enacted too swiftly and without sufficient scrutiny.

Parliamentary Government

The *parliamentary system* of democracy, also known as **parliamentary government,** is the most widely used form of democracy in the world today.

In most parliamentary systems of democracy, the term "government" is used in its narrow sense: it refers to the head of government (usually called the *prime minister* or *premier*) and the various ministers of the executive branch (foreign minister, finance minister, etc.). The head of government is the chief executive decision maker in the country. Many parliamentary regimes also have a *ceremonial head of state*: a monarch or president who possesses few, if any, real decision-making powers and whose main job is to symbolize the country's unity or the continuity of its history.

There are numerous versions of parliamentary government, and virtually every country that has this form of democracy has one or more unique features that are not to be found in other parliamentary systems in quite the same way. Nevertheless, the basic institutions of parliamentarism tend to be widely shared. Simply put, the defining principle of parliamentary government is that *the government is selected in a two-step process:*

1. **The people elect the national legislature.**
2. **The national legislature (usually the lower house in bicameral legislatures) elects or approves the government.**

In this system, there is no separation of powers between the legislative and executive branches as in the United States; rather there is a **fusion of powers** between the legislature and the executive. To put it another way, *the government in a parliamentary system stems from the legislature and is formally accountable to it.* This fusion of powers and accountability are achieved in the following ways:

- As just indicated, *the legislature elects (or approves) the government.* In most examples of

FIGURE 9.2   **Parliamentary Government**

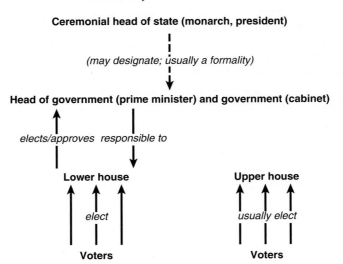

the parliamentary system, the people do not directly vote for the prime minister; they vote for candidates running for the national legislature, who in turn have the opportunity to vote for (or approve) the prime minister and cabinet.

- *The government must present and defend its policies before the legislature.* Typically the prime minister and other cabinet ministers must regularly appear before the legislature to present their policies and defend them in open debate. They may also have to answer questions posed by members of the legislature in open session. In the United States, by contrast, the president is not required to answer questions in Congress but is required only to deliver an annual "state of the union" message explaining his policies.
- *The legislature can vote the government out of office.* Just as the legislature "makes" the government by voting it into office, it can also "unmake" the government by voting it out of office. Typically it exercises this prerogative through a *vote of confidence.*

A **vote of confidence** is a showdown vote in the legislature to determine if the government still has the support (confidence) of a voting majority of legislators. If the government loses this vote it must usually resign and the legislature must vote a new government into office. If it cannot, the people must vote for a new legislature.

The essential features of parliamentarism just outlined provide for a system of *governmental dependence on the legislature* that differs fundamentally from the U.S. system of separation of powers.

Let's clarify how typical parliamentary systems of government work by providing a few examples of *how the legislature elects or approves the government.* Several outcomes are possible, and we'll focus here on three of them. They are (1) *single-party majoritarian government;* (2) *majority coalition government;* and (3) *minority government.*

Single-Party Majoritarian Government   In a **single-party majoritarian government,** *one party wins an absolute majority of seats in the national legislature and forms the government.* (An *absolute majority* means 50 percent plus one.)

An illustration is the British election for the House of Commons of 1997 (see table 9.1). In these

TABLE 9.1

British House of Commons Elections, 1997

(659 Seats)

Party	No. of Seats	% of Seats
Labour	419	63.6
Conservatives	165	25.0
Liberal Democrats	46	7.0
Eight others	29	4.4

British Prime Minister Tony Blair answering questions in the House of Commons.

elections the Labour Party won 419 of the 659 seats in the House, or 63.6 percent of the total. After the House assembled following the popular elections, the Labour Members of Parliament (MPs) used their majority to support a government consisting entirely of Labour Party ministers, led by Prime Minister Tony Blair. The other parties in the House assumed the role of *opposition parties.*

With the Labour Party possessing 179 more seats than the combined total of the opposition parties, Mr. Blair's majoritarian government was now in the position of being able to pass its legislative proposals into law with relative ease. However, this enviable position requires the willingness of Labour MPs to maintain **party discipline.** *Party discipline is maintained when the parliamentary deputies of a particular party vote together unanimously as a bloc.* Party discipline is more likely to occur in parliamentary systems than in the United States, where a tradition of greater individuality and independence on the part of members of Congress flourishes. Even though unanimous party discipline in Britain by no means occurs all the time, it still occurs more often than in the United States.

As long as the governing party manages to "whip" its legislative delegation into concerted action, a single-party majoritarian government can exhibit remarkable *efficiency:* it can get its legislative proposals passed quickly and smoothly. Lacking the votes against a highly disciplined governing party, the opposition parties simply cannot muster a majority to defeat the government's bills. In the case of Britain, single-party majoritarian governments typically manage to win passage of 97 percent of the bills they propose in the House of Commons, an extraordinarily high degree of governmental efficiency.

What happens, however, if *no* party succeeds in winning an absolute majority of legislative seats? We then have a **hung parliament.** The alternatives are a *majority coalition government* or, failing that, a *minority government.*

Majority Coalition Government   A **coalition government** *consists of two or more parties that agree to share cabinet posts, usually in order to form a voting majority in the legislature.* An example derives from the results of the elections to the Bundestag, Germany's lower house, in 1998.

As we can see in table 9.2, no party won an absolute majority of the Bundestag's 669 seats (i.e., 335 seats). How, then, can a government be formed? In this case the Social Democrats cut a deal with the Greens to form a coalition government. The Social Democrats, being the larger of the two coalition partners, took the most important cabinet position, that of *chancellor.* (In Germany the head of government is called the chancellor rather than prime minister.) Of the remaining fifteen cabinet slots, nine went to Social Democrats, including the key ministries of finance, justice, and defense. For their part, the Greens got four cabinet posts, including that of foreign minister, which is frequently regarded as the second most prestigious cabinet position after the head of government. By joining forces to govern the country, the Social Democrats and the Greens together had 51.5 percent of the seats in the Bundestag, a slender majority. As long as their respective Bun-

TABLE 9.2

German Bundestag Elections, 1998

(669 Seats)

Party	No. of Seats	% of Seats
Social Democrats	298	44.5
Christian Democrats	245	36.7
Greens	47	7.0
Free Democrats	44	6.6
Party of Democratic Socialism	35	5.2

destag delegations maintain party discipline, the bills the coalition partners propose to the legislature will safely win passage.

Quite clearly, the Greens have good reason to feel satisfied with this arrangement. With only 7 percent of the seats in the Bundestag they managed to capture a considerable share of power in the national government. This example illustrates one of the most characteristic features of coalition government: *it provides small parties with an opportunity to participate in the executive branch of government.* Rather than being relegated to the status of a weak opposition party in the Bundestag with little influence on the course of government policy, the Greens negotiated their way into the pinnacle of policy making power, the cabinet. Their continuing presence in the government means that they will be able to exert direct influence on practically every major political issue facing the country.

By its very nature, coalition government invariably involves ongoing negotiations among the parties that take part in it. The policies pursued by the cabinet are usually the product of agreements and bargains that are struck between the coalition partners. In the example shown here, the Social Democrats and the Greens must usually agree on the bills they propose to the legislature as well as on other decisions their government makes in the day-to-day task of running the national government. Coalition government is government by bargaining par excellence.

What are the chief advantages and disadvantages of coalition government?

One advantage is that coalitions *expand representation in the executive branch of government.* As our example illustrates, coalition governments can permit a small party like the Greens to participate directly in the executive branch of state decision making, giving the people who voted for that party, constituting only about 7 percent of the electorate, a far greater influence on what their government does than if the Greens were simply a minuscule opposition party in the national legislature.

Another advantage of coalition governments is that *they increase the level of bargaining and compromise in the executive branch of government.* By compelling the coalition partners to constantly work together on the policies they pursue, coalitions promote the democratic ideals of negotiation and accommodation. Unlike single-party majoritarian governments, which allow one party to monopolize the executive branch as well as the legislative agenda, coalitions force the largest party to take account of the concerns and preferences of other parties. In the process they provide a mechanism for bridging over the divergences and conflicts that separate the diverse elements of the electorate that these parties represent. At least in principle, coalition governments may increase the likelihood that politics will follow the path of moderation and compromise rather than the dominance of a single party's point of view.

A third advantage of coalition government is its *flexibility and adaptability.* As we've seen, the parliamentary form of democracy permits the legislature to unmake governments as well as make them. If the parties that form a governing coalition have a falling out and cannot patch up their political disagreements, it may be possible to form a new coalition government *without having to wait for the next elections.* The leaders of the various parties have a chance to cobble together a new majority coalition. This happened in Germany in 1982, for example, when the existing coalition government of the Social Democrats and Free Democrats fell apart over irreconcilable differences. A new coalition government was soon formed by the Christian Democrats and Free Democrats, with Helmut Kohl as chancellor. This coalition survived several subsequent elections and governed until 1998, giving Kohl sixteen years in power.

As it happens, the disadvantages of coalition government are closely related to its advantages. Whereas the inclusion of more than one party in a coalition cabinet expands the level of representation in the executive branch, the involvement of too many parties may prove unwieldy. As a general

rule, the greater the number of parties represented in a coalition government, the more difficult it is to reach common accord on policies and decisions. The German examples we have just examined are fairly simple ones involving two-party coalition governments. But some democracies have multiparty coalitions involving three or more parties. Throughout much of the 1970s, 1980s, and 1990s, for example, Italy was governed by a succession of coalition governments consisting of four to nine parties. Prolonged negotiations, stalemate, and policy turmoil were often the result. Multiparty coalitions can sometimes produce considerable governmental inefficiency. It is simply harder for two or more parties to formulate policies and implement decisions as efficiently and effectively as a single party that commands a majority of the legislature's seats.[3]

Another potential disadvantage is that small parties may gain a level of influence in the government that far outweighs their share of electoral support. As we saw in the German case, the Greens in 1998 acquired key cabinet positions even though they garnered only 7 percent of Bundestag seats. While some people may applaud a political system that allows a minority party to make its way into the highest reaches of decision-making power, others may regard such a prospect as unfair because it confers excessive influence on parties with small, sometimes very small, constituencies. Of the par-

Coalition government: Italian Prime Minister Massimo D'Alema (with moustache) is flanked by ministers representing his eight-party coalition upon taking office in October 1998. The fractious coalition, which grew to nine parties, fell apart in April 2000 but was reassembled under a former prime minister, Giuliano Amato. Amato's new government was Italy's 58th since 1945. Most have been coalition governments.

ties that participated in Italy's numerous multi-party coalition governments, three won less than 5 percent of the national vote each. In 1981–82, Italy's prime minister—the most powerful political figure in the country—came from a party that had captured only 1.9 percent of the vote! Does the distribution of such enormous governmental power to very small parties stretch the limits of fairness in democratic representation?

A third disadvantage derives from the very flexibility and adaptability of coalition government that we highlighted earlier as one of its advantages. Whereas the institutions of parliamentary democracy and coalition government can be valuable tools enabling party leaders and legislators to remove ineffective governments, there often exists the potential for abusing these opportunities. In some democracies, governing coalitions fall apart and must be replaced fairly frequently, a phenomenon known as **governmental instability.** Once again, Italy provides a cautionary example of what can go wrong in a parliamentary democracy. Between 1945 and mid-2000, Italy had no fewer than fifty-eight governments! A large number of them were coalitions involving three or more parties. Some of these multiparty cabinets lasted no more than a few months or even weeks. Other countries have also had periods of turbulent governmental instability.[4]

Minority Government What if no party has an absolute majority of seats in the legislature, and the leaders of the various parties cannot come to terms on forming a coalition government that enjoys the backing of the majority of legislators? Under these difficult circumstances a *minority government* may have to be formed. As its name implies, a **minority government** *consists of one or more parties whose delegates do not constitute a majority of the legislative house.* Since it takes a voting majority to pass bills into law, how can such a government legislate? There are several possibilities.

One possibility is a **parliamentary alliance.** In this case, *two or more parties agree that they will not share cabinet posts, but their legislators will vote together to support the government and pass legislation.* Britain provides an example. In 1976 the Labour Party government of Prime Minister

James Callaghan lost its majority when several Labour members of Parliament switched parties. Callaghan then got the Liberal Party, which had thirteen members in the House of Commons, to support his government in exchange for joint consultation on all bills brought up for a vote. This arrangement eventually broke down, but Callaghan managed to work out a similar parliamentary alliance with other parties. Agreements of this kind can be quite unstable, as Callaghan found out in 1979 when he lost a vote of confidence in the Commons by only one vote. His government thereupon resigned and new parliamentary elections had to be held.

If a minority government cannot get help from other parties through the formation of a parliamentary alliance, it may still be able to survive by garnering the support of other parties in the legislature *on a vote-by-vote basis* as each piece of legislation comes up for parliamentary consideration. Sweden's government elected in 1998 provides an example (see table 9.3). Sweden's Social Democrats formed a single-party minority government. They managed to pass most of their legislation with votes from the Left Party and the Greens. But these three parties did not agree on everything, and sometimes the Social Democrats had to seek the votes of other parties in order to pass certain types of bills into law. Obviously, a minority government's dependence on other parties in the legislature—whether in a parliamentary alliance or on a vote-by-vote basis—can give the cooperating parties a considerable amount of negotiating power, enabling them to extract rewards and benefits from the

TABLE 9.3

Swedish Riksdag Elections, 1998		
(349 Seats)		
Party	No. of Seats	% of Seats
Social Democrats	131	37.5
Moderates	82	23.5
Left Party (Communists)	43	12.3
Christian Democrats	42	12.0
Center Party	18	5.2
Liberals	17	4.9
Greens	16	4.6

Source: Inter-Parliamentary Union, *Chronicle of Parliamentary Elections,* vol. 32.

government that they might not otherwise receive if the governing party possessed its own voting majority. If this ongoing negotiating process bogs down, the result can be gridlock. The U.S. system of government is therefore not the only type of democracy that is gridlock-prone.

A third possible way a minority government can govern is to ask the opposition parties to *abstain* from voting against it whenever it presents its bills to the legislature for a vote. In most democracies, all that is needed to confirm a government or pass a bill into law is *a majority of those present and voting.* If some legislators abstain on a given vote or are not present in the chamber when the vote takes place, their "non-votes" are not counted as votes against the government or against a particular piece of legislation. As you might expect, minority governments of this type are usually highly unstable; the abstaining parties may not be willing to tolerate for very long a government in which they do not participate or from which they derive few, if any, benefits. More generally, minority governments constitute a fragile basis for stable rule over the long run, whichever form they may take. Nevertheless, they are a relatively common occurrence in today's parliamentary systems.

But what if the parties in the legislature are unable to form *any* government, whether a majoritarian or a minority government? In that case their only recourse is to go to the voters and ask them to elect a new legislature.

Anticipated Elections   Every democracy requires elections to the national legislature at regular intervals. In the United States, elections are held every two years for the entire House of Representatives and one-third of the Senate. In Britain, elections to the House of Commons must take place every five years. The German Bundestag has a four-year statutory term, and so on. In contrast to the United States, however, most parliamentary government forms of democracy permit the possibility of holding parliamentary elections *prior to* the expiration of the legislature's full term in office. The British, for example, do not necessarily have to wait five years before holding elections to the House of Commons; elections to the Commons can take place before the expiration of this statu-

tory term. And once these elections occur, a new full five-year term for the newly elected House of Commons begins. Similar possibilities obtain in other parliamentary democracies.

Parliamentary elections that take place before the expiration of the legislature's full term are called **anticipated elections.** (They are also informally known as **snap elections.**) Anticipated elections play an important role in realizing the potential of representative democracy. They provide the voters with a valuable mechanism for registering their opinions and influencing political decision makers more often than would be the case if no such mechanism existed. And because they tend to be called at especially critical junctures in the nation's political life, during a national crisis or in the midst of severe political gridlock, snap elections permit the citizens to have a say in the resolution of the problem in a timely and orderly fashion.

Under what circumstances, then, are anticipated elections most likely to take place? The most frequent occasions are the following:

- *No government can be formed in the national legislature.* As explained earlier, it is possible that no single party possesses a majority of seats in the legislature, and it proves impossible to form a majority coalition government or a minority government. In some instances the government loses a vote of confidence, and the legislators are unable to form a new one. Faced with total gridlock, the nation's political leaders now have no choice but to call the voters to the polls to elect a new parliament.
- *Public pressure demands immediate elections.* Suppose there is a major crisis and the existing government is in trouble. Polls show that public confidence is waning considerably. Even key leaders of the governing party or parties begin calling for change. Under these circumstances the government may feel pressured by public opinion to resign and call new elections, allowing the people an opportunity to vote for a new legislature. Even though the government is *not obliged by law* to call new elections just because the public demands them, it may do so anyway if it feels it can no longer govern effectively.

  For example, in the early 1990s the Italian government was jolted by such shocking revelations of corruption that it responded to the public's disgust by calling anticipated elections in 1994. Because corruption continued even after these elections, another round of snap elections took place only two years later.

- ***The government wants snap elections so as to solidify a parliamentary majority.*** Sometimes an existing government will want to call anticipated elections because public opinion polls show that, if elections are held right away instead of a year or more later, the governing party (or parties) would win. Every politician knows that the public is fickle and political fortunes cannot be predicted. A government that enjoys popular favor today may lose it next month or next year. Consequently it may be in the government's interest to call snap elections while it still enjoys enough public support to be reelected.

British Prime Minister Margaret Thatcher, for example, called snap elections in 1983, one year ahead of schedule, to capitalize on her rising popularity following Britain's victory over Argentina in the Falklands War. Her party, the Conservatives, increased its House of Commons majority from 53 percent to 61 percent.

To be sure, most politicians understand that they risk alienating the voters if they abuse their right to call anticipated elections. Voters may react angrily if they feel they are being called out to vote too frequently or that the political elites are not trying hard enough to form a workable government. A number of democracies have rules that limit the number of times snap elections may be held within a given period of time. With or without such rules, political leaders tend to call them fairly rarely, with a keen eye to the public mood.

Presidential-Parliamentary Democracies

The third type of modern democracy to be sketched out here is the mixed **presidential-parliamentary system**.[5] The essence of this institutional arrangement is that *it possesses both a president with significant decision-making powers and a prime minister with responsibilities to the national legislature.* In other words, this system has *two executive decision makers:* the president and the prime minister. Figure 9.3 is a graphic model of this system, typified by contemporary France and Russia.

In some cases, as in France and Russia, the president has even greater constitutional powers than the president of the United States, while the legislature has fewer powers than the U.S. Congress. The French or Russian president, for example, may issue decrees or other executive decisions

FIGURE 9.3   Presidential-Parliamentary System

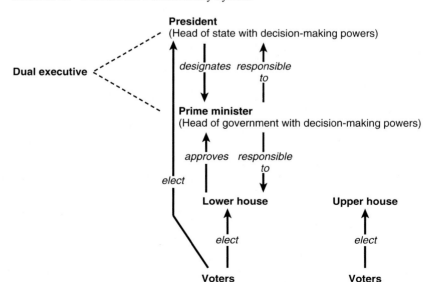

without parliamentary approval. He may even possess the authority to declare a state of national emergency and govern with little or no parliamentary check on his authority. The parliament, for its part, can be constitutionally forbidden to propose or pass laws in certain areas that are the exclusive preserve of presidential or cabinet authority. In France, for example, legislators are not allowed to propose bills that would require the government to raise or reduce state expenditures, a provision that severely limits the French legislature's "powers of the purse."

The main purpose of this type of regime is to expedite the process of making governmental decisions. By conferring a significant measure of legal authority on the president, it may be possible to avoid the protracted wrangling that often ensues when lawmaking is dominated by legislators. Presidential-parliamentary democracies are thus intended above all to maximize the *efficiency* of the decision-making process and the *stability* of executive authority. France adopted this system in 1958 precisely in order to avoid the persistent instability and gridlock that had plagued its parliamentary system of government from 1946 to 1958. Russia adopted its own variant of this system in 1993–94 with a view to managing the difficult transition from communism to democracy through strong executive power. President Boris Yeltsin, who was committed to democracy, wanted a free hand to make fundamental political and economic reforms that were opposed by the legislature's majority of communists and other opponents of change.

The danger arises, however, that a president with too much power may abuse it, perhaps threatening the very principles of negotiation, accommodation, and compromise on which democracy ultimately rests. Yeltsin's critics, for example, accused him of wielding quasi-dictatorial powers by unilaterally issuing decrees and other authoritative decisions without sufficient parliamentary consultation. Various French presidents have also been denounced as excessively secretive and authoritarian. Presidential-parliamentary regimes tend to walk a fine line between stable, efficient rule on the one hand and the abuse of executive power on the other.

Meanwhile, an efficient decision-making process firmly concentrated in the president's

hands may not always come about in practice. In addition to electing the president, the voters also elect the legislature. If the president represents one political party and the majority of legislators represent rival parties, gridlock may ensue. It can even happen that the president and the prime minister represent opposing parties, a prospect that can severely complicate the process of decision making at the highest executive levels of national government. In both France and Russia, the president may name the prime minister but the legislature has the right to reject the president's choice. As a consequence, the president may decide to name a prime minister of an opposing party so as to satisfy the legislative majority.

France has experienced this problem several times since the 1980s and most recently since 1997. President Jacques Chirac is a conservative, but the legislature elected in 1997 is dominated by his arch-rivals, the Socialists. Chirac had little choice but to appoint Socialist leader Lionel Jospin as prime minister. The two opposing political figures are condemned by France's constitutional system to cooperate in order to avoid prolonged gridlock and paralysis. Ironically, while the mixed presidential-parliamentary system is designed to streamline executive decision making, it can sometimes end up by severely complicating it.

Comparisons

Of the three types of democracy we have just examined, which one is "the best"? Seeking an unequivocal answer to this question is an exercise in futility. All three systems have advantages and disadvantages. The U.S. system of checks and balances prevents the domination of any single branch of government but risks the hazards of divided government and gridlock. Parliamentary government can at times function more efficiently and flexibly than the U.S. system, but these advantages are most likely to occur when one party enjoys an absolute majority of seats. When this condition does not prevail, majority coalition governments and minority governments can sometimes bring just as much gridlock as in the United States, if not more. Finally, presidential-parliamentary systems may at times ensure stable and effective government, but they can run roughshod over the legislature and risk crossing the thin line that separates presidential democracy from outright authoritarianism. At other times, the decision-making powers of the presidency in this system can shrink considerably if opposing parties control the legislature and the president has to deal with his chief opponent as prime minister.

Every system of government exists in the real-world context of an individual country's unique blend of historical, economic, social, and other characteristics. No two countries are ever exactly alike, and their political institutions are bound to emerge and develop in accordance with their own distinctive features. The U.S. system of separation of powers has evolved over more than two hundred years in a nation whose experiences have been very different from those of Europe, Latin America, and other parts of the world. The factors that account for the durability of this system in the United States may not be present in other countries, where other types of democracy may be more suitable or desirable.

Similarly, the factors that account for the way parliamentary government works in Britain are quite different from those that affect its operation in Japan, Israel, India, or elsewhere. The attributes of the mixed presidential-parliamentary system may be appropriate in some countries at particular stages in their history, but not at other times or in other countries. These national particularities will stand out more clearly when we examine the ways parliamentarism and the presidential-parliamentary system work in specific countries in later chapters.[6]

ELECTORAL SYSTEMS

Regular elections constitute one of the most indispensable components of modern democracy. Not all democracies have the same electoral systems, however. *There are different ways of counting the votes.* As a consequence, *there are different ways of making the votes count* in terms of who wins governing power and who does not.

Vote counting is an aspect of political science that has attracted close attention for centuries. It poses some tantalizing theoretical puzzles while at the same time exerting a profound effect on the way political power is distributed in the real world of politics. One of the most intriguing conundrums centers on *Condorcet's paradox and Arrow's general possibility theorem,* which are discussed in the appendix at the end of this chapter. The rest of this section will focus on several electoral systems that are currently in use around the world.

First we'll look at two methods for electing a president: the *direct election* system used in France, Russia, and some other countries, and the *electoral college* system used in the United States. Next we'll look at two methods for electing a chamber of the national legislature: the *single member district/plurality* system and *proportional representation.* These respective electoral systems by no means exhaust the range of vote-counting methods that are in use in the world today or that have been used in the past. By the same token, there are a number of electoral systems that have been proposed but never tried. With all their variants, however, the systems we describe here are the most widely used electoral systems in today's democracies.

Electing a President

In some democracies, the process of electing a president is straightforward: the people vote directly for individual candidates. In France and Russia this electoral process can be decided in a single election, or it may require two rounds of voting. In the first round of balloting, virtually any number of candidates may run, subject to certain requirements for candidacy. If one candidate gets an absolute majority of popular votes (50 percent plus one vote) in the first round, that person is declared the winner. If no one gets an absolute majority, a second round of balloting is held a week or two later between the top two finishers of the first round. The winner of this runoff election is elected president.

This direct-election system tends to give voters a wide assortment of choices in the first round; in effect, it amounts to a national primary election in which all eligible candidates run on the same day. This system also compels the voters to choose between two individuals in the event that a second round is necessary. If one's favored candidate does not survive the first round, the voter must decide whether to vote for one of the two remaining candidates or not vote at all. The results of recent presidential elections in France and Russia show that this system encourages a fairly large turnout in round one and a similar (or even higher) turnout in round two (see table 9.4). At least in France, it also guarantees that the person elected president is the choice of an absolute majority of those who turn out to vote. The Russians have an opportunity in both rounds to cast a vote *against* the candidates.

The U.S. system is considerably more complicated. Many of the framers of the Constitution did not want the direct election of the president by the voters because they were skeptical about the political wisdom of the population; they preferred a system that gave the final say in choosing the chief executive to a politically sophisticated elite. They therefore introduced a procedure in which voters in each state choose presidential *electors,* who in turn elect the president. The number of electors assigned to each state varies with the size of its population and equals the number of delegates it sends to the House of Representatives plus two more.[7]

Several weeks after the popular elections take place, the chosen electors assemble separately within each state as the **electoral college** and vote for the president. To be elected, the winning candidate must win an absolute majority of the total number of votes in the electoral college. Today there are 538 electoral college votes; the winning majority is 270 votes.

TABLE 9.4

Direct Election Systems in France and Russia

French Presidential Elections, 1995

Round 1 (April 23) (Turnout: 76.4%)			Round 2 (May 7) (Turnout: 77.7%)	
Candidate	**Party**	**% of Vote**	**Candidate**	**% of Vote**
Lionel Jospin	Socialist	23.3	Chirac	52.6
Jacques Chirac	Rally for the Republic	20.8	Jospin	47.4
Edouard Balladur	Rally for the Republic	18.6		
Jean-Marie Le Pen	National Front	15.0		
Robert Hue	Communist	8.6		
Arlette Laguiller	Trotskyite	5.3		
Philippe de Villiers	Struggle for Values	4.8		
Dominique Voynet	Greens	3.3		
Jacques Cheminade	Federation for a New Solidarity	0.3		

Russian Presidential Elections, 1996

Round 1 (June 16) (Turnout: 69%)			Round 2 (July 3) (Turnout: 69%)	
Candidate	**Party**	**% of Vote**	**Candidate**	**% of Vote**
Boris Yeltsin	(No party affiliation)	34.8	Yeltsin	53.8
Gennady Zyuganov	Communist	32.1	Zyuganov	40.3
Alexander Lebed	Congress of Russian Communities	14.7	Against both	4.8
Grigory Yavlinsky	Yabloko	7.4		
Vladimir Zhirinovsky	Liberal Democratic Party	5.8		
Svyatoslav Fyodorov	(No party affiliation)	0.9		
Mikhail Gorbachev	(No party affiliation)	0.5		
Martin Shakkum	Russian Popular Socialist Party	0.35		
Yuri Vlasov	(No party affiliation)	0.2		
Vladimir Bryntsalov	(No party affiliation)	0.16		
Against all candidates		3.0		

In the early history of the republic, the electors had considerable latitude to vote for their own preferred candidate for president. As the system evolved, the voters in each state acquired the opportunity to vote for competing slates of electors and it became increasingly expected that the electors would vote for the candidate they are "pledged" to support. Nowadays the voters pull a lever next to the name of their preferred choice for president. In effect they are voting for the electors pledged to that candidate. The vote taken by the college of electors has become a formality. The electors rarely vote for someone other than the person who has won the majority of popular votes in their respective states even though, in most states, they are not bound by law to do so.

Another peculiarity of this system is that, in most states, whoever wins the highest popular vote total within each state automatically wins *all* that state's electoral votes. The U.S. presidential election system thus consists of *winner-take-all* elections in almost all the fifty states plus the District of Columbia. To illustrate: in the 1996 elections, President Clinton won 48 percent of the popular vote in Florida; Robert Dole won 42.3 percent of the votes in that state; and Ross Perot captured 9.1 percent. Having garnered the highest number of votes, President Clinton won *all* of Florida's twenty-five electoral votes. Some people have questioned this system's fairness, arguing in favor of a *proportional* distribution of electoral votes in each state. Under a proportional arrangement, President Clinton would have been entitled only to 48 percent of Florida's electoral votes (12 votes), Senator Dole would have been entitled to 42 percent (11), and Perot would have received 9 percent of the state's electoral votes (2). If each candidate were to get a share of electoral college votes in proportion to his or her share of the popular vote within each state, the distribution of votes in the electoral college would be much closer than it is under the current system.[8]

As table 9.5 shows, a candidate can win the presidency by winning a popular majority in just eleven states plus the District of Columbia. Even if that candidate does not win a single popular vote in any of the other states, he or she will still win 270 electoral college votes.

In the U.S. system it is quite possible for a candidate to win *less* than an absolute majority of popular votes and still be elected president. This result is particularly likely when there are more than two candidates running in the general election. In 1996, Bill Clinton won the presidency with 70.4 percent of the votes in the electoral college (379), but he won only 49.2 percent of the national vote. Bob Dole won 40.7 percent of the popular vote and 29.6 percent of the electoral college votes (159), while Ross Perot won 8.4 percent of the popular vote and no electoral college votes. It is even possible to be elected president in the college of electors and *lose* the nationwide popular vote to a competing candidate. This result occurred twice in American history, in 1876 and 1888.[9]

Legislative Elections

As we pointed out in chapter 6, a country's national legislature is either *unicameral,* consisting of only one house, or *bicameral,* consisting of two. There are several different methods for electing these legislative chambers. The two methods we'll examine here—the *single member district/plurality* method and *proportional representation*—each has several different variants. In this chapter we'll simply describe the main principles of these two electoral systems using a few illustrative examples, but

TABLE 9.5

Minimum Number of States Needed to Win 270 Electoral College Votes	
State	**Electoral Votes**
California	54
New York	33
Texas	32
Florida	25
Pennsylvania	23
Illinois	22
Ohio	21
Michigan	18
New Jersey	15
Massachusetts	12
Indiana	12
District of Columbia*	3
TOTAL:	270

*The following states also have three electoral votes each: Alaska, Delaware, Montana, North Dakota, South Dakota, Vermont, and Wyoming.

we'll defer a more detailed explanation of how they work in specific countries to later chapters.

The Single Member District/Plurality Method   In the **single member district/plurality** electoral system, the country is divided into electoral districts for elections to a particular legislative chamber. The United States, for example, is divided into 435 electoral districts for the House of Representatives. Britain is now divided into 659 districts for elections to the House of Commons. *One person is elected to represent each district; hence the term single member district (SMD).*

One advantage of this system is that, with only one representative per district, the voters should have an easier time identifying their legislative deputy than would be the case if their district were a *multimember district.* A multimember district sends two or more representatives to the national legislature. Single member districts are supposed to be more personalized than multimember districts, thereby promoting greater citizen awareness of politics and greater accountability on the part of the elected representative to his or her constituency. In actual fact, most Americans do *not* know the name of their representative, but they cannot blame their ignorance on the complexity of their electoral system. It's actually quite simple.

If there are only two candidates running in each district, the winner automatically wins by an absolute majority (50 percent plus one vote). This result frequently occurs in the United States, where most Congressional races are traditionally limited to a Democrat competing against a Republican. In Britain and several other countries that have the SMD voting system, however, three or more candidates routinely compete in each district. In some of these races the winning candidate will win an absolute majority of the votes cast, but it is not neces-

sary to win an absolute majority to be elected the district's representative. *A majority—the highest number of votes among the competing candidates—is sufficient to win.* The candidate who wins the highest number of votes in this system is often said to be "first past the post." In the hypothetical British example shown in table 9.6, Jean Smith, the Labour Party candidate, is the winner with 37.5 percent of the vote in her district.

The other candidates simply lose. *The SMD/plurality electoral system is a "winner take all" system.* France has a two-round variant of this system.

This electoral system's main advantages lie in its relative simplicity and the chances it offers to promote name recognition on the part of incumbent representatives and their challengers. But it has some potential problems. For one thing, *the SMD/plurality system can lead to a disparity between a party's share of the vote on a nationwide basis and its share of the seats in the legislature.* To understand this possibility, simply consider the outcome of a hypothetical race for one seat in the U.S. House of Representatives. In our example, the Republican candidate gets 51 percent of the votes cast and the Democrat gets 49 percent. There are no other candidates running in this district. The Republican is elected to Congress; the Democrat will have to wait two more years for another opportunity to campaign for the seat.

Now suppose that this result, by odd coincidence, occurs in *all 435 House districts.* If we add up all the votes cast throughout the country for the House of Representatives, it is evident that the Republican candidates together captured 51 percent of the vote nationwide while the Democratic candidates together garnered 49 percent. Because the Republican candidate won each House contest, however, the Republicans end up with *all 435* House seats; the Democrats get none. The bot-

TABLE 9.6

Hypothetical Election in a British Electoral District (House of Commons)			
Candidate	Party	No. of Votes	% of Vote
Jean Smith	Labour	12,000	37.5
Jack Jones	Conservative	10,000	31.3
Martha Brown	Liberal Democrat	8,000	25.0
George Martin	Green	2,000	6.2

tom line is that the Republicans have won slightly more than half the national vote but 100 percent of the seats; the Democrats have won slightly less than half the vote but come away with no representation in the House at all. Table 9.7 displays this result.

Obviously this is an extreme example that is not likely to occur any time soon. But it illustrates a general point: under the SMD system, a significant difference between a party's share of the national vote and its share of legislative seats *can* occur. Table 9.8 provides a real example.

Note that, in the 1992 elections to the House, there was a difference of 8.5 percent between the Democrats' share of all votes in the 435 House races combined (50.8 percent) and the percentage of these races they actually won (59.3 percent). That's a fairly wide disparity. Likewise there was a disparity of 5.1 percent between the Republicans' share of the vote for all House races combined (45.6 percent) and their percentage of seats in the House (40.5 per-

cent). Even wider disparities have occurred in other years. A particularly glaring example of this phenomenon occurred in the 1997 elections to the British House of Commons. The Labour party won 43.3 percent of the national vote, but 63.6 percent of the seats! (See table 9.9.) At times the anomalies of the SMD system can be truly bizarre, as the following figures show.

HOW ANOMALIES CAN OCCUR IN THE SMD SYSTEM

Consider a state that elects three members to the U.S. House of Representatives. In each race, a Democrat runs against a Republican. Conceivably, voter turnout and the margin of victory could vary considerably from one district to another, resulting in the following hypothetical result:

	Candidate	Votes
1st District	Democrat	100,000
	Republican	10,000
2nd District	Democrat	50,000
	Republican	50,020
3rd District	Democrat	10,000
	Republican	20,000
Totals	Democrats	160,000
	Republicans	80,020
		240,020

As you can see, the three Democrats together captured approximately two-thirds of the votes, but the Republicans won two of the three districts. Anomalies of this sort have actually occurred in real elections.[10]

Another characteristic problem of the SMD/plurality electoral system is that *it tends to punish small parties.* In order to win a significant share of

TABLE 9.7
Hypothetical Election to the U.S. House of Representatives

Party	% of Total Vote Nationwide	% of Seats Won
Republicans	51	100
Democrats	49	0

TABLE 9.8
Elections to U.S. House of Representatives, 1992

	% of Popular Vote Nationwide	% of Seats Won
Democrats	50.8	59.3
Republicans	45.6	40.5
Others	3.6	(1 seat)

TABLE 9.9
Recent Elections to the British House of Commons

Party	1992			1997		
	% of Popular Vote	% of Seats	No. of Seats	% of Popular Vote	% of Seats	No. of Seats
Conservatives	42.8	51.7	336	30.7	25.0	165
Labour	35.2	41.7	271	43.3	63.6	419
Liberal Democrats	18.3	3.1	20	16.8	7.0	46
Others	3.7	3.7	24	9.3	4.4	29

seats in the U.S. House of Representatives or the British House of Commons, a party must be able to field viable candidates throughout the country, in virtually all districts. Parties that are not large enough to mount such extensive campaigns are not likely to win many legislative seats. The SMD system, in other words, is a major reason why the United States has a two-party system. Other parties are too weak within the individual districts, as well as nationally, to elect their candidates to the House.

Elections to the British House of Commons provide a vivid illustration of how difficult it is for small parties to win a share of parliamentary seats commensurate with their share of the popular vote. Note in table 9.9 that in 1992 and 1997, the Liberal Democrats, Britain's third-largest party, won nearly 20 percent of the vote nationwide but a mere 3 percent of the seats in the Commons in 1992 and 7 percent in 1997. (That is, they won only 3 percent of the 651 individual district races in 1992 and 7 percent of 659 races in 1997.) Their voter support was spread out widely across the country, but was sufficiently concentrated to win a plurality in only a few districts. Other parties fared even more poorly.

One of the chief problems of the SMD/plurality system, then, is that *a result that is fair at the local level may turn out to be unfair at the national level.* "Winner take all" may be a fair way to elect someone to represent your district in the national legislature. But when all the votes are counted nationwide, there may be a significant gap between the parties' respective share of legislative seats and their share of the national vote. Statistical measures of these disparities show that they can remain quite significant over many years. The proportional representation system is designed to overcome this problem.

Proportional Representation   *Under* **proportional representation** *(PR), a party's share (percentage) of its seats in the legislature exactly or approximately equals its share of the popular vote nationwide.* To put it very simply, if a party gets 25 percent of the popular vote in legislative elections, it will get 25 percent (exactly or approximately) of the seats in the legislature. Various statistical formulas are employed to ensure these results. There are numerous variants of the PR principle. Most of those in use today are approximate PR systems. In the **party list** variant, parties draw up lists of candidates, rank-ordering their names in accordance with their political prominence. Typically, if a party is entitled to 200 legislative seats, the first 200 people on its list will get the seats.[11]

Prior to 1994, Italy had a PR system for elections to its lower house, the Chamber of Deputies. The results of the Italian elections of 1992 provide an instructive illustration of the PR system (see table 9.10). The first thing to observe in these results is the close approximation between each identified party's share of the national vote and its share of the seats in the Chamber of Deputies. For several parties the two numbers are the same; for others they differ by only 3 percent (in the case of the Christian Democrats) or less. Each party, in other words, wins a share of legislative seats *in proportion to* its share of the national vote. We do not see the wide disparities in these two figures that are possible—and that sometimes actually occur—in the SMD/plurality system.[12]

The next observation, and perhaps the most striking one in this example, is the large number of parties elected to the Chamber. Indeed, *PR can lead to a fairly wide proliferation of political parties represented in the legislature.* Under these conditions, it is not likely that a single party will win an absolute majority of legislative seats. As a consequence, *PR often results in a multiparty coalition government or a minority government.* If the parties that participate in these arrangements get along and have the best interests of the voters at heart, such a system can work smoothly in establishing stable and effective governments. As we've already noted, however, multiparty governments can also be highly unstable and inefficient. One of the drawbacks of PR, therefore, is that it increases the chances of instability and inefficiency.

In the case of Italy in 1992, negotiations among the various parties led to the formation of a four-party coalition government consisting of the Christian Democrats, the Socialists, the Social Democrats, and the Liberals. Together they comprised a slim majority of the Chamber's 630 deputies (52.5 percent). These same four parties had been coalition partners since the 1970s, at times with the Republicans constituting a fifth partner. Under this system, very small parties like the Social Democrats and the Liberals not only succeeded in winning parliamentary seats, they also managed as coalition partners to gain a share of cabinet posts and thus a direct

TABLE 9.10

Elections to Italy's Chamber of Deputies, 1992

(630 Seats)

Party	% of Vote Nationwide	% of Seats	No. of Seats
Greens	2.7	2.5	16
La Rete (Anti-Mafia party)	1.8	1.9	12
Communist Refoundation	5.6	5.6	35
Democratic Party of the Left (reform Communists)	16.1	16.9	107
Socialist Unity Party	13.6	14.6	92
Social Democratic Party	2.7	2.5	16
Liberal Party	2.8	2.7	17
Republican Party	4.4	4.3	27
Christian Democratic Party	29.6	32.7	206
Northern League	8.6	8.7	55
Italian Social Movement/ National Right	5.3	5.4	34
Others (combined)	6.3	2.1	13

Source: Inter-Parliamentary Union, *Chronicle of Parliamentary Elections and Developments,* vol. 26.

role in government decision making. They also got a proportionate share of jobs in the country's vast state bureaucracy.

PR can therefore be a blessing for small parties by providing them with a share of seats in the legislature that is roughly equivalent to their share of popular support. Unlike the SMD/plurality system, which punishes small parties by making it very difficult to translate their popular mandate into equivalent legislative gains, PR is more faithfully representative of the popular will. Its advocates therefore exalt it as a fairer system of democratic representation than the SMD/plurality system is. If Britain had PR, proponents would point out, the Liberal Democrats, who got 16.8 percent of the vote in 1997, would have received roughly the same percentage of seats in the House of Commons. And if the United States were to adopt PR, there would probably be an increase in the number of parties from which the voters could choose. PR systems are seldom, if ever, two-party systems.

Critics of PR contend that it can lead to such a large number of parties in the national legislature that governing becomes next to impossible. Many Italians came to precisely that conclusion after nearly five decades of chronic governmental instability and endemic corruption. The four-party coalition cabinet that was formed after the 1992 elections became embroiled in a massive corrup-

tion scandal whose roots could be traced back nearly four decades. Intense public pressure eventually forced the government to resign and ultimately led to the complete restructuring of Italy's electoral system. In 1994 a new system was introduced that combined PR with the SMD/plurality method. Only one-fourth of the Chamber's 630 seats were elected under PR in that year and the remaining three-fourths were chosen under SMD. The express purpose of this change was to reduce the unwieldy number of parties elected to the Chamber in hopes of ending the repetitive cycle of unstable and corrupt coalition governments. In fact, the new electoral system accomplished at least some of these desired results. The main parties regrouped, forming three large blocs in the Chamber of Deputies. This result provided clear evidence that the nature of the electoral system can be an independent variable having a direct impact on the number of political parties in representative institutions as well as on their strategic behavior.

Some democracies with PR systems have found a way to cut back on the number of parties elected to the legislature. A **hurdle** can be used to require a party to win a certain percentage of the national vote in order to acquire legislative seats. Parties falling below this hurdle usually do not get any seats. Sweden has a 4 percent hurdle, for example, and Germany has a 5 percent hurdle. Italy's PR system prior to 1994 had no hurdle, but a 4 percent hurdle was introduced in 1994. The introduction of a hurdle can definitely reduce the number of parties elected to parliament.

Another criticism that is often leveled at PR is that it tends to be more impersonal than the SMD system. Whereas the voters in an SMD system have a chance to identify the competing candidates by name and only have to remember the name of the one and only person elected to represent their district, PR elections are usually less personalized. In most PR systems the voters vote for a party, not an individual candidate. Each party provides a list of the candidates it puts up for election but the names on these lists are not likely to be highly publicized in the media. Except for the most prominent leaders in each party, candidates for the legislature in most PR systems are not likely to have a high degree of name recognition among the voters. In addition, some countries with PR systems have multimember districts, with as many as eight or ten legislators elected to serve each district. While some voters may like having a multiplicity of representatives catering to their district's needs, others may find it difficult to recall the name of any of them. It may therefore be more difficult to hold individual legislators accountable to their local constituents in such circumstances.

Germany tries to get around these problems by combining PR with the SMD system. Half of the Bundestag's seats are elected by PR, the other half by SMD. A statistical formula ensures that the final distribution of seats in that chamber approximates PR. Russia also uses a combination of PR and SMD in electing its lower house, the State Duma.

At times PR can be more effective than SMD in promoting the election of women and minorities. In a party-list PR system, a party can simply add candidates from these groups to its list of prospective legislators. If the party wins 200 seats, and 100 women and minority members are rank-ordered among its top 200 candidates, those women and minority candidates enter the legislature. In an electoral system of this type, the party rather than individual candidates typically finances the election campaign. By contrast, winning a single-member district seat in a legislature like the U.S. House of Representatives may require individual candidates to raise substantial amounts of money to promote their name recognition, a reality that

often disadvantages female or minority candidates for Congress.

In sum, the main advantages of PR are (1) its *fairness* in translating popular support for political parties into equivalent shares of legislative seats; (2) its ability to *help small parties*—and perhaps women and minorities—to win a fair share of legislative seats; and (3) its tendency to *enhance voter choice* by providing the electorate with a wide array of parties from which to choose. PR's disadvantages include (1) its tendency to promote the *proliferation of a large number of parties*; (2) its tendency thereby to increase the likelihood of *hung parliaments, governmental instability, inefficiency* and *ineffectiveness*; and (3) its *impersonal character*.

Just as we cannot identify with any confidence "the best" institutional form of representative democracy, it is equally difficult to pick either the SMD/plurality system or PR as the better legislative electoral system. As we've seen, both systems have advantages and disadvantages. Most important, how these systems work in actual practice tends to differ from country to country. In some democracies the SMD/plurality system may produce election results that disadvantaged parties regard as unfair. But SMD does not necessarily lead to wide disparities between the popular vote and the distribution of legislative seats all the time. In the 1994 elections to the U.S. House of Representatives, the Republicans won 51.1 percent of the national vote and got 53.3 percent of the seats; the Democrats won 46.8 percent of the vote and got 46.4 percent of the seats.

To understand the impact of electoral systems on the actual course of political events, therefore, we need to combine a firm theoretical understanding of how these systems *can* work with detailed empirical examinations of how they actually *do* work in different democracies.[13] One question is immensely relevant to average citizens in all democracies: do voters turn out at the polls at consistently higher rates under one of these systems as opposed to the other? Theoretically, one would think that the PR system would attract more voters than plurality systems on the grounds that PR gives the voters a greater chance to elect representatives of their favorite party into the legislature. Under PR, a party can win seats and perhaps cabinet ministries even if it gets less than 10 percent of the total vote. Under plurality systems, as in the United States or Britain, the two largest parties are likely to win the overwhelming majority of the seats. PR systems thus tend to entice a greater number of parties to run candidates, giving the voters a wider array of choice on election day than they are likely to get under a plurality system.

Following these assumptions, we'll hypothesize that PR electoral systems tend to result in higher voter turnout rates than plurality systems on a fairly consistent basis. Does the available evidence support this supposition?

HYPOTHESIS-TESTING EXERCISE: Do PR Systems Have Higher Turnout Than Plurality Systems?

HYPOTHESIS
Proportional representation produces higher voter turnouts than plurality systems in legislative elections.

VARIABLES
The **dependent variable** *is voter turnout.* The **independent variables** are *PR* and *plurality voting systems.*

EXPECTATIONS
If our hypothesis is correct, we would expect to find that democracies with PR will have consistently higher turnout rates than those with plurality systems.

EVIDENCE
Table 9.11 is a list of twenty-two countries that have held democratic elections for at least the past forty years. Most

of them have retained the same parliamentary electoral system throughout the decades, the chief exceptions being France and Italy. Though the various PR systems differ in specific details, in principle they are sufficiently similar to justify grouping them together for comparative purposes. The same is true of the plurality systems.

It is immediately apparent that a large number of countries with PR systems have average turnout rates of 79 percent or higher; only two of the states with plurality systems attract more voters. Turnout in the PR countries from 1945 to 1997 averages out to 78 percent; in the plurality countries the average is 69.5 percent. These figures are consistent with our hypothesis.

The cases of France and Italy are especially instructive. Under the IVth Republic, from 1944 to 1958, France had a PR system. It switched to a plurality system under the Vth Republic starting in 1958. Average turnout rates were higher under PR (72.2 percent) than under the plurality system (65.3 percent). Italy had the highest average turnout rates in the world when it had a PR system with no hurdle. In those years, from 1948 to 1992, the Italians turned out to vote at an average rate exceeding 92 percent. In 1994 and 1996 it used a different system, in which 75 percent of the deputies were elected under a plurality system and the remaining 25 percent under PR. Turnout in those two elections averaged 89 percent. The experiences of France and Italy thus conform to our expectations.[14]

CONCLUSIONS
Higher average turnout rates for PR systems are obviously the rule. Nevertheless, we should not lose sight of

TABLE 9.11

Turnout in PR and Plurality Electoral Systems

PR Systems		Plurality Systems	
Country	Average Turnout, 1945–1997	Country	Average Turnout, 1945–1997
Italy	92.5%	New Zealand	86.2%
Iceland	89.5	Australia	84.4
Austria	85.1	United Kingdom	74.9
Belgium	84.9	Canada	68.4
Netherlands	84.8	France, Vth Republic	65.3
Denmark	83.6	India	60.6
Sweden	83.4	United States	48.3
Germany	80.6		
Israel	80.0		
Norway	79.8		
Finland	79.0		
Ireland	74.9		
France, IVth Republic	72.2		
Luxembourg	64.1		
Switzerland	49.3		

Source: International Institute for Democracy and Electoral Assistance, *Voter Turnout from 1945 to 1997: A Global Report.*

some interesting details. Notice that average turnout rates are higher in New Zealand, Australia, the United Kingdom, and Canada—countries with variants of the plurality system—than in Japan, Luxembourg, and Switzerland, which have variants of PR. And Italy's turnouts in 1994 and 1996, when it was predominantly a plurality system, were markedly higher than the long-term trends in almost all other PR countries. Plurality systems thus do not *always* have lower turnout rates than PR systems. Our overall evidence is therefore *mixed*.

If we dig into some data not shown here, we can occasionally find significant variations in voter turnout within the same country, despite the fact that no change has occurred in its electoral system. In Switzerland, for example, turnout has plunged from 63 percent in 1951 to 35.7 percent in 1995. In the United States, turnout for House elections is typically higher in years when a presidential election takes place than in off years (see figure 3.4).[15] Germany's electoral system combines PR *and* SMD/plurality: though the final result is always approximate proportional representation, voters may be lured to the polls at least in part to vote for a single member to represent their voting district.

These and other departures from the general validity of our hypothesis serve as reminders that virtually every generalization has its exceptions and that a correlation between two variables does not by itself explain *why* it occurs. People vote—or stay at home—for all sorts of reasons. Although people show a general tendency to mark their ballots in PR systems at higher rates than in countries with plurality systems, it would be a mistake to assume that electoral systems alone account for voter turnout. Perhaps we should remind ourselves of another generalization: more often than not, multicausality is more likely to explain the complex phenomena of political reality than is reductivist monocausality.

KEY TERMS
(Underlined in the text)

Separation of powers
Checks and balances
Divided government
Parliamentary government
Fusion of powers
Vote of confidence
Single-party majoritarian government
Party discipline
Hung parliament
Coalition government
Governmental instability
Minority government
Anticipated (snap) elections
Presidential-parliamentary system
Electoral college
Single member district/plurality electoral system
Proportional representation
Hurdle

APPENDIX

Condorcet's Paradox and Arrow's General Possibility Theorem

The Marquis de Condorcet (kon-dor-say), an eighteenth-century French philosopher and mathematician, was one of the first to point out the following paradox of voting:

If three individuals are faced with three different choices (such as competing candidates for election or alternative policies for dealing with a particular problem), it may be impossible to determine the will of the majority.

Condorcet deduced this conclusion by considering how three people (I, II, and III, respectively) might prioritize their preferences for choices A, B, and C:

I prefers A to B and B to C (and thus A to C);
II prefers B to C and C to A (and thus B to A);
III prefers C to A and A to B (and thus C to B).

Which choice does the majority prefer? Two out of three prefer A to B and B to C. We may therefore conclude that a majority prefers A to C. Does this mean that the majority wishes to eliminate C as an acceptable choice? Evidently not, since two out of the three individuals (viz., II and III) prefer C to A! Condorcet's paradox thus follows logically from the premises of the problem. On the basis of deductive logic, Condorcet showed that when the public is divided in the manner just described, majority rule is impossible and gridlock inevitable.

Nearly two centuries later, Kenneth Arrow, a Nobel Prize–winning American economist, elaborated on this paradox and applied it to the problems communities face when trying to make choices that will satisfy the economic preferences of the population. In his book *Social Choice and Individual Values*,[16] Arrow showed with rigorous deductive logic that, when faced with at least three alternative proposals for providing for society's economic welfare under plausible real-world conditions, the community may be unable to come up with a clear majority for any of the three available choices. Once again, gridlock ensues. Building a tightly linked chain of axioms, conditions, theorems, and definitions, Arrow further deduced that, when this happens, **either it may be impossible to make any decision at all, or the policy choice must be imposed on the public dictatorially** (that is, by political leaders acting on their own). Arrow called this conclusion the "general possibility theorem."

> **Arrow's theorem explains why, in a democracy based on the principle of majority rule, it may at times be impossible to make political decisions except by violating that very principle. It predicts that, under certain conditions, democracy will lead either to hopeless gridlock and non-decision, or else to some form of non-democratic decision making. The theorem is thus explanatory and predictive.**

Of course, the conditions posited by Condorcet and Arrow need not always occur. Sometimes the public may speak with a clear majority in favor of a single choice. But *if* the public is divided in accordance with the voting priorities laid out by Condorcet, Arrow's logic shows that either gridlock or dictatorial decision making *must* ensue.

These conclusions have obvious implications for the ability of democracies to function effectively. At the same time, it is worth noting the method Condorcet and Arrow used to arrive at their conclusions. Both theorists used *deductive logic.* Neither of them examined any particular cases of democratic gridlock empirically. Their conclusions followed in logical succession from their premises, providing excellent examples of deduction as applied to politics.

NOTES

1. Aristotle, *The Politics,* rev. ed., trans. T. A. Sinclair and Trevor J. Saunders (London: Penguin, 1981), bk. 4, sec. 11–12, pp. 264–72.
2. Charles Louis de Secondat, Baron de Montesquieu, *The Spirit of Laws,* 2 vols., trans. Thomas Nugent (New York: Colonial Press, 1900), especially pt. 2, bk. 11. On his influence, see Paul Merrill Spurlin, *Montesquieu in America 1760–1801* (New York: Octagon, 1969).
3. William H. Riker suggests that coalition partners often find that it is their own best interest to share the spoils of a coalition government with as few parties as possible. They therefore tend to favor a "minimum winning coalition" as opposed to one that maximizes parliamentary support. See *The Theory of Political Coalitions* (New Haven, Conn.: Yale University Press, 1962).
4. See, for example, Michael Laver and Norman Schofield, *Multiparty Government: The Politics of Coalition in Europe* (Oxford: Oxford University Press, 1991).
5. Some scholars call this system the *semi-presidential system.* We prefer the term *presidential-parliamentary system* because it more closely approximates the reality of a truly mixed system in which the president, no matter how constitutionally powerful, must still share power with a legislature and a prime minister, no matter how constitutionally weak.
6. For debates on these issues, see, for example, Juan J. Linz, "The Perils of Presidentialism," and "The Virtues of Parliamentarism," in *The Global Resurgence of Democracy,* 2nd ed., ed. Larry Diamond and Marc F. Plattner (Baltimore, Md.: Johns Hopkins University Press, 1996), 108–126 and 138–145; Donald L. Horowitz, "Comparing Democratic Systems," ibid., 127–133; Seymour Martin Lipset, "The Centrality of Political Culture," ibid., 134–137; and the essays in Arendt Lijphart, ed., *Parliamentary versus Presidential Government* (Oxford: Oxford University Press, 1992). See also Lijphart's study, *Patterns of Democracy: Government Forms and Performance in Thirty-Six Countries* (New Haven, Conn.: Yale University Press, 1999); and *The Failure of Presidential Democracy,* ed. Juan J. Linz and Arturo Valenzuela (Baltimore, Md.: Johns Hopkins University Press, 1994).
7. In the early years of the Republic, most states did not even hold popular elections to select their presidential electors. As late as 1800, ten of the sixteen states chose their electors by majority vote of the state legislature; only two states held statewide elections in which the eligible electorate could vote for presidential electors. In the nineteenth century it gradually became customary throughout the country for the people to vote for the electors in their respective states. See Stanley Elkins and Eric McKitrick, *The Age of Federalism* (New York: Oxford University Press, 1993), 741.
8. In the event that no candidate wins 270 votes in the electoral college, the Constitution prescribes that the House of Representatives then elects the president. In this eventuality, each state gets only *one* vote, which means that each state's delegation in the House must agree on one candidate. Whoever wins a majority of the fifty votes is elected president.

9. In 1876, Hayes (Republican) won 48 percent of the popular vote and 285 electoral college votes, beating Tilden (Democrat), who won 51 percent of the popular vote but only 184 electoral college votes. In 1888, Harrison (R) won 47.8 percent of the popular vote and 233 votes in the electoral college, defeating Cleveland (D), who got 48.6 percent of the popular vote but 168 electoral votes. In 1824, Andrew Jackson won a plurality of the popular vote (41.3 percent) and enough electoral college votes to win the presidency. Three opposing candidates split the remaining popular vote.

10. In 1984, for example, California elected forty-five members to the U.S. House of Representatives. When all the votes for these races were added up, the Democratic candidates collectively won 49.1 percent of the statewide popular vote while Republican candidates together got 49.4 percent. (Third party candidates won the remaining 1.5 percent of the total vote.) However, Democrats won 60 percent of the forty-five district races and Republicans 40 percent. In the same year, Florida sent nineteen members to the House in Washington, D.C. On a statewide basis the Republican candidates collectively won 53.4 percent of the popular vote and Democratic candidates 46.6 percent. But Democrats were victorious in twelve of the nineteen districts (63 percent of the districts) while Republicans won the remaining seven (37 percent of the districts). These disparities occurred because voter turnout and the margin of victory varied from district to district.

11. For an explanation of various statistical methods for distributing seats in proportional representation systems, see *Electoral Systems: A World-wide Comparative Study* (Geneva: Inter-Parliamentary Union, n.d.), 7–11. The same publication explains variants of other electoral systems as well.

12. "Disproportionality" in voting systems—the difference between a party's share of seats in the legislature and its share of the popular vote—is consistently higher in plurality systems than under proportional representation. Statistical calculations in which 1.0 equals the lowest level of disproportionality show that Italy's system scored an average of 1.1 over a period of three decades, while Britain's plurality system averaged 19.5 and those of Canada, Australia, and New Zealand together averaged 10.7. See Arend Lijphart et al., *Electoral Systems and Party Systems* (Oxford: Oxford University Press, 1994).

13. For a debate on parliamentary electoral systems, see the essays by Lijphart, Lardeyret, and Quade in Diamond and Plattner, 146–77. See also Rein Taagepera and Matthew Soberg Shugart, *Seats and Votes* (New Haven, Conn.: Yale University Press, 1989).

14. The Italian constitution requires voting as a "civic duty." Until 2000, citizens who failed to vote in two successive legislative elections could be stricken from the electoral rolls of eligible voters. An indeterminate number of Italians may thus have turned out to vote over the years out of a sense of obligation. Enforcement of the sanctions tended to be lax, however, and it is likely that Italy's electoral system has had a greater impact on turnout than the legal obligation to vote.

15. *Voter Turnout from 1945 to 1997: A Global Report on Political Participation* (Stockholm, Sweden: International Institute for Democracy and Electoral Assistance, 1997). The website for this organization is <www.int-idea.se>.

16. Kenneth J. Arrow, *Social Choice and Individual Values*, 2d ed. (New Haven, Conn.: Yale University Press, 1951).

CHAPTER 10

CONDITIONS FOR DEMOCRACY AND DEMOCRATIZATION

Ten Conditions—Poland—Romania

Why is it that some countries succeed in establishing democracies and sustaining them over long periods of time, whereas others cannot even build a functioning democracy or keep one for very long? What must countries do in order to make a successful transition from a non-democratic regime to an enduring democracy? These are among the oldest riddles of politics. They also relate with dramatic urgency to the world we live in.

In this chapter we'll look at a number of factors that have helped account for the success of some of the oldest democracies in the world, such as the United States and Britain. These same factors provide guidelines for countries that are now engaged in the difficult but crucially important process of democratization. **Democratization** *refers to the process of building a democracy following the collapse of a non-democratic regime.* It is a *transition process* from one form of government to a very different one.

In today's world there are numerous democratization processes taking place: in Latin America and Africa, where democracies are replacing discredited military regimes or one-party dictatorships; in Russia and other parts of the former Soviet Union as well as in East-Central Europe, where democracy is gaining a foothold following decades of communist party rule; in Asia, in places like the Philippines, South Korea, Taiwan, and Indonesia; and in other parts of the world as well. In some of these cases, democracy is making a comeback following earlier attempts that ended in failure. Brazil, Argentina, and Chile are examples. In other cases democracy is literally being built from scratch, on the basis of virtually no prior history of democratic governance. Russia is a prime example.

In still other countries there have been recent stirrings of support for democracy but authoritarian regimes continue to wield power, often by ruthlessly suppressing democratic tendencies. China is an illustrative case, but not the only one.

Of course, the hope of democracy's advocates is that the democratization processes now going on around the world will succeed and that countries on the verge of democracy will find a way to overcome authoritarian rule. The ultimate aim of all these efforts is the **consolidation** of democracy. Countries that embark on the democratization process need to complete it by building a strong and lasting democracy that withstands the tests of time. Nations cross the dividing line between democratization and consolidation when their institutions are so widely accepted and their democratic practices are so ingrained that their populations and elites—including the military and former dictatorial parties—cannot imagine replacing democracy with an authoritarian government. Democracy thus becomes "the only game in town." One indication that this threshold is within reach might be the successful completion of two or three fair elections. Inevitably, the road from the earliest phases of democratization to the full achievement of a consolidated democracy is a long one, requiring decades of perseverance and hard work. The factors we enumerate in this chapter can help countries proceed from authoritarianism to democratization, and from democratization to the consolidation of a lasting democracy. Success, however, is by no means a sure thing.

TEN CONDITIONS FOR DEMOCRACY

The ten factors that follow do not constitute a magic formula capable of guaranteeing that a democracy will come about or, if it does, that it will survive over the long run. Every country must find its own path to a democratic system based on its own idiosyncrasies. Very few successful democracies or democratizing countries will possess all the factors on our list. Some, in fact, may even display certain characteristics that are precisely the opposite of our presumptive conditions for democratic government, yet they may nevertheless succeed in building and sustaining other democratic structures and processes.

Rather than constituting a foolproof recipe for "how to build a democracy," therefore, what follows is simply a list of **independent variables** in **hypotheses** that we can formulate about how democracies emerge and why they endure. In each case our **dependent variables** are *the emergence and consolidation of democracy*. And in each case our chief **expectation** is that the independent variables promote processes that are conducive to the emergence and long-term survival of democracy. This chapter is therefore an extended **hypothesis-testing exercise** that tests some variables against relevant evidence. Our basic assumption is that each of the ten independent variables on our list *increases the chances* for successful democratization and democratic consolidation. Conversely, we hypothesize that the absence of these factors weakens the prospects for democracy. Obviously, we cannot subject these hypothe-

ses to an exhaustive test in these few pages, but a cursory look at how they relate to two newly democratizing former communist countries in East-Central Europe—Poland and Romania—may clarify the forces that promote, or obstruct, the development of democracy.

1. State Institutions

First and foremost, a successful democracy requires a functioning state that has sovereignty over a defined territory and is viewed as legitimate by its population. As Juan Linz and Alfred Stepan have pointed out in their comprehensive study of democratization, this phenomenon of "*stateness*" is a fundamental prerequisite of democratic development. "Without a state," they note, "there can be no citizenship; without citizenship, there can be no democracy."[1] Countries where significant elements of the population want autonomy or complete independence and do not accept the legitimacy of the existing central government—as in Yugoslavia on the eve of its dissolution in the early 1990s or Russia during the war with separatists in Chechnya—are off to a rocky start in the democratization process.

Just as important, a functioning democracy needs governmental institutions that will ensure *popular sovereignty* and basic *civil rights and liberties*, much as we characterized them in chapter 8. At the very least, the state must be organized on the basis of the *rule of law*. Those who govern must be *accountable* to the population, with fair, competitive elections permitting the *removability* of key officials on a regular basis. The *transparency* of the governing process must permit the citizenry to keep a watchful eye on state officials so as to detect corruption and punish those who perpetrate it. The *judiciary* must be independent of political manipulation by the executive and legislative branches. The *bureaucracy* must be bound by legal procedures, while at the same time possessing sufficient resources to assist elected officials in the policy making and policy implementation processes. The *military* must abide by the rules of the game of democratic governance and accept civilian controls. The lawmaking process must be reasonably *efficient* (timely) and *effective*, successfully addressing the country's problems.

Countries that organize their state institutions in accordance with these core values and procedures take a vital first step toward the development and consolidation of democracy. Every successful democracy resides on the foundation stones of democratic state institutions, as the history of the United States, England, and the nations that built stable democracies after World War II (such as West Germany, Italy, Japan, and India) emphatically attests. By contrast, countries whose governments do not consistently adhere to these basic democratic precepts, observing them only partially or periodically, risk losing democracy entirely. The strong arm of the military, for instance, has extinguished democracy for prolonged periods in countries like Brazil, Argentina, Nigeria, and South Korea. The thirst for dominant power on the part of democratically elected heads of government has also led to democracy's dissolution on more than one occasion. Evidence that can be gleaned from around the world over long stretches of history appears to be amply *consistent* with the hypothesis that thoroughly democratized state institutions, rather than partially or inconsistently democratized ones, are vitally necessary to the stability and long-term success of democracy. *Democratic state building* is thus a primary task of newly democratizing countries.

The consolidation of democratic institutions is by no means automatic, however. It is not enough to write a constitution setting up governmental institutions that, on paper, appear to be democratically structured. To give their democracy life and make it work, those who hold state office must behave in strict conformity with democratic precepts, and important elements in society must want democracy to succeed. Once established, democratic state institutions need to be nurtured and adapted to changing conditions if they are to endure. A democratically organized state is the indispensable precondition to democracy, but to understand how it emerges and how it evolves we must look at the other conditions for democracy on our list.

2. Elites Committed to Democracy

Democracy, we are often told, is government by the people. But as we noted in chapter 8, modern democracies are more accurately described as government *by elites* who are *accountable* to the people. This counterintuitive notion may contradict our commonsense concept of democracy as a fundamentally mass phenomenon, but in reality all governments, including today's democracies, are run on a day-to-day basis by elites. The success, indeed the very existence, of democracy therefore depends to a considerable degree on the attitudes and behavior of society's political and social elites.

Obviously those who pursue politics as a profession must take the lead in fostering democratic principles. At the very least these *political elites* must scrupulously adhere to the laws and norms of democracy, resisting temptations to dominance and corruption. A capacity for bargaining and compromise is essential. But many theorists would argue that the art of *leadership* in a democracy requires much more. Ideally, those who aspire to political leadership in democracies need to rise above the routine transactions of everyday politics, with its deal making and vote counting, by inspiring the population to widen their perspectives on the meaning of democratic rights and values and to surmount internal differences. Morally uplifting leadership of this quality is especially vital when there is public resistance to more democracy (as occurs when the majority favors discrimination against minorities) or when broad popular support is needed to meet an especially difficult challenge (such as war or major economic problems).[2]

Truly great leadership always has a moral dimension. The Macchiavellian notion that the ideal ruler "should know how to do evil" and instill fear in the citizenry has no place in democratic governance. The tasks of democratization and consolidation, in particular, require leadership skills of the highest magnitude in view of the enormous political, economic, and attitudinal changes they impose on the population. Countries that lack capable leaders during these critical phases risk losing their precious opportunity to build democracy altogether.

Political elites are not the only ones who must abide by the ground rules of democracy if a democratic polity is to develop and flourish. The term *"elites"* does not apply solely to political leaders. Virtually all professions and organizations have leading figures who constitute an elite by virtue of their lofty administrative positions or widely respected achievements. Many of them play a direct or indirect role in their country's political life. Business elites, military elites, religious elites, ethnic elites, media elites, and academic elites, among others, have special responsibilities within their respective spheres of activity when it comes to observing the principles and ideals of democratic behavior. Although these political and social elites may comprise no more than 1 percent to 5 percent of a country's population, when they overstep the bounds of democratic restraint and assert their own dominance or when they influence their followers to turn in anti-democratic directions, democracy itself is at risk. But when they emphatically throw their weight behind democracy, its chances for survival rise appreciably.

One of the greatest ironies of political life is that not only are elites *compatible* with democracy, as long as they are fully committed to democratic institutions and procedures; they are *indispensable* to it. An even greater irony is that *elites can at times be even more democratic than the masses.* In an eye-opening study conducted in the late 1970s, political scientists found that American political and legal elites—including community leaders, lawyers, and judges—were generally more supportive of freedom of speech, freedom of association, and other liberties guaranteed in the Bill of Rights than was the general public.[3] Other studies reveal that elites in various democracies often provide crucial support for welfare programs and democratic values aimed at enhancing economic and political equality for the masses. Without such elite support, the masses would be worse off.[4]

While the attitudes and actions of society's elites are of fundamental significance at every stage of a democracy's evolution, there is evidence that they are particularly relevant in its earliest stages. It was the commitment to political and economic liberty on the part of America's founding fathers, a highly select political and economic elite, that set the United States on its initial course toward the full-blown mass democracy it was to become. It was the determination of Frederik W. de Klerk, the leader of the predominantly white National Party, and Nelson Mandela, the leader of the largely black African National Congress, to come to terms on establishing a multiracial democracy that brought about

F. W. de Klerk and Nelson Mandela at Mandela's inauguration as president of South Africa, May 10, 1994.

South Africa's first truly democratic elections on the basis of "one person, one vote" in 1994. It was an undisguised alliance between business elites and the military high command that kept democracy at bay in a number of Latin American countries through much of the 1970s and 1980s, and it was the forbearance of these same elites that permitted a return to civilian democracy in Argentina, Brazil, Chile, and several other states in the region. And it was reform-minded communist party leaders in countries like Russia, Hungary, and Lithuania who were instrumental in moving their nations from communism to democracy.

These and countless other examples are *consistent* with the hypothesis that political and social elites have a decisive impact on how democracy develops, or whether it develops at all. They confirm the *theory of democratic elitism,* which asserts that real-world democracies involve a combination of mass participation and, most importantly, elites devoted to political liberty.[5]

3. National Wealth

We examined the correlation between national wealth and democracy at considerable length in chapter 4. That evidence is *mixed*. While national wealth definitely tends to increase the prospects for the development and maintenance of democracy, there are relatively wealthy countries that are not democracies and some poor ones that have succeeded in building and sustaining democratic institutions and practices.

4. Private Enterprise

The connection between private enterprise and democracy reflects the hypothesis that economic freedom promotes political freedom. People who own their own businesses or who work in privately owned companies, according to this hypothesis, will want to have a say in how the government treats them. They will especially want a say in how the government deals with property rights, taxes, business regulations, and so on. "Having a say" in what the government does and holding it accountable is what popular sovereignty is all about. In this conception, democracy emerges as a mechanism for protecting property rights. The reverse side of this hypothesis contends that the absence of economic liberty promotes authoritarianism. When the government controls the economy, it reduces the opportunities for citizens to organize themselves and take care of their economic needs independently of the state, effectively snuffing out citizen controls on state power.

One of the most influential studies of these tendencies is Barrington Moore's *Social Origins of Dictatorship and Democracy.*[6] Moore argued that democracy emerged in Britain and the United States, the chief incubators of modern democracy, largely because of the early appearance in those countries of a successful capitalist elite, the *bourgeoisie,* who made private industry and agriculture the dominant elements of the economy. They also demanded a say in the governance of their respective countries in order to ensure the state's protection of their property rights. By contrast, countries that failed to develop a strong entrepreneurial class did not produce successful democracies until the second half of the twentieth century, if at all. Historically, countries like Germany, China, and Russia had a comparatively weak private business class and an undeveloped commercial agricultural

class in the nineteenth and early twentieth centuries. Instead they had a land-poor peasantry and powerful state intervention in most facets of economic life. Japan also had a landless peasantry, while its powerful business elite was closely tied to the imperial state.

As a consequence, Moore observed, Russia and China fell to the communists, Germany got a fascist dictatorship, and Japan came under an aggressive military elite prior to World War II. Moore concluded that a thriving capitalist class is essential to the emergence of democratic institutions. He summed up this point in the pithy phrase, "No bourgeois, no democracy." Stated another way, Moore's thesis is that private enterprise stimulates the growth of a middle class that does not depend directly on the state for its livelihood. As we'll see in the next section, the middle class itself can provide essential backing for a democratic regime.

While there is ample evidence consistent with these hypotheses, there is also a considerable amount of evidence indicating that private enterprise does not necessarily promote democracy. Quite a few countries have had a thriving private sector in tandem with repressive political institutions. In some cases the owners of large corporations have actively supported non-democratic political authority, as exemplified at various times in Latin American countries like Mexico, Argentina, Brazil, and Chile and in Asian states like Singapore and the Philippines. Communist China today combines a vibrant private sector with unrelenting one-party dictatorship. It is still not entirely evident that the expansion of private enterprise in that country is stimulating pressures for democracy; to some extent it may actually be buttressing communist rule. In post-communist Russia the rapid introduction of private enterprise has been accompanied by the emergence of a small clique of politically influential multimillionaires and, simultaneously, by a drastic decline in living standards for large segments of the population. Some of the most disadvantaged people have responded to their plight by rejecting democracy itself, as have some entrepreneurs.[7]

The evidence is therefore so mixed as to be *inconclusive.* While capitalism has acted to promote democratic tendencies in some countries, it has retarded, undermined, or suppressed them in others.

5. A Middle Class

A related hypothesis suggests that countries that are sharply divided into a small class of rich people and a large mass of poor, with no substantial middle class between them, are not likely to establish democracy. The rich will use their control of the economy to dominate the poor, while the poor will be mainly interested in expropriating the rich. Presumably, each of these opposing classes would be willing to use authoritarianism to impose its will on the other. A middle class, according to this hypothesis, is more favorable to democracy because its members seek to establish their own economic security on the basis of private enterprise, the rule of law, and an accountable government. These ideas are as old as Aristotle and as timely as the new millennium.

Who constitutes the middle class? As we observed in chapter 2, one way of defining a social class is by applying objective criteria, such as annual household income thresholds, and by assigning people to such categories as "upper class," "middle class," and "poor" on the basis of where they fall within the established income parameters. In many countries the middle class is large enough to be further differentiated into "upper middle," "middle middle," and "lower middle" echelons. In countries with a business sector, at least part of the middle class earns its livelihood by owning or working for private enterprises. The bourgeoisie, as it is traditionally defined, refers to those segments of the middle and upper classes that are connected to the private sector. But the middle class is often larger than just the bourgeoisie; it invariably includes middle-income people who work for the state (such as bureaucrats and public school teachers) and for non-profit organizations (such as private universities and hospitals).

There is substantial historical and contemporary evidence linking the middle class with attitudes favorable to democracy. The democratic tendencies that blossomed in Britain, the United States, and France in the eighteenth and nineteenth centuries were largely the product of middle-class pressures against decaying monarchies and economically stagnant aristocracies. To this very day the middle class is the backbone of democracy in all three countries as well as in other democracies that have emerged and flourished in the twentieth century. In recent years key elements of the middle class have also played a leading role in militating for civil rights and democratic procedures in Latin America and in countries like South Korea and Taiwan, where military regimes or one-party governments have held sway for decades. In former communist countries like Russia, where the middle class still consists largely of state employees, a new middle class tied to the emerging private sector is just beginning to make its appearance. Thus far it appears to favor democracy.

But does the middle class always support democracy? Instructively, there is evidence that large elements of the middle class can turn their backs on democratic institutions and throw their support to dictators if they feel that democracy is jeopardizing their well-being. Such was the attitude of millions of middle-class Germans who were devastated by a succession of economic crises in the 1920s and early 1930s, when Germany had a democratic system of government. Having concluded that democracy itself was the source of their woes, major segments of the middle class voted for Hitler and the Nazis. "No prosperity, no democracy" may be a widespread middle-class attitude in other democracies as well. Even if a sizable middle class supports democracy in a given country, there is no guarantee that its support alone can bring democracy about where it does not already exist or sustain it where it does exist. In many cases democracy may require the backing of other classes as well, both rich and poor.

On balance, then, the evidence for this hypothesis is *inconclusive*. While there is unmistakable evidence that the middle class has helped promote democracy in a number of instances, there is also evidence that this class may turn away from democracy if its material well-being is imperiled.

6. Support of the Disadvantaged for Democracy

According to this hypothesis, the commitment of society's elites and the middle class may greatly enhance the prospects for democracy, but if society's most disadvantaged elements feel they are left out of the democratic process or have nothing to gain from it, they could pose a serious threat to the country's democratic institutions and processes. Typically, the "disadvantaged" consists of the poorest members of the population, a group that in some countries comprises millions of people clinging desperately to survival. But other groups can also be counted among society's economically or socially disadvantaged, such as women and minorities. If democracy offers no real hope of overcoming poverty or systematic discrimination, how can it claim to represent all the people inclusively? One result may be mass indifference on the part of the destitute and the oppressed. More ominously, seething mass discontent could provide a base of support for anti-democratic political movements and might even erupt into politically motivated violence. These problems are magnified if the downtrodden comprise a sizable segment of the population.

Evidence relating to this hypothesis comes from a variety of countries at various stages of their historical development. Britain, for example, managed to solidify democracy while significantly expanding mass participation in the late nineteenth and early twentieth centuries by gradually giving the working class the right to vote. As a consequence the workers, who constituted the largest and poorest segment of British society, accepted democracy as the only legitimate method for seeking redress of their grievances, rejecting violent revolution and dictatorship. The inclusion of Britain's masses into the democratic system helps explain why communist and fascist parties never found much of a following there. In France and Germany, by contrast, the development of democracy was slower and more turbulent than in Britain. The vast majority of workers in these countries had reason to feel shut out of the political process. The result was a greater sense of disillusionment with democracy on the part of large elements of the working masses, a sense of alienation that in the twentieth century found expression in significant working-class support for communist or fascist parties. Millions of workers supported the communists or Nazis in Germany prior to World War II, while the French Communist Party was one of the largest communist parties in Western Europe after the war.

The support of underprivileged groups for democracy is by no means automatic, however, even when they are given opportunities to take part in the democratic process. Much depends on how effectively elected governments deal with their problems, especially those spawned by the economic marketplace. Private enterprise may stimulate extraordinary economic growth and thereby foster democratic tendencies on the part of those who profit by it. But the market economy can also produce prolonged slowdowns and deep depressions, persistent unemployment, inflation, acute poverty, and long-term financial insecurity. Those most affected by these hardships will usually look to their government for relief. To maintain mass support for democracy, therefore, elected governments must provide a panoply of social welfare measures designed to help the disadvantaged cope with economic distress. Unemployment and disability insurance, education and job training, food and medical assistance, public housing, retirement pensions, and other welfare benefits are considered essential to securing the allegiance of underprivileged groups to democracy.

Democracy collapsed in Germany in the early 1930s in part because of the government's failure to rescue millions of Germans from the ravages of the Great Depression. By contrast, democracy survived in the United States in part because Franklin D. Roosevelt's New Deal convinced the majority that the government was earnestly trying to address their problems. Since the end of World War II, the *welfare state* has become an essential concomitant of democracy, even in the world's most prosperous countries.

In less industrialized countries, where the disadvantaged are often inhabitants of impoverished rural areas or overcrowded shanty towns, democracy usually falters whenever mass support for it is lacking. In Russia and China, the communists managed to take power in large part by securing their grip on the peasant masses, initially promising to satisfy their land hunger only to crush whatever hopes they may have harbored for democratic political and property rights. And in a host of less developed countries in today's world—whether in Africa, Latin America, or Asia—democracy tends to be weak or nonexistent where the masses of the population, mired in poverty and bereft of education, are either unable to organize broad-based democratic movements or unwilling to support democratic parties that do not adequately address their needs. It tends to be stronger where democratic parties and interest groups go out of their way to appeal to the underprivileged and make determined efforts to deal with their problems when in government.

While admittedly sketchy, the evidence presented here appears to be generally *consistent* with the notion that the support of the disadvantaged is critical for democracy. Unless these segments of the population believe they can improve their lot by supporting democratic movements and parties, democracy will probably rest on shaky foundations. In countries where destitute or oppressed masses have no opportunity to support democracy or simply refuse to do so, democracy may not succeed for anyone.

7. An Active Civil Society and a Democratic Political Culture

The term "civil society" refers to *the population organized into associations independently of the state.* These associations can assume all sorts of purposes. Some may be overtly political, such as political parties, voter leagues, and other organizations directly involved in electoral politics. Parties have a special responsibility in mediating between the political elites and the people. Parties that do not accept the rules of democratic politics pose a constant threat to democracy. And parties that are so internally divided or uncertain of where they stand make it very difficult for voters to know what to expect from the politicians they elect. Stable democracy requires effectively organized, well-led parties capable of inspiring the voters' confidence and of competently managing the state once elected.

Civil associations with a political purpose also include interest groups that devote at least part of their time to influencing public officials. Trade unions, business associations, ethnic and religious organizations, and single-issue organizations such as those advocating or opposing abortion rights, gun control, and the like—these and similar groups typify politically oriented interest groups. Other civil associations, such as parent-teacher associations, may be less directly political while still taking an interest in public policies that affect them.

And some private associations may have no political agenda at all, such as choral groups or bowling leagues. What matters in all these organizations is that citizens form them on their own, without any prompting or interference by government.

The more the citizenry is involved in such private associations, according to a widely held hypothesis, the more likely they will succeed in maintaining democracy. By freely entering into groups and associations, the hypothesis assumes, individuals learn habits of organization, cooperation, and trust that are vital to the sustenance of democratic institutions and procedures, creating patterns of interaction that link society together at the grassroots level. In the process, they learn how to deal with many of the community's problems on their own, independently of government. Civil society is thus a primary source of a **democratic political culture,** *a pattern of widely shared attitudes and values supportive of democratic institutions and procedures.* It is the social web that underlies democratic government, making it possible to limit the state's power and keeping it accountable to a self-organized citizenry.[8]

In his famous treatise on democracy in America in the 1830s, Alexis de Tocqueville placed special emphasis on the broad range of private organizations and associations that knitted Americans together in the early decades of their republic. This burgeoning network of business groups, religious societies, temperance leagues, and other forums for citizen-to-citizen contact outside the formal boundaries of government was, in his view, of fundamental importance in accounting for the success of the new nation's bold democratic experiment. Self-reliance and voluntary cooperation, he hypothesized, were in fact vital to the success of any democracy, providing a social bulwark against a tyrannical or domineering state. "The morals and intelligence of a democratic people would be in . . . danger," he argued, ". . . if ever a government wholly usurped the place of private associations. . . . In democratic countries knowledge of how to combine is the mother of all other forms of knowledge." Tocqueville asserted that the clearest and most precise law controlling human society was centered on voluntary associations: "If men are to remain civilized or to become civilized, the art of association must develop and improve among them."[9]

In the 1990s another political scientist painted a more unsettling portrait of the state of American civil society. In a widely publicized article with the intriguing title "Bowling Alone: America's Declining Social Capital," Robert Putnam provided statistical evidence of a steady decline in membership in all sorts of private associations in the United States, from PTAs to bowling leagues, starting in the late 1960s. Putnam hypothesized that this downward trend in associational life was a major factor contributing to plummeting levels of trust in America's governmental institutions. The result, Putnam wrote, is the growing "disarray" of American democracy.[10]

While Putnam's hypothesis has stimulated considerable debate, few observers would question that a vibrant civil society has played a major role in building and sustaining democracy in America. Much the same can be said for a number of other successful democracies, such as Britain, France, Germany, and Italy. As a general rule, there is considerable corroborative evidence linking a civil society with democracy. Countries with a strong civil society are said to have "social capital" that can be "spent" on achieving the community's goals effectively and on preserving democracy in times of crisis. But this link is more likely to prevail when society's civil associations accept the rules and norms of democracy as a matter of principle, not just for tactical gains. There is also strong evidence correlating a democratic political culture with successful democracy, but it can take a long time before a newly democratizing country's population learns democratic attitudes and behaviors and internalizes them to the point where they become second nature. On the whole, however, the evidence is *consistent* with the hypothesis.

8. Education and Freedom of Information

According to this hypothesis, the prospects for democracy rise with society's education levels: the more educated the populace, the greater the support there will be for democratic values and procedures. Conversely, societies with high levels of illiteracy and a poorly educated populace are less likely to create or sustain democracy. Relatedly, democracy requires the free flow of information and freedom of expression. Without the ability to discuss politics openly and debate contending points of view, it will be difficult for proponents of democracy to get organized under a dictatorship, a factor that may stall or completely prevent a democracy from coming into being. Even after democratic institutions are set in place, the level of citizen participation in political life will depend to a considerable degree on the ready availability of relevant facts about the community's affairs and on opportunities for public discussion and citizen education about complicated political and economic issues.

Governments must therefore be willing to provide adequate information to the public, and there must be ample sources of independent information and analysis provided in newspapers, on radio and television, and at various other forums for political discussion. Just as important, the citizens must avail themselves of these multiple sources of information. Democracy cannot be built on ignorance. People have to know and understand what is going on and what their choices are.

There is considerable evidence in support of this hypothesis. When democracy emerged in Britain and the United States, for example, it was pushed forward primarily by society's most highly educated elites. British and American universities in the eighteenth and nineteenth centuries permitted the study of political philosophy and encouraged rigorous debate. In addition, the British monarchy permitted a considerable amount of press freedom and open political discussion, a factor that was critical to the expansion of Parliament's role in Britain and to the spread of democratic ideas in the American colonies. Conversely, democratic tendencies in these centuries were stultified in countries like Russia, Japan, and China, where the study of political philosophy was not encouraged and where oppressive state censorship smothered the open exchange of information and ideas. Meanwhile, in today's world, the most successful democracies tend to have higher literacy and secondary school graduation rates than non-democracies do.

Even when educational opportunities are widened and increasing numbers of people finish high school or enter universities, much depends on the *content* of what is taught and discussed. The Soviet Union, for example, greatly expanded educational opportunities for the masses, but the free discussion of political ideas was strictly forbidden. The academic study of politics, history, economics, and sociology conformed rigidly to the government's official interpretations of Marxism. And as we'll see in chapter 13, those interpretations often diverged substantially from Marx's own ideas. The Soviet censorship system imposed yet another stifling weight on the development of democratic ideas. The state-controlled media provided a steady dose of carefully contrived propaganda that could not be openly questioned.

Many other dictatorships have exhibited similar patterns of restricted education and official censorship. Whether they can endure in the new millennium, with political information and open discussion accessible across national boundaries via the Internet, e-mail, and satellite television, is a fascinating question.

As a general rule, there is a close correlation between democracy, on the one hand, and high educational levels and multiple sources of information on the other. Moreover, democracy itself promotes both education and open media. Democracy can therefore be both an effect and a cause of a well-educated populace and multiple sources of information. In either case, there is substantial evidence *consistent* with our hypothesis that these variables are causatively connected.

9. A Homogeneous Society

Some people contend that democracy is most likely to endure when it rests on a socially homogeneous society. By contrast, fragmented societies that are torn by deep ethnic, religious, class, or other divisions are assumed to provide too unstable a foundation for steady democratic governance.

Without doubt, the contemporary world is not lacking in deeply polarized societies that have found it virtually impossible to establish democratic institutions or maintain them for very long. The former Yugoslavia is a glaring example. A list of additional examples would be a long one. Information gathered by Freedom House analysts show that mono-ethnic countries, in which a dominant ethnic group comprises at least two-thirds of the population, are twice as likely to be rated as "free" (i.e., democratic) as multiethnic countries.[11]

And yet there is compelling evidence that contradicts the homogeneity hypothesis. Some countries have found ways to make democracy work despite serious social cleavages. The United States is just one example. The United Kingdom forged and expanded democracy in spite of sharp conflicts among the English, Irish, Welsh, and Scots. India, a country riven by powerful religious and regional conflicts, has managed to maintain free speech, regular elections, and other core features of democracy for all but a few years of its history as a modern independent country. And as we saw in chapter 8, the Netherlands successfully dealt with its various social divisions through the mechanism of consociational democracy. Few successful democracies in today's world, in fact, are without social cleavages of one kind or another, at times quite severe. Conversely, in Japan and Germany, where there was a relatively high degree of ethnic homogeneity, democracy did not succeed until after it was imposed by the victorious occupation powers after World War II.

Thus the homogeneity hypothesis is at best *inconclusive*. While social polarization may make it more difficult for democracy to flower and mature, it does not by any means make it impossible. Some societies find ways to bridge over their social divisions through democratic mechanisms. Evidence from the oldest and largest democracies in the world is inconsistent with the hypothesis. In fact, in some cases the reverse may be true: social heterogeneity may at times *increase* the likelihood of democracy, because it provides the most acceptable methods for a highly divided people to reconcile their differences and live peacefully together.

10. A Favorable International Environment

The conditions for democracy we have examined thus far are located within individual countries. But at times the external environment can have a significant impact on the prospects for democracy's emergence and subsequent development. It was not by accident, for example, that countries as diverse as the United States and India embarked on democracy from the earliest moments of their modern history as independent states. Both had previously been British colonies, and the native elites who took up the reins of government in these countries after independence had already acquired an understanding of democratic ideas and practices from the British. Canada, Australia, and New Zealand are also stable democracies whose roots go back to British domination. Of course, not all former British colonies have turned out to be stable democracies. Most have not, as the fate of Pakistan, Singapore, and a number of African countries attests. Nevertheless, British democratic traditions have had palpable and lasting effects on several countries. In stark contrast to Britain's democratizing influences, the Soviet Union smothered democracy in East-Central Europe for more than forty years after World War II by imposing repressive communist dictatorships on the region.

War and its consequences can sometimes exert a withering effect on democracy. War generally requires firm centralized leadership and an influential role for the military command in the highest political councils. Under these circumstances there may be little room for interparty squabbling, an intrusive free press, or the open expression of public opinion. Some governments that intend to launch aggressive wars, like Hitler's Germany or Mussolini's Italy, have little use for democracy. Others that regard the threat of war as a real possibility may be similarly predisposed against internal democratic procedures, though not all countries involved in dangerous international conflicts have succumbed to the temptation of militaristic authoritarianism. The United States and its West European allies, for example, maintained their democratic institutions throughout the Cold War despite the hair-trigger nuclear standoff with the Soviet Union. Democracy has also managed to thrive in Israel in spite of that country's prolonged confrontation with neighboring adversaries. But other countries under siege have not been so fortunate.

Global economic conditions can at times exert an equally profound impact on the prospects for democracy in particular countries. The Great Depression of the early 1930s was a major contributing factor in the collapse of Germany's democracy and the rising popularity of the Nazis. In our own day and age, the chances for a successful transition to democracy in countries that have lately cast off dictatorship in Latin America, Africa, or

Asia may depend in considerable measure on the willingness of the economically advanced democracies to provide timely economic assistance or to open up their markets to mutually beneficial trade. The European Union is playing a crucial role in East-Central Europe by holding out the possibility of eventual EU membership to the region's former communist states.[12]

The evidence is thus *consistent* with the hypothesis. But experience shows that, while external influences may be important, ultimately no foreign government or combination of governments is likely to prove capable of creating or propping up democratic institutions and habits in countries where the domestic conditions for democracy are unfavorable. Ultimately, the sources and nutrients of democracy must be homegrown if democracy is to germinate and blossom to its full potential.[13]

How do these conditions for democracy, summarized in table 10.1, help us understand real-world cases of democratization? The following brief overviews of Poland and Romania provide some insights into democratic transition processes in two East-Central European countries that in 1989 began emerging from decades of communist dictatorship.

TABLE 10.1

Conditions for Democracy	
Independent Variable	**Evidence Is Mainly . . .**
1. State institutions	Consistent
2. Elites committed to democracy	Consistent
3. National wealth	Mixed: generally consistent, but with major exceptions
4. Private enterprise	Inconclusive: evidence for and against
5. Middle class	Consistent
6. Support of the disadvantaged	Consistent
7. Civil society and democratic political culture	Consistent
8. Education and freedom of information	Consistent
9. Homogeneous society	Inconclusive: evidence for and against
10. Favorable international environment	Consistent

FIGURE 10.1   East-Central Europe

POLAND

The crackdown was swift. On December 13, 1981, the Polish government under General Wojciech Jaruzelski (Ya-ru-ZEL-ski) declared a state of martial law and banned the 10-million strong trade union "**Solidarity.**" Solidarity's charismatic leader, a factory electrician named Lech Walesa (Lek Va-WEN-sa), was placed under arrest, along with other prominent leaders of the movement. It appeared that the Polish people's challenge to communist rule, the most successful in the entire communist world, was finished.

Less than eight years later the tables were turned. More precisely, Walesa and his colleagues were seated at a large round table on equal terms with Jaruzelski and other state officials to discuss a historic transfer of power. The government's attempt to smash popular support for Solidarity had failed, the economy was on the verge of collapse, and international pressures from the West for substantial change were mounting. The Round Table Agreement, signed in April 1989, provided for the first real contested elections in Poland since the imposition of communist rule by the Soviet Union following World War II. Although the agreement allowed the communists to keep a majority of the seats in the Sejm, the lower house of the Polish legislature, Solidarity candidates roundly defeated their communist rivals in head-to-head contests for the remaining seats as well as for the newly created upper house, the Senate.

These election results struck the rest of communist-controlled East-Central Europe like a thunderbolt. The fact that Polish communist authorities had permitted elections to take place at all, not to mention their results, sent unmistakable signals throughout the Soviet-dominated region that communist rule was on its last legs. Even more astonishing, the fact that the Soviet Union had allowed these events to occur without interference was unprecedented. Throughout the Cold War, Soviet leaders had reacted vigorously to all serious challenges to communist party domination in their East-Central European domain. When workers staged anti-government protests in communist East Germany in 1953, when Hungarians rose up in support of democratic freedoms in 1956, and when reform-minded communists came to power in Czechoslovakia and granted greater freedom of expression and other liberties in 1968, Moscow had dispatched troops and tanks to suppress these revolts with ruthless determination. Now in 1989, a new Soviet leadership under Mikhail Gorbachev was far more sympathetic to political reforms in East-Central Europe than its predecessors. Gorbachev's main priorities were to end the costly Cold War and reinvigorate the floundering Soviet economy, preferably with the West's aid. He knew that military intervention in Poland would only provoke the West's indignation, dashing these plans.[14]

Once it became clear that communist authority was sputtering, people throughout East-Central Europe boldly followed in Poland's footsteps. A mass exodus from East Germany and spontaneous demonstrations against the communist regime in the summer and fall of 1989 induced the East German government on November 9 to open the Berlin wall, the dreaded barrier that had separated democratic West Berlin from communist East Berlin since 1961. The complete collapse of the communist East German regime ensued the following year, after pro-democracy parties won a resounding electoral victory. The day after the wall was opened, a reform-oriented Communist Party clique in Bulgaria ousted the old-guard dictator who had governed the country since 1964. Less than a week later, people began taking to the streets in Czechoslovakia to demand the resignation of the communist government. With no signs of support from Moscow, the communists simply gave up and handed power to democratic forces led by Vaclav Havel, a playwright who had been arrested repeatedly for his outspoken anti-communist views. In December, demonstrations occurred in Romania against the harsh communist dictatorship of Nicolae Ceausescu (Chow-SHESS-koo). A revolt within his own party resulted in his removal from office and execution. And in March 1990 the Hungarian communists were unseated in elections won by more pronouncedly democratic parties.

It was not long before the communists lost their remaining vestiges of power in Poland. In 1990, Walesa was elected president, and the following year a new parliament was returned with a non-communist majority. Poland's transition to democracy was now in full swing. What do our ten conditions for democracy tell us about the Polish experience?

1. State Institutions

Poland began its transition process with widespread popular support for the country's existing boundaries. For a country with a long history of boundary problems, this consensus was significant.[15] No national minority groups seriously challenged the central government's legitimate authority to govern the country. Hence Poland, unlike Yugoslavia or Russia, was not saddled with "stateness" problems such as secession or civil strife as it embarked on democratization.

Another aspect of its initial transition from communism to democracy was the manner in which it was accomplished. As we've seen, the transition occurred on the basis of a *negotiated agreement* between the ruling communist authorities and their main opponents, the Solidarity movement. The Round Table pact resulted from mutual compromises that initially led only to a partial victory for Solidarity. Jaruzelski remained in power as president for another year, and fully contested elections to the Sejm did not take place until the end of 1991. Nevertheless, the negotiated nature of the arrangement meant that both sides would refrain from violence, an important achievement. It also established a precedent for further negotiations, which in Poland led to the communists' assent to the elections of 1990 and 1991 and their agreement to quietly step down from power upon their defeat. These results, too, were no mean achievements.[16]

The Round Table talks also set up the framework for Poland's post-communist institutional structure. Poland adopted a modified form of the French-style presidential-parliamentary system, a system it ratified with few changes in its new constitution of 1997. The president is directly elected by the people and has real decision-making powers, but fewer than the French and Russian presidents. The Sejm elects the prime minister, who forms the government. Walesa wanted even greater presidential power to appoint and dismiss the prime minister (as in France and Russia) but opponents of such a powerful presidency blocked his proposed change.

The Sejm is elected by a variant of proportional representation. In the 1991 elections there was no hurdle. As a consequence, some thirty parties won representation in the lower house, making it difficult to form stable governments. This fragmentation of the Sejm complicated the transformation process, imposing delays on the process of economic reform. To rectify the problem, a hurdle was imposed for the 1993 parliamentary elections. Since then, individual parties have had to win at least 5 percent of the vote nationwide to be represented, while two or more parties running jointly must clear an 8 percent national hurdle. Following this change, only seven parties or party-blocs were elected in 1993 and five in 1997.

Pro-democratic parties have successfully taken over the bureaucracy and taken control over the military from communist-era authorities. Transparency has been observed, with minimal corruption. (One prime minister was ousted when his contacts with Soviet and Russian spy agencies became known.) The country seems to be handling the processes of democratic state building successfully.

2. Elites Committed to Democracy

There seems to be little doubt that Poland's post-communist elites are fully committed to the democratic process. Of particular significance in this respect is the transformation of Poland's communists. While the hard-core communist leaders of the pre-1989 era have largely faded from the political scene, a new party known as the Democratic Left Alliance was established by reform-minded former communists. It is thoroughly devoted to democratic principles and market economics. It also favors Poland's entry into NATO and the European Union and has little in common with post-communist Russia. In 1995 this party's leader, Alexander Kwasniewski (Kvash-NYEV-ski), defeated Lech Walesa for the presidency. Another party with ties to the communist era, the Agrarian Party, is also committed to the democratic process. The Solidarity movement splintered into a multiplicity of currents and small parties once democratization began, but all emphatically favor democracy. In 1997 they formed a bloc of parties known as the Solidarity Electoral Alliance and won 43.7 percent of the seats in the Sejm, forming a coalition government with the business-oriented Freedom Union party. The Catholic church hierarchy, the military, the business community, and other key social elites are all squarely behind the democratization process.

3. National Wealth

None of the former communist countries of East-Central Europe was in good shape economically when the democratic transformation processes commenced in 1989–90. All of them lagged significantly behind the United States and Western Europe in terms of industrial and agricultural production, technological development, and general living standards. Poland's chronic economic woes were a primary source of mass discontent with communist rule. In addition, by 1989 the government had run up a $39 billion debt owed to lending institutions around the world.

Over the course of the 1990s, Poland's economic situation improved considerably, though serious problems remain. Its gross domestic product grew by an annual average of 4.5 percent in the 1990s, the highest growth rate among all the former communist states of the region. (By comparison, it grew only 1.8 percent a year during the 1980s, the last decade of communist rule.) The growth rate exceeded 5 percent in 1997–98, and its gross national product topped $150 billion. Its per capita gross national product of $3,900 in 1998 fell within the upper-middle income range and appears sufficient to sustain a democracy. Much of Poland's international debt was forgiven by its creditors, including banks and foreign governments. Poverty is still widespread, however, with one-fourth of the population living below the government's official poverty line in the mid-1990s and 15 percent living on less than $2 a day. While Poland is still not wealthy by Western standards, its post-communist economy has shown a significant capacity to grow. Because many Poles identify democracy itself with economic prosperity (as indicated in table 8.2), the economy's successes appear to be solidifying public support for democracy.[17]

4. Private Enterprise

One of the most ambitious tasks undertaken by Poland's post-communist leadership, perhaps second in importance only to the task of building democratic institutions itself, is that of building a successful private sector. Broad support for private enterprise in Poland has deep roots in the communist period. In 1956 the communist authorities acquiesced in popular demands for private agriculture and agreed to permit it, enabling Poland's large farm population to escape the forced collectivization of agriculture that other communist regimes imposed on the people under their rule. (Collectivization involved the takeover of land, livestock, and produce by communist state authorities.) Various small businesses were also allowed, such as privately owned restaurants.

Since the early 1990s Poland has made significant strides in privatizing large parts of the economy. Most of its state-owned industries from the communist era have been sold off to private owners or, if economically defunct, liquidated entirely. By the late 1990s, about 90 percent of domestic investment came from the private sector. The pace and extent of privatization have not been uncontested, however. Some political parties have wanted a slower pace than others, fearful that privatization may raise unemployment because of downsizing and factory closures. Disagreements have emerged between coalition partners over this issue, but despite delays, the process has gone forward. The disagreements have largely centered on the speed, scope, and method of privatization, not on privatization per se. Most important, the creation of a large private sector has not seriously threatened the democratic process.

Like Hungary, the Czech Republic, and other former communist states, post-communist Poland has devised its own privatization model, reflecting its specific economic and social circumstances as well as its political bargaining processes. As living standards improve for those who own private businesses or are employed in them, private enterprise appears to be solidifying support for democracy.[18]

5. The Middle Class

Just as the creation of a modern private sector is a relatively recent development in Poland, so too is the creation of a western-style middle class. When the communists were in power, Poland's equivalent of a middle class consisted mostly of state employees with white-collar jobs and moderate income levels. Bureaucrats, academics, doctors, and others engaged in fields requiring higher education and intellectual rather than purely physical labor comprised the vast majority of this social group. The owners of private businesses and some of their employees were also part of this communist-era middle class. Large numbers of this class opposed communist rule (except, of course, the most committed party officials). Since the onset of democratization and the privatization process there has developed a new segment of society connected with the emerging private sector. Together with the state-sector middle class, which still exists in substantial numbers, they constitute Poland's new middle class. As the hypothesis predicts, this larger middle class appears to be providing solid backing for the democratic process.

6. Support of the Disadvantaged for Democracy

Under communism, many if not most Poles considered themselves economically disadvantaged. Shortages of food, clothing, and other basic necessities were frequent. A promising economic upswing in the early 1970s proved short-lived; living standards stagnated or declined in subsequent years. The cost of living remained relatively low because of government subsidies for food, health care, transportation, and the like, but strikes and demonstrations broke out on several occasions when the government announced price increases. A general dissatisfaction with the quality of material life was a pervasive feature of Polish life throughout the communist period, joining with opposition to the dictatorial political system and historical antipathy to Russian imperialism as a chief source of the population's animus against communist rule. Those at the bottom rungs of the social pyramid, including factory workers, miners, and other manual laborers, depended heavily on the state for their jobs and welfare benefits, but for the most part they opposed the non-democratic political system. It was ordinary factory workers who formed Solidarity.

Since the democratization process began, Poland's less advantaged groups have largely thrown their support behind the democratic process. The main concern of many of them is that the privatization of the economy will result in higher unemployment as the new private owners seek to trim costs and raise profits by laying off workers. Factories that cannot compete effectively in the world marketplace or find investors willing to modernize them at times shut down completely. Poland's large farm community, comprising 28 percent of the population at the end of the 1990s, also faces an insecure future, since the prospect of joining the European Union will require more efficient farming. So far, however, these concerns have been expressed through political parties, interest groups, and other democratic institutions and procedures.

Poland's disadvantaged proved to be a major source of support for democracy under the communists, and despite their unease over various economic issues, they provide major support for the democratization process today. To retain their loyalty, however, elected governments will have to maintain a basic level of welfare benefits while working to raise the country's overall economic prospects. A decline in voter turnout as the 1990s progressed may be indicative of mounting frustration among various segments of the population, especially those whose economic fortunes have not substantially improved since communism fell.

7. Civil Society and a Democratic Political Culture

Perhaps more than any other single factor, the formation of Solidarity as an organized mass movement staunchly opposed to communism made Poland unique among all communist-ruled countries. In no other state did the population mobilize itself so successfully against communist dictatorship. As an association organized by the people independently of the state, Solidarity was a stellar example of what civil society entails. What began as a small group of factory workers conducting an illegal strike in 1980 quickly mushroomed into a broad-based popular movement involving industrial workers, farmers, and white-collar state employees united in their opposition to the communist authorities.

Backed into a corner by the movement's popularity, the government legalized Solidarity at the end of 1980. But once it became clear that the communist

Lech Walesa, his arm raised in a victory salute, stands in front of a Solidarity banner at a Catholic mass in 1987. Though the communists were still in power, 100,000 Poles defiantly demonstrated their support for Solidarity.

party was losing control over the country, its leaders banned the movement a year later. Undeterred, Solidarity's leaders kept the organization alive underground, sustained by the support of the overwhelming majority of the population. It continued to organize strikes. Finally in 1989, the ruling authorities, now consisting of pro-communist military officers rather than party's discredited civilian leadership, came to the round table, setting in motion the events that ultimately led to communism's demise.[19]

Solidarity's bold defiance of communist rule was by no means unprecedented in Poland. Polish antipathy to communism, intensified by a long history of resistance to Russian domination, manifested itself repeatedly during the long decades of the Cold War. Partisans fought a civil war against

the communists after World War II. In 1956, spontaneous strikes broke out among Polish factory workers, prompting Moscow to grant political and economic concessions. Students and intellectuals staged protests in the 1960s. More strikes occurred in the 1970s. Throughout all these years, right up to the very end of communist domination, Poland's Catholic church stood out as an institutional alternative to the communist party. Upward of 90 percent of Poland's population attended mass regularly, expressing not only their religious devotion but also their political rejection of atheistic communism. Frequently the church hierarchy would act as an intermediary between Polish society and the communist authorities, at times winning important concessions from the ruling party. The church was thus another organized agent of civil society in communist Poland, playing a far more active role in this regard than religious leaders in other communist states.

In sum, communism collapsed in Poland in large measure because the Poles created a vibrant civil society in opposition to it. In the process they decisively rejected the legitimacy of the dictatorship and forged a democratic political culture, amassing wide support for the principles of citizen participation in the political process, the accountability of the government to the people, freedom of expression, and other defining hallmarks of democracy. Because the Poles scored these achievements while the communists were still in power, they were already well advanced on the road to democracy when communist rule finally ended.[20]

Since then, both civil society and democratic attitudes have developed further. A plethora of citizen organizations, both political and nonpolitical in nature, have sprouted up, providing continuing support for the core ideas and values of democracy.

8. Education and Freedom of Information

The extraordinary advances of civil society in Poland when the communists ran the country were accompanied by greater freedom for academic research and mass communications than most other countries in the Soviet bloc enjoyed. By the 1960s and 1970s, Polish social scientists were conducting the most politically sensitive public opinion surveys in communist East-Central Europe. These polls revealed massive opposition to the communist political system and support for democratic pluralism. Much of this information was widely circulated, providing an outlet for the expression of mass opinion. In spite of the official censorship system, Polish intellectuals were able to exchange controversial views and travel to the West. "Flying universities" independent of the state educational system provided courses and discussion forums on political topics that were strictly taboo in other communist countries. Once Solidarity came into the picture there was a veritable explosion of mass circulation newspapers, journals, and other publications openly critical of the communist regime. The imposition of martial law restricted some of these activities, but much of it continued illegally. These educational and informational accomplishments were of inestimable value in bringing about the collapse of communist authority in Poland and ushering in the democratization process.[21]

By the end of the 1990s, 85 percent of Poland's media were privately owned. About 3,000 newspapers were in circulation. Though state-owned television and radio stations are active, they are subject to democratic controls. There are now more than a hundred private radio stations and ten commercial TV stations.

9. A Homogeneous Society

Polish society today is ethnically homogeneous: 98 percent of the population of 39 million consists of Poles. (Some three million Polish Jews perished in the Holocaust during World War II, virtually the entire Jewish population of the country.) Approximately 1 percent consists of ethnic Germans. (After World War II, parts of Germany were incorporated into Poland.) The overwhelming majority of Poles are Roman Catholics. While social homogeneity is no guarantor of democracy, at least the challenges of democratization in Poland are not complicated by ethnic hatreds or warring religions. Ethnic minority parties are exempt from the 5 percent electoral hurdle. Differences over the proper role of the Catholic church in Polish political life abound, with some favoring a central role for Catholic education and doctrines and others preferring a greater separation of church and state. But these conflicts are considerably less intense than the deadly religious feuds of the Balkans or Northern Ireland. Class differences are evident as some Poles are profiting from the economic transformations while others are being left behind, but poverty levels are not as great as in Russia or other poor countries in the region. All told, the relative homogeneity of Polish society seems to help the democratization process.

10. A Favorable International Environment

International factors were critical in Poland's transformation from communist rule to a newly democratizing state. As already noted, Gorbachev's willingness to permit elections there in 1989 and 1990 represented a radical break with the past practice of Soviet leaders. Without Moscow's acceptance of the Polish communist party's defeats at the hands of Solidarity, it is doubtful that democracy would have triumphed in the region. International support for Solidarity was also a crucial factor. Moral support expressed by the United States and various West European governments kept world attention focused on the organization during the years of martial law. Of particular importance was the support for Solidarity voiced by Pope John Paul II, who was a Polish cardinal before his elevation to the papacy. The pope's trips to his homeland drew throngs numbering in the millions and constituted a direct challenge to the communist authorities.

The quest for a stable democracy in the 1990s was accompanied by several facilitating factors in the international environment. The European Union signed several agreements with the Polish government prior to entering into formal negotiations with it on eventual membership. In 1999, Poland entered the North Atlantic Treaty Organization (NATO), along with the Czech Republic and Hungary. Loans from the International Monetary Fund and other international lenders and aid contributors have provided welcome economic assistance, though not all of it was used wisely.[22] Direct investment by foreign firms and investors rose from $89 million in 1990 to nearly $5 billion in 1997, the highest figure in East-Central Europe.

In sum, Poland's democratization process has been aided by salutary factors in virtually all ten conditions on our list. Romania's experience, however, has been more problematic.

ROMANIA

All of a sudden the crowd turned on the dictator. In the middle of an ordinary propaganda speech delivered to what was supposed to be a well-controlled group of Romanians, Nicolae Ceausescu stopped speaking. Clearly he could not believe his eyes and ears. Instead of shouting "Ceausescu and the people," as crowds had done on hundreds of previous occasions in accordance with the carefully orchestrated rituals of communist rule, people began chanting "Ceausescu the dictator!" Stunned by this unprecedented display of spontaneous anger, Ceausescu departed from his script and tried to placate the mob with promises of higher wages and better living conditions. But the unthinkable had happened: the man who had been the "sultanistic" boss of Romania for thirty-four years, wielding extraordinary personal power, had suddenly lost his ability to intimidate. As he frantically struggled to make himself heard, the televised transmission of the event was cut off.

Romanian dictator Nicolae Ceausescu addressing a crowd in Bucharest.

The next day, hundreds of thousands of Romanian citizens flooded Bucharest, demanding Ceausescu's ouster. Senior military officers joined the uprising and arrested the tyrant and his wife. A shadowy group of Communist Party political figures announced the formation of a "National Salvation Front Council," pledging themselves to pluralist democracy. Three days later, on December 25, Ceausescu and his wife were summarily executed following a hastily arranged trial behind closed doors. It appeared to all the world that Romania was following in the footsteps of the rest of East-Central Europe: communism, it seemed, was finished and democracy triumphant.

But were they? For the next seven years, Romania was led by President Ion Iliescu, a former communist official who had been part of a Communist Party faction opposed to Ceausescu. Unlike Walesa or Havel, he was never an anti-communist dissident. The crowd's vilification of Ceausescu on that fateful day, it later turned out, was not entirely a spontaneous popular explosion. Many of the people who shouted down the dictator had been assembled by Iliescu's faction, which took advantage of the population's widespread antipathy to Ceausescu in order to seize power for themselves. The Romanian "revolution" of 1989 was thus a factional coup by communist leaders superimposed upon the genuine anti-Ceausescu sentiments of the masses.

Thus the National Salvation Front (NSF) did not start out as a mass-based anti-communist organization like Poland's Solidarity but as an anti-Ceausescu conspiracy within the dictator's own party. Quite a few of its members retained deep misgivings about liberal democracy and private enterprise. Until they were voted out of power at the end of 1996, Iliescu and other politicians formerly connected with the communist regime pursued political and economic reforms only half-heartedly. The more pronouncedly democratic leaders who came after them, while determined to accelerate the reform process, have had to contend with the fact that Romania lagged well behind Poland, Hungary, and the Czech Republic in the pace and scope of democratization and economic liberalization. On all ten counts, Romania has had a difficult time meeting the main conditions for democracy and its smooth consolidation.

1. State Institutions

Romania entered the post-Ceausescu era with a potentially serious "stateness" problem. Approximately 1.7 million of its 23 million citizens are ethnic Hungarians. Most of them live in Transylvania, an area that belonged to Hungary before 1920. Tensions between the Hungarian minority and the Romanian government were present throughout the decades of communist rule, but Ceausescu and his predecessors kept them under tight control. Only in the last days of Ceausescu's regime did Hungarian frustrations erupt into mass protests. The first major anti-Ceausescu demonstrations occurred in mid-December 1989 in the Transylvanian town of Timosoara. Ceausescu's security forces quelled the disruptions, but some two thousand people were killed. After he was removed from power, the new leaders realized they had to address the concerns of the Hungarian minority in order to prevent a possible secessionist movement and to secure their full acceptance of the governing authorities in Bucharest. In 1996 Romania signed a friendship treaty with Hungary in which the two neighbors agreed to respect each other's borders. Romania further agreed to respect the right of its Hungarian citizens to maintain their identity, but ruled out full autonomy for Transylvania. While the issue of minority rights is still a contentious one in Romania today, the prospect of a civil war or the breakup of the Romanian state appears remote.

The first efforts to establish democratic state institutions and procedures were also problematic. Iliescu's government repeatedly violated cardinal principles of the rule of law. The Ceausescus' trial was a mockery of democratic jurisprudence. When students staged demonstrations in 1990 calling for more rigid standards of democratic legality, Iliescu brought coal miners into Bucharest to pummel the demonstrators and trash the headquarters of opposition parties. His government's control over the state-owned media and its refusal to grant the opposition parties adequate air time or access to printing presses enabled Iliescu to win two elections to the presidency, in 1990 and 1992. These same advantages permitted his followers to outpoll their opponents in elections to the national legislature. While some democratic reforms did take place, change was slow and only partial. The judiciary was often manipulated by the executive branch, and corruption was rampant. Iliescu, after all, had taken power as a communist adversary of Ceausescu, not as a democratic champion of liberty.

Because Iliescu wanted strong presidential powers, Romania's post-Ceausescu political system was modeled on the French presidential-parliamentary system. Iliescu exercised his prerogatives with quasi-authoritarian firmness. The legislature was kept relatively weak, and it was so divided in the Iliescu years that it was difficult, at times impossible, to pass urgently needed reform legislation.

In 1996 Iliescu was defeated in his third bid for the presidency by a bona fide proponent of democracy, Emil Constantinescu, the leader of the multiparty Democratic Convention of Romania. The Convention also bested Iliescu's party in elections to the parliament and formed a majority coalition with two other democratically oriented parties. The prime ministers appointed by Constantinescu have sought to institutionalize the rule of law and eliminate corruption with greater vigor than their predecessors did.

2. Elites Committed to Democracy

The collection of small parties that form the Democratic Convention of Romania is firmly committed to expanding and stabilizing democracy. So, too, are the Convention's main parliamentary allies of the late 1990s, the Social Democratic Union and the Hungarian Democratic Federation of Romania. The other large parties voice support for democracy but the extent of their commitment is questionable. After the National Salvation Front broke up, the former Communist Party led by Iliescu merged with smaller parties to form a new grouping, the Party of Social Democracy of Romania. The past performance of Iliescu and his backers when they were in power suggests that their devotion to democratic principles is partial at best. The remaining two parties elected to the legislature in 1996 are rabidly nationalist. The Party of Romanian National Unity and the Greater Romania Party espouse anti-Hungarian and anti-Semitic views that are utterly at variance with the values of tolerance, compromise, inclusion, and equality that are fundamental to democracy. These two parties together won 9 percent of the vote in 1996.

Since assuming office, President Constantinescu and his parliamentary supporters have moved to reduce corruption and strengthen democratic state institutions. The task of reforming the bureaucracy and widening the independence of the judiciary has been daunting, however, and progress has been slow. The military is under civilian control. Trade unions have extended their membership and embraced democracy but strikes have occasionally turned violent. Romania's business elites are still weak. The religious hierarchy, consisting predominantly of Orthodox prelates, has largely stayed out of politics, but some clerics have spoken out in favor of democratic liberties. As the new millennium dawned, the task of building broad-based elite support for democracy in Romania was still in its embryonic stages, certainly less advanced than in Poland.

3. National Wealth

The Romanian economy under Ceausescu was one of the poorest in Europe. Decades of mismanagement, exacerbated by the dictator's autocratic control over the country's economic activities, resulted in abysmal levels of industrial production, a stunted agricultural sector, periodic electrical brownouts, lethal levels of pollution, and the virtual collapse of international trade, especially with the West. When Iliescu assumed power, Romania's per capita gross national product was lower than Poland's. The government had paid off most of its international debts, but only because of Ceausescu's draconian austerity measures that relegated Romanian consumers to the lowest living standards in the Soviet bloc.

By the end of 1998, Romania's per capita gross national product stood at $1,390, one of the lowest among the former communist countries of the region. Between 1995 and 1998 its GNP actually contracted 15 percent. Living standards remain among the lowest in Europe, plummeting 20 percent in 1997 as Constantinescu's massive economic reform program got under way. While these realities may not preclude the development of democracy, they surely heighten the pressures on pro-

democratic authorities to improve the economic situation so as to cultivate and retain popular support for democratic governance.

4. Private Enterprise

Under Ceausescu, the state controlled virtually the entire economy. Since the onset of the post-Ceausescu era, leading state officials starting with Iliescu have proclaimed their commitment to reducing the state's share of economic activity and creating a successful private sector. Progress in these directions has been slow. By 1992 the private sector comprised only 30 percent of the economy, and progress remained slow through the rest of the decade. The International Monetary Fund has provided economic assistance, but only on condition that Romania accelerate privatization and cut the state's budget deficits. Even after Constantinescu came to power on a program devoted to stimulating privatization, his first prime minister was forced out of office for bungling the process.

Despite its expected benefits, privatization comes at a high price for workers and managers displaced by the country's economic transformation. Most of Romania's factories are so dilapidated that private investors, both domestic and foreign, have little interest in buying them, though foreign investment has risen since 1997. But when private owners cut their work force in the process of modernizing their newly acquired businesses and when plants close down because no one wants them, the resulting unemployment inevitably creates social discontent and political problems. Time will tell whether the effort to bring Romania's antiquated economy up to the standards of the rest of Europe, a task likely to take decades, will reinforce or undermine the consolidation of democracy.

5. A Middle Class

As in other countries of the Soviet bloc, the middle class in Romania under communist rule consisted almost entirely of state employees: bureaucrats, teachers, scientists, and the like. So repressive was Ceausescu's tyranny, however, that these people had little chance to develop a class identity or to pressure the state, however meekly, for higher pay or other privileges enjoyed by their counterparts in Poland. Intellectuals were subjected to considerably more stringent controls in Romania than in Poland, with no outlets to publish ideas that did not faithfully parrot the official ideology and with far fewer opportunities to travel abroad for professional purposes. (Even travel to Poland and Hungary was restricted.) Dissatisfied but dispirited, the middle class under Ceausescu was too cowed to launch a subversive movement for democracy.

In the 1990s the emergence of a new middle class, consisting of people employed in the state sector as well as those in the budding private sector, has been slow. Whether this class assumes a greater sense of its own identity and links its future with democracy will ultimately depend on the performance of the economy. If its members have reason to believe that their living standards are improving under democratic conditions, their support for democracy will presumably deepen. But if their material well-being shows no signs of a turn for the better, it is quite possible that Romania's middle class will lapse into political apathy, depriving democracy of a crucial source of support.

6. Support of the Disadvantaged for Democracy

As in Poland, most people in Romania had grounds to feel economically disadvantaged under communism; indeed all the more so, as Romania's economic conditions were worse than Poland's. But whereas Polish workers challenged the authorities with strikes, often wringing concessions from panicky communist leaders fearful of a mass outburst against them, Romania was so subdued by Ceausescu's totalitarian police state that open resistance was rare. The only serious strikes occurred in 1977 when coal miners demanded better working and living conditions. The government made a few economic concessions but also used its security forces to quash the rebellion and kill the strike's organizers. There were no further efforts by the country's impoverished masses to challenge Ceausescu's rule until 1989.

Since then the poorest elements in Romanian society—predominantly factory workers, miners,

and peasants—have exhibited inconsistent support for democratization. Many voted for Iliescu and his political allies. Ominously, some have resorted to violence to vent their frustrations at the slow pace of change. Coal miners wreaked havoc in Bucharest in 1991. In early 1999 some twenty thousand miners, incensed at the government's plans to close down more than a hundred unproductive mines, began a lengthy march toward Bucharest, clashing repeatedly with police along the way. As the authorities made military preparations for a bloody confrontation, a deal was worked out with the miners encamped only 100 miles from the capital city. The agreement was not likely to satisfy either side for very long, as Romania's parlous economic situation will require the government to trim economic losses in the mining areas, inevitably resulting in more wage squeezes and unemployment. Many factories are subjected to the same pressures. Whether those whose jobs are affected by these economic policies will be willing to support the democratically elected governments that enforce them is a major question facing Romania's slowly germinating democracy. So, too, is the issue of mass poverty. In the mid-1990s, more than 70 percent of the population earned the equivalent of less than $2 a day. In addition, Romanian women have tended to be more disadvantaged than their Polish counterparts, both during and after communism.[23]

7. Civil Society and a Democratic Political Culture

When we compare the role of civil society under communist rule in Poland and Romania, it is evident that the two countries were on diametrically opposite ends of the spectrum. Whereas Poland had an especially active civil society, Romania under Ceausescu had none. Not only were there few strikes, but the only effort to create an independent trade union was met with an instant crackdown and the disappearance of its organizer. The Orthodox church, traditionally the largest organized religion in Romania, was never allowed to play the kind of intermediary role that the Catholic church played in Poland. Romanian scholars and scientists had fewer chances to travel abroad. All conversations with foreigners had to be reported to the authorities, a regulation that was not in force in most other neighboring communist countries.

Human rights groups were prevented from getting organized, and the country's few dissidents labored in desperate isolation, with no chance to spread their ideas via an underground network of activists. When Ceausescu ordered women to undergo gynecological examinations in an effort to prevent abortions, and when thousands of unwanted children (many of them afflicted with AIDS) filled Romania's orphanages, there were no organizations in Romania to take up their cause.

Since the advent of democracy, a civil society has begun to spring up. New political parties have come into existence. Several trade unions have formed, along with ethnic, human rights, environmentalist, feminist, and other advocacy groups. Whether these groups all favor democracy, however, is still an open question. When parties do not accept basic democratic principles and values and when interest groups resort to violence or other non-democratic practices, civil society is not necessarily conducive to democratic consolidation. It is therefore still too early to tell if Romania's nascent civic organizations will nurture the democratic political culture that must underlie any successful democracy.

8. Education and Freedom of Information

Under Ceausescu, the content of education was rigidly controlled. Even communist doctrine in Romania was heavily laced with Ceausescu's own ideological contributions, a collection of banalities. So strict was the state's suppression of free information that typewriters had to be licensed by the police.

Although Iliescu manipulated the state-owned media when in power, since his departure there has been a reorganization of the state-owned broadcast network. A number of private radio and TV stations now exist and there is an abundance of independent newspapers, magazines, and journals. Press freedoms are increasingly respected, though laws against defaming political leaders can sometimes be used to intimidate journalists. The trend, however, is clearly favorable to a more open

education system and the free flow of information, both of which promote democratization.

9. A Homogenous Society

As already noted, Romania has a large Hungarian minority that openly displayed its long-suppressed discontent under Ceausescu in December 1989, precipitating the dictator's demise less than two weeks later. Hungarians in post-communist Romania are still the victims of ethnic slurs and discrimination. So, too, are Romania's Roma population (Gypsies), believed to number 1 to 2 million.[24] The two Romanian ultranationalist parties openly deride both groups, along with Jews and international capitalists. Hungarians have formed their own party, however, which joined the coalition government formed after the 1996 elections. In addition, various non-governmental organizations have sprung into existence to defend the rights of minorities.

Language conflicts have arisen since democratization began, with Hungarians demanding the right to instruction in their own language in a number of university departments, demands that were opposed by various Romanian politicians. Many Hungarians, in fact, want their own educational system in Transylvania, with instruction in Hungarian at all levels. Whether these and other ethnic tensions help promote or undermine tolerance and fair play in Romania is another open question that the coming years will answer.[25]

10. A Favorable International Environment

By the time the Romanian public was willing to risk open defiance of Ceausescu in December 1989, communist rule had essentially collapsed in all the other East-Central European states belonging to the Soviet alliance. With no support from Moscow, whose leaders he had frequently antagonized, Ceausescu was isolated not only at home but internationally as well. The international environment was thus propitious for his removal from power.

Since the initiation of the democratization process, the outside world has been helpful, but less so in Romania than in Poland, the Czech Republic, or Hungary. The Iliescu government's sluggish approach to economic reform imposed significant delays on the international community's readiness to provide assistance. Since 1997, however, things have picked up, as the International Monetary Fund, foreign governments, and private investors have increased their financial support. Foreign direct investment went from zero in 1990 to $1.2 billion by 1997. In 1999 the European Union agreed to begin negotiations with Romania on full membership, though the process is likely to take years. NATO has turned down Romania's request for full membership, though President Clinton during a visit in 1997 said that future membership is a possibility as long as the country proceeds along the paths of democratic and economic transformation.

The starkly contrasting cases of Poland and Romania provide insights into the prospects for democracy in other former communist countries in East-Central Europe. Hungary and the Czech Republic have largely reflected Poland's pattern. Though all three countries have their specific peculiarities, they are the most politically and economically advanced states in the region. Slovakia (which split off from Czechoslovakia in 1993) and Bulgaria have come closer to Romania's pattern of slower progress toward democratic consolidation and market-oriented economic reforms.[26]

IS DEMOCRACY INEVITABLE?

At a time when the United States was the only functioning democracy in the world, Alexis de Tocqueville was highly ambivalent regarding the prospects for democracy elsewhere. In the opening pages of *Democracy in America* he expressed buoyant optimism, convinced that the gradual progress of political equality and democratic governance, at least in America and Europe, was ordained by God. Later in the book he struck a more cautious tone, acknowledging that it was "hard to make the people take a share in government." Democracy would therefore have to compete with absolutist monarchy as one of two systems of government vying for the allegiance of humanity. Given these two choices, Tocqueville emphatically favored democracy.[27]

As the nineteenth century rounded to a close, another astute observer of both American and Eu-

ropean politics, Woodrow Wilson, heralded democracy's eventual triumph over monarchy with even greater conviction than Tocqueville. The rise of mass education, Wilson averred, was already having a noticeable impact on the spread of democratic ideas and institutions in a number of countries. These trends promised to "reduce politics to a single pure form by excluding all other governing forces and institutions but those of a wide suffrage and a democratic representation."[28] Several decades later, as president of the United States, Wilson would justify U.S. involvement in World War I as an opportunity to "make the world safe for democracy."

In more recent years the hypothesis that democracy's ultimate victory over authoritarianism is inevitable has been reaffirmed by Francis Fukuyama, an American political scientist. In a widely discussed article and a subsequent book, Fukuyama argued that the collapse of communism in East-Central Europe and the Soviet Union signaled the failure of the last remaining ideological challenge to liberal democracy. (The other main challenge to democracy in the twentieth century, fascism, had already been defeated in World War II.) While a variety of authoritarian regimes still held sway around the globe, Fukuyama believed that these lingering despotisms were bereft of any appealing ideas that might attract a mass following.

Above all they cannot offer what every individual, in Fukuyama's view, cherishes above all else in social life: recognition by others as an equal human being. Only democracy can respond to these innermost yearnings of the human spirit, he maintains, because only democracy provides opportunities for participation in the life of the community on the basis of equal dignity and respect. Its ultimate spread around the world will therefore constitute the "end of history," in the sense that no better political alternative will come about.[29]

Addressing the question of democracy's future from a more empirical perspective, Samuel Huntington has taken a less sanguine view of the inevitability of democracy's worldwide success. In *The Third Wave*, published in 1991, Huntington observed that, since the advent of the mass suffrage in the United States, there have been three great "waves" of transitions to democracy around the world. Once established, however, democracy has not always endured. The first two waves were each followed by a "reverse wave," in which at least some of the countries that had managed to build a democracy failed to keep it, reverting instead to some form of authoritarianism. The possibility of a third reverse wave in our own day and age is a distinct possibility.

According to Huntington, the first wave extended from 1828 to 1926. During that period some thirty-three countries adopted at least the rudimentary components of democracy such as male suffrage by secret ballot and the accountability of the government to an elected legislature. Around 1922, however, a reverse trend began taking shape as democracy collapsed in a number of these very countries. By 1942, eleven states had succumbed to fascism or some other brand of dictatorial rule.

As World War II ground to its conclusion, a second wave of democratization got under way. This process started with the reintroduction of democracy in Italy and Germany and its introduction in Japan after the war; it gained momentum with the extension of democracy to a growing number of developing countries. This second wave of democratization lasted approximately from 1943 to 1962 and embraced forty-one countries that either failed in a previous attempt to establish stable democracy or joined the democratic camp for the first time. As before, however, democracy did not manage to take root and flourish in every case. A second reverse wave set in around 1958 and continued through 1975. All told, twenty-two states lapsed into authoritarian rule during the second reverse wave.

The **third wave** of democratization began in 1974 with the emergence of democratic institutions in Portugal. Over the next twenty years or so democracy mushroomed in more than forty states, culminating in the collapse of the Soviet Union and the transition of several of the USSR's constituent union republics to independent democracies.

Has a third reverse wave already started? Between 1987 and 1995, the number of electoral democracies in the world rose astronomically from 69 to 117. By the start of 1999, that number held steady at 117; though there was no further increase, there was no decrease, either.[30] While a few

new democracies or reconstituted democracies slipped back into non-democratic rule in the 1990s (such as Peru, where President Alberto Fujimori assumed dictatorial power, and Kenya, where the ruling party staged fraudulent or manipulated elections), there has been no massive reverse wave. Still, the process of democratization in a host of countries is far from complete, a fact that underscores the fragility and unpredictability of democratic governance.

So is democracy inevitable? "Time is on the side of democracy," Huntington asserted on the final page of his book. But the thrust of his analysis alerts us to the reality that democracy is far from poised to conquer the globe anytime soon.[31]

Be that as it may, the prospects for democracy are probably much better in the world we live in than ever before in human history. For all its weaknesses and imperfections, democracy has much to recommend it over the coercive stability of dictatorships. It still offers humanity greater opportunities for freedom, dignity, and self-realization than does any other form of government yet devised. "Indeed it has been said," Winston Churchill once observed, "that democracy is the worst form of government—except all those other forms which have been tried from time to time."

KEY TERMS
(Underlined in the text)

Democratization
Consolidation
Civil society
Third wave
Solidarity

NOTES

1. Juan J. Linz and Alfred Stepan, *Problems of Democratic Transition and Consolidation: Southern Europe, South America, and Post-Communist Europe* (Baltimore, Md.: Johns Hopkins University Press, 1996), 28.
2. James MacGregor Burns, *Leadership* (New York: Harper and Row, 1978). See also F. G. Baily, *Humbuggery and Manipulation: The Art of Leadership* (Ithaca, N.Y.: Cornell University Press, 1988) and Ann Ruth Wilner, *The Spellbinders: Charismatic Political Leadership* (New Haven, Conn.: Yale University Press, 1984).

3. Herbert McCloskey and Alida Brill, *Dimensions of Tolerance* (New York: Russell Sage Foundation, 1983). See also Thomas R. Dye and Harmon Ziegler, *The Irony of Democracy*, 8th ed. (Pacific Grove, Calif.: Brooks/Cole, 1990).

4. For a cross-national comparison of the United States, Japan, and Sweden, see Sidney Verba et al., *Elites and the Idea of Equality* (Cambridge, Mass.: Harvard University Press, 1987).

5. Peter Bachrach, *The Theory of Democratic Elitism* (Boston: Little, Brown, 1967).

6. Barrington Moore, *Social Origins of Dictatorship and Democracy* (Boston: Beacon, 1966).

7. One Russian businessman said, "If people tell me that for the sake of symbolic democracy I must give up my property—well, democracy is not worth that much to me." *Financial Times*, November 7, 1995.

8. Jean L. Cohen and Andrew Arato, *Civil Society and Political Theory* (Cambridge, Mass.: MIT Press, 1994); Chris Hann and Elizabeth Dunn, *Civil Society: Challenging Western Models* (London: Routledge, 1996); John Keane, *Civil Society: Old Images, New Visions* (Stanford, Calif.: Stanford University Press, 1998); Thomas Janoski, *Citizenship and Civil Society* (Cambridge, England: Cambridge University Press, 1998); Avishai Margalit, *The Decent Society*, trans. Naomi Goldblum (Cambridge, Mass.: Harvard University Press, 1996); Donald W. Shriver, *An Ethic for Enemies: Forgiveness in Politics* (New York: Oxford University Press, 1995).

9. Alexis de Tocqueville, *Democracy in America*, ed. J. P. Mayer, trans. George Lawrence (New York: Harper and Row, 1966), pt. 2, 513–17.

10. Robert D. Putnam, "Bowling Alone: America's Declining Social Capital," *Journal of Democracy* 6, no. 1 (January 1995): 65–78, and *Bowling Alone: The Collapse and Revival of American Community* (New York: Simon and Schuster, 2000).

11. Of eighty-eight countries ranked by Freedom House as "free" in 1998–99, sixty-six were mono-ethnic. Out of 114 mono-ethnic countries, 66 (58 percent) were "free" ("democratic" in this book's terminology); 22 (19 percent) were "partly free" ("partly democratic"); and 26 (23 percent) were "not free" ("authoritarian"). Of seventy-seven multiethnic countries (in which no ethnic group comprised at least two-thirds of the population), twenty-two were "free" (29 percent), thirty-one were "partly free" (40 percent); and twenty-four were "not free." See *Freedom in the World 1998–1999* (New York: Freedom House, 1999), 9. For the criteria defining "free," "partly free," and "not free" countries, see chapter 4, endnote 2 (pp. 93–94).

12. In 1997 the EU invited Poland, the Czech Republic, Hungary, Slovenia, and Estonia to begin formal negotiations on admission into the EU. In 1999 the EU indicated its willingness to start similar negotiations with Slovakia, Romania, Bulgaria, Latvia, and Lithuania.

13. For arguments advocating external support for democracy, see Joshua Muravchik, *Exporting Democracy: Fulfilling America's Destiny* (Washington, D.C.: American Enterprise Institute Press, 1991).

14. The Soviet Union's allies in East-Central Europe were East Germany (the German Democratic Republic), Poland, Czechoslovakia, Hungary, Romania, and Bulgaria. Together with the USSR they formed an alliance called the Warsaw Treaty Organization, or Warsaw Pact.

15. Poland was partitioned by Prussia and Austria in 1772, 1792, and 1795. Following the third partition, Poland ceased to exist as an independent state. In 1831, Russia suppressed a national uprising and annexed most of Poland. The Russians squelched another uprising in 1863. The country was reconstituted in 1918, but its eastern and western boundaries changed both during and after World War II. The USSR annexed about one-third of Poland's territory in the east but gave Poland new lands at Germany's expense in the west. In 1990, Poland and Germany signed a treaty confirming their existing boundary.

16. Linz and Stepan characterize this transition as a "pacted transition." See *Problems of Democratic Transition and Consolidation*, 264 ff.

17. The data are in the World Bank's *World Development Report 1999/2000* (New York: Oxford University Press, 1999).

18. For a comparative study of privatization processes, see David Stark and Laszlo Bruszt, *Postsocialist Pathways: Transforming Politics and Property in East Central Europe* (Cambridge, England: Cambridge University Press, 1998).

19. Timothy Garton Ash, *The Polish Revolution: Solidarity* (New York: Charles Scribner's Sons, 1983) and, by Jadwiga Stanizkis, *Poland's Self-Limiting Revolution*, ed. Jan T. Gross (Princeton, N.J.: Princeton University Press, 1984) and *The Dynamics of the Breakthrough in Eastern Europe: The Polish Experience* (Berkeley: University of California Press, 1991).

20. On civil society under communism in East-Central Europe, see Vladimir Tismaneanu, *Reinventing Politics* (New York: Free Press, 1993).

21. Jane Leftwich Curry, *Poland's Journalists: Professionalism and Politics* (Cambridge, England: Cambridge University Press, 1990).

22. On the problems arising from Western economic advice and assistance, see Janine R. Wedel, *Collision and Collusion: The Strange Case of Western Aid to Eastern Europe* (New York: St. Martin's Press, 1998).

23. On the status of women in East-Central Europe in the communist era, see *Women, State and Party in Eastern Europe,* ed. Sharon L. Wolchik and Alfred G. Meyer (Durham, N.C.: Duke University Press, 1985); in the democratic transition process, see *Women and Democracy: Latin America and Central and Eastern Europe,* ed. Jane S. Jaquette and Sharon L. Wolchik (Baltimore, Md.: Johns Hopkins University Press, 1998).

24. *Evaluation of the Gypsy Population and of Their Movements in Central and Eastern Europe and in Some OECD Countries* (Paris: Organization for Economic Cooperation and Development, 1993).

25. Zsuzsa Csergo, *Language and Institutional Legitimacy: A Comparative Study of Romania and Slovakia* (Ph.D. diss., George Washington University, 2000).

26. Linz and Stepan, *Problems of Democratic Transition and Consolidation,* 235–365; Vladimir Tismaneanu, *Fantasies of Salvation: Democracy, Nationalism, and Myth in Post-Communist Europe* (Princeton, N.J.: Princeton University Press, 1998).

27. Tocqueville, *Democracy in America,* 12, 314–15.

28. Woodrow Wilson, *The State* (Boston: D.C. Heath, 1889), 603.

29. Francis Fukuyama, "The End of History?" *The National Interest,* no. 16 (summer 1989): 3–18, and *The End of History and the Last Man* (New York: Free Press, 1992).

30. *Freedom in the World 1998–1999,* 5.

31. Samuel P. Huntington, *The Third Wave* (Norman: University of Oklahoma Press, 1991).

CHAPTER 11

PEOPLE AND POLITICS

Voters—Parties—Interest Groups—
Dissidence—Revolution

MASS PARTICIPATION IN DEMOCRACIES

One of the central premises of democratic theory is that citizens will take full advantage of their opportunities to participate actively in political life, making their views known to the governing authorities and holding them fully accountable for their actions. Contrary to these expectations, however, most people who live in democracies choose not to participate very much. One study of political participation in the United States conducted in the 1960s labeled 30 percent of the adult population "apathetics" because they knew virtually nothing about politics. Another 60 percent were labeled "spectators" on the grounds that they paid some attention to politics, though they varied in degree. Many spectators paid only minimal attention to political goings-on. Only about 5 percent to 7 percent could be termed "gladiators" who actively participated in political campaigns in presidential election years; in other years this group of political activists would typically fall to 1 percent to 2 percent of the population. Counting the gladiators and the most politically active spectators, only about 20 percent of the population regularly engaged in discussions about political issues; they were labeled "opinion leaders." These figures have remained substantially the same right up through the 1990s.[1] In other democracies, too, most people do not get actively involved in political life.

Nevertheless, as a general rule a large number of citizens, quite often the majority, will turn out to vote in periodic elections. Voting is the main form of mass participation in virtually all democratic countries. Voter turnout rates differ from country to country, however. As table 11.1 indicates, the United States on average ranks next to the bottom of twenty-two major democracies, and at the very bottom in off-year Congressional elections.

Why don't people who have the privilege of democratic participation take advantage of it? One explanation was hypothesized by Mancur Olson in his acclaimed book, *The Logic of Collective Action*[2].

THE LOGIC OF COLLECTIVE ACTION

According to a traditional assumption about democracy, people who are free to engage in open political activity will take advantage of this opportunity by organizing or joining groups that seek to exert pressure on state decision makers in behalf of some common group interest or demand. Indeed, such interest groups (or pressure groups) are a common feature of modern democracy.

Even in non-democratic regimes, it is often assumed that a population that is severely repressed by the government will sooner or later rise up and revolt. History is full of examples of such outbursts. While most of

TABLE 11.1

Electoral Turnout in Selected Democracies

The figures show average turnout, measured as a percentage of the voting age population, in countries that have had fair elections to the lower house of parliament since at least the 1950s.[*]

Country	1950s	1960s	1970s	1980s	1990s
Australia	83	84	85	83	83
Austria	89	90	88	87	78
Belgium	88	87	88	89	84
Canada	70	72	68	67	60
Denmark	78	87	86	85	81
Finland	76	85	82	79	72
France	71	67	67	64	60
Germany	84	82	86	79	73
Iceland	91	89	89	90	88
India	61	59	61	63	59
Ireland	73	74	82	76	71
Israel	79	82	81	81	83
Italy	93	94	94	93	90
Japan	74	71	72	71	61
Luxembourg	62	70	71	63	61
Netherlands	88	90	85	82	75
New Zealand	91	84	83	86	80
Norway	78	83	80	83	76
Sweden	77	83	87	86	83
Switzerland	61	53	43	40	38
United Kingdom	79	75	74	74	73
United States	49	56	46	46	43
Presidential years	57	62	54	52	52
Off years	43	48	41	38	37

[*]Turnout for *registered* voters tends to be somewhat higher in all countries and significantly higher in the United States (see figure 3.4). Data for the 1990s extend through 1997.
Source: Voter Turnout for 1945 to 1997: A Global Report on Political Participation (Stockholm: International Institute for Democracy and Electoral Assistance, 1997), and this organization's website, <www.int-idea.se>

them were crushed by the overwhelming power of the state, in a few cases the forces for change produced a real revolution, overturning the prevailing system of government.

The reasoning behind such activity seems rather obvious: people who are dissatisfied and who believe that the state should do something to redress their grievances will band together and take appropriate "collective action" (whether through legal democratic procedures or through illegal or violent activities) to get the government to do something for them. Intuitively, such behavior seems perfectly reasonable and rational.

But is it? In ***The Logic of Collective Action***, Mancur Olson suggested that people in large groups usually do *not* behave this way. Rather than join in collective action with like-minded citizens, even people with serious grievances usually do nothing. Personal inaction is often preferred to collective action.

Olson argues that such inaction is a *rational choice* for the individual. Most social scientists define **rationality** as *behavior aimed at maximizing gains and minimizing costs or risks.* Thus the rational "economic man"—*homo economicus*—acts to make money, not lose it. As applied to the logic of collective action, Olson hypothesizes that the average person will reason as follows when making up her or his mind about whether to get involved in some sort of group political activity:

- The costs and risks of such action may be too high (one will have to sacrifice time, comfort, or perhaps money, and one may even run the risk of being jailed, beaten, or killed if the activity is illegal).
- If a group has already been formed to militate in behalf of the individual's interests, one's own contribution may not be all that necessary anyway ("If 10,000 are demonstrating in the streets or signing petitions, what difference will one more make?").

- If the group fails to change government policy favorably, those engaged in the collective action gain exactly what those who did not engage in it get: nothing. But if the group succeeds, the non-participant shares in the collective gains equally with the hardy activists who bore the costs and risks of action (lower taxes, extra social security benefits, a more responsive government, and so on).

This logic is particularly applicable in the case of *collective goods:* material or nonmaterial goods that are shared by large segments of the community rather than being divisible among individuals. Social security increases, national security, and an improved environment are examples.

Given these considerations, Olson maintains that most people will opt to be nonparticipating "free riders" who let others do the dirty work of political activity for them. Inaction is more likely than collective action. "The paradox," Olson concludes, "is that . . . large groups, at least if they are composed of rational individuals, will *not* act in their group interest." This conclusion is strikingly counterintuitive, since it contradicts the common-sense assumption that rational people will take action in their own-self interest if given the opportunity to do so.

Although the *degree* of political participation in democracies can vary considerably, the *forms* of mass democratic participation are generally the same. Typically they include *elections, political parties,* and *interest groups.* Let's examine these and a few additional modes of popular participation and look at some relevant hypotheses on these topics.

Elections

Political scientists are keenly interested in elections. In fact, the scientific study of elections has its own name: **psephology,** a term that comes from the Greek word for pebble. (In ancient Greek city-states, people voted by depositing colored pebbles into "vote" containers.) We are particularly interested in finding *patterns* in electoral behavior. What types of people, for example, vote for the various parties competing for power? One answer to this perennially topical question is that, as a general rule, wealthier people tend to vote for the more conservative parties (such as the Republicans in the United States, the Conservative Party in Britain, or the Christian Democrats in Ger-

many), and the less well-to-do tend to vote for left-of-center parties especially concerned with social welfare (such as the Democrats in the United States, the Labour Party in Britain, or the Social Democratic Party of Germany). As with any frequently observed pattern, however, there are bound to be exceptions. In fact, voting patterns in most democracies are affected by a plethora of factors. While income levels frequently play a major role in influencing how people vote, so do additional variables such as party identification, education level, ethnicity, religion, gender, age, ideology, and other factors.

In addition, sometimes there are certain legal or institutional factors that may affect voter turnout. In the United States, for instance, people must voluntarily go to a registration place and register in order to be eligible to vote. In most other democracies, voter registration procedures are easier and less time-consuming. One scholar showed that U.S. registration requirements reduced voter turnout by at least 10 percent compared with other democratic countries (see figure 3.4).[3] Attitudinal factors may also affect voting behavior. For example, people who trust the government to govern effectively are more likely to vote than those who have less trust and a lower sense of their own political "efficacy," in other words, their ability to have some impact on what the government does.[4] In sum, scientific studies of elections and electoral behavior must take account of a lot of variables.

Do Voters Know What They're Doing? It is a standing premise of democratic theory that voters need to be aware of what they are doing when they vote. Without a minimum level of political comprehension on the part of the electorate, the act of voting may be meaningless and the very notion of popular sovereignty illusory. Democracy thus rests on the assumption that voters are rational. Are they?

As we noted in our account of the logic of collective action, social scientists define **rationality** as *behavior aimed at maximizing one's benefits and minimizing one's risks and losses.* A **rational choice**, therefore, is a *choice or decision that is consciously calculated to maximize gains and minimize risks and losses.* In political science, economics, and other social sciences, **rational choice**

theory *hypothesizes that people generally behave in these ways.*

To put it schematically, voters may be defined as rational if they

1. know what their own priorities are (lower taxes, less crime, a cleaner environment, and the like);
2. gather as much information as they can about the various candidates and understand their positions on the issues;
3. understand what the likely consequences will be if this or that candidate gets elected; and
4. vote for those candidates who are most likely to satisfy those priorities once in office.

Some rational choice theorists have maintained that voters are truly rational only when they seek to promote their own material self-interests. This rather narrow definition stresses personal selfishness as an essential ingredient of rationality. Voters with this type of orientation are rational if they vote for candidates who would lower their taxes or increase their social security payments, for example; they are not interested in the general welfare of the community. Other theorists take a broader view of rationality, maintaining that one can still be considered rational even if one's election-day priorities place community goals rather than personal ones at the top of the list. Thus if a voter wants to promote environmental safety or national security, that person may be considered a rational voter as long as she votes for candidates who openly espouse such goals. Even in these cases, such community-minded individuals would still gain some personal advantage if their broad general-welfare goals are achieved (such as clean air or a stronger national defense). Of course, individual voters may not gain many benefits at all if the candidates they vote for lose. What matters in rational decision making is the *conscious intention* of maximizing one's benefits, not the end result, over which individual voters do not have much control.

One theory of voting behavior has suggested that voters do in fact act rationally. The choices they make when deciding how to vote, in this view, are just as rational as the choices consumers make when shopping. In a famous study published in 1957, Anthony Downs suggested that voters in democracies think and act pretty much like consumers in a market economy: they know what type of product they want, they shop around and gather information about alternative models, they look at how the available products will affect their wallet, and they make a rational selection based on what is best for them. Thus each citizen, Downs hypothesized, "casts his vote for the party he believes will provide him with more benefits than any other." Politicians, for their part, behave like sellers, rationally adjusting their "product lines" (their policies and campaign promises) so as to attract the most "buyers" (voters). Democratically elected governments and opposition parties, Downs said, will always act in their own self-interest: they will espouse only those policies that maximize votes, whether or not such policies are good for society in some ideal sense.[5]

Downs explained the logic of electoral behavior in purely theoretical terms. But a landmark empirical study based on election returns and interviews with voters provided considerable evidence that most Americans were anything but rational in their actual voting activity. *The American Voter*, a comprehensive analysis of elections in the late 1940s and 1950s undertaken by a team of political scientists at the University of Michigan, showed that most Americans did not vote on the issues at all. The single most important variable accounting for how the majority of Americans voted in this period was *party identification*. Those who identified themselves as Democrats tended generally to vote for Democratic Party candidates, and those who identified themselves as Republican tended to vote accordingly. Only about 20 percent of the electorate changed their long-term loyalties from one party to another. The study also showed that the vast majority of voters, between two-thirds and three-fourths of the total, could not recognize much of a difference between the two major parties on the issues despite all the efforts by Republican and Democratic candidates to make their disagreements explicit. Most strikingly, the researchers also found that an extremely small proportion of the electorate, only 2.5 percent to 3.5 percent, thought about politics in coherent ideological terms, such as "liberal" or "conservative" orientations. The latter finding was especially noteworthy because most American politicians tended to orient themselves along a liberal-conservative dimension.[6]

Subsequent studies by members of the Michigan group largely corroborated this depiction of the American voter as essentially uninformed and non-ideological, with little appreciation of the policy implications of the candidates' positions. In a study of the political belief systems of Americans, for example, Philip E. Converse found that they consisted mainly of what he called *nonattitudes*. These are political opinions that are inconsistent, contradictory, and subject to unpredictable fluctuations over time.[7] Another political scientist suggested that only about 20 percent of the U.S. citizenry are reasonably well-informed about political issues, a group known as the **attentive public.** By contrast, the **mass public** has considerably less political knowledge. Additional studies have portrayed most British and French voters in a similar light.[8]

Students of U.S. voting behavior in more recent decades have somewhat altered this unflattering portrait of the average American citizen. While acknowledging that very few voters meet the criteria for rationality defined earlier, some scholars argue that high levels of political knowledge and analytical sophistication may not be necessary for voters to make up their minds in a reasonable fashion. Most voters, they contend, have a "gut" understanding of the candidates and issues, derived in part from campaign slogans and other cues they get from politicians and the media. These simple understandings, based on information shortcuts rather than on extensive reading and analysis, are good enough for them to make electoral choices that are logically consistent with their own political preferences, however vaguely they may be articulated. Without being perfectly rational, most voters, according to this view, are not entirely irrational, either. They act in accordance with a kind of **limited rationality** (also called *low-information rationality* or *bounded rationality*).[9]

Scholars examining voting behavior in Europe have uncovered evidence that European voters also have a greater appreciation of the issues than was earlier assumed, and they vote accordingly. These studies further show that in countries like Germany, Italy, and the Netherlands, voters tend to be more ideologically sophisticated and consistent than the average American voter.[10]

Political Parties

Political parties are the main mechanism for providing the voters with a menu of candidates and programs from which to make their electoral choices. As a consequence, parties are indispensable to the functioning of contemporary democracies. But parties also exist in non-democratic countries as well. Hitler's Germany, the Soviet Union, Communist China, and a host of other authoritarian countries have been governed by a political party that typically bans all competing parties and monopolizes state power. Any understanding of political parties must take account of the variety of roles parties can play under different political conditions and systems.

Political parties *are organizations that seek to place their designated representatives in governmental positions.*

This definition is broad enough to include several different types of political parties. For example:

- *Competitive political parties* accept democratic principles and compete for governmental positions through the electoral process in democracies.
- *Anti-regime parties* do not accept the rules and principles of the existing system of government but seek instead to overturn them in a revolution. Sometimes anti-regime parties compete in democratic elections, but their goal is not to promote democracy but to gain power, with the ultimate intention of destroying democracy. The Nazi Party and the German Communist Party in Germany's inter-war democracy (1918–33) are examples.
- *Power-monopolizing parties* monopolize governmental power in authoritarian regimes. The Nazi Party during Hitler's dictatorship, the Communist Party of the Soviet Union, the Chinese Communist Party, and a host of other ruling parties in "one-party regimes" fit this description.[11]

One thing that all three party types have in common is that they *seek governmental power.* Whether in the legislature, the executive branch, local government, or some other state institution;

whether through democratic electoral procedures or through force and intimidation, parties exist mainly to obtain the power to make authoritative decisions. We'll spend the rest of this section looking primarily at competitive parties, since these are the ones that promote mass participation in democracies.

Particularistic and Catch-all Parties   Another distinction that is commonly made when categorizing political parties is that between *particularistic* and *catch-all* parties.

   Particularistic parties *are parties that confine their appeal to a particular segment of the population.* When modern political parties emerged in nineteenth-century Europe and America, they often had a rather narrow appeal. Conservative parties tended to reflect the attitudes of the aristocratic upper classes and the wealthier members of the business class, while working-class parties sought their votes almost exclusively from the laboring masses in urban industrial centers. Agrarian parties promoted the interests of farmers. These parties were defined essentially by their *social class* base. Other particularistic parties had a predominantly religious outlook. These so-called *confessional* parties usually sought the votes of Protestants or Catholics in countries with deep religious animosities. In Ireland and the Netherlands, for instance, Protestants and Catholics set up their own rival parties, and in nineteenth-century Germany a Catholic party was established to defend the interests of Catholic Germans. Other parties were organized to promote the interests of national or regional minorities, and still others sought to drum up support for some specific issue: voting rights for women, free trade, a ban on alcohol. Particularistic parties of various sorts still exist in many democracies today.

   By contrast, **catch-all parties** *are parties that seek to widen their base of popular support as much as possible.* Their primary aim is to win elections and take over the government. Accordingly they try to catch all the votes they can, drawing them from a diversity of social classes, religions, ethnic groups, and other segments of the population. In the process they usually loosen their commitment to specific groups or principles and adopt more flexible positions capable of broadening their mass appeal. Sometimes catch-all parties are criticized for being so vague about where they stand that the voters can't tell where they stand at all. But it is only by diluting their political consistency and opening their arms to all comers that they can amass the vote tallies they need to outpoll the other parties. Thus catch-all parties tend to be middle-of-the-road, moderate parties. They steer clear of the left and right political extremes, preferring instead to cast a wide net on either side of the political center.

   According to one widely held hypothesis, catch-all parties are more supportive of stable democracy than are particularistic parties.[12] Catch-all parties, it is argued, promote moderation and compromise across social classes and other groups in society because they are so inclusive. Particularistic parties stick to their own narrow interests in a conflictual and uncompromising posture. Evidence from democracies in North America and Western Europe provides considerable support for this proposition. Virtually every generalization has its exceptions, however, and so does this one. One of the most viscerally anti-democratic parties in history, the German Nazi party, increasingly became a catch-all party as it fought its way to power through the electoral process in the late 1920s and early 1930s. With stunning rapidity the Nazis increased their share of the national vote from just 2.6 percent in 1928 to more than 37 percent by the summer of 1932. On their way to becoming the most popular party in democratic Germany, the Nazis made every effort to capture votes from the upper, middle, and working classes, from urban voters and rural voters, from women as well as men, from Protestants and Catholics, and from every age group eligible to vote. Though the Nazis did better among some of these voter categories than others, both their intentions and their electoral successes distinctly marked them as an anti-regime, authoritarian catch-all party.[13]

Responsible Party Government   In order for electoral democracy to work effectively, according to some theorists, three essential things must happen. First, the competing parties need to clarify as explicitly as possible what they would do if they are elected to positions of governmental responsibility. Thus *each party must formulate a coherent program* and spell it out to the voters in advance of election day, specifying where it stands on economic policy, social welfare policy, foreign policy, and so on. Candidates running for office need to reinforce these messages in their campaign appearances. Second, *the voters need to compare the competing programs carefully and vote for the candidates most representative of their own views.* And third, on taking office *the victorious party must translate its campaign programs and promises into governmental action.* This three-step model of **responsible party government** is depicted in figure 11.1.

Various theories of democracy suggest that this model represents the best way of converting citizen demands into effective government action. Obviously, it places a considerable degree of responsibility on parties, voters, and governments to think seriously about political issues and act decisively. As it happens, political realities in most democratic countries rarely conform to the model of responsible party government. Let's examine some of the obstacles that may stand in its way.

Internally Fragmented Parties One problem arises when a political party is internally divided. In some cases these divisions may reflect fundamental differences that endure over long periods. Some parties, for example, may have a left wing that favors higher taxes and more welfare spending and a right wing that favors lower taxes and less welfare spending. These fissures may in turn reflect the diverse social bases of the party. Parties that court votes from a diversity of ethnic groups, religions, income levels, geographical regions, and the like are bound to experience internal divisions rooted in the competing interests of these different groups. In other cases disagreements within the party may center on immediate, short-term issues. In the 1960s and early 1970s, for example, the Democratic Party in the United States was divided over the Vietnam War into "hawks," who favored continuing military intervention, and "doves," who wanted an early withdrawal from the conflict. And in some instances a party may be di-

vided over competing loyalties to rival politicians who seek to lead the party.

Internal divisions of these kinds often complicate the process of what political scientists call *interest aggregation.*[14]

> **Interest aggregation** *is the process by which political parties gather together (aggregate) the various interests, priorities, and opinions of their leaders and constituents and shape them into common goals and policy proposals.*

The interest aggregation process represents step 1 in the responsible party government model shown in figure 11.1. Some parties perform it more effectively than others. In just about all political parties in today's democracies, however, it is a complicated task that usually involves a considerable amount of negotiation and bargaining among the political elites who guide the party's fortunes. In the United States, it is further affected by the primary election system, which gives the voters a chance to choose among competing orientations and politicians *within* their favored party. Most other democracies do not have primaries, but instead nominate their candidates at meetings of party activists or by mail. The more complex the process of internal interest aggregation, the more difficult it will be for the party to speak with a clear, unified voice to the voters.

As a consequence, the programs that parties present to the voters may be so vague or internally inconsistent that it's hard to tell exactly what the party will actually do if elected to office. Large catch-all parties are especially prone to these problems. It is quite common in the United States, for example, for candidates nominated for the presidency to casually ignore, or openly repudiate, the "platform" of general principles and specific proposals that is officially adopted at the party's nominating convention.

Voter Ignorance and Shifting Party Alignments Step 2 of the responsible party government model assumes

FIGURE 11.1 Responsible Party Government Model

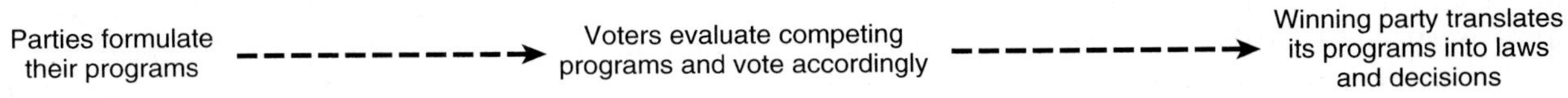

Parties formulate their programs – – – – – – → Voters evaluate competing programs and vote accordingly – – – – – – → Winning party translates its programs into laws and decisions

that voters have a sufficient comprehension of political affairs to make intelligent decisions in the voting booth. As we've seen, however, average voters in most democracies are not very well informed on the issues. They may not have the time or sophistication to evaluate the programs and proposals advanced by the competing parties at election time. In the Congressional elections of 1996, to take another recent example from the United States, the Republicans went to the voters with an explicitly formulated ten-point program called the *Contract With America*. Polls conducted during the campaign showed that a majority of voters could not identify this document.

To complicate matters, in some democracies political parties are having an increasingly difficult time holding a stable core following of voters. *Party loyalty* is in decline in many democracies. In the United States, voter identification with the Democrats and Republicans, so prominent in the 1950s and 1960s, has diminished considerably since then.[15] In Western Europe, party loyalties in the 1960s were very close to what they were in the 1920s. Although they still remain strong in many cases, they have become looser in a number of European countries, and new parties have come into the picture.[16] Party loyalties have also weakened in Japan, India, and other democracies.

Voters who consistently identify themselves with one political party and vote for its candidates from one election to the next are called *partisan voters*. Sometimes certain identifiable groups in society, such as various socioeconomic classes, religious groups, or ethnic groups, have a general tendency to support a favorite party over long periods of time. This phenomenon is called **stable partisan alignment**: the same social groups vote for the same party time after time. But when large numbers of voters disengage their established loyalties to their favorite party and become less partisan and more independent, **partisan dealignment** is said to occur. Partisan dealignment means that once-solid supporters of a particular party no longer vote for that party's candidates automatically. They may vote for certain of its candidates depending on the stance they take on various issues, or they may gravitate to another party, or they may switch back and forth between parties from one election to the next.

Voters who move back and forth in this way are called **swing voters.**

Under conditions of partisan dealignment, the bonds linking voters and parties become more fragile and temporary, and it becomes more difficult for parties to produce long-term programs that will attract a long-term following. By having to make frequent shifts and revisions in their programs to attract increasingly fickle and unpredictable voters, parties find it harder to represent their constituents' views in a stable fashion and support policy initiatives that may take many years to translate into effective governmental action. In short, party dealignments further complicate the task of establishing responsible party government.

Sometimes the voters may change their habits even more radically. When a large bloc of voters that traditionally votes for one party massively shifts its support to a rival party and sticks with that party over prolonged periods, **party realignment** takes place. In the United States, Southern white Protestant males were once solid Democrats. Since the 1970s, however, they have moved in large numbers to the Republicans. Whereas partisan *dealignment* means simply a *loosening* of traditional party loyalties on the part of *individuals, realignment* means an *enduring shift* from one party to another on the part of large *social groups*. Realignments represent major changes in a society's electoral patterns, in some cases placing new obstacles in the path of responsible party government.

Divided Government or Coalition Government   After the elections take place, it's up to the elected officials to translate their programs and promises into authoritative actions (step 3 of the responsible party government model). This process can be strewn with hazards, however. In some democracies, such as the United States, France, and Russia, the voters may elect a president of one party and a legislative majority of a rival party or parties. As such cases of *divided government* frequently demonstrate, it is usually more difficult to convert the competing proposals of rival parties into government actions than it is to convert the proposals of just one governing party. To cite one example: in 1988, George Bush was elected to the U.S. presidency pledging that he would not raise taxes. "Read my lips: no new taxes!" Bush declared at the Republican convention. Although this pledge was the most widely publicized theme in Bush's election campaign, the Democratic majority in the Congress subsequently compelled President Bush to raise taxes. In later years a Republican congressional majority similarly prevented President Clinton from fulfilling various campaign pledges.

In democracies that have a parliamentary system of government, as we explained in chapter 9, two or more parties may be forced to form a *coalition government* or a *parliamentary alliance* in order to form a working majority in the legislature. Once again, the more parties that are involved in the decision making process, the more difficult it is *for any individual party* to give the voters what it promised. Legislation and executive decisions under these conditions must reflect carefully constructed deals and compromises among the governing parties. Sometimes no stable governing majority can be formed, paralyzing the decision-making process.

In these instances, legislatures and governments are divided *because the people who elected them are divided.* Hence the inability of individual parties to deliver on their campaign promises is not necessarily due to the ineptitude or venality of the politicians, but to the political fragmentation of the electorate.

Lack of Party Discipline Another reason why victorious political parties, once elected, may not be able to give their constituents exactly what they promised is that their legislators in the national parliament may not observe *party discipline* when voting on legislation. **Party discipline *means that the party's entire legislative delegation votes together* unanimously *on bills that come up for a vote.***

Party discipline is traditionally somewhat low in the United States. Members of Congress have usually financed their own election campaigns and are not financially dependent on their party. In addition, the American system of separation of powers gives members of Congress an institutional independence from the presidency. As a result, presidents may not be able to convince legislators in their own party to go along with their policies, as Bill Clinton learned in 1994 when he could not convince a Democratic majority in Congress to pass his health care reform proposals. (See

the section titled *Interest-Group Pluralism in the United States* later in this chapter.)

Party discipline is relatively higher in parliamentary democracies like Britain and Germany. Even in these countries, however, the unity of the party's legislative delegation may occasionally break down as individual legislators diverge from their party leadership on roll call votes.

While the ideal of responsible party government can be very difficult to achieve in well-established democracies, it can be even more elusive in newly democratizing countries. Russia and most of the other states that once formed the Soviet Union have had little or no prior history as democracies. As a consequence, new parties must be built from scratch. Brand new parties are also coming into being in Eastern Europe. In countries that are making the transition from authoritarianism to democracy in Latin America, East Asia, Africa, and elsewhere, new parties must be formed from the ground up or, in some cases, re-formed on the remains of parties that once existed under earlier democratic regimes. It will most probably take quite a few years before these parties solidify into stable organizations with fairly coherent political orientations, widespread voter recognition, and a core of loyal voters. Some will probably fall by the wayside. If these fledgling democracies are to take root, however, parties will have to play a major role in forging vital links between the population and the state.

Party Systems The term **party system** *refers to the number of parties within a country, their ideological orientations, and various other general patterns.* We'll consider just two variable features of party systems here: the *number* of parties to be found within a given system, and the ideologically based distinction between *centripetal and centrifugal* party systems.[17]

The Number of Parties Some democracies are dominated over prolonged periods by one party. These are called **dominant-party systems.** Japan, for example, was governed uninterruptedly by the Liberal Democratic Party (LDP) from 1955 to 1993. Although other parties ran against the LDP in freely contested elections, they were not able to win a parliamentary majority until the LDP suffered severe losses in voter support in the 1990s because of corruption scandals. Mexico was governed by the Institutional Revolutionary Party (PRI) from 1929 until 2000, when Vicente Fox, a challenger from a rival party, won the presidential election. Although several parties had increased their share of the vote from the 1970s onward, the PRI remained Mexico's dominant party until it lost the all-important presidency to Fox.

Very few countries have a predominantly **two-party system.** The United States, of course, is one of them. While third parties have cropped up now and then on the national scene, they have not fared very well in getting their candidates elected to Congress or the presidency.[18] Some people regard Britain as having a two-party system. To be sure, the Conservative and Labour parties have taken turns running the government since World War II without having to take on other parties as coalition partners. But several other parties also exist in the United Kingdom that regularly elect representatives to Parliament and they occasionally play an important role in shaping the government's policies. Britain might more appropriately be called a **few-party system.** Few-party systems typically have about three to five important parties. Contemporary France, Germany, Japan, and Canada also fall into this category.

Still other countries have real **multiparty systems.** Multiparty systems typically have six or more parties that play a significant political role, electing their candidates to the national legislature, participating in coalition governments or parliamentary alliances, providing critical support in key legislative votes, or obstructing government actions they don't like. The Scandinavian countries, Russia, Poland, Israel, and Italy provide examples of multiparty systems.

HYPOTHESIS-TESTING EXERCISE: Duverger's Law

HYPOTHESIS

What causes the variations in the number of parties to be found in various democracies? The question is of more than academic interest. Public opinion polls in recent years have shown that as many as 60 percent of Americans are dissatisfied with their two-party system

and favor the creation of more parties to widen their range of electoral choice. Can a change in the nation's vote-counting procedures produce the desired result?

The central hypothesis that bears on this issue suggests that the *number of parties* (the **dependent variable**) depends largely on the *nature of the electoral system* (the **independent variable**). In one specific variant of this thesis, the French political scientist Maurice Duverger contended that *single-ballot plurality* electoral procedures just about always produce *two-party systems.* These two variables are so frequently correlated that, in Duverger's view, their pairing constitutes a veritable law of social science; hence it is known as *Duverger's law.*[19] Examples include the electoral systems used to elect the House of Commons in the United Kingdom and the systems used in the United States to elect the House of Representatives and the Senate. A related hypothesis holds that *proportional representation* produces *multiparty systems.* Does the evidence support these propositions?

VARIABLES

In the first hypothesis, the **independent variable** is the *single-ballot plurality* electoral procedure, and the **dependent variable** is a *two-party system.* In the second hypothesis, the **independent variable** is *proportional representation*, and the **dependent variable** is a *multiparty system.*

EXPECTATIONS

If the hypotheses are correct, we'd expect the evidence to show that (1) single-ballot plurality systems are associated with countries dominated by two parties, and (2) proportional representation is invariably associated with a multiplicity of competing parties.

EVIDENCE

Evidence from the United States offers the strongest confirmation for the first hypothesis, Duverger's law. Elections to the House of Representatives and the Senate involve a plurality system for determining the winner. In each of these winner-take-all contests, the winner is the person who gets the most votes, even if she falls short of an absolute majority (50 percent plus one). (In presidential elections, the candidate who wins the most votes within each state usually wins all of that state's electoral college votes.) These U.S. elections are all *single-ballot* procedures: the voters do not come back to the polls a week or two after the first round of voting in order to select surviving candidates in a second-round runoff election. (France and Russia have such two-ballot procedures and thus are not covered by Duverger's law.) In conformity with our expectations, the U.S. political system has been dominated by the Democrats and Republicans for more than a century. Other parties have had a difficult time winning elections at the national level (and even at most state and local levels).

Britain's situation is a bit more complicated. Unquestionably, two parties—Labour and the Conservatives—have dominated British politics in the postwar period, a fact consistent with Duverger's law. But smaller parties have continued to win seats in the House of Commons, and at times they have played a crucial role in determining how Britain is governed. Following two elections in 1974, neither Labour nor the Conservatives won enough seats to ensure a sizable majority. The Labour party presided over two minority governments at various times over the next several years and was required to make deals with several smaller parties in order to ensure a voting majority in the House of Commons. When this support was withdrawn in 1979, the Labour government collapsed. While these incidents have been the exception to an otherwise protracted period of two-party dominance, they demonstrate that the British party system is not as consistently controlled by two parties as the U.S. system is.

Duverger's law would lead us to expect that Italy would develop a two-party system following the transformation of its electoral system in the 1990s from proportional representation to a partial single-ballot plurality system. (In the elections of 1994 and 1996, 75 percent of the seats in the Chamber of Deputies were chosen on the basis of a single-member, district plurality system and the remainder by PR.) Although a consolidation of Italy's numerous parties has indeed occurred, a two-party system has not yet emerged. Instead, three large blocs of parties were formed after the electoral reform, and the parties composing them have thus far retained their separate organizations and, in most cases, a core following. It is still too early to tell if Italy will eventually develop a two-party system, though Duverger himself acknowledged that countries with deep-seated multiparty traditions may take a long time to shrink down to two parties after adopting a single-ballot plurality voting system.

Additional evidence contradicting Duverger's law comes from India, where a single-ballot plurality system once supported the dominance of a single party, the Congress Party, which governed uninterruptedly from 1947 until the 1980s. Since then, a variety of parties have not only won seats in the legislature, they have also participated in governments. India has never had a consistent two-party system.

As to the hypothesis correlating proportional representation with multiparty systems, there is considerable evidence in its support. Germany's pre-Nazi Weimar Republic, where PR reigned in elections to the lower house, had more than twenty parties at various points in its brief history from 1919 to 1933. Scandinavian countries tend to have about a half dozen parties significantly involved in cabinet formation or lawmaking. Sixteen parties were elected to Italy's parliament in 1992. Poland's parliament had thirty parties and factions represented in the lower house, the Sejm, as a result of the 1991 elections. Other examples could be added. As Duverger noted, "it is certain that proportional representation always coincides with a multiparty system." No country in the world combines PR and a two-party system.

Once again, however, there are some variations. The principle of proportional representation can be applied in dozens of different ways. A variety of statistical formulas can be used to calculate the final distribution of parliamentary seats; the candidates can be elected at large or in multimember districts; several alternative vote-counting techniques can be employed—these and other technical details can result in different results in different countries. Some countries with proportional representation have managed to keep the number of viable parties relatively small by erecting a minimum-vote hurdle. In these countries a party must get a minimum percentage of votes nationwide (typically 4 or 5 percent) in order to be represented in the national parliament. Germany's 5 percent hurdle has resulted in a political system dominated for most of the postwar period by two large parties (the Social Democrats and the Christian Democrats), with only one or two smaller parties winning the remaining parliamentary seats (the Free Democrats and, since the 1980s, the Greens). Poland's introduction of a hurdle cut the number of parties in the legislature substantially, from thirty to seven. Other countries with PR also use hurdles to keep the number of parties within reasonable limits.

CONCLUSIONS

On balance, the evidence bearing on both hypotheses is *mixed.* Evidence from the United States and Britain is mostly consistent with Duverger's law. But Britain's party system is not an exclusively two-party system, and evidence from countries like Italy and India challenges the law's claims to universality. (Duverger himself, it should be noted, acknowledged that the single-ballot plurality election procedure "does not necessarily and absolutely" lead to two-party systems in all situations. Only as a general tendency, he stipulated, can it be considered a "law.") The evidence concerning proportional representation is also *mixed:* most of it supports the proposition that PR leads to a multiparty system, but ways can be found to reduce this effect. Duverger himself recognized that the party-multiplying tendencies of PR can vary from one country to the next.[20]

If the United States were to change its electoral laws by adopting proportional representation, would parties other than the Democrats and Republicans be more likely to win elections than under the current laws? The evidence we have considered here, along with empirical studies conducted by scholars like Duverger, tell us that the answer is probably *yes*. How many parties can win which elections, however, is another question, one whose answer depends in part on the specific form a PR system would take. Even then, to win elections a party must ultimately attract voters, a prospect that hinges on far more variables than just the nature of the electoral system. In the final analysis, the question of which parties win elections in a democracy may depend in large part on the electoral systems, but numerous other factors intevene as well.

We must also ask whether a multiplicity of parties in the Congress would necessarily enhance the efficiency of U.S. lawmaking procedures or the effectiveness of legislation in addressing the country's problems. Would the United States necessarily be better off if there were three or more parties in the national legislature? Keep in mind that the United States is not a parliamentary system; hence the parties in Congress could not combine to form coalition governments, as parties in countries that combine parliamentary government with PR can do. Proportional representation tends to have the greatest impact on the executive branch when coalition governments are formed. Moreover, the phenomenon of divided government in the United States already makes for an occasionally difficult and time-consuming lawmaking process when the president is of one party and the Congressional majority is of the other. Would the U.S. system of government be any *less* difficult if the president had to deal with two or more opposition parties in Congress rather than just one? Would the president court allies in a multi-party Congress by inviting members of other parties into the cabinet, in effect constituting a U.S.-style coalition government? How any electoral system actually works thus depends to a considerable degree on the institutional relationship between the legislature and the executive branch. A PR electoral procedure in the American separation-of-powers system would inevitably have different results than in a parliamentary system, but some intriguing new governmental practices could emerge as a result.

Is there an *optimum* number of political parties? Political scientists have long debated this question, arguing the pros and cons of alternative party systems. Albert Hirschman, an economist with a keen sensitivity to political realities, argues for a few-party system in his book, *Exit, Voice, and Loyalty*.[21] Like some other theorists, Hirschman strikes an analogy between politics and economics.

EXIT, VOICE, AND LOYALTY

What happens when voters are dissatisfied with the candidates their party nominates for office? Albert Hirschman argues that disgruntled voters are very similar to consumers dissatisfied with the quality of the cars being produced by their favorite auto manufacturer. Voters, like consumers, have essentially two choices: *voice* and *exit.*

If they exercise the **voice** option, they speak up and express their complaints. Voters will contact their party representatives, attend party meetings, or take other vocal actions to prompt the party into nominating better candidates or adopting different policy positions. Consumers will write to the manufacturer to voice their disappointment with the latest car models or perhaps speak out at stockholders' meetings. These efforts may bring positive results, leading to more acceptable politicians or improved automobiles.

If they exercise the **exit** option, voters stop voting for the party they have traditionally supported; they switch their allegiance to another party or perhaps stop voting altogether. If their original party gets the message and improves its candidates or policy orientation, some voters who have left the party may come back. But others may exit permanently. Similarly, dissatisfied car buyers may exercise their exit option by buying their next car from a different manufacturer.

The choices that voters and consumers make depend on their degree of *loyalty* to their original party or car company. If they are very loyal, such as the dyed-in-the-wool Democrat or the faithful Mustang enthusiast, they will probably delay exiting until they have exhausted every possible attempt to change things by raising their voice. If their loyalty to the organization is not so great, they will probably make an early exit. In politics, Hirschman points out, a certain amount of party loyalty is beneficial for the entire political system if it induces dissatisfied citizens to be energetic and creative in raising their voices to effect desirable change. Parties that listen to their constituents are often better for democracy than unresponsive ones.

But too much loyalty to a political party provides its leaders with no incentive to improve its candidates or ideas, thereby risking its continuing deterioration. Sometimes a party will listen to its followers only when they begin deserting it at the polls. Both voice and exit, therefore, are important *feedback mechanisms* that alert party leaders to mistakes that are ruining the organization. These same considerations apply to corporations whose products "ain't what they used to be" in the eyes of consumers.

Hirschman concludes that the optimal political system is the one we have labeled a *few-party* system. (Hirschman does not specify any particular number of parties but he seems to mean about three to five.) Such a party system is able to provide fairly balanced opportunities for both voice and exit. People have real options if they wish to exit, but they are likely to do so only after first exercising their voice in an attempt to improve their original party. As long as these parties have distinct but bridgeable differences and accept the rules of democracy, this type of system is likely to produce parties that are responsive to the voters and capable of forming viable governments.

A two-party system like the United States has is not as desirable, in Hirschman's view. It doesn't provide voters with enough alternatives for exit if they are no longer comfortable voting for the party they've habitually supported. If the second party is also unpalatable, these voters may stop voting entirely. Voice therefore plays an inordinately important role in American party politics. But voice is usually exercised by the small number of people willing to take an active part in party affairs. Many of these activists tend to be either more liberal or more conservative than the average voter, resulting in candidates for office and party platforms that do not reflect the centrist tendencies of most American voters.

At the other extreme, multiparty systems provide too many opportunities for exit. People are therefore tempted to desert their accustomed party too quickly, passing up the opportunity to fight for its improvement. Some people may flit from one party to another, producing a system with a large number of small and internally weak parties that cannot count on keeping or enlarging a solid base of supporters. Weak parties can result in weak governments.

Centripetal and Centrifugal Party Systems These terms pertain to the tendencies of party systems to have either predominantly *moderate* or *extremist* parties. *A* **centripetal** *party system is one that favors moderate, centrist parties rather than extremist ones.* The term derives from the Latin for "cen-

ter seeking." In a centripetal system, the main parties and the majority of the electorate tend toward the center of the political spectrum, making consensus possible. The United States, Britain, and contemporary Germany are a few examples. By contrast, a **centrifugal** *("center fleeing") party system is one in which the leading parties and large numbers of voters tend toward the extremes of right or left.* Germany's Weimar Republic (1919–33) is a prime example. During the last few years of its existence, increasing numbers of voters deserted the centrist parties, which favored democracy, and flocked to the German Communist Party on the extreme left and Hitler's Nazi Party on the extreme right. (See figure 11.2 on page 256).

Interest Groups

Interest groups *are organizations that speak up for the interests and demands of particular groups of people, often with the aim of influencing the state to do something in their behalf.*

Interest groups provide another means of mass participation in democratic political systems. They promote the aims of specific segments of the mass public by exerting pressure on political parties, candidates, and government officials themselves. In the terminology developed by Almond and Powell, interest groups perform the function of **interest articulation.** That is, they *articulate* the interests, demands, and desires of various groups in society. *Political parties and interest groups are called* **intermediate organizations:** they are located *in between the population and the state.* At least in democracies, one of their aims is to enable citizens to influence state actions.

At the same time, some interest groups serve the interests of various elites in society. Interest groups that articulate the views of corporate executives, doctors, lawyers, and other narrowly defined groups represent smaller segments of society than do those with a broader mass base, such as groups that speak up for factory workers, the elderly, or a particular ethnic group. Interest groups are thus vehicles for both elite *and* mass interest articulation.

Not all interest groups are interested exclusively in political activities. In many cases they try to promote their group interests without recourse to government involvement. Trade unions, for example, may work out their problems over pay and

FIGURE 11.2   Centripetal and Centrifugal Party Systems

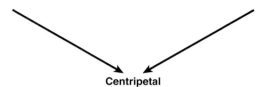

| Centripetal | Centrifugal |

working conditions through direct interactions with company executives, employing negotiations, strikes, and other bargaining techniques. In political science we are mainly interested in the *political* activities of interest groups. When trade unions or business associations ask the state to take their side in a labor dispute or in support of specific governmental economic policies, their actions become decidedly political. In the United States and some other democracies, many interest groups have *lobbies,* which work directly to influence government policy, usually by establishing contacts with government decision makers.[22]

A Typology of Interest Groups   Political scientists have proposed several different categories for distinguishing among different types of interest groups. The ones presented here borrow some terminology from other scholars while also making some refinements in their definitions for the sake of clarifying what interest groups are.[23]

Associational interest groups are organizations that speak up for specific segments of a country's population who share common problems and goals. They are most likely to be found in democracies, which permit freedom of association, rather than in authoritarian states, which usually do not allow such groups to be established independently of state control. Associational interest groups display considerable variety. Some articulate the *economic* interests of their supporters, such as trade unions and business associations. Others may represent ethnic groups (such as the National Association for the Advancement of Colored People), gender and sexual preference groups (the National Organization for Women; the Gay Alliance), religious groups (the Christian Coalition) and specific-issue groups (the National Rifle Association).

Private institutional groups are mainly nongovernmental organizations that are organized primarily for some purpose other than political action. Private corporations, such as Exxon or General Motors, and established religious institutions, such as the Roman Catholic Church or the Anglican Church, are examples. Like associational groups, these private groups may also have lobbying offices to represent their interests in contacts with public officials.

Unlike associational interest groups and private institutional interest groups, not all groups that seek to promote their political interests are well organized. Sometimes a particular segment of the population that shares a common identity—such as an ethnic minority, the adherents of a particular religion, or people who have the same occupation or live in the same area—may spontaneously come together on an ad hoc basis to express a particular grievance or seek some immediate goal. Such groups are called **nonassociational interest groups.** Examples include African Americans who boycotted white-owned businesses in the 1960s to protest racial discrimination in southern towns; consumers who took part in a nationwide letter-writing campaign to urge Congress to pass laws prohibiting the manufacture of dangerous toys; and citizens who band together to pressure their local government into improving traffic safety at a deadly intersection. Once the problem is resolved, nonassociational groups frequently dissolve. Sometimes, however, they form more permanent associational groups or merge with existing ones.

Another type of unorganized interest group is the **anomic group.** Anomic groups spring up spontaneously to give vent to the anger or frustrations of the population. Their defining characteristic tends to be sudden outbursts of protest activity, occasionally accompanied by violence. (The term comes from the ancient Greek word for "lawlessness," *anomia.*) Spontaneous demonstrations, riots, and wildcat strikes are examples of anomic behavior.

FIGURE 11.3   Trade Union Membership Around the World

Union membership as percentage of employees.

EUROPE

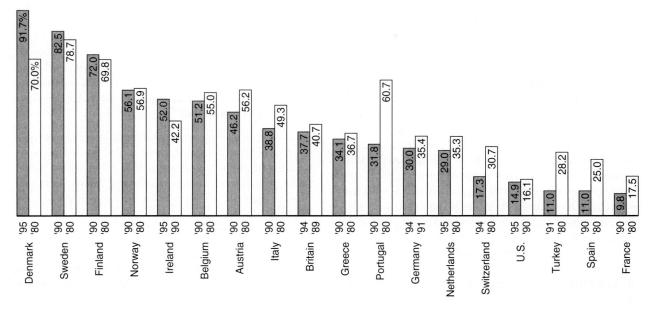

ASIA, PACIFIC, AFRICA

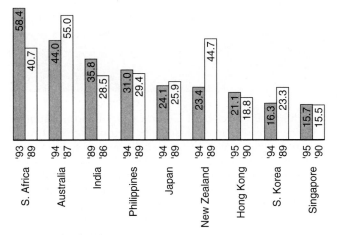

LATIN AMERICA

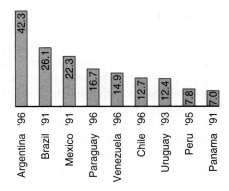

NOTE: Membership numbers for some countries
may be inflated because workers belong to more
than one union.

Source: National governments; International Labor Organization.

New social movements consist of segments of the population who share common identities and goals along with the belief that the established political parties and interest groups have not adequately represented their interests. Women, gays, environmentalists, and peace advocates, among others, have formed social movements of this kind in various democracies, especially since the 1960s and 1970s. In some cases these movements have spawned new associational interest groups. Quite often, however, individuals may feel part of the movement without belonging to any specific organization connected with it (such as the feminist movement). The aims of many of these movements are often pointedly political, as people who identify with them may vote for candidates favorable to the movement's cause, initiate lawsuits motivated by its concerns, or engage in some other activity aimed at influencing public opinion or getting state authorities to take action.[24]

No consideration of interest groups can be complete without a reference to groups in society that do *not* clearly articulate their common interests. Even in flourishing democracies, there may be segments of society with identifiable political interests that, for one reason or another, do not succeed in building interest groups or call attention to their grievances through anomic behavior. An example consists of people who are not covered by any kind of medical insurance in the United States. By 1999 this segment of the population surpassed 44 million people. Their problems are acknowledged by political leaders in both major parties, but they have no formal organization or other mechanism of their own for collectively articulating their concerns. The lack of an effective interest group of this kind helps explain why the U.S. government has been slow to legislate a satisfactory solution to the problem of the uninsured. Countries all over the globe have their own examples of unorganized social groups that are not able to articulate their political needs effectively. Day workers, child laborers, abused or oppressed women—these and other politically voiceless people, numbering in the millions, confirm the enormous importance of interest groups precisely because they do not have them.

Pluralism and Corporatism   Precisely *how* interest groups function can differ markedly from one country to another. One distinction that students of interest groups frequently make is that between *pluralism* and *corporatism.*

As we noted in chapter 5, **pluralism** is a concept of democracy that asserts that political power in most democracies is not monopolized by one particular social group (such as big business) or by a tightly interconnected combination of groups who form a unified power elite. Rather, political power is dispersed among a *plurality* of groups and interests. When applied to interest groups, pluralism emphasizes

- *freedom of association,* which means that people are free to organize their own interest groups
- *competition for influence,* which means that interest groups on different sides of an issue freely compete for the attention of legislators and other authoritative decision makers and seek to influence their actions

This model of **interest-group pluralism** is best exemplified by the United States. To get a clearer picture of how interest-group pluralism actually works, let's look at the Clinton administration's attempt to get Congress to pass a major health care reform bill in its first term.

INTEREST-GROUP PLURALISM IN THE UNITED STATES
The Politics of Health Care Reform, 1993–94

"This year," President Clinton proclaimed in January 1994, "we will make history by reforming our health care system." With this nationally televised announcement, the president launched the final phase of his campaign to get Congress to pass a major reform of the nation's health care system. The president's proposal called for universal health insurance, to be provided entirely by private insurance companies. This proposal aimed at insuring some 37 million Americans who lacked any kind of health insurance, along with millions more who had inadequate or only temporary coverage. To finance the program, the federal government would require most employers to pay for 80 percent of their employees' insurance premiums. Tobacco taxes would be raised to help fund federal subsidies to the poor so that they could buy their own insurance policies. Federal law would prevent anyone from being denied insurance coverage. The U.S. government would impose explicit limits on the insurance companies' ability to increase their prices for health insurance. The government would also require insurance-purchasing cooperatives to be formed, aimed at driving down health care prices. The U.S. government's role in the entire process was to be supervised by a new federal agency, the National Health Board.

The administration's proposal, presented to Congress in October 1993, was spelled out in a 1,342-page bill. Even before the bill was drafted, various opponents of the proposal had already mounted their first efforts to turn public opinion and Congressional attitudes against it. The Health Insurance Association of America (HIAA), an interest group representing the main private health insurance companies, sponsored a series of television commercials that portrayed "Harry and Louise," a fictitious middle-class couple, wrestling with a massive copy of Clinton's plan and criticizing its proposals for significant U.S. government involvement in the nation's health care system. The ads were aired nationally on the Cable News Network and were also targeted more narrowly on audiences in Washington, D.C. and fifteen states where key members of Congress resided. Over the ensuing year HIAA spent $15 million on television, radio, and print commercials against the Clinton proposal.

As the bill came under the intense scrutiny of Congressional committees in 1994, the television and newspaper advertising blitz intensified. By the summer of 1994, as the bill neared final Congressional consideration, some forty-nine groups had spent a total of $50 million on broadcast and print ads intended to sway opinions either for or against the administration's proposals.[25] The ads opposed to the Clinton plan proved especially effective in changing public attitudes. In October 1993, 51 percent of Americans favored Clinton's proposal. By January only 48 percent favored the president's bill, a figure that plummeted to 42 percent in September. As we've noted, the 37 million uninsured Americans had no interest group of their own. There was also considerable public ignorance about the Clinton proposal. One poll taken in January 1994 revealed that 69 percent of senior citizens knew very little or nothing about the plan's provisions.

Meanwhile, the peculiarities of the U.S. political system added to the president's difficulties. The Democrats controlled both houses of Congress. By the summer of 1994 there were 256 Democrats in the House of Representatives, 178 Republicans, and one independent. The Senate had 56 Democrats and 44 Republicans. But the Democrats were not able to maintain party unity. The spirit of Congressional individualism strongly asserted itself as several Democrats came out with their own health care reform proposals that deviated from the Clinton plan. Five separate Congressional committees, each chaired by a Democrat, conducted hearings on health care and debated alternative proposals. For their part, the Republicans offered no alternative bill. With no clear consensus on a health plan of their own, Republican members of Congress were content to let the Democrats' proposals die.

Over the years, various segments of the health and insurance industry had spent a considerable amount of money cultivating influence in Congress. According to one estimate, these companies gave a total of $40.1 million to the campaign war chests of U.S. senators over a fifteen-year period. Three senators had each received more than a million dollars; 28 others each received more than a half million. All 100 senators serving in 1994 had received contributions from this lobby, ranging from $3,000 to more than $1.25 million.[26]

Ultimately it was Congress that had the final word on health care in 1994. As more Democrats pulled away from the administration's legislation, the Republican leadership announced that it would not back a compromise bill. In late September the two parties agreed to abandon any further attempt at health care reform in 1994. In the end, groups opposing Clinton's proposal had spent $46.1 million in the campaign to defeat his proposal. By the end of the decade, the number of Americans without medical insurance rose to 44.3 million.[27]

In contrast to the U.S. variant of pluralism, **corporatism** represents a different approach to involving interest groups in the policy process. Defined in very broad terms,

> **corporatism** *is a system of formal interest-group participation in the state's decision-making processes.*

Different versions of corporatism have existed in a diversity of countries at different periods of time and in different political systems. It has been variously conceptualized and embraced by the Roman Catholic Church, fascist dictatorships under Mussolini and Hitler, military dictatorships in Latin America, authoritarian regimes in Portugal and Mexico, and modern democracies like Austria, Germany, and Sweden. These and other proponents of corporatist methods share some ideas in common but diverge, at times considerably, in their application of those ideas.

One of the most widely shared commonalities of corporatist thinking is the notion that *leading representatives of the key groups in society—especially business and labor—should negotiate directly with government officials to work out the country's principal economic and social welfare policies.* We'll confine ourselves in this chapter to sketching out a very generalized model (an *ideal type*) of modern corporatism as it works in several democracies today (though democracies differ in their application of corporatist ideas to their specific circumstances). Along the way we'll highlight some salient differences between corporatism and U.S.-style pluralism.

Corporatism in contemporary democracies (sometimes called **neo-corporatism**) typically consists of the following institutions and procedures:

1. The main groups in society involved in economic production—notably industry, labor, and agriculture—form large interest groups that represent a large proportion, sometimes the majority, of the people in their respective sector. These large interest groups are called **peak associations.** A peak association for labor will thus represent a high percentage of the country's factory workers. The peak associations tend to be *hierarchically organized;* that is, their national leaders exercise considerable influence over the rank and file at local levels. (In the United States, such peak associations are rare; each industry tends to have its own labor unions that bargain with employers. The AFL-CIO, American labor's large umbrella organization, does not engage in corporatist-style bargaining.)

2. Leaders of the main peak associations, especially those representing the business sector and labor, meet on a relatively regular basis with representatives of the state, who are usually from the executive branch rather than the legislature. The executive branch representatives may include the prime minister, other cabinet ministers, their deputies, or key bureaucrats in relevant ministries. Under corporatism, the executive branch plays a more important role in dealing with business and labor groups than the legislature does. (In the United States, Con-

gress tends to play a more active role than the president in dealing with interest groups.)

3. Together these representatives of the main peak associations and the state work out deals on such economic issues as taxes, wages, working conditions, social welfare benefits, and the like. (In the United States, the government usually does not get involved in brokering agreements between unions and employers on wages or working conditions.)

4. Once agreements are worked out, the business and labor negotiators go back to their respective groups and solicit the reactions of their members. If the rank and file does not accept the agreements, they may have to be renegotiated. But the leaders of the peak associations frequently exert pressure on the membership to go along with the deals they have worked out in the tripartite negotiations on the grounds that they are the best possible under present circumstances.

5. If appropriate, the national legislature ratifies the agreed-upon arrangements by passing them into law. In parliamentary systems, the government can usually count on commanding the parliamentary majority to facilitate this procedure. Quite often the parliament's role is limited to voting on a "done deal."

6. The peak association leaders then urge their respective members to carry out the agreements. If they fail, the agreements may have to be renegotiated.

Compared with the freewheeling style of American pluralism, neo-corporatism is typically a more orderly and regularized process. Bilateral and tripartite negotiations among business, labor, and government are often an ongoing process. However, corporatism can also be a more *closed* process than pluralism is. The negotiations tend to take place behind closed doors, centered in the executive branch of government. It is not always as open a process as those fought out in the legislature, under the open glare of television cameras. At the same time, corporatist negotiating procedures generally are not as competitive as in the United States, where competing interest groups seek to influence public opinion and legislators

FIGURE 11.4   Models of U.S.-Style Interest-Group Pluralism and Neo-Corporatism

PLURALISM

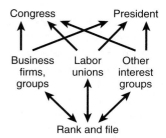

NEO-CORPORATISM

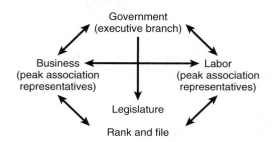

through expensive media campaigns or other pressure tactics ("write your Congressman" campaigns and the like). Under corporatism, the main peak associations tend to have exclusive negotiating rights for their respective segment of society when dealing with the state. For its part, the state expects the associations to make sure that their members adhere to whatever agreements they jointly reach.[28]

Proponents of corporatist procedures argue that they provide the government with an effective way of keeping the economy running smoothly, based on constant negotiations with business and labor leaders who are armed with broad negotiating powers. (For a description of neo-corporatism in Germany, see chapter 18.) In the United States, by contrast, the government has less direct influence over business or labor. Critics of the American system charge that the U.S. economy is less coordinated and less efficient as a result.

Patron-Client Relationships

Patron-client relationships, or **clientelism,** represent another set of ties between political elites and the population. In contrast to mass electoral politics and large-scale interest-group activity, patron-client relationships generally operate on a smaller, more personalized scale. Their origins are rooted in the personal ties that developed in preindustrial societies between local authorities and ordinary villagers or peasants in need of advice, favors, or perhaps a job from authoritative figures. The pa-

trons in these relationships could be the village mayor, a respected landowner, or other local notables who did not necessarily hold official governmental positions. Their clients were those who came forward, hat in hand, with a favor to ask. Patrons who did favors for a large number of clients could accumulate considerable personal power and prestige in the local community.

With the advent of urban industrialism in the nineteenth century and the expansion of electoral democracy that accompanied it in the United States and certain parts of Europe, patron-client relationships moved into the big cities and became politicized. Now it was political figures, particularly those connected with vote-generating urban political machines, who became patrons for all sorts of clients struggling to make a life for themselves in the intimidating maze of mass society: local residents trying to climb out of poverty, recent arrivals from rural hinterlands, immigrants from near and far. With their hands on the apparatus of city, regional, and occasionally national government, politicians and their well-connected associates dispensed jobs, contracts, and other favors to a widening clientele. In exchange for these considerations, the clients provided their patrons with a highly cherished reward: votes. This style of political activity became especially prevalent in the United States and Italy.[29]

Patron-client networks of various types continue to exist today in a number of countries. Quite often it is a powerful political party, one with access to government funds and jobs, that is the principal patron in these relationships. In quite a few cases these relationships are marked by bribery, favoritism, and other forms of corruption. The Congress Party of India, the Institutional Revolutionary Party of Mexico, the Liberal Democratic Party of Japan, and various parties in Greece, Italy, the Philippines, and elsewhere are characterized by "clientelistic" relationships of one sort or another. Even some authoritarian ruling parties seek a certain measure of popular support by playing patron to favored client groups, whether in the population or within the government bureaucracy. China's Communist Party, for example, has been cultivating clientelistic ties with members of the country's private business sector with the dual aim of promoting economic growth and discouraging pro-democracy sentiments among business people. [30]

MASS PARTICIPATION IN AUTHORITARIAN REGIMES

Authoritarian regimes usually do not allow much, if any, free political participation by the people. Some of them may have the trappings of democracy, such as elections, parties, interest groups, and news media, but the population's ability to use these mechanisms is rarely free; it is typically controlled by the ruling authorities themselves. In a sense, then, mass participation does exist in many non-democratic political systems, but it is usually controlled or channeled from above. It is therefore called **coercive participation.** The people, having no parties or interest groups of their own to represent or articulate their desires, are reduced to an atomized "mass society": an amorphous crowd with no effective organizations to express or aggregate their interests and thus no direct way to influence the actions of the state.[31]

Nevertheless, the Nazis and the communists, along with certain other authoritarian governments in the past as well as today, have seen to it that the masses do participate in various political activities under the state's direction. Some of these non-democratic regimes have staged **uncontested elections.** The population is asked (and in some cases compelled) to vote for specified candidates to a national legislative body or some local legislature. For each legislative seat there is typically only one candidate, someone chosen by the ruling authorities; the voters have no real choice. In most of these cases, the legislature so elected is of little importance, since the main political decisions are made elsewhere, by the higher-ups in the state's executive machinery. Both the electoral process and the elected organs are purely *symbolic* in nature: the symbols of democracy are present but not the reality. The ruling authorities use these procedures mainly to manipulate and control the public, giving the masses they rule a false sense of participating in the affairs of state. Prior to 1989, the Soviet Union and the former communist states of East-Central Europe all had uncontested (or mostly uncontested) elections and powerless legislatures based on this model. Contemporary states using similar procedures include the People's Republic of China, Cuba, Iraq, and Iran.

Another form of mass participation utilized in at least some authoritarian states is **mass mobilization.** In addition to being called out to vote in phony elections, the people may also be compelled to take part in mass demonstrations and parades organized by the government, listen to propaganda speeches at their school or place of work, or lend a hand in special barnstorming work projects in the factory, on the farm, or out on construction sites. The Nazi and communist regimes excelled at these mobilization procedures.

To be sure, it can also happen that authoritarian regimes may enjoy a measure of mass support. Quite a few dictatorships have openly cultivated popular appeal by providing the masses with improvements in their economic welfare, by enhancing their national pride through military conquests or nationalistic propaganda, or by various other means. In some cases these regimes may actually succeed in building a broad base of popularity. One example was the government of Juan Perón, an army colonel who openly cultivated the laboring classes in Argentina through an array of social welfare measures. Though he won elections in 1946, 1951, and 1973, he presided over a corrupt authoritarian government that has been described as a form of "popular authoritarianism."[32] Nazi Germany, the Soviet Union, and other authoritarian regimes have also attempted to curry mass support with varying degrees of success.

Such overtures to the mass population by political elites is known as *populism.* Actually, **populism** has two meanings. When it springs from the people themselves, populism means *mass anti-*

elitism. It expresses the people's hostility to the overweening power of elites. Sometimes these sentiments can spark significant political activity, like the Populist Party organized in the 1890s by American farmers and workers opposed to the power of big business. When the source of populist ideas is the political elites, populism means *elite efforts to cultivate the support of the disadvantaged masses.* Elite-driven populism routinely occurs in democracies as politicians seek to drum up votes among the downtrodden by promising to alleviate their poverty. But it can also occur in authoritarian regimes as dictators try to curry mass support, or at least acceptance, by providing the masses with various welfare benefits to alleviate their plight.

It does not always work. Communist leaders in the USSR and East-Central Europe sought to keep their populations quiet through an unwritten "social contract" stipulating, in effect, that the people would refrain from challenging the regime politically while the regime would provide economic and social amenities in return. Communism failed at least in part because the ruling authorities, saddled with stagnating economies, did not keep their end of the bargain.

If a non-democratic regime's leaders are truly unpopular and if people categorically reject the political system, they can simply revolt. Anti-regime behavior of this kind takes two basic forms: *dissidence* and *revolution.* Both are risky.

Dissidence

Dissidence *is anti-government behavior that falls short of actually toppling the regime.* It can take many forms, from the distribution of leaflets and other peaceful activities to overt acts of terrorism. While dissidents may nourish the hope that their small sparks of personal opposition will ignite a general conflagration, they are often willing to take extraordinary risks even if they realize that a mass uprising is not an immediate likelihood. Surveillance, incarceration, and torture are often their grim rewards.

Political dissidence is by no means confined to advocates of democracy. Some may wish to replace one form of dictatorship with another. A number of the most prominent political dissidents

in recent decades, however, have been outspoken proponents of democratic liberty, courageously taking up the cause of human freedom and dignity against incalculable odds. Here are just a few examples:

- **Aung San Suu Kyi,** winner of the 1991 Nobel Peace Prize for her efforts to bring democracy to Myanmar (Burma), was placed under house arrest by the dictatorial regime of Gen. Ne Win in 1989. Under intense international pressure the regime formally released her in 1995, but she has remained under tight surveillance.
- **Nelson Mandela,** the South African champion of racial equality, was jailed for twenty-seven years before reaching an historic agreement with white leaders that gave non-whites the vote in 1994.
- **Kim Dae Jung,** a fearless advocate of democracy in South Korea during three decades of authoritarian rule, spent sixteen years in prison, in exile, or under house arrest before being elected president in 1997.
- **Lech Walesa,** an electrician who led illegal strikes against Poland's communist government in 1980, spearheaded the creation of Solidarity, the communist bloc's only non-communist trade union. Though Solidarity was temporarily banned and Walesa arrested, in 1989 it pressured the communist regime to hold elections and subsequently give up power. Walesa served as post-communist Poland's first president from 1990 to 1995.
- **Vaclav Havel,** an acclaimed Czechoslovak playwright, was repeatedly jailed by the communist authorities in the 1970s and 1980s before becoming the first president of post-communist Czechoslovakia.
- **Wei Jingsheng,** known as the father of China's democracy movement, emerged as one of the country's boldest champions of democracy in 1978, when communist authorities briefly allowed people to express their political opinions on posters attached to "Democracy Wall" in Beijing. His open denunciation of communist rule led to a fifteen-year prison term the following year. Wei was rearrested in 1994 and later sentenced to fourteen years imprisonment. In 1997 he was freed and sent to the United States.

Vaclav Havel

- **Wang Dan** was at the top of the Chinese regime's most-wanted list at the age of twenty for his leadership role in the 1989 student demonstrations for democracy in Beijing's Tiananmen Square. Following his arrest he spent four years in prison. Upon his release in 1993 he continued his pro-democracy activities, only to be arrested again. The communist authorities released him to the United States in 1998.
- **Andrei Sakharov,** the father of the Soviet H-bomb, was exiled to the isolated city of Gorky in the 1970s for his pro-democracy views. After being freed by Soviet reformer Mikhail Gorbachev, he was an outspoken champion of democracy during the USSR's final years.

Revolution

<u>Revolution</u> *usually means the overthrow of one system of government and its replacement by a different system.* Such fundamental changes in a nation's political regime are often accompanied by profound changes in the political attitudes of the masses and elites, a phenomenon often referred to as a **cultural revolution.**

Successful revolutions are rare. The American revolution of the 1770s and 1780s, the French revolution unleashed in 1789, the Russian revolution of 1917, the Chinese revolution that started in 1911

Wang Dan addresses students during the 1989 pro-democracy demonstration in Tiananmen Square.

with the collapse of the Manchu dynasty and culminated in the communist takeover of 1949, and the Iranian revolution that toppled the Shah in 1979 are major examples in modern history. More recently, the collapse of communism in the Soviet Union and East-Central Europe and the swing toward democracy in these countries surely qualify as true revolutions. The transformations from authoritarian rule to democracy now taking place in a number of other countries around the world may also be considered revolutionary.

When do revolutions take place? The enormous scholarly literature on revolutions provides several explanations. All of them stress the importance of mass opposition to the existing government and a widespread yearning for something better as a critical element. While political activists—*revolutionary elites*—invariably lead revolutions, they cannot succeed without establishing some kind of rapport with the masses.[33]

One set of explanations looks at the *psychological sources* of revolutionary violence. Some, for example, regard revolutionary activity as a rational choice, arguing that the "logic of collective action," which views most people as politically passive, may not always apply. The people's discontent may be so great that they are willing to shake off their passivity and actively participate in anti-regime activity, even if they run the risk of being arrested or shot. Such behavior may be quite rational if there appears to be a "once-in-a-lifetime" chance to get rid of a despised government, the risks are tolerable, and the chances of success look good. Calculations like these may account for the popular uprisings in East-Central Europe that destroyed communism.[34] The other set of explanations concentrates on the *social and political conditions* of revolutionary situations. Any comprehensive understanding of the causes and outcomes of revolutionary tumult requires us to combine both types of analysis.

Many of the most compelling psychological studies of revolution are rooted in *frustration-aggression theory,* which argues that people turn to violence when they are repeatedly or consistently frustrated in their attempts to achieve their goals. James C. Davies, for example, hypothesized that revolutions are not likely to occur simply because people are poor or oppressed, as common sense might lead us to expect. He made the counterintuitive argument that revolutions are most likely when large numbers of people have experienced recent improvements in their living conditions but are suddenly confronted with a sharp reversal of fortunes as the economy takes a downward turn. In these circumstances, the "rising expectations" that people experienced under favorable economic conditions are rudely frustrated and replaced with fears of reverting back to the deplorable conditions that prevailed before the improvements. The result is a rapid increase in violent behavior, which eventually targets the political regime itself.[35] Poland went through fluctuations of this sort when promising economic gains arising from expanded international trade in the early 1970s were quickly frustrated when the global economy went into a recession because of rising oil prices. Sharp declines in Polish living standards triggered the mass unrest that eventually toppled the communist regime.

One of the most influential students of mass violence and revolutionary psychology is Ted Robert Gurr. His widely read book *Why Men Rebel* centers on *relative deprivation* as the main source of frustration that, at least in some cases, sparks mass violence and can lead to a real revolution. Relative deprivation occurs when people perceive a gap between what they feel rightfully entitled to and what they feel they are actually capable of getting and keeping under existing circumstances. If they are continually frustrated in their efforts to satisfy their basic political, economic, or social goals and if there are no alternative ways of satisfying them, the likelihood rises that they will engage in some form of collective violence against others. Ultimately these frustrations can lead to exceptionally high magnitudes of *political* violence aimed directly at the governing authorities.[36] Other psychological studies have focused on "revolutionary personalities" and individual revolutionaries.[37]

Another category of research on revolutions focuses on the social, economic, and political realities (or "structures") that exist when revolutionary activity explodes. Karl Marx theorized that when a country has achieved an advanced stage of capitalism, society becomes split between a small but wealthy and politically dominant business class (the bourgeoisie) and a large mass of workers and unemployed. Once they fully understand their predicament and achieve "class consciousness," the workers will stage a revolution and wrest control of the economy from the bourgeoisie. Marx's theory of inevitable revolution was not confirmed by subsequent historical events, however.

A more recent structural approach explores the causes of the French, Russian, and Chinese revolutions and finds striking political and social similarities among all three cases. At the political level, the prerevolutionary state in France, Russia, and China consisted of a decaying absolutist monarchy that could no longer cope with the pressures posed by stronger foreign rivals. At the socioeconomic level, all three countries experienced violent rebellions by peasants who had become fed up with their inferior economic and social status. Finally, in each of the three cases the revolutionaries mobilized the masses and, upon taking power, set up a powerful centralized state with an intrusive bureaucracy. Authoritarian rule, not democracy, was the immediate result.[38]

Revolutionary activity has by no means subsided in our times. During the 1980s and early 1990s, for example, a fanatical guerilla movement known as the Shining Path conducted a systematic terror campaign in Peru in an effort to take over state power. As many as 25,000 people were killed during the prolonged insurrection. The movement suffered a severe blow in 1992 when its leader was captured and sentenced to prison. Colombia has witnessed a decades-long attempt by revolutionaries to topple the central government. By 1999 the rebels were in control of as much as half the country. Revolutionaries with a political agenda based on Islamic fundamentalism have been active in contemporary Egypt, Algeria, and several other Middle Eastern countries.

What have been the *causes* of these revolutionary activities? In Peru, it appears that economic factors were predominant in explaining why various Peruvians supported Shining Path. Most came from impoverished urban and rural backgrounds, and the movement grew during a period of severe hardship for the Peruvian economy, especially for the poor classes.[39] Colombia's rebels started out as Marxists bent on social revolution, but their aims appear to have degenerated more recently to the simple pursuit of power and economic control over the territory they occupy, plus access to the lucrative drug trade. Economic deprivation may animate many of the Muslim fundamentalists in Egypt and Algeria, but these movements seek far more than economic transformations. They are driven largely by religious beliefs that proclaim the necessity of organizing society and the state in strict conformity with the precepts of Islamic law. Religious belief, which in this case functions as an *ideology* with avowedly political aims, is thus a causative variable of revolutionary action in the Egyptian and Algerian cases.

KEY TERMS
(Underlined in the text)

Logic of collective action
Rationality and rational choice
Psephology
Limited (bounded) rationality
Particularistic parties
Catch-all parties
Responsible party government model
Interest aggregation
Stable partisan alignment
Partisan dealignment
Swing voters
Party realignment
Exit, voice, and loyalty
Centripetal and centrifugal party systems
Interest group
Interest articulation
Interest-group pluralism
Corporatism and neo-corporatism
Patron-client relationships (clientelism)
Coercive participation
Mass mobilization
Populism
Dissidence
Revolution

NOTES

1. Lester W. Milbraith, *Political Participation* (Chicago: Rand McNally, 1965). See also the second edition, coauthored with M. L. Goel (Chicago: Rand McNally, 1977). See also Sidney Verba and Norman H. Nie, *Participation in American Politics* (New York: Harper and Row, 1972); Michael M. Gant and Norman R. Luttbeg, *American Electoral Behavior: 1952–1988* (Itasca, Ill.: F. E. Peacock, 1991).

2. Mancur Olson, *The Logic of Collective Action* (Cambridge, Mass.: Harvard University Press, 1965).

3. G. Bingham Powell, "American Voter Turnout in Comparative Perspective," *American Political Science Review* 80, no. 1 (March 1986): 17–43. For a discussion of turnout in the United States, see Gant and Luttbeg, *American Electoral Behavior*. For a comparative study, see Sidney Verba, Norman H. Nie, and Jae-on Kim, *Participation and Political Equality: A Seven-Nation Comparison* (London: Cambridge University Press, 1978), 190–91, 234–68.

4. Public opinion surveys in the United States show declining levels of trust in government and personal efficacy. For example, asked how often one trusts the government in Washington to "do what is right," 15 percent of Americans said "always" in 1964, 2 percent in 1980, and 4 percent in 1988; 62 percent said "most of the time" in 1964, 23 percent in 1980, and 36 percent in 1988; 22 percent said "some or none of the time" in 1962, 73 percent in 1980, and 58 percent in 1988. When asked to agree or disagree with the statement, "People like me don't have any say about what the government does," 29 percent agreed in 1964, 39 percent in 1980, and 45 percent in 1988; 69 percent disagreed in 1964, 59 percent in 1980, and 54

percent in 1988. The rest did not know or had no opinion. Reported from National Election Studies in Gant and Luttbeg, *American Electoral Behavior*, 128.

5. Anthony Downs, *An Economic Theory of Democracy* (New York: Harper and Row, 1957). In later years Downs conceded that this depiction of voter rationality in terms of purely material self-interest was "rather narrowly focused." Voters, he later wrote, could still be rational if they espoused general welfare goals for the community. Indeed, Downs's later work emphasizes that democracy's survival requires selfless dedication to such principles as tolerance and liberty for all. See "Social Values and Democracy," in *The Economic Approach to Politics: A Critical Reassessment of the Theory of Rational Action*, ed. Kristin R. Monroe (New York: HarperCollins, 1991), 143–70.

6. Angus Campbell, Philip E. Converse, Warren E. Miller, and Donald E. Stokes, *The American Voter* (Chicago: University of Chicago Press, 1960).

7. Angus Campbell et al., *Elections and the Political Order* (New York: Wiley, 1966); Philip E. Converse, "The Nature of Belief Systems in Mass Public," in *Ideology and Discontent*, ed. David E. Apter (Glencoe, Ill.: Free Press, 1964).

8. David Butler and Donald Stokes, *Political Change in Britain*, 2d ed. (New York: St. Martin's Press, 1974); Philip E. Converse and Georges Dupeux, "Politicization and the Electorate in France and the United States," *Public Opinion Quarterly*, no. 26 (1963): 1–23.

9. See, for example, Samuel L. Popkin, *The Reasoning Voter* (Chicago: University of Chicago Press, 1991).

10. Hans-Dieter Klingemann, "Measuring Ideological Conceptualization," in *Political Action*, by Samuel Barnes et al. (Beverly Hills, Calif.: Sage, 1979); Dieter Fuchs and Hans-Dieter Klingemann, "The Left-Right Schema," in *Continuities in Political Action*, by M. Kent Jennings and Jan van Deth (Berlin: De Gruyter, 1989). See also Russell J. Dalton, *Citizen Politics: Public Opinion and Political Parties in Advanced Industrial Democracies*, 2d ed. (Chatham, N.J.: Chatham House, 1996); Russell J. Dalton, Scott Flanagan, and Paul Allen Beck, eds., *Electoral Change in Advanced Industrial Democracies: Realignment or Dealignment?* (Princeton; N.J.: Princeton University Press, 1984).

11. This definition of "party" is based on the work of Kenneth Janda. See his book *Political Parties: A Cross-National Survey* (New York: Free Press, 1980), 5, and his essay "Comparative Political Parties: Research and Theory," in *Political Science: The State of the Discipline II*, ed. Ada W. Finifter, (Washington, D.C.: American Political Science Association, 1993), 163–91.

12. On catch-all parties, see Otto Kirchheimer, "The Transformation of the West European Party Systems," in *Political Parties and Political Development*, ed. Joseph LaPalombara and Myron Weiner (Princeton, N.J.: Princeton University Press, 1966), 177–200.

13. Thomas Childers, *The Nazi Voter* (Chapel Hill: University of North Carolina Press, 1983); Richard F. Hamilton, *Who Voted for Hitler?* (Princeton, N.J.: Princeton University Press, 1982).

14. Gabriel A. Almond and G. Bingham Powell Jr., *Comparative Politics: A Developmental Approach* (Boston: Little, Brown, 1966) and *Comparative Politics: System, Process, Policy* (Boston: Little, Brown, 1978).

15. Between 1952 and 1964, about 75 percent of American voters identified themselves fairly strongly with either the Democrats or the Republicans. This percentage of "partisan" party identifiers dropped to about 61 percent by the mid-1970s. (Paul Allen Beck, "The Dealignment Era in America," in Dalton, Flanagan, and Beck, *Electoral Change in Advanced Industrial Democracies*, 243.) The percentage of American voters identifying themselves as "independents" rose from 5 percent of the electorate to 11 percent in 1988. The rate at which Democrats or Republicans defect from their party to vote for the opposing party's presidential candidate shows no clear pattern between 1952 and 1988; defection rates vary from election to election. See Gant and Luttbeg, *American Electoral Behavior*, 63–74.

16. Seymour M. Lipset and Stein Rokkan, eds., *Party Systems and Voter Alignments: Cross-National Perspectives* (New York: Free Press, 1967), 50. On changes occurring in the 1970s, see Dalton, Flanagan, and Beck, *Electoral Change in Advanced Industrial Democracies*. On the persistence of party loyalties in Britain, Germany, and the Netherlands, see Bradley M. Richardson, "European Party Loyalties Revisited," *American Political Science Review* 85, no. 3 (September 1991): 751–75.

17. For a detailed study, see Giovanni Sartori, *Parties and Party Systems* (Cambridge: Cambridge University Press, 1976).

18. In recent decades several individuals have run for president as independents, including George Wallace (who got 13.6 percent of the vote in 1968), John Anderson (6.6 percent in 1980), and Ross Perot (18.9 percent in 1992 and 8 percent in 1996). None ever established a viable political party capable of effectively challenging the dominance of the Democrats or Republicans. See Steven J. Rosenstone, Roy L. Behr, and Edward H. Lazarus, *Third Parties in America* (Princeton, N.J.: Princeton University Press, 1984).

19. Maurice Duverger, *Political Parties*, 2d English ed., rev., trans. Barbara and Robert North (London: Methuen, 1959), 217. See also Duverger's *Party Politics and Pressure Groups*, trans. David Wagoner (New

York: Crowell, 1972), and *Introduction à la politique* (Paris: Gallimard, 1964).

20. Writing in the 1950s, Duverger said that the introduction of a single-ballot plurality electoral system in West Germany and Italy would "unquestionably" produce a two-party system. "However," he continued, "the brutal application of the single-ballot system in a country in which multipartism has taken deep root, as in France, would not produce the same results, except after a very long delay. The electoral system works in the direction of bipartism; it does not necessarily and absolutely lead to it in spite of all obstacles. The basic tendency combines with others which attenuate it, check it, or arrest it. With these reserves we can nevertheless consider that dualism of parties is the 'brazen law' (as Marx would have said) of the simple-majority single-ballot electoral system." Duverger, *Political Parties*, 228. For his views on PR and multiparty systems, see ibid., 245–55.

21. Albert O. Hirschman, *Exit, Voice, and Loyalty* (Cambridge, Mass.: Harvard University, 1970).

22. By the mid-1990s there were about 14,000 lobbyists in Washington (*Washington Post,* November 30, 1995). See also John R. Wright, *Interest Groups and Congress* (Boston: Allyn and Bacon, 1996), 23.

23. One of the earliest studies to detail the importance of interest groups in the United States was Arthur Bentley, *The Process of Government* (Bloomington, Ind.: Principia Press, 1949). Another classic is David B. Truman, *The Governmental Process* (New York: Alfred A. Knopf, 1971).

24. Russell J. Dalton and Manfred Keuchler, eds., *Challenging the Political Order: New Social and Political Movements in Western Democracies* (New York: Oxford University Press, 1990); Aldon D. Morris and Carol McClurg Mueller, *Frontiers in Social Movement Theory* (New Haven, Conn.: Yale, 1992).

25. *Washington Post,* July 19, 1994, p. A6. For examples of full-page ads in the same newspaper in 1994, see March 13, p. A11; March 16, p. A15; March 17, p. A20; and July 21, p. A27.

26. For a list, see *Washington Post,* August 15, 1994, p. A17.

27. *Washington Post,* October 11, 1994, p. A6; and October 4, 1999, p. A1. For a critical analysis of interest groups in the United States, see Jonathan Rauch, *Demosclerosis: The Silent Killer of American Government* (New York: Times Books, 1994).

28. For a good introduction to corporatism in theory and practice, see Peter J. Williamson, *Varieties of Corporatism* (Cambridge: Cambridge University Press, 1985) and *Corporatism in Perspective* (London: SAGE, 1989); and Alan Cawson, *Corporatism and Political Theory* (Oxford: Basil Blackwell, 1986). See also Philippe C. Schmitter, "Still the Century of Corporatism?" *Review*

of Politics 36 (1974): 85–131; Schmitter and Gerhard Lehmbruch, *Trends Towards Corporatist Intermediation* (Beverly Hills, Calif.: Sage, 1979); Lehmbruch and Schmitter, *Patterns of Corporatist Policy-Making* (Beverly Hills, Calif.: Sage, 1982); Peter J. Katzenstein, *Corporatism and Change: Austria, Switzerland, and the Politics of Industry* (Ithaca, N.Y.: Cornell University Press, 1984).

29. Theodore J. Lowi, *At the Pleasure of the Mayor: Patronage and Power in New York City, 1898-1958* (London: Macmillan, 1964); P. A. Allum, *Politics and Society in Post-War Naples* (Cambridge: Cambridge University Press, 1973).

30. Margaret M. Pearson, *China's New Business Elite* (Berkeley: University of California Press, 1997).

31. A classic work on this subject is William Kornhauser, *The Politics of Mass Society* (Glencoe, Ill.: Free Press, 1959).

32. Jeane J. Kirkpatrick, *Leader and Vanguard in Mass Society: A Study of Peronist Argentina* (Cambridge, Mass.: MIT Press, 1971); Lars Schoultz, "The Socio-Economic Determinants of Popular-Authoritarian Electoral Behavior: The Case of Peronism," *American Political Science Review* 71, no. 4 (December 1977): 1423–46.

33. For introductory overviews, see Peter C. Sederberg, *Fires Within: Political Violence and Revolutionary Change* (New York: HarperCollins, 1994), and A. S. Cohen, *Theories of Revolution: An Introduction* (London: Thomas Nelson, 1975).

34. On revolution and collective action, see Michael Taylor, ed., *Rationality and Revolution* (New York: Cambridge University Press, 1988).

35. James Chowning Davies, "The J-curve of Rising and Declining Satisfactions as a Cause of Revolution and Rebellion," in *Violence in America,* rev. ed., ed. Hugh Davis Graham and Ted Robert Gurr (Beverly Hills, Calif.: Sage, 1976), 415–36.

36. Ted Robert Gurr, *Why Men Rebel* (Princeton, N.J.: Princeton University Press, 1970). See also Ivo K. Feierabend et al., eds., *Anger, Violence, and Politics* (Englewood Cliffs, N.J.: Prentice Hall, 1972) and Fred R. von der Mehden, *Comparative Political Violence* (Englewood Cliffs, N.J.: Prentice Hall, 1973).

37. E. Victor Wolfenstein, *The Revolutionary Personality: Lenin, Trotsky, Gandhi* (Princeton, N.J.: Princeton University Press, 1971); Bruce Mazlish, *The Revolutionary Ascetic: Evolution of a Political Type* (New York: Basic Books, 1976); Erik H. Erikson, *Gandhi's Truth: On the Origins of Militant Nonviolence* (New York: Norton, 1969).

38. Theda Skocpol, *States and Social Revolutions* (Cambridge: Cambridge University Press, 1979).

39. Cynthia L. McClintock, "Why Peasants Rebel: The Case of Peru's Sendero Luminoso," *World Politics* 37, no. 1 (October 1984): 48–84; David Scott Palmer, ed., *Shining Path of Peru* (New York: St. Martin's, Press, 1992).

CHAPTER 12

POLITICAL CULTURE AND POLITICAL PSYCHOLOGY

DEFINING POLITICAL CULTURE

It is generally recognized that in the United States, certain basic attitudes about political life are widely shared. Americans tend to be rather proud of their political system, for example: they revere their Constitution, prizing it as one of the greatest political documents ever devised. At the same time, their attitudes toward politicians are rather ambivalent. While Americans generally treat their political leaders with civility, they can be highly critical of politicians and even quite cynical about them.

Americans are also pretty ambivalent about government in general. There is a prevailing aversion to "big government" and excessive governmental intrusion in people's lives. In fact, many Americans do not have a particularly high regard for government. Though only a few Americans are intensely angry about their government, trust in government officials has declined appreciably since the 1960s.[1] Many people regard the government as inefficient and wasteful and hold the private business sector in higher esteem as more effective than politicians or bureaucrats. Most Americans value individual responsibility and personal initiative over excessive reliance on the state. Most favor equality (or equity) of opportunity rather than a state-enforced equality of condition.

In fact, most Americans just don't care about politics all that much. As we noted in the previous chapter, voter turnout in the United States is lower than in most other Western democracies. Still, most Americans perceive themselves as law abiding and have a high respect for law and order. They decisively reject violence as a legitimate form of political action. The vast majority pay their taxes, though most Americans dislike high taxes and would much prefer to see them reduced rather than raised.

Americans value hard work, believing that people are entitled to earn as much money as they can. Private enterprise, while not without problems, is viewed positively by most Americans as basically successful, even though many of them regard large corporations as excessively powerful and impersonal. Socialism is taboo. By and large Americans tend to be distrustful of excessive power in any form, whether it is the power of government, large corporations, or "special interests" representing powerful groups in society.

Nevertheless, most Americans believe that it is proper for the government to help take care of people who cannot help themselves. There is a consensus that such large government programs as Social Security, Medicare, and welfare for poor children or for those unable to work are necessary. Some observers maintain that Americans in recent decades have become so accustomed to expecting various government benefits that an "entitlement" mentality has set in. While they may object to big government in principle, they favor it in practice as long as they can derive some gain from it.

Most Americans favor compromise. They like to get things done, and a refusal to compromise is regarded as a barrier to effective action. Quite a few Americans have become fed up with the two main political parties in recent years because they believe that Democratic and Republican politicians are more interested in opposing each other than in reaching effective agreements that can help the country. This willingness to compromise helps make for moderation in American political life. Most Americans think of themselves as moderates or centrists. Even those few who regard themselves as liberals or conservatives tend to shun the more extreme tendencies of these competing orientations. Political radicalism of any kind is generally frowned upon.

Of all the political values Americans hold, freedom usually tops the list. Typically this means freedom from excessive governmental interference, but it is more than that. To most Americans, freedom means that they can come and go as they please and express themselves as they wish, that there are practically no barriers to what they can accomplish, and that the future is full of possibilities. Most Americans are relatively optimistic about the future; there is a continuing belief that all are entitled to fulfill "the American dream": to own one's own house, earn a rising income, and enjoy the pleasures of life, a value extolled in the Declaration of Independence as "the pursuit of happiness." Most Americans claim they are basically satisfied with their lives.

Americans are also generally tolerant of the freedoms of fellow Americans, and they have a general commitment to "fair play" and equity. Their tolerance has limits, however. Although there has been substantial progress in the area of racial and ethnic tolerance over the past three decades, racial antagonisms persist, and many heterosexuals are intolerant of homosexuals.

On the whole, Americans trust one another and can work together to achieve common goals. A high degree of interpersonal cooperation undergirds American society, giving rise to all sorts of civic, business, cultural, philanthropic, and other associations and volunteer organizations. But many American also experience a tension between their desire for freedom and individualism, on the one hand, and close community bonds on the other. Interpersonal trust, moreover, is declining, especially among younger Americans, as is participation in voluntary associations.

Most Americans are religious. To a greater extent than people in most other democracies, they believe in God, attend church regularly, and are profoundly influenced by religious beliefs and moral teachings.

To be sure, not all Americans subscribe to all these notions. Public opinion survey data, however, show that large numbers of them do, often a majority. In most respects, these surveys have displayed considerable consistency over the last several decades.[2]

The attitudes toward politics that were just described are representative of what political scientists would call the prevailing **political culture** of the United States.

> <u>Political culture</u> *is a pattern of beliefs, values, expectations, and—above all—attitudes that people have with respect to authority, society, and politics.*

Political culture reflects the ways people think and feel about politics. It consists of clusters of attitudes about government and social relations that are shared by large proportions of a country's population, quite often the majority. It includes some core values that people have, especially those relating to political ideals and social relations. In some cases, the *ideas of liberal democracy* are the main source of these values, as in the case of freedom, private enterprise, and equality of opportunity. In other cases *religion* is a source of values. Many widely shared values in the United States have been shaped by the Judeo-Christian heritage. Similarly, Confucianism has exerted a profound influence on prevailing moral and social values in many Asian countries, and Islam has had an equally powerful impact on the political culture of numerous countries in the Middle East, Africa, and various parts of Asia.

One's *family* and the larger *society* are also sources of the values people hold. The **political socialization** process can be looked upon as *the process whereby individuals learn about politics and the political culture of their society.* They learn these things first from their own family (the *primary agent of socialization*) and then from the larger society and its *secondary agents of socialization,* such as peer groups, schools, churches, places of employment, and the like.

In addition to reflecting widely shared values, political culture includes the understandings people have about politics within their respective countries as well as the unwritten "rules of the game" of political life, such as rules about what is acceptable and unacceptable. (In some countries, giving public officials gifts in exchange for favors is acceptable, in others it is condemned as corruption.) It includes people's *expectations* about what is likely or unlikely in politics. (In the United States, people expect elections to take place regularly and do not expect the military to seize power. In other countries the public's expectations may be quite different.) It includes their own opinions about what is right and wrong in political life. In short, political culture involves a combination of values, understandings, expectations, and opinions that shape mass attitudes toward political life. While some regard political culture as a nebulous concept, since it consists of so many disparate elements, many political scientists believe that it is a real phenomenon of mass psychology that can be empirically verified in studies of public opinion.[3]

Most countries have a *dominant political culture,* a collection of attitudes that is broadly shared by the political elites and a large proportion of the population. These dominant or prevailing attitudes frequently cut across different social classes, ethnic groups, and other social strata. The attitudes we have just described as elements of the dominant political culture in the United States are broadly representative of "middle America"—the white middle class.[4] To be sure, not everyone in the United States shares all of them. A majority of African Americans have different attitudes than most whites on a host of racial questions, for example. Nevertheless, they share quite a few basic attitudes with whites, including support for the Constitution, individual freedom, private enterprise, equality of opportunity, the importance of education and hard work, and belief in God.[5]

Many if not most countries also have one or more *political subcultures.* A **political subculture** *is a political culture that deviates from the dominant culture in key respects.* In the United States, for ex-

ample, not everyone agrees with the dominant attitudes of American political culture. Many poor and uneducated people, for example, feel more or less permanently alienated from the American political and economic systems. They may feel a fundamental dissatisfaction with life in general and a sense of being trapped in their circumstances. In some instances these orientations are combined with a hostile attitude toward authority, intolerance of different ethnic groups, and a sense that one has nothing to compromise. In the most extreme cases these attitudes may lead to a flaunting of the law and perhaps a tendency to violence. As table 12.1 on page 272 indicates, the United States has a very high murder rate compared to other economically developed democracies. Many other countries have political subcultures of their own that coexist with the dominant culture.

Studies of Political Culture

The concept of political culture has a venerable tradition. Plato and Aristotle both attached considerable importance to the basic attitudes people have about authority, about how social relationships should be conducted, and about the role government should play in people's lives. Some of these cultural attitudes, they maintained, favor democracy, while others are incompatible with democratic self-government.

Alexis de Tocqueville placed cultural values and attitudes at the forefront of his famous analysis of democracy in America. In place of our contemporary term "political culture," he used *mores,* a generic term meaning the broadly shared customs and manners of a society. Tocqueville defined mores as "the whole moral and intellectual state of a people," and he was particularly interested in *political* mores, those "habits of the heart" and "mental habits" that helped shape the political behavior of Americans. In his view, American political mores were characterized above all by the love of liberty, an attitude he believed was propagated by both the Protestant and Catholic religions in America, by the educational system, and by the family, with women playing an especially important role. In addition, Tocqueville believed that Americans had a basic good sense about political life that came from generations of experience with

TABLE 12.1

**Annual Homicide Rates
in Selected Countries, 1990s**

Country	Year	Homicide Rate (per 100,000 population)
South Africa	1995	75.30
Estonia	1994	28.21
Brazil	1993	19.04
Mexico	1994	17.58
Philippines	1996	16.20
United States	1997	6.80*
Northern Ireland	1994	6.09
Argentina	1994	4.51
Hungary	1994	3.53
Finland	1994	3.24
Portugal	1994	2.98
Israel	1993	2.32
Italy	1992	2.25
Scotland	1994	2.24
Canada	1992	2.16
Slovenia	1994	2.01
Australia	1994	1.86
England and Wales	1992	1.78
Singapore	1994	1.71
South Korea	1994	1.62
Switzerland	1994	1.32
Sweden	1993	1.30
Denmark	1993	1.21
Austria	1994	1.17
Germany	1994	1.17
Greece	1994	1.14
France	1994	1.12
Netherlands	1994	1.11
Norway	1993	0.97
Spain	1993	0.95
Japan	1994	0.62
Ireland	1991	0.62

*United States in 1993: 9.93.

Sources: For South Africa and the Philippines, United Nations Crime and Justice Information Network <www.uncjin.org>. For the United States in 1997, *FBI Uniform Crime Report, 1997.* For all others, *International Journal of Epidemiology* 27: 216.[6]

social cooperation and local self-government at the village level. He also noted their general "restraint," "moderation," and "self-command."

In fact, Tocqueville regarded these attitudinal factors as even more important in accounting for the success of American democracy than the Constitution and other legal pillars of the U.S. governmental system. "Laws are always unsteady when unsupported by mores," he wrote. "Mores are the only tough and durable power in a nation." With-

out the proper attitudes and habits on the part of the population, Tocqueville clearly implied, even the most brilliantly conceived democratic institutions would inevitably rest on shaky foundations.[7] Other students of early American history have also underscored the impact of cultural factors on political developments. Gordon S. Wood, for example, notes that changes in attitudes toward authority relationships in the family accompanied the American colonies' break from Britain, with more liberal attitudes replacing the traditional patriarchal household.[8]

The German sociologist Max Weber was also a keen student of political culture. He believed that political and economic institutions could not be understood solely on their own terms. Cultural attitudes deriving from such nonpolitical sources as religion, the family, and rules of logic can also have a profound impact on political and economic reality. In one of his most famous works, *The Protestant Ethic and the Sprit of Capitalism,* Weber wondered why Protestants tended to dominate the German economy at the turn of the twentieth century, occupying the most important corporate executive positions to a far greater extent than Catholics did. Weber located the answer in the contrasting emphases of Protestant and Catholic asceticism. Both religions traditionally preached an ascetic life style ("plain living"). But whereas Protestants starting with Martin Luther placed a high value on personal involvement in worldly activities along with saving one's wealth, medieval Catholic doctrine attached a higher value to withdrawing from the worlds of commerce and politics in favor of worshiping God in monasteries. Protestant asceticism, in Weber's view, was more conducive than Catholic asceticism was to economic activity, thrift, and the accumulation of wealth. Though the value of asceticism itself declined over the centuries for average Protestants and Catholics, many of the social and economic attitudes they generated remained. In other works Weber showed how father-dominated households formed the basis of "patriarchal" societies with an authoritarian political elite, and how the logic of legal reasoning provided the basis for the rule of law and the modern state.[9]

A ground-breaking study of political culture was published in 1963 by Gabriel Almond and

Sidney Verba. Entitled *The Civic Culture,* the study examined political culture in five countries (the United States, Britain, West Germany, Italy, and Mexico).[10] Based on responses to a host of questions about politics, the authors concluded that the populations of each of these countries could be divided into three groups:

1. *Participants,* who are generally knowledgeable about politics. Participants have positive feelings about their governmental system and regard that system as legitimate and worthy of support. They vote regularly and may also get involved in other forms of political activity.
2. *Subjects,* who are less knowledgeable about what is going on in politics. Subjects evince relatively little pride in their political institutions, vote rarely, and have little confidence in their ability to get results out of government, but they are law abiding and can be quite deferential in their attitudes toward governmental authority.
3. *Parochials,* who know practically nothing about politics, especially at the national level. Their world is usually confined to their local community or village. They are basically alienated from their government and apathetic, with very low confidence in their ability to get government officials to help them or to effect political change.

Almond and Verba concluded that all the countries they studied consisted of a mixture of participants, subjects, and parochials. The countries differed, however, with respect to the relative size of the three categories in proportion to the population. At the time the studies were conducted, in the late 1950s, the United States had a high proportion of participants and subjects. Mexico and Italy had high proportions of subjects and parochials, while Britain and Germany fell in between.

Almond and Verba hypothesized that democracy would be most stable in countries possessing what they called a **civic culture,** that is, a combination of fairly large numbers of participants and subjects together with a smaller number of parochials. In their view, democracy did not require a population consisting entirely of politically active participants. Too many activists, they argued, might destabilize the political system. Democracy would be most stable if, in addition to political activists, the population also included subjects and parochials who did not make too many political demands and who quietly accepted the existing political arrangements. They believed that the United States and Britain most closely approximated this ideal mixture, with the United States having a somewhat larger proportion of active participants and Britain a somewhat larger proportion of subjects with deferential attitudes toward the country's elites and political institutions.

Like Tocqueville, Almond and Verba affirmed that a successful democracy requires more than just democratic governmental institutions and laws; it also requires a compatible political culture. "Unless the political culture is able to support a democratic system," they wrote, "the chances for the success of that system are slim." By contrast, the authors hypothesized that authoritarian governments of various kinds (such as communist countries and military dictatorships) would rest on a cultural foundation of subject and parochial attitudes. Politically active participants would be a small minority in such countries, confined mainly to the ruling elite and their most determined opponents. Advocates of the importance of political culture arguments thus contend that authoritarian governments do not rule on the basis of force alone. They stay in power at least in part because large segments of the population share certain attitudes and beliefs supportive of authoritarian rule.

The Civic Culture had been widely discussed by political scientists ever since its initial appearance. While some scholars have questioned the authors' assumptions and conclusions, others have supported their basic contention that attitudes and feelings do play a major role in explaining why some countries have stable democracies and others do not.[11] Let's look at some examples in the following hypothesis-testing exercise.

HYPOTHESIS-TESTING EXERCISE: Does Political Culture Matter?

HYPOTHESIS

The hypothesis to be tested asserts that political culture is a factor that affects the existence or success of democracy independently of other factors such as political institutions or economic realities.

VARIABLES

In this hypothesis, the **dependent variable** is the existence or success of *democracy* and the **independent variable** is *political culture*.

EXPECTATIONS

If the hypothesis is correct, then we would expect to find that countries with successful democracies have a political culture characterized by high levels of interpersonal trust and cooperation. Conversely, we would expect that countries in which these and related attitudes are not widely shared by the populace are either not democracies at all or have unstable, ineffective democracies. We would further expect to find that these cultural factors exercise an impact of their own on democracy independently of such other variables as political institutions or levels of wealth. In testing the hypothesis empirically, we would expect to find evidence of these attitudes in public opinion surveys and various forms of behavior, such as public involvement in voluntary associations.

EVIDENCE

In three major books and other works devoted to testing this hypothesis, Ronald Inglehart has found considerable evidence that high levels of interpersonal trust and voluntary participation in cooperative associations are strongly correlated with stable democracies. Countries that lack these cultural attributes tend to be less successful at building or maintaining stable democratic institutions. While admitting that the cultural factors associated with democracy are often correlated with high levels of national economic development, Inglehart notes that "wealth alone does not automatically bring democracy." By the same token, he notes that "democracy is not attained simply by making institutional changes or by clever elite-level maneuvering." Rather, cultural factors play a role of their own in affecting democracy's prospects.[12]

In another recent study, Robert Putnam and his associates examined various explanations of why some regions of Italy have very effective governments while other regions do not. They found that economic factors were not the principal explanatory variables. The critical difference rested on a key aspect of political culture, namely, the extent to which people trusted one another enough to cooperate in forming cooperative associations. Regions with a history of social trust and cooperation were more successful at making democracy work than were those characterized by high levels of suspicion and non-cooperation.[13]

Unfortunately, there is little or no public opinion survey data available in non-democratic countries. Public attitudes thus cannot be systematically examined in these cases. However, there is ample historical evidence that many authoritarian states have had low levels of participation in private voluntary associations.

CONCLUSIONS

In a study of some forty-three countries, Inglehart concluded that "political culture does seem to be a central factor in the survival of democracy," with a general tendency for successful democracies to be undergirded by the cultural attitudes identified in the hypothesis. Putnam and other scholars have also uncovered evidence that political culture can be an important independent variable explaining why democracy works well in some instances but less effectively (or not at all) in others. These findings are largely *consistent* with the hypothesis. But there have been very few works that have tested the hypothesis with the empirical thoroughness of Inglehart and Putnam, and more work needs to be done to see if evidence seriously contradicting their findings can be found.

Conceptualizing Political Culture

In order to make the concept of political culture clearer, let's consider a number of different patterns of attitudes and values about political and social life that can exist in different countries. We'll divide these attitudinal patterns into three clusters: (1) *attitudes toward authority*; (2) *attitudes toward society*; and (3) *attitudes toward politics*, especially *the state*. Within each of these clusters, we'll look at specific dichotomies (i.e., paired opposites) that form the outer extremes of possible attitudes people may have. We should recognize, however, that many people, perhaps the majority, do not share these extreme attitudes, but are located at various points in between them. Hence we should conceptualize the various attitudes people have toward a given object (such as the government) in terms of a *continuum*, a line of gradations between one polar extreme and the other. Let's clarify these notions with specific examples.

Attitudes Toward Authority One possible dichotomy that describes attitudes toward authority is the **submissive-rebellious** dichotomy (figure 12.1). At one extreme, people can be highly submissive toward authority (whether in the family or in the political community). Often this atti-

FIGURE 12.1   Continuum of Attitudes Toward Authority

Submissive	Deferential	Interactive	Alienated	Rebellious

FIGURE 12.2   Continuum of Attitudes Toward Society: Conflictual/Cooperative Dimension

Highly conflictual	Somewhat conflictual	Mixture of conflict and compromise	Highly consensual

tude is tinged with fatalism and resignation (e.g., "Nothing can be changed; it is God's will."). At the other extreme are those who reject authority altogether and seek to rebel against it. But there are various way stations in between. Without being humbly submissive, people can be **deferential** toward authority, like the "subjects" in Almond and Verba's analysis. These people willingly respect authority but do not seek to deal with it directly. Moving along the continuum, people can be **interactive** with authority: they can share in making the decisions that affect their lives. This interactive attitude is characteristic of what Almond and Verba would call "participants."

Next along the continuum we find **alienated** attitudes toward authority. Alienated people are too discontented to be obligingly submissive or quietly deferential, and they are generally quite cynical about the authority patterns under which they live. But if they do anything at all to express their alienation, the actions they take will usually be sporadic, halfhearted, and ultimately, ineffective (such as persistently showing up late for work or refusing to vote). At the opposite extreme on this continuum, people with **rebellious** attitudes toward authority are so hostile to the ruling powers that they try to take effective action against them. In political life, rebels may undertake such dissident behavior as publicly denouncing the government, or they may actively seek to overthrow it, whether violently or through nonviolent resistance. Highly traditional political cultures, such as Middle Eastern sheikdoms, tend to have a large number of submissive and deferential citizens. Democracies thrive on an interactive citizenry, though some people may feel alienated. Any country with a large number of rebels is probably experiencing violent discontent or civil war.

Attitudes Toward Society   One continuum of this type is delineated by the **consensual-conflictual** dichotomy (figure 12.2). At one end of the line we find people with highly cooperative attitudes toward other individuals and social groups. They exhibit high levels of tolerance, interpersonal trust, and willingness to compromise. At the other end we find highly conflictual attitudes toward other individuals and social groups, defined by correspondingly low levels of tolerance, interpersonal trust, and propensity to compromise. The continuum shows various gradations in between. Yugoslavia, wracked by ethnic cleansing in the 1990s, and Lebanon, with a plethora of religious groups embroiled in prolonged civil strife in the 1980s, are examples of highly conflictual political cultures. Japan exemplifies a highly consensual one: political decisions typically have to meet with a broad social consensus before they can be finalized. The United States, Canada, the West European democracies, and other successful democratic states generally display a mixture of conflict and compromise, with the conflicts typically dealt with through the democratic process rather than through violence.

Another dichotomy we can expect to find in people's attitudes toward other people is the **collectivist-individualist** dichotomy (figure 12.3). At the far right end, the most extreme individualists have an "everyone-for-himself" mentality. Proponents of *economic individualism* reject government assistance and seek to take care of themselves and their immediate families entirely on their own. If they fail in these efforts, they proudly reject handouts or charity. Such extreme types expect every one else in society to behave the same way. Proponents of what may be called *expressive individualism* believe that all individuals should have the right to say what they want and live as they please, with scant regard for the larger society. Whether stressing economic or expressive individualism, extreme individualists place the individual at the center of society.

At the left end of this continuum are extreme collectivists who discount individual rights and freedoms in favor of group rights and group activities. Just as extreme individualists may be willing to tolerate a high level of social inequality, extreme collectivists seek to achieve as much egalitarianism as they can in all facets of social life: equality of opportunity, wealth, education, power, and so forth. In the middle are those who seek a balance between the welfare of the individual and the welfare of the larger community.

Historically, the United States has gravitated somewhat toward the individualist side of this dichotomy, an attitude reflected in the old nostrum, "The government that governs least, governs best." Russia has generally gravitated toward the collectivist side. One hypothesis that will merit repeated testing in the coming years is that individualist cultures are more likely to favor market economies than are collectivist cultures, which would tend to favor strong state intervention in the economy in order to promote social equality.

Attitudes Toward the State   The main dichotomy in this cluster of attitudes is the **permissive state–interventionist state** dichotomy (figure 12.4). At one end are those who favor a weak government that permits people the widest possible freedom to do what they want. The most extreme permissivists want no governmental interference of any kind in the economy (no taxes!), a minimal government role in maintaining law and order, no national obligation to defend the country, indeed,

very few government intrusions of any kind. The most extreme permissivist is basically an anarchist. As one moves along the continuum, one finds increasing levels of support for various governmental tasks, starting with such elemental ones as the maintenance of law and order, regulation of transportation facilities, delivery of the mail, and control over the national defense.

At the other end of the continuum are those who favor maximum governmental intervention in all facets of life, including control over the economy and the regulation of social conflicts. Political elites who favor such an interventionist state may do so, at least in some cases, in order to maximize their own power over the population or over the economy. But ordinary citizens may also prefer an interventionist state, usually because they want the state to protect them against economic fluctuations, ill health, destitution in old age, or other possible hardships, whether natural or human-made. Proponents of the interventionist state may be willing to give up some of their personal freedoms in exchange for the state's assistance. Of course, there are less extreme variants of this protectivist attitude as one moves back toward the center of the continuum.

Various questions have been asked of citizens in different countries to ascertain their attitudes toward the state. The next two tables show how wide the range of opinion can be among some of the world's economically advanced democracies. Table 12.2 reflects attitudes on the question of whether it should be the state's responsibility to reduce income disparities. Table 12.3 shows different levels of trust in their respective national political institutions on the part of citizens in the European Union. Figure 12.5 shows a general tendency toward declining trust in a number of established democracies.

FIGURE 12.3   **Continuum of Attitudes Toward Society: Individualist/Collectivist Dimension**

Extreme collectivism	Balance of individualism and collectivism	Extreme individualism

FIGURE 12.4   **Continuum of Attitudes Toward the State**

Permissive state	Balance of permissiveness and interventionism	Highly interventionist state

The continua of attitudes shown in Figures 12.1 through 12.4 make ample room for political sub-cultures within a given country. Whereas the majority of the population may cluster around the middle of the spectrum along the authority continuum, favoring interactive relations with the decision makers, some people in the same country may be alienated from the dominant elites or political majority, or may even be actively rebellious. Similarly, whereas a few people may favor "rugged individualism," most segments of society may not. The point is, almost every country will have people whose attitudes can be located at different points along the attitudinal spectrums. At the same time, many countries will show majorities huddled around the midpoint. In short, we should conceive of each country's political culture as consisting of a combination of attitudes on a variety of dimensions. In most cases it would be an oversimplification to suggest that we can locate an entire country at a precise point along any of the spectrums we have shown in this chapter.

We can hypothesize that some combinations of attitudes will be more supportive of stable democracy than others are, while alternative combinations can be expected to yield different results. For example, at least hypothetically we can assume that:

- Societies with (1) high levels of interactive attitudes toward authority, (2) a high level of consensual attitudes toward society, (3) intermediate levels of individualism and collectivism, and (4) roughly balanced support for permissiveness and intervention on the part of the state will be more likely to sustain a stable democracy than will societies whose majorities deviate from these standards.
- Societies with (1) a high level of alienated or rebellious attitudes toward authority, (2) high levels of conflictual social attitudes and individualism, and (3) high levels of support for a permissive, weak state are likely to be embroiled in continuing civil conflict.
- Societies with (1) high levels of submissiveness or deference to authority, (2) high levels of social consensus and collectivism, and (3) wide support for an interventionist state are likely to be fairly stable authoritarian states of one kind or another.

Of course, these alternative combinations of attitude mixtures by no means exhaust all the possibilities. We may find some other mixtures as we look directly at specific countries.

TABLE 12.2

Attitudes Toward the State in Selected Democracies (1987)

Percentage who say they "agree" or "strongly agree" that it is the state's responsibility to reduce income disparities between those with high incomes and those with lower incomes.

Italy	82%
Austria	81
Hungary	80
Netherlands	65
Britain	64
Germany	61
Australia	44
Switzerland	43
United States	29

Source: International Social Survey Program.

TABLE 12.3

Trust in Political Institutions in EU Countries, 1999

Average percentages of people who "tend to trust" the civil service, the national parliament, the national government, and political parties in their home country.

Netherlands	56%	Denmark	43%	Sweden	34%
Luxembourg	51	Ireland	39	United Kingdom	34
Austria	45	Greece	38	France	32
Portugal	44	Spain	38	Belgium	26
Finland	43	Germany	37	Italy	25

Source: Eurobarometer, no. 51 (spring 1999).

FIGURE 12.5   Political Confidence, Annual Percent Change

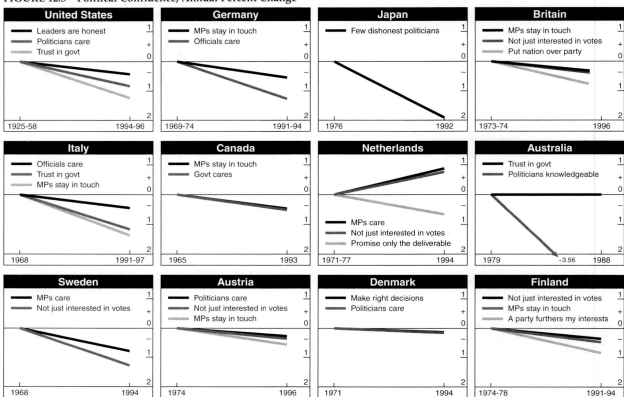

Wording in questions varies slightly

Source: The Economist, July 17, 1998.

Do Political Cultures Change?

Although most systematic studies of political culture have revealed considerable continuity in the way particular populations think about politics, political culture is rarely static. Attitudinal change is real; all political cultures evolve. In some cases such changes take place slowly, shifting only every two generations or more. But in other cases they occur a bit more rapidly. As noted in chapter 2, members of every generation tend to be influenced by the political events of their youth. More generally, people learn about their political culture and change it through the process of political socialization. When succeeding generations basically adopt the political attitudes of their parents with little or no change, obviously change in political culture

will be slight. But when key segments of a particular generation adopt political attitudes at variance with those of the preceding generation, a country's political culture can change accordingly.

A good example of such generational change occurred in West Germany after World War II. In 1953, some eight years after the defeat of Nazi Germany, only about half the population said that democracy was the best form of government. With the passing of the older generation and the emergence of younger people who grew up after the war, support for democracy rose appreciably. In 1972, 90 percent of West Germans favored democracy.[14] Other countries offer similar examples of such generational changes in basic attitudes. Similar changes are occurring right before our eyes in the formerly communist countries of Russia,

Poland, the Czech Republic, and others. Attitudes toward authority, society, and the state are in flux, sometimes wildly so. While some people in these countries cling to old habits of mind and behavior and long for a restoration of strong political authority and a state-controlled economy, others (especially younger people) are ready to experiment with democracy and private enterprise.[15]

Culture Shifts in Modernizing and Postindustrial Societies   Another shift in attitudes has occurred since the 1960s in many Western democracies. As Ronald Inglehart has shown, an increasing percentage of citizens in the United States and Western Europe in the 1960s and 1970s shared what he called "**post-materialist**" **values.** Instead of being motivated primarily by the need for financial security, as was the case with previous generations, a large number of citizens who came of voting age in these years, particularly those who had a secure economic background and higher education, tended to vote or engage in other forms of political behavior on the basis of broader concerns about the welfare of the community. The goals of urban renovation, environmental protection, and other community-wide considerations increasingly took precedence over personal wealth as a source of political behavior. Subsequent decades showed slight variations in these attitudes in particular countries.[16]

In a subsequent work, Inglehart undertook a sweeping investigation of the hypothesis that "economic, political and cultural change go together in coherent patterns that are changing the world in predictable ways." With an insightful look at the historical record and an analysis of recent survey data from forty-three countries, Inglehart found substantial evidence consistent with modernization theory and what he calls "postmodernization."

- **Modernization theory** contends that, as societies progress from largely agricultural economies to industrialization, the attitudes and values of the population shift as well. A preoccupation with survival under conditions of acute scarcity gives way to a quest for personal economic advancement. Maximizing one's material security and wealth becomes a top priority.

   As people pursue these economic goals, they seek greater political influence. Whereas pre-modern societies tend to have authoritarian regimes, the rising prosperity and education levels that accompany industrial modernization promote greater mass political participation. Industrialism and the value changes accompanying it thus promote democracy.

- **Postmodernization.** In the most economically advanced societies of the late twentieth century, industrial economies developed into postindustrial economies. The service sector—consisting of government, education, banking and finance, retail stores, and all sorts of consumer services—has replaced manufacturing as the main source of economic growth and employment. Personal and national incomes have risen appreciably. A well-funded welfare state now guarantees minimal living standards for the less fortunate as well as various other benefits for all (medical insurance, social security pensions, etc.).

   Under these "postmodern" conditions of rising prosperity, the main priorities of a growing portion of the population shift from maximizing material wealth to maximizing nonmaterial forms of personal well-being: a satisfying job, a clean environment, more leisure time, and other postmaterialist values. Politically, these values entail less reliance on the state and declining deference to authority. People want less government intervention in their lives; voters show greater independence at election time, loosening their traditional ties to the major political parties. Socially, people who embrace postmaterialist values also exhibit looser religious attachments and greater acceptance of women's rights, homosexuality, and abortion. Ironically, though their living standards are high, people with postmaterialist values have higher expectations and tend to display fairly high levels of dissatisfaction with their governments.

Inglehart's findings show that countries in today's world vary in ways that can be predicted by these modernization and postmodernization processes. The economically advanced democracies of North America and Western Europe show the highest levels of citizens with postmaterialist values. Poorer countries like Nigeria and India, where the struggle for survival is still a compelling necessity for millions of people, exhibit lower levels of postmaterialism and greater concerns for basic material security. The contrast between materialist and postmaterialist values is most strikingly evident in countries experiencing rapid economic change. In Japan and South Korea, where economic growth has soared astronomically in the past several decades, dramatic intergenerational differences are observable in a variety of attitudes. On the whole, young people are embracing postmaterialist values while their elders retain the materialist attitudes they adopted when they were young. The former communist countries of Russia and East-Central Europe have also undergone rapid economic change in recent years, though the hope of future improvements has often been accompanied by precipitate declines in living standards. People who have been materially damaged in these fluctuations tend to be more interested in material security than in postmaterial ideals.

Countries caught in the throes of a grave political and economic crisis may diverge even more widely from postmaterialism, retreating into what Inglehart calls an "authoritarian reflex." In largely premodern societies, this reflex may take the form of religious fundamentalism or "nativism," a traditional form of tribalism or nationalism. In more industrialized countries it can lead to a longing for powerful secular rulers along with outbursts of hypernationalism, as in Yugoslavia under Milosevic. In all these cases, Inglehart concludes, economic transformations, political change, and cultural attitudes interact in highly complex ways, displaying reciprocal patterns of causation.[17]

A Clash of Civilizations?   Samuel Huntington has advanced the hypothesis that the main source of conflict in the contemporary world is neither ideological nor economic but cultural in nature, centered in a "clash of civilizations." Defining a civilization as the broadest level of a person's identity, Huntington divides the world into seven civilizations: Western, Confucian, Japanese, Hindu, Slavic-Orthodox, Latin American, and African. Each one is rooted in a distinct blend of history, culture, and—most important—religion. With the disappearance of the ideological rivalries of the Cold War, the principal "fault lines" in world politics are drawn at the borders of these cultural communities. Though nation-states will endure and the processes of economic globalization will go forward, Huntington believes that

the values and political ideals of these disparate civilizations are sufficiently different as to complicate global cooperation and stimulate sharp antagonisms. Under these circumstances, he argues, the West must stick to its core democratic values but repudiate the idea that the defining features of Western civilization—Christianity, the rule of law, pluralistic democracy, individualism, and the separation of church and state—are universally applicable. "The belief that non-Western people should adopt Western values, institutions and cultures is, if taken seriously, immoral in its implications," he writes. Instead of foisting these values on the world or expecting economic and technological progress to create a single, Western-oriented global culture, Huntington urges the United States to concentrate on solidifying Western unity while encouraging international acceptance of cultural diversity and coexistence. Otherwise, he warns, "The next world war, if there is one, will be a war between civilizations."[18]

PSYCHOLOGICAL FACTORS: ARE PEOPLE RATIONAL?

Humans are rational beings, the Greek philosophers assured us. And yet the path of human history is strewn with evidence of humankind's irrationality: brutal wars and civil violence, political movements based on hatred and fear, bizarre examples of "popular delusions and the madness of crowds."[19] Even routine election campaigns in stable democracies are rarely devoid of emotional appeals, whether blatant or subtle, to people's passions, anxieties, or prejudices.

As students of human behavior, political scientists must be sensitive to psychological factors in political life. What people believe and how they behave in the realm of politics are invariably the result of how they *perceive* political reality. Indeed, perceptions are often more important than reality itself as a guide to behavior. And since perceptions are a product of the mind, they can be just as deeply influenced by irrational factors—emotions, illogic, paranoia, and other obstacles to rational thought—as by our highest faculties of reason and reflection. The work of Sigmund Freud (1856–1939), the founder of psychoanalysis, has sensitized us to the possibility that human actions can be the product of subconscious factors of which we are not immediately aware, such as sexual impulses or deeply buried childhood traumas. Moreover, even our most conscious analytical endeavors can be subject to reasoning errors of all sorts.

Anyone interested in politics should therefore pay close attention to the work of psychologists whose findings tell us something about the ways people behave in politics, whether as individuals or as groups. Among the classics in this field are several older works that sought to account for the horrors of Nazism. In *The Authoritarian Personality*, for example, a group of psychologists and political analysts probed the personality factors that inclined certain types of people to be particularly receptive to fascist or racist propaganda. Such variables as a rigid adherence to conventional values, a low tolerance of ambiguity, a reliance on superstition as opposed to scientific logic, and gullibility as opposed to independent critical judgment emerged as the leading characteristics of the "antidemocratic personality."[20] Erich Fromm's *Escape from Freedom* is another work of this kind.[21]

One analysis of human perceptions that has intriguing implications for political behavior is the **theory of cognitive dissonance.** Leon Festinger, a social psychologist, conducted experiments showing that many people, when faced with information that contradicts some deeply held opinion, preference, or bias, find ways to ignore or explain away the undesirable messages. Rather than altering their views in a rational fashion to take account of the facts before their eyes, they steadfastly cling to their cherished beliefs. They also go out of their way to avoid information they suspect will be "dissonant" with what they are used to believing. The mass public and political decision makers alike are prone to these misperceptions.[22]

Irrationality was a major theme of several early investigators of political psychology. Harold Lasswell, for example, argued that professional politicians sought political power primarily for irrational reasons. Power seekers, he maintained, pursued power to overcome low self-esteem brought on by physical handicaps, economic deprivation, or childhood difficulties such as unloving or excessively demanding parents.[23] Other scholars have also drawn attention to irrational elements in political life.[24]

Rational Choice Theory

In recent decades, a number of political scientists have been more interested in the concept of *rationality*. As we have seen in previous chapters, political scientists define **rationality** as *behavior that is calculated to maximize one's gains and minimize one's losses and risks.* In the past several decades they have elaborated a mode of political analysis known as **rational choice theory** (or *rational actor theory*). Rational choice theory in political science is mainly derived from economics. It stems from those economists who view human beings as motivated in their economic behavior primarily by material self-interest, in other words, by the desire to acquire money and other possessions aimed at enhancing their material well-being. In the jargon of economics, such individuals seek to "maximize their utilities": they seek to acquire as many materially useful goods as they can so as to come out with a net gain rather than a net loss.

When applied to politics, rational choice theory states that people tend to behave in political life essentially as follows:

- They are motivated by material self-interest, consciously seeking to maximize their gains and minimize their costs and risks.
- They know what their goals are, and they order their preferences in accordance with their priorities.
- They have fairly complete information about pertinent political realities as well as an ability to understand the options available to them and to calculate the likely consequences of alternative courses of action.
- They make conscious choices designed to bring about the maximum expected payoff; that is, they select the "best" available policy option or vote for the "best" candidate in accordance with their defined priorities and goals.

To what extent do these conceptions of rationality conform to reality?

Empirical studies provide lots of evidence showing that many voters, quite often the majority, are indeed motivated by pocketbook issues: they pull the voting lever for those candidates they believe are most likely to improve their material circumstances. But not all voters act this way.

Some vote for candidates who promise to clean up the environment or strengthen the nation's military power, even though they realize that such costly programs may end up *reducing* the voters' personal material welfare by raising their taxes or boosting the cost of living. Voters holding postmaterialist values or advocates of a strong defense will be more inclined to act on their perception of what is good for the local community or the country as a whole rather than on their personal economic self-interest. Of course, what is good for one's country is also good for oneself. Hence "self-interest" need not be defined solely in material terms; one can have a *self*-interest in a better community, however one may conceive of that goal.

Even voters who are primarily concerned with their own wallets may differ in their perceptions of how to maximize their material gains. Some may be interested in short-term gains, like immediate tax cuts or welfare benefits, even though such measures may worsen general and personal economic conditions in the long run. Other voters may be willing to forego short-term economic advantages in hopes that their sacrifices this year (such as higher taxes or lower welfare benefits) will improve the economy—and their own economic prospects—several years down the road. The rational choice model does not enable us to predict which of these two variants of material self-interest the voters will choose.

Similar considerations apply to politicians. Political figures driven by pure self-interest are more likely to be attracted by power than by riches, but power is not the same thing as material gain. Of course, one should never discount the possibility of enriching oneself through political corruption. Happily, there also exist politicians whose careers are motivated by high standards of public service, placing the public's interests ahead of their own.

In sum, material self-interest does motivate political behavior in many instances, but by no means all.[25]

Critics of rational actor theory have also questioned its second premise, namely, that people know what their goals are and pursue them in accordance with a fairly well thought-out order of priorities and preferences and a thorough knowledge of relevant facts. As we saw in chapter 11, voters tend to have precious little information about the candidates and issues they vote on. And as we saw in chapter 6, political leaders and bureaucrats charged with making important decisions are also frequently in the dark when selecting policy options. How, then, can people make rational choices in a state of ignorance?

Some scholars assert that they cannot; in their view, the rational choice model therefore collapses on its own unrealistic assumptions. But others have sought to rescue the model by modifying it. In their view, people do not need *full* information to make rational decisions. Voters and decision makers can find ways to make choices and decisions based on the limited information they possess. In this realm of *bounded rationality*, rationality is limited ("bounded") by the lack of information, but it does not disappear altogether.[26] In any event, rational choice theorists and their critics have stimulated a vigorous debate about the psychology of political behavior that has enlightened both theorists and practitioners alike.[27]

Game Theory

In an effort to understand the dynamics of how people make choices and decisions in political life, whether they are merely voters or high-powered officials, some political scientists employ an analytical technique called *game theory*. Game theory was initially devised in the 1940s by John von Neumann, a mathematician, and Oskar Morgenstern, an economist, in an effort to explain in abstract terms how business executives make strategic decisions in a competitive market economy.[28] Political scientists began exploring the implications of game theory for political behavior. Since the essence of politics is conflict, many political interactions, including competition between parties, ethnic groups, or rival countries, can be likened to competitive games.

Some games are called <u>**zero-sum games**</u>. These are games in which *one player's loss is the other player's gain in equal measure.* If I jump two of your checkers, your loss is –2 and my gain is +2. The sum equals zero. Real-life examples of zero-sum games would include situations in which an invading country grabs a piece of another country's territory; a political party attracts a specific number of another party's traditional voters; or a certain amount of money in the national budget is transferred from one program (military procurement) to another (aid to education). Zero-sum games usually reflect all-out conflict.

Other games take account of more complicated realities. So-called **mixed-sum** or **variable-sum games** are those in which *the sum of the players' gains and losses does not equal zero.* My loss, for example, may be greater than your gain. This would occur if my party loses a million voters, your party gains half of them, and the other half don't vote. When three or more players are involved, the relative spread of gains and losses can be mixed in all sorts of ways.

In addition, some theoretical games allow for the possibility of *cooperation* between competing players, an outcome that often occurs in real-life situations. If people are rational in the sense that they always act in their own self-interest, *is conflict more rational than cooperation?* Will people always choose to get the better of their opponents? Or can cooperation also be rational, even if one is cooperating with a competitor or enemy? One of the most widely studied games that tackles these questions is **Prisoner's Dilemma,** which is presented in the appendix to this chapter.

It is worth rounding out this discussion of psychological and cognitive influences on politics by pointing out that some scholars have probed the biological roots of social and political behavior. Perceptive observers like Edmund O. Wilson and Roger D. Masters have explored some of the extraordinary links that connect evolutionary processes with human social relationships and political organization.[29]

KEY TERMS
(Underlined in the text)

Political culture and subculture
Political socialization
Civic culture
Post-materialist values
Modernization theory
Postmodernization
Cognitive dissonance
Rational choice theory
Zero-sum game
Mixed-sum or variable-sum game

APPENDIX
Prisoner's Dilemma

Two partners who collaborated in an armed robbery are arrested. The police put them into separate cells. The prosecutor would like to convict them both, but there are no witnesses to the crime who can identify them. To get a conviction, the prosecutor needs the testimony of the robbers themselves. In separate conversations, she offers each prisoner the same deal: "If you squeal on your partner and say he's guilty, but your partner keeps silent, I'll set you free and give you a $25,000 reward; your partner will get fifty years in the slammer. But if he squeals on you and you keep silent, he goes free and gets the money, and you will get fifty years. If each of you accuses the other, I'll get two convictions, and in thanks, I'll see to it that each of you gets only ten years. If you both keep silent, I'll have to set you both free, but neither one of you will get any reward." If you are one of the prisoners, what is your "rational choice"?

Note the underlying premises of the game. First, whatever choice you make, the outcome will not be determined entirely by your decision. It will also be determined by what your partner does. Second, you cannot be certain in advance what your partner will do, and you cannot communicate with him. Third, your partner is just like you: a criminal, not Mother Teresa. Can you trust him? Can you figure out what *his* rational choice will be?

In order to visualize the various options before you and their potential consequences, it is useful to construct a *decision matrix* (figure 12.6). The matrix consists of four boxes that correspond to the four possible decision outcomes: (1) you both squeal; (2) you keep silent but your partner squeals; (3) you both keep silent; (4) you squeal but your partner keeps silent. Inside each box are two numbers. The numbers are purely arbitrary, but they represent the *relative value* to you and your partner of the possible consequences of your decisions. Since the best outcome for you (or your partner) would be to go free with the $25,000 reward, let's assign that outcome a value of +100. The worst possible outcome for you (or your partner) would be to get a fifty-year prison sentence; let's assign this worst outcome a value of –100. The other possible outcomes lie in between these extremes. Let's say that

FIGURE 12.6

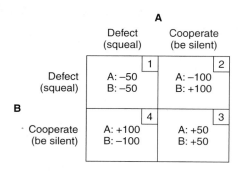

a ten-year sentence is worth –50, and going free without the reward is worth +50.

You are Prisoner A and your partner is Prisoner B. To translate the decision options just mentioned into the jargon of game theory, we'll call squealing on one's partner "defection" and keeping silent "cooperation."

In Box 1, you and your partner both squeal on each other (i.e., you both "defect"). Thus you both end up with ten-year prison terms (–50 each). In Box 2, your partner squeals (defects) and you keep silent (cooperate). As a result, your partner gets the maximum payoff (+100) and you end up with the maximum punishment (–100). (To put it another way, B gets the better of the two possible positive outcomes and you get the worse of the two possible negative outcomes.) In Box 3, you both keep silent. You are both set free, but you get no reward. Each of you ends up with +50. Finally, Box 4 is the reverse image of Box 2: you defect by squealing, while your partner cooperates by keeping silent. Consequently, you get +100 and your partner gets –100.

The prosecutor has made her offers, and you and your partner are now deliberating what to do. From the prosecutor's standpoint, does this game have a "solution" that she can predict? Is there a single choice whose potential consequences offer the highest possible gain at the lowest possible risk?

Consider your options. If you choose to defect (i.e., squeal), depending on what Prisoner B does, you will end up with either –50 (Box 1) or +100 (Box 4). If you choose to cooperate (keep silent), you will end up with either –100 (Box 2) or +50 (Box 3). Most game theoreticians, playing the pros-

ecutor's role, would say that the rational choice would be for you to defect. Defection offers the highest possible gain (+100) and the less costly of the two negative outcomes (–50). By contrast, cooperation offers the lower of the two positive outcomes (+50) and the more costly of the negative outcomes (–100). If you are rational, therefore, you will choose to defect. So will your partner. From the prosecutor's vantage point, the rational "solution" to the game is Box 1. She can reasonably predict that you and your partner will both squeal.

Viewed in political terms, the chief implication of Prisoner's Dilemma is that *it is more rational for each individual to be uncooperative than cooperative.* If this is indeed the case, it would follow that political conflict is inevitable and cooperation virtually impossible. This conclusion appears to hold even if *individual* rationality leaves both players *worse* off than they would be if they had cooperated. Hence the dilemma.

How valid are these conclusions? As game theorists themselves are aware, Prisoner's Dilemma is likely to lead to the solution of mutual defection only if it is played once or a few times. But real-life political interactions rarely involve a single, one-shot decision. Remember, politics is a *process:* it usually involves an ongoing series of interactions, decisions, reconsiderations, and new decisions. Moreover, the two prisoners in the game were not allowed to communicate with each other. But in actual practice, people usually do communicate; even enemies negotiate. Hence it is at least possible that the rational tendency to be uncooperative, as reflected in Prisoner's Dilemma, can be overcome through repeated interactions and communications among individuals, groups, or countries in conflict. Repeated plays of the game are called *iterations*.

When Prisoner's Dilemma is played out in a laboratory setting, it frequently turns out that players A and B start out by defecting, but they increasingly cooperate the more they play the game. They learn that when *both* defect, neither one gets +100; both get jail time (–50). With more iterations they learn to trust each other and come to realize that, if both cooperate, both will get out of prison (+50). The result of *mutual cooperation,* therefore, is a positive payoff for each player; the result of mutual defection is a cost for each one. Still, both players are always aware that cooperation carries huge risks: if you cooperate and your partner suddenly defects, you could end up with the worst possible outcome.

The main point of Prisoner's Dilemma as applied to politics is simply this: it graphically demonstrates why cooperation is so difficult to achieve by showing how conflict can be a *rational choice*. It also demonstrates that, over time, people can *learn* that the benefits of cooperation can outweigh the risks of continued conflict. Many theorists regard Prisoner's Dilemma as an accurate representation of real-life conflictual situations. It has been used to understand the underyling dynamics of intractable ethnic and religious conflicts, the Cold War, the Arab-Israeli dispute, arms races, and a variety of other political confrontations. It has also found applications in business, psychology, and biology.[30]

NOTES

1. In 1964, 22 percent of Americans said they distrusted the federal government. This figure climbed to 62 percent in 1976 and 73 percent in 1980 before dropping to 58 percent in 1988. Cited in Michael M. Gant and Norman R. Luttbeg, *American Electoral Behavior* (Itasca, Ill.: F. E. Peacock, 1991), 144. A poll taken in 1995 revealed that 45 percent of Americans were "satisfied but not enthusiastic" about the way their federal government works, and 41 percent were "dissatisfied but not angry." Only 3 percent were "enthusiastic" and 9 percent were "angry." See *Washington Post*, May 18, 1995, p. A12.

2. Donald J. Devine, *The Political Culture of the United States* (Boston: Little, Brown, 1972); Herbert McClosky and John Zaller, *The American Ethos: Public Attitudes Toward Capitalism and Democracy* (Cambridge: Cambridge University Press, 1985); Robert N. Bellah et al., *Habits of the Heart: Individualism and Commitment in American Life* (Berkeley: University of California Press, 1985); Gary Wills, *A Necessary Evil: A History of American Distrust of Government* (New York: Simon and Schuster, 1999). See also the attitudinal orientations of various clusters of Americans in the survey conducted by the Kaiser Family Foundation, *The Washington Post*, and Harvard University entitled *Why Don't Americans Trust the Government?* (Menlo Park, Calif.: Henry J. Kaiser Family Fund, 1996). On the intellectual history of contending political cultures in the United States, see Richard J. Ellis, *American Political Cultures* (Oxford: Oxford University Press, 1993).

3. For a survey of different definitions of political culture, see John R. Gibbins, "Contemporary Political Culture: An Introduction," in *Contemporary Political Culture*, ed. John R. Gibbins (London: Sage, 1989), 1–30.

4. Herbert J. Gans, *Middle American Individualism* (New York: Free Press, 1988).

5. Some of these views are discussed in Lee Sigelman and Susan Welch, *Black Americans' Views of Racial Inequality* (Cambridge: Cambridge University Press, 1991).

6. E. G. Krug, K. E. Powell, and L. L. Dahlberg, "Firearm-Related Deaths in the United States and 35 Other High- and Upper-Middle-Income Countries," *International Journal of Epidemiology* 27, no. 3 (April 1998): 214–21. On the difficulties of comparing homicide statistics cross-nationally, see William J. Chambliss, *Power, Politics, and Crime* (Boulder, Colo.: Westview, 1999), 32–62.

7. Alexis de Tocqueville, *Democracy in America,* ed. J. P. Mayer, trans. George Lawrence (New York: Harper and Row, 1966), 165, 274, 287–89, 291, 297–301, 309.

8. John Adams remarked that "the source of the revolution" against England was the "systematical dissolution of the true family authority." See Gordon S. Wood, *The Radicalism of the American Revolution* (New York: Alfred A. Knopf, 1991), 145–68.

9. Max Weber, *The Protestant Ethic and the Spirit of Capitalism,* trans. Talcott Parsons (London: Routledge, 1992). This work was first published in 1904 and 1905. See also H. H. Gerth and C. Wright Mills, eds., *From Max Weber: Essays in Sociology* (New York: Oxford: 1946).

10. Gabriel Almond and Sidney Verba, *The Civic Culture* (Boston: Little, Brown, 1963).

11. Gabriel A. Almond and Sidney Verba, eds., *The Civic Culture Revisited* (Boston: Little, Brown, 1980).

12. Ronald Inglehart, *Culture Shift in Advanced Industrial Society* (Princeton, N.J.: Princeton University Press, 1990) and *Modernization and Postmodernization* (Princeton, N.J.: Princeton University Press, 1997). The quotes are on page 215 in the latter work.

13. Robert D. Putnam, *Making Democracy Work: Civic Traditions in Modern Italy* (Princeton, N.J.: Princeton University Press, 1993). Putnam's findings corroborated the results of an earlier work on Italian political culture by Edward C. Banfield, who found that high levels of distrust among families undermined the effectiveness of local government. See *The Moral Basis of a Backward Society* (New York: Free Press, 1967).

14. Kendall L. Baker, Russell J. Dalton, and Kai Hildebrandt, *Germany Transformed: Political Culture and the New Politics* (Cambridge, Mass.: Harvard University Press, 1981), 24; David Conradt, "Changing German

Political Culture," in Almond and Verba, *The Civic Culture Revisited*, 212–72.

15. The question of cultural change is also addressed in Cynthia McClintock, *Peasant Cooperatives and Political Change in Peru* (Princeton, N.J.: Princeton University Press, 1991).

16. Ronald Inglehart, *The Silent Revolution: Changing Values and Political Styles Among Western Publics* (Princeton, N.J.: Princeton University Press, 1977).

17. Inglehart, *Modernization and Postmodernization*.

18. Samuel P. Huntington, *The Clash of Civilizations and the Remaking of the World Order* (New York: Simon and Schuster, 1996). Huntington's prior article in *Foreign Affairs* 72, no. 3 (summer 1993): 22–49, is published along with rejoinders in *The Clash of Civilizations? The Debate* (New York: W. W. Norton, 1993). See also "The West Unique, Not Universal," *Foreign Affairs* 75, no. 6 (November–December 1996): 28–46.

19. Charles Mackay, *Extraordinary Popular Delusions and the Madness of Crowds* (Boston: L. C. Page, 1932).

20. T. W. Adorno et al., *The Authoritarian Personality* (New York: Harper and Bros., 1950). See also Bob Altemeyer, *Right-Wing Authoritarianism* (Winnepeg: University of Manitoba Press, 1981) and *Enemies of Freedom* (San Francisco: Jossey-Bass, 1988). For a review of subsequent studies on this topic, see Jos D. Meloen, "A Critical Analysis of Forty Years of Authoritarianism Research: Did Theory Testing Suffer from Cold War Attitudes?" in *Nationalism, Ethnicity, and Identity*, ed. Russell F. Farnen (New Brunswick, N.J.: Transaction, 1994), 127–65.

21. Fromm argued that industrial capitalism and population growth in nineteenth- and twentieth-century Europe produced a society of lonely and insecure individuals, overwhelmed by the impersonal forces of factory discipline, overcrowded cities, giant corporations, and distant government officials. The freedoms of democracy and the market economy produced an inner sense of dependence and anxiety. To escape these psychological burdens, millions of Germans and Italians turned to fascism in hopes of gaining greater security and an attachment to a larger cause—the nation. In democracies, Fromm argued, the same impersonal forces drive people into the false sense of security offered by mass conformity. See *Escape from Freedom* (New York: Holt, Rinehart, and Winston, 1941).

22. Leon Festinger, *A Theory of Cognitive Dissonance* (Stanford, Calif.: Stanford University Press, 1957); Robert Jervis, *Perception and Misperception in International Politics* (Princeton, N.J.: Princeton University Press, 1976).

23. Harold D. Lasswell, *Power and Personality* (New York: W. W. Norton, 1948) and *Psychopathology and Politics* (New York: Viking, 1960).

24. Neil J. Kressel, *Political Psychology: Classic and Contemporary Readings* (New York: Paragon House, 1993); Fred I. Greenstein, *Personality and Politics* (Chicago: Markham, 1969); Carol Barner-Barry and Robert Rosenwein, *Psychological Perspectives on Politics* (Englewood Cliffs, N.J.: Prentice Hall, 1985); Richard Hofstadter, *The Paranoid Style in American Politics* (New York: Knopf, 1965); and Robert S. Robins and Jerrold M. Post, *Political Paranoia* (New Haven, Conn.: Yale University Press, 1997).

25. For a review of these issues, see Kristin R. Monroe, ed., *The Economic Approach to Politics: A Critical Reassessment of the Theory of Rational Action* (New York: HarperCollins, 1991).

26. Herbert A. Simon, *Administrative Behavior* (New York: Free Press, 1976), originally published in 1947; and *Models of Bounded Rationality,* 2 vols. (Cambridge, Mass.: MIT Press, 1982).

27. Another early source of rational actor theory is James A. Buchanan and Gordon Tullock, *The Calculus of Consent* (Ann Arbor: University of Michigan Press, 1962). See also George Tsebelis, *Nested Games: Rational Choice in Comparative Politics* (Berkeley: University of California Press, 1990); William H. Riker and Peter C. Ordeshook, *An Introduction to Positive Political Theory* (Englewood Cliffs, N.J.: Prentice Hall, 1973). For criticisms of rational actor theories, see Monroe, *Economic Approach to Politics;* and Donald P. Green and Ian Shapiro, *Pathologies of Rational Choice Theory* (New Haven, Conn.: Yale University Press, 1994).

28. John von Neumann and Oskar Morgenstern, *Theory of Games and Economic Behavior* (New York: Wiley, 1944).

29. See Edward O. Wilson, *Sociobiology* (Cambridge, Mass.: Harvard University Press, 1975), and *On Human Nature* (Cambridge, Mass.: Harvard University Press, 1978). See also Roger D. Masters, *The Nature of Politics* (New Haven, Conn.: Yale University Press, 1989).

30. Jon Elster has commented that politics is about "ways of transcending the Prisoner's Dilemma." See "Some Conceptual Problems in Political Theory," in *Power and Political Theory*, ed. Brian Barry (London: Wiley, 1976), 249. For elaborations on Prisoner's Dilemma, see Anatol Rapoport and Albert M. Chammah, *Prisoner's Dilemma* (Ann Arbor: University of Michigan Press, 1965); and Robert Axelrod, *The Evolution of Cooperation* (New York: Basic Books, 1984).

CHAPTER 13

IDEOLOGY

In virtually every country in the world, political ideas have played a vital role in shaping the kinds of government that have evolved over time as well as the ways people behave in political life. Perhaps because of their ubiquity in such a wide variety of settings, political ideas and the terminology used to express them can be a source of considerable confusion. As we've pointed out before, such terms as "liberalism," "conservatism," "social-ism," and the like can take on different meanings, depending on the historical or country-specific context in which they are used. One of the central purposes of this chapter is to clear up some of this conceptual ambiguity.

To begin with, the term "ideology" itself is used in different ways. In its most informal, everyday usage, ideology frequently means little more than a person's general political orientation. When people say, "Ideologically, I'm a Republican" or "Feminism is my ideology," they often mean simply that they identify with the Republican party or feminist causes in a general way, without neces-sarily subscribing to a carefully elaborated theory of politics or a point-by-point programmatic guide to political action. This generic meaning of the word is the one that tends to be used in ordinary political discourse by most average citizens. But politicians, activists, political scientists, and others who take a more avid interest in politics usually have a more formal understanding of ideology. In its formal definition, **ideology** *is a coherent set of ideas that typically includes*

1. *a theory about political relationships and the role of the state*
2. *a notion of what constitutes political legiti-macy and the highest political values*
3. *an action program indicating the goals, ideals, policies, and tactics to be pursued by the state, political elites, and the masses*

This second definition involves a more systemati-cally thought-out ideological orientation than the first definition does.

Although ideologies are created by sophisti-cated thinkers and are grasped in their entirely by very few people, they can exert a profound impact on mass political behavior. Political elites are often quite successful at attracting large followings by getting a few key points of their ideologies across to the masses. Most people living in established democracies have not read the works of John Locke or James Madison, but they have learned in the course of their political socialization that democracy entails the right to vote and various other rights and freedoms. Average Muslims are not scholars of the Koran and may have little or no understanding of the complicated doctrinal feuds that have marked their religion's history. Still, they may be swayed by Islamic clerics to adopt any of a variety of political attitudes ranging from extreme hostility to the non-Islamic world to considerably more tolerant positions.

Throughout history there have been relatively few political orientations sufficiently coherent to be regarded as ideologies. Most flourished in the twentieth century, which is often called "the century of ideologies." In this chapter we'll focus on four of them: **liberalism, socialism, fascism,** and **Islam.** The sharp differences among these ideological orientations have fueled some of the most bitter conflicts in human history. People have fought and died over ideological beliefs by the tens of millions.

All four ideologies have variants. Sometimes these variations are very similar to one another. Liberals and conservatives in the contemporary United States, for example, are in basic agreement on the Constitution and on the nature of the economy as a mixture of private enterprise and state intervention. But in other cases the diverse tendencies within an ideology can be so disparate as to constitute distinctive ideologies in their own right. At times these internal variants have sparked intense conflict between their adherents, resulting in prolonged debates and in some cases bloody feuds over the ideology's "correct" interpretation. The socialist tradition, for example, produced two fundamentally different strains: Soviet-style communism and Western-oriented social democracy. Islam has produced several competing doctrinal and political orientations.

Any attempt to understand comparative politics in the contemporary world must explore the ideological sources of political life. We must also consider the implications of ideology for the immediate future. Some scholars assert that the intense ideological conflicts of the twentieth century are dying out. Have we reached the "end of ideology"? We'll examine this hypothesis at the end of the chapter.

LIBERALISM

In today's world, **liberalism** *essentially means democracy.* Because this book devotes three full chapters to democracy, we do not need to devote many pages here to a detailed discussion of liberal ideology. It is nevertheless useful at this point to clarify the diverse shadings of meaning that the term "liberalism" has acquired over the course of its historical evolution.

In its oldest and broadest definition, **liberalism** *refers to a system of government that guarantees liberty.* This was the original meaning of the term as it emerged in the late seventeenth and early eighteenth centuries in Great Britain and as it developed over the course of the eighteenth, nineteenth, and early twentieth centuries, particularly in Britain, America, and France. In its earliest manifestation, liberalism posed a direct challenge to government by absolute monarchs and aristocracies, expressing the basic idea that the power of the state should be limited and that certain freedoms should be granted to the people by law. From the outset, the essence of liberalism was its opposition to tyrannical state power. It regarded the citizenry, not God, as the source of legitimacy.

For its earliest advocates, like Locke, Madison, and Thomas Jefferson, liberalism did not imply mass democracy based on universal suffrage. The early liberals espoused a highly elitist concept of liberalism based on the view that only a small segment of the people, consisting predominantly of wealthy, educated, white males, was sufficiently enlightened to govern society and ensure the implementation of basic civil rights and liberties. They tended to favor a limited suffrage, with the right to vote confined primarily to men of property.

For many early liberals, moreover, the concept of liberalism was two-dimensional: it had both political and economic components. Whereas political liberalism emphasized the concept of government by consent of the governed, economic liberalism stressed the notion that the state should strictly limit its role in the economy, leaving the bulk of the nation's economic activities in the hands of private individuals and companies. Early economic liberalism championed a *free-enterprise* economy. It sought to dismantle the vast edifice of taxes, state monopolies, feudal estates, and other forms of governmental or aristocratic domination of economic life that were common under most monarchical regimes. In their place it favored freely operating businesses and commercial farming.

As liberal ideas evolved over the course of the nineteenth and twentieth centuries, the notion that a liberal political order requires mass democratic participation gradually asserted itself. Universal adult suffrage finally became a reality during and after World War I as females gained the right to vote in Britain (1918), Germany (1919), and the United States (1920). A host of countries adopted universal voting rights after World War II. As a consequence, liberalism as a political ideology today is synonymous with modern democracy.

The concept of economic liberalism also changed over time, especially during the second half of the twentieth century. Whereas early conceptualizers of economic liberalism advocated only the barest minimum of government involvement in the economy, since World War II most proponents of private enterprise have accepted the view that governments should play a significant role in national economic life. Instead of advocating a completely free-enterprise economic system, they accept a *partially* free-enterprise system. Today's economic liberals acknowledge that governments must raise taxes, regulate banks and stock markets, promote economic growth, and provide various social welfare measures for the population such as education, unemployment insurance, and pensions. While many of them may wish to keep the government's economic activity as limited as possible, most economic liberals today accept a far greater degree of government interference in the economy than their counterparts would have permitted in earlier eras.

Hence we can make a general distinction among economic liberals between *classical liberals,* who favored virtually no governmental intervention in the economy, and *neo-classical liberals,* who favor private enterprise but admit that governments need to play a major role in national economic life. In today's world, classical liberals are a vanished breed.

Liberalism and Conservatism in the United States

The interacting concepts of political and economic liberalism resulted in several different strands of liberalism in the contemporary world. In the United States, for example, the term "liberalism" as used in everyday parlance has a narrower, more specific meaning than the generic ones just described.[1] Lib-

President Franklin D. Roosevelt

eralism in the United States is a variant of the liberal tradition that can be called *social-welfare liberalism.* **Social-welfare liberalism** *means active government intervention in the economy and society for the purpose of promoting economic growth, community welfare, and social justice.* With its stress on government activism, this conception of liberalism took shape in Franklin D. Roosevelt's New Deal. Assuming office in 1933 at a time when American political traditions precluded massive governmental interference in the private sector, Roosevelt boldly broke precedent and launched sweeping measures to combat the Great Depression. In the process, proponents of federal government activism in the United States became known as "liberals" mainly because they favored a liberal (i.e., permissive) interpretation of the Constitution's injunction to "promote the general welfare."

As a general rule, American social-welfare liberals support private enterprise as the basis of the national economy. They are not socialists, because they do not favor abolishing private enterprise or drastically limiting its scope in favor of a predominantly state-controlled economic system. However, most social-welfare liberals in the United States would favor government intervention in the private economy in order to promote various social goals. Such measures would include taxing wealthier citizens in order to raise funds for anti-poverty programs or general welfare purposes, such as public education; imposing environmental regulations on private businesses; and using the powers of the law to combat racial or gender discrimination in the private sector. Historically, American liberals have tended to side with the labor movement in labor-management disputes. They have generally made their home in the Democratic Party.

Conservatism in the United States is the heir to the classical liberal tradition of minimal government interference in the economy. During the New Deal decades, many rock-ribbed conservatives viewed Roosevelt's interventions in the economy as heresy. As time went on, and many New Deal programs such as Social Security and the regulation of the private banking system proved their popularity, most conservatives came to accept the notion that the government must play an expanded role in the modern American economy. Nowadays the differences between liberals and conservatives in the United States are considerably less acute than in the 1930s. With respect to economic issues, they tend to be mainly differences of degree rather than differences of principle. Contemporary conservatives (or *neo-conservatives*) do not reject government interventionism in principle but tend toward skepticism about its effectiveness in dealing with poverty or ameliorating other social conditions. As a general tendency, conservatives prefer more limited government activism, less government spending, and greater freedom for the private sector. They tend to side with the business sector in labor-management relations. In recent decades, modern liberals and conservatives have also differed on such value issues as abortion and school prayer, with "cultural conservatives," often connected with the Christian right, more inclined to take pro-life and pro-prayer positions than liberals are. Conservatives have generally gravitated to the Republican Party.

Even these differences can be blurred depending upon the individual. Some contemporary American liberals take conservative positions on particular issues (favoring a balanced budget or discouraging abortion, for example) while some conservatives may adopt liberal points of view on various issues (for example, by opposing discrimination or favoring legal abortion). There are also wide areas of liberal-conservative agreement on various foreign policy issues. These converging viewpoints help moderate political conflict in the United States.

Liberalism and Conservatism Around the World

The term "liberalism" also has two meanings in many countries outside the United States, roughly similar to those employed in the American context. Throughout much of the world, the first meaning of liberalism is its traditional one: as a generic political orientation, liberalism favors political and economic freedom as opposed to authoritarianism and socialism. In countries where democracy is just emerging, as in Russia, or where it is not permitted to exist, liberalism is frequently understood in this fundamental sense.

Its second connotation roughly approximates the more specific meaning that the term liberalism has acquired in twentieth-century U.S. politics. Like social-welfare liberals in the United States, many politicians and political parties that label themselves "liberal" in Canada, Western Europe, and elsewhere combine staunch support for private enterprise with attitudes favoring a certain amount of state intervention to improve general living conditions. European liberals, for example, constitute a centrist movement positioned in between the more conservative parties on their right and the working-class-oriented social democratic parties on their immediate left.

Conservatism also assumes different meanings in different contexts. In its most literal meaning, conservatism means resistance to any kind of change unless absolutely necessary. In the famous words of Sir Edward Grey, "When it is not necessary to change, it is necessary not to change." If change must come in order to save the country or preserve certain essential values, then it should be gradual rather than abrupt or revolutionary. Accordingly, "conservative" can apply in literal terms to anyone who wishes to conserve things as they are, whether the prevailing system of government is a monarchy, a communist dictatorship, or a flourishing democracy. For **Edmund Burke** (1729–1797), considered the founding father of British conservative thought, the constitutional order of monarchy, Parliament, and church had

Edmund Burke

proven its legitimacy in Britain over the course of centuries. The accumulated wisdom of tradition, in his view, should not be thrown over in a headlong rush to revolution.[2]

In democratic countries, today's conservatives favor democracy. Let's label conservatives in modern democracies *democratic* (or *pro-democracy*) *conservatives.* Within this group we can observe both widely shared similarities and salient differences. Political leaders like former President Ronald Reagan and Senator Phil Gramm in the United States, former Prime Ministers Margaret Thatcher and John Major in Britain, former Chancellor Helmut Kohl of Germany, President Jacques Chirac of France, and Prime Minister Yoshiro Mori of Japan are all regarded as democratic conservatives. As a general rule, all of them attach a high priority to promoting private enterprise. European and Japanese conservatives, however, tend to favor a more interventionist state than is typically the case with American conservatives. The notion that "the government that governs least, governs best" is a quintessentially American notion; conservatives in other democracies around the world traditionally place a higher value on a strong state. Even so, individual conservative politicians will differ in applying these general principles.

Some democracies have anti-democratic tendencies that are labeled "ultra-conservative" or "reactionary." Their proponents typically espouse authoritarian forms of government (such as monarchy or fascism), or they are avowedly racist or chauvinistic. Unlike the pro-democracy conservatism we have just described, these orientations cannot be regarded as part of the liberal democratic tradition.

Christian Democracy

In a number of European and Latin American countries, Christian Democracy constitutes a distinctive branch of the liberal-democratic tradition. Its origins lie in the political orientations of the Roman Catholic Church. Although the Church hierarchy was initially hostile to democracy, in the late nineteenth and early twentieth centuries it became increasingly alarmed at the spread of anti-religious and materialistic political doctrines throughout Europe, particularly in countries with a sizable Catholic population. Church authorities were especially disturbed at the rise of socialist and communist parties, with their outspokenly anti-religious views. At the same time, Church leaders were equally distraught at the materialistic excesses of modern capitalism. More generally, the Vatican hierarchy feared that intense class conflict between the poor, the rich, and the middle class would rip apart the fabric of society, making it vulnerable to the appeals of atheistic ideologies. It would also divide Catholics throughout Europe into mutually antagonistic social classes.

To prevent these occurrences, the Church felt it advisable to promote the establishment of Catholic-oriented political parties wherever possible, especially in Italy. After World War II most Christian Democratic parties in Europe and Latin America no longer had formal ties with the Church, but their roots in Catholic doctrine continue to color some of their political positions on issues like abortion or divorce. Some Christian Democratic parties, like Germany's, combine Catholics and Protestants.[3]

SOCIALISM

The origins of twentieth-century socialist movements are to be found in nineteenth-century Europe. Socialism emerged as a reaction to the excesses of the industrial revolution and free enterprise. Over the course of the nineteenth century, the spread of manufacturing in Britain, France, Germany, and several other countries rapidly blighted the cities and countryside with grimy factories and squalid slums. Men, women, and children toiled long hours for meager wages. For much of the century, governments did virtually nothing to regulate working hours, safety standards, or child labor. Business owners were free to deal with their work force as they wished. Health care and unemployment insurance either did not exist at all or were grossly inadequate. The vast majority of the working class, lacking basic educational opportunities, faced a desperate future with scant hope of improving their lot. Peasants who owned little or no land of their own labored under similarly arduous circumstances for their landlords.

These conditions spawned several variants of socialist ideology. In the first half of the nineteenth century a number of socialist thinkers devised elaborate plans for replacing the free-enterprise system (capitalism) with an entirely different economic system in which the workers, or the people as a whole, would collectively own the factories, farms, mines, and other productive enterprises. Common ownership of the economy (or "communism") would thus replace private ownership. While the schemes proposed by these imaginative thinkers differed in detail, they agreed on one essential point: capitalism was an exploitative and unstable economic system that had to be replaced by a more humane society based on the values of equality and community. These thinkers came to be known as *utopian socialists,* a term that derived from Sir Thomas Moore's design for an ideal society in his book, *Utopia,* published in 1516. Efforts to establish ideal socialist communities largely failed in Europe, however, and in some cases their adherents journeyed to the United States, creating utopian societies in Texas, Indiana, New Jersey, and other states. Most of these experiments also proved short-lived.[4]

A more enduring approach to socialism was elaborated by **Karl Marx** (1818–1883). Marx was significantly influenced by the utopian socialists, but in the course of his long career as an ideologist he developed a far more complicated system of thought that incorporated elements of philosophy, history, economics, sociology, and political theory. Marx turned out to be the principal intellectual source of twentieth-century socialism. Though his complex ideas were interpreted in different ways by his contemporaries and subsequent generations, Marx himself shared with the utopian socialists the basic notion that capitalism was inherently flawed and had to be replaced by common ownership of the economy by the working masses.

In its original nineteenth-century conception, therefore, <u>socialism</u> was understood as *a political and economic system in which private enterprise (capitalism) is abolished and replaced by some form of common ownership of factories, farms, and other productive enterprises.* Most nineteenth-century theorists, including Marx, made no sharp distinction between "socialism" and "communism" and used these words interchangeably.

Marxism

Summarizing Marx's thought is no easy task. The following brief sections convey some of its essential points without underestimating its complexity, ambiguity, and internal inconsistencies.

History Has Direction   Marx was born in Trier, Germany. His father's family name was originally Levi, and both of Karl's grandfathers were rabbis. Karl's father, a freethinker, abandoned Judaism, changed the family name, and saw to it that his children were baptized Christian. Young Karl became an atheist at an early age, however, eventu-

Karl Marx

ally denouncing religion itself as "the opiate of the masses."[5] After spending a year studying law at Bonn University in 1835–36, Marx moved to Berlin and began reading philosophy in earnest. He quickly became attracted to the ideas of one of the most influential figures in modern philosophy, Georg Wilhelm Friedrich **Hegel** (1770–1831). Marx was particularly intrigued by Hegel's philosophy of history.

Hegel maintained that human history has an identifiable direction and purpose. He argued that the long-term progression of history moves in accordance with a process he called the *dialectic*. For Hegel, the dialectic meant that history advances through recurring clashes between opposing forces. Conflicting religious beliefs, philosophical ideas, forms of government and society, modes of artistic expression: over thousands of years, these and other elements of the human drama were always and everywhere in contention. The progress of humanity from one historical epoch to the next thus always involves conflict. Hegel termed these ongoing conflicts "contradictions."

Hegel further believed that these contradictions arose because virtually everything creates its own opposite. Just as intense joy produces tears, and masters "create" slaves, every development in humankind's historical evolution—ideas, institutions, technologies, and so on—produces contrary developments. "Contradiction is the root and movement of all life," he wrote, noting that life from its very inception contains the germ of death. To clarify these notions, Hegel's followers labeled the predominant features of any given moment of history as the *thesis.* These predominating beliefs, political institutions, art forms, and the like produce contrary tendencies, called the *antithesis.* Over time the clash between thesis and antithesis produces a *synthesis,* which involves a mixture of some parts of the thesis and some parts of the antithesis. Every successive stage of history contains bits and pieces of the past while at the same time constituting something new. And each synthesis becomes a new thesis that produces a new antithesis, leading to a new synthesis, and so on. In Hegel's terminology, some things are "canceled" while other things are "preserved"; in the process, humanity is "lifted up" to progressively higher stages of historical development. Figure 13.1 illustrates this dialectical movement of history.

Hegel firmly believed that humanity would eventually reach a final synthesis, a state of perfection beyond which there would be no more conflicts. While he was vague about the details, he implied that humankind was close to reaching this final stage of its development in the very time and place in which he lived, namely, Prussia in the early nineteenth century. At that time, Prussia was a predominantly Protestant country governed by a monarchy; it had neither democracy nor socialism. Furthermore, Hegel believed that this strife-torn but inexorable path of the dialectic toward human perfection was guided to its ultimate destination by God.

As a student barely out of his teens, Marx was captivated by Hegel's vision of the dialectical process of history. But as an atheist, Marx could not accept Hegel's assumption that God presided over the dialectical process. Hegel was a philosophical *idealist* in the sense that he believed in

FIGURE 13.1 Hegel's Dialectical Conception of History

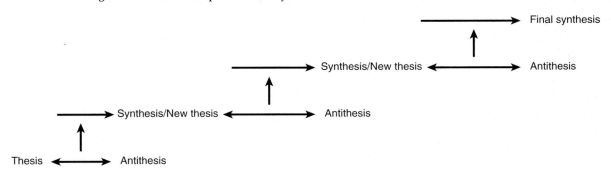

spiritual, or "ideal," forces like the deity. But Marx was a philosophical *materialist* who rejected spiritual essences. For materialists, human beings and the ideas they create are purely material substances. Marx found support for his materialistic inclinations in the writings of another German philosopher, Ludwig Feuerbach (1804–1872), who summed up his materialist outlook in the clipped phrase, *"Der Mensch ist was er isst"* ("Man is what he eats").

By the time Marx finished his doctoral dissertation at the age of twenty-three, he had devised his own philosophy of history known as *dialectical materialism*. It was a combination of Hegel's concept of the dialectical progression of history with the materialistic notion that purely material forces, not God, control this dialectical process. But what were these material forces?

Economics and Class Conflict as the Motor Forces of History   Although Marx was steeped in philosophy, he was less interested in sublime abstractions than in social realities. "The philosophers have only *interpreted* the world, in various ways," he wrote. "The point, however, is to *change* it." Pledging himself to a "ruthless criticism of everything existing," Marx moved to Paris and began his first major treatise on political economy in 1844.[6] In these early manuscripts Marx concluded that it was *economic* factors that constituted the primary material sources of human action. Private property, in particular, stood out as a principal cause of *alienation,* which Marx described as "the self-estrangement of man from himself." He reasoned that as long as there is private ownership of productive enterprises, the workers are engaged in producing objects that do not belong to them. Their employers sell these commodities and pocket the profits, remunerating the workers with wages barely sufficient to keep them alive. The workers are therefore "alienated" from the very products of their labor. The only way out of this inhuman predicament, Marx announced, was communism.

Over the next several years Marx was to refine his central notion that the principal motive forces in society and politics were economic in nature. He was joined in this endeavor by **Friedrich Engels** (1820–1895). The son of a wealthy German indus-

trialist, Engels spurned the family business and became a socialist in his youth.[7] The two became lifelong collaborators, though Marx was the creative thinker while Engels contented himself with popularizing his friend's more abstruse ideas. One of their most famous tracts was the Communist *Manifesto,* written in 1847 at the request of a group of German communists and published the following year. In this and subsequent works, Marx developed two critical ideas that defined what dialectical materialism meant in practice.

The first of these ideas was the notion that *economic relations condition everything else that happens in human affairs.* All economies, Marx asserted, are based on certain material "means of production," which include factories, land, technology, and most important, the human labor force. All economies also have distinctive "relations of production," which are the social relationships that exist among individuals and groups involved in the production process. Under conditions of slavery, the relations of production centered on the relationship between masters and slaves. In nineteenth-century industrial capitalism, the relations of production centered on the interactions between private employers and the work force. The means of production and the relations of production together form what Marx called the *base* of society.

This economic base, in Marx's theory, affects virtually every other facet of human existence, including the type of government a country has and the predominant themes of its art and literature as well as its prevailing beliefs and social conventions. Taken together, these social realities constitute what Marx called the *superstructure* of society. For Marx, the economic base determines, or at the very least conditions, the superstructure. To put it more narrowly, economics determines, or at least significantly influences, politics. In essence, whoever controls a nation's economy also controls its political system, including all state institutions as well as the prevailing political attitudes and behavioral patterns of the population. Thus the state is always manipulated by those who possess economic power.[8] (See figure 13.2.)

The second idea that was critical to Marx's concept of dialectical materialism was *class conflict.* Marx maintained that whenever there is private ownership of the means of production, social

FIGURE 13.2   Marx's Concept of Base and Superstructure

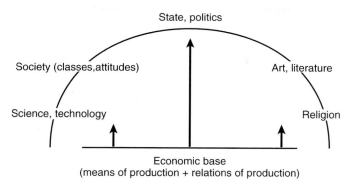

classes come into being. The relationships between the main social classes under conditions of private property, in Marx's view, are invariably antagonistic. "The history of all hitherto existing society," he wrote in the *Manifesto*, "is the history of class struggles."[9] Thus in the ancient world, the slave-master class and the slave class were locked in hostile confrontation. In nineteenth-century Europe, wherever capitalism was the dominant mode of production, the capitalist class confronted the working class.

When referring to the capitalist class in the industrializing countries, Marx used the term **"<u>bourgeoisie</u>."** The term derived from *bourg*, the old German and French word for town or city. (Industrial capitalism in Marx's time was largely an urban phenomenon.) The bourgeoisie consisted of entrepreneurs who owned factories and other productive enterprises, together with other private businesspeople who stood to profit from providing their services in a free-enterprise economy: bankers, lawyers, accountants, and the like. Marx used the term **"<u>proletariat</u>"** when referring to the industrial working class, which consisted mainly of factory laborers. This term came from the Latin *proletarius*, referring to a member of the non-property-owning lower class of ancient Rome. In Marx's conceptualization, these two classes were destined to clash, much like the thesis and antithesis in Hegelian philosophy. True to the laws of the dialectic, the bourgeoisie creates the very class that will destroy it. By building factories, the capitalists in effect create the working class. "What the bourgeoisie therefore produces, above all," Marx wrote, "is its own grave-diggers."

As industrial capitalism matures over time, he believed, the "contradictions" inherent in the relationship between bourgeoisie and proletariat inevitably intensify. The rich grow richer while the poor get poorer. The most successful capitalists drive their competitors out of business, a process Marx called *monopolization*. As a consequence, the bourgeoisie shrinks in size, concentrating society's wealth in very few hands. The middle class, consisting of small, independent property owners—shop owners, artisans, small farmers, and the like—are also victimized by the relentless pursuit of capitalist competition. Crushed by aggressive large-scale businesses, the middle class literally disappears, sinking into the working class. As the ranks of the proletariat swell beyond the capitalist system's ability to employ them, the unemployed grow into a vast "reserve army of the proletariat." Bereft of any stable source of income, they constitute what Marx called the *lumpenproletariat*, the "proletariat in rags."

Meanwhile, the capitalist elite uses its control over the state to reinforce its subjugation of the proletariat. For Marx, the state is always an instrument of class domination. "Political power," says the *Manifesto*, "is merely the organized power of one class for oppressing another." In capitalist societies, "The executive of the modern state is but a committee for managing the common affairs of the bourgeoisie." In Marx's view, electoral democracy in capitalist societies is a sham that holds out no hope for the working class; it is nothing more than a "bourgeois democracy," thoroughly manipulated by the capitalist class for its own benefit. Legislatures, political parties, politicians—all do the bidding of the captains of industry. Britain, where Marx lived from 1849 until his death in 1883, impressed him as a prime example of such a capitalist-dominated parliamentary system.

Eventually, the proletariat comes to comprise the vast majority of the population wherever advanced capitalism has developed to its full potential. Only about 10 percent of the population ends up owning private businesses. Under these circumstances, the capitalist economic system is no longer able to sustain itself; the capitalists are outnumbered. Time is then ripe for revolution and socialism.

In sum, Marx's concept of dialectical materialism held that the *material forces* driving the dialectical movement of history were *economic conditions,* while the *dialectical clash of opposites* consisted mainly of *class conflicts.*

The Socialist Revolution   In the *Manifesto,* Marx and Engels declared that the capitalist bourgeoisie is destined to be overthrown in a working-class revolution. Reduced to a small minority of the population, the bourgeois class, despite its extraordinary wealth and political power, is incapable of holding back the mounting tide of proletarian resentment. The proletariat, imbued with growing "class consciousness," ultimately takes matters into its own hands, undertaking "the forcible overthrow of all existing social conditions" in a spontaneous revolutionary outburst. Through the dialectical clash of bourgeoisie and proletariat, humanity is then "lifted up" to the higher historical plane of communism.

Once installed in power, Marx and Engels predicted, the working class dismantles the entire capitalist system. Private ownership of the means of production is forever abolished, the capitalist "expropriators" are expropriated. The workers themselves take possession of factories, farms, and other productive enterprises, reorganizing economic life for the benefit of the people as a whole. With the dissolution of private property and its transformation into "the property of all members of society," all class distinctions then cease to exist. The economic exploitation of one class by another is no longer possible. The proletariat scrupulously refrains from setting itself up as a new dominant class. Communism, in Marx's grand vision, is a truly classless society.

Finally liberated from capitalist oppression, the working masses find true freedom. For Marx, freedom above all meant freedom from economic exploitation. When the burden of working for exploitative employers is removed, the people are at last free to develop their own personalities and talents to their maximum potential.

Most important, Marx and Engels affirmed that the abolition of private property is accompanied by the abolition of the "bourgeois" state. Indeed, the seizure of state power will be the first task of the revolutionaries. Having captured the main institutions of government, the proletariat then uses its command of the state to wrest all economic power from the bourgeoisie. This process of removing the control of industry and agriculture from the hands of the bourgeoisie occurs by degrees, however, and may require a certain amount of time. In various writings Marx and Engels said that, in some cases, the workers may have to establish a "dictatorship of the proletariat" to supervise the gradual takeover of economic power from the capitalists. Neither Marx nor Engels ever said how long the dictatorship of the proletariat would last, but they implied that it would be brief, perhaps no longer than a year. Once the proletarian state completes its primary tasks of dissolving private property and establishing a socialist economy, the dictatorship of the working class comes to an end.[10]

In fact, once the capitalists have been deprived of their economic power, *government itself ceases to exist as a political institution.* The state, as Engels crisply put it, *"dies out."* While there may still be an "administration" in communist society to take care of basic services, the state is no longer an instrument of class domination. It has no real political power. By abolishing private property, the victorious working class abolishes class conflict; and by abolishing class conflict, which is the driving force of politics, it abolishes politics itself. Under communism, in other words, private property, social classes, conflict, a class-controlled state, political power, and politics itself all disappear.[11]

While politics withers away in communist society, economic conditions vastly improve. Marx and Engels prophesied that the great mass of the population would respond to their new-found freedom with a tremendous burst of creativity and productive energy. Although everyone would be expected to work, they would work for society as a whole, not for greedy capitalists. The result would be a superabundance of socially useful goods from which everyone would ultimately benefit. As time goes on and the socialist economy expands, it becomes increasingly possible to distribute the goods of society according to the principle "From each according to his ability, to each according to his needs." In this so-called higher phase of communism, people contribute to the economy whatever they can, and they get back whatever they need.[12]

Marx and Engels thus portrayed socialist society (that is, communism) as an idyllic utopia. In Hegelian terms, communism was Marx's vision of the final synthesis in the long dialectical march of human history. Beyond a few generalities about a classless, stateless society, however, the two founding fathers of modern socialist ideology had very little to say about how communism would actually work. They left no blueprint indicating how the socialist economy would be organized, though they never suggested that a communist state would control the economy. Nor did they outline a communist "constitution," since there would be no politicized government. They blithely assumed that, without any class conflicts to divide them, the people themselves would find ways to manage their common affairs harmoniously.

Scientific Socialism   In the *Manifesto,* Marx and Engels proclaimed that the destruction of capitalism and the victory of the proletariat were inevitable. For Marx, the inevitability of socialism was ordained by the immutable laws of History, whose secrets he believed he had discovered. Just as Hegel had discerned the laws of dialectical development and just as Charles Darwin had discovered the laws of biological evolution, Marx maintained that he had uncovered the laws governing humanity's social development. On these grounds Marx always insisted that his theories of dialectical materialism were "scientific." So conceived, History was the source of communism's legitimacy.

Accordingly, Marx asserted that the entire course of humankind's historical development, from the most primitive preindustrial societies to the highest stage of communism, was governed by the laws of economic determinism. These laws, moreover, were immutable; no one could change them or get around them. Accordingly, Marx sketched out an outline of human history that was divided into five distinct phases of historical development. Each phase was defined by the prevailing modes of economic production. Inevitably, whenever there was private ownship of the means of production, class conflict was bound to occur.

According to Marx's outline of history, summarized in table 13.1, each successive phase is characterized by a higher, more sophisticated form of economic and social organization. Thus at the dawn of civilization, with cave dwellers and forest people sharing the land, a classless "primitive communism" holds sway. As the centuries unfold, the world of ancient Egypt, Greece, and Rome, characterized by class struggles between masters and slaves, gives way to medieval Europe, with aristocratic feudal landowners confronting impoverished serfs and a rising business class, the bourgeoisie. At approximately the same time, China and other parts of Asia are characterized by a mode of production in which a central state organizes vast hydraulic (i.e., water-management) projects, harnessing the rivers to irrigate the land and, not incidentally, to impose the government's authority on a widely dispersed agricultural society. The fourth stage of history is Marx's own time and place: nineteenth-century Europe. Characterized by industrial capitalism and the fierce struggle between the bourgeoisie and proletariat, this stage witnesses extraordinary scientific and technological achievements but is doomed from the start to explode in a working-class revolution. Communism, the fifth stage of human history, would be the final stage, marking humanity's arrival at a state of veritable social perfection.

Marx did not believe that humanity would traverse all these successive stages simultaneously. The march to socialism would take place in one country at a time, at different rates of speed depending on local conditions. Because Britain, France, and Germany were the most industrially advanced capitalist economies in Europe in his lifetime, Marx believed that socialist revolutions would occur in those countries first. He realized, however, that no two countries are alike. Countries

TABLE 13.1

Phase	Mode of Ownership of the Means of Production	Dominant Mode of Production	Class Conflict
Phases of Historical Development According to Marx and Engels			
1. Primitive communism	Family/tribal use of land	Communal subsistence agriculture	None
2. Slavery (ancient world)	Communal-state ownership; some private property	Communal-state agriculture and industry	Masters vs. slaves
3. Feudalism (Medieval Europe)	State-feudal ownership of land; emerging private industry and commerce	Feudal agriculture	Feudal aristocracy vs. serfs and emerging bourgeoisie
Asiatic mode of production	Communal-state ownership	State-managed hydraulic projects	None
4. Capitalism (nineteenth-century Europe, United States)	Private	Industrial capitalism	Bourgeoisie vs. proletariat
5. Communism	Communal	Communal industry and agriculture	None

outside of Europe would not necessarily follow the same historical trajectory as Europe's evolution from feudalism to capitalism to communism.

Nevertheless, both Marx and Engels believed that, as a general rule, industrial capitalism was a necessary precondition to the construction of a successful socialist society over the long term. They did not believe that predominantly agricultural societies were ripe for socialist development, and so they dismissed peasants as incapable of mounting a true socialist revolution. They disparaged rural life as "idiocy." Only the industrial working class had the "class consciousness" necessary to create a stable and enduring socialist society.

The question of whether predominantly agricultural societies were capable of experiencing a socialist revolution was a controversial one. Russia, for example, was just beginning to industrialize by the late nineteenth century. The vast majority of its population consisted of impoverished peasants, while a capitalist bourgeoisie had not yet formed itself as a dominant class. When asked by Russian socialists if a revolution could occur in Russia on the basis of rural socialist communities, Marx and Engels replied that a revolutionary upheaval in preindustrialized Russia was indeed possible, but they cautioned that a socialist society would last in Russia only if socialism also came about in the industrially advanced capitalist countries of Europe. In their view, a peasant-based so-

cialism could not succeed on its own; it would need assistance from more industrially advanced socialist countries in order to survive.[13]

These "scientific" predictions would prove wrong. In actual fact, the proletarian revolutions Marx and Engels foresaw as imminent in Britain, France, and Germany in the 1840s never took place in these countries. Communist revolutions did not occur until the twentieth century. Ironically, they triumphed in precisely those countries where industrialism and capitalism were largely undeveloped and where a modern bourgeoisie was weak or absent. Countries like Russia, China, and Cuba were predominantly agricultural societies when the communists came to power.

The triumph of what came to be known as *Soviet-style communism* (or *Marxism-Leninism*) in these countries represented only one strand of Marx's legacy, however. In another irony of history, the advanced capitalist societies of Western Europe, which Marx's "laws" regarded as primed for revolution, did not experience revolution at all. Instead they developed socialist movements that combined socialist economics with ballot-box democracy, a combination known as *social democracy*.

Soviet-Style Communism

When communism triumphed in Russia in 1917, it did so under circumstances significantly different from those predicted by Marx and Engels. As we have just seen, Marx and Engels believed that advanced industrial capitalism with a large working-class majority was a precondition for any successful socialist revolution. Russia was still an overwhelmingly agricultural society in 1917, however. Marx had depicted the revolution as a largely spontaneous upheaval carried out by the masses; he did not portray it as an organized conspiracy led by a handful of revolutionary leaders. And yet, communism came to Russia precisely as a well-orchestrated coup d'état engineered by a highly centralized political party, the Bolsheviks. It was this party, which soon came to be known as the Communist Party, that defined the essence of Soviet-style communism.

The party's principal creator was **Vladimir Ilyich Lenin** (1870–1924). An avid student of Marx's writings from his teenage years, Lenin placed his own stamp on the Marxist tradition by adapting its core ideas to Russia's specific conditions. Arguing that Marxism was not an inalterable dogma but a flexible body of thought capable of diverse applications, Lenin retained Marx's hostility to capitalism and his commitment to socialist revolution but he abandoned, reinterpreted, or adjusted other aspects of Marx's ideology to conform with Russian realities in the early twentieth century.

Lenin's single most important contribution to Marxist theory, as expostulated in *What Is To Be Done?* (1902), was the notion that the industrial working class in modern Russia and Europe was not capable of launching a spontaneous mass revolution on its own; it had to be led to socialism by a party of professional revolutionaries. Experience had already shown that, instead of risking a potentially disastrous uprising, most workers were content to form trade unions and to seek negotiated compromises with their capitalist employers. But trade unionism, argued Lenin, amounted to acceptance of capitalism; only its complete destruction could liberate the workers from capitalist exploitation. If the workers would not destroy capitalism on their own, a "party of a new type" would have to be formed whose primary task would be to organize and carry out a violent revolution at the first sign of weakness in the capitalist ruling class. This party would be the "vanguard of the proletariat," acting as its "organizational weapon."[14]

For Russia's rulers, that critical moment of weakness occurred amid the turmoil of World War I. With minimal resistance, Lenin's Bolsheviks, organized into a small militia, seized official buildings that had been abandoned by an unpopular government in November 1917. It took a brutal civil war that extended into 1921 before the Bolsheviks had vanquished all their opponents. From that point onward, Russia's Communist Party monopolized power in what subsequently became known as the Soviet Union (or USSR, the Union of Soviet Socialist Republics).

The key idea of <u>**Leninism**</u> is *the primacy of the communist party.* It is the party that leads the revolution; it is the party that governs the country once the revolution has eliminated its foes. Lenin's definition of the "dictatorship of the proletariat" was distinctly different from Marx's conception of a temporary government in the hands of the masses. "The dictatorship of the proletariat," Lenin affirmed, "is the dictatorship of the party." Far from being a temporary phenomenon, the Communist Party exercised dictatorial rule over the Soviet Union until December 1991, when its power collapsed and the USSR itself disintegrated.

For much of its reign, the party leadership utilized all the coercive mechanisms at its disposal to enforce its will, at times resorting to mass murder. **Joseph Stalin** (1878–1953), who succeeded Lenin following a power struggle within the party hierarchy, brutalized Soviet society by imprisoning millions in concentration camps, killing off the cream of the party elite, and intimidating workers, peasants, intellectuals, and others into submission through the unremitting use of violence. His successors over the remaining decades of Soviet rule were not as overtly murderous as Stalin on a mass scale, but until the late 1980s they did not shrink from using severe coercive measures to ensure compliance with their dictates.

In another sharp departure from Marx's tenets, Soviet rulers erected a powerful state to undergird their dominance. Instead of "dying out," the state swelled into a gargantuan bureaucratic arm of Communist Party rule. The Soviet state was a highly politicized state, moreover; it consisted of party and governmental institutions that joined in propagandizing the population, repressing dissent, and implementing policies over which the people had little or no influence. Its top officials constituted a privileged elite that enjoyed benefits denied to the mass public. This enormous party-state governing apparatus also planned and operated virtually all economic activity in the USSR, a system known as a *centrally planned economy.* (We'll discuss central planning at greater length in chapter 14.)

At no point in its history did the Soviet Union approach the stateless, egalitarian utopia that was Marx's conception of communism. The USSR was called "communist" only because it was governed by the Communist Party. The same can be said for other "communist" countries that came into being after the USSR. These included China, where the Chinese Communist Party took power in 1949 following a long civil war; Poland, Hungary, and other East-Central European nations on which the USSR imposed communist party rule after World War II; Cuba, where Fidal Castro's communists won a revolutionary struggle in 1959; and others such as North Korea and Vietnam. All were the heirs, not just of Marx, but also of Lenin. Hence twentieth-century communism, defined in terms of communist party dictatorship, was rooted in the ideology of *Marxism-Leninism.*

Social Democracy

The second main inheritor of Marx's legacy was **social democracy.** One of the chief incubators of the social democratic tradition was the Social Democratic Party of Germany (known by its German initials as the SPD). Founded in 1875, the SPD became Germany's largest political party by the turn of the century, capturing 27 percent of the vote in 1898. Its backbone was the German working class, a disparate mass of mostly blue-collar workers with an acute consciousness of their subaltern status in German society. Deprived of economic power through the absence of collective bargaining rights, German workers began forming trade unions to compel employers to negotiate with them, using strikes as their main weapon. Deprived of political power by the kaiser's authoritarian regime, workers looked mostly to the SPD to win them a share of participation in the affairs of government. The ballot box became their main political weapon. In militating for both economic

and political power, most German workers shunned the path of revolution, sharply contradicting Marx's predictions of an inevitable proletarian uprising.

One SPD leader, **Eduard Bernstein** (1850–1932), drew the implications of this contradiction between Marxist theory and working-class practice with bold clarity. A trade union organizer from Berlin, Bernstein spent several years in England as a political exile. During that time he came into contact with a group of British socialists, the Fabians, who advocated a gradualistic, democratic approach to reducing the economic power of the country's capitalist elite by widening the role of state intervention in the economy. Upon returning to Germany he published a small book, *Evolutionary Socialism,* in 1898. It marked his emergence as the theoretical godfather of social democracy.

The book was a point-by-point refutation of key tenets of Marx's thought. The capitalist class, Bernstein noted, was not growing smaller in number, as Marx had forecast, but more sizable. The middle class, far from sinking into the proletariat, was growing larger and more prosperous. The working class, instead of becoming steadily poorer, was to some extent better off than in previous decades (though it was still at the bottom of the social heap). Instead of shrinking down into just two classes—the bourgeoisie and the proletariat—society was becoming more variegated and complex. Moreover, the catastrophic collapse of capitalism did not appear to be imminent, either in Germany or anywhere else. And most controversially of all, Bernstein stated that the destruction of capitalism and the establishment of a classless communist society were by no means historically inevitable. Marx, he wrote, had not scientifically proven the inevitability of socialism; he had merely assumed it.

For Bernstein, the immediate aim of the socialist movement should not be to mount a violent revolution but to promote democracy. Bernstein defined democracy as "the absence of class government," a political system "where a political privilege belongs to no one class as opposed to the whole community." At the time Bernstein was writing, Germany was anything but a democracy. Although the kaiser's government permitted contested elections to a national parliament, that body had few real powers. Bernstein advocated univer-

FIGURE 13.3   Legacies of Marxism

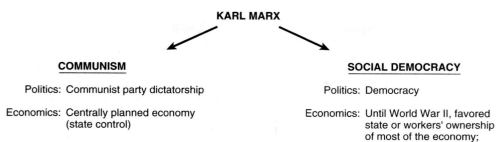

KARL MARX

COMMUNISM

Politics: Communist party dictatorship

Economics: Centrally planned economy
(state control)

SOCIAL DEMOCRACY

Politics: Democracy

Economics: Until World War II, favored
state or workers' ownership
of most of the economy;
after World War II, favored
mixture of private enterprise
and welfare state

sal suffrage, proportional representation, equal rights for all citizens, and parliamentary control over legislation. He emphatically rejected both the kaiser's militaristic dictatorship as well as Marx's "dictatorship of the proletariat." He regarded compromise and moderation as indispensable elements of democratic government.

So defined, democracy for Bernstein was "the indispensable precondition to the realization of socialism." As to socialism itself, Bernstein conceived of it as a "cooperative society," combining worker-owned producers' associations, consumer cooperatives, trade unions, and other institutions organized for the benefit of the whole population and guided by the principle of majority rule. Bernstein opposed the creation of a centrally planned economy operated by the state, regarding it as impossibly unwieldy.

Over the next several decades, the SPD's commitment to political democracy intensified. The party was a mainstay of democratic government during Germany's ill-fated Weimar Republic (1918–1933), which died an early death at the hands of Hitler and the Nazis. After World War II a revived SPD became one of the two largest parties in West Germany, a status it still enjoys today in unified Germany. (Chancellor Gerhard Schroeder is an SPD leader.) Meanwhile, starting in the 1950s the SPD began retreating from its earlier commitment to economic socialism. It accepted private enterprise and the market as the principal mechanisms of economic production. It has sought to promote the interests of the working class and other constituents by working within the capitalist system through democratic processes.

Other social democratic parties emerged in the industrialized nations of Europe and have undergone a roughly similar historical evolution. Most of them started out as particularistic parties based largely in the industrial working class. Although workers and trade unions still provide the main constituency for most of these parties, many of them have broadened their electoral base to incorporate elements of the middle class. In the process they became catch-all parties. Most significantly, after World War II these social democratic parties progressively abandoned or modified their earlier demands for the liquidation of capitalism and its replacement by some form of economic socialism. Like the SPD, most social democratic parties in today's industrially advanced democracies accept private enterprise and the market economy. Today, social democracy in most democracies is practically indistinguishable from American *social-welfare liberalism*, though many European social democrats favor a larger welfare state than do most U.S. liberals.

It should be noted that despite high levels of industrialization, the United States never developed a successful social democratic party that favored the state's takeover of factories and other productive enterprises.[15]

Socialism in the Developing World

The varieties of socialism are multiplied when we look at socialist ideas in the developing countries. In Asia, Africa, the Middle East, and Latin America, various forms of socialism have been articulated and adapted over many decades to fit social and economic conditions that are quite different from those that prevailed in nineteenth- or twentieth-century Europe. In most instances, these variants of socialism emerged in countries with little or no industrialization. A proletariat in the European sense has either been very small or nonexistent. Not surprisingly, some of the most creative socialist theorists and political activists in the less economically advanced part of the world have not based their ideas on Marxism. Instead they have looked into local traditions and circumstances to find a suitable inspiration for their own approach to socialist thought and action.

One of the most influential Third World socialists was **Julius K. Nyerere** (1922–1999), the principal theoretician of what became known as "African socialism." A British-educated Christian from Tanzania, Nyerere conceived of socialism more as an "attitude of mind" than as a formal set of doctrines and institutions that were everywhere the same. He rejected Marx's notions of class struggle and the necessity of achieving capitalism as a precondition for socialism. Nyerere devised a Tanzanian variant of socialism rooted in long-standing tribal customs that emphasized the individual's responsibility to the community and the community's responsibility to care for the individual. Out of this tradition he derived the concept of *ujamaa*, or "familyhood." In this conceptualization, socialism was viewed as an extension of the basic family unit. Under Nyerere's leadership as president of Tanzania for more than twenty years, the government abolished private ownership of land and instituted a system of communally owned rural property, touting "self-reliance" as the country's main economic goal.[16] Several African nations-states embarked on roughly similar paths in the 1960s and 1970s. Over time, however, a number of them, including Tanzania, were forced by economic realities to curtail or abandon their lofty goals of agricultural self-sufficiency and full economic equality. Some have reintroduced market economic mechanisms.[17]

Another source of non-Marxist concepts of socialism was the Middle East. A revolution led by Colonel Gamel Abdel Nasser deposed the king of Egypt in 1952 and installed a new regime led mainly by military officers. Nasser elaborated a form of "Arab socialism" that placed heavy emphasis on governmental direction of the economy. These measures were accompanied by efforts to anchor the ideology of Arab socialism in the religious traditions of Islam.[18] Fairly similar concepts of Arab socialism were elaborated in the 1960s in Syria, Iraq, and Libya. As in Nasser's Egypt, they tended to emphasize the state's responsibility for guiding the economy. They also went hand in hand with strong authoritarian governments. The popularity of socialism in the Middle East has waned in recent decades, however, in part because of pressures to open these economies up to market forces and in part because of the collapse of the Soviet Union, which was an occasional ally of several states in the region.

In Latin America, socialist movements have frequently tended to have a Marxist background. Some have been Soviet-oriented communist parties, some have espoused violent revolutions of one kind or another (at times with the support of Fidel Castro's communist regime in Cuba), and still others have been social democratic in orientation. One notable example of a radical social democrat was Salvador Allende, who was elected president of Chile in 1970. Allende's Socialist Party was committed to democracy but was equally committed to redistributing the nation's wealth from the rich to the poor and to nationalizing large privately owned corporations, including copper mines owned by U.S. companies. Although Allende was not a Soviet-style communist, Chile's Communist Party was part of his governing coalition. Irked by Allende's socialist economic policies and his friendly gestures toward the Soviet Union and Castro's Cuba, the Nixon administration conspired with Allende's domestic opponents to undermine his government. In 1973 a military coup led by Gen. Augusto Pinochet and abetted by the CIA ousted the socialist coalition. Allende was killed in the assault, and democracy itself was extinguished in Chile for the next sixteen years.

FASCISM

Historically, <u>**fascism**</u> is mainly a European phenomenon that emerged between the two world wars. Its most successful manifestations occurred in Italy, where Benito Mussolini's National Fascist Party held power from 1922 until 1943, and in

Benito Mussolini and Adolph Hitler

movements in today's world also represent extreme responses to social or economic problems for which democratic solutions are either inadequate or completely unacceptable to certain segments of society. Ethnic diversity and long-term unemployment are typical of the problems that spark neo-fascist resentments, particularly among poorly educated white males.

Reduced to its basic elements, fascist ideology consists of the following four points: *hypernationalism, racism, totalitarianism,* and *mass mobilization* through propaganda and coercion. To be sure, not all fascist movements have shared all these defining characteristics. The features enumerated here form a composite "ideal type" of fascism extracted mainly from the experiences of inter-war Italy and Germany.

Germany, where Adolph Hitler and the Nazis ruled between 1933 and 1945. Fascist movements also existed in other European countries during the inter-war period, including France, Hungary, and Romania, but they did not acquire the extraordinary grip on power achieved by their Italian and German counterparts.[19] Fascist-like movements and ideas have also emerged in other parts of the globe in the decades before and after World War II, including the present day. The American Nazi Party, neo-Nazi skinheads in Europe, and white-supremacist Afrikaner groups in South Africa are often singled out as examples of quasi-fascist or neo-fascist organizations in the contemporary era.

In most instances, fascism is a response to a specific combination of problems that face certain societies at a particular juncture in their historical development. Italy and Germany after World War I were especially ripe for the kinds of ideas and emotional appeals articulated by fascist demagogues. Both countries had emerged from defeat feeling humiliated and betrayed, and both had to confront overwhelming economic problems. In both countries, moreover, democracy failed to provide adequate remedies for the nation's misfortunes. Growing numbers of Italians and Germans came to the conclusion that democracy itself was the principal problem. In most instances neo-fascist

Hypernationalism

Fascism is rooted in an extreme version of nationalism called *hypernationalism*. Nationalism is the notion that the members of one's nation (or "people") must act together to achieve certain collective goals. In its fascist variant, the nation is exalted as the supreme political value. This conception of nationalism is far more intense than patriotism, which means love of one's country. For many fascists, love of one's own country requires hatred of others, particularly those marked as implacable enemies.

National glory and self-assertion therefore assume the highest priority on the political agenda of most fascist movements. Mussolini was determined to establish an Italian empire through the conquest of Ethiopia in 1936 and other territorial acquisitions during World War II. Hitler sought to subdue all of Europe and the Soviet Union by force of arms, with the express intention of creating a fascist "New Order." **Chauvinism,** which is strong aversion to anything foreign, is a typical component of the fascist worldview.

Whereas militant nationalism characterizes fascist attitudes toward the outside world, national unity is often the chief priority at home. For Mussolini, Hitler, and other fascists, internal divisiveness breeds external weakness; hence democracy is intolerable precisely because it promotes national discord. Democratic debate and free competition for power inevitably mean that the nation is constantly at war with itself, its domestic fissures deepened by open conflict among social classes, religions, regions, and other segments of the country. Democracy, in this view, is a prescription for national powerlessness, a condition no fascist could possibly accept. In one way or another, other fascist or neo-fascist movements have also placed a high premium on national strength in relations with foreign governments and on national unity at home. But not only is fascism characterized by its devotion to the nation, it is also frequently distinguished by the way it defines the nation.

Racism

At least some fascist and neo-fascist movements have defined the nation primarily in terms of race. Concepts of racial purity and superiority were especially characteristic of German fascism under Hitler. The notion that the Germans were members of a pure-blooded "Aryan race," an utterly fabricated idea, was a central tenet of Nazi doctrine. Nazi ideology exalted the Germans as a race of "supermen" and denigrated most other racial categories as "subhumans."

Jews were treated with particular contempt. Anti-Semitism assumed ferocious proportions in Nazi doctrine. After World War I, Nazi propagandists used the Jews as scapegoats for Germany's political and economic ills even though Jews comprised less than 1 percent of Germany's population. By the late 1930s the Nazi state had instituted a number of racial laws aimed at publicly humiliating German Jews and depriving them of their means of livelihood. During World War II the determination of Hitler and his principal henchmen to proceed with "the final solution of the Jewish problem" throughout Europe resulted in the Holocaust, the annihilation of some 6 million Jews throughout Europe and the Soviet Union and the infliction of untold suffering on millions of survivors. Anti-Semitism has been a characteristic feature of most other fascist or neo-fascist movements as well, though not all these movements have been as fanatically or blatantly anti-Semitic as the Nazis.[20]

Anti-Semitism is by no means the only form of racism to be found in fascist or quasi-fascist movements. The Nazis denounced just about all racial or ethnic groups not explicitly identified as "Aryan." Depending on local circumstances, racism has also been a defining characteristic of fascist-like movements in other countries as well, spawning hatred and even violence against immigrants and indigenous members of target ethnic groups. Hatred of homosexuals and the physically and mentally handicapped was also part of the Nazi worldview.

Totalitarianism

Fascist ideology demands a powerful state. The very word "fascism" derives originally from the Latin *fasces*, which in ancient Rome was a staff consisting of a bundle of rods bound together around an axe. The *fasces* would be held aloft on ceremonial occasions as a symbol of national unity and the state's authority.

Once ensconced in office, Mussolini and Hitler established strong totalitarian states. Totalitarianism is an exceptionally intrusive form of authoritarianism in which the state monopolizes control not only over all institutions of government but also over the educational system, the media, science, and the arts, leaving little room for private liberty. Youth groups and even organized religions also come under the watchful eye of the state. Mussolini bluntly asserted that "for the Fascist, all is in the State and nothing human or spiritual exists, much less has value, outside the State. In this sense, Fascism is totalitarian."[21]

The fascists of Italy and Germany also used state mechanisms to secure their control over the economy. Unlike communists and social democrats of that era, who favored abolishing private enterprise, the fascists were willing to permit private firms to do business and make profits. These businesses were subject to all sorts of state regulations, however. To ensure that privately owned companies conducted their operations in accordance with the government's priorities, especially the large industrial concerns, Italian and German authorities created special state institutions, which they called "corporations," in which leading representatives of the business community would meet on a regular basis with state officials to coordinate economic goals and operations. The government established similar "corporations" to represent the labor force, though all trade unions and other labor organizations were abolished except for those operated by the state or the fascist party. "Corporations" representing agriculture and other sectors of the economy were similarly organized. This system of **state corporatism** served the central purposes of facilitating the state's supervision of the economy and, not incidentally, of organizing the economy for war.[22]

The fascist concept of totalitarianism, at least in its Italian and German variants, was also characterized by the concept of a *party-state.* The state and the fascist party were fused. The Italian fascists' motto, "Everything inside the state, nothing outside the state, nothing against the state," above all meant that the state and the National Fascist Party were one.[23] Hitler's dictatorial state and the Nazi Party were similarly intertwined, with the Nazis monopolizing virtually all official state institutions.

Mass Mobilization
Through Propaganda and Coercion

Traditional authoritarian regimes, like the old monarchies of Europe, China, and Japan, made little effort to court popularity. The Italian and German fascist parties, by contrast, were authoritarian movements that made decisive efforts to cultivate mass support. Although they rejected democracy as a goal, prior to taking power they took full advantage of electoral democracy to build a wide constituency. Mussolini and Hitler were charismatic orators whose speeches transfixed millions. Their parties proved highly effective at organizing parades, rallies, and other media events to galvanize a mass following. The breadth of their appeal, moreover, was multiclass in nature. Though the Italian and German fascist movements started out in the 1920s with a pronounced working-class orientation, over time they drew support from farmers, the large middle class, and even the wealthiest strata of society. The Nazis, for example, raised their share of the electorate from 3 percent in 1928 to more than 37 percent by the summer of 1932, becoming the largest party in Germany.

In addition to using democratic mechanisms to achieve power, Italian and German fascists freely engaged in coercive techniques in their rush to build and consolidate mass support. The glorification of violence against political opponents was another core element of fascist ideology. Mussolini's fascist party explicitly defined itself as a "militia." From its earliest years it included "squads" (*fasci*) of black-shirted toughs whose task was to beat up political rivals and fight their way into local city halls, seizing power by force. In October 1922, tens of thousands of armed fascists were massed on the outskirts of Rome, poised for a final assault on the Italian government itself. To avoid a massacre, the king of Italy, acting under his constitutional authority to designate the head of government, named Mussolini the country's new prime minister. The next day the fascist militia staged a victory parade in the streets of the capital city, an event known as the "march on Rome." The Nazis also employed force in their march to power. Hitler set up a militia in brown shirts, which developed into the notorious SA, the so-called Storm Troopers. By 1932, on the eve of the Nazi takeover of power, there were more than four hundred thousand Storm Troopers. In January 1933, German President Hindenburg appointed Hitler the country's new chancellor.

Efforts to mobilize the population, both peaceful and violent, became all the more extensive after the conquest of power. Fascist Italy and Germany were mass mobilization regimes, resolved to enlist maximum popular support and stifle all opposition. Both regimes organized continuous propaganda campaigns designed to stir up popularity, appealing not only to national pride but also to the darkest anxieties, prejudices, and yearnings for vengeance on the part of the Italian and German populations. They also engineered massive employment programs and other efforts to improve the economic welfare of large elements of the population. And they did not hesitate to use violence against real or imagined political opponents, with secret police, concentration camps, and torture employed with intimidating effect.

Some scholars contend that fascism was an "epochal" phenomenon unique to inter-war Europe. Nevertheless, it is far too early to consign fascism to the graveyard of history. At least hypothetically, fascist ideas may find a popular resonance wherever other forms of government, including democracy, fail to address the basic needs of the population for economic security, national pride, and social order. It remains at least conceivable that fascist ideology, or some variant of it, may succeed in mobilizing support wherever conditions favor its distinctive blend of intense nationalism, racism, powerful state authority, mass mobilization, and militant violence.[24]

RELIGION AS POLITICAL IDEOLOGY: ISLAM

Throughout history, religions have often articulated explicit political messages. The Roman Catholic church was a dominant political force in medieval Europe, conferring divine legitimacy on kings and emperors through papal anointment. Protestantism challenged the papacy's exclusive right to legitimize Christian political authorities. The Church of England, Lutheran princes in Germany, Calvinist communities in Switzerland, Puritans in the American colonies—these and other Protestant churches and sects explicitly mixed religion and politics. In today's world, most countries with a Christian majority, mainly in Europe and North America, are democracies that have established a formal institutional separation between church and state. Even so, as a practical matter religion and politics remain closely linked in the attitudes of many citizens and political leaders in a number of contemporary democracies, especially over such controversial issues as abortion, divorce, and public schooling. In Russia, meanwhile, the Russian Orthodox Church was a powerful prop supporting a succession of tsarist governments that ruled Russia for nearly a thousand years before the Communist Revolution of 1917. Severely persecuted under the Communists, Russian Orthodoxy has reemerged as a political force in post-communist Russia, often espousing nationalist views. Various forms of what is known as Eastern Orthodoxy assume an important political role in countries like Romania, Serbia, and Greece.

Outside the Christian world, religion and philosophical traditions have become intertwined with politics in a variety of ways. In China and other parts of East Asia, the philosophy of Confucianism inculcated a deep respect for authority along with other values that undergirded imperial rule for

centuries; its principles still influence political attitudes throughout the region. In India, Mohandas Gandhi succeeded in forging Hinduism and Indian nationalism into a potent political force that gained India's independence from Great Britain in 1947. Israel was founded in 1948 on the basis of *Zionism,* the political ideology that proclaims the right of Jews around the world to establish a Jewish state in the Holy Land. Buddhism, animism, and other religious traditions have also been involved in politics, whether directly or indirectly, at different times in different places.

One of the most politically active religions has been Islam. From its origins in the Middle East in the seventh century down to the present day, Islam has taught its believers that religion is invariably connected with politics. The concept of the Muslim "nation," known in Arabic as the *umma,* regards all the world's Muslims as constituting a political community as well as a religious one. Islamic law, known as the **Shariah,** not only sets forth a code of conduct applicable to the relationship between the Muslim faithful and God *(Allah),* it also prescribes proper behavior in the realms of economics and political action. Traditional Islamic teaching requires the establishment of an Islamic state in which the law of God, as expressed in the Shariah and other holy sources, becomes the law of humankind.

Islamic religious doctrine may therefore be regarded as a political ideology because it makes no sharp distinction between church and state. It regards divine law as higher than any human-made law and exalts the Islamic state as the ideal temporal state. It prescribes moral ideals such as justice, socioeconomic equality, and charity as the principal sources of social obligation. And it requires the Muslim community to defend the faith against all enemies, religious and political.

As in the case of most of the world's great religions, the central precepts of Islam have been interpreted and practiced in a variety of ways. One of the oldest divisions within Islam is that between **Sunni** Muslims and **Shiite** (or *Shiah*) Muslims, a distinction that has important political ramifications in today's world. Both sects accept the Prophet Muhammad, born in Mecca in 570, as the founder of Islam, esteeming him as the last in a line of prophets that includes Adam, Abraham,

Moses, and Jesus. Both believe that God sent the Archangel Gabriel to transmit a collection of divine revelations to Muhammad in Arabic. These revelations were later gathered together by Muhammad's companions in the *Koran* (or *Quran*), which all Muslims revere as their holiest book. Sunnis and Shiites differ, however, over the authority of Muhammad's successors.

Muhammad did not name a successor, or caliph, to assume his position as the spiritual and political leader of the Muslim community. After his death in 632, rival Muslim groups staked conflicting claims to his succession. A majority believed that Muhammad's successors should be elected by his closest companions. This group became known as "Sunnis," a term designating "those who follow the words and deeds of Prophet Muhammad." The Sunni majority succeeded in electing the first four caliphs, all of whom had been among Muhammad's closest followers. The fourth caliph to be so elected was Ali, Muhammad's son-in-law.

A minority group, however, opposed the principle of elections and insisted that God had intervened directly by instructing Muhammad to name Ali as the very first caliph. This group became known as the "Shiites," a term referring to the partisans of Ali. Shiites do not regard the first three elected caliphs as legitimate. They regard Ali and his son Hussein as the true successors of Muhammad and confer on them the title of *imam,* a term that implies that they were chosen by God and endowed with religious and political infallibility.

As Islam rapidly spread from the Arabian peninsula to Syria, Iraq, and Iran and then to Spain and northern Africa, fierce infighting divided the Muslim religious and political leadership. Ali and Hussein were murdered by Islamic rivals, and the breech between Sunnis and Shiites widened. In addition to differing over Muhammad's succession, the two sects parted company over a number of doctrinal matters as well. These fissures still exist. About 85 percent of Muslims today are Sunnis, the remaining 15 percent mostly Shiites. Iran and Iraq have Shiite majorities, while most other predominantly Muslim countries have a Sunni majority.

The diversity of contemporary Islam is heightened by the size of the Muslim community and its geopolitical dispersion. Today approximately one billion Muslims live under a multiplicity of political regimes. The division of the modern world into sovereign nation-states, now almost two hundred in number, has made it virtually impossible for Muslims to form a united community under a single Islamic state. More than forty countries have a Muslim majority. Very few, however, are governed in strict accordance with Islamic law. Iran and Saudi Arabia are the prime examples, though Iran is governed by Shiite clerics and Saudi Arabia is ruled by a royal family, the Saudis, who are Sunnis. Despite their political and religious differences, both governments implement the Shariah. The world of Islamic politics also includes governing officials who do not enforce Islamic law but preside over secular (non-religious) governments. In addition, there are prominent individuals and organized groups that espouse one variant or another of Islamic ideology.

One scholar, Mir Zohair Husain, has identified four main orientations in contemporary Islamic thought and practice. Each orientation has a distinct set of ideas on the relationship between religion and politics.

- *Fundamentalists* strongly advocate the creation of Islamic states wherever possible, to be governed in accordance with a puritanical interpretation of Islamic law. They condemn secularization and tend to be extremely hostile to Western political and cultural influences. The more extreme fundamentalists have engaged in terror campaigns against secularized Muslim leaders, Israel, the United States, France, and other targeted enemies. These violent extremists interpret the Muslim concept of *jihad*—the notion that Muslims must strive for personal morality and community responsibility—in martial terms, advocating a "holy war" against hostile non-Muslims. Examples of fundamentalists include such Iranian leaders as Ayatollah Ruhollah Khomeini, who ruled the country from 1979 to 1989, and most of his successors. Fundamentalist groups that have engaged in terror tactics include the Islamic Group, a collection of more than forty factions in Egypt; *Hamas* (Zeal) and *Hezbollah* (Party of God), whose targets are primarily Israelis; and the Islamic Salvation Front, which has sought to overthrow the government of Algeria. In 1995 Sheik Omar Abdel-Rahman, an Egyptian cleric, was convicted along with nine other fundamentalists of plotting a "war of urban terrorism" in the United States that included the World Trade Center bombing in New York two years earlier.

- *Traditionalists* also favor the creation of Islamic states and share the Fundamentalists' anti-secular and anti-Western attitudes. One of their main differences with the fundamentalists concerns the role of the Muslim clergy. Traditionalists tend to be clerics, whereas many of the most politically active fundamentalists are not. Consequently most traditionalists would like to see the clergy govern Islamic states rather than non-clerical Muslims. Many traditionalists also tend to be less fanatical than fundamentalists in taking action against secularized Muslim political leaders.

- *Modernists* are often devout practicing Muslims who favor an Islamic state. While opposing secularization in theory, however, they tend to tolerate it in practice. Modernist Muslims believe that Islam needs to incorporate certain non-Islamic political ideas, such as liberal democracy or socialism, in order to adapt itself to the modern world. Many modernists would also favor a less hostile relationship with the West that would permit economic and political cooperation. They criticize fundamentalist and traditionalist Muslims for being inflexible, doctrinaire, and backward-looking rather than progressive and realistic.

- *Pragmatists* are even more secularized than modernists. Many do not even practice Islam, though some observe the faith privately while refusing to allow their religious beliefs to influence their political views. Some pragmatists favor Western democracy, while others favor secular forms of authoritarianism.[25]

One of the most pressing questions facing many countries with large Muslim populations concerns the compatibility of Islam and Western-style liberal democracy. Of the four orientations just described, it would appear that fundamentalist and traditional Muslims would be less likely to favor liberal institutions and freedoms than modernist and pragmatic Muslims. We can therefore hypothesize that democratic institutions stand a better chance for success under modernist or pragmatic Muslim leaders than under intolerant fanatics or dogmatic theocrats.[26] However, Islamic countries have not been successful at building democracy. Of forty-three countries with a Muslim majority, at the end of the 1990s only seven were electoral democracies and only one (Mali) was rated as "free" (i.e., democratic). By contrast, seventy-nine of the eighty-eight "free" countries were predominantly Christian, and another was Israel.[27] If democracy succeeds in Indonesia, where elections were held in 1999 for the first time since the 1950s, it will embrace the most populous Muslim country in the world.

The following sketches of a few representative countries in the Islamic world provide an indication of its political diversity.

Turkey.   Upon the collapse of the centuries-old Ottoman Empire, Turkey was reconstituted as a republic in 1923 under the guidance of **Mustafa Kemal Ataturk** (1881–1938). Kemal Ataturk was firmly committed to a secular state, enforcing a strict separation of government and religion. Since his death the army has been the guardian of "Kemalist" secularism. Though it has permitted electoral democracy at various times, it has occasionally stepped in and taken power directly. The

Kemal Ataturk

military last restored democratic procedures in 1983, but in 1997 it broke up a government led by the Welfare Party, an outspokenly Islamic organization that was the largest party elected to the parliament. The military rejected Welfare's attempts to expand Islamic education and to introduce various reforms favored by large segments of the population, which is 99.8 percent Muslim. After banning the Welfare Party, the military permitted a new Islamic party to be formed under tight restrictions.

Egypt. As president of Egypt since 1981, Hosni Mubarak has based his rule on a largely secular organization, the National Democratic Party, and on the crucial support of the Egyptian military. While courting Muslim popularity by using the state media to broadcast Islamic religious programs, Mubarak has harshly persecuted Muslim groups bent on toppling his government and setting up a more purely religious Islamic state. Many Egyptian Muslims have condemned Mubarak for his handling of the economy, with its extremes of wealth for a few and poverty for the masses, and for his cooperation with Israel and the United States. But in 1999 he staged his fourth "yes-no" referendum on his rule, once again winning more than 95 percent of the vote. No opposition candidates were permitted to run against him, and opposition forces boycotted the vote. Mubarak's predecessor, Anwar al-Sadat, also pursued secular policies and in 1981 was assassinated by members of the extremist Muslim group *Al-Jihad* (The Holy Struggle).

Algeria. A former French colony that won its independence in 1962 after a prolonged war, Algeria has been wracked by a brutal civil conflict pitting the secular military government against Islamic forces led by the Islamic Salvation Front (FIS). Between 1991 and 1999 an estimated one hundred thousand people were killed. In 1992 the government canceled the second round of national elections after the FIS scored major victories in the first round. More fighting ensued, but in 1999 there were new elections. The military regime's favored candidate, Abdelaziz Bouteflika, was elected after the main Islamic candidates withdrew, charging the government with fixing the elections. Bouteflika vowed to restore peace, and his peace plan later in the year was endorsed in a referendum by more than 80 percent of war-weary voters who turned out in large numbers.

Pakistan. Established as an independent state when British India was divided in 1947, Pakistan has a 97 percent Muslim majority. Military governments, mostly with a secular orientation, have governed the country for about twenty-five years, alternating with unstable democracies. In 1997 the Pakistan Muslim League won a large parliamentary majority and formed a government. Tensions with India, a predominantly Hindu country, intensified in 1998 and 1999 as the two neighbors engaged in nuclear weapons tests and resumed their territorial dispute over the province of Kashmir. In the fall of 1999 Gen. Pervaiz Musharraf led a military coup that ousted the civilian government.

THE LEFT-RIGHT SPECTRUM

Now that we've surveyed a number of ideologies, we can present a more detailed left-right political spectrum than the one in chapter 2. In view of the complexities of political reality, however, the traditional left-right political spectrum as presented in figure 13.4 should be taken with a grain

FIGURE 13.4 The Left-Right Spectrum

of salt. Though anarchism is placed on the extreme left, some extreme right-wing groups in the United States are so anti-government that they come close to advocating anarchism. Soviet-style communism (as in the former USSR or contemporary China) is placed on the left because of its historical associations with revolutionary socialism. It is virtually indistinguishable from fascism in several key respects, however. Both communist and fascist regimes have been one-party totalitarian regimes with a highly nationalistic foreign policy. Military regimes, for their part, come in left-wing socialist variants (in which the military leaders take up the cause of the working class or the poor) and right-wing variants (in which the military is aligned with a conservative ruling elite). Religiously oriented states, like fundamentalist or traditionalist Islamic states, are placed on the right because of their reactionary tendency to implement religious and political doctrines as they were propounded more than thirteen hundred years ago; but to the extent that they implement social welfare programs for the masses, they resemble the welfarist tendencies of the socialist left.

These and other intersections across the political spectrum have prompted some observers to suggest that political reality is more accurately represented by a horseshoe (figure 13.5) than by a straight line. The horseshoe depicts the proximity of left and right extremism. Ultimately, both of these graphic representations tend to oversimplify matters. As with virtually every major political phenomenon, ideology must be studied on a comparative basis in order to bring into sharp focus the similarities and differences to be found across place and time.

FIGURE 13.5   A Political Horseshoe

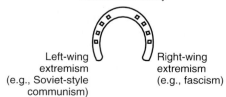

Liberal democracy

Left-wing   Right-wing
extremism   extremism
(e.g., Soviet-style   (e.g., fascism)
communism)

HYPOTHESIS-TESTING EXERCISE: The End of Ideology?

HYPOTHESIS

Using different arguments, a number of scholars have hypothesized that the era of fierce ideological conflict is over.

Hypothesis 1

Daniel Bell, for example, has argued that fundamental changes occurring in the economies of most advanced capitalist countries since World War II have undercut the basis of the historic ideological clash between capitalism and socialism. Instead of being dominated by industrialism, with its emphasis on manufacturing and manual labor, the economies of the United States, Japan, and most West European countries are now driven by the service sector, consisting of financial services (banks, stock markets); consumer services (stores, restaurants, and the like); health and legal services; and so on. Education and technology have become the driving forces of economic advancement. Once a country employs more than half its work force in the service sector, it can be considered a *postindustrial economy.* Under these circumstances, the size of the blue-collar labor force declines relative to white-collar service employees. At the same time, a growing number of better-paid workers think of themselves as middle class rather than working class. As a consequence, Bell argues, the classic confrontation between the capitalist bourgeoisie and the industrial proletariat essentially dies out. Political life inside the postindustrial democracies increasingly revolves around moderate middle-class parties instead of the sharply antagonistic parties of the traditional left and right.[28]

Hypothesis 2

A related but more recent "end-of-ideology" hypothesis maintains that the forces of technological advancement and economic globalization since the 1970s have undermined the traditional dichotomy between capitalism and socialism on a global scale. Most of the extraordinary technological innovations of the past several decades, especially in the computer and telecommunications industries, were pioneered by private companies. One of the principal reasons why the Soviet Union collapsed, according to this hypothesis, was that its centrally planned socialist economy proved incapable of keeping up with the accelerated pace of high technology advancement in countries with private enterprise. Meanwhile, the private-enterprise economies long ago ceased being "capitalist" in the sense in which Karl Marx and many of his followers in subsequent generations understood the term. Historically, capitalism meant that the state allowed private companies maximum freedom to do what they pleased; if government played any role at all, in the traditional Marxist view, it was to side with the bourgeoisie against the working masses. But the economies of the United States, Japan, and Western Europe today are *mixed economies* in which the state plays a major role, at times assisting private firms and at times regulating their activities. These countries, moreover, are all *welfare states* in which the workers have collective bargaining rights and the government provides a host of welfare benefits to the general population, such as education, unemployment, health insurance, health care, pensions, and the like. They are also mass democracies.

The second hypothesis therefore asserts that the mixed-economy democracies have proven their superiority as the contemporary world's most stable and successful economic system, clearly outperforming Soviet-stye socialism and virtually all other authoritarian governments. As a consequence, there is a growing global consensus on the desirability of the democratic mixed-economy model as the optimal form of political and economic organization. Over time, by implication, all other ideological rivals to this model will lose support and die out.

VARIABLES

In these closely related hypotheses, the **dependent variable** is the *end of ideological conflict*, both within countries and among the nations of the world. The **independent variable** in Hypothesis 1 is *postindustrialism*. In Hypothesis 2 it is *the superiority of mixed-economy democracies* to all other ideological rivals.

EXPECTATIONS

If the hypotheses are true, we would expect to find that conflict between proponents of capitalism and socialism has died out in postindustrial economies, both domestically and globally. Bell's hypothesis would have us find that in postindustrial democracies, traditional labor-oriented leftist parties and business-oriented right-wing parties have been superseded by centrist parties sharing a broad consensus on political and economic issues. The second hypothesis projects a global increase in the number of countries becoming mixed-economy democracies and a decline in competing ideological orientations such as communism, fascism, religious ideologies, and others.

EVIDENCE

The evidence required to put these hypotheses to a systematic test is so vast that it is impossible to fulfill the task here. The most we can do for now is mention a few facts that touch on the hypotheses and their expectations.

In support of Bell's hypothesis, it is evident that political life in virtually all postindustrial democracies in today's world no longer revolves around capitalist parties committed to unregulated capitalism and labor-oriented parties committed to socialism. Since the end of World War II, and in some countries even earlier, the parties that attract the most votes have tended to be centrist parties that accept a broad political consensus on the mixed economy and the welfare state. This ideological consensus is typically shared by the largest conservative parties (which still tend to favor the business sector) as well as by the leading social democratic parties (which still tend to represent the labor movement). All these countries also have a sizable middle class, and in some cases manual workers consider themselves members of this class. Moreover, in most of these countries, assertive communist parties seeking state control of the economy have either died out or joined in the general consensus.

Nevertheless, within this broad consensus on the nature of the economy there is ample room for conflict. The clash between business-oriented conservative parties and labor-oriented social democratic parties continues to be one of the liveliest sources of political contention in most postindustrial democracies. Conflicts over tax policy, wages, workers' benefits, unemployment, and the like still spark serious political contention in most economically advanced democracies. It is also the case that pronouncedly anti-capitalist communist or leftist parties and extremely nationalistic or racist neo-fascist parties can still be found in a number of today's postindustrial democracies, though they rarely get more than 15 percent of the vote.

The second hypothesis, which posits a rise in mixed-economy democracies worldwide and a general decline in rival ideologies, finds support in the fact that the centrally planned economies of the former Soviet Union and the communist-ruled states of East-Central Europe fell far behind the mixed-economy democracies in developing advanced technologies and maintaining economic growth. As the hypothesis would lead us to expect, Soviet-style communist planning is now being replaced in these countries by private enterprise and other features of the modern mixed economy. Even China, which continues to be governed by a powerful communist party, abandoned central planning in the 1980s and now has a considerable amount of private enterprise. A growing number of less developed countries in Asia, Latin America, Africa, and the Middle East, as well, have made substantial changes in their economic systems since the 1980s, reducing the degree of state domination of the economy and expanding opportunities for private enterprise. In quite a few cases these economic changes have been accompanied by efforts to establish democracy.[29]

On the other side of the ledger, it is also true that ideological opposition to the prevailing Western model of the mixed-economy democracy continues to exist in various parts of the world, in some instances quite vociferously. In Russia, for example, the triumph of private enterprise and democracy is still by no means assured. The Russian Communist Party, with its outspoken criticisms of the private sector, remains a significant force in Russian politics, as do extreme nationalistic forces. China openly advertises its own model, combining private enterprise with stern authoritarian rule. The desirability of combining private enterprise with some form or another of authoritarian rule has a wide following in other East Asian countries as well. In addition, as we have seen, Muslims around the world have advanced their own ideological alternatives to Western political and economic models. The more extreme of these alternatives reflect a categorical rejection of Western ideas as "satanic." One scholar, Benjamin Barber, characterizes the clash between contemporary Islam and the technologically advanced democracies in terms of "Jihad versus McWorld."[30] Finally, it cannot be casually assumed that no new ideological orientations will arise in the future. A large proportion of the world's population lives in abject poverty; the blessings of the modern mixed-economy welfare state have eluded them. As Kenneth Jowett has observed, new political ideas and "movements of rage" may yet emerge from these desperate conditions or from other political landscapes where Western ideas are deemed inappropriate or downright unacceptable.[31]

CONCLUSIONS

The sketchy evidence we have just summarized is quite *mixed*. On balance, the evidence bearing on Bell's hypothesis is mostly consistent with his proposition that postindustrial economies tend to reduce internal ideological conflict between traditional socialist and capitalist orientations. Even so, political conflicts between business and labor remain high on the agendas of most postindustrial democracies. Globalization often intensifies these conflicts by throwing people out of work when their companies move abroad to take advantage of cheaper labor, lower taxes, or other incentives. The evidence relating to the second hypothesis is still inconclusive. While there seems to be a "wave" of democracy and private enterprise billowing around the world, the long-term success of these efforts is by no means a certainty. Islamic ideology and other orientations still pose a challenge to Western political and economic ideas.

KEY TERMS
(Underlined in the text)

Ideology
Liberalism
Conservatism
Socialism
Marxism
Bourgeoisie
Proletariat
Leninism
Social democracy
Fascism
Chauvinism
State corporatism
Shariah
Sunni
Shiite

NOTES

1. For a widely read analysis, see Louis Hartz, *The Liberal Tradition in America* (New York: Harcourt, Brace, and World, 1955).
2. For a biography of Burke, see Conor Cruise O'Brien, *The Great Melody* (Chicago: University of Chicago Press, 1992). See also Burke's critique of the French Revolution, *Reflections on the Revolution in France* (1790).
3. Stathis N. Kalyvas, *The Rise of Christian Democracy in Europe* (Ithaca, N.Y.: Cornell University Press, 1996).
4. On utopian socialism, see Edmund Wilson, *To the Finland Station* (Garden City, N.Y.: Doubleday, 1940); Robert Heilbroner, *The Worldly Philosophers*, 6th ed. (New York: Simon and Schuster, 1992); and Charles Nordhoff, *The Communistic Societies of the United States* (New York: Hillary House, 1960), first published in 1875.
5. "Contribution to the Critique of Hegel's *Philosophy of Right:* Introduction" (1843), and "On the Jewish Question" (1843), in Robert C. Tucker, ed., *The Marx-Engels Reader* (New York: Norton, 1972), 12, 24–51.
6. *Economic and Philosophic Manuscripts of 1844*, excerpted in Tucker, *The Marx-Engels Reader*, 53–103. This work was not published in full until 1932.
7. Engels's first book, *The Condition of the Working Class in England in 1844*, describes in grim detail the sordidness of working-class life in Manchester and other industrial centers. Excerpts are in Tucker, *The Marx-Engels Reader*, 429–35.
8. "The mode of production of economic life conditions the social, political and intellectual process in general." From *A Contribution to the Critique of Political Economy*, Tucker, *The Marx-Engels Reader*, 4. See also Melvin Rader, *Marx's Conception of History* (New York: Oxford University Press, 1979).
9. *Manifesto of the Communist Party*, in Tucker, *The Marx-Engels Reader*, 335.

10. Marx, "The Class Struggles in France 1848–1850" (1850), cited in Tucker, *The Marx-Engels Reader*, 406; *Critique of the Gotha Program* (written in 1875, published in 1891), ibid., 395. See also Engels's introduction to the republication in 1891 of Marx's *The Civil War in France* (1871), ibid., 537.

11. Engels would later reinforce this point, affirming that once the working class eliminates the economic basis of class conflict, "the government of persons is replaced by the administration of things . . . The state," he insisted, "is not 'abolished'. *It dies out.*" This formulation became known as the doctrine of "the withering away of the state." See Engels, *Socialism: Utopian and Scientific* (1880), Tucker, *The Marx-Engels Reader*, 635.

12. *Critique of the Gotha Program* (1875), Tucker, *The Marx-Engels Reader*, 388.

13. Engels, "On Social Relations in Russia," (1875), Tucker, *The Marx-Engels Reader*, 589–99; Marx and Engels, preface to the Russian edition of the *Manifesto* (1882), ibid., 333–34.

14. V. I. Lenin, *What Is to Be Done?* in *The Lenin Anthology*, ed. Robert C. Tucker (New York: W. W. Norton, 1975), 12–114.

15. Bernstein wrote that the United States "apparently contradicts everything that the socialistic theory has hitherto advanced." In 1906 a prominent German sociologist addressed this curiosity. See Werner Sombart, *Why Is There No Socialism in the United States?* trans. Patricia M. Hocking and C. T. Husbands (White Plains, N.Y.: M. E. Sharpe, 1976). The American Socialist Party fielded presidential candidates between 1900 and 1932 but its candidates never obtained a million votes. For a biography of the party's last major leader, see W. A. Swanberg, *Norman Thomas, the Last Idealist* (New York: Scribner, 1976).

16. Julius K. Nyerere, *Ujamaa—Essays on Socialism* (London: Oxford University Press, 1968).

17. For an early account, see William H. Friedland and Carl G. Rosberg Jr., eds., *African Socialism* (Stanford, Calif.: Stanford University Press, 1964).

18. Abdel Moghny Said, *Arab Socialism* (London: Blandford Press, 1972).

19. Stanley G. Payne, *A History of Fascism, 1914–1945* (Madison, University of Wisconsin Press, 1995).

20. Meir Michaelis, *Mussolini and the Jews* (London: Oxford University Press, 1978).

21. Benito Mussolini and Giovanni Gentile, "The Doctrine of Fascism," in *Italian Fascisms from Pareto to Gentile,* ed. Adrian Lyttlelton, trans. Douglas Parmee (New York: Harper and Row, 1973), 42. See also Herman Finer, *Mussolini's Italy* (New York: Grosset and Dunlap, 1965), 198, 201. This classic work was first published in 1935.

22. On Mussolini's progression from socialism to fascism, see A. James Gregor, *Young Mussolini and the Intellectual Origins of Fascism* (Berkeley: University of California Press, 1979).

23. Ernst Nolte, *Three Faces of Fascism,* trans. Leila Vennewitz (New York: Mentor, 1969), 282.

24. One leading scholar of fascism, A. James Gregor, has argued that fascist ideas may be found even in political movements that are not openly identified as fascist, including communist parties in Asia and Latin America and radical groups in the United States. Fascism and twentieth-century communism, he argues, are not mutually exclusive but share certain things in common, especially nationalism, totalitarianism, and mass mobilization. See *The Fascist Persuasion in Radical Politics* (Princeton, N.J.: Princeton University Press, 1974).

25. Mir Zohair Husain, *Global Islamic Politics* (New York: HarperCollins, 1996). See also Edward Said, *Orientalism* (New York: Vintage, 1979); Edward Mortimer, *Faith and Power* (New York: Vintage, 1982); Bernard Lewis, *The Political Language of Islam* (Chicago: University of Chicago Press, 1988); John L. Esposito, *Islam,* 2d ed. (New York: Oxford University Press, 1991), and *The Islamic Threat: Myth or Reality?* (New York: Oxford University Press, 1992).

26. On the relationship between Islam and democracy, see Leonard Binder, *Islamic Liberalism* (Chicago: University of Chicago Press, 1988).

27. *Freedom in the World 1998–1999* (New York: Freedom House, 1999), 11.

28. Daniel Bell, *The End of Ideology,* rev. ed. (New York: Free Press, 1961), *The Coming of Post-Industrial Society* (New York: Basic Books, 1973 and 1999), and *The Cultural Contradictions of Capitalism* (New York: Basic Books, 1976). See also Chaim I. Waxman, ed., *The End of Ideology Debate* (New York: Simon and Schuster, 1969).

29. Daniel Yergin and Joseph Stanislaw, *The Commanding Heights* (New York: Simon and Schuster, 1998).

30. Benjamin R. Barber, *Jihad Versus McWorld* (New York: Times Book, 1995).

31. Kenneth Jowett, *New World Disorder* (Berkeley: University of California Press, 1992), 275–77.

CHAPTER 14

POLITICAL ECONOMY
Laissez-Faire—Central Planning— Mixed Economies—Welfare States

Politics and economics are intimately interrelated. Whether it is a matter of taxes, budget deficits, health care programs, or foreign trade, economic issues are invariably the stuff of intense political controversy and governmental decision making. Especially in today's tightly woven interdependent world, a sound understanding of economics is more than just useful: it's a survival skill. Consider the following example of how international relationships affect the value of our money.

A TOURIST'S GUIDE TO INTERNATIONAL ECONOMICS

Most countries have their own currency: the U.S. dollar, the Japanese yen, and the Swiss franc are among the most widely used currencies in the world. Most members of the European Union share a common currency, the euro. Just like stocks and bonds, currencies are bought and sold on world markets by banks and other private currency traders. Nearly *one trillion* dollars' worth of currencies change hands around the globe on a typical business day. And just like stocks and bonds, currencies change their relative value as a result of these global transactions.

A currency's value—its price relative to other currencies—can often be affected by *political* as well as economic considerations. If currency traders believe that Country X may experience political instability or tur-

moil such as an unpredictable new government or a civil war, they may sell off their holdings of that country's currency, buying up the currencies of more politically stable countries instead. They may do the same thing if they believe that Country X is about to experience major economic difficulties. When a country's currency is being sold in large quantities in world currency exchanges, its value relative to stronger, more desirable currencies drops, or *depreciates,* significantly.

The result of **currency depreciation** (or **currency devaluation**) can be felt instantly by tourists visiting the country whose currency is declining in value. Suppose you are an American tourist visiting Mexico. When you arrive, the Mexican peso is valued at 3.5 to the dollar. At this rate, you buy 350 pesos for $100. After a few days of dining and shopping, you need more pesos. But in the meantime, Mexico experiences a currency crisis as international traders begin a massive sell-off of pesos. The next time you go to a bank to exchange your dollars, you find to your delight that the peso is now valued at 5 to the dollar. For $100 you can now get 500 pesos in exchange. Your dollar is worth more relative to the peso than it was when you arrived. If the peso continues to slide in value, you may be able to extend your stay or buy more items, since each dollar exchanged buys more Mexican goods and services than it did upon your arrival. Mexicans involved in the tourist trade eagerly welcome your additional expenditures. Like you, they stand to benefit from the peso's devaluation.

For many Mexicans, however, the peso's depreciation brings unwelcome consequences. Mexicans who buy imported goods from the United States such as computers or autos must now pay out more pesos per dollar's worth of purchase. A $1,000 American-made computer cost 3,500 pesos before the currency crisis; it now costs 5,000 pesos following the Mexican currency's devaluation. At the new rate of exchange, a Mexican consumer or businessperson may decide that it's too expensive to buy the computer at the higher peso price. In that case, the U.S. computer exporter loses a sale. For a U.S.-based company that sells a lot of goods south of the border, the peso's decline may result in a severe loss of customers. The business may be forced to lay off workers or may even go bankrupt.

Imagine the impact of the peso's decline on billions of dollars' worth of economic transactions between the two countries. (In 1998, U.S. exports to Mexico totaled $79 billion and Mexican exports to the United States totaled $94.7 billion.) Large numbers of tourists, consumers, and businesses on both sides of the border are directly affected by the shift: some positively, others negatively. *In virtually every case of currency depreciation, there are winners and losers* (see table 14.1). Those who are economically disadvantaged will exert pressure on the Mexican and U.S. governments to do something about the peso's decline. The economic issue now becomes a political issue: people want governments to take action.

What can governments do in this situation? The most immediate option is for governments to *intervene in world currency markets* by buying pesos. Like stocks, the value of a currency rises the more it is purchased. If the U.S. and Mexican governments spend millions of dollars from their treasuries to buy pesos, the value of the peso will likely rise. It may not go all the way back from 5 to the dollar to 3.5, but at least it will move closer to the latter figure. Most important, the object of the governments' intervention is to *stabilize* the peso so that it will not fall or rise wildly, but will retain a fairly stable and predictable value against the dollar and other world currencies.

The case just outlined is not fictitious. At the end of 1994, the Mexican peso began falling in value against the U.S. dollar exactly as described. Within a few months the peso plunged from 3.45 to 8 to the dollar. To halt the peso's slide, the Mexican government spent millions of U.S. dollars in its possession (its dollar *reserves*) to buy pesos on world markets. The U.S. government joined with other governments in providing the Mexican government with a $38 billion rescue package to strengthen its economy, in hopes of making the peso more attractive to currency buyers. Though the peso's value rose in response to this assistance, it fell once again in the fall of 1995.

The peso's sudden deterioration had profound political consequences for both Mexico and the United States. In Mexico it triggered a severe economic crisis. The prices of imported goods rose dramatically, hurting businesses and consumers. Prices in 1995 were more than 40 percent higher than the previous year. As many as one million people were thrown out of work in 1995 alone because their employers could no longer afford to pay them. The country's domestic economic growth fell; interest rates skyrocketed to as much as 100 percent. A significant increase in violent crime in Mexico City and other parts of the country was attributed to rising economic frustration. Predictably, Mexicans from all walks of life looked to their government to help them. In the United States, the Clinton administration and the Republican-controlled Congress worked out a response to the Mexican situation because American businesses and consumers have an interest in a stable, fairly valued peso. Approximately seven hundred thousand jobs in the United States depended on trade with Mexico. The United States also had an interest in helping Mexico avoid potentially violent internal unrest as well as a rise in illegal immigrants coming across the U.S. border.

But as the peso fell, Mexico's exports rose more than 30 percent over the next few years. Sales to the United States, which buys 80 percent of the country's export goods, got an additional boost from the North American Free Trade Agreement (NAFTA), which reduces trade barriers between the United States, Mexico, and Canada. The steep rise in Mexico's export industry

TABLE 14.1
Winners and Losers in a Currency Devaluation

As the Mexican peso depreciates relative to the U.S. dollar . . .

Winners	Losers
U.S. purchasers and importers of Mexican goods and services	Mexican purchasers and importers of U.S. goods and services
Mexican sellers and exporters to U.S. buyers	U.S. sellers and exporters to Mexican buyers

helped stabilize the economy and boosted growth rates considerably starting in 1996. While wages for industrial workers and other aspects of Mexico's economy deteriorated as a result of the currency evaluation, exports and other sectors improved. Winners as well as losers were still in evidence in Mexico several years after the peso's dramatic fall.

Economics is the study of how people and societies choose to use and allocate the scarce resources at their disposal, such as natural resources, human-made goods, and human services. Accordingly, economists examine such things as the way prices are determined, the impact of taxes, and such other phenomena as production, inflation, unemployment, and the causes of economic growth and decline.

Like political science, economics is a behavioral science: one of its main ambitions is to examine the ways individuals and organizations behave when making economic choices and decisions. And like at least some political scientists, many economists employ **rational choice theory,** the notion that people generally act on the basis of calculated self-interest to maximize their gains and reduce their costs or risks. Thus *homo economicus*—economic man—is a rational actor who is able to figure out how to increase his wealth and minimize his losses. Viewed from the larger perspective of an entire society, however, a collection of individual and corporate rational actors may not necessarily produce economic results that maximize everyone's welfare. What is rational for you may be bad for me. If you decide to raise prices for the goods you sell me, you are increasing my costs. Sometimes decisions that are rational for an individual or a particular company may prove harmful for the larger community. If a factory keeps its costs down by refusing to use expensive pollution control devices, the pollutants its chimneys belch into the air not only damage the public's health but raise the community's health care costs in the process. Conversely, it can also happen that economic decisions that are rational for the community as a whole may be deleterious for particular individuals or groups. If the government, for example, decides to trim its budget deficit by raising your taxes, you may not personally appreciate the rationality of its choice.

In short, the economic activities of individuals, private enterprises, and governments very often produce negative consequences for others. Of course, there are times when public and private economic policies benefit just about everyone to a greater or lesser degree. A growing economy can afford better roads, more medical research, cleaner air. In these cases, everyone wins. But all too often there are losers as well as winners. This outcome is especially likely when the resources people want—money, land, jobs, and so on—are limited in quantity, an all-too-common occurrence. As a consequence, the allocation of scarce resources in society can sometimes be a zero-sum game. That is, it may be impossible to improve one person's welfare without reducing the welfare of someone else.[1] In other commonly occurring cases a decision that may improve your welfare in the long run (balanced budgets, for example) may worsen it in the short run (higher taxes).

In these and other social relationships that arise out of economic interactions, conflicts over "who gets what" often result. Whenever conflict occurs over economic issues and the state is expected to deal with them, economics is joined with politics. Every economic system, moreover, is "political" in the sense that it is embedded in laws and procedures that are sanctioned by the state. Whether it is a private-enterprise system, socialism, or some other mode of economic organization, the state invariably makes laws that determine how the economy works in practice. Economics is therefore always inseparable from politics.

> **Political economy** *is the study of how communities pursue collective economic goals and deal with conflicts over resources and other economic factors in an authoritative way by means of government.*

In other words, *political economy is about the relationship between the economy and the state and about the various ways people try to use the state to improve their economic welfare.*

Viewed in the most general terms, political economy is interested in two broad sets of questions: (1) *How does economics affect politics?* and (2) *How does politics affect economics?* In question 1, economics is the *independent variable* (i.e., the cause or influencing factor) and politics is the *dependent variable* (i.e., the effect). Here's an example:

1. *Economics affects politics.* It frequently happens in democracies that many voters, sometimes a majority, "vote their pocketbooks": they vote for candidates who appear most likely to improve their economic well-being. Empirical evidence in the United States shows that, since World War II, incumbent presidents usually win reelection if the economy grows by about 4 percent or more in the four quarters preceding the election.[2]

In question 2 the variables are reversed: politics is the independent variable and economics is the dependent variable. Here's an example:

2. *Politics affects economics.* In 1996 and 1997, President Bill Clinton signed bills passed by the Republican-dominated majority in Congress designed to balance the annual federal government budget by 2002. This legislation, hammered out in long negotiations that required the Democrats and Republicans to compromise their differences, is credited with promoting one of the longest periods of sustained economic growth and high employment in decades.

Because economic transactions and political activity go on all the time, *the relationship between politics and economics is frequently interactive.* That is, economic variables affect political variables, which in turn affect economic variables, which then affect political variables, and so on. A central purpose of political economy is to clarify these interacting relationships.

One of the most important of these relationships is the relationship between *states* and *markets.* Such terms as "markets," "the market economy," and "market forces" refer mainly to the private sector. They apply broadly to the production, buying, and selling of goods and services by private companies and individuals, with prices and salaries determined largely by the forces of supply and demand rather than by government fiat. Political economy examines such questions as, How do government policies affect market forces, and vice versa? Should governments control or regulate the economy, or should markets have fairly free rein? Can there be an acceptable balance between states and markets?

The answers to these questions, whether of an empirical or prescriptive nature, will vary from country to country and are often grist for the mill of incessant debate within individual countries.[3]

Because political economy encompasses a wide range of specific issues, we'll spread out our conceptual treatment of this topic over two chapters. This chapter looks first at some basic terminology in economics. It then examines three systems of political economy: *laissez-faire capitalism, central planning,* and *mixed economies.* Each one entails a different theory of the relationship between the state and the economy. A prime example of a mixed economy is the modern *welfare state,* which is discussed in the last section of this chapter. The next chapter focuses on countries engaged in early stages of economic development.

SOME BASIC ECONOMIC CONCEPTS

In order to grasp the main issues of political economy, an understanding of a few central concepts in economics is essential. The definitions in the accompanying box are by no means intended as a substitute for a course in economics. Our aim here is simply to provide some rudimentary information about basic economic phenomena and analytical terminology with a view to enhancing your understanding of politics.

BASIC ECONOMIC CONCEPTS

The **Gross National Product (GNP)** refers to the *total amount of goods and services produced by a country's economy in a specified time period.* It measures not only what the country's economy is producing at home, but also the income earned by the country's residents from their investments and businesses overseas. The income earned by foreigners from their investments in the host country is subtracted from the latter figure. Thus if the domestic economy of country X generated $10 trillion worth of income at home last year, and residents of X earned $2 trillion abroad, while foreigners earned $1 trillion from their investments in X, then X's GNP last year was $11 trillion.

The **Gross Domestic Product (GDP)** is just the *total output in goods and services of a country's domestic economy.* It does not include the income of residents earned abroad, nor does it take account of the income of

Stacks of *Reichsmark* bills were needed to make simple purchases as the German currency's value rapidly depreciated in the great inflation of 1922–23.

foreigners from investments within the country's borders. Because it excludes these latter two figures, the GDP is considered a more accurate measure than the GNP of what an economy is actually producing at home through the efforts of its own citizens.

Economic growth refers to *increases in a country's GNP or GDP over a specified period of time.* If a country's national or domestic income falls below the previous period's figure, it experiences *negative growth.*

Inflation means *steadily rising prices.* The **inflation rate** measures the extent to which the average price for goods in one time period exceeds average prices in some previous period. If the average price for a typical "market basket" of a society's goods and services in 1999 was 10 percent higher than the average price for those same goods in 1998, then the annual inflation rate for 1999 was 10 percent.

Inflation has several different causes. One is an excess in a country's supply of money in circulation. As a result, the money's value declines (or *depreciates*): a single dollar buys less and less. The expression, "Too many dollars chasing too few goods," captures this problem. To remedy it, the government must stop printing more money or significantly reduce the amount it is printing. Governmental decisions affecting the money supply are the main concern of *monetary policy.* **Monetarism** is an economic theory that emphasizes the links between a country's money supply and such phenomena as inflation and economic growth. One of its most influential exponents has been **Milton Friedman,** a Nobel Prize winner.

Prolonged inflation can be ruinous. When the inflation rate tops 10 percent to 15 percent per year, governments are usually expected to step in and solve the problem. Their efforts are not always successful. Between 1987 and 1991, the annual inflation rate averaged more than 1,000 percent in Argentina and Brazil and more than 2,000 percent in Peru. In 1993 Ukraine had an inflation rate of 8,000 percent. In 1923, Germany's inflation rate topped 1 billion percent! Inflation of this magnitude is called **hyperinflation,** which is usually defined as an inflation rate that exceeds 50 percent per month. Failure to reduce runaway inflation can jeopardize a government's ability to stay in power. Inflation can therefore be just as much a political problem as an economic one.

The **central bank** is the national government's official bank. In the United States it is the Federal Reserve System. In most countries the central bank's main tasks are to determine how much money to print and to provide loans to private (commercial) banks. Central banks may also engage in open market transactions such as buying and selling government bonds. These various actions often have the effect of raising or lowering the nation's inflation rate.

For instance, when private banks borrow cash from the central bank for their own lending and investment operations, the central bank charges them interest. If inflation is undesirably high, the central bank may raise the interest rate it charges to commercial banks. The central bank's interest rate is called the *discount rate* or the *bank rate.* Through this action the central bank can indirectly raise commercial interest rates throughout the economy. If the commercial banks must pay higher interest to the central bank, they cover this added expense by charging their own customers higher interest rates for personal or business loans. Higher commercial interest rates discourage prospective borrowers. As interest rates go up, fewer people are willing to take out personal loans for college tuition, auto purchases, home mortgages, or other big expenditures, and fewer businesses are willing to borrow heavily to expand their operations. Less money gets circulated in the economy, the demand for goods declines, and inflation falls. But as a result of this "tight money" policy, business in general may also fall off and unemployment may rise.

Conversely, the economy could be in a recession or a depression. The difference is mainly a matter of degree. A **recession** is a period of low growth, zero growth, or negative growth, resulting in declining business activity, rising unemployment, and perhaps some bankruptcies. A **depression** is much more severe, with prolonged negative growth, massive unemployment, and widespread bankruptcies. In these situations inflation is typically low or nonexistent; prices tend to fall. To stimulate the economy, the central bank may reduce the discount rate or take other action to make money more available to businesses and consumers. If successful, this "easy money" policy revives business activity and reduces unemployment, though prices may rise in the process.

A trade-off exists between inflation and employment: governmental policies aimed at keeping inflation low may at times increase unemployment, while policies aimed at stimulating business and increasing employment opportunities may sometimes increase the inflation rate. The aim of most governments is to sustain both high employment and low inflation simultaneously, but this dual objective is sometimes hard to achieve. Governments therefore frequently have to make difficult policy choices that may adversely affect certain segments of the population for at least the short term, if not longer. Because central banks can have such a powerful influence on the economy, their policies often trigger political conflict.

The question of who controls the central bank is therefore crucial and profoundly political. Some central banks are fairly independent of the executive and legislative branches of government and enjoy ample latitude to make tough decisions that may be good for the economy but unpopular, such as raising interest rates. (The U.S. Federal Reserve bank is an example.) Other central banks are less independent of political decision makers and may have less freedom to make politically unpopular decisions.

A **budget deficit** occurs when a government spends more than it takes in. When expenditures equal revenues, the government has a **balanced budget.**

The **national debt** is the amount of money a government owes as the result of a budget deficit at the end of the fiscal year or as the result of accumulated budget deficits over a period of years. The government owes the debt to people from whom it has borrowed money to pay its bills. In order to meet its expenditures from one year to the next, a government that cannot earn sufficient revenue from taxes or other sources must borrow the necessary sums from private lenders or other governments. Like any commercial borrower, the government must pay its creditors interest on the loans, thus raising the amount it owes even more.

One way governments borrow money is to issue bonds (like U.S. Savings bonds) or treasury bills ("T-bills"). The purchasers are reimbursed, with interest, after a specified period of time. Usually people will buy these bonds only if they have confidence in the government's ability to pay them back, along with the promised interest. Governments that cannot evoke such confidence from potential lenders are in real trouble. They may have to apply to other governments or international lending institutions to bail them out of their debts.

One of the negative consequences of a large and enduring national debt is that it requires the indebted government to pay ever-increasing sums in interest payments. (Paying interest in periodic installments is called **debt servicing.**) In addition, by borrowing huge amounts of cash from bond purchasers, the government is soaking up money that would otherwise remain in people's hands, to be spent by consumers or invested by businesspeople. Persistent government borrowing, in other words, deprives the national economy of funds that could be more productively utilized, through consumer spending and business investment, to boost economic growth. Some economists recommend that no government should ever allow its deficits to exceed a certain amount (say, 3 percent of GDP per year). Nevertheless, as long as a government's creditors remain confident that they will be paid, governments can go on borrowing indefinitely.

> The U.S. government ran consecutive annual budget deficits from 1969 through 1998. By the end of that period the national debt stood at $5.4 trillion, requiring budgetary outlays in excess of $243 million to service the debt in 1998, an amount that consumed 14.7 percent of the federal budget. Thanks to a booming economy, the United States finally realized a budget surplus in 1999.

Ultimately, there are only two ways to reduce budget deficits and the national debt: slash government spending or raise revenue such as taxes. (For especially large debts, both may have to be done simultaneously.) Obviously, these choices can be quite painful for large segments of the population. Even though it may be rational for the country as a whole to undertake these measures, individuals who might be economically hurt by reduced government spending or higher taxes will consider it rational for themselves to oppose such measures. The result, of course, is serious political conflict. In sum, deficits and debts are the results of *political* choices, not just purely economic ones.

Fiscal policy *is tax policy.* The term derives from the "fisc," a synonym for the state treasury. There are many ways taxes can be levied. One of the most common political controversies surrounding tax questions centers on the fairness of the tax burden. **Progressive income taxes** are generally considered to be fair because they *take a rising proportion of income as income rises.* The rich must pay at a higher rate than lower-income households do. Critics of this system charge, however, that a "soak the rich" tax policy hinders overall economic growth and employment opportunities because it deprives the most well-endowed consumers and investors in the economy of money they could use to buy goods and services or invest in productive businesses.

Regressive taxes *take a decreasing percentage of income as income rises.* There are several types. **Sales taxes,** for example, are generally regressive in nature. If everyone in a certain jurisdiction (such as Alabama or France) is subject to the same sales tax rate (say, 10 percent) for certain categories of goods, lower-income people will pay out a higher portion of their income for these taxes than will wealthier people, especially if such necessities as food and clothing are taxed. Low-income people have to spend most of their earnings, whereas the rich can afford to save or invest a portion of their income, and what they do not spend is not subject to sales taxes.

In the United States the federal government has at times imposed national sales taxes on such things as gasoline, alcoholic beverages, and cigarettes. In addition, the fifty states have the right to impose statewide sales taxes. Local communities in the United States, such as cities and counties, also have certain tax powers, as in the case of real estate taxes.

Many countries in Western Europe and elsewhere have a national **value added tax** (VAT) on certain types of goods and services. The VAT is a national sales tax imposed at every point in the production and marketing process of specified goods. Ultimately it is the final consumer who ends up paying the entire tax. By the mid-1990s the average VAT rate was about 20 percent in most countries belonging to the European Union, though the actual rate varied with the item.

Finally, a **flat tax** taxes everyone's income at the same rate (say, 20 percent), regardless of their wealth. In the United States, a national flat tax has been proposed in recent years by both liberal and conservative candidates for president, but never adopted.

LAISSEZ-FAIRE CAPITALISM

The form of political economy with the least amount of governmental interference is known as **laissez-faire** capitalism. *Laissez-faire* (less-ay fair) means "let do" or "leave alone" in French. In effect, the state leaves private individuals alone in their economic activity and lets them do whatever they want. **Capitalism** means private ownership of businesses, in other words, **private enterprise.**

In a completely pure laissez-faire economy, private enterprise is really *free* enterprise: the government plays little or no role in restricting private economic activity. People are free to make as much money as they can by whatever means, subject perhaps to a few laws regulating contracts and penalizing criminal behavior. In such a system there are no taxes to be paid, no health or safety regulations to be concerned about, and no laws requiring employers to pay their employees minimum wages, limit their working hours, or provide them with paid vacations. There are no laws regulating child or female labor. In its most extreme variant, laissez-faire capitalism can be quite beneficial to entrepreneurs, allowing them to concentrate on the rigors of economic competition and the laws of the marketplace. But it can be extremely detrimental to workers and other employees, leaving them unprotected against the demands of their employers. Laissez-faire capitalism prevailed in the United States, Britain, and a few other countries during Karl Marx's lifetime.

Laissez-faire capitalism in its purest form is the most unregulated variant of a market economy. *A* **market economy** *is an economic system in which prices are determined mainly by supply and demand.* The government, in other words, does not control the price system. The prices of goods and services are established by "what the market will bear": by the independent decisions of sellers and buyers, each seeking to get the most for their money in a market characterized by open competition between businesses. One of the first exponents of this type of economic system was **Adam Smith,** the first major theoretician of laissez-faire capitalism.

ADAM SMITH
(1723–1790)

The year 1776 produced two classic manifestos of political and economic liberty: the Declaration of Independence of the American colonies, and Adam Smith's monumental work, *An Inquiry into the Nature and Causes of The Wealth of Nations* (or *The Wealth of Nations,* for short). Thomas Jefferson's Declaration launched the American Revolution. Smith's treatise launched an intellectual revolution, providing the most detailed theoretical explanation up to that time of how a freely operating market economy might function and of how it could constitute the most effective possible mechanism for expanding national wealth. Smith's book was a passionate plea for the removal of virtually all governmental restrictions on private enterprise. Just as Jefferson proclaimed America's

Adam Smith

political independence from the British crown, Smith insisted on the British economy's independence from the crown's intrusive intervention.

One of Smith's original insights was the notion that labor was more than just common drudgery necessary to sustain life, a view harbored by many economists of his day. He argued that, when liberated from excessive governmental restraints, work produces wealth. Not only does a free economy provide the best means of enhancing the wealth of individuals; Smith argued that it also promotes the wealth of entire nations.

The idea for which Smith is perhaps most famous is that the pursuit of every individual's economic self-interest ultimately increases the wealth of society as a whole. Personal gain enhances the common good. Smith believed that individuals are motivated basically by the quest for social status and material wealth in their economic undertakings. Without intentionally striving to do so, however, acquisitive private entrepreneurs end up promoting the general welfare. "It is not from the benevolence of the butcher, the brewer, or the baker that we expect our dinner," he wrote, "but from their regard to their own interest." In a celebrated image, Smith said that the self-interested economic decisions of individuals would lead to the enlargement of society's welfare as if guided to that end by an "invisible hand." The enterprising individual, he wrote,

neither intends to promote the public interest, nor knows how much he is promoting it. (He) intends only his own gain; and he is in this, as in many other cases, led by an invisible hand to promote an end which was no part of his intention. . . . By pursuing his interest, he frequently promotes that of the soci-

ety more effectually than when he really intends to promote it.

Smith therefore recommended that private self-interest be given free rein and that all governmental impediments to "perfect liberty" in economic life be removed.

The freely operating market economy, in Smith's view, would not lead to chaos. On the contrary, it would be a self-sustaining mechanism that would regulate production, prices, wages, and even population through a spontaneous combination of incentives and restraints. The profit motive would stimulate production, but competition would keep prices in check, since consumers would seek the best bargains. Firms that produced more than they could sell might face disaster; hence the market would discourage overproduction. As profits mounted, workers would earn higher wages. Better living conditions and the prospect of a brighter future would encourage people to have more children. A larger population would mean a larger work force, hence more production and consumption. At the same time, an abundance of available workers would allow employers to reduce the wages they offered, thereby discouraging future overpopulation. While Adam Smith was too much of a realist to expect an earthly paradise, he believed that the market economy, if left unhindered, would function with clockwork regularity to maximize the welfare of all. He also believed that the market was a better form of social regulation than an all-powerful government.

At the time Smith was writing, Britain's economy was a complicated mixture of private enterprise and government regulations and monopolies, many of them in place since medieval times. Like other European monarchies of the period, Britain was heavily influenced by the century-old doctrine of *mercantilism*. **Mercantilism** was the notion that *the state should expand its direct role in the economy and control foreign trade for the purpose of maximizing national wealth and power.* Smith rejected mercantilism. In his view, the government's involvement in the economy had only retarded England's economic growth. "It is the highest impertinence and presumption . . . in kings and ministers," he wrote, "to pretend to watch over the economy of private people." Smith denounced royal authorities as "the greatest spendthrifts" in society and praised the hard work and frugality of private individuals for having "maintained the progress of England toward opulence and improvement."

The Wealth of Nations still stands as the veritable bible of **classical economic liberalism.** Nevertheless, Smith has often been misinterpreted as a proponent of unrestrained personal greed and a kind of free-market anarchy, devoid of any governmental role at all. In fact Smith strongly maintained that the market economy presupposed a moral order characterized by human benevolence and self-restraint and by a legal system that would effectively punish wrongdoing.

In an earlier work, *The Theory of Moral Sentiments* (1759), Smith acknowledged that avarice and ambition, when left unchecked, produce "tumult" and injustice. Civilization is possible, he believed, only when personal selfishness is restrained by sympathy for all human beings, "that general fellow feeling which we have with every man merely because he is our fellow creature." People must also have a sense of fair play and a conscience capable of feeling remorse and shame at the mistreatment of others. To keep people honest, Smith added, the state must rigidly enforce a strong code of justice. "Justice," he wrote, "is the main pillar that upholds the whole edifice." Without it, "civil society would become a scene of bloodshed and disorder" and "must in a moment crumble into atoms."

Smith therefore insisted that even the most competitive, ruggedly individualistic economy had to be based on the principle that no one should be allowed to harm another person and that all human beings deserved to be treated with "love, respect, and esteem." He also stated in this important earlier work that the "invisible hand" would eventually produce economic equality. In Smith's view, the main beneficiaries of laissez-faire capitalism ultimately would not be a small entrepreneurial elite but the population as a whole.

Moreover, Smith argued in *The Wealth of Nations* that the state should provide public works that were too unprofitable for private capitalists to undertake (such as roads, bridges, and canals) as well as public education. Smith also expressed concern that "the laboring poor"—the majority of the population—might be reduced to a state of "mental mutilation" from their exertions. He therefore expected the state to provide cultural activities to prevent the masses from being spiritually and intellectually "deformed."

In the end, Adam Smith was the prophet of modern capitalism. But he did not advocate personal greed for its own sake. The expansion of the wealth of society and its widespread distribution were his overriding economic ideals.[4] Were his theories valid?

HYPOTHESIS-TESTING EXERCISE: Was Adam Smith Right?

HYPOTHESIS AND VARIABLES

In Smith's hypothesis that laissez-faire capitalism promotes the wealth of society and economic equality more effectively than state-dominated economies, the **dependent variables** are *national wealth* and *economic equality;* the **independent variables** are *laissez-faire capitalism* and *state-dominated economies.*

EXPECTATIONS

Accordingly, we would expect laissez-faire economies to produce higher levels of national wealth and equality than state-centered economies do.

EVIDENCE

Over the course of the two centuries following Smith's *Wealth of Nations,* capitalism and the market economy became the dominant economic system in much of Western Europe and in the United States. In keeping with Smith's predictions, the wealth of the predominantly capitalist nations expanded significantly. The United States, Britain, France, and other laissez-faire economies generally outperformed economies with higher levels of government intervention. However, Smith's faith in the laissez-faire market system reflected excessive optimism about its ability to provide an equal, or even fair, distribution of goods and services. As the nineteenth century progressed and the industrial revolution advanced in the most dynamic economies, national wealth increased but large segments of the population, in some cases the majority, were mired in poverty. Especially in Europe, which lacked the wide open spaces and other opportunities available to citizens of the United States for upward socioeconomic mobility, the divisions between rich and poor deepened. The ranks of the middle classes increased, but many of these people—shopkeepers, artisans, small farmers, and the like—clung to a precarious existence that alternated between prosperity and bankruptcy.

Smith also failed to foresee with sufficient clarity the extraordinary fluctuations between periods of growth and periods of decline that market economies exhibited. Instead of working with clock-like regularity, free-market capitalism tended to oscillate between spectacular expansions and severe depressions, often triggered by financial panics or stock market crashes. These "boom and bust" tendencies became known as the *business cycle* and soon came to be regarded as a normal fact of economic life. Moreover, Smith's assumption that a widely shared code of ethics, backed by the law, would guarantee that no one would be personally or materially harmed by the free-market economy turned out to be naively idealistic. In fact, the development of capitalism in nineteenth-century Europe was brutal in its impact on the masses, who were left largely unprotected by the state.

In the twentieth century, the Great Depression tolled the death knell of laissez-faire in most countries where it reigned supreme. The result in most economically advanced democracies was the mixed economy and the modern welfare state. In today's world there are no countries with a purely laissez-faire economy; to varying degrees, governments are involved in all contemporary economic systems.

CONCLUSIONS

The evidence is therefore quite *mixed.* Although it is largely consistent with Smith's general prediction that laissez-faire economies would generate national wealth more successfully than state-dominated economies, it is quite inconsistent with Smith's assumption that laissez-faire would eliminate poverty and, over time, produce relative equality.

Within decades of Smith's dreamy vision of the wealth of nations, a new generation of British economists described the free-market economy in considerably harsher terms. **David Ricardo** (1772–1823) argued that private entrepreneurs had little choice but to squeeze their workers to produce everything they possibly could at the lowest possible wages. In no other way, he maintained, could productive capitalists amass the funds they needed for further investment and business expansion. Ricardo's *iron law of wages* stipulated that the development of the economy, and hence the creation of future employment opportunities, required this pitiless "capital accumulation" process at the expense of the impoverished labor force.[5]

Thomas Malthus (1766–1834) maintained that, whereas population grew in a geometric progression (2, 4, 6, 8, . . .), food supplies grew in an arithmetic progression (1, 2, 3, 4, . . .). Consequently, prudence dictated that the masses should not be encouraged by high wages to have lots of children. Excessive overpopulation, according to his calculations, would ultimately outstrip food supplies and provoke mass starvation. It was therefore better to keep working-class wages relatively low. Malthus's calculations turned out to be overly pessimistic, but his dire predictions prompted one contemporary to label economics "the dismal science."[6]

Social Darwinism represented another school of thought that drew stark conclusions from the social divisions created by the progress of capitalist economics. Stimulated by the British social thinker **Herbert Spencer** (1820–1903) and the American

economist **William Graham Sumner** (1840–1910), the social Darwinists argued that, just as animal species had evolved by a process of natural selection, humanity also develops in accordance with the grim law of the "survival of the fittest." (It was Spencer, not Charles Darwin, who coined this term.) Society as a whole would advance only if it encouraged and rewarded individual economic achievement. Spencer firmly opposed all attempts by the state to assist the poor or even educate them. "The whole effort of nature," he wrote, "is to get rid of such [people], to clear the world of them, and make room for better." Sumner, a Yale professor, similarly opposed governmental intervention on behalf of the weak, arguing that the survival of the fittest was "the law of civilization."[7]

Social Darwinist logic made great strides not only among Britain's entrepreneurial elites but in the United States as well. The American economy reflected the principles of laissez-faire capitalism right from its origins. By the late nineteenth century, vast fortunes were accumulated as railroad magnates, steel and oil tycoons, and other infamous "robber barons" plied their trade without the burdens of labor laws or meddlesome governmental regulations. Federal income taxes barely existed until the Sixteenth Amendment to the Constitution was ratified in 1913. Only with Franklin D. Roosevelt's New Deal did laissez-faire economic theory, which had failed to halt the Great Depression, lose its grip on economists and policy makers in the United States. In Europe, meanwhile, the most vocal opponents of laissez-faire economics were socialists who favored abolishing capitalism entirely. In Western Europe, the socialist movement became more moderate over time, as social democratic parties came around to favoring the mixed-economy welfare state. In Russia, however, socialism took on the far more radical form of the centrally planned economy.

THE CENTRALLY PLANNED
ECONOMY (CPE)

The Russian communists seized control of the central government in the autumn of 1917. Over the next several years they consolidated their rule in a bloody civil war against their main opponents. After a brief period in which private enterprise was permitted, the Soviet government under Joseph Stalin began taking charge of the economy in the late 1920s. With rare exceptions (such as tiny family-owned plots of land), all factories, farms, stores, and services came under the all-encompassing control of government agencies. A mammoth planning bureaucracy was erected to organize the production of all manufactured goods. Agriculture was "collectivized" and subjected to bureaucratic supervision. The prices of all products and services were dictated by the planning authorities, whose decrees completely supplanted the market economy's laws of supply and demand. Legally binding plans were issued by the government every year requiring factories and farms to meet official production quotas, usually specified in terms of quantities of goods (pairs of shoes, tons of hay, etc.). A five-year plan set production targets over a longer term.

Beginning with Stalin and continuing under his successors right up to Mikhail Gorbachev in the second half of the 1980s, the Soviet Union had a **centrally planned economy (CPE)**. The distinguishing feature of this type of system is *the fusion of the state and the economy.* Unlike those systems of political economy that permit a private sector to enjoy a certain degree of economic freedom from state interference, the CPE in its purest form permits no such freedom. The state and the economy are merged into an integrated whole. In effect, the state "owns" the economy. Economic decisions are always governmental decisions. It is government, not private individuals or companies, that determines what should be produced and in what quantities, how these goods should be distributed, and at what price. Because the state, in effect, commands the entire economic process, the CPE is also called a **command economy.**

In Soviet theory, a fully planned economy was expected to be far more rational in the production and allocation of goods than was a capitalist economy. The market, according to the communists, was chaotic, with countless private individuals and firms making countless decisions in their own personal interest. It wasted resources on unnecessary production and led to inflation, unemployment, inequality, bankruptcies, and depressions. A planned economy, they felt, would avoid these pitfalls. By placing control of the entire economy in the hands of central planners, Soviet officials assumed they could manage the production and distribution process with far greater efficiency and stability than market-driven capitalists could. In their view, growth would be higher and faster than under capitalism, and distribution would be fairer.

Not insignificantly, a planned economy would also facilitate the political elite's control over the population. One of the essential purposes of the state planning system was to stamp out all opportunities for individuals and groups to be independent of Communist Party rule. The extinction of economic freedom was deliberately intended to reinforce the extinction of political freedom.

Industrial production in the Soviet Union grew dramatically in the 1930s under the new planning system. The output of steel, coal, electricity, and other vital elements of an industrial economy rose at breakneck speed, elevating the Soviet Union from a backward agricultural country to an industrial giant in less than a decade. Agricultural production suffered, however, as the collectivization process, in which landholders were forced to hand over their fields, crops, and farm animals to the state, created havoc in the countryside. Millions of people perished in the process as Stalin's regime used brutal force to impose its will on the rural masses. Additional setbacks occurred during World War II, as the German invasion in 1941 and three years of continuous fighting resulted in the destruction of seventeen hundred Soviet cities and towns and the devastation of the agricultural economy.

The Soviet economy gradually revived after the war, prompting communist officials in the early 1960s to make ambitious claims about overtaking the U.S. economy in the next ten years. Nikita Khrushchev, Stalin's successor, boasted that the Soviet Union would achieve Marx's vision of pure communism by 1980. By that time, he declared, the USSR would have the world's most productive economy and highest living standards, its benefits shared equally by a contented population.[8]

Far from accomplishing that grandiose goal, the Soviet economy fell increasingly behind its mixed-economy competitors. Upon assuming the leadership of the Communist Party of the Soviet Union in 1985, Mikhail Gorbachev denounced his predecessors' years in power as an "era of stagnation."

Between 1978 and 1985 the Soviet economy had experienced zero growth. Poor harvests had forced the Soviets on several occasions to import grain from the United States and other countries. As the United States, Japan, and Western Europe charted new directions in high-technology development, the Soviet Union fell three to four computer generations behind world standards. The cumbersome central planning bureaucracy, with its slow standard operating procedures and indifference to profits, proved no match for the rapid production techniques of private companies competing in global markets.

Over the next several years, Gorbachev tried to come up with a new formula for rescuing the central planning system, including the adoption of a modicum of private enterprise, but he never succeeded in devising a more effective economic mechanism. As production and living standards continued to decline, disillusionment with central planning became increasingly widespread. In late 1991, Gorbachev gave up power and the Soviet Union itself ceased to exist. Starting in January 1992, Russia—now an independent country—began moving toward a mixed economy with the introduction of substantial private enterprise and market mechanisms for determining prices. Though the state continues to play a major role in the Russian economy, the centrally planned economy is a thing of the past.

Similar developments have taken place in East-Central Europe. After the USSR imposed communist party dictatorships on Poland, Hungary, Czechoslovakia, and other countries in the region, all these states built their own versions of central planning. As in the USSR's case, the results were disappointing: none proved capable of catching up with Western production achievements, living standards, or technological innovations. Various attempts to reform the CPE failed. As communism itself gave way to democracy at the start of the 1990s, the post-communist countries of East-Central Europe embarked on the privatization of state-owned companies and the introduction of market forces. Thus far, most of these countries have been quite creative in developing various combinations of public and private economic activity.[9]

For its part, China began dismantling its central planning system long before Russia or East-Central Europe. The Chinese Communist Party leadership itself inaugurated privatization measures and market reforms starting in the late 1970s. Over the course of the following decade, most of China's industrial enterprises and farms came into private hands. Oddly enough, these massive economic transformations took place in spite of the fact that the communists retained their grip on power, harshly repressing all demands for democracy.

We'll examine the privatization process in Russia and China at greater length in subsequent chapters. For now, we can note that in these and other countries, the transition from central planning to a mixed economy has been a profoundly political process, involving conflicts over the nature of the privatization process as well as its effects on economic growth, employment, and other politically sensitive economic issues. The fate of democracy itself hangs in the balance.

One hypothesis that stands out as particularly relevant in these circumstances states that the process of economic privatization promotes democratization. Its underlying premise is that economic freedom promotes political freedom: a private enterprise economy creates social groups (such as businesspeople and an upwardly mobile work force) who wish to preserve and expand their freedom to do business by keeping government intervention limited and by making sure that they have a say, through the electoral process and other democratic procedures, in the decisions governments make. The principal expectation of this hypothesis is that, if the economic liberalization process succeeds, democracy will succeed in Russia and East-Central Europe, and it may even successfully challenge communist rule in China.

A contrary thesis is less optimistic. It suggests that the privatization process in formerly communist countries and China ultimately undermines support for democracy. If the economic transformations now under way produce unacceptable levels of inflation, unemployment, inequality, or corruption, large segments of the population and political elites may turn against economic change and, simultaneously, against political change as well. Some may long nostalgically for the "good old days" under central planning when, despite that system's disadvantages, life was more stable and predictable and prices for most basic goods, when available, were cheaper. Driven to despair by economic adversity, many people may demand a strong authoritarian government to impose order on a society they perceive as careening into chaos.

In between these extreme scenarios of triumphant success and catastrophic failure lies a third hypothetical alternative: the dual processes of marketization and democratization may inch along at a rocky pace, with alternating successes and failures, advances and retreats. Though the economic and political transformation processes present great difficulties, the populations and political elites of these countries in this scenario together manage to "muddle through," achieving at least some degree of both market economics and democracy.

Whatever happens, it can be confidently anticipated that the development of stable market economic mechanisms and democratic institutions and practices will be a long process, requiring perhaps decades of concerted social and political action. The hypotheses just presented, as well as other ones applicable to these developments, will have to be continually put to the test as time goes on.

MIXED ECONOMIES

The most widely adopted economic system in the world today is neither laissez-faire capitalism nor full-scale socialism but something in between: the *mixed economy.*

A <u>mixed economy</u> *combines both private enterprise and state involvement in the country's economic affairs.*

There is considerable variety in the forms a mixed economy can take. No single model is faithfully copied by all mixed-economy countries.

For one thing, countries may differ in the relative *degree* of capitalism and state intervention they have. Some grant wider latitude than others to the private sector while holding governmental intervention within bounds (or at least trying to do so). The United States is a good example. Even though the role of federal, state, and local governments in the U.S. economy is considerable, the Unite States exhibits relatively less state intervention than do most other advanced industrial economies. A comparison of such factors as the percentage of GDP taken up by central government expenditures and by tax revenues illustrates the point (see table 14.2).

Mixed economies may also differ in the *forms* of state intervention that they employ. In some cases the government's economic involvement is largely indirect. That is, the state allows private enterprise and market mechanisms to play the main role in the national economy but seeks to influence or adjust private behavior so as to advance certain national economic goals. The central bank, for example, may influence commercial bank interest rates in order to rein in inflation or stimulate growth, or the government may raise or lower taxes in order

TABLE 14.2
Expenditures and Tax Revenues as a Percentage of GDP in Selected Economically Advanced Democracies, 1997

Country	Central Government Expenditures as to % GDP	Central Government Tax Revenues as % of GDP
Canada	20.8	n.a.*
Denmark	40.0	33.7
France	44.6	39.2
Germany	32.1	26.7
Italy	45.4	42.2
Netherlands	46.0	42.7
Sweden	43.2	36.9
United Kingdom	36.4	33.4
United States	20.7	19.8

*Not available

Source: World Bank, *World Development Report 1999/2000.*

to advance political or economic goals. In these and other instances of indirect intervention, the state does not directly own enterprises outright but confines its role to influencing or regulating the private sector.

One of the most widely utilized forms of indirect state intervention in the economy consists of a set of policy mechanisms known collectively as *Keynesianism*. **Keynesianism *refers to the state's use of fiscal and monetary measures and public spending to promote growth in an economy dominated by private enterprise.*** Its main architect was perhaps the most influential economist of the twentieth century, **John Maynard Keynes**.

JOHN MAYNARD KEYNES
(1883–1946)

Keynes (canes) was born in Britain the year Karl Marx died. As a young man he studied economics at Cambridge University at a time when the teaching of economic theory there had not advanced very far beyond the doctrines of Adam Smith and David Ricardo. In the course of a vigorous and colorful life surrounded by artists and writers, Keynes made a major contribution of his own to economic theory, providing an original alternative to both socialism and laissez-faire.

The laissez-faire tradition Keynes inherited as a student stressed the notion that a free-market economy was a self-regulating mechanism. It would provide steady growth and full employment, its proponents hypothesized, as long as government did not interfere with its operations. The chief stimulus to Keynes's revision of classical economic theory was the Great Depression. The Wall Street stock market crash of October 1929 shattered the foundations of the U.S. economy and exacerbated the problems of other capitalist economies, resulting in bankruptcies, plummeting economic growth, and skyrocketing unemployment around the world. As the years ground on with little improvement, governments as well as the private sector appeared to be at a loss as to how to resolve the crisis. The conventional wisdom of laissez-faire confidently predicted that market forces would generate a recovery in the long run. As Keynes drily observed, however, "In the long run we're all dead."

He argued that the best way to stimulate economic growth during a depression was to increase total spending—that is, *aggregate demand* for goods and services—throughout the economy. As soon as more money was

spent for these things, businesspeople would amass enough profits to expand their operations and hire new workers. Unfortunately, Keynes observed, individual consumers do not have much money to spend in a depression. With millions unemployed, much of the population is more likely to be reduced to penury. Starved for customers, businesses stagnate or go bankrupt. Keynes thus reached a startling conclusion: *a free-market economy does not possess the mechanisms needed to recover from a depression on its own.*

If consumers, banks, and businesses do not have sufficient money to spend in the economy so as to spark a recovery, who does? Governments, Keynes replied. By spending additional funds from the national budget, over and above the amounts already being spent, governments can inject spendable money into the economy and thereby "prime the pump" of the private sector. The state can take this action by directly purchasing goods and services from private businesses (such as highway construction equipment or weaponry) or by hiring people for such things as military service or public works projects, such as building dams or sweeping streets. By putting cash in the hands of consumers and businesses, Keynes argued, governments would enable individuals to buy more things, thereby increasing the demand for goods, and enable businesses to increase production and hire more employees. Economic recovery would then be under way.

Keynes laid out these ideas in *The General Theory of Employment, Interest, and Money*, published in 1936. By that time, Franklin D. Roosevelt's New Deal had already begun implementing some of them, such as the mass hiring of unemployed workers through the Public Works Administration and the Civilian Conservation Corps. But in Keynes's opinion, the Roosevelt administration was not spending enough to pump the country out of the depression. Only when the U.S. government engaged in much more massive public spending during World War II did the depression in the United States come to an end.

One problem that disturbed some economists and government officials was that, during the depression, the United States and other governments were already running budget deficits. Keynes's call for even more budgetary expenditures in spite of the deficits was viewed as heresy by classical theorists, who faithfully adhered to the maxim that sound economic policy required balanced budgets. Once again Keynes challenged the accepted wisdom. He asserted that in certain compelling circumstances such as a depression, governments may have to engage in deficit spending in order to improve the overall economy.

Deficit spending is spending by governments even though there is a budgetary deficit that cannot be balanced through ordinary revenue sources (such as taxes). To finance this excess spending, governments must borrow money from individuals or other lenders and pay them interest, thus building up the national debt.

Keynes believed that the money governments spent over budget would eventually come back to the national treasury in the form of enhanced tax revenue, collected from increasingly profitable businesses and a rising number of well-paid employees as the recovery widens and the economy grows.

While some of his early critics accused Keynes of being a socialist, in fact he always looked upon the private sector as the main source of economic growth and employment. In his view the state's proper role was to stimulate private enterprise, not replace it. He regarded Marxism as "scientifically erroneous."

After World War II, Keynes's principles of government intervention won growing acceptance. By the 1960s the United States, Western Europe, and other countries were routinely using Keynesian mechanisms to "fine-tune" their economies and regulate the business cycle. In more recent decades, however, the economic experiences of many advanced capitalist economies have prompted considerable debate about the pertinence of Keynes's theories. Many contemporary economists argue that national debts have reached such astronomical heights in some countries that additional deficit spending may only hamper future economic growth. A number of economists and public officials also believe that capitalist economies are generally better off with less government intervention rather than more. A number of them cite the warnings of another major theorist, **Friedrich von Hayek** (1899–1992), that excessive government involvement in the economy is "the road to serfdom."[10] Most would agree that we now live in a "post-Keynesian" era in which many of the economic problems we face require solutions different from those Keynes proposed.

Whatever one thinks about Keynes's theories, one thing is certain: virtually all governments and economists in the capitalist world we live in reject laissez-faire. Today the center of political debate is not over the question of *whether* governments should intervene in the economy, but *how much*. By providing a feasible alternative to both laissez-faire capitalism and all-out socialism, Keynes and like-minded economists produced a revolution in economic thinking whose general tenets are widely accepted. Consequently, the so-called *neo-liberals* of the contemporary world regard private enterprise and the market as the most effective forms of economic organization, but admit that governments have a major role to play in today's complex economies.[11]

In addition to employing indirect forms of economic intervention, governments may also engage in more direct forms of activity in mixed economies. In some countries the state may directly own certain enterprises, whether as full owner or as a shareholder in partnership with other investors. These state-owned firms in mixed economies are usually called **public enterprises** or **para-statal enterprises.** Sometimes they are monopolies, the sole provider of a particular good or service (such as electricity or railroads). But sometimes they compete with other firms in the domestic or international market, selling such things as autos, banking services, or air travel. To turn a profit, therefore, they must pay just as much attention to quality control and pricing strategy as private companies do. Such internationally known firms as Air France and Rolls Royce have been owned by the state, along with giant companies in Italy, Spain, Sweden, Brazil, Mexico, and other countries.

The chief difference between public enterprises and private firms is that the managers and work force of public enterprises are employed directly by the state and the earnings of state-owned companies go into the national treasury. Such enterprises may also receive loans or other forms of financing directly from the state budget.

Like most other aspects of economic activity, public enterprises can ignite sharp political controversies. Their proponents regard them as an effective way to combat unemployment and earn revenue for the national treasury so as to help finance general budgetary outlays. Opponents of public enterprises, by contrast, argue that state-owned companies might be less efficient and competitive than private firms. If they do not turn a profit, they may have to be bailed out with state subsidies, thereby draining the national treasury. In some cases public enterprises may become nests of corruption, with state sector managers acquiring money illegally, perhaps in collusion with politicians who protect them. Scandals of this kind have rocked Italy and France in recent years.

These and other arguments against public enterprises have convinced many of their opponents to push for their privatization. **Privatization** *means the transfer of state-owned enterprises to private ownership.* (It is the opposite of **nationalization,** *which is the transfer of privately owned firms to state ownership.*) The privatization issue has unleashed a storm of political controversy in Britain, France, Russia, Brazil, India, and other countries in recent years.[12]

Another variant of direct state intervention in mixed economies is *bureaucratic coordination* of the economy. In bureaucratically coordinated economies, the state plays a direct and constant role in coordinating the activities of private firms (and, perhaps, the labor market as well) for broad national purposes. Such purposes might include promoting economic growth, distributing social welfare benefits, enhancing international competitiveness, or implementing a military strategy. These direct efforts are typically more intrusive than the indirect measures governments may use to affect the economy, such as the Keynesian mechanisms described earlier. There are several different variants of bureaucratic coordination in mixed economies, as the following examples illustrate:

- Contemporary Japan and South Korea have aggressively competitive private firms that cooperate closely with state agencies to promote exports. Such agencies as the Ministry of Finance and the Ministry of International Trade and Industry wield very important bureaucratic power in the Japanese economy, as do their counterparts in South Korea.
- Germany, Austria, and other countries have corporatist systems that involve continuing discussions and coordination among business organizations, labor unions, and government. (On corporatism, see chapter 11.)
- France has a system of "indicative planning" through which the state and private enterprises coordinate general guidelines and expectations of economic development.
- Various African countries have state-managed purchasing boards and other bureaucratic institutions that help coordinate agricultural development or other economic activities.

Whether guided by indirect or direct methods of state intervention, mixed economies cannot escape politics. This is especially the case nowadays because most countries are *welfare states.* Most welfare states today are mixed economies. While some are

authoritarian regimes, the most highly developed ones are in the economically advanced democracies.

WELFARE STATES

Broadly defined, the welfare state *is a form of political economy in which the state assumes responsibility for the general welfare of its population,* especially its most vulnerable elements, through spending on such items as education, housing, health care, pensions, unemployment compensation, food subsidies, family allowances, and other programs.

The term *welfare state* came into vogue in Britain in the 1930s and 1940s. Though it is largely a 20th-century phenomenon, its roots reach into the previous century. As laissez-faire capitalism advanced and the working-class population expanded, a number of European political theorists and politicians began groping for ways to maintain robust economic growth while at the same time confronting the appalling poverty of the working class and the unemployed.

In Britain the path to the modern welfare state was long and circuitous. One of its early intellectual forebears was **Jeremy Bentham** (1748–1832). Bentham was a philosopher whose basic premise was that humanity is motivated in all its actions by the pursuit of pleasure and the avoidance of pain. As an ethical principle, he believed that whatever promoted pleasure or happiness was good and whatever caused pain or suffering was bad. In Bentham's view, all human actions were to be judged in terms of their utility in maximizing happiness and relieving suffering.

Bentham is perhaps most famous for his statement that the principal aim of government should be to promote "the greatest happiness of the greatest number." He therefore believed that governments should "augment the happiness of the people" more than they diminished it. "The business of government," in short, was "to promote the happiness of society." To this end, Bentham maintained that the chief obligation of government was to provide certain services to the population, including basic physical security against crime and foreign enemies, economic subsistence, and the legal protection of property rights, personal reputation, and private contracts.

Bentham strongly believed that democracy provided the most effective means for achieving these goals, inasmuch as monarchies and other authoritarian regimes invariably promoted the happiness of a privileged minority. Only by participating in a democracy would people be willing to make the personal sacrifices necessary to enlarge the community's overall well-being. In advancing these views, Bentham advocated neither socialism nor laissez-faire. Private business activity, in his view, was necessary to increase society's wealth. The state, however, was expected to intervene in the economy to ensure a minimum standard of living and to reduce inequality. These fundamental principles would later become the ideological cornerstones of the twentieth-century welfare state.[13]

Another progenitor of the welfare state was **John Stuart Mill** (1806–1873). Mill was the son of a prominent Scottish political writer who was a close friend of Bentham's. Mill's essays *On Liberty* (1859) and *Considerations on Representative Government* (1861) established his reputation as a democratic theorist of the first rank. As a member of the House of Commons he championed a variety of liberal causes, including equal political rights for women.

It was his youthful interest in political economy, however, that launched Mill on a lifelong quest for an economic system that combined free enterprise and a measure of government involvement in the economy. His masterwork, *The Principles of Political Economy*, first appeared in 1848, the same year Marx and Engels published their communist *Manifesto*. Mill's work pointed in a fundamentally different direction from revolutionary socialism, however. Over seven successive editions of the book, Mill's preference for private enterprise and market mechanisms remained unshakable. Laissez-faire, he wrote, "should be the general practice: every departure from it, unless required by some great good, is a certain evil." He also regarded restrictions on economic competition, as advocated by socialists, as "evil." Communism, he prophesied, would "grind all down to a tame uniformity of thoughts, feelings, and actions."

Nevertheless, Mill was equally outspoken in his objections to a completely unrestrained free market. Among the departures from it that he considered justifiable, Mill advocated such things as state-funded education, public works, restrictions on child labor, and limited governmental assistance to those unable to work. He also supported the right of workers to organize trade unions and go on strike. To remedy the social inequalities produced by capitalism, Mill favored stiff inheritance taxes aimed at preventing the concentration of wealth in a handful of families. He also favored producers' cooperatives that would compete in the marketplace under the ownership and management of the workers themselves. These ideas flew directly in the face of the British elite's laissez-faire inclinations. Over time, however, Mill's ideas sensitized Britain to the possibility of finding a middle ground between the extremes of unregulated capitalism and revolutionary socialism. Though many of his ideas were considered radical in their day, Mill helped clear the way intellectually for the modern welfare state.[14]

Ironically, it was the highly conservative ruling elite of nineteenth-century Germany that introduced some of Europe's first major social welfare programs. In the 1880s the kaiser's authoritarian government introduced the industrialized world's first government-financed health and accident insurance for workers and its first state-managed pension program. The kaiser and his ministers were no socialists. Their chief incentives for providing social welfare benefits to Germany's working masses were to stave off a potential socialist revolution and to reduce popular support for the Social Democrats.

The Emergence of the Modern Welfare State: Germany, Sweden, and the United States

In a few countries the twentieth-century welfare state began taking shape in the decades between World War I and World War II. After the kaiser's departure following Germany's defeat in 1918, the German Weimar Republic (1919–1933) took the unprecedented step of incorporating generous welfare benefits into the constitution as legally guaranteed social rights. These included the right to a job or unemployment insurance, decent housing, allowances for families with newborn children, comprehensive health insurance, and collective bargaining rights for workers and their trade unions. To help pay for these advantages, private businesses were heavily taxed.

Unfortunately for proponents of democracy, the entire Weimar system collapsed as the German economy was battered by astronomical inflation in the early 1920s and by a wave of bankruptcies and rising unemployment with the onset of the Great Depression in the early 1930s. Moreover, business, labor, and agricultural leaders were never able to agree on a mutually acceptable balance of economic policies. The failure of the Weimar Republic's political economy provided a perfect opportunity for the Nazi Party under Adolph Hitler to take advantage of widespread frustrations and gain power. While establishing one of the most tyrannical dictatorships ever known, the Nazis also established their own version of the welfare state, one that placed the economy firmly in the hands of a brutal, war-driven elite.

A far more salutary development occurred in Sweden. As the Great Depression took a heavy toll on Sweden's export-oriented economy, leaders of parties and interest groups representing agriculture, labor, and big business made a concerted effort to iron out their conflicts in a grand "historic compromise." In the process, they saved Swedish democracy and established "a model for what all of Europe would do after 1945."[15] Today Sweden and other Scandinavian countries are "cradle-to-grave" social welfare systems, with the state providing a broad spectrum of benefits to workers, farmers, and the sizable middle class.

Across the ocean, Franklin D. Roosevelt's New Deal was forging a new model for the political economy of the United States, one whose basic parameters would also set a pattern for the postwar period. Prior to Roosevelt, the U.S. government had provided only minimal social welfare benefits, mainly to war veterans.[16] The prevailing laissez-faire orthodoxy dictated against governmental interference in the economy and especially against deficit spending. Roosevelt himself initially accepted this view, but later vowed to try anything that might work to bring the U.S. economy out of the depression. Guided by no preconceived blueprint, FDR and his "brain trust" launched a wide assortment of measures aimed at soaking up unemployment and reinvigorating the economy. Public works programs, the Tennessee Valley Authority, the Social Security system, and the Wagner Act, which provided legal support for trade unions, were all products of New Deal interventionism. So, too, was the National Recovery Administration (NRA), a corporatist body intended to pull together representatives from business, labor, agriculture, and government in an effort to regulate wages, prices, and production.[17]

Although the NRA was declared unconstitutional by the Supreme Court and although FDR's critics denounced the New Deal as "creeping socialism," quite a few of Roosevelt's programs remained in place long after the end of his administration. Most important, the New Deal established the legitimacy of significant governmental intervention in the U.S. economy. Though various presidents in subsequent decades objected to what they regarded as excessive levels of government spending and other forms of intervention, none objected to the *principle* of intervention, not even staunch conservatives like Ronald Reagan. The New Deal thus laid the foundations of the U.S. postwar welfare state.

The Postwar Welfare State

The heyday of the welfare state in the economically advanced democracies occurred in the first three decades after World War II. In 1945, Britain's Labour Party won its first majority in the House of Commons. Under Prime Minister Clement Attlee, the Labour government enacted a series of major welfare measures and nationalized several private corporations. (The owners were compensated.) The centerpiece of Labour's legislation was the National Health Service, which guaranteed free medical and dental care to all British citizens while preserving private care for those willing to pay for it. Although the Conservative Party, which had traditionally campaigned against such measures, returned to power in 1951, it did not abolish the National Health Service, which remains a broadly popular institution to this day.

West Germany's Federal Republic, which was created after World War II under the aegis of U.S. British and French occupation authorities, moved under fairly conservative governments led by Chancellor Konrad Adenauer, a Christian Democrat, to establish a welfare state defined by Christian Democratic leaders as a "social market economy." This concept encapsulated the Christian Democrats' commitment to both competitive market capitalism and a concern for general social welfare as embodied in such programs as universal health insurance, family allowances, various benefits for industrial workers, and tuition-free public education all the way through graduate school. West Germany's Social Democratic Party (the SPD) has generally favored an even wider extension of the country's social welfare system.

Most other industrially advanced countries also expanded their welfare programs after World War II. In most cases, the social and political underpinnings of the welfare state were the same. *From its inception, the democratic welfare state has been based on compromises made by representatives of labor, agriculture, and the business sector as mediated and enforced by a democratically accountable state.* The specific agreements reached in Western Europe soon after World War II are sometimes known as the *postwar settlements.*

Particularly rapid expansion of the welfare state took place between 1960 and 1975. This period witnessed fairly continuous economic growth in the advanced democracies. It was during these decades that the economies of the United States, Canada, Japan and most of Western Europe completed their transformation from industrial economies to **postindustrial economies.** Postindustrial economies are characterized by the fact that more than half the work force is engaged in the service sector of the economy rather than in manufacturing or agriculture. The service sector consists of such fields as banking, insurance, and other economic services; government service; management; the medical professions; scientific research; consulting; education; and a broad range of consumer services such as restaurants, health clubs, entertainment, and the like. Postindustrial economies place a particularly high premium on education or specialized training as the principal means to individual economic advancement. Unlike predominantly agricultural economies or traditional industrial economies centered on manufacturing—both of which are based mainly on physical labor— postindustrial economies are *knowledge-based economies.* They therefore require a fairly large measure of government support of educational opportunities for the population.

As the economically advanced democracies blazed the trails of postindustrialism from the 1960s onward, their governments became increasingly committed to promoting not only education but a host of other programs designed to enhance the welfare of the population and the growth of the economy. Most of these governments utilized Keynesian tax and spending policies designed to keep growth rates climbing while maintaining high levels of employment. As national wealth grew, the amount of money available for social welfare programs rose apace. Government expenditures on an array of social programs in most of these countries rose from 10 percent to 20 percent of GNP in the 1950s to between one-fourth and one-third of GNP in the mid-1970s.[18] The so-called **Keynesian welfare state** became the dominant mode of political economy throughout the economically advanced world of democratic states.

Not only have government welfare programs assisted the poor and the working class, who benefit from such things as unemployment insurance, food stamps, public housing, and various income assistance programs aimed at providing a social safety net of minimally acceptable living conditions, but they have also benefited the middle class and even the upper class. In various welfare states, people from all income levels have taken full advantage of expanding educational opportunities, health insurance, retirement pensions, and other state-sponsored programs. In countries such as the United States, special tax breaks, such as write-offs for interest paid on home mortgages or other loans, have constituted a form of social welfare benefit for middle- and upper-class property owners, amounting to tens of billions of dollars annually in lost revenue to the national treasury.

Moreover, both left-wing parties and mainstream conservative parties have tended to agree on the basic idea of the welfare state, though they might disagree on the extent or form of government funding for social welfare measures. Most of these parties in Western Europe, North America, and Japan have recognized that government-funded welfare measures are widely popular and that their electoral fortunes often depend on their ability to provide social benefits to key segments of the population. The main differences among these various political parties and governments have generally been a matter of degree, not principle. The gamut has extended from the extensive welfare systems of Sweden and other Scandinavian countries (commonly known as the *Swedish model*) to the less all-encompassing, though still significant, welfarism of the United States. Japan, despite its considerable national wealth, has been the least committed to social welfare expansion among the industrially advanced countries through most of the postwar period.[19] (See table 14.3.)

To be sure, welfare programs cost money. Some populations have been willing to shoulder higher tax burdens than others. Table 14.4 shows the top tax rates in eleven democratic welfare states. Note that the United States is a comparatively low-tax country.

Farewell to the Welfare State?

Starting in the mid-1970s, doubts about the sustainability of the welfare state began spreading in Western Europe and North America. In October 1973, the world's leading oil exporting countries, spearheaded by several Middle Eastern states, announced the immediate quadrupling of petroleum prices. The sudden price hike dealt a staggering blow to the energy-hungry industrialized democracies, resulting in runaway inflation and a sharp contraction of economic production and foreign trade. The steady economic growth that had underwritten the expansion of social welfare spending in the 1960–75 period could no longer be counted on in the future. The result in many of these countries was a relatively new phenomenon dubbed *stagflation,* an unusual combination of economic stagnation and high inflation. (Classical economic theory predicted that, when the economy goes into a recession, prices should fall, not rise.)

Keynesian prescriptions for fine-tuning the national economy, which had registered some visible successes in the previous decade, no longer appeared to work. The budgetary deficits that many advanced industrial democracies had been running up as government welfare programs proliferated now threatened to get out of hand. Burgeoning national debts only fueled further inflation, while large segments of the population demanded ever-higher government-funded pensions, health benefits, and other forms of assistance to help them keep up with the rising cost of living. But government treasuries

TABLE 14.3

Government Social Spending as Percentage of GDP

Country	1980	1990	1995
Belgium	24.6	25.6	27.1
Canada	13.2	17.6	18.2
Denmark	27.5	28.1	32.0
France	23.5	26.7	30.0
Germany	23.7	23.2	28.0
Italy	18.4	23.0	23.7
Japan	9.9	11.2	13.8
Netherlands	28.5	29.7	27.8
Sweden	29.8	32.2	33.0
United Kingdom	18.3	19.5	22.5
United States	13.4	13.5	15.8

Source: OECD, *Social Expenditure Data Base 1980–1996.*
Government social spending refers to expenditures on such items as pensions, health care, unemployment compensation, education, family allowances, income maintenance, and the like.

TABLE 14.4

Highest Marginal Tax Rates, 1998

Individual Income

Country	Top Tax Rate (%)	On Income Over ($)	Top Corporate Tax Rate (%)
Belgium	55	65,547	39
Canada	29	41,370	38
Denmark	58	—	34
France	—	—	33
Germany	53	66,988	30
Italy	46	181,801	37
Japan	50	230,592	38
Netherlands	60	51,373	35
Sweden	31	27,198	28
United Kingdom	40	44,580	31
United States	40	278,450	35

Source: World Bank, *World Development Report 1999/2000.*

were no longer prepared to meet these demands as the decline in economic activity brought in diminishing tax revenues and necessitated rising amounts of compensation for the growing ranks of the unemployed (see table 14.5 and figure 14.1).

Throughout the 1980s and into the 1990s, the idea gained currency in the economically advanced democracies that governments could no longer afford the high deficits and weighty tax burdens typically produced by the modern welfare state. Conservative and centrist political elites

TABLE 14.5

Government Budget Surpluses and Deficits as a Percentage of GDP in Selected Democratic Welfare States

Country	1985	1990	1995	1998
Canada	–7.3	–4.5	–4.5	1.3
Denmark	—	1.0	–2.3	1.0
France	–2.9	–1.6	–4.9	–2.9
Germany	–1.2	–2.1	–3.3	–2.0
Italy	–12.4	–11.2	–7.7	–2.7
Japan	–0.8	2.9	–3.6	–6.0
Netherlands	–3.6	–5.1	–3.7	–0.7
Sweden	–3.8	4.2	–7.0	1.9
United Kingdom	–2.9	–1.5	–5.8	–2.7
United States	–3.2	–2.7	–1.9	1.7

Source: OECD Economic Outlook, June 1999.

FIGURE 14.1   Gap Between Public Spending and Public Revenue in Major Industrial Countries* (as Percent of Gross Domestic Product)

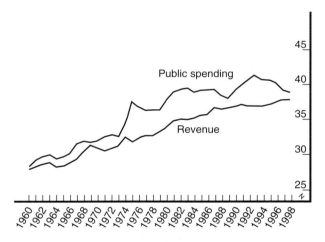

*Data are from the United States, Japan, the Federal Republic of Germany, France, Britain, Italy, and Canada.
Source: The Economist, September 11, 1999.

and a growing segment of public opinion increasingly affirmed that greater reliance needed to be placed on the private sector and market forces to spur economic growth and thereby increase employment opportunities. For many people, the welfare state—and government intervention in the economy more generally—seemed to have reached their limits. In the 1980s, conservatives like President Ronald Reagan and British Prime Minister Margaret Thatcher spoke out forcefully in favor of greater reliance on the private sector and

less reliance on government. In 1991, the leaders of the twelve West European countries that then constituted the European Community (the forerunner of today's fifteen-member European Union) agreed to restrict their annual budget deficits to no more than 3 percent of GDP as a precondition for adopting the euro. That restriction, along with other criteria, continues to require tough budget control measures on the part of most EU countries.

In spite of belt-tightening policies in a number of countries over the past two decades, the welfare state remains both viable and popular. As table 14.3 shows, government social welfare expenditures are still considerable (though their share of GDP varies across countries) and tax revenues still comprise a large share of gross domestic product in most of the welfare states on our list (table 14.2). The welfare state has endured even though national debts have tended to come down. Indeed, social welfare spending remains broadly popular in most economically advanced democracies, a fact even conservatives acknowledge. In Britain, government welfare spending actually *increased* between 1979 and 1992 under Prime Minister Thatcher, due in part to higher spending for unemployment compensation during the recessions that took place in the Thatcher years. President Reagan *raised* Social Security payments in the 1980s. Public opinion surveys have confirmed the continuing popularity of a broad assortment of government-funded social benefits among a majority of citizens in the economically advanced democracies. At times these welfarist attitudes coexist with support for cutting budget deficits and reducing taxes, a combination of attitudes that leaves politicians with the difficult challenge of doing more with less.[20]

The Politics of Welfare States

The difficulties most democratic welfare states encounter in coming up with the money needed to meet continuing public demands for welfare services have prompted some serious soul-searching about the nature of the state's proper role in economic affairs. More fundamentally, it has also raised some provocative questions about the very nature of contemporary democracy itself.

One disturbing hypothesis suggests that today's mass democracies make such overwhelming demands on their governments for benefits of various kinds that the results can only be uncontrollable budget deficits. These deficits, in turn, stifle economic growth by breeding abnormally high interest rates or inflation, or both. Modern welfarist democracies are therefore by nature self-defeating: they prevent the very increases in national wealth that are needed to meet rising public demands for governmental assistance.

At the same time, the argument continues, democracies place such inordinate pressures on elected officials to "deliver the goods" (better schools, more health care, higher pensions, increased poverty relief, etc.) that politicians cannot get elected unless they make promises that are inevitably unrealistic. Candidates competing in electoral contests seek to outdo one another in making fantastic promises, a process known as *overbidding*. Once elected, political leaders then find that they cannot deliver the goods as promised to the constituents who voted for them because of inescapable budgetary constraints or other adverse economic conditions over which they have little or no immediate control, such as sluggish growth rates, high inflation, or a weak international economy.

In fact, many elected officials find themselves locked into automatic spending commitments for programs already enacted into law. These commitments can consume the lion's share of the national budget, leaving precious little money available for new programs. In the United States, the funds available for discretionary spending (that is, money that can be spent at the discretion of the President and Congress) typically amount only to about a third of the federal budget. The remaining two-thirds is already committed to mandatory payments for Social Security, Medicare, and other social welfare measures, plus interest payments on the national debt.

In addition to confronting demands for more benefits, political leaders must frequently confront demands for lower taxes. It is not uncommon that demands for tax relief are raised by the very people who insist on more government assistance for themselves. Mass democracies seem to have no shortage of citizens who feel entitled to various welfare benefits but who are always ready to shift the burden of paying for them to someone else.[21]

As a consequence, democracy once again proves itself to be self-defeating: voters make demands that their government cannot fulfill and for which they are not willing to pay. They take out their frustrations by turning against the incumbent leaders and shifting their support to challengers who make unrealistic promises of their own ("More gain, less pain"). To save themselves, the incumbents may feel compelled to outbid their opponents by providing instant rewards or grandiose pledges to their constituents at election time—tax cuts, higher pensions, and the like—even though the economy can ill afford such favors. Incumbents thus have an interest in promoting a favorable *political business cycle*, using the powers of their office to tilt economic policy in directions that will enhance their chances for reelection. Irrespective of whether the incumbents are victorious or the vote goes to their opponents, the cycle of broken promises and voter discontent just begins anew.

While elected officials may try to sway voters by tampering with the economy at election time, some analysts doubt that they have sufficient short-term control over the economy to do so effectively.[22] Nevertheless, there is some evidence that many voters at election time are more likely to be swayed by economic conditions than by other factors impinging on their vote. As we noted earlier, incumbent U.S. presidents are likely to win reelection if the economy has grown by at least 4 percent during the four quarters preceding the election.

There are several variants of these generalizations about the corruptive nature of democratic welfare politics and the "entitlement mentality" accompanying it. One that surfaced in the mid-1970s hypothesized that the increase in mass political participation that had taken place in the United States and various West European countries over the preceding fifteen years (through the enfranchisement of eighteen-year-olds and the increased activism of minority groups), along with the rise in welfare spending that occurred in the same period, had overloaded governments with demands they could not fulfill. The result was a "crisis of governability." Frustrated by the inability of elected leaders and bureaucratic agencies to respond to their demands, growing numbers of citizens in these countries showed signs of having less trust in their governments. Paradoxically, the natural functionings of democracy—mass participation and open interest articulation—were undermining the authority of democratically elected governments in the eyes of the population.

One exponent of this view, Harvard's Samuel Huntington, argued that these trends could lead to a reduced sense of efficacy among the electorate ("My vote means nothing!"), resulting in less participation in voting and other forms of democratic activity over time. To combat this "distemper of democracy," Huntington recommended greater moderation in the demands people make of their governments. Otherwise, he prophesied, democracy itself—particularly in the United States—might be placed in jeopardy as a consequence of its own overindulgence and excesses. "Democracy will have a longer life if it has a more balanced existence," Huntington concluded, arguing that there are "potentially desirable limits to the indefinite expansion of political democracy."[23]

Another set of hypotheses concerning the self-destructive tendencies of modern democratic welfare states was advanced by Mancur Olson. Building on the propositions he developed in *The Logic of Collective Action* (see chapter 11), Olson argued in *The Rise and Decline of Nations* (1982) that one of the main variables that accounts for stunted economic growth and the ungovernability of certain democracies is the existence of small special-interest groups that exert an excessively powerful influence over political and economic decision makers. Whereas large groups—such as consumers, taxpayers, the middle class, and so on—are not likely to form effective organizations to promote their interests, small groups (business cartels, sector-specific trade unions, health insurance providers, and the like) are far more likely to do so. As a consequence they acquire a degree of organizational power for collective action that is disproportionately greater than their share of the population.

In modern democratic welfare states, these groups pressure governments into providing their members with special privileges and benefits at the expense of society as a whole. Ironically, these narrowly based pressure groups are more likely to exist in countries that have had a long history of stable democracy, such as Britain and the United States. Successful democracies, in essence, breed

the very political forces that undermine an elected government's ability to govern in behalf of all the people. The result, almost inevitably, is the ungovernability of democracies.[24]

Obviously, one implication of this line of thought is that democratic welfare states are courting disaster as long as politicians and the people who vote for them think only of themselves and steadfastly reject the costs, sacrifices, compromises, and risks of a more responsible concern for society's current and future welfare. Democracy, in short, is its own worst enemy.

Other critics of the welfare state point out that it has failed to stamp out poverty, guarantee job security, or eliminate class conflict. Though they vary in degree, virtually all the democratic welfare states of the contemporary world continue to experience the problems of hard-core poverty, unemployment, and fairly wide disparities in personal incomes and family wealth. Because today's highly advanced postindustrial economies are particularly dependent on highly educated professionals and a technically skilled work force, income gaps between different socioeconomic classes increasingly reflect gaps in education levels (see figure 14.2).

Welfare states are also maligned for encouraging excessive dependency on government handouts, a phenomenon that may induce some people to live off welfare payments instead of holding down a steady job. Efforts in the United States,

TABLE 14.6

Unemployment in Selected Democratic Welfare States (as a Percentage of Civilian Labor Force)					
Country	1980	1985	1990	1995	1998
Belgium	9.3	10.4	6.7	9.9	9.5
Canada	7.5	10.5	8.2	9.5	8.3
Denmark	—	—	7.7	7.2	5.1
France	5.8	10.1	9.0	11.7	11.7
Germany	2.6	7.2	4.8	8.2	9.4
Ireland	—	16.9	13.4	12.3	7.8
Italy	5.6	8.5	9.1	11.9	11.9
Japan	2.0	2.6	2.1	3.2	4.1
Spain	10.5	21.7	16.2	22.9	18.8
Sweden	2.0	2.9	1.7	8.8	8.3
United Kingdom	6.2	11.5	7.1	8.7	6.3
United States	7.2	7.2	5.6	5.6	4.5

Source: OECD Economic Outlook, June 1999.

FIGURE 14.2   Education and Earnings in the United States
Source: The U.S. Census Bureau.

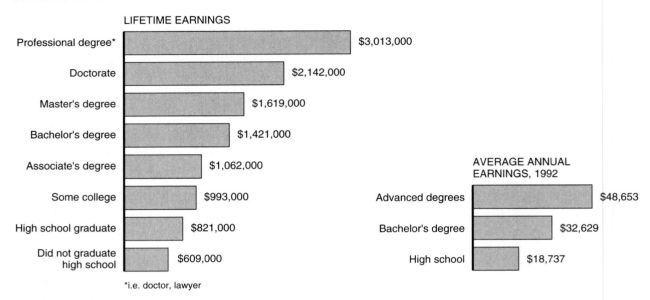

LIFETIME EARNINGS

Professional degree*	$3,013,000
Doctorate	$2,142,000
Master's degree	$1,619,000
Bachelor's degree	$1,421,000
Associate's degree	$1,062,000
Some college	$993,000
High school graduate	$821,000
Did not graduate high school	$609,000

*i.e. doctor, lawyer

AVERAGE ANNUAL EARNINGS, 1992

Advanced degrees	$48,653
Bachelor's degree	$32,629
High school	$18,737

PERCENT OF AMERICANS WITH:

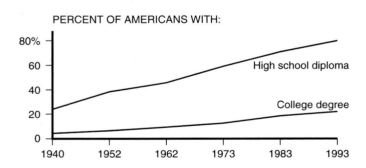

High school diploma

College degree

Britain, and other countries in recent years to require impoverished welfare recipients to work in exchange for welfare benefits (or instead of them) reflect the frustration of many taxpayers who believe that income maintenance programs for the able-bodied poor are often abused. "Workfare" programs of this kind are sometimes hampered, however, by a paucity of well-paying jobs for poorly educated or unskilled workers.

Still, many political observers argue that the modern democratic welfare state, for all its faults, is the most stable and humane system of political economy humankind has ever developed. It has

vastly expanded humanity's ability to govern itself, conferring the rights of open political participation and accountability on virtually the entire population. It has combined the freedoms of private enterprise with the security of a social safety net that has all but eliminated the terrors of permanent impoverishment and misery. It has balanced the power of wealth with the power of organization for labor, minorities, and other less privileged groups. It has provided educational opportunities and community services that were undreamed of only a few generations ago. While admitting that the welfare state's detractors may have some valid points, many of its defenders would say that no superior alternative presently exists or is ever likely to exist. In this view, the democratic welfare state constitutes a model that many countries in the world are striving to emulate, especially former communist countries and others that are now in transition from authoritarianism to democracy.

KEY TERMS AND NAMES
(Underlined in the text)

Currency depreciation (devaluation)
Political economy
GNP
GDP
Inflation
Central bank
Recession
Depression
Budget deficit
National debt
Debt servicing
Fiscal policy
Value added tax (VAT)
Laissez-faire
Market economy
Adam Smith
Centrally planned (command) economy
Mixed economy
John Maynard Keynes
Privatization
Nationalization
Welfare state

NOTES

1. The term *Pareto optimum* refers to a state of economic equilibrium in which no one's welfare can be improved without reducing someone else's welfare. It was named after the Italian political economist Vilfredo Pareto (1848–1923).
2. Since 1948 the only exceptions to this rule occurred in 1956, when President Eisenhower was reelected despite 1.4 percent growth in the previous twelve months, and 1976, when President Ford was defeated despite 4 percent growth (*The Economist*, May 27, 1995, pp. 25–26).
3. See Herman M. Schwartz, *States Versus Markets* (New York: St. Martin's Press, 1994); and Martin

Staniland, *What Is Political Economy?* (New Haven, Conn.: Yale University Press, 1985).
4. Adam Smith, *The Wealth of Nations* (Chicago: University of Chicago Press, 1977). For recent studies, see Jerry Z. Muller, *Adam Smith in His Time and Ours* (Princeton, N.J.: Princeton University Press, 1993); Ian Simpson Ross, *The Life of Adam Smith* (Oxford: Clarendon Press, 1995); and Athol Fitzgibbons, *Adam Smith's System of Liberty, Wealth, and Virtue* (New York: Oxford University Press, 1995).
5. David Ricardo, *The Principles of Political Economy and Taxation* (New York: E. P. Dutton, 1948). This work was first published in 1817.
6. Thomas Malthus, *An Essay on the Principle of Population* (New York: Oxford University Press, 1994). This work was first published in 1798.
7. Cited in Richard Hofstadter, *Social Darwinism in American Thought*, rev. ed. (New York: George Braziller, 1959), 41, 57.
8. See the *Program of the Communist Party of the Soviet Union*, issued in 1961.
9. David Stark and Laszlo Bruszt, *Postsocialist Pathways* (Cambridge: Cambridge University Press, 1998).
10. Friedrich von Hayek, *The Road to Serfdom* (Chicago: University of Chicago Press, 1956).
11. On Keynes, see Robert Lekachman, *The Age of Keynes* (New York: Random House, 1966); Robert Skidelsky, *John Maynard Keynes: A Biography*, 2 vols. (New York: Viking/Penguin, 1994). For essays on Smith, Malthus, and Keynes, see D. D. Raphael et al., *Three Great Economists* (New York: Oxford University Press, 1997).
12. Daniel Yergin and Joseph Stanislaw, *The Commanding Heights: The Battle Between Government and the Marketplace That Is Remaking the Modern World* (New York: Simon and Schuster, 1998); Harvey Feigenbaum, Jeffrey Henig, and Chris Hamnett, *Shrinking the State: The Political Underpinnings of Privatization* (Cambridge: Cambridge University Press, 1998).
13. For a sampling of Bentham's writings, see Bhikhu Pradesh, ed., *Bentham's Political Thought* (London: Croom Helm, 1973).
14. For a comprehensive interpretation, see Alan Ryan, *J. S. Mill* (London: Routledge and Kegan Paul, 1974). For a psychohistory that relates Mill's ideas and personality to his relationships with his father and his wife, see Bruce Mazlish, *James and John Stuart Mill* (New York: Basic Books, 1975).
15. Sheri Berman, *The Social Democratic Movement* (Cambridge, Mass.: Harvard University Press, 1998); Peter Gourevitch, *Politics in Hard Times* (Ithaca, N.Y.: Cornell University Press, 1986), 34.
16. Theda Skocpol, *Protecting Soldiers and Mothers: The Political Origins of Social Policy in the United States*

(Cambridge, Mass.: Harvard University Press, 1992).

17. Robert F. Himmelfarb, *Survival of Corporatism in the New Deal Era, 1933–1945* (New York: Garland, 1994).

18. Cited in Christopher Pierson, *Beyond the Welfare State?* (University Park: Pennsylvania State University Press, 1991), 128.

19. For an analysis of different types of democratic welfare regimes, see Gøsta Esping-Andersen, *Three Worlds of Welfare Capitalism* (Princeton, N.J.: Princeton University Press, 1990).

20. Pierson, *Beyond the Welfare State?* 168–78. See also Paul Pierson, *Dismantling the Welfare State? Reagan, Thatcher, and the Politics of Retrenchment* (Cambridge: Cambridge University Press, 1994).

21. Shortly after the November 1994 Congressional elections in the United States, a survey asked voters to list their chief priorities for the new Congress. The top priority, selected by 62 percent of those surveyed, was protecting Medicare and Social Security. The second most widely named priority, mentioned by 60 percent of the survey respondants, was reducing government spending (*The Washington Post*, November 28, 1994, p. A12).

22. James E. Alt and K. Alec Chrystal, *Political Economics* (Berkeley: University of California Press, 1983), 103–25.

23. Michel Crozier, Samuel P. Huntington, and Joji Watanuki, *The Crisis of Democracy* (New York: New York University Press, 1975).

24. To remedy the situation, Olson urged the repeal of all special-interest legislation or regulation and the breakup of small, narrowly based interest groups. In their place, he called for larger interest organizations ("encompassing organizations") that represent broader segments of the population, such as "peak associations" that speak up for vast segments of labor, business, or other elements of society rather than smaller subgroups within these sectors. See *The Rise and Decline of Nations* (New Haven, Conn.: Yale University Press, 1982).

CHAPTER 15

THE POLITICS OF DEVELOPMENT

South Korea—India

The **<u>developing countries</u>** consist of more than 150 states spread across the globe from Latin America to Africa, from the Middle East to East Asia. Together they are home to 85 percent of the world's population. These countries are also sometimes referred to as the "Third World," a term coined by a French economist in the 1950s. Although it had never been common previously to speak of the "First World" as a euphemism for the economically advanced democracies or to refer to the communist states as the "Second World," it was universally understood that the Third World applied to just about every other country on the planet. Confined largely to the southern hemisphere, the Third World is also known collectively as "the South," in contrast to North America, Europe, and Japan, known collectively as "the North." "North-South relations" are relations between the more economically advanced countries and those that are less developed.

Like most blanket terms, such designations as Third World or the South cover a far greater variety than they imply. In fact, the nations of the developing world exhibit an extraordinary diversity of political systems, social structures, and even levels of economic development. Some are (or have been) democracies. Others are authoritarian regimes of various types, such as traditional monarchies or military dictatorships. Some are fairly homogeneous when it comes to the ethnic composition or religious beliefs of the population; others consist of socially heterogeneous populations. In economic terms, a few developing countries are relatively rich, most are poor, and quite a few are in between.

At the same time, most developing states share certain basic features that distinguish them from the economically advanced democracies and the former communist countries of East-Central Europe and the USSR. Most—but not all—have experienced a colonial past (see table 15.1). Few states in these regions managed to escape long-term colonization by the imperialist powers. Even some that avoided colonial rule came under short-term domination by outside powers at one time or another in their history.

Another commonality that most developing states share is their relative economic inferiority to the industrially developed democracies. Hence they are frequently called *less developed countries* (LDCs). But here, too, there are exceptions, and there is some overlap with states typically categorized in the First or Second World. For example, several Middle Eastern countries are rich in oil reserves or other economic assets. In 1999, three of them—Kuwait, Qatar, and the United Arab Emirates—were ranked among the world's high-income countries, while Saudi Arabia and Libya were in the upper-middle-income category. Their economies contracted significantly in the 1990s,

TABLE 15.1

Colonization Patterns

Region or Country	Colonizing Powers	Period of Decolonization
Latin America	Spain, Portugal	1810–1820s
Caribbean	Britain, France, Denmark, the Netherlands, United States	1950s–1970s
Africa	Portugal, Britain, France, Germany, Belgium, Italy	1950s–1960s
Middle East; North Africa	Turkey, Britain, France, Spain, Italy	1920s; 1940s–1950s
India; Pakistan	Britain	1947
Southeast Asia	France, Britain, the Netherlands, Japan	1945–1950s
Korea; Taiwan	Japan	1945
Philippines	United States	1946
Pacific Islands	United States, France, Japan	1945–1980s

TABLE 15.2

Population and Annual Per Capita GNP in Selected Oil-Producing States

Country	Population (in millions, 1998)	Per Capita GNP (1998)
Richest Oil-Producing States		
Kuwait	2.0	Estimated high-income
Qatar	0.5	Estimated high-income
Saudi Arabia	21.0	Estimated high-income
United Arab Emirates	2.7	$18,220
Other Selected Oil-Exporting States		
Ecuador	12.0	$1,530
Gabon	1.2	3,950
Iran	62.0	1,770
Iraq	22.3	Estimated lower-middle
Libya	5.3	Estimated upper-middle
Mexico	96.0	3,970
Nigeria	121.0	300
Venezuela	23.0	3,500

Sources: World Bank, *World Development Report 1999/2000.*

however, as world petroleum prices fell below their high-water marks of the 1970s and early 1980s. Still, they are comparatively prosperous by Third World standards. A number of other countries in the developing world are also oil exporters, but because of their larger populations or other factors they are not as well off as the leading Middle Eastern petroleum producers (see table 15.2).

NEWLY INDUSTRIALIZING COUNTRIES (NICs)

Yet another category of developing countries consists of a small number of relatively successful economies known as the **newly industrializing countries (NICs)**. Several of them are in East Asia:

South Korea, Taiwan, Singapore, Indonesia, Thailand, and Malaysia. (Vietnam, Kampuchea, and the Philippines tend to lag behind.) Hong Kong used to be grouped with these East Asian NICs when it was under British authority, but in 1997 it reverted to Communist China. The largest non-Asian countries typically categorized as NICs are Brazil, Mexico, and Argentina. In 1998 these countries had per capita national incomes ranging from $680 (Indonesia) to $30,060 (Singapore).

The NICs are characterized above all by the fact that, since the 1950s and 1960s, they have significantly industrialized their economies. They have also expanded the postindustrial service sector, and some have moved into high-technology production. To varying degrees they have been quite

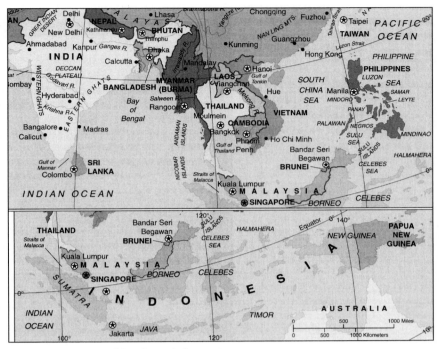

FIGURE 15.1   Map of Southeast Asia

successful, but several were severely shaken by the global financial crisis that started in East Asia in 1997 and spread across the globe over the next several years. (See chapter 1, "The Global Financial Crises of 1997–99: Asia, Russia, and Brazil.") The most successful East Asian NICs, once grouped with Japan as the "Asian Tigers" during nearly thirty years of spectacular economic growth, were particularly hard hit by the crisis. Of the Latin American NICs, Brazil's economy was the most severely affected by Asia's financial turmoil.

In addition to sharing certain economic features, all these countries have had problems building stable democracies. What accounts for their inability to sustain democratic institutions and practices in spite of their relative economic success? We'll take up this question as it concerns Mexico and Brazil in chapter 23. The next section is a brief look at South Korea.

SOUTH KOREA

With the defeat of Japan in 1945, thirty-five years of imperial Japanese rule over Korea came to an end.

An agreement between the United States and the Soviet Union divided the country at the 38° parallel. The United States intended the division to be temporary, but Soviet and North Korean leaders, and even South Korean political elites, would not agree to reunifying the country on the basis of free elections. Under Moscow's aegis, North Korea became the People's Republic of Korea, a rigid communist dictatorship led for nearly forty years by Kim Il Sung. Upon Kim's death in 1994, power devolved upon his fifty-two-year-old son, Kim Jong II.

In 1948, South Korea became the **Republic of Korea.** The United States initially hoped that the new republic would develop stable democratic institutions. But the country's first leader, Syngman Rhee, disappointed these hopes, ruling largely through the bureaucracy, the military, and the police. When North Korean troops invaded South Korea in June 1950, setting off a bloody three-year conflict, the United States had little choice but to tolerate Rhee's autocratic rule. The Cold War conflict against North Korea and its communist allies, the Soviet Union and China, took precedence over democratization in South

FIGURE 15.2   Map of Asia Showing South Korea

Korea. The war proved very costly: 1.3 million South Koreans were killed and the economy was devastated. More than 33,000 American troops lost their lives in the conflict.

Syngman Rhee retained power until 1960. Corruption at the highest levels, rigged elections, and lackluster economic performance triggered student riots that year, forcing Rhee's resignation. The leaders who were elected to replace him vowed to attack political corruption, but they were unable to maintain political order. In May 1961, the South Korean military seized power in a coup d'état, putting a quick end to the democratic aspirations of Prime Minister Myong Chang's Second Republic. Major General Park Chung Hee, the new ruler, promised an eventual return to civilian rule, but he prohibited thousands of pro-democracy politicians from participating in political life, and his government broke up the existing labor unions.

American pressure to restore democracy prompted Park Chung Hee to hold elections in 1963. After formally retiring from the military, Park defeated several rivals for the presidency. A new constitution establishing South Korea's Third Republic soon followed. Although it appeared to guarantee democratic procedures, in fact Park ruled with a firm authoritarian hand, backed by the re-

pressive apparatus of the military and the Korean Central Intelligence Agency (KCIA). Park's government responded harshly to student demonstrators and parliamentary opponents of his policies.

Nevertheless, Park also sought to court popular favor by significantly improving South Korea's economic performance. An improved economy, he believed, might enhance his dictatorial regime's legitimacy in the eyes of the population.

Prior to the mid-1960s, Park and his predecessors pursued an economic strategy known as *import substitution*. This policy attempted to compensate for South Korea's economic weakness and its dependence on the outside world by building up its own manufacturing base, especially for consumer goods that would otherwise have to be imported from abroad. In a country still devastated by the Korean War, imports could be quite expensive. Most of them had to be paid for in hard currencies, such as U.S. dollars, which were in short supply. Moreover, South Korea was still largely an agricultural country. Import substitution, it was assumed, would promote domestic industrialization.

But this inward-looking strategy had costs of its own, including budget deficits and inflation. Starting in the mid-1960s, therefore, Park Chung Hee's government abandoned import substitution and shifted to a strategy of *export-led growth*. The state's formidable powers were now turned systematically to converting the Republic of Korea into one of the most dynamic trading nations in the world.

The government initiated a series of financial incentives, such as tax breaks and low-interest loans, to South Korea's top fifty private companies, the *chaebol*, to encourage them to orient their production to world markets. The government placed particular emphasis on cultivating about a dozen high-technology firms. Meanwhile, Park's regime continued its suppression of the labor movement. Real wages (wages adjusted for inflation) did not grow at all between 1959 and 1967 for most workers. Though they began to edge up thereafter, they remained significantly below average Japanese and West European wage levels. The South Korean government also maintained tight restrictions on trade unions, limiting their right to strike and cramping their freedom to negotiate directly with private businesses.

In purely economic terms, the strategy worked. Exports rose from $56.7 million in 1962 to $17.5 billion in 1980, manufacturing boomed, and national income reached new heights, with annual growth rates averaging more than 9 percent a year. The population grew from 25 million in 1960 to 40 million by the early 1980s, with the bulk of the work force increasingly engaged in manufacturing or services rather than agriculture. South Korean companies like Hyundai, Sanyo, Samsun, and Kia became internationally respected trademarks.

The magnitude of the country's economic growth relative to other developing countries was dramatically illustrated by the meteoric upsurge of its gross national product. In 1950 South Korea's per capita GNP was about $100, slightly lower than India's and Ghana's. By 1990 it was $3,600 and in 1998 it was $7,970. India's per capita GNP in 1998 was $430, Ghana's $390.

These impressive economic achievements coincided with considerable political repression and periodic turmoil, however. The Third Republic's constitution forbade the president from serving more than two terms in office. After winning reelection in 1967, Park Chung Hee sponsored a constitutional amendment permitting him to run for a third term. Although he was reelected in 1971, Park barely defeated a pro-democracy reformer, **Kim Dae Jung,** who garnered 46 percent of the vote.

Determined to solidify his powers, Park declared martial law, banned all political parties, and shut down the universities. He then engineered a new constitution, which was approved in a referendum at the end of 1972. The institutions of the new Fourth Republic were decidedly authoritarian. Direct elections to the presidency were abolished and the legislature and the judiciary got weaker. Emergency measures and presidential decrees severely restricted the rights of citizens to criticize the government. Kim Dae Jung was kidnapped by state police agents in 1973 and remained under arrest for six years.

Despite the regime's overpowering repressiveness, popular sentiment for democracy continued to simmer under the surface. The ruling elites feared a potential uprising, but they became increasingly divided among themselves. Sharpening rivalries in the top leadership exploded in October 1979, when the head of the KCIA assassinated President Park. The event released an outpouring of pent-up popular discontent over the govern-

ment's suppression of civil freedoms, democratic accountability, and the rights of organized labor.

But expectations for democracy were dashed once again as the military quickly reasserted its dominance, declaring martial law. General Chun Doo Hwan assumed power and brutally suppressed a massive public protest in Kwangju in May 1980; hundreds died in the melee. Chun's government promulgated a new constitution, inaugurating South Korea's Fifth Republic. Like its predecessors, the new governing document affirmed strong executive authority. Over the next several years new restrictive measures were imposed on the press and labor movement, wages were scaled down, and "reeducation" camps were set up for the regime's opponents. The U.S. government and international human rights organizations repeatedly condemned South Korea for violating basic civil rights. Chun won a presidential election in 1981 only after imprisoning or banning his chief rivals. Kim Dae Jung was arrested again and sentenced to death, but he was later allowed to leave for the United States, where he remained for two years.

Despite South Korea's continuing conquest of international markets, the next years of dictatorial rule and active state coordination of the economy exacted a heavy price from workers, civil servants, farmers, and even some private businesses. These developments only intensified public pressures for democratic reforms. Catholics and Protestants, whose numbers were proliferating in a country traditionally dominated by Confucian and Buddhist beliefs, were particularly vocal in demanding constitutional change. Elements of the country's growing middle class, buoyed by rising prosperity and educational opportunities, demanded a greater say in how they were governed. And students, a perennial source of political activism against military rule, bravely staged demonstrations against Chun's dictatorship. Their opposition grew all the more embittered with the disclosure in 1987 that a Seoul National University student had been tortured to death by the police. Despite the regime's repressive administration, a democratically minded civil society continued to grow.

Chun promised to relinquish power after the completion of his seven-year term. But he picked Roh Tae Woo, a military crony, to run as his successor. The announcement of Roh's candidacy sparked a firestorm of protest. Student demonstrations turned violent in several cities. Roh calmed the situation by proclaiming his acceptance of the opposition's demands for civil liberties, direct presidential elections, and amnesty for political prisoners.

The presidential election that took place in December 1987 was a four-way race that Roh won with a plurality of 36.6 percent. The pro-democracy opposition lost the contest because its two most prestigious leaders, Kim Dae Jung and Kim Young Sam, both insisted on running against Roh Tae Woo. The "two Kims" got 27 percent and 28 percent of the vote, respectively.

The Sixth Republic that came into being with the 1988 constitution was more respectful of democratic liberties than any previous South Korean government, with the exception of the short-lived Second Republic of 1960–61. In 1992, the democratic opposition parties won a major victory in parliamentary elections. In the same year, the pro-democracy reformer Kim Young Sam was elected to the presidency with 42 percent of the vote. Optimism about South Korea's prospects for a truly comprehensive, stable democracy was now higher than ever before, uplifted by a widespread feeling that the country's "economic miracle" would last indefinitely. Within a few short years, however, hopes for a broader democracy were rudely disappointed while the economy plunged into an unanticipated abyss.

Although Kim Young Sam took office pledging to eliminate official corruption, widen the rights of trade unions, and reduce the *chaebol*'s excessive power in the South Korean economy, he failed to accomplish any of these goals. Executives of the leading companies continued to get preferential treatment from key governmental and bureaucratic officials, often exchanging payoffs for valuable favors. Promises to increase the number of trade unions and strengthen their bargaining rights came to naught. Plans to introduce long overdue economic reforms, such as stricter oversight of the country's poorly managed banks, were stalled in the national legislature.

Even more ominously, South Korea's high-flying economy got caught in the crosswinds of the financial turmoil spreading from Japan, Thailand, and other countries in the region. International economic turmoil combined with structural weaknesses in the South Korean economy to precipitate the collapse of eight large *chaebol* in 1997. President Kim Young Sam's son was implicated in a massive financial scandal and sentenced to three years in prison. The country found itself mired in $180 billion in foreign debts. As Asia's problems worsened, investors pulled large amounts of capital out of South Korea. In an effort to stave off impending disaster, the government negotiated a $57 billion rescue package with the International Monetary Fund at the end of 1997, accepting IMF demands for a major overhaul of its financial institutions and economic policies.

As South Korea's economic troubles peaked, elections were held in December 1997. Kim Dae Jung, the courageous champion of democracy, won the presidency with 40 percent of the vote. Assuming office at a time of grave economic peril, the new president appeared to have sufficient popular support to undertake necessary reforms. Some of them were bound to be painful for workers and other constituents, since the effects of globalization on the South Korean economy will probably result in job layoffs and long-term changes whose outcome cannot be foreseen with certainty. Inevitably, the future of democracy in South Korea will depend significantly on how its current government addresses these challenges.[1]

KIM DAE JUNG'S ADVICE TO YOUTH

Shortly after his election to the presidency at the age of 74, Kim Dae Jung told reporters: "I nearly faced death four times, I was imprisoned for six years, I was in exile or under house arrest for ten years, and although I was tempted, I never gave in to the pressures. I fought for my cause and I finally won. And I think this gives good lessons to young people who are trying to live upright lives. When you believe in something, you must pursue it."[2]

HYPOTHESIS-TESTING EXERCISE: Conditions for Democracy in South Korea

How do South Korea's experiences match up against the ten conditions for democracy we enumerated in chapter

TABLE 15.3

Political Developments in South Korea

Period	Constitution	Leader	Regime Type
1948–60	First Republic	Syngman Rhee	Civilian authoritarian
1960–61	Second Republic	Chang Myon	Democratic
1961–73	Third Republic	Park Chung Hee	Military and civilian authoritarian; limited democratic procedures
1973–80	Fourth Republic	Park Chung Hee	Military and civilian authoritarian; repressive
1980–87	Fifth Republic	Chun Doo Hwan	Military and civilian authoritarian
1987–92	Sixth Republic	Roh Tae Woo	Military and civilian quasi-democratic
1992–98		Kim Young Sam	Democratic
1998–		Kim Dae Jung	Democratic

Kim Dae Jung

10? In the following hypothesis-testing exercise, we'll test each of these *ten conditions* as **independent variables** for their impact on *democracy in South Korea,* which is the **dependent variable.** We expect that the presence of these conditions enhances democracy's chances, while their absence reduces them.

1. STATE INSTITUTIONS
Right from the start, South Korea has had a "stateness" problem. The division of Korea into two states has imposed severe political hardships on South Koreans, not only during the 1950–53 war but ever since. The country has had to maintain a sizable military force and constant vigilance against a potentially aggressive North Korean communist regime. In 1998 South Korea spent 3.4 percent of its GNP on the military, a hefty figure that exceeded the relative military outlays of Britain (3 percent), France (3.1 percent) and Japan (1 percent) and fell only

slightly lower than that of the United States (3.8 percent). This permanent security problem has given the South Korean military an exceptionally prominent role in the country's political life, providing a convenient pretext for authoritarian rule. Even today, tough internal security laws result in hundreds of arrests of people accused of consorting with North Korea. A ray of hope for closer ties between North and South Korea suddenly burst through the gloom in their relations in June 2000, when Kim Jong Il, Communist Korea's reclusive leader, invited South Korean President Kim Dae Jung to North Korea. The unprecedented encounter resulted in general agreements to widen economic ties and eventually reunite the two states. Reunification, if it comes, is not expected to take place anytime soon, however.

For all but a few years of its history, South Korea has been governed under non-democratic state institutions. Its leaders routinely ignored the rule of law and indulged in blatant corruption. Even under Kim Young Sam, an outspoken advocate of democracy, violations of the rule of law and official corruption were not entirely eliminated. His government frequently ignored constitutionally established procedures and proved both inefficient and ineffective in dealing with the country's mounting economic problems. His successor, Kim Dae Jung, has thus far shown greater respect for constitutional democracy, awakening hopes that democratic state institutions can finally be stabilized for the first time since South Korea's foundation.

2. ELITES COMMITTED TO DEMOCRACY
Quite clearly, South Korea's political, military, and economic elites have not supported democracy during most of the country's history. While various party leaders and other prominent South Koreans have expressed their support for democracy, until the 1990s they were not able to exercise effective political power. Democracy's future will require strict adherence to democratic procedures and values not only on the part of political

leaders, but also South Korea's military, bureaucratic, and business elites.

3. NATIONAL WEALTH

South Korea's experience from the 1960s until the early 1990s flies in the face of the proposition that national wealth by itself promotes democracy. While most of the wealthier countries in the world are stable democracies, as we saw in chapter 4, there are some notable exceptions. South Korea has been one of them. Its extraordinary rise to one of the richest nations in the world coincided with stern authoritarian rule. The recent collapse of its economy took place under the quasi-democratic regime of Kim Young Sam. As we shall note in the fifth point, however, South Korea's rising national wealth contributed to the growth of a middle class, elements of which have supported democratic reforms.

4. PRIVATE ENTERPRISE

Here, too, South Korea's political evolution until recently has been largely inconsistent with the hypothesis. In chapter 10 we noted quite a few examples of non-democratic governments that have tolerated, and in some cases actively cultivated, private enterprise. Hitler's Germany, Latin American military dictatorships, and contemporary China are prominent examples. Until its gradual shift to democracy in the 1990s, South Korea's high-growth economy was predicated on a close connection between authoritarian governments and highly favored corporations, especially those belonging to the *chaebol.* This intimate relationship between the state and the private sector has constituted the essence of the South Korean economic model, a model borrowed in large part from Japan. Direct investments and credits from the state treasury, generous tax breaks, lax supervision of business practices, and other favors from government authorities have been the defining characteristics of this system, sometimes characterized as ***crony capitalism.*** Even Kim Young Sam's partially democratic government maintained the model's essential features. While the results until the late 1990s were hugely successful in economic terms, their implications for democracy have been predominantly negative. As Robert Garran has observed, the state's heavy intervention in the economy "created an almost seamless web of interconnections between top players in government, politics, finance and business—a process that entrenched corruption and cronyism."[3] It thus appears that President Kim Dae Jung's efforts to build democracy in South Korea will require a new relationship between the state and the private sector as well.

5. A MIDDLE CLASS

As South Korea's economy has grown, so has its middle class. Support for pro-democratic parties and interest groups has come to a significant extent from this rising social sector, consisting of people connected to both the private and public sectors. Whether those members of the middle class who are favorably disposed to democracy maintain their support in the future, however, may depend on their economic fortunes as President Kim Dae Jung leads the country through the financial crisis and a difficult political and economic reform process.

6. SUPPORT OF THE DISADVANTAGED FOR DEMOCRACY

South Korea's less privileged classes, consisting mainly of low-paid factory and farm workers, have provided varying degrees of support for democracy. Industrial workers have offered considerable support for trade unions, which have consistently called for democratic reforms. Agricultural workers have tended to be less overtly organized into pro-democratic groups. How these groups behave in the future may depend on how well they fare under the current democratic government's efforts to surmount the country's economic difficulties and deal with a host of domestic and international pressures. Workers who demand job security may be disappointed, as South Korea's economic restructuring may result in bankruptcies and other changes that tend to promote unemployment. (Unemployment rose from 2.6 percent in 1997 to more than 7 percent in 1999.) In 1997 the legislature abolished the country's lifetime employment guarantees, a move that permits firms to fire unneeded workers. The measure cannot help but heighten working-class anxieties. Kim Dae Jung's leadership skills will be seriously tested as he seeks to retain the loyalties of his supporters under conditions of economic adversity. Women have also been subjected to economic and social disadvantages, arising largely out of traditional cultural attitudes and practices. A growing feminist movement is pinning its hopes on democracy for widening opportunities for women in South Korea's business and political spheres.

7. AN ACTIVE CIVIL SOCIETY AND A DEMOCRATIC POLITICAL CULTURE

Even during the most repressive periods of military rule, many South Koreans boldly confronted the government in open demonstrations, strikes, and other forms of civil protest. Students, trade unions, and other citizen groups, many functioning illegally, kept alive the fires of an active civil society in these years, often running serious risks of arrest or violent death. Pro-democracy political parties also existed under authoritarian regimes, at times clandestinely. Since 1992, these and other elements of civil society have been allowed to operate more freely. Their activities have significantly contributed to building a democratic political culture among large segments of South Korea's population.

8. EDUCATION AND FREEDOM OF INFORMATION

The military regimes vastly increased educational opportunities for all South Koreans. Between the early 1960s and the late 1980s, secondary school attendance rose from about 30 percent to nearly 90 percent of the population, while university-level enrollments increased from 6 percent to 36 percent. The authorities recognized that a well-educated work force was a necessity for a sophisticated high-tech economy. Although the regime sought to keep a tight lid on politically controversial publications and academic courses, it permitted scholars and students to travel abroad and gain access to Western ideas. Students were frequently the most demonstrative foes of military rule and vocal advocates of democratic reforms. Many businesspeople and ordinary citizens were also free to travel outside the country. A strict censorship prevented real press freedom, but news about domestic and foreign developments circulated through various illegal and semi-legal channels. Since the advent of democratic reforms, academic and press restrictions have been lifted, though Kim Young Sam's government enforced various laws limiting the free expression of certain politically sensitive opinions. Kim Dae Jung's government has been more permissive with respect to freedom of expression.

9. A HOMOGENEOUS SOCIETY

South Korea's society is ethnically homogeneous. This reality, however, has not made it any easier for the country to build and maintain democracy for most of its history. In recent decades there has been growing religious heterogeneity, with Christians now constituting 49 percent of the population and Buddhists 47 percent. Many South Korean Christians have been quite supportive of democracy.

10. A FAVORABLE INTERNATIONAL ENVIRONMENT

South Korea's military regimes managed to keep a tight grip on power for decades in spite of U.S. preferences for democracy. American pressures for democratic change were not especially intense during the height of the Cold War in the 1950s and 1960s, however, as the confrontation with North Korea required a firm U.S. commitment to reliable South Korean governments and their military command. Favorable international economic conditions from the 1960s to the end of the 1990s, moreover, proved highly conducive to South Korea's economic expansion but not very conducive to democracy. More recently, the global financial crisis has created a shaky foundation on which to build a solid democratic government. While the International Monetary Fund's substantial rescue loan should provide Kim Dae Jung's government with welcome financial support, the structural reforms the IMF has attached as conditions to this money may antagonize businesses, bureaucrats, and workers who lose out in the process, at least until the economy rebounds. On all these accounts, the international environment has not especially favored democracy in South Korea. Democracy's global resurgence, however, may provide some general sustenance to pro-democracy forces there.

South Korea is by no means the only small country in East Asia to combine rapid economic growth with authoritarian politics. Others include the following:

- **Singapore,** an island smaller than New York City, achieved the ninth highest per capita GNP in the world by the late 1990s. Between 1965 and 1990, its export-driven economy thrived under the no-nonsense rule of Lee Kuan Yew, who believed that discipline is more important than democracy when it comes to promoting economic development. "Every time anybody starts anything which will unwind or unravel this orderly, organized, sensible, rational society, and make it irrational and emotional," he once stated, "I put a stop to it without hesitation." His hand-picked successor, Goh Chok Tong, has also attacked liberal democracy. Though opposition parties may compete in elections, the ruling People's Action Party makes use of the state's formidable powers to suppress them by muzzling the press, harassing political opponents, and spreading patronage, money, and social welfare benefits to its supporters.[4]

- **Malaysia** averaged 5.7 percent annual growth rates from the mid-1980s to the mid-1990s under Mahathir Mohamad, another harsh critic of democracy and devotee of the "Asian development model," with its close ties between government and business. Like other countries in the region, Malaysia was severely affected by the late-1990s financial crisis.[5]

- **Thailand** had the world's highest growth rates between 1984 and 1995, averaging 8.4 percent annually. A corrupt elected government fell victim to a military coup in 1991, which sustained the country's rapid growth until the currency collapsed in the summer of 1997, setting off a wave of currency devaluations in the region. As the economy disintegrated, middle-class demonstrators took to the streets demanding democratic reforms. A new democratic constitution was passed and a new government took power that quickly won plaudits for its bold economic reforms. Unemployment has tripled, however, and in 1998 the economy contracted by almost 8 percent. The military keeps a watchful eye on the situation and poses a latent threat to democracy in a country with a long history of coups d'état.

- **Indonesia** is a largely Muslim country boasting the world's fourth largest population (207.4 million in 1998). Until 1997 it was governed under President Suharto, who took power in a 1965 military coup. After growing at a robust 6 percent per year between 1985 and 1995, Indonesia's economy went into a tailspin during the 1997 Asian financial crisis. Students and other protestors mounted angry demonstrations, forcing Suharto's resignation. In 1999 the first democratic elections in more than forty years brought to power a pro-democracy president, Abdurrahman Wahid, a Muslim intellectual.

While Singapore and Malaysia were still under authoritarian governments as the century came to a close, the experiences of South Korea, Thailand, and Indonesia indicated that longings for democracy were widespread in spite of the fact that these countries had made enormous economic strides under authoritarian regimes. The 1997 financial crisis detonated demands for a more accountable democracy in South Korea and for the replacement of non-democratic regimes in the other two countries. These events indicate that popular support for democracy may actually *intensify* during an economic crisis. Time will tell, however, if the new democratic governments in these countries can retain this support during the painful process of economic reform, which may be accompanied by higher unemployment and slower rates of growth.

UNDERDEVELOPED COUNTRIES

Although the Newly Industrializing Countries are considered developing countries, most countries in the developing world are considerably worse off. Quite a few middle-income countries have major

pockets of poverty, especially those in the lower-middle-income range. But the most severely impoverished are the "low-income" countries. In 1998 the World Bank counted sixty-three countries in the low-income group, each with a per capita GNP of $760 or less. Including the world's two most populous countries, China and India, they comprised more than half the globe's population, with a combined total of more than 3.5 billion people in 1998. As many as 1.5 billion of them subsist at the barest margins of survival on less than $1 a day. That bellweather figure of absolute poverty was higher than in 1987, when it stood at 1.2 billion, and it is expected to rise to 1.9 billion by 2025 if current trends of population growth and economic stagnation persist.[6]

Income statistics tell only part of the story. Other indicators reveal the tragic dimensions of the poorest countries' predicament with even greater harshness:

- People living on less than $1 a day are five times more likely to die before the age of five than are those living on more than that amount.
- As many as 100 million people have no permanent shelter.
- About 800 million people are malnourished. Thirteen million to 18 million people die every year from malnutrition, a figure that averages out to forty thousand per day. Approximately three-fourths of these victims are under the age of five. Global food supplies, which doubled between 1975 and 2000, will have to double again by 2035 to keep up with population growth.
- Millions of malnourished children who manage to survive into adulthood have suffered irreparable brain damage because of insufficient protein during their early years.
- About 14 million people die every year from vaccine-preventable diseases.[7]

Moreover, the economic chasm between the rich and poor has been widening steadily. The income gap between the richest third of the nations of the world and the poorest third, measured in terms of average per capita GNP, grew from about eleven to one in 1970 to just short of twenty to one by 1995. And as we noted in chapter 1, the combined annual income of the world's poorest 2.5 billion people equals the net worth of the world's richest 225 people.

However we choose to draw the dividing lines between middle-income and low-income nations, the fact is undeniable that a large number of developing countries suffer from **underdevelopment.** "Underdeveloped" economies are somewhat different from "undeveloped" economies. Undeveloped economies are ready to grow, like the United States in the mid-nineteenth century. Underdeveloped economies suffer from chronic, seemingly eternal low growth and mass poverty. The distinctions between various stages of economic development were clarified by Walt Rostow in a book that was highly influential in the 1960s.[8]

Why haven't the chronically underdeveloped countries been able to develop their economies? This pressing question has generated a wide range of answers. The following overview presents a few independent variables that students of economic development have used in their efforts to explain the persistence of underdevelopment in different settings. The list is by no means exhaustive or detailed, however, and is certainly no substitute for an in-depth study of the complexities of economic development.

Population

Some of the world's poorest countries are teeming with tens of millions of people with inadequate food, housing, medical care, or employment. Poverty in such cases often means the barest level of subsistence. All too frequently, the most unfortunate fall even below that minimum standard. If they do not die in infancy or childhood, they can be condemned to a life of sheer torpor.

People may of course decide how many children to have on the basis of economic realities, religious convictions, or purely personal considerations, but population can also be an explosive political issue. Some governments have intervened directly in population dynamics by fashioning policies aimed at curbing population growth. China's communist leadership decreed in 1979 that no couple living in an urban area should be allowed to have more than one child; rural couples may have more than one child only under specified circumstances. Forced sterilization has been imposed on millions of Chinese men, a policy that has enraged international human rights and religious organizations. India's government-sponsored birth control programs,

TABLE 15.4

Countries with a Population over One Hundred Million, 1998 and 2050			
Country	1998 Population (in millions)	Country	Expected Population in 2050 (in millions)
China	1,256	India	1,529
India	982	China	1,478
United States	274	United States	349
Indonesia	206	Pakistan	346
Brazil	166	Indonesia	312
Pakistan	148	Nigeria	244
Russia	147	Brazil	244
Japan	126	Bangladesh	213
Nigeria	106	Ethiopia	169
		Democratic Republic of the Congo	160
		Mexico	147
		Philippines	131
		Vietnam	127
		Russia	121
		Iran	115
		Egypt	115
		Japan	105
		Turkey	101

Source: United Nations Population Fund, *6 Billion: A Time for Choices. The State of World Population 1999,* <www.unfpa.org>.

which include sex education and official encouragement for voluntary sterilization, is regarded by many observers as inadequate and ineffective. Poor implementation of the Indian government's policies at various administrative levels are often singled out as one of the reasons behind the country's failure to rein in its population explosion. Other governments have also proven ineffective in stemming population growth, and some have not even attempted to do so in an organized fashion. The controversies of population politics were in full view at the International Conference on Population and Development, held in 1994 under the auspices of the United Nations.

Sociocultural Explanations

Some analysts attribute economic underdevelopment to social and institutional structures and to the cultural attitudes and modes of behavior that accompany them. One such school of thought was first conceptualized by Max Weber earlier in this century and later adapted by American social scientists in the 1950s and 1960s. It makes a fundamental distinction between *modern* and *traditional* societies.

Modern societies are characterized by a complex social structure consisting of differentiated, specialized professions (doctors, farmers, mechanics, etc.) and organized associations (trade unions and other interest groups), all interacting with one another over a relatively wide geographic area. They also tend to have a network of well-developed governmental institutions, including highly organized bureaucracies and a fairly sophisticated system of laws that regulate political, economic, and social interactions. Modern societies are heavily centered in urban areas and are characterized by fairly high rates of literacy and education.

Traditional societies, by contrast, tend to consist of extended families engaged in primary economic activities, such as subsistence agriculture, within a fairly small area. They display little or no professional differentiation, since one person may perform multiple tasks (farmer, medicine man, priest). There are few, if any, organized associations. They also have much simpler institutional structures. Government, to the extent that it is organized at all, is typically built around elites who wield power arbitrarily, demanding the population's deference while freely engaging in all sorts

of corruption. Most people in traditional societies live in rural areas. Very few are educated or even literate.

Whereas modern societies tend to be secular (even though they may permit religious freedom), rationally organized, and attuned to scientific logic, traditional societies tend to attribute natural phenomena to supernatural forces over which human beings have little control. In modern societies, religion and science coexist. In traditional societies, religious belief or superstition substitutes for scientific rationality. As a consequence, modern societies are able to apply science to the production of sophisticated technology, while traditional societies must make do with fairly primitive technology.

Whereas modern societies are based on impersonal rules that apply to everyone, such as legal codes and the laws of the economic marketplace, social and political relationships in traditional societies are more personalized, with a high value placed on face-to-face relations and personal favoritism. Modern societies are dynamic; change is the norm. Traditional societies are highly conservative and resistant to change; people know their place in the existing social hierarchy and are expected to stay there. Quite often, a sense of resignation precludes even the possibility of change.

Scholars who stress these and related distinctions between modern and traditional societies are often exponents of **modernization theory,** which contends that economic underdevelopment cannot be overcome until the society in question abandons its traditional social and institutional structures, along with their accompanying attitudes and behavioral patterns. Countries as diverse as India, Burma, and specific African and Middle Eastern states have been variously viewed as possessing distinct features of traditional society that appear to obstruct their economic development.[9]

The modern versus traditional society dichotomy is not without its critics. Some maintain that the distinction is too sharp, arguing that it is possible for some countries to retain certain elements of their own traditional society while simultaneously adopting specific aspects of modern society. A number of critics accuse Western social scientists of ethnocentric bias because they equate modern societies with Western societies. By placing American or West European concepts of modernity on a pedestal as the preferred ideal, they argue, Western advocates of modernization theory implicitly denigrate non-Western approaches to political and economic life and overlook the possibility that individual countries will be able to find their own path to economic growth, independent of their would-be tutors in the West. Another criticism suggests that some less developed countries have already advanced well beyond the simple social and political structures of traditional society but still remain economically undeveloped. Other explanations of economic backwardness are therefore necessary.[10]

Domestic Economy Explanations

After World War II, most of the nations of Asia and Africa that had been colonized by Britain, France, and other European powers in the eighteenth and nineteenth centuries gained their independence. The process was known as **decolonization.** Flush with their newly won independence, the leaders of many of these decolonized states embraced one form or another of what they generally called socialism. For a number of the freshly independent states, socialism above all meant two things: (1) opposition to Western neo-colonialism, and (2) a powerful role for the state in organizing the national economy.

"Neo-colonialism" and *"neo-imperialism"* were the terms used by many Third World leaders to denounce what they regarded as attempts by Britain, France, the United States, or other Western states to try to dominate their economies and dictate their political orientations even after the formal termination of colonial rule. These anti-Western attitudes often included a fierce determination on the part of Third World political leaders to reject the market-oriented economic approaches of the advanced capitalist states and to forge their own homegrown models of economic development. Anti-colonialism thus implied anti-capitalism. Third World socialism was a strategy consciously aimed at reinforcing independence from the West. In several developing countries, businesses or other property privately owned by Europeans or Americans were expropriated by the state, often without compensation.

In addition to having a distinctly anti-Western bias, socialism in many developing nations meant that the state would play a galvanizing role in guiding the process of national economic development. Throughout the developing world, especially in the decades extending from the 1950s to the 1980s, a considerable number of political leaders and economists subscribed to the view that a state-centered socialist system would promote economic development far more rapidly and far more equitably than free-market capitalism. Denouncing capitalism as greedy and exploitative, they called for state economic plans aimed at systematically expanding the nation's wealth and alleviating the misery of the vast majority of the population. Many of them also placed a sharp emphasis on economic self-reliance and spurned trade relations with the West.

State-dominated economic systems of one type or another today remain an attractive alternative to Western-style private enterprise for many political leaders and intellectuals throughout the developing world. Over the course of the 1980s, however, calls for enhancing private enterprise and introducing market mechanisms made a strong resurgence not only among Western governments and international organizations such as the World Bank and the International Monetary Fund, which were already predisposed to neo-liberal economics, but also among a growing number of political figures, economists, and private citizens in developing countries.

This widening interest in market economics stemmed in part from the failure of a number of heavily state-managed economies to grow. Political elites in Bolivia, India, Tanzania, and other countries reached the conclusion that excessive government involvement in the economy had not stimulated growth but retarded it. An effort to privatize at least some government-controlled enterprises followed. Another source of the surge in neo-liberal reforms in various developing countries was the strong support for private enterprise around the world that came from the Reagan administration in the United States and the Thatcher government in Britain. Both leaders were ideological conservatives, boisterously supportive of the private sector and chary of intrusive government involvement in the economy. Yet another source of the change in attitude toward capitalism was the undeniable success of the East Asian NICs, at least until the late 1990s. Finally, the collapse of the Soviet Union and its communist empire in Eastern Europe took the wind from the sails of many Third World socialist movements, particularly those that depended on financial or military support from Moscow and its allies. The future will determine whether the latest trends toward privatization and market economics will succeed in spurring greater economic growth in developing countries and in spreading the effects of growth to the whole population.

International Explanations

As we have repeatedly emphasized, what happens *within* nations is very often affected by what happens *between* nations, and vice versa. Not surprisingly, some explanations as to why certain countries experience significant economic growth while others do not are rooted in the interconnection between internal factors and external ones.

One explanation of this kind is associated with Raul Prebisch, an Argentine economist who served for many years as the head of the United Nations Economic Commission for Latin America. Prebisch and others like him have maintained that one of the chief causes of economic underdevelopment is the prevailing structure of the international economy. Specifically, most Third World countries are at a permanent disadvantage because the *terms of trade* for their imports and exports favor the rich nations of the world. In other words, the products that most poor nations must import (such as energy, technology, autos, and other manufactured goods) cost more than the products they can sell in world markets (which often consist of raw materials or cheap manufactures). The result is lingering economic backwardness. To remedy the situation, Prebisch and economists who make similar arguments have demanded a complete restructuring of the international trading system. In the 1970s they called for the negotiation of a New International Economic Order, based on preferential concessions by the advanced states of the North in order to compensate the poorer countries of the South. Although some of Prebisch's recommendations have been

adopted by various economically advanced states in their trade ties with LDCs, the radical reordering of the world trading system he advocated has not come about.[11]

Another international explanation for Third World poverty is **dependency theory.** This theory asserts that the advanced capitalist countries of the North dominate the world economy and constitute its "core" (or "metropolis"). The poor countries are relegated to the "periphery" of the world capitalist system. They are treated as mere satellites of the rich industrialized nations and remain economically dependent on them. One variant of this theory asserts that capitalists in the core countries sometimes succeed in making alliances with capitalist entrepreneurs and other groups in particular developing countries. The result is a "dual economy" within such countries: a relatively well-to-do capitalist elite with international connections coexists with poverty-stricken masses who are cut off from such privileged contacts. Those involved in these capitalist Third World enclaves, in turn, frequently ally themselves with repressive right-wing dictatorships at home in an effort to suppress the local labor movement and enrich themselves. In many cases these ruling elites cooperate with giant transnational corporations in exploiting the local economy. International economic dependency, in short, has palpable political consequences at home in many "peripheral" countries.

There are several variants of dependency theory, most of them espoused by Marxist scholars. However they may differ in their details, their essential point is the same: economic underdevelopment in the Third World is the result of the deliberate economic exploitation of the South by the rich states of the North. It is this notion more than any other that constitutes the core belief of "Third Worldism" as a political ideology.[12]

The dependency hypothesis has touched off a lively debate. Some of its critics insist that it is domestic factors—whether social, cultural, economic, or political in nature—that are the main causes of underdevelopment in Third World countries. Others stress an interaction of domestic and international variables but reject the dependency theorists' depiction of these connections. The neo-liberal critique of dependency, for example, affirms that countries that orient their national economy toward active involvement in international trade are more likely to experience growth than countries that cut themselves off from the global economy, whether for ideological reasons (e.g., anti-capitalism) or others. As one might expect, neo-liberals point to the Asian NICs as prime examples of export-oriented growth. At the same time, they criticize inward-looking economies based on excessive import substitution or political hostility to trade with the capitalist world as paragons of domestic economic stagnation.[13]

Over the course of the 1990s the neo-liberal approach won acceptance among a growing number of governments in the developing world. By the end of the decade, 110 developing countries were members of the World Trade Organization, compared with only sixty-five members of the WTO's predecessor, the General Agreement on Tariffs and Trade (GATT), in 1987. The WTO members from the developing world accounted for 20 percent of world trade. While the ideas of economic liberalization and participation in the global trading order have won widening approval in principle, however, many developing country elites express serious reservations about their practical implementation. The forces of globalization can bring economic destabilization just as readily as they provide jobs, investment, and other economic benefits, they point out, and the rich countries continue to dominate the global trading order, often preaching the advantages of trade liberalization while denying entry into their countries to unwanted exports from the developing world. Still, the trend toward greater liberalization and participation in the world economy has been emphatically established by a large number of developing nations in the past decade, and it appears likely to continue well into the new millennium.

Domestic Political Explanations

Another set of hypotheses accentuates domestic political factors as important independent variables that help explain economic performance. One study, for example, compared the development experiences of more than forty Third World countries between 1950 and 1980. Although the study was conducted by a team of economists, it concluded that political factors were just as important, and

sometimes even more important, than economic factors in accounting for the success or failure of a country's efforts to develop its economy. Economically successful countries tended to exhibit long-term political stability and continuity of leadership, growth-oriented economic policies pursued by the government, competent administrative personnel, and a cohesive sense of nationhood on the part of the population. Countries lacking these attributes tended to fare poorly when it came to promoting economic growth.[14]

The relationship between economic development and politics is often a complex one, however. As Samuel Huntington pointed out in his influential study, *Political Order in Changing Societies,* there is always a dynamic interaction between socioeconomic modernization and political development, but the results may vary. As a developing country embarks on the path of modernization and independence, political participation on the part of the masses tends to increase. Literacy, higher education, and urbanization expand, promoting mass political activism. In order to gain popular support, political leaders seek to mobilize the masses, organizing them into supporting various political ideas and programs. At the same time, the state makes a conscious effort to promote the country's economic development. Social change, economic change, and mass political mobilization are the order of the day. These processes typify what Huntington calls *political modernization.*

How the state and other political institutions deal with these changes is problematic. The process of building effective institutions is what Huntington calls *political development.* Successful political development requires the creation of interest groups and political parties that are capable of expressing and aggregating popular demands in a representative fashion and of channeling these demands into concrete and realistic policy proposals that governments can act upon. It also requires effective governmental institutions—executives, legislatures, bureaucracies, and so on—that can make decisions efficiently and implement them effectively. Only by being responsive to the newly activated masses can these political associations and institutions hope to gain popular legitimacy. If they succeed, the result can be long-term political order and steady economic growth.

Successful political development is not a simple trick, however. Social, economic, and political modernization may explode with such force that it rapidly outpaces the ability of political associations and institutions to keep up with the demands being placed on them. Modernization, in other words, has a destabilizing effect on interest groups, parties, and governments. If these political organizations fail to respond to the avalanche of popular demands suddenly cascading upon them, the results can be devastating: social frustration, political violence, revolutionary upheaval, or the imposition of repressive authoritarian rule can conceivably follow. If political development fails to keep pace with modernization, the result can be long-term political and economic decay. "The primary problem in politics," Huntington states, "is the lag in the development of institutions behind social and economic changes." In sum, Huntington argues that economic growth does not take place in a political vacuum. It can best flourish in a context of political order and stability, rooted in legitimate political institutions.[15]

One of the implications of Huntington's study is that, in modernizing countries, political order may be more difficult to achieve in a democracy than in an authoritarian regime. Democracies encourage political participation, and participation increases the demands people place on their governments. But too many demands can make it all the more difficult for the state to concentrate its attention and resources on developing the economy. As a consequence, the political elites of developing countries may find it in their own best interest, and in the interests of economic development more generally, to limit popular participation and govern on the basis of more authoritarian methods. Deciding how much participation to allow, or how to regulate or stifle it, is no easy choice, as Huntington notes. Until the "third wave" of democracy gathered momentum in the 1980s, most Third World leaders rejected Western-style liberal democracy in favor of more authoritarian methods of controlling or mobilizing the population.[16]

Indeed the question of whether authoritarian states or democracies are more effective at promoting rapid economic growth is still one of the most contentious political issues of modern poli-

tics. The authoritarian camp derides democracy as hopelessly inefficient. Economic growth, its adherents proclaim, is faster, more extensive, and more enduring when the central government takes charge of the country's productive forces. Many of them would also argue that democratic rights and liberties are not even all that popular under conditions of economic underdevelopment. If given a choice between improved living standards and political freedom, they contend, most destitute people will prefer improved living standards. The right to vote means nothing, in their view, to populations whose bellies are empty.

In stark opposition to these voices, democracy's advocates insist that democratic government is not only superior to authoritarianism on moral grounds; it is actually more effective when it comes to generating and sustaining economic growth. Advancing this claim in theoretical terms, Mancur Olson argued that democracies are more successful than despotic governments at guaranteeing property rights, which are a verifiably important catalyst of economic growth. Democratic accountability also ensures that elected officials do not confiscate society's wealth for themselves, as despots are wont to do, but leave a large share of money and resources in the hands of economically productive entrepreneurs and investors.[17]

Whatever the moral or practical merits of democracy may be, in actual fact the record of democracy in the less developed countries is a troubled one. Chapter 4 provides extensive data relating levels of national wealth to varying degrees of democracy. As the tables show, the lower we go down the economic pyramid, the less likely we are to encounter democracy. Of all the lower-middle and low-income countries listed there, only two—Costa Rica and India—have managed to sustain free democratic political institutions for most of the period from 1950 to 1995. Even India suffered a severe setback when Prime Minister Indira Gandhi suspended democracy and ruled dictatorially for several years (see later in this chapter). In 1998, however, India moved up from the ranks of the "partly democratic" to join the "democratic" states, thus bringing the number of people living in democracies at the start of 1999 to nearly 2.4 billion (40 percent of the world's population). In the previous year only 1.27 billion lived in countries classified as democracies (21.7 percent of global population).

If we look at democracy's reach by regions within the developing world, certain patterns are unmistakable. Latin America and the Caribbean region have chalked up quite a successful record, and Asia had the next best mix of democracies and partial democracies. Africa's performance was less successful, with more authoritarian regimes than democracies or partial democracies. The Middle East had the least successful track record: there were no electoral democracies in the Arab world.[18]

What can less developed countries do to enhance the prospects for democracy? A recent comparative study of democracy in the developing world has produced some insightful generalizations about the many factors that impinge upon a nation's efforts to build stable democratic institutions and processes. They bear a close resemblance to the ten conditions for democracy we listed in chapter 10.[19]

The following thumbnail portrait of India can provide a bit more perspective on the triumphs and travails of democracy in one of the poorest countries of the developing world.

INDIA

"At the stroke of midnight, while the world sleeps, India will awake to life and freedom." With those words, Jawaharlal Nehru proclaimed India's inde-

pendence, which took effect, after centuries of foreign domination, on August 15, 1947.

As independent India's first prime minister, Nehru inherited the world's second most populous nation after China. Nearly 350 million people formed a vast mosaic of religions, languages, classes, and castes, squeezed into an area only about a third the size of the United States. Prior to independence, the country consisted of more than 500 states and subdivisions, most with their own distinct traditions and social patterns. Out of this tangled human web Nehru was determined to shape the structures of an enduring democracy and lay the groundwork for steady economic development.

The challenge was daunting. India's freedom was accompanied by fierce bloodletting between its two largest religious groups, Hindus and Muslims. The confrontation was the result of the breakup of British India into two separate states, India and Pakistan.

Jawaharlal Nehru (left), India's first-post-independence prime minister, and Mohandas Gandhi

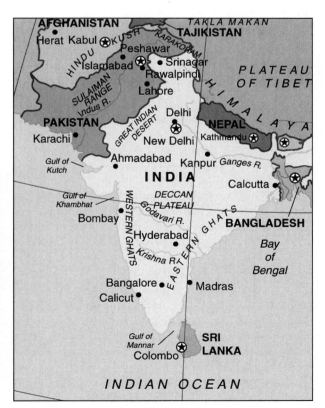

FIGURE 15.3   Map of South Asia

After gaining their first foothold in India in 1614, the British gradually extended their domains on the South Asian subcontinent over the course of the seventeenth and eighteenth centuries, ousting Portuguese, French, and Dutch settlers in the process. In 1858, when it officially became a crown colony, British India extended from the borders of Iran and Afghanistan in the north to the southern tip of the subcontinent, opposite the island of Ceylon (now Sri Lanka), another British possession.

Throughout these centuries, the British were at best tolerated but never fully accepted by the population as the legitimate rulers of India's destiny. In 1885, a small group of nationalists formed the Indian National Congress, an organization intended to give Indians a greater say in their own affairs and, eventually, freedom. For the next several decades the Congress was largely ineffectual, its membership confined to the country's urbanized, educated elite and its small middle-class following. When **Mohandas Gandhi** became the organization's leader, however, the Congress took on the character of a surging mass movement rooted in India's populous rural villages.

As a young lawyer, Gandhi had worked in South Africa, using western legal concepts and his own doctrine of *satyagraha* (moral persuasion) in an effort to obtain civil rights and racial justice for the country's Indian minority. After returning to India in 1915, Gandhi began employing the same techniques of persuasion and nonviolent agitation to rouse India's masses against British rule. He organized several demonstrative campaigns of civil disobedience in the 1920s and 1930s, including his famous salt march, a 240-mile trek to the Indian Ocean, where he clutched a handful of salt in defiance of British regulations requiring payment of a salt tax. Gandhi was arrested, and the event became an international sensation. Over the next seventeen years, Gandhi stood out as the charismatic political and spiritual leader of India's impoverished masses and an inspiration throughout the world to oppressed groups seeking to overcome domination through nonviolent means. His followers called him *Mahatma* (Great Soul).

Although a devout Hindu, Gandhi believed strongly in religious tolerance and the national unity of India's diverse peoples. He had no desire to see British India partitioned into separate states after independence. Islamic leaders led by Mohammed Ali Jinnah, however, insisted on the formation of a separate state composed mainly of Muslims. The British authorities agreed. After intensive negotiations it was decided to partition Punjab and Bengal, two northern provinces located 900 miles apart. Each was divided roughly evenly into Muslim and Hindu populations. Portions of these provinces were split off from India to form the new nation-state of Pakistan. One part of Punjab became West Pakistan and a part of Bengal became East Pakistan. The border regions of Kashmir and Jammu were hotly contested and the boundary line still remains unratified. The partition plan resulted in the uprooting of more than ten million people, as Hindus moved to the Indian side of the border and Muslims moved to Pakistan. Periodic outbursts of violence between the two groups in 1947 and 1948 resulted in hundreds of thousands of casualties. Gandhi himself was assassinated by Hindu fanatics infuriated at his efforts to accommodate the Muslims.[20]

Following these unpropitious beginnings, Nehru focused his attention on the political and economic modernization of India. An ardent nationalist and a descendant of the country's select Brahmin caste, Nehru had spent seven years in Britain, where he was educated at Harrow and Cambridge University and admitted to London's prestigious Inns of Court. Although determined to win India's freedom from British rule, he was a great admirer of Western democracy and socialist conceptions of economic justice. He presided over the adoption of India's 1950 constitution, which adopted British-style parliamentary democracy.

Succeeding Gandhi as the leading figure in the Indian National Congress, Nehru helped shape the organization into a political party capable of representing not only India's elites and middle class but also its poor, uneducated masses. Under his guidance, the Congress Party quickly dominated India's emerging political system. Aided by a single-member-district, plurality electoral system, the Congress Party in the 1952–67 period managed to convert a popular vote ranging from 45 percent to 48 percent of the ballots into control of about 75 percent of the seats in the Lok Sabha, the lower house of the national parliament. (It got roughly similar shares in the 1980s.) In these years the Congress Party evolved into a large grassroots movement as well as the principal party of government at the national level. Its success appeared to be just what Samuel Huntington would have ordered for a country in the throes of modernization: an effective political organization responsive to the newly mobilized masses.[21] Nehru's charismatic leadership and the Congress Party's early dominance helped legitimize India's democratic system among a majority of its citizens. Voter turnout for national elections has averaged about 60 percent of eligible voters since the 1960s.[22]

But neither Nehru nor the party was able to resolve India's two most haunting problems: the immense scope of its economic underdevelopment and the potential explosiveness of its social and regional diversity. Either of these challenges would be enough to keep democracy at bay, or destroy it, in most any other country.

Two years after Nehru's death in 1964, India faced a severe food shortage that compelled the government to appeal to the outside world for immediate assistance. India remained dependent on food imports until 1978. Since then the country has been relatively self-sufficient in food supplies despite a burgeoning population. Nevertheless, poverty has remained ineradicable. The Nehru government's economic strategy of achieving "self-sustained growth" through a combination of private enterprise and government planning yielded some significant gains in national income. But it set India on a course of import substitution and escalating government involvement in the economy that led to waste and inefficiency. India's industrial growth rates have lagged behind those of other developing countries, such as China, South Korea, and Mexico. Early plans to revitalize the agricultural economy were never seriously implemented. India's rural villages, where 85 percent of the population still resides, remain mired in backwardness, with 40 percent of the country living in absolute poverty.

Intense social divisions provide a continuing source of political conflict. While socioeconomic divisions are one source of turmoil, cleavages along religious, ethnolinguistic, and caste lines play an important role of their own.

Today's India is still a predominantly Hindu country: 83 percent of the population adheres to this ancient faith. Muslims comprise about 11 percent of the populace. Even after the partition of British India in 1947–48, some 50 million Muslims remained in India; today they number more than 160 million. Approximately 2 percent of Indians are Sikhs, the adherents of a Hindu sect that branched off from traditional Hinduism some five hundred years ago. Christians of various denominations comprise 2.4 percent of the population, and a host of other religions have smaller groups of followers.

Ethnolinguistic distinctions are even more abundant. Though Hindi and English are the main official languages, the constitution recognizes fourteen other official languages. There are twenty-four languages spoken by at least a million people each, and over sixteen hundred dialects. These divisions lead to considerable regional diversity and fragmentation. India's federal structure now consists of twenty-five states and seven union territories, and local distinctions within these subdivisions abound. Separatist movements have flared up in Punjab (with its large Sikh population), Assam and Nagaland in the northeast, in the border areas of Kashmir and Jammu, and elsewhere.

The ties of caste also exert a profoundly divisive effect on Indian society, even though Nehru's government abolished the caste system in legal terms. With deep roots in Hindu cosmology, more than a thousand castes still exist, separated by doctrines and traditions that forbid contact between members of specified castes. A prevailing hierarchy differentiates higher castes from lower ones, with millions relegated to the lowest caste of Untouchables, a group Gandhi sought to dignify by calling them *harijans* (children of God).

Thus far, India's democracy has proved sufficiently resilient to withstand the acute challenges posed by these economic and social realities. The maintenance of democratic procedures and political stability has not been very consistent, however.

In 1966 Nehru's daughter, Indira Gandhi (who was no relation of Mohandas Gandhi's), became prime minister. Three years later, deep divisions within the Congress Party over policy issues and personalities split the organization into two parties, one loyal to Mrs. Gandhi and the other opposed to her. Prime Minister Gandhi used her control over political patronage to build a new

Congress Party concerned mainly with winning elections rather than serving as the country's prime force for national political integration, as it had in the past.

Meanwhile, long-standing tensions with Pakistan reached a boiling point. In 1971, as 10 million refugees streamed into India in an attempt to flee a civil war, Mrs. Gandhi ordered the Indian army into East Pakistan to put a decisive end to Pakistani control of the area. The Pakistani army quickly surrendered, and with India's blessing, East Pakistan became an independent country, Bangladesh.

On the heels of this triumph, Mrs. Gandhi and her Congress allies won a smashing victory at the polls. In 1975, however, a court invalidated the 1971 elections on the grounds that civil servants had openly aided Mrs. Gandhi's reelection campaign in violation of the constitution. Besieged with demands for her resignation, the prime minister instead declared a state of emergency and suspended normal democratic procedures. She had her chief political opponents arrested and imposed strict censorship on the press. Two years of repressive emergency rule followed. India's fragile democracy appeared finished.

In 1977 Mrs. Gandhi lifted the state of emergency and allowed parliamentary elections. Her Congress Party was soundly defeated, garnering only 34 percent of the vote and a mere 28 percent of parliamentary seats. But the new government of M. R. Desai's Janata Dal Party did not last long. With an emotional appeal to India's masses, Mrs. Gandhi led Congress to a decisive comeback. In 1980, her party won two-thirds of the seats in the lower house.

Religious tensions reached new heights in 1984 when Sikh militants demanding greater autonomy for the state of Punjab ensconced themselves in the Golden Temple, a sacred Sikh shrine, and began using it as a base for terrorist operations. Mrs. Gandhi dispatched the Indian army to dislodge the terrorists; more than a thousand Sikhs lost their lives in the raid. The tragedy created an outpouring of resentment among India's 14 million Sikhs. Several months later, Prime Minister Gandhi was assassinated by two Sikh bodyguards. An organized massacre of Sikhs in New Delhi ensued.

The Congress Party then named Indira's son, Rajiv, as prime minister. Rajiv led the party to an impressive electoral victory later in the year. From the outset, however, his government was plagued by mounting sectarian violence in Punjab. Rajiv also failed to heel festering divisions within the Congress Party, which became increasingly factionalized. His efforts to reduce the heavy hand of the government in India's economy also fizzled. By 1985, central government expenditures amounted to more than 35 percent of GNP, up from about 19 percent in 1960. Elections in 1989 swept the Congress Party from power in the aftermath of a kickback scandal, but the next two prime ministers could not establish a stable base of power in the fractionalized parliament. Fresh elections were ordered in 1991, and during a campaign appearance, Rajiv was assassinated by Tamils linked to Sri Lankan guerilla movements. Tamil resentments at the Indian government stemmed from India's unsuccessful military intervention in Sri Lanka several years earlier as well as from ethnic animosities in the southern Indian province of Tamil Nadhu, where the Tamil population was a source of resistance to central government authorities.

The next prime minister, P. V. N. Rao, formed a new Congress-led government following the elections. One of Rao's principal ambitions was to reduce the state's role in the economy by promoting an extensive privatization program. Despite some progress toward this goal, the state's share of the economy remained large. Meanwhile, India's smoldering religious tensions erupted once again as more than 150,000 Hindu fundamentalists demolished a sixteenth-century mosque cherished by Muslims, claiming that it occupied a holy Hindu site. The incident, occurring in the town of Ayodhya, was inspired by the rightist India People's Party (*Bharatiya Janata Party,* or BJP), a stridently pro-Hindu organization. Some seventeen hundred people were killed as sporadic confrontations between Hindus and Muslims flared up over the next two weeks. Anti-Muslim violence in Bombay and elsewhere in early 1993 produced an additional thousand casualties. Corruption scandals aggravated Rao's difficulties, along with persistent unemployment and inflation. In the 1996 parliamentary elections the Congress Party suffered a major defeat, with the BJP winning a plurality of seats in the Lok Sabha but not enough to form a government on its own.

The remaining years of the decade witnessed a succession of weak minority governments. In the 1996 elections, Congress's share of seats fell from 47.5 percent to 25.7 percent, rising only to 30.1 percent in the snap elections of 1998. The BJP and its allies raised their share from 21.5 percent in 1991 to 35.4 percent in 1996 and 46.2 percent in 1998. Following the 1998 elections, a BJP-led minority government was formed under Atal Bihari Vajpayee (VAJ-pie), a moderate in a party noted for its fanatical pro-Hindu attitudes. Vajpayee backed away from the BJP's earlier pledges to build a Hindu temple on the site of the old Ayodhya mosque, but sought to awaken national pride through a series of nuclear weapons tests several months after taking office. The underground explosions provoked Pakistan into conducting its own nuclear tests and prompted considerable international concern at the prospect of a nuclear confrontation between the two arch-rivals. Conflicts over Kashmir, most of which is in India, intensified these tensions, and fighting broke out in the summer of 1999 as Pakistani troops invaded the area. Despite India's internal political turmoil, its army evicted the intruders.

In 1999 Vajpayee's multiparty minority government fell apart and lost a vote of confidence. Since no new governing coalition could be stitched together, Indian voters were called to the polls for the third time in as many years. As its new leader the Congress Party chose Sonia Gandhi, Rajiv's widow and an Italian by birth. The choice was roundly criticized by numerous opponents of the Congress Party, and even some Congress members questioned the appropriateness of selecting a non-Indian female as the country's potential next prime minister. "Every drop of my blood says this is my country," Gandhi replied. The elections were spread out over four weeks and provoked sporadic outbursts of violence; more than three hundred people were killed in campaign-related incidents. Only half the eligible electorate voted, an unusually low turnout. When the vote counting was over, Vajpayee and his coalition partners had managed to win a plurality of seats in India's Lok Sabha; but with only a third of the total, they fell far short of a majority. Both the BJP-led coalition and the Congress party lost seats, while several regional parties, reflecting the enormous importance

TABLE 15.5

India's Lok Sabha, 1999 (543 seats)

Parties	Seats (1998)	% of Seats
BJP and two other parties	182 (194)	33.5
Indian National Congress	112 (141)	20.6
Communist Party of India (Marxist)	32 (32)	5.9
Six regional parties	112 (78)	20.6
Others	105 (98)	19.3

of local issues in Indian politics, increased their share of votes in parliament.

The final result was an even more fractionated lower house than before the elections. Vajpayee, reelected prime minister, formed a government consisting of the BJP and twenty-three smaller parties. With the BJP leadership so dependent on so many partners, the outlook for prolonged political stability did not appear to be bright. Nationalist pressures on the government remained high, though Vajpayee voiced hopes for a modus vivendi over Kashmir and other conflicts with Pakistan, whose government was taken over by military leaders in the fall of 1999.

For her part, Sonia Gandhi, who ran for the Lok Sabha in three districts (a practice that is allowed in India), won reelection and vowed to work for women's rights. Her daughter, Priyanka, is viewed by many observers as the Congress Party's next leader.

India and the Ten Conditions for Democracy

How does our list of ten conditions for democracy help us understand India's improbable success as a democracy, or its potential for a future breakdown of democratic governance?

1. State Institutions On the face of it, India appears to be saddled with insurmountable weaknesses in its institutional structures. Fissiparous tendencies rooted in the country's ethnolinguistic and religious heterogeneity are institutionalized in its federal system and exacerbated by separatist movements, creating an enormous "stateness" problem. Disputes with Pakistan over the Kashmir border complicate matters. Extensive official corruption eats away at public support for state officials and politicians, as do persistent inefficiency and ineffectiveness at all levels of government. Hundreds of state-level legislators and some forty members of the Indian parliament turned out to have criminal records in the 1990s, as did more than a thousand candidates for office who had been convicted of murder, rape, extortion, and other crimes. Political gang warfare wreaks havoc on the electoral process; killings and kidnapings are common in some areas. Police and military personnel routinely abuse their authority, engaging in torture, rape, "disappearances," and murder against insurgents, Sikhs, members of the lower castes, and other victims. Illegal detentions, the wanton destruction of property, and other abuses have been documented. The judicial arm of the state, while independent, is burdened by a backlog of 30 million cases.

And yet, the central government has thus far managed to hold India's explosive parts together without an all-out civil war or the outright secession of any of its states. Most important, the electoral process retains an enduring legitimacy in the eyes of most Indians. Though turnout is declining at the national level, it still exceeds turnout rates in U.S. congressional elections; political life is lively at the state and local levels. While Indians may evince disillusionment with the political leaders their democracy serves up and while the recourse to political violence occurs with alarming frequency, elite and mass support for democracy in principle is widespread. The traditions of parliamentary government adapted from Britain remain intact, and though political contestation is often fierce, no political parties or insurrectionary movements appear poised to impose an authoritarian alternative on the entire country.

2. Elites Committed to Democracy The creators of modern India—Gandhi, Nehru, and their immediate successors—were uniformly committed to democracy, as were most of the elites at the head of the country's major ethnolinguistic and religious groups. Arend Lijphart, who pioneered the concept of *consociational democracy* with respect to countries torn by social strife (see chapter 8), has argued that

the consociational model, which stresses the importance of power sharing among the elites representing the main conflicting social groups, explains why democracy has endured in India in spite of its teeming social diversity. Lijphart argues that even when India was governed under the Congress Party's large parliamentary majorities, key elements of the consociational model were present. Power sharing among the core elites and cultural autonomy for diverse linguistic groups were fully in evidence, at least until the late 1960s.

Subsequently, a breakdown in power-sharing arrangements occurred as Congress lost its grip on the political system. Not surprisingly, Lijphart observed, violent political contestation heated up. Even so, Indian elites were careful to retain a sufficient level of power sharing among the country's diverse groups to keep democracy from falling apart entirely. (Indira Gandhi's two-year period of emergency rule in the 1970s was the exception.) In Lijphart's view, it is these consociational power-sharing efforts, despite their varying degrees of intensity, that best account for the success of Indian democracy.[23]

The fragmentation of India's party system has accelerated since Lijphart published his analysis; the Congress Party continues to lose support and its main rival, the BJP, is unable to fashion a working majority of its own. It would appear that consociational power sharing has diminished in recent years. Nevertheless, the elites who dominate India's political parties and social groups do not appear willing to replace it with a non-democratic system. Though it may be increasingly difficult to achieve in practice, some form of consociational democracy, centered on inter-elite accommodation, still seems to be the political model most Indian leaders favor in principle. As long as a commitment to this principle endures, democracy itself may endure, strife-torn and turbulent though it may be.

3. National Wealth As we observed in chapter 4, India stands out as one of the chief exceptions to the rule correlating national poverty with non-democratic regimes. With a per capita GNP of a mere $430 in 1998, India is one of the poorest countries in the world by this measure. In the mid-1990s, 87.5 percent of the country's vast population was living on less than $2 a day, and 47 percent were subsisting on less than $1 a day. Women and children are especially damaged by the ravages of poverty. Government programs designed to reduce the causes and effects of chronic underdevelopment have had little impact. At the same time, India's gross national product of $421.3 billion was the eleventh highest in the world in 1998. Its GDP grew at an average rate of 5.8 percent in the 1980s and 6.1 percent from 1990 to 1998, impressive results by any standard. Thus India's economic status is an ambivalent one: its economy produces considerable aggregate wealth, but not enough to raise the boats of its immense population. On balance, however, it would appear that India's massive and chronic levels of poverty would be highly inconsistent with the long-term survival of democracy. Other factors therefore have to account for India's success, and they will also have to assume responsibility for preserving Indian democracy in the future.

4. Private Enterprise   Efforts to promote private enterprise intensified in the 1990s, especially under Rao's government. These trends ran counter to the high levels of government intervention that had characterized India's mixed economy since Nehru's days. Private sector development has been quite vibrant; a number of government-owned firms have been privatized, and the sums invested in India's stock market nearly tripled in the 1990s. At the same time, the state retains a strong economic presence: central government spending actually rose as a percentage of GDP between 1980 (10.8 percent) and 1997 (14.7 percent). The national government ran a succession of deficits, amounting to 4.9 percent of GDP in 1997. Taxes are high, with the top rate of 40 percent affecting all incomes over $5,059 a year. Barriers to private-sector development remain. Be that as it may, neither the persistence of state interventionism nor the growth of private sector development appears to have affected Indian democracy in any negative way, while proponents of both approaches tend to favor democratic methods for obtaining their goals.

5. A Middle Class   India's middle class is estimated at 25 percent to 30 percent of the popula-

tion. In a country with a billion people, that's a sizable segment of society. In conformity with our hypotheses, the Indian middle class has provided a large and consistent bloc of support for democracy. To be sure, many middle-class Indians are gripped by the same ethnolinguistic and religious fervor that characterizes large elements of the rest of the population. On the whole, however, the overwhelming majority of them appear to favor democracy over any authoritarian modes of government, even though they may object to the way democracy works in everyday practice.

6. Support of the Disadvantaged for Democracy   If endemic poverty is to constitute a serious threat to democracy, the masses must be mobilized against it as an unacceptable form of government. Thus far, however, no political movement has managed to whip up an organized protest of the poor against democracy. Here again, the ambiguities of the Indian case are apparent. While there may be widespread discontent on the part of India's masses at the way their problems have been dealt with by the elected elites, there has been no substantial backlash on their part against electoral democracy itself. On the contrary, political activism is increasingly energized in many of the all-important states in India's federal system. Women, the victims of the "feminization of poverty" in India, have entered voting booths and run for office at growing rates, in some states pulling even with men.[24]

In most cases, however, it is apathy and resignation rather than revolutionary unrest that mark the political attitudes of India's destitute masses. In a culture suffused with Hinduism, the eternal mysteries of karma and divine intervention assume a far greater immediacy in the lives of the multitudes than the mundane practicalities of politics. On a less ethereal plane, the simple struggle to survive from one day to the next leaves little time to care about elections and party programs. While *support* for democracy may not be the consequence, there is little in the way of mass *opposition* to it, either. Deference to existing political authority is far-reaching. Between India's rising cadres of political activists and its long-suffering, acquiescent millions, there arises little in the way of an organized threat to electoral democracy from the poverty-stricken masses.

7. Civil Society and a Democratic Political Culture   In a country as large and variegated as India's, torn as it is by so many unresolved conflicts, it should not be surprising to find starkly contrasting cultural realities. A thriving civil society shares the social landscape with a notoriously uncivil, violent-prone society. Boisterous political activism coexists with deference and resignation. Attitudes and behaviors conducive to democracy must contend with a variety of ethnic, religious, social, and political subcultures that brazenly flaunt the values of tolerance, compromise, trust, and other moral underpinnings of a democratic political culture. Many people involved in the process of electoral democracy, while subscribing to democratic values in principle, simply use the procedures of democracy to extract gains for their own camp while resolutely seeking to undermine their opponents' chances of achieving a just measure of benefits for themselves. While millions of Indians, and many members of the political elite, are dedicated to national harmony and the extension of democratic rights to all, many others view the game of democracy in strictly zero-sum terms (my gain is your loss).

To some extent, the cause of civil society in India has made some noteworthy advances in recent years. Women's rights groups are proliferating, a major development in a country where the abuse of women is rampant. (Suicides and killings over dowries are common phenomena; rape and partner abuse go widely unprosecuted; child prostitution and the mistreatment of prostitutes are flagrant; and the legal rights of women are generally undeveloped.) Human rights organizations have also become more active, focusing on such issues as the exploitation of children in the work force and the abuses committed by government authorities. Trade unions are organized and energetic. These signs of a vigorous civil society constitute a powerful bulwark against any potential effort by authoritarians to extinguish deeply cherished democratic rights and freedoms and deprive the Indian people of their rights of political participation. But they must contend with contrary forces that reject the ground rules of social cooperation and constantly tear at its fabric.

8. Education and Freedom of Information   Here, too, India's record is a ganglion of contradictions.

The country can boast of large numbers of college graduates and recipients of graduate and professional degrees. Many college grads remain unemployed for years, however. Illiteracy is a mass phenomenon, affecting one-third of males over age fifteen and more than 60 percent of females.

India's press freedoms are secure: national and local newspapers and magazines thrive. There is no censorship. Journalists have been physically attacked for their political views, however. The Indian government holds a monopoly on domestic television broadcasting, but foreign-based networks have been allowed to broadcast in recent years.

9. A Homogeneous Society   Obviously, India is the very opposite of a homogeneous society. As the previous pages have indicated, it is the dissatisfactions of the country's various ethnolonguistic and religious groups that have placed Indian democracy on a rocky foundation from its very inception. And it is the violent tendencies of the most fanatical members of these various groups that have posed the gravest threat to Indian democracy, a threat that has become more menacing over the past ten years. If India is to survive as a democratic state, it will be in spite of its rich and volatile social diversity.

10. A Favorable International Environment   India's external environment is also a source of both negative and positive influences on its democratic order. Its tormented relationship with Pakistan inevitably has an impact on the delicate ties between Hindus and Muslims in India itself. The ardent nationalism voiced by many BJP followers and other Hindu nationalists takes aim above all at neighboring Pakistan, but it has a domestic focus as well, viewing Muslims with suspicion and scorning the Congress Party and others for allegedly failing to provide adequate support for Hindus against their rivals. India's status as a nuclear power, while a source of pride for most Indians, has prompted warnings by opponents of nuclear saber-rattling that the country should not pursue a potentially dangerous militarism. (India is not a signatory of the Nuclear Non-Proliferation Treaty.) India also has a long-standing border conflict with China. Otherwise, its external rela-

Conclusions

Writing in 1970, a prominent Indian political scientist suggested that India's chief problem was not that political institutionalization was lagging behind economic modernization, as postulated in Huntington's hypothesis about the roots of political decay. Rather, the danger was the reverse: the country's sophisticated political institutions—such as its parliamentary mode of government and the Congress Party—might fail to provide sufficient economic and social modernization.[25] The events of the ensuing decades have indeed confirmed these fears of lingering economic backwardness and intense social conflict. But political institutions have also decayed.

Writing in 1990, another Indian political scientist warned that the failure of India's political organizations to deal with persistent poverty and deep-seated social frictions was creating a veritable "crisis of governability." The Congress Party had disintegrated into a collection of cliques concerned solely with winning elections; political elites were more concerned with their own political power than with strengthening governmental institutions; and various social groups were increasingly mobilized for the purpose of winning control over local and national governmental bodies, with the express aim of wringing special benefits from them. While socioeconomic problems were more intense than ever, political factors thus appeared to be just as significant, if not more so, in explaining India's mounting political violence, regional separatism, and governmental ineffectiveness.[26]

Will India's democracy survive? The question has sparked a decades-long debate between optimists and pessimists.[27] Both must come to grips with the extraordinary complexities of a country that combines high-tech modernity with timeless traditionalism. In the 1960s India developed the capability to produce nuclear weapons. In 1980 it launched the first in a series of space satellites. In 1994, an outbreak of pneumonic plague occurred in the rat-infested city of Surat. Prior to the epidemic, the city government had no program for eliminating the rodents because they are worshiped by Hindus as the companions of Ganesh, an elephant-headed god.[28]

KEY TERMS AND NAMES
(Underlined in the text)

Developing countries
NICs
Kim Dae Jung
Underdevelopment
Modernization theory
Decolonization
Dependency theory
Mohandos Gandhi

NOTES

1. On South Korea, see Sung-Joo Han, "South Korea: Politics in Transition," in *Politics in Developing Countries*, ed. Larry Diamond, Juan J. Linz, and Seymour Martin Lipset (Boulder, Colo.: Lynne Rienner, 1990), 313–50; Stephan Haggard, *Pathways from the Periphery* (Ithaca, N.Y.: Cornell University Press, 1990), 51–75, 130–38; Nigel Harris, *The End of the Third World* (London: Penguin, 1986), 31–45; Robert Garran, *Tigers Tamed* (Honolulu: University of Hawaii Press, 1998), 119–36; Dennis L. McNamara, ed., *Corporatism and Korean Capitalism* (London: Routledge, 1999).

2. *Washington Post*, January 9, 1998. On Kim Dae Jung and the 1980 protests, see *The Kwangju Uprising*, Henry Scott-Stokes and Jai Eui, eds. (Armonk, N.Y.: M. E. Sharpe, 2000).

3. *Tigers Tamed*, p. 123.

4. Cited in Haggard, *Pathways from the Periphery*, 106; Harris, *End of the Third World*, 61; *The Economist*, August 27, 1994, and January 11, 1997. Goh praised voters for having "rejected Western-style liberal democracy and freedoms" after his party was re-elected in 1997 (*Washington Post*, January 3, 1997).

5. Alasdair Bowie, *Crossing the Industrial Divide: State, Society, and the Politics of Economic Transformation in Malaysia* (New York, N.Y.: Columbia University Press, 1991).

6. World Bank, *World Development Report 1999/2000* (New York: Oxford University Press, 1999).

7. For an overview, see ibid., and Robert J. Grifiths, ed., *Annual Editions: Developing World 98–99*, 8th ed.

(Guilford, Conn.: Dushkin/McGraw-Hill, 1998). See also the annual *Human Development Report* published by the United Nations Development Program, available at <www.undp.org>.

8. In *The Stages of Economic Growth,* first published in 1960, Rostow looked at the economic evolution of the United States and the leading West European countries and divided their development into five known stages: (1) *traditional society,* which in Europe existed prior to the seventeenth century; (2) a *transitional* phase during which the preconditions for takeoff were established; (3) the *takeoff* stage, in which sustained levels of economic growth became the normal condition (a period reached in Britain at the end of the eighteenth century and in the United States around the 1840s); (4) the *drive to maturity,* a long period of economic and technological expansion, and (5) the age of *mass consumption,* initiated in the United States around World War I and developed to its logical conclusion there and in Western Europe in the 1950s. At this point, a sixth stage— *beyond consumption*—begins. (Contemporary analysts would identify this sixth stage with postindustrial society.) Most Third World countries today are still stuck in the transitional stage. In 1990, Rostow identified ten countries that had embarked on the "drive to maturity" by taking advantage of the latest advancements in technology. See W. W. Rostow, *The Stages of Economic Growth,* 3d ed. (Cambridge: Cambridge University Press, 1990).

9. Daniel Lerner, *The Passing of Traditional Society* (New York: Free Press, 1958); David E. Apter, *The Politics of Modernization* (Chicago: University of Chicago Press, 1965); Cyril E. Black, ed., *Comparative Modernization: A Reader* (New York: Free Press, 1976).

10. For a critical appraisal, see Irene L. Gendzier, *Managing Political Change: Social Scientists and the Third World* (Boulder, Colo.: Westview, 1985). An early study that recognized a mixture of the traditional and the modern in developing countries is Gabriel A. Almond and James S. Coleman, eds., *The Politics of the Developing Areas* (Princeton, N.J.: Princeton University Press, 1960). Ronald Inglehart supports modernization theory in *Modernization and Postmodernization* (Princeton, N.J.: Princeton University Press, 1997), 7 ff. (his views are summarized in chapter 12).

11. Joseph L. Love, "Raul Prebisch and the Origins of the Doctrine of Unequal Exchange," *Latin American Research Review* 15, no. 3 (1980); Mahbub ul Haq, *The Poverty Curtain: Choices for the Third World* (New York: Columbia University Press, 1976).

12. For examples of dependency theory see Andre Gunder Frank, *Capitalism and Underdevelopment in Latin America* (London: Penguin, 1970) and *Critique and Anti-Critique* (New York: Praeger, 1971). On the capitalist world-system, see Immanuel Wallerstein, *The Capitalist World-Economy* (Cambridge: Cambridge University Press, 1979) and *The Politics of the World-Economy* (New York: Cambridge University Press, 1984). For review essays, see James A. Caporoso, "Dependency Theory: Continuities and Discontinuities in Development Studies," *International Organization* 34, no. 4 (autumn 1980): 605–28, and Tony Smith, "Requiem or New Agenda for Third World Studies?" *World Politics* 37, no. 4 (July 1985): 532–61.

13. For examples of neo-liberal views on the Third World, see "A Survey of the Third World," *The Economist,* September 23, 1989.

14. Lloyd G. Reynolds, *Economic Growth in the Third World* (New Haven, Conn.: Yale University Press, 1985).

15. Samuel P. Huntington, *Political Order in Changing Societies* (New Haven, Conn.: Yale University Press, 1968).

16. Samuel P. Huntington and Joan M. Nelson, *No Easy Choice: Political Participation in Developing Countries* (Cambridge, Mass.: Harvard University Press, 1976).

17. Mancur Olson, "Dictatorship, Democracy, and Development," *American Political Science Review* 87, no. 3 (September 1993): 567–76. Elsewhere, Olson argues that narrowly based political or social groups can impede economic development. India's caste system is one example relevant to the Third World. See *The Rise and Decline of Nations* (New Haven, Conn.: Yale University Press, 1982).

18. Of thirty-three developing countries in the Americas, twenty-three were "democratic" in early 1999 and nine were "partly democratic." Only one—Castro's Cuba—was still "authoritarian." Of thirty-seven developing countries in Asia, eighteen were "democratic," nine "partly democratic" and ten "authoritarian." Of fifty-three African countries, nine were "democratic," twenty-one "partly democratic" and twenty-three "authoritarian" (43 percent of the total). The twelve countries belonging to the Commonwealth of Independent States, which includes all but three republics of the former Soviet Union, contained seven "partly democratic" states and five "authoritarian" ones. Out of thirteen developing countries in the Middle East (exclusive of North Africa), three were "partly democratic" and ten "authoritarian." See *Freedom in the World 1998–1999* (New York: Freedom House, 1999), 10–11. In this book we substitute "democratic" for the Freedom House designation "free," "partly democratic" for "partly free," and "authoritarian" for "not free."

19. Larry Diamond, Juan J. Linz, and Seymour Martin Lipset, eds., *Democracy in Developing Countries,* (Boul-

der, Colo.: Lynne Rienner, 1988), and *Politics in Developing Countries,* 2d ed. (Boulder, Colo.: Lynne Rienner, 1995). See also Larry Diamond, *Developing Democracy* (Baltimore, Md.: Johns Hopkins, 1999), and Stephan Haggard and Robert R. Kaufman, eds. *The Political Economy of Democratic Transitions* (Princeton: Princeton University Press, 1995).

20. On Gandhi and the origins of independent India and Pakistan, see Larry Collins and Dominique Lapierre, *Freedom at Midnight* (New York: Simon and Schuster, 1975). For a biography of Gandhi by a prominent psychologist, see Erik H. Erikson, *Gandhi's Truth* (New York: W. W. Norton, 1969). See also Richard Attenborough's epic film *Gandhi.*

21. Myron Weiner, *Party Building in a New Nation: The Indian National Congress* (Chicago: Chicago University Press, 1967).

22. Samuel J. Eldersveld and Bashiruddin Ahmed, *Citizens and Politics: Mass Political Behavior in India* (Chicago: University of Chicago Press, 1978).

23. Arend Lijphart, "The Puzzle of Indian Democracy: A Consociational Interpretation," *American Political Science Review* 90, no. 2 (June 1996): 258–68.

24. *The Sun,* Baltimore, September 30, 1999.

25. Rajni Kothari, *Politics in India* (Boston: Little, Brown, 1970), 433.

26. Atul Kohli, *Democracy and Discontent: India's Growing Crisis of Governability* (Cambridge: Cambridge University Press, 1990). See also Satish Saterwal, *Roots of Crisis: Interpreting Contemporary Indian Society* (Thousand Oaks, Calif.: Sage, 1996).

27. For a more optimistic analysis that does not minimize India's problems, see Jyotirindra Das Gupta, "India: Democratic Becoming and Combined Development," in Diamond, Linz, and Lipset, *Politics in Developing Countries,* 218–69.

28. *Washington Post,* September 27, 1994.

PART TWO

COUNTRIES
AND LEADERS

CHAPTER 16

THE UNITED KINGDOM OF GREAT BRITAIN AND NORTHERN IRELAND

Population (1999): 58.3 million

Area: 94,251 square miles
(smaller than Oregon)

Source: U.S. Central Intelligence Agency.

TONY BLAIR TAKES OFFICE

The elections to the House of Commons of May 1, 1997, ushered in a new era in British politics. After eighteen years of Conservative Party rule, the Labour Party won a resounding victory under the leadership of Tony Blair. Blair, an energetic forty-three, did not have long to wait before assuming office. The very next morning, Prime Minister John Major promptly moved out of his official quarters at Number 10 Downing Street and submitted his resignation to Queen Elizabeth II at Buckingham Palace in a ceremony known as the "kissing of hands." Less than an hour later, Blair held his own private audience with the queen, who formally invited him to serve as her new prime minister. These encounters were largely ritualistic. Although the monarch formally retains the legal authority to name the head of "Her Majesty's Government," in practice the rules of modern British democracy require her to desig-nate the individual chosen by the political party that controls the House of Commons.

As millions of television viewers looked on, Blair and his wife got out of the limousine escorting them from the royal palace to walk the final half-block to their family's new residence on Downing Street. Addressing a crowd of well-wishers, Blair reiterated the central theme of his campaign when he referred to the Labour Party as the "New Labour" party. "We ran as New Labour and will govern as New Labour," he proclaimed, an assertion that echoed his repeated pledges over the previous months that the Labour Party had changed significantly under his direction from the party it had been in the past.

Founded at the start of the twentieth century, the Labour Party once stood primarily for the British working class and the most economically disadvantaged segments of the population. Its leaders tended to espouse full employment, welfare benefits, and other measures that often required high taxes and various regulations on private enterprise. They also advocated the takeover of large private corporations by the state, a process known as the *nationalization* of private enterprise. These attitudes and policy choices reflected Britain's history as a country with deeply rooted class distinctions, where millions of people identified themselves as "working class" and saw little chance of rising into the prosperous echelons of the middle class, and virtually no chance of entering the privileged world of the super-rich upper class. Many of them looked to the Labour Party as the chief defender of low-income families and industrial trade unions against the uncertainties of the economic marketplace.

Under Blair's stewardship, Labour began distancing itself from these leftist tendencies, edging closer to the center of the British political spectrum. Following his selection as party leader in July 1994, Blair convinced key elements in the party to abandon Labour's high-tax inclinations and to assume an outspokenly pro-business orientation. To this end the party formally renounced its historic commitment to the principle of nationalizing the country's main industries. Blair also abandoned the rhetoric of class conflict, speaking instead of "one nation and one society." In the process, Blair and his supporters managed to dilute the influence of Britain's trade unions, traditionally the backbone of the party, on

Tony Blair greets supporters.

Labour's internal decision-making procedures. Instead of appealing mainly to Britain's manual workers and low-salaried white-collar employees, Blair wanted New Labour to reach out more effectively to Britain's populous middle class. Only by attracting more middle class votes, he believed, could the party gain a majority of seats in the House of Commons and reclaim control of the government, which it had failed to do in the punishing elections of 1979, 1983, 1987, and 1992. The Conservative Party had won all these previous contests, the first three under the leadership of Margaret Thatcher and the last under her successor, Mr. Major.

For Americans observing British politics in the 1990s, these developments had a curiously familiar ring. Tony Blair's efforts to move Labour from the left of the spectrum to the center were strikingly reminiscent of Bill Clinton's attempts to lead the Democrats in a roughly similar direction starting with the 1992 presidential campaign. Blair's invocations of "New Labour" consciously echoed Clinton's description of himself as a "New Democrat." While both men believed that government should provide assistance to those unable to take care of their own basic needs, such as food and health care, they favored more vigorous efforts to shift people off welfare dependency and into steady jobs, preferably in the private sector. And while both sought to preserve their parties' historic links with organized labor and the underprivileged, they also made determined efforts to court the middle class, renouncing "tax-and-spend" policies. These and other resemblances were more than coincidental. Blair deliberately patterned himself on Clinton, cultivating close personal ties between Labour Party leaders and Clinton associates and borrowing heavily from the Clinton camp's election campaign experiences.[1]

In a wider sense, Blair and Clinton were both looking for what they called a **"third way,"** that is, a combination of effective social welfare policies for people in need of government assistance and a vigorous commitment to private sector growth, low inflation, balanced budgets, and moderate levels of taxation. They and other advocates of the third way saw this approach as different from the priorities of conservatives like Ronald Reagan and Margaret Thatcher, who favored more drastic cuts in welfare spending and a greater reliance on market forces, and different

as well from the views of more left-wing Democrats and Labourites who favored considerably more welfare spending even if it meant higher taxes and sizable budget deficits.[2] These domestic policy similarities carried over into the foreign policy domain, as Blair and Clinton coordinated their strategies in the Yugoslavia crisis and maintained close U.S.-British cooperation in a variety of international issues.

At the same time, Blair and his New Labour allies entered office facing a number of specifically British problems, such as the following:

- *Constitutional reform.* The British constitution is not a single written document but a vast collection of laws and practices that have accumulated over centuries. In addition to calling for a written constitution, proponents of reform have called for the adoption of a U.S.-style bill of rights, a new parliamentary electoral system, and an end to voting privileges for hereditary members of the House of Lords, among other changes.

- *Devolution.* Although it is commonplace to speak of "Britain" when referring to the country we are examining in this chapter, a practice we shall follow, its proper name is **the United Kingdom of Great Britain and Northern Ireland** (the **UK**). Great Britain consists of England, Scotland, and Wales. Northern Ireland is juridically separate from the Republic of Ireland, which is an independent country. The four regions of the UK all elect members to the House of Commons and are under the queen as head of state. For much of its history, the UK has been a *unitary state,* with political decision making centered in national institutions located mostly in London. **Devolution** means the transfer of more decision-making power to local institutions in Scotland, Wales, and Northern Ireland, a change Blair favored. Indeed, the new prime minister assumed power facing mounting pressures for a settlement of the intractable conflict between Catholics and Protestants in Northern Ireland.

- *The European Union.* In the Treaty of Maastricht of 1992, the EU pledged itself to building an economic and monetary union based on a common currency, the euro. Britain's ambivalent attitudes toward expanded cooperation with its EU partners had sharply divided the Conservative Party and posed immediate challenges for Tony Blair.

These and other issues in contemporary British politics have a long history, in some cases stretching back centuries. Together they have sparked every type of conflict we identified in our definition of politics in chapter 2, including conflicts over

- *Power:* Who has governed Britain? How have contending social groups, parties, and interest groups influenced the state and its policies?
- *Resources:* How has the country's wealth been owned and distributed? What roles have the state and markets played in the British economy?
- *Social identity:* How have class, regional, and religious conflicts affected British politics?
- *Ideas:* How did British democracy develop? What does "socialism" mean in Britain?
- *Values:* Should Britain attach a higher priority to individual freedom or to community welfare? How tolerant are the British?

These issues also raise questions of a comparative nature. Why, for example, did Britain develop a stable democracy much earlier in its history than most other countries? How do its political institutions differ from those of the United States? How have the UK's leaders coped with economic problems similar to those that challenge numerous governments around the world, such as competing domestic pressures for welfare benefits and lower taxes, for reducing unemployment as well as preventing inflation, for meeting public sector obligations while encouraging private sector initiative? Do the pressures of regionalism in Scotland, Wales, and Northern Ireland threaten to break the United Kingdom apart, in the same way that regional separatism threatens the unity of countries like Canada?

Questions like these cannot be answered without a close look at Britain's past. Let's begin with its long road from monarchy to democracy.

HISTORICAL BACKGROUND: THE EVOLUTION OF BRITISH DEMOCRACY

In some countries, democracy came about as the result of a fairly sudden turn of events. Examples include the American revolution, the periodic swings from military rule to democratic governance that have taken place in various Latin American nations, and more recently, the outbursts of democracy in Russia and East-Central Europe that accompanied the collapse of communism. In contrast to these and other revolutionary transformations, democracy developed in Britain in a slow, piecemeal fashion that took centuries to unfold. Evolution, not revolution, has characterized the British democratic experience.

Following the collapse of the Roman Empire in the fifth century, England was governed by a succession of monarchs until the middle of the seventeenth century. While most of them ruled with military force and other forms of coercive power, from the middle ages onward there was a growing tendency to justify the crown's legitimacy according to the **divine right of kings,** the doctrine asserting that the monarch derived his or her power from God and not from the people. The concept of divine right provided the legal basis for **sovereign monarchy,** or **absolutism,** which meant that the monarch was the supreme political authority in the land and enjoyed the right to absolute power. Rarely, however, did the crown sit easily on the English monarch's head. Claims to sovereign authority by no means always resulted in unassailable rule or smooth transitions from one monarch to the next on the basis of inherited succession. Challenges to individual claimants to the throne, as well as to royal authority itself, were frequent and sometimes violent. Over the span of centuries, rivalries over the coveted English crown fueled dynastic wars with France and Spain as well as civil wars, palace intrigues, and strategic marriages involving both native and foreign-born noble families.

The first real break with the principle of monarchy occurred in the 1640s, when civil war led to the defeat of the royal army, followed by the trial and decapitation of King Charles I. In 1649, England was declared a republic for the first time in its history. Oliver Cromwell, a commoner rather than a nobleman, ascended to power and ruled as "Lord Protector" under the country's first written constitution. Shortly after Cromwell died, the monarchy was restored in 1660. A monarch has served as Britain's official head of state ever since, though with diminishing real power.

Other countries have also experienced extended periods of sovereign monarchy. For hundreds of years France, Spain, Germany, Russia, China, and Japan, to mention only a few, were governed by kings, queens, or emperors who asserted their

TABLE 16.1

England's Royal Families and Selected Monarchs

House of Wessex (Anglo-Saxons), 802–1066
Alfred the Great, 871–899

Normans and Plantagenets, 1066–1327
William I (the Conqueror), 1066–1087

Houses of Lancaster and York, 1327–1485

Tudors, 1485–1603
Henry VIII, 1509–1547
Elizabeth I, 1558–1603

House of Stuart and House of Orange, 1603–1714
Charles I, 1625–1649
[Republic, 1649–1660]
Charles II, 1660–1685
James II, 1685–1688
William III (Orange), 1689–1702

Hanoverians, 1714–1837
George III, 1760–1820

House of Saxe-Coburg, 1837–1914
Victoria, 1837–1901

Windsors, 1914–
George VI, 1936–1952
Elizabeth II, 1952 to present

royal preeminence over all other institutions and political forces within their respective realms. In stark contrast to these countries, England began moving as early as the thirteenth century toward a less autocratic form of monarchical power. When viewed in comparative perspective, England's gradual evolution to democracy under the aegis of monarchy stands out as one of very few examples of such a transition. What accounts for it?

As we saw in our discussion of conditions for democracy in chapter 10, the forging of a successful democratic system usually requires a constellation of favorable factors, not just one or two. Britain began developing most of these conditions at exceptionally early stages in its history. They included:

- Parliament, a *state institution* of paramount importance that fostered *elites* opposed to royal absolutism and dedicated to the rule of law
- English nationalism, which took a form that proved especially favorable for the creation of a democratic *political culture*
- *private enterprise*, which promoted *national wealth* and the development of a democratic *middle class*

- political parties that embraced democracy rather than anti-democratic ideologies, bringing *disadvantaged* groups like the working class into the democratic fold. Trade unions and other elements of *civil society* also promoted democratic practices
- a system of *education*, centered in elite universities like Oxford and Cambridge, that fostered freedom of thought, scientific inquiry, and artistic creativity.

Meanwhile, the British have found ways to deal with a number of serious challenges that at various times have threatened to place democracy in jeopardy or severely limited its scope.

- From its very inception the United Kingdom has suffered from a *stateness* problem: it was formed by force, with England compelling Wales, Scotland, and Ireland to join it in forming a unified state. The consequences of the UK's coercive foundation and the resulting national *heterogeneity* of its population are still being addressed through the Blair government's devolution policies.
- Britain's *elites*, though committed to Parliament, took a long time to permit popular sovereignty, granting the vote to the mass citizenry only in the twentieth century.
- Glaring socioeconomic inequalities produced fairly rigid class distinctions that still leave many Britons feeling *disadvantaged* and excluded from the full range of political and social opportunities democracy is expected to provide.
- A frequently tumultuous *international environment* has included more than two centuries of imperialism, two world wars, the Cold War and the complicated post-cold war order.

The Mother of Parliaments

Parliament began in England as an extension of monarchical rule. In 1212 and 1213, King John summoned various clergymen, barons, knights and other prominent personages "to speak with us concerning the affairs of our realm." The term "parliament" derives from the French *parler*, "to speak." From the outset, however, these elites displayed a marked interest in protecting their own powers and liberties as prelates of the Catholic Church or as leaders of England's counties and villages. In 1215 they prevailed upon King John to sign **Magna Carta** (the Great Charter), a document specifying their rights in such matters as taxation, judicial appointments and private property. Magna Carta plainly implied that there were limits to the king's sovereign power and that the monarchy was not above the law. A Parliament summoned in 1265 included representatives of the common elements of society—the equivalent of the middle classes—rather than just the upper ranks of the nobility and church.

These ideas and practices took hold during the fourteenth century as a succession of monarchs called Parliament into session with growing frequency and acknowledged its responsibility in providing advice and passing legislation. In the process the institution became divided into two houses. The "lords spiritual and temporal" consisted of bishops and other members of the cloth, along with earls, dukes, and various members of the country's higher nobility. The "commons" consisted of knights and other elements of the so-called lesser nobility, together with "burgesses," who were prominent citizens from local communities. Typically the crown summoned the **House of Lords** into session by personal invitation and appointed many of its members to lifetime noble ranks (peerages), some of them with rights of inheritance. The **House of Commons** was usually elected by local property-owning elites in counties and towns. By the late 1370s it was generally accepted that no statutes could be issued without parliamentary consent. The House of Lords was developing into England's highest court, while the Commons acquired the right to approve taxes.

Over the next two centuries Parliament became a permanent fixture of England's governmental system. Even Cromwell relied on parliamentary support, and it was Parliament that restored the monarchy after his death.[3]

Despite its importance, Parliament remained constitutionally subordinate to the crown until the late seventeenth century. England's monarchs insisted that their reliance on parliamentary consent in no way compromised the principle of sovereign monarchy or the doctrine of divine right. They viewed Parliament as an instrument of monarchical rule, not as a democratic substitute for it. Most members of Parliament shared this notion until

the dramatic events of 1688–89 brought about a fundamental reordering in the balance of constitutional power in England.

James II, a Catholic, assumed the throne in 1685. England was by now a predominantly Protestant country, however. Its Protestant Reformation had begun in the 1530s when King Henry VIII broke with the Roman Catholic Church and established the Church of England (or Anglican Church), with himself as its head. (To this day the British monarch is still the official head of the Anglican Church, which is the country's *established church*.) During his first few years as king, James II managed to antagonize virtually all the leading elements of English society through his efforts to restore Catholics to the political prominence they had once enjoyed before the Reformation and through his determination to assert royal powers in the face of widespread opposition to autocratic rule. Acting with extraordinary boldness, the king's opponents invited the Dutch monarch William of Orange to invade England and take power. William was married to James II's daughter Mary, and his own family had distant ties to the English aristocracy. Just as significant, he was a Protestant who proclaimed his willingness to respect the rights of Parliament and the established liberties of English society. Upon William's arrival in England at the end of 1688, King James fled into exile. A special parliamentary assembly thereupon declared that James had abdicated the throne. It then bestowed the monarchy jointly on King William and Queen Mary. For the first time in English history, Parliament had deposed one monarch and elected another. A declaration of parliamentary rights issued in early 1689 explicitly forbade the crown from suspending the laws of the land without Parliament's approval.

These events, occurring without bloodshed, are celebrated as England's **Glorious Revolution.** They established a solid precedent for *parliamentary supremacy*, which evolved over the following centuries into the foundation stone of modern British government. **Parliamentary supremacy** *means that Parliament, not the crown, the courts, or any other institution, is the supreme authority in the British political system.*[4]

Over the course of the eighteenth and nineteenth centuries, Parliament persistently whittled away at the monarch's remaining powers. In the process, Britain's system of government became a **constitutional monarchy,** a system in which the monarch performs the largely symbolic functions of a ceremonial head of state while day-to-day decision making rests firmly in the hands of a prime minister and cabinet, backed by their supporters in Parliament. "The monarch reigns but the government rules" became the standard characterization of this system.

Today, despite the fact that Parliament and the cabinet are by far the most important decision-making institutions in the land, the monarch possesses a few traditional political prerogatives that have not been formally abolished. Specifically, the crown retains the legal authority to call parliamentary elections and name the prime minister. Every election to the House of Commons is consequently preceded by an election proclamation by the monarch, and every change of prime minister requires the "kissing of hands" and a formal designation ceremony. The fact that the queen now takes these and other actions upon the advice of the leadership of the House of Commons rather than on her own initiative indicates that Parliament has the upper hand in practice. But Parliament has not abrogated these monarchical privileges in legal theory. In the official language of British constitutional law, the basis of Britain's system of government consists of "the queen (or king) in Parliament." In other words, the monarch is part of Parliament, along with its two houses.

Parliament today not only stands politically supreme over a constitutional monarchy; it is also Britain's highest judicial authority. The United Kingdom never developed a Supreme Court like the United States, or a European-style constitutional court, empowered to declare acts of Parliament unconstitutional. Laws passed by Parliament are thus not subject to judicial review and can be amended or abolished only by Parliament itself.

Meanwhile, the balance of power between Parliament and the **government** (the cabinet plus additional ministers) has undergone its own evolution. By the nineteenth century it was evident that the Parliament's legislative powers and the cabinet's executive powers had become *fused.* Under the influence of increasingly assertive prime ministers and the rise of political parties, Britain in the nineteenth century possessed an institutional framework in which:

(1) the qualified electorate voted for the House of Commons, whereupon

(2) the Commons advised the monarch in selecting the prime minister, held the government accountable for its actions, and enacted bills into law.

The Commons also acquired the right to dismiss governments and form new ones, while the prime minister acquired the right to advise the monarch to dissolve the Commons and order new elections. Because Parliament was housed in Westminster Palace, this system of government became known as the **Westminster system.**[5] (See figure 16.1.)

The *fusion* of parliamentary and executive powers constitutes the essence of **parliamentary government,** a form of government that differs fundamentally from the American system's *separation* of Congressional and presidential powers.[6] Chapter 9 describes this system in general terms. We'll examine how it works in contemporary Britain later in this chapter.

Two additional developments occurring over the nineteenth and twentieth centuries strengthened the democratic aspects of this evolving system: the expansion of the franchise and the ascendancy of the Commons over the House of Lords.

Just as it took centuries for Parliament to become the institutional bedrock of democracy, it also took Britain a long time to confer the right to vote on all its adult citizens. Only in the twentieth century was the franchise extended to virtually all adult males and females.

- Prior to 1832, only males who met stringent property-owning requirements had the right to vote, a group constituting only 5 percent of all adults over the age of twenty-one.
- The Great Reform Act of 1832 extended the franchise to about 7 percent of the adult population, while continuing to limit it to men of property.
- Another voting reform passed in 1867 eased these qualifications somewhat, enabling a segment of Britain's urban working class males to vote for the first time. Still, only about 16 percent of the total adult population was allowed to vote.
- In 1884 the franchise was widened to include all males over age twenty-one who owned a home, a group comprising about 28 percent of people in that age group.

FIGURE 16.1   Britain's Parliamentary Government

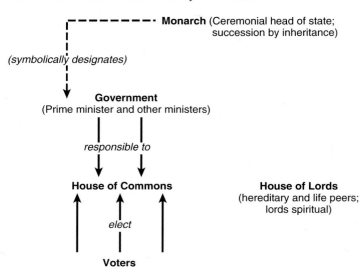

• Only in 1918, under the impact of the widely shared sacrifices of World War I, were most property qualifications eliminated for males over age twenty-one. At the same time, women obtained the right to vote for the first time, a triumph due in part to the critical role women played in the work force during the Great War. The international environment thus promoted democracy in Britain in the war years. Female suffrage also came about because of decades of militant campaigning for enfranchisement by Britain's "suffragettes." Initially, however, only women over age thirty gained the right to vote; it was not until 1928 that the female voting age was lowered to age twenty-one.

• Though virtually all adults over age twenty-one were now able to vote, university graduates and various business owners still enjoyed the right to cast *two* votes in parliamentary elections. This plural voting privilege was not abolished until 1948, when the Representation of the People Act formally established the principle of "one person, one vote" throughout the United Kingdom.

• In 1969 the voting age was lowered to age eighteen, and in 1985 about 4 million British citizens overseas were granted voting rights.

Some individuals, such as the royal family and other titled peers, still have no right to vote.[7]

The gradual extension of the suffrage was accompanied by the increasing authority of Parliament's elected body, the House of Commons, over the House of Lords. Until the early twentieth century the House of Lords retained the right to approve all bills passed by the Commons before they could become law. Because the House of Lords was an unelected body representing the aristocracy and the Anglican Church hierarchy, it constituted the last bastion of non-democratic rule in a country that was increasingly opening itself up to democratic influences and procedures. In 1911 the Lords lost their veto privilege, retaining little more than the right to delay the enactment of legislation by up to two years. In 1949 their ability to delay legislation was reduced to one year. In 1999, Tony Blair's government effected another major reform of the upper house, to be described later in this chapter.

Nationalism and Political Culture

A contributing factor in the development of British democracy was the particular brand of nationalism that accompanied Parliament's institutional evolution. As we noted in chapter 7, **nationalism** *is an idea that emphasizes the distinctiveness of one's nation (or people) and articulates certain national interests, purposes, or goals for action,* self-government being the most important. In modern nation-states, the "nation" typically consists of the population of an entire country, or at least its vast majority. Nationalism tends above all to stress the unity of the national community, rooted in a common *national identity* that seeks to bind the people together on the basis of such things as a common ethnic heritage or shared beliefs and values.

In some countries the development of nationalism had pronouncedly anti-democratic accents. Japan, Russia, and Germany stand out as prominent examples. The development of nationhood in these countries, extending from medieval times until well into the twentieth century, was orchestrated largely by aristocratic elites who had no intention of sharing power with elected parliaments. The military establishment, rather than legislative bodies, was their favored institutional partner. In England, by contrast, nationalism from its inception was understood by the country's politically active elites and broad segments of the population in terms that promoted democratic ideals.

In an insightful comparative analysis of the origins of nationalism, Liah Greenfeld points out that England was the first country to develop a modern national consciousness.[8] This national self-conception emerged in the sixteenth century, spurred on by both religious and political developments. One of its chief catalysts was the Protestant Reformation. By 1600, the majority of English people were Protestant, adhering to a church that explicitly defined itself as "Anglican." Protestantism, in short, was a defining element of the English nation, shaping not just the country's most prominent religious orientation but its basic national identity. Not surprisingly, as the Reformation unfolded, English hostility to largely Catholic countries like Spain and France intensified, provoking nationalistic animosities to foreigners throughout Catholic Europe.

As Greenfeld notes, however, nationalism in England involved far more than just religious affiliation or distrust of foreigners. Right from its origins, it was infused with a specific political content. Nationalism arose at a time when Parliament was already well established as a vital component of English government, with widespread support among nobles and commoners, among Catholics as well as Protestants. The English concept of national identity included the notion that the English people were free and equal individuals under the law, with the right to participate in politics and government. The political values of individual freedom, equal dignity, and self-government—values that are at the heart of modern democracy—became defining characteristics of the English nation. Over time, Anglicanism lost its importance as a critical element of English nationalism but political factors retained their decisive impact. Ultimately, what defined the English nation more than anything else was *the way the English governed themselves*. English nationalism, in short, was defined in part by democratic principles.

It therefore gave rise to a political culture that proved highly conducive to the expansion of democracy. As we saw in chapter 12, **political culture** refers to *a pattern of beliefs, values, expectations and—above all—attitudes that people have with respect to authority, society, and politics*. In their classic study of political culture, Gabriel Almond and Sidney Verba described Britain in the 1950s as having a *civic culture*: that is, a cluster of attitudes favoring the rule of law, individual liberty, equal human dignity, and political moderation. They also pointed out that the British tended to be more deferential to established authority than did people in other democracies like the United States. Though these deferential attitudes appear to have declined in more recent decades, the basic contours Britain's civic culture, including a vibrant civil society, remain largely the same today.[9]

Private Enterprise and the Middle Class

Another variable that promoted the development of English democracy was the emergence of private agriculture and other business enterprises owned and operated by individuals, families, and corporations independently of the state and its chief partner, the centuries-old aristocracy. These economic processes stimulated the emergence of a property-owning middle class, centrally located in Britain's social pyramid between the wealthy aristocratic elite and the masses of poor peasants and laborers. By acquiring land or businesses of their own, these ambitious entrepreneurs acquired a personal stake in how they were governed. They wanted a say in shaping the laws of the land, especially laws regarding taxes, contracts, and other regulations affecting private property. By electing sympathetic representatives to the House of Commons they not only advanced their own economic interests; they simultaneously promoted the principle of representative self-government. In their view, the defense of property rights required the assertion of political rights.

An early catalyst to private business activity was the growth of commercial agriculture in the sixteenth and seventeenth centuries. Following his rupture with the papacy, Henry VIII ordered the liquidation of large estates owned by monasteries and other Catholic religious orders. Much of this land was taken over by individuals who converted their shares into private farms. In approximately the same period, laws were promulgated eliminating the medieval tradition allowing peasants and other non-landowners to plant crops and graze animals for personal consumption on lands designated as community property. Many of these common lands were broken up into private farms and enclosed by fences to keep out the landless poor. This "enclosure movement," which lasted until the first decades of the nineteenth century, drove tens of thousands of poor peasants off the land, often depriving them of their main source of food. Though the process was brutal and frequently violent, its main result was that—unlike Russia, China, and some other countries—Britain entered the late nineteenth century unencumbered by a large, landless peasantry whose discontent might serve as a source of revolutionary ferment. Instead the country's rich green countryside was cultivated by wealthy estate owners and a rising middle class of commercial farmers. These rural property owners ultimately promoted England's democratization through their support of Parliament and their insistence on voting rights for themselves, along with other legal privileges and freedoms.

The ranks of the propertied middle class swelled with the expansion of private manufacturing and other commercial activities in the sixteenth to eighteenth centuries. Along with the rise of entrepreneurship in these years there came a growing demand for lawyers, bankers, accountants, and other professionals capable of providing specialized services to private enterprise. By 1800 the English middle class had firmly established itself as the driving force behind a dynamic market economy. As its contributions to the wealth of the country be-

came increasingly indispensable, its influence on Parliament and government decision making grew apace. The social historian Barrington Moore maintained that, without such a capitalist bourgeoisie, there can be no democracy. Countries that failed to develop large-scale private agriculture and industry before the twentieth century—like Japan, Russia, and China—generally failed to develop democracy until much later, if at all.[10]

The expansion of capitalism in Britain was by no means without problems, however. Large numbers of landless peasants, laborers, and others who made up the uneducated mass of British society found it difficult to climb out of the bottom of the social heap in spite of the new opportunities the market economy opened up. Even the middle class itself led a precarious existence, as the volatile dynamics of the marketplace produced bankruptcies, inflation, and recessions alongside incalculable personal fortunes and rising national wealth.

These conflicting tendencies intensified in the nineteenth and early twentieth centuries as Britain's industrial revolution, which had taken off in the late 1700s, well ahead of other European countries, flourished and matured. In an economy increasingly functioning according to laissez-faire principles, with minimal government involvement, industrial capitalism generated a huge working class whose fate was determined almost entirely by employers bent on raising profits at all costs. Subsistence-level wages, long working hours, and unsanitary living conditions became the unalterable lot of millions of men, women, and children, with little or no state assistance or protection. Britain's overseas empire, on which the sun never set from Africa and India to Hong Kong and the Caribbean, provided some outlet for those wishing to start a new life in the colonies. But the empire did little to alter the grim realities of poverty for the overwhelming majority of workers and their families who stayed behind.[11]

On top of all this, Britain's aristocratic elite, the descendants of blue-blooded families whose lines stretched back centuries, managed to maintain their lofty status at the apex of British society. Though they had ceded place to the business class as the principal creators of England's wealth in the eighteenth and nineteenth centuries, their hereditary titles, accumulated riches, and superior educational attainments at universities like Oxford and Cambridge gave them a social preeminence and political influence that far exceeded their numbers.

The result of these economic and social transformations was a society that by the nineteenth century, if not earlier, was demarcated by increasingly rigid class distinctions. The "class system" became synonymous with social reality throughout Britain (especially in England, where industrialization was the most pronounced). The social class into which one was born largely determined one's life chances, including educational prospects, occupation, and income. Except for remarkably ambitious and talented individuals who managed to pull themselves out of deprivation, upward social mobility into the middle class proved difficult; more difficult, to be sure, than in the United States at comparable periods. For most people, the class they entered at birth would in all likelihood be the class their children and grandchildren remained in all their lives. Even the middle class itself became increasingly stratified as industrial capitalism developed in the late nineteenth and early twentieth centuries. Successful owners of large businesses formed an upper middle class whose wealth at times rivaled the inherited millions of the aristocracy, while small businesspeople and white-collar workers occupied lower rungs on the middle-class ladder, at times veering on poverty.

Inevitably, such stark class stratification engendered intense conflicts: conflicts over money, jobs, living conditions, and basic fairness. And just as inevitably, these conflicts over "who got what" in British society could not help but become politicized. The privileged upper crust, the plucky middle classes, and the downtrodden workers all looked to the British state for protection and benefits.

In the mid-nineteenth century, Karl Marx predicted that any society dominated by the capitalist bourgeoisie was bound to have a government completely in its thrall. Under these conditions, the exploited working masses—the *proletariat*—would eventually take matters into their own hands and stage a revolution, expropriating political as well as economic power from their masters. Their victory would set the stage for socialism, permanently eradicating private enterprise and "bourgeois democracy." In laying out this scenario, Marx had England in mind above all. England was farther

advanced along the road of laissez-faire industrial capitalism than any country in the world, with the possible exception of the United States. And yet, contrary to Marx, the proletarian revolution never occurred there, nor did democracy die.

On the contrary, both capitalism and democracy have flourished in the United Kingdom down to the present day. They have continued to survive in spite of persistently sharp class divisions in contemporary British society. What accounts for these results? One of the main reasons why Marx's prognostications did not come true can be found in the ideological development of Britain's leading political parties.

The Rise of Political Parties

Since the end of World War II, British politics has been dominated by two parties, the Conservative Party and the Labour Party. A third one, which now calls itself the Liberal Democratic Party, has played a less important role but still attracts a wide following. Several other parties also exist, but their electoral support is much smaller than that of the three main parties, all of which have roots in the past.

Modern political parties emerged in Britain in the nineteenth century. The two parties that dominated the latter half of the 1900s—the Conservatives and the Liberals—could trace their origins to earlier political orientations rooted in the religious and constitutional disputes of the two previous centuries. The **Conservatives** descended primarily from the **Tories,** a moniker they informally retain today. In the seventeenth and eighteenth centuries the Tories were identified by their devotion to absolutist monarchy, aristocratic rule, the House of Lords, and the established Anglican Church. The Liberals' chief antecedents were the Whigs, who tended to favor a more limited monarchy, one whose power would be reined in by the House of Commons acting on the principle of government by consent of the governed. Although the terms "Tory" and "Whig" were originally insults leveled by each side's detractors, in actual practice the two orientations shared certain positions in common.[12] A majority of both groups favored a monarchy of real stature, an authoritative role for Parliament, Protestantism as opposed to Catholicism, and government by propertied elites rather than mass democracy. Both strove to avoid a recurrence of the Civil Wars of the 1640s and recoiled in horror at the French Revolution. These commonalities helped set British politics on a course of moderation, consensus, and compromise that endures to this day.

Party development remained embryonic in the first half of the nineteenth century. Organization was so weak and ideological orientations so fluid that partisan loyalties tended to shift with the issues of the day. The Tories, who began referring to themselves as Conservatives in the 1830s, were divided into competing factions, as were the Whigs. By the end of the century, party ideology and organizational structure began to solidify. The Conservatives under the leadership of Benjamin Disraeli emerged as the chief advocate of the landed aristocracy, while the Liberals under leaders like William Gladstone stepped forward as the main party of the urbanized, business-oriented middle class, championing laissez-faire and free trade. Even these distinctions, however, reflected general tendencies rather than strict demarcations. Most important, both parties accepted the existing constitutional framework of a limited monarchy, cabinet accountability to Parliament, and a restricted franchise confined to property-owning males. At a time when France, Germany, Russia, and Japan experienced authoritarian rule undergirded by the military, Britain's leading parties were wedded to parliamentary government and entertained no thought of military authoritarianism.[13]

At the same time, both Conservatives and Liberals feared the mounting resentments of the working class. Britain's proletariat grew steadily in the nineteenth century. Early government efforts to alleviate their plight did little more than reduce working hours for women and children to about sixty per week. The Poor Law of 1839 actually *decreased* state expenditures on the destitute. None of this legislation addressed the fundamental problem, which was the workers' lack of political power, a weakness that left them completely subservient to their employers. To redress this imbalance, a working-class group known as the Chartists was formed in 1838. Their "Charter" of demands called for universal male suffrage, the secret ballot (as opposed to open elections by show of hands), and salaries for members of Parliament so that politicians other than the superflu-

ously wealthy could afford to hold office. Two petitions to Parliament expressing these wishes were decisively rejected, as neither the Conservatives nor the Liberals in the reign of Queen Victoria were prepared to open the floodgates of democracy to the masses. Both parties were strongly committed to preserving the property rights of land and factory owners. The resulting social conflicts occasionally sparked violence, as strikes, lockouts, and worker demonstrations led to bloody police crackdowns. Most workers, however, hewed the path of peaceful democratic change. Collaboration with sympathetic Liberals like Gladstone yielded a few gains, such as the legalization of trade unions and the right to strike in 1871. But the predominance of business interests in Liberal ranks precluded the critical breakthrough to mass suffrage.

It was therefore incumbent on the workers' movement to establish a party of its own. Accordingly, in 1900 the leaders of several worker-oriented groups held a conference in London and formed the "Labour Representation Committee." After electing twenty-nine candidates to the House of Commons in 1906, this organization renamed itself the **Labour Party.**

From its inception the new party's main source of support came from Britain's trade unions. By 1900 some 1.2 million workers were affiliated with the Trades Union Congress, an umbrella organization formed by smaller unions representing railway workers, factory laborers, miners, and other industrial occupations. Another early source of Labour support consisted of intellectuals, artists, and other middle- and upper-class sympathizers of the labour movement who objected on ethical grounds to laissez-faire capitalism's exploitative tendencies. Though their ranks were small, with only a few thousand activists divided into several groups, they exerted a substantial influence on informed political opinion by virtue of their publications and social prominence. One of these groups, the Fabian Society, included such notables as playwright George Bernard Shaw and social critics Sidney and Beatrice Webb.[14]

What is perhaps most significant about the various founding elements of the Labour Party is that their overwhelming majority decisively rejected Marxism, anarchism, and other ideologies calling for violent revolution and the creation of an entirely new social and political order. Most of them believed that working-class demands for political participation and economic justice could be accommodated within the framework of parliamentary democracy and peaceful industrial development under the aegis of the British state. While many of the Labour Party's founders called themselves "socialists," most understood this term to mean a system in which national and local government agencies would play a greater role in the economy for the benefit of the working class, without necessarily eliminating private enterprise altogether. Though many believed that the state should take over the main factories, mines, utilities, and other privately owned industries, very few advocated the wholesale government absorption of all the farms, stores, and other small- and medium-sized businesses that gave millions of British families a personal stake in private property. Only a minority of British socialists favored the gigantic state-run centrally planned economy that the Soviet Union was to set up in the 1930s. Quite a few continued to favor cooperation with the Liberal Party on certain issues, the so-called Lib-Lab orientation.

Just as significant, the early Labourites were true social democrats who believed in ballot-box democracy. They categorically rejected dictatorship. Many of them even professed their loyalty to the monarchy, as long as the crown did not interfere in the workings of Parliament. Far from opposing democracy, the Labour Party and its adherents wanted to extend its blessings to the working masses through universal male and female suffrage. Moreover, a large number of Labour leaders and voters resisted Marxism because its atheistic tenets conflicted with their strong religious convictions.[15] In short, the Labour Party helped enfold Britain's poorest classes into the democratic process. As a result, Britain did not develop a large alienated working class that felt left out of the mainstream of democratic politics. By contrast, France, Germany, and a number of other countries entered the twentieth century with many discontented workers who became radicalized and ultimately supported anti-democratic parties like the communists and fascists.

Another comparison worth noting is that the Labour Party envisioned a much greater economic role for the state than the Democratic Party in the United States tended to favor. Though both parties had deep roots in the labor movement, Labour's call for the nationalization of private companies was not echoed by Franklin Roosevelt's New Deal, which sought instead to revive private economic activity rather than replace it with government ownership. In advocating the takeover of at least some private enterprises by the state, Labour was more socialist than the Democrats ever were.

As the Labour Party gained strength, the Conservatives and Liberals underwent their own evolution in the direction of greater democracy for all. It was a Liberal government under Prime Minister David Lloyd George that conferred voting rights on most males and females in 1918, and it was a Conservative government that expanded female suffrage in 1928. In the 1930s, as the Great Depression wracked the British economy, several Labour leaders joined with Liberals and Conservatives in forming a broad coalition government. Another three-party national unity coalition governed Britain during World War II under Prime Minister Winston Churchill. (Churchill was a Conservative who had once belonged to the Liberal Party.) These crucial developments forged an unshakable consensus among the main parties of the left (Labour), right (Conservatives), and center (Liberals) that the British system of government must consist of ballot-box democracy under a limited monarchy. The three main parties also developed a consensus on Britain's economic system, embracing the general principle that it should be a mixed economy that combined private enterprise with state intervention aimed at stimulating growth and providing for the welfare of the population. Fatefully, this wide consensus on democracy and the mixed economy was precisely what eluded Germany, Italy, Spain, Russia, Japan, and a host of other countries in the first half of the twentieth century, resulting in fierce dictatorships and two world wars. By contrast, Britain emerged from the First and Second World Wars with its democracy strengthened.

British Politics Since World War II

Consensus on the fundamental principles of British democracy and political economy has by no means prevented real differences from emerging among the main parties when it comes to the specifics of government policy. Since World War II, Labour and the Conservatives have sparred vigorously over how Britain's mixed-economy welfare state should be managed, while the Liberals underwent profound transformations over this very issue. The question of what role the state should play in the economy has arguably been the single most contentious issue in postwar British politics.

Labour and the Welfare State, 1945–51 In July 1945, slightly more than two months after Germany's surrender, British voters ousted Churchill's government and swung massively to the Labour Party. With 48 percent of the popular vote and a 146-seat majority in the House of Commons, Labour formed its first majoritarian government under Clement Attlee and used its mandate to break new ground in expanding the state's role in the economy. Between 1946 and 1949 the Attlee government nationalized the Bank of England, civil aviation, and the iron and steel industries, along with the country's coal mines, railroads, gas and electricity utilities, and long-distance trucking companies. The owners of these businesses were compensated out of state revenues. In addition, the Labour government established the **National Health Service (NHS),** providing virtually free medical care for the entire population. (Private medical care and health insurance remained available for those willing to pay for it.) Other welfare measures included a vastly extended state-funded insurance program to cover unemployment, job-related accidents, maternity allowances, and pensions for widows and retirees, plus direct income assistance for the poorest families. To maintain full employment at a time when Britain's economy was still recovering from the hardships of World War II, the Labour government utilized Keynesian tax-and-spend principles. By 1950 the Labour Party had succeeded beyond all expectations in laying the foundations of Britain's large postwar welfare state, adapting to the realities of British capitalism its long-standing commitment to a social democratic conception of economic democracy.[16]

Conservative Acceptance of the Welfare State Despite the unprecedented scope of Labour's nationalizations and welfare measures, Conservative and Liberal politicians generally went along with most of them. Both parties had introduced their own welfare schemes prior to World War II, albeit on a considerably smaller scale.

Accordingly, when the Conservatives were voted back into power in 1951, they did not set out to reverse everything that Attlee's government had accomplished. Though they reprivatized the iron and steel industries and long-distance trucking, they kept the other nationalized companies firmly in state hands. Under prime ministers Winston Churchill (1951–55), Anthony Eden (1955–57), Harold Macmillan (1957–63), and Alec Douglas-Home (1963–64), a succession of Conservative governments significantly expanded spending on the National Health Service, public housing, education, and other welfare services. As one wag put it, "Labour gave us free teeth and the Tories didn't pull 'em out!" To prevent strikes, these Conservative governments acceded to a number of trade union demands for higher wages and other benefits, even though the unions were the principal financial and electoral backers of the Labour Party. And like the previous Labour government, the Conservatives used Keynesian mechanisms such as tax incentives and direct government spending to promote economic growth and reduce unemployment.

While continuing to present themselves as the party most favorable to private business and the middle class, the Conservatives in these years amply demonstrated their adherence to Britain's "postwar settlement," which combined private enterprise with a significant amount of state intervention in the economy. Conservative acceptance of this expansive state role in fact reflected a broad popular consensus in Britain at this time on the need for "collective," that is, state-centered, solutions to national problems as opposed to private initiatives centered in the economic marketplace. The period of British politics extending from 1945 through the 1970s has been aptly described as "the collectivist age," with the value of community welfare predominating over free-market individualism in public and elite opinion to a greater extent than in the United States.[17]

After losing to Labour in the elections of 1964, the Conservatives were voted back into power in 1970. Prime Minister Edward (Ted) Heath assumed office with a pledge to preserve the essentials of the welfare state while scaling back some of its more costly programs. Heath also believed that some of Britain's largest trade unions were abusing their right to strike and should be obligated to keep their agreements with private companies.

Heath's initial attempts to curtail state intervention in the economy and curb trade union power underwent a sharp reversal in 1972, however. At the start of the year, unemployment reached one million. At the same time, the coal miners' union declared a nationwide strike for higher wages. Several attempts to reach a settlement fell through, and violence flared up as picketers prevented coal and oil supplies from reaching electric power plants. Strikes by shipbuilders and dockworkers intensified the crisis. By the end of the year, electricity output had dwindled to such low levels that the government declared a state of emergency and put Britain on a three-day work week to conserve energy. Brownouts and heating fuel shortages made for a dark and cold winter.

In the face of these challenges, Heath abandoned his previous attempts to confront the unions and instead sought a long-term accommodation based on corporatist principles. (*Corporatism* is a system of institutionalized bargaining among the leaders of government, business, and labor. See chapter 11.) He called on the Trade Unions Congress to join with the government and the main interest group representing the business community, the Confederation of British Industry, in negotiating a series of agreements on pay scales, prices, and production. In exchange for regular but limited increases in union members' incomes and curbs on inflation, the unions were asked to call off the strikes and ensure a peaceful and productive work environment. The miners and other unions rebuffed the offer, and Heath called new elections for February 1974 in the midst of a rapidly deteriorating economic situation. "Who governs Britain?"—the unions or the government?—was a central issue of the campaign.

The result was a defeat for the Conservatives but a less than satisfactory victory for the Labour Party. Labour emerged as the largest party in the House of Commons but lacked an overall voting majority. Harold Wilson thereupon formed a minority Labour government, but he called new elections in October 1974 that gave his party a slender three-vote majority.

Labour Divided   Ever since its halcyon days under Attlee's first government, the Labour Party leadership had been split into two increasingly divergent camps. The party's left wing remained faithful to the ideals of economic socialism. Their adherents favored the nationalization of major industries, government spending to ensure full employment, and generous welfare benefits to be paid for by imposing high taxes on private businesses and upper-income individuals. The leftists attached a higher priority to expanding the welfare state than to any other items of the budget, including defense. Their main supporters were Britain's unionized workers.

The other Labour group consisted of moderates who shared the left's commitment to the welfare state and trade unionism but warned that government spending needed to be kept within certain limits so as not to generate skyrocketing budget deficits and a mounting national debt. Too much government spending and excessive taxation, they feared, might jeopardize Britain's international economic position and place intolerable pressures on corporations and taxpayers, ultimately resulting in job layoffs and disgruntled middle-class voters. Labour moderates also supported U.S. foreign and defense policies during the Cold War, even though they necessitated significant levels of British military spending.

The first signs of a split between the left and moderate wings of the Labour Party surfaced during Attlee's postwar governments as the costs of Labour's welfare programs soared. (The construction of the welfare state under Attlee would have been impossible without a $3.75 billion loan from the U.S. government.[18]) As a combination of economic problems brought Britain to the brink of bankruptcy in the late 1940s, several party leaders began urging cutbacks in the sums devoted to the NHS and other welfare programs. These proposals were regarded as heresy by other leaders who viewed free medical and dental care and other welfare benefits as Labour's irrevocable contribution to the British people. Though the party survived the 1950 elections with its majority intact, Attlee's second government fell apart the following year amid acrimonious feuding between the party's two wings. Unable to govern, Attlee called snap elections in 1951, which the Conservatives won.

The rift between the Labour left and the moderates intensified over the following years as the Conservatives mounted successive election victories in 1955 and 1959. It was only partially healed when Labour regained power in 1964 under the leadership of Harold Wilson. Wilson, the Oxford-educated son of a factory employee, had been an outspoken representative of the party's left wing in earlier years, but he pursued more moderate policies as prime minister. A witty debater and skilled parliamentarian, he vigorously supported the welfare state and the trade unions but was constrained under Britain's mounting economic difficulties to cut welfare spending in certain areas and to impose a wage freeze on workers. His introduction of a bill to mandate a vote of all trade union members before a strike could be declared, and to require a one-month cooling-off period before beginning a strike, angered key trade union leaders, several of whom wanted a free hand to call strikes without polling the full membership. Wilson withdrew the bill in the face of their protests. His support for the U.S. government's prosecution of the war in Vietnam may have reaffirmed Britain's loyalty as a NATO ally but it tarnished his image among Labour's anti-war left wing.

At the same time, Wilson won plaudits on the left, and among most Labour moderates as well, for renationalizing the steel industry and increasing spending on the National Health Service, public housing, education, and other welfare programs. Corporation and other taxes were raised to pay for these expenditures. His decision in 1967 to devalue the pound (from 2.80 to 2.40 to the dollar) helped stimulate British exports, providing some relief for the country's worsening unemployment problems. And as the Beatles, miniskirts, and "swinging London" exploded Britain's stodgy image as a bastion of social conservatism, Wilson's Labour Party enacted laws legalizing abortion, decriminalizing homosexuality between consenting adults, and easing requirements for divorce. Thanks to these measures, along with his reputation for honesty and competence, Wilson held the Labour Party together as it won a new majority in 1966 and seemed poised for yet another victory when he called snap elections in 1970. Unexpectedly, however, the favorable public opinion polls on which Wilson relied turned out to be wrong. To everyone's surprise, the Conservatives came back to power under Ted Heath.[19]

It was during the 1970s that Labour's internal fissures reopened over two perennially controversial issues: the trade unions and state intervention in the economy. The rise of trade union militancy during Heath's government was cheered by those on the left who believed that Britain's working class was fully justified in demanding a greater share of the nation's wealth, especially at a time of rising unemployment. But Labour moderates insisted that the economy could not function unless the unions accepted limits on their wage demands and strike activities. Accordingly, when Wilson reassumed office in 1974 he called for a "social contract" in which the unions would agree to wage restraint in return for government price and rent controls, subsidies for basic foods, and other welfare measures. This policy succeeded in calming Britain's troubled industrial relations for the next two years, providing Wilson with a favorable opportunity to announce his retirement.

His successor was James Callaghan, a Labour MP since the Attlee years. "Sunny Jim" was quickly forced to shoulder the burdens of the British economy's continuing slide when, in 1976, the pound's depreciating value against other currencies required financial assistance from the International Monetary Fund. The IMF imposed stringent spending and borrowing limitations on the British government, necessitating sharp cuts in welfare expenditures that did not sit well with the Labour left. As the economy subsequently perked up, union leaders grew restive under the government's recommendation that wage increases be limited to 5 percent. Several of the larger unions were now dominated by Marxists who were determined to use the strike weapon to assault the capitalist system. Their followers, though a small minority among the Labour Party's active membership, were increasingly successful in winning a foothold in the party's local and national decision-making bodies, posing a direct challenge to the moderates and, more pointedly, to Callaghan's government. The pressures on Callaghan intensified during the winter of 1978–79—the "winter of discontent"—as a series of strikes by truck drivers, trash collectors, and other workers inconvenienced the general public, prompting widespread fears that the unions were out of control.[20]

Britain's labor unrest was but one symptom of a persistent economic slump. Unemployment, inflation, and growth levels that compared unfavorably with other countries in Europe over the course of the 1970s persuaded many observers that Britain was sinking into irreversible decline. The combination of economic maladies afflicting the once-mighty empire became known as "the English disease." The government's failure to revive the economy and contain trade union militancy led many to conclude that Britain was ungovernable.[21]

As Callaghan wrestled with these troublesome long-term trends, his own troubles were exacerbated by dwindling support in the House of Commons. Defections from Labour ranks and defeats incurred in by-elections (which take place upon the death or retirement of a Commons member) deprived the party of its majority in 1977. In order to save his minority government, Callaghan formed a parliamentary alliance with the Liberal Party, which had thirteen seats. The "Lab-Lib" alliance lasted barely a year. In a last-ditch effort to secure a voting majority, Callaghan cut deals with the Scottish Nationalist Party and its Welsh counterpart, which together held fourteen seats. But this new parliamentary alliance was shaken after government-sponsored referendums on devolution in Scotland and Wales failed. With rumors flying that Callaghan's government and its allies no longer commanded a voting majority in the House, the Conservatives supported a no-confidence motion. The tense showdown came late in the evening of March 28, 1979. By the slimmest of margins, 311–310, Callaghan's government was defeated, setting the stage for new elections to the House of Commons only six weeks later.[22]

The result was a convincing victory for the Conservatives, whose magnetic and combative leader was to serve as Britain's prime minister for the next eleven years: **Margaret Thatcher**.

PROFILE: Margaret Thatcher

"I am a conviction politician," Margaret Thatcher affirmed before a roaring throng of Conservative Party faithful as the 1979 election campaign got under way. Comparing herself to Old Testament prophets who spurned consensus and passionately pursued their own

Margaret Thatcher

convictions, the Conservative standard-bearer served notice that she did not intend to be bound by the prevailing consensus of postwar British politics. That consensus rested on the notion that it was the obligation of the British state to maintain full employment, expand social welfare benefits, subsidize or take over large corporations facing bankruptcy, and accommodate trade union demands so as to prevent crippling strikes. It also rested on Keynesian principles of government intervention in the economy. One by one, Thatcher repudiated each of these tenets of British collectivism. Refusing to exalt the state as the mainstay of the British economy, she emphatically favored markets.

- Instead of confirming the state's responsibility for full employment, she placed her faith in the private sector as the principal motor force for job creation.
- While affirming support for the main institutions of the British welfare state, including the National Health Service, she vowed to scale back the soaring costs of welfare by attacking the "culture of dependency." In her view, too many able-bodied citizens preferred government handouts to individual responsibility and hard work.
- Rather than bail out unprofitable industries with taxpayers' money, Thatcher vowed to let private corporations assume full responsibility for their insolvency, even if that meant going out of business and dismissing their work force. No government, she believed, could overturn the rules of the marketplace. Privately owned companies needed to trim costs and expand

sales, while state-owned companies needed to cease draining the national treasury. Only then, she argued, would the economy grow and job opportunities proliferate on a sustained basis. Far from favoring the nationalization of private enterprises, Thatcher called for the *privatization* of nationalized enterprises. She also vowed to promote an "enterprise culture" aimed at encouraging entrepreneurism in a country that, in her view, was permeated with a socialist mentality placing excessive reliance on the state.

- Instead of placating trade unions in an attempt to avoid strikes, Thatcher declared her readiness to confront union leaders whenever their demands were economically unjustifiable or their actions illegal. She insisted that wage increases had to be tied to worker productivity. Inordinate wage hikes, she maintained, placed companies in jeopardy by making their products too expensive to be competitive, ultimately producing more unemployment. Illegal actions such as violent demonstrations and the destruction of property had to be met with fines and other penalties. And Thatcher favored greater democracy within trade unions, requiring union leaders to poll their membership before calling strikes. In her view, it was the militancy of a few avowedly Marxist union leaders, not the rank and file, that accounted for Britain's turbulent labor-management relations.

- In a sharp critique of Keynesianism, Thatcher disavowed the principle of boosting government expenditures in an effort to stimulate economic activity. Excessive state spending, especially when accompanied by budget deficits, led to high taxation and inflation, ultimately stifling economic growth. In place of Keynesian ideas, Thatcher embraced *monetarism*, the notion that inflation is fueled by an excess of money placed in circulation by the state's currency authorities. She condemned the "easy money" policies of previous governments and vowed to keep tight reins on the treasury's printing presses. For Thatcher, the battle against inflation took a higher priority over the battle against unemployment, at least in the short run.

These views constituted, in Thatcher's words, a "root-and-branch" reversal of the guiding assumptions of British politics. They also reflected a neo-liberal view of economic democracy, one that stressed the liberties of the marketplace and the opportunities of a "people's capitalism" against the Labour Party's more welfarist, egalitarian approach to economic democracy. Thatcher's outspoken decisiveness and buoyant optimism about Britain's possibilities at a time of mounting pessimism captured the mood of a growing number of British voters. In May 1979 the Conservatives won a forty-three-seat majority in the House of Commons, and Margaret

Thatcher became the first female prime minister in British history.

The daughter of a small-town shopkeeper, Thatcher (née Roberts) was born in 1925 and grew up in a modest flat located above the family grocery store. Her introduction to politics came in childhood, sparked by her father's election to several local offices. Following in his footsteps, Thatcher was a true-blue Conservative from the start. Unlike most Conservative politicians, however, she did not come from the privileged upper crust of British society but from the lower middle class, a social stratum whose fortunes bordered on poverty during the Great Depression. It was during this period that young Margaret learned the values of hard work, thrift, and the need for all the members of the community to help one another without engaging in bitter class conflict or expecting much assistance from the government. Working in her parents' store, she developed the view that business was creative and fun rather than harsh and alienating. "There is no better course for understanding free-market economics than life in a corner shop," she later wrote.

With the aid of scholarships and donations from her community, Thatcher went to Oxford and studied chemistry. Her love of science had to compete with her strong political inclinations, and she quickly got involved in the Conservative Party's student organization. Upon being elected its president she caught the eye of party professionals and was invited to attend the party's annual national conference. Shortly after graduation in 1947 she realized that she wanted to be a member of Parliament. After losing her first two electoral contests in 1950 and 1951, she settled into married life with Dennis Thatcher, a wealthy businessman, while raising twins, studying law, and keeping up a busy schedule of meetings and discussions within Conservative Party circles.

In 1959 she was invited by the Conservative organization of the suburban London constituency of Finchley to compete for the party's nomination. Although she did not live there, she was eligible to represent Finchley because British law does not require members of Parliament to reside in the district they represent. To be nominated to run in parliamentary elections, prospective Conservative candidates must first win the approval of the party selection committee of the district (or *constituency*) in which they wish to run. They must then win final approval at an "adoption meeting" attended by any dues-paying Conservatives in the constituency who wish to attend. Unlike the United States, Britain does not have primary elections in which the general public votes for their respective party's nominees. Thatcher bested three rivals at the Finchley selection meetings and, despite reservations by some local Conservatives about nominating a female, overwhelmingly won endorsement at the adoption meeting. In the general elections to the House of Commons held three months later, Thatcher outpolled her Labour and Liberal opponents and became a member of Parliament for the first time. In eight subsequent elections she was never defeated.

A tireless worker, Thatcher rose quickly up the ranks of the party leadership. In 1961 she became a parliamentary aide to the minister for pensions and national insurance, in effect becoming a junior minister. In 1970 Prime Minister Ted Heath appointed her to her first cabinet post as education secretary. But it was the experience of the Heath government that set her on a course at loggerheads with prevailing Conservative Party adherence to consensus politics. She regarded Heath's decision to change his free-market policies in 1972 in an effort to come to terms with the strike-prone unions as a mistake. Vowing never to make such a U-turn, Thatcher declared shortly after taking office, "You turn if you want to; the lady's not for turning."

In 1975 Thatcher was elected by Conservative members of Parliament as their party's new leader. Under her leadership the Conservatives won convincing majorities in the House of Commons in 1979, 1983, and 1987. (Their share of the popular vote, however, remained around 42 percent, as shown in this chapter's appendix.) Her overall record was a mixed bag of successes and disappointments.

- *Inflation.* One of Thatcher's biggest successes was her struggle against inflation. In 1980 Britain's inflation rate was 21 percent; by 1982 it was down to 5 percent and in 1986 it fell to 2.5 percent. Her government did not manage to control the money supply as much as it had hoped, however.

- *Growth.* Economic growth rates increased modestly in the 1980s by about 1.9 percent, higher than the previous decade. Business profits and real wages also rose under Thatcher's stewardship, but the gap between rich and poor widened.[23] So, too, did the gap between the prosperous southern parts of Britain and the declining north.

- *Trade unions.* The Thatcher government won its biggest battle with trade union militancy when it faced down a yearlong strike in 1984–85 by the National Union of Mineworkers, led by the Marxist Arthur Scargill. It also secured legislation holding unions responsible for illegal actions and expanding democratic voting procedures within the unions. By the end of the decade the number of hours lost to strikes had dropped appreciably. At the same time, trade union membership fell, and union leaders lost the substantial bargaining power they once had. Nevertheless, a substantial number of British workers supported Thatcher's policies, and the Conservatives

won 37 percent of the working-class vote in the 1987 elections.

- *Privatization.* More than twenty-five state-owned companies were sold, in whole or in part, to private bidders. They included British Petroleum, British Airways, British Telecom, and the Jaguar, Rolls Royce, and Rover auto firms. The sales reaped more than £25 billion for the treasury, though critics charged that the sale prices were too low.

- *Unemployment.* The Achilles heel of Thatcher's administration, unemployment soared from 5 percent when she assumed office to more than 10 percent from 1982 to 1987, with more than 3 million people out of work. (In the same years, unemployment was only slightly lower in the European Community but averaged about 7 percent in the United States and 2.6 percent in Japan.) Unemployment began edging downward in 1988, falling to 5.5 percent in 1990.

- *Spending and taxes.* Although one of Thatcher's top priorities was a reduction in government expenditures, state spending actually *rose* during her tenure in office, both in money terms and as a percentage of gross domestic product. Her government's failure to rein in spending was due to rising outlays for unemployment compensation, pensions, defense, public safety, and various welfare measures, including the National Health Service. Though the government kept its commitment to lower income tax rates, it raised the value-added national sales tax from 8 percent to 15 percent. Annual budget deficits averaged 1.3 percent of GDP, a figure lower than in the U.S. but higher than France or Germany.

- *Social issues.* Although she favored abortion rights and the legality of homosexuality, she called for a restoration of the death penalty and favored caning as a proper punishment for convicted offenders. (Neither capital punishment nor caning were reinstituted during her tenure.) She touched off a storm of controversy with her remark that "there is no such thing as society." Rather, she said, there are individuals and families, and they should "look to themselves first" rather than to the state for help in solving their problems. Her campaign to change British political culture by inculcating the values of the "enterprise culture" in place of collectivist values met with only modest success. However, her policy of encouraging low-income families in public housing to buy their homes from the state proved highly popular in the working class.

- *Foreign policy.* Thatcher achieved an international reputation as the "iron lady" for her toughness in foreign policy.
  - In 1982 she sent the British fleet to repel Argentina's invasion of the Falkland Islands, a small territory

off the Argentine coast that had been governed by Britain for nearly 150 years. The successful operation resulted in the collapse of Argentina's military dictatorship and a Conservative landslide in the snap elections of 1983.

- A staunch opponent of communism, Thatcher reaffirmed Britain's alliance with the United States and other NATO allies, strengthening the UK's defense posture in the process. She had an especially close partnership with President Ronald Reagan, who shared most of her beliefs, and played a critical diplomatic role in the West's dealings with the Soviet Union when Mikhail Gorbachev sought to end the Cold War.

- Her feisty defense of British sovereignty led to frequent conflicts with other members of the European Community. Thatcher spearheaded the EC's successful efforts to establish a single European market in which private enterprise could flourish. However, she believed that European integration should permit the widest possible latitude for the independent policies of member states. She scoffed at the federalist vision of a supranational "United States of Europe," in which major policy decisions would increasingly be made by politicians and bureaucrats at EC headquarters in Brussels.

Describing herself as "single-minded" and fiercely devoted to principle, Thatcher never shied away from a bruising political fight. Not only did her policies provoke harsh attacks by Labour and other opposition parties, but they could also spark objections within Conservative ranks. Not infrequently her own cabinet ministers or Conservatives in the House of Commons spoke out against her economic or foreign policies. While occasionally willing to compromise, Thatcher more often pursued a take-charge leadership style, sacking colleagues who crossed her and mobilizing her loyal grassroots following among Conservative activists in support of her agenda. In 1990, however, the acrimony of opponents within her own party reached the boiling point.

In that year Britain was in an uproar over the Thatcher government's proposal for a new scheme for local taxation. In an effort to make sure that everyone except the very poor contributed to local finances, the government proposed supplementing the existing real-estate tax system with a head tax on individuals, whose names were to be taken from the registry of voters. Dubbed the "poll tax," the plan provoked widespread public disapproval and the vocal hostility of many Conservative politicians. More than 60 percent of the country opposed it and Thatcher's approval ratings plunged to the lowest levels ever seen for a British prime minis-

ter. Taking advantage of her weakness, two Conservative leaders announced they would challenge Thatcher at the annual vote of Conservative members of the Commons to select the party's leader.

Though Thatcher had handily won these elections in past years, usually without opposition, this time she fell short of the minimum votes necessary to win on the first ballot. Convinced that her position was hopeless, she withdrew from the second ballot and announced her resignation as prime minister on November 28. With her support, John Major outpolled her principal rivals and was elected to succeed her as Conservative Party leader. In a subsequent vote in the House of Commons, Major was confirmed as prime minister.

After eleven and one-half years in office, Margaret Thatcher was ousted by her own party's parliamentary delegation. Nevertheless, as the dominant figure in British politics in the 1980s, her successes and failures were bound to leave a lasting imprint on the 1990s and beyond.[24]

John Major's Governments, 1990–97   John Major's modest background made him a most unlikely Conservative Party leader. In contrast to the aristocratic pedigrees or upper-middle-class affluence of the Tory elite, Major's family teetered on the brink of poverty. He grew up in run-down neighborhoods like Brixton, one of the most racially mixed areas of London. An uninspired student, Major quit school at sixteen and spent the next twenty years in routine administrative jobs, mostly in the banking sector. But he also developed an interest in politics, inheriting his father's Conservative loyalties. After two unsuccessful attempts, he was elected to the House of Commons in the 1979 Conservative landslide. Major quietly worked his way up the party's leadership ranks, winning appointment to two high-level cabinet positions in succession in 1989. Though he was never particularly close to Thatcher, she supported him in the 1990 party leadership struggle, enabling him to become prime minister at the age of forty-seven.

Major brought palpable changes in style and policy. His cheerful smile quickly marked him as a less contentious figure than his predecessor was. A pragmatic consensus-seeker rather than a headstrong ideologue, he consulted representatives of all the diverse currents within his party and included a number of them in his cabinet.

John Major

Although Major shared Thatcher's aversion to inflation and other aspects of her economic orientation, he departed from her policies in several areas. One of his first decisions was to abandon the poll tax, a move that won him plaudits among the Conservative Party faithful as well as the general public. He also underscored his government's commitment to improving social services more explicitly than Thatcher did, confirming his government's commitment to the National Health Service and producing a "Citizens' Charter" that spelled out what the citizenry had the right to expect from government agencies. Major was also more vocal than Thatcher in his support for improved race relations and gay rights. He opposed the death penalty, dreamed of a "classless society," and appointed more women to cabinet posts and other high offices than his predecessor did.[25]

Though lacking in charisma and saddled with a severe recession that began shortly after he assumed office, Major led the Conservatives to their fourth straight electoral victory in April 1992. The win was largely unexpected, as the Labour Party under the new leadership of Neil Kinnock was beginning to shed its image as a left-wing movement dominated by militant trade union leaders. Polls conducted right up to voting day showed the Conservatives and Labour neck-and-neck, with the outcome pointing to a hung parliament in which no party would enjoy a voting majority. But as the campaign came down to the wire, Major convinced a growing number of voters that an economic recovery was under way and that the Conservatives would prove more competent at sustaining it than the Labour Party would. The Conservatives lost forty seats, but contrary to the forecasts, they managed to retain a twenty-one-seat majority in the House of Commons.[26]

As things turned out, this majority did not remain solidly behind Major. The newly reelected prime minister soon found himself ensnared in the issue that most sharply divided the Conservative Party: Europe.

Several months after the elections, world currency traders began massively selling British pounds, fearing that they were overvalued in relation to other currencies such as the U.S. dollar and the German Deutschemark (or "D-mark"). Britain at this time was a member of Europe's Exchange Rate Mechanism (ERM), an agreement among Western Europe's largest economies to keep their currency exchange rates within certain limits, or "bands." The British pound, for example, was set at an average of 2.95 D-marks. Whenever currency traders brought the exchange rate too high above this price (e.g., 2.85 D-marks per pound) or too far below it (e.g., 3.3 D-marks per pound), under the ERM the British or German government would buy its own currency in world markets to bring the exchange rate closer to the optimum level of 2.95. In September 1992 the assault on the pound, fueled by concern about Britain's recession and other economic woes, forced the government to spend more than £10 billion to prop up the pound's value. Appeals to the German government for assistance proved unavailing, as Germany's central bank shared the view that the pound was overvalued.

In a stunning policy reversal, Major's government announced its withdrawal from the ERM. Not only did this decision represent a humiliating admission of the UK's economic weakness, but it also demonstrated that Britain could not necessarily count on Germany or its other European partners to come to its rescue in times of acute economic stress. These implications of the UK's withdrawal from the ERM worried Conservative "Euroskeptics" like Margaret Thatcher, who believed that Britain was already losing its independence by cooperating too closely with its continental European allies. Major spent his next five years in office gamely struggling to maintain party unity in the face of severe internal discord over European issues.[27]

In November 1991, leaders of the twelve countries that comprised the European Community at that time held a summit in the Dutch town of Maastricht and agreed to substantially increase their economic and political integration over the decade. Their principal aim was economic and monetary union (EMU), to be anchored in the creation of a single European currency (the euro) and a European central bank to manage it. A treaty to this effect was signed in February 1992. In 1993, with a view to the eventual achievement of these and other cooperative goals, the European Community changed its name to the European Union (EU).

From the outset, Major let his European partners understand that his government was in no position to commit itself to abandoning the pound in favor of an all-European currency. Moreover, he had signed the Maastricht Treaty only after negotiating Britain's right to opt out of the clauses pertaining to European monetary union. He also refused to accept the EU's "Social Chapter," which granted Europe's workers greater rights and welfare benefits than they currently enjoyed in Britain. Major also had doubts about the treaty's sections on establishing a "common foreign and security policy," something he feared would loosen Britain's close political and military ties with the United States. And he vigorously protested the EU's decision to ban the sale of British beef in the other member states following an outbreak of "mad cow" disease, arguing that EU authorities in Brussels were punishing Britain unfairly.[28] Despite these reservations, however, Major himself was nowhere nearly as reluctant to join in the European integration process as the more diehard anti-Europeanists within his own party. He believed that Britain's long-term economic interests required closer trade and financial ties to its EU partners over the coming years, a view strongly endorsed by the pro-European wing of his party.

On a succession of key votes in the Commons on the Maastricht Treaty, as many as twenty-six Conservatives voted against the Major government's bills calling for the treaty's adoption. Major went to extraordinary lengths to impose party dis-

cipline on the defectors. At one point he "withdrew the whip" from eight obstinate Maastricht opponents. In the House of Commons, each party has a "whip" whose job is to make sure that all the party's members of Parliament vote together on important bills. "Withdrawing the whip" means that members who defy their leadership on these votes are no longer invited to participate in meetings of the party's parliamentary delegation or other important activities. After losing a crucial vote on the Maastricht Treaty by 324–316, Major staged a vote of confidence to determine whether his government still enjoyed the support of the Commons majority. He won in spite of wide defections from Conservative ranks, thanks to support from Northern Ireland's Protestant party. With public opinion running two to one against Britain's joining a common European currency, Major promised to hold a national referendum on the issue before making a final decision on it.[29]

By 1995 Major was so exasperated at the opposition to his European policies among fellow Conservatives that he resigned as party leader and demanded a vote by the party's House of Commons delegation to reelect or remove him. He won handily, but the internal divisions in his party remained unhealed. Major's woes were exacerbated by a series of scandals. Though the prime minister vowed to go "back to basics" in conducting an efficient and honest government, a dozen cabinet officials were forced to resign for financial misconduct, sexual embarrassments, or other improprieties. Meanwhile, a number of Conservative losses in by-elections, coupled with the defection of several Tories to other parties, reduced the Major government's majority in the Commons to zero by the end of 1996. When the elections of 1997 rolled around, Major and the Conservatives were in no shape to present themselves to the voters as a unified party. Although the economy was perking up, the Conservatives' political luster was tarnished.[30] Just as significant, they now faced a rejuvenated Labour Party headed by its most popular leader in decades: **Tony Blair.**

PROFILE: Tony Blair

From his family background to his political predilections, Tony Blair was never a typical Labour Party politician.

Unlike such previous party leaders as Harold Wilson, James Callaghan, and Neil Kinnock, Blair did not stem from the working class but from a relatively well-off middle-class family. His father, a lawyer and university lecturer, was a Conservative Party activist whose moderately Tory views were to exercise a lifelong influence on Tony's political outlook. With the aid of a scholarship, Tony went off to a private boarding school at the age of thirteen and entered Oxford in 1972 to study law. It was only after graduation three years later that he joined the Labour Party.

Born in 1953, Anthony Charles Lynton Blair came of age in the late 1960s and early 1970s, a time of political activism and social rebellion for British youth as it was for the Vietnam War generation of young Americans. Blair was both an eager participant in the cultural enthusiasms of that era as well as a serious young man in search of a guiding political philosophy. A moderately rebellious teenager (he once ran away from school), he became the lead singer of a rock band, Ugly Rumors, while at Oxford. (The name was taken from the back cover of a Grateful Dead album.) But a more serious strain had already taken shape in his personality. When he was ten years old, his father suffered a debilitating stroke, an event that impressed upon young Tony the uncertainties of life. (Blair's mother was to die of cancer only weeks after his graduation from Oxford.) While at the university he deepened his religious faith, entering the Church of England in his second year. Like many students in those years, Blair was also looking for ways to make a positive impact on society, promoting the post-materialist values of compassion and community welfare in place of self-centered material success. He found a moral compass in the writings of John Macmurray, a little-known Scottish philosopher.

Macmurray rejected the central tenet of classical political and economic liberalism that human beings are individuals first and creatures of society only secondarily. This view, extolled by John Locke, Adam Smith, and other liberal thinkers, exalts individual freedom as the bedrock of political liberty and personal acquisitiveness as the source of "the wealth of nations." Macmurray reversed these priorities by affirming that humans achieve their identity primarily by relating to others rather than by maximizing self-interest. People are fundamentally social animals, he wrote, and their ties to the community must therefore take precedence over their quest for personal freedom and private gain. Macmurray combined these views with a strong attachment to Christian ethics and an abiding belief that the family constitutes the primary basis of all stable social relations.

Unlike Marx or twentieth-century socialists, Macmurray repudiated class conflict and placed little emphasis on big government as the principal guarantor of social well-being. On the contrary, his insistence that families and communities must help one another and that individuals must assume personal responsibility for contributing to the general welfare reflected the views of traditional British conservatives like Edmund Burke. They also anticipated the views of American and British "communitarians" in the 1990s, who have argued that community welfare must go hand-in-hand with personal responsibility and that the state cannot be expected to resolve all of society's problems.

Upon graduation, Blair could perhaps best be described as a Christian ethical socialist or communitarian. He combined a moral commitment to social welfare and compassion for the needy with a traditionalist's attachment to God, family, and individual responsibility to the larger community. This combination of "welfarist" and conservative values has defined Tony Blair's "third-way" political viewpoint down to the present day.

After leaving Oxford, Blair moved to London and began studying for bar exams in the law offices of a prominent Labour Party activist. It was there that he met Cherie Booth, who had just graduated at the top of her class in law at the London School of Economics. The daughter of a television actor, Cherie was already involved in Labour Party activities. Soon after getting married, they both decided to run for the House of Commons. Tony failed in his first two attempts to secure a nomination in local Labour Party organizations, but in 1982 he was selected as the Labour candidate in a by-election. The constituency was staunchly Conservative, however, and Blair went down to defeat. One year later Blair got another chance to throw his hat in the ring when, after five ballots at the local adoption meeting, he won the nomination of the Labour Party's organization in Sedgefield. This constituency was located in a former mining area in northeastern England near Durham, where Blair had grown up. It had a long tradition of electing Labour candidates to Parliament. In the 1983 elections Blair won his seat, but the overall results were a disaster for Labour. Margaret Thatcher led the Conservatives to a decisive victory in the wake of Britain's triumph over Argentina in the Falklands War. Cherie fell victim to the Conservative tide, losing her bid for election to Parliament.

At age thirty, Blair was the youngest Labour member of the newly elected House of Commons. But his youth proved no barrier to rapid advancement; Blair's rise up the party's leadership ranks was meteoric. An articulate and affable communicator, Blair proved more effective than other Labour leaders in convincing the party faithful that fundamental changes had to be made in Labour's ideological orientation if it ever hoped to recapture power. In the process he abandoned his own leftist positions on several issues and accommodated himself—and the party—to selected aspects of Thatcherism.

The 1980s were a decade of disarray within the Labour Party. Following the Conservatives' win in 1979, the leadership passed from the moderate James Callaghan to Michael Foot, who had been a leader of the party's left wing since the 1940s. Under his stewardship the rules for electing the party's leader were substantially changed. In previous years only Labour members of the Commons had the right to choose the head of the party, a practice similar to the Conservatives' procedure. Labour's new rules, adopted in 1981, established an "electoral college" that allotted 40 percent of the vote to trade unions, 30 percent to Labour members of the Commons and the European Parliament, and 30 percent to dues-paying party members. This "bloc vote" approach was designed to enhance the influence of Labour's left wing on the party's leadership and policies.

Blair opposed this leftward drift, but the left's ascendancy resulted in a 1983 election manifesto that called for more nationalizations of private enterprises, massive state spending to ensure full employment, and the elimination of Britain's nuclear weapons. In addition, the Labour left staunchly opposed Thatcher's attempts to restrain militant trade unions. This election program proved disastrous at the polls. The party's share of the vote plunged to 27.6 percent (down from 37 percent in 1979) and Labour lost sixty seats in the House of Commons.

In addition to losing voters, the party also began losing some of its leaders. In 1981, thirty Labour MPs, including four former cabinet ministers, bolted from the party and announced the creation of a new one, the Social Democratic Party (SDP). The new organization soon formed a partnership with the Liberal Party, which was now a considerably smaller and less influential political force than it was during its glory days before World War II. The "Alliance," as the partnership was called, won more than 25 percent of the vote in 1983, wooing centrist voters who opposed both the Labour left and Thatcher's brand of Conservatism. (In 1988, under new leadership, the Alliance was reconstituted as the Liberal Democrats.)

Despite his misgivings, Tony Blair remained in the Labour Party and took an active role in altering its course. Rather than "exit," he used his "voice" to change things within the party (see in chapter 11 the section titled "Exit, Voice, and Loyalty"). Blair vigorously supported Neil Kinnock, who replaced Foot as party leader after the 1983 elections. Kinnock understood that the party faced catastrophe unless it tacked

closer to the political center. Under his leadership Labour backed away from its traditional commitment to full employment at all costs and accepted several of Thatcher's policies, including certain privatization decisions and several of her measures aimed at curbing trade union militancy. Blair supported these shifts, and Kinnock in return raised him from relative obscurity in the back rows of the Labour Party's parliamentary delegation to the front benches occupied by its more prominent members. Although the proponents of a more moderate Labour Party were now in the ascendancy, their efforts were not enough to overtake the Conservatives. Labour won back some voters in 1987 and 1992 but lost both elections.

After the 1992 defeat, Kinnock stepped down and the party leadership fell on Joseph Smith, another moderate. Smith succeeded in getting the party to change its procedures for electing the party leader. The electoral college established in 1981 was replaced with a new one that gave equal weight to trade unionists, members of Parliament and the European Parliament, and ordinary party members. The reform eliminated the preferential infuence of the unions in Labour's leadership selection process. Blair welcomed the change and called for even greater democracy within the party in choosing its leaders, candidates, and policies. His stature in the party was now considerable. As a member of Labour's leadership team in the House of Commons, he sparred with Conservative cabinet ministers in parliamentary debates and won growing public recognition as the party's best television performer. He also earned grudging respect from Conservative politicians for his understanding of the issues and his moderate stances.

In the spring of 1994, Blair got an unexpected opportunity when Smith died suddenly of a heart attack. The party's new election procedures played in Blair's favor as public opinion polls showed him enjoying a solid lead among trade unionists, parliamentarians, and party members over other aspirants for the leadership post. In July 1994 Blair was formally elected Labour's new leader. As head of the party's delegation in the Commons, he regularly questioned John Major about his policies and delighted in exposing the divisions within his government on Europe and other issues.

Blair also pressed for more reforms in his own party aimed at broadening its base of potential voters. With his prodding a special Labour Party conference in April 1995 voted to reword Clause IV of the party's constitution, which had committed the party to seek "the common ownership of the means of production, distribution, and exchange." This phrase, drafted in 1917, reflected the party's early vision of socialism, with the state taking control of much of the economy. Though this goal was subsequently abandoned in practice, its formal elimination in 1995 was intended by Blair and his followers as another signal to the voters that the Labour Party, now dubbed "New Labour," had decisively broken with its past as a socialist party dominated by trade unions.

Other changes in style and substance followed. In adopting a more accommodating attitude toward business, in affirming the need to keep inflation and taxes low, and in several other areas of domestic and foreign policy, Blair pulled the Labour Party closer to Conservative positions. He deftly balanced these shifts with assurances that a Blair government would be more attentive to community welfare and social fairness than the Conservatives. Accordingly, he pledged to raise spending on education and job retraining and vowed to be "tough on crime and tough on the causes of crime, too."

With a keen eye to American politics, Blair identified Bill Clinton as a kindred spirit. Even before his selection as Labour Party leader, one of Blair's closest advisors worked on Clinton's election campaign in 1992 and learned a number of useful electioneering techniques. Blair himself journeyed to the U.S. in 1993 to meet with Clinton aides. Clinton's "New Democrat" approach, which stressed education and training for workers as well as tax breaks and other benefits for the middle class, struck a responsive chord in the Blair camp.

Blair's efforts to reposition his party closer to the center of the political spectrum was not without controversy, however. Like Clinton, Blair sought to distance himself from the established trade unions without rupturing his ties with them completely. He knew that 4½ million union members had the right to vote in Labour Party leadership elections. He also knew that, in the United Kingdom as in the United States, union members and non-unionized workers alike had reason to worry about job security at a time of accelerating economic globalization. Labor organizations on both sides of the Atlantic looked to their governments to protect their jobs, but Blair—again like Clinton—believed that an open global trading system ultimately creates more jobs and greater national wealth than protectionist trade barriers do. Blair further believed that the interests of all Britons, including workers, would be best served through closer ties to the European Union. On this issue, too, he encountered resistance in Labour ranks. While Labour may not have been as deeply divided as the Conservatives over Europe, key party leaders as well as large elements of the rank and file remained skeptical of the EU, fearing that the single European market and EU institutions in Brussels give large private corporations a greater say than labour organizations in Europe's economic affairs.

In sum, Blair's determination to shift the Labour Party to the center amounted to a major redefinition of the party's ideological self-conception, especially when compared to the 1980s. In his words, "Socialism . . . is not about class, or trade unions, or capitalism versus socialism. It is about a belief in working together to get things done." This watered-down conceptualization was criticized as vague, but it was a far cry from the markedly state-centered, trade-unionist view of British socialism historically associated with the Labour Party. It reflected Blair's search for a third way between the extremes of free-market individualism and big-government collectivism.

While many Labourites expressed reservations about Blair's policies, most supported him because he was the most electable leader the party had put forward in years. He did not disappoint. Labour won 43 percent of the vote in 1997 and ended up with a commanding 63.6 percent of the seats in the Commons, one the most decisive electoral triumphs in British history.[31]

Now that we have surveyed British political developments since World War II, what generalizations can we make about them? What explains why British voters have swung back and forth between Labour and Conservative governments? What explains why these parties and the governments they have formed have adopted the policies we have just described?

One of the oldest hypotheses about voting behavior suggests that people tend to vote in accordance with their class interests. People in the lower levels of the income pyramid can thus be expected to vote for labor- and welfare-oriented parties, while those in the upper echelons vote for conservative parties that pledge to keep taxes low and protect private business freedoms. A related hypothesis suggests that parties shape their policy proposals with particular ideological goals in mind, such as expanding social welfare or promoting private enterprise. In carrying out these goals parties appeal above all to core followers—such as a particular social class—and give them what they want when in government.

How well do these two hypotheses explain voting patterns and what governments do in Britain? Let's test them in the following exercises.

HYPOTHESIS-TESTING EXERCISES:
Social Class and Ideology in British Politics

HYPOTHESIS 1

Social class best explains election outcomes in Britain.

VARIABLES

The **dependent variable** is *election outcomes*. On what is it dependent? The **independent** (or explanatory) **variable** is *social class.*

EXPECTATIONS

If this hypothesis is correct, then we would expect the evidence to show that: (1) working-class voters and others at the lower end of the socioeconomic pyramid vote consistently for the Labour Party; (2) upper-income people tend to vote consistently for the Conservatives; and (3) the middle class splits its vote, with the less affluent strata tending toward Labour and the more affluent voting Conservative.

EVIDENCE

"Class is the basis of British party politics," a political scientist wrote in the 1960; "all else is mere embellishment and detail."[32] Indeed, class-based voting patterns were especially evident prior to World War II and up until the 1960s. Between 1945 and 1970, for instance, the Conservatives won a solid 60 percent or more of the votes of nonmanual (white-collar) voters, while Labour won similarly large shares of the manual working-class vote. However, there is also evidence indicating that the impact of social class on voters' preferences is not nearly as one-sided and consistent as our hypothesis would lead us to suspect. For example:

- Even in the 1945–70 period, a substantial number of manual workers (25 percent or more) voted Conservative, the so-called "working-class Tories." Labour won more than a fifth of the white-collar vote in this period. While much of that support came from the lower end of the income scale, some of it came from well-to-do voters who shared Labour's aim of improving life for the less advantaged classes even if it meant higher taxes for themselves.[33]
- In the 1970s there was mounting evidence of *party dealignment:* a growing number of voters were breaking away from their traditional party loyalties. Labour won a diminishing share of its core working-class fol-

lowing, in part because of disappointment at the Labour government's performance in 1964–70. The Conservatives suffered defections as well, and more voters cast ballots for the Liberals or local parties in Scotland, Wales, and Northern Ireland.

- The heightened ideological confrontations of the Thatcher years sparked more changes. While the Tories held steady at about 42 percent of the vote, they won growing support from manual working-class voters and low-income public housing residents. These votes reflected working-class support for Thatcher's opposition to militant trade union leaders who called strikes without balloting the membership, and for her efforts to help public housing residents purchase homes from the government. In 1983, Labour won only 47 percent of the manual working-class vote; 30 percent went to the Conservatives. The Liberals and their allies, meanwhile, won more middle-class votes from the Conservatives and a growing share of manual workers (22 percent in 1983).
- The 1997 election witnessed a large swing of middle-class voters to Labour and sizable defections from the Conservatives.

CONCLUSIONS

The Evidence is *mixed.* British elections since 1945 demonstrate that social class indeed accounts for a substantial amount of voting behavior. The Conservatives have always managed to attract at least half the white-collar vote, and above a certain income level their share of electoral support invariably rises the higher one goes up Britain's income pyramid. The Labour Party, for its part, has always won at least 40 percent of the manual working-class vote. Nevertheless, British voters have not consistently voted in strict accordance with their social class. When manual workers—especially trade union members—vote Conservative or Liberal rather than Labour, their behavior contradicts the expectations of our hypothesis. So, too, does the behavior of well-off voters for the Labour Party.

These unexpected voting patterns turn out to be even more variegated when we delve into the complexities of what "class" means. Throughout most of the postwar period a majority of Britons have identified themselves as "working class": more than 80 percent in the 1950s, around 70 percent in the 1970s and 1980s, and more than 60 percent in the 1990s. But these subjective class identities do not always conform to the objective classifications of class devised by social scientists, which are typically based on income levels or occupations. Some people who may call themselves "working-class" may have "middle class" occupations (such as supervisory or technical personnel) and vote Conservative at higher rates than manual workers do. Conversely, some people in white-collar positions typically categorized as middle class by researchers (such as junior level office managers, bureaucrats, or teachers) may vote Labour at higher rates than do more senior white-collar workers such as business executives.

The facts also show that, especially since the 1970s, many voters have not maintained consistent party loyalty. Rather, a growing percentage of them have voted for parties that reflect their own attitudes on the issues of the day. This increase in "issue voting" contradicts the notion that voters rarely think for themselves at election time and automatically vote for the same party time and again. Today only about half of British voters are steadfastly faithful to either Labour or the Conservatives (compared with about two-thirds in the 1960s). The other half exhibits little or no long-term loyalty to any party, especially "floaters" (or "swing voters") who switch parties routinely depending on the candidates and the issues. Public opinion polls taken during election periods increasingly indicate that a majority of the voters tend to favor the winning party's stance on most of the issues at the heart of the campaign. In the 1980s, the majority favored the Conservatives' approach to the economy, law and order, trade union militancy, and related controversies. In 1997 most people tended to favor Tony Blair's approach to the main issues of the day.

A significant number of British voters thus exhibit a degree of "bounded rationality" (or "low-information rationality"). Though they may not be fully informed about all the issues, they know enough to make up their own minds, choosing candidates and switching parties in accordance with their own interests and ideals. These considerations may reflect their economic class interests ("Under which party will I be better off?"), but they may also reflect other personal priorities such as religious beliefs, regional loyalties, post-materialist values, and the like.

In sum, *class matters* in British elections, but it does not by itself explain their results. While there is a lot of evidence of class voting that is consistent with the hypothesis, there is a considerable amount that is inconsistent with it. Given this mixed evidence, it would be wrong to say that class alone determines British election outcomes.[34]

HYPOTHESIS 2

Class-oriented ideologies account for the policies favored by the competing parties as well as the decisions they have made when in government.

VARIABLES

The **dependent variables** here are *party and government policies*. What accounts for them? The proposed **independent variable** is *class-oriented ideologies*.

EXPECTATIONS

If the hypothesis is correct, we would expect to find that (1) party programs tend to reflect class-based ideologies fairly consistently. Thus, Labour can be expected to favor the nationalization of private firms to maintain full employment, along with welfarist, pro-union policies in order to appeal to its working-class base. The high taxes needed to pay for these measures would fall mainly on the upper classes and private corporations. For their part, the Conservatives can be expected to favor lower taxes, less welfare spending, and greater freedom for private business, policies sure to appeal to its core followers in the business sector and the upper reaches of the socioeconomic pyramid. In addition, we would expect to find that (2) once installed in government, both parties consistently translate their electoral programs into law.

EVIDENCE

Like the first hypothesis, this one contains a grain of truth. Throughout its history, Labour has been the party of "big government," with a pronouncedly welfarist orientation directed at its core working-class and lower middle-class followings. The Conservatives have stepped forward as the party of the upper classes and private enterprise. Once again, however, there is considerable evidence that contradicts the expectations of the hypothesis. Neither party has demonstrated ideological consistency in the postwar period, and neither has been able to carry out all the main elements of its program while in power. In some cases they ended up doing precisely the *opposite* of what they promised the voters.

- Both parties have been internally divided through most of the postwar decades. Labour has been divided into a socialist left wing and more moderate elements. Conservatives have been divided into those who strongly favor private enterprise and want considerably less government interference in the economy—like Thatcher and her supporters—and those who support these goals in principle while favoring various welfare programs, the nationalization of some firms, and compromises with the unions (like Heath). *A divided party makes for less ideological consistency.* In the 1990s, the leaders of both parties distanced themselves from the more outspokenly ideological wings of their respective parties. Blair steered a wide path from the Labour left, while Major and his successor, William Hague, proved more moderate than the hard-core Thatcherites.

- Both Labour and the Conservatives have had to reach out beyond their core constituencies in order to win elections. Most important, both have had to appeal to the broad middle class, people whose incomes are in between the bottom 10 to 20 percent of the socioeconomic pyramid and the top 10 percent to 20 percent. As a general rule, most members of this large intermediate group want *both* government welfare programs from which they benefit (such as education and medical care) *and* a limited tax burden. Some work for the public sector and others for the private sector.

As Britain's economy has expanded since World War II, the size of its middle class has grown.[35] Consequently, both parties have been pressured into abandoning ideologies that appeal only to a narrow class-based core constituency. To be elected, both have had to strike a balance between government spending on popular programs and reasonable limits to budget deficits, taxes, and inflation. In sum, *the middle class tends to reject ideological extremes, favoring moderate, centrist political leaders.*

- Neither Labour nor the Conservative party has been able to enact a consistent ideological program while in government. Despite their achievements, the first Labour governments after the war had to scale down their socialist programs because of escalating budget deficits. Similarly, Wilson and Callaghan were compelled to trim government spending and fend off trade union demands when Britain's position in the international economy deteriorated. Thatcher ended up raising government spending and taxes in spite of pledges to the contrary. Major failed to keep Britain in the Exchange Rate Mechanism. In these and other cases, British governments have had to alter key aspects of their governing programs under powerful budgetary and international pressures.

CONCLUSIONS

The evidence for our second hypothesis is *mixed.* The Labour and Conservative parties have a long history of appealing to different social classes; not surprisingly, the basic thrust of their respective policy orientations has reflected—and continues to reflect—these class-based constituencies. Nevertheless, there is compelling evidence against the notion that these parties have maintained ideological consistency. The growth of the middle class has been especially important in diluting their more extreme ideological inclinations. The replacement of Margaret Thatcher by John Major and the election of Tony Blair blurred the ideological distinctiveness of the two parties even further in the 1990s. The Conservatives and Labour constitute catch-all parties whose policy differences are mainly a matter of nuance and detail rather than sharply clashing political visions. The leaders of both parties appear primarily concerned with winning power and exercising it with moderation and technical competence. This pragmatic approach to governing seems to reflect the post-Thatcherite consensus shared by most Britons, one that favors a generous but efficient welfare state along with low inflation and a dynamic private sector.

At the same time, the evidence contradicts our expectation that British governments make their decisions mostly on ideological grounds. While each party of course has its own agenda, one that may at times be highly ideological, once in power it can be forced to back away from its best-laid plans and take actions it deems unpalatable but unavoidable. Britain's experience demonstrates how *governments must live under constraints,* democracies in particular. They cannot always do what they want to do. Politically, they are constrained by what the public will tolerate. Economically, they are constrained by budgetary and international realities. These and other constraints make it difficult to pursue ideologically consistent policies in today's world.

BRITISH DEMOCRACY TODAY: PARTIES, ELECTIONS, AND STATE INSTITUTIONS

Parties and Elections

Political parties are vital to the electoral process in all democracies, but especially so in a parliamentary system of government. British parties are more centrally organized than are parties in the United States and play a more direct role in defining policy goals, nominating candidates for office, conducting election campaigns, and coordinating legislative and government activities. The three largest parties—Labour, the Conservatives, and the Liberal Democrats—are particularly well organized. Each has a national headquarters and bureaucracy, representatives in Parliament (the "parliamentary party"), and local organizations in all House of Commons districts in Great Britain (the "constituency parties"). (Neither Labour nor the Liberal Democrats are organized in Northern Ireland, while the Conservatives have only a token following there.) Unlike the Democrats and Republicans in the United States. these parties also have dues-paying members. *Only those members whose dues are paid up are allowed to vote in constituency elections to nominate candidates for the House of Commons.*

The Party Leader All the main parties in the United Kingdom have explicit procedures for choosing the party leader, who is the person most likely to become prime minister should the party win a majority of seats in the Commons. By contrast, the two main U.S. parties do not have a formal chief. While a serving president is usually regarded as the leader of his party, he does not carry this title officially. The party that does not occupy the White House may be even less certain as to who its "leader" actually is. Both the Republicans and Democrats have a national committee, but its chair is mainly concerned with fundraising and does not serve as the party's chief spokesperson on policy matters or as its next presidential candidate.

Just as important, Britain's parliamentary system requires any prospective prime minister to be a member of Parliament, preferably of the Commons. It is therefore unthinkable that a British politician could become leader of one of the main parties or rise to "the top o' the greasy pole" as head of government without parliamentary experience. Several have also served in the cabinet prior to assuming party leadership. Perhaps the least experienced party leader in recent times is William Hague, who was elected to head the Conservatives in 1997 following Major's resignation. At age thirty-five, Hague had served in Parliament only eight years before his election. One reason for his selection was that the Labour Party's substantial majority in the Commons convinced many Conservatives that the next parliamentary elections would probably not be held until 2001 or 2002, giving Hague several years to prove his mettle and enhance his qualifications as a prospective prime minister.[36] However, it is quite possible for a political figure in the United States to have no experience whatsoever in national government, either in Congress or the cabinet, and still win election to the highest office of the land. Presidents Carter, Reagan, and Clinton are recent examples.

Meanwhile, British prime ministers are elected by a much smaller group of voters than are U.S. presidents. In Britain, the party leader's name appears on the ballot only in one House of Commons district (constituency). In 1997, Tony Blair was the Labour candidate for Parliament in Sedgefield, nowhere else. Voters living in other constituencies who might favor Blair for prime minister would have to vote for the Labour Party candidate running in their own constituency and hope that Labour candidates win a majority of these single-member constituency contests. By contrast, all American voters have a chance to choose among the competing candidates for president in the general elections.

Another striking distinction between the British and American systems is that *party professionals* play a paramount role in selecting the leaders of the two largest parties in the UK. Not only do U.S. parties lack a formal leader, but also their presidential nominees are increasingly chosen by *voters* in primary elections rather than by professional politicians or activists. As Jimmy Carter and Bill Clinton showed, it is quite possible for a candidate who is virtually unknown outside his home state in January to get elected to the presidency in November. The British system is considerably less hospitable to such "outsiders."

Every year the Labour Party and the Conservatives hold a conference at which their leaders make major pronouncements and party activists debate policy alternatives. The Liberal Democrats convene twice yearly for these purposes. By contrast, American parties hold national conventions only every four years, mainly to nominate their candidates for president and vice president. Nowadays the presidential nominee usually has the nomination sewn up weeks before the convention meets, thanks to victories in the primary elections held earlier, Al Gore and George W. Bush effectively sealed their respective nominations several months before their party conventions in 2000. Policy debate at U.S. political conventions is rare.

British Parties   Though the three largest British parties share several organizational features in common, they differ in details. The **Conservatives,** who have been formally known as the "Conservative and Unionist Party" ever since the days when they favored the union of Ireland with Great Britain, tend to be more centralized than Labour or the Liberal Democrats. They confer greater authority on their leader and MPs. (The term **"MP"**— **"Member of Parliament"**—can apply to members of either the Commons or Lords, but typically refers to the former.) The selection of party leader is entrusted solely to Conservative members of the House of Commons.[37] Once elected, the Conservative leader has considerable latitude to enunciate party policy, though consultations with other party leaders and junior MPs are frequent.

There is no official figure on the number of Conservative Party members. It was estimated at around 750,000 in the early 1990s but plunged to around 400,000 by the end of John Major's government.[38] The party sets no fixed amount for dues, but it needs an average of £6 (about $10) annually per member and counts on its well-heeled loyalists to contribute more.

The Conservatives finished out the 1990s in a state of drift, still divided on Europe and uncertain of their domestic policy course. Though party chief Hague accused Blair of "holding a dagger at the heart of what it is to be British," and promised a "commonsense revolution" against him, many Tories believe that Blair owes his success to his deft pilfering of their ideas.

The **Labour Party** has about 350,000 members, a figure that reflected a rise in over 100,000 new members after Blair assumed the leadership. In addition, more than 4 million members of trade unions that are formally affiliated with the Labour Party are entitled to vote as individuals for the party leader under current procedures. Annual dues range from a few pounds for workers, students, and pensioners to £15 ($24) as the minimum contribution for most everyone else.

Labour employs a more democratic process than the Tories when selecting its leader and formulating policies. Under the rules adopted in 1993, the leader and deputy leader are chosen by an electoral college consisting of trade unionists, members of the Commons and the European Parliament, and dues-paying party members. The vote of the three groups is weighted one-third each. When Blair was elected in 1994, he got 52.3 percent of the trade unionists' votes, 60.5 percent of the MPs, and 58.2 percent of the dues-paying members; his final count averaged out at 57 percent. As long as he serves as prime minister, Blair cannot be subjected to reelection as Labour's leader unless the party's annual conference demands it. Should he die while in office or become "unavailable," the cabinet would select one of its members to serve as prime minister until the party's electoral college chooses a new chief.

Labour's leader has less discretion in setting party policy than his Conservative counterpart.

The annual Labour Party conference traditionally decides party policy. Half of its twelve hundred members represent trade unions, and the other half come from constituency parties. Blair has tried to enhance his freedom of maneuver by establishing a smaller "national policy forum" in the party to discuss policy issues. A National Executive Committee, consisting of twenty-six prominent party members, controls Labour's bureaucracy and influences policy discussions.

The **Liberal Democrats,** formally known as the "Social and Liberal Democratic Party," do things slightly differently from the two larger parties. The party was formally established in 1988, the result of the merger of the two "Alliance" parties, the Social Democrats and the Liberals. With only about 70,000 paid members, the Liberal Democrats elect their leader by means of a mail-in ballot of the membership. Paddy Ashdown was elected in 1988 and was followed in 1999 by Charles Kennedy. Party members are asked to contribute £15 annually, though the minimum contribution is set at only £2.50. The Liberal Democrats have a largely middle-class following, but they have often been successful at picking up Labour voters as well as Conservatives when people are dissatisfied with their erstwhile favorite party.

Several minor parties also field candidates for the Commons, but not in all constituencies. They tend to have weak organizations dominated by a few leaders, with little or no dues-paying membership. The more successful of these parties are based outside of England. The **Scottish National Party** (SNP), founded in 1934, advocates independence for Scotland. It won 22.1 percent of the Scottish vote in 1997 and six seats in the House of Commons. Its main competitor is the Labour Party, which won fifty-six of Scotland's seventy-two Commons seats. The **Welsh Nationalist Party** (Plaid Cymru), founded in 1925, wants more autonomy for Wales (but not outright independence) and greater use of the Welsh language. It polled 9.9 percent of the Welsh vote in 1997 and won only four of the forty seats reserved for Wales in the House of Commons. Northern Ireland's parties reflect that region's tortuous history of sectarian strife between Protestants and Catholics. In the 1997 elections for eighteen seats in the Commons, the "Unionist Bloc," an alliance of Protestant parties led by the **Ulster Unionist Party** and the **Ulster Democratic Party,** garnered slightly more than half the Northern Irish vote and won thirteen seats. The Catholic "Nationalist Bloc," consisting of the **Social Democratic and Labour Party** and **Sinn Fein** ("We Ourselves"), the political wing of the Irish Republican Army, won about 40 percent of the vote and five seats in Parliament. The nonsectarian **Alliance Party** won 6.5 percent of the vote in the region but no seats in the Commons. A number of smaller parties collectively won about 8 percent of the Northern Irish vote but no seats.

Other parties fielding candidates primarily in England are quite small and uniformly unsuccessful at electing MPs. In 1997 the largest of these was the **Referendum Party,** which was founded in late 1995 by an eccentric billionaire, Sir James Goldsmith, a staunch opponent of European integration who called for a referendum on Britain's relationship with the EU. The well-funded party put up candidates in more than five hundred constituencies but won only 2.6 percent of the vote and no seats in Parliament. (Goldsmith died in 1998.) Another anti-EU party, the **UK Independence Party,** contested fewer than two hundred constituencies in 1997, garnering only 0.3 percent of the total vote and no seats. Other small parties in 1997 included the environmentalist **Green Party** (0.2 percent of the vote); the ultra-left **Socialist Labour Party** (0.2 percent); and at approximately 0.1 percent of the vote each, the **Liberal Party,** consisting of die-hard Liberals who refused to join the Liberal Democrats, the ultra-right **British National Party,** the **Natural Law Party,** devoted to the teachings of Mahareshi Mahesh Yogi, and the anti-abortionist **Prolife Alliance.** Most of these parties ran candidates in fewer than sixty-five constituencies; none won any seats in the House of Commons. Very few independents run for Parliament, and in 1997 as in most prior election years, none was elected.

Absent from the scene in the 1990s was Britain's **Communist Party,** which was one of the smallest and least successful communist parties in Western Europe. Its share of the vote after 1945 was consistently below 1 percent; from 1950 onward it had no representation in Parliament. In November 1991 the party dissolved, just one month before the collapse of the Soviet Union. The Communists'

historic failure highlights the Labour Party's dominance of the British left and stands out in marked contrast to the highly successful communist parties of postwar France and Italy.

Elections to the House of Commons: The Nomination Process   One of the first things candidates for elective office must do in most democracies is obtain the official nomination of a political party (unless, of course, one chooses to run independently). In the United States, not only candidates for the presidency but also aspirants to the Senate and the House of Representatives—along with contestants for state and local offices—must usually take part in primary elections to win their party's nomination to compete in the general elections several months later. Again, it is the *voters* who select the nominees of their respective parties in these primaries.

Like most parliamentary democracies, *the United Kingdom does not have primary elections.* Rather, each party has its own "in-house" procedures for choosing its nominees to compete in the general elections to the House of Commons. In the three largest parties it is the *party activists and dues-paying party members in each constituency* who select their party's nominee. In the smaller parties that have few, if any, dues-paying members, the nomination process tends to be controlled even more tightly by professional party elites.

Nomination procedures are relatively similar in the Conservative and Labour parties, as our profiles of Margaret Thatcher and Tony Blair illustrated. People who wish to run for Parliament are typically interviewed by a party's selection committee in the constituency they wish to represent. (Unlike U.S. members of Congress, MPs do not have to reside in the constituency they represent.) If a constituency is considered fairly safe for one of the parties and the nomination is up for grabs, quite a few apply, sometimes between twenty-five and a hundred. But if an incumbent MP is popular or if a challenging party is not likely to win, there will usually be far fewer applicants for the nomination. The selection committee screens the applicants and draws up a short list, normally consisting of between two and ten applicants. This all-important short-list decision is invariably taken by a very small group of people; constituency selection committees generally consist of only about a dozen local activists in the Conservative Party and around twenty in the Labour Party.

Once prospective nominees have made the short list, they appear before an adoption meeting of the local constituency membership. (Conservative Party constituency associations often have a further screening of the short-list candidates, only one or two of whom may be presented to the full constituency membership for final approval.) In the Conservative and Labour parties, these nomination meetings are rarely attended by more than 200 dues-paying members; in most cases only about 50 to 150 show up to vote.[39] Assuming a generous average turnout of 160 voting members in each constituency, what this means is that *slightly more than 100,000 people in each of Britain's two largest parties participate in the nomination process for more than 650 House of Commons seats.* The Liberal Democrats' nominees are chosen by some 70,000 members in a postal ballot. Far fewer people are eligible to take part in the nomination process in the smaller parties. With about 44 million eligible voters in the UK in 1997, it appears that *fewer than 1 percent of British voters participated in the party nomination process* for the House of Commons in that year. In the United States, about 30 to 40 percent of eligible voters typically participate in primary elections for the House of Representatives. While many Americans belittle these turnouts as lamentably low, they are considerably higher than in Britain and other democracies that do not have primaries.

Meanwhile, the central headquarters of the main parties plays its own role in the selection process. The dossiers of prospective nominees for Parliament are usually scrutinized by the central office, and some applicants are personally interviewed. While the national headquarters rarely imposes a candidate of its own choosing on a local constituency, all candidates nominated by the constituency parties must be approved by the party's central organs. As a consequence, candidates for Parliament—as well as serving MPs—tend to be more dependent on their national party leadership than are candidates for Congress in the United States, who compete in primary elections on their own initiative and raise most of their own campaign funding. If a party's national leadership refuses its endorsement of a prospective candidate,

that person will not be able to run for Parliament as the party's official nominee. No similar process of interference by the Democratic or Republican national committee exists in the United States, giving candidates and elected members of Congress greater independence from their party leadership than their British counterparts enjoy.

Campaigns and Campaign Financing Another salient difference between British and American electoral processes is that the UK does not specify the timing of general elections very far in advance of their occurrence. The U.S. Constitution designates the first Tuesday after the second Monday in November every two years for House and Senate elections and every four years for presidential elections. In Britain the prime minister may ask the queen to call elections to the House of Commons at any time. While British law requires parliamentary elections to take place at least every five years, prime ministers may call anticipated ("snap") elections before the expiration of Parliament's full five-year term. If public opinion polls look favorable for the government, the motivation to call a snap election is especially high. In fact, snap elections are the rule rather than the exception in Britain. Since 1918, John Major's second government (1992–97) has been the only one in peacetime to serve out its full term. Except for the crisis years of 1935–45, all other prime ministers called snap elections.

Once the prime minister gets the queen's symbolic approval and announces the date of the elections, an official campaign period begins that has important legal consequences. Typically the election occurs about three to four weeks after the prime minister's announcement, though Major set a forty-five-day campaign in 1997. Parliament is formally "dissolved" in that period and ceases to meet; hence no new legislation can be enacted. In the United States, Congress and the president may continue to work on legislation during election campaigns and often do so with an eye to influencing voters.

Once the campaign is under way, the main parties issue an election "manifesto" that outlines the policies they promise to pursue if elected to form the government. The formulation of these manifestos is taken more seriously by British parties than by the two largest parties in the United States. In the United States a special committee debates and drafts a party "platform" at the start of the presidential nominating convention. The platform may then be debated and adopted by vote of the full convention. Presidential candidates in both parties, however, are notorious for completely ignoring the platform in the ensuing campaign and have been known to bluntly assert their refusal to be bound by it.

Strict spending rules apply during the official campaign period in the UK. It is only during these weeks that parties and candidates may spend money for advertising and related election purposes. Most of the advertisement money is for handouts and billboards, since *British law forbids paid political ads on television or radio*. The British Broadcasting Corporation (BBC) provides each party with a limited amount of free air time during the campaign period, while the national treasury picks up the tab for campaign mailings. In the United States, candidates and parties may spend as much money as they want on their campaigns at any time and may usually buy as much national or local broadcast time, and postage, as they can afford. Moreover, there is no officially designated campaign period in the United States. Aspirants to the presidency often declare their candidacy eighteen months or more before the presidential election, as do many Senate and House hopefuls. Presidential primaries begin in January, making for a lengthy campaign season.

One of the most significant differences between British and American elections is that, ever since the passage of the Corrupt and Illegal Practices Act in 1883, British law places limits on how much may be spent on behalf of *individual candidates* running for the House of Commons. While the precise amount varies from one election to another and depends in part on the number of voters in each constituency, candidates in the 1990s were allowed to spend no more than about £7,500 on average—about $10,000. Most candidates spent less. In the United States, individual candidates now spend about $1 million in contested primary and general elections to the House of Representatives. The cost of running for the U.S. Senate or the presidency is, of course, vastly higher.

British law places no legal limits, however, on the amount the *parties* may spend on their national campaigns during the election period. In recent years these costs have soared, especially as British parties have adopted American election techniques such as hiring expensive ad firms, distributing glossy literature, and the like. Traditionally, the Conservative Party has tended to have the most money at its disposal, thanks to generous contributions from corporations and wealthy supporters. Labour's funding has mainly come from friendly trade unions. Both parties massively outspend the Liberal Democrats and other rivals.

In 1992 and 1997, Labour managed to match the Conservatives' war chest, and Blair was successful at attracting more contributions from businesspeople than his party usually received in the past. Although the amounts spent by British parties do not come proportionally close to what American parties spend, both the Conservatives and Labour found themselves saddled with debt in the 1990s. Moreover, both parties have inevitably found themselves beholden to their chief benefactors, whether they are interest groups or individuals. In British politics as in U.S. politics, money talks. One of Blair's first controversies as prime minister flared up when a wealthy business contributor was given a special exemption from laws banning tobacco advertising.

In 1998 a committee tasked by Blair to examine campaign financing proposed public disclosure of all contributions over £5,000 ($3,100), a cap of £20 million ($12.4 million) on total party spending, and an increase in public campaign funding, among other suggestions.[40]

All candidates in parliamentary elections are required to put up a deposit of £500. If they fail to garner at least 5 percent of the vote in their constituency, they forfeit the deposit, which reverts to the national treasury. In most cases their party will pay for lost deposits, another indication of the financial ties linking the candidates to the party they represent.

Thus far no British general election has been accompanied by a head-to-head television debate of the main party leaders. As we shall see later in this chapter, however, party leaders engage in direct televised exchanges every week on the floor of the House of Commons, a practice known as "prime minister's question time." The leaders of these parties are therefore quite well known to the public long before the election takes place.

Voter Registration and Turnout Unlike American voters, British citizens are not required to go to a designated location to register to vote. The U.S. registration system has a dampening effect on the number of eligible voters who actually vote. In Britain, voters may register by mail, and election authorities may conduct a door-to-door canvass of some residences before an upcoming election to make sure that all citizens eligible to vote are on the registry. While this system may miss about 9 percent of potential voters, it manages to register a higher proportion than the U.S. system does.

Voter turnout in Britain has remained consistently higher than in the United States, in spite of the fact that the two countries have similar election procedures for the lower house. Since 1945, turnout in fifteen elections to the House of Commons has averaged 74.4 percent of eligible voters. The 1997 turnout of 69.4 percent was the lowest. In the United States, turnout in the 1998 elections to the House of Representatives was 36 percent. (For a comparison of turnout rates, see chapter 11.) Turnout in U.S. presidential races also falls far short of British averages.

The Electoral System The electoral system used to elect the House of Commons is the **single member district (SMD)/plurality** method. There is only one round of elections: hence it is a *single-ballot* procedure. The United States employs the same system for elections to the House of Representatives. (France uses a two-ballot SMD procedure, with a second round of runoff elections to the lower house of parliament occurring one week after the first round.)

The United Kingdom is divided into more than six hundred electoral districts (constituencies); in 1997 there were 659. There is no fixed number of constituencies, nor is there a precise limit on the size of their population. To ensure relative fairness in representation, a Boundary Commission is empowered to redraw constituency boundaries based on population every eight to twelve years. As in the United States, the drawing of district boundaries is a contentious political issue, as a party may lose or gain seats depending on how the lines are drawn. In recent years the English constituencies have tended to represent about 68,000 voters each, with lower numbers in Scotland, Wales, and Northern Ireland. In the United States, each of the 435 seats in the House of Representatives represents, on average, 450,000 eligible voters, but the actual figure varies by state.

One person is elected to represent each district in a winner-take-all contest. Since at least three candidates compete in most UK districts, the victor does not have to earn an absolute majority of the votes cast (more than 50 percent) to win; *a plurality suffices.* Each candidate's name is listed on a paper ballot, followed by her or his party affiliation (see figure 16.2). Britain does not use voting machines. In the example in table 16.2, Casale was "first past the post" with 42.8 percent of the vote.

As we saw in chapter 9, one of the chief results of the SMD/plurality system is that it sometimes produces a disparity between a party's percentage of the total vote and its percentage of the seats in the legislature. In Britain these disparities can at times be very wide, generally much wider than in the United States. One of the most glaring examples is the Parliament elected in 1997. With slightly more than 43 percent of the popular vote, the Labour Party won more than 63 percent of the seats—a twenty-point disparity! The Conservatives' share of

TABLE 16.2

Wimbledon Constituency Election to House of Commons, 1997			
Candidate	Party	Votes	% of Votes
Abid	Referendum	993	2.1
Casale	Labour	20,674	42.8
Davies	Prolife Alliance	326	0.7
Goodson-Wickes	Conservative	17,684	36.6
Kirby	Mongolian BBQ	112	0.2
Stacey	Rainbow Dream	47	0.1
Thacker	Green Party	474	1.0
Willott	Liberal Democrat	8,014	16.6

FIGURE 16.2   Sample Ballot for House of Commons Election, Wimbledon Constituency, May 1, 1997

VOTE FOR ONE CANDIDATE ONLY

......./....................

COUNTERFOIL

WIMBLEDON CONSTITUENCY

1 MAY 1997

1

ABID

Hameed Zayer Abid
5 Simpson Road, Ham, Richmond, Surrey, TW10 7TU

The Referendum Party Candidate

2

CASALE

Roger Mark Casale
17 Lingfield Road, Wimbledon, London, SW19 4QD

The Labour Party Candidate

3

DAVIES

Sophie Amanda Helen Davies
20 Eagle Wharf Court, Lafone Street, London, SE1 2LZ

Prolife Alliance

4

GOODSON-WICKES

Charles Goodson-Wickes
37 St James's Place, London, SW1A 1NS

The Official Conservative Party Candidate

5

KIRBY

Matthew Giles Kirby
24 Calonne Road, London, SW19 5HJ

Mongolian Barbeque Great Place To Party

6

STACEY

Graham Leonard Stacey
4 Ridgway Place, Wimbledon, London, SW19 4EP

The Rainbow Dream Ticket Leisure Party

7

THACKER

Rajeev Kumar Thacker
5 Melrose Road, Merton Park, London, SW19 3HF

Green Party

8

WILLOTT

Alison Leyland Willott
40 Elm Walk, Raynes Park, London, SW20 9ED

Liberal Democrat

seats in the Commons was also higher than their share of the national vote in every election from 1979 to 1992. In another anomaly, the governing party actually won *fewer* votes nationally than its main rival in the elections of 1951 and February 1974. (See the table on British elections in the appendix to this chapter.)

While victorious parties have good reason to cheer the results of the British electoral system, less successful parties feel it discriminates against them. *The SMD/plurality system punishes small parties.* What matters in this system is not the percentage of votes a party gets nationwide, but *how many districts* its candidates win. A small party may have a substantial following spread throughout the country, but its candidates may amass enough votes to win only in a small number of constituencies. The Liberal Democrats and their predecessors, the Alliance and the Liberal Party, provide telling examples (see this chapter's appendix). Not surprisingly, they have called for a *proportional representation* system to replace the SMD/plurality system.

Proportional representation (PR) *means that a political party is entitled to a share of legislative seats that is proportional to its share of the popular vote nationwide.* Thus a party that gets 30 percent of the vote would automatically get about 30 percent of the seats. If Britain were to adopt PR, it could probably count on a significant reordering of its governing processes. In all likelihood it would be more difficult for one party to win an absolute majority of seats in the House of Commons. Hung parliaments, in which no party enjoys a majority, would be more common. Single-party majoritarian governments—which have been the norm in Britain since World War II—would accordingly give way to majority coalition governments or minority govern-

ments. While a PR system may provide greater fairness in representing the voters in Parliament, it would also make governments more difficult to form and perhaps more internally divided and unstable as well. A more equitably representative Commons, in short, could increase the chances for governmental gridlock if coalition or parliamentary alliance partners cannot get along. (See chapter 9 for a fuller discussion of PR, coalition governments, and minority governments.)

If Britain had used the "party list" form of proportional representation in the 1997 elections, with a requirement that a party win at least 5 percent of the vote to earn any seats, the House of Commons would look quite different from its actual composition under SMD, as table 16.3 demonstrates. The 1997 vote under PR would have produced a hung parliament. To get elected prime minister, Tony Blair probably would have been compelled to cut a deal with the Liberal Democrats, forming either a majority coalition government (in which Labour and the Liberal Democrats would share cabinet posts) or a parliamentary alliance (in which the two parties would agree to form a voting majority in the Commons while Labour organized a minority government).

In sum, Britain's single-ballot, single member district/plurality electoral system is one of the main reasons why British politics tends to be dominated by the two largest parties. (This reality is consistent with *Duverger's law;* see chapter 11.) Many observers, in fact, describe Britain as having a two-party system. But other parties are also involved in the political process, indeed considerably more than in the United States. At times these other parties can play a vital decision-making role. As we have seen, Callaghan's government relied on sup-

TABLE 16.3

Distribution of Seats under SMD and PR Systems, 1997

Party	Actual Results under SMD/plurality			Under PR	
	% of Vote	Seats	% of Seats	Seats	% of Seats
Labour	43.3	419	63.6	300	45.5
Conservative	30.7	165	25.0	208	31.6
Liberal Democrats	16.8	46	7.0	113	17.2
Others	9.3	29	4.4	38	5.8

Source: David Butler and Dennis Kavanagh, *The British General Election of 1997* (New York: St. Martin's Press, 1997), p. 319.

port from the Liberals and non-English nationalist parties, while Major required the votes of Northern Irish MPs to get his legislation on the Maastricht Treaty passed and to survive a vote of confidence. Thus it would be inaccurate to describe Britain's party system as similar to the more pronouncedly two-party system that prevails in the United States. Accordingly, we describe the United Kingdom as having a *few-party* system: it has more than two parties, but fewer parties actively involved in the government than one would find in *multiparty* countries like Italy, where four or five parties have routinely joined in governing coalitions or parliamentary alliances. If Britain were to adopt PR, three or more parties would probably play a greater role in government than they do today.

In 1998, a commission studying the British electoral system recommended a reform under which 80 percent of the Commons would be elected in single-member districts, but under new rules that would ensure that the winner receives an absolute majority of votes cast, not just a plurality. The remaining 20 percent of Commons seats would be elected on a proportional representation basis in each of the United Kingdom's four regions. Blair promised a referendum on the voting system before any changes are made.[41]

Parliament

The State Opening of Parliament is one of the most resplendent events of British political life. Normally it takes place every autumn as Parliament begins a new session, but it also occurs when a new government assumes office soon after parliamentary elections. Garbed in flowing robes and bearing the Imperial State Crown, the Queen strides into the House of Lords, accompanied by peers of the realm in ornate attire. After she ascends her throne, the sergeant-at-arms knocks on the door of the House of Commons with a black rod and formally commands its members to join Her Majesty. With both houses assembled, the monarch then delivers the Queen's Speech, which outlines the legislative priorities her government will pursue in the coming session. While custom prescribes the ceremonial aspects of the occasion, the speech is written entirely by the government. Over the next several days its contents are sub-

jected to a vigorous debate as the two houses get down to business.

Commons: The Legislative Process   In order to become law, all bills must be passed by a majority of those present and voting in both the House of Commons and the House of Lords. A bill introduced in one house may not be considered in the other until it is passed; unlike the U.S. Congress, the two British houses do not consider similar legislation simultaneously. Members of both houses have the right to debate bills proposed by the government and, within certain limits, to propose legislation and amendments of their own. The procedures for voting on legislation are also roughly the same in both houses. As the democratically elected house, however, the Commons enjoys important prerogatives not accorded the Lords. These include above all the right to elect the government and hold it directly accountable, voting it out of office if a majority of the Commons no longer has confidence in the prime minister and cabinet.

Once installed in office, the government takes the initiative in drafting most of the legislation and shepherding it through Parliament. In Britain, as in most other parliamentary democracies, the legislative process ultimately rests on the principle of *party discipline.* That is, all the members of a party's parliamentary delegation are expected to

Elizabeth II delivers the "Queen's Speech" before Parliament.

vote together unanimously on most pieces of legislation. Should a government's support in the Commons fall below 50 percent on key bills, it could be forced to resign. Consequently, government "whips" stay in close contact with the party's parliamentary membership to ensure a bloc vote, especially on bills the government deems crucial, such as the budget or high-priority manifesto promises.[42]

The concept of party discipline applies no less to opposition parties than it does to the governing party. MPs who vote against their leadership's clearly enunciated position can be penalized, whether by being excluded from party meetings or, in the most extreme cases, by being denied the right to run for reelection as the party's official candidate. Occasionally a party's leaders will relax party discipline and allow their colleagues to vote as they wish on matters of conscience, such as abortion, the death penalty, or gun control. And it sometimes happens that members of Parliament will defy their leadership and vote against its legislation, a reality John Major frequently encountered. As a general rule, however, British legislators maintain party unanimity about 90 percent of the time, far more often than members of Congress. For reasons we've already noted, British legislators tend to be more dependent on their national party leadership than Congressional members are.

Once the government has readied a bill, it announces its topic to the Parliament in a first reading. The bill is then debated on the floor of the House in a second reading. Depending on the issue, debates in the House of Commons can be soporifically dull, with few members in attendance, or emotionally charged and bristling with partisan invective. The layout of the Commons lends itself to face-to-face exchanges between the governing party and the parties representing "Her Majesty's loyal opposition." The Speaker of the House presides from a raised chair, facing a center aisle. Since 1992 the Speaker has been Betty Boothroyd, a Labour MP whose position necessitates strict impartiality.[43] Five rows of green benches rise on either side of the aisle. The benches to the Speaker's right are occupied by the governing party, those to her left by the opposition parties. The seating arrangements are said to date from the sixteenth century, when the Com-

mons met in St. Stephen's chapel, seated in choir stalls located on opposite sides of the altar. A ceremonial rod, the mace, is visible on a table when the House is in session.

In the front rows of each side sit the parties' top leaders. The government's front benches are typically occupied by its ministers, at times led by the prime minister in person. The front benches of "parties opposite" are occupied by their respective leading personalities. Whenever the Conservative or Labour Party is in opposition, its front benches are taken up by members of the **shadow cabinet,** each of whom is assigned a portfolio corresponding to a cabinet post. (Other opposition parties are too small, and too unlikely to take power, to have their own shadow cabinets.) The leader of the chief opposition party is the shadow prime minister, whose main task in Parliament is to challenge the governing prime minister. The shadow defense minister keeps tabs on the government's minister of defense, the shadow foreign secretary "shadows" the cabinet's foreign secretary, and so on. Should a reversal of fortune bring the opposition party into power, the shadow cabinet will be ready to take office, its members having already immersed themselves in the details of their portfolios while in opposition. The U.S. Congress has no shadow cabinet.

Behind the front benches sit the **backbenchers,** ordinary MPs who have no spot in the government or shadow cabinet. Though they are fully cognizant of their duty to observe party discipline, they tend to be more than simply complacent followers of their party's leadership. Backbenchers have opinions of their own, and they must also consider the interests of the constituencies they represent. Government leaders must therefore conduct frequent consultations with their backbench supporters to make sure that bills under consideration meet with their approval. Opposition leaders must also seek to harmonize their policy positions with their backbenchers' wishes.[44]

After the first debate on a bill, a vote is taken. If a majority supports it, the bill then moves to a committee for detailed scrutiny. British parliamentary committees lack the authority, staff, and financial resources that U.S. Congressional committees possess. Most of Congress's work takes place in permanent committees with specific areas of competence, such as the Senate Foreign Relations Committee or the House Judiciary Committee. These committees may conduct open hearings on legislation or government policy, questioning outside experts or representatives of interest groups who seek to influence Congressional action. Some committees interrogate cabinet secretaries and other high-level executive branch officials on a regular basis. Congressional committees also have investigatory powers, with the right to subpoena witnesses and probe executive branch activities. By contrast, until the 1980s the House of Commons had no similar permanent committees. Instead it had "standing committees," which are ad hoc bodies formed to consider specific bills, disbanding once their work is done. Standing committees still play an important role in the parliamentary process, but since 1980 the Commons has also established more than a dozen "departmental select committees" patterned on the U.S. model, albeit with less intrusive investigatory powers.

It is in the standing committees that most bills are examined and amendments proposed. Government ministers and MPs loyal to the governing party's position generally have the upper hand in these committees. As a result, amendments to government-drafted bills are less frequent than in the U.S. Congress, where legislative proposals—even those with strong presidential endorsement—are often significantly amended before going to the floor for a final vote.

Once the bill comes out of committee in a form the government is willing to accept, it then goes before the whole House for a third reading and the decisive vote. If an initial voice vote is too close to call, a "division" takes place. Members of the house then divide into two lobbies located just outside the chamber. Those voting "aye" scurry into one lobby, those voting "no" into the other. No abstentions are recorded. The Speaker appoints "tellers" to count the votes as each MP files past them. Faithful to tradition, Parliament has resisted the use of electronic voting devices.

Throughout the legislative process, the government's priorities predominate. Well over 90 percent of all government-drafted bills are passed into law, often unamended. Even the most controversial measures are often passed quite rapidly. The Attlee government, for example, proposed

seventy-five bills in 1945–46. All of them passed in one year, including such sweeping measures as the creation of the National Health Service and the nationalization of several major companies. In 1997, the Blair government's bill to ban all handguns was enacted by the House of Commons shortly after it was introduced (see below). In the United States, by contrast, Congress has never passed universal health insurance legislation, and it took six years to pass the Brady bill, a handgun regulation measure considerably less comprehensive than Britain's total ban on such weapons. As a general rule, Britain's parliamentary system, resting on the fusion of government and parliamentary majority, is more efficient at passing legislation than is the U.S. separation-of-powers system. Especially when compared with periods of divided government in the United States, when the president represents one party and the Congressional majority the other, British lawmaking is considerably less susceptible to gridlock.

Individual members of the Commons and Lords have the right to propose their own legislation, called "private members' bills," but only as long as the primary purpose of these bills is not to spend money or raise taxes. The government must approve virtually all spending and taxation legislation. Most private members' bills die, especially if the government is not willing to support them. British MPs thus have considerably less latitude for independent legislative initiative than do members of Congress.[45]

BRITAIN BANS HANDGUNS

The tranquility of Dunblane, a town in Scotland, was suddenly shattered on March 13, 1996 when a local man known to be emotionally unstable entered a school carrying four legally owned handguns and opened fire. Sixteen children and a teacher lay dead before the gunman turned a .357-magnum revolver on himself. The public outcry that followed the massacre induced John Major's government to introduce legislation proposing a partial ban on handguns. Major's bill outlawed the in-home possession of handguns larger than .22-caliber—about 80 percent of all legally owned handguns—and imposed tight restrictions on storing handguns in gun clubs. Some Conservatives favored a more sweeping ban, but by applying pressures to observe party discipline the government secured the bill's passage in February 1997.

Labour Party leaders voted for the bill but argued that it did not go far enough. Labour's 1997 election manifesto pledged legislation to extend the ban to all handguns, and five weeks after the Blair government took office its bill was ready for a vote in the House of Commons. In addition to banning the possession of small-caliber handguns (.22-caliber or less) at home, Blair's bill tightened restrictions on the use of handguns for sport, making it illegal for British marksmanship teams to practice in Britain. (A special government dispensation would allow handgun competitions to take place in Britain in such international events as the Commonwealth Games or the Olympics.) Handgun owners would be compensated for their weapons at market value on turning them in to the authorities.

Proponents of the bill admitted that the total handgun ban might not prevent violent crime or stop another Dunblane tragedy from occurring. "But what we can do is everything we can to make it less likely," a Labour deputy argued. Another argument raised in the bill's favor was that Britain needed to resist the emergence of an American-style "gun culture" as evidenced in rising gun-related crime and violent movies. (Though the figure is growing, about 3,500 crimes involving handguns are committed each year in Britain, compared with about a million in the United States.) In addition, the bill's advocates could point to overwhelming popular support for Blair's proposal, with polls showing as many as 83 percent of the British public favoring the total ban. (In the United States, support for banning the production or ownership of firearms varies from 20 percent to 40 percent.)

Though Britain has no written or unwritten constitutional right to gun ownership, opponents of the bill argued that its restrictions on the use of handguns for sport barred activities that were previously considered legal. Several Conservative MPs questioned the wisdom of requiring British shooting teams to practice abroad. The bill's opponents also argued that the ban on handguns would probably do little to reduce violent crime, since only about 200,000 handguns were officially licensed by the government and their owners tended to be law-abiding citizens. Approximately one to two million handguns were thought to be held illegally, however, and most crimes were committed with illegally owned weapons. As a consequence, the bill's opponents contended, the handgun ban would punish average citizens but was not likely to induce criminal elements to turn in their weapons.

After these and other arguments for and against the bill were aired, the Commons passed the Blair government's bill on June 11, 1997 by a vote of 384–181. Both the Labour and Conservative parties allowed a free vote, permitting their members to vote their conscience instead of maintaining party discipline.[46]

Parliamentary Questions   One of the most distinctive features of British politics is the practice of allowing members of the Commons to address questions directly to the prime minister and other government ministers. More than 50,000 queries are submitted in writing by MPs in an average year, and most receive a written response. The most controversial inquiries, however, usually surface in open session during the periods devoted to the ministerial **question time.** By custom, the prime minister and other government ministers must appear before the Commons on a regular basis to answer questions posed by the members. Prime minister's question time now takes place once a week for thirty minutes. (Blair's predecessors took questions in two fifteen-minute sessions weekly.) The highly charged atmosphere surrounding the prime minister's grilling guarantees a packed chamber, with many members obliged to remain standing since the benches cannot accommodate the full House. Since 1989 the proceedings have been aired live on television.[47]

MPs who wish to ask a question must submit a written notice in advance of the session. The submissions are then drawn in lottery fashion to determine the order of questioning. Only about a dozen backbenchers will be able to raise a question in the allotted time, since the leaders of the two main opposition parties are given precedence in confronting the prime minister with several questions, often on different topics. The Speaker recognizes each questioner in turn, struggling to maintain order amidst the noisy bellowing and heckling that typically accompany a sharply worded question. After each question the prime minister rises to a lectern, the "despatch box," and delivers a response. Prime ministers do not know the content of the questions in advance, so their staff prepares them for a variety of likely queries. Still, no amount of preparation can substitute for the cool nerves, quick wit, and debating agility required to answer—or artfully evade—a succession of hostile queries addressed by opposition leaders and backbenchers.

Members of the prime minister's own party also ask questions, usually of a friendly nature designed to elicit a glowing account of the government's achievements. On occasion, however, party disunity shows through when backbenchers raise questions indicating their dissatisfaction with their leader's policies.

Margaret Thatcher said that no head of government is as accountable as the British prime minister, largely because of the rigors of question time. No U.S. president has ever had to withstand the grueling ordeal of open questioning in Congress. The U.S. Constitution requires only that the chief executive submit to Congress an annual "state of the union" report. George Washington and the Congress discussed a questioning procedure but it was never instituted.

PRIME MINISTER'S QUESTION TIME: BLAIR VERSUS HAGUE

[The following exchange between Prime Minister Blair and Conservative leader William Hague took place in the fall of 1998, on the eve of the release of a report by the Jenkins Commission on whether Britain should adopt proportional representation. Hague took aim at Labour Party divisions on the issue, including Blair's lack of enthusiasm for PR.]

Hague: Madame Speaker, the prime minister committed himself at the election to a referendum on the voting system in this Parliament. Is he still committed to it?

Blair: Madame Speaker, we have made it clear that we will state our position when the Jenkins Committee reports tomorrow.

[Laughter, shouts from Conservative benches]

Hague: What's wrong with yes or no? What is wrong with answering a question in this House with a yes or no? And doesn't that answer reveal that he's got himself into something that he doesn't know how to get out of? And he's now got the foreign secretary—wherever he is—passionately in favor of PR, and he's got the . . . leader of the House of Commons passionately against PR, and he's got himself passionately concerned to avoid answering the question . . .

[Shouts on both sides]

Speaker: Order! Order! Mr Hague . . . Order!

Blair: Madame Speaker, as indeed I said just a few days ago, we have always envisaged having a referendum in this Parliament, but we have also said that we will wait for the Jenkins Commission to see what precise system of voting change that they propose . . .

Hague: How is it . . . that he now *envisages* keeping a promise but he's going to wait to see whether he's going to do it? [Laughter] . . . Even he has to laugh at the silliness of his own answers! [Laughter; shouts] Isn't it time that he stop blundering into constitutional upheavals without knowing what they'll lead to? And aren't there higher priorities for any government, with jobs being lost every day, with hospitals facing a crisis this winter? These are the real people's priorities, and shouldn't he be dealing with those instead of trying to gerrymander a system that has served our country well?

[Shouts on both sides]

Blair: Madame Speaker . . . as for the people's priorities, since this government came to power, we've reduced the unemployment levels we inherited from the Conservatives! 400,000 extra jobs! [Shouts of approval from Labour benches] A hundred thousand children in class sizes that are reduced from where they were under the Conservative government! Under this government, after years of rising waiting lists [for hospital services], waiting lists *falling* under a Labour government! And under this government—thanks to the New Deal—140,000 young people off the dole! That is this government addressing the mess inherited from the Conservative government!

[Shouts of approval from Labour benches]

Other government ministers must also go before the Commons and answer questions, each appearing about once a month. Unlike the prime minister, who is responsible for all the government's policies, the other ministers are questioned primarily on their specific area of responsibility. Even so, the cut and thrust of the process can be unnerving. In 1983 a Conservative undersecretary suffered a collapse and died on the spot while being grilled by Labour MPs.

Votes of Confidence Perhaps the most compelling indication of the executive's accountability to Parliament resides in the Commons' right to remove the government in a vote of confidence. A confidence motion may be posed either by the opposition (as in 1979) or by the government itself, as in 1994 when Prime Minister Major sought to determine whether his government still enjoyed majority support. The procedure has been used quite sparingly, however. Since 1885 only two British governments have actually been defeated in a confidence vote. Both were Labour minority governments: Ramsay MacDonald's in 1924 and Callaghan's in 1979. This record is remarkable when compared with the more frequent defeats that governments in other democracies have suffered in confidence votes, and it testifies to the enduring stability of British politics.

Members of the House of Commons What types of people get elected to the House of Commons? A glance at the professions of the members elected in 1997 reveals some unmistakable patterns (see table 16.4). Conservative MPs come predominantly from the professions and the business sector, while the Labour delegation includes a large number of manual workers and teachers. Lawyers comprised 11 percent of the Commons in 1997, compared with 36 percent in the U.S. House

of Representatives and 55 percent in the Senate. A disproportionate number of MPs in the 1990s graduated from Oxford or Cambridge, though fewer than in the past. Until 1979 more than half the Conservatives in the Commons studied at the elite "Oxbridge" universities.

The representation of women has undergone slow but observable change over the years. In the seven Parliaments elected between 1964 and 1983, women held as few as nineteen seats and no more than 28 (2.9 percent and 4.3 percent of the total membership, respectively). In 1987 the figure jumped to forty-one members (6.3 percent) and edged a bit higher in 1992. In an effort to increase the number of women in Parliament, Labour in the 1990s adopted a candidate selection procedure aimed at electing women to half the party's seats in the Commons in future elections. In 1997, 121 women were elected (18.5 percent of the total), of whom 101 were in the Labour Party and fourteen were Conservative. (For a comparison of female representation in various legislatures around the world, see table 2.3 on page 42.)

The House of Commons has not been very representative of the United Kingdom's non-white minorities. Britain's history as a colonial power resulted in the creation of the **British Commonwealth of Nations** in 1919. The organization initially sought to regulate relations between the United Kingdom

TABLE 16.4

Professional Backgrounds of Members of House of Commons and U.S. House of Representatives			
UK House of Commons (elected 1997)		**U.S. House of Representatives (elected 1998)**	
Profession	% of Members	Profession	% of Members
Business	24	Law	36
Education	19	Business	36
Law	11	Public service and politics	24
Party employees	10	Education	19
Journalists, publishers	8	Agriculture	5
Manual workers	6	Real estate	4
Trade union officials	6	Medicine	3
Civil service and local government	2	Law enforcement	2
Farmers and laborers	1	Journalism	2
Medicine	9	Engineering	2
Other or no information available	12	Health care	1
		Technical, skilled labour	1
		Other	<1

Totals exceed 100 percent because some members reported more than one profession.
Source: Chronicle of Parliamentary Elections and Developments (Geneva: Inter-Parliamentary Union), vol. 31, p. 211, and vol. 32, p. 226.

and its colonies, but as Britain relinquished control over most of its dominions it evolved mainly into a forum for promoting economic cooperation. Today the Commonwealth has fifty-two members, most of which are independent states. Until the 1960s, residents of Commonwealth countries had the right to settle in the UK with full citizenship rights. But rising immigration in the 1950s and 1960s, especially from India, Pakistan, Africa, and the Caribbean, sparked resentment among large numbers of white Britons. In 1968 Wilson's Labour government restricted automatic entry rights only to Commonwealth residents who had a parent or grandparent born in the UK. Conservative governments under Heath and Thatcher imposed still more restrictions on immigration.

By the late 1990s there were some 3.6 million non-whites living in the UK, about 6 percent of the population. Between 1929 and 1987 there were no non-white members of the Commons. Non-white representation in the Commons rose only slightly in 1992 and 1997. Public opinion polls consistently show that large majorities of blacks, Asians, and even whites regard Britain as a racist society. Blair admitted before a hushed Commons in 1999 that "racism still exists in our society" after a report accused the London police and other British institutions of "institutional racism."

Members of the Commons are less well paid than their counterparts in other economically advanced democracies. They now earn about $80,000 a year, while members of the U.S. House of Representatives make a little over $140,000.

The House of Lords At the start of 1999 there were 1,294 members of the House of Lords. In accordance with centuries-old custom, the membership has traditionally included various bishops of the Church of England and so-called hereditary peers, who may bequeath their membership to an heir. In early 1999 there were twenty-six "Lords spiritual" and 759 hereditary peers (including sixteen women). Laws were passed in 1876 and 1958 permitting the creation of "life peers," who serve in the House of Lords only for the duration of their lifetime without the right to pass their membership on to their successors. Life peers are named by the queen on the advice of the prime minister, usually as a reward for exemplary achievement in political or professional life. In the first months of 1999 there were 500 life peers (eighty-seven women), including former prime ministers Harold Wilson and Margaret Thatcher and the composer Andrew Lloyd Webber.

Most members of the non-clerical "Lords temporal" are affiliated with a political party. In early 1999 there were 477 Conservatives, 176 Laborites, and sixty-eight Liberal Democrats. There were also more than three hundred "cross-benchers" who did not align themselves with any party. Attendance at Lords sessions has often been spotty; traditionally, only a minority of members would show up on an average business day, while a few "backwoodsmen," usually from remote parts of Britain, rarely participated at all.

In 1999, the Blair government prevailed upon the Lords to accept a drastic change: the ranks of hereditary peers were reduced to ninety-two members. Those permitted to stay on had to be elected by their colleagues in a special vote; the rest were required to relinquish their cherished parliamentary seats, abandoning to history a patrimony that in some cases stretched back to the fifteenth and sixteenth centuries. Additional reforms were expected the following year, subjecting the venerable House to radical restructuring and a diminished legislative role.

Until these changes take effect, however, the House of Lords at the start of the new millennium still has the right to vote on legislation passed by the Commons as well as to propose and pass legislation of its own. In the event that the two houses cannot agree on a particular piece of legislation, a compromise is usually worked out. But if no compromise can be reached, the Lords under current procedures may not kill a bill already passed by the Commons. Laws enacted in 1911 and 1949 permit the Lords only to delay the passage of legislation they do not accept, in some cases for no more than one month and in others for up to a year. If the Lords fail to pass the disputed bills within the allotted time, they automatically become law. The House of Commons has invoked this automatic enactment provision only once since 1949. How the next round of reforms would affect these procedures had yet to be determined in mid–2000.

While its legislative importance has progressively diminished, the House of Lords continues to stand at the apex of Britain's legal system. It is the supreme court of appeal for the entire country in civil cases, and for England, Wales, and Northern Ireland (not Scotland) in criminal cases. This juridical function is carried out by a special Appellate Committee, which consists of Lords who have had high-level judicial experience. It also includes the Lord Chancellor, who is the Speaker of the House of Lords. Most of the Appellate Committee's work is carried out by the so-called Lords of Appeal in Ordinary, or "Law Lords," a small group of life peers who have been specifically selected for membership because of their judicial expertise. They are the only salaried members of the House.

One of the most controversial cases before the Law Lords in recent years concerned Gen. Augusto Pinochet, the former military dictator of Chile. In 1998 Pinochet was in Britain for medical treatment when the Spanish government requested his extradition to stand trial for ordering the murder of political opponents in the 1970s and 1980s. Relatives of many of these victims now resided in Spain and other European countries. The Law Lords ruled in favor of extradition, but in early 2000 the Blair government pronounced Pinochet medically unfit to stand trial and allowed him to return to Chile.[48]

The Government

In a parliamentary system, the **government** refers to the chief decision-making body of the executive branch. It is used in the same way people refer to a president's administration in the United States. In Britain the government consists of about a hundred individuals, *all of whom must be members of Parliament.* Most are members of the House of Commons, but some also come from Lords.

The Cabinet The most prestigious twenty or so government ministers constitute the cabinet. Its leader is the prime minister, who also bears the titles of First Lord of the Treasury and Minister for the Civil Service. Most cabinet ministers are formally known as secretaries of state, though a few have more high-sounding titles such the Chancellor of the Exchequer, who is responsible for the budget, and the Lord Chancellor, who is the United Kingdom's chief justice. Each cabinet member assumes responsibility for a particular functional area, such as foreign affairs, health, or trade and industry, and most preside over a department of civil servants engaged in the bureaucratic tasks of policy planning and implementation within their respective domains. By tradition, two or three cabinet ministers are members of the House of Lords, but the prime minister and all others belong to the Commons.[49]

Although it is customary—and correct—to say that Britain's political system rests on the principle of parliamentary sovereignty, in actual practice the government tends to exercise more authoritative power than Parliament does. As noted earlier in this chapter, the government dominates the legislative process, taking the initiative in proposing most bills and invoking party discipline when they come up for a vote. While the Parliament may always hold the government accountable for its actions and retains the right to remove it from office in a confidence vote, on a day-to-day basis it is the government that steers the legislature's activities rather than the other way around.

The prime minister, moreover, steers the government. The head of government possesses an impressive array of powers, all of which derive from customary practice and are not codified in legal statutes. These include the right to appoint and dismiss other cabinet members and top bureaucratic officials, or change their positions, without having to secure Parliament's approval. (The U.S. president may appoint cabinet members and many other officials only with the Senate's approval.) Some observers have suggested that the British prime minister's powers amount to an "elective dictatorship." While there is more hyperbole than accuracy in this characterization, the fact remains that Britain's prime minister usually has more powers of initiative and greater control over the cabinet and the legislative process than do most heads of government, including the president of the United States.

Leadership styles have varied among Britain's prime ministers. Some have been dynamic leaders determined to seize the policy-making initiative and impose their preferences on their cabinet and party. Others have been more consensus oriented, seeking to balance and coordinate the diverse opinions expressed by other party leaders and the various groups and constituencies connected with their party. Thatcher and Blair are examples of dynamic initiators; Attlee and Major tended to be consensus seekers. Other prime ministers have combined aspects of both leadership styles to varying degrees.

British cabinets tend to meet far more regularly than do cabinets in the United States and to assume a greater collective role in debating and deciding government policy. U.S. presidents tend to conduct full cabinet meetings only rarely, preferring instead to meet with specific cabinet members on issues related to their particular areas of responsibility. In Britain the entire cabinet usually meets once a week. While its deliberations are secret, the memoirs of former ministers and occasional leaks to the press reveal that it is a lively institution whose leading members speak up on a range of issues, even those not immediately concerned with their particular functional responsibilities. Budget debates can be especially intense, as the various ministers defend their own department's claims to financial appropriations. The prime minister is not formally bound to follow the cabinet's preferences on any issue, but even a strong-willed leader like Thatcher or Blair cannot stray too far from the cabinet's wishes without risking a potential loss in leadership authority.

Once a decision is made and the prime minister enunciates it, the principle of *collective responsibility* demands that all cabinet minsters fall into line behind the policy in their public statements.

The Civil Service　Visitors to Parliament and No. 10 Downing Street soon find themselves on an imposing boulevard called **Whitehall.** Along its wide expanse are some of the most important ministries and agencies of the British government. Just as "No. 10" is synonymous with the prime minister and "Westminster" with Parliament, "Whitehall" connotes the country's bureaucracy, or *civil service.* From the Foreign Office to departments concerned with local government, Britain's civil service is a vital part of the executive branch, playing a critical role in the formulation and execution of the government's policies.

Like many bureaucracies, the civil service is both indispensable and maligned. No prime minister or cabinet official can do without the expertise of its professional cadres, many of whom have devoted their entire careers to specific policy issues. Quite often an experienced civil servant will know more about a policy matter than the cabinet minister or agency chief who supervises that office. Tensions sometimes arise when the prime minister or cabinet ministers are determined to pursue a policy initiative at variance with the preferences of the senior civil servants who advise them. Although they are expected to be politically neutral, following the government's lead in policy matters and dutifully carrying out its decisions, highly experienced civil servants may on occasion disagree with the government's policy and seek to alter its course, primarily through articulate persuasion rather than bureaucratic sabotage. (A witty television show called *Yes, Minister* has spoofed these stratagems.) As in many other bureaucracies around the world, Whitehall at times exhibits a preference for incremental decision making rather than bold new departures from existing policies. (On incremental decision making, see chapter 6.)

Conflicts of this type are relatively rare, as British civil servants typically make every effort to accommodate the wishes of the elected government. But they are more likely to occur in Britain than in the United States. The president has the right to fill some two to three thousand plum positions at the highest levels of the American federal bureaucracy, thus ensuring compliance with presidential policy preferences throughout the executive branch. The prime minister may fill far fewer. Career civil servants occupy most of the remaining posts. About seven hundred officials comprise the Higher Civil Service, a prestigious elite heavily populated with "Oxbridge" graduates, mostly males. These highly influential career civil servants owe their positions to professional accomplishment within the bureaucracy, including success in competitive mid-career examinations, rather than to political patronage. From their ranks a smaller group of about sixty to seventy are selected as "permanent secretaries," a uniquely British "elite of the elite" of career bureaucrats who work intimately with government ministers. While it is sometimes criticized as a bastion of elitism with little direct accountability to the population, Britain's civil service also wins wide praise as a model of bureaucratic professionalism and incorruptibility.[50]

Prime Minister Thatcher periodically encountered frictions with civil servants opposed to her policy agenda. She dealt with them by pressuring the civil service to fill high-level vacancies with personnel more attuned to her thinking. She also complained of the bureaucracy's size, reducing its personnel from more than 700,000 when she took office to about 560,000 by the time she left. By the late 1990s the civil service had fewer than 500,000 employees. Blair has been even more aggressive in bringing in his own network of policy advisors from outside the established civil service ranks.[51]

The Monarchy

Although its power has been whittled down to practically nothing and its prerogatives are largely ceremonial, Britain's thousand-year-old monarchy nevertheless fulfills an important function in British politics: it provides a living symbol of the long continuity of the country's history and the unshakeable durability of its people and institutions. In virtually every country in the world, political symbols retain an importance far exceeding their practical contribution to the routine processes of governing. The national flag, monuments to great leaders or fallen soldiers, historically noteworthy buildings—these and other treasures are deeply cherished as signposts of a people's common identity and collective history. Countries like Britain that have retained a ceremonial monarchy attach a high value to its symbolic significance.

In recent years the British royal family has suffered a number of widely publicized indignities and tragedies. The marital troubles of the queen's sons, Princes Charles and Andrew, were splashed across the tabloid media for the world to see. A fire ravaged part of Windsor Palace. In 1997 the popular Princess Diana was killed in an auto accident in Paris, not long after her divorce from Charles. And Queen Elizabeth II was personally subjected to criticism for her aloofness from the general public. Nevertheless, both the queen herself and the monarchy as an institution continue to enjoy wide popularity in Britain. By the end of the 1990s approximately 70 percent of Britons favored retaining the monarchy. Some would see this loyalty as evidence of continuing deference to aristo-

cratic authority in British political culture. The British aristocracy is not nearly as powerful as it was before World War II, however. Moreover, mounting criticism of the royal family's lavish lifestyle has led to reductions in the amount of public revenue devoted to its upkeep, and in 1992 the queen agreed to pay income taxes.[52]

While the monarch's principal duties remain largely ceremonial, the weight of tradition still holds a high place in British political life. Moreover, the distinction between the monarch's *formal legal* powers under Britain's unwritten constitution and her *actual decision-making* powers remains fuzzy in a number of areas. Constitutionally, the monarch is part of Parliament. She retains the formal legal authority to designate the prime minister, dissolve Parliament, and call parliamentary elections. No act of Parliament may take effect as law until the monarch signs a document of Royal Assent. The monarch is the nominal commander-in-chief of the armed forces and the head of the British Commonwealth.

In actual practice, the monarch is not a *voting member* of Parliament like the members of the Houses of Commons and Lords. Her right to designate the prime minister is limited by the majority party's right to recommend its preferred designee. Her rights to dissolve Parliament and call elections are formalities that are superseded by the prime minister's prerogatives. She cannot refuse her Royal Assent without creating a grave constitutional crisis. (Not since 1707 has a British monarch refused to assent to an act of Parliament.) In actuality it is the government that directs the armed forces in war and peace and sets policy on the Commonwealth.

Nevertheless, circumstances could arise in which the monarch's formal legal powers might assume real decision-making significance. Suppose, for example, that the British electorate returns a hung parliament, such as the one that would have resulted in 1997 if a system of proportional representation had been in effect (see table 16.3). What would happen if the leaders of the largest parties could not agree on a prime minister to be recommended to the monarch? In that case the queen or her successor might take the initiative in designating a member of Parliament—perhaps the leader of one of these parties—to try to form a government acceptable to the Commons. In all likelihood, the monarch would not take such action without a broad political consensus on its desirability. Still, if a PR electoral system were to be instituted in the United Kingdom, it could open up prospects for a practical decision-making role for the monarch in nominating a potential head of government for Parliament's approval.

POLITICAL ISSUES IN TODAY'S BRITAIN

Northern Ireland   The relationship between England and Ireland has been troubled for centuries. English monarchs launched their first attacks on the region in the twelfth century and reaffirmed their hegemony some two hundred years later in another wave of invasions. It was England's Protestant Reformation, however, that injected religious passions into what had previously been a power struggle for control over Ireland's territory and population. After breaking with the Vatican, Henry VIII declared himself King of Ireland. While the overwhelming majority of the Irish remained faithful to the Catholic Church, England in the early seventeenth century began uprooting Irish Catholic landowners in the northern province of Ulster and replaced them with English and Scottish Protestants. In 1801, under English pressure, Ireland joined England and Scotland in the United Kingdom. (Scotland had already joined with England in forming the United Kingdom in 1707.)

Former U.S. Senator and Northern Ireland mediator George Mitchell (seated, center) with Nobel Peace Prize recipient John Hume (left), chairman of the Northern Ireland peace talks, and Sinn Fein Leader Gerry Adams.

Irish opposition to English domination remained intense, especially among Catholics. While famine produced mass starvation and drove millions to the United States starting in the mid-nineteenth century, a succession of insurrections fueled an increasingly violent independence movement. On Easter Monday 1916, an uprising by Irish nationalists in Dublin and elsewhere was put down with heavy casualties on both sides. By 1920 a veritable war was under way between England and Ireland, with advocates of independence flocking to such groups as Sinn Fein (shin fain), founded in 1917, and the Irish Republican Army (IRA), a militia organized in 1919. Finally in 1922, the British government permitted the creation of a self-governing Irish Free State in southern Ireland, where Catholics had a majority. Six Ulster counties with a Protestant majority remained in the United Kingdom and became known as Northern Ireland. In 1949 the Irish Free State changed its name to the Republic of Ireland (also known simply as Ireland).[53]

Tensions between Protestants and Catholics in Northern Ireland continued without letup. In 1969 they erupted into violence, prompting Prime Minister Callaghan to authorize British troops to restore calm. Hopes for a speedy truce proved illusory. For much of the next three decades, cities like Belfast and Derry were carved into barricaded camps, with pitched battles and random violence commonplace. Occasionally the conflict spilled over into London and other parts of England as bombings and assassination attempts occurred with frightening unpredictability. In 1972 the British government suspended Northern Ireland's local legislature and imposed direct rule on the region. Meanwhile, the population balance shifted. Though Catholics constituted 43 percent of Northern Ireland's 1.6 million people, they acquired a majority in four of the region's six counties.

It was not until the late 1990s that widespread yearnings for peace induced Protestant and Catholic leaders to come to terms. More than 3,200 people had been killed since 1969. A twenty-one month negotiation process, chaired by U.S. Ambassador George J. Mitchell and strongly promoted by President Clinton, culminated on April 10, 1998, with a draft accord. The so-called Good Friday agreement won the endorsement of more than 71 percent of voters in Northern Ireland and 94 percent in Ireland when put to a referendum the following month. The accord created a Northern Ireland Assembly to take over local affairs, replacing the British government's direct rule. It also contained a vaguely worded provision requiring Protestant and Catholic paramilitary groups to give up their weapons.

Disagreements over the accord's implementation imposed new delays on the peace process, and in the fall of 1999 Mitchell (who had since retired as ambassador) returned to Northern Ireland to bring the parties back to the negotiating table. The impasse was quickly broken, and in late November a twelve-member cabinet was formed to manage Northern Ireland's local affairs. The new government consisted equally of Protestant and Catholic leaders, some of whom were former guerilla fighters and implacable enemies. It is responsible to the 108-member Assembly seated in Stormont, just outside Belfast. On December 2, the British government formally declared the devolution of local authority from the House of Commons to Northern Ireland's Assembly and government. While remaining in the United Kingdom, Northern Ireland assumed responsibility for local schools, public transportation, finance, and other matters. The central government in London retained its overall authority over taxation, foreign policy, and other national issues. On the same day, the Republic of Ireland renounced the articles of its constitution claiming jurisdiction over Northern Ireland's six counties and agreed that only the people of Northern Ireland may decide if they wish to leave the UK and merge with the Republic of Ireland. It is unlikely that such a referendum will occur anytime soon.

Nor is it likely that good will between the former combatants will come about easily. In February 2000, the British government temporarily suspended the new Northern Irish government when IRA hard-liners delayed handing over their weapons, as required by the accords, and Protestant hard-liners threatened to back out. Several months later the weapons issue edged closer to resolution. Though Ireland's wars of religion might be nearing their end, many years will have to pass before ancient enemies can establish mutual trust.[54]

Devolution in Wales and Scotland   Like Ireland, Wales and Scotland were also conquered and

forced to unite with England. The English subdued Wales at the end of the thirteenth century and proclaimed a formal union in 1536. Scotland was also invaded in the late thirteenth century, but it took several centuries marked by sporadic fighting before it was officially united with England. Nearly forty years after this merger took place, a Scottish uprising led by "Bonnie Prince Charlie" of the royal House of Stuart was decisively defeated by English forces in 1746.

Once incorporated under the English crown and Parliament, Wales and Scotland became part of Britain's unitary state. By the 1960s, however, rising national sentiment in both areas provoked demands for greater autonomy from London and the creation of locally responsible legislative and executive bodies. In Scotland there were calls by leaders of the Scottish National Party for outright independence. After the failure of previous governments to devolve decision-making authority from the center to local organs, the Blair government presented the people of Scotland and Wales with new devolution proposals. In September 1997 nearly 75 percent of Scottish voters approved the plan, which called for the establishment of a Scottish legislature in 2000 along with a chief executive known as the first minister. The 129-member unicameral assembly, elected by proportional representation, is empowered to make laws in such areas as education, health care, housing, criminal justice, and transportation and possesses limited powers to vary tax rates. In elections to the Scottish legislature held in 1999, the Labour Party won fifty-six seats and formed the new administration in coalition with the Liberals. The pro-independence Scottish National Party finished second with thirty-five seats, a result with potentially major consequences for Scotland's future status in the United Kingdom should sentiment favoring independence rise.

Shortly after the referendum in Scotland, Welsh voters gave a less enthusiastic endorsement to Blair's devolution plans for Wales. Slightly more than 50 percent approved the creation of a Welsh legislature, albeit one with less power than its Scottish counterpart. The new assembly will be able to affect the British government's spending priorities in Wales, however. Popular pressures for more autonomy are not as strong in Wales as in Scotland, though the Welsh language enjoys equal legal status with English. In elections held in 1999 to the sixty-seat assembly, Labour won twenty-eight seats and Plaid Cymru, the nationalist party, won seventeen.

In another devolution measure, Blair won approval from the voters of London for the establishment of its first-ever elected mayor. (London's elected city council had been abolished under the Thatcher government.) The elections took place in 2000.

The Economy   After slightly more than two years in office, the Blair government could boast that the nation's economy was growing at a modest rate (about 1 percent in 1999) while unemployment (at about 6 percent) and inflation (a shade over 2 percent) remained low. It could also claim it had kept its election manifesto promises in a number of economic and social policy areas. Its legislative achievements included new spending measures for education, child care, and the National Health Service; a windfall utilities tax to fund employment programs for youth and the long-term unemployed; a cut in corporation taxes; and various anti-crime measures. To help defray the government's higher education expenses, students attending Oxford, Cambridge, and other publicly funded institutions were required to pay tuition in 1999 for the first time. Blair's initial efforts to trim welfare spending in several categories ran into opposition among left-leaning Labour MPs but passed with Conservative support. Blair's government is banking on expanded technology investment to spur future growth.

HEALTH CARE IN THE UK: THE NATIONAL HEALTH SERVICE

Created in 1948, the **National Health Service (NHS)** provides free medical and dental care for all people residing in the UK, though fees are charged for some procedures and people must pay for medications not regarded as essential to personal health (such as Viagra). The NHS is funded largely out of general government revenues. Approximately 85 percent of Britons make use of it. Private medical insurance and treatment remain available for those wishing to pay for it, and by the late 1990s about 12 percent of the population had private health insurance.

The NHS includes a large network of hospitals and clinics organized under local authorities. Doctors and dentists are self-employed and are paid a government-set fee each year for each patient who registers with them. With health care consuming about one-eighth of total government expenditures annually, NHS officials are under considerable pressure to keep costs down. Health care is consequently rationed. Many patients must wait up to a year or more for surgery for non-life-threatening maladies, and certain local NHS authorities refuse to provide free cosmetic surgery or procedures to treat a growing list of "non-medical" problems such as varicose veins or impacted wisdom teeth. Moreover, the British government tends to spend proportionately less on health care than do certain other economically advanced countries. Between 1990 and 1997 it spent an average of 5.7 percent of its GDP on health, most of it on the NHS. In the same period the Japanese government spent the same percentage, the U.S. government spent 6.6 percent of its GDP on health, France 7.7 percent, and Germany 8.1 percent. When private spending on health is added to public spending, Britain in the mid-1990s spent $1,300 per capita on health care while other countries in its economic category spent an average of $2,071, with the United States spending $3,830. Costs are expected to soar, however, as Britain's population ages and more expensive treatments become available.

Though the NHS remains popular in principle, public dissatisfaction with the care it provides is rising. In its first two years in office, the Blair government raised NHS funding about 1 percent but cut spending for some items and retained various market elements introduced by the Conservatives.[55]

Europe   By the late 1990s, about a third of all British legislation and 70 percent of its business law were decided by the European Union in Brussels, not by Parliament. With opinion surveys revealing widespread opposition to the euro as well as considerable public ignorance about the EU and the lowest levels of attachment to Europe among all the EU countries, the Blair government moved slowly but unmistakably in the direction of closer cooperation with Britain's European partners. (Polls also revealed that more than 40 percent of the English—a hefty plurality—believe that the EU will have more influence over their lives by 2020 than Parliament or local government organs will.)[56] After confirming that the United Kingdom would not adopt the euro until sometime around 2002, and only after a referendum, Blair's cabinet began taking preparatory steps aimed at readying Britain for eventual adoption of the new European currency.[57] It also formally affirmed Britain's adherence to EU human rights law, an action that effectively gives the country a bill of rights whose provisions supersede traditional British law. In the 1999 elections to the European Parliament, conducted under proportional representation, the Conservatives—with an outspokenly Euroskeptic message—outpolled Labour by nearly 8 percent.

For their part, the Conservatives remained bitterly divided on European issues. Party chief William Hague delivered blistering attacks on Blair's European policy, but his views were in turn rejected by Conservative political figures like Kenneth Clarke, who favor closer ties with the EU and the adoption of the euro. As in years past, one of the central objections of Euroskeptics to closer European integration was the fear that Britain's revered parliamentary traditions could be overwhelmed by the EU bureaucracy in Brussels, resulting in a "democratic deficit."[58]

BRITAIN AND THE FOUR FACES OF DEMOCRACY

Along with the United States, the United Kingdom is one of the modern world's two oldest continuously functioning democracies. Its success reflects the evolutionary development, over more than three hundred years, of the four faces of democracy we enumerated in chapter 8. And yet it was only in the twentieth century that the British people acquired the full rights of popular sovereignty (Face I) through the extension of the franchise to all adult men and women. Though a wide range of civil rights and liberties (Face II) have been afforded the citizenry through the gradual development of legal practices and understandings, there is still no codified British bill of rights.

While compromise and cooperation have long been defining values of British political culture, a tradition whose roots go back to the aristocracy's sense of *noblesse oblige* ("nobility obliges"), the struggle to inculcate democratic values in the entire population goes on. Though there have been commendable strides in the direction of religious and ethnic

tolerance and in the development of a multiracial society on British soil, the inclusion of non-whites in the political process is far from complete, historic tensions between the English and the Scots and Welsh persist, and the fires of religious hatred in Northern Ireland are just beginning to show signs of dying down. Few countries in the world, however, have mastered the challenges of building a universally shared democratic value system (Face III).

It is with respect to economic democracy (Face IV) that Britain has charted a pioneering effort among the world's democracies. After World War II it created one of the most extensive welfare states ever seen, the product of the Labour Party's concept of socialism and the Conservative Party's initial acceptance of consensus politics. Under Margaret Thatcher, the Conservatives veered decisively in the direction of market capitalism. But this rightward turn did not entirely abandon welfarist policies. It also reflected, at least to some extent, Thatcher's personal conception of a people's capitalism that would bring the privileges of home ownership and stock acquisition to a broader segment of the populace, including the working class. These two alternative notions of economic democracy—the welfarist and the capitalist—have perhaps been debated more explicitly in Britain than in most democracies, including the United States.

Despite its long lineage, British democracy is still evolving as the new millennium arrives. With change on the horizon or under discussion with respect to the electoral system, devolution, civil rights, the currency, and other matters, the United Kingdom continues to forge new directions in areas of vital importance to the functioning, and at times the very definition, of democracy. The readiness of the British people to meet these challenges while adhering to their time-tested devotion to the rule of law offers vivid testimony to democracy's capacity for adaptation and creative development and to its vitality as an ever-ripening political idea.

KEY TERMS AND NAMES
(Underlined in the text)

Third way
Devolution
Divine right of kings
Sovereign monarchy (absolutism)

Magna Carta
House of Lords
House of Commons
Glorious Revolution of 1688
John Major
Constitutional monarchy
Westminster system
Conservatives (Tories)
Labour Party
Margaret Thatcher
Tony Blair
MP
Shadow cabinet
Backbenchers
Question time
British Commonwealth of Nations
Government
Whitehall
National Health Service

FOR DISCUSSION: WHAT WOULD YOU DO?

1. If you were a British citizen, to which party would you belong? Would you be a dues-paying party activist and regularly attend party meetings?
2. Would you have favored the 1997 legislation to ban all handguns?

3. Would you favor the National Health Service? Would you be willing to pay higher taxes to expand it?
4. If you were asked to choose in a referendum between retaining the current electoral system or adopting proportional representation, how would you vote?

FOR FURTHER READING

In addition to the titles in the notes, consult the following:

Robert Blackburn, *The Electoral System in Britain* (New York: St. Martin's Press, 1995).

Vernon Bogdanor, *Politics and the Constitution* (Aldershot, UK: Dartmouth, 1996).

Eric Evans, *Thatcher and Thatcherism* (New York: Routledge, 1997).

Leonard Freedman, *Politics and Policy in Britain* (White Plains, N.Y. Longman, 1996).

Philip Giddings and Gavin Drewry, eds., *Westminster and Europe* (New York: St. Martin's Press, 1996).

W. H. Greenleaf, *The British Political Tradition*, 2 vols. (London: Methuen, 1983).

David Judge, *The Parliamentary State* (London: Sage, 1993).

Joel Krieger, *British Politics in the Global Age* (Oxford; Oxford University Press, 1999).

Paul Mitchell and Rick Wilford, eds., *Politics in Northern Ireland* (Boulder, Colo.: Westview, 1999).

APPENDIX

House of Commons Elections, 1945–97							
	Percentage of Popular Vote				Percentage of Seats		
	Conservatives	Labour	Liberals, Alliance, Lib. Dems	Others	Conservatives	Labour	Libs., Alliance, Lib. Dems	Others
1945	39.8	48.3	9.1	2.7	33.3	61.4	1.9	3.4
1950	43.5	46.1	9.1	1.3	47.8	50.4	1.4	0.3
1951	48.0	48.8	2.5	0.7	51.4	47.2	1.0	0.5
1955	49.7	46.4	2.5	1.1	54.8	44.0	1.0	0.3
1959	49.4	43.8	5.9	1.0	57.9	41.0	1.0	0.2
1964	43.4	44.1	11.2	1.3	48.3	50.3	1.4	—
1966	41.9	47.9	8.5	1.6	40.2	57.6	1.9	0.3
1970	46.4	43.0	7.5	3.1	52.4	45.7	1.0	1.0
1974 (Feb.)	37.8	37.1	19.3	5.8	46.8	47.4	2.2	3.6
1974 (Oct.)	35.8	39.2	18.3	6.7	43.6	50.2	2.1	4.1
1979	43.9	37.0	13.8	5.3	53.4	42.4	1.7	2.5
1983	42.4	27.6	25.4	4.6	61.1	32.2	3.5	3.5
1987	42.3	30.8	22.6	4.6	57.9	35.2	3.4	3.5
1992	41.9	34.4	17.8	5.8	51.6	41.6	3.1	3.7
1997	30.7	43.3	16.8	9.3	25.0	63.4	7.0	4.4

Kenneth O. Morgan, ed., *The Oxford History of Britain* (Oxford: Oxford University Press, 1988).

Philip Norton, *The British Polity*, 3d ed. (New York: Longman, 1994).

Martin Pugh, *State and Society: British Political and Social History, 1870–1992* (New York: Arnold, 1994).

Joseph Ruane and Jennifer Todd, *The Dynamics of Conflict in Northern Ireland* (Cambridge: Cambridge University Press, 1996).

Stephen P. Savage and Lynton Robins, eds., *Public Policy Under Thatcher* (New York: St. Martin's Press, 1990).

Anthony Seldon and Stuart Ball, eds., *Conservative Century* (New York: Oxford University Press, 1994).

Paul Silk and Rhodri Walters, *How Parliament Works*, 3d ed. (London: Longman, 1995).

Joel D. Wolfe, *Power and Privatization* (New York: St. Martin's Press, 1996).

John W. Young, *Britain and the World in the Twentieth Century* (New York: Arnold, 1994).

Nikolaos Zahariadis, *Markets, States, and Public Policy: Privatization in Britain and France* (Ann Arbor: University of Michigan Press, 1995).

WEBSITES

General websites with links to a wide variety of British topics include <www.britain-info.org>, <www.opengovernment.gov>, <www.ukpol.co.uk>, and <www.searchuk.com>. Parliament can be accessed at <www.parliament.uk>. Information on prime minister's question time, along with links to the main parties, can be obtained via <www.cspan.org>. The Labour Party's website is <www.labour.org.uk>, and the Conservatives' is <www.conservative-party.org.uk>. Hansard's transcripts of parliamentary debates can be accessed at <www.parliament.the-stationary-office.co.uk/pa/cm>.

NOTES

1. Paul Anderson and Nyta Mann, *Safety First: The Making of New Labour* (London: Granta, 1997).

2. Tony Blair, *The Third Way* (London: Fabian Society, 1998); Anthony Giddens, *The Third Way: The Renewal of Social Democracy* (Cambridge, UK: Polity Press, 1999).

3. R. G. Davies and J. H. Denton, eds., *The English Parliament in the Middle Ages* (Manchester: Manchester University Press, 1981); Conrad Russell, *The Crisis of Parliaments* (London: Oxford University Press,

1971). King Charles I's determination to rule without Parliament in the 1630s provoked intense opposition and helped precipitate the Civil Wars of the 1640s and his own execution in 1649.

4. Stuart E. Prall, *The Bloodless Revolution: England 1688* (Madison: University of Wisconsin Press, 1985).

5. One historian notes that in the years between 1832 and 1867 Britain changed "from a system in which the Crown was the dominant influence in Parliament to a system in which the mass electorate began increasingly to call the tune." See Robert Blake, *Disraeli* (New York: St. Martin's Press, 1967), 259. Though the monarch today still formally names the prime minister, by 1834 the monarch could no longer appoint a head of government unacceptable to the Commons majority.

6. For a classic description of Britain's governmental system in the latter half of the nineteenth century, with comparisons with the United States, see Walter Bagehot, *The English Constitution* (Brighton, UK: Sussex Academic Press, 1997).

7. See Dick Leonard, *Elections in Britain Today: A Guide for Voters and Students*, 3d ed. (New York: St. Martin's Press, 1996), 12–23. On the suffragettes, see George Klosko and Margaret G. Klosko, *The Struggle for Women's Rights* (Upper Saddle River, N.J.: Prentice Hall, 1999); Barbara Winslow, *Sylvia Pankhurst* (New York: St. Martin's Press, 1996); and Jo Vellacott, *From Liberal to Labour with Women's Suffrage: The Story of Catherine Marshall* (Montreal: McGill-Queen's University Press, 1993).

8. Liah Greenfeld, *Nationalism: Five Roads to Modernity* (Cambridge, Mass.: Harvard University Press, 1992), ch. 1.

9. Gabriel Almond and Sidney Verba, *The Civic Culture* (Boston: Little, Brown, 1963). On the decline of deferential attitudes in British political culture, see Dennis Kavanaugh, "Political Culture in Great Britain: The Decline of the Civic Culture," in Gabriel A. Almond and Sidney Verba, eds., *The Civic Culture Revisited* (Boston: Little, Brown, 1980), 124–76.

10. Barrington Moore, *Social Origins of Dictatorship and Democracy: Lord and Peasant in the Making of the Modern World* (Boston: Beacon, 1966).

11. Eric Hobsbawm, *Industry and Empire* (London: Penguin Books, 1990); E. P. Thompson, *The Making of the English Working Class* (New York: Pantheon, 1964).

12. Originally, a "tory" was an Irish Catholic outlaw. In the seventeenth century the term was abusively applied by opponents of King James II to those who supported his rule and the claims of his Catholic heirs to the throne on the grounds of inherited legitimacy. A "whig" (or "whiggamore") was a Scottish

horse thief. It was applied to Scottish Presbyterians and others who wanted Parliament to prevent James, a Catholic, from succeeding to the throne, even though he was the legitimate heir. Thus the Tories became identified initially with the traditional principle of royal inheritance and the Whigs with the principle of Parliament's right to alter the succession.

13. For biographies that provide extensive accounts of the times, see Blake, *Disraeli*; Stanley Weintraub, *Disraeli: A Biography* (New York: Truman Talley/Dutton, 1993); Roy Jenkins, *Gladstone: A Biography* (New York: Random House, 1997); and Philip Magnus, *Gladstone* (New York: E. P. Dutton, 1964).

14. The Webbs were cofounders of the London School of Economics and Politics. See Norman and Jeanne MacKenzie, *The Fabians* (New York: Simon and Schuster, 1977).

15. Henry Pelling and Alastair Reed, *A Short History of the Labour Party*, 11th ed. (New York: St. Martin's Press, 1996); Stanley Pierson, *Marxism and the Origins of British Socialism* (Ithaca, N.Y.: Cornell University Press, 1973).

16. Kenneth O. Morgan, *Labour in Power 1945–1951* (Oxford: Oxford University Press, 1986); Jim Fyrth, ed., *Labour's High Noon: The Government and the Economy 1945–51* (London: Lawrence and Wishart, 1993).

17. Samuel Beer, *British Politics in the Collectivist Age* (New York: Vintage Books, 1969).

18. The United States charged a 2 percent interest rate on the loan and attached various trade and currency conditions. Britain paid back the loan ahead of schedule. See Morgan, *Labour in Power*, 144–51.

19. Harold Wilson, *A Personal Record: The Labour Government 1964–1970* (Boston: Little, Brown, 1971) and *The Governance of Britain* (New York: Harper and Row, 1976); Ben Pimlott, *Harold Wilson* (New York: HarperCollins, 1991).

20. Howard R. Penniman, ed., *Britain at the Polls 1979* (Washington, D.C.: American Enterprise Institute, 1981); Richard Coopey and Nicholas Woodward, eds., *Britain in the 1970s: The Troubled Economy* (London: University College of London, 1996).

21. For a cultural explanation of Britain's economic decline in these years, see Martin J. Wiener, *English Culture and the Decline of the Industrial Spirit, 1850–1980* (Cambridge: Cambridge University Press, 1981).

22. Callaghan was deserted by an erstwhile supporter from a Northern Ireland Catholic party and lost the vote of a dying Labour member who was too ill to take part. For his account, see James Callaghan, *Time and Chance* (London: Collins, 1987), 558–63.

23. In 1979 the bottom tenth of the population shared 4.1 percent of the national income while the top tenth got 20 percent of it. By 1991 the bottom tenth's share was only 2.5 percent while the top tenth's share had grown to 26 percent. Income inequality grew faster in the United Kingdom in the 1980s than in any other economically advanced democracy except New Zealand.

24. Margaret Thatcher, *The Path to Power* (New York: HarperCollins, 1995) and *The Downing Street Years* (New York: HarperCollins, 1993); Hugo Young, *The Iron Lady* (New York: Farrar, Strauss, and Giroux, 1989); Dennis Kavanagh, *Thatcherism and British Politics*, 2d ed. (New York: Oxford University Press, 1990); Christopher Johnson, *The Economy Under Mrs. Thatcher, 1979–1990* (London: Penguin, 1991); David Butler, Andrew Adonis, and Tony Travers, *Failure in British Government: The Politics of the Poll Tax* (New York: Oxford University Press, 1994).

25. Anthony Seldon, *Major: A Political Life* (London: Weidenfeld and Nicolson, 1997). Major declared, "I am utterly committed to the NHS." (*The Economist*, January 21, 1995). Chancellor of the Exchequer Kenneth Clarke stated, "This government will never take part in any attempt to dismantle the welfare state. . . . We want to see a better welfare state." (*Financial Times*, December 4/5, 1993).

26. Anthony King et al., *Britain at the Polls 1992* (Chatham, N.J.: Chatham House Publishers, 1993).

27. For Major's own account, see *John Major: The Autobiography* (London: HarperCollins, 1999).

28. The EU banned the sale of British beef in March 1996 after an outbreak in the United Kingdom of bovine spongiform encephalopathy, a disease fatal to cows and potentially fatal to humans. Over the next five years British farmers were required to destroy nearly 3 million head of cattle and lost some $5 billion in sales. EU agriculture ministers voted in November 1998 to lift the ban.

29. Martin Holmes, ed., *The Eurosceptical Reader* (New York: St. Martin's Press, 1996).

30. After Major pulled Britain out of the ERM in 1992, the pound depreciated in value relative to other currencies. This devaluation made it cheaper for foreigners to buy British pounds as well as British goods, thus boosting sales of British exports abroad. In addition, Britain's central bank—the Bank of England—enabled commercial banks to reduce their interest rates, making it easier for businesses and consumers to borrow money. The lower interest rates, which fell from an average of 10.5 percent in 1992 to 6 percent by 1997, stimulated business expansion as well as consumer purchases of cars,

housing, and other goods and services. Meanwhile, inflation remained at 3.5 percent or below in 1992–97 while unemployment dropped from around 10 percent to 6.5 percent.

31. John Rentoul, *Tony Blair* (London: Little, Brown, 1995); Jon Sopel, *Tony Blair: The Modernizer* (London: Bantam, 1995).

32. Peter G. J. Pulzer, *Political Representation and Elections in Britain,* 3d ed. (London: Allen and Unwin, 1975), 102.

33. Eric A. Nordlinger, *The Working-Class Tories* (Berkeley: University of California Press, 1967).

34. For a confirmation of this conclusion, see John Bartle, "Left-Right Position Matters, But Does Social Class? Causal Models of the 1992 British General Election," *British Journal of Political Science* 28 (1998): 501–29.

35. When asked to identify their profession, respondents identified themselves as follows:

	1964 (%)	1992 (%)
Group 1 Higher Salariat (upper-grade professionals)	7.0	11.6
Group 2 Lower Salariat (junior-grade professionals)	12.3	16.3
Group 3 Routine clerical	16.5	24.2
Group 4 Petty bourgeoisie (small business owners)	6.6	7.1
Group 5 Foremen and technicians	7.6	4.8
Group 6 Skilled manual workers	17.8	10.9
Group 7 Unskilled manual workers	32.4	25.1

Note the rise in the middle-class categories (Groups 1–4) and the decline in working-class categories (Groups 5–7). This categorization of professions was devised by James H. Goldthorpe, *Social Mobility and Class Structure in Modern Britain,* 2d ed. (Oxford: Clarendon Press, 1980). The figures are reported in Andrew Adonis and Stephen Pollard, *A Class Act* (London: Penguin, 1998), 8.

36. Born in 1961, Hague chaired his local Young Conservatives organization at age sixteen and was invited to address a Conservative national conference while still in his teens. Following in the footsteps of Margaret Thatcher, he became president of the Oxford University Conservative Association several years later. He was also president of the Oxford Union, the university's prestigious debating society, and studied at the INSEAD business school in France. After working

in the private sector in the 1980s, he was elected to Parliament from Richmond in a 1989 by-election. After a succession of junior-level positions with the Chancellor of the Exchequer and the department responsible for social security and the disabled, he was appointed to John Major's cabinet in 1995 with responsibility for Wales. Following the Conservatives' defeat and Major's resignation in 1997, he was elected leader of the Conservative Party.

37. Under current procedures this election is supposed to take place annually, though Thatcher did not have any challengers until 1989. If the election is contested, the incumbent or a challenger can win on the first ballot only by getting an overall majority *and* by outpolling the runner-up by at least 15 percent of all the members of the parliamentary party. Thatcher failed to clear this hurdle in 1990 but Major managed it when he insisted on a reelection vote in 1995. On the second ballot an absolute majority suffices to win. Major was elected on the second ballot in 1990 and Hague was elected on the third ballot in 1997.

38. Paul Whitely, Patrick Seyd, and Jeremy Richardson, *True Blues: The Politics of Conservative Party Membership* (Oxford: Clarendon Press, 1994); David Butler and Dennis Kavanagh, *The British General Election of 1997* (New York: St. Martin's Press, 1997), 26.

39. Leonard, *Elections in Britain Today,* 97.

40. *The Economist,* October 17, 1998.

41. *The Economist,* October 31, 1998.

42. The term "whip" has two meanings. In addition to referring to the persons charged with keeping a party's legislative delegation in line, a whip also refers to the message sent by the party leadership to its MPs indicating the relative importance it attaches to bills coming up for a vote. Bills of relatively minor importance are underlined once; more significant bills are underlined twice or three times. MPs who vote against a "three-line whip" risk severe disciplinary action by the party leadership.

43. By tradition, the Speaker is an MP who is acceptable to all the major parties and observes impartiality in conducting Commons meetings. An inter-party agreement allows the Speaker to run for reelection to the Commons without opposition. The Speaker may vote only to break a tie.

44. For a detailed study of the various roles played by MPs, see Donald D. Searing, *Westminster's World* (Cambridge, Mass.: Harvard University Press, 1994).

45. Between 1987 and 1992, only sixty-five private members' bills passed while 519 failed.

46. *Washington Post,* October 17, 1996 and June 12, 1997. For the text of the debate in the House of Commons on Blair's bill on June 11, 1997, go to <www.parliament.the-stationary-office.co.uk/pa/cm>.

47. A taped broadcast of prime minister's question time is aired weekly in the United States by the C-SPAN network.

48. Two panels of Law Lords took up the case. The first panel ruled by three to two that murder and torture by governments are crimes under international law, thus rejecting Pinochet's claim that he was immune from prosecution for deeds he committed while serving as Chile's head of state. That ruling was nullified after it turned out that one of the judges had ties to Amnesty International, which was involved in the case against Pinochet. A second panel of seven different Law Lords later restricted Pinochet's liability to crimes committed after 1988, when the International Torture Convention became binding on the United Kingdom, Spain, and Chile. Following the second ruling, a British magistrate ruled that Pinochet could be extradited to Spain for prosecution. See *The Economist,* March 27, 1999. The government's decision to allow Pinochet to return home was based on an evaluation by a panel of physicians.

49. When Sir Alec Douglas-Home became prime minister in 1963 he was a member of the House of Lords. He thereupon renounced his title and subsequently won a seat in Commons in a by-election.

50. Peter Hennessy, *Whitehall* (London: Fontana, 1994); Richard Pyper, *The British Civil Service* (Hemel Hempstead, U.K.: Prentice Hall, 1995); Peter Barberis, *The Elite of the Elite: Permanent Secretaries in the British Higher Civil Service* (Aldershot, U.K.: Dartmouth, 1996).

51. See the series of articles on Blair's "new establishment" in *The Economist,* August 7, August 14, August 21, August 28, and September 4, 1999.

52. By the late 1990s the royal family received approximately $14 million a year from the national budget. On the aristocracy, see David Cannadine, *The Decline and Fall of the British Aristrocracy* (New Haven, Conn: Yale University Press, 1990).

53. Jonathan Bardon, *A History of Ulster* (Belfast, U.K.: Blackstaff, 1992).

54. On the peace process, see George J. Mitchell, *Making Peace* (New York: Alfred A. Knopf, 1999); and Jack Holland, *Hope Against History: The Course of Conflict in Northern Ireland* (New York: Henry Holt, 1999).

55. *The Economist,* March 15, 1997, and October 18, 1997; World Bank, *World Development Report 1999/2000* (New York: Oxford University Press, 1999), 242–43.

56. *The Economist,* November 6, 1999.

57. Polls taken in 1997 showed that 75 percent of Britons knew little or nothing about the EU and only 2 percent considered themselves well informed (*Financial Times,* August 4, 1997). A 1999 survey found that only 37 percent of the British felt "very attached" or "fairly attached" to Europe, and 57 percent "not very" or "not at all" attached. The EU average was 56 percent in the former category and 40 percent in the latter (*Eurobarometer,* Report 51 [spring 1999]: 9).

58. Geoffrey Evans, "Euroscepticism and Conservative Electoral Support: How an Asset Became a Liability," *British Journal of Political Science* 28 (1998), 573–90.

CHAPTER 17

FRANCE

Population (1999): 59 million

Area: 176,460 square miles
(about two-thirds the size of Texas)

Bretagne = Brittany
Bourgogne = Burgundy
Source: U.S. Central Intelligence Agency.

"COHABITATION"
AND THE ELECTIONS OF 1997

As the results of the first round of voting rolled in, it was obvious that **President Jacques Chirac** had miscalculated. On April 21 he had taken advantage of the formidable powers of the French presidency by dissolving the lower house of the legislature, the National Assembly, and calling new elections one year ahead of schedule. His aim in these snap elections was to win a new majority for his conservative party, the French People's Rally, and its allies. A victory in 1997 would extend the conservatives' dominance of the legislature for five more years, allowing Chirac and his partners to build on their spectacular success in the 1993 legislative elections and continue their efforts to trim budget deficits, boost the private sector, and prepare the country for the adoption of Europe's new currency, the euro.

Public opinion polls seemed to justify Chirac's optimism. While the French did not appear ready to return as large a conservative majority as in 1993, when Chirac's coalition won a commanding 84 percent of Assembly seats, the conservatives held a steady ten-point lead over their arch-rivals, the Socialists, throughout most of the five-week campaign. Politics is full of surprises, however, and polls showed as many as 40 percent of the voters still undecided only a week before election day. Unexpectedly, the Socialists and their allies on the left wing of the French political spectrum outpolled the conservative parties in round 1, held on May 25. But the final shape of the new National Assembly was still in doubt.

France has a **single member district** election system for the National Assembly. The country is divided into more than five hundred election districts, and one person is elected to represent each district. The U.S. House of Representatives and the British House of Commons are also elected in single member districts. But unlike the U.S. and UK systems, the French variant of this system involves a two-round process. Candidates for the National Assembly must win an absolute majority of votes (50 percent plus one) in their respective districts in order to be elected in round 1. In districts where no one captures an outright majority, a second round is held a week later for all contestants who

garnered at least 12.5 percent of first-round votes. The winners in round 2 are decided on a plurality basis: whoever gets the most votes within each district wins. In 1997 more than 80 percent of the Assembly's 577 seats were decided in the second round, held on June 1.

The left's second-round victory was convincing. The Socialists won 38.9 percent of the popular vote and ended up with 246 seats (42.6 percent of the National Assembly). Smaller leftist parties, including communists, ecologists, and others, captured 6.3 percent of the vote and seventy-four seats. Altogether the left had won 320 seats, a 55.5 percent majority. This total represented an astonishing comeback after the left's disastrous defeat of 1993, when the Socialists and other leftist parties captured a meager 13.8 percent of Assembly seats. The turnabout was equally striking from the right wing's perspective, only in reverse. In four years the conservatives saw their delegation in the National Assembly shrink from 484 seats to 257. It was their worst defeat in nearly forty years.

Once again, as in the four previous legislative elections, most French voters had voted against the parties in control of the lower house. But even though a majority appeared to have repudiated the conservatives' austerity budgets and other policies, Jacques Chirac was still president. *The president of France is elected directly by the people, not by the legislature, and at that time served a seven-year term.* Chirac was elected in 1995 and could be expected to stay in office until 2002. The left's National Assembly victory in 1997 thus set the stage for *divided government:* a president representing one political orientation and a legislative majority consisting of the opposite orientation. Students of American government are all too familiar with this arrangement. Bill Clinton, a Democrat, had to deal with a Republican majority in Congress for six of his eight years in office.

France's political system is more complicated than the U.S. system, however. The United States has a single executive (the president), who presides over the cabinet and is responsible for the government's policies. France, by contrast, has a mixed **presidential-parliamentary system** of democracy. This system establishes *two* decision-making executives. In addition to having a powerful president, the French system also has a prime minister. One of the president's duties is to *appoint the prime minister.* While the president is free to name anyone he wants, the National Assembly has the authority to reject the prime minister by majority vote. In making his selection, the president must be sensitive to the wishes of the legislative majority, taking pains to appoint someone who will meet its approval. In 1997, Chirac bowed to the realities dictated by the legislative election results and named **Lionel Jospin** (zho-span), the leader of the Socialist Party and his chief political opponent, as prime minister. Jospin, in turn, formed a cabinet that reflected the freshly elected leftist majority. His first coalition government consisted of eighteen Socialists, three communists, and five other left-wing politicians.

The French constitution requires the president, who is *head of state,* and the prime minister, who is *head of government,* to share power. Both have major responsibilities for domestic and foreign policy. When the two executives come from opposing sides of the political spectrum, one from the left and the other from the right, the French call this situation **cohabitation.**

To put things in comparative perspective, if the United States had the French system, President Clinton probably would have appointed Newt Gingrich, the most prominent Republican in the House of Representatives, as *prime minister* of the United States following the Republicans' 1994 victory that gave them control of the House. Gingrich, not Clinton, would have formed the cabinet, in all likelihood filling it with Republicans. Both men then would have had to "cohabitate" by sharing responsibility for domestic and foreign policy. After Gingrich's retirement following the 1998 elections, Clinton probably would have appointed another Republican leader to replace him, since the Republicans retained their House majority.

Obviously, the task of governing France can be more difficult during periods of cohabitation than when the president and the National Assembly majority are on the same political wavelength. A conservative president wants a conservative Assembly majority, permitting him to appoint a friendly conservative prime minister. The same goes for Socialists and their allies on the left. Cohabitation threatens gridlock. Actually, ever since 1958, when the current French constitution took

effect, cohabitation has been the exception rather than the rule. It occurred for the first time in 1986–88, when the Socialist leader **François Mitterrand** was president and the legislative majority was conservative. (Mitterrand appointed his rival Chirac as prime minister.) It happened again from 1993 to 1995, following the conservatives' legislative rout of the Socialists. (In those years Mitterrand appointed Edouard Balladur, a member of Chirac's party, as prime minister.) In all other years France has been governed by a president, prime minister, and legislative majority that shared the same general ideology, whether conservative on the right or social democratic on the left.

The cohabitation of Chirac and Jospin promised to be prickly. The two men held very different views on a range of issues facing the country. Chirac was committed to reducing state expenditures for various welfare benefits, with a view to bringing the government's annual budget deficits into line with European Union guidelines. With France's approval, the EU had agreed that the euro could not take effect at the end of the 1990s unless all the countries wishing to adopt it reduced their yearly deficits to no more than 3 percent of GDP. To meet this goal, Chirac reached into his own party and tapped Alain Juppé (zhoo-pay) as his first prime minister in 1995, charging him with the task of setting limits to the state's pension benefits and other costly welfare programs. The two like-minded executives also favored the privatization of various state-owned enterprises, reflecting conservative preferences for stimulating economic growth through the private sector rather than by expanding the state's role in the nation's economy.

But Juppé's budget-slashing proposals ran into serious trouble at the end of 1995, when a wave of strikes and demonstrations greeted his plans to tighten eligibility requirements for pensions, increase public health fees, and introduce other measures designed to lower state expenditures. The prime minister's popularity ratings plummeted steadily over the following year, culminating in the voters' rejection of the conservative parties and their turn to the Socialists in 1997.

The Socialists, for their part, were historically committed to a powerful role for the state in promoting growth, expanding welfare, and creating jobs. Under former president Mitterrand, who served two consecutive terms from 1981 to 1995, Socialist governments had nationalized a number of large private companies. Jospin railed against the "hard capitalism" of Ronald Reagan and Margaret Thatcher and praised Bill Clinton and Tony Blair for repudiating it. During the 1997 campaign he called for a "new economic humanism," promising to pursue European monetary union without sacrificing social welfare. The Socialist standard-bearer was particularly troubled by France's persistent unemployment problem. Under a succession of Socialist and conservative governments, the ranks of the unemployed had swollen from 2 million in 1981 (7.2 percent of the work force) to more than 3 million in 1997. Juppé's promise in 1995 to create 700,000 new jobs by the end of the following year had fallen far short of its target. By 1997, France's jobless rate of 12.8 percent was one of the highest in Europe. As the campaign took shape, Jospin vowed to create 750,000 new jobs for young people over a five-year period, half of them in the public sector and the other half in private enterprise. The Socialists also called for a thirty-five-hour work week, a proposal conservative leaders opposed. Jospin also promised to stop the privatization of state-owned French firms.

Many of the problems facing the Chirac-Jospin combination at the turn of the millennium are similar to those confronting other economically advanced democracies. The need to stimulate economic growth, combat unemployment and inflation, cut budget deficits, expand education, finance pension funds, provide the welfare programs voters want, keep taxes within acceptable limits, and deal with the forces of globalization—these are familiar challenges throughout the world. So is the task of finding political agreement on an acceptable balance between the state (the public sector) and markets (the private sector). This is a particularly salient issue in France, where the state has traditionally enjoyed a paramount place in the economy. And like many other countries, France faces the thorny problem of balancing the freedom of employers to hire and fire workers and determine their wages and benefits with the rights of workers to count on a decent income, job security, health care, and other necessities. Indeed, relations between the government, private enterprise, and trade unions are especially complicated in France, a country with a history of deep class cleavages and sharp ideological clashes between the socialist left and the capitalist right.

Compared with the United States, the French state plays a larger role in the economy, both directly and indirectly. French government expenditures in 1998 took up 54 percent of the country's GDP, as against slightly more than 30 percent in the United States. French corporations must pay considerably higher taxes and social security contributions than American firms, and they often face greater restrictions on their ability to lay off workers. French workers tend to work shorter hours, enjoy more paid vacation days, and retire earlier than their American counterparts, and they are more likely to go on strike. Unemployment is higher than in the United States (11 percent as opposed to about 4 percent in 1999). The French are subjected to higher tax rates but receive more generous educational and welfare benefits. Public education is basically tuition free, straight through graduate school. The government makes sure that virtually all French citizens have health insurance, whereas the United States in 1999 had 45 million people without it. The French political spectrum includes more parties, including a few extreme parties of left and right. And French workers, students, and other citizens are more likely to take to the streets by the hundreds of thousands to demonstrate their disapproval of pending legislation or government decisions, especially on economic and education issues. They often make state

FIGURE 17.1   Unemployment Rates in France, 1981–1996 (in millions)
Source: Le Monde Hebdomodaire, May 10, 1997.

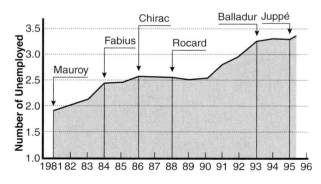

officials back down, successfully pressuring them to abandon or modify their policies.

In addition to tackling various economic problems, the French today are searching for ways to expand the participation of women in political life while dealing with an increasingly diverse population. Though female representation in the National Assembly doubled in 1997 from thirty-two to sixty-three, and Jospin appointed eight women to his twenty-six-member cabinet, French women remain significantly underrepresented in the nation's elective and administrative offices.[1] The country's ethnic composition, meanwhile, displays an increasingly heterogeneous pallet as immigrants and asylum seekers from Africa, the Middle East, and Asia—many of them from former French colonies—have streamed into France in recent decades in search of political freedom and economic opportunity. The multiethnic composition of France's World Cup–winning soccer team of 1998 reflected this growing diversity. At the same time, racism, religious animosity, and competition for jobs and welfare benefits have intensified, giving rise to restrictive immigration legislation and avowedly anti-immigrant political movements. More long-standing internal divisions exploded in April 2000, when a bomb shattered a McDonald's in Brittany. A nationalist movement known as the Breton Revolutionary Army, which favors an independent Brittany and opposes globalization, was suspected as responsible for the blast.

On top of its economic and social agenda, France is still contending with long-standing constitutional issues. The country's presidential-parliamentary system of government, while constituting a model for Russia, Poland, and other democracies, presents an intriguing array of advantages and pitfalls. Written in 1958 under the direction of **General Charles de Gaulle,** one of the dominant political figures of the twentieth century, the French constitution was designed to stabilize decision-making authority by vesting it in an exceptionally powerful president while systematically limiting the authority of the national legislature. Though the system has functioned in accordance with these intentions over most of its history, cohabitation can dilute the president's authority considerably. It can also limit the prime minister's freedom of action by subjecting him or her to unwelcome presidential oversight.

After the 1997 legislative elections, President Chirac found himself in a far weaker position than he enjoyed during his first two years in office, when the Assembly supported him with an overwhelming conservative majority. And Lionel Jospin, who led the left to an impressive victory only one month after British voters swept the Labour Party into power, found himself in a weaker position than his ideological cousin, Tony Blair. Whereas Blair does not have to share power with a constitutionally powerful head of state because the queen's duties are largely ceremonial, Jospin must coordinate many of his actions with his political nemesis, President Chirac. This duality of executive power was plainly visible around the world during the Kosovo conflict in 1999. Since both President Chirac and Prime Minister Jospin have foreign policy responsibilities, both men had to coordinate France's position as a NATO member throughout the crisis. Coordination is imperative in numerous other policy areas as well. Without it, government decision making in France can break down, conceivably resulting in political paralysis. Ironically, political paralysis is precisely what France's current constitution was designed to prevent.

Meanwhile, in September 2000 French voters approved a referendum reducing the president's seven-year term to five years, starting in 2002. The constitutional reform would permit people to vote for the president and the National Assembly in the same year on a regular basis, perhaps reducing the likelihood of divided government and cohabitation in the future.

Questions for Analysis While addressing a number of central issues in French politics, this chapter will highlight the country's efforts to deal with the main sources of political conflict that we enumerated in chapter 2:

- *Power:* Who has held power over the course of French history? How does the French constitution distribute decision-making powers? How have French leaders used their power? What are some of the distinguishing characteristics of French political elites?

- *Resources:* What are the respective roles of the state and the private sector in managing the economy? How has France dealt with chronic unemployment and other economic challenges?
- *Social identity:* How have the French dealt with conflicts arising from religious and ethnic diversity?
- *Ideas:* Which are the chief ideological orientations in French politics? What do such terms as "left," "right," "socialism," "communism," and "conservatism" mean in the French context?
- *Values:* How consensual (or conflictual) is French political culture? How tolerant are the French?

Because so many aspects of French politics today cannot be understood without an appreciation of their historical roots, we'll begin by surveying some key events in the development of French democracy, drawing some instructive comparisons along the way.

HISTORICAL BACKGROUND: THE EVOLUTION OF FRENCH DEMOCRACY

As we noted in chapter 16, British democracy evolved in a long process that stretched from the origins of Parliament in the 1200s to the full flowering of universal suffrage in the twentieth century. To be sure, this development did not take place in a continuous straight line; monarchical absolutism, civil wars, and other factors cast numerous obstacles in democracy's path. Nevertheless, Britain on the whole experienced a relatively stable progression toward mass democracy after establishing the principle of parliamentary supremacy in 1688.

The French democratic experience was considerably more spasmodic. Instead of a fairly steady evolution, France experienced a convulsive revolution. The French Revolution that began in 1789 was far more radical and violent than Britain's Glorious Revolution a hundred years earlier. Instead of paralleling Britain's gradual expansion of democratic rights in the nineteenth and twentieth centuries, French democracy suffered a succession of failures, giving way to authoritarian regimes of various types. And instead of developing a single concept of democratic governance, like Britain's parliamentary system, France tried out several democratic constitutions before settling on its current variant of the presidential-parliamentary model.

In tracing France's tortuous road to stable democracy, we can point to several factors on our list of conditions for democracy that we presented in chapter 10 that distinguish the French political tradition from Britain's. They include the following:

- a long history of non-democratic *state institutions*, characterized by a strong centralized state and weak parliamentary traditions
- the prolonged influence of authoritarian *elites*
- a prominent role for the state in promoting *national wealth* despite substantial *private enterprise*, especially in non-democratic regimes
- a concept of French nationalism that, at least until the Revolution, centered on the state and its authority rather than on the people and their liberties, retarding the emergence of a moderate democratic *political culture*
- a *middle class* that did not constitute a steady source of support for democracy but divided its sympathies between democratic and various non-democratic orientations
- prolonged difficulties integrating the working class, the country's main *disadvantaged* class, into democracy, resulting in the political alienation of many workers and the emergence of revolutionary socialist parties
- a turbulent *international environment* that at various times suppressed, destroyed, or threatened to destroy democracy

Though France has traditionally had more ethnic and religious *homogeneity* than the United Kingdom, and developed an elite system of higher *education* at about the same time as England, these factors alone were not capable of overriding the other factors that made democratic stability much more difficult for the French to achieve than it was for the British. Let's look at these factors in greater detail.

The French State

"L'Etat c'est moi" ("I am the State"). This famous utterance is attributed to King Louis XIV, who reigned from 1651 to 1715. Though perhaps apocryphal, it aptly indicated where power resided in France. A succession of monarchs had ruled the country since the late tenth century, with the Bourbon dynasty establishing itself in 1589. Fancying

himself the "sun king," Louis XIV was determined to fortify royal authority through a firm application of the principle of the *divine right of kings:* the notion that God—not the people—was the source of the government's legitimacy. The kingdom he inherited from his father, Louis XIII, was already anchored in centralized state institutions built around the monarch, his chief ministers, and an expanding cadre of professional bureaucrats. It was during the elder Louis's reign (1610–1643) that France outpaced England and other European monarchies in laying the foundations of the modern state, creating an embryonic model of central bureaucratic authority and military command that was destined to be adapted by most European powers over the course of the next two centuries. Under Louis XIV, the sinews of the French state were strengthened even further and the monarch's autocratic powers enhanced. His heir, Louis XV, allegedly expressed his own lack of faith in the ability of the French people to govern themselves by haughtily predicting, "*Après mois, le déluge*" ("After me, the deluge").[2]

This pioneering exercise in state creation was the handiwork of three successive chief ministers to the crown. Cardinal *Richelieu,* the "grey eminence" behind Louis XIII's throne, assumed virtually full control of the monarchy's domestic and foreign policies. Although he was a prelate of the Catholic Church, Richelieu was ruthlessly devoted to the establishment of a secular state whose principal purposes were the triumph of royal absolutism at home and the expansion of French power abroad. He forcefully asserted the central government's authority over previously autonomous local governments in various parts of France. He also put the French army and navy under more rigorous central control and laid the groundwork for an administrative elite increasingly selected on the basis of professional competence rather than aristocratic connections. His shrewd diplomacy and military conquests made France the preeminent power in Europe, while his mercantilist international trade policy multiplied the nation's wealth.

Upon his death in 1642, another cardinal, *Giulio Mazarin,* took over as Richelieu's handpicked successor. As the young Louis XIV's principal advisor, Mazarin followed in his predecessor's footsteps in expanding the French monarchy's power against both internal and external challengers. He also trained his successor, *Jean Baptiste Colbert,* who proved equally devoted to expanding the powers of the royal government while serving as the king's finance minister from 1661 to 1683.[3]

In marked contrast to England, the assertion of royal dominance in France was accompanied by the absence of an assertive national parliament. England's Parliament started carving out substantial shares of authority for itself in the fourteenth century, gradually but relentlessly establishing its two houses as co-responsible with the monarch for the governance of the realm. Over the next centuries its authority grew. During the 1640s, as France underwent the transition from Louis XIII to Louis XIV, England's Parliament convicted King Charles I of treason and ordered his execution. During the civil wars and Oliver Cromwell's dictatorship that framed this event, Parliament endured. Just as significant, Parliament took the initiative in restoring the monarchy after Cromwell's death. More significant still, it was Parliament that deposed King James II and conferred the crown on William of Orange in the Glorious Revolution of 1688. That bold action, taken at the height of the sun king's absolute power in France, substituted parliamentary sovereignty for the divine right of kings and turned out to be a giant step on the path to mass democracy in twentieth-century Britain.

Initially, the French national legislature advanced even more rapidly than England's Parliament in the direction of democratic representation. It originated in 1302, when King Philip IV invited a number of prominent personages to confer with him in Paris. The one-day meeting took place in Notre Dame cathedral. Those invited included members of what were known in medieval society as "estates." The First Estate consisted of the nobility, the Second Estate consisted of the Roman Catholic clergy, and the Third Estate consisted of the populations of cities, towns, and rural villages. In essence, the Third Estate encompassed the people of France. Their representation in France's nascent national parliament, which became known as the "States General," constituted the first attempts by the French monarchy to address the population as a whole rather than just the aristocratic and ecclesiastic elites. The next meeting of the States

General, held in 1308, included more than five hundred delegates, perhaps as many as half of them coming from the Third Estate.

Over the course of the fourteenth century, meetings of the States General occurred more frequently as the royal government asked it to approve taxes and sought its counsel during the Hundred Years War with England (1337–1453). In the process, the Third Estate assumed even greater prominence in governmental deliberations than England's equivalent body, the House of Commons, at this time. Its representatives tended to come disproportionately from the country's emerging middle class rather than from the peasantry, which comprised the bulk of the population. In 1357 they compelled the king to agree in writing to permit the States General to meet whenever its members wished and to accept its oversight of most of the royal government's activities. This agreement, spelled out in the "Great Ordinance," in principle handed over to the French parliament effective control over the country's governmental affairs. It went much further than Magna Carta (1215) or the medieval English Parliament did in establishing the bases of a *constitutional monarchy*, a system in which a national legislature sets limits to the monarch's power. If the Great Ordinance had been followed, France might have achieved in the fourteenth century what Britain did not accomplish until the late seventeenth century.

The French crown was not ready to concede power so rapidly, however. The king quickly disavowed the Great Ordinance, and successive French monarchs called the States General into session with diminishing frequency. After 1439 it did not meet again until 1614. Louis XIV and his immediate successors had no use for it, and the next meeting of the States General was not called until 1789. By that time, popular demands for representation in government had been suppressed for so long that, when at last given a chance for expression, they exploded in a revolutionary frenzy.

The Revolution The **French Revolution** was such a shattering series of events that it redefined the significance of almost everything that had come before it in the country's political history. Centuries of royal absolutism, the absence of par-

liamentary representation, a disaffected nobility with little influence over the monarch and his ministers, financial mismanagement, an unfair tax system, festering urban and rural poverty—these and a multiplicity of additional factors can all be viewed as antecedent causes of the Revolution. Just as powerfully, the Revolution could not help but stamp an indelible imprint on much of what followed it.

The sorry plight of the government's finances compelled the crown in 1789 to convene the first meeting of the States General in 175 years. Without some form of popular approval, there was little likelihood that King Louis XVI would get the new taxes his lavish administration required. (A major source of the crown's debt was the financial support it had given the American Revolution against England, France's arch-rival.) From the outset the newly assembled parliament was led by the largely middle-class deputies elected to represent the Third Estate. Shortly after convening, most of the Third Estate's 600-member delegation demanded a constitutional monarchy. The king relented, and the States General quickly reconstituted itself as a unicameral National Assembly. Also known as the Constituent Assembly, the legislature immediately set about the task of drafting France's first written constitution. Its preamble was a "Declaration of the Rights of Man," which enshrined private property along with "resistance to oppression" and citizen participation in the law making process as fundamental civil rights. It formally granted citizenship to all French males over age twenty-five and extended voting rights to those citizens who could meet various property qualifications. "Liberty! Equality! Fraternity!"—the battle cry of the Revolution—filled the air.

At this juncture in the summer of 1789, France appeared to be moving steadily toward a moderate constitutional monarchy roughly similar to Britain's. But more radical elements, organized mainly in political clubs known as the Jacobins, favored abolishing the monarchy altogether and establishing a republic.[4] The Jacobins quickly took political control of the capital city, aided by the poorest classes of Paris, whose smoldering discontent erupted in mass outbursts such as the storming of the Bastille prison on July 14, 1789. (The anniversary is still celebrated as France's national holiday.)

Over the next three years, relations between the crown and the Assembly deteriorated. Finally in August 1792, Jacobin elements orchestrated an insurrection in Paris that drove the king from power. A new legislature was elected the following month. Known as the Convention, its members were considerably more radical than the deputies elected to the first National Assembly of 1789 or its successor, elected in 1791. One of the Convention's first acts was to declare France a Republic in September 1792. (In its most literal sense, a *republic* is a form of government without a monarch, and a *republican* is an opponent of monarchy.)

The Convention's members were not always in full agreement. The assembly was divided into extreme radicals, who were seated to the left of the speaker of the house; more moderate elements, seated to the speaker's right; and a majority of delegates in the center whose views were indeterminate or tended to shift. These seating arrangements gave rise to the terms "left," "right," and "center" in politics. Though a minority, the left proved highly effective in swaying the Convention's votes. Known as "the Mountain," its delegates persuaded the Convention to put the king on trial. Out of 721 deputies, 394 voted to condemn Louis XVI to death. He died on the guillotine in January 1793.

The king's execution set in motion an orgy of bloodletting known in French history as "the Terror." Over the next year and a half, some twenty thousand "enemies of the people" met their grim fate on the guillotine or in front of execution

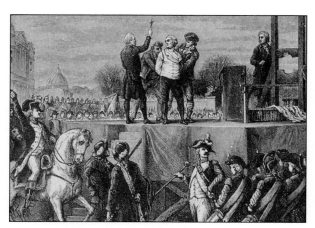

The execution of King Louis XVI, 1793

squads. They included members of the nobility as well as Catholic priests and nuns, victims of the Revolution's anti-clericalism. Outbursts of anti-revolutionary activity were ruthlessly suppressed in various parts of France. The Revolution also began consuming revolutionaries. Factional struggles broke out between its most zealous adherents and advocates of a more moderately ordered republic devoted to social peace and respect for property rights. Even heroes of the Revolution died on the scaffold.

As the Terror unfolded, the power of the central government intensified. Initially the Convention drafted a new constitution that would have created a powerful unicameral legislature, universal suffrage, and a comprehensive bill of rights. Though the document won overwhelming endorsement in a referendum, it was never implemented. In its place, the radical revolutionaries established a twelve-member Committee of Public Safety that exercised harsh dictatorial rule. In addition to conducting its reign of terror, the Committee sent out "national agents" to impose the central government's will on local governments. The term **Jacobinism** became synonymous with *a highly centralized form of government.*

The trend toward greater centralization continued even after more moderate factions seized power in July 1794. The next group of revolutionary leaders, solidly middle class and committed to private property rights, abolished the Committee of Public Safety, executed its leaders, and put an end to the Terror. But they also set up a strong executive government of their own, known as the Directory. Five Directors were selected by a Council of Five Hundred to govern the country. Voting rights were restricted and parliamentary powers withered.

Though it imposed a measure of tranquillity on an exhausted nation, the Directory could not establish an enduring government. In 1799 it gave way to yet another strong-willed authoritarian regime as General Napoleon Bonaparte grabbed power with the support of the French military. Napoleon's coup d'état effectively terminated France's decade of revolution. It had begun with lofty dreams of democracy, defined in the context of eighteenth-century Europe as constituting a limited monarchy, an elected national legislature, qualified male suffrage, and private property rights. Within a few years the Revolution had degenerated into dictatorship, fanaticism, and civil strife. The elimination of royal absolutism led not to democracy but to new forms of centralized state power.[5]

After the Revolution: From Napoleon to the Vth Republic   Napoleon accentuated these centralizing tendencies. After proclaiming himself "First Consul" of France at the start of his rule, he assumed the crown of Emperor in 1804. A brilliant military commander whose armies brought most of Europe under French domination, Napoleon took an equally domineering approach to domestic affairs. He organized a secret police. He pioneered the use of plebiscites to cultivate popular support for his dictatorship. In three such referendums he won the approval of 99 percent of the voters, though the voting procedures were manipulated by the authorities and the official tallies were surely suspect. Another innovation was the creation of a corps of **prefects** charged with ensuring the central government's control over more than eighty administrative departments into which France had been divided during the Revolution. The prefecture system endured with only minor changes until the 1980s, undergirding France's long tradition as a **unitary state.** A unitary state emphasizes the central government's primacy over local governments. It contrasts with *federalism,* which combines central government authority with significant decision-making powers for local officials. Even today, despite reforms granting more powers to local governments, France retains the defining features of a unitary state.

Napoleon's authoritarian rule lasted only as long as his military prowess ensured French dominance in Europe. His army's defeat in 1814 by an alliance of European powers destroyed his regime. Napoleon was sent off into exile, and the victorious allies, whose governments all had monarchs, collaborated with French royalists in restoring the Bourbon monarchy to France. A spirited attempt by Napoleon to reclaim power foundered on the battlefield of Waterloo in 1815, and the Restoration was confirmed. The new king, Louis XVIII (a brother of Louis XVI), agreed to a constitution permitting an elected legislature, but his regal powers were substantial. After he died in 1824, his brother Charles X tried even more vigorously to reestablish a sovereign monarchy similar to the *ancien régime* (old regime) that had existed before the Revolution.

But the clock of history could not be turned back to the eighteenth century. Popular agitation resulted in his replacement in July 1830 by a constitutional monarchy under King Louis-Philippe of the house of Orleans. Reigning as the "citizen-king," the new monarch was content to leave affairs of state in the hands of middle-class politicians allied with the country's property owners and its rising business elite. Prime Minister François Guizot explicitly exhorted the country's businessmen, "Gentlemen, get rich!"

In kaleidoscopic fashion, one regime succeeded another. Louis-Philippe's so-called July Monarchy lasted only until 1848, when working-class uprisings forced his departure and swept into power a new government devoted to the Revolution's principles of liberty, equality, and fraternity. Alas, France's IInd Republic proved to be as ill-fated as the Ist Republic of the 1790s. The new republic's leaders proved unable to fulfill their promises to hire the unemployed and improve social welfare. The frustrated working class rose in rebellion once again, and the government resorted to military force to put down the upheaval. With the specter of revolution hanging over the country, the military seized power at the end of 1850 under the leadership of Napoleon's nephew, Louis-Napoleon. A new period of authoritarian rule ensued as the IInd Empire reasserted the state's undisputed authority. Like his uncle, Louis-Napoleon (also known as Napoleon III) sought mass approval in manipulated plebiscites but could not survive military defeat. When the French army suffered disaster in the Franco-Prussian War of 1870–71 and Louis-Napoleon was captured, France found itself without a government yet again.

As in 1848, the vacuum was filled in 1870 by devotees of democracy. The IIIrd Republic got off to a shaky start, marked by the bloody suppression of a revolutionary uprising in Paris, but it eventually righted itself, promulgating a new constitution in 1875. Its parliamentary system expanded male suffrage, fostered the growth of political parties, and guaranteed civil rights and freedoms, sparking a renaissance in the arts and sciences. But while the IIIrd Republic enjoyed the longest run of any French regime since the Revolution, lasting until 1940, it was no model of governmental stability. Between the 1870s and 1940 it produced no fewer than 108 governments! In the same period Britain had fewer than thirty governments and the United States had seventeen presidents. Vilified by monarchists on the right and revolutionary socialists on the left, at several junctures the IIIrd Republic teetered on collapse.[6]

With the sudden defeat of French forces at the hands of Hitler's army in 1940, the IIIrd Republic perished and France fell under the grip of Nazi occupation. Initially, the Germans divided the country roughly in half, imposing direct rule in the north and organizing a puppet government under accommodating French officials in the south. The puppet regime, headquartered in Vichy, was headed by Marshal Philippe Pétain, a World War I hero who agreed to collaborate with the occupiers in hopes of mitigating the rigors of Nazi rule. The occupation split France into antagonistic camps. *Collaborationists* assisted the Germans; *resistants* took extreme risks in organizing underground opposition to Nazi rule. In 1942 the Germans disbanded the Vichy government and took control of southern France for the remainder of the occupation.

Nazi rule finally ended in 1944 as American and British forces joined with the troops of "Free France" under General de Gaulle in driving out the Germans. De Gaulle thereupon installed himself as chief of a Provisional Government whose principal purpose was to preside over the elaboration of a new constitution. It took two years to accomplish this task, and de Gaulle retreated into retirement once it became clear that his own constitutional design would not win approval. The **IVth Republic,** formally inaugurated in 1946, was a parliamentary system with a ceremonial presidency and a bicameral legislature. From the outset it was dogged by governmental instability: a parade of twenty-two coalition governments struggled to exercise power over the next twelve years. Like other unstable French republics before it, the IVth Republic ultimately fell apart, the victim of its internal conflicts and external disasters.[7]

After failing to reimpose colonial rule on Vietnam and other parts of Indochina after World War II, the IVth Republic's leaders decided to suppress an Arab independence movement in Algeria that began in 1954. Algeria had come under French control starting in 1830, and its European minority looked to the French government for protection against the Arab majority. The war ground on inconclusively, splitting French society as devastatingly as the Vietnam War was later to divide Americans. In May 1958 a group of French generals in Algeria, disgruntled at the government's reluctance to prosecute the war more aggressively, staged a mutiny. The IVth Republic quickly crumbled. A majority of National Assembly delegates voted to confer power on de Gaulle, who came out of retirement with the determination to reorganize the state under a new constitution. The result was the **Vth Republic,** whose presidential-parliamentary system was approved in a referendum at the end of 1958. With only a few alterations since then, the Vth Republic's constitution remains in force today.

Conclusions   The key points that emerge from the preceding historical account, summarized in table 17.1, are the following:

- France has experienced an extraordinary multiplicity of political regimes over the past 200-odd years. Since the start of the Revolution in 1789 it has had eleven different governmental regimes and fifteen constitutions. This *regime instability* (or *constitutional instability*) contrasts quite starkly with the far less turbulent constitutional development of Britain and the United States.
- French regimes have tended to alternate between more or less democratically organized *republics* and *authoritarian regimes* of one kind or another.
- The authoritarian strain in French politics has been much stronger than in the United Kingdom or the United States, and its manifestations have often been accompanied by a powerful governing role for *military* leaders. At times French dictators have drummed up mass approval in plebiscites.
- The first four French republics themselves proved to be highly unstable, exhibiting various

TABLE 17.1

French Constitutional Regimes

Until 1789	Sovereign monarchies	1848–1850	IInd Republic
1789–1792	Constitutional monarchy	1851–1870	IInd Empire (Napoleon III)
1792–1799	Ist Republic	1870/75–1940	IIIrd Republic
1793–1794	—Committee of Public Safety	1940–1944	German occupation
1794–1799	—Directorate	1940–1942	Vichy regime
1799–1804	Consulate (Napoleon Bonaparte)	1944–1946	Provisional governments
1804–1814	Ist Empire (Napoleon I)	1946–1958	IVth Republic
1814–1830	Quasi-sovereign monarchy	1958 to present	Vth Republic
1830–1848	Constitutional monarchy		

types of what may be called *governmental instability*. Here, too, the contrast with Britain and the United States is striking.

- There has been a continuing tradition of *centralized state authority* throughout French history. While the powers of the central government were especially pronounced under authoritarian regimes, even the republics have maintained the institutions of a *unitary state* and refrained from reconstituting France as a federation. To be sure, the United Kingdom has also been a unitary state until recently, but its central authorities frequently have had to take special measures, both coercive and conciliatory, in dealing with Northern Ireland, Scotland, and Wales. The devolutionary policies of Tony Blair's government are moving the UK decidedly closer to a federal system. The United States has been a federation since 1789.

French Nationalism

Just as the development of French state institutions diverged sharply from Britain's, French nationalism also displayed palpable differences with British conceptions of national identity. Over the course of the sixteenth and seventeenth centuries, the term "nation" in England became associated with the people rather than the state and with Parliament as opposed to an all-powerful monarchy. English Protestantism stimulated these developments. Over time, English nationalism became synonymous with a nation of free individuals governing themselves through parliamentary representation.

As the sociologist Liah Greenfeld has shown, French nationalism until shortly before the Revolution revolved overwhelmingly around the state and its crowning authority, the monarchy. Especially during the height of the monarch's absolute power in the seventeenth century, "the nation" referred mainly to the royal government rather than the people. In this spirit, French kings regarded their primary obligation as enhancing the power and glory of the state rather than increasing the freedoms and welfare of the population, as in England. The people were relegated to the status of servile subjects. Although French Protestants, the Huguenots, espoused a more populist concept of nationalism and took up the cause of those who were subjugated by royal authority, they never succeeded in taking political power. The only Protestant king of France, Henry IV (1589–1610), converted to Catholicism. Protestantism in France thus failed to play the politically liberating role it played in England.[8]

The Revolution made decisive changes in French national consciousness. More than anything else, the Revolution signified the French people's assertion of their right as citizens to constitute the French nation. The word "national," as used in such terms as "National Assembly" and "national defense," placed the people of France squarely in the center of the country's political and social life. Popular sovereignty replaced sovereign monarchy. Still, Greenfeld notes that, even during the Revolution, the French conception of popular nationalism continued to differ from Britain's. While the British conceived of their nation as consisting of individuals, the French tended to think of "the people" as a collective entity. In the British idea, individuals formed the nation; in France, the people as a whole formed the nation. This subtle distinction mirrored John Locke's devotion to individual liberty and Jean-Jacques Rousseau's preference for collective liberty. It was to have long-term implications for political culture. In greater proportions than in Britain or the United States, political elites of both the right and left in France have tended to look to the state more than to private enterprise or society as the chief source of responsibility for the country's economic well-being. The terms "Colbertist" and "Jacobin" are still applied to French politicians who favor a strong state, a concept known as *étatisme* (statism). While governmental powers in France have been frequently subject to limitations, especially when a democratic constitution is in effect, the French state has nonetheless tended to enjoy greater prominence than in other democracies like the United States and Britain.[9]

Social Class and Democracy

Among the many factors that impeded France's advance toward stable democracy, the political roles played by elites and various social classes stand out as particularly prominent. Once again, a comparison with Britain is instructive.

The Nobility In Britain, the nobility contributed to the evolutionary unfolding of democratic institutions and practices because, right from the start, it formed a vital component of Parliament. In the twentieth century the House of Lords, the aristocracy's parliamentary preserve, was willing to accept significant limitations on its legislative powers, ceding pride of place to the House of Commons and thus widening popular democracy. Titled peers have occasionally served as prime ministers or in other cabinet posts, at times promoting such things as the extension of voting rights, the expansion of the welfare state, or other populist democratic policies. Because they were cut in on British democracy, Britain's aristocratic elites supported it.

The French nobility tended to be cut out of political developments, shunted aside by absolutist monarchs adamantly opposed to sharing power with a national parliament. Feeling neglected and powerless under the monarchy, some nobles joined the Revolution in 1789. (The Marquis de Lafayette, who fought in the American Revolution, was typical.) Far more nobles died on the

guillotine, however. From then on, what remained of the French aristocracy was politically marginalized, depriving French democracy of a prominent source of elite support.

The Middle Class The various elements of the British middle class made indispensable contributions to democracy in England, promoting Parliament along with the Conservative and Liberal parties as the main vehicles for achieving their class interests. The relationship between the middle class and democracy was more complicated in France. By 1789, centuries of exclusion from governmental power had created a split in middle-class ranks between moderates willing to settle for a constitutional monarchy and radicals determined to wipe out the detested monarchy forever. After the Ist Republic was established in 1792, a further split occurred among the largely middle-class Jacobins, as one faction unleashed the Terror and their more temperate rivals replaced them with the Directory. Neither group advanced the cause of stable democracy.[10]

Over the course of the nineteenth century, the French middle class was split between those who favored a republic and more democracy (largely to protect their own property rights) and those who believed that their economic interests were best protected under authoritarian regimes. When democracy finally steadied itself in the IIIrd Republic (1870–1940), it was dominated by middle class politicians and their followings.[11]

During World War II, the French middle class found itself split once again. While the majority of the population stayed aloof from political action and concentrated on coping with the daily realities of the German occupation, French fascism and the resistance movement both had middle-class support. The two republics that came after World War II have been solidly middle class in orientation. Middle-class elites and parties have dominated political life, including most of the leaders and voters of the Socialist Party, the main party of the French left.

France's middle class has thus traveled in two political directions: while providing crucial support for democratic institutions at various times, it has been has been less consistent in its support for democracy than was Britain's middle class.

The Working Class The political role of the working class in France presents additional striking differences with the British experience. The industrial working class was the main disadvantaged social class in France and Britain in the nineteenth and twentieth centuries. Class conflict between workers and capitalists has been sharp in both countries, but Britain managed much earlier than France to contain these conflicts within the structures of parliamentary democracy. Significantly, it was Britain's middle-class parties, the Conservatives and the Liberals, that extended the franchise to working-class voters. But it was the establishment of the Labour Party at the start of the twentieth century that most decisively incorporated Britain's working class into democracy. Britain's Communist Party never gained much support, and the country's trade unions—even those led by radical socialists—have tended to support Labour rather than more extreme parties.

A number of events in French history made for a more radicalized segment of the labor movement than in Britain, with results that are visible to this day. As industrialization intensified in the 1820s and subsequent decades, French manual laborers had to contend with the same wretched conditions as their British counterparts. Especially after the July Monarchy came to power in 1830, the government firmly supported the profit-maximizing ambitions of the capitalist elite. The blatant exploitation of the French working class fueled a rage that boiled over in February 1848. As workers took up arms, King Louis-Philippe fled the country and his regime disintegrated.

The IInd Republic was forged in the crucible of this workers' revolution. Its leaders immediately vowed to ameliorate working-class conditions through various welfare measures, including the creation of public sector jobs for the unemployed. The government's promises outran its financial capacities, however. As many as 100,000 workers applied for the jobs, but the state could afford to hire only about 10,000. Short of cash, the IInd Republic canceled the employment programs after several months. In their frustration, workers took to the barricades once again, this time arming themselves against a democratically oriented republic that was ostensibly on their side. Fatefully, it was precisely this republic that crushed the uprising in

July 1848, leading many workers to feel betrayed by democracy itself.

An even bloodier sequence of events occurred in 1871, with similar implications for French democracy. As Emperor Napoleon III's government collapsed and France capitulated to Prussia, opponents of the makeshift new regime took control of several parts of Paris and created their own government. Proclaiming themselves the "Commune" of Paris, the insurrectionists included working-class revolutionaries and their supporters who sought to establish a socialist society. The leaders of the nascent IIIrd Republic, determined to impose their authority on the entire country, dispatched troops to put down the insurrection. As many as fifteen thousand people lost their lives in a bloodbath marked by atrocities on both sides. When the smoke had cleared, the Commune was liquidated, but large numbers of working-class citizens and their sympathizers once again felt subjugated by a French government that professed democratic ideals.[12]

In the wake of these events, several socialist parties were formed in France to militate for workers' rights. In 1905 various socialist organizations merged to form a single party that joined the "Socialist International," a group of European socialist parties. The party called itself the "French Section of the Socialist International," known by its French initials as the **SFIO**. Many of its members were social democrats: like Britain's newly established Labour Party, they disavowed revolutionary violence and dictatorship and instead favored improving the lot of workers through ballot-box democracy and trade union activity. In 1920, proponents of a more radical approach to socialism organized the **French Communist Party (PCF).** Its founders were a disparate group of ideological socialists and pacifists, but the Soviet government in Moscow used its influence to help a pro-Soviet faction take over the party leadership. From the mid-1920s until the late 1980s, PCF leaders generally provided faithful support for Soviet dictates and preferences. They opposed NATO and maintained a consistently hostile attitude toward the United States throughout the Cold War. The French Communists also dominated a trade union federation, the General Confederation of Labor (CGT), and frequently used it to call strikes and demonstrations against French businesses and governments.

In 1936, as the Great Depression boosted unemployment in France, the SFIO and the PCF won an electoral victory in the lower house of the French parliament that permitted the establishment of a Socialist-dominated government. Known as the *Popular Front*, the IIIrd Republic's first left-wing government produced a spate of laws providing for unemployment compensation, state sector jobs, trade union bargaining rights, paid vacations, and other measures benefiting the country's most disadvantaged groups. France's equivalent of President Franklin D. Roosevelt's New Deal lasted only about a year, however. By 1937, more conservative, pro-business parties used their influence in the legislature's upper chamber to block further reforms. Once again, many French workers had reason to feel let down by French democracy.

This long history of working-class radicalism and disaffection from democratic governments helps explain why France, in contrast to Britain, ended up with a comparatively large Communist Party that was allied with the Soviet Union and militantly hostile to private enterprise. Although PCF leaders increasingly expressed their adherence to democratic principles after World War II, they remained ominously vague in their characterizations of what a "socialist democracy" would look like if they were given the opportunity to establish one in France. During the IVth Republic, from 1946 to 1958, the French Communist Party was the country's largest political party, routinely capturing about 25 percent of the vote in elections to the national legislature. Some 2 million workers were affiliated with the communist-dominated trade union organization, the CGT.

In 1979 the French Communists could still garner 20 percent of the ballots. The party's vote has dwindled since then, however. In 1988 it got only 6.8 percent; in 1997, 3.8 percent. Nevertheless, French Communists continue to play an active role in French politics. In the 1997 parliamentary elections they obtained 6.4 percent of the seats in the National Assembly and three of its leaders were invited by Prime Minister Jospin to participate in his first government. The party's leader, Robert Hue, voiced sharp disapproval of NATO's bombing campaign in the Kosovo conflict two years later, a position decidedly at variance with Jospin's approval of NATO's policy. For its part, Britain's Communist Party never got more than 1 percent of the vote after World War II.

Consequences   The clash between left and right has thus tended to be sharper in France than in Britain, reflecting a somewhat more antagonistic confrontation between the working class and the business community. In the 1970s this situation prompted a French sociologist to describe France as a "stalled society," incapable of resolving its economic disputes because both sides have a fear of face-to-face negotiations. As a consequence, the French government has often had to play a mediating role between business and labor.[13] Inevitably, those in power tend to side with those who elected them, the conservatives supporting business leaders (known collectively as the *patronat*) and the Socialists and their allies supporting labor.

The confrontational nature of labor-management relations in France reflects a more general tendency toward conflict and contention in French history than in British history. As Charles Tilly points out in *The Contentious French*, France has witnessed a plethora of politically motivated disorders over the past four centuries, largely in reaction to the expansion of the state and the growth of capitalism.[14] (As Charles de Gaulle put it, "How can you govern a nation that has 246 kinds of cheese?") Whereas British political culture has generally emphasized moderation, pragmatic problem solving, and compromise in dealing with its problems, France's more conflictual political culture has placed a greater emphasis on ideological differentiation, demands for radical change, and negotiating intransigence. These attitudinal predispositions have mellowed in recent decades, but a penchant for mass protest remains a vital part of French political culture, as the strikes and demonstrations of 1995 indicated.

Politics in the Vth Republic

Since its origins in the IVth Republic's fatal crisis of 1958, France's Vth Republic has been dominated by two exceptional political leaders: Charles de Gaulle and François Mitterrand. As the Republic's founder, de Gaulle was not only the source of its constitution but of a political movement—**Gaullism**—that still bears his name. (Contemporary Gaullists like Jacques Chirac are known as **neo-Gaullists** because they have adapted and modernized de Gaulle's seminal ideas.) Mitterrand was the organizer of France's Socialist Party, the party of Prime Minister Lionel Jospin. Any effort to appreciate French politics under Chirac and Jospin must begin with a close examination of these powerful influences on their respective political orientations (see the accompanying boxes).

PROFILE: Charles de Gaulle

"All my life," wrote Charles de Gaulle, "I have formed a certain idea of France." Guided by a profound sense of history, the man who was to lead France through some of its darkest hours was keenly aware of the fierce divisions that constantly threatened to tear the country apart. But he never deviated from his conviction that "France cannot be France without grandeur."

In a career that stretched from the battlefields of the First World War to the unrest that rocked Paris in 1968, de Gaulle dedicated his life to rescuing France from international humiliation and fratricidal strife. He seems to have had an early premonition of his destiny. At age fifteen he wrote an essay describing how "General de Gaulle" would one day save France from ignominious de-

Charles de Gaulle (left) greets Gen. Raoul Salan in Algeria in 1958, shortly before assuming the presidency. Salan was a leader of the military coup that precipitated the collapse of the IVth Republic and was later convicted of plotting to overthrow de Gaulle's Vth Republic.

feat. "I did not doubt," he later wrote of his adolescence, "that France would have to go through enormous trials, that the whole point of life consisted of one day rendering her some conspicuous service." At various times when no one else appeared capable of rallying the nation to combat its enemies or prevent a headlong plunge into civil war, de Gaulle spoke of embodying in his own person the legitimacy of national political authority. In his own mind, de Gaulle *was* France.

FROM WAR TO WAR

Born in 1890 into a Catholic family of modest means, de Gaulle decided in boyhood to pursue a military career. In 1910 he entered the French Military Academy at St. Cyr, France's equivalent of West Point. At six feet four inches in height, he struck an imposing figure. Upon graduation he came under the command of Philippe Pétain, a man whose fate was to be linked to de Gaulle's for more than three decades. As World War I broke out in August 1914 and German troops swarmed into Belgium and France, Lieutenant de Gaulle quickly found himself in the thick of the fighting. Wounded in three separate engagements, he was taken prisoner and spent most of the war in German captivity, risking escape five times. Marshal Pétain emerged from the war a national hero, having beaten the Germans in the critical battle of Verdun in 1916.

After the war de Gaulle returned to St. Cyr as a history professor and attended the Ecole de Guerre (War Academy) in Paris, the training ground of the country's military elite. He soon distinguished himself as an original strategic thinker and a literary stylist of considerable talent. In addition to writing a history of the French army at Pétain's behest, de Gaulle authored a treatise on leadership that uncannily foreshadowed the leadership style he was to adopt in subsequent decades. A wise leader, he counseled in *The Edge of the Sword* (1932), must always maintain a certain distance from his followers and cultivate an air of mystery. "People have little respect for someone they know too well," he warned. Another work brought him into direct conflict with the military brass. After World War I, French strategists adopted a defensive doctrine built around the "Maginot line," a heavily fortified barrier designed to block a potential German invasion. De Gaulle archly criticized this static approach in 1934, arguing for a mobile defensive force more heavily reliant on tanks, planes, and other mechanized weapons. Though he won over a number of France's leading politicians to his ideas, Pétain and the military hierarchy persuaded the IIIrd Republic's governments to keep the Maginot line intact.

The merits of de Gaulle's advice became painfully evident in the spring of 1940, when Adolph Hitler's armies rapidly devastated French forces. Ironically, the

Germans used the very tactics of mechanized warfare de Gaulle had advocated for France. French commanders recognized their mistake and called on de Gaulle to mount an effective defense, but it was too late. With millions of panicked French citizens fleeing the German advance and half the army taken prisoner, Marshal Pétain assumed control of the government and capitulated. Germany's conquest of France had taken only six weeks. Under Hitler's harsh terms, France was initially divided in two. The northern part of the country, including Paris, came under the direct control of German occupation authorities. In the south, the Germans temporarily allowed Pétain to set up a new French state headquartered in Vichy. Like many French people, Pétain believed that the IIIrd Republic had been too politically divided to preserve the nation's security. Though the Vichy government had no real independence and was forced to comply with German wishes, Pétain hoped that it could reduce the severity of German domination and initiate a long process of French national rebirth under authoritarian rule. Many of Vichy's officials and supporters, meanwhile, were openly hostile to democracy and sympathized with fascism. A number of them took part in the roundup of French Jews for deportation to Nazi concentration camps.[15]

De Gaulle drew precisely the opposite conclusions from France's catastrophe. Rejecting any thought of surrender, he repaired to England in hopes of reorganizing French armed resistance to the Germans in conjunction with Winston Churchill's government. In the first of a series of stirring radio broadcasts from London, de Gaulle on June 18 declared that France's defeat was not final. With an overseas empire, British assistance, and the "unlimited use of the vast industries of the United States," he assured the French that they were not alone. Speaking "in the name of France" the next day, de Gaulle declared that all Frenchmen still under arms had the "strict duty of refusing to carry out the enemy's conditions." In effect, he dismissed Pétain's government as illegitimate. "At that moment," he later wrote in his memoirs, "it was for me to assume the country's fate, to take France upon myself."

For de Gaulle the war years alternated between loneliness and adulation, despair and triumph. From his London redoubt he created a new French government, known informally as Free France and later as the Provisional Government. A number of IIIrd Republic politicians and military leaders spurned Vichy and acknowledged de Gaulle as their chief. Over the next four years de Gaulle galvanized a Free French army numbering 115,000 troops, based mostly in Britain and in French colonies in Africa, the Middle East, and Southeast Asia. Free French forces fought the Germans in North Africa

and Italy. A growing resistance movement in France answered to him as the country's true leader. Captured Resistance fighters were known to utter "Long live de Gaulle!" as their final words before execution.

Despite these rising manifestations of legitimacy accorded him by French men and women, de Gaulle had a difficult time dealing with his closest allies. Churchill supported Free France, but his failure to inform de Gaulle in advance of certain U.S. and British military operations fueled the General's greatest anxiety, that France would not be treated as an equal by the United States and Britain. President Franklin D. Roosevelt stoked these fears by casually dismissing de Gaulle as an overblown egotist. During the first years of the war the United States maintained diplomatic ties with the Vichy government, and it subsequently preferred dealing with another overseas French general, Henri Giraud, instead of de Gaulle. Churchill interceded with FDR in de Gaulle's behalf but Roosevelt persistently refused to recognize the Free France movement until the German occupation of France was practically over.

In laying out his plans for the postwar order, the U.S. president informed de Gaulle that the future would be dominated by the United States, Britain, the Soviet Union, and China; there was no room for France in his grand design. On the contrary, until the war's final stages Roosevelt favored an occupation regime for France, with U.S. forces set to occupy French territory as liberators. On the eve of the D-Day invasion of Normandy in June 1944, the United States and Britain still withheld formal recognition of de Gaulle's Provisional Government as the legitimate government of France. When de Gaulle complained bitterly to Churchill, the prime minister testily replied, "Every time I have to choose between you and Roosevelt, I shall always choose Roosevelt." The wartime alliance left de Gaulle with a lifelong vision of collusion between the "Anglo-Saxons" (the Americans and the British) to keep France down, a humiliating affront he would never accept.

Despite these conflicts, de Gaulle remained a loyal partner of the anti-Hitler coalition. Several hundred thousand French forces took part in the country's liberation alongside U.S. and British troops in the summer and fall of 1944. In July, following de Gaulle's triumphal visit to the United States, the Roosevelt administration finally accorded his Provisional Government tentative recognition, which it formalized in October.

THE PROVISIONAL GOVERNMENT AND THE IVTH REPUBLIC

As soon as French troops entered Paris in August, General de Gaulle assumed the reins of power. With Pétain under arrest,[16] the only possible challenge to his authority was the French Communist Party (PCF), which had thousands of armed resistance fighters at its disposal. While some communists appeared poised to seize power by force, de Gaulle neutralized the threat by inviting PCF leaders into his government.

From the outset, the new government's main tasks were to reinvigorate France's shattered economy and establish a stable democracy. In addressing the first of these challenges, de Gaulle conferred primary responsibility for stimulating economic activity on the French state. Although he rejected Marxist ideology and socialist rhetoric, de Gaulle was suspicious of capitalism. He believed that one of France's chronic problems was excessive hostility between the country's profit-driven capitalist elite and the masses of poorly paid workers, many of whom gravitated to the Communist Party in hopes of abolishing private enterprise completely or, at the very least, exerting maximum pressure on the business sector to improve their wages and working conditions. In an effort to reduce class conflict, de Gaulle favored a "social" economic policy that permitted considerable private enterprise but remained sensitive to working-class needs. State management of the national economy was central to this program.

During the first year of de Gaulle's postwar government the state nationalized most of the energy industry, a large part of the banking sector, the railroads, and transport companies like Air France and Renault autos. Additional reforms expanded social security, provided family allowances for new children, and gave workers a say in the companies that employed them. For the rest of his life, de Gaulle remained a strong believer in state direction of the economy. Known as **dirigisme,** this policy stops short of full-scale socialism by allowing ample room for private enterprise. But it encourages state ownership of various enterprises and state coordination of the country's economic activity through planning mechanisms and other forms of intervention in the marketplace.

It was in the political sphere, however, that the Provisional Government concentrated its energies. De Gaulle was firmly committed to democracy, but he did not want France to return to the governmental instability of the IIIrd Republic. He deplored the "regime of the parties" that, in his view, had only heightened France's social and ideological divisions rather than bringing the nation together. He therefore favored a constitution that would counterbalance the powers of the legislature with a strong executive, endowed with real decision-making powers. In de Gaulle's conception, this chief executive would be the "arbiter" and "guide" of French politics, standing above the political parties and social classes as a truly national figure representing the best interests of France as a whole. Needless to say, he conceived of this supreme role for himself.

De Gaulle was fully conscious of his unique role in French history. On the one hand, he was a military man in a country with a long tradition of authoritarian military rule. On the other, he repudiated dictatorship and staunchly supported democracy. In effect, de Gaulle was a bridge linking the two warring traditions of French political history: the tradition of authority, order, and stability historically represented by the monarchy, the army, and the Catholic church; and the tradition of "liberty, equality, fraternity" associated with the Revolution and subsequent republican regimes. In the past, France had never succeeded in combining democracy with stability. De Gaulle believed that the only way to achieve a stable democracy was to anchor democratic institutions in a powerful presidency that would guarantee firm and decisive governance. A strong and stable government at home, moreover, was for de Gaulle the precondition of an active foreign policy that would place France in the front rank of the world's most powerful countries.

To his chagrin, the Constituent Assembly elected in October 1945 for the purpose of writing a new constitution did not share his vision. The communists emerged as the largest party in France, winning 26.1 percent of the vote. Two other parties with roots in the IIIrd Republic—the social democratic SFIO and the middle-class Radical Party—joined the Communists in favoring a return to parliamentary government without the super-executive proposed by de Gaulle. Recognizing that the Assembly would never draft the constitution he wanted, de Gaulle resigned in January 1946 and retreated to his war-battered estate in Normandy. "Since I cannot govern as I wish, that is to say fully," he declared, *"I'm leaving!"* From his self-imposed exile, however, de Gaulle cast a long shadow over French politics. When the IVth Republic's constitution was finally written and submitted to the voters later that year, he denounced it as "stupid." He was convinced that British-style parliamentary government was ill-suited to France and doomed to certain failure.

Events were to prove him right. The IVth Republic witnessed a steady succession of revolving-door governments. The lower house of the legislature, elected by proportional representation, was divided among five main parties and several smaller ones. The Communist Party usually had the largest delegation, but most of the other parties refused to deal with it because of its implacable pro-Soviet orientation at a time of mounting Cold War hostilities. (France was a charter member of NATO in 1949, an alliance the communists vehemently denounced.) De Gaulle and his followers established their own party dedicated to criticizing the IVth Republic's deficiencies. Governments tended to be coalitions consisting of three or more parties. No sooner would the coalition partners cobble an agreement on one policy than they fell apart over others. In all, twenty-two governments came and went over a twelve-year period. One of them lasted only two days, another merely one. "Immobilism" became the watchword of the IVth Republic.

The system's demise came in 1958, precipitated by events in Algeria, the most important of France's overseas colonies. One of the most difficult questions confronting postwar France was what to do about the French Empire. In 1947, Britain granted full independence to its largest colonial possessions, India and Pakistan. But de Gaulle and the IVth Republic governments that followed him decided to retain control of France's imperial domains. This fateful choice resulted in a protracted struggle in Vietnam, where local communists as well as non-communists fought to rid their country of French domination. Unable to sustain the fight, France reached a negotiated settlement with the Vietnamese in 1954 that put an end to its political presence in Indochina. The United States took France's place in the region when it agreed to protect South Vietnam against the communist-run government of North Vietnam.

No sooner had the French withdrawn from Vietnam than a new independence movement flared up in Algeria. By virtue of its proximity to France and the presence of more than a million Europeans among its inhabitants, Algeria was France's most prized colonial dominion. The Europeans were outnumbered by twelve million Arabs, however, and in the fall of 1954 an Arab insurgency took arms against French forces. Though a majority of France favored preserving Algeria's colonial status at this time, as did a number of politicians like François Mitterrand, military leaders in Algeria believed that the floundering coalition governments in Paris were incapable of providing the support they considered necessary for a decisive military victory. In May 1958 they decided to take matters into their own hands.

In a calculated act of insubordination, they engineered the military takeover of France's official government facilities in Algeria. They also proclaimed their own "Committee of Public Safety" to govern the colony. At the heart of the generals' strategy was the hope that their mutiny would precipitate the downfall of the IVth Republic and motivate their trusted military comrade, General de Gaulle, to come out of retirement and form a "Government of Public Safety" in Paris. Though de Gaulle was informed of the generals' plans, there is no evidence that he participated in the planning of their revolt or approved of its execution. In any event, many IVth Republic leaders admitted that only he had the stature and experience needed to resolve the crisis. De Gaulle did not miss this unexpected opportunity to return to center stage. On May 15, two days after the generals' mutiny, he issued a statement rebuking the IVth Republic for twelve years of "degradation" and affirming his readiness for action:

> Not so long ago the country, in its depths, trusted me to lead it in its entirety to its salvation. Today, with the trials that face it once again, let it know that I am ready to assume the powers of the Republic.

The IVth Republic's president, exercising his right to designate the prime minister, thereupon invited de Gaulle to form a new government. De Gaulle agreed, but only on condition that he be granted exceptional powers to govern France by decree for six months, during which his government would have the authority to formulate a new constitution for the voters' consideration. After an intense debate, a large majority of the IVth Republic's lower house accepted de Gaulle's terms. In an extraordinary admission of their ineffectiveness, they voted to abolish the IVth Republic itself. Among those voting against de Gaulle's assumption of power was a future president of the next republic, François Mitterrand.

Though the generals in Algeria assumed that de Gaulle's return signaled a more aggressive approach to crushing the Algerian independence movement, de Gaulle himself provided no such assurances. In a quick trip to the troubled colony immediately after assuming office, he was deliriously embraced by Algeria's European population, especially after assuring them, "I have understood you." As it turned out, de Gaulle intended this phrase to be deliberately enigmatic. In his heart he had already made up his mind that, in an era of decolonization, France would have no choice but to grant Algeria's Arab majority their independence. It was only a matter of time. Moreover, de Gaulle categorically rejected the generals' suggestions that he establish a dictatorship in France. He had no tolerance for a coup d'état and firmly warned the military to obey his orders. In de Gaulle's view, only his firm presence at the helm of the French government could prevent a descent into chaotic civil war and preserve democracy.

DE GAULLE AND THE CONSTITUTION OF THE VTH REPUBLIC

For the time being, de Gaulle enjoined the army in Algeria to continue the war against the independence movement. Though he intended eventually to seek a negotiated settlement, he needed to keep the French military occupied and the Algerian rebels on the defensive while he got on with the business of framing a new constitution. For this task he assembled a small group of experts led by Michel Debré, a trusted advisor and former member of the French parliament. De Gaulle himself took an active role at every stage in the elaboration of the document. The final draft reflected a combination of a powerful presidency, which was de Gaulle's highest priority, and a prime minister and government who would be answerable to the legislature, as favored by parliamentarians like Debré. Thus the Vth Republic constitution was to have two executives, each with significant decision-making authority.

The *president* was conceived as a national arbiter, ensuring "the regular functioning of the governmental authorities, as well as the continuity of the state." In foreign affairs the president is "the guarantor of national independence" and commander-in-chief of the armed forces. In its initial draft, the new constitution called for the president to be elected to a seven-year term by a special electoral college, consisting of some eighty thousand elected political leaders from around the country. In 1962 the constitution was amended to provide for the president's direct election by the people in a process that permits two rounds of voting. To be elected in the first round, the candidate with the most votes must capture an absolute majority of those who turn out to vote. If no one gets more than 50 percent, a runoff election takes place two weeks later between the top two finishers of the first round. This system ensures that the president is elected by a majority of the voting public.

Among the powers in the president's arsenal, the new constitution conferred on the head of state the right to *name the prime minister;* the right to *chair cabinet meetings;* the right to *dissolve the lower house* of the legislature (the National Assembly) and *set anticipated elections;* the right to *call national referendums,* putting questions directly to the voters; and the right to *declare a state of emergency* and govern by executive decrees during that period.

The *government,* for its part, is authorized to "determine and direct the policy of the nation." The constitution says that the *prime minister,* as head of government, "shall direct the operation of the government" and is responsible for national defense. The prime minister and government may be forced to resign if the National Assembly passes a motion of censure against them (a vote of no-confidence). Thus they are responsible to the National Assembly. But the prime minister can also be pressured by the president into resigning. And the president may fire other members of the cabinet and replace them if the prime minister agrees. Thus in practice the prime minister and cabinet are also responsible to the president, not just to the National Assembly.

As conceived by its framers, the new constitution's creation of a dual executive was not expected to be troublesome. The president, it was widely assumed, would lay out broad policy guidelines and ensure overall political stability, while the prime minister would take charge of day-to-day governmental activities. But early critics of the proposed constitution, including François Mitterrand, were quick to criticize de Gaulle for seeking excessive decision-making authority. Some warned that the high-powered presidency amounted to an "elected dictatorship," and accused de Gaulle of "Bonapartism"—a reference to Napoleon's military autocracy. The French Communists were especially hostile to the draft. But the yearning for order and stability was widespread throughout France, especially in the throes of the Algerian crisis. When it was submitted to the people for their judgment in September 1958, de Gaulle's constitution was approved by 79 percent of the voters, a landslide of unprecedented proportions in French democracy. Two months later, de Gaulle's party and its conservative allies outpolled the left-wing parties in elections to the new republic's first National Assembly, ensuring an invincible parliamentary majority in favor of de Gaulle's constitution. And in December, de Gaulle won 78.5 percent of the votes cast in the electoral college established to select the president. In January 1959 he took the oath of office and moved into Elysée Palace, the president's home. He was 68.

De Gaulle appointed Debré as his first prime minister. Although the two men saw eye-to-eye on most issues, and although Debré had considerable latitude to conduct the government's domestic policy, from the beginning it was evident that de Gaulle viewed the presidency as the central decision-making office in the Vth Republic. At times he would announce policy initiatives without even informing Debré in advance. When de Gaulle no longer regarded Debré as politically useful, he made him resign in 1962 and replaced him with another loyal servant, Georges Pompidou. De Gaulle presided imperiously over the government's weekly meetings, typically leaving the assembled ministers too intimidated to speak up. "True, there was a government which 'decides the policy of the nation'," de Gaulle later wrote. "But everyone knew that it would proceed from my choice and act only with my blessing."

When he ordered a referendum in 1962 asking the people to approve the direct popular election of the president, de Gaulle's critics charged that he ignored the constitution's provision requiring him to obtain parliamentary approval before holding a referendum. The legislature thereupon voted to censure Pompidou's government, an act that required the prime minister's resignation. Incensed at the National Assembly's presumptuousness, de Gaulle promptly reappointed Pompidou and dissolved the Assembly, calling new elections. In 1965, when he ran for reelection, de Gaulle barely bothered to campaign. To his surprise he failed to win an absolute majority in the first round. As a result he was forced into a second round with his most serious challenger, François Mitterrand. After campaigning more vigorously, he defeated Mitterrand by 54.6 percent to 45.4 percent.

ALGERIA

Only once did de Gaulle resort to invoking the emergency powers outlined in Article 16 of the constitution. The festering Algerian situation provided the catalyst.

Once the Vth Republic's new institutions were securely in place, de Gaulle announced in September 1959 that he would allow the Algerians to decide for themselves in a referendum how they wished to be governed. Since the vast majority were Muslims bent on independence from France, de Gaulle's decision meant that France would no longer insist on a "French Algeria," but would agree to permit an "Algerian Algeria." The announcement sparked riots in Algeria several months later, with French generals openly inciting European Algerians to ignore de Gaulle and take over the Algerian government. Stung by the brazen attempt of key military leaders to stage a coup d'état in the colony, de Gaulle went on television in military dress and delivered one of his most powerful speeches. He forcefully reaffirmed his decision to permit self-determination for the Algerians and reminded the French people that he had personally embodied "national legitimacy" for twenty years. He then declared: "I am the supreme authority. It is I who bear the destiny of the country in my hands. I must, therefore, be obeyed by all French soldiers." De Gaulle's display of command convinced most troops in Algeria to abandon their rebellious commanders. The coup attempt quickly fizzled and some of its leaders were arrested.

But the crisis was not over. Disenchanted French generals and their followers in Algeria and France formed an underground conspiracy, the Secret Army Organization (OAS), dedicated to assassinating de Gaulle. In April 1961 a group of generals tried once again to seize power in Algeria by force. At the same time, French police uncovered OAS plans for the military takeover of the French government in Paris. Rumors of a landing by insurgent paratroopers gripped the country. In another riveting television appearance in full military uniform, the president announced that he was invoking Article 16 of the constitution, vowing to "take whatever steps seem to me to be required by the circumstances." Once again, his ringing assertion of authority had a magnetic effect. Large numbers of French paratroopers and other soldiers who had been poised for action instantly deserted their rebellious commanders. The insurgency dissolved and several of its plotters surrendered to French authorities.

As required by the constitution, the parliament continued to meet throughout the duration of the national emergency. Its powers, however, remained in doubt, since Article 16 does not specify exactly what, if anything, the legislature may do during the emergency period. Appeals to President de Gaulle by François Mitterrand and other legislators to clarify the situation were met with majestic silence. The public, meanwhile, solidly backed de Gaulle. Polls showed that 84 percent

trusted him to resolve the crisis. Several months after the declaring the state of emergency, de Gaulle announced it was over. No French president since him has ever invoked Article 16.

Later in that same year, de Gaulle and his wife narrowly escaped calamity as a detonating device exploded near their car. The assassin was subsequently apprehended, but violence by OAS sympathizers accelerated in Algeria and France throughout the following year. De Gaulle nevertheless persisted in his Algerian policy. In March 1962, French and Algerian negotiators meeting in Evian agreed on a peace accord providing for a referendum on the colony's status. To legitimize the accord democratically, de Gaulle ordered a separate referendum in France. More than 90 percent of those who went to the polls in France approved the Evian agreements. As the Algerian majority moved toward independence, the OAS intensified its efforts to prevent it. OAS marksmen on at least two occasions came within inches of shooting de Gaulle, at one point shattering his car windows with gunfire. Several OAS leaders were arrested and either executed or exiled. But others remained underground, including some prominent political leaders who had been close to de Gaulle during World War II.

DE GAULLE'S "POLICY OF GRANDEUR"

Once the Algerian question was settled, de Gaulle turned to foreign policy matters that, in his eyes, were far more important. "France is not really herself unless in the front rank," he wrote in his memoirs. This meant above all that France must never allow itself to be a mere follower of the "Anglo-Saxons," especially the United States. De Gaulle therefore devised a foreign policy designed to enhance French freedom of maneuver in foreign affairs, while at the same time remaining a member of the NATO political alliance and a dedicated foe of Soviet imperialism. In a series of measures that irked President Lyndon B. Johnson's administration, de Gaulle withdrew French military forces from the unified NATO military command in Europe, which was always headed by an American general, and compelled the United States and NATO to remove their troops and facilities from French soil. The United States, he asserted, could not be counted on to keep its word to defend Europe in the event of a Soviet attack. France therefore required its own nuclear arsenal and the freedom to determine when to use it, independent of NATO military planners. While withdrawing from NATO's *military* component, de Gaulle made sure that France remained in NATO's *political* decision-making bodies, where it would have a say in the alliance's overall diplomatic and strategic direction. That arrangement was still in effect in 2000.

In addition, de Gaulle openly criticized the U.S. war effort in Vietnam, refrained from joining the United

States in backing Israel in the June War of 1967, and established diplomatic relations with Communist China at a time when the United States refused to do so. In pursuing his own diplomatic initiatives with the Soviet Union and the communist states of East-Central Europe, he hoped to establish himself as a bridge between East and West during the Cold War rather than as a mere tool of Washington's worldwide anti-communist policy. He assiduously courted West Germany in hopes of distancing it from its preferential ties with the United States. And in 1963 he vetoed Britain's application for membership in the European Community, the forerunner of the European Union, on the grounds that the UK was simply a "Trojan horse" promoting American domination in Europe. In place of a federal Europe, centered in supranational decision-making organs in Brussels, he favored a "Europe of countries," in which the main decisions would always be taken by the organization's member governments. De Gaulle was a proud defender of French national sovereignty and opposed surrendering control over his country's political fate to European technocrats.

While these and other initiatives antagonized American and British policy makers, de Gaulle remained a reliable ally in times of crisis. He stood firm against Soviet pressures on Berlin when tensions surrounding that city heated up, and he vigorously supported the United States during the Cuban missile crisis of 1962. Despite his problems with Roosevelt and Johnson, de Gaulle got on well with Presidents Eisenhower, Kennedy, and Nixon. Years later, British Prime Minister Margaret Thatcher would embrace de Gaulle's vision of a "Europe of countries" as the cornerstone of her opposition to a federated European Union.

De Gaulle fully realized, of course, that his policy of promoting French grandeur abroad required political unity and economic strength at home. With the "bold support of the nation," he had written years earlier, "I could promise that no one would ignore or defy the will of France." But precisely these preconditions blew up in his face in 1968, when French students, intellectuals, and working people suddenly burst into spontaneous protests at the existing political order. The resulting threat of chaos confronted de Gaulle with his last major crisis.

1968

The extraordinary events of 1968 began with a series of small protests by students dissatisfied with conditions in several of the country's large public universities. During the 1960s the student population had risen from 200,000 to more than 500,000, but the French government had not expanded facilities fast enough to accommodate the increases. Libraries and laboratories were overcrowded and lecture halls were so inadequate that thousands of students were forced to listen to their lectures on radio. Most students had no contact with their professors and felt ignored by incommunicative university administrators. In March a few dozen students led by Daniel Cohn-Bendit, a charismatic redheaded idealist later dubbed "Danny the Red," took over some lecture halls at the University of Paris campus in the suburb of Nanterre. As the protests continued, the dean closed down the campus on May 2. The next day, sympathetic students at the Sorbonne in central Paris tore up paving stones and erected barricades. The government ordered the police to clear the area. Quite a few students were brutally beaten and a number were arrested. From this point on, the protests escalated wildly and the brutality of the police inflamed public opinion.

Within a week, students had taken over most of the Latin Quarter, the location of the Sorbonne and other universities. Pitched battles with the police grew increasingly violent as de Gaulle's government refused to negotiate. Students threw stones and Molotov cocktails, the police used truncheons and tear gas. In one overnight exchange nearly four hundred students were wounded and a hundred cars set ablaze. As de Gaulle remained stonily silent and his ministers appeared befuddled, some 300,000 students and political opponents of de Gaulle's regime staged a massive demonstration, with many shouting for the president's resignation. De Gaulle responded by casually leaving the next day on a planned trip to Romania.

On that very day, the protests entered a new phase as factory workers at a state-owned factory staged a wildcat strike. This spontaneous action set in motion a nationwide strike movement involving industrial workers and white-collar employees throughout France. Within weeks some 10 million French people were on strike. Factories and offices closed, public services virtually ceased, and the nation's transportation system came to a standstill. Most workers had little in common with the students. Cohn-Bendit and other student leaders spoke of destroying the Vth Republic and replacing it with a utopian society whose precise contours they admittedly could not define. "Take your dreams for reality!" was one of their slogans; many drew their inspiration from Mao Zedong, the leader of Communist China. But the striking workers were mainly interested in bread-and-butter issues, not revolution. A slowdown in the French economy over the previous year had reduced their purchasing power and boosted unemployment.

With the entire country sliding toward anarchy, de Gaulle cut his trip short and returned home. "In five days," he thundered at his ministers, "ten years of struggle against rottenness in the State have been lost.

What a fine state you'll all be in when I'm no longer here!" In a television address aimed at restoring order, the embattled president offered to hold a national referendum on reforming the university's structures and allowing greater "participation" by workers in the management of their places of employment. But unlike his previous attempts to meet a crisis with a rousing speech, this time his words had no effect. More violence followed as protestars stormed through Paris and riot police gave them battle.

In an effort to stem the strike movement that threatened to paralyze the country, the government agreed to a major increase in the minimum wage and a reduction in working hours, along with other concessions and proposals for worker "participation." The leaders of the French Communist Party's trade union organization, the CGT, agreed to the deal and recommended its approval by the rank and file. To their dismay, however, workers at several large factories rejected it and refused to go back to work. With this bitter disappointment, the French government was at wit's end. François Mitterrand announced his availability for the presidency in the event de Gaulle resigned. Ominously, Prime Minister Pompidou ordered tanks to take up positions at the gates of Paris. And de Gaulle confided to an aide that he was about to "fall to pieces." And then, suddenly, the general disappeared.

On May 29, de Gaulle informed Pompidou that he was returning to his estate in Normandy to think things over, but he did not reveal his true intentions. "I want to plunge the French people, including the government, into doubt and anxiety," he told his son-in-law, "in order to regain control of the situation." It turned out that de Gaulle had flown secretly across the border for a meeting with General Jacques Massu, commander-in-chief of French troops in West Germany. Though Massu had once opposed de Gaulle's Algerian policy, the two generals respected each other. In an agonized conversation, de Gaulle considered going into retirement, but Massu talked him out of it, assuring him of the army's backing. His spirits revived, the aging president mustered his forces for one more attempt to call France to order.

The following afternoon, President de Gaulle calmly addressed the country on radio. "As the possessor of national and republican legitimacy," he intoned, "I have a mandate from the people and I shall fulfill it." The president then announced that he was dissolving the National Assembly and setting new elections. Warning that France was threatened with a totalitarian dictatorship, de Gaulle placed the blame for the country's chaotic situation squarely on the French Communist Party and hinted obliquely at using military force in the event that the electoral process was thwarted. Shortly after he spoke, a crowd that swelled to more than 500,000 people filled the boulevards of Paris in a massive display of support for de Gaulle. The atmosphere of revolutionary chaos was suddenly broken.

Over the next several weeks, Pompidou took charge of the government's election campaign, placing heavy emphasis on the alleged threat by the French Communists to seize power. In actual fact, the Communist Party leadership wanted nothing to do with the uncontrollable student movement and was looking for a compromise solution to the wildcat strikes.[17] The electoral ploy worked, however, as millions of French people longed for a restoration of social peace. The results of the elections of June 23 and 30 were a triumph for de Gaulle's party and its allies on the right. They won 360 of the National Assembly's 485 seats. Mitterrand's social democratic grouping lost half its seats and so did the communists. As workers returned to their jobs, the student revolt quietly dissipated in the fine spring weather.[18]

De Gaulle had once more worked his charismatic magic on the people of France, rescuing the country from the brink of disintegration. But at 78, he was not inclined to seek any more titanic challenges. The 1968 events had exposed severe divisions in French society as well as weaknesses in its economy, severely undercutting his foreign policy ambitions. French business leaders opposed his scheme for worker participation. And by the following year, with calm restored, there was a growing feeling in the electorate that France no longer needed him. Sensing that the time had come to exit the scene, de Gaulle turned a referendum on reforming the Senate in April 1969 into a referendum on himself. He announced that he would quit if his proposal were defeated. When the results showed 53 percent against his proposed reform, he resigned the presidency the following day. He thereupon withdrew to his Normandy estate to resume the writing of his memoirs and to enjoy his retirement with his wife. While at home on November 9, 1970, de Gaulle suffered a ruptured blood vessel and died in less than an hour.

DE GAULLE'S LEGACY

De Gaulle was a man of many contradictions. Arrogant and resolute in his use of personal power, he remained incorruptible and free from the taint of scandal. Like the Boutbon monarchs, he believed that he personified the French state and that the deluge would surely follow him. And yet he reined in these authoritarian instincts with a principled commitment to popular democracy. Though he occasionally violated the spirit of democracy and even the letter of his own constitution, de Gaulle more than once saved democracy in France from its challengers of both right and left. He detested the routine transactions of everyday parliamentary politics but felt a personal connection with the people of France that went over the heads of ordinary politicians. When he spoke "in the name of France," as he often did, he embodied in his own way Rousseau's principle of the "general will." (His detractors would say that "the general will is the General's will!") Though conservative in social matters, in 1944 he gave French women the vote for the first time. His economic policies transcended the traditional categories of left and right, socialist and capitalist. And in an age of impersonal economic forces and mass social movements, he showed how the fortunes of an entire nation can at times rest on the shoulders of a single individual.

Since his death, no one in France has assumed de Gaulle's mantle as one of the world's most extraordinary political leaders. But his towering presence continues to hover over French politics. "Gaullism" became a synonym for strong presidential authority at home and foreign policy activism on the world stage. Not only have these basic tenets come to be shared by Gaullists and neo-Gaullists favorably disposed to the General's contributions to French politics, but they have also been adapted in varying ways by political leaders who once opposed de Gaulle, such as Mitterrand. To a considerable extent, most of France today accepts the Gaullist consensus that the Vth Republic's constitution should remain in force essentially as it is and that France needs to play a role of its own in world affairs, independent of the United States while at the same time allied with it. And while left and right in today's France may argue over how to manage the relationship between private enterprise and the labor force, there is a wide consensus around de Gaulle's view that the state must play a large role in the French economy for the benefit of all. Finally there has emerged in recent decades a growing consensus on the need to put aside the uncompromising attitudes and visceral divisions of the past, which de Gaulle always decried as a source of national weakness, and to forge greater unity of purpose and cooperation among the forces of French society and political life.

While France has changed considerably since Charles de Gaulle's lifetime, its state institutions and prevailing political attitudes remain deeply affected by his powerful imprint.[19]

De Gaulle's Conservative Successors: Pompidou and Giscard d'Estaing

After de Gaulle's resignation, a special presidential election brought **Georges Pompidou** to the Elysée Palace. (The constitution does not provide for a vice president to fill out the term of a president who vacates the office. The president of the Senate takes over temporarily, but new presidential elections must be held within thirty-five days.) Pompidou had been a close associate of de Gaulle's since the liberation of France at the end of World War II. A brilliant student, he started out as a literature teacher and later became a successful banker, eventually rising to prominence as an executive in the Rothschild Bank. Pompidou proved invaluable to de Gaulle as his chief assistant during the crucial months of 1958, when the General governed by decree and presided over the drafting of the Vth Republic's constitution. He was tapped by de Gaulle once again in 1962 to replace Michel Debré as prime minister. He served the president dutifully in this position, deferring to de Gaulle in matters of the highest political importance.

Until he assumed the presidency, Pompidou lacked a wide political following of his own. In 1962 he became the first—and thus far the only—prime minister in the Vth Republic to lose a vote of confidence in the National Assembly, but de Gaulle immediately reappointed him. Pompidou remained in that post throughout the 1968 crisis, making crucial decisions when de Gaulle appeared to lose his grip. After de Gaulle regained his self-confidence and called snap elections, Pompidou masterminded the Gaullists' electoral landslide. De Gaulle thereupon dismissed his faithful lieutenant from the government and chose a new prime minister, Maurice Couve de Murville.

When de Gaulle retired, Pompidou declared his candidacy. With the French left in disarray in 1969, he won a comfortable victory against a centrist challenger, Alain Poher. Though he was a confirmed Gaullist, he soon put his own stamp on the Gaullist tradition. His economic policies deviated slightly from the de Gaulle's insistence on intrusive state controls. As a man of the private sector, Pompidou gradually tilted the government's policies in the direction of greater freedom for private enterprise. At the same time, he made sure that the state continued to coordinate the economy's direction through the loose "indicative planning" procedures implemented under de Gaulle. His foreign policy diverged from de Gaulle's through his adoption of more positive attitudes toward the United States and Britain. He favored closer cooperation with NATO (though not a complete return to the alliance's integrated command) and withdrew France's veto of Britain's entry into the European Community. With the approval of French voters in a referendum, Britain entered the EC in 1972.

A devastating illness prevented Pompidou from serving out his full seven-year term. Upon his death in 1974, fresh presidential elections were held that signaled major shifts in the French political landscape after sixteen years of Gaullist dominance. No candidate won an absolute majority in the first round. Significantly, the Gaullist party's candidate, Jacques Chaban-Delmas, finished third. The top two contenders who vied in the runoff election were **Valéry Giscard d'Estaing** (Zhee-scar Day-sta*ng*) and François Mitterrand. Giscard was a conservative who had served as finance minister under de Gaulle. Though his policy predilections were close to those of de Gaulle's followers, he had his own small political party that rivaled the Gaullists for the center-right vote. Mitterrand was a veteran of the IVth Republic and an outspoken foe of de Gaulle's Vth Republic constitution. His appearance in the 1974 presidential contest appeared more promising than his quixotic 1965 candidacy against de Gaulle because the diverse forces of the French left were now more united than they had been in decades. In 1971 Mitterrand had won the leadership of a new French Socialist party, and the following year he successfully negotiated a "Common Program" with the French Communist Party for governing France together. The 1974 presidential elections thus presented French voters with a stark choice between opposing left-right visions of how the country should be governed and how its economy should be organized. When all the votes were counted, Giscard d'Estaing narrowly beat Mitterrand, 50.7 percent to 49.3 percent.

Giscard's presidency was largely uneventful, at least when compared to the tumultuous 1950s and 1960s. His government secured the passage of a liberal abortion law, lowered the voting age to eighteen, and promoted women's rights. It also reinstituted the guillotine for capital punishment. Like Pompidou, Giscard mended fences with the United States but refrained from reentering NATO's military command structure. He promoted European unity, forging France's links with

West Germany and Britain. Giscard's governing style reflected his emphasis on technocratic competence, especially in monetary and fiscal matters. He openly criticized de Gaulle's regal distance from the French population, but aside from an occasional appearance in a restaurant and other carefully orchestrated contacts with ordinary people, Giscard maintained a quasi-aristocratic bearing that earned him a reputation for snobbery. He jealously guarded the powers of the presidential office and kept the National Assembly in its subordinate position.

Ultimately the most important event affecting France during Giscard's administration had already occurred in 1973. Following the Arab-Israeli war in October, the governments of the world's leading oil-producing countries decided to vastly increase the prices they charged foreign oil companies for crude petroleum. Within months, world oil prices were four times higher than before the October Mideast war. The 1973 oil shock was followed by still more oil price hikes over the decade, and their cumulative impact wreaked havoc on economic activity around the world. During the first years of Giscard's presidency, France was on the verge of overtaking West Germany as the most successful economy in Western Europe. But as the effects of the oil crisis took their toll, the French economy reeled. Economic growth stagnated and inflation soared, an increasingly contagious global phenomenon that economists dubbed *stagflation*. Government action seemed powerless to arrest the disturbing trends.

Giscard's first prime minister, Jacques Chirac, increased government spending in an effort to stimulate the economy by Keynesian methods. When that approach failed, Giscard replaced Chirac with Raymond Barre, a professor and former trade minister hailed by his admirers as "the best economist in France." Barre reversed the government's course and clamped a tight lid of austerity on the budget, but problems remained. By the time Giscard's term ended in 1981, France was staggering under a 10 percent inflation rate and an unemployment figure of 7.2 percent, the highest in decades. More than 1.5 million people were out of work.[20]

The stage was now set for a reprise of the Giscard-Mitterrand duel for the presidency. This time, however, France's waning economic fortunes played into the hands of the challenger from the left.

PROFILE: François Mitterrand

"Anyone who does not accept a rupture with the established order and capitalist society cannot be a member of the Socialist Party," François Mitterrand exclaimed before the party faithful in 1971. "Revolution is rupture. Our base is class confrontation. The real enemy is the monopoly of money—the money that corrupts, buys, crushes!"

The speech rang out like a revolutionary call to arms. It filled the assembly hall with phrases that had defined the French left since the nineteenth century. Mitterrand made it very clear that if the Socialist Party were elected to govern France, the country could expect some radical changes in its political and economic structures. A year later, Mitterrand and the Socialists joined with the French Communist Party (PCF) in adopting a "Common Program of the Left" that specified in considerable detail the kinds of changes they proposed to introduce. The Vth Republic's constitution would be rewritten: its powerful presidency would be cut down to size and the powers of the legislature enhanced. Nine of the country's largest private conglomerates would be nationalized by the state, along with other private companies. Workers would get a boost in the minimum wage and other benefits. Taxes would be raised on the rich to pay for a variety of social programs. Military spending would be cut.

François Mitterrand

In 1981, Mitterrand was elected president of France on campaign pledges closely patterned on the Common Program. His "110 Proposals" promised major constitutional and economic alterations. But within two short years the left's program was in shambles. Mitterrand's hopes of jump-starting economic growth and slashing unemployment through bold government action ended in failure. His decades-long crusade against the Vth Republic's high-powered presidency was abandoned. An austerity policy strikingly similar to Barre's abruptly replaced robust government spending. And in 1986 Mitterrand had to face a revived conservative majority in the National Assembly, a predicament that prompted him to appoint his Gaullist adversary, Jacques Chirac, as prime minister. Chirac immediately set about reversing the nationalizations and other policies Mitterrand and the Socialists had instituted with such euphoric optimism only a few years earlier. Before the end of his first term as president, the socialism Mitterrand had fought for seemed dead.

How had this happened? And what did Mitterrand's experience mean for the idea of socialism in France and the future of the left? The Mitterrand years provide a telling tale not only about one of the country's most important political leaders, but more broadly about the nature of ideology and the ability of governments to accomplish their goals in an advanced democracy like France. It also provides the background of France's current government under Lionel Jospin, Mitterrand's successor at the helm of the Socialist Party.

YOUTHFUL ADVENTURES

François Mitterrand did not begin his career on the left. On the contrary, his upbringing and education shaped him as a conservative. Born in 1916, Mitterrand was raised in a pious Catholic family of small-business people in provincial France. He attended religious schools and lived in a Catholic boarding house while studying law and political science in Paris in the 1930s. Though he drifted away from the practice of Catholicism as a young man, he preserved a number of values associated with Catholic social teachings about brotherhood and social equality. Like most French politicians of his generation, his outlook was also profoundly shaped by the traumas of World War II. Mitterrand joined the army in 1939, and when the Germans stormed into France the following year he was wounded in battle, captured, and shipped off to prisoner of war (POW) camps in Germany. He escaped after eighteen months and stealthily made his way home. His family resided in the southern part of France where Marshall Pétain's government, based in Vichy, now had administrative control under the Germans' watchful eyes. At a time of limited opportunities, Mitterrand took a position as a minor functionary in the Vichy administration's bureau for the resettlement of war prisoners. His new position, his widening circle of friends in the Vichy regime, and his occasional publications in political newspapers marked him as a man of the right and—according to some accounts—a sincere devotee of Pétain. Mitterrand's own statements about this period of his life tended to be less than revealing.[21]

While working in the Vichy bureaucracy, Mitterrand sought out the anti-German resistance movement that was sprouting up in various parts of the country. For a time he worked for Vichy and the resistance simultaneously, leading a risky double life. Mitterrand quit his government job in early 1943 and went underground, eventually assuming the leadership of a resistance organization consisting of former French prisoners of war. At age twenty-seven, he journeyed abroad clandestinely to meet with General de Gaulle in hopes of obtaining assistance for his group. Their relationship got off to a bad start and never improved. De Gaulle was determined to keep the French resistance movement under his own authority and ordered Mitterrand to merge his organization with another one headed by de Gaulle's nephew. Mitterrand initially refused, but on returning to France complied with the General's directives.

Shortly after Paris was liberated in 1944, Mitterrand was appointed by de Gaulle's Provisional Government to a secondary position in the new ministry for POWs. When de Gaulle spotted him at a meeting of state officials, he greeted Mitterrand by scornfully exclaiming, "What, you again?" That rebuke left a lasting impression of bitterness on Mitterrand's attitudes toward the General. Several months later de Gaulle took Mitterrand to task after a violent demonstration by POWs for more state assistance. The violence was orchestrated by communist agitators and Mitterrand had disapproved of it, but de Gaulle held him responsible.

THE MAN OF THE REPUBLIC

In 1946 Mitterrand won election to the newly established Republic's lower house of parliament. His political orientation at this time was still more center-right than leftist. His party belonged to a group of small centrist parties favoring less intervention by the state in private enterprise and freedom for Catholic schools to operate without undue government interference. Both positions were traditionally associated with the right in France and hotly contested by the left. Mitterrand was never a Marxist. Hence he did not join the main social democratic party, the French Section of the Socialist International (SFIO), and he staunchly opposed the communists.

Soon after taking his parliamentary seat, Mitterrand at the age of thirty was invited into the cabinet. Over the ensuing years he served as a minister in eleven of the Republic's twenty-two governments, ultimately rising to such high-level positions as minister of justice and minister of the interior. Despite the Republic's reputation for governmental instability and immobilism, Mitterrand approved of the constitution and relished the parliamentary game. He also staked out positions that would later prove embarrassing. During the Algerian conflict, for example, he affirmed that "Algeria is France" and voiced support for military action. Even after Algeria became independent, Mitterrand expressed regret that "Algeria is leaving us." He similarly regretted the decolonization of France's African dependencies. Years later, he would adopt very different attitudes as a champion of the developing world's independence.

THE CHALLENGER

It was his stance against de Gaulle in the spring of 1958 that established Mitterrand as an early opponent of the Vth Republic. As leading officials of the beleaguered Republic turned to de Gaulle to lead them out of the Algerian impasse, Mitterrand sharply confronted the General at a meeting of political leaders and later voted against granting him extraordinary powers to write a new constitution. Although he promised to rally to him if de Gaulle succeeded in establishing "a new form of democracy," Mitterrand feared that dictatorship would be the most likely result of de Gaulle's return to power. Over the next several years Mitterrand became France's most outspoken critic of de Gaulle's regime. He vocally opposed virtually all of de Gaulle's policies, especially the use of referendums and the constitutional amendment establishing the direct election of the president by the people. Both procedures, in Mitterrand's view, circumvented parliamentary democracy and threatened to establish a popular authoritarianism. In 1964 Mitterrand published a broadside entitled *The Permanent Coup d'Etat*, which systematically attacked de Gaulle's use of personal power as a form of dictatorial rule.

The following year, Mitterrand decided to challenge de Gaulle in the Vth Republic's first popular election to the presidency. He stitched together a loose coalition of center-left parties and his own political organization, which was more of a club than a party. He also convinced the Communist Party leadership to back him. Although he was a lifelong opponent of communist doctrine and deplored the PCF's symbiotic connection to the Soviet Union, Mitterrand knew that it would be impossible to beat de Gaulle without the votes of PCF followers, who accounted for close to a fourth of the electorate. To everyone's surprise, de Gaulle failed to win an absolute majority in the first round of voting. Mitterrand finished a strong second and won a chance to face de Gaulle in a head-to-head runoff election. Though he lost to the General, Mitterrand won a major symbolic victory by garnering nearly 45 percent of the vote.

After the 1965 elections, Mitterrand was increasingly looked upon as the left's main presidential contender. But there was considerable uncertainty as to what the left actually stood for. The old-guard leaders of the venerable SFIO were mostly moderates who favored a significant role for the state in economic affairs but shied away from radical anti-capitalist rhetoric or grandiose schemes for nationalizing more private businesses. Some had even come to terms with de Gaulle's constitution. The communists, for their part, were vehemently anti-capitalist and loyal to Moscow. Mitterrand himself provided little enlightenment on what the left would do once in power; he did not really think of himself as a socialist and rarely talked about socialism prior to the 1965 presidential race. He had never associated himself with the industrial working class. In the mid-1960s Mitterrand's ideological messages were inscrutably vague. "The Left," he said, "is whatever fights for individual liberties, for justice, for social equality. . . . The Left means love between peoples."

Within a few years Mitterrand's rhetoric would become considerably more specific in its demands and far more radical in tone. The events of 1968 provided a major stimulus to these leftward shifts. In the midst of the crisis, Mitterrand had overplayed his hand by calling for de Gaulle's resignation and announcing his own candidacy for the Elysée Palace. De Gaulle's resuscitation and the right's stunning victory in the hastily called parliamentary elections were a rude shock for Mitterrand personally and for the left-wing parties collectively. At the same time, the student unrest and the parallel nationwide strike movement convinced Mitterrand and his followers that beneath the surface of French society there was a widespread yearning for radical political and economic change. Mitterrand believed that if the left could tap these longings and express them in a clearly articulated political program, the conservatives' grip on power could be overturned.

The left's electoral catastrophe of 1968 prompted a reorganization of its party structures. The SFIO renamed itself the Socialist Party in 1969. Taking advantage of infighting between the party's moderates and its more radical wings, Mitterrand managed to get himself elected as the party's new chief at a conference of Socialist activists in 1971. While striving to keep the party's conflicting factions together, he moved toward a more pronouncedly anti-capitalist position. His conviction that the left could not take power without the votes of Communist Party supporters reinforced these ideological adjustments. The socialists and communists reached agreement on the *Common Program of the Left* only after

arduous negotiations, with concessions coming from both sides. Ever since the 1920s, these two groups had never trusted each other: the Socialists were committed to ballot-box democracy while the Communists dutifully supported the USSR's single-party dictatorship. By 1972 both sides were ready to cooperate, and the Common Program spelled out a series of measures designed to weaken the hold of private enterprise on the French economy without entirely destroying it. Mitterrand, however, was under no illusions about the Communists' trustworthiness as political partners. His aims were purely electoral. Shortly after signing on to the Common Program he declared that he hoped to entice three out of five Communist voters to defect to his Socialist Party!

In bolstering his appeal to left-wing voters, Mitterrand heated up his rhetoric. "I have become convinced that the economic structure of capitalism is a dictatorship," he told one interviewer. "The mutation we are proposing," he later wrote, "must culminate in the abolition of capitalism. . . . There can be no coexistence between socialism and capitalism." In *The Rose in the Fist*, a book whose title described the Socialist Party's emblem, he reinforced the Common Program's call for major constitutional reform. Mitterrand wanted to reduce the president's term in office to five years, curtail the use of presidential referendums, and eliminate the emergency powers of Article 16, which he called "the dictatorship article." Mitterrand also called for permitting the prime minister to enjoy the full powers granted by the constitution and for strengthening the powers of the National Assembly.

To Mitterrand's consternation, the left failed to take control of the National Assembly in the elections of 1973 and 1978. The Communists effectively scuttled the unity of the left in 1978 once it became evident that they were losing voters to the Socialists. Mitterrand suffered a more personal disappointment in 1974, when he lost his presidential bid to Giscard d'Estaing. It was not until 1981 that Mitterrand's—and the left's—time had come.[22]

A TROUBLED PRESIDENCY

Like the previous presidential elections, the 1981 contest did not produce a victor with an absolute majority in round 1. The second ballot saw Mitterrand narrowly defeat Giscard d'Estaing by 51.8 percent to 48.2 percent. Ten days later Mitterrand took office and quickly exercised one of the president's most important prerogatives: he announced the dissolution of the conservative-dominated National Assembly. Riding a crest of popularity, Mitterrand's Socialist Party defied most predictions and won nearly 55 percent of the seats, giving it full control of the lower house. A small leftist party allied with the Socialists added to their total of parliamentary support. Fortunately for Mitterrand, the socialists would not need the parliamentary votes of the Communist Party in order to govern. Nevertheless, in an effort to reduce frictions with the PCF and curry its support, the new president invited four communists to join the cabinet in minor ministerial posts.

Mitterrand selected Pierre Mauroy as his first prime minister and Lionel Jospin as the Socialist Party's new chief. The new government moved rapidly to fulfill the party's campaign pledges. Within their first two years in power the Socialists fully nationalized eight major conglomerates, including some of the country's leading firms in telecommunications, electronics, chemicals, steel, and airplane construction. The nationalized companies accounted for about a fifth of France's industrial production and brought the number of workers in French public enterprises to nearly one-fourth of the total industrial work force. The state also bought controlling ownership of a large pharmaceutical company and a weapons manufacturer, and it nationalized thirty-six banks. The nationalizations cost the state some 39 billion francs (about $8 billion). Several of the newly nationalized firms lost money over the next several years and had to be bailed out with infusions of cash from the national treasury before they became profitable.

To improve the lives of French workers, the Mitterrand-Mauroy government raised the minimum wage nine times between 1981 and 1983; added a fifth week of paid vacation to the four weeks established by the Popular Front government in 1936; reduced working hours for most categories of workers from forty hours a week to thirty-nine, while requiring employers to pay their workers for forty hours; enhanced trade union bargaining rights; cut the minimum retirement age from sixty-five to sixty; and raised pensions. Private businesses were compensated by the state for about half the added expenses these and other laws would impose on them. In addition, the government increased family allowances and provided new funding for rent subsidies for the poor, assistance to struggling farmers, and aid to the part-time unemployed. After a year and half in power the bill for the government's new social welfare programs came to 1 billion francs (about $500 million). To finance them the government in 1982 imposed a wealth tax on large fortunes and the following year it raised the average income tax rate from 42 percent to 44 percent. (The average income tax rate in the United States was about 35 percent.)

These measures reflected not only the French left's aversion to capitalism and its devotion to bettering the lives of workers and the less fortunate; but also Mitterrand's lifelong belief that money was the root of evil and that people had a moral obligation to help those in need. Moreover, Mitterrand agreed with the Socialist

Party's more left-leaning economic advisors that the best way to combat France's rising unemployment was to increase government spending. This policy was not so much Marxist in inspiration as Keynesian. It derived from Keynes's notion that governments can "reflate," or "prime the pump," of a sluggish economy by spending money and thereby raising the overall demand for goods and services. Mitterrand's reflationary policy was the opposite of the deflationary (budget-cutting) policies Margaret Thatcher sought to pursue in Britain.[23]

As it happened, this economic strategy turned out to be ill-timed. France was not an island unto itself; it was unavoidably caught in the snares of globalization. France was the world's fifth largest economy, its fourth largest trading nation, and a pivotal member of the European Community. International economic conditions in the early 1980s were not conducive to the free-spending policies of Mitterrand's new government, which vastly increased budget deficits and the national debt. These policies aggravated France's inflation rate, making the French franc overvalued in relation to the currencies of countries with lower inflation, notably West Germany, France's main trade partner. Acknowledging this reality, Mitterrand's administration had to devalue the franc three times in relation to the deutschemark in its first two years in office. Furthermore, Mitterrand's initial economics team assumed that the world economy, still staggering from the oil price hikes of the 1970s, would begin to grow again, raising world demand for French exports. They placed special hopes on the U.S. and West German economies, but neither of them took off as rapidly as anticipated.

Other international factors also worked against the French economy, including growing competition from Japan in the global market for autos and electronics. French competitiveness in world markets was declining. To make matters worse for the Socialists, wealthy French people and businesses began shifting their money overseas in order to escape the widening tax net. This capital flight deprived the economy of money that could be used to increase the demand for goods at home. Finally, by 1983 it was evident that the government's Keynesian spending programs and its nationalization of private corporations were simply not succeeding in reducing unemployment.

Buffeted by these economic exigencies, the Mitterrand government slammed the brakes on its costly programs and reversed course. It froze wages and prices, cut subsidies to nationalized companies, laid off employees, imposed fees on various social services, and raised taxes. Though the Socialists described these and other painful decisions as a temporary "parenthesis" in the pursuit of socialism, and insisted that their new policy of "rigor" had nothing in common with Giscard d'Estaing's "austerity," in fact President Mitterrand and his ministers were compelled by events to pursue a conservative austerity policy for most of the next dozen years. Moderate Socialists who opposed the unrelenting anti-capitalism of the party's left wing increasingly made themselves heard. Though Mitterrand's heart belonged on the left, he appointed a succession of Socialist prime ministers who shifted the government's policies toward promoting private sector development. "Profit" and "entrepreneurism" replaced "regulation" and "nationalization" in the Socialist vocabulary.

In 1984 Mitterrand replaced Mauroy with Laurent Fabius, at age thirty-seven the youngest French prime minister since before the Revolution. After a period of "cohabitation" with Jacques Chirac from 1986–88, Mitterrand chose as his next head of government Michel Rocard, a technocrat who was the president's chief rival within the Socialist Party. In 1991 he replaced Rocard with Edith Cresson, the country's first female prime minister. She was followed in less than a year by Pierre Beregovoy, another Socialist moderate. In addition to meeting little success in stimulating the economy, all these Socialist ministers suffered serious political problems. Fabius was implicated in the government's failure to prevent national health authorities from selling blood they knew to be contaminated with the AIDS virus. (He was exonerated in 1999 and joined Lionel Jospin's second cabinet the following year.) Rocard did not have a Socialist majority in the Assembly and had to make deals with rival parties. Cresson was treated shabbily by the male political establishment but exacerbated her problems through administrative ineptitude. Beregovoy was charged with accepting an inappropriate loan and committed suicide.

The Socialists' popularity suffered further losses when the government proposed incorporating the country's large Catholic school network into a single secularized state educational system. The proposal angered Catholics, who organized a demonstration of a million people in Paris against it. Mitterrand withdrew the plan, but that decision only angered its proponents on the left. In addition, the Socialists were perceived by a growing segment of the public as soft on crime at a time of mounting criminality. (Their decision to abolish the death penalty drew mixed reactions.) A series of financial scandals tarnished their image as a party of clean government.

In spite of all these difficulties and the Socialist Party's declining electoral fortunes, Mitterrand himself held on to power. In 1988 he defeated Jacques Chirac for the presidency by 54 percent to 49.5 percent. An instinct for flexibility and increasing ideological ambivalence helped ensure his political survival. After Chirac's Gaullists and their allies in Giscard's party won control of the National Assembly in 1986, Mitterrand appointed Chirac as prime minister and ultimately accepted the conservatives' plans to privatize more than sixty state-controlled companies. Polls showed that the vast majority of French people wanted the two rivals to get along and maintain governmental stability. Mitterrand was re-elected in 1988 largely because he was now viewed as an avuncular unifier of the nation; he stopped talking about "socialism" and offered no major policy initiatives of his own. In his final two years in office (1993–95), he once again acceded to the priorities of a conservative government under Prime Minister Balladur and acquiesced in a new round of privatizations. Meanwhile, he all but gave up the pursuit of constitutional reform. The man who had been an incessant critic of de Gaulle's presidential authority declared after assuming office in 1981 that he would exercise the "full powers" of the constitution, later asserting that they "suited" him. Though he continued to speak out in favor of reducing the presidential term to five years and other changes, nothing was done about it during his tenure.

A number of Mitterrand's achievements were broadly popular, not just among those who benefited from Socialist welfare measures. These included his efforts to loosen the state's monopoly on radio and television stations and to decentralize the country's decision-making structures somewhat by granting greater powers to local authorities. His strong support for European integration also won him plaudits. He maintained close ties with Germany and supported the European single market and other integrative initiatives promoted by another French Socialist, Jacques Delors, who was president of the European Commission during the Mitterrand years. Still, the public's doubts about the euro, the EU's common currency, ran high. In a 1991 referendum, barely 51 percent of French voters approved the Maastricht Treaty.

MITTERRAND'S LEGACY

Though time will cast a wider perspective on his presidency, it appears for now that Mitterrand's most important legacy was his acceptance on behalf of the French left (or at least a substantial part of the left) of both capitalism and the Vth Republic's constitution. A country that for more than a century had been split between socialists on the left and advocates of private enterprise on the right, with each side having its uncompromising extremists, edged closer during the Mitterrand years to a consensus on its political economy. While the left still favors state intervention to promote the welfare of the bottom sectors of the social pyramid, most of its leaders now also accept the need to promote growth in the private sector. Rabid anti-capitalism is in decline. And while the right emphasizes capitalist enterprise, its main leaders also accept government responsibility for the welfare state. In addition, the French Communist Party by the 1990s was a shadow of what it had been in the 1970s. French intellectuals in the Mitterrand decades became considerably less enamored of Marxist theory than they were in the 1950s and 1960s. A number of participants in the events of 1968 abandoned their youthful revolutionary fervor and became ardent anti-Marxists. ("Danny the Red" Cohn-Bendit won election to the European Parliament.) Finally, Mitterrand's acceptance of the Vth Republic meant that he had come to terms with his old adversary, Charles de Gaulle. Indeed, his aloof presidential style and his delight in the trappings of the office prompted frequent comparisons between Mitterrand and his grand predecessor.

In 1996, François Mitterrand died after a long battle with prostate cancer. (It was later revealed by his physician that he had suffered from the disease throughout his presidency.) In the end, his main political contribution to French politics was his willingness to compromise some of the differences between right and left, Gaullists and anti-Gaullists, Catholics and secularists. His willingness to abandon the state-centered socialism he embraced as a presidential candidate significantly reduced the influence of ideology on French politics and brought the Socialist Party closer to the political center. In the process, he established a precedent for the regular alternation of power between center-left and center-right

parties. Just as significant, his readiness to share power in cohabitation with Chirac's government headed off a potentially debilitating constitutional crisis. Ironically, the Vth Republic's most ardent critic ended his career by stabilizing its institutional arrangements, bringing moderation, stability, and "normalcy" to French politics. In a country wracked through much of its history by stormy conflict, this was no mean achievement.[24]

FRENCH STATE INSTITUTIONS

France's presidential-parliamentary system involves a mixture of presidential authority, a responsible prime minister and government, and a weak but nevertheless important legislature. The basic structure of the system is modeled in figure 17.2.

The Executive   The preceding biographical sketches contain considerable information about the offices of the president and prime minister in the Vth Republic. Table 17.2 summarizes key features of these offices.

As we have seen, the relationship between the president and the prime minister can vary considerably with personalities and political circumstances. *The constitution's text is not a precise guide to actual practice when it comes to determining which of these two officials has the greater decision-making authority.* Executive

FIGURE 17.2   France's Presidential-Parliamentary System

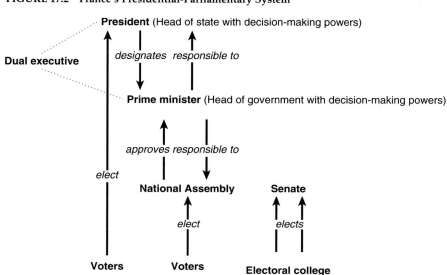

TABLE 17.2
France's Dual Executive

President

Election	Elected by the people. Candidates must be born or naturalized French citizens, at least twenty-three years old, nominated by 500 elected officials (legislators, mayors, etc.). Winning candidate must get absolute majority of voters turning out in first or second round. Until 2002, presidents served a seven-year term, with no limit on the number of terms. In 2000, the presidential term was reduced to five years, starting in 2002.
Powers	Head of state ("the highest authority of the state"). Likely to be de facto chief decision maker (except in periods of cohabitation).
	Commander of armed forces. Presides over higher councils and committees of national defense.
	Names the prime minister. De facto power to force prime minister to resign (except under cohabitation).
	With prime minister's approval, may appoint and dismiss other cabinet ministers.
	Chairs cabinet meetings.
	May veto government ordinances and decrees.
	May dissolve National Assembly and call new elections, which must take place within twenty to forty days. May not dissolve Assembly again for one year.
	May *not* veto bills passed by Parliament but may ask the deputies to reconsider legislation.
	May send messages to Parliament.
	On the proposal of the government or the two legislative chambers, may submit questions to the voters in referendums on bills dealing with "the organization of the public authorities," European Union agreements, or international treaties requiring ratification.
	May declare a state of national emergency under circumstances specified in Article 16 and govern by decree.
	Can be indicted (impeached) only for high treason. Indictment requires an absolute majority of each house of Parliament in an open vote. If indicted, president is tried by the High Court of Justice, composed of various members of both houses of Parliament. Not legally accountable for any other actions performed in office.

Prime Minister

Selection	Designated by the president.
Powers	Head of government. PM "shall direct the operation of the government," which in turn "shall determine and direct the policy of the nation." Likely to be chief decision maker in periods of cohabitation, subject to agreements with president.
	Responsible for national defense. The government "shall have at its disposal . . . the armed forces."
	Makes appointments to civil and military posts. The government is responsible for the civil service.
	May replace president as chair of national defense committees and, under exceptional circumstances, may chair cabinet meetings.
	May seek parliamentary "investiture," that is, vote of approval by National Assembly upon presenting the government and its program.
	May be dismissed by National Assembly, subject to provisions concerning vote of censure (see later in this chapter).

power in France is often shared on the basis of ad hoc arrangements, especially in periods of cohabitation. All five presidents of the Vth Republic have tended to regard foreign affairs and security policy as their "reserved domain" of responsibility. But all five have intruded into domestic matters as well. While they granted their prime ministers a certain latitude to pursue their own initiatives in economic and social policy, the extent of this ministerial freedom has varied considerably.

Acting under the constraints of cohabitation, for instance, Mitterrand allowed Chirac and Balladur greater freedom to conduct policies at variance with his own preferences than either he or any of his predecessors in the presidency would have allowed a prime minister of his own party. President Chirac has similarly allowed Prime Minister Jospin a great deal of leeway to elaborate the government's domestic agenda, even though it differs from Chirac's priorities. Conversely, cohabitation

TABLE 17.3

French Presidential Elections (Second Round Percentages)							
1965	De Gaulle	54.5	1974	Giscard d'Estaing	50.8	1988	Mitterrand	54.0
	Mitterrand	45.5		Mitterrand	49.2		Chirac	45.9
1969	Pompidou	57.6	1981	Mitterrand	51.8	1995	Chirac	52.6
	Poher	42.4		Giscard d'Estaing	48.2		Jospin	47.4

has also encouraged prime ministers to inject themselves in the conduct of the country's foreign policy. Prime Ministers Chirac (1986–88), Balladur (1993–95), and Jospin (since 1997) all prevailed upon their respective presidents to be permitted to participate in major diplomatic meetings and in the foreign policy decision-making process.

In sum, the Vth Republic's arrangements for executive power are more complicated than in the United States, where the president is the sole chief executive, or in the United Kingdom, where the prime minister has ample authority to lead the government. The French dual executive creates real problems of power sharing. Thus far, French leaders at the highest levels have found ways to deal with these complications without paralyzing the French system of government through intractable disagreements or prolonged indecision. How France's political system works thus depends as much on the personalities of the leaders as it does on the strictures of the law or the pull of ideology.[25]

The Government The American term "cabinet" refers to the various cabinet secretaries who run the main departments of the U.S. government or who enjoy similarly high status. In France the cabinet is called the *government* and its members are known as *ministers*. In the language of the Vth Republic's constitution, the government is formally called the *Council of Ministers*. Normally the government consists of *full ministers*, who are the most important figures, and *junior ministers* of somewhat lesser rank.

One of the distinctive features of the Vth Republic is that the government is responsible to *two* authorities, not just one. It is delicately positioned between the president and the National Assembly and is formally accountable to both of them. Both the president and the Assembly have explicit or implied rights to choose and dismiss the prime

minister and other cabinet ministers. In Britain, by contrast, the government is responsible only to the House of Commons.

The constitution gives the president the authority to name the prime minister. It does not expressly say that the president also has the right to *dismiss* the prime minister, stating only that the head of state "terminates the functions of the prime minister when the latter presents the resignation of the government." Presumably, therefore, the prime minister (PM) can always resign but the president has no constititional authority to compel him or her to do so. Nevertheless, every president of the Vth Republic has removed prime ministers they no longer wished to see in office, replacing them with more preferable successors. Sometimes a president wants a new PM in order to try out new policies or give the government a fresh look. On occasion a president has sought to deflect public indignation at his own failures by sacking the prime minister as a scapegoat. Whatever the reasons, French presidents at various times have simply told the PM to resign.

This procedure does not present any problems as long as the president and the prime minister belong to the same party or ideological group. De Gaulle's ministers fully understood that they served at the pleasure of the General, and Socialist prime ministers similarly understood that President Mitterrand was their chief. Thus far, however, no president has asked for a prime minister's resignation in times of cohabitation. Strictly speaking, Prime Ministers Chirac and Balladur would not have been required to step down solely upon President Mitterrand's request, nor may President Chirac on his own authority fire Prime Minister Jospin. But if a prime minister were to refuse presidential pressure to resign, a serious crisis could very well ensue.

As to picking the other cabinet members, the constitution grants the president the right "to appoint and dismiss" them, but only "on the proposal of the prime minister." This stipulation implies that the prime minister initiates the actual selection process and then seeks the president's approval. Here again, actual practice has often diverged from the letter of the law. All five presidents have at times taken it upon themselves to appoint their own preferred choices to various cabinet positions. In these cases the prime minister is expected to consent to the president's selections. As might be expected, the president's ability to impose cabinet choices on the prime minister diminishes considerably under cohabitation. In these awkward circumstances the premier chooses the cabinet, though the president's primacy in foreign and defense policy tends to be respected. During the precedent-setting first cohabitation of 1986–88, President Mitterrand insisted on the right to veto Prime Minister Chirac's choices for foreign minister and defense minister. Chirac complied when Mitterrand rejected his first picks, appointing ministers more acceptable to the president.

Censure   In addition to being responsible to the president, the government is also formally responsible to the National Assembly. Most important, the Assembly has the right to vote the prime minister

TABLE 17.4
Fifth Republic Prime Ministers

President de Gaulle:
  Debré (1959–62)
  Pompidou (1962–68)
  Couve de Murville (1968–69)
President Pompidou:
  Chaban-Delmas (1969–72)
  Messmer (1972–74)
President Giscard d'Estaing:
  Chirac (1974–76)
  Barre (1976–81)
President Mitterrand:
  Mauroy (1981–84)
  Fabius (1984–86)
  Chirac (1986–88)*
  Rocard (1988–91)
  Cresson (1991–92)
  Beregovoy (1992–93)
  Balladur (1993–95)*
President Chirac:
  Juppé (1995–97)
  Jospin (1997 to present)*

*Cohabitation.

and government out of office in a vote of "censure," the French equivalent of a vote of no-confidence. The Vth Republic's provisions for the censure procedure are very exacting. De Gaulle and the constitution's framers were determined to avoid the experience of the IVth Republic, whose legislature was able to depose a government relatively easily by majority vote, thereby contributing to the regime's gnawing instability. In order to topple a government in the Vth Republic, the National Assembly must meet the following conditions:

1. A censure motion must be signed by at least 10 percent of the Assembly.
2. The vote may not take place until after a forty-eight-hour "cooling off" period.
3. The motion is adopted only if it is passed by a majority of the full Assembly (289 out of 577). A majority of *those voting* is insufficient; abstentions do not count.

If the censure motion passes, the prime minister must submit his or her resignation to the president, along with that of the rest of the government. Presumably, the president must then select a new PM. In 1962 President de Gaulle flouted this provision when he reappointed Prime Minister Pompidou immediately after the Assembly passed a censure motion against Pompidou's government. To add insult to injury, de Gaulle then sent the Assembly packing and called snap elections. The 1962 incident was the only case of a successful vote of censure against a government in the Vth Republic, though more than thirty censure motions have been filed. If a censure motion fails to obtain the necessary majority, its signers may not introduce another one in the same legislative session except under special circumstances.

If the prime minister wishes, she or he may ask the Assembly for a vote of confidence on the government's initial program or on a general declaration of its policies. Although this procedure is not mandated by law, most prime ministers have sought an early vote of support of this kind shortly after assuming office. Known as *investiture,* this practice is followed in a number of parliamentary systems (in effect, the legislature vests power in the government). Alternatively, a government that has already been in power for some time may ask the Assembly to approve its policy orientations. Prime ministers who make such a request typically want to force a divided Assembly to clear the air and decide if the majority backs the government or not. If a government fails to muster a majority in the Assembly on a vote of investiture or a policy declaration, it must resign.

Question Time   As in Britain, French government ministers—including the prime minister—are required to answer questions posed by members of Parliament. Questions periods are held every week in both the National Assembly and the Senate. Most of the questions are in written form, as are most of the ministerial responses. Since 1989 a weekly oral interrogation of a minister or deputy minister has taken place in the Assembly. Thus far, however, the Vth Republic has not followed the British custom of requiring the prime minister to answer questions spontaneously every week. The president is never required to appear before Parliament.

Cabinet Membership   The size of the cabinet has varied from as few as twenty-four members to as many as forty-nine. So, too, has its composition. Typically the cabinet includes political leaders from the parties forming the Assembly majority. It may also include other individuals trusted by the president, such as technocrats who have no significant leadership role in a political party but who bring a special expertise to their cabinet portfolio. Some cabinet members, including prime ministers, are graduates of the **grandes écoles,** France's elite graduate schools. Pompidou and Fabius, for example, graduated from the Ecole Normale Superieure, the most prestigious institution for future academics. Giscard and others graduated from the Ecole Polytechnique, founded by Napoleon to train engineers and technicians. Quite a few ministers and deputy ministers, not to mention two presidents, have been products of the **National Academy for Administration** (*Ecole Nationale d'Administration,* or **ENA**), an institution established under de Gaulle after World War II to train the country's policy elite. Its graduates are known as *Enarques* and include Giscard d'Estaing, Fabius, Chirac, Rocard, Balladur, Juppé, and a roster of the country's top political and business leaders.[26]

De Gaulle, Pompidou, and Giscard d'Estaing typically presided over governments consisting of Gaullists and members of Giscard's party. Mitterrand's first prime minister, Pierre Mauroy, had a cabinet comprised mainly of Socialists, but four communists and a few ministers from smaller leftist parties also held cabinet posts. The communists walked out of the next government headed by Laurent Fabius, leaving the Socialists and their smaller allies in command. During the first cohabitation government, Prime Minister Chirac struck a careful balance between people from his own party and Giscard's.

Perhaps the most fragile governments were the ones headed by the Socialists between 1988 and 1993. The Socialist Party managed to win more seats than their conservative rivals in the 1988 elections to the National Assembly, but fell short of a majority, winning only 276 seats. To achieve a voting majority (289), Socialist prime ministers had to woo votes from other parties. In order to garner the support of friendly Giscardiens for their new pro-business policies, Mitterrand and Prime Minister Rocard gave cabinet posts to several people from the center-right parties. The next two cabinets, under Cresson and Beregovoy, had similar problems.

As noted earlier, Jospin's first coalition government in 1997 consisted of eighteen Socialists, three Communists, and five other leftists, including ecology-oriented politicians. In March 2000 he formed a new cabinet with thirty-three members, including twenty-four Socialists, four Communists, two Greens, and three from smaller left-wing parties.

Incompatibility Clause   Although most cabinet ministers are chosen from the parliamentary ranks of the parties, the Vth Republic's constitution specifically forbids members of the government from simultaneously serving as elected deputies to either the National Assembly or the Senate. The so-called *incompatibility clause,* which makes cabinet service incompatible with membership in Parliament, was designed to reduce the government's dependence on the legislature and give it greater autonomy than it enjoyed under the IVth Republic. Members of the French Parliament who are invited to join the cabinet must relinquish their legislative seats. This provision is the exact opposite of the British system, which *requires* cabinet members to serve simultaneously as members of Parliament. It is nonetheless permissible, however, for a member of the French government to hold other official positions at the same time. Quite a few government ministers work simultaneously as mayors, members of town councils, regional government officials, and the like. In the past there have been cabinet ministers holding as many as five posts at the same time! In 1987 a new law took effect limiting this "accumulation of positions" (*cumul des mandats*) to no more than two, and further revisions were proposed in 2000.

Meetings   The French cabinet usually meets once a week, far more regularly than the U.S. cabinet does. The president typically chairs these meetings, though the prime minister fills in on occasion. How the government reaches its decisions usually depends on the preferences of the president (and, in some cases, the prime minister). De Gaulle tended to lecture his ministers on his policies, stifling discussion. Other presidents have tended to be more open to debate. In most cases, it is one of the two principal executives—the president or prime minister—who takes the lead in deciding the government's policy. France is not governed by majority rule in the cabinet. Once the government's policy is enunciated, the cabinet as a whole is expected to take collective responsibility for it in public.

Parliament

The bicameral French Parliament (*Parlement*) consists of the *National Assembly*, its lower house, and the *Senate*, the upper house.

The National Assembly   The **National Assembly** currently has 577 deputies. As noted at the start of this chapter, each deputy is elected in accordance with a two-round variant of the single member district (SMD) electoral system. An absolute majority is required to win in the first round, a plurality suffices in the second. This system replaced the proportional representation system of the IVth Republic, which de Gaulle scorned because it resulted in a proliferation of parties in the legislature. None of them came even close to holding a majority of seats, thus requiring the parties to patch together coalition cabinets that invariably proved unsustainable. The SMD system makes it more difficult

for small parties to get elected and easier for a single party to capture a majority of seats. While this outcome may result in more stable governments, it comes at the price of scrupulously fair representation. The SMD system often leads to disparities between a party's share of the popular vote and its share of legislative seats. In the Vth Republic's first legislative elections in 1958, for example, the Gaullists and their allies received 37.5 percent of the vote but won 66 percent of the Assembly districts in mainland France. In 1993 the Gaullists (RPR) and their main center-right allies, the UDF, together won 54 percent of the second-round vote but 80 percent of the Assembly districts (seats).[27] (See table 17.5. For an explanation of electoral systems, see chapter 9.)

One of the unique features of the two-round electoral system is that it encourages parties that field competing candidates in round 1 to cooperate in round 2. If, for example, the socialist and communist candidates split the left-wing vote in the first round, the left stands a better chance of beating the Gaullist and centrist candidates in the second round if the communist candidate withdraws and the communist party calls on its voters to support the socialist candidate (see table 17.6). Second-round electoral alliances of this kind are common on both the left and right, though they require an agreement between party chiefs at the highest levels. In this system of *désistement* (withdrawal), the candidate who receives the lesser share of votes in round 1 will typically agree to "desist" from running in round 2 in favor of the candidate from the allied party. Parties so incompatible that they cannot come together in this manner are disadvantaged (like the National Front and the Green Party in table 17.6).

The deputies elected to the National Assembly typically come from a wide range of career backgrounds. In the Assemblies elected in 1988, 1993, and 1997, only about 5 percent have been career politicians. By far the largest profession represented has been teachers (27.5 percent in 1988, 13 percent in 1993, 25.7 percent in 1997). Most of them are socialists, reflecting the exceptionally high levels of support the teaching profession and intellectuals provide the socialist party. Health professionals make up between 7 percent and 10 percent of the total and are divided among the

TABLE 17.5

National Assembly, 1993 and 1997 (577 Seats)

	1993				1997			
	% of Vote (Round 1)	% of Vote (Round 2)	Seats	% of Seats	% of Vote (Round 1)	% of Vote (Round 2)	Seats	% of Seats
Left:								
Socialist Party (PS)	17.6	28.7	54	9.4	23.5	38.6	246	42.6
Other left*	2.7	3.3	16	2.8	4.3	4.3	29	5.0
Communist Party (PCF)	9.2	4.6	23	3.9	9.9	3.7	37	6.4
Greens**	7.6	1.7	—	—	6.8	1.6	8	1.3
Extreme left	1.8	0.1	—	—	2.5	—	—	—
Right:								
RPR (Neo-Gaullists)	20.4	28.3	247	42.8	15.7	22.7	139	24.1
UDF (Center-Right)	19.1	25.8	213	36.9	14.2	21.0	109	18.9
National Front	12.4	5.7	—	—	14.9	5.7	1	1.7
Other right	5.0	3.6	24	4.2	6.7	2.4	8	1.4
Others	4.2	—	—	—	1.4	—	—	—

*1993: Presidential Majority and Left Radicals; 1997: Socialist Radical Party and various left
**Includes Greens and Ecology Generation in 1993; Greens only in 1997.
Source: Inter-Parliamentary Union, *Parliamentary Elections and Developments,* vols. 27 and 31.

TABLE 17.6

Electoral Alliances in a Hypothetical National Assembly District

Candidates	Round 1*	Electoral Alliances	Round 2
Dupont (Socialist)	20%	Socialist + Communists:	34%
Lapierre (Communist)	14%	Lapierre drops out	
Laurent (Gaullist)	16%	Gaullists + UDF:	30%
Leroy (UDF**)	14%	Leroy drops out	
Rougemont (National Front)	23%	None	23%
Daniel (Green)	13%	None	13%

*Candidates must get at least 12.5 percent in round 1 to run again in round 2.
**UDF, Union for French Democracy, is an alliance of several center-right parties.
The Socialist Dupont wins the seat. Note that the National Front candidate would have won in round 2 if no electoral alliances had been formed. The Gaullist-UDF candidate (Laurent) would have won if the socialists and communists had failed to agree on a common second-round candidate. In actuality, not all communist voters will necessarily vote for the socialist in round 2, nor will all UDF voters necessarily vote for the Gaullist candidate. Some first-round voters may not even turn out in the second round. And it sometimes happens that two parties (e.g., the Gaullists and the UDF) will agree on joint *first*-round candidates.

Socialists and the main conservative parties. High-level government officials and bureaucrats also get elected to the Assembly in fairly large numbers (around 9 percent). Lawyers are less well represented in the French Assembly than in the U.S. Congress or the British House of Commons, averaging about 5 percent. People with business backgrounds are also less in evidence in France, though their share of the Assembly rose from 2.9 percent in the left-dominated Assembly of 1988 to 6 percent after the Gaullist-centrist landslide of 1993. Workers account for only about 1 percent of the deputies, fewer than those represented in Britain's Labour Party delegation in the House of Commons (see table 16.4 on page 412).

Senate The **Senate** has 321 members. All are elected to a nine-year term by a special electoral college that represents local governments throughout France. More than 100,000 mayors, city council members, and departmental officials comprise the bulk of the electoral body's membership; the

TABLE 17.7

Professional Backgrounds of National Assembly Members Elected in 1997 (% of total)

Teachers	26%
Liberal professions	21
Judges, civil servants, public sector employees	17
Private sector employees	17
Employers and self-employed (including farmers)	11
Retired and other professions	10

Total exceeds 100 percent because some deputies reported more than one profession.

Source: Chronicle of Parliamentary Elections and Developments, vol. 31.

577 members of the National Assembly make up the rest. Historically, the upper house of the French legislature has usually been dominated by local "notables" and rural interests, a phenomenon that has not substantially changed. Though the center of political gravity remains Paris and though economic modernization has reduced the agricultural work force from more than 30 percent at the end of World War II to about 6 percent today, a large segment of the population continues to reside in small towns and rural communities. Moreover, many city dwellers maintain sentimental attachments to their provincial roots. French farmers and vintners, whose exports are enjoyed around the world, exercise considerable political influence and are among the chief beneficiaries of the European Union's Common Agricultural Policy. The Senate speaks up for these cultural and economic forces, representing the provincial areas Parisians call *la France profonde*—"deep France."[28]

Most senators tend to be conservative and anti-socialist in their political leanings. Nevertheless, they frequently objected to de Gaulle's haughtiness and opposed some of his policies. In a bid to reduce the Senate's influence, de Gaulle proposed a reform of its electoral college system and a diminution of the Senate's right to co-legislate with the National Assembly. He resigned when the voters rejected these proposals in the 1969 referendum. Since then, the Senate majority has largely supported de Gaulle's conservative successors and often fought to block Socialist legislation. The Senate normally works with the Assembly in drafting common language for bills their members propose.

But if the Senate objects to government-drafted legislation, the government can get around these obstacles by bringing its bills directly before the Assembly for a decisive vote. Thus the French Senate may be able to delay the passage of legislation but not block it completely. (Similarly, the British House of Lords may also delay but not kill legislation.)

Parliament's Limitations The French Parliament's principal distinction is the relatively narrow scope of its importance compared with legislatures in most other democracies. One of de Gaulle's chief purposes in 1958 was to downgrade the Parliament of the Vth Republic, eliminating the principle of parliamentary supremacy that formed the basis of the IVth Republic's unstable political system. As a consequence, the Vth Republic's constitution specifically identifies the policy areas in which Parliament has competence to legislate. All other governmental matters are reserved to the "rule-making" authority of the executive branch, which may issue decrees or ordinances without parliamentary approval. The constitution also spells out additional limits on Parliament's decision-making powers.

Items that fall within Parliament's legislative purview include nationality issues, criminal law, the electoral system, tax rates, and the nationalization of private enterprises. It may also pass civil rights legislation, as the constitution does not contain an enumerated bill of rights.[29] Additionally, Parliament may "determine the fundamental principles" of such things as the organization of the country's national defense, local government, education, property rights, commercial law, and labor law, though the details of these matters may be subject to the government's intervention. Parliament has the exclusive right to declare war and ratify most international treaties.

Aside from possessing these and a few other specified powers, France's Parliament is severely restricted by the overriding authority of the president and the prime minister's government. These restrictions affect both the substance of the law and the procedures used to make it. Here are some examples:

- The government, not Parliament, sets the agenda of bills to be considered and their order of priority. It can also limit the time allotted for parliamentary consideration of legislation. (In the United Kingdom, the government and Parliament jointly work out the agenda and calendar, though the government's wishes usually prevail. The U.S. Congress controls its own agenda and calendar.)

- While members of Parliament have the right to initiate bills, so does the government. Government bills take priority over private members' bills in parliamentary deliberations and have a far greater likelihood of being passed. Typically, fewer than 25 percent of the bills passed during the term of a legislature will have been introduced by legislators independently of the government. (Much the same can be said about Britain. All legislation in the United States is proposed by members of Congress, though some of it may be at the behest of the administration.)

- Members of the French Parliament have no right to introduce legislation or propose amendments to bills that entail an increase or reduction in public expenditures. Only the government may propose spending bills or amendments. (The same is essentially true in the UK, but not the United States) As a practical matter, the French government can define a wide range of policy issues as spending bills, since virtually every undertaking by the state involves expenses.

- Finance bills, including the annual budget bill, must be passed by the two houses of Parliament within seventy days. Otherwise, they automatically become law by government decree. (Neither Britain nor the United States imposes a time limit on finance bills or provides for their automatic enactment by decree.)

- The government may attach the question of confidence to any bill or part of a bill. In these circumstances, the bill becomes law automatically, *without* a parliamentary vote. The only way Parliament can block such a bill is to pass a censure motion against the government in accordance with the procedures outlined earlier. In effect, the government may adopt a law on its own authority and dare the Assembly to vote it out of office! This "provocation" procedure has been utilized about seventy times by various prime ministers since 1958, always with success. (No similar provision exists in the United States or the United Kingdom.)

- Under special circumstances, the government may ask Parliament to refrain from passing legislation on matters that are normally reserved to the legislature's lawmaking competence, permitting the government to enact measures in these areas by decree. (Britain has roughly similar "statutory instruments." Though the U.S. presidents may issue "executive orders" in certain areas, they cannot ask Congress to give up its legislative prerogatives.)

- The government may limit Parliament's right to propose amendments to bills after they are introduced and may compel Parliament to vote only on amendments proposed by the government. (This so-called "blocked vote" procedure does not exist in Britain or the United States.)

- All legislation goes through parliamentary committees, but they have minimal decision-making powers. Committees may not introduce bills intended to alter the purpose of government bills. By declaring a bill urgent, the government can reduce the time allotted to committee consideration of pending legislation. (Parliamentary committees are also fairly weak in Britain but are more powerful in the United States. In the 1990s French parliamentary committees gained the right to query cabinet ministers about relevant legislation, as in the United States.)

In sum, the French Parliament is much weaker than the legislatures of Britain, the United States, and indeed most other democracies. Its deputies exhibit rather high rates of absenteeism and comparatively low levels of independence from their respective party leaders. Nevertheless, the partisan composition of the Parliament, and particularly of the National Assembly, ultimately determines which parties can form a viable government. In periods of cohabitation, this reality confers on France's legislature a decisive political importance.

The Constitutional Council

What happens if the executive branch and the legislature cannot agree whether a piece of legislation falls within the lawmaking competence of Parliament or the decree-making privileges of the government? The Vth Republic constitution provides for a **Constitutional Council** to adjudicate such controversies. At the request of either the government or Parliament, the Council must hand down a definitive ruling within eight days. In addition, the Council has the authority to rule on the constitutionality of so-called "organic laws" that are under consideration in Parliament. Organic laws relate to the operation and legal authority of state institutions. Parliament may not enact any measure in this sensitive area if the Constitutional Council decides it is incompatible with the constitution. In Britain, by contrast, Parliament is supreme: it has the exclusive right to enact bills into law without judicial oversight.

When the Vth Republic was first established, de Gaulle and his associates wanted the Constitutional Council to act as yet another brake on parliamentary initiative. Rather than applying judicial checks and balances on both the executive and legislative branches like the U.S. Supreme Court does, the Council was conceived by the Republic's framers essentially as a check on the legislature, not on the executive. Three of its nine members are appointed by the president of France, including the head of the Council, who alone is empowered to break tie votes. The other six are appointed by the presiding officers of the National Assembly and the Senate. These nine members serve one nine-year term each, but former French presidents become members of the Council for life. In keeping with the framers' intentions, most Council rulings have in fact supported the government and run against the preferences of the parliamentary opposition.

Another difference between the Constitutional Council and the U.S. Supreme Court is that the Council has less extensive powers of *judicial review*, which is the authority to invalidate laws as unconstitutional. The Supreme Court may review laws already in existence, for example, but the Constitutional Council must confine its rulings to draft laws that have not as yet taken effect. Moreover, only the central government or members of Parliament may bring cases before the Council, not local officials or private citizens as in the United States. Nevertheless, since the 1970s the Council has issued a number of decisions widening the civil liberties of the population as against the authority of the state. And in 1974 the constitution was amended to allow sixty National Assembly deputies or sixty Senators the right to bring cases before the Council. Until then, only the president, the prime minister, and

the two speakers of Parliament had this privilege. The change has allowed opposition legislators to initiate proceedings, resulting in more cases as well as more rulings that have run against the government's preferences. Both the conservative parties and the Socialists have availed themselves of the extended opportunities to challenge government decisions.[30]

The Civil Service

Ever since the middle ages, the French state has sought to solidify its control over the country through a powerful administrative bureaucracy in Paris. The authority of the civil service not only to implement the law of the land but also to create it through bureaucratic regulations grew stronger in the nineteenth century as Parliament's authority remained comparatively weak. Today the French civil service still wields significant power in virtually every aspect of the country's economic and social life. The scope of its activities extends from economic planning and financial affairs to the worlds of education, scientific research, health care, foreign policy, and host of other areas. Its personnel, especially some ten thousand functionaries in the highest echelons, enjoy considerable prestige as highly competent policy professionals. Many of them were educated at ENA or other selective graduate schools, and quite a few are socially and politically well connected. In every sense of the word, the top layers of the French civil service constitute a true political elite.

One of the distinguishing characteristics of the French civil service is its close interaction with private enterprise. To a far greater extent than in the United States, Britain, or many other democracies, the top managers of state agencies and the directors of major private corporations in France often share similar educational and social backgrounds and switch back and forth from the public sector to the private. A disproportionately large number of them have attended one of the *grandes écoles*. Although a number of these elite academies are publicly funded and tuition-free, and the students may even be paid a stipend, many of those who take the entrance exams tend to come from upper-class or upper-middle-class families in the Parisian "higher bourgeoisie."[31]

A job in the state bureaucracy is often the stepping-stone to a career in private enterprise. Ambitious civil servants who acquire expertise in finance, management, or some other field of relevance to private business are often lured away to well-paying positions in France's leading companies. The reverse pattern can also occur. When the French government nationalized a large number of firms under Mitterrand in the early 1980s, the managerial personnel who ran them under state ownership were in a number of cases the same people who managed them when they were privately owned. Thus the distinction between the public and private sectors in France tends to be fairly loose.[32]

The government's economic planning system provides another point of contact between the state and the private sector. The General Planning Commission (*Commissariat générale du plan*) interacts on a regular basis with government officials and private business executives to lay out broad goals and guidelines for the country's economic development and to exchange mutually useful information. Though the importance of the planning process has diminished somewhat in recent years, it remains a critical link between the state bureaucracy and the private sector.

Although the French civil service reinforces France's reputation as a "strong state," like all bureaucracies it does not always function in accordance with the highest standards of administrative rationality. Inter-agency rivalries, informal lines of communication, "satisficing," and other forms of bureaucratic irrationality are invariably present. And those charged with administering laws enacted by elected officials can find ways to delay or sabotage their implementation if they choose to do so. Nevertheless, in a country where some 5 million people are employed in the public sector—nearly one-fourth of the total work force—the civil service inevitably looms large as a vital component of the French state.[33]

Local Government and Decentralization

The trends underlying France's long history as a unitary state administered from Paris, while predominant, have not gone uncontested. From its earliest foundations as a national entity, France has always been composed of a diversity of regions, some with their own traditional languages or dialects (such as Brittany, the Basque area, and Alsace). Paris and other large cities experience many of the problems of modern urban centers, while more than twenty thousand small towns still dot the French countryside. Many people living in these areas have sought greater powers for their local governments to manage their own affairs with greater freedom from the central state. The French Revolution, in particular, unleashed pressures for the decentralization of the central government's power in addition to contrary tendencies toward strong centralization. Over the following two centuries, the centralizing tendencies invariably won out. Mitterrand's election to the presidency, however, promised a fresh approach to decentralization.

France is divided into twenty-two "regions" (counting Corsica), ninety-six mainland and four overseas "departments," and more than 36,700 "communes" ranging from large cities to rural villages.[34] In 1982 the Socialists enacted a decentralization scheme that increased the powers of various subnational governments without dismantling the decisive predominance of the central state. The reform weakened the traditional powers of France's prefects, who had been since Napoleon's time the central government's agents in the various departments. No longer were they expected to impose the central government's will on the localities; instead they were to function in a consultative capacity, facilitating communication between the center and the rest of the country. Greater authority was now devolved upon elected councils at the communal, departmental, and regional levels. (The Socialists also changed the title of prefect to "commissioner of the Republic," but when the conservatives regained control of Parliament in 1986 they changed it back to prefect.)

These subnational bodies now received the green light to impose various local taxes and assume wider responsibility for local matters in such areas as transportation, the environment, and various economic and welfare functions. In addition, over the ensuing years, cities like Lyons and regions bordering Germany and Switzerland won greater authority to promote cross-border economic cooperation, often with encouragement from the European Union. Jospin's government has acted to permit wider official usage of local traditional languages, such as Breton in Brittany.

Despite these changes, the national government continues to control the bulk of France's tax collections and public spending. It also monopolizes the administration of the entire educational system and plays the predominant role in transportation, the environment, and social welfare. Decentralization is greater than it was before the Socialist reforms, but the girders of the French unitary state remain intact. Meanwhile, France does not experience mass separatist tendencies as powerful as those present in Quebec or Scotland, though nationalist movements in Brittany that favor greater autonomy or full independence are fairly active.[35]

Political Parties

Typically, more than thirty political parties and groupings put up candidates for office in France, giving voters a wide array of electoral choices. (In 1997 there were forty-eight in the first round of voting.) The two-round SMD electoral system for elections to the National Assembly keeps most of them from winning a greater share of seats than they might otherwise get under proportional representation (PR). The National Front, for example, won 15 percent of the first-round vote in 1997 and 5.6 percent of the second-round vote, but ended up with only one seat. Nevertheless, there are more parties represented in the National Assembly today than in the U.S. Congress or the British House of Commons.

What explains this efflorescence of parties and independents? For one thing, France's SMD system makes it possible to win with only 12.5 percent of the vote in the first round and a mere plurality in the second. As a consequence, candidates in three-person races can win with less than half of the second-round vote. (In 1997, 18 percent of the second-round races involved three candidates.) In addition, the French penchant for casting political issues in ideological terms and the persistence of a diversity of class, religious, cultural, and other identities—in spite of vast economic and social changes over the past fifty years—encourages the formation or endurance of parties dedicated to distinct ideological orientations or the interests of specific segments of the electorate (such as ecology-oriented voters). Tellingly, in 1997 most victorious small-party candidates won their

races with an absolute majority in the second round.[36] Another factor accounting for the wide range of parties in France is that PR is used in elections to regional, departmental, and municipal councils as well as to the European Parliament. PR gives parties a share of elected positions at these supranational and subnational levels that is roughly equivalent to their share of the vote, thus giving small parties an incentive to field candidates.

French parties tend to be categorized as belonging to political "families" of the left and right. The main leftist party (the socialists) and the main right-wing parties (the Gaullists and the Union for French Democracy) tend to be moderate in their policy orientations, avoiding the extremes of all-out socialism or all-out laissez-faire capitalism. They are also dedicated to democratic principles and the institutional framework of the Vth Republic. These large parties, along with several moderate smaller ones, hug close to the political center, where most of the voters cluster. Hence the Socialists may be considered a center-left party, while the Gaullists and UDF parties are center-right parties. The communists and a few small leftist parties are situated to the left of the socialists, while the anti-immigrant National Front is an extreme right-wing party.

The Right   The "right" in French politics is a term burdened with heavy historical connotations. From the time of the Revolution to World War II, the French right was mainly associated with authoritarianism, imperialism, and in some cases, anti-semitism. Its principal exponents were monarchists, Bonapartists, the military, the Catholic church hierarchy, the upper classes, and others who never accepted the Revolution. After World War II the right was redefined by de Gaullle and his followers to embrace democracy and the civil liberties promised by the Revolution. Today's center-right parties are "conservative" to the extent that they oppose socialism, embrace private enterprise, and champion French nationalism (though the term "conservative" is not used as widely in France as in the United States or Britain).

The Neo-Gaullists   Today the Gaullist (or neo-Gaullist) party is the largest party of the center-right. Known since 1976 as the **Rally for the Republic** (*Rassemblement pour la République*, or **RPR**), it has undergone several name changes since the movement was founded by de Gaulle in the 1940s.[37] As we've seen, the essence of Gaullism is its devotion to the constitutional principles of the Vth Republic. Its economic orientations have tended to vary over time from de Gaulle's unapologetic statism to the more pro-business policies of his successors. Today there are several discernible currents within the party. Some of its leaders favor a more integrated European Union while others are more skeptical. Some are concerned that France has admitted too many immigrants and have voiced understanding for the attitudes of the National Front; others have emphatically rejected any association with the Front or its positions. And some are more enthusiastic than others about economic liberalization, privatization, balanced budgets, and globalization. President Jacques Chirac, the most prominent Gaullist since Pompidou, personifies these conflicting strands of contemporary neo-Gaullism. At one time or another he has been on opposite sides of a number of pressing issues facing the country.

PROFILE: Jacques Chirac

Upon being elected chief of the Gaullist party in 1974, Jacques Chirac assumed the daunting task of redefining Gaullism in the absence of de Gaulle. His challenge has been to remold an organization forged by a hero in times of crisis into a "normal" party, one that is primarily concerned with the routine problems of governing in more tranquil, non-crisis conditions. While Chirac has largely succeeded in this effort, he has had to deal with the consequences of his own oscillations on economic policy and European integration, as well as challenges to his leadership and policy views from within the RPR.

Born in 1932, Chirac grew up in comfortable circumstances, the son of the chief financial officer of a large state-owned aviation company. He experienced World War II as a boy and had vaguely leftist leanings in his teenage years. Though a voracious reader, he craved adventure and took a job aboard a commercial ship that plied the Mediterranean. Called home by his father to resume his studies, Chirac entered the Institute for Political Studies in Paris, where his classmates included future prime minister Michel Rocard and other ambi-

tious contemporaries. In 1953 Chirac spent the summer in the United States, taking courses at the Harvard Business School and working at the local Howard Johnson's. With friends he hitchhiked to California, then made his way to Dallas, New Orleans, the deep South, Washington, and New York. It was such a memorable experience that he returned the following year to do research on the port of New Orleans.

Still uncertain about his career, Chirac passed the stiff entrance exams for the National Academy for Administration (ENA) but delayed his matriculation so as to fulfill his military obligation. It was 1956 and the Algerian war was raging. Convinced that Algeria should remain French, Chirac took an immediate liking to military life, volunteering for dangerous operations. After returning to France he completed the rigorous ENA curriculum, finishing sixteenth in his class. In 1959 he returned to Algeria as a junior administrator and over the ensuing year came to accept de Gaulle's position in favor of Algerian independence.

In 1962 a friend managed to get Chirac a position on Prime Minister Pompidou's staff. He quickly established a reputation for competence and high energy, winning Pompidou's praise as "my bulldozer" for his ability to get things done. By 1967 he was ready to enter the political lists on his own, winning election to the National Assembly. But he quickly gave up the seat to take a succession of junior ministerial positions. As the cabinet secretary responsible for the budget, Chirac reported to Finance Minister Giscard d'Estaing and briefed President de Gaulle. After Pompidou became president, he served as Minister of Agriculture and Minister of the Interior.

Jacques Chirac

Pompidou's death in 1974 marked a major turning point for Chirac as well as for the Gaullist movement. When Jacques Chaban-Delmas, one of de Gaulle's loyal followers, declared his candidacy for the presidency, Chirac and other Gaullist party figures refused to back him, fearing that he would not be an effective candidate against François Mitterrand. Chirac discreetly supported Giscard d'Estaing, whose bid for the presidency required votes from Gaullist ranks. When Giscard knocked out Chaban in round 1 and narrowly defeated Mitterrand in round 2, he rewarded Chirac by naming him prime minister. Later that year, Chirac was elected by the Gaullist party's central committee as its new chief.

Though Chirac and Giscard were both conservatives, their personalities and political ambitions were bound to clash. Aloof and aristocratic, Giscard firmly believed in the primacy of the presidency and subjected his prime minister to petty humiliations. It was Giscard, not Chirac, who picked the majority of the cabinet ministers. Emotional and populist, Chirac headed the largest party on the right, far larger than Giscard's Republican Party. Without the support of the Gaullists, Giscard would not have been able to govern. The two men also differed on economic policy. Rising unemployment induced Giscard to stray from his pro-market preferences on taking office and to favor new infusions of government spending to prime the pump of the economy. Chirac eagerly embraced this position, arguing that French traditions required the state to take action against recession and unemployment. In the 1970s Chirac favored a statist economic policy and claimed that the Gaullist party was a party of the "national left." Giscard was by nature uncomfortable with this approach, fearing excessive inflation. Increasing tensions over economic policy combined with personal rivalries to drive the two men apart. In 1976 Chirac resigned as prime minister.

Determined to remain a national political figure, Chirac was elected mayor of Paris the following year. More important, he retained his position as chief of the RPR, the Gaullist party. In 1981 his ill-feelings toward Giscard induced him to run against the president in the first round. Chirac took only 18 percent of the vote against Giscard's 28 percent, and Mitterrand went on to win the presidency. Chirac's next chance to assume national office came in 1986, when the RPR and Giscard's followers won a three-seat majority in the National Assembly. Acknowledging the new right-wing majority, President Mitterrand took the historic step of inviting Chirac to serve as his next prime minister. It was the Vth Republic's first experience of cohabitation.

The two men scarcely knew each other except as political foes, but each made efforts to get along. Mitterrand granted Chirac wider latitude in his role as head of government than most former presidents had permitted prime ministers of their own political party or ideological persuasion. Indeed, Chirac got on better with Mitterrand than he had with Giscard. While Mitterrand insisted on retaining presidential primacy in foreign and defense policy, a demand Chirac honored, the prime minister was able to select his own cabinet members. From the outset his government launched a series of initiatives that reversed some of the Socialists' most important achievements. Wheras the Socialists had nationalized private companies, Chirac and his RPR-UDF cabinet set out to privatize some sixty-five state-owned firms. Ever since 1981, Chirac had begun distancing himself from his earlier state-centric views on the economy and, under the influence of President Reagan in the United States and Prime Minister Thatcher in the UK, increasingly extolled the benefits of the private sector. His aim was to widen mass participation in capitalism by increasing the number of small stockholders investing in private companies, a goal the initial privatizations fulfilled.

Chirac's government also reduced the wealth tax the Socialists had imposed on the most affluent citizens and cut taxes for lower income brackets as well. Mitterrand tried to block or delay some of these measures, incurring Chirac's anger, but most of them went through. At the same time, Chirac continued to believe that the state needed to retain major responsibilities in guiding the economy. He never went as far as Reagan or Thatcher in denouncing state economic intervention. He presumably understood that most French people at the time placed a higher value on equality than on economic liberty (see figure 8.4 on page 188).

The presidential election calendar put an end to two years of cohabitation in 1988. Inevitably, Chirac and Mitterrand squared off as the principal leaders of their respective camps. Mitterrand won the final duel in the second round with a convincing 54 percent of the vote. Upon being reelected, Mitterrand dissolved the National Assembly and ordered new elections. When the right-wing parties lost their slender majority, Chirac retreated to his mayor's office. He had to wait another five years before the Gaullists and their allies in the UDF were able to reclaim power at the national level. As unemployment rose and the Socialists became embroiled in a series of financial and campaign funding scandals, the RPR and UDF won an overwhelming victory in the 1993 legislative elections, capturing 84 percent of the seats.

At this point Chirac stepped back and allowed Edouard Balladur, a friend since the Pompidou years, to become prime minister as Mitterrand and the right embarked on their second experience of cohabitation. Once again a Gaullist-UDF government set about privatizing state-owned companies, including banks, insurance companies, communications firms, and other valuable economic assets. The balance in the relationship between the state and the private sector tilted decidedly in the latter's direction during these two periods of cohabitation. Still, French business leaders, to a greater extent than their counterparts in the United States or Britain, continued to look to the state for guidance concerning the economy's overall direction.[38] But unemployment maintained its steady rise and Balladur's government, like the Socialists, was tarnished by financial scandals. A reform of election campaign financing in 1988 had failed to prevent corruption.[39] The government was also forced to withdraw controversial bills in the face of mass protests. The entire French political elite increasingly became the target of the citizenry's distrust.

The second period of left-right cohabitation came to an end in 1995 with the conclusion of Mitterrand's second term. Jacques Chirac once again found himself poised to stake his claim on the presidency, the post he had coveted since his earliest years in politics. To his dismay, however, it was not just Lionel Jospin who now stood in his way; his most pressing challenge came from within his own party, from Edouard Balladur. Although Balladur had been Chirac's chief political counselor, he was convinced that the Gaullist party chief was not sufficiently popular to win a presidential election. When Balladur announced his intention to run for the presidency, the Gaullist camp became split between his supporters and Chirac's. The UDF, still nourishing bitter memories of Chirac's relations with Giscard, lent most of its electoral support to Balladur. After a tense campaign in which the two Gaullist candidates split the center-right vote, Chirac barely nudged out Balladur in the first round, 21 percent to 18 percent. The split allowed Jospin to emerge as the front-runner with only 23 percent of the vote. The RPR and UDF pulled together in round 2, enabling Chirac to defeat Jospin by 52.6 percent to 47.4 percent.

Jacques Chirac was now president of France. He inherited the massive RPR-UDF majority that had been elected to the National Assembly in 1993, with three more years to run before the next regularly scheduled Assembly elections. But after appointing his fellow Gaullist, Alain Juppé, as prime minister, Chirac quickly ran into trouble. Like his attitudes on the economy, Chirac's position on European integration had wavered over the years. In the past he had counterbalanced his support for Europe with warnings of excessive federalism and bureaucratism in Brussels, which in his view diminished French national sovereignty. On becoming president, he was compelled to follow the European

Union's criteria for creating the euro. Under Mitterrand, France had assumed the obligation of reducing its annual budget deficit to no more than 3 percent of GDP and of cutting its substantial national debt. It also sought to keep inflation down in an effort to keep the franc in a stable balance with the German mark. Chirac, like Mitterrand, was caught in the webs of globalization emanating from European economic integration.

To comply with these requirements, Juppé announced new budgetary austerity measures in November 1995. With a view to overhauling the country's state pension system, which was deeply in arrears, he called for raising the eligibility for full pensions from thirty-seven and a half years of employment to forty. He also raised fees for hospital treatment and other forms of health care and increased health insurance premiums for the unemployed and retirees. In a separate move, the government also announced plans to cut costs in the railway system. These and related measures, which were sprung on the populace with little or no explanation, sparked the most widespread outpouring of mass protest since 1968.

A half million public sector workers went on strike on the first day, and additional strikes over the following weeks by workers in urban transport, the railways, airports, the postal system, gas and electric utilities, telecommunications, hospitals, and the civil service brought normal life to a halt. Demonstrations in Paris and other cities brought hundreds of thousands into the streets. Juppé's initial reactions to these events were coldly dismissive, reflecting an arrogance many people regarded as typical of the French governing elite. But as economic paralysis loomed, Juppé was forced to enter into negotiations with the trade unions and public sector employees in an effort to reach a compromise. Some of his austerity plans had to be curtailed or canceled. As Juppé's approval ratings plunged, President Chirac struggled to distance himself from his premier, but his own popularity crumbled as well.

Chirac and Juppé did not recover from these and other early blunders. Fearing that the center-right's popularity would sink even lower by 1998, the year of the next regularly scheduled National Assembly elections, Chirac decided in 1997 to call snap elections a year ahead of time. His hope was to retain a large enough majority for the RPR and its allies to pursue their policies of budget cutting and privatization for five more years. His calculations proved wrong, and in June 1997 the left under Jospin's Socialists retook control of the lower house. Now it was Chirac's turn as president to accept the reality of an opposing parliamentary majority. In naming Jospin prime minister, Chirac launched the Vth Republic's third experience with cohabitation. Once again, the awesome constitutional powers of the presidency were about to be eclipsed by a constitutionally powerful prime minister. Despite their differences, however, Chirac and Jospin managed to get along rather well, and both enjoyed high popularity at the start of the new millennium.[40]

The RPR is a broad-based catch-all party. Although its main base of support comes from the middle classes, it continues to appeal to about 30 percent of the working class, though its share of that constituency has dropped off since the 1980s. Practicing Catholics, businesspeople, and the elderly tend to vote for the RPR in large proportions. It ended the 1990s in disarray, however, as divisions over Europe and other issues decimated its leadership. Charles Pasqua, a former justice minister, bolted the RPR and formed a more outspokenly anti-EU organization. Philippe Séguin, another ex-minister, resigned as party chief. At the end of 1999 the party chose a woman as its new president, Michèle Alliot-Marie, in hopes of redefining Gaullism and reestablishing its unity.

The Union for French Democracy The **Union for French Democracy** (*Union pour la démocratie française,* or **UDF**) is a group of small center-right parties and individuals who have banded together to promote their strongest candidates at election time. Founded in 1978 at the instigation of President Giscard d'Estaing, the UDF has consisted variously of about four or five parties and political clubs. The UDF's initial raison d'être was to support Giscard's presidency. From its inception it has also pursued the longer-term goal of establishing a unified political movement located in between the Gaullists and the Socialists, an aim that has motivated its activities since the end of Giscard's term in 1981. Animosities toward Chirac have helped sustain the UDF's existence as a separate force, but its principal problem is that its main constituencies are similar to those courted by the Gaullists: the middle and upper classes, businesspeople, and Catholics. Still, the UDF won a respectable 25.8 percent of the second-round vote in 1993 and 21 percent in 1997. Its electoral agreements with the Gaullists have enabled many UDF candidates to win National Assembly seats, since in recent years the two partes have agreed to back common candidates even in the first round of Assembly elections.[41]

The UDF leadership changed hands in the 1990s as Giscard's hold over the movement weakened. François Bayrou took over the leadership in 1998, boasting that the UDF's outspokenly pro-EU stance makes it "the most pro-European party in Europe." A succession of splits in the UDF after the 1997 elections has proliferated the divisions plaguing the French center-right.[42]

The National Front Perhaps the most controversial party in France is the **National Front** (*Front national,* or **FN**). The party was established in 1972 when several extreme right-wing factions got together and chose **Jean-Marie Le Pen** as their leader. Le Pen had already achieved notoriety as a right-wing parliamentary deputy in the IVth Republic. Having fought earlier in Indochina as a paratrooper, he left the legislature and fought in Algeria to keep the colony in French hands. In 1965 he managed the presidential campaign of a former Vichy official who sought to rally arch–right-wingers who despised de Gaulle because of his opposition to Pétain and his decision to grant Algeria independence. Though Le Pen's candidate won scarcely more than 5 percent of the vote, the extreme right did not die out. A collection of Vichyites, anti-Semites, fundamentalist Catholics, die-hard proponents of French imperialism, and theorists of European racial and cultural superiority were resolved to combine their efforts in a new party with a direct appeal to the voters. The Front became their organization and Le Pen, a combative stump speaker, was their man.

The large influx of foreign immigrants provided a burning issue that the FN seized in making its first electoral breakthroughs. Buoyed by the expanding French economy, immigrants streamed into France in the 1960s and early 1970s. Though many were Europeans, a large number were Arabs from the Mahgreb countries (the former North African colonies of Algeria, Tunisia, and Morocco). The rate of immigration slowed down somewhat in the late 1970s, but by the following decade there were more than 4 million immigrants in all, comprising about 8 percent of the population. Of these, about 35 percent came from the

Mahgreb, virtually all of them Muslim. Mahgrebis accounted for an even larger share of foreigners under age thirty. Immigrants from other countries boosted the Muslim population in France today to an estimated figure of between 2.5 and 4 million.

Most Muslims employed in the French economy are unskilled workers, with a large number unemployed. While some French voters view them as competitors for jobs and welfare benefits, the main problem is cultural: many non-Muslims, whether French in origin or immigrants of European extraction, find it difficult to accept Muslims as French citizens. (Since the late 1960s more than 60 percent of French survey respondents have said that there are "too many" North Africans in the country. In 1999, 51 percent said there were "too many Arabs" and 40 percent admitted to being racist.[43]) Until the 1990s, foreigners could become naturalized citizens fairly routinely after five years of residency, while their children born in France automatically acquired citizenship at age eighteen, subject to residency requirements. Le Pen made it clear that the existence of a large foreign element in France was unacceptable.

With a stridently chauvinist program, the FN won 11 percent of the vote in elections to the European Parliament in 1984. In 1988 Le Pen shocked the political mainstream by polling 14.4 percent of the first-round vote for the presidency. In 1995 he increased his presidential support to 15 percent, winning more than 4.5 million votes. And in a succession of elections to the National Assembly, the FN has seen its share of the first-round vote rise from 9.7 percent in 1986 to 15.1 percent in 1997.[44] In the process, Le Pen sharpened his anti-foreigner rhetoric, proposing a fifty-point program calling for a total ban on new immigration, job discrimination in favor of the French, the dismantling of ethnic ghettos, the ineligibility of immigrants and their families for various welfare benefits, a revision of the naturalization process, and the revocation of naturalization for various immigrants granted citizenship in the past. He also called for the expulsion of foreigners already residing in France.

The FN's success cannot be explained exclusively by its anti-immigrant stance. The party's bigotry also extends to Jews. In 1987 Le Pen touched off a storm of controversy with his state-ment on national radio that the Nazi gas chambers were just "a point of detail" in World War II. (There are about 750,000 Jews in France.) The FN has also reached out to a wider constituency concerned about high taxation, unemployment, crime, AIDS, globalization, and other woes afflicting French society. It routinely attacks the Socialists, Communists, Gaullists, and UDF parties as the "gang of four" responsible for these problems. Its wide electoral base encompasses blue- and white-collar workers, small business owners, affluent voters, and young people. By the late 1990s, 25 to 30 percent of French voters had voted for the FN at least once.

Thrown off guard by the FN's electoral inroads, the main parties of the left and right have equivocated in their responses. The Socialists openly decry the party's racism, but Mitterrand declared that the number of immigrants exceeded the "threshold of tolerance." In 1989 the Socialist government was thrown into embarrassment when three Muslim high school girls insisted on wearing head scarves in school. Prominent Socialist Party officials and intellectuals denounced the gesture as a blow to the secularization of the school system, a century-old priority of the French left, but Education Minister Lionel Jospin allowed the scarves to be worn. (Subsequently, the Council of State ruled that individual schools had discretion to decide whether head scarves were permissible.) The communists, for their part, distributed campaign literature portraying immigrants in negative stereotypes in a bid to keep working-class voters from switching to the FN.

The mainstream right-wing parties have felt especially threatened by the National Front. Chirac deplores racism, but in seeking to sympathize with anti-immigrant voters in 1991 he publicly described Muslims and blacks as living in public housing with numerous wives and children while enjoying extensive welfare benefits without working. "If you add to that the noise and smell," Chirac went on, it was understandable why the French were upset. When Edouard Balladur established a Gaullist-UDF government in 1993, his interior minister, the RPR's Charles Pasqua, removed the right of automatic French citizenship from children born in France of non-French parents. They were now required to apply for naturalization after age sixteen and go through a probationary period free from political activity.

These and other measures, known as the "Pasqua laws," placed new restrictions on immigrants but did not appreciably reduce the numbers obtaining French citizenship. Pasqua also stated that the Gaullist party's values were not all that different from those of the National Front, though not all Gaullists agreed with him. On assuming the presidency in 1995, Chirac cracked down on illegal immigrants, evicting a number of them them from public housing and increasing the number of deportations. Various UDF leaders, including Giscard d'Estaing, have also spoken out against the immigrant population so as not to be outflanked by the National Front. This get-tough attitude toward immigrants, however, has not measurably reduced electoral support for the FN. Some center-right leaders have openly attacked Le Pen. Prime Minister Juppé, for example, lambasted him as "racist, antisemitic and xenophobic."

In 1998, Le Pen was convicted of using violence against a female Socialist candidate in the 1997 parliamentary election campaign. In the same year, Le Pen's rivals provoked a split in the National Front. Bruno Mègret, the FN's number two, claimed the leadership of the National Front, denouncing Le Pen's reluctance to collaborate with more moderate right-wingers. With a master's degree from Berkeley and a Greek-Jewish wife, Mègret is more suave than Le Pen but espouses the same bigotry toward immigrants, calling for their expulsion in order to save French civilization and insisting on preferential treatment for ethnic French. The FN's electoral fortunes fell sharply in 2000; the party captured only 5.7 percent of the vote in elections to the European Parliament. With its blatant racism, xenophobic nationalism, and occasional hints of taking power by force, the French extreme right has many of the telltale markings of fascism.[45]

Other Rightists   The 1997 elections also yielded eight additional rightist Assembly members. Several are known for their opposition to closer French integration into the European Union, such as Philippe de Villiers, who ran for the presidency in 1995. Whereas left-wing anti-EU parties tend to regard the European Union as a capitalist organization that disadvantages workers and consumers, their right-wing counterparts object to the loss of French national sovereignty that the euro and other aspects of European integration entail.

The Left

The Socialists   The main party of the French left today is the **Socialist Party** (*Parti socialiste*, or **PS**). Although it is customary to identify socialism with the industrial working class and the underprivileged more generally, the PS has never been a predominantly workers' party or a party of the poor. Ever since its foundation in 1970, it has mainly been a middle-class party, attracting those segments of the French middle class who attach a high priority to enhancing social welfare and civil rights for the population as a whole. The party's core voters as well as its dues-paying members and candidates for office include a high proportion of teachers, professors, civil servants, doctors, and other white-collar professionals. Despite the harsh anticapitalist rhetoric of the early Mitterrand years, the PS has also drawn a significant number of votes from private business people and managerial personnel. Less than half its constituency is working class, with most of it consisting of better-paid skilled workers rather than unskilled laborers.

Its main trade union support comes from the two non-communist federations, the Workers' Force (*Force Ouvrière*, or FO) and the traditionally Catholic-oriented French Democratic Confederation of Labor (*Confédération française démocratique du travail*, or CFDT). Neither of these union organizations maintains formal institutional links with the Socialists, however, and trade union membership in general has declined appreciably since the 1980s.[46] On the whole, the French Socialist Party has been considerably less connected with industrial workers and trade unions than the British Labour Party is.

Ideologically, the party has undergone a major transformation from the state-centered, anti-business socialism of its first dozen years to more accommodating attitudes toward private enterprise since the Mitterrand government's policy turnabout of 1983. Still, the party remains divided between those who wish to place even more confidence in the private sector and those who wish to retain a stronger role for the state in regulating capitalism and enlarging social welfare benefits. Since becoming prime minister in 1997, Lionel Jospin has pursued a middle course that combines the pursuit of private-sector growth with a welfare orientation that is more state-centered than that of his British counterpart, Tony Blair.

PROFILE: Lionel Jospin

Lionel Jospin was born into a Protestant family in 1937. His father was an activist in the SFIO, and his own political passions were already visible in his teens: in 1956 he was an ardent opponent of the war in Algeria and an equally impassioned critic of the Soviet destruction of the Hungarian people's uprising against communist rule that took place in the autumn of that year. He became active in France's largest student organization and joined a small leftist grouping. He was also an accomplished basketball player. As a young man Jospin climbed the same ladder into the French political elite as many other ambitious members of his generation. After attending the Institute for Political Studies in Paris and completing his military service, he entered the National Academy for Administration (ENA) in 1963. His first assignment upon graduation was in the Ministry of Foreign Affairs. He appeared to be headed toward a stellar diplomatic career when the events of 1968 convinced him to resume political activism. While teaching economics and running a business department at the Paris-Sceaux University of Technology, where he remained a faculty member for eleven years, Jospin joined the newly founded Socialist Party in 1971.

Lionel Jospin

His rise up the party's ranks under François Mitterrand's leadership was swift. By 1973 he was a member of the party's Executive Bureau and one of its national secretaries with responsibility for shaping its positions on vocational training. Two years later he became the party's secretary for Third World affairs and in 1979 assumed responsibility for its foreign policy orientation. Mitterrand's confidence in Jospin won him the task of chairing meetings of the party's executive committees in the party leader's absence. As the Socialists embarked on the delicate path of forging an electoral alliance with the Communists, Mitterrand entrusted Jospin with the negotiations. Though the unity of the two left-wing parties ultimately fell apart, Jospin was instrumental in helping Mitterrand win the presidency in 1981. From the start of the campaign until 1988, Jospin was First Secretary of the Socialist Party.

Jospin entered the cabinet as minister for national education, youth, and sport at the start of Mitterrand's second term in 1988. In 1993, however, he lost his parliamentary seat in the Socialists' electoral debacle, and in the same year resigned his position as the party's leader. His dismay at the fratricidal infighting among Socialist leaders, which was exacerbated by the policy reversals, electoral defeats, and corruption scandals of Mitterrand's administration, prompted his resignation. But the following year he was enticed to rejoin the leadership ranks and in 1995 announced his candidacy for the Socialist Party's nomination for the presidency of France. In a ballot conducted among party members, Jospin won 65 percent of the vote and captured the nomination. His first-round plurality in the presidential elections, comprising 23 percent of the vote, stunned the Gaullists, whose votes were divided between their two feuding leaders, Jacques Chirac (21 percent) and the prime minister, Edouard Balladur (18 percent). Chirac bested Jospin in the runoff, 52.6 percent to 47.4 percent.

But only four years later, Jospin led the Socialists to a spirited comeback. With his designation as prime minister in 1997, he quickly wrested the policy-making initiative from President Chirac, demonstrating once again that, in periods of cohabitation, the reins of power in the Vth Republic can pass decisively from the president to the head of government.

JOSPIN AS PRIME MINISTER

During the 1997 election campaign, Jospin espoused a leftist program, attacking the EU's criteria for the euro as too stringent and vowing to put an end to the conservatives' privatization program and to vastly increase state spending to create new jobs. He also pledged to institute a thirty-five-hour work week to open up more job opportunities for the unemployed. But not long after taking office, Jospin backtracked on some of these positions and turned out to be far more flexible than his rhetoric suggested.

Instead of halting the privatization process, Jospin's government by the end of 1999 had reaped more revenue in stock sales of state-owned firms than all five previous governments put together, including those led by Gaullists like Balladur and Juppé. The sale of large shares of Air France, France Telecom, Aerospatiale, and other public enterprises brought more than 180 billion francs into the treasury (about $36 billion), more than double the figure of Jacques Chirac's government of 1986–87. In addition, Jospin's unwillingness to inject the government in merger negotiations involving formerly state-controlled banks and oil companies represented another marked departure from the past practice of previous French governments (including conservative ones).

Jospin also backed away from earlier hints that he might boost government deficit spending beyond the limit of 3 percent of GDP imposed by the EU's agreement on monetary union. He cut spending enough to keep the deficit below 3 percent and announced plans to reduce it further, to 1 percent, by 2002. He also asserted that it was no longer possible to regulate the economy through administrative measures, another brusque departure not only from Socialist rhetoric but from traditional French policies stretching all the way back to de Gaulle's first postwar government. In 2000 he readied a series at tax cuts. These shifts reflected the mounting pressures of globalization on the French economy, stemming from European monetary union and the need to remain competitive in international markets.

At the same time, Jospin insisted that he remained a "democratic socialist." He refrained from co-signing a document with Tony Blair and German chancellor Gerhard Schroeder on the "third way," which seeks to redefine European social democratic parties in more centrist terms. Jospin summarized his position by saying, "Yes to the free-market economy; no to the free-market society." In this vein he secured the passage of his government's work week reduction legislation in 1998 and 1999, with the vigorous support of Martine Aubry, minister for employment and solidarity. The laws require private companies with more than twenty workers to reduce their work hours to an average of thirty-five per week while paying their workers for thirty-nine hours. Similar provisions were expected to affect smaller companies starting in 2002, while negotiations were under way to extend the thirty-five-hour week to France's 4.5 million public sector employees. The purpose of these regulations was to free up more working hours for the unemployed. Companies that manage to increase their work force are given a small government bonus ($1,500 a year for each job created). The laws were vigorously opposed by Chirac and the center-right opposition parties as well as by business owners, many of whom quickly found loopholes enabling them to thwart the regulations' principal purposes. Some people who felt they would be adversely affected by the changes staged strikes and protests. In March 2000, however, the government said that 180,000 full-time jobs were already being created or saved since the initial legislation was passed in 1998.[47]

In addition to steering a middle course on the economy, Jospin has pursued a mixture of leftist and more conservative positions on other issues as well. True to the Socialists' commitments to social and political inclusiveness, Jospin—whose wife is a feminist philosopher—succeeded in increasing the representation of women in the Parliament and cabinet. Prior to the 1997 campaign he decreed that one-third of Socialist Party candidates for the National Assembly had to be women. His government also introduced a constitutional amendment guaranteeing women "equal access" with men in seeking elective office; it won wide bipartisan support in both houses of the legislature. Jospin's government secured passage of a bill extending equal family rights to gay couples and unwed heterosexuals; it granted citizenship rights to 80,000 immigrants; and it permitted the use of local languages like Breton, Alsatian, and Provençal in public schools.

In a more conservative vein, Jospin has proceeded with military reforms initiated by the Gaullists with a view to ending the draft. He has cracked down on crime and pledged to cut corporation taxes. He also joined with Chirac in ensuring active French participation in NATO's Kosovo bombing campaign in spite of opposition from communists and Greens in his cabinet. Jospin and Chirac also cooperated in managing France's trade disputes with the United States and its relations with its EU partners. His success in getting along with Chirac has resulted in high public approval ratings for both figures. At the same time, Jospin has sought to retain the loyalty of the left wing of the Socialist Party, along with his communist and Green coalition partners, while in practice moving in the pragmatic, centrist directions articulated by Blair and Schroeder.

Respected as a man of integrity, Jospin thus far has been unscathed by personal scandal, unlike other Socialist leaders in recent years. But at the end of 1999 he had to accept the resignation of his influential finance minister, Dominique Strauss-Kahn, when charges were brought accusing him of illegally accepting funds on behalf of the Socialist Party from a government social security fund for students. Nevertheless, Jospin ended the century with wide public support and a rosy economic outlook. Unemployment was edging just below 11 percent and economic growth was 2.7 percent while inflation was under 2 percent. If these trends continued, he would be well-poised for another presidential bid in 2002.

The Communists The **French Communist Party** (*Parti communiste francais,* or **PCF**) has seen its fortunes wane appreciably in recent decades. The party suffered major losses in the 1968 elections when the Gaullists conducted a pointedly anti-PCF campaign. The communists lost even more voters in the early 1980s as Mitterrand's Socialists chipped away at their working-class base. The anti-immigrant National Front party has tried to lure erstwhile communist voters from their party allegiances, deftly playing on working-class resentments of immigrants who were perceived as competing for jobs and welfare benefits. In addition, the PCF's trade union partner, the CGT *(Confédération génerale de travail),* has experienced a sharp decline in membership and political clout since the 1970s as the French economy has shed jobs in industrial manufacturing and placed growing reliance on a modernized private sector. Finally, the collapse of the Soviet system of government in 1991 left the PCF without a clear ideological compass.

Battered by these challenges, the communists in 1994 picked a new chief, Robert Hue, to replace Georges Marchais, who had dominated the party since 1972. Hue was more open to public debate within the PCF than his autocratic predecessor but he ran into trouble over allegations of financial improprieties. In 2000 the PCF reorganized itself, selecting a woman, Dominique Gradot, as its president. The party faces an uphill struggle as its traditional source of support, the unskilled industrial working class, continues to shrink. Today the PCF's support still remains concentrated in industrial and mining regions, especially the factory areas outside of Paris, which are known as the "Red Belt" because of the party's decades-long control of local governments.

Small Leftist Parties The National Assembly elected in 1997 also includes two small left-wing parties now allied with the Socialists. The **Radical-Socialists** (*Parti radical-socialiste,* or **PRS**) is a recently reconstituted party with roots in the IIIrd Republic. The **Citizens Movement** (*Mouvement des Citoyens,* or **MDC**) is led by Mitterrand-era cabinet minister Jean-Pierre Chevènement. A left-wing Socialist, Chevènement opposed Mitterrand's austerity policies after 1982 and French participation in the Persian Gulf War of 1990–91. He broke from the PS and formed the Citizens Movement in 1992 as a left-wing party opposed to the Maastricht Treaty. He has continued to favor an actively interventionist, welfare-oriented state while serving as minister of the interior in Jospin's first and second cabinets.

Several ecology-oriented parties and independents are also associated with the left. The largest of these groups is the **Green Party,** which in 1997 won 3.6 percent of the first-round vote and entered the National Assembly for the first time with six seats. Dominique Voynet, the Greens' leader, joined Jospin's first cabinet as minister for the environment. The 1997 elections also returned two independent "ecologists" and nine "diverse left" deputies. Rivalries between the leaders of the two main ecology parties have divided the ecological movement. Finally, there are several left-wing mini-parties and groupings (*groupuscules*) that failed to win parliamentary seats, including Trotskyites and anti-EU organizations.

Interest Groups

France has a wide assortment of interest groups ranging from well-established associational groups such as labor unions, business associations, farmers' organizations and the like to less structured nonassociational groups that come together to militate for particular issues. Groups arising from new social movements such as those concerned with women's issues, gay rights, and immigrants are also highly active. France's long tradition of open contestation and mass protect makes for a highly participant political culture, as the following account demonstrates.

FRANCE AND GLOBALIZATION

"We're making it the trial of globalization," the speaker declared, to the delight of forty thousand demonstrators assembled outside the courthouse of Millau, a rustic town surrounded by one of France's most productive farm regions. For the supporters of José Bové, a sheep farmer whose trial was about to begin on a sunny day in June 2000, the statement was no exaggeration. Bové and nine co-defendants found themselves at the epicenter of a major controversy in France's trade relations with the United States. At issue were not only billions of dollars in economic ties between the two countries, but also the larger question of how—or whether—a trading nation like France can resist the pressures of globalization in such areas as biotechnology and transnational business.

Bové and his fellow defendants were on trial for smashing a local McDonald's restaurant while it was under construction the previous summer, causing $100,000 in damage. Freely admitting their responsibility, Bové and his friends described their action as a "festive dismantling" of the burger franchise. McDonald's is widely perceived around the world as a symbol of American culture and corporate expansionism, and the attack was intended as an act of retaliation against the United States. Earlier, France had taken the lead in urging its European Union partners to ban the import of hormone-treated American beef. In response, the Clinton administration slapped a 100 percent tariff on a variety of European food imports, specifically targeting such French delicacies as foie gras, Dijon mustard, and premium cheeses. José Bové was personally affected: his sheep produce milk for Roquefort, the popular blue cheese that was high on the United States tariff list.

The EU's ban on hormone-treated beef from the United States reflected deep misgivings on the part of many Europeans about the safety of chemically or genetically modified food and plants. Arguments for and against the genetic alteration of organisms, a technology that is making rapid strides in the United States, have animated debates both within the nations of Europe—including France—and between the European Union and the United States. Advocates of genetic alteration maintain that it will significantly increase world food production, stimulate the development of drought- and salt-resistant plants, and curtail reliance on pesticides. Its opponents counter that it will reduce biodiversity by favoring certain forms of plant life over others while spreading resistance to antibiotics in bacteria. Critics of genetic modification also maintain that it will boost the power of multinational agrobusinesses at the expense of small farmers. In the spring of 2000, the European Parliament voted to permit genetic food alteration. That decision was sharply criticized by Dominique Voynet, France's environment minister, who vowed to "completely protect the safety of consumers and the environment" from genetic tampering with the food supply.

The issues raised in the Bové case tapped a wellspring of popular support for the globally conscious crusader throughout France. (Bové, who grew up in California while his parents studied at Berkeley, was among the opponents of globalization who staged demonstrations in Seattle at the 2000 World Trade Organization meetings.) While interest groups representing French farmers and environmentalists voiced their specific grievances, including Bové's Peasant Confederation, more spontaneous expressions of support came from citizens opposed to globalization in general and to American junk food in particular. Even President Chirac and Prime Minister Jospin, sensing the public mood, expressed general understanding for Bové's concerns. The attack on McDonald's provided grist for the mill of those French people who are wary of excessive American influence. (A 1999 poll revealed that 60 percent of the French regard the United States as militarily, economically, and culturally too powerful.) The incident also provided a focal point for a number of France's highly energized interest groups and political activists, highlighting some defining features of French political life in the process.[48]

HYPOTHESIS-TESTING EXERCISE: Do Institutions Determine Behavior?

HYPOTHESIS

The mixed presidential-parliamentary system established under the constitution of the Vth Republic has enhanced stability in French political life by creating a strong executive and a relatively weak parliament. It has also promoted policy consistency, the predictability of government actions, and an effective governing process capable of resolving the nation's problems. Political institutions thus shape the behavior of state officials, constraining them to act in certain regularized and predictable patterns.

VARIABLES

The **dependent variables** are *political stability, consistency, and predictability* along with *governmental effectiveness*. On what are they dependent? The **independent variable** is the *presidential-parliamentary system of the Vth Republic.*

EXPECTATIONS

If the hypothesis is true, then we would expect to find that (1) France has had more political stability under the Vth Republic than under the IVth Republic; (2) the Vth Republic's presidential-parliamentary system has provided for consistency and predictability in government policy with minimal interference from the legislature; and (3) governments in the Vth Republic have effectively resolved some of the most pressing problems facing the country.

EVIDENCE

(1) The French experience shows that political stability is not necessarily guaranteed by the constitution. As we've seen, France was rocked in the 1960s by a succession of potentially catastrophic crises, from the threat of military coups during the Algerian imbroglio to the events of 1968. What is remarkable is that the Vth Republic survived these crises. Was its survival due to the structure of its state institutions, as prescribed by the constitution? The answer would seem to be a qualified yes. The power and prestige that the constitution confers on the presidency enabled President de Gaulle to take a series of measures to preserve democracy and make authoritative (and at times unpopular) decisions with a decisiveness that political leaders in the IVth Republic lacked. But our answer must be qualified by the fact that de Gaulle himself was an exceptional man, a charismatic leader endowed with extraordinary personal support among the vast majority of the French people, especially during crises. A constitution may provide for specific presidential powers, but it cannot by itself create a respected leader.

Still, the Vth Republic's institutional arrangements put an end to the succession of unstable coalition governments that characterized the IVth Republic. Though some cabinets have consisted of representatives of two or more parties (such as the current one under Jospin), they have not been as dependent on a fractious parliament as IVth Republic governments invariably were. Only one Vth Republic government has ever lost a vote of confidence. The result has been greater longevity for Vth Republic governments. These facts are consistent with the expectations of the hypothesis.

(2) While stability has increased under the Vth Republic, there has been less consistency and predictability than the constitution initially appeared to provide. For one thing, the dual executive system does not always function consistently or in predictable ways; much depends on the policy orientations and personalities of the president and prime minister. De Gaulle generally insisted on the primacy of the president over the prime minister, though he was willing to accord his PMs some latitude on matters in which he did not take a prevailing interest. Giscard d'Estaing and Prime Minister Chirac had a difficult relationship, ultimately falling out over policy differences and political rivalry. Cohabitation, of course, magnifies the likelihood of policy inconsistency and unpredictability.

In these circumstances the National Assembly decisively intrudes on the executive branch. Because it can topple the government by a vote of censure, it can require the president to select a prime minister acceptable to the legislative majority and thereby impose that majority's policies on the president. While serving as prime ministers under President Mitterrand, Chirac and Balladur took policy initiatives completely at variance with Mitterrand's preferences, in many cases undoing the Socialists' crowning legislative achievements. Jospin has similarly favored measures opposed by President Chirac (such as the thirty-five-hour work week and the use of local languages).

Thus the Vth Republic's constitution has established the bases for both a *strong executive* as well as a *divided executive*. While its institutions provide a framework that sets limits to what elected officials may do, these institutions do not compel presidents and prime ministers to agree on policy initiatives or even to cooperate with each other to ensure a smooth governing process. Far from "constraining" elected officials to act in specified ways, the Vth Republic's constitution provides for a makeshift relationship between the country's two leading executives that varies with personalities on an ad hoc basis. Furthermore, the constitution cannot prevent an individual leader from changing his or her mind and reversing policy course, as Giscard d'Estaing, Mitterrand, Chirac, and Jospin all did at one time or another. In contrast to the expectations of our hypothesis, policy consistency and predictability are *not necessarily* enhanced by the Vth Republic's institutions.

(3) As to governmental effectiveness, the record in France—as in most other countries, regardless of their constitution—is mixed. Under de Gaulle's firm presidential authority, the Vth Republic's constitution enabled France to take several important measures that the far weaker governments of the IVth Republic proved incapable of undertaking: the decolonization of Algeria, the reassertion of France's international prestige, the elimination of the threat of a military coup d'état. De Gaulle's successors also had sufficient latitude to promote their own priorities, such as European integration. But the economic record is more complicated. For all its political problems, the IVth Republic compiled a creditable record of economic successes over time. The first decades of the Vth Republic were also generally successful, leading some people to describe the 1944–74 period as "the thirty glorious years" of economic growth.

Since then, however, the economy has become harder to manage effectively. Despite noteworthy achievements in modernizing France's technological infrastructure, maintaining growth, and reducing inflation, presidents and prime ministers in more recent decades have not been very effective in lowering the unemployment rolls. Neither leftist approaches favoring increased state spending nor conservative approaches favoring the private sector have been effective. These failures apparently have nothing to do with the nature of the constitution; they reside in structural problems rooted in the French economy (such as the tax system and the population's age structure) and in the larger global economic system. The Vth Republic's constitutional framework may thus enhance governmental effectiveness in some areas, particularly those that are responsive to strong executive authority, but it cannot raise the likelihood of success in all areas of state activity.

CONCLUSIONS

The evidence bearing on our hypothesis is therefore *mixed*. While generally promoting governmental stability in stark contrast to the IVth Republic, the Vth Republic's presidential-parliamentary system has not always enhanced policy consistency or predictability. While permitting greater governmental effectiveness in some policy domains, it has proven ineffective (or perhaps irrelevant) in others. In sum, the experience of the Vth Republic demonstrates that the institutional arrangements of a written constitution may establish a general framework within which public officials must act, but they cannot always constrain political leaders to behave in predictable patterns. How French presidents and prime ministers deal with each other and the national legislature may depend on personalities, the shifting whims of the electorate, or other extra-constitutional realities. The French experience also shows that even the most carefully crafted constitution may not always work in accordance with its framers' intentions.

FRANCE AND THE FOUR FACES OF DEMOCRACY

As we've seen, France took a long and winding road to stable democracy. The threat of authoritarianism hung over French politics until well into the 1960s. In 1997, 75 percent of survey respondents agreed that the National Front constituted a "danger for democracy" and 48 percent believed that democracy in France was working badly. In recent years approximately 30 percent of eligible voters have abstained from voting in national legislative elections. Nevertheless, France since the end of World War II has essentially met the basic criteria for Face I of democracy, that of popular sovereignty. It has also largely secured the fundamental rights and liberties of Face II.

It is Face III—democracy as a value system—that is a source of problems, in France as in many other democracies. The values of tolerance, nondiscrimination, and fair play are perhaps the hardest aspects of democracy to achieve, and the French

are still wrestling with them today. Their task is all the more difficult because the problems centering around Muslims and other immigrants are bound up with the more fundamental question of "who is French?" A nation whose majority has been long accustomed to defining "French-ness" in ethnic terms must now confront the problems of ethnic diversity and citizenship on a larger scale than ever before.

As to Face IV, socioeconomic democracy, the French have pursued two approaches to improving the economic well-being of the population and dealing with income disparities: one centered in the state, the other in the private sector. The two approaches are not entirely mutually exclusive. A general consensus between the mainstream parties now prevails on the principle of combining the two approaches, a fact that blurs the historic distinctions between right and left in French politics. (In 1999, 86 percent saw no difference between Socialist and conservative governments.[49]) The combined approach can claim a mixture of successes and shortcomings. It has made France the fourth largest economy in the world while providing a vital social security net for the population. At the same time, glaring socioeconomic inequalities remain. While France has taken major strides since World War II in making economic welfare a defining component of democracy, it must still contend with the challenges of growth, efficiency, and equality in an increasingly competitive global environment.

While these realities present France with an imposing array of challenges as it heads into the twenty-first century, one thing is certain: in changing its political institutions and practices in the past thirty years, the country has achieved demonstrable successes in overcoming its historic legacy of internal strife and instability. The achievements of the French political system at the end of the twentieth century appear to provide a solid basis for confronting the tasks of the next one.

KEY TERMS AND NAMES
(Underlined in the text)

Jacques Chirac
Presidential-parliamentary system
Lionel Jospin
Cohabitation
François Mitterrand

Privatization
De Gaulle
French Revolution
Jacobinism
Prefects
IVth Republic
Vth Republic
SFIO
French Communist Party (PCF)
Gaullism and neo-Gaullists
Dirigisme
Grandes écoles
National Academy
  for Administration (ENA)
National Assembly
Senate
Rally for the Republic (RPR)
Union for French Democracy (UDF)
National Front (FN)
Socialist Party (PS)

FOR DISCUSSION: WHAT WOULD YOU DO?

1. If you were a French citizen, to which party (if any) would you belong? Would you favor or oppose cohabitation?
2. What changes to the constitution would you favor, if any?
3. Should the government widen social welfare and hire the unemployed, even if it means raising taxes? Or should it cut taxes and confer more responsibility on individuals and businesses?
4. Would you favor the thirty-five-hour work week (with pay for thirty-nine hours)?
5. Would you favor policies designed to restrict immigration and the rights of immigrants, or policies aimed at facilitating immigration and widening immigrants' rights?
6. Where do you stand on the issue of France and globalization?

FOR FURTHER READING

In addition to the titles in the notes, consult the following:

Fernand Braudel, *The Identity of France*, 2 vols., trans. by Siân Reynolds (London: Collins, 1988).

Alistair Cole, *French Politics and Society* (London: Prentice Hall, 1998).
Henry W. Ehrmann and Martin A. Schain, *Politics in France*, 2d ed. (New York: HarperCollins, 1992).
Michael S. Lewis-Beck, ed., *How France Votes* (New York: Chatham House, 2000).
William Safran, *The French Polity*, 4th ed. (White Plains, N.Y.: Longman, 1995).
Anne Stevens, *The Government and Politics of France*, 2d ed. (New York: St. Martin's Press, 1996).
Ronald Tiersky, *France in the New Europe* (Belmont, Calif.: Wadsworth, 1994).

WEBSITES

General websites with links to numerous political topics include <www.info-france-usa.org>, <www.diplomatie.fr>, and the French search engine, <www.nomade.fr>.

NOTES

1. Women hold down 57 percent of public sector jobs but only 7 percent in the senior ranks. Out of eighty-eight university presidents, in 1999 only four were women, while there were only five females among 109 state prefects (*Washington Post*, March 1, 1999).
2. Andrew Lossky, *Louis XIV and the French Monarchy* (New Brunswick, N.J.: Rutgers University Press, 1994); Olivier Bernier, *Louis XIV: A Royal Life* (Garden City, N.Y.: Doubleday, 1987).
3. Joseph Bergin, *Cardinal Richelieu* (New Haven, Conn.: Yale University Press, 1990); Richard Bonney, *Political Change in France Under Richelieu and Mazarin 1624–1661* (Oxford: Oxford University Press, 1978); Ines Murat, *Colbert*, trans. R. F. Cook and J. Van Asselt (Charlottesville: University of Virginia Press, 1984).
4. The Jacobins (JACK-o-bins) took their name from an order of friars who were established in the church of St. Jacques (i.e., St. Jacob) in Paris. The Jacobins held meetings in the dining hall of the church convent.
5. The literature on the French Revolution is voluminous. For thorough overviews, see Simon Schama, *Citizens* (New York: Knopf, 1989); William Doyle, *The Oxford History of the French Revolution* (Oxford: Oxford University Press, 1989); and Emmet Kennedy, *A Cultural History of the French Revolution* (New Haven, Conn.: Yale University Press, 1989).
6. The Third Republic's first president, Marshal Patrice MacMahon, was a monarchist who tried to re-establish authoritarian rule. Electoral victories by

pro-Republic forces in 1876 and 1877 prevented him from succeding and he resigned. In the late 1880s General Georges Boulanger, "the man on horseback," almost took power in a coup. See James Harding, *The Astonishing Adventure of General Boulanger* (New York: Scribner, 1971) and William D. Irvine, *The Boulanger Affair Reconsidered* (New York: Oxford University Press, 1989). Between 1894 and 1906 the Dreyfus Affair, which took its name from a Jewish officer unjustly accused of treason, triggered an intense struggle between the Republic's authoritarian opponents and "Dreyfusards" who supported democracy. Dreyfus served years of hard labor on Devil's Island, a penal colony off the coast of French Guyana, before being exonerated. See Jean-Denis Bredin, *The Affair: The Case of Alfred Dreyfus,* trans. Jeffrey Mehlman (New York: G. Braziller, 1986).

7. Jacques Fauvet, *La IVe République* (Paris: Fayard, 1959).

8. Liah Greenfeld, *Nationalism: Five Roads to Modernity* (Cambridge, Mass.: Harvard University Press, 1992), 89–188.

9. Sudhir Hazareesingh, *Political Traditions in Modern France* (Oxford: Oxford University Press, 1994).

10. For an analysis of the Revolution stressing the role of social classes, see Barrington Moore, *Social Origins of Dictatorship and Democracy* (Boston: Beacon, 1969), 40–110. Moore argues that the destruction of the French nobility removed a class that, in some other countries, supported fascism in the twentieth century. He also notes that the peasantry and bourgeoisie were each split in their attitudes toward democracy and capitalism, resulting in less solid support for democracy than in England.

11. Sanford Elwitt, *The Making of the Third Republic* (Baton Rouge: Louisiana State University Press, 1975).

12. Edward S. Mason, *The Paris Commune* (New York: Macmillan, 1930). For Karl Marx's views on the Commune, see *The Civil War in France*, in *The Marx-Engels Reader,* Robert C. Tucker ed. (New York: W. W. Norton, 1972), 526–76.

13. Michael Crozier, *The Stalled Society* (New York: Viking, 1974).

14. Charles Tilly, *The Contentious French* (Cambridge, Mass.: Belknap, 1986). See Also Philip G. Cerny, *Social Movements and Protests in France* (New York: St. Martin's, Press, 1982).

15. Robert O. Paxton, *Vichy France* (New York: Knopf, 1972); Michael R. Marrus and Robert O. Paxton, *Vichy France and the Jews* (New York: Basic Books,

1981). See also the film by Marcel Ophuls, *Le chagrin et la pitié (The Sorrow and the Pity).*

16. Pétain was tried for treason and sentenced to death, but was pardoned by de Gaulle.

17. See the analysis by Richard Johnson, an American student who witnessed the 1968 events, in *The French Communist Party Versus the Students* (New Haven, Conn.: Yale University Press, 1972).

18. Alain Touraine, *The May Movement,* trans. Leonard F. X. Mayhew (New York: Random House, 1971); Alain Schnapp and Pierre Vidal-Naquet, *The French Student Uprising, November 1967–June 1968,* trans. Maria Jolas (Boston: Beacon, 1971). For a fictionalized account, see the novel by James Jones, *The Merry Month of May* (New York: Delacorte, 1971).

19. Charles de Gaulle, *The Complete War Memoirs of Charles de Gaulle,* trans. Jonathan Griffin and Richard Howard (New York: Simon and Schuster, 1959) and *Memoirs of Hope,* trans. Terence Kilmartin (New York: Simon and Schuster, 1971). See also Jean Lacouture, *De Gaulle: The Rebel 1890–1944,* trans. Patrick O'Brien (New York: W. W. Norton, 1993) and *De Gaulle: The Ruler 1945–1970,* trans. Alan Sheridan (New York: W. W. Norton, 1993); Charles Williams, *The Last Great Frenchman: A Life of General de Gaulle* (New York: Wiley, 1995); Robert O. Paxton and Nicholas Wahl, *De Gaulle and the United States* (Providence, R.I.: Berg, 1994).

20. Valéry Giscard d'Estaing, *French Democracy,* trans. Vincent Cronin (Garden City, N.Y.: Doubleday, 1977); J. R. Frears, *France in the Giscard Presidency* (London: Allen and Unwin, 1981).

21. Mitterrand was often accused of covering up his early right-wing views and Pétainist leanings. See, for example, Pierre Péan, *Une Jeunesse française: François Mitterrand 1934–1947* (Paris: Fayard, 1994). See also Catherine Nay, *The Black and the Red: François Mitterrand, the Story of an Ambition,* trans. Alan Sheridan (New York: Harcourt Brace Jovanovich, 1987). For Mitterrand's account of his political development, see *Ma part de verité* (Paris: Fayard, 1969).

22. For Mitterrand's thoughts on the 1970s, see *The Wheat and the Chaff,* trans. Richard S. Woodward, Helen R. Lane, and Concilia Hayter (New York: Seaver, 1982). For an account of the "union of the left," see George Ross, *Workers and Communists in France* (Berkeley: University of California Press, 1982).

23. For a comparison, see Peter Hall, *Governing the Economy: The Politics of State Intervention in Britain and France* (Oxford: Oxford University Press, 1986).

24. Julius W. Friend, *The Long Presidency: France in the Mitterrand Years, 1981–1995* (Boulder, Colo.: Westview, 1998); Mairi Maclean, ed., *The Mitterrand Years*

(New York: St. Martin's, Press, 1998); Anthony Daley, ed., *The Mitterrand Era* (New York: New York University Press, 1996); Alistair Cole, *François Mitterrand* (London: Routledge, 1994); Wayne Northcott, *Mitterrand: A Political Biography* (New York: Holmes and Meier, 1992); George Ross et al., eds., *The Mitterrand Experiment* (New York: Oxford University Press, 1987); Jean Lacouture, *Mitterrand: une histoire de Francais,* 2 vols. (Paris: Seuil, 1998).

25. Robert Elgie, *The Role of the Prime Minister in France, 1981–91* (New York: St. Martin's, Press, 1993); Leslie Derfler, *President and Parliament* (Boca Raton: Louisiana State University, 1983); William G. Andrews, *Presidential Government in Gaullist France* (Albany: State University of New York Press, 1982).

26. ENA graduates only about eighty students a year, Ecole Polytechnique about three hundred. By 1999, six out of eight previous prime ministers were ENA graduates, two out of the three most recent presidents, and more than half of Jospin's top cabinet ministers. Two out of three chairmen of the top forty companies listed on the French stock exchange had graduated from either ENA or the Ecole Polytechnique. (*The Economist,* June 5, 1999).

27. In 1986 Mitterrand and the Socialists changed the electoral law back to proportional representation. Although the Gaullists and their allies won a majority of National Assembly seats that year, they ended up with fewer seats than they would have won under SMD. Chirac's government thereupon changed the election system back to SMD in time for the 1988 parliamentary elections. The Socialists won control of the Assembly in those elections, winning more seats than they would have received under proportional representation.

28. Out of a total population of 59 million in 1999, only about 15 million live in France's ten largest cities (9 million in Paris). There are more than twenty thousand communes having a population of fewer than five hundred people. On "deep France," see Richard Bernstein, *Fragile Glory: A Portrait of France and the French* (New York: Plume, 1991). On the agriculture lobby, see John Keeler, *The Politics of Neocorporatism in France* (New York: Oxford University Press, 1987).

29. The preamble affirms the "attachment" of the French people to the Declaration of the Rights of Man of 1789 and to the rights listed in the preamble to the Fourth Republic's constitution. Article 2 states that the Fifth Republic ensures "the equality of all citizens before the law, without discrimination of origin, race or religion."

30. John Bell, *French Constitutional Law* (Oxford: Clarendon Press, 1992); Alec Stone, *The Birth of Judicial Politics in France: The Constitutional Council in Comparative Perspective* (New York: Oxford University Press, 1992).

31. Even though the French public educational system is practically tuition-free right through graduate school, young people from the provinces and from lower-middle-class or working-class families do not apply to the elite academies in significant numbers. Socialist attempts to encourage more applicants from these groups in the 1980s were not very successful.

32. Ezra N. Suleiman, *Elites in French Society* (Princeton, N.J.: Princeton University Press, 1978); Harvey Feigenbaum, *The Politics of Public Enterprise: Oil and the French State* (Princeton, N.J.: Princeton University Press, 1985).

33. In addition to 2.6 million national and local government employees, the figure of 5 million includes schoolteachers and professors along with employees of the railroads, public hospitals, public enterprises, utilities, and other state-run concerns. The civil service has its own administrative court, the *Council of State.* Consisting of more than two hundred high-level civil servants, this body adjudicates problems arising from regulations issued by the French governmental bureaucracy.

34. France maintains four "overseas departments" (*départements d'outre-mer,* or DOMs): Guadeloupe, Martinique, and Guyana in the Caribbean and the island of Réunion in the Indian Ocean. It also has three "overseas territories" (*territoires d'outre-mer,* or TOMs): French Polynesia, New Caledonia (near Australia), and the Pacific islands of Wallis and Futuna. In addition, it possesses two "territorial collectivities": St. Pierre-et-Miquelon, located next to Canada, and Mayotte, located near Madagascar. These overseas areas, which are not considered part of "metropolitan France," elect twenty-two seats in the French National Assembly. The Mediterranean island of Corsica is part of metropolitan France. It has enjoyed a special autonomous status since 1982 and elects four deputies to the National Assembly.

35. Vivien A. Schmidt, *Democratizing France: The Political and Administrative History of Decentralization* (Cambridge: Cambridge University Press, 1990).

36. In 1997 all seven Citizens Movement candidates elected to the Assembly won an absolute majority of votes in the second round, as did twelve out of thirteen winning candidates of the Radical-Socialist Party, eight out of nine victorious "diverse left" deputies, and five out of eight victorious ecology candidates. All eight "diverse right" deputies won with an absolute majority, one in the first round and the others in the second. Less than 20 percent of the Assembly races had three candidates in round 2, of

which seventy-six involved National Front candidates competing against both left and center-right opponents. There were no races with more than three candidates in the second round. For the election results, see *Le Monde*, June 3, 1997.

37. The first Gaullist party, the French People's Rally (the *Rassemblement du peuple francais*, or RPF), lasted from 1947 to 1953. In 1958 the Gaullists reconstituted themselves as the Union for the New Republic (*Union pour la nouvelle République*, the UNR), then changed their party's name again in 1968 to the Union for the Defense of the Republic and, subsequently, the Democratic Union for the Republic (*Union démocratique pour la République*, or UDR).

38. Vivien A. Schmidt, *From State to Market? The Transformation of French Business and Government* (Cambridge: Cambridge University Press, 1996).

39. A campaign funding law passed in 1988 provided for partial public funding of campaigns, but failed to eliminate secret funding from private sources. A 1995 reform barred political contributions by private corporations. Neither of these measures prevents undisclosed sums from flowing to the main parties.

40. Franz-Olivier Giesbert, *Jacques Chirac* (Paris: Seuil, 1987); John Tuppen, *Chirac's France, 1986–88* (New York: St. Martin's, Press, 1991); Jean-Marie Colombani, *Le President de la République* (Paris: Stock, 1998); Raphaëlle Bacqué and Denis Saverot, *Seul Comme Chirac* (Paris: Grasset, 1998); Patrick Jarreau, *Chirac: la Malédiction* (Paris: Stock, 1998).

41. The 109 UDF deputies elected in 1997 consisted of five individuals who ran solely under the UDF label (including Giscard d'Estaing and Barre); eleven "direct adherents" of the UDF; forty-three connected with the "Democratic Force" group, led by Francois Bayrou; forty-one members of the Republican Party, led by Francois Léotard; six members of the Popular Party for French Democracy, led by former foreign minister Hervé Charette; and three members of the Radical Party, led by Thierry Cornillet.

42. The Republican Party changed its name to "Liberal Democracy" under the new leadership of Alain Madelin, a free-market enthusiast, and split off from the UDF in 1998. A smaller group split from Madelin's party and formed a new grouping connected with the UDF.

43. *The Economist*, June 5, 1999.

44. Thanks to the use of proportional representation in 1986, the FN earned thirty-five Assembly seats. The reintroduction of the SMD system in 1988 made it more difficult for the party to translate its votes into seats.

45. Peter Fysh and Jim Wolfreys, *The Politics of Racism in France* (New York: St. Martin's, Press, UK: 1998); Jonathon Marcus, *The National Front in French Politics* (Basingstroke, Macmillan, 1995); Françoise Gaspard, *A Small City in France: A Socialist Mayor Confronts Neofascism* (Cambridge, Mass.: Harvard University Press, 1995).

46. In 1975 only 23 percent of the French labor force belonged to unions; by 1992 this figure was down to less than 10 percent. See Mark Kesselman, "Does the French Labor Movement Have a Future?" in *Chirac's Challenge*, ed. John T. S. Keeler and Martin A. Schain (New York: St. Martin's Press, 1996), 143–65.

47. *The Economist*, April 3, 1999; *Le Monde hebdomodaire*, December 18 and 25, 1999, January 15 and 22, February 5, and April 8, 2000.

48. *Washington Post*, July 1, 2000; *The Economist*, July 8, 2000; *Le Monde hebdomodaire*, April 29, 2000. The poll results are in *The Economist*, June 5, 1999. Bové and eight co-defendants were found guilty by the lower court in September 2000. He was sentenced to three months in jail but vowed to appeal the verdict.

49. *The Economist*, July 31, 1999.

CHAPTER 18

GERMANY

Population (1999): 82 million   Area: 137,826 square miles
(about the size of Montana)

THE REVOLUTION OF 1989–90

Most people could not believe their ears when they heard the announcement. Unexpectedly, on the evening of November 9, 1989, one of the leaders of East Germany's communist regime declared in a televised press conference that East German citizens would henceforth receive immediate and unconditional permission to travel abroad. The statement seemed to represent a complete reversal of three decades of stringent communist controls over the travel rights of the East German population. News of the announcement spread rapidly throughout the country: "Did you hear? Is it possible?" Crowds quickly gathered on the eastern side of the Berlin wall to see if the official declaration was really true. For several hours they waited while the border crossings remained shut. Then around midnight, the guards calmly opened the barriers and let them out. A revolution was under way.

Ever since August 1961, when the East German authorities began building the makeshift barriers they subsequently fortified into a massive concrete wall, the two parts of Berlin had been blocked off from each other. The wall ran twenty-seven miles across the center of what used to be the capital of Germany, and it circled around the perimeter of West Berlin. Armed East German border guards surveyed the barrier from control towers, shooting anyone who tried to escape to the western side. Approximately a hundred-sixty fatalities attested to their marksmanship. A no-man's-land of mines

Berlin celebrates the opening of the wall in front of the Brandenburg Gate, 1989.

and barbed wire kept all but the most audacious from getting anywhere near the eastern side of the wall. (About five thousand people succeeded in escaping through those barriers.) For years only a small number of East Berliners received permission to visit the western part of the city, mostly elderly pensioners or individuals attending a funeral or some special family event. West Berliners were rarely allowed into East Berlin at all until the 1970s. Subsequently, they and other outsiders usually had to go through time-consuming border control procedures in the eastern sector before being allowed in, and their passports were carefully scrutinized on their way out.

The same stiff regimen applied to East Germany as a whole, which surrounded the divided city of Berlin. The country's boundaries with its communist neighbors, Poland and Czechoslovakia, were vigilantly patrolled by border guards, while its sensitive border with West Germany was sealed off by yet another wall, guarded like the Berlin wall by sharpshooters, mines, and other obstacles. East Germans were rarely allowed to get out except under special circumstances or to visit other communist countries. Foreigners had to follow strict visa regulations when traveling inside East Germany.

The division of Germany was one of the most traumatic and dangerous aspects of the Cold War. It resulted from the agreement of the Western allies and the Soviet Union to split Germany into western and eastern occupation zones following Hitler's defeat, which occurred in May 1945, and to impose a similar east-west division on Berlin. In principle, these divisions were supposed to be temporary; the victorious combatants spoke of eventually reestablishing a single, unified German government. Their failure to agree on the political nature of such a government, however, produced the divisions that, for the next forty years, appeared to be permanent. The Western allies—the United States, Britain, and France—favored democracy and private enterprise and moved to create a democratic state in their West German occupation zones. Known as the **Federal Republic of Germany** (the **FRG**), and informally as **West Germany,** it came into existence in 1949 and established its capital in Bonn. The Soviet Union created a dictatorship in its eastern occupation zone under trusted German communists. The

German Democratic Republic (the **GDR**, or **East Germany**) was also formally established in 1949.[1] West Germany assumed de facto control over West Berlin and the East German authorities took control over East Berlin.[2]

Over the ensuing decades, divided Germany and divided Berlin gave almost literal meaning to the "iron curtain" that was said to divide the communist part of Europe from the West after World War II. It separated families, partitioned some 80 million Germans into two ideologically antagonistic states, and created a powder keg of confrontation in the heart of Europe that on several occasions threatened to explode into nuclear war. Berlin was especially sensitive. Located deep inside East Germany, 110 miles from the West German border, it was surrounded by over 300,000 Soviet troops based in the GDR. In 1948 the Soviet government under Joseph Stalin decided to test the West's willingness to defend West Berlin by imposing a military blockade on the road and railway corridors linking the city to West Germany. The Western allies responded by airlifting food and other vital supplies to the West Berliners, a strategy that induced Stalin to call off the blockade a year later. Neither side wanted war, but tensions ran high.[3]

The 1961 crisis was precipitated by an accelerating exodus of East Berliners to the West. Until that summer, there were no physical barriers dividing the two parts of the city; hundreds of thousands of Berliners routinely shuttled between West Berlin and East Berlin every day. But the freedom of East Berliners to go to West Berlin provided them with an easy escape route to West Germany and, from there, to the rest of the world. (The East German government had already closed off its longer border with West Germany.) Between the end of the war and mid-1961, nearly 3 million East Germans who did not wish to live under communism took advantage of this opportunity, depleting the GDR of one-seventh of its initial population. By summer this population hemorrhage had accelerated to 100,000 per month. To stop it, the East German authorities, with Soviet collusion, began constructing what became the Berlin wall. The United States and its allies moved troops into position in West Berlin but did not intrude into the Soviet sector to tear down the barriers.[4] For the next twenty-eight

years, the wall's hulking presence appeared to be an irremovable feature of the German landscape. But all that began to change on the night of November 9, 1989.

For several months the communist party rulers of East Germany had grown increasingly nervous. Their grip on the population, tightened by the most pervasive surveillance network in the communist bloc, was weakening. In 1989 as in 1961, people were leaving East Germany in droves. Ironically, their escape route now was in the east. Thousands of East Germans on vacation in neighboring communist-ruled Hungary took advantage of that country's recently opened border with Austria and simply walked or rode to freedom, their possessions stuffed in a few suitcases. Similarly, East German vacationers in Czechoslovakia, a more rigidly governed communist state than Hungary, swarmed into the West German embassy in Prague and pressured the West German and Czech authorities to agree to let them leave for West Germany. These actions by allied communist governments mortified East Germany's leaders, but there was little they could do about it. Between July and October, more than 120,000 found a way to leave East Germany.

Things got more intense in the fall, as antiregime demonstrations began taking place in East German cities like Leipzig and Dresden. They started slowly at first, with a few brave protesters daring to voice open criticism of one of the most fearsome police states in the world. Once it became clear that the East German authorities were not prepared to crush the protests with overwhelming force, as they might have done in the past, growing numbers of people were emboldened to take to the streets. By October, demonstrations were a weekly occurrence. Clearly rattled, the communist party leadership decided to replace Erich Honecker, who had led the GDR for eighteen years, with a younger leader in hopes of convincing the population of its readiness for change. But the protest movement intensified. In early November more than a million people gathered peacefully in East Berlin in an unprecedented show of opposition to the regime's dictatorial practices.

None of this would have happened without the forbearance of the Soviet Union. But far from cracking down on these massive displays of anti-communist activity, Moscow had inadvertently precipitated them. Once Mikhail Gorbachev assumed the Soviet leadership in 1985, winds of change began blowing from the Kremlin across the entire communist bloc. Gorbachev was a communist reformer. He fully understood that the USSR and the communist states of Central and Eastern Europe were deeply mired in economic and technological inferiority to the West and Japan. He also had no illusions about the fact that the Soviet system of repressive government and state-centered socialism were to blame for the communist world's predicament.

But the Soviet leader also fervently believed that the Soviet system could be fixed. With more "openness" and public debate, with more "democratization" within the Communist Party, and with a "restructuring" of its political and economic institutions, Gorbachev maintained that the communist system of one-party government and a socialist economy could be modernized and made to work more effectively. It did not need to be completely replaced with Western-style democracy and capitalism. The challenge, in Gorbachev's vision, was to find new reform-oriented communist leaders to lead the USSR and the other communist states in the right direction. The rigid old-guard leaders of East Germany, in his view, were clearly not up to the task. "History punishes those who come too late," he pointedly warned them. Gorbachev hoped that reform-oriented communists like himself would rise to the top in the East German leadership.

Gorbachev had an additional reason to oppose the use of force against the East German leadership's challengers. His entire strategy of reforming the Soviet system was predicated on favorable relations with the United States and its allies. The Cold War, with its exorbitant military expenditures and other costs, had to be ended so that the USSR and its allies could shift their resources to rebuilding their flagging economies. Gorbachev also hoped that friendlier ties with the West and Japan might result in some economic assistance. The use of coercion to suppress demonstrators or stop them from emigrating to the West would inevitably dash these hopes. As a consequence, Gorbachev quietly stood by as

more than forty years of Soviet hegemony in East-Central Europe slipped through his fingers over the course of 1989. Communist reformers in Hungary tore down their "iron curtain" with Austria, while Poland's communist leaders came to an agreement with the Solidarity trade union leaders on free elections. Those elections virtually removed the Polish communists from power. These developments could not help but have an impact on East German citizens. If the Soviets, Hungarians, and Poles could have change, they felt, why can't we?

It was in the context of these swirling events that the East German leadership, in a desperate attempt to calm the population and restore order, decided to ease the detested travel restrictions. They probably had no idea that, in doing so, they were opening a floodgate.[5] Reports of the opening of the Berlin wall spread over Germany within hours and shocked the entire world the next day. Recognizing that the wall could no longer be sustained, the East German authorities in the following days opened more checkpoints. By the hundreds of thousands, people who had never seen the western part of the city—and thought they might never see it—calmly stepped across what was once an impenetrable frontier. The barriers along the East German-West German border were also opened. As a state of almost delirious mass euphoria gripped the country, more than five million East Germans crossed the inter-German borders in the first four days after the wall's opening.

The opening of the Berlin wall triggered a chain of events that occurred so rapidly that political leaders in all the countries with a stake in Europe could barely keep up with them. While leaders of the two German states cautiously spoke of "stability" and long-term "reform," most East Germans wanted radical change immediately. While Prime Minister Thatcher and President Mitterrand, evoking memories of World War II, warned that a unified Germany might be too powerful, the rapid disintegration of East Germany's communist regime made unification inevitable. And while the United States and the USSR debated the implications of the German events for European security, East Germany's currency collapsed and people in both German states demanded elections in the GDR. In March 1990, free elections were held there for the first time, with dozens of newly formed parties participating. The fledgling party organizations connected with West Germany's three largest parties—the Christian Democrats, the Social Democrats, and the Free Democrats—handily won more than 75 percent of the East German vote. Their chief goal was the same: the dissolution of East Germany as a separate state and its incorporation into the Federal Republic.

On October 3, 1990—less than one year after the opening of the wall—the two Germanies were unified into an enlarged Federal Republic of Germany. The consequences of this revolutionary development are still among the most salient issues facing Germany today.[6]

GERMANY TODAY

As Germany enters the new millennium, it must still contend with the political fallout and economic costs of absorbing the former East Germany into the FRG. Both tasks have been fraught with problems.

Politically, many eastern Germans—particularly older ones who came of age in the GDR—retain attitudes associated with the former communist country's political culture. Instead of learning the "rules of the game" of a Western pluralistic democracy, with its emphasis on bargaining, compromise, and tolerance, they underwent their political socialization under an authoritarian state that preached intolerance of opposing points of view. It is perhaps not surprising that some have stopped voting in the period since unification while others have gravitated to extremist movements that scorn democratic values and foment intolerance toward foreigners and minorities. In addition, people who were socialized in the GDR became accustomed to its state-run socialist economy and relatively well-provisioned welfare state, with communist authorities assuming responsibility for assigning jobs and setting low prices for most basic needs. Since unification, many East Germans have had difficulty coping with a market economy. The GDR's collapse suddenly forced them to assume responsibility for finding work and managing their finances on their own, an unsettling new reality for many people. Quite a few former East Germans who op-

posed the repressiveness of that country's dictatorship still miss its paternalistic welfare system. As a consequence, many of them today vote for the **Party of Democratic Socialism (PDS),** the successor of the GDR's ruling communist party, which is highly critical of Western capitalism and nourishes nostalgia for the all-encompassing government, cheaper prices, and simpler life of the old communist system.

Yet another political problem stems from the reluctance of many West Germans to accept their new fellow citizens. The forty-year division of Germany created two different societies with two different mentalities. Resentments on both sides abound. A significant number of *Wessis* ("Westies"), who live in the former West Germany, look down upon the *Ossis* ("Easties") as too alien in their attitudes and too demanding in their requests for economic assistance to be regarded as truly equal compatriots. Many *Ossis* feel discriminated against and rejected by smug and self-contented *Wessis*. While Germany achieved political unification as a state in 1990, the unification of its political culture remains a continuing process. "The wall in people's minds" still exists. In 1999, ten years after the opening of the Berlin wall, public opinion polls revealed that 22 percent of Germans, if given the opportunity, would favor turning back the clock to the division of Germany, even if it meant bringing back the wall. More than half (57 percent) said it would take another ten years before the Germans constitute "one people." Still, the overwhelming majority of both eastern and western Germans viewed unification in positive terms, despite its problems, and would not wish to bring back the past. Polls also showed that a majority of eastern Germans want both the freedoms of individual responsibility and the security of government-funded social programs and saw no incompatibility between the two.[7]

In addition to these political problems, the economic costs of unification have been staggering. East Germany's economy was in shambles when unification took place. Its factories were hopelessly antiquated, its telecommunications system and transportation networks barely serviceable, its housing dilapidated. Its consumer sector produced goods that fell far below world quality standards and its wage scales lagged considerably behind

West German norms. The need to embark immediately on the long process of bringing eastern Germany's economy up to western German levels was imperative. Accordingly, the German government created a Trust Agency in 1990 to sell off industrial plants, buildings, and other properties previously owned by the East German state. Within three years it sold off more than 12,000 properties to private investors; but by the end of 1994 more than 3,500 concerns were in such deplorable condition that they had to be closed down.

In addition, the government of the Federal Republic invested 1 trillion deutschemarks (more than $500 billion in today's terms) in eastern Germany during the 1990s in an effort to modernize its communications and transportation infrastructure, restructure its educational system, and establish new government institutions. A large chunk of this money has been used to provide jobs or unemployment compensation for eastern Germans thrown out of work by the liquidation of the GDR's enterprises, government bureaucracy, and military. (In the first few years after the 1989 revolution, the east German labor force contracted by almost 60 percent, while unemployment throughout Germany rose from 9.5 percent to 15.5 percent.) New wage contracts were negotiated for east German workers, at times through the intermediation of the government in Bonn. To pay for these and related expenditures, new taxes had to be imposed on the population, with West Germans footing most of the bill. The average income tax rate rose from about 43 percent to 50 percent. Meanwhile, private German companies in western Germany have invested huge sums of their own money in eastern Germany, spending as much as $150 billion in a single year on new factories, housing construction, and other projects.

The challenges of unification have unfolded in a wider context of social diversification, economic restructuring, and political change throughout Germany.

Social Diversification

For much of their history, Germans have defined themselves largely in ethnic terms. Being "German" has traditionally meant that one is linked by blood ties to fellow Germans, has lived on German territory, and speaks German (or one of its local dialects) as one's native language. Of course, as we noted in chapter 6, ethnic concepts of nationalism are ultimately based on a *belief* in common biological ancestors; such beliefs are largely mythical, however, since there is no proof that any national group in the world has maintained an unbroken lineage from its earliest ancestors. Over the centuries, the Germanic tribes intermingled with Slavs, Scandinavians, Romans, and other groups in the region. Their descendants also mixed with a variety of ethnic groups. Nevertheless, the widespread belief in a shared biological bond has historically provided the basis of German national identity. Consequently, a person was *born* a German and could not *become* a German.

Reflecting this ethnic concept of national identity, Germany's citizenship laws were traditionally based on the principle of *jus sanguinis*—the law of blood—as opposed to *jus soli*, the law of soil. (*Jus soli* confers national citizenship on those who are born on the country's territory, regardless of blood ties, as in the United States.) By the 1990s, however, the changing ethnic composition of Germany's population prompted a reconsideration of the country's citizenship laws.

The impetus for change stemmed from the 1960s, when the booming West German economy required the importation of more than 2 million foreign workers. Along with new arrivals from Yugoslavia, Greece, Portugal, and other nearby European countries, "guest workers" were invited in particularly large numbers from Turkey, a NATO ally with a large unemployed work force. While a number of Turks returned home with their accumulated savings, many more stayed in Germany, raising their children in neighborhoods that soon acquired a predominantly Turkish character. By 1998 there were more than 2.1 million Turks living in Germany, nearly 30 percent of all resident aliens in the country. Many were born there and grew up attending German schools and speaking German fluently. In addition, foreigners from numerous other countries from around the world, some of them escaping political persecution or economic hardships, took up residency in Germany in the 1970s, 1980s, and 1990s.

By the end of the decade Germany had about 1.5 million refugees. The conflicts that followed the disintegration of Yugoslavia brought a particularly large refugee flood, rising to 330,000 by 1996. Unification itself added still more foreigners, as people from the Soviet Union and other parts of the disintegrating communist bloc sought a better life in Germany just as the former East Germany was being integrated into the Federal Republic. Some of these people were ethnic Germans whose families had lived for centuries in Russia or Eastern Europe. Since 1990 more than a million of them have emigrated to Germany and claimed German citizenship under special provisions in the country's constitution.

By the late 1990s, some 7.4 million foreigners were living in the Federal Republic. Half of them had lived in Germany for more than ten years, and about 100,000 children are born in Germany every year to non-citizens.

Under German law at the time, most of these foreigners and their children born in Germany stood little chance of becoming naturalized German citizens. For many Germans, disturbed at the rising numbers of foreigners, these laws were perfectly acceptable. Quite a few Germans were especially opposed to citizenship for the Turkish Muslims, a religious minority in a predominantly Christian country. But pressures from foreign residents as well as from a growing segment of Germans themselves induced the government to change the citizenship laws. At the start of 2000, a new citizenship law took effect that eases the ability of non-native Germans to acquire the full rights of German citizenship.

The old law, which was based on a 1913 statute enforcing the principle of *jus sanguinis,* confined German citizenship strictly to people born of German parents. The new law retains this right for ethnic Germans while adding the principle of *jus soli,* which bases citizenship on one's place of birth. The change permits children born in Germany of non-German parents to acquire German citizenship *at birth,* so long as at least one parent has legally resided in Germany at least eight years. In addition, the naturalization laws applying to foreigners who were not born in Germany have eased as well. In the past, a resident alien needed to live in Germany fifteen years before applying for citizenship; as of 2000, the waiting period is reduced to eight years.

These changes have not been greeted with universal approval. While millions of Germans are ready to live in a more ethnically diverse society, many others are concerned about the problems of integrating so many non-Germans in a country with a sordid history of racism. A small minority of ultranationalists have engaged in wanton acts of violence against foreigners in recent years. Many of these incidents have occurred in the former East Germany, where unemployed youths have had a difficult time coping with the turmoil of reunification.[8]

Economic Restructuring

After World War II, the West German government devised a blueprint for combining a vigorous private sector with a generous government-financed welfare state, a combination it called the *social market economy.* Stimulated by Marshall Plan assistance from the United States, the FRG experienced an "economic miracle" by the late 1950s. Over the next decades, West Germany's burgeoning export sector and thriving domestic economy secured its place as the fourth largest economy in the world behind the United States, the Soviet Union, and Japan. With the USSR's collapse, Germany became the world's third largest economy. It is the world's second largest trading nation, with a trade volume higher than Japan's. These successes have provided a substantial tax base to finance a growing array of state-funded or state-managed welfare programs for the population. They include tuition-free education through graduate school, universal health insurance and a state-funded hospital system, retirement pensions, family allowances, and a network of spas and vacation retreats for workers. In addition, the German state has provided substantial subsidies for the arts, scientific research, housing, transportation, and other amenities. Social welfare spending was proportionately higher in Germany than in the United States and other economically advanced democracies throughout the 1960s and 1970s (see table 18.1). It has risen steadily from a little more than 20 percent of GDP in 1960 to more than 34 percent by the late 1990s.

Germany's economic system has rested on a broad political consensus. The main political parties of the center-right (the Christian Democrats), the center-left (the Social Democrats), and the center

TABLE 18.1

Central Government Social Welfare Spending* as a Percentage of GDP, 1960–1980

	1960	1970	1980
Federal Republic of Germany	20.5	23.5	30.8
United Kingdom	13.8	18.5	22.0
United States	10.9	15.7	20.7
Japan	8.0	9.3	16.9

Source: Organization of Economic Cooperation and Development, cited in Jan-Erik Lane et al., *Political Data Handbook OECD Countries* (Oxford: Oxford University Press, 1997).
*Social welfare spending includes expenditures on education, health, pensions, unemployment compensation, and sickness, maternity, and temporary disablement benefits.

(the Free Democrats) have largely agreed on the general principles of the social market economy, usually confining their disagreements to specific details.

By the 1990s the costs of these programs were becoming harder for the economy to bear. Starting in the 1970s, the German government's yearly expenditures increasingly outran its revenues. The accumulating national debt created by these annual budget deficits rose fivefold between the early 1980s and late 1990s. In the process, the amount of money the government has had to pay out every year in interest payments on this debt has quadrupled, consuming 26 percent of the budget by 1999.[9] (The comparable U.S. figure was just less than 15 percent.)

The enormous costs of unification since 1990 have substantially increased these burdens. So, too, have the costs of globalization. The Maastricht agreement of 1991–92 committed the Federal Republic and its European partners to setting strict limits to their annual budgetary deficits and national debts as preconditions to establishing the common European currency, the euro. The German government was in the forefront of EU members pushing for these stringent requirements. Meanwhile, changes in the world economy have curtailed German exports in some areas while opening up new opportunities for German businesses to cut their operating expenses by shifting some of their operations abroad. The relatively high costs of providing benefits to German workers out of company revenues have prompted large corporations like

Daimler-Chrysler, BMW, and others to expand plants or open new ones in East-Central Europe and the developing world, where labor costs are considerably lower. Employment opportunities in Germany have diminished as a result. Unemployment has risen appreciably in recent years, from less than 7 percent in 1990 to 10.5 percent in 1999, adding rising unemployment compensation expenditures to the existing problems of the cash-strapped government budget. Most of this unemployment was in the former East Germany, where 18 percent of the work force was unemployed in 1999.

By the end of the decade, a growing number of politicians from all the mainstream parties were calling for more serious efforts to trim government spending and restore a measure of balance to the country's public finances. Business leaders were particularly vocal in demanding limits to the money they were required to allocate for their employees' welfare benefits, often amounting to more than 40 percent of labor costs. But any decision to cut social benefits, or even to cut the rate of future increases in social benefits to lower levels, is bound to be unpopular with those who have become accustomed to receiving them. German workers, for example, want to remain the best paid in the world. East German workers, who are paid about $10 an hour less on average than their western counterparts, want the same pay scales and benefits as west German workers as soon as possible. Not surprisingly, opposition to drastic cuts in government spending has arisen from several quarters, creating serious leadership problems for the country's political elites. How does an elected leader in a democracy persuade the people to accept austerity measures when they don't want to? How much latitude (or *autonomy*) do leaders have from public pressure when they deem it necessary to take actions that are widely unpopular?

Political Change

The social and economic problems now confronting Germany have coincided with political changes of considerable magnitude. In the fall of 1998, a new German government was elected to office. Led by Chancellor **Gerhard Schroeder,** it was a coalition government consisting of Schroeder's **Social Democratic Party of Germany** (*Sozialdemokratische partei Deutschlands,* known in the

English-speaking world by its German initials, **SPD**) and the **Greens,** an environmentally oriented party. The SPD-Green alliance followed sixteen years of coalition governments consisting of the other mainstream parties, the **Christian Democrats** and the **Free Democrats.** Those center-right governments were led by Chancellor Helmut Kohl, one of the longest-serving heads of government in the history of modern democracy (1982–1998).

Although the SPD had traditionally championed the cause of Germany's working class and less privileged and had fought hard to widen the benefits of the welfare state for the bottom half of the socioeconomic pyramid, Schroeder announced that he favored serious belt-tightening measures designed to rein in government spending. Like Bill Clinton in the United States and Tony Blair in Britain, Schroeder belongs to a center-left party but favors budget-cutting and pro-business policies more typically associated with conservative parties. Just as Clinton defined himself as a "New Democrat" and Blair proclaimed the advent of "New Labour," Schroeder speaks of creating a **"new center"** *(neue Mitte)* in Germany. All three political leaders have sought to move their parties from the left side of the political spectrum closer to the center, a shift that means moving from a tradition of generous government welfare spending, relatively high taxes, and a tolerance of annual budget deficits to a policy favoring more limited government intervention in the economy, lower taxes, and balanced budgets. At the same time, all three leaders have sought to retain an effective role for government programs in alleviating poverty, providing adequate health care and social security, and protecting the public against abuses by profit-driven private companies. Various advocates of this centrist approach call it the "**third way**": it seeks a middle ground between high-spending welfarism on the left and unfettered market capitalism on the right. In 1999, Schroeder joined with Tony Blair in drafting a document spelling out the centrist orientation of the third way, advancing it as a new theoretical point of departure for Europe's social democratic parties.[10]

The Clinton administration managed to turn the U.S. economy around from the high federal budget deficits of the 1980s and early 1990s to the surpluses of the second half of the decade, a suc-

cess accomplished in conjunction with a Republican Congress after 1992. After two and a half years in office, Blair had also achieved a number of his goals, aided in large part by a thriving British economy. But Schroeder's first year in power was paved with difficulties. A split inside his own party placed immediate obstacles in his path. Oskar Lafontaine, the chairman of the Social Democratic Party and the leader of its left wing, assumed the all-important economics ministry in Schroeder's cabinet and openly disagreed with the chancellor's budget-tightening policies. Whereas Schroeder advocated long-term reductions in government spending, Lafontaine favored higher levels of spending in order to stimulate economic growth in accordance with Keynesian theories. When a group of powerful business leaders warned the chancellor of dire economic consequences if welfare entitlements were not trimmed down, Schroeder reaffirmed his policy and Lafontaine promptly quit the cabinet in March 1999. The Social Democratic Party's activists and voters themselves were split into pro-Schroeder and pro-Lafontaine wings.

Schroeder's difficulties were compounded by the necessities of sharing power. The elections to Germany's lower house, the *Bundestag,* held in September 1998 returned a hung parliament: that is, no party acquired an absolute majority of seats. Schroeder's Social Democrats emerged as the largest party with 298 seats, or 44.5 percent of the total. To form a government Schroeder reached out to the Greens, who won 7 percent of the Bundestag's 669 seats, and invited it to share cabinet ministries in a coalition government. A relatively young party founded in the late 1970s, the Greens were committed to radical changes in Germany's environmental policies. In particular, they wanted to close down the country's nineteen nuclear power plants and replace them with nonnuclear energy.

After several weeks of painstaking negotiations following the elections, Schroeder and the Greens came to terms on a joint government program. But it was not long before problems between the two partners arose. Schroeder backtracked from his pledge to consider the closure of the nuclear power installations, deferring any decision on the matter for several years. A number of Green parliamentary deputies and party activists, feeling betrayed, called on their party leaders to quit the cabinet.

In the spring of 1999 the Kosovo conflict added new challenges. The Greens were traditionally pacifists, staunchly opposed to U.S. nuclear weapons on German territory and reluctant to commit German troops to international peacekeeping operations. With the formation of the SPD-Green coalition government in 1998, one of the Greens' top leaders, Joschka Fischer, became foreign minister. An anti-NATO pacifist in his younger years, Fischer had modified his position over time. As the NATO bombing campaign got under way in Serbia in late March 1999, he stepped forward as one of its most outspoken advocates. Though he managed to convince most of his party to go along with the military campaign, not all the Greens approved of his position. The successful completion of the NATO mission after seventy-eight days of bombardments, resulting in the withdrawal of Serbian troops from Kosovo, eased these pressures somewhat, but Chancellor Schroeder and the Greens still did not always see eye-to-eye on government policies. Whether the coalition will in fact last the full four years of the Bundestag's term, ending in 2002, is a frequently posed question.

Battered by charges of drift and indecisiveness, Schroeder saw his approval ratings slip to only 31 percent, a slide of ten points during his first year in office. Meanwhile, his arch-rivals—the Christian Democrats—staged a rapid comeback. In 1999 they won several state-level elections, giving them a voting majority in the upper house of the German legislature. (We'll explain how this system works later in this chapter.) As a consequence, Chancellor Schroeder found himself in a position not unlike that of President Clinton. Just as Clinton had to deal with a Republican Congress, Schroeder had to deal with an upper house in the hands of his opponents. A German version of *divided government* was in place, constricting the chief executive's options and setting the stage for potential gridlock.

As the 1990s ended, another change of potentially historic magnitude took shape as Helmut Kohl admitted to supervising an illegal slush fund for his party, the Christian Democrats, while serving as chancellor. The revelation threatened to rip apart one of Germany's most powerful parties, tearing away at the trust its voters placed in its leaders.

Democracy and Political Conflict in Germany

Many of the problems Germany is encountering today mirror previous experiences of national disunity, economic hardships, and challenges to democracy from both left and right-wing extremists. Dealing with the after-effects of national division, for instance, is nothing new: the German people have a long tradition of being divided into separate states. A unified German state was not established until 1871, centuries after the creation of centralized states in Britain and France. The division of Germany into separate states that occurred after World War II was thus a variation on an old theme. So too is the current effort to forge a common national identity out of Germans accustomed to separate political systems.

Similarly, the challenges to German democracy posed today by the extreme right or left also have roots in Germany's past. Germany did not adopt a liberal democratic constitution until after its defeat in World War I. The so-called Weimar Republic proved a colossal failure, lasting only from 1919 to 1933. Overburdened with economic disasters and opposition to democracy itself on the part of large segments of the political elite and the population, it gave way to Adolph Hitler's Nazi dictatorship. Over the next twelve years the Nazi regime lit the fires of racial oppression at home and military aggression across the continent of Europe, plunging hundreds of millions of people into the nightmare of World War II and subjecting Jews and other outcasts to systematic extermination.

To be sure, times have changed and German democracy today is nowhere nearly as endangered as it was in the fragile Weimar Republic. On the left, the Party of Democratic Socialism is tame by comparison with its communist predecessors, while the rabidly anti-foreigner parties of the extreme right are nowhere nearly as popular as the Nazis in the 1930s. The country's democratic values are widely shared among the populace. The economy, for all its problems, is still one of the most successful in the world. Relations with Germany's partners in the European Union, its neighbors in Central and Eastern Europe and its main transatlantic ally, the United States, are overwhelmingly positive. Nevertheless, the problems of building a common German national identity, dealing with ethnic diversity, fashioning a successful economic model, and defining Germany's role in the world are problems that, in different ways, have haunted Germany before. History matters deeply in today's Germany: traumatic recollections of the country's earlier failures and transgressions are frequently discussed in public forums and form a vital part of the national political culture. With an eye to the past, many Germans today express anxiety about the future, fearing the changes that lie ahead.

In the midst of these simmering issues, in 1999 the Federal Republic of Germany transferred its capital from Bonn to Berlin, reclaiming for its seat of government the vast metropolis located squarely in the center of Europe. The era of the "Berlin Republic" had now begun. In this chapter we'll examine the historical context and political foundations of Germany's newly unified nation, focusing on the five sources of political conflict we discussed in chapter 2:

- *Power:* Who has governed Germany? How is power distributed among Germany's political institutions today? How much political influence do trade unions and business associations have in Germany?
- *Resources:* How have economic developments affected the evolution of German politics over the years? What kinds of economic and social welfare reforms are now in view?
- *Social identity:* Who is a German? That is, how is Germany dealing with the challenge of building a common identity among east and west Germans, and how is it addressing the issue of citizenship for ethnic minorities?
- *Ideas:* What are some of the legacies of fascism and communism in today's Germany? How stable is German democracy, and who are its main challengers?
- *Values:* How has German political culture changed over time, moving from one that supported authoritarianism to one based on more democratic values?

HISTORICAL BACKGROUND: GERMANY'S DIFFICULT PATH TO DEMOCRACY

Perhaps the most striking feature about German history prior to World War II is that, unlike Britain and France, Germany failed to develop a sustain-able democracy. That fact is particularly curious, considering that the Germans enjoyed roughly the same level of economic development as citizens in those countries, making Germany one of the three wealthiest and most productive nations in Europe. The Germans' religious and intellectual traditions were just as rich: until Hitler took power, Catholicism, Protestantism, and Judaism co-existed, however precariously, while a constellation of geniuses made brilliant contributions to philosophy, science, literature, music, technology, and other fields of creative endeavor. Germany's first democratic constitution, that of the ill-fated Weimar Republic, was perhaps the most progressive constitutional document the world had yet seen. Even so, democracy did not begin to strike lasting roots on German soil until it was implanted by U.S., British, and French occupation forces in West Germany after 1945.

What accounts for this remarkable failure of democratic ideas and institutions to take hold from within Germany itself? Several factors on our list of conditions for democracy in chapter 10 stand out as especially noteworthy:

- the ambivalence of liberal ideology in eighteenth and nineteenth-century Germany, which could not overcome *state institutions* characterized by authoritarian governments and a weak parliamentary tradition
- the weakness of support for democracy among German *elites* and the *middle class*
- a preference for a state-dominated economy rather than *private enterprise*
- the anti-democratic and ethnic biases of German nationalism, contributing to a non-democratic *political culture*
- a "*stateness*" problem marked by the relative lateness of the creation of a central German state, a process that was finally accomplished by forces opposed to democracy
- difficulties promoting *national wealth* because of the absence of a central German state before 1871, the high costs of World War I, and severe economic problems during the Weimar Republic
- the existence of a large number of *disadvantaged* workers, some of whom gravitated to anti-democratic parties like the Communists and the Nazis

- a violent *international environment* promoted by the hypernationalism of German elites

Although pre-Hitler Germany had a relatively *homogeneous* population and a superb system of *education* for its elites, these factors alone were not sufficient to build or sustain a democracy. Let's briefly survey these explanatory variables.

The Weakness of German Liberalism

As chapter 16 points out, the origins of democracy in Britain stretch all the way back to the emergence of Parliament in the Middle Ages. In the late seventeenth century, British democracy took ideological shape in the thought of John Locke and scored a major constitutional triumph with the adoption of the doctrine of parliamentary supremacy. In the following century Adam Smith laid down the conceptual bases of economic liberalism, making what turned out to be a major contribution to the theory and practice of liberal democracy. As we saw in chapter 18, democracy burst open in France in the Revolution that began in 1789. In varying degrees, support for democratic ideas could be found within all the major segments of French society, from aristocrats and the middle class to the urban poor and the peasant masses. Similarly, democracy in the United States originated in the democratic institutions and practices of the colonies, with broad support from all social classes.

When these seminal events in the history of democracy took place, Germany had a real "stateness" problem: it did not even exist as a nation-state. Prior to the French Revolution, the German people were divided into more than 1,790 principalities, duchies, city-states, and other governmental entities, each asserting independence from the others. Despite some consolidation, by the early nineteenth century there were still over three hundred German mini-states, most no bigger than towns or rural counties. Virtually all of them were ruled by a prince, a duke, or some other noble lord. Some were predominantly Protestant, others Catholic. The division of Christendom had in fact started in Germany with Martin Luther and the Protestant Reformation in the sixteenth century, and one of its immediate effects was to reinforce the political division of the German people into a multiplicity of states.

Not until 1848 did German liberalism make its grand entry. In that year the first popular elections ever held among the Germans produced an assembly whose purpose was to discuss political reform and the possible formation of a unified German government. Some eight hundred delegates from thirty-eight sovereign German states met in St. Paul's church in Frankfurt for nearly a year. But their deliberations came to nought. While the more outspoken liberals on the left advocated British-style parliamentary supremacy, conservatives on the right insisted on a supreme monarch. While left-wing liberals called for universal male suffrage, right wingers preferred a limited suffrage based on property qualifications. Consensus was equally difficult to achieve on religious and economic issues, nor could the delegates agree on the fundamental question of *how* to organize a unified German state under a central government.

In the end, the Frankfurt assembly stitched together a compromise draft constitution calling for the creation of a national German parliament that would share power with a monarch. But its divided members failed to agree on the principle of parliamentary supremacy and could not specify exactly how the new parliament and the king were to share power. The Frankfurt delegates were equally vague about the "basic rights" the German people would in principle enjoy in the proposed new state. When the assembly presented its patchwork document to the king of Prussia in 1849 and invited him to become the first king of a united Germany, he brusquely dismissed the offer. Neither he nor any other reigning German aristocrat wanted anything to do with parliamentarism, however watered down. The Frankfurt assembly thereupon disbanded, never to meet again. The king later ordered his troops to break up the liberal movement in Prussia.

The failure of political liberalism to gain a foothold in eighteenth- and nineteenth-century Germany reflected the narrow social base of its support. In Britain and France, various members of the nobility were willing to go along with parliamentarism; in the German principalities there was considerably less support for constitutional monarchy among the reigning royal houses. In Britain and France the rising middle class, eager to secure its fortunes in private commerce and agriculture, exerted effective pressure for popular sovereignty. But in Germany at that time the commercial middle class was weaker. Of greater significance was the so-called "middle stratum" *(Mittelstand)* of society, whose members consisted mainly of intellectuals and people employed by the state rather than by private enterprise. They included bureaucrats, professors, jurists, and other state employees. Though this class was the principal source of liberal ideas in Germany, many of its members espoused an elitist conception of liberalism that was less interested in limiting the powers of the state than in placing a strong state in their own hands. They were also less interested in electoral politics and the practical problems of coalition building and governing than in philosophical concepts of reason and intellectual freedom. They also tended to frown on the commercial classes; indeed, German liberals largely rejected Adam Smith's concepts of economic liberty and placed greater faith in a protective state that would dominate the economy. The Anglo-American notion that economic liberty goes hand in hand with political liberty was foreign to German liberalism.

Finally, many if not most German liberals of the nineteenth century had little tolerance for mass democracy. The workers and peasants who constituted the bulk of the population had virtually no place in their vision of a liberal state. For their part, Germany's downtrodden classes of peasants and urban workers were considerably less active in militating for democracy than were their counterparts in France at the time of the Revolution. Cries of "Liberty! Equality! Fraternity!" were decidedly less audible in German than in French.

In sum, early-nineteenth-century German liberalism was more ambivalent and less pragmatic than its British or American variants and considerably weaker in its social bases of support than in England, America, or France. The result was comparatively tepid support for popular sovereignty, representative democracy, limited government, or enumerated civil rights and liberties.[11]

German Nationalism

German nationalism took a form that was similarly unsupportive of democratic institutions and liberties. As Liah Greenfeld has shown, English national-

ism was infused from its earliest phases in the sixteenth and seventeenth centuries with democratic values that derived from the country's long parliamentary traditions and the concepts of religious individualism nurtured by English Protestantism. To be English was to be a free and equal member of a self-governing society. French nationalism placed a greater emphasis on the authority of the state than did English nationalism and on collective liberty (the "general will") as opposed to individual liberties; but by the time of the Revolution the French nation became synonymous with liberty, equality, and fraternity, values that ultimately promoted democracy in France's turbulent nineteenth and twentieth centuries. In Germany, by contrast, nationalism arrived later and had little to do with democratic values.

Until the early nineteenth century, Greenfeld notes, the notion that the Germans constituted a single, unified nation barely existed. The fragmentation of the German people into numerous political sovereignties promoted narrow local identities and retarded the development of an overarching German national consciousness. People tended to think of themselves as Bavarians, Prussians, Austrians, Saxons, Hanoverians, and the like rather than as "Germans." Germany's Protestant Reformation, moreover, did not have the same liberating effect on elite or mass attitudes as did England's Reformation, at least not in its formative phases. Martin Luther did not conceive of the German people in democratic terms as separate from the noble princes and lords who ruled them in their various sovereign domains, nor did he promote a common German national identity. Only later did certain strands of German Protestantism promote such democratic values as individualism, equality, and capitalist entrepreneurship.[12]

When nationalist ideas finally took discernible shape in Germany, they arose in the first decade of the nineteenth century as a response to Napoleon's invasion of German territory and his defeat of Prussia, the strongest of the German states, in 1806. The absence of a unified German state with a large standing army prevented a concerted military response to the French incursions, prompting a number of Germans to call for greater national unity. These appeals were often accompanied by fierce hostility to France, firmly resisting French attempts to topple the crowned heads of Europe. As a consequence,

German nationalist ideas in this decisive period tended to reject the French Revolution's notions of liberty, equality, and fraternity as well as Napoleon's efforts to redraw the map of Europe with a mass-based conscripted army. Anti-British sentiments also filtered into the nationalist yearnings of a number of German patriots, reflecting and reinforcing their anti-democratic biases.

From that point on, German nationalism developed very rapidly in the nineteenth century. Initially, its main advocates tended to be writers and thinkers, professors and journalists: In other words, intellectuals rather than more practically oriented people like political organizers or entrepreneurs. Some of them, Greenfeld points out, coupled their clarion calls for national unity with unabashed assertions of the intellectual and moral superiority of the German people *(Volk)* over all other nations of the world, stressing the alleged purity of the German language and German blood. In Greenfeld's view, these assertions were essentially racist in nature. At the same time, she argues, those Germans who coupled their nationalist outpourings with appeals for democracy frequently understood "democracy" as necessitating the complete subservience of the individual to the nation as a whole. Such a notion was wholly at variance with the concepts of individual rights and freedoms that are normally considered indispensable to democracy. In effect, it amounted to a rejection of real democratic values and an embrace of dictatorial authority.[13]

These anti-democratic tendencies in German nationalist thought found their reflection in the realm of political culture, severely retarding the spread of democratic values among German elites and the wider population. Moreover, the inability of German liberals to produce a united Germany based on a democratic constitution had a long-term practical impact on the Germans' inability to couple nationalism with democracy. By the time German national sentiment gathered sufficient force in the second half of the nineteenth century to bring about a unified German state, the leaders of the unification process were anything but democratic.

The Creation of the German State

Germany is an example of a "late state": it came together under a single central government much later than Britain or France (or even the United States). Late-blooming states tend to share common problems, as the experiences of Germany, Italy, and Japan show. Until the last third of the nineteenth century, all three countries were internally fragmented; the central government was either weak (as in Japan) or nonexistent (as in Germany and Italy). All three countries centralized their governing institutions at approximately the same time, in the 1860s–70s. And all three felt a need to accelerate their economic development as rapidly as possible so as to catch up with the successful great powers. As a consequence, they all relied heavily on the central government to guide the economy, even though private companies were allowed to thrive.

In addition, the governments of these three late states felt compelled to make special efforts to mold a new sense of national identity and loyalty to the central government among their people in place of regional or local identities. People had to be taught to think of themselves as "Germans," "Italians," or "Japanese." Intense nationalism was the result, accompanied by militarism and chauvinistic propaganda. Ultimately these tendencies took the form of imperial aggression abroad and, by the 1920s and 1930s, a fiercely anti-Western fascism. While Germany, Italy, and Japan were very different in many other respects, dictatorship and hypernationalism triumphed and democracy suffered in all three states.

Indeed, when the Germans dealt with their "stateness" problem by finally coming together as a single nation-state in 1871, it was not democracy that forged their unity but military force. After the liberals' failure to unite the various mini-states under an elected national parliament, the banner of national unity was picked up by the most powerful German state of them all, the kingdom of Prussia. Centered in the plains surrounding Berlin, Prussia under the Hohenzollern dynasty had clawed its way into the ranks of Europe's most important powers over the course of the eighteenth century. By the 1860s it possessed a nascent industrial economy and, most important, one of the largest and most disciplined armies on the continent. It also had a dynamic leader who was determined to create a unified German state under the Prussian monarchy: **Otto von Bismarck.** As chancellor (prime minister) of Prussia, Bismarck—a son of the Prussian nobility—had little use for democracy. On the contrary, he declared his intention to unite the Germans by "blood and iron" rather than by ballots. Bismarck and his followers regarded national disunity as a source of national weakness. Their principal object was to galvanize Germany into a great power capable of competing with the British and French empires on the world stage.

Bismarck led Prussia into three wars that ultimately resulted in the formation of Germany's first modern state. In 1864 Prussia attacked Denmark and came away with two provinces, Schleswig and Holstein, that remain part of Germany today. In 1866 the Prussians trounced Austria, a rival power that had its own hopes of leading the German people to national unity. And in his boldest stroke, Bismarck led Prussia to victory over France in the Franco-Prussian War of 1870–71. As these wars convincingly demonstrated the effectiveness of Prussian might, Bismarck fanned the passions of German nationalism and won the agreement of more than twenty smaller German states to join together under the Prussian monarchy to form a single Germany. Ironically, the glittering ceremony attending this historic occasion did not take place in Berlin but in newly conquered France: in January 1871 the German Empire (or *Reich*) was proclaimed in the palace of Versailles, where King Wilhelm of Prussia was crowned Emperor *(Kaiser)* of Germany.

The new central government that Bismarck now created seemed to have the outward appearances of a democracy. A national legislature, the *Reichstag,* was seated in Berlin; all German males had the right to elect its deputies. In fact, however, the Reichstag's powers were severely limited and Bismarck's purposes were purely manipulative. One of his principal aims was to keep the liberal movement divided by encouraging the formation of rival parties and factions. Bismarck largely succeeded in this ambition, as the liberals never managed to overcome their differences over the nature of democracy and the role of private enterprise; they suffered diminishing public support over time. As parliamentary deputies, moreover, they did not have much power. Under the constitution, the Reichstag had no right to unseat the government; the chancellor, as head of government, was

solely responsible to the kaiser, not to the legislature. (In Britain and France at this time, the reverse was the case: the prime minister and his government were responsible to the legislature and could be voted out of office.) Whenever the Reichstag showed any signs of opposing his policies, Chancellor Bismarck simply ignored or circumvented its actions. The kaiser's Germany was an authoritarian state, firmly controlled by the Prussian nobility and its main institutional arm, the military.

Not surprisingly, the German state played a prominent role in the economy. Private enterprise was allowed to flourish, with vast industrial concerns churning out iron and steel while millions of small-scale entrepreneurs ran their shops and farms. But unlike Britain, the United States, and France, capitalism in Germany did not succeed in promoting democratic institutions and practices. Most industrialists cooperated with state authorities in supplying what the kaiser's regime wanted most: a well-equipped army and navy, an extensive railroad network, and a modern economic infrastructure, all of which were dedicated to enhancing Germany's military prowess and diplomatic influence. Far from favoring mass democracy, the country's leading industrialists joined with the aristocratic owners of Prussia's large rural estates in providing support for the kaiser's dictatorial regime, an alliance known as the "marriage of iron and rye."

For their part, a large portion of Germany's small and medium-sized business owners—the backbone of the middle class—were in principle favorable to democratic institutions but were neither able nor willing to organize effective opposition to the prevailing order. Many middle-class Germans, in fact, took pride in the international glory their country had achieved under the kaiser. Finally, many of Germany's most prominent intellectuals and artists looked down on politics as unworthy of their attention and refrained from taking up the cause of democratic values.

The most impassioned proponents of democracy in the kaiser's Germany were the Social Democrats. Founded in 1875, the Social Democratic Party of Germany (SPD)—the party of Gerhard Schroeder—quickly emerged as the main advocate for the country's main disadvantaged group, the industrial working class. As German industry expanded, so did the ranks of factory workers, seamstresses, coal miners, and others engaged in the day-to-day rigors of manual labor. Like their counterparts in Britain, France, and other industrializing countries at this time, Germany's workers were relegated to a life of grinding physical toil, squalid living conditions, and the demoralization that comes with prolonged economic exploitation and political powerlessness. Facing sixty to seventy hours of work every week, with subsistence wages and inadequate educational or health facilities, millions of German men, women, and child laborers found themselves chained to the lowest levels of the social pyramid, with virtually no opportunity to rise into the middle class. When the new German state was founded, no government programs existed to alleviate the plight of the working masses or the unemployed. The Social Democratic Party's mission was to change this situation radically.

At the time of its foundation, the SPD represented a merger of two wings of Germany's socialist movement. One wing derived from the ideas of Karl Marx and favored a violent revolution to overturn the existing political and social order; it placed working-class solidarity ahead of German national solidarity and sought to unite the workers of the world against capitalism wherever it existed. The other wing was less keen on revolution and preferred a more orderly path to a new society, one that would respect German national sentiments. Over the ensuing decades the latter wing won out. Known as the "revisionists," the more moderate German Social Democrats revised Marx's doctrines by spurning revolutionary violence in favor of ballot-box democracy. They also favored trade union activity and negotiations with the captains of industry rather than the complete destruction of the capitalist order. The revisionists' main theoretician was Eduard Bernstein, a Berlin trade unionist who adopted the moderate, pragmatic, and democratic outlook of British socialists while living in political exile in England. (On Bernstein's views, see chapter 13.)

Working-class support for the Social Democrats crystallized rapidly. Even elements of the white-collar lower middle class rallied to the SPD's banner, including shop workers, secretaries, civil servants, and others who identified themselves as "working class." Fearing that the rise in working-class discontent and political consciousness might lead to revolutionary outbursts, Chancellor Bismarck announced the industrialized world's first major government welfare programs for workers. In the 1880s Germany introduced health, accident, and disability insurance along with a state-funded retirement pension system. These programs failed to stem popular support for the Social Democrats, however, and a temporary ban on the SPD proved no more effective. By 1898 the SPD was the largest party in Germany, winning more than 27 percent of the vote for the Reichstag. In 1912 the party won 34.8 percent.

As the most vociferous exponents of change in Germany, the Social Democrats kept up a constant barrage of criticism of the kaiser's government. In place of authoritarianism they called for parliamentary democracy; in place of profit-driven capitalism they called for a socialist economy based on workers' control of enterprises and state-managed welfare programs; and in place of militarism and global imperialism they espoused pacifism, disarmament, and international cooperation. But despite their sizable support among Germany's voters, their efforts to alter the kaiser's regime failed. Indeed, in a dramatic turnabout, the Social Democratic leadership rallied to the kaiser's side in the feverish first days of World War I. Vowing that they would never leave the fatherland in the lurch, the party's Reichstag delegation voted for war credits in August 1914, knowing full well that German workers would soon be making war on their British, French, and Russian working-class comrades. For the SPD, as for most Germans, the spirit of nationalism was overpowering. (The same was true for the British Labour Party and French Socialists.) Democracy in Germany would have to wait until the end of the most brutal conflict the world had ever seen.

The Weimar Republic

After four years of carnage,[14] and with the collapse of the German army imminent, the kaiser abdicated and fled the country. On hearing the news, the leader of the Social Democratic Party proclaimed a republic from the balcony of the Reichstag. The date was November 9, 1918. Two days later, Germany surrendered. With the sudden disappearance of the entire governmental structure that had ruled the country since its inception in 1871, power in Germany was up for grabs.

Power, like nature, abhors a vacuum. Into the void there charged a number of competing aspirants for control of the German state. Communists tried to launch a spontaneous revolution, but their venture was quickly countered by paramilitary forces led by senior army officers. As the revolutionary left fought pitched battles with the militaristic right over the following chaotic months and with both groups fundamentally opposed to democracy, a makeshift German government managed to stage elections to a constitutional assembly in early 1919. The assembly met in Weimar, the home town of Goethe and the symbolic heart of German culture. After six months of intense deliberation, the assembled delegates adopted a new constitution. The **Weimar Republic** was born, so called because of the birthplace of its constitution. Germany was at last a democracy.

The constitution adopted at Weimar in 1919 was in some respects the most democratic in the world at that time. It gave all men and women over age twenty-one the right to vote, securing a victory for women's suffrage that surpassed Britain, the United States, and most other democracies.[15] It also enumerated a number of legally guaranteed economic and social rights that were not to be found in the constitutions of other democratic states. These included the constitutional right to a job or unemployment compensation, decent housing, comprehensive health insurance, allowances for the "protection of motherhood," and a retirement pension. Private property rights were also protected by the constitution, but the owners of private enterprises were obligated to "serve the common good." The state reserved the right to take over privately owned property in the interest of the community (with compensation for the owners). Workers earned a host of new rights, including "equal rights" with their employers in regulating wages and working conditions. In short, the Weimar constitution's framers strove to institute not just popular sovereignty and civil rights (Faces I and II of democracy), but also a measure of economic democracy (Face IV).

The structure of the national government was also novel. The constitution created a mixed *presidential-parliamentary* democracy, which today's French and Russian constitutions strikingly resemble. The president of the Republic was directly elected by the people and possessed real decision-making powers. In a risky departure from standard democratic practice, however, the Weimar constitution gave the president extraordinary powers to suspend basic civil rights and liberties during an emergency and to exercise virtually dictatorial authority. As things turned out, the Republic's last president flagrantly abused this authority and used it to rule the country by decree, eventually turning the government over to Hitler and the Nazis.[16]

The Weimar constitution established a bicameral national legislature. The lower house, the Reichstag, functioned much like the British House of Commons: it held the head of government (i.e., the chancellor) and the rest of the cabinet accountable. Thus the Reichstag could topple the government in a vote of no-confidence, forcing either the formation of a new cabinet or anticipated elections in which the voters would select a new Reichstag.

The electoral system used for popular elections to the Reichstag was proportional representation, with no minimum hurdle. This system allowed a multiplicity of small parties, many of them with less than 5 percent of the vote, to win Reichstag seats. Like most PR systems, Weimar's variant had both positive and negative features. On the positive side, it gave voters a wide range of electoral choice—in some elections thirty or more parties would put up candidates—and it was scrupulously fair in granting each party a share of Reichstag seats approximately equal to its share of the national vote. (A dozen parties or more would typically win Reichstag representation.) To this extent, the electoral system was highly democratic and provided greater fairness in representation than the single member district systems in use in Britain and the United States. On the negative side, however, Weimar's PR system resulted in such a wide proliferation of parties in the legislature that it became extremely difficult to form stable governments. No party ever won an absolute majority of seats, making coalition governments inevitable. The inability of the coalition partners to stick together proved one of the downfalls of the Weimar system. (On proportional representation and single member district voting systems, see chapter 9.)

The problems that eventually proved fatal for Germany's fledgling democracy began accumulating right from the start. Economic disasters topped the list. The Republic started life under conditions of severe unemployment. Millions of soldiers, beaten and humiliated, straggled home from the front to find the civilian economy in no shape to employ them. For many, the opportunity to work for right-wing paramilitary organizations was their only hope for remuneration and a measure of self-respect. As time went on, large numbers of these angry and demoralized troops gravitated to the Nazis' brown-shirted militias, enabling Hitler and his followers to intimidate their opponents in the streets. Meanwhile, German workers returned from the war to face even more impoverishment than before, a prospect that drove many of them to support the Communists and other groups militating for a socialist revolution.

Germany's economic woes were aggravated by a steep bill for war reparations imposed by the victorious powers. In 1921, Britain, France, and the United States demanded the payment of $33 billion in gold marks, to be paid out in installments starting immediately. The reparations only aggravated an inflation rate that was already spinning out of control. As the German government printed money around the clock, prices rose more than 300 percent per month. The average inflation rate for 1922–23 was over 1 billion percent! Deft financial maneuvers by the government finally brought the inflationary spiral under control, but millions of Germans in all social classes were financially ruined. The middle class was especially hard hit. Instead of constituting a bastion of support for democracy as in the United States and Britain, large numbers of the middle class in Germany turned away from the Weimar democratic regime and flocked to the Nazis or other anti-democratic groups.

After the Wall Street stock market crash of 1929, the Great Depression spread economic misery around the globe. Germany was devastated. Banks and other businesses plunged into bankruptcy while unemployment skyrocketed, exceeding 30 percent of the work force by 1932. Neither the state treasury nor employers could afford to keep up with rising demands for unemployment compensation, reducing millions to abject poverty.

Farmers, small business owners, and people in virtually every other sector of the economy were also driven to despair.

These mounting economic and social crises took place in a political environment in which support for democracy remained feeble. The absence of democratic traditions in Germany deprived the Weimar Republic of a solid foundation, while the unrelenting assaults it took from friends and foes alike prevented it from achieving sustained stability. Initially, the Republic started out with a broad base of popular support. The three political parties most committed to democracy—the Social Democrats, the Center Party (a largely Catholic-oriented organization), and the middle-class German Democratic Party—together captured more than 75 percent of the vote in 1919. A fourth party, backed by business circles, soon joined their ranks. Leaders of these parties formed a succession of coalition governments, but their common commitment to democracy could not overcome their differences on a host of issues, from economic policy to foreign policy. Conflicts between the representatives of business and labor were particularly intense. To complicate things, all four parties were each *internally* divided on how to deal with the problems besetting the country. Compromise was not a widely shared political value. Other democratic values associated with Face III of democracy, such as trust and tolerance, were also in short supply.

Hence these shaky coalition cabinets frequently fell apart and had to be painfully stitched together again, only to succumb to more bickering and breakups. Between 1919 and 1933, Germany had twenty-two governments. Many of them were *minority governments:* that is, they did not have the support of a majority of Reichstag delegates. As a consequence, they could be easily toppled in no-confidence votes posed by their adversaries. The ineffectiveness of these governing coalitions in addressing Germany's problems progressively eroded their electoral base. By 1924 the combined popular vote for the four main pro-democracy parties fell to 48.8 percent, a minority of the electorate. In 1930 their support dipped to 44.6 percent, and in the fall of 1932, in the last elections held before Hitler came to power, it plummeted to 35 percent.

The electoral fortunes of the anti-democratic parties rose apace. On the left, the German Communist Party increased its electoral support from only 2 percent in 1920 to nearly 17 percent in 1932. During this period its leadership passed into the hands of a pro-Soviet faction, dedicated to abolishing democracy and private enterprise in Germany and establishing a communist dictatorship modeled on the USSR. To this end the Communists organized repeated strikes and demonstrations against the Republic's political and economic power structure.

On the right, most hard-line conservatives who opposed democracy initially cast their support to the Nationalists (formally known as the German National People's Party). This party was essentially a throwback to the kaiser's era. It longed for the restoration of strong authoritarian rule and a powerful military establishment, while harboring bitter resentment of the Western powers for defeating Germany and imposing humiliating surrender terms on the German people. The Nationalists doubled their vote in the first six years of the Republic, peaking at 20.5 percent in late 1924. Their most revered figure, Field Marshal Paul von Hindenburg, was elected president of Germany in 1925 and handily reelected in 1932. At first, Hindenburg endeavored out of patriotic loyalty to keep Germany's new democratic system afloat. In his heart and soul, however, he remained a man of the old regime, a Prussian aristocrat devoted to the army. As the depression took its devastating toll, Hindenburg used his emergency powers to govern the country by decree, ignoring the Reichstag and relying on a coterie of arch-conservative cronies.

It was **Adolf Hitler** and his National Socialist German Workers Party, or **Nazis** for short, who picked up a growing share of the right-wing nationalist vote over time. But the Nazis' support among the German people was by no means confined to the old-guard conservatives. Hitler himself was neither a Prussian (he was born in Austria), an aristocrat (his background was lower middle class), nor a high-ranking officer (he was a corporal in World War I). But he nourished a fiery German nationalism, fueled by fierce hatred of Britain, France, and the United States and their democratic systems of government. He was also a rabid anti-Semite. Driven by demonic energy and endowed with spellbinding oratorical skills, Hitler built up

the Nazi party from obscurity to mass popularity in only a few years. With just 3 percent of the vote in 1924 and 2.6 percent in 1928, the Nazis capitalized on the widespread misery generated by the depression and captured more than 37 percent in the summer of 1932, by far the highest vote ever won by any party in the Weimar Republic. The Nazis were now the largest party in Germany.

Electoral support for the Nazis came from virtually every corner of German society. The upper crust, the sizable middle classes, and even a substantial minority of workers (about 25 percent) gave the Nazis their vote. The Nazis won about a third of the urban vote and did even better in rural areas. They were very popular among older voters and had a growing following among Germany's youth. And despite their glorification of violence, they ultimately attracted more female voters than male voters.[17] Hitler's inflammatory oratory combined with the most well-organized election campaign machine in Germany to make the Nazis the most successful catch-all party in the Weimar Republic. (A *catch-all party* is one that seeks to win as many votes as it can rather than concentrating its appeal on a particular segment of the electorate. See chapter 11.) Unlike most catch-all parties, however, the Nazis were no friends of democracy but its vehement opponents. They took skillful advantage of the Weimar Republic's democratic institutions to destroy democracy itself. They also built up their own uniformed militia, numbering 400,000 by 1932, to beat up political rivals and threaten the Republic with a potential coup d'état.

In the summer of 1932, more than half of Germany's voters (51.6 percent) voted either for the Nazis or the Communists, the two most stridently anti-democratic parties in the country. Having few options left, President Hindenburg named Hitler chancellor of Germany in January 1933. The president and his entourage thought they could keep the upstart corporal under control, but Hitler proved more than their match. By the end of the year democracy was essentially extinguished and Germany was in the grip of a totalitarian fascist dictatorship.[18]

The Fascist Regime

As we indicated in our discussion of fascist ideology in chapter 13, the Nazi world view was grounded in *hypernationalism* and *racism*. The German people (*Volk*) were conceived in crackpot anthropological terms as the "Aryan race" and "the master race," while non-Aryans—especially Jews and Slavs—were vilified as "sub-humans." (Hitler's alliances with Mussolini's Italy and fascist Japan required the Nazis to mute their anti-Latin and anti-Asiatic bigotry for political reasons.) Shortly after the Nazis took power, German Jews, who represented only 0.9 percent of the population, were accused of ruining the country and subjected to strict limitations on their economic and educational activities. They were also compelled to suffer public harassment and indignities orchestrated by the regime. Gypsies, homosexuals, and the mentally retarded were also targeted for abuse. Once World War II began, these and other groups deemed genetically inferior were packed off to extermination camps and systematically slaughtered.

Nazi rule took the form of a *totalitarian dictatorship*. A single party, the Nazis, monopolized state power; all other parties were outlawed. Hitler exercised supreme personal authority over the party and the state. The Nazi party-state regulated virtually every aspect of social life in Germany; its control was virtually total. The educational system, the arts, the media, scientific research, and other aspects of social and intellectual life all came under Nazi supervision.

The state also assumed responsibility for coordinating the economy, though private enterprise was allowed to exist. Nazi governmental authorities set up committees, called "corporations," in which state representatives would meet with leaders of the country's largest businesses as well as with individuals handpicked by the regime to "represent" farmers, workers, and other segments of the economy. This system, known as *state corporatism*, enabled the Nazi party-state to impose its priorities on the country's private entrepreneurs. Since Hitler and his adjutants were bent on war, their highest economic priority was to build up a vast military machine, a goal they succeeded in accomplishing in violation of the provisions of the 1919 Versailles Peace Treaty that placed strict limits on Germany's military capacity. State corporatism also enabled the regime to regulate the labor force. All trade unions and other organizations representing workers or farmers were abolished except for those run by the Nazis.

Taken together, these characteristics of fascist rule made Nazi totalitarianism considerably more repressive and intrusive than the kaiser's regime, imposingly authoritarian though it was.

Another defining feature of German fascism was *mass mobilization*. Right from their earliest days as a political party in the Weimar Republic, the Nazis under Hitler's firm direction were determined to cultivate broad popularity. They devoted considerable attention to propaganda, using every means at their disposal—marches, rallies, posters, fliers, party newspapers, radio, and film—to drum up mass support. Once they took over the German state, their control over the media and schools permitted them to intensify these propaganda efforts enormously. In addition, the Nazis created a host of organizations—youth organizations, war veterans groups, and the like—to instill their ideas in the population. Hitler's rhetorical ability to inflame nationalistic passions energized these efforts.

Indeed, prior to the dark days of World War II, the Nazis enjoyed considerable popular support within Germany. (They were also widely popular in Austria, which Germany annexed in 1938.) The Nazis' well-orchestrated propaganda efforts were not solely responsible for this success. By brazenly flouting the Versailles Treaty, Hitler restored pride to millions of Germans seething with rancor from their wartime defeat and postwar humiliation. In addition, the Nazi government put a decisive end to the political instability and social chaos of the Weimar Republic. While the Republic's supporters were appalled at the demise of democracy, millions of other Germans were gladly ready to give up their democratic liberties in exchange for political and social tranquillity. Given a choice between freedom and order, many people preferred order. The longing for a strong state and dutiful obedience to official authority were integral elements of German political culture at that time.[19] The Nazis appealed to these attitudes. In elections held in March 1933, shortly after Hitler was named chancellor and under conditions marked by Nazi suppression of opposing parties, the Nazis won 44 percent of the vote: not a majority, but still a substantial figure.

Perhaps most important, the Nazis achieved popularity by arresting Germany's economic slide.

With tight control over the state budget, they rapidly addressed the unemployment problem by hiring people for public works projects and—not incidentally—for service in the military or in Nazi party organizations. Orders for military matériel and other equipment reinvigorated German industry and kept factories humming, creating jobs for workers and managers. Inflation was brought under control. The Nazis also introduced a series of welfare measures to assist the most vulnerable parts of the population. In sum, the Nazi economy represented a kind of militarized Keynesian welfare state: the state stimulated growth and soaked up unemployment by spending large sums of money in the economy (in accordance with Keynes's prescriptions), and much of this money was spent for military purposes (in accordance with Nazi priorities). The years 1936–39 were perhaps the best years the German economy had ever seen up to that point. (On Keynesianism, see chapter 14.)

Finally, the Nazis gained popularity by engineering a social revolution. Germany's old political elites, heavily populated with aristocrats and the scions of distinguished families, were summarily pushed aside by the Nazis to make way for less pedigreed Germans. The Nazi leaders were overwhelmingly from the middle classes, especially the lower middle class. Once ensconced in power, they opened up positions in the swelling party and state bureaucracies as well as in the army, the educational system, and other institutions to people like themselves.[20]

It was World War II that ultimately destroyed Hitler's "thousand-year Reich," devastating the German economy and inflicting misery and fear on the population. Initiated with Germany's invasion of Poland on September 1, 1939, the war delivered control over virtually all of continental Europe to Hitler and Mussolini before the Nazi military juggernaut was finally vanquished in 1945 by the combined efforts of the United States, the USSR, Britain, and Free France. (As Japan's ally, Hitler had declared war on the United States after Pearl Harbor in 1941.) More than 50 million lives were lost in the European theater of the conflict; tens of millions more were uprooted. At the end of the war Germany itself was dismembered: the Soviet Union annexed part of its territory and gave other parts to Poland and Czechoslovakia. The remaining area was then divided among the four victorious allies into occupation zones, which in 1949 were consolidated into the two separate German states.

As Germans nervously entered the postwar era, uncertain of their political fate, they could look back on the first half of the twentieth century as a succession of catastrophes. Their traumatic experiences could not help but have a powerful impact on their postwar attitudes. Two world wars imprinted an instinctive pacifism on millions of Germans, along with a reluctance on the part of many of them to engage in any display of nationalist sentiment. The tribulations of the Weimar Republic, constituting a paradigm of a failed democracy, left many Germans with a lasting fear of inflation and unemployment, along with an object lesson in what happens when political leaders refuse to compromise their differences. As a consequence, political culture in postwar Germany—particularly in democratic West Germany—was marked by anti-militarism, an embarrassed reticence about patriotism, a strong aversion to economic instability, and a prevailing inclination to political consensus and compromise. Moreover, until the 1960s most Germans wanted little to do with politics; they focused on their jobs and families, leaving political matters in the hands of their new democratic leaders. These attitudes profoundly shaped the development of the Federal Republic.

DEMOCRACY IN THE FEDERAL REPUBLIC OF GERMANY

The Formation of Parties

As American, British, and French authorities settled into their respective Occupation zones in 1945, their first task was to lay the foundations for democracy in a country that had just experienced twelve years of Nazi dictatorship. Many Nazi chieftains were put on trial for war crimes in Nuremberg, but thousands of lower level bureaucrats, jurists, and others involved in the administration of the fascist regime had to be dealt with. Initially the Western occupiers embarked on a program of "de-Nazification" to purge all those who had taken part in the Nazi system from the new governmental organs that were being created. This wholesale dismissal of everyone even remotely connected with the fascist government soon proved impracticable, however; there were not enough untainted administrators or judges to fill the positions that needed to be filled in the new administrative system. As a consequence, the West German bureaucracy and court system included many former Nazi Party members or sympathizers for several decades. Fortunately, the vast majority of them adjusted their actions to the new democratic order imposed on them by the victorious Western powers.

Of course, it was at the highest levels of political authority that the future of German democracy depended. It was therefore imperative to set up an effective system of competitive, pro-democracy political parties. With some notable exceptions, quite a few political figures from the Weimar era had come to terms with Hitler and the Nazis. Germany's ambivalent liberals—the group that ever since 1848 had oscillated between Western-style democracy and authoritarianism—were largely discredited, as their principal leaders had cast their lot with Hitler or anti-democratic nationalists at the end of the Weimar Republic. A new liberal party was formed in 1948, the **Free Democratic Party** (*Freie demokratische partei*, or **FDP**), under leaders thoroughly committed to democracy. Though small, this party—also known as the "liberals"—has played a critical role in the Federal Republic down to the present day.

The leadership of the **Social Democratic Party of Germany** was less corrupted by capitulation to fascism. Several of its most prominent figures spent a large part of the Nazi period in prisons or concentration camps; others fled the country. At the end of the war, Kurt Schumacher emerged from imprisonment and took over the reins of the SPD hierarchy. A passionate social democrat who took that designation literally, Schumacher wanted both economic socialism and ballot-box democracy. He believed that a middle path had to be found between American-style capitalism and Soviet-style dictatorship. Accordingly, he set the SPD on a course in favor of a powerful role for the state and workers in managing a welfare-oriented socialist economy, while advocating competitive elections and civil liberties as a bulwark against fascism, communism, or any other dictatorial ideology. Though his party later abandoned his socialist economic doctrines, Schumacher helped reestablish the SPD as one of German democracy's staunchest supporters.[21]

During the Weimar Republic, two parties appealing mainly to Catholic voters had provided relatively consistent support for democracy: the Center Party and its Bavarian affiliate, the Bavarian People's Party. After the war, two new parties were established that directed their appeal to West Germany's Catholics and Protestants. The two confessions had roughly equal shares of the population. After experiencing the brutality of fascism and war, many Germans were ready to support parties that subscribed in a general way to such Christian principles as fellowship and reconciliation. (Some Social Democrats still evinced a hostility to religion that derived from their origins in nineteenth-century Marxism.) One of these new parties, the **Christian Democratic Union** (*Christlich-demokratische Union,* or **CDU**) set up operations everywhere in West Germany except Bavaria, the largest of West Germany's constituent states. Konrad Adenauer, a respected Center Party politician who had served as mayor of Cologne from 1917 until the Nazi takeover in 1933, came out of retirement to head the CDU.

Bavaria, with its state capital in Munich, had a largely Catholic population; it proudly guarded its dialects, its traditional modes of dress, and other distinctly German cultural traditions along with a vibrant sense of independence. (Fittingly, a popular song about Bavaria is sung to the tune of "Deep in the Heart of Texas.") Bavarian politicians wanted to set up their own wing of the newly founded Christian Democratic movement, the **Christian Social Union** (*Christlich-soziale Union,* or **CSU**). The two parties have generally cooperated as one party and are usually referred to as the "CDU/CSU." The CSU tends to be more conservative than the CDU, however, and rivalries between their leaders occasionally produce frictions. Unless otherwise specified, the term "Christian Democrats" refers to the CDU and CSU together.

Other parties also came to the fore in the first years after Germany's defeat, including a Communist Party, but it was these three—the Christian Democrats, the Social Democrats, and the Free Democrats—that were to dominate politics in the Federal Republic right up to the present.

The Basic Law and the Federal Republic of Germany's Institutional Framework

As World War II came to a close in 1944 and 1945, the allies in the anti-Hitler coalition had no clear notion of what to do with Germany after the war other than to impose their own control over it. One plan hatched by a senior member of President Franklin D. Roosevelt's cabinet, Treasury Secretary Robert Morgenthau, actually called for converting Germany into a pastoral country, with no industrial base that might be used to create another war machine. The French wanted Germany carved up into small, weak regions. Although the United States, Britain, France, and the Soviet Union eventually agreed on the demarcation of their respective Occupation zones (along with the division of Berlin, a special case), it became increasingly apparent by 1947 that the Soviet Union and the three Western powers were at loggerheads over a wide range of issues in the postwar world.

The ideological clash between Western democracy and market economics, on the one hand, and Moscow's communist-party dictatorship and centrally planned economy, on the other, was irresoluble. Harsh ideological rhetoric inflamed the atmosphere. Additionally, the Soviet government's imposition of communist regimes on the countries of Central and Eastern Europe that were under the control of the Soviet army created growing consternation in the West, which had hoped for democracy in Poland, Hungary, Czechoslovakia, and other nations in the region. Kremlin threats against Iran, Turkey, and other countries sparked Western resolve to defend them against a possible Soviet takeover or invasion. As tensions mounted, it became apparent that there could be no agreement on creating a single, unified German government. No formal peace treaty could be signed between the victors of World War II and the vanquished, similar to the Versailles Peace Treaty that had concluded World War I, because there was no agreement on *which* German government would sign it. Germany was doomed to being divided between the powers that had defeated it.

In 1948 the three Western Occupation governments took a major step toward the creation of a separate West German state by establishing a common currency for all three of their zones. The Soviets responded by blockading the land passages between West Germany and West Berlin, provoking the West to respond with the Berlin airlift of 1948–49. As the crisis heated up, the Western powers in July 1948 ordered the German authorities under their control to convene an assembly to write a constitution for a West German government. Most Germans were considerably reluctant to take this step, fearing that a separate constitution for West Germany would dash all hopes of eventually reestablishing a single German state with the borders it had in 1937, before Hitler annexed Austria and parts of Czechoslovakia.[22]

Bowing to Allied pressures, the elected leaders of the various regions into which West Germany was divided at the time themselves selected the members of the constitutional assembly. Thus the body that drafted the Federal Republic's founding document was not elected by the people (unlike the assembly that convened in Weimar in 1919). After nine months of deliberation, the assembled delegates produced a document they called a **"Basic Law"** (*Grundgesetz*); they shunned the term "constitution" (*Verfassung*) on the grounds that only a reunited Germany could have a permanent constitution. The Basic Law was meant to be temporary, pending reunification. Contrary to the preferences of the Occupation authorities, the Germans did not submit the Basic Law to the West German voters for their approval, again on the grounds that only a reunited German people could vote to legitimize its most important governing instrument. Article 146 stipulated that the Basic Law would expire upon the unification of the Germans and their approval of a "constitution" in a free vote. Rather than submit the Basic Law to only part of the German people in a referendum, its framers secured its ratification by members of the various regional legislatures.

On May 23, 1949, the Basic Law went into effect and the Federal Republic of Germany was formally proclaimed in the Western Occupation zones. To this day the Basic Law has never been submitted to the voters for their approval. Consequently, some Germans are now calling for its replacement by a full-fledged constitution that would gain its legitimacy in a national referendum.

In another sign of the Basic Law's intended temporariness, its framers established Bonn as the Federal Republic's capital. The choice of this small, dreamy town instead of a large city like Frankfurt or Munich reflected their hope that Germany's division would not last very long and that, sooner or later, Berlin would once again stand proudly as the capital of a large, united Germany. Even the buildings selected to house important institutions like the parliament and the chancellor's office were modest quarters that could be easily left behind when the time came to move to Berlin. In addition, the Federal Republic proclaimed the Basic Law's validity for *all* Germans, including those in communist East Germany and other parts of former German territory. West Germany's main political parties were all in agreement that the Soviet-imposed communist dictatorship in East Germany was completely illegitimate and that eventual reunification should be a national goal.

A Federal System

In keeping with the centuries-old German tradition of fragmentation into numerous regions and cities, the Basic Law established the Federal Republic as a federal system. *Federalism* is a political system that combines a meaningful central government with a multiplicity of regional or local governments that have specific real powers. (The United States is an obvious example.) Even the kaiser's monarchical regime had respected the particularisms of various regional governments, giving them substantial latitude in determining how to implement the laws decided upon by the central government. Indeed, Hitler's dictatorship was the most highly centralized German government that ever existed. After the devastating fascist experience, the Allied Occupation powers and most Germans themselves had no desire to recreate a powerful central government.

The original Basic Law established eleven **Laender** (lender), a term rendered in English as "**states**" (as in, "The United States has fifty states."). Three of these states are actually large cities (Berlin, Hamburg, and Bremen). Each *Land* (state) has its own legislature, known as the *Landtag* (State Diet), elected every four or five years by the state's voters. (Similarly, every state in the United States has its own elected legisla-

ture.) The elections are usually staggered; rarely do more than two of them occur on the same day, with some occurring in different years.

All these state legislatures are unicameral except Bavaria's, which has two houses. The majority party (or parties) of each newly elected legislature elects a state government, whose chief bears the title of "minister-president" *(Ministerpraesident)*. Each minister-president is roughly analogous to an American governor, though they are elected differently and the extent of their legal powers differs. The position of minister-president is an important one in German politics, at times serving as a stepping stone to higher office. Just as several U.S. presidents like Bill Clinton, Ronald Reagan, and Jimmy Carter were previously governors, several German chancellors and candidates for that position once served as minister-presidents of individual German states. Unlike American governors, however, most minister-presidents serve simultaneously as members of the German federal legislature, thus participating in national government. Presidents Carter, Reagan, and Clinton had never held national office before assuming the presidency.

From the very beginning, the Basic Law conferred extensive powers on each state to regulate education, the administration of justice, the police, and the mass media, including radio and television, within its territory. (In constitutional law, the legal powers accorded the regional subunits of a federal system are known as "reserved powers," i.e., they are *reserved* to the subunits.) In addition to having these considerable reserved powers, the states were given the right to supervise the administration of *federal* laws—laws enacted by the Federal Republic's national legislature and central government—within their respective jurisdictions. Since virtually every law touching on domestic affairs in Germany has an administrative component, the states have their hand in practically every aspect of government administration. Most taxes imposed by the federal government, for instance, are actually collected by the states. Though the fifty states in the United States also have extensive reserved powers, they do not have such sweeping rights to administer federal laws and regulations as their German counterparts do.

The only major policy areas where the states play little or no role concern Germany's international dealings, such as foreign and defense policy. Even in foreign affairs, however, the states are expanding the scope of their authority. In 1992 the Basic Law was amended to give the states a major role in shaping the German government's policies toward the European Union. Fearing that the process of European unification might give EU authorities in Brussels excessive powers to interfere in their internal state affairs (for example, by imposing regulations on their broadcast media), the *Laender* won the right to veto any agreement the German government might conclude with the European Union that intrudes on their local powers.

With the collapse of the communist government of the German Democratic Republic, East Germany was united with the rest of the Federal Republic in 1990 on the basis of a provision in the Basic Law that permitted the incorporation of new states into the FRG. After the 1990 elections in East Germany demonstrated overwhelming popular support for unification, the GDR was reorganized into five states. These five states then entered the Federal Republic in a procedure roughly similar to the way various territories once "joined the union" of the United States of America. Some political forces in both eastern and western Germany objected to this procedure, arguing that Article 146 of the Basic Law mandates a new German constitution and a national referendum on it when unification takes place. Former anti-communist East German dissidents have joined with western German Greens and Social Democrats in demanding a new constitution, but their proposals were blocked by their opponents, the Christian Democrats, in the mid-1990s.

The Federal Republic now consists of sixteen states (Laender). The former East Germany is often referred to as "the five new states." Local governments in Germany at the county and municipal levels within these states are heavily dependent on money transferred to them from the federal and state budgets.[23]

The Bundesrat

Perhaps the most striking evidence of the political power of Germany's sixteen states is the special role they play in constituting the upper house of the Federal Republic's national parliament. This house is known as the Federal Council, or **Bundesrat.**

The Bundesrat directly represents the states. It is chosen *by the state governments;* unlike the U.S. Senate, its members are *not* directly elected by the people of each state. What this means in practice is that the *majority party (or parties) within each state legislature* selects the state's representatives in the Bundesrat (because it is this legislative majority that forms the state government). Thus if the Christian Democrats have the majority of seats in the state legislature of Hesse, they will establish Hesse's government and pick its minister-president. That government will in turn send Christian Democrats to represent Hesse in the Bundesrat. If the Social Democrats and Greens have a combined majority of seats in Hamburg, they will form a coalition government to govern this large city-state, and their government will select people of its own choosing to represent Hamburg in the Bundesrat. The opposition parties in these state legislatures have no role in selecting their state's Bundesrat deputies.

Each Bundesrat delegate votes on instructions from his or her state government and has no personal freedom in deciding how to vote in that chamber. Bundesrat deputies thus have vastly less independence than do U.S. senators, who may vote as they see fit.

Though each state is represented, the Bundesrat's voting procedures are not based on "one state, one vote." Because Germany's sixteen states come in different sizes, the Bundesrat uses a *weighted voting* procedure. The largest states, with a population of more than 7 million each, are each entitled to six votes in the Bundesrat. States with between 6 and 7 million inhabitants are each entitled to five Bundesrat votes; those with more than 2 million people are entitled to four votes; all the rest are entitled to three votes each. Thus the sixteen states that comprise the Bundesrat together dispose of a total of sixty-nine votes, distributed proportionately by size. If the four largest states, with six votes each, choose to vote together, their twenty-four votes are enough to block the passage of any bill requiring a two-thirds majority. In these circumstances the four largest states can use their weighted votes to block action favored by the twelve smaller states. Even so, the Bundesrat's malapportionment favors the smaller states.[24]

Each state may send as many representatives to the Bundesrat as it has votes; but each state deputation must vote together as a bloc. Thus, if Bavaria sends six deputies to the Bundesrat, all six must vote in unison as instructed by the Bavarian state government. In practice, a large number of deputies sent to the Bundesrat by their state governments are not elected state legislators but are civil servants working in their state's bureaucracy. Such people tend to be technical experts on the policy issues they are likely to vote on (such as budgetary matters, education, the environment, and so on). Sometimes a state's Bundesrat delegation will be instructed not to vote at all. If the state government is a coalition between two parties (say, the Social Democrats and the Christian Democrats) and the partners cannot agree on certain pieces of legislation that come up for a vote in the Bundesrat, they may instruct their delegation in that body to abstain from voting.

Table 18.2 lists Germany's sixteen states, along with their populations and state capitals, the number of votes they are entitled to in the Bundesrat, the parties that governed them in early 2000, and the names of their respective minister-presidents at that time.

What can the Bundesrat do? First and foremost, the Basic Law gives the upper house a *veto power* over all bills whose passage into law would re-quire the state governments to implement their provisions. In the formative years of the Federal Republic, it was assumed that very few bills of this type would come up. Since the 1970s, the scope of the states' authority to execute federal laws has expanded considerably. Nowadays, almost two-thirds of all federal legislation requires the Bundesrat's approval, including tax measures, educational reforms, environmental laws, the regulation of cable television, and the like. If a bill is specifically designated as one that *requires* Bundesrat approval, the Bundesrat can veto it by majority vote even if the bill has already passed the lower house, the Bundestag.

This legislative power has major political significance, as the government of Chancellor Gerhard Schroeder soon found out. In a series of state legislative elections in 1999, the Christian Democrats won or maintained a role in five state governments, giving them a majority of votes in the Bundesrat. As a result, Schroeder was forced to shape many of his government's policies with a view to their potential reception in an upper house dominated by his adversaries. Such issues as citizenship rights, economic policy, and other questions over which the Social Democrats and Christian Democrats disagreed now had to be either compromised or shelved.

TABLE 18.2

Germany's Sixteen States

State (*Land*)	Population (millions, 1999)	State Capital	Bundesrat Votes	Government mid-2000	Minister-President
North Rhine-Westphalia	17.3	Duesseldorf	6	SPD, Greens	Clement (SPD)
Bavaria	12.1	Munich	6	CSU	Stoiber (CSU)
Baden-Wuerttemberg	10.4	Stuttgart	6	CDU, FDP	Teufel (CDU)
Lower Saxony	7.8	Hanover	6	SPD	Glogowski (SPD)
Hesse	5.9	Wiesbaden	5	CDU, FDP	Koch (CDU)
Saxony*	4.6	Dresden	4	CDU	Biedenkopf (CDU)
Rhineland-Palatinate	4.0	Mainz	4	SPD, FDP	Beck (SPD)
Berlin	3.5		4	CDU, SPD	Diepgen (CDU)
Schleswig-Holstein	2.8	Kiel	4	SPD, Greens	Simonis (SPD)
Saxony-Anhalt*	2.7	Magdeburg	4	SPD, Greens	Hoeppner (SPD)
Brandenburg*	2.6	Potsdam	4	SPD, CDU	Stolpe (SPD)
Thuringia*	2.5	Erfurt	4	CDU, SPD	Vogel (CDU)
Mecklenburg-West Pomerania*	1.8	Schwerin	3	SPD, PDS	Ringstorff (SPD)
Hamburg	1.7		3	SPD, Greens	Runde (SPD)
Saar (or Saarland)	1.1	Saarbruecken	3	CDU	Mueller (CDU)
Bremen	0.7		3	SPD, CDU	Scherf (SPD)

*Formerly part of communist East Germany.

The Bundesrat also gets to vote on some bills that do not directly affect state governments, such as foreign or defense policy. On these issues, a negative Bundesrat vote can be overridden by a vote in the Bundestag. Thus the Bundesrat's approval is not required on *all* legislation. (In the United States, by contrast, the Senate's approval is required for all legislation.) Still, the Bundesrat can block even these kinds of bills. For example, if the Bundesrat *by two-thirds majority* rejects a bill that does not *require* its approval, the Bundestag can pass it *only with a two-thirds majority* of its own. If it fails to do so, the bill is dead.

The Bundesrat also exercises its influence in party committees, where draft legislation is often amended before it goes up for a final vote. In addition, Bundesrat deputies may initiate legislation (always acting on their state government's instructions, to be sure). In sum, the Bundesrat gives Germany's sixteen state governments a direct role in the national parliament that the fifty state governments in the United States do not possess. It forces the central government in Berlin to pay close attention to the wishes of each state's elected officials, injecting a considerable measure of decentralization into Germany's federal system. So important are the states in Germany's political decision-making process that one student of German affairs has called the Federal Republic's central government a "semi-sovereign state," in large measure because it must constantly share power with the *Laender*.[25]

For all its influence, however, the Bundesrat takes a back seat to the other federal legislative chamber, the Bundestag, when it comes to forming the German government and holding it accountable to the voters' elected representatives. The Bundestag is really the main locus of parliamentary action in the Federal Republic.

The Bundestag

The **Bundestag**—or Federal Diet—is the lower house of the national legislature. In most respects it functions much like Britain's House of Commons or the lower house in other parliamentary systems. Although, as its title implies, the Federal Republic has a federal structure, its system of national government is a variant of British-style *parliamentary*

government. That is, (1) *the people elect the lower house of the legislature*, and (2) *the lower house holds the government accountable* and retains the right to vote the government out of office. (See chapter 9 for a description of parliamentary government.)

The Bundestag's Electoral System   Bundestag elections take place at least every four years, though anticipated elections may be called before the expiration of the full four-year term. Members of the Bundestag are elected through a combination of the two main systems for electing a legislature: *the single member district (SMD) system and proportional representation (PR). Half the members are elected by SMD, the other half by PR.* Once all the votes are counted, a formula is used to ensure that the final distribution of Bundestag seats approximately resembles proportional representation. This dual system is sometimes called a *personalized proportional electoral system.*

The election takes place in 328 electoral districts, each averaging about 240,000 inhabitants and about 165,000 voters. The more populous states thus have more electoral districts than the smaller ones, as in the United States. Voter registration is automatic when a citizen registers with the local authorities on taking up residence, as required under German law; it is usually confirmed by a mailed registration form. Virtually everyone over age eighteen has the right to vote.

On election day, each voter gets two votes on the election ballot (see figure 18.1). The first vote—called the "district" vote—lists the *candidates by name* on the left column, along with their respective party affiliations. The voter chooses one candidate, just as in the United States when voting for the House of Representatives or in the United Kingdom when voting for the House of Commons. There are 328 members of the Bundestag elected in this first vote (i.e., a single member for each electoral district); each of these seats is known as a "direct mandate."

The second vote—called the "party list" vote—is the proportional representation part of the election. In the right column, the ballot lists the major *parties* within each state (SPD, CDU or CSU, FDP, etc.). Beneath the name of each party are the names of several of its most prominent leaders to assist the voters in identifying the parties; each party keeps a much longer list of candidates

FIGURE 18.1 German Sample Ballet

Source: Münster Statistical Office. "You Have 2 Votes": The left column lists candidates by name for the single member district vote and the right column lists parties for the proportional representation vote, along with the names of prominent party leaders.

Stimmzettel

für die Wahl zum Deutschen Bundestag im Wahlkreis 307 Suhl - Schmalkalden - Ilmenau - Neuhaus

am 27. September 1998

Sie haben 2 Stimmen

hier 1 Stimme
für die Wahl
eines/einer Wahlkreis-
abgeordneten

hier 1 Stimme
für die Wahl
einer Landesliste (Partei)
- maßgebende Stimme für die Verteilung der Sitze insgesamt auf die einzelnen Parteien -

Erststimme

1	**Nolte,** Claudia Diplom-Ingenieur, MdB Ilmenau Oehrenstöcker Landstraße 106	**CDU**	Christlich Demokratische Union Deutschlands	
2	**Gleicke,** Iris Diplom-Ingenieur, MdB Schleusingen Zeile 1	**SPD**	Sozialdemokratische Partei Deutschlands	
3	**Zimmer,** Gabriele Sprachmittlerin, MdL Nahetal-Waldau Am Sportplatz 6a	**PDS**	Partei des Demokratischen Sozialismus	
4	**Hotop,** Reinhard kaufmännischer Angestellter Schleusingen Langes Tal 14b	**GRÜNE**	BÜNDNIS 90/ DIE GRÜNEN	
5	**Wilhelm,** Bernd Unternehmer Schmalkalden Auergasse 23	**F.D.P.**	Freie Demokratische Partei	
6	**Dr. Latussek,** Paul Diplom-Ingenieur Ilmenau Erlenstraße 14	**BFB -** **Die Offensive**	BUND FREIER BÜRGER - OFFENSIVE FÜR DEUTSCHLAND, Die Freiheitlichen	
14	**Mayer,** Wolfgang Lehrer Erfurt Johannesstraße 158	**DSU**	Deutsche Soziale Union	

Zweitstimme

	CDU	Christlich Demokratische Union Deutschlands Claudia Nolte, Manfred Grund, Bernward Müller, Vera Lengsfeld, Norbert Otto	1
	SPD	Sozialdemokratische Partei Deutschlands Christoph Matschie, Gisela Schröter, Wieland Sorge, Iris Gleicke, Gerhard Neumann	2
	PDS	Partei des Demokratischen Sozialismus Dr. Ruth Fuchs, Gerhard Jüttemann, Rosel Neuhäuser, Carsten Hübner, Kersten Naumann	3
	GRÜNE	BÜNDNIS 90/DIE GRÜNEN Katrin Göring-Eckardt, Rudolf Keßner, Gisela Hartmann, Dr. Matias Mieth, Elke Boullon	4
	F.D.P.	Freie Demokratische Partei Dr. Karlheinz Guttmacher, Gerhard Peter, Martin Henning, Hans-Joachim Wiegand, Eva Treuler	5
	BFB - **Die Offensive**	BUND FREIER BÜRGER - OFFENSIVE FÜR DEUTSCHLAND, Die Freiheitlichen Dr. Paul Latussek, Günther Steinert, Dirk Geyer, Kati Lange, Harry Drechsler	6
	DVU	DEUTSCHE VOLKSUNION Gerhard Frey, Gerhard Konrad, Klaus Deckert, Kurt Hoppe, Margitta Männich	7
	GRAUE	DIE GRAUEN - Graue Panther Dr. Ehrentraud Matz, Arno Butscher, Ruth Piehler, Peter Wöllner, Gertrud Buttlar	8
	REP	DIE REPUBLIKANER Dr. Heinz-Joachim Schneider, Matthias Ritter, Gudrun Otto	9
		Feministische Partei DIE FRAUEN Mechthild Ziegenhagen, Ursula Häusler, Barbara Sabine Heimann, Eleonore Sömmer, Christine Körber	10
	Pro DM	Initiative Pro D-Mark - neue liberale Partei Klaus Gebhardt, Bernd Schöbel, Stefan Pischner, Gerhard Otto, Martin Klimek	11
	FORUM	NEUES FORUM Matthias Büchner, Dr. Viktor Rimbakowsky, Dieter Kohl, Matthias Röder, Matthias Baumann	12
	ödp	Ökologisch-Demokratische Partei Karl-Edmund Vogt, Clemens Roschka, Waltraud Döring, Franz-Josef Mai, Ulrich Weißbrodt	13

whose names do not appear on the ballot. This list of candidates is known as the "state list" *(Landesliste)*. But it is the *party as a whole* that the voter checks when exercising her or his second vote.

It is thus possible for a voter to split the ticket by voting, say, for a Social Democratic candidate in the first vote and for the Free Democratic Party in the second. In the 1990s, slightly more than 15 percent of the voters engaged in ticket splitting, usually in hopes of producing a coalition government between two favored parties (CDU-FDP, SPD-Greens, etc.).

The proportional representation (second) vote ultimately determines how many Bundestag seats each party will get. Prior to the elections, the law sets the minimum number of seats the next Bundestag must have. In recent years this figure has been 656 seats (i.e., 2 times 328 districts). Each party is entitled to a share of Bundestag seats comparable to its share of the *popular vote nationwide in the second vote.* Thus, for example, if a party wins 40 percent of the total second vote on a nationwide basis, it is entitled to 40 percent of the Bundestag seats (i.e., 262 out of 656 seats). Its final representation in the Bundestag is thus *proportional* to its share of the national vote. At the same time, each party keeps the seats its candidates won in the first vote (the single member district vote). If the same party in our example won 100 of these first vote contests, it is entitled to 162 more seats from the second vote in order to bring its total to 262. Those 162 seats are filled by candidates selected by party leaders and activists within each state from their state list (the *Landesliste*), and they are listed in order of their political prominence within the party.[26] Thus if an important leader of the party fails to win a single member district seat, she will probably be near the top of the second vote list in her state and will thus win election to the Bundestag (see table 18.3).

Sometimes it happens that a party wins a larger percentage of first vote district contests within a particular state (say, 45 percent of the single member district mandates in Hesse) than its share of the total vote nationwide in the second vote (e.g., 40 percent). When this occurs, Hesse's Bundestag delegation is enlarged to allow the party to keep all 45 percent of the seats it won there. These extra seats are known as "overhang mandates" *(Ueberhangmandate)*. In 1998 the SPD won thirteen overhang mandates in this way. As a result, the size of the Bundestag was increased from 656, its legally established minimum, to 669.[27]

Although this system seems complicated, its aims are actually quite simple. It seeks to provide the advantages of *candidate recognition,* which is supposed to come with a single member district system in which individual candidates are presented to the voters by name. At the same time, it provides *fairness in party representation,* ensuring that each party gets a share of Bundestag seats roughly equal to its share of the national vote. As we noted in chapter 9, single member district systems sometimes result in a disparity between a party's share of the vote and its share of legislative seats; PR is designed to eliminate, or at least minimize, this disparity. Proportional representation may also promote the representation of women in the Bundestag because it enables the parties to include as many female candidates on their state lists as they wish. These candidates usually do not have to raise their own campaign funds, contrary to candidates for Congress in the United States. Women comprised 30.9 percent of the Bundestag in 2000, as opposed to 12.9 percent of the U.S. House of Representatives (see table 2.3 on page 42).

To be sure, PR can bring disadvantages of its own. It can encourage so many parties to field candidates and enable so many of them to win seats that the legislature can end up splintered into a dozen parties or more, some of them representing as little as 3 percent of the electorate or less. In these

TABLE 18.3

Hypothetical Election Result for a Party			
A Number of first vote "direct mandates" won	**B** % of popular vote nationwide in second (party list) vote	**C** Number of seats entitled to (% of second vote × 656)	**D** Seats won from second vote (C − A)
100	40%	262 (40% × 656)	162 (262 − 100)

TABLE 18.4

Bundestag Elections, September 27, 1998 (656 Seats in Principle, Increased to 669)

Party	District Mandates Won (First Vote)	% of Vote Nationwide (Second Vote)	Final Number of Seats*	% of Seats
SPD	212	40.9	298	45.4
CDU/CSU	112	35.1	245	36.6
Greens	0	6.7	47	7.0
FDP	0	6.2	43	6.4
PDS	4	5.1	36	5.4
Twenty-seven others	0	5.9	0	0
TOTALS	328	(100%)**	669	(100%)**

*Seats won in second vote, plus overhang mandates and the distribution of seats unfilled by parties that failed to clear the 5 percent hurdle.
**Rounded off.
Source: Federal Returning Officer, Federal Statistical Office, FRG.

circumstances, it is unlikely that a single party will emerge with a majority of seats, making coalition building necessary, with all its potential for divided, unstable governments. The Weimar Republic provides a classic example of proportional representation run amok. In order to prevent a repetition of those traumatic years and to keep very small parties from fractionating the Bundestag, the West German government in the 1950s imposed a 5 percent minimum hurdle: a party must win at least 5 percent of the second vote nationwide in order to be represented in the Bundestag.

Because of the hurdle, the Bundestag for much of its history has included only the three main parties (CDU/CSU, SPD, and FDP). Since the 1960s, several extreme right-wing parties have repeatedly failed to clear the hurdle. The Greens surmounted it for the first time in 1983 with 5.6 percent, but failed in 1990 with only 4.8 percent. Since then they have rebounded, clearing the hurdle in both 1994 and 1998. After unification, the Party of Democratic Socialism (PDS), the successor to East Germany's former ruling communist party, managed to win Bundestag seats in 1990 and 1994 thanks to provisions in the electoral laws circumventing the 5 percent hurdle rule.[28] The PDS scraped over the hurdle in 1998, winning 5.2 percent.

In 1998, thirty-three parties competed in the elections, but only six of them cleared the 5 percent hurdle and won seats in the Bundestag. The remaining twenty-seven parties collectively garnered only 5.9 percent of the second vote nationwide. What happens to the Bundestag seats they would have won if there were no hurdle (5.9 percent of 656, or thirty-nine seats)? They are distributed to the winning parties, each getting a percentage of seats equivalent to its share of the second vote.[29]

Once all the Bundestag seats are distributed in accordance with these provisions, the final result is *approximate proportional representation,* as indicated in the 1998 election results shown in table 18.4. Voter turnout tends to be quite high, usually 80 percent or more.

Forming the Government   Once elections have taken place, the Bundestag's first order of business is to set up a government. The Basic Law authorizes the president of the Federal Republic, the country's ceremonial head of state, to formally propose someone to serve as **chancellor,** or head of government. Like the queen of the United Kingdom, however, the German president has little choice but to designate the person whose party is in the strongest position in the Bundestag to form a government that will be backed by the majority of its members. (We'll have more to say about the presidency in the next section.) If one party holds an absolute majority of the seats, then it will be able to form a majoritarian government with no need to rely on coalition partners. Although majoritarian governments are the norm in Britain, in the Federal Republic there has never been one: *every government since 1949 has been a coalition government.*[30] But unlike the Weimar Republic, which had a succession of weak *minority* coalition governments, the Federal Republic has enjoyed considerably more stability: all of its coalition governments have started out with the voting support of a majority of Bundestag deputies.

It is up to the parties and their top leaders to work out terms for a governing coalition. During the 1998 elections, there was speculation that if the Social Democrats won the largest number of seats, they would probably turn to the Greens as their coalition partners; but some speculated that the SPD leadership might alternatively approach the Christian Democrats. Although the SPD and the CDU/CSU are rivals, in the 1960s they set aside their differences to form a government known as the "Grand Coalition." At the time of the 1998 elections the Social Democrats and Christian Democrats jointly ran smaller Grand Coalition governments in several *Laender*. But as the election returns came in, Christian Democratic leaders made it clear that they had no desire to establish a Grand Coalition at the national level, nor were many Social Democrats so inclined. With the SPD holding a large plurality of seats in the new Bundestag (44.5 percent), President Roman Herzog, a Christian Democrat, called on Gerhard Schroeder to form a government. After several weeks of bargaining, the SPD came to terms with the Greens, resulting in Germany's first "red-green" coalition government at the national level.

After the coalition partners have agreed to form a government, the Bundestag holds a formal vote for chancellor. Invariably this vote falls along straight party lines, with the coalition partners voting favorably to ensure a majority for the new head of government and the minority parties asserting their opposition. After this investiture, the chancellor names the cabinet ministers, usually on the basis of a previous agreement between the coalition parties. The junior partner in most coalition governments is assigned the post of foreign minister, generally considered the second most prestigious position after the chancellor, and several other cabinet ministries as well. Once the government is in place, the chancellor presents a formal "government declaration" (*Regierungserklaerung*) to the Bundestag, a policy address indicating the government's main priorities.

The size of the cabinet varies from one government to the next, ranging from as few as sixteen to as many as twenty or more. Schroeder's cabinet in 1999 had sixteen members counting himself. It included eleven Social Democrats, four Greens, and one member without party affiliation. Unlike

Britain, the German cabinet rarely debates policy issues collectively or takes decisions that may go against the chancellor's preferences. Germany's so-called "chancellor democracy" gives the head of government wider discretion than in Britain to pursue his own priorities. Ultimately, however, the chancellor must take account of his coalition partners' wishes. If a disgruntled junior party pulls out, the senior party will either have to find new allies or resign. So far this has happened only once in the Federal Republic, in 1982 (see later in this section). Nevertheless, the government's dependence on party alignments in the Bundestag makes for a close fusion of the executive branch and the legislature.

One of the chief ways the Bundestag holds the government accountable is by open debate and by enabling its members to pose questions directly to cabinet ministers. As in Britain, most of these questions and their responses are in written form. But Germany has also adopted a modified version of Britain's question time: an hour is set aside on a regular basis to enable members of the Bundestag to pose oral questions to cabinet ministers or their representatives. An additional hour can be devoted to oral questioning upon the request of the deputies. Unlike Britain, where the prime minister must face questions in the House of Commons every week, Germany does not require the chancellor to undergo an oral grilling in the Bundestag on a weekly basis. Still, even the chancellor must answer oral questions from time to time. Important Bundestag sessions are often broadcast on live television, and the tenor of debate, while courteous, can be sharp.[31]

The most effective form of government accountability to the Bundestag centers in the vote of confidence. As in other parliamentary systems, the Bundestag has the right to vote the government out of office. As noted earlier, governments in the Weimar Republic were routinely held hostage to confidence votes because many of them were minority governments: in a showdown vote, they could not count on a majority of Reichstag delegates to support them. In the Federal Republic, by contrast, there have been no minority governments. In practice, then, a government in the Federal Republic can be toppled in a confidence vote only if it loses its majority in the Bundestag through defections from its own ranks or if a coalition partner decided to pull out of the cabinet. Even then, the Basic Law imposes strict conditions under which a vote of confidence can be used to unseat the government. In what is called the **constructive vote of confidence,** the opposition must not simply form a voting majority against the government: *it must also be ready to form a new government under a new chancellor within forty-eight hours of the vote.*

In view of these obstacles, the confidence procedure has been used only twice in the entire history of the Federal Republic. In 1972, the SPD-FDP coalition government under Chancellor Willy Brandt enjoyed a slender majority in the Bundestag. But as a crucial vote approached on controversial treaties with the Soviet Union and its allies, rumors circulated that several FDP Bundestag deputies opposed to the treaties would vote against the government, perhaps depriving it of its majority. Eager to pounce on this possibility, the Christian Democrats posed the question of confidence and declared that their leader would be ready to form a new government. A tense secret ballot resulted in a tie vote, with two abstentions; the no-confidence motion failed.

Ten years later, another SPD-FDP government, under Chancellor Helmut Schmidt, came apart at the seams after months of wrangling between the two coalition partners over economic and foreign policy issues. The leadership of the Free Democratic Party decided to withdraw from the coalition in the fall of 1982 and announced its readiness to switch partners, joining with the Christian Democrats in forming a new government. When the constructive vote of confidence was held, the deal was already set: the Christian Democrats and Free Democrats voted against Schmidt's government, forcing him to resign. They immediately set up a CDU/CSU-FDP coalition government under Chancellor Helmut Kohl, the leader of the CDU. Kohl presided over a series of Christian Democrat-Free Democrat governments for the next sixteen years, until 1998.[32]

As long as the governing coalition parties stick together and maintain their Bundestag majority, it is therefore virtually impossible to unseat a German government. The result has been considerable government stability, *in spite of coalition cabinets.* Of course, this stability requires the party leaders to get along and agree on the main lines of domestic and foreign policy. After World War II, with the horrendous experience of conflict and recrimination between the Weimar Republic's parties hauntingly in mind, the main parties in the Federal Republic went out of their way to narrow their differences and achieve consensus on such fundamentals as the nature of the political system, the structure of the "social market economy," and relations with the United States and other nations of the world. As a consequence, Social Democrats, Christian Democrats, and Free Democrats have been able to form coalition governments with one another interchangeably.

Government stability in the Federal Republic also requires fairly strict *party discipline:* all the members of a party's Bundestag delegation are expected to vote in unison, except on special occasions when the party leadership allows its deputies to vote as they wish. Party discipline is higher in Germany than in the United States. The result is relatively smooth sailing through the Bundestag for bills drafted by the government. Roughly 85 percent of government bills pass the lower house, as opposed to about 40 percent of legislation introduced by individual members. Thanks to party discipline, Chancellor Kohl was able to maintain his coalition government with a mere ten-vote majority from 1994 to 1998.

Another factor that serves to facilitate the legislative process in Germany centers on the unusually close relationships between the cabinet, the Bundestag, and the civil service. To begin with, most cabinet ministers and their deputy ministers are themselves members of the Bundestag; they are therefore well acquainted with the procedures and norms of parliamentary practice. By contrast, some U.S. presidents, like Carter, Reagan and Clinton, had never served in Congress and came to power with little appreciation of its customs. The same has been true of many U.S. cabinet secretaries. Moreover, a sizable number of Bundestag deputies tend to come from the civil service. U.S law prohibits civil servants from running for office while holding down their bureaucratic positions, but Germany permits it; it even allows civil servants to get promoted within the government bureaucracy while serving in the legislature. Another large group of Bundestag deputies tends to come from trade unions, business associations, and other non-governmental interest groups involved in the policy-making process. Upward of 70 percent of the Bundestag thus has considerable experience in government or interest groups, giving them professional expertise in their various policy specialties.

Campaign Financing   Campaign financing is often one of democracy's weak spots. In some countries like the United States and Japan, campaign expenses for individual candidates and party organizations are so costly that they require unceasing efforts to raise funds from wealthy private contributors, businesses, trade unions, and other sources. The entire political process risks being corrupted by the inordinate influence of big contributors. Virtually every major democracy in recent years has experienced scandals of one kind or another associated with illegal or unethical campaign funding.

The Federal Republic of Germany has sought to reduce the undue influence of large donors by providing substantial funding for parties out of state revenues. In accordance with the most recent revision of its campaign financing laws that took force in 1994, the German government gives each party 1.3 deutschemarks (DM) for each vote it received in the previous elections, up to 5 million votes. It provides 1 mark for each vote above 5 million. (One deutschemark in 1999 was worth about 38 U.S. cents.) In addition, it gives every party a half deutschemark for every one it raises on its own through dues, publications, and other means. To qualify, a party needs to have gained at least 0.5 percent of the vote in the last election. Membership dues and contributions to parties by corporations and individuals are tax deductible up to a maximum amount (DM20,000; about $7,600). Neither candidates nor parties may purchase radio or television advertising time; the stations are required by law to provide the parties free air time during the designated campaign period. Campaign spending by all the parties together in a given campaign must not exceed DM230 million. These regulations apply to all Bundestag, Landtag, and European Parliament elections. They are considerably stiffer than current campaign finance laws in the United States.[33] Even so, former chancellor Helmut Kohl landed in considerable trouble, as we shall see later in this chapter, when it was revealed after he left office that he had maintained an illegal slush fund during his years as chancellor.

The Presidency

As we've indicated, the federal **president** is Germany's head of state. The position is largely cere-monial, analogous to that of the British monarch. Germany's president in no way possesses the powers of the president of the United States, France, or Russia. The occupant's principal duty is to select a party leader to form a government after a Bundestag election, upon the chancellor's resignation, or following the government's defeat in a constructive vote of confidence. This task is usually ritualistic, as the person to be designated as the next chancellor has invariably been predetermined by the alignment of parties in the Bundestag.[34]

Nevertheless, the president can still play a significant role in German politics. As a figure who is supposed to represent Germany as a whole and stand above the fray of partisan conflict, the president may exercise a moral authority that transcends the day-to-day skirmishes over policy issues. Two of Germany's most recent presidents—Richard von Weizsaecker (1984–94) and Roman Herzog (1994–99), both Christian Democrats—won international acclaim with powerful speeches reminding Germans of their obligation never to forget the moral turpitude of the Hitler years.

The federal president is not elected by the people but by a special Federal Convention (*Bundesversammlung*). This body consists of both the Bundestag and the Bundesrat, plus an equal number of delegates elected by the sixteen state legislatures. The dominant party or governing coalition is usually able to get its candidate elected, but at times the three main party groups—Christian Democrats, Social Democrats, and Free Democrats—reach agreement on an individual they hold in high esteem. Two presidents have come from the ranks of the small Free Democratic Party: Theodor Heuss, the Federal Republic's first president (1949–59), and Walter Scheel, a widely popular FDP leader (1974–79). Both were elected with the backing of one or both of the larger parties. Von Weizsaecker was unopposed by the Social Democrats. The Federal Republic's other past presidents have included Heinrich Luebke (1959–69), a Christian Democrat; Gustav Heinemann (1969–74), a Social Democrat; and Karl Carstens (1979–84), a Christian Democrat. In May 1999, the Social Democrats and Greens combined to elect Johannes Rau, a former SPD chancellor candidate against Helmut Kohl. The president serves a five-year term and may be reelected only once.

The Federal Judiciary

The Basic Law established an elaborate court system, crowned at the federal level by several superior courts. These include the Federal Supreme Court (*Bundesgerichtshof*), which is Germany's highest court of appeals in ordinary civil and criminal cases, and specialized courts concerned respectively with administrative law, labor law, financial law, and social affairs. By far the most important of these high courts is the **Federal Constitutional Court** (*Bundesverfassungsgericht*). From its inception the Constitutional Court was endowed with the power of *judicial review:* the right to interpret the Basic Law and to strike down as unconstitutional laws passed by the parliament and actions taken by the government. With this considerable discretionary authority, the Federal Constitutional Court has been called the most powerful judicial body in Europe; in some respects its authority surpasses that of the U.S. Supreme Court.[35] (Britain has no comparable supreme court, while France's Constitutional Council has substantially more limited powers.)

Seated in Karlsruhe, the Federal Constitutional Court consists of sixteen justices, most of them former judges or eminent constitutional scholars. Half are appointed by the Bundestag, the other half by the Bundesrat. Each house must confirm a nominee for the Court by two-thirds vote, a supermajority deliberately intended to require the approval of the two largest parties, the Christian Democrats and the Social Democrats. Germany's political leaders have sought to ensure a scrupulous balance on the Court between adherents of the two parties, along with an occasional Free Democratic Party member. Even the main left and right factions *within* the main parties are often represented on the Court. Once seated, however, the justices are expected to be nonpartisan, delivering their rulings on the basis of complete political independence. The Court is divided into two eight-person "senates," each of which is responsible for specific categories of constitutional issues. The president of the Court presides over the first senate, the vice president over the second. All justices serve a maximum twelve-year term.

In assuming ample powers to interpret the Basic Law, the Federal Constitutional Court broke with a long tradition in German legal theory known as "positivism." That doctrine held that the laws were so clearly written and detailed that they did not need much interpretation by the courts. Germany's judges thus had little latitude to define the scope of the law through interpretative rulings, but were expected to rigidly apply the state's official interpretations. As a consequence, many of them blindly followed the antidemocratic legal strictures laid down by the kaiser's imperial government and, later, by Hitler and the Nazis. In explicitly conferring on the Constitutional Court the responsibility for defending the Basic Law's guarantees of human dignity, liberty, justice, and a number of enumerated human rights, the founders of the Federal Republic wanted a clean break with the past and endowed the court with special responsibilities for defending democracy.

Unlike the U.S. Supreme Court, Germany's Constitutional Court does not hear cases. Instead it is asked to rule on constitutional issues upon the request of the federal government, state governments, or one-third of the members of the Bundestag. Individual citizens may also bring complaints before the Court if they believe their constitutional rights have been violated. The Court itself decides which of these thousands of requests it wishes to adjudicate. Not only does it possess the right to invalidate, approve, or attach conditions to laws already passed; it may also rule on "differences of opinion and doubts" about pending legislation if so requested. Within its vast scope of authority, the Court may rule on jurisdictional disputes between different branches of government and may even rule on sensitive foreign policy matters—areas the U.S. Supreme Court usually avoids on the grounds that they are "political" issues best left to the Congress and the president.

Among the plethora of landmark decisions the Constitutional Court has handed down, one of its most controversial was its invalidation of Germany's 1992 post-unification abortion law, which had departed from the Federal Republic's statute outlawing abortions and adopted East Germany's practice of permitting them. Without banning abortions entirely, the Court called for greater measures to protect the unborn (such as counseling for pregnant women) and abolished funding for abortions through the national health insurance system. In light of this ruling the legislature passed a new law in 1995 permitting abortions in the first trimester but requiring counseling aimed at the "protection of unborn life." The court practically rewrote Germany's campaign financing statues in 1992, ruling in favor of more public funding for campaign expenses and imposing tighter limits on tax-exempt donations. It also rewrote Germany's electoral laws so as to widen the opportunities for the former East Germany to win seats in the Bundestag in the crucial 1990 elections. In other decisions affecting the electoral system, it affirmed the validity of the 5 percent hurdle but struck down legislation permitting foreign residents to vote in state and local elections.

In 1990 the court upheld an artist's right to take liberties with the German flag on grounds of freedom of expression. In 1998 it declined to take up the complaint of a citizen who claimed that his rights were being violated by smokers. Among its foreign policy rulings, the Court upheld the Federal Republic's treaties with the Soviet Union and East-Central Europe in 1973, an issue hotly contested by Christian Democrats, and affirmed the government's decisions to deploy military forces in Somalia and Bosnia in 1993.

The Bundesbank

Another important German state institution is its Federal Bank, the **Bundesbank.** Like so many other institutions in the Federal Republic, it was created with the disastrous experiences of the Weimar Republic and fascism firmly in mind. One of its key features is its considerable independence from the government and parliament. Its freedom of action in dealing with Germany's monetary policy and its ability to influence commercial interest rates is even greater than that of the U.S. Federal Reserve System, the Bank of England, or central banks in most other democracies.

With its headquarters in Frankfurt, the Bundesbank is governed by a seven-member directorate, headed by the Bank's president, and a council. The directorate is appointed by the president of Germany upon the government's recommendation; the council is appointed by regional government bank representatives designated by the Bundesrat. Once appointed, these officials typically act as Germany's guardians of fiscal conservatism, at

times clashing with the chancellor over economic policy. The Bundesbank has a well-deserved reputation for tenaciously combating inflation, a duty it regards as especially important in light of the Weimar Republic's record of devastating inflationary spirals. Keeping inflation down requires a tight lid on the printing of money and, at appropriate times, interest rate hikes aimed at encouraging people to take their money out of circulation by investing it in savings banks. It also requires the government to keep its budget as close to balanced as possible, a policy the Bundesbank heartily endorses. The Bundesbank has been perhaps the most successful central bank in the world over the past several decades in smothering inflationary tendencies (though its critics accuse it of tolerating too much unemployment as a result).

The Bundesbank's international prestige has been so great that Germany's main partners in the European Union have accorded it a leading role in setting conditions for the EU's currency, the euro. Virtually all EU countries have followed its guidelines in pursuing anti-inflationary, budget-trimming policies. Fittingly, the European Central Bank—the EU's supranational organ that supervises the euro—is located in Frankfurt, not far from the Bundesbank.

PARTIES AND POLITICS IN THE FEDERAL REPUBLIC

Building a Democratic Political Culture

The Federal Republic started out in an environment marked by considerable skepticism about democracy. In a public opinion survey taken in 1951, West Germans were asked, "When in this century do you think Germany has been best off?" Perhaps unsurprisingly, only 2 percent named the current period. Barely two years after the formation of the Federal Republic, West Germany was still reeling, economically and psychologically, from the war's devastation. But only 7 percent named the Weimar Republic, Germany's previous democracy. No fewer than 45 percent of the respondents identified the kaiser's empire before the start of World War I in 1914 as Germany's best period, while 42 percent said Germans had lived best under Hitler before the start of World War II

(1933–39). Another survey taken in 1953 asked whether democracy was the best form of government for Germany; only half the respondents said yes. Another survey conducted in these years revealed that more than a third of West Germans would have supported a bid by a new Nazi party to seize power or would have remained indifferent if it occurred. Another third favored restoring the kaiser's monarchy.

Clearly, democracy had to prove itself to most West Germans. Over the course of the late 1950s and 1960s, however, mass attitudes swung overwhelmingly in democracy's favor. By 1970, 90 percent of West Germans said that democracy was the best form of government for Germany. This shift in the country's political culture was no doubt promoted by the Federal Republic's economic successes. Thanks to Marshall Plan assistance from the United States, effective government actions, and the hard work of millions of Germans, the Federal Republic experienced an economic "miracle" that extended from the second half of the 1950s until well into the next decade. Germans in every social class benefited from the boom, including workers at the lower end of the socioeconomic pyramid as well as the large and growing middle class. The West German government's concept of the "social market economy" provided ample room for private enterprise, but it also ensured welfare benefits and social protections for workers and others positioned in the less advantaged rungs of society.

By 1959, 42 percent of survey respondents named the contemporary period as the time when Germans lived best, while support for the Nazi era dwindled to 18 percent. Those identifying the Federal Republic as Germany's best period rose even further over the following years, reaching 62 percent in 1963 and 81 percent in 1970. Nostalgia for Hitler or the kaiser waned dramatically; by 1970 these bygone eras were fading fast in historical memory, esteemed by only 5 percent of the population each as the time when Germans lived best. As older Germans passed from the scene, their children and grandchildren acquired a much greater respect for democracy and the prosperity it had brought them in the postwar period. Some twenty-five years after the end of World War II, not only had West Germany undergone a profound transformation of its political and economic

systems, it had also witnessed one of the most thoroughgoing transformations in political culture ever documented.[36]

The Federal Republic's political institutions have buttressed support for democracy. The Basic Law provides an extensive list of basic civil rights. Article 20 defines the Federal Republic as "a democratic and social federal state" and gives citizens the right to "resist any person or persons seeking to abolish the constitutional order," if no alternative to armed resistance exists. The next article explicitly bans all political parties whose adherents "seek to abolish or impair the free democratic order" or to endanger the Federal Republic's existence. In the 1950s the Federal Constitutional Court upheld the government's right to ban the German Communist Party and a neo-Nazi party on these grounds. Article 9 prohibits any association that is "directed against the constitutional order or the concept of international understanding."

With Germany's dark past providing an ever-present shadow over much of its development, the Federal Republic has managed not only to survive but to thrive. As the following brief outline of its political evolution shows, the Federal Republic has been characterized by considerable political stability, a broad consensus on political and economic fundamentals among its main political parties, and a record of considerable economic achievement over the long term, despite periodic downswings.

The Adenauer Era (1949–63)

Few politicians typified the longing for stability most Germans felt after the war more than **Konrad Adenauer.** Born in 1876, Adenauer was in his early seventies when he was encouraged by Western occupation authorities to assume the leadership of the newly formed Christian Democratic Union. He was one of a small number of conservative politicians untainted by cooperation with the Nazis. As mayor of Cologne from 1917 to Hitler's takeover in 1933, Adenauer had spent the Nazi period in seclusion, tending his rose garden. In his critical role as West Germany's first chancellor, *der Alte* (the old man) exuded a sense of grandfatherly tranquillity, which masked a steely determination to alter the course of Germany's domestic and foreign policies decisively.

Konrad Adenauer

Starting in 1949, Adenauer formed a succession of coalition governments with either the Free Democratic Party or smaller, short-lived groupings such as the German Party or the Free People's Party. Though he favored private enterprise, like many Christian Democrats he also had a strong welfarist orientation, based in Christian doctrine. (Adenauer was Catholic, and the CDU was a confessional—i.e., religiously oriented—party.) Hence he tempered his support for market economics with support for equitable compensation for West German workers and various social welfare guarantees. Although he was a conservative who vigorously opposed the Social Democrats' more radical socialism of the 1950s, Adenauer favored a role for German workers in sharing responsibility with their employers in determining wages, working hours, and other company policies, a concept known as *co-determination* (*Mitbestimmung*). Under his leadership a watered-

down variant of co-determination was instituted in the coal and steel industries.[37]

Adenauer was particularly interested in foreign policy. Though he joined with most other West German politicians in advocating the country's reunification, his first priority was to integrate the Federal Republic firmly into the West, even if it meant renouncing a potential agreement on reunification with the Soviet Union. He therefore formed a close partnership with France, starting with a joint coal and steel community in 1952. West Germany helped form the six-member European Economic Community in 1958 (the forerunner of the European Union), and Adenauer enjoyed a close personal rapport with President Charles de Gaulle. At the same time, Adenauer worked closely with the United States, engineering the creation of a new German army and its integration into NATO in 1955.[38]

It was his success in piloting West Germany's economic revival that won him the most plaudits, however. When he retired from the chancellorship in 1963 at the age of 87, he ceded his place to Ludwig Erhard, the man most responsible for designing the Federal Republic's social market economy. Erhard served three years as chancellor. By the mid-1960s the wind was beginning to go out of the economy's sails. As a recession set in, West Germany's workers, heretofore among the most moderate in Europe when it came to wage demands and strike activity, began to grow restive on seeing their gains in living standards slow down. In an unprecedented move, several Christian Democratic leaders proposed sharing power with their arch-rivals, the Social Democrats, in an effort to head off an economic crisis that might bring unsettling social and political consequences. The result was the Grand Coalition government.

The Grand Coalition (1966–69)

Prior to joining the Grand Coalition cabinet, the Social Democrats went through some major ideological transformations. Under Kurt Schumacher's guidance, the SPD espoused domestic and foreign policies that clashed diametrically with Adenauer's social market economics and his alliance with the United States. Schumacher was a doctrinaire socialist who rejected capitalism in favor of state ownership of productive enterprises and a paramount role for workers' councils in running factories and other places of work. Though he despised communism and refused to collaborate with the Soviets, he was on equally unfriendly terms with the United States. Schumacher was a passionate German nationalist dedicated to reunifying the country in its pre-1938 borders as soon as possible. He fully understood that Adenauer's efforts to integrate the Federal Republic into the West virtually precluded early reunification. Schumacher and the SPD therefore rigorously opposed Germany's postwar rearmament and its adherence to the Atlantic alliance.

Other voices could be heard within the SPD, however, and after Schumacher died in 1952 they became increasingly influential. Recognizing that the majority of West German citizens did not favor the party's socialist orientations and fearing that the party was doomed to garnering little more than a third of the vote unless it changed its tune, the Social Democratic leadership held a special conference in the town of Bad Godesberg in 1959 and made some major doctrinal changes. They formally accepted private enterprise and the market as the underlying bases of the Federal Republic's economy. They agreed to work within the structure of market mechanisms to improve the lot of the working class through non-confrontational measures designed to promote cooperation between business and labor. In essence, the Social Democrats now accepted the "social market economy." They also explicitly renounced their previous anti-religious biases (a stance that derived from Karl Marx's atheistic tendencies) and assured Germany's believers that they would be welcome in the Social Democratic Party. (A number of SPD leaders and numerous followers were devout Protestants.) These changes were followed in 1960 by a decision to accept West Germany's rearmament and its membership in NATO. With the completion of these ideological about-faces, the Social Democrats became acceptable partners in the eyes of most Christian Democrats.[39]

It was one of the most conservative of the Christian Democratic leaders who broached the startling idea of a Grand Coalition: Franz-Josef Strauss, the feisty leader of the Christian Social Union (CSU), the CDU's Bavarian sister party. Strauss reckoned that the SPD might be useful in

taming working-class discontent while the economy righted itself, but he ultimately hoped that the Christian Democrats would get enough credit for the anticipated recovery that the voters would return them to power in the next elections. As things worked out, it was the Social Democrats who stepped forward as the most dynamic partner in the Grand Coalition. The chancellor, Kurt-Georg Kiesinger, was a Christian Democrat; but the chief credit for the economy's rebound went to the Social Democratic finance minister, Kurt Schiller.

Perhaps the most prominent member of the cabinet was another Social Democrat, Foreign Minister **Willy Brandt.** Brandt had fled Germany during the Hitler years, adopting Norwegian citizenship. Though his anti-Nazi credentials were above reproach, some Germans on the right considered him a traitor to the fatherland. Brandt made a rapid rise up the SPD's leadership ranks after the war, serving as mayor of West Berlin in 1961 at the time the wall was built. Like many other Social Democrats, Brandt was revolted at the nation's division and longed to see Germany restored to unity in a peaceful, democratic Europe. As foreign minister he undertook some new initiatives to entice the communist countries of East-Central Europe to consider the possibility of peaceful unification, but his forays came to naught. The Soviet Union made it clear that it would not let Poland, Czechoslovakia, or other states under its control take any action on Germany's status independently of Moscow.

In 1969, the Grand Coalition ran its course as the electoral cycle mandated elections to a new Bundestag. Though the tally was close, the SPD managed to form a "small coalition" with the Free Democrats thanks to a tenuous twelve-vote majority over the Christian Democrats. Brandt became chancellor and Walter Scheel, the FDP's reform-minded leader, became foreign minister.

Brandt in Power (1969–74)

With Brandt's ascendancy, the West German government embarked on its most active pursuit of unification since the founding of the Federal Republic. While keeping the Federal Republic firmly planted in NATO and West European supranational institutions, Brandt devised a new "eastern policy" *(Ostpolitik)* that directly approached the Soviet Union and engaged the East German leadership in face-to-face negotiations, steps regarded as heresy by previous West German governments. In 1970 his government concluded a "renunciation of force" agreement with the Soviets, pledging to resolve all disputes peacefully. Similar treaties followed with communist Poland and Czechoslovakia. All these treaties were consciously aimed at proving West Germany's commitment to reconciliation with the nations Hitler's Germany had brutalized during the war. The SPD-FDP coalition's ulterior motive was to convince the USSR and its allies in the region that they had nothing to fear from a peace-loving, united German state.

Brandt fully assumed that, even with these agreements, Germany's reunification was a long way off, perhaps decades away. In the interval he sought immediate relief for the thousands of German families on either side of the Berlin wall and the inter-German frontier who were forcibly separated by a very real iron curtain. East Germany's hard-line communist leadership intensely resisted making major concessions to the West Germans, but under Soviet pressure they relented. In 1972 the two German states agreed to a sweeping set of new regulations that greatly facilitated the ability of West Berliners and other West Germans to visit East Germany. (Alas, East Germans did not win any substantial new rights from their government to visit West Germany.) In yet another set of negotiations, the USSR came to terms with the United States, Britain, and France in formally guaranteeing unhindered passage on the access routes between West Germany proper and West Berlin, thereby removing a source of dangerous frictions.

For these efforts, Brandt won the Nobel Peace Prize in 1971. His place in history was assured the following year when his treaties passed muster in the Bundestag, narrowly surviving the opposition of the Christian Democrats and a few defectors from the governing coalition parties. (The Federal Constitutional Court affirmed their constitutionality.) Brandt's political luster did not last very long, however. In 1974 it was revealed that an East German spy was working on his staff; the spy's wife was also nabbed for espionage. Though Brandt

Willy Brandt kneels at the memorial commemorating the victims of Nazi atrocities in Warsaw's Jewish ghetto, 1970. Brandt was the first West German chancellor to visit Poland after the Nazi occupation.

had been unaware of their true identity, he took responsibility for the mishap and resigned.[40]

Schmidt's Governments (1974–82)

Brandt's successor was **Helmut Schmidt,** a Social Democrat with a razor-sharp intellect and special expertise in economics and defense policy. Schmidt acquired his fairly conservative version of Social Democratic ideology during the war, through contacts with Labour Party members while he was a prisoner of war in British captivity. He assumed office at a time when his financial skills were critically challenged. In 1973, the world's leading oil producing nations quadrupled the price of oil, triggering a global economic crisis. The United States, Western Europe, and Japan sputtered into recession and suffered an unusual combination of diminishing growth and high inflation, a phenomenon dubbed *stagflation.* Oil prices edged up even higher throughout the decade, only to double again in 1979. As the leader of the SPD's right wing, Schmidt favored relatively austere budget-tightening policies designed to dampen inflation. He also maintained close ties with the leaders of West Germany's trade unions,

Helmut Schmidt

traditionally the SPD's most reliable supporters, and with leading members of the business community, a connection reinforced by the business-oriented Free Democrats. These consultations paid off, as the unions kept their wage demands within limits and big business strove to maintain production, holding unemployment in check. While inflation rates in other countries spiraled into double-digits, the Federal Republic held the line at about 7 percent. It also enjoyed a peaceful labor environment, with few strikes.

Schmidt's attempts to hold the line on government spending did not sit well with the SPD's left wing, which favored higher spending on social welfare. The party's youth organization, the Young Socialists, or Jusos (yuzos), favored even more radical policies aimed at imposing higher taxes on corporations and wealthy individuals and redistributing the nation's wealth to ensure greater socioeconomic equality. (Future Chancellor Gerhard Schroeder was the head of the Jusos from 1978 to 1980, and certain members of his cabinet were Jusos during these years.) Though Schmidt spurned these suggestions, he was under considerable pressure to provide more assistance to the SPD's working-class and lower-middle-class electorate.

Schmidt's defense policies provoked even greater consternation within the party's left-wing ranks. In the late 1970s the Soviet Union racheted up the arms race by installing a new generation of guided missiles, equipped with deadly nuclear warheads, within minutes of West German territory. Schmidt responded by convincing the United States and other NATO partners to develop new counter-missiles of their own in an effort to get the Soviets to reach an agreement that would restore the nuclear balance in Europe at lower levels of

missile deployments. In 1979 NATO agreed to start developing its counter-weapons, some of which would be based on West Germany's densely populated territory. The NATO decision unleashed one of the most virulent crises of the Cold War. It also touched off a wave of protest within West Germany, as hundreds of thousands of people took to the streets in large demonstrations against the missiles. The effects of the crisis were particularly tumultuous inside the Social Democratic Party, as left-wingers—like Schroeder—and a growing number of moderates joined the opposition to Schmidt's counter-missile scheme. Schmidt himself became increasingly isolated within his own party.[41]

Conflict with his coalition partners, the Free Democrats, exacerbated Schmidt's difficulties. Although the FDP maintained its governing coalition with the Social Democrats during the 1980 elections, within a year the two parties were squabbling over economic policy. While Schmidt wanted to stimulate economic growth through Keynesian methods by cutting taxes for average taxpayers and raising government spending, however modestly, the Free Democrats preferred deeper cuts in welfare spending and tax breaks focused on the business sector. The FDP's leader, Foreign Minister Hans-Dietrich Genscher, was also worried that the SPD's internal splits might weaken Schmidt's resolve to deploy the new NATO missiles. He also feared that the FDP itself might fall below the 5 percent hurdle unless it took drastic steps to solidify its image.

In a reversal of alliances, the FDP in the fall of 1982 announced that it was withdrawing from Schmidt's government and was prepared to form a new governing coalition with the Chistian Democrats. The FDP's strategic location in the center of the West German political spectrum, squarely in between the Christian Democrats to its right and the Social Democrats to its left, enabled this party to be the indispensable partner in a string of coalition governments starting in the earliest years of the Federal Republic. In spite of averaging only about 12 percent of the vote, the FDP contributed dozens of cabinet ministers to West German governments and had an impact on the country's domestic and foreign policies that far exceeded its small following. Its maneuverability proved effective once again, as its turnabout in 1982 caused

Schmidt's government to lose a constructive vote of confidence in the Bundestag. It was immediately replaced by a new coalition consisting of the Christian Democrats and the Free Democrats. Genscher retained his post as foreign minister, and the chancellorship passed to one of the most devoted leaders of the CDU, **Helmut Kohl**.

PROFILE: Helmut Kohl

"Dear fellow citizens!" At those simple words, thousands of East Germans who had gathered in front of a church in Dresden broke out into spontaneous cheers. They had just heard the chancellor of the Federal Republic of Germany directly address them as though they were citizens of the same country. The moving scene took place in December 1989, scarcely more than a month after the opening of the Berlin wall. In what has been described as the best speech of his career, Helmut Kohl repeatedly used the terms "we" and "our" when speaking to the crowd, assuring them of his commitment to achieving the unification of the two Germanies. Within less than a year, his promise was fulfilled.

Kohl's historic reputation as "the chancellor of German unity" represented an unexpected personal triumph for a politician whose career had been all but written off as finished on more than one occasion. An unprepossessing man who lacked Adenauer's stature, Brandt's charisma, or Schmidt's intellectual acuity, Kohl repeatedly rebounded from defeat and turned out to be the Federal Republic's longest-serving head of government.

Helmut Kohl

Born in the Rhineland in 1930, Kohl grew up in a Catholic and staunchly anti-Nazi household, the son of a civil servant. He was too young for military service during the war, but was forced to endure the regimentation of Hitler's youth movement. His eighteen-year-old brother was killed in action and his father was pressed into military service in his fifties. In later years, Kohl would say that he had been blessed with "the grace of late birth," meaning that he was too young to have been implicated in the misdeeds of Nazi Germany. Soon after the war ended, young Helmut embarked on his lifelong political path. He joined the newly established Christian Democratic Union at the age of sixteen. The following year he showed precocious signs of his dedication to European integration when he co-founded a group called "Europe-Union." While studying law and completing a doctoral dissertation over the following years, Kohl rapidly advanced up the ladder of the CDU party organization in his home state, the Rhineland-Palatinate. In 1969 he was elected the state's minister-president, its highest office. Kohl's noteriety in national politics rose apace. In the same year he was elected the CDU's deputy chairman at the party's national congress. He also served as a member of the Bundestag.

In his first major setback, in 1971 Kohl lost a bid to become chairman of the CDU, its most important position. Luckily for him, the post was open again only two years later, and Kohl won the job with 520 votes out of 600 cast by the CDU professionals and activists authorized to elect the party chief. Traditionally, the CDU chairman is the Christian Democrats' candidate for chancellor in the next elections. In 1976, Kohl's leadership brought the Christian Democrats to within a few seats of an absolute majority in the Bundestag; but their showing was not enough to unseat the SPD-FDP coalition government led by Chancellor Helmut Schmidt. Kohl planned to try again for the chancellorship in 1980. However, he lost out in a leadership struggle to Franz-Josef Strauss, the Bavarian CSU chief who was his chief rival within the Christian Democratic movement. With the aggressively conservative Strauss at the head of the CDU/CSU ticket, the Christian Democrats suffered a serious decline at the polls and Schmidt's SDP-FDP government once again returned to power.

At this point Kohl and the Christian Democrats appeared to be at their lowest ebb. But the Free Democrats' decision to pull out of their coalition with the Social Democrats gave them an unanticipated opening. As the FDP switched partners, Kohl was elected chancellor by the Bundestag on October 1, 1982. He then arranged for snap elections to be held six months later so that the public could render its verdict on the new government, which was not the one the majority of voters had elected in 1980. The Christian Democrats and their FDP allies won a solid Bundestag majority, ensuring their government's survival.

From 1982 until 1998, Chancellor Kohl played a criti-cal role in some of the most pathbreaking events of the postwar era. One of his first decisions was to go ahead with the controversial deployment of the new NATO missiles in Germany starting in 1983, in spite of sub-stantial public opposition. The Soviet Union strenu-ously objected to the deployments, but in 1985 a new leadership team under Mikhail Gorbachev took power in the Kremlin. Kohl and Gorbachev soon struck up a close working relationship that blossomed into a real friendship. Their mutual respect and common desire for an end to Cold War tensions made a vital contribu-tion to improving the NATO alliance's ties with the USSR. In a startling turnabout, Gorbachev and the NATO countries agreed in 1987 to dismantle and de-stroy all the intermediate range missiles they had just installed in the European area over the previous ten years, removing in one bold stroke a major source of East-West frictions. The Kohl-Gorbachev connection also smoothed the way to improvements in Bonn's ties with the German Democratic Republic. Kohl met on several occasions with East German leaders, and his government agreed to provide East Germany with vari-ous forms of economic assistance in exchange for con-cessions facilitating people-to-people contacts and bor-der crossings between the two Germanies.

While pursuing better ties with the Federal Repub-lic's eastern neighbors, Kohl took major steps to solidify relations with its western allies. He accorded special at-tention to France, meeting on a regular basis with Presi-dent François Mitterrand, another trusted interlocutor. He played a leading role in boosting West European in-tegration by putting Germany's weight behind such measures as the Single European Act of 1986, which set the groundwork for a common market among the mem-ber states, and the Treaty of Maastricht of 1992, which led to the euro and the European Central Bank later in the decade. Kohl also got on well with the three Ameri-can presidents whose administrations coincided with his years in office. His relationship with President Rea-gan survived a delicate controversy in 1985, when Rea-gan agreed to go ahead with a scheduled visit to a war cemetery in Bitburg even after it was disclosed that for-mer Nazi storm troopers were buried there. (Kohl was not aware of the Nazi grave sites when the visit was planned, but he urged Reagan not to cancel the trip de-spite vocal objections on both sides of the Atlantic.) Kohl was in Reagan's presence in West Berlin in 1987 when the American president rhetorically addressed the Soviet leadership with the appeal, "Mr. Gorbachev, tear down this wall!" Kohl's ties with President Bush as-sumed a special importance during the complicated ne-gotiations leading to Germany's unification. Kohl also

enjoyed friendly ties with President Clinton, treating him on one visit to a favorite Rhineland delicacy, stuffed pig gut.

It was Kohl's center-stage role in the unification process, however, that proved his greatest triumph. Like many Germans, the chancellor was initially taken aback by the unanticipated opening of the inter-German bor-ders in November 1989. His first reaction was a ten-point program that envisaged a carefully phased process of co-operation between the two Germanies over a ten-year period. But the plan was quickly overtaken by a wave of popular pressure in East Germany for immediate unifi-cation, which occurred a year later. Kohl's bonds with Gorbachev were critical in winning the Soviet leader's acceptance of the newly united Germany's membership in NATO. His ties with Mitterrand and other European leaders served to allay the fears of many Europeans that an enlarged Germany would be so powerful that it would seek to dominate the region. Kohl assured them that his aim was "a European Germany, not a German Europe." In pursuing his foreign policy initiatives, Kohl worked closely with two successive FDP foreign minis-ters, Hans-Dietrich Genscher and Klaus Kinkel.

In December 1990, Kohl led the CDU-FDP coalition to a resounding victory in the first Bundestag elections to be held in unified Germany. The chancellor had con-vincingly portrayed himself during the campaign as an enthusiastic champion of unification, and the CDU did exceptionally well in East Germany. His opponent, the SPD's Oskar Lafontaine, spent the campaign warning of the costs and other potential problems of integrating eastern Germany into the Federal Republic, giving the impression that his support for reunification itself was weak. As it happened, Kohl had to recognize after being reinstated as chancellor that reunification would cost much more money than he had led the voters to believe. His campaign promises of "blossoming landscapes" in East Germany proved embarrassingly unrealistic during the arduous post-unification decade.

In his next term Kohl made major efforts to consult with Germany's state governments, business associa-tions, trade unions, and even the Social Democrats in an effort to build as large a consensus as possible on bearing the costs of modernizing eastern Germany's economy. (The implications of these efforts for Ger-many's neo-corporatist system are discussed later in this chapter.) But rising discontent in both parts of Germany fostered by the consequences of unification led many political analysts to predict Kohl's defeat in the 1994 elections. Once again, however, he con-founded the doomsayers. Kohl's simple manner res-onated with millions of middle-class German voters, and the Christian Democrats and Free Democrats eked out a narrow Bundestag majority. In 1994 Kohl was elected chancellor for the fifth time, albeit by the slender margin of 338 to 333 Bundestag members.

Kohl's next four-year term was marked by continuing efforts to build up the east German economy while contending with mounting unemployment, exploding social welfare costs, and a troubling loss of economic dynamism. It was also highlighted by his government's indispensable role in guiding the process of monetary union among qualified members of the European Union. With a mixed record of achievements and difficulties, the embattled Kohl went before the voters once again in 1998, only to lose out to a new coalition consisting of the Social Democrats and the Greens. After sixteen years at the helm of the Federal Republic, the chancellor of German unity stepped down.[42]

Taking his place in the ranks of the Bundestag opposition parties, Kohl found himself at the center of controversy once again as the decade came to a close. After investigations revealed that various contributors had provided large sums of cash to the Christian Democrats illegally, Kohl admitted that he had operated a secret party slush fund the entire time he was chancellor and had accepted $1 million in illegal campaign contributions from sources he refused to identify. But in testi-mony before a parliamentary committee in June 2000, Kohl vehemently denied providing favors in exchange for money. He also denied allegations that former French President François Mitterrand had funneled millions to Kohl's 1994 election campaign in appreciation for Kohl's help in arranging the sale of an east German oil refinery to a French company. Despite these denials, an official investigation found that computer files relating to a variety of alleged illegal payments to Kohl and his party had been systematically destroyed before he left office. "I have no knowledge of any bribery," Kohl protested. But the image of the "chancellor of German unity" was already badly tarnished.

The SPD-Green Coalition

The formation of the SPD-Green coalition following the September 1998 elections broke new ground in German politics. It marked the ascendancy of Germany's postwar generation to the highest rungs of power. Gerhard Schroeder, the new chancellor, was born in 1944. He belongs to a generation that grew up in a democratic country,

TABLE 18.5

Governments of the Federal Republic of Germany			
Governing Coalition	Chancellor (Party)	Came to Power Following . . .	Opposing Chancellor Candidate (Party)
CDU/CSU, FDP, DP[1]	Adenauer (CDU)	Elections, 1949	Schumacher (SPD)
CDU/CSU, FDP, DP, G[2]	Adenauer	Elections, 1953	Ollenhauer (SPD)
CDU/CSU, FDP, DP/FVP[3]	Adenauer	Elections, 1957	Ollenhauer
CDU/CSU, FDP	Adenauer	Elections, 1961	Brandt (SPD)
CDU/CSU, FDP	Erhard (CDU)	Adenauer retirement, 1963	
CDU/CSU, FDP	Erhard	Elections, 1965	Brandt
CDU/CSU, SPD	Kiesinger (CDU)	Coalition change, 1966	
SPD, FDP	Brandt (SPD)	Elections, 1969	Kiesinger (CDU)
SPD, FDP	Brandt	Elections, 1972	Barzel (CDU)
SPD, FDP	Schmidt (SPD)	Brandt resignation, 1974	
SPD, FDP	Schmidt	Elections, 1976	Kohl (CDU)
SPD, FDP	Schmidt	Elections, 1980	Strauss (CSU)
CDU/CSU, FDP	Kohl (CDU)	Coalition change, no-confidence vote, 1982	
CDU/CSU, FDP	Kohl	Elections, 1983	Vogel (SPD)
CDU/CSU, FDP	Kohl	Elections, 1987	Rau (SPD)
CDU/CSU, FDP	Kohl	Elections, 1990	Lafontaine (SPD)
CDU/CSU, FDP	Kohl	Elections, 1994	Scharping (SPD)
SPD, Greens	Schroeder (SPD)	Elections, 1998	Kohl

[1]DP = *Deutsche Partei* (German Party)
[2]G = All-German bloc
[3]FVP = *Freie Volkspartei* (Free People's Party)
Source: Muenster Statistical Office.

bearing no guilt for the collapse of democracy in the Weimar period or the crimes of Nazism. Joschka Fischer, the Greens' principal leader, was born in 1948. Precisely how these generational realities will affect German politics and the conduct of foreign policy has been the subject of intense speculation. Conceivably, a generation untainted by fascism may be less reluctant to assert Germany's national interests in world affairs than were its predecessors, who generally refrained from appearing excessively nationalistic. But such a resurgence of national assertiveness need not occur. Germany's new leaders—especially Social Democrats and Greens—may retain a basic aversion to displays of national self-interest or independence from Germany's allies in NATO and the European Union. Their vital contribution to NATO's Kosovo operations appear to confirm the latter tendency.

Another pathbreaking aspect of the red-green coalition government is its ideological coloration. After sixteen years of conservative rule under Helmut Kohl, the torch of power passed to a group of individuals whose past political activism marked them as the most left-leaning leaders the Federal Republic has yet seen. Will their leftist inclinations result in abrupt departures from established economic and social policies? The ideological turnabouts of Gerhard Schroeder suggest otherwise.

PROFILE: Gerhard Schroeder

"I am not 'center'," Gerhard Schroeder wrote in 1986. "I am left, and I will remain so. The center is an imaginary idea—and I regard the SPD as a party that is to the left of this imaginary idea." Twelve years later, addressing the party congress that would nominate him as the SPD's candidate for chancellor, he quoted Willy Brandt's admonition, "Whoever wants to obtain a majority and power in Germany must win over the center." Pledging himself to building a "new center," Schroeder succeeded in restoring the Social Democrats to power for the first time since the collapse of Helmut Schmidt's government in 1980.

Fatefully, it was Schmidt who was responsible for attracting Schroeder to the Social Democratic party in the first place. His eloquence and effectiveness as a minister in the Hamburg government in the early 1960s inspired the nineteen-year-old's admiration and gave his politi-

Gerhard Schroeder stands before banner proclaiming, "Germany United Fatherland".

cal instincts direction. Though still pursuing his high school diploma, Schroeder was already politically active and driven by an intense determination to succeed. A difficult childhood fueled these ambitions. Though he was born at the tail end of the Hitler era, he did not entirely escape the war's ravaging effects: his father was killed in battle only a few days after his birth. Raised by a loving mother who needed welfare assistance to supplement her earnings as a cleaning lady, Gerhard grew up in extreme poverty. With his stepfather hospitalized with tuberculosis, he had to assume family responsibilities for his mother and sisters at an early age. He dropped out of school at age fourteen and went to work as a sales clerk, a decision that usually relegated impoverished Germans to a lifetime of menial jobs. But Schroeder was determined to pursue his education; he attended night school and managed to earn his high school baccalaureate degree *(Abitur)* with a view to studying law.

The hardships of his youth also provided a powerful stimulus to get involved in politics. "My past, of which I am very proud, helped me find my way," Schroeder later confided. "I wanted to improve my situation. But I didn't want to do it so much for myself; I wanted it for others. And that's why I went into politics."

After completing his law studies at the University of Goettingen, thanks in part to scholarships from a foundation with ties to the Social Democrats, Schroeder achieved notoriety as a leftist lawyer willing to take on controversial cases involving former terrorists, gay pastors, and political activists who had run afoul of the law. In all these cases his aim was not to defend illegal activity but to make sure that people were not denied their constitutional rights just because they were viewed as political extremists.

Germany experienced a sudden outpouring of leftist activism in the late 1960s and early 1970s, as Marxist-oriented students shook the foundations of the country's postwar passivity and challenged the sacred cows of the Federal Republic's political establishment: capitalism, the NATO alliance, and a silent refusal to subject the Nazi past to a critical examination. The more radical elements formed an "extra-parliamentary opposition" that demanded an end to capitalism and a fundamental (though vaguely formulated) transformation of the Federal Republic's political institutions. The Social Democratic Party's youth organization—the Jusos—was caught up in this generational movement, and Schroeder was a member of its left wing. From the outset, however, he was more interested in practical politics than in Marxist theory, and he had nothing to do with the violent proclivities of the most extreme radicals.

Still, he took an active part in denouncing capitalism, the Vietnam war, and Germany's decision to install new NATO missiles in response to the Soviet missile buildup of the late 1970s. The latter issue brought him into direct conflict with Chancellor Schmidt, the principal architect of the NATO policy. In 1978, just as the missile issue was provoking mass demonstrations and heated debate, Schroeder was elected chairman of the Jusos. Though Schmidt had been his youthful role model, Schroeder took part in the SPD's internal revolt against him over the missile issue, a revolt that so weakened Schmidt's government that it fell apart in 1980, bringing Helmut Kohl to power. Schmidt felt so betrayed by his party that he never attended another SPD congress until 1998, when he was ready to embrace a significantly more moderate Gerhard Schroeder as party leader.

In 1980, Schroeder won his first election to the Bundestag, where he cut a youthful figure clad in a sweater rather than the standard suit and tie. From his earliest days in elective office, he was resolved to become chancellor. With this ultimate prize firmly in mind, he ran as the SPD's candidate for minister-president of the state of Lower Saxony in 1986, shocking the party's established leaders by calling for the elimination of Germany's nuclear power plants after the Chernobyl disaster in the Soviet Union. Though the SPD lost the election, Schroeder's nuclear position brought him closer to the Greens at a time when the idea of SPD-Green collaboration was still contested inside both parties. Four years later, he led the SPD to a plurality in Lower Saxony and forged a coalition government with the Greens. In two subsequent elections, in 1994 and 1998, Schroeder led the Social Democrats to victory in Lower Saxony, enabling the party to govern the state without coalition partners. It was in these years, as the chief of one of Germany's most populous states, that Schroeder made his

mark as an effective leader—a "doer"—and moderated his views, winning the confidence of key members of the business community. He looked back on the anti-capitalist leanings of his Young Socialist days as a period of "cluelessness."

Schroeder did not shrink from controversial positions, however. In 1990, as Germans indulged in the euphoria of unification, he joined with the party's new leader, Oskar Lafontaine, in warning of the serious economic and social costs of too rapid a unification process. Both leaders saw to it that their respective Bundesrat delegations voted against the unification treaty, a decision that was widely perceived as a vote against unification itself. Lafontaine and the SPD went down to a crushing defeat to Kohl's Christian Democrats in the post-unification Bundestag elections, in large measure because of their lukewarm support for the unification process.

After losing a bid for the SPD leadership to Rudolf Sharping in 1993, Shroeder won the party's overwhelming endorsement in 1998, just a few months before the impending Bundestag elections. Describing himself as a man of the middle and buoyed by the previous year's success of Tony Blair in Britain, he vowed to govern from the center. His success in leading the Social Democrats into a governing coalition with the Greens marked the culmination of a long process of political self-definition and a restless quest for power for a man from humble origins.[43]

It also marked a turbulent new beginning in Schroeder's career. No sooner did he take up his post as chancellor when the accumulated problems of the German economy shook his government to the core. Schroeder entered office with a mixture of neo-liberal views favoring private sector expansion and traditional Social Democratic positions favoring an active role for government in fostering education, research, technology development, and social justice for the less advantaged. The new chancellor was also looking for ways to tame the uncontrolled forces of globalization through international agreements that would stabilize financial investments and discourage investors from rapidly pulling massive amounts of money out of countries whose economies are at risk. His finance minister and old political ally, Oskar Lafontaine, shared most of these views but favored larger infusions of government spending as a means to boosting overall demand and eventually reducing unemployment, a classic Keynesian recipe.

Several months after the Schroeder government went to work, a group of influential German business leaders warned the chancellor that they would shift their investments out of the country unless he took decisive action to lower hourly labor costs, which were among the highest in the world, reduce corporate tax burdens, and take other measures to provide a more profitable business environment. Schroeder indicated his willingness to go along with these ideas, whereupon Lafontaine quit the government and launched a broadside attack on Schroeder's policies.[44] The feud split the SPD and deprived Schroeder of a solid basis of party support. With his popularity ratings falling amid perceptions of drift and indecisiveness, Schroeder formulated a package of economic measures in the fall of 1999 that was bound to sharpen the debate.

Joschka Fischer and the Greens

Joschka Fischer, the foreign minister, has undergone political transformations of his own. Fischer joined the Greens in 1982, only a few years after the party was founded. The Greens emerged in the late 1970s as an outgrowth of several citizens movements, known generically as *new social movements,* that took up the causes of environmentalism, women's rights, and other issues that, in their view, were not being properly addressed by the mainstream parties and interest groups. The people who formed the Greens were particularly concerned with preserving a green environment: they focused special attention on Germany's nuclear power plants and on the presence of American nuclear weapons on German territory. The United States had begun stationing nuclear weapons in the Federal Republic in the 1950s, and the prospect of still more nuclear-armed missiles in the Soviet-

NATO arms race of the late 1970s and 1980s provoked an outpouring of pacifist sentiment among the Greens and their followers.

Led initially by a group of young people that included Petra Kelly, whose father was American, the Greens appealed mainly to younger (under thirty-five), educated, middle-class voters with post-materialist values. They scored their first electoral successes in 1981 and 1982, winning seats in several state legislatures. In 1983 they cleared the 5 percent hurdle and sent their first delegates to the Bundestag. Dressed casually in sandals and jeans, Green deputies stood out in striking contrast to the more traditionally attired political establishment, creating a scene that highlighted the country's political and generational diversity.

But the Greens themselves were not immune to differences of viewpoint within their own ranks. Two wings split the party. The "fundamentalists" (dubbed *Fondis*) tended to oppose industrialization per se as ecologically threatening; they also opposed coalescing with the Social Democrats. The "realists" (*Realos*) favored tighter environmental safeguards without dismantling German industry and spoke in favor of cooperating with like-minded Social Democrats in state and local governments (and, potentially, at the national level). In 1985 the realists won a tactical victory as they led the party into a governing coalition with the SPD in the state of Hesse. But the fundamentalists made a comeback the following year when the Chernobyl nuclear power plant explosion in the Soviet Ukraine stoked public anxieties. In 1986 the Greens' platform called for the liquidation of all of West Germany's nuclear energy plants and its immediate withdrawal from NATO. Carrying these ideas to the voters in the Bundestag elections of 1987, the Greens raised their vote to 8.3 percent.

The sudden unification of Germany in 1989–90 caught the Greens unprepared for the emotional outburst of national sentiment that accompanied the opening of the Berlin wall and the collapse of East Germany. Most Greens abhorred nationalistic displays, and their delegates refused to join in the singing of the national anthem that spontaneously broke out in the Bundestag when word came on November 9, 1989, that the East German authorities were prepared to open the borders. One Green leader suggested that the massive surge of East Germans across the newly opened borders was

Joschka Fischer

motivated by nothing more than a desire to purchase bananas and other comestibles not readily available in East Germany. When the treaties formalizing Germany's unification came up for a vote, the Green delegation voted against them. These anti-unification positions were not shared by most Green voters, however, and in the 1990 Bundestag elections the Greens fell below the 5 percent hurdle (4.8 percent in West Germany and 3.9 percent overall), losing its representation in the lower house.[45]

Following this defeat, Joschka Fischer led the realist wing in taking control of the party. The Greens came around to accepting Germany's unification and formed a merger with Alliance '90, one of the citizens groups opposed to communist rule that had helped spearhead the revolution in East Germany. The Greens also accepted NATO. Fischer himself abandoned his initial opposition to German participation in NATO military activities in the Balkans after a visit to mass grave sites in Bosnia. When the possibility arose in 1998 to enter the national government for the first time as a coalition partner of the Social Democrats, Fischer and other Green leaders hammered out a common governing program with Schroeder and the SPD. It unequivocally affirmed Germany's attachments to NATO and the European Union, called for a major overhaul of the country's finances, and pledged "to get out of atomic energy as quickly as possible," with "irreversible" legislation to this effect to be passed during the legislature's four-year tenure. During the Kosovo crisis of 1999, Fischer emphatically backed the NATO air campaign.

But the Greens remain internally divided on a number of issues, and their leaders do not always see eye-to-eye with Chancellor Schroeder. Several Green members of the Bundestag openly condemned the NATO air war over Kosovo. Differences divide Greens from the former West Germany from those who come from East Germany over such issues as trials for former East German communist leaders and cooperation with the Party of Democratic Socialism, the successor of the former communist party of the German Democratic Republic. East German Greens generally take a more outspokenly anti-communist position than do their western counterparts. Finally, many Greens are disappointed at Schroeder's decision to postpone into the distant future a decision to decommission Germany's nineteen nuclear power plants. Whether the red-green coalition would survive until the next Bundestag elections, set for 2002, was thus an open question.

NEO-CORPORATISM AND GERMANY'S POLITICAL ECONOMY

As we've observed, one of the most striking differences between Germany's postwar democracy and the disastrous Weimar Republic was the determination of the country's elites after World War II to strive for consensus on major political, economic, and social issues. The founders of the Federal Republic not only came to terms on the constitutional principles codified in the Basic Law; over time they also forged a consensus on the nature of the economy and social justice. Over the course of the 1960s and 1970s, the Federal Republic's elites enhanced the cooperative aspects of their economic system by anchoring it in a decision-making process known as *neo-corporatism.*

As explained in chapter 11, **corporatism** *is a form of formal interest-group representation in the state's decision-making processes.* The form of corporatism that developed in West Germany after World War II was democratic in nature and featured several elements sufficiently distinct from other forms of corporatism that it came to be labeled __neo-corporatism.__

The basic idea is simple: representatives of the main business associations and trade unions—known as "peak associations"—sit down with government officials on a regular basis and map out the main lines of the country's economic and social welfare policies. Wage parameters, working conditions, paid vacation time, welfare benefits, profit margins—these and other labor-management issues are heavily influenced, and often largely determined, by these tripartite negotiations. The aims of corporatism in a democracy are to widen participation in the economic decision-making process and to reinforce socioeconomic stability by giving everyone a sense of where the economy should be heading over the coming year or so.

The Social Democrats, the main party of the working class, were particularly supportive of neo-corporatist mechanisms and expanded their scope when leading the federal government in the 1970s. They have been especially sensitive to the demands of the **German Federation of Labor**

(*Deutscher Gewerkschaftsbund,* or **DGB**), the large peak association of the labor movement that consists of sixteen major trade unions and has some 8 million members. At the time, even Christian Democrats and Free Democrats went along with neo-corporatism, since their backers in the business community benefited from the system's virtual guarantee of a productive work force, moderate wage demands, and few strikes. These parties have close ties with peak associations representing big business (such as the **Federation of German Industry,** or **BDI**) as well as those representing smaller businesses and agricultural interests.[46]

In contrast to the stormy business-labor relationships that rocked Britain, France, and other European countries in the 1970s, the Federal Republic was an island of labor peace in that decade. But in the 1980s, after Helmut Kohl became chancellor, the government began backing away from corporatist procedures, preferring instead to rely on market forces to work themselves out without undue state interference. To some extent the coalition parties, which enjoyed strong support from the business community, were influenced by the free-market doctrines of Margaret Thatcher and Ronald Reagan, though they did not go quite so far in attacking the principle of government involvement in the economy.

Once the Berlin wall opened and German reunification suddenly presented itself as an unanticipated reality, many observers predicted that neo-corporatism would make even further retreats, possibly disappearing entirely under a host of new problems. The neo-corporatist patterns of cooperation and consultation, they hypothesized, would increasingly give way to sharp conflicts between western Germany and eastern Germany, between business and labor, and between the competing political parties. Has this hypothesis proven correct?

HYPOTHESIS-TESTING EXERCISE: Neo-Corporatism in Germany

HYPOTHESIS

According to the hypothesis, unification should cause a decline in neo-corporatist decision-making procedures in Germany.

VARIABLES

The **dependent variable** is Germany's *neo-corporatist decision-making procedures.* On what is it dependent? The hypothesis identifies the *unification* of West and East Germany as the **independent variable** that is presumably having an effect on neo-corporatism, causing it to decline or even die out.

EXPECTATIONS

Proponents of the hypothesis expected a number of things to happen as a result of the unification process. Among other consequences, they believed that the collapse of East Germany's economy would create major frictions between business and labor. With large numbers of East German workers thrown out of work by the liquidation of defunct communist-era enterprises, most of them would be forced to work for less money than West German workers. West German businesses would then rush into East Germany to take advantage of the cheaper labor costs, perhaps depriving West Germans of their jobs. Trade unions would militate for fairer treatment of workers in both parts of Germany. It was also expected that these sharpening business-labor tensions would spill over into party politics: the pro-business Christian Democrats and Free Democrats could be expected to take the private sector's side, while the Social Democrats and the Party of Democratic Socialism would support the workers. Extremist parties of left and right might polarize the political system even further by playing upon the public's anxieties and animosities. Interparty cooperation, an important element of German neo-corporatism, would therefore disintegrate.

Under these circumstances, prophets of corporatism's demise also expected Kohl's government to be even less inclined than in the past to mediate these disputes. Rather, they expected his government to deal with the problems of unification by trying to impose its own solutions on the labor movement and on the opposition parties as well as on the five new East German states, which would be too poor and weak to exert much influence. The final result, according to these observers, would be less corporatist consultation and a greater centralization of power in the hands of Kohl's government. They further believed that Germany's central government would not even consult with the country's state governments as much as it had in the past.

EVIDENCE

As an insightful study has shown,[47] labor tensions definitely grew in both eastern and western Germany as unemployment followed in the wake of unification. However, the consequences were just the opposite of those predicted by exponents of the hypothesis. Instead of centralizing its power and taking a solidly pro-business stance, the Kohl government actually reinforced corporatist practices. Once it became clear that the economic costs of unification were going to be higher than Kohl had anticipated, and once eastern German Christian Democrats convinced the chancellor that their party would lose votes if they did not address eastern Germany's discontented population, Kohl moved to achieve a broad consensus on a "solidarity pact" that would siphon large sums of money to the east's troubled economy. Between September 1992 and March 1993, no fewer than forty meetings took place in Kohl's office alone as the government made an energetic effort to find common ground among Germany's main economic interest groups, party leaders, and state governments.

Instead of taking a uniformly pro-business stance, Kohl convinced the leaders of several of Germany's leading business associations to provide funds for the eastern German economy and to buy capital equipment from east German factories so as to keep them operating as long as possible. While west German businesses stood to profit from the transformation of the east's economy in the long run, Kohl and his key cabinet ministers got them to make some sacrifices in the short run. Kohl also negotiated with the heads of important trade unions and won their agreement to moderate the wage demands of west German workers. In exchange, Kohl promised to keep as many communist-era eastern German factories in operation as long as possible, in spite of their low quality standards, rather than putting them out of business all at once and aggravating unemployment. Both sides gave ground in these talks, without yielding on other disagreements. (The unions wanted the government to raise wages in eastern Germany to western levels as rapidly as possible, but the government resisted this step, arguing that east German workers were still considerably less skilled and less productive than their western German counterparts.)

Just as important, Kohl's CDU/CSU-FDP government entered into direct talks with the Social Democratic leadership. The SPD now controlled the Bundesrat, requiring Kohl to come to terms in order to get elements of his solidarity pact passed into law. At the SPD's insistence, Kohl withdrew his plans to cut welfare benefits. In return, the SPD agreed to withdraw its call for new taxes on the rich in the following year. Kohl also consulted with the state governments and cut a deal with them that reduced their contributions to the unification funds. Rather than centralizing the government's power at the expense of the states, the unification process reinforced the bargaining power of the states. Germany's central government remained a "semi-sovereign state," and the Kohl government confirmed its acceptance of the Federal Republic's tradition of cooperative federalism.

Ultimately, Kohl's government did cut welfare spending, reneging on its promises to the Social Democrats. But

Kohl and his coalition partners were also compelled by the mounting costs of unification to give up their resistance to the SPD's calls for a tax hike. The government and parliament approved a 7.5 percent "solidarity tax" surcharge on German taxpayers to help pay for the surging costs of propping up East Germany's economy. Since average tax rates in Germany were already around 44 percent, many Germans now had to pay about half of their income in taxes. After winning a mere ten-vote majority in the Bundestag in 1994, the CDU/CSU-FDP coalition government was in no position to adopt an all-out confrontationist stance when addressing the severe problems stemming from unification. Cooperation and consultation with the business community, the trade unions, the opposition parties, and the state governments proved vital as painful and politically unpopular decisions had to be made.

CONCLUSIONS

The preponderance of the evidence is largely *inconsistent* with the hypothesis that Germany's unification could be expected to undermine neo-corporatism. On the contrary, it has served to reinforce it, especially in the 1992–93 period and even afterwards.

During his initial year in office, Chancellor Schroeder appeared to favor neo-corporatist procedures in dealing with the acute economic problems facing his government. He kept up a busy round of consultations with labor and business representatives in an attempt to win concessions from both groups and to forge a general national consensus on the painful decisions he wants to make in restructuring the country's economy.

POLITICAL ISSUES IN TODAY'S GERMANY

As Germany moves into the new millennium, it confronts a challenging array of problems that touch on the most basic aspects of its political system, its economic and social well-being, and its very identity as a nation-state. The following is a partial list of these problems.

Restructuring the Economy

Germany must simultaneously deal with massive unemployment, a huge national debt, and an annual debt-servicing obligation that, in Schroeder's estimation, threatens to make the German government "incapable of political action." It also faces escalating social welfare expenditures; and one of the highest corporate and individual tax burdens among the world's economically advanced democracies. In announcing what Schroeder called the largest economic reform project ever undertaken in the Federal Republic, the German government in 1999 launched plans to create an "Alliance for Jobs" aimed at widening long-term job prospects and developing a short-term crash program to create 100,000 new jobs immediately for young people. The "Alliance" is a neo-corporatist venture involving the intimate collaboration of government, business, and trade union representatives. Unemployment fell to 3.9 million in 2000.

The government also announced plans to trim the national debt by DM 150 billion ($28.5 billion) by 2003. Reaching this goal requires major spending cuts in virtually all ministries of the federal government, reducing the funds available for social welfare benefits, government-backed student loans, retirement pensions, pay increases for government personnel, and a host of other traditionally well-funded budget items. But persuading the population to make the prescribed sacrifices will require consummate leadership skill as well as a citizenry that is willing to engage in "followership." In 1999, large losses for the SPD in state elections and public demonstrations against the proposed austerity measures did not bode well for Schroeder's government. At the end of the year, however, his austerity package won approval in the Bundestag.

In an effort to bring tax relief to Germany's businesses, the government in 2000 announced plans to cut corporate tax rates substantially, with a view to freeing up more money for investment and to making German companies more competitive in the global economy. In addition, employers are getting a reduction in their non-wage obligations to their employees. Tax rates for individuals are also set to fall. By 2005, tax cuts for businesses and individuals were expected to total $30 billion. Tax relief of this magnitude, however, will bring the government substantially lower revenues, thus necessitating more budget cuts in the future.

The Consequences of Unification

In a speech on the tenth anniversary of the opening of the Berlin wall, Chancellor Schroeder ac-

knowledged in late 1999 that, though much had been accomplished in integrating the former East Germany into the Federal Republic, much more still needed to be done. Major expenditures by the German government and private investors will still be necessary over the coming decades to revitalize eastern Germany's economy and lift it up to western German standards. In addition, Germans on both sides of their once impenetrable borders will have to deal with the lure of extremist parties among people who have been materially disadvantaged and psychologically jolted by the unification process. East Germans will need to come to terms with officials of the former communist state, including their highest leaders and the dreaded political police, some of whom have been subject to prosecution in the Federal Republic. And "the wall in people's minds" will have to come down if Germans of east and west are to feel that they are truly equal citizens of the same country.

Ethnic Diversity

As we noted at the beginning of this chapter, new citizenship and naturalization laws went into effect in 2000. These reforms and related changes will go a long way to giving a substantial number of Germany's 7.4 million foreigners and their descendants the right to become German citizens, with full voting rights and other privileges, should they so choose. While it is still difficult to tell how many will avail themselves of that opportunity, the recent changes reflect the fact that Germany is a multiethnic country, with non-Germans constituting 9 percent of the population.

To be sure, not all Germans are ready to accept this reality. Dealing with ethnic diversity will require efforts to combat violence and discrimination aimed at the foreign-born and their descendants. In 1998 there were more than 700 recorded violent offenses against foreigners committed by people with extreme right-wing orientations, a figure lower than in the previous year (790) but higher than in 1996 (624). The Federal Office for the Protection of the Constitution has recorded more than 50,000 right-wing extremists, of whom more than 8,000 (mostly skinheads) are considered militant and prone to violence. Many of them are concentrated in the former East Germany, where unemployment and other pangs of the unification process have generated mass frustration and "Germany for Germans" attitudes. Two right-wing nationalist parties, the Republicans *(Republikaner)* and the German People's Union *(Deutsche Volksunion,* or DVU), are currently under official surveillance by German authorities as potentially anti-constitutional parties.[48]

International Commitments

Despite its internal travails, Germany remains one of the most influential and prosperous countries in the world. Its imports and exports combine to make it the globe's most active trading nation after the United States. Its status in the European Union as a major source of funding for EU programs and a source of monetary stability in support of the euro make it the linchpin of European integration. Its support for the EU's enlargement is vital to the incorporation of perhaps as many as a dozen new members in the coming years, mostly from neighboring Central and Eastern Europe. And its role as a partner of the United States in NATO is critical to the functioning of the alliance and its reliability as a guarantor of peace in Europe and even in regions beyond Europe's borders, such as the Persian Gulf. Balancing the difficult processes of change at home with these heavy global responsibilities will surely test Germany's leaders, as well as its people, for quite some time.

The Crisis of the Christian Democrats

Helmut Kohl's admission that he had managed an illegal party fund during his chancellorship, and a welter of allegations about millions more in bribes and unlawful payments to Kohl and the Christian Democrats, profoundly damaged the CDU's credibility and created a serious upheaval within its ranks. Kohl's successor as CDU chief, Wolfgang Schaeuble, only made matters worse when he subsequently admitted to lying about a $50,000 contribution from an arms dealer. In the spring of 2000, the CDU chose a new leader, Angela Merkel, a former physicist and pro-democracy activist from East Germany. As the first woman to head the party, Merkel immediately confronted the challenges of restoring voter confidence and staving

off the party's bankruptcy in the face of more than $20 million in fines.

GERMANY AND THE FOUR FACES OF DEMOCRACY

Viewed against the panoramic canvas of the last two centuries, Germany has come a long way toward building a stable and prosperous democracy. Against the weight of its authoritarian traditions and aggressive tendencies, it has achieved singular successes in meeting some of the defining criteria of all four faces of democracy. In the decades since the end of World War II it has guaranteed the prerequisites of popular sovereignty (Face I) through a representative parliamentary democracy, combining real voter choice and alternation in power with long-term political stability. The Basic Law explicitly states that all state authority emanates from the people (Article 20), and it includes special provisions against anti-democratic parties and movements. The unification process has extended these sovereign political rights to more than 15 million people who once lived under communist domination in East Germany. Ironically, perhaps the most visible violation of popular sovereignty in Germany is that the Basic Law itself has never been submitted to the people for their approval, a lacuna many Germans wish to rectify with a new, post-unification constitution.

Postwar Germany has also secured the basic rights and liberties associated with Face II of democracy. The Basic Law enumerates these rights and freedoms, in some cases with even greater specificity than does the Bill of Rights of the U.S. Constitution. (The right to form trade unions, own private property, and enjoy freedom of movement, for example, are stated explicitly in the Basic Law. Germany provides no constitutional right to bear arms, and handgun laws are stricter than in the United States.) Press freedoms, which are also explicitly guaranteed, are enjoyed by one of the largest newspaper readerships in the world. Religious freedoms are also guaranteed, though a strict separation of church and state is not mandated. On the contrary, the government has played a special role in helping the established churches collect "church taxes" and in permitting religious instruction in state-funded schools.[49]

The values associated with Face III of democracy have also been accorded special consideration in postwar Germany. The generally accepted necessity to overcome the brutalities of past nondemocratic regimes, especially those perpetrated by Nazi Germany, has imbued postwar Germany's political elite with a special responsibility to inculcate the values of tolerance, mutual respect, and cooperation in the population. The very first article of the Basic Law begins with the affirmation, "The dignity of man shall be inviolable. To respect and protect it shall be the duty of all state authority." The values of peace and justice in the world are extolled in the very next sentence. Article 3 mandates equality before the law, including the equality of men and women. It distinctly prohibits prejudice and favoritism on grounds of sex, race, religious and political opinions, and other personal characteristics. Moreover, the quest for consensus and compromise on the part of Germany's main party leaders has made a contribution of inestimable value to the Federal Republic's political stability and the effectiveness of its governmental and economic institutions.

Of course, no amount of rhetorical eloquence or constitutional law can guarantee that people will never be intolerant of others or will never seek to circumvent or undermine the central values of democracy. Manifestations of anti-foreign sentiments and recurrent outbursts of violence against residents not regarded as purely German provide ample testimony to that reality. Nevertheless, such attitudes and behaviors are considered extremist in today's Germany, the outbursts of a marginalized minority. The overwhelming majority of the population accepts the core democratic values associated with Face III of democracy, while government agencies, religious bodies, and other organizations have organized a variety of programs to promote harmony among the country's increasingly diversified population. That fact is truly remarkable when viewed against the institutionalized racism of the Nazi era.

Finally, postwar Germany has taken a number of steps in the direction of economic democracy (Face IV). Private enterprise and market competition constitute the foundation stones of the country's economic system. The Federal Republic defines economic democracy as incorporating private property rights; it does not seek to be a socialist democracy that repudiates or severely limits the private business sector. Though Article 15 of the Basic Law permits the government to nationalize privately owned natural and human-made resources, German leaders have not sought to create a largely state-run economy. Nevertheless, right from the Federal Republic's inception, its political elites, including those in such business-oriented conservative parties as the Christian Democrats and Free Democrats, have sought to temper the freedoms of the market with state-sponsored programs designed to limit socioeconomic inequality and powerlessness.

The concepts of the "social market economy" and "co-determination," however limited their actual scope, have played a role in balancing market forces with social welfare protections and at least some input by workers in the private sector. Germany's neo-corporatist procedures have reinforced these efforts by giving trade union representatives a direct role in the policy-making process. The redistribution of tax revenues to the poorer states and to less advantaged elements of the population has helped reduce economic inequality. As a result of these and other practices, Germany today has less inequality than does the United States or certain other economically advanced democracies. The main source of inequality now is that between western Germany and the former East Germany. But the efforts of the German government, businesses, and taxpayers to even out these differences as rapidly as possible have been extraordinary. Though these efforts will not bear fruit for quite some time, they nonetheless testify to the importance of socioeconomic fairness in German political culture and behavior.

In sum, Germany has made remarkable strides in the postwar era in building and sustaining a viable democracy. While pressing economic and social problems will certainly challenge the country's elites and citizenry in the coming years, it is not likely that democracy itself will be in serious jeopardy.

KEY TERMS AND NAMES
(Underlined in the text)

Party of Democratic Socialism (PDS)
Gerhard Schroeder

Social Democratic Party of Germany (SPD)
Greens
Otto von Bismarck
Weimar Republic
Adolph Hitler
Nazis
Free Democratic Party (FDP)
Christian Democratic Union (CDU)
Christian Social Union (CSU)
Basic Law
States (*Laender*)
Bundesrat
Bundestag
Chancellor
President
Federal Constitutional Court
Bundesbank
Konrad Adenauer
Willy Brandt
Helmut Schmidt
Helmut Kohl
Joschka Fischer
Neo-corporatism

FOR DISCUSSION: WHAT WOULD YOU DO?

1. If you were a German citizen, to which party (if any) would you belong?
2. Do you favor the Schroeder government's austerity policies, or would you prefer higher government spending to jump-start the economy and expand social welfare benefits?
3. Should voting rights be granted to foreign residents?
4. If you were German, would you favor a more active international diplomatic role for Germany, even if it means engaging military forces?

FOR FURTHER READING

In addition to the titles in the notes, consult the following:

Clay Clemens and William E. Paterson, eds., *The Kohl Chancellorship* (London: Frank Cass, 1998).
David P. Conradt, *The German Polity*, 6 ed. (White Plains, N.Y.: Longman, 1996).
Russel J. Dalton, *Politics in Germany*, 2 ed. (New York: HarperCollins, 1993).

Lewis J. Edinger and Brigitte L. Nacos, *From Bonn to Berlin* (New York: Columbia University Press, 1998).
Derek Lewis and John R. P. McKenzie, *The New Germany* (Exeter, U.K.: Exeter University Press, 1995).

WEBSITES

The main website with political material on Germany in English, along with numerous links, is <www.germany-info.org>.

NOTES

1. John H. Backer, *The Decision to Divide Germany* (Durham, N.C.: Duke University Press, 1978); Norman M. Naimark, *The Russians in Germany* (Cambridge, Mass.: Belknap, 1995); Henry Krisch, *German Politics Under Soviet Occupation* (New York: Columbia University Press, 1972); Ann L. Phillips, *Soviet Policy Toward East Germany Reconsidered* (Westport, Conn.: Greenwood, 1986).
2. The juridical status of Berlin was complicated. The four-power agreements provided that all of Berlin would be under the joint control of the four occupation authorities. The United States, Britain, and France adhered to that position. The Soviets and East Germans, however, claimed East Berlin as the capital of the German Democratic Republic, a position the three Western powers rejected. The West German government claimed that West Berlin belonged to the Federal Republic of Germany, a position that was also rejected by the U.S., British, and French governments.
3. W. Phillips Davison, *The Berlin Blockade* (Princeton, N.J.: Princeton University Press, 1958).
4. Curtis Cate, *The Ides of August* (New York: Evans, 1975); Robert M. Slusser, *The Berlin Crisis of 1961* (Baltimore, Md.: Johns Hopkins University Press, 1973).
5. Subsequent accounts by the key decision makers indicated that their instructions were misinterpreted and that the wall was to be opened the next day. Günter Schabowski, *Der Absturz* (Berlin: Rowohlt, 1992); Egon Krenz, *Wenn Mauern fallen* (Vienna: Paul Neff, 1990).
6. Robert Darnton, *Berlin Journal, 1989–1990* (New York: W.W. Norton, 1991); Charles S. Maier, *Dissolution* (Princeton, N.J.: Princeton University Press, 1997); Jeffrey Gedmin, *The Hidden Hand* (Washington, D.C.: AEI Press, 1992); Gert-Joachim Glaessner, *The Unification Process in Germany* (New York: St. Martin's Press, 1992); Elizabeth Pond, *Beyond the Wall* (Washington: Brookings Institution, 1993); Konrad H. Jarausch, *The Rush to German Unity*

(New York: Oxford University Press, 1994); Philip Zelikow and Condoleezza Rice, *Germany Unified and Europe Transformed* (Cambridge, Mass.: Harvard University Press, 1995); Angela E. Stent, *Russia and Germany Reborn* (Princeton, N.J.: Princeton University Press, 1999).

7. Survey data on unification tends to vary somewhat, but stable opinion patterns are discernible. A survey conducted by the Konrad Adenauer Foundation in the summer of 1999 found that three out of four eastern Germans regarded the advantages of unification as outweighing the disadvantages, and 94 percent said they would not wish to relinquish the democratic freedoms they acquired after unification. A survey conducted by the Allensbach Institute for Public Opinion Research in the same period found that 8 percent of eastern Germans and 14 percent of westerners would favor a return to the pre-unification period. Monthly surveys conducted by the same institute since 1990 reveal that, as a general tendency, between 60 percent and 65 percent of eastern Germans and 50 percent of western Germans regard unification as a source of happiness, while 20 percent of easterners and 30 percent of westerners describe it negatively as a source of "concern." Reported in <www.germany-info.org>; Wolfram Brunner and Viola Neu, "Freiheit oder Gleichheit" (St. Augustin, Germany: Konrad Adenauer Foundation, 1999); Elmar Brähler and Horst-Eberhard Richter, "Deutsche—zehn Jahre nach der Wende," *Aus Politik und Zeitgeschichte*, supplement B 45/99 to *Das Parlament*, 1999; *Frankfurter Allgemeine Zeitung*, September 15, 1999.

8. William A. Barbieri Jr., *Ethics of Citizenship: Immigration and Group Rights in Germany* (Durham, N.C.: Duke University Press, 1998).

9. *Der Spiegel*, September 13, 1999, 96–110.

10. For the text, consult the Labour Party website, <www.labour.org.uk>. French prime minister Jospin declined to sign the document but shared some of its views.

11. James J. Sheehan, *German Liberalism in the nineteenth Century* (Chicago: University of Chicago Press, 1978); Leonard Krieger, *The German Idea of Freedom* (Chicago: University of Chicago Press, 1957).

12. Luther wanted Christian princes to practice the general principles laid out in the Bible, but he accepted the prevailing view that their authority derived from God (not the people). See Joshua Mitchell, "Protestant Thought and Republican Spirit: How Luther Enchanted the World," *American Political Science Review* 86, no. 3 (September 1992); 688–95. On later developments, see Max Weber, *The Protestant Ethic and the Spirit of Capitalism*, trans. Talcott Parsons (London: Routledge, 1992). For Weber's views, see chapter 12.

13. "German national consciousness was unmistakably and distinctly racist from the moment it existed," Greenfeld writes, "and the national identity of the Germans was essentially an identity of race, and only superficially that of language or anything else." German concepts of democracy in this period, she continues, "meant nothing but the total submersion of the individual within the collectivity (in the latter instance—the nation), renunciation of every particular interest, and unconditional service of the collective self by each in its proper place." Liah Greenfeld, *Nationalism: Five Roads to Modernity* (Cambridge, Mass.: Harvard University Press, 1992), 369.

14. The Great War took an estimated 10 million lives and left about 30 million wounded. It claimed 10 percent of France's male population and 9 percent of British males under age forty-five. Out of 11 million German troops mobilized, 1.8 million were killed and 4.2 million were wounded. Russia, Austria-Hungary, Italy, and other combatants also took heavy casualties. The United States, whose troops entered the fray in the spring of 1918, suffered 11,500 deaths and 206,000 wounded.

15. In Britain, all males over age twenty-one and women over thirty won the right to vote in 1918. The voting age for British women was not lowered to twenty-one until 1928. Women did not have the right to vote throughout the United States until 1920, with the passage of the Nineteenth Amendment to the Constitution. Until then, American women could vote only in about a dozen states. Though France and Italy had universal male suffrage in 1919, women in both countries did not gain the right to vote until the 1940s. New Zealand was the first to give its female citizens the vote (1893).

16. Article 48 of the constitution stipulated that when "public security and order are seriously disturbed or endangered," the president had the authority to "take the necessary measures necessary for their restoration, intervening in case of need with the help of the armed forces." In these circumstances, the president could abrogate such constitutional guarantees as the inviolability of personal liberty and domicile, the secrecy of private correspondence, and the rights of free speech, assembly, association, and private property. Article 48 also provided that the Reichstag could rescind the president's emergency powers, but it never did.

17. Richard F. Hamilton, *Who Voted for Hitler?* (Princeton N.J.: Princeton University Press, 1982); Thomas Childers, *The Nazi Voter* (Chapel Hill: University of North Carolina Press, 1983).

18. Sheri Berman, *The Social Democratic Movement* (Cambridge, Mass.: Harvard University Press, 1998); Anton Kaes, Martin Jay, and Edward Dimendberg, eds., *The Weimar Republic Sourcebook* (Berkeley: University of California Press, 1994).

19. Erich Fromm, *Escape from Freedom* (New York: Holt, Rinehart, and Winston, 1941); Bertram Schaffner, *Fatherland: A Study of Authoritarianism in the German Family* (New York: Columbia University Press, 1948); T. W. Adorno et al., *The Authoritarian Personality* (New York: Harper and Bros., 1950).

20. Kurt Dietrich Bracher, *The German Dictatorship* (New York: Praeger, 1970); David Schoenbaum, *Hitler's Social Revolution* (New York: W. W. Norton, 1980).

21. Lewis Edinger, *Kurt Schumacher* (Stanford, Calif.: Stanford University Press, 1965).

22. In addition to being divided into West Germany and East Germany after the war, Germany lost a considerable amount of territory to its eastern neighbors. The Soviet Union, whose armies occupied the region, gave some parts of Germany to Poland, including the cities of Danzig (now Gdansk) and Stettin (Szczecin) and the industrial region of Silesia. The USSR annexed the city of Königsberg and its surrounding region, renaming it Kaliningrad. It is still part of Russia. The Soviets also restored the Sudetenland to Czechoslovakia. In 1938 Hitler had annexed this region, with its large German population, winning British and French acceptance of his action at the Munich conference.

23. Local government in Germany is based on some 16,000 cities, towns, and villages; all have elected councils and have various responsibilities for schools, fire safety, sanitation, and other activities. All but about 100 of these communities (*Gemeinden*) fall within county (*Kreis*) administrations. Though local and county governments may raise some of their revenue locally, most if it comes in the form of grants from the federal and state governments.

24. The smaller states have more Bundesrat votes per capita than the larger ones do. The state of Bremen, for example, has one Bundesrat vote for about every 235,000 people in its jurisdiction, while the most populous state, North Rhine-Westphalia, has one Bundesrat vote for every 2.8 million inhabitants. The Bundesrat is thus malapportioned in favor of the smaller states: it is not based on the principle of "one person, one vote." The U.S. Senate, in which small states like Rhode Island and large ones like California each get two votes, is also malapportioned in favor of the less populous states.

25. Peter Katzenstein, *Policy and Politics in West Germany: The Growth of a Semi-Sovereign State?*

(Philadelphia: Temple University Press, 1987). Also Uwe Thaysen, *The Bundesrat, the Länder, and German Federalism* (Washington, D.C.: American Institute for Contemporary German Studies, 1994).

26. Like most democracies outside the United States, Germany does not have a primary election system that enables voters to select the nominees of the various parties. Instead, the parties themselves choose their candidates and Bundestag representatives. While these candidate selection processes differ somewhat from one party to another, in virtually all of them the process is dominated by hard-core party activists who attend meetings regularly or sit on important party committees.

27. In 1998 the SPD won one overhang mandate in Hamburg and the rest in the former East Germany (three in Brandenburg, two in Mecklenburg-Western Pomerania, three in Thuringia and four in Saxony-Anhalt). In each state, the SPD won a larger number of Bundestag seats through its first vote district victories than it was entitled to by virtue of its second vote showing, namely, 40.9 percent share of the second vote nationwide.

28. The 1990 elections, the first after unification, had special one-time-only rules that allowed parties in the former East Germany to win Bundestag seats without strictly adhering to the 5 percent hurdle rule. Another provision of the electoral laws that has been in effect for decades but rarely used is the "three-mandate waiver" rule. If a party fails to clear the 5 percent hurdle *but wins at least three first vote district mandates*, the hurdle clause is waived and it is entitled to a share of Bundestag seats in proportion to its share of the second vote. In 1994 the PDS won only 4.4 percent of the second vote nationwide, but it won four district mandates. As a consequence, it was awarded a total of thirty seats, a figure roughly proportionate to its second vote share.

29. The Bundestag seats that parties falling below the 5 percent hurdle would have won in its absence are distributed to the parties that clear the hurdle, in proportion to their share of the popular vote. For example, if a party wins 3 percent of the vote, it would be entitled in a pure PR system with no hurdle to 3 percent of the Bundestag seats (e.g., twenty out of 656). In 1998 the SPD won 40.9 percent of the second vote and was therefore entitled to 40.9 percent of the thirty-nine seats unclaimed by the parties that fell below the hurdle (i.e., sixteen seats).

30. In 1957 the Christian Democrats won a slim majority of Bundestag seats and could have formed a majoritarian government on their own, but they chose

to form a coalition with a smaller partner, the short-lived Free People's Party (FVP).

31. Bundestag investigative committees also serve as a legislative check on the government by probing the cabinet's decisions or allegations of incompetence or malfeasance. But the fact that these committees are dominated by the very parties that constitute the government tends to limit the scope of their inquiries.

32. Following the formation of the Kohl government in 1982, the CDU/CSU-FDP coalition wanted to gain the voters' approval in snap elections. However, the Basic Law permits anticipated elections to be held only when no majority government can be formed or when a government loses a constructive vote of no-confidence. In order to permit these elections to be held before the next regularly scheduled elections set for 1984, the government had to stage-manage a feigned defeat in a constructive vote of confidence. New Bundestag elections thereupon followed in March 1983, returning the Christian Democrat–Free Democrat majority.

33. Campaign financing for federal elections in the United States is regulated under the Federal Elections Campaign Act of 1971, which was toughened in 1974 and 1976. It provides for partial funding of presidential elections with public funds contributed voluntarily by taxpayers. It also limits campaign contributions from individuals to $25,000 a year and forbids contributions from the treasuries of corporations and trade unions. The law places no limits on the sums that can be donated to candidates or parties by "political action committees" set up to assist favored candidates or parties. A bill prohibiting most contributions to political parties passed the House of Representatives in September 1999, but failed to clear the Senate. It was estimated that as much as $300 billion might be raised for the presidential and Congressional elections in 2000.

34. In the event that the parties cannot agree on a chancellor, the president may have some discretion in picking someone of his or her own choice; even then, however, the Bundestag majority would have to agree. The president co-signs all bills before they become law, but has no veto power; the signature is usually automatic. One of the presidency's dormant powers is to declare a state of legislative emergency if so requested by the government and the Bundesrat. Under these circumstances, the government—not the president—would govern by decree. No such emergency has ever been declared in the Federal Republic.

35. Donald Kommers, *The Federal Constitutional Court* (Washington, D.C.: American Institute for Contem-porary German Studies, 1994), and *The Constitutional Jurisprudence of the Federal Republic of Germany* (Durham, N.C.: Duke University Press, 1989).

36. David P. Conradt, "Changing German Political Culture," in *The Civic Culture Revisited*, ed. Gabriel A. Almond and Sidney Verba (Boston: Little, Brown, 1980), 212–72; Kendall L. Baker, Russel J. Dalton, and Kai Hildebrandt, *Germany Transformed* (Cambridge, Mass.: Harvard University Press, 1981).

37. Germany has not adopted *parity co-determination,* which would give labor and management equal representation in running private firms, despite support for it among many Social Democrats and others on the left.

38. Konrad Adenauer, *Memoirs,* trans. Beate Ruhm von Oppen (Chicago: H. Regnery, 1966); Arnold J. Heidenheimer, *Adenauer and the CDU* (The Hague: Martinus Nijhoff, 1960); Terrence Prittie, *Konrad Adenauer, 1876–1967* (Chicago: Cowles, 1971); Hans-Peter Schwarz, *Konrad Adenauer,* trans. by Louise Willmot (Providence, R.I.: Berghahn, 1995).

39. Edinger, *Kurt Schumacher;* Douglas A. Chalmers, *The Social Democratic Party of Germany* (New Haven, Conn.: Yale University Press, 1964).

40. Willy Brandt, *My Life in Politics* (New York: Viking, 1992), and *People and Politics: The Years 1960–1975,* trans. J. Maxwell Brownjohn (Boston: Little, Brown, 1978); Barbara Marshall, *Willy Brandt: A Political Biography* (New York: St. Martin's Press, 1997).

41. Helmut Schmidt, *Men and Powers: A Memoir,* trans. Ruth Hein (New York: Random House, 1989); Jonathan Carr, *Helmut Schmidt: Helmsman of Germany* (London: Weidenfield and Nicholson, 1985).

42. Karl Hugo Pruys, *Kohl, Genius of the Present,* trans. Kathleen Bunten (Chicago: Edition q, 1996).

43. This profile is based on Volker Herres and Klaus Waller, *Gerhard Schröder: der Weg nach Berlin* (Munich: Econ and List, 1998).

44. For Lafontaine's views on Schroeder following his resignation from the cabinet, see his book, *Das herz schlägt links (The Heart Beats on the Left)* (Munich: Econ, 1999). For a review, see *The Economist,* October 23, 1999. On the SPD's situation during the Kohl years, see Fritz Scharpf, *Crisis and Choice in European Social Democracy* (Ithaca, N.Y.: Cornell University Press, 1991). For an analysis of Germany's economic and political predicament in this period from a neo-liberal perspective, see *The Economist,* February 6, 1999.

45. Gene E. Frankland, *Between Power and Protest: The Green Party in Germany* (Boulder, Colo.: Westview Press, 1992).

46. In addition to BDI *(Bundesverband der deutschen Industrie),* the business community's peak associations

include the Federation of German Employer Associations (BDA) and the German Industrial and Trade Conference (DIHT). Germany's 2.5 million farmers are represented mainly by three highly influential associations that together call themselves the "Green Front" (though they are not related to the Green Party). They are the Farmer's League, the Association of Agricultural Chambers, and a cooperative organization, the *Raiffeisenverband*.

47. Razeen Sally and Douglas Webber, "The German Solidarity Pact: A Case Study in the Politics of the Unified Germany," *German Politics* 3, no. 1 (April 1994): 18–46.

48. The *Republikaner* have been in existence since the 1980s but have never elected any candidates to the Bundestag. In 1998 they got 1.9 percent of the vote, and they claimed 15,000 members. The DVU claims up to 18,000 members and received 1.2 percent of the vote in 1998.

49. The state recognizes several large religious organizations as "corporations in public law." These include the Evangelical (Lutheran) Church, Germany's largest Protestant denomination, and the Roman Catholic Church; each has about 28 million members, comprising about two-thirds of the population. Others include the Central Council of Jews in Germany, the Greek and Russian Orthodox Churches, and the Seventh Day Adventists. (Germany does not recognize the Church of Scientology as a public corporation.) Germans who choose to register as adherents of one of these religious "corporations" pay the government a surcharge on their income tax, currently about 9 percent. The government then distributes most of these funds to the churches according to the number of their respective adherents, retaining a certain amount to cover administrative costs. In return, the churches make vital contributions to the population, operating hospitals, day care centers, and nursing homes and providing humanitarian assistance to developing countries.

CHAPTER 19

JAPAN
Dean W. Collinwood

Population (1999): 126.2 million

Area: 145,882 square miles
(slightly larger than California)

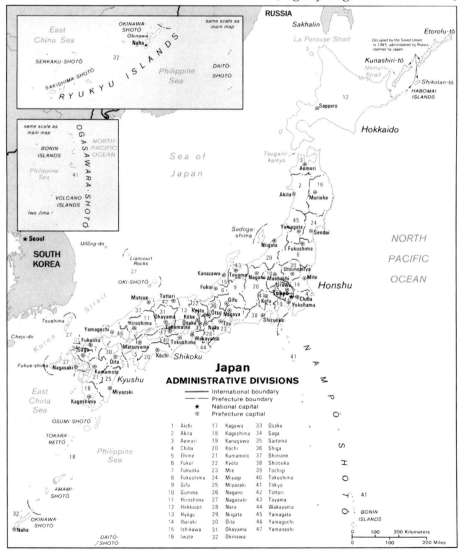

Japan
ADMINISTRATIVE DIVISIONS

—————— International boundary
— · — · — Prefecture boundary
★ National capital
⊙ Prefecture captial

1	Aichi	17	Kagawa	33	Ōsaka
2	Akita	18	Kagoshima	34	Saga
3	Aomori	19	Kanagawa	35	Saitama
4	Chiba	20	Kōchi	36	Shiga
5	Ehime	21	Kumamoto	37	Shimane
6	Fukui	22	Kyōto	38	Shizuoka
7	Fukuoka	23	Mie	39	Tochigi
8	Fukushima	24	Miyagi	40	Tokushima
9	Gifu	25	Miyazaki	41	Tōkyō
10	Gumma	26	Nagano	42	Tottori
11	Hiroshima	27	Nagasaki	43	Toyama
12	Hokkaidō	28	Nara	44	Wakayama
13	Hyōgo	29	Niigata	45	Yamagata
14	Ibaraki	30	Ōita	46	Yamaguchi
15	Ishikawa	31	Okayama	47	Yamanashi
16	Iwate	32	Okinawa		

Source: U.S. Central Intelligence Agency

543

EARTHQUAKES AND PARALYSIS IN THE 1990s

When all the votes were finally counted, the result was stunning. In a rare occurrence in Japanese politics, the prime minister and his cabinet had lost a vote of confidence in the House of Representatives, the lower house of Japan's parliament. On June 18, 1993, by a vote of 255 to 220, the House deprived the government of seventy-three-year-old Prime Minister Kiichi Miyazawa of its majority, forcing his resignation. Even more shocking, thirty-nine members of Miyazawa's own party, the Liberal Democratic Party (LDP), had joined with the opposition parties in voting against him. This split in the LDP's ranks not only sealed Miyazawa's fate, it signaled an earthquake in Japan's political system.

Ever since their party was founded in 1955, the Liberal Democrats had won every national election and formed every government. The opposition parties were so weak that they barely counted. The LDP's dominance of the country's political institutions not only included its sway over the cabinet and the two houses of parliament (known together as the Diet), it also extended over Japan's powerful bureaucracy and most of its local governments. Under the LDP's one-party rule, Japan had risen from wartime defeat and initial postwar poverty to the exalted status of the world's second largest economy after the United States. In 1993 it had a $132 billion global trade surplus, $50 billion of it with the United States. As the economic powerhouse of Asia, Japan fueled the growth of virtually every country in the region. But by the early 1990s the Japanese economy was in crisis and the LDP in disarray. The party's breakup in the Miyazawa no-confidence vote raised the possibility that Japan would soon have a non-LDP government for the first time in thirty-eight years. As Miyazawa, following custom, bowed politely to the House following his defeat and slowly left the chamber, it was evident that change had come not just to his own government, but to the prevailing patterns of Japan's political system.

What caused this shred in the fabric of Japanese politics? One factor was the dismal state of the economy. After establishing itself as the world's most active trading nation and catapulting over such strong economies as those of Britain, France, and Germany during the 1960s and 1970s, Japan suffered the sudden collapse of a number of its most important financial institutions. Japanese banks had made hundreds of billions of dollars in bad loans to corporations and investors with no ability to repay what they had borrowed. The magnitude of these unpaid debts sent shock waves through the economy in Japan and the rest of Asia.[1] But a second factor had an even more devastating effect on the Liberal Democrats' grip on power: corruption.

Only a few months before Miyazawa was forced to endure the fatal vote of no-confidence, the LDP was jolted by the arrest of Shin Kanemaru, one of its most powerful politicians, on charges of tax evasion. Revelations of corruption on the part of LDP leaders were nothing new. Over the previous decades the Japanese had become accustomed to one scandal after another involving bribery, kickbacks, and other forms of corruption on the part of Liberal Democratic Party officials, legislators, cabinet ministers, and even prime ministers. In 1989, for example, two prime ministers in succession were forced to resign, the first for receiving illegal donations from a major Japanese corporation (the Recruit Company), the second for alleged improprieties with a geisha whom he paid to be his mistress. But the arrest of Shin Kanemaru in March 1993 was the straw that broke the camel's back as far as public opinion was concerned.

At age seventy-eight, Kanemaru was the Liberal Democrats' top behind-the-scenes power broker. His influence could make or break LDP politicians as they grappled their way up the ladder of political power. A long list of Liberal Democratic cabinet ministers owed their positions to Kanemaru's nod. His influence remained undiminished despite his 1992 admission that he had received more than $4 million in illegal campaign contributions, a scandal that forced his resignation from the Diet. The following year, the public and many LDP politicians were further disillusioned with the news that investigators had uncovered some $750,000 in gold ingots hidden under the floorboards of his house, plus millions of dollars in cash and bonds stashed away in his homes and offices. Kanemaru died in 1996 before he could be brought to trial, but for a growing number of Japanese, the corruption of the LDP's patriarch typified the party itself and the government it had monopolized for nearly four decades.

Not all Liberal Democrats were corrupt, to be sure. But efforts to reform the party's practices invariably foundered on the staunch opposition of LDP politicians whose careers had profited from illicit behavior. Miyazawa himself, only days before his ouster, was forced to withdraw a reform plan that unleashed a storm of indignation among party officials determined to resist change. But the widespread public hunger for a reordering of the Japanese political system was now irrepressible.

One month after Miyazawa's resignation, new elections were held for the House of Representatives. The weeks preceding the vote witnessed a frenzy of party realignments. Several dozen LDP parliamentarians quit the party and helped form new ones. Hundreds of thousands of Japanese citizens, normally known for their political quiescence, got involved in clubs and associations organized over the preceding year to promote political change. People spoke excitedly of the "Heisi Revolution," referring to the name of the current emperor's reign, and of political *risutora*, the Japanese pronunciation of "restructuring," a term borrowed from Michail Gorbachev's reforms in Russia. Many other Japanese citizens, however, were either so confused by the turmoil, or perhaps so fed up with politics, that they stayed away from the polls; only two out of three eligible voters turned out, about 5 percent fewer than in most previous elections.

Nevertheless, when election day came on July 18, the result was a watershed in Japanese politics. For the first time since 1955, the Liberal Democrats lost their lower house majority, winning only 44 percent of the seats. Power passed to a seven-party coalition government headed by Morihiro Hosokawa, a fifty-five-year-old politician who once served as a regional governor. No LDP members were invited into his cabinet. Just as astounding, a woman—Takako Doi, a Socialist—was elected speaker of the House, quite a feat in a parliament with 98 percent male membership.

The grandson of a former prime minister, Hosokawa had begun his career in the Liberal Democratic Party but bolted it because of the leadership's resistance to reform. In 1992 he organized the Japan New Party. Dynamic and photogenic (he

Morihiro Hosokawa

once played a samurai in a movie), the popular Hosokawa took office amid high hopes for a new beginning in Japanese politics. One of his first acts as prime minister was to issue a formal apology to the world for Japan's "acts of aggression and colonial rule" during World War II, a gesture previous LDP governments had been reluctant to make. His first major piece of legislation was a reform bill that called for the complete overhaul of Japan's lower house electoral system and for significant restrictions on campaign financing. When the bill was rejected by the upper house of the Diet, still dominated by old-guard Liberal Democrats, Hosokawa made compromises to save its essence. The compromises calmed the nerves of politicians accustomed to harmony and consensus in political bargaining—a defining feature of Japanese political culture—and the watered-down reforms cleared both houses in 1994.

But Hosokawa's government did not finish out the year. When Liberal Democrats accused him of improperly using a $970,000 loan for political purposes and an investment consultant publicly charged him with lying to the Diet about a large stock purchase, he resigned rather than undergo a politicized public investigation. Hosokawa's successor, another former LDP member, lasted only a few months as his multiparty government squabbled over economic reforms. By the middle of 1994, scarcely a year after the "restructuring" elections, the Japanese government was in a state of paralysis. Its standing in the world, which waited impatiently for a revival of the once mighty Japanese economy, declined. The non-LDP coalition parties proved incapable of governing and broke up. Their failure reopened the door to the Liberal Democrats, who returned to power as the coalition partners of none other than the Socialists, their arch-rivals since the 1950s.

This curious combination of the two parties that were the biggest losers of the 1993 elections did not improve matters. The new prime minister was a genteel seventy-year-old Socialist with no clearly articulated program for governing the country. After six more months of political drift and economic decline, Japan's government changed hands once again in January 1996. This time a Liberal Democrat, Ryutaro Hashimoto, took over as prime minister, restoring the highest political office in the land to the party most voters had repudiated less than three years earlier.

"Business as usual" quickly set in. Within a matter of months Hashimoto's government was embroiled in a financial scandal. As his approval ratings plummeted rapidly, the prime minister called snap elections in hopes of cobbling together a workable majority in the House of Representatives. And so in October 1996 Japanese voters went to the polls again, albeit with considerably less enthusiasm than in 1993. Only 59 percent bothered to cast their ballots, a postwar low. The number of people identifying with any of the parties, traditionally more than 80 percent, sank to half the electorate.

The campaign period, which by law may last only twelve days in Japan, had all the elements of a traditional Japanese election process. Typically, candidates in small rural towns and large cities like Tokyo don white gloves to symbolize their devotion to clean government and they make as many personal appearances as possible. Many of them will drive around in vans draped with large-print campaign slogans and equipped with powerful microphone and loud-speaker systems. Stopping in front of train stations or busy intersections, microphone in hand, they will address everyone who happens by. The sound volume will be so loud that no one will escape hearing at least part of their speeches. Each candidate may give four or five such speeches a day during the campaign. Meanwhile, members of the candidate's *koenkai*, or support group, including relatives and friends, will be making speeches and telephone calls on behalf of their favorite contender and gluing posters to hundreds of makeshift campaign billboards.

In 1996, for the first time, individual candidates were allowed to run television advertisements. (In previous elections only the national party organizations could do so.) Inevitably, these expenditures drove up the costs of running for office rather than reducing them. In spite of the 1994 reforms that placed limits on the amount of funds individual candidates could raise, the cost of the average campaign rose from an average $500,000 for a single Diet seat in previous elections to between $1 million and close to $3 million, often exceeding the $1 million price tag of the most expensive campaigns for the U.S. House of Representatives.

Other aims of the 1994 Hosokawa reforms also fell short of their original intent. Hopes of promoting a U.S.-style two-party system, with the Liberal Democrats vying against a large opposition party, proved unreachable. More than a half-dozen parties put up candidates in 1996, and the LDP's most serious rival, the New Frontier Party, was a new upstart party created only two years earlier. The reformers' hopes of encouraging more meaningful debate on the issues during election campaigns also met with disappointment, as most candidates resorted to blaring sound trucks and vague slogans, often laced with vituperative attacks on their opponents. Things became so acrimonious that the largest parties filed suit against each other for violating the new campaign law's prohibition on mudslinging. And hopes of bringing new blood into the political elite were only partially fulfilled. While the number of first-time candidates and females rose somewhat, roughly 30 percent of those elected had fathers or grandfathers in previous Japanese parliaments. (For LDP deputies, the figure was 50 percent.)

When the votes were tallied, the LDP ended up with 48 percent of the 500 seats in the House of Representatives. Though short of an absolute majority, the Liberal Democrats took advantage of their opponents' inability to agree on an alternative cabinet and established a minority government under Hashimoto. To pass its bills into law, the new cabinet bargained for the votes of two smaller parties and several independents. For all practical purposes, Japan's political system had reverted back to the one-party dominance of the LDP. And the LDP, for its part, reverted to its old ways of doing business. New scandals came to light, and Hashimoto's efforts to revive the economy had little effect. In 1998, the voters administered another sharp rebuke to the LDP during elections to Japan's upper house, the House of Councillors. Although the prime minister is responsible to the lower house and not the upper chamber, Hashimoto accepted responsibility for the voters' disaffection and resigned.

In his place as head of government stepped another Liberal Democrat, Keizo Obuchi. Obuchi enlarged his government's parliamentary support in the fall of 1999 by inviting two smaller parties, the New Komeito party and the New Conservative party, to form a coalition cabinet with the Liberal Democrats. His efforts to revive the economy were just beginning to bear fruit and his popularity ratings were starting to climb when he suffered a stroke in April 2000. Within days the party bosses who steered the Liberal Democrats' fortunes met behind closed doors and picked a relative unknown, **Yoshiro Mori,** as Japan's new prime minister. Mori's selection represented another throwback to the LDP's traditional practices. A longtime party loyalist with no mass following or policy agenda of his own, Mori was chosen primarily because the leaders of the Liberal Democrats' various factions wanted to reach a quick consensus, not because he stood out as a commanding leader. In an effort to rally public support for the new government, Mori called new parliamentary elections for June 25, 2000—several months ahead of schedule. Though Mori's approval ratings were below 20 percent,

LDP leaders were confident that the party itself remained fairly popular, especially in rural areas.

Their calculations proved right, but just barely. The Liberal Democrats lost thirty-eight seats but remained by far the largest party in the House of Representatives. (The full results are shown later in this chapter, in table 19.7.) Soon after the election, the LDP leadership once again agreed on Mori as prime minister and reestablished a coalition government with the New Komeito and the New Conservative parties. How long Mori would remain in office was uncertain, however, as his personal popularity remained minimal.

DEMOCRACY AND POLITICAL CONFLICT IN JAPAN

Clearly, the 1990s were a tumultuous period in Japanese politics that combined fundamental transformations with the familiar patterns of previous decades. Corruption and waning public trust in government officials were plainly visible. At the same time, profound changes in party structures, the electoral system, and the willingness of voters to become actively involved in promoting reform demonstrated that the pulse of democracy in Japan was beating at an accelerated rate.

It was not always so. For nearly 2,000 years Japan's government was, like those of most other Asian countries, anything but an electoral democracy. Though political parties and a legislature appeared in the last decades of the nineteenth century, Japan did not become a democracy until after its defeat in World War II in 1945, when American Occupation authorities essentially imposed a democratic constitution on the country. Until then, Japan was governed by a long succession of authoritarian regimes.

Even today, some observers of Japanese politics raise the question of just *how* democratic the country really is. The dominance of a single political party, the Liberal Democratic Party, for more than forty years; the overweening power of the central bureaucracy; the pernicious influence of corruption; and a number of other factors have prompted concern that Japan is not very democratic when viewed against the criteria set forth in chapter 8.

In this chapter we shall examine the question of how democratic Japan is today. We will also look at how the Japanese have dealt with the five sources of political conflict we outlined in chapter 2:

- *Power:* Which parties, social groups, and individuals have wielded political power in Japan? Are Japanese political elites today more powerful than in other democracies? Have Japanese leaders abused their power through corrupt practices?
- *Resources:* How did Japan rise from the catastrophe of World War II to become the world's second-largest economy? Why has the economic "bubble" burst in recent years?
- *Social identity:* Can Japan be considered a largely homogeneous society, undisturbed by conflicts over race, religion, social class, and other identities that make for intense conflict in other societies?
- *Ideas:* What do terms like "conservatism" and "socialism" mean in Japan? To what extent have ideologies influenced the behavior of voters and political parties or movements? Is there a Japanese (or Asian) model of democracy that is different from Western democracy?
- *Values:* What are some of the characteristic features of Japanese political culture? Do the Japanese have essentially the same value structure as other economically developed democracies, or are they significantly different on key questions?

Let's begin with an exploration of Japan's long-delayed acceptance of democracy.

HISTORICAL BACKGROUND OF JAPANESE POLITICS: WHY NO DEMOCRACY?

The Role of the Emperor in Japanese Government

The common image of an all-powerful king who controls his country with an iron fist or rules by whim does not fit the role of the emperor in Japanese history. Indeed, the Japanese language did not even have a word for "leader" until the late nineteenth century, when Western influences made themselves felt. The emperor (*tenno;* literally "heavenly sovereign") was anciently thought to have had the ability to communicate with the gods

on behalf of his people.[2] Indeed, Japanese emperors ruled by divine right, claiming their political legitimacy as descendents of the Sun Goddess, whose grandson supposedly came to earth around 660 B.C. to bestow authority on Japan's ruler. Accordingly, the emperor annually performed rituals in which he petitioned the gods for a good rice harvest. Even today the emperor keeps a small rice paddy on the imperial palace grounds in Tokyo where he performs such rituals. The emperor's role was more like that of religious high priest than a head of state. In fact, the details of running the country, or even making policies, were considered beneath the emperor's dignity. Ministers or other representatives of the emperor wielded actual power. Sometimes affairs of state were handled by regents or emperor substitutes; at other times, military generals called **shoguns** ruled. In certain periods the shoguns appointed their own ministers or regents who became the de facto rulers of the country. Ministers, regents, or shoguns usually developed their own power bases, including armies, away from the official center of imperial power in the central Japanese city of Kyoto and were virtually sovereign in their own geographic domains or fiefs—not unlike lords in feudal England.

Much of Japanese political history, therefore, is a record of battles between rival extended families or clans, each attempting to elevate itself (or maintain itself) to a level just below that of the emperor himself (or herself in ancient times[3]). Who was actually running the country was often hard to determine. Sometimes a regent or substitute for the shogun ruled in the shogun's name, while the shogun ruled in the name of the emperor's substitute regent, who ruled in the name of the emperor, who actually had very little power to delegate in the first place, and who ruled in the name of the gods. Thus, in practice, the country's government was usually a military dictatorship built on a thin theocratic foundation. A pure *theocracy* is government by religious authorities, and while Japan was never a true theocracy, its early history contains evidence of the strong influence of religion in government.

There have been about 125 emperors, although the first fourteen who reigned before A.D. 300 are considered legendary by most scholars. The current emperor, **Emperor Akihito,** assumed the of-

Emperor Akihito

fice after his father, **Emperor Hirohito,** died in 1989. Occasionally, some emperors actually tried to become real players in governance or unexpectedly found themselves holding more political power than they had anticipated. Between A.D. 645 and 806, for example, the emperors of Japan, copying the Tang dynasty in China, directly ruled the country and established a centralized, highly bureaucratized, hierarchical system of government.

Similarly, in the late 1800s, Japanese "imperial loyalists" who believed in the Confucian philosophy that the emperor should be the actual ruler of the country succeeded in ridding Japan of the rival shoguns and restored the emperor to a position of power. Confucius, a Chinese intellectual and minor political figure, lived from 551 to 479 B.C. and taught that the anarchy he saw around him could best be solved by having paternalistic kings ruling over a society based on respect and hierarchy. Following this philosophy, Japanese reformers began

what was soon called the **Meiji Restoration** of 1868. It was called "Meiji" because that was the reign-name chosen by the emperor of the time, and it was called a "restoration" because, for the first time in hundreds of years, the emperor was being restored to his "rightful" position as actual ruler. The reforms of that period ultimately led Japan into the modern world politically. It will be valuable to review these changes in greater detail.[4]

Part of the push for direct imperial rule in the 1800s came from those who believed in the Confucian doctrine of benevolent monarchy. Others, however, were not as interested in "restoring" an emperor as in bringing an end to 250 years of strict rule by one shogun family, the powerful Tokugawa family. But there was yet another important source of discontent. As has often been the case since those times, foreign pressure, or *gaiastu*, was perhaps the most powerful precipitant of political change in the 1800s. In 1853, U.S. naval commander Matthew C. Perry sailed into Tokyo Bay in his "black ship," which was equipped with modern military technology and other gadgetry from America's newly industrializing economy. Perry demanded that Japan open its country to trade and allow transport vessels to dock and resupply. As they had done to almost all such demands for over 250 years, the Japanese resisted at first, but when Perry demonstrated the power of his weapons by firing into Tokyo Bay and by showing some of Japan's leaders the modern technology he had on board, people suddenly realized that Japan was too weak to resist or remain isolated any longer from the rest of the world. The shoguns reluctantly opened the country to trade from abroad.

But some Japanese wanted much more than that. As we noted, the leaders of some of the feudal clans were tired of being dominated by the Tokugawa family, which had ruled in the name of the emperor since 1600. Moreover, they had come to believe that the feudal Tokyo Shogunate was holding back the country's development. With a relatively weak central government, political authority in Japan was dispersed among a multiplicity of local clans, feudal lords (the *daimyo*), and members of an elite military caste known as the **samurai.** The reformers thought that restoring the emperor to a position of real power would allow him to reduce or even eliminate the power of these local figures and shoguns and modernize the country as a single, united entity. National disunity, in their view, was a source of national weakness.

The ensuing rebellion by the four feudal clans that wanted change was resisted by many of the others. Some of this resistance was violent, and for the next five years the newly established Meiji central government found itself suppressing uprisings in many parts of society, by samurais, farmers, and others. Prevailing over all these opposition groups, the new government officially abolished feudal or clan authority in 1871 and in 1876 eliminated the samurai class with its various status privileges. The clan fiefdoms were replaced by prefectures under central government control, and the emperor moved from Kyoto to Tokyo (formerly known as Edo), the city from whence the shoguns had ruled for centuries.

Interestingly, it was approximately in these same years that Germany gathered its various parts into a single state under a central government, as did Italy. Japan, Germany, and Italy were thus latecomers compared to Britain and France in creating a strong centralized state. Some scholars argue that such "late states," because they had to catch up to the most powerful countries as rapidly as possible, were especially prone to using strong government authority to coordinate their economic modernization. In addition, late states like Japan, Germany, and Italy engaged in external aggression in the twentieth century in order to build up empires to compete with Britain, France, and the United States and to forge a sense of common national identity at home vis-à-vis the outside world.

Also falling under the axe of the new Meiji rulers was the Tokugawa family's strict control over the lives of ordinary citizens. Under the Tokugawa shogun prior to 1868, the boundaries between social classes had been strictly enforced, with rules of behavior for each class. These rules prevented people from even imagining how life might be for them if they were richer or more educated (or poorer and less educated). For instance, children of farmers could play with dolls that were dressed only in farmers' clothing; it was against the rules for poor children to have dolls dressed like samurais or other elites.

Likewise, the shoguns had prevented the growth of a solid middle class by putting restrictions on what merchants and other business owners could do. For instance, successful merchants in Tokyo who attempted to build additional floors onto their homes were ordered to remove them; no one should look or behave above his or her assigned social class. The absence of a large urban middle class was probably a factor that prevented the development of democracy in Japan. As the experience of Britain, the United States, France, and other countries has demonstrated, a middle class rooted in private enterprise can exert enormous pressures for civil rights and liberties, especially property rights and the right to vote.

Once the Meiji government began promoting Japan's economic modernization, a section of the merchant class prospered under the regime's authoritarian practices and supported the ruling authorities, even at the expense of forsaking democracy. Meanwhile, the Meiji state fostered the creation of large economic conglomerates called **zaibatsu**. These were cartels of private companies that depended heavily on the government for investment funds and other forms of assistance, establishing an exceptionally close bond between big business and the Japanese state that endures to this day. Modern-day companies like Mitsubishi and Mitsui got their start in this formative period. The zaibatsu leaders had little taste for democracy, however, and decisively lent their support to a repressive Japanese state.[5]

The former Tokugawa regime had attempted to rein in the feudal lords who owned most of Japan's agricultural property. No matter how far away from the capital they lived, these lords were regularly required to spend half a year in Tokyo, where the ruling shogun could keep an eye on them. Moreover, forcing them to maintain two households and to travel frequently to Tokyo with their large entourages of assistants and servants was costly and prevented the domain lords from amassing excessive wealth—wealth that might have fueled an anti-Tokugawa rebellion. Once in power, the Meiji leaders abolished these practices and dismantled many other social rules that had kept people "in their place" for more than 250 years. However, they also enacted many new strict regulations (such as restrictions on publications and on public assembly) that had the effect of strengthening the central government at the expense of the provinces.

The Rise of Party Politics

Some people violently (but unsuccessfully) resisted the powerful Meiji oligarchs; others, especially disgruntled former samurai, rural landowners, and urban intellectuals, attempted to preserve their privileges or prevent their further decline by forming political associations—the precursors of political parties. The appearance of these new organizations was extremely significant. It meant that, for the first time, men of influence were making at least a small effort to ascertain what the population wanted out of government. The one cause that got the most attention was democracy.

When the emperor was restored to power in 1868, he was only fourteen years old and completely unprepared to govern. Those who had masterminded the overthrow of the feudal system constituted themselves as an autocratic inner circle around him. In the emperor's name they issued declarations on all aspects of political life, shifting yet more power away from the former fiefdoms and toward the central government. For those who had ruled their own local domains for hundreds of years with near sovereignty, these autocratic fiats were a bitter pill to swallow.

Moreover, there was no unanimity of opinion within the Meiji leadership itself. When internal dissension caused some Meiji elites to resign their posts in the new government, they retaliated by creating political parties. Beginning in 1874, several proto-parties were formed that had as their goal the establishment of a parliamentary democracy, complete with a constitution. Intellectuals were behind these parties, as were some merchants, but many of those pushing for democracy were former domain leaders and disaffected former samurai who saw a constitution as the only realistic way to prevent the new central government from taking even more power away from the provinces. The predecessor of today's Liberal Democratic Party was formed in 1874 by, among others, Taisuke Itagaki, who had been a member of the Meiji government but who had resigned in frustration at the anti-democratic policies of the Meiji leadership.

Debate among the educated elite of Meiji society produced varied opinions on the preferred structure of government: some leaders favored a British-style government, others the French model, and still others the Prussian or German model. Many of the Meiji leaders had studied these various forms of government firsthand during official tours of Europe and America in the 1870s and 1880s.[6] In 1872, for example, a delegation of 111 government leaders and students led by Tomomi Iwakura (including the first Japanese women to travel abroad[7]) visited the United States, stopping in various cities to observe American society and government. Sent by the Meiji government to attempt to revise trade treaties with the United States, the delegation tried to absorb as much American political culture as possible. These highly independent and well-educated Japanese leaders were probably way ahead of the mainstream Japanese population in their interest in Western-style democracy, but with the era of isolation finally at an end, many ordinary Japanese saw these travelers as harbingers of good news and a new life, whatever that might be. The account of their tour of America and Europe was devoured by Japan's reading public at the time.

The delegation was fascinated by the new transcontinental railroad (Japan still had no railroads), by the steel bridges and high-rise buildings of Chicago and Philadelphia, and by the sheer size of the United States. On one stop in Salt Lake City, where they stayed for three weeks, the group collected copies of Utah's territorial constitution and other government policy documents, observed sessions of the legislature, visited schools and colleges, inspected the U.S. troops stationed there, and spent many hours with politicians and social and religious leaders to discuss the state's tax system and its agricultural policies, parliamentary procedures, police system, religion, and many other features of American life.[8]

One very active participant in these discussions was thirty-two-year-old Hirobumi Ito, the man who would subsequently draft Japan's first constitution and become its first prime minister. After more than fifteen years of studying European and American governmental systems and debating their suitability to Japan, Ito and other democracy advocates drafted a European-style parliamentary constitution. He favored the European models because, among other reasons, most European constitutions allowed for a monarch, whereas the U.S. Constitution did not.

In 1889, twenty-one years after the Meiji rebellion, the parties pushing for a constitutional government finally prevailed, and a new constitution was promulgated. It took effect upon a declaration by the emperor, not by a vote of the people, for Japan had not yet moved that far along the road toward democratic government. Moreover, the constitution established the emperor as the sovereign voice in matters of government. The Meiji Restoration, it must be emphasized, was an *aristocratic* revolution, not a democratic one. It was engineered by upper-class samurai and other authoritarian political elites, not by mass social forces opposed to monarchy and favorable to democracy like those that propelled the French Revolution. It would be some thirty years before mass workers' parties such as the Japan Communist Party and the Japan Socialist League were attempted. In 1889, however, Japan was still far from a democracy. Indeed, the first election in Japan did not take place until 1890, and even then only half a million people (about 1 percent of the population) were allowed to vote because suffrage was restricted to males who paid a certain amount of taxes. (Of course, the right to vote was similarly restricted to property-owning males in nineteenth-century Britain, France, and the United States.) Universal manhood suffrage was not instituted in Japan until 1928, and women did not get the vote until after World War II.

Despite its distance from the ideal democratic model, the first Japanese constitution was extremely significant because, during its making, the Japanese began to learn how to organize themselves politically to advance their goals. Between 1874 and 1890 several political parties or associations were formed: the Public Party of Patriots (later the Liberal Party); the Freedom and People's Rights Movement; the Constitutional Reform Party; and the Constitutional Liberal Party. Most of these parties were created by governmental elites who had become dissatisfied with the centralized nature of the new Meiji government and wanted to restore some of the rights formerly enjoyed in the provinces. Those in charge of the Meiji government soon came to realize that they had no alternative but to create parties of their own—"bureaucrats' parties" as they were called—to distinguish them from the so-called "popular parties." Unlike the western democracies, the commoners or ordinary people in Japan were not major players in the early years of party formation, although they contributed to pressure for reform by engaging in various forms of civil disobedience. Despite their origins at the hands of elites, the new parties were a significant step in the direction of mass democracy because parties, by their vary nature, require reaching out for the support of like-minded people.

It is important to note that the constitution did not specifically mention political parties. Cabinet ministers, including the prime minister, were not selected on the basis of which party had received the largest share of the vote. Indeed, members of the House of Peers (the upper house) were appointed by the emperor entirely from among the imperial family and other nobles, while members of the House of Representatives took office as independents, not as representatives of any political party. Cabinet positions were rotated among members of the four clans that had effected the Meiji imperial restoration, and it was not until 1918 that the first non-pedigreed commoner became prime minister. But party influence steadily increased while clan influence waned. Indeed, the headlong rush by the Meiji government to industrialize Japan and catch up to the West produced so many labor problems that still more political parties were created, including the Social Democratic Party and the Japan Socialist Party, which did, indeed, have roots in the common people.

It is also important to note that the Japanese parliament in this period had very little real decision-making authority. Its purpose was mainly consultative, providing the cabinet officials who exercised real power in Japan with advice and respectful criticism. It therefore closely resembled the German Reichstag organized in the 1870s under the stern authoritarian rule of the kaiser and his chancellor, Otto von Bismarck. It was considerably less powerful than the British Parliament, which rested on the bedrock principle of parliamentary supremacy, or the U.S. Congress, with its extensive lawmaking powers exercised in conjunction with the president.

Conflict between the Military and the Civilian Government

Resistance to the rise of party politics came from some of the top Meiji oligarchs and the old clan-dominated bureaucracy (i.e., some of the former feudal elites), and particularly from the military, which was led by former samurai. As it happened, the beginnings of parliamentary government in Japan in the late 1800s and early 1900s coincided with the rise of Japanese nationalism and military aggression against its neighbors in Asia.[9] If the Japanese had learned one thing from the Western nations, it was that the powerful countries of the 1800s were expansionists. They understood that countries like England, France, Holland, and others had tried, whenever possible, to extend their power and national security by subduing weaker nations militarily and subjugating them politically. Even the United States, which had been founded in open opposition to the idea of empire, would soon take control of Hawaii (1893), followed by the Philippines, Puerto Rico, and Guam (1898). Japan realized very quickly that if it wanted to avoid the dismemberment of its territory by Western powers, which were already carving up China, it would need to build a credible military of its own—one capable not only of protecting itself but also of subduing other nations.

To prepare for expansionism, Japanese leaders had carefully observed the military structure of many Western countries. Officers from France were imported to revamp the Japanese army, while British naval officers were brought in to reorganize the navy. Universal military service for Japanese men was inaugurated in 1872. Bolstered by the belief that Japan had now caught up to the West in terms of military preparedness, the Japanese military launched an active campaign to acquire an empire for Japan. The military took over Okinawa and the Ryukyu Islands in 1879, Taiwan and the Pescadores in 1895, southern Manchuria and Sakhalin Island in 1905, and Korea in 1910. In acquiring this vast amount of real estate, the Japanese military had handily defeated the armed forces of both China and Russia. After some fifty years of development and westernization, Japan was finally recognized worldwide as a formidable force in Asia.

Not everyone in Japan was initially pleased with the militarization of the country. By the early 1890s a major battle for resources was under way inside the government. Some Meiji-era party leaders (especially those not connected with the four clans that launched the 1868 Meiji rebellion) preferred that Japan spend its resources on its social rather than its military infrastructure. Pressure from these leaders produced a national education system in 1871 (using the United States as a model) and a new criminal code (using France as a model). But the military, which had been given enormous power in the new constitution, and indeed was not even required to answer to the Diet, was successful in enlisting support for its motto of "Enrich the Country, Strengthen the Military." Whereas in 1891 and 1892 some of the political parties had successfully forced the resignation of cabinets that had tried to expand the budget for military purposes, by 1894, when Japan was poised to take over Taiwan, most of the opposition to militarization and expansionism had been obliterated in a cloud of nationalistic fervor. The hawks had won the resource allocation debate.

By the 1930s the military had been able to elevate itself to a position of dominance in Japanese governance. Among the reasons for this situation was the universal conscription law of 1872. The former samurai elite who took charge of the military after 1868 took full advantage of conscription to indoctrinate the entire male population with the values of militarism. Military education, including infantry exercises for students from junior high school through university, became mandatory parts of the curriculum. The worldwide economic depression of the 1930s also presented a strong challenge to the civilian government, as did instability in China. Thus the Japanese people, who had always tolerated a high level of militaristic control of their lives during the era of the shoguns, now found their civilian government reduced to the status of a virtual puppet of the army and navy. Those who resisted the state's militarization often found their lives in danger, as was the case with Prime Minister Tsuyoshi Inukai in 1932. While attempting to keep the army under control and to block its expansionist designs on China, Inukai was assassinated by military officers.

Military control of the country was further strengthened by the February 26 Incident. In 1936, some fourteen hundred soldiers led by junior officers staged a coup d'état in Tokyo. Seizing the center of the city, they killed several top government officials, including the minister of finance, and attempted to kill the prime minister. Their goal was to have the prime minister replaced by a general loyal to their cause. The attempt was eventually suppressed by other units of the military under direct orders of the emperor, but—ironically—the incident actually ended up increasing the military's influence in Tokyo. Under the guise of maintaining public order, the military persuaded the cabinet to increase its budget (and thus its general visibility) and to impose strict censorship on the media. Thus from the 1930s until the end of World War II in 1945, the cabinet came under the direct control of uniformed generals or their military collaborators.

In the 1940s several efforts were made to subsume all political parties into one large, totalitarian unit called the Imperial Rule Assistance Association (IRAA). Seen by many as the Japanese equivalent of Hitler's Nazi Party, with branches organized all over the country, the military-inspired IRAA was never completely successful in obliterating the influence of civilian political parties. Nonetheless, during the Pacific War years, political parties were virtually eliminated, and it was the army, navy, and air force that held real power in the country. As to Emperor Hirohito, who reigned from 1926 to 1989, no one knows exactly how involved he was in supporting or promoting the militarization of Japan, although many believe he was far more involved than he appeared to be at the time. It is likely, however, that once again, as during the era of the shoguns, it was primarily the military, using the emperor's name and legitimacy, that established and implemented Japan's policies of military aggression overseas and the suppression of civilian government at home.

For many years, the Japanese military machine seemed unstoppable. Troops swarmed over Manchuria, China, in 1931 and much of southeast Asia in 1941. In 1942, under prime minister and general **Hideki Tojo,** Japan launched devastating, simultaneous attacks on the Philippines, Malaya, and Hawaii. By mid-1942, Japan controlled a vast territory from Korea and eastern China in the north, to Indonesia in the south and far out into the islands of the Pacific. This area was what the Japanese leadership called the "Greater East Asian Co-prosperity Sphere," but to the victims of Japanese aggression, the term was just window dressing for nothing less than brutal domination by the "Nazis of Asia."

The luck ran out for the Japanese upon the entry of the Allies, especially the United States, in the war against them in 1942. Island by island, country by country, the Japanese were pushed back in bloody battles costing thousands of military and civilian lives. In the Allied attack on Okinawa, for example, 110,000 Japanese soldiers were killed as well as 150,000 Japanese civilians and at least 50,000 Americans. Air raids on the Japanese islands proper ended with the atomic bombing of the cities of Hiroshima and Nagasaki in August 1945, after which the emperor, in a dramatic radio announcement, declared surrender.

Japan and the Conditions for Democracy

In sum, Japanese history prior to the end of the Second World War exhibited precious few of the conditions for democracy enumerated in chapter 10. *State institutions* and *political elites* were thoroughly authoritarian. *National wealth* was low compared to the leading Western countries, while *private enterprise* was dominated by cartels that were highly dependent on the imperial state. The long-suppressed *middle class* remained politically weak. The *disadvantaged* classes of peasants and urban workers occasionally staged protest actions but were not sufficiently organized to effect democratic change from below. *Civil society* was undeveloped, with mass-based political parties largely eclipsed by state-oriented bureaucratic parties.

Japan's *political culture* was shaped by Confucian attitudes emphasizing social harmony, consensus, and hierarchy rather than democratic contestation, individual liberty, or constitutional limits to state power. *Education* was an elitist privilege and the government was able to manipulate the *flow of information.* Japan's *international environment* was characterized by centuries of isolation followed by decades of aggressive imperialism, both of which reinforced the political influence of the military. Of all the conditions on our list, only Japan's ethnic *homogeneity* might have proved helpful in sustaining a democracy, but by itself it could not create democratic institutions and behaviors where few, if any, existed. It took the complete destruction of Japan's imperial system by U.S. forces in World War II to bring democracy to Japan.

BUILDING JAPANESE DEMOCRACY

The Occupation Begins

In August 1945, thousands of tired, hungry, and demoralized Japanese lined the streets of cities throughout Japan to watch their conquerors—the Allied forces—arrive to take over their country. Although most Japanese today agree that losing the war was the best thing that could have happened to Japan, at the time, the **Occupation** was regarded with both fear and a begrudging envy. "What will they do to us?" the people worried, and "What is it that they have or know that gave them the power to defeat our divinely led country?"

The answers to these questions came quickly. Led by U.S. Gen. Douglas MacArthur, some 5,500

General Douglas MacArthur and Emperor Hirohito during the U.S. Occupation

occupation officials, mostly American, began remaking Japan in their own image. They were backed by 150,000 Occupation troops.[10] Although the Occupation regime allowed the emperor to remain as Japan's symbolic head of state, it removed virtually all his authority. Emperor Hirohito, who had no alternative but to cooperate with the Occupation authorities, issued a statement declaring that he did not rule by divine right, contradicting a notion the Japanese had long been taught to believe. Occupation leaders also swept some 200,000 war-era political and military leaders from office and went on to dismantle the military and police apparatus, change the educational and legal systems, introduce sweeping land reforms, weaken the power of the zaibatsu (the business cartels), and encourage the formation of labor unions. Most significant is that they threw out the Meiji constitution of 1889 and replaced it in 1947 with a new constitution modeled heavily, though not exclusively, on the British and U.S. systems of government.

Japan's Constitution

The new constitution declared that sovereignty resides with the Japanese people and that the emperor, with no powers related to government, derives his position as symbol of the state "from the will of the people," not from heaven. It established the equality of the sexes in marriage and other matters. It guaranteed various freedoms, such as those of speech, religion, assembly, private property ownership, voting in secret elections, and so on. One significant feature was that it declared that the Japanese people would "forever renounce war," the only such declaration by any country in the world (the famous Article 9).[11] Subsequent legislation gave women the vote for the first time in Japanese history and lowered the voting age to twenty.

The will of the people was to be expressed through a Westminster-style bicameral parliament, the **Diet**, with an elected **House of Representatives** (the lower house) and an elected **House of Councillors** (the upper house). The lower house would select a prime minister who, as head of government, would choose the cabinet. The prime minister and a majority of cabinet members would be chosen from elected members of the Diet (who retain their seats while serving in the cabinet) and must be civilians. Terms of members of the House of Representatives were set at four years (unless the House were to be dissolved earlier for some reason) and those of the House of Councillors at six years. The initial electoral regime for the House of Representatives established multimember parliamentary districts, but that system was changed in the 1994 reforms (see later in this chapter). Half the members of the House of Councillors are elected every three years by popular vote for a six-year term that is not terminated upon dissolution of the House of Representatives. In the event the House of Representatives is dissolved, a general election must be held within forty days to reconstitute the Diet. A bill becomes law when it is passed by both houses of the Diet, and it can become law even when the House of Councillors initially rejects it, as long as it is subsequently passed by two-thirds of the members of the House of Representatives.

The power of prefectural and municipal governments was designed to be weaker than those powers in a federal system, giving the Japanese central government a stronger hand over the forty-seven prefectures and other regional units than, say, the central government has over the states in the United States. An independent judiciary with a Supreme Court and lower courts was also established to adjudicate laws. The Supreme Court, consisting of fourteen judges plus a chief justice, was given the power of judicial review to rule on the constitutionality of laws. The emperor appoints the

chief justice upon receiving a designation from the cabinet, and the remaining justices are appointed by the cabinet and reviewed by voters in a general election. They must retire at age seventy.

The postwar Occupation lasted seven years, until 1952. At its end, the nation was on the road to economic recovery, sovereignty had been handed over to the Japanese people, and Japan had been reaccepted by the world community as a legitimate nation. The Occupation's reforms had catalyzed the formation of new political parties as well as an explosion of new labor unions (some 5 million workers had joined unions by 1946). Let's review these developments in more detail.

Political Parties in Postwar Japan

The years immediately following World War II were times of turbulence for Japan's political party system. Aspirants for political office created new parties that echoed what the U.S. government wanted and at the same time reflected the people's desire for change from the militarism of the past. Party names that implied change, such as "progressive" and "liberal," were popular. So were names suggesting an important feature of Japan's political culture, the tendency toward communal or group rather than individual action, as reflected in party names like "socialist," "cooperative," and "communist." New parties created by 1952 (many with direct links to prewar parties) are listed in table 19.1.

With many former political leaders purged by the Occupation, the new and reconstituted parties

TABLE 19.1
Parties Created During the Postwar Occupation (1945–52)

Japan Communist Party: established in 1945 with prewar roots
Japan Socialist Party: established in 1945 with prewar roots
Japan Liberal Party: established in 1945 from a faction of an earlier party established in 1900
Japan Progressive Party: established in 1945 from a faction of an earlier party established in 1900
Japan Cooperative Party: established in 1945 with no prewar links
Democratic Party: established in 1947 with roots in Japan Liberal and Democratic Liberal Parties
People's Cooperative Party: established in 1947 with roots in Japan Cooperative Party
Worker-Farmer Party: established in 1948 with roots in Japan Socialist Party
Shakai Kakushinto: established in 1948 with roots in Japan Socialist Party
Democratic Liberal Party: established in 1948 with roots in Japan Liberal Party
Liberal Party: established in 1950 with roots in several other newly formed parties
People's Democratic Party: established in 1950 with roots in several other newly formed parties
Kyodoto: established in 1952 with roots in several other newly formed parties
Japan Reform Party: established in 1952 with roots in People's Democratic Party

had to draw their leadership from outside the old ruling elites, particularly from the ranks of the business community and the retired bureaucracy. The close relationship that the business community and bureaucracy currently maintain with the Liberal Democratic Party stems, in part, from this Occupation-era necessity (and, in part, from the government-business relationship established during the late 1800s).

After ten years of postwar deal making and power positioning by all parties, a new stability took hold in 1955 that would continue more or less unchanged and unchallenged for nearly forty years. Two parties came to the fore in the Diet: the **Liberal Democratic Party** (**LDP**) and the **Japan Socialist Party** (**JSP**).

The LDP, despite its left-sounding name, was a conservative party that had been formed from two other business-oriented conservative parties; it could trace its roots back to the Public Party of Patriots established in 1874 during the early Meiji Restoration. Party leaders used the term "liberal" in its original sense, as supportive of democracy and private enterprise. From its inception the LDP favored business and economic growth over other issues. It was not as concerned with remilitarization and national pride as it was with reigniting the economy and rebuilding the country's industrial infrastructure. To this end, and in keeping with Japanese traditions, the Liberal Democrats placed heavy emphasis on the need for close collaboration between the largest private corporations and the Japanese government. Their support for extensive state involvement in the private sector distinguishes them from conservative parties in the United States and Britain, which have tended to favor less government intervention and more independence for private enterprise.

The LDP also curried the favor of the farm vote by providing subsidies for rice and strenuously resisting the importation of less expensive foreign rice. In foreign policy, LDP leaders favored friendly cooperation with the United States and supported the U.S.-Japan Security Treaty of 1954 that allowed thousands of U.S. troops to be stationed at numerous military bases throughout Japan. Aided by the support of middle-class white-collar "salarymen" as well as the farmers of the countryside, the LDP took control of the government and guided Japan through its stunning economic recovery and rise to world prominence.

The Japan Socialist Party assumed the role of chief opposition party. Like the LDP, it too was created in 1955. The JSP traced its roots back to the Socialist Study Society of 1898. It saw itself as the party of ordinary people, a position reflected in the titles of its precursor parties: the Socialist Masses Party, the Japan Proletarian Party, the Labor-Farmer Party, the Japan Commoners' Party, and others with similar left-sounding titles. Despite its "masses" approach, it never garnered enough seats in the House of Representatives to serve as more than an annoyance to the powerful LDP until the late 1980s, as we shall see later in the chapter. In fact, the JSP was never socialist in the sense of favoring less capitalistic approaches to economic life. Many of its supporters were hardly distinguishable in their economic views from those supporting the LDP, except perhaps in their desire to resist joining the establishment.

In the 1950s, many Japanese hoped that the LDP and the JSP would form the backbone of a British-style two-party system that would bring needed stability to Japanese politics. They hoped that these two parties, with their slightly different philosophies of government, would periodically rotate in and out of government like the Conservative and Labour parties in Britain. As it happened, however, the LDP ended up controlling the government for four decades and running the country more or less as a one-party state. The 1960s saw the rise of the **Clean Government Party,** or **Komeito,** a Buddhist religion-based party, but it would not become a major player for nearly three decades. Renamed **New Komeito** in 1999, it became part of an LDP-led coalition government—much to the dismay of the majority of the population. Since the 1930s, when the military used religion to advance its control of the government, many Japanese have remained leery of any close church-state relationships. Extreme right-wing groups wanting the return of Japan's era of military bravado were never able to excite the interest of the war-weary population. Thus the LDP reigned virtually unchallenged.

Some have argued that the LDP's long dominance of Japanese politics and governmental power diminished democracy, because it narrowed the voters' alternative choices to parties with little chance of winning and prevented real alternation in power. But others countered that, despite the absence of a strong opposition in the Diet for several decades, the conservative LDP in fact represented a variety of viewpoints, since the party itself was a combination of many interests. This raises the issue of *habatsu*, or intra-party **factions** or cliques.

In a style reminiscent of ancient samurai and the lords they vowed to protect at all costs, the LDP and other parties in Japan are comprised of a number of factions, each headed by a powerful, experienced politician. This prominent politician establishes patron-client relationships with younger, less powerful members of the Diet who support him in Diet debates, in voting on bills, in campaigning, and in other ways. In return, he helps find influential positions for his *habatsu* members and helps them get reelected by distributing donated money for use in their campaigns. Younger members find the money, in particular, to be crucial to their chances of election, because it is with such funds that they pay for the labor and support of their *koenkai*, or support groups.

At any one time, there may be as many as a dozen factions within a single political party. The number of members per faction could be as few as three or four and as many as one hundred or more. Generally, the more members in a faction, the more powerful that faction. The leaders of powerful factions have the best chances of becoming prime minister or heading powerful ministries in the cabinet such as the Ministry of Finance, the Ministry of International Trade and Industry, or the Foreign Ministry. Generally speaking, decisions about top posts are made with social harmony in mind. That is, cabinet posts are usually distributed in such a way that there is at least one representative from each major faction. When necessary, cabinet members will be replaced for no substantive cause and even after only short tenures in office just to satisfy the power-sharing demands of the *habatsu*.

During the forty years of LDP dominance of the cabinet, when inter-party conflicts were subdued because of the insurmountable power of the LDP, the voting public focused its attention on factional distribution in government in the same way that voters in other countries were paying attention to the number of seats held by differing parties. Despite efforts to reform the factional system, factions continue to play a major role in Japanese party politics. Unfortunately, if the public thought that a fair distribution of cabinet posts by faction was a way to allow varied voices to be heard in the halls of the Diet, they were mistaken. Factions have never been primarily about political ideology, but rather about money and the distribution of power—two of the major sources of conflict in all political systems.

Japan's faction-ridden party system, dominated by a single party, brought a measure of political stability for four decades. But in addition to preventing alternative voices from being heard, it also fostered rampant corruption. In Japan as in other democracies, the longer a party stays in power without effective challengers with a real chance of unseating its leaders, the greater the temptations to corruption are likely to be. By the 1960s, parties looking to capture non-LDP centrist voters and brandishing such names as the "Clean Government Party" and the "Democratic Socialist Party" emerged to challenge the dominance of the LDP. The influence of these parties was minimal, however, until the late 1970s and early 1980s, when LDP corruption captured the headlines, and voters started to cast serious glances at the new aspirants for power.

The Results of One-Party Dominance

The years of one-party LDP rule produced a thick web of behind-the-scenes collusion between big business, political parties, and the bureaucracy (sometimes referred to as the "iron triangle"). So powerful was the influence of the big business elite—known as the *zaikai*—that it could impose its will on the LDP leadership, virtually dictating the selection of prime ministers and other cabinet officials. Buying the votes of politicians became standard practice.[12] Although insiders were aware of the situation, the public got its first extensive exposure to its leaders' dishonesty around the time of the 1976 general election. As is often the case in Japan, the news came from outside the country.

During hearings in the U.S. Senate Committee on Foreign Relations, Lockheed Aircraft Corporation revealed that it had paid millions of dollars in illegal payments to politicians worldwide in return for promises of aircraft purchases by various foreign governments. Prominent among those so paid was Japanese Prime Minister **Kakuei Tanaka**.[13] Tanaka was eventually tried and convicted in Japan, while the corruption scandal mushroomed as reporters found hard evidence of bribery payments from a variety of corporations to many LDP leaders. In addition to the Lockheed Scandal, there was the Recruit Scandal that brought down Prime Minister Takeshita, the Kyowa Scandal, the Sagawa Kyubin Scandal that tarnished LDP strongman Shin Kanemaru, and many others.[14]

PROFILE: Kakuei Tanaka

On July 7, 1972, fifty-four-year old Kakuei Tanaka walked across the Niju Bridge into the Imperial Palace in Tokyo to receive the emperor's confirmation as the new prime minister of Japan. His elevation to the highest political office in the land was one of the most unusual in Japanese history. Japan is a nation that reveres education, but Tanaka had not only not graduated from college, he had not even finished high school. Born in 1918 and raised in the hinterlands of Niigata Prefecture by a dissolute father who had gambled away the family income, the new prime minister's image had also long been tarnished by his marriage thirty years earlier to a divorcée (he was twenty-four years old at the time and she was thirty-one), and by his having to manage his first reelec-

Former Prime Minister Kakuei Tanaka with his daughter.

tion campaign from jail because of his arrest for bribery only a year after his first election to parliament.

Just two years and five months after his assumption of the prime ministership, Tanaka resigned his office amid a swirl of media exposés that alleged bribery involving fantastic sums of money. His resignation came just four months after the resignation of U.S. President Richard Nixon in 1974 and carried an impact in Japan not unlike that of Nixon's resignation in the United States. The following summary of Tanaka's political career will shed light on the central role of "money politics" and on the place of factions, or *habatsu,* in Japan's political system.[15]

Tanaka started his adult life as a construction worker and contractor. His wife was the daughter of a construction company owner and subsequently inherited the company. During World War II he made substantial money on projects in Korea and then used those funds after the war to successfully run for national office as a representative from Niigata in 1947. Although positioning himself as a conservative, he favored policies that helped blue-collar workers like himself. In return for their votes, he saw that his prefecture's constituents were blessed with new roads, tunnels, and other large construction projects. When Tanaka was arrested for bribery in his first year in office, it was because voters, especially owners of small, blue-collar businesses, gave him their strong support—and apparently illegally gave him their money—because he had decided to vote against the then-Socialist government's attempt to nationalize the coal mines. Eventually his political support group, or *koenkai,* numbered over 95,000 members.

Cleared of the coal mine bribery charge, Tanaka advanced inside the conservative party and was eventually chosen for several cabinet posts. While minister of finance (one of the most powerful posts in Japanese politics), he revealed his approach to government by making it clear to the highly educated bureaucrats under him that he, not they, was in charge of Japan's finances. He knew by personal experience how to make money buying and selling land and buildings, and he often impressed his staff with his ability to grasp the details of such transactions. As minister of finance, his job was to oversee the buying and selling of government properties and the appropriation of massive sums for public works such as freeways and railroads. During his tenure, it is clear that he not only increased his own prefecture's share of government largess (it rose from fifth place to first place out of forty-seven prefectures and similar regional units); he also found ways to line his own pockets. Shadow companies with which he was involved would often buy up land just before it was to be purchased by the government for some public works project. Tanaka had clearly used his political offices to make himself a very rich man. But he had also helped make Japan a very rich country.

As minister of international trade and industry, he started or encouraged such massive projects as the new Tokyo International Airport in Narita, the undersea tunnel linking Hokkaido island with the main island of Honshu, an atomic power plant, a bullet train line to his prefecture, two major highways, and many others. How did he accomplish all this? He used the notorious factional *habatsu* system.

Shortly after Tanaka entered politics, he aligned himself with the Sato faction in the Liberal Democratic Party. Factions or political cliques organized around a senior politician are almost parties within a party, and Eisaku Sato's faction was one of the strongest ever. It supported Sato as prime minister for a tenure of eight years—the longest in Japanese history. Sato, a former bureaucrat, was the younger brother of a previous prime minister and became prime minister himself in 1964, just as Japan's economy was poised to overtake the economies of France, Britain, and Germany. With the Sato faction's financial help, Tanaka was elected to the Diet again and again until he eventually became prime minister. Tanaka found ways, apparently often illegal ways, to gather large sums of money that he disbursed to up-and-coming Diet members (and many plum bureaucrats) until he had created his own faction of loyal subordinates. Once he became a cabinet member, he saw to it that his own faction members received plum cabinet posts. For instance, in the 1970s, seven ministers of construction and four ministers of posts and telecommunications were in Tanaka's faction, as was the minister of transportation. Tanaka was so unabashed about buying support for his projects—he believed that money was the key to success in government—that he is alleged to have given substantial gifts of money to *every* member of the Diet in 1974!

Under a cloud of media exposure about his shady financial dealings, Tanaka resigned as prime minister in late 1974. But his influence as head of the Tanaka faction remained undiminished. Though he was later forced to resign his membership in the Liberal Democratic Party, he remained the strongest LDP faction leader during the 1980s, and his faction remained the largest of all factions. For ten years after his own resignation as prime minister, other leaders of his faction succeeded him in that high office, placing large numbers of the faction's members in the cabinet. Tanaka himself remained a Diet member even after he gave up his cabinet posts and actively recruited new subordinates, probably in hopes of staging a political comeback. But two events kept him from achieving that goal.

The first was the Lockheed Scandal. As the U.S. Senate investigation revealed, several members of the Japanese government, including Kakuei Tanaka while serving as prime minister, had received large sums of bribery money from the Lockheed Aircraft Corporation in return for their support for the purchase of Lockheed jet aircraft by Japanese airline companies. The sale required the approval of the Ministry of Transportation. More than a dozen people were directly paid off, with Prime Minister Tanaka receiving a $2 million bribe for his support for the deal.

The Japanese government eventually indicted sixteen people (with five more politicians implicated but not indicted for various reasons). All but one were convicted. Tanaka, who had by that time been out of the prime minister's office for nine years, was fined and sentenced to four years in prison. But he appealed his conviction (as did the others) and did not actually serve any time. Moreover, he refused to resign his seat in the Diet. He apparently felt that he had been doing the same thing many other politicians had done and that his approach to governance was, in effect, normal politics in Japan. The opposition, however, demanded a vote on his removal from office. Prime Minister Yasuhiro Nakasone, whose cabinet was peopled by Tanaka faction members, refused to allow the vote, whereupon all the opposition parties boycotted the Diet for over a month, forcing the prime minister to call an election in December 1983.

Although the LDP lost heavily and barely retained a majority in the lower house, Tanaka ran as an independent and was returned to office in 1983—for the fifteenth time—with the highest number of votes he had ever received in his entire political career. Once again, voters in his district, recognizing the pork barrel benefits Tanaka had brought home to them, gave their favorite son their strong support on election day. All the other LDP factions lost heavily, but Tanaka's faction remained more or less unaffected, with six of his faction members receiving seats in the new cabinet and with Tanaka and his faction in control of picking the next prime minister.

The election had proven once again that Tanaka, with the largest and wealthiest faction in the Diet, was the most powerful politician in the country. He was often referred to as the "shadow shogun" because of his ability to dictate the course of Japanese politics from behind the scenes whether in or out of office, whether a member of the ruling party or not, and whether convicted of serious crimes or not. With the passage of a little more time, he might have reclaimed the post of prime minister. But fate willed it otherwise. Two years after his resounding election victory, Kakuei Tanaka, at age sixty-seven, suffered a paralyzing stroke that hospitalized him and ended one of the most extraordinary political careers in Japanese history. He officially retired from politics in 1990.

By the late 1980s, these scandals had so disillusioned the electorate that, for the first time in decades, opposition parties felt they had a chance to actually defeat the LDP. Especially hopeful was the Japan Socialist Party led by Takako Doi. Not only did the JSP benefit from LDP corruption, but Doi was a woman—indeed, the first woman to ever head a major party in Japan. That fact alone brought unusual attention to the JSP. Using this unique opportunity (as well as public anger over the LDP's introduction of a 3 percent consumption tax), the JSP actually defeated the LDP in the upper house in the 1989 elections, spurring many disgruntled LDP members to bolt the party and create "study groups" or other precursors of change in the country's party system. New parties sprang up overnight: the Japan New Party, the New Harbinger Party, and the Renewal Party, to name a few. Japanese civil society entered a period of vigorous activity. Suddenly, voters had more than a dozen parties from which to choose candidates. The spate of new choices seemed to overwhelm even the voters' initial interest in

Doi's Socialists. For the first time since 1955, the LDP was in trouble.

JAPAN'S POLITICAL ECONOMY: FROM "JAPAN INC." TO THE "BUBBLE"

Adding to the LDP's problems in the late 1980s and early 1990s was the collapse of the "bubble economy." Beginning in the late 1950s, Japan's economy began a dramatic recovery from the ashes of war. By 1961 annual growth was over 14 percent, more than three times that of most other industrialized economies. With the LDP at the helm, Japan vaulted into second place among the world's economies, overtaking Canada (1960), Britain and France (mid-1960s), West Germany (1968), and the Soviet Union (1991) for that honor.[16] The economy made a dramatic shift from reliance on agriculture to high-quality industrial production, and by the late 1960s the United States was purchasing about one-third of all of Japan's exports, making Japan America's single most important trading partner.

By the 1980s the economy was so successful that governments the world over were sending experts to Japan to study its industrial management style and other factors they imagined had contributed to the country's phenomenal success.[17] So strong was the economy that Japan's overseas direct investments,

TABLE 19.2

Japan's LDP Prime Ministers, 1954–93		
Prime Minister	**Term of Office**	**Reasons for Rotation out of Office**
Ichiro Hatoyama	1954–56	Resigned after concluding treaty with USSR, of which some business leaders disapproved
Tanzan Ishibashi	1956–57	Illness
Nobusuke Kishi	1957–60	Resigned after mishandling renewal of controversial U.S.-Japanese security treaty
Hayato Ikeda	1960–64	Illness
Eisaku Sato	1964–72	Ousted by Tanaka in intra-party struggle
Kakuei Tanaka	1972–74	Corruption
Takeo Miki	1974–76	Resigned
Takeo Fukuda	1976–78	Defeated in intra-party vote by Masayoshi Ohira
Masayoshi Ohira	1978–80	Resigned after no-confidence vote against him
Zenko Suzuki	1980–82	Resigned
Yasuhiro Nakasone	1982–87	Resigned
Noboru Takeshita	1987–89	Resigned after recruit bribery scandal
Sousuke Uno	1989	Resigned after sexual misconduct allegations
Toshiki Kaifu	1989–91	Resigned after failure to pass reform bills
Kiichi Miyazawa	1991–93	Resigned upon vote of no-confidence

plus loans and economic aid, were energizing the entire Asian region, while its economic model of close ties between the state and private corporations was adapted by South Korea, Singapore, Taiwan, and other countries in the region.[18] In 1988, Japan's investments in enterprises in foreign countries (mostly North America) totaled $47 billion. Foreign investment assumed a higher percentage of GNP in Japan than in the much larger United States. In 1993, with an outlay of $11.3 billion, Japan became the world's largest financial aid donor, with 65 percent of its aid going to the Asian region. In the 1990s, Japan was exporting 10 percent of all products exported worldwide (the U.S. share was 13 percent) at a value of $339.5 billion.[19] Unfortunately, Japan was only importing about 6 percent of world imports, creating balance of trade deficits with many countries, especially the United States—a source of continuing friction. Still, the phenomenal expansion of Japan's export sector was one of the leading catalysts of economic globalization during the 1970s and 1980s.

How much of this meteoric economic growth can actually be credited to the LDP is unclear, for many factors seemed to be at play.[20] For example, Japan's business conglomerates, the zaibatsu, had been broken up by the Occupation authorities after the war. This move allowed new businesses to get started. Moreover, much of Japan's physical infrastructure (roads, factories, railroads, and the like) was destroyed during the Allied bombing. This destruction turned out to be a blessing in disguise, for it permitted Japan to build modern factories equipped with the latest technologies.

Of course, no rebuilding could have been accomplished without massive amounts of capital. In Japan's case, its former enemy became its biggest benefactor. The United States, believing that Japan could serve as a counterweight to China and other emerging communist nations in Asia, provided substantial reconstruction aid. Major Japanese corporations such as Sony got their start with such foreign assistance. It also did not hurt that, at the very moment Japan needed capital, the Korean War erupted next door in 1950. U.S. military funds in the early 1950s helped many Japanese companies get started, including Mazda Motors, which made Jeeps for the Korean War effort.

Of major significance to the country's economic recovery was the Japanese government's lack of expenditures on its own military. Because the post–World War II constitution forbade the Japanese nation from ever again building a war capability, the government was able to redirect funds that "normal" countries usually spend on defense to such areas as education, public works, and support of new industries. Almost everyone, however, agreed that Japan needed some kind of self-defense force, even if it would not have the capability of projecting itself militarily outside of Japan. The problem was how to build such a force without violating Article 9 of the constitution. Eventually, under Prime Minister Miki in 1976, the government established a defense spending limit of 1 percent of GNP. Compared to the United States at the time (6 to 7 percent) Britain (about 5 percent), and France (about 4 percent), that seems like a small amount. But the size of Japan's economy became so large in the 1980s that the 1 percent figure translated into over $10 billion per year in actual defense dollars, giving Japan one of the largest defense budgets in the industrialized world.[21]

Nevertheless, the Japanese government preferred to focus its attention on economic growth rather than on military preparedness, and thus Japanese industry came to look upon the government as a facilitator rather than a controller of private enterprise. With government support, Japanese industry began an export-oriented growth strategy that privileged gaining market share over realizing immediate profits. The government became an active player in selecting and supporting industries it felt had a good chance of succeeding.

For example, the Ministry of International Trade and Industry would regularly target a particular industry, say, steel, container ships, automobiles, and so on, for rapid growth through government support. If necessary, it would impose import controls on foreign products in those sectors, thereby protecting Japanese industry from competition. The export strategy of most companies was to obtain growth in market share rather than to pull in immediate profits. Thus, products were priced lower than similar products elsewhere. Japanese investors seemed comfortable waiting for the day when their company's product would dominate the market and then, finally, yield high stock dividends. By contrast, American investors seemed to want immediate profits, and thus the product price had to be high. This situation gave Japanese products the upper hand and caused tremendous consternation in U.S. industry, especially in such sectors as automobiles and steel manufacturing. By 1994, the Japanese were exporting so much more than they were importing that there was a worldwide trade surplus in Japan's favor in excess of $120 billion per year. Moreover, the Japanese had come to believe that foreign-made products were often inferior to Japanese-made ones and therefore did not pressure the government to eliminate protectionist measures.

Adding to the strength of Japan's economy was a relatively mild tax burden. Industries targeted for growth were often given tax breaks, and even personal income tax was not burdensome. In 1998, Japan's highest marginal individual income tax rate was 50 percent, but it did not take effect until one's income reached more than $230,000, a higher figure than most economically advanced democracies (see table 14.4 on page 334). Japan's bottom personal income tax rate has been among the lowest in the industrialized world, as table 19.3 indicates.

Social factors in which the government had no hand also contributed to the success of the Japanese economy. For instance, workers were used to working six days a week and then saving a large portion of their paychecks. With personal savings rates as high as 25 percent at times, compared to only 3 percent in the United States, banks always had enough funds on hand to make loans for new business start-ups. Workers were also exceptionally loyal to their companies, working overtime without pay and rarely resorting to union activity to resolve disputes. In return for this loyalty, the

TABLE 19.3

Personal Income Tax Lowest Rate (%), 1992	
New Zealand	24
Australia	20
Sweden	20
United Kingdom	20
Germany	19
Canada	17
United States	16
Japan	10

Source: Revenue Statistics of OECD Member Countries 1965–1993, OECD, 1994.

larger companies promised lifetime employment to their workers and adopted a benevolent, paternalistic stance toward them. It should be noted, however, that smaller companies were never able to promise lifetime employment and that even in larger companies there was always more movement into and out of companies, especially by younger workers, than was commonly thought.

Although there were a number of factors that the government did not control and that contributed to high growth, such as the traditional respect for education and hard work, it cannot be denied that the government worked diligently to promote economic development. Its approach could be described as an imperfect mixture of some of the principles of Adam Smith and John Maynard Keynes. The Japanese leadership believed that private property and capitalism should be the basis of the economy, but they also believed that the state is obligated to guide the development of free enterprises. Consequently, the LDP and the bureaucracy actively worked with the private sector to select industries most likely to achieve dramatic growth. They then provided plenty of capital to those industries and continued to give administrative guidance as necessary. They also quickly erected trade barriers such as import quotas whenever they felt a selected industry was under attack from outside competitors. Thus, despite the reforms initiated by the Allied Occupation in the 1940s, the Japanese government still permitted and encouraged a cartel-like economic structure in certain segments of the economy (today usually referred to as *keiretsu* rather than zaibatsu).

The result of these and other factors (including Japan's reliance on the United States to provide much of its defense, and the infusion of money that the Korean War brought into the country) was that Japan's economy grew at an amazing 10 percent a year on average for many years—the fastest growth rate of any country in the world. From small shop owners to corporation presidents, everyone benefited from the economic miracle. So cozy was the government with private enterprise that outsiders began to refer to the whole country as "Japan Inc.," a criticism that suggested that Japan's industries and government were one and the same. But this criticism—leveled by foreign companies that were having a hard time breaking into the strong Japanese market—was misplaced if not downright wrong. Compared to many economies in Europe, for example, the Japanese economy was quite "free." The Japanese had never tried to nationalize major industries as in Britain, France, Germany, and Italy, to name a just few "capitalist" countries. In France, for instance, the government until the 1980s controlled most of the insurance companies, whereas in Japan, insurance companies received strong administrative guidance from the government but were never owned or controlled by it.

Commonly known as **state-guided capitalism**, the Japanese economic model produced tremendous immediate results, but it also contributed to serious long-term blunders. Determined to keep every state-assisted company afloat no matter what, the government encouraged struggling companies to simply get more loans from private banks and keep going rather than let the free play of the market determine which companies or product lines would survive and which ones would fail. When the banks agreed to make loans to risky companies, they were, of course, putting their own survival at risk. The banks always assumed that, like the companies, they too would get government help if they needed to be bailed out.

By the late 1980s, however, the pile of bad bank loans was too high for even the Japanese government to handle. A decade later, the Ministry of Finance had to admit that Japanese banks were still holding 35 trillion yen (about $3 billion) in bad loans. Inflated real estate prices aggravated the problem, which was caused in part by land speculation resulting from Prime Minister Tanaka's plan to start major construction projects throughout Japan's previously undeveloped regions. Many Japanese companies had invested heavily in real estate and had used the assumed value of their land holdings to persuade banks to give them loans for industrial expansion or to support unprofitable but hard-to-sell product lines or simply to invest in the burgeoning stock market. But property values fell rapidly in a sudden "correction" when the Bank of Japan increased interest rates in 1989. When stock prices plummeted in 1990, wiping out $2.3 trillion in investor money, investors no longer had money to pay back the

large loans they had taken out. Dozens of companies went bankrupt and many businessmen committed suicide in disgrace.

Japan's economic woes were exacerbated by faulty decisions taken by the government's powerful bureaucracy. Bureaucrats in the Ministry of Finance and the Ministry of International Trade and Industry, for example, did not always do their homework when it came to recommending strategies to the private sector. For instance, one of the reasons that Japan trails the United States and many other countries in the development of computer software and other information industry products is that the bureaucrats strongly advised Japanese industry in the 1970s to give its attention to mainframe supercomputers rather than personal computers, a serious miscalculation. Both the early successes of these ministries and their recent missteps demonstrate the immense impact of "administrative guidance" on the Japanese economy.

The Japanese Bureaucracy

Starting with the Meiji Restoration of 1868, a new Japanese prime minister and cabinet has taken office every sixteen months, on average. Many prime ministers have been able to hold on to power for only a few months before the winds of political change have driven them from office. One of the shortest tenures was that of Prime Minister Tsutomu Hata, who took office on April 25, 1994 only to leave just nine weeks later. Even during the thirty-eight-year heyday of LDP rule, factional politics inside the party resulted in relatively frequent changes at the top or the reshuffling of cabinet portfolios (see table 19.2). Given such a high level of turnover and considering that many cabinet posts are given to politicians who have no particular knowledge of, or even interest in, the ministry over which they preside, it is not surprising that unelected bureaucrats within the various ministries wield real power. In effect, they run the government. Japan's elected officials—Diet representatives, cabinet members, and even prime ministers—often find that they have very little actual role in the determination of government policy. Until recently, cabinet ministers were generally not even questioned directly in the Diet, but were represented instead by bureaucrats. (The British practice of subjecting the prime minister to questions by members of parliament was not introduced until late 1999.) In Japan, the people's will and that of the nation's elected representatives often take a back seat to the priorities of the bureaucracy.

As in Britain and France, bureaucrats in Japan are often selected from the best universities—in Japan it is predominantly the University of Tokyo—and are required to take rigorous civil service examinations. Passing these exams brings public respect and guaranteed careers in government. Japanese traditions reinforce the prestige of the civil service. Historically, Japanese bureaucrats often came from aristocratic families and worked directly for the emperor. It was often said that, whereas Japanese politicians worked for themselves, the bureaucrats worked for the nation and were therefore above the pettiness of politics.

With the advantage of these historical precedents, today's bureaucrats have built for themselves a mammoth empire that has resisted numerous reform efforts and that seems to push forward consistent policies regardless of which political party is in power. As in France, and unlike in the United States and a handful of other democracies, in Japan the bureaucracy is where things happen. The Japanese bureaucracy is smaller than the bureaucracies to be found in some other industrialized nations, but at 5 million full-time employees, it is a powerful force in Japanese society. Let's examine the current ratio of elected officials to bureaucrats.

At the national level, voters currently elect 626 members of the Diet to represent them. By contrast, there are 1,146,950 other central government personnel working in the various ministries, none of whom is elected by the people.[22] Thus there are approximately 1,830 bureaucrats for every one elected official at the national level. For regional and local political offices, voters elect about 35,000 people. But running the various towns, cities, and prefectures are almost 3.3 million bureaucrats, for a ratio of ninety-three unelected bureaucrats for every one elected official. Combining the national, regional, and local totals produces a ratio of 124 bureaucrats for every one elected official. These figures do not include part-time personnel (thousands of them), nor do they include officers and employees (620,000 people) of the 115 public corporations, nor any of the eight privatized public corporations, nor any of

the some 250 deliberative councils which are attached to various ministries. (Public corporations are government-created agencies that function like private for-profit corporations.)

Efforts to control, reform, or reduce the size of the bureaucracy have usually failed. But in 1999, the Diet passed legislation that will alter many features of the bureaucracy for the first time in decades. By January 1, 2001, the number of ministries and agencies will be reduced from twenty-two to thirteen; bureaus within ministries will be reduced from 128 to ninety-six; advisory bodies to ministries and agencies will be reduced from 211 to eighty-nine; and many of the public corporations will be given more autonomy. Significantly, the total number of government officials must be reduced by 20 percent by the end of 2010. Under the new reforms, the grip of the Ministry of Education on the ninety-nine national universities and the many national research laboratories will be loosened, allowing more independent research but also increasing the likelihood that universities and research institutes will compete more vigorously among themselves for funding.

One ministry that has gained international fame for its role in guiding Japan's economic growth— the **Ministry of International Trade and Industry (MITI)**—will be renamed the Ministry of Economy and Industry and will be given more responsibility for the growth of small and medium-sized businesses. As the prime protector and promoter of Japanese industry since 1949, MITI has no exact parallel anywhere in the world, and although it is relatively small, it has tremendous influence through its ability to approve or deny new technological developments, including imports, and to influence the business community through the placement of many of its retired top leaders in the management ranks of Japan's large business conglomerates. Counterpart organizations such as the U.S. Department of Commerce have never had the power or influence of MITI, nor would the U.S. business community welcome such a role for it, preferring instead a business style less encumbered (and also less facilitated) by government.

Occupying top honors as ministries go is the **Ministry of Finance,** often considered the most powerful government ministry in the world of economically advanced democracies. Every year the Finance Ministry hires the highest-scoring graduates from Japan's top universities (mostly the University of Tokyo). Sometimes seen as a conservative ministry when compared with the expansionist MITI, the Ministry of Finance has actually played a vital role in forecasting potential growth areas for the economy and regulating banking and taxation. Perhaps most important is its role as final decision maker for budget requests from all the other ministries. All other ministries must submit annual budget requests to the Finance Minister in time for the start of the new fiscal year each April. This gives the ministry a powerful hand in guiding the economy as it sees fit.

CASE STUDY OF A JAPANESE MINISTRY

Another way to understand the bureaucracy in Japan is to examine the workings of just one ministry. Let's look at the Ministry of Agriculture, Forestry, and Fisheries. Of course, only one cabinet minister (almost always an elected Diet member[23]) heads this ministry, but the ministry employs over 44,041 civil servants assigned to 155 divisions (branch offices, agencies, centers, laboratories, etc.).[24] A brief review of even a partial list of the various divisions reveals the breadth of coverage and the depth of detail with which national ministries involve themselves in the lives of citizens: National Research Institute of Vegetables, Ornamental Plants, and Tea; National Livestock Breeding Center; Fertilizer and Feed Inspection Station; Animal Quarantine Station; National Center for Seeds and Seedlings; National Food Research Institute; National Institute of Fruit Tree Science; Food and Marketing Bureau; Private Forest Department; National Salmon Resources Center; National Research Institute of Aquaculture; Center for Quality Control and Consumers Service; and National Farmers Academy.

In addition to the above divisions within the ministry itself, the Ministry of Agriculture, Forestry, and Fisheries has attached to it twelve public corporations. A sample of these corporations includes the Japan Racing Association, the Farmers' Pension Fund, the Water Resources Development Public Corporation, the Forest Development Corporation, and several others.

Furthermore, the Ministry oversees thirteen deliberative "councils" that gather information and advise the ministry on matters in its portfolio. A sample of these includes the Veterinary Affairs Council, the Sweetening

Resources Council, the Agricultural Mechanization Council, the Fruit Industry Promotion Council, the Research Committee for Agricultural and Forestry Standard, and several others. There are 250 such councils attached to the various central government ministries.

This extensive network of ministerial divisions, public corporations, and councils, each with its own regulations, allows the Ministry of Agriculture, Forestry, and Fisheries to control its constituents through a system called "administrative guidance." In other words, whenever a member of the public or a private company or organization—say, a farmers' association—wishes to begin or expand a venture that would fall under the purview of the Agriculture Ministry, the project must be approved by one or more of the subsections of the Ministry. This approval process may require numerous applications and frequent visits to one or more of the Ministry's offices. During such visits, ministry officials have many opportunities to set parameters, explain regulations, require modifications or deletions of part of the project, and so on. In this way, citizens' projects, though perhaps quite unique at first, are ultimately made to fit the mold of ministry policies and procedures.

Organizations that cooperate fully with ministry directives, especially private sector companies, may find themselves in the fortunate position of having a ministry official come to work with them after retirement from the ministry. Bureaucrats often retire in their early fifties and seek employment in the private sector, where they can receive more than twice their civil service salary. The company benefits by having on its staff a former ministry official with "insider" influence. This system of retirement to selected private sector organizations is called *amakudari,* or "descent from heaven," meaning that the official comes from above with his powerful government connections to work in and assist the private sector while at the same time keeping the company in compliance with the bureaucracy's wishes. Similar practices occur in France, another country with an especially influential state bureaucracy and close state-business connections.

Japanese civil servants, especially the twenty thousand or so who constitute the core elite, are aware that their education at the best universities in Japan and their power as government officials give them special advantages. They believe that their viewpoint from the pinnacle of power is more objective and just than that of special interest groups or narrow specialists—and certainly better than that of the elected politicians who are nominally their superiors, but whom they sometimes scorn. Traditionally, many high-level bureaucrats were descended from the Tokugawa-era samurai families. The public image these elites created relative to their dedication, hard work, self-sacrifice, and impartiality has remained a fixture of the Japanese bureaucracy ever since. As long as the government has worked well, the public has had little reason to challenge these traditional claims of superiority.

In recent years, however, the bureaucratic veneer has begun to crack.[25] Not only have disgruntled government bureaucrats written scathing exposés about wild parties, lazy workers, and gross inefficiencies, but the general public has become aware that many bureaucrats are simply neither as competent nor as impartial as once thought. Far from making decisions on the basis of the general good, central bureaucrats in Japan have been found to be highly susceptible to bribery from the private sector and from regional and municipal officials. Today's newspapers regularly carry stories about *kankan settai,* that is, the practice of local and regional officials spending citizens' taxes on lavish drinking parties and other entertainments, including expensive overseas travel, in order to curry favor with central government officials. Important financial decisions, such as the provision of huge bank loans to certain businesses, have been found to be based on personal friendships (sometimes called "crony capitalism") rather than on credit-worthiness, a factor that contributed to the collapse of the bubble economy in 1989 and 1990.

Japanese bureaucrats are not known for their attention to the demands of consumer groups or environmental groups, but they seem to respond quickly to big business producer groups such as the Japan Chamber of Commerce and Industry, the Japan Association of Corporate Executives, and the Federation of Economic Organizations *(Keidanren)*. With nearly 1,000 corporate members and 120 industry-wide associations as Keidanren members, this big business group carries enormous weight inside the government. It has influenced bureaucrats and elected officials to ig-

nore or vote against proposals that would have preserved the environment and protected consumers. In fact, it was at the insistence of the Keidanren in 1955 that the two largest conservative political parties merged to form the Liberal Democratic Party.

Perhaps even worse than unfair influence, graft, and corruption are the growing number of cases in which government officials have shown poor judgment at the expense of the citizens they are supposed to serve. One such case was a potentially disastrous leak at a nuclear power plant in 1997. Rather than inform the public immediately, the bureaucrats decided to keep absolute silence, even though such a decision potentially endangered the lives of many people.[26] In another case, HIV-tainted blood was allowed to be sold and used for blood transfusions with the knowledge of bureaucrats from the Ministry of Health. (Curiously, a similar incident occurred in France in the 1980s.) These cases, plus charges of corruption and incompetence against the Ministry of Finance (some of whose officials were arrested in highly publicized police raids) and other ministries, have severely tarnished the image of the central bureaucracy in recent years.

The Bursting Bubble

The problems that accumulated in Japan's economy in the late 1980s and early 1990s—the collapse of the banking system, the precipitate fall in real estate prices, bureaucratic miscalculations, and related troubles—produced a serious recession from which Japan has not yet recovered. The high cost of living hit Japanese consumers hard: by the mid–1990s a bag of white rice cost $40 compared to the U.S. price of about $7. And because of Japan's pivotal role in today's globalized economy, its economic crisis inevitably had a ripple effect on other economies around the world, spawning financial crises in Asia, cutting the profits of companies doing business with the Japanese, and sending stock prices tumbling on Wall Street and other stock exchanges around the world. The high-flying economic system that once appeared insuperable is increasingly viewed by many Japanese and outside observers as a bubble that has burst. Many are questioning its basic premises and casting about for new ideas to re-form it. Has Japan's vaunted economic model failed?[27]

HYPOTHESIS-TESTING EXERCISE: The Japanese Economy

HYPOTHESIS AND VARIABLES

According to the tenets of economic liberalism, governments that utilize free-market approaches to economic development will produce more wealth for society than will those that try to dominate the economy through state control or excessive government regulation of the economy.

The **dependent variable** is *wealth,* and the competing **independent variables** are *market capitalism* and *a state-controlled economy.*

EXPECTATIONS

We would expect that Japan's economy would have generated more wealth during the period from 1945 to the present, when a form of market capitalism was the rule, than any period prior to that time, especially the Edo or Tokugawa periods (1600–1868), when the military shoguns attempted to control every aspect of the feudal economy. The style of market capitalism in Japan is a modified version of liberal principles. It combines completely unfettered and unassisted enterprises in large segments of the economy with state-assisted enterprises that receive preferential treatment in financing and protection from outside competition. None of these state interventions, however, has ever reached the level of state domination of the economy that prevailed in the pre-1868 period or even the level of intervention that a number of West European governments engaged in during the 1960s and 1970s. We would also expect to find lower growth or related problems in areas of the economy where market principles are violated.

EVIDENCE

By the mid–1960s, the Japanese economy under its combination of market liberalism and state-guided capitalism was poised to overtake the economies of several European countries. Today, despite over a decade of economic recession and even some years of negative economic growth, the Japanese economy is still the second largest in the world, behind the United States. (In 1997, Japan's GNP was nearly $4.8 trillion, compared to $7.7 trillion for the United States. On a per capita basis, Japan was second in the world while the United States was sixth.) In recent years, the Japanese have generated so much wealth that Japan has been able to assist the devel-opment of economies all over the world; indeed Japan is a larger donor of foreign aid than the United States, giving out some $10 billion a year. Some countries, especially in Asia, have received so much Japanese aid money that a large portion of their own gross domestic product is actually the spillover of Japanese wealth.

By contrast, during the Tokugawa era, the Japanese shoguns prohibited all foreign trade except out of one port in Nagasaki, which they controlled themselves. Except for Holland, countries formerly trading with Japan were not allowed even to enter Japan's ports. Furthermore, the shoguns forced their subordinate daimyos, or domain lords, to spend alternating years living in Tokyo, an expensive practice that drained their resources and forced many of them to borrow heavily from rice merchants and samurai. As a result of these controls the economy grew weaker by comparison to its counterparts in Europe and North America. By the mid–1800s, the Japanese realized that their economy and their military were no match for the West, and they had to begin a painful re-structuring process.

When weak spots are found in the modern Japanese economy today, it is often at precisely those places where the Japanese have violated market principles in favor of state control. For instance, for many years the government owned and controlled the national railway system. After decades of such control, the system was found to have 277,000 more employees on its payroll than it needed and to have accumulated a public debt in excess of $257 billion. The government eventually resolved the problem by privatizing the system. Likewise, the government has made it a practice for years to provide "administrative guidance" to a variety of industries—that is, to select certain industries for growth and then support them, even at the expense of a truly free market. When lagging sales produced crises in these selected industries, the government encouraged banks to prop up the industries with large loans based on weak collateral. In short, they violated the principle of the free market by supporting companies or products that the consumers did not want. That was one of the causes of the prolonged recession of the 1990s and further evidence that the Japanese economy suffered precisely at those points where the government violated market principles.

CONCLUSIONS

On the whole the evidence is largely *consistent* with our hypothesis. Though postwar Japan has hardly been a laissez-faire economy with no government intervention, its blend of free enterprise, market mechanisms, and state assistance for dynamic private firms has produced far more rapid growth than did the more state-dominated economic strategies that its leaders employed in the past.

POLITICAL CHANGE IN THE 1990s

The 1993 Elections

Just as the LDP had been praised for its role in revitalizing the economy, it was now blamed for its inability to restore it to health. As in other societies, the population rightly perceived that the economy and politics are closely intertwined. And as we saw in the beginning of this chapter, corruption reared its ugly head again in the Shin Kanemaru affair, when police raids on the property of the LDP kingmaker unearthed millions in ill-gotten money. In 1993, following the Diet's ouster of Prime Minister Miyazawa, a growing number of former LDP voters decided that it was now time to exit the party rather than raise their voices to try to change it from within.[28] So too did a growing number of LDP politicians, many of whom quit the disgraced party and formed new ones.

In addition to the **Japan New Party,** founded in 1992 by Morihiro Hosakawa, two more parties sprang up just before the elections: the **Japan Renewal Party** (Shinseito), led by former LDP leaders Tsutomu Hata and Ichiro Ozawa, and the **New Harbinger Party** (also translated as the New Party Pioneer), led by another ex-LDP Diet member, Masayoshi Takemura. A number of other parties provided additional choices for the Japanese electorate. On the left were the **Japan Socialist Party** (which wished to be known in English as the **Social Democratic Party**) and the **Japan Communist Party.** In the center were two offshoots of the Socialist Party, namely, the **Democratic Socialist Party** and the **United Social Democratic Party** (Shaminren). Both parties were more moderate than the Socialists, most of whose leaders still rejected the security alliance with the United States. Another centrist group, the **Komeito,** had ties to a Buddhist movement. Several smaller parties and independent candidates complemented the electoral menu.

The results of the 1993 elections (which had the lowest voter turnout in three decades) represented a stinging repudiation of the Liberal Democrats, but no other party emerged as a clear alternative (see table 19.4).

Upon losing control of the lower house, the LDP was forced to turn power over to a broad coalition of old and new opposition parties. In a state of disbelief, the party that had governed Japan without interruption since 1955 now retreated to its new place in the opposition. Although still the largest single party, it had lost control of both houses of the Diet and was no longer able to control its membership.

The hung parliament that followed the 1993 elections ushered in a period of instability and uncertainty that discomfited many Japanese and foreign governments. Over the next three years the country had four prime ministers (see table 19.5). Lacking clear direction, the post-1993 coalition governments had little success in tackling the country's mounting economic problems and declining global position. Hosokawa's reformist cabinet, which assumed power immediately after the elections, made good on its promises of electoral

TABLE 19.4

House of Representatives Election Results, 1990 and 1993 (512 seats in 1990; 511 in 1993)				
	1990		1993	
Party	Seats	% of Vote	Seats	% of Vote
Liberal Democratic Party	275	46.1	223	36.6
Social Democratic Party	136	24.4	70	15.4
Japan Renewal Party	—	—	55	10.1
Komeito	45	8.0	51	8.1
Japan New Party	—	—	35	8.0
Democratic Socialist Party	14	4.8	15	3.5
Japan Communist Party	16	8.0	15	7.7
Other Parties	5	1.0	17	3.3
Independents	21	4.1	30	5.9

TABLE 19.5

Japan's Governments, 1993–2000

Prime Minister (Party)	Governing Parties	Term of Office
Morihoro Hosokawa (Japan New Party)	7-party coalition	July 1993–April 1994
Tsutomu Hata (Japan Renewal Party)	5-party coalition	April–July 1994
Tomiichi Murayama (Japan Socialist Party)	3-party coalition	July 1994–Jan 1996
Ryutaro Hashimoto (LDP)	LDP minority government	January–October 1996
Ryutaro Hashimoto	LDP minority government	October 1996–July 1998
Keizo Obuchi (LDP)	LDP minority government	July 1998–October 1999
Keizo Obuchi	3-party coalition	October 1999–April 2000
Yoshiro Mori (LDP)	3-party coalition	April 2000–present

reform but dissolved amid hints of scandal. Disagreements over tax policy and other issues plagued the next two coalition cabinets before the Liberal Democrats returned to power in an unlikely partnership with the Socialists in January 1996 under Ryutaro Hashimoto. Corruption and indecisiveness continued to have a wearying effect on domestic public opinion, and there was a widening sense around the world that government in Japan had ground to a halt.

In a desperate attempt to head off mounting criticism and hopeful of establishing a more secure basis for governing without coalition partners, Hashimoto dissolved the House of Representatives and called anticipated elections in the fall of 1996. The constitution requires elections to be held within forty days after the dissolution of the lower house. (The upper house is never dissolved.) The House of Representatives is formally dissolved when a dissolution edict from the emperor (actually decided by the cabinet), wrapped in purple paper, is opened and read by the speaker. With the completion of this ceremony, the 1996 race was on.

The Electoral Reforms Take Effect

The campaign was fought under the new electoral laws enacted in 1994. Under the previous system, Japan's House of Representatives was elected in multimember districts. The country was divided into 129 districts; depending on the district's size, between two and six deputies were elected to represent it in the House. The candidates' names did not appear on the ballot, so voters had to write in their selections. This system required Japanese politicians to do everything they could to enhance

their name recognition. Incumbents running for reelection thus had an incentive to deliver highly visible pork-barrel projects to their districts, a practice that at times encouraged corruption in the legislative process. All candidates felt the need to spend lavishly on campaign advertising. (Brazil has a similar system, with roughly similar results.) Ultimately, the pre-1996 electoral system reinforced the Liberal Democrats' lock on power. As the governing party, it had the power to allocate government-funded projects to districts represented by LDP deputies. And as the party with the greatest access to wealthy corporate contributors, the LDP could afford to field several candidates in each district, several of whom might win. By the 1980s it was estimated that running an election campaign for a seat in the Japanese House of Representatives could be five times as costly as running for the U.S. House, with an average reported expenditure of $2.5 million. Prior to 1996, none of this money was allowed to be spent on individual television advertising.[29] Candidates in the larger districts, where five or six Diet representatives were chosen, could win a seat with as little as 20 percent of the vote.

In an attempt to reduce the LDP's advantages and open up the election process to other, less well-funded parties, Prime Minister Hosokawa proposed a sweeping reform of the electoral system as well as stiff limitations on campaign funding. His proposal called for reducing the size of the House from 511 to an even 500 seats and for instituting a two-ballot election process. In the compromise bill that was eventually passed into law, it was agreed that 300 seats would be elected in single member districts (SMD) on a winner-take-all basis; the remaining 200 would be elected according to proportional representation (PR). For the PR vote, the country was divided into eleven new districts, with parties required to win at least 2 percent of the vote in those districts.

This new system is roughly similar to the dual SMD/PR method for electing the lower house of parliament now in use in Germany and Russia. It seeks to combine the name recognition factor of single member districts, where candidates run by name, with the fairness in representation afforded by proportional representation, which allows even small parties to win representation in the lower house. The 2 percent hurdle in each district is aimed at preventing a proliferation of mini-parties. On election day, each voter gets two ballots: one showing the names of individual candidates, the other showing a list of the competing parties. The voter selects one candidate and one party. Voters are therefore free to split their vote, choosing, say, an LDP candidate on the single member ballot but marking the Japan Socialist Party on the proportional representation list.[30] For years, rural districts have been favored by the multiseat system, but the new SMD/PR system was likely to alter the balance of power away from the rural areas. This may give political advantages to parties whose constituencies are urban workers—a fact not lost on the LDP, which continues to mull over possible revisions of the 1994 reforms. The public, however, wants the LDP to leave things alone for awhile and see how the new system will work before attempting any reforms.

Every Japanese adult age twenty-five or older has the opportunity to run for the House of Representatives. In practice, however, only those who can command large sums of money or who enjoy the advantage of coming from already established political families (sometimes called the "elected nobility") usually succeed at the polls. Hosokawa's original proposals for curtailing campaign funding were fairly stringent. He wanted to ban all donations to individual candidates, requiring donors to make their contributions only to a party's national organization. In negotiations with the Liberal Democrats, Hosokawa retreated from that position and agreed to allow individual candidates to receive up to $4,500 per private sector corporate donor. Obviously, candidates with nu-

merous corporate donors would be able to receive many times that figure, a reality likely to benefit the well-connected Liberal Democrats. (The compromise reform law phased out *all* contributions to individual candidates starting in 1999.) The reform required the disclosure of the source of any donations above $450. (Under the previous system, disclosure was required for donations above $9,000.) It also enabled parties to receive campaign funding from the state. The earlier practice of restricting the official campaign period to twelve days was retained.

The 1994 reform of the electoral system has not pleased everyone. Indeed, after the 1996 elections, the LDP, the Liberal Party, and the New Komeito Party began to float ideas for change; each hoped for a return to some version of multiseat constituencies. But public opinion favors continuing the current system for several more elections until its merits or demerits can be fully evaluated.

The 1996 Elections

The House of Representatives election of October 20, 1996, took place in a period of flux unprecedented in the lifetime of many Japanese voters. Every week, it seemed, some new political group was freshly born or was joined together from the remains of former parties. And every month it seemed that new alliances were announced, many of which, for ideological reasons, would have been judged unworkable from the start had the electorate taken the time to evaluate them. Voters were bewildered by the sudden array of new parties, most of whose ideological positions were unclear at best. More than a dozen parties, along with a similar number of independent candidates, sought votes in 1996. These factors help explain the unusually low turnout for the 1996 vote, with only 59.7 percent of the eligible voters going to the polls, the lowest turnout in postwar Japan.

The largest new party to take part in the elections was the **New Frontier Party,** an amalgam of nine former parties that was put together in 1994 by two former Liberal Democratic politicians, Ichiro Ozawa and former prime minister Tsutomo Hata. In 1995 Ozawa, an energetic proponent of political and economic reform, bested Hata in an election to choose the party's leader. (In a new twist on party leadership selection procedures, which are usually controlled by party elites in Japan, New Frontier allowed all adult citizens to vote for its leader upon payment of a $10 contribution. More than 1.6 million people took part in the vote.) The final results indicated a good showing for New Frontier, which captured 156 seats. But this tally was not enough to outdo the Liberal Democrats, who came in first with 239 seats.

Nor was it enough to create a real two-party system, as the authors of the 1994 electoral reforms had wished. Several other parties also won seats in the new legislature, preventing the Liberal Democrats from governing with an absolute majority of seats (see table 19.6). With 47.8 percent of the total seats in the House of Representatives, Prime Minister Hashimoto had to cut deals with smaller parties in order to retain control of the government and pass his bills into law. With the agreement of the Socialists and the small Sakigake Party, along with a few independents, Hashimoto put together a parliamentary alliance that enabled the Liberal Democrats to form a single-party minority government. In full command of the cabinet once again, the LDP was back on top of the Japanese political system.

Aftermath of the 1996 Elections

Hashimoto's new government found it difficult to take decisive measures to overcome Japan's economic malaise. As a man who had earned his stripes as a tough negotiator in trade talks with the United States, Hashimoto was not inclined to push for radical changes in the tax code, banking regulations, and other aspects of the Japanese economy that Ameri-can government officials and economists advised the Japanese to undertake. In 1998, Japanese voters expressed their dismay at the slow pace of change by dealing the Liberal Democrats a rude blow in elections to the Diet's upper house, the House of Councillors.[31] Stung by this shock, Hashimoto decided to resign, even though he was not obligated to do so. His successor was **Keizo Obuchi,** a member of the same powerful faction as former Prime Minister Tanaka (originally the Sato faction, but now called the Takeshita faction). Obuchi became the eighty-fourth prime minister in Japan's history.

An orthodox conservative, Obuchi was one of the least popular contenders for the office of prime minister. Although he was a well-known politician, having served in the Diet since the age of twenty-six and having held high-profile positions such as foreign minister, most people believed that he possessed neither the vision nor the dynamism to lead Japan out of its decade-long economic stagnation. Moreover, the policy issues Obuchi seemed most interested in, such as getting Russia to return the northern islands it has occupied since World War II or maintaining the U.S.-Japan security arrangement (see later in this chapter), did not seem as urgent as jump-starting the economy and reforming government. By late 1999, Obuchi's approval rating had nose-dived to just 32 percent. One major complaint against him was his inclusion of the Komeito Party in a three-party coalition government with the LDP and the newly created **New Conservative Party** in October of that year. A political offshoot of a Buddhist denomination known for its strong-arm tactics (the *Sokka Gakkai*), Komeito had been part of the New Frontier Party in the 1996 elections. When

TABLE 19.6

House of Representatives Elections, 1996 (500 seats: 300 chosen by SMD, 200 by PR)			
Party	Total Seats (%)	SMD Seats	PR Seats
Liberal Democratic Party	239 (47.8)	169	70
New Frontier Party	156 (31.2)	96	60
Democratic Party	52 (10.4)	17	35
Japan Communist Party	26 (5.2)	2	24
Social Democratic Party	15 (3.0)	4	11
Sakigake	2 (0.4)	2	0
Other	1 (0.2)	1	0
Independents	9 (1.8)	9	0

New Frontier subsequently broke up, Komeito reconstituted itself as **New Komeito.** But it was still too closely linked to religion to be trusted by the average Japanese voter. Obuchi countered that including New Komeito was politically necessary if the LDP, still weakened in numbers and political clout, was to be able to pass Diet legislation. In general, the voting public expected Obuchi's government to solve the problem of bad loans by Japan's major banks and revitalize the economy, something he had not accomplished by the start of new millennium. Obuchi's strategy was to stimulate growth by pumping large amounts of government money into the economy through generous spending on public works projects and other programs. He put the reform of Japan's fiscal system on hold, postponing tax increases that some critics considered urgent in view of the rising national debt resulting from the government's lavish spending measures. However, signs of the economy's slow recovery were sprouting up when Obuchi suffered a debilitating stroke in April 2000; he died several weeks later.

In his place the kingpins of the Liberal Democratic Party installed Yoshiro Mori, a little-known figure whose principal merit was his acceptability to the party's various factions. (Mori himself belonged to the same faction as Obuchi.) Mori promised to continue Obuchi's economic strategy but he soon found himself the butt of criticism for some embarrassing gaffes. In one widely reported comment, Mori asserted that Japan is "a divine country with the emperor at its center." He soon apologized for any "misunderstanding" this remark may have caused and insisted that it did not contradict the postwar principle that sovereignty resides with the Japanese people. Mori did not explicitly retract his earlier statement, however.

The 2000 Elections

With the next elections to the House of Representatives due to be held before the end of 2000, Liberal Democratic Party politicians decided to schedule them at the end of June. Their hope was that the LDP's continuing popularity among large segments of the electorate, especially in rural areas where it traditionally ran strong, would be sufficient to overcome Mori's lack of mass appeal. (Mori's popularity ratings hovered between 12 and

Prime Minister Yoshiro Mori

19 percent.) They also hoped that the government's massive public works and welfare programs would be gratefully rewarded with votes.

The results of the elections of June 25, 2000, as shown in table 19.7, were no cause for rejoicing for the Liberal Democrats: they lost a considerable number of seats. (Though they had won 239 seats in the previous elections of 1996, their ranks subsequently swelled to 271 when the New Frontier Party fell apart and a number of its deputies gravitated to the Liberal Democrats.) The public's continuing disaffection was evident in the 60.5 percent turnout, only slightly higher than the record low turnout of 1996. But the final tally was good enough to enable the Liberal Democrats to reconstitute their coalition government with New Komeito and the New Conservative party. With the size of the House reduced from 500 to 480, the Liberal Democrats won 233 seats (48.5 percent of the total). New Komeito won thirty-one seats

TABLE 19.7

House of Representatives Elections, 2000 (480 seats: 300 chosen by SMD, 180 by PR)			
Parties	**Total Seats (%)**	**SMD Seats**	**PR Seats**
Governing coalition parties:			
Liberal Democratic Party	233 (48.5)	177	56
New Komeito Party	31 (6.5)	7	24
New Conservative Party	7 (1.5)	7	0
Opposition parties:			
Democratic Party	127 (26.5)	80	47
Liberal Party	22 (4.6)	4	18
Japan Communist Party	20 (4.2)	0	20
Social Democratic Party	19 (4.0)	4	15
Small parties and independents	21 (4.4)	21	0

(6.5 percent) and the New Conservatives won seven seats (1.5 percent). The largest opposition party, the Democratic Party of Japan, increased its representation from fifty-two seats in 1996 to 127 seats. The Social Democratic Party (also known as the Japan Socialist Party) improved its showing from fifteen seats in 1996 to nineteen. The Liberal Party, a new party led by Ichiro Ozawa following the break-up of his New Frontier Party, debuted with twenty-two seats.

Yoshiro Mori emerged from the elections as the renewed choice of the consensus-conscious LDP faction leaders and was duly reinstated as prime minister. He vowed once again to continue the economic policies that he inherited from his predecessor. But a scandal was brewing that threatened to tarnish the Liberal Democrats with fresh charges of corruption. A former LDP construction minister was arrested a few days after the elections and accused of receiving $285,000 in kickbacks, reviving fears that a Liberal Democratic government might once again be immersed in corruption charges.

One of the few signs of change to emerge from the June 2000 elections was a slight increase in the number of females elected to the lower house. Thirty-five women won seats in the House of Representatives, as compared with twenty-three in the previous Diet. In spite of the increase, Japan still has one of the world's lowest percentages of women serving in the lower house of a nationally elected parliament (7.3 percent). Ironically, Japan's reformed electoral system is part of the problem: 300 of the 480 House members are elected in single member districts. The SMD system places a premium on name recognition, inducing politicians to spend large amounts of money on their campaigns to make themselves known to the public. Few women in Japanese political life possess the organizational and financial backing needed to meet this challenge. Single member districts also favor incumbents who can remind the electorate of the government benefits they have secured for their constituencies while serving in the legislature. Following Mori's reelection, the LDP selected Mrs. Chikage Ogi, the leader of the New Conservative Party, as minister of construction. But her cabinet appointment represented a questionable political victory for Japanese women, inasmuch as no male political figures wanted the scandal-tainted post.

It would be an understatement to say that Japanese party politics today remains in a state of flux. The situation is likely to produce unexpected electoral consequences for many national elections into the future. Many people speculate on what impact, if any, the end of multiseat constituencies will have on the faction system, especially within the LDP. Perhaps it is too early to tell, but it appears that the faction system has, indeed, weakened somewhat and that what used to be factional (within-party) friction is becoming *inter-party* friction. But factions have a long history in Japan, and should the LDP return as a single-party government in the future, it is likely that factions will continue to play an important role.

While local races have remained more stable, they have not been entirely immune to the vagaries of national-level party politics and may themselves yield new shifts of power in the coming years. In addition to the national elections, voters also periodically vote for the governors of Tokyo and Osaka as well as some 35,000 local and prefectural government officials. The prefectural system was established during the 1870s when the Meiji government replaced the 260 feudal domains with more centrally administered units, eventually numbering forty-seven. Historically, the prefectures had little power compared to the central administration. But during the Allied Occupation, legislation was passed that allocated some tasks to local government, and further attempts to empower local governments were made in the late 1990s.

CLUES TO ATTITUDES AND BEHAVIOR: IDEOLOGY, POLITICAL CULTURE, AND SOCIAL CLASS

Does Ideology Matter?

Most Japanese voters do not engage in issue-based political discussion during election campaigns; rather, they evaluate the personality and influence potential of their candidates very carefully. They expect, however unrealistically, to personally meet their favorite for office, and they take that personal relationship very seriously. With personality and personal relationships prevailing in Japanese voters' minds as the key qualifications for office, coherent political ideologies play a less important role as determinants of Japanese voting behavior.

Similarly, ideology is of little significance in explaining the recent rush to create new political parties. Despite the confusion catalyzed by the end of absolute LDP dominance, one thing is very clear to Japanese voters as well as to outside observers: profound differences in political philosophy do not seem to constitute the basis for new party formation or party membership. Indeed, just as U.S. President Bill Clinton was frequently criticized for abandoning Democratic Party principles in favor of his own reelection, Japan's political parties, heedless of their public reputation as "conservative," "liberal," "reform," and so on, were often found to be "stealing" planks from one an-

other's platforms for political expediency. Indeed, many politicians seemed to ignore ideology altogether in their rush to create an organization—any organization—that could topple the LDP.

Ideology, Political Culture, and Class Identity in Historical Perspective

In short, ideology in today's Japan is less significant than it was in the pre–World War II period. In the 1920s and 1930s a number of ideology-based parties emerged, some of which emphasized the needs of the working classes and drew upon the increasingly popular terminology of socialism and communism. With names like the Labor-Peasant Party, the Japan Proletarian Party, and the Japanese Communist Party, these organizations, many of them short-lived, solicited membership on the basis of political theories or beliefs about the nature of "just" societies. In addition, a number of parties were established to promote the cause of liberal democracy, an ideological orientation that sharply contradicted the prevailing authoritarianism of the ruling elites.

In earlier periods of Japanese political history, more than today, political conflict seemed to stem from differences in fundamental ideas and values. Advocates of equality and democracy clashed with the guardians of social hierarchy and imperial rule. That era, called the Taisho Era after the Emperor Taisho, who reigned from 1912 to 1926, covered the years just before World War I until the Great Depression of the 1930s. It was a most unusual time for Japan. Not only did it witness unprecedented ideological conflict, it was also characterized by major changes in the country's mass political culture. The Japanese people had historically thought of themselves as obedient to those above them in the social hierarchy. The impact of Confucianism, imported from China in the fifth century, had created a political culture that stressed respect for authority and deference to the political elites, while Buddhism encouraged a certain detachment from worldly conflict, a passivity that facilitated unfettered leadership by top aristocrats.

But the Taisho Era was remarkably unruly, with various segments of society engaged in passionate debates about equality, democracy, and other core political concepts and values. At times these disagreements turned violent. The conflicts began with a bang in 1913 when a popular protest movement of journalists, opposition parties, and others surrounded the Diet building in Tokyo and demanded the resignation of the prime minister for violating the principles of democratic government. The demonstrators raided pro-government newspaper offices and set fire to police stations. Naming themselves the "Movement to Protect Constitutional Government," the protesters persisted until the prime minister resigned, the first such resignation forced by a popular movement in Japanese history.

With the wartime economy booming, the labor movement began to strengthen. Not only did workers demand a more equitable distribution of company profits, they also wanted recognition as valuable players in society. It was the first time in Japanese history that the masses felt they had a chance to "be somebody." Disgruntled workers organized hundreds of work stoppages, and when the government wanted to raise the price of rice, as many as two million workers and housewives took to the streets in protest. Like workers in other countries at the time, Japanese workers were fighting over core identity issues—in this case, their role in the new social class structure. Shedding their past deference to established authority, many Japanese dared to be openly contentious.

When the economic boom ended after World War I and employers began to lay off workers or reduce their wages, the masses would have none of it. Workers and leftist intellectuals organized the Japan Federation of Labor in 1921 and the Japan Communist Party in 1922. Liberal intellectuals argued forcefully to the alarmed elite that the era of privileges and special recognition for the upper classes was over. Realizing that there was no way to contain this clash over values, the ruling elites reluctantly began to make concessions. The government passed a minimum wage law, a tenant-landlord law, and most significant, a universal voting law that gave the vote to all males over age twenty-five.

But just as the political left was making headway, the political right, with far more resources at its command, also began to organize. Its representatives in the Diet rushed through new "anti-subversion" laws that gave the police the right to suppress intellectuals and workers. The Japan Communist Party, which favored abolition of the monarchy, was forced underground and severely suppressed in the 1930s.

While workers in the cities were becoming radicalized, rural peasants were organizing themselves into unions to demand rent reductions on farmland. But the farmers' movement showed little strength at the polls, and many farmers' complaints were muted by land reforms initiated in 1939. In the rural areas, the government increased the inculcation of conservative, even militaristic, values in the minds of elementary school children. Respect for imperial institutions and the positive value of social hierarchy were key elements in the students' required moral education. Although the Taisho Era is often referred to as one of popular awakening, in the end the forces of right-wing extremism prevailed, manipulating popular attitudes and setting the stage for the militarization of the government in the 1930s and Japan's wholesale aggression against its neighbors.

During the war years of the 1940s, the military-dominated government virtually abolished all political parties and suppressed, but did not completely extinguish, popular movements that did not support the war effort. When that unhappy era of propaganda and forced obedience to the imperial state ended, the population as a whole seemed less inclined to join any organization that espoused a strong ideological line, whether religious, social, or political. There was a brief flirtation with left-wing parties and radical labor unions during the Allied Occupation (1945 to 1952), but the Japanese people for the most part seemed far more committed to practicality than principle. At war's end, they were physically and emotionally exhausted and disillusioned with government. More than anything else, they wanted stability and normalcy.

Political Attitudes and Social Class in Postwar Japan

After the war, a broad consensus developed around the core values of pacifism, democracy, equality of opportunity, private enterprise, and active state intervention in the economy. The Liberal Democratic Party, for all its faults in succumbing to corruption, epitomized these values. With the chief ideological struggles of the past now decisively resolved in favor of democracy, ideology lost its earlier prominence as a source of political conflict. Today, only the Japan Communist Party, which has barely 5 percent of the lower house seats (and sometimes no seats in either house of the Diet) seems to be considered enough of an outsider ideologically that the other parties avoid it when seeking coalition partners.

Every country has a collection of individuals or small groups that seem to have perpetual complaints about the government of the day, no matter what it is. Japanese people are used to hearing speakers on the sound trucks of right-wing militarists as they blast each government for its pacifism. And the world watched in amazement as the radical religious group, the Aum Shinrikyo, attempted to kill thousands of passengers in ruthless subway gas attacks. But these groups are small and generally not well organized, and they typically gather only the anger or disgust of mainstream society rather than its support.

Even the nagging question of the 1950s and 1960s about whether or not Japan should build and maintain a strong military organization (the LDP essentially said yes, and the Socialists and Communists said no) seems to have evaporated. The Japanese public seems comfortable with a 1 percent cap on military expenditure, even though they know that the size of the economy has meant that the seemingly small percentage has, in fact, propelled Japan into the top category of nations in terms of actual money spent on military preparations. And although many Japanese were opposed, the Miyazawa government in 1992 was able to pass legislation that allowed Japanese military personnel to participate in United Nations peacekeeping operations in Cambodia.

In the wake of the weakening of LDP dominance, the world has watched in amazement as conservatives have teamed up with Socialists and as reform parties have joined ranks with establishment parties in order to form one government after another. Japan's only Socialist premier, Tomiichi Murayama, who governed from 1994 to 1996, did a complete about-face on taking office and repudiated his party's decades-long opposition to Japan's national anthem and military forces and its pacifistic opposition to the security partnership with the United States. The relatively non-ideological atmosphere has not appeared to bother Japanese voters, most of whom seem more interested in a candidate's connections than in his or her convictions. Says one scholar, "nobody in the provinces really cares whether a politician is nominally a socialist or a conservative (or, for that matter, honest): what counts is whether he gets results in pressuring the central government to send some resources to the region."[32] Like the United States and the West European democracies, Japan has experienced the "end of ideology" in the postwar period.

Even social class differences, which are often the basis for political party membership in many countries and which influenced party formation in the 1920s, have not generally produced sharp ideological conflicts in postwar Japan or coalesced into party structures. As some have suggested, this phenomenon reflects the fact that Japanese society is "vertical": each person, however high or low on the socioeconomic scale, feels obligations to those above or below him.

This verticality is particularly evident in the structure of labor unions. Whereas in most countries labor unions constitute a strong symbolic statement of workers' feelings of separateness from the owners and managers of corporations, in Japan they are "company unions." That is, the labor union is an in-house organization with an office inside the company and a budget provided by the company for certain activities and with membership coming only from within the company. Labor leaders feel an obligation to management and vice versa. Organizing an industry-wide strike would be very difficult since union membership does not extend industry-wide.

On the managerial side, managers who can create harmony *(wa)* are considered more praiseworthy leaders than those who are good at winning every contest. As spoofed in the popular 1980's American movie, *Mr. Baseball*, even managers of professional sports teams would prefer their team to *just barely* win, so that the opposing team will not be demoralized and disharmony created. In this way, it is believed, the system as a whole can keep happily working for years, and that goal is more important than winning. This very Japanese concept of *wa* is generally shared by most of the population and constitutes a core element of the nation's political culture. It venerates social harmony and broad consensus as more important values than individualism and self-assertion. That is why, when major political conflict erupts in Japan, it is likely that, behind the scenes, major changes in social relationships are underway, as happened during the Taisho Era.

In addition to the moderating influence of verticality and *wa* in Japanese society, the social class structure today benefits from the Occupation reforms after World War II. Determined to eliminate any source of potential challenge to the rule of law from the military or business conglomerates, the Occupation authorities redistributed large land holdings, broke up many of the business cartels (zaibatsu), and implemented many other social reforms that elevated the status of women and others. As a result of these and subsequent developments, Japanese society today has fewer obvious social class markers than ever in its history, and the vast majority of citizens consider themselves to be members of the affluent middle class. Japan also experiences less socioeconomic inequality than the United States, Britain, or several other economically advanced democracies. While an income gap assuredly exists between the richest and the poorest, it is narrower than in most other economically advanced democracies. By the mid-1990s a mere 2 percent of Japanese households had incomes below $16,000 per year, and only 2 percent had incomes above $160,000. Everyone else was in the middle, with half of the country's households making an average annual income of between $35,000 and $75,000. Even Japan's top business executives earn considerably less than their American counterparts, a fact the late Sony executive Akio Morita pointed out in criticizing corporate practices in the United States. The top executives at Toyota and Honda earn little more than $300,000 a year, a pittance compared to America's corporate millionaires.

The current Japanese level of social equality is the result not only of modern cultural attitudes created in part by the Occupation but also of deliberate efforts by the Japanese government since the end of World War II. Despite their pro-business ethos, the Liberal Democrats established a system designed to reduce inequality by imposing heavy taxes on the wealthiest citizens (who often pay 50 percent of their income in taxes) and on corporations (37.5 percent), while providing substantial government subsidies to the poor and keeping taxes low for most people. Critics of this policy claim that the country's difficult economic situation will require some changes in these practices, including lower business taxes and fewer subsidies. And everyone is worried about the increasing size of the elderly population. How can society support people who are forced to retire at age fifty-five or sixty and live another thirty years? Japan has the longest life expectancy of any country in the world, and projections show that in 2025, more than 25 percent of the population will be over age sixty-five. Many people worry that Japan's elderly will come to constitute a massive underclass. In 2000, Prime Minister Mori proposed raising the normal retirement age to seventy.

Meanwhile, widely shared Japanese social attitudes, stressing strong family ties, respect for authority, and the importance of education, act as cultural brakes on heavy government spending. Some 922 students out of every 1,000 graduate from high school (compared to only 757 out of 1,000 in the United States). Despite the high price of land and housing, nearly 60 percent of the Japanese own their own homes (compared to 54 percent in France and 64 percent in the United States). Only about 1 percent of the population is on welfare, as families often care for their own. Drug addiction is uncommon, resulting in a low crime rate. Fewer than twenty people are killed by gunfire in Japan in an average year, compared with more than 100 per day in the United States in the late 1990s, counting murders, suicides, and accidents. The low rate is likely due to Japan's strict gun control laws: handguns are illegal, and the use of guns for hunting and sports is strictly regulated. Unwed mothers account for only 1 percent of births (though the abortion rate is traditionally high); the literacy rate is 99.9 percent.[33]

These statistics implicitly explain why the Japanese government does not have to foot a huge bill for crime prevention, or the penal system, or poverty-stricken children, or literacy programs. The nagging recession of the 1990s eventually produced an unemployment rate of 4 percent—an unusually high rate for Japan, which usually boasts a rate of only about 2 percent (compared to an exceptionally low 4 percent in the United States in 1999 and 10 percent in Canada). Homeless people have started camping out in train stations, much to the consternation of officials. But these problems are mild in Japan compared to many other societies where the family structure is less supportive. The government continues to provide some of the same benefits found in West European welfare states, such as tuition-free education through college for those able to pass the rigorous entrance exams into the government-funded universities (but not the private universities), as well as universal health insurance in cooperation with industry and private citizens.

About 6 percent of the Japanese are employed in agriculture (3 percent in the United States), over 23 percent are employed in manufacturing, and another 23 percent are employed in the service industries. The Japanese average wage exceeds that of most industrialized countries: $20 per hour compared to $12 in the United States, $9 in Britain, and $14 per hour in Germany. Moreover, the relative level of worker satisfaction is revealed in the small annual number of work days lost to labor strikes: only 112 days lost in Japan in 1993, compared to 3,981 days in the United States, 649 days in the United Kingdom, and 593 days in Germany.

Consensus and Conflict in Contemporary Japan

Despite the powerful webs of consensus that knit Japanese society together, distinct political differences nevertheless exist that occasionally solidify into action (though probably less frequently than in other democracies). Sometimes they can break out into violent conflict. Japanese students, for example, have at times staged mass demonstrations in support of such causes as opposition to Japan's security ties to the United States. Rough clashes with the police have ensued, but many of the 1960's demonstrators have now taken their places in the corporate world, and there is little student activism today.

A particularly acute display of public discontent surfaced in the 1970s, when the government announced its intention to build the new Narita international airport in the Chiba area, located one hour east of Tokyo. An idyllic location, with rice paddies and forests surrounding small hamlets,

the area was seen by environmentalists and rice farmers as the worst possible place to construct an airport. Demonstrations, riots, and even homemade rocket attacks on airport construction workers revealed deep-seated anger at government policy. Protected by police in head-to-toe battle gear, construction workers were able to complete the massive project, and the government got its way, although not without serious damage to its image. Today, some politicians are calling on the government to once again permit international flights to land at the old Haneda airport in Tokyo proper.

Such outbursts are rare in Japan. The broad thrust of public opinion gravitates away from extreme ideological positions and inclines toward immediate issues affecting one's livelihood or neighborhood. Interest group articulation tends to be local rather than national, and thus has little ultimate effect on government policy. Consumer movements are particularly short-lived. As one observer has correctly noted, the Japanese are not concerned with "the broad constitutional, environmental or personal liberty issues that tend to interest intellectuals" in other countries.[34] Whether this will always remain so is an open question. Indeed, in recent years, with the public increasingly disaffected from the formal political party process, the atmosphere may become increasingly conducive to the growth of issue-based interest groups. Moreover, as Japanese culture as a whole becomes more heavily influenced by the individualistic mindset of the West as opposed to the "good-of-the-whole" philosophy of Confucian-influenced Asian societies, it may be that the Japanese will increasingly find it "natural" to forcefully express their opinions and desires for change.

To be sure, there are other topics that could be cited as sources of disharmony and potential springboards for single-issue party formation. Some are even picked up as issues by existing political parties. Pollution is one example. During the 1970s, the LDP realized that environmental problems were becoming so severe that voters might punish the party at the polls. New regulations were created that helped improve air and water quality and thus reduced pressure on the government. Another example is the treatment of minorities, especially Koreans and the indigenous Ainu, who have been subjected to both social and governmental discrimination for years. Eventually the LDP loosened some onerous regulations regarding Koreans. But it is government corruption and public demands for greater account-ability on the part of civil servants that have spawned the only real drive for new party creation in recent years. A number of Diet members have or-ganized anti-corruption "study groups" as precur-sors to actual parties while the topic of corruption has dominated political debate in recent years.

Meanwhile, several controversial international issues animate political debate in Japan today without necessarily providing a basis for the for-mation of new parties. Indeed, the LDP and other leading parties are internally divided over how best to deal with them. Some of the most sensitive of these issues center on relations with the United States, Russia, and Japan's Asian neighbors. A brief overview of some current foreign policy is-sues throws considerable light on the close interac-tion of domestic politics and international rela-tions in contemporary Japan.

CONTEMPORARY ISSUES

The U.S.-Japan Security Treaties Issue

After Japan's defeat in World War II, the occupying forces under Gen. Douglas MacArthur effected a complete demilitarization and disarmament of the country, after which the various participating na-tions signed a peace treaty with Japan. Many Japa-nese, glad to have the war come to an end, adopted the position that Japan should be a neutral power, like Switzerland, with no military treaties with other countries. Many Japanese went even further and opposed the reestablishment of the military in any form. The Japan Socialist Party made that phi-losophy one of the key points of its party platform in the 1940s and 1950s. Article 9 of the new Japa-nese constitution also reinforced this position when it declared that Japan would renounce war forever. The LDP has favored building a strong self-defense force while relying on the U.S.-Japan security agree-ments to provide its primary security umbrella.

However, the outbreak of the Korean War in 1950 and the increasing Cold War antagonism between the West and its allies and the Soviet Union and its allies convinced the Occupation authorities that Japan needed its own self-defense forces and had to be an ally of the West. Various treaties and agree-

ments were thus signed between 1951 and 1960 that allowed the United States military to occupy over 100 former Japanese military bases in Japan and to keep tens of thousands of U.S. troops stationed there. Japan was permitted to build its small "Self-Defense Force," and the United States agreed to de-fend Japan in the event of outside attack.

From these military bases the United States exe-cuted its war against the Chinese-supported North Koreans during the Korean War of 1950–53. But as time went on, the presence of so many American troops on Japanese soil created serious problems. Unruly off-duty soldiers got into trouble with local inhabitants, and the noise of jet night-training mis-sions annoyed residents near the bases. For many, the presence of the troops was a sign that Japan was still an occupied country without complete sovereignty.

The Liberal Democratic Party supported the signing, and subsequent re-signing, of the security and base treaties. The opposition parties, led by the Japan Socialist Party, generally did not. In 1960, when the original treaty came up for re-newal, the LDP engineered a vote on the treaty issue late at night when most opposition members of the Diet had gone home. This provoked mas-sive street demonstrations all over Japan and forced the cancellation of the visit of U.S. President Dwight D. Eisenhower to Japan. The prime minis-ter resigned, but the treaties remained in force and the demonstrations continued.

One clause of the treaty allowed Japan to end its adherence to it in 1970 if it wished. In anticipation of that opportunity, university students, organized into the "All-Japan Student Union," took to the streets, using sharpened bamboo poles as spears to battle police and creating such unrest that many universities were closed for months. In violent demonstrations that echoed the anti–Vietnam War protests exploding all over the United States and other countries at the time, students deplored the fact that nuclear-armed U.S. naval vessels were probably docking in Japan. They claimed that this was an affront to their nuclear-free, pacifist beliefs, which had resulted from the atomic bombings of Hiroshima and Nagasaki during World War II. They also decried the "puppet" relationship that they claimed the United States had forced on Japan and that the conservatives in government had accepted. Public anger was defused somewhat when the United States agreed to vacate some of the bases in the more heavily populated areas (they were turned over to Japan's Self-Defense Forces or turned into parks) and to return the island of Okinawa to Japanese control.

It was agreed that the United States could continue to rent most of the bases already in use on Okinawa, constituting some 25 percent of the island's surface. This situation, in turn, eventually provoked a rare confrontation in Japan: a challenge to central government authority by a prefectural government. After an Okinawan schoolgirl was raped by two U.S. soldiers in 1995 (there have been many other less well-known attacks on civilians by U.S. soldiers), the governor of Okinawa demanded that the U.S. give up its use of the island as its main military outpost in Asia and send its thirty thousand troops elsewhere. Closing down the bases became a priority of his local administration's policy. Once again, protesters hit the streets, this time led by their own governor. Using the strong powers of central authority granted it by the constitution, the government in Tokyo made it clear that it alone—not the governor of Okinawa—would negotiate changes in the security agreement with the United States.

Adjustments were eventually made that helped minimize the annoyance of the bases to the local citizens, but the security treaty remained, as did the bases. The Japanese people seem to have accepted the status quo, but the issue of the treaties and military bases and Japan's right to defend itself without the involvement of outside military entanglements always remains just below the surface of political debate in Japan. Today the Self-Defense Force is relatively small, numbering only 156,000 troops (compared to 2.3 million troops in the People's Republic of China). But as the United States increases its pressure on Japan to shoulder more security responsibilities in the Asian-Pacific region, it is likely that military development and the related issue of Japan's non-war clause of its constitution will receive even more attention in the future.

The Northern Territories Dispute

To the north of the island of Hokkaido lie several small but politically important islands: Kunashiri, Etorofu, Shikotan, and the Habumai islands. Called the **Northern Territories** by the Japanese, these islands have been claimed by Japan but occupied by Russia since the end of World War II. Russia claims it has a legal right to the islands and that all Japanese claims to them were forfeited at the signing of the San Francisco Peace Treaty in 1951 (which, ironically, Russia did not sign). Japan, on the other hand, says that none of the islands in question was included in the treaty. As a result of this stalemate, Japan and Russia have never signed a peace treaty to formally conclude World War II between them, and Japanese relations with Russia remain cool.[35]

In the early 1990s, with the Soviet Union's economy in tatters and the communist system's complete collapse imminent, the Kremlin's leaders seemed more willing than before to settle accounts with Japan, in return for much needed financial assistance. In 1991 Soviet President Mikhail Gorbachev declared his intention to settle the issue by the year 2000. But upon the demise of the Soviet Union later that year, the issue took on nationalistic overtones, with hardliners in the Russian government seeing the loss of the islands as a further blow to the international prestige of their country.

Nevertheless, in 1998, following on the heels of a similar meeting five months earlier, Russian President Boris Yeltsin held a short summit in Japan with Japanese Prime Minister Ryutaro Hashimoto. The Russian president seemed interested in moving forward toward a resolution of the now fifty-year old problem, and of course there was no doubt that the Japanese wanted the islands back. Japanese citizens with a special interest in the islands—such as those having deceased family members buried there—had long been staging demonstrations against Russia's foot-dragging. But if the Japanese wanted a resolution and the Russians wanted a resolution, why was the problem still unsolved as of mid-2000?

The answer lies in the aphorism that "international politics is merely domestic politics writ large." Japan is united by a broad nationwide consensus on the return of the islands, but Russia is not. Some Russian leaders seem to understand the need to return the islands, but as it happens, the majority of the Russian people (70 percent) are opposed to the return of the islands to Japan, as are many Russian legislators. Although these opinions must clearly weigh on the mind of any Russian politician interested in solving the problem, an even greater obstacle lies within the Russian bureaucracy. Different Russian ministries are negatively affected by the proposed return of the islands. For instance, Russian fishing boats complain to the Fisheries Ministry that access to their source of livelihood will be stopped by the return of the islands to Japan. The Defense Ministry sees the potential return of the islands, which bases Russian submarine and other military installations, as a blow to the security of Russia in the Far East (probably an exaggerated claim, now that the Cold War is over). And the Russian Foreign Ministry, which tries to handle all the competing interests from other ministries while dealing with opposing views inside its own bureaus, ended up being heavily criticized by other ministries when it tried to resolve an earlier dispute over the safety of Japanese fishermen in the Northern Territories. It would appear that if the Japanese government really wants to get back its islands, it must first sort out what is going on inside the Russian bureaucracy.

Japan and Its Asian Neighbors

Although the Taiwanese generally are at peace with their history as a colony of Japan, the rest of Asia continues to view Japan dimly. In the 1970s the Indonesians staged violent demonstrations against the visit of the Japanese prime minister; the mainland Chinese complain every time Japan improves its military capability; and the Koreans have little good to say for their neighbors to the east. The animosity runs both ways, and many Japanese look down on those of Southeast Asian or Korean descent. Even Koreans who have lived in Japan for generations and are Japanese in virtually every respect are often required to give their fingerprints when applying for a visa, whereas the Japanese are not.

Memories of Japan's aggression in World War II have not yet died out in Asia. Although Prime Minister Hosokawa apologized for Japanese aggression in 1993, the Diet did not pass a resolution to this effect for two more years. Even then, nationalist LDP politicians objected to an unambiguous "apology" and replaced that word with an expression of "re-

morse" in the resolution, which was primarily directed at the nations of Asia that had suffered under Japanese occupation. The Japanese government has never apologized to the United States for the attack on Pearl Harbor, which is still widely regarded in Japan as a legitimate wartime response to hostile U.S. actions and rivalry in the Pacific.

Yet Japanese overseas direct investment and development assistance have increasingly won the praise of Asian leaders in recent years. Singapore, for instance, has openly praised the Japanese economic model, and few in Asia would deny that the infusion of Japanese yen into their economies has transformed the region. In a recent year, out of twenty countries in the Pacific Rim, thirteen listed Japan as their most important or second most important trading partner. Indicative of the growing respect for Japan are the large numbers of Asian students who choose to study the Japanese language, correctly believing that it will be useful as a tool for business.

JAPAN AND THE FOUR FACES OF DEMOCRACY

We conclude by returning to the question we raised at the start of this chapter: *how democratic is Japan?*

With respect to Face I of democracy, it is clear that the Japanese system of government is far from the ideal of "government of the people." More pointedly, it has even strayed from the fundamental principle of government by elites *accountable* to the people. To be sure, since the end of the Occupation, the Japanese people have enjoyed the right to vote for their national and local government officials in free, open, and competitive elections. To that extent, Japan has fulfilled the minimum requirements of an electoral democracy. It was a majority of Japanese voters who repeatedly returned the Liberal Democratic Party to power for nearly four decades, passing up the opportunity to elect its opponents. As long as the economy boomed and life was basically good, most Japanese felt they had little reason to vote for change.

But the flagrant violation of the public trust by corrupt LDP officials constituted an indisputable abuse of power, making a mockery of the most elementary principles of popular sovereignty and elite accountability. The corrosive power of money in the electoral and policy-making processes has often flouted the general public interest and the will of the citizenry. The extraordinary power of unelected bureaucrats has escaped democratic controls by the people and their elected legislative and governmental representatives. And until the formation of a host of new parties in the 1990s, the main opposition parties were so dogmatic or limited in their appeal that they failed to offer the mass of the population an acceptable alternative to the Liberal Democrats. These and similar realities of Japanese politics have tarnished postwar Japan's struggle to be a full democracy, representative of its people. To their credit, however, a large number of Japanese political elites and growing numbers of ordinary citizens have taken concerted action in recent years to change the system's most repugnant features. Their efforts, while perhaps only partially successful thus far, provide vivid testimony that the spirit of popular sovereignty and representative democracy is very much alive in a country habituated to one-party rule for most of its postwar history.

As to Face II, Japan has done a reasonably good job in maintaining basic political and civil liberties. During the 1950s and 1960s, for example, when students took to the streets in massive demonstrations, some people wondered if the government would take advantage of the unrest to curtail the freedom of assembly rights guaranteed in the 1947 constitution. But the courts upheld the constitutional rights of citizens to assemble. Similarly, the press, as well as private citizens, has been able to print articles in strong opposition to government or government policies, usually without fear of retaliation. The courts have been generally cautious in ruling on cases where basic human rights would be curtailed. Many residents of Japan feel that their level of personal freedom is greater than in other democracies—in part due to gun control and the relatively low violent crime rate and the resulting ability to walk the streets day or night with less concern for personal safety. They believe that "freedom" has gone too far in many countries of the west; they believe there is sometimes greater freedom within structure.

Face III of democracy centers on democratic values. Among the most important of these values, the Japanese score heavily with respect to consensus and compromise. Japanese cultural traditions attach a high value to social harmony, resulting in a rela-

tively high level of civility in the country's political life. The need for consensus can sometimes be dysfunctional, however, as when it allows elements of the political elite or Japanese society to block necessary reforms or changes. With respect to the value of tolerance, the Japanese tend to be divided. A large number are tolerant of the small non-Japanese minorities in their midst and are open to sincere cooperation with foreign governments and businesses. But traditional attitudes of intolerance and chauvinism, striking deep chords in the national psyche, are still very much present. Southeast Asians, for example, are not treated with the same civility as Americans or Europeans. While marriages of Japanese with non-Japanese are generally looked down upon, Japanese-Caucasian marriages are more acceptable than, say, Japanese-African marriages.

Finally, Japan has made enormous strides since the war to achieve a modicum of economic democracy, which is Face IV of democracy. While the country has by no means achieved real income equality, it has widened equality of opportunity through a superior educational system and professional advancement based on merit, while at the same time producing a level of income differentiation that is less unequal than in many economically advanced democracies. Its principal shortcoming with respect to Face IV, as noted earlier, is the relative absence of effective democratic checks on the bureaucratic elite's power in the all-important domain of economic decision making.

Thus we conclude by affirming that, for all its problems, Japan *is* a democracy containing many of the structures and values found in the major industrialized democracies of Europe and North America. It is also obvious that the Japanese people much prefer this system to anything they have experienced in more than two thousand years of history. Not very long ago Japan was so withdrawn from the world that even its own citizens who managed to travel abroad were not allowed to return home for fear they would contaminate the population with unacceptable ideas from overseas. An even shorter historical distance takes us back to a period of military dictatorship at home and ruthless aggression abroad. Today the Japanese can rightfully boast of having democratic institutions that are still just a distant dream in the minds of would-be democrats in many emerging countries of Asia and elsewhere around the world. If such a country can make a dramatic turnabout and establish a democratic system within a relatively few short years, then perhaps those nations that have suffered under internal and external oppression for so long can also make a new start.

KEY TERMS AND NAMES
(Underlined in the text)

Yoshiro Mori
Shoguns
Emperor Akihito
Emperor Hirohito
Meiji Restoration (1868)
Samurai
Zaibatsu
Occupation
Diet
House of Representatives
House of Councillors
Liberal Democratic Party (LDP)
Japan Socialist Party (Social Democratic Party)
Factions
Kakuei Tanaka
State-guided capitalism
Ministry of International Trade and Industry (MITI)
Social Democratic Party
Northern Territories

FOR DISCUSSION:
WHAT WOULD YOU DO?

1. If you were a Japanese citizen, which party (if any) would you belong to?
2. If you were a Japanese voter, would you vote for corrupt politicians as long as they delivered benefits to your district?
3. Would you vote for a party or candidates other than the Liberal Democrats, knowing that your choices would probably have to form a coalition with other parties?

FOR FURTHER READING

In addition to the titles in the notes, consult the following:

Asahi Shimbun Publishing Company, *Asahi Shimbun Japan Almanac* 1998.

Roger Buckley, *Japan Today,* 3d ed. (Cambridge: Cambridge University Press, 1998).

John W. Dower, *Embracing Defeat: Japan in the Wake of World War II* (New York: W. W. Norton, 1999).

Purnendra Jain and Takashi Inoguchi, eds., *Japanese Politics Today: Beyond Karaoke Democracy?* (Melbourne: MacMillan Education Australia, 1997).

Japan External Trade Organization, *Handy Facts on U.S.-Japan Economic Relations* (Tokyo: JETRO, 1998).

Takako Kishima, *Political Life in Japan: Democracy in a Reversible World* (Princeton, N.J.: Princeton University Press, 1991).

Kodansha International, *Japan: Profile of a Nation,* (Tokyo: Kodansha, 1994).

Richard McGregor, *Japan Swings* (St. Leonards, New South Wales, Australia: Allen and Unwin, 1996).

Nippon Steel Corporation, *Nippon: The Land and Its People,* 2d ed. (Gakuseisha Publishing, 1984).

Yung H. Park, *Bureaucrats and Ministers in Contemporary Japanese Government* (Berkeley, Calif.: Institute of East Asian Studies, 1986).

J. A. A. Stockwin, *Japan: Divided Politics in a Growth Economy* (New York: W. W. Norton, 1975).

WEBSITES

An all-purpose site with hyperlinks is the Japan Information Network site, <www.jin.jcic.or.jp>. The English language edition of *The Japan Times* can be reached at <www.japantimes.co.jp/topnews.html>. See also the site of the Japan Policy Research Institute, <www.nmjc.org/jpri>.

NOTES

1. For more on the Asian financial crisis of the 1990s, see Dean W. Collinwood, *Japan and the Pacific Rim,* 5th ed. (Guilford, Conn.: Dushkin/McGraw-Hill, 1999), 12–13.
2. *Nippon Tateyoko [Japan As It Is]* (Tokyo: Gakken, 1997), 171.
3. Women have reigned as empresses ten times in Japanese history. Most reigned between the years A.D. 500 to 800, although one reigned as recently as the mid-1700s. For more, see *Japan: An Illustrated Encyclopedia* (Tokyo: Kodansha, 1993), 337.
4. W. Scott Morton, *Japan: Its History and Culture,* 3d ed. (New York: McGraw-Hill, 1994), 149–80.
5. Barrington Moore, *Social Origins of Dictatorship and Democracy* (Boston: Beacon, 1969), 228–313. Moore argues that democracy was stultified in Japan by an alliance of agrarian landlords and the big business

industrialists of the zaibatsu. Both groups favored repression rather than democracy. The landlords sought to keep the peasant masses in their place, a task they were able to accomplish because the cultivation of rice could proceed in traditional ways without extensive economic modernization and social change. The industrialists sought to keep the urban working class in check. Small and medium-sized urban capitalism in Meiji Japan was too weak to produce a pro-democratic bourgeoisie comparable to the ones that developed in Britain, the United States, and France. As Moore puts it, "no bourgeois, no democracy." The ultimate result by the 1930s was a Japanese variant of fascism, infused with such national traditions as the warrior spirit of the samurai, emperor-worship, and hatred of foreigners.

6. In 1860, the Edo Shogunate organized a tour to the United States for top government leaders. The trip directly exposed government officials to democratic forms of government for the first time in Japanese history, but many of the Edo officials were displaced by the Meiji revolution.

7. One of these women later returned to Japan and established Japan's first university for women, Tsuda Juku Daigaku, in western Tokyo.

8. Dean W. Collinwood, Ryoichi Yamamoto, and Kazue Matsui-Haag, *Samurais in Salt Lake: Diary of the First Diplomatic Japanese Delegation to Visit Utah, 1872* (Salt Lake City: U.S. Japan Center, 1996).

9. Koichi Kishimoto, *Politics in Modern Japan*, 4th ed., (Tokyo: Japan Echo, 1997), 19–24.

10. J. A. A. Stockwin, *Governing Japan*, 3d ed. (Malden, Mass.: Blackwell Publishers, 1999), 36–53.

11. See Kishimoto, *Politics in Modern Japan*, 161–170, for a complete English version of the constitution of 1947.

12. For an analysis of money and politics, see Karel van Wolferen, *The Enigma of Japanese Power* (New York: Random House, 1989).

13. Chalmers Johnson, *Japan: Who Governs? The Rise of the Developmental State* (New York: W. W. Norton, 1995), 184 ff.

14. Stockwin, *Governing Japan*, 57–58.

15. Johnson, *Japan: Who Governs?* 183–211.

16. Briefly in 1995, the Japanese economy technically was larger than that of the United States, but everyone knew it was just a figment of the gyrating currency exchange rates rather than a real achievement. In terms of purchasing power, the average Japanese consumer has about 70 percent of the buying power of the average U.S. consumer.

17. For more on Japan's phenomenal economic rise, see Ezra F. Vogel, *Japan as No. 1: Lessons for America* (Tokyo: Charles E. Tuttle, 1979).

18. For more on Japan's influence on Asia and the world, see Nishigaki Akira and Shimomura Yasutami, *The Economics of Development Assistance: Japan's ODA in a Symbiotic World* (Tokyo: LTCB International Library Foundation, 1998); Walter Hatch and Kozo Yamamura, *Asia in Japan's Embrace: Building a Regional Production Alliance* (Cambridge: Cambridge University Press, 1996); and Dennis J. Encarnation, *Rivals Beyond Trade: America Versus Japan in Global Competition* (Ithaca, N.Y.: Cornell University Press, 1992).

19. Japan Institute for Social and Economic Affairs, *An International Comparison* (Tokyo: Keizai Koho Center, 1983).

20. Collinwood, *Japan and the Pacific Rim*, 27–28.

21. Japan Institute for Social and Economic Affairs, *An International Comparison*.

22. *Organization of the Government of Japan* (Tokyo: Institute of Administrative Management, Prime Minister's Office, 1999).

23. Occasionally, high-ranking civil servants are given cabinet posts, but the appointment of non-Diet members to the cabinet is a rarity in Japan, as in most parliamentary systems.

24. Some civil servants working in this ministry may actually receive their pay from another branch of government but may be assigned to work temporarily in this ministry.

25. Taichi Sakaiya, "The Myth of the Competent Bureaucrat," in *Japan Echo* (February 1998): 25–30. For an opposite view, see Peter Drucker, "In Defense of Japanese Bureaucracy," in *Foreign Affairs* (September/October 1998): 68–80.

26. A more serious nuclear plant accident occurred in September 1999, but this time the government was more forthcoming about the danger to the public.

27. For a critical review of Japan's rise to power, see van Wolferen, *The Enigma of Japanese Power*.

28. On the concepts of exit, voice, and loyalty, see chapter 11.

29. *Washington Post*, October 19, 1996.

30. For a description of the SMD and PR electoral systems, see chapter 9.

31. The House of Councillors is one of the two chambers of the Japanese Diet. Originally an appointive body, the House of Councillors today is elected by popular vote. Every three years, half of the 252 Councillors are elected to a six-year term. One hundred seats are filled via proportional representation, and 152 seats are filled based on prefectural districts. Terms of office of Councillors are not terminated even in the event the House of

Representatives is dissolved. Japanese citizens age thirty or older may stand for election to the House of Councillors (age twenty-five for the House of Representatives).

32. Johnson, *Japan: Who Governs?* 186.

33. *Washington Post*, May 4, 1997 and March 16, 1997.

34. Stockwin, *Governing Japan*, 111.

35. "Russia and Japan: What Next?" in *Japan Echo* (August 1998): 19–30. The Russians have claimed that the specific Kuril Islands that they occupy were given up by Japan at the end of World War II.

CHAPTER 20

ISRAEL

Nathan J. Brown

Population (1999): 6,145,000

Area: 7,992 square miles[1]
(about the size of New Jersey)

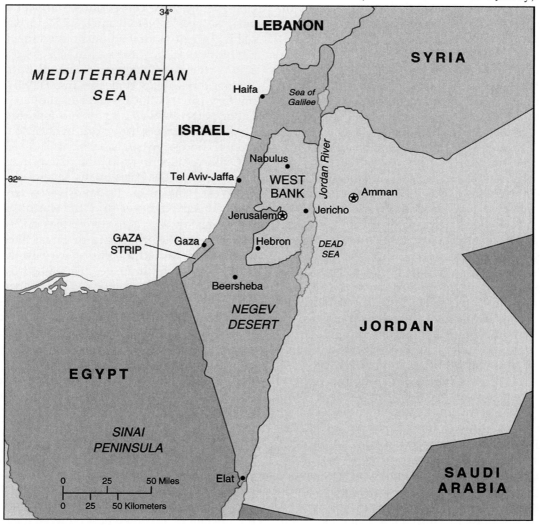

On the evening of November 4, 1999, Prime Minister **Ehud Barak** ignored the warnings of Israeli security services and stepped forward to address a rally of tens of thousands of fellow citizens in the center of Tel Aviv. It was only seven months since Barak had addressed another crowd that had gathered spontaneously at the same place to celebrate his electoral victory. But most minds that November evening were on bullets, not ballots. Precisely five years earlier, Barak's mentor and predecessor, Yitzhak Rabin, had been shot dead on the very spot. The assassin, a student named Yigal Amir, claimed that Rabin was a traitor and had to die. Rabin's supporters charged that Amir had not acted in a vacuum and that the assassination had been encouraged by wild and irresponsible rhetoric from opposition leaders attacking Rabin's policy of negotiating peace with the Palestinians.

Barak's speech at the rally passed without incident. But the refrain he led the crowd in chanting— "We are not afraid!"—was a clear reminder of the painful events of the previous seven years. In 1992, Rabin had taken office after leading his Labor Party to a narrow but decisive victory. Rabin's peace policies deeply divided the country, but most were horrified at the assassination. Shimon Peres, Rabin's successor, called snap elections in 1996 to take advantage of the wave of sympathy. In a great upset, Binyamin Netanyahu, one of Rabin's outspoken opponents, defeated Peres.

When he passed from the position of opposition critic to prime minister, Netanyahu found himself in an impossible position. Detested by Rabin's followers and distrusted even by many of his own allies, Netanyahu proved incapable of leading the country in any clear direction. His government consisted of a coalition of several parties that were themselves divided over the content and pace of Israel's negotiating position. While some were willing to proceed with the agreements Rabin had negotiated, albeit with minor changes, others remained categorically opposed to making any serious concessions to the Palestinians, including those already worked out. Unable to implement the agreements or abandon them, Netanyahu's coalition disintegrated, forcing him to call a new round of elections in April 1999. Changing their minds once more, Israeli voters elected Ehud Barak, a man who modeled his career and policies

after Rabin. For the third time in seven years, the Israeli electorate had opted for a dramatic change in the country's political direction.

Barak was prepared to deliver dramatic change, but he soon found himself in as much trouble as Netanyahu when it came to coping with a fractious, multiparty coalition government. In order to include a diversity of opinion in his cabinet and secure a voting majority in Israel's parliament, Barak assembled a six-party government consisting of two leftist parties, a centrist party, two conservative religious parties, and a small conservative party representing Jews from the former Soviet Union. (The three conservative parties had previously served in Netanyahu's cabinet.) Barak himself had spent more than thirty-five years in the Israeli army, participating in numerous operations against the hostile states on Israel's borders and against the stateless Palestinians. Having left the military for a political career in the left-of-center Labor party, he was now determined to secure a long-term peace settlement, even if it required painful concessions on Israel's part.

Once installed in office, the new prime minister transferred to the Palestinians several portions of the **West Bank** of the Jordan River, a territory Israel had occupied ever since the war of June 1967. The decision was a controversial one, as some Israelis—including some of Barak's coalition partners—regarded the entire West Bank as their country's rightful heritage, bequeathed by God to the Jewish people in biblical times. Other Israelis favored retaining the territory for nationalist or security reasons rather than on religious grounds.

Barak also hinted at a willingness to return virtually all of the **Golan Heights** to Syria—another territory acquired in the 1967 war. Barak had fought in the battle to take that sensitive border area, the source of numerous clashes between Israeli and Syrian forces before 1967. The suggestion of a withdrawal set off bitter criticisms, not merely from the 17,000 Israelis who had settled on the Golan Heights, but even from some of Barak's supporters who considered the territory too strategically important to give back. The talks between Israel and Syria eventually broke down in the spring of 2000, but not before the differences between the two sides had narrowed close to the vanishing point. The death in June 2000 of Hafez Assad, Syria's leader for three decades, and his replacement by his son Bashar, led some observers to expect that a deal might soon be in the offing.

Even more daringly, in May 2000 Barak withdrew Israeli troops from Lebanon. Ever since 1982, when Israel invaded the country on its northern border, Israeli soldiers had occupied parts of Lebanon in an effort to keep out Palestinian guerillas and other groups bent on launching attacks on Israeli territory. During the 1999 election campaign, Barak had promised to pull the troops out if he was elected, but most Israelis assumed that he wanted to do so only after first coming to terms with Syria. (Syria had many of its own troops in Lebanon.) When the talks with Syria collapsed prior to Hafez Assad's death, Barak ordered a unilateral withdrawal, making good on his campaign pledge.

In what promised to be his boldest stroke of all, Barak flew to the United States in July 2000 to join with President Bill Clinton and Yasser Arafat, the Palestinian leader, to discuss a comprehensive peace settlement. Before departing for the president's Camp David retreat, away from the prying eyes of the world press, Barak discovered that even a decision to enter such talks—much less a real agreement—could bring his government to the brink of collapse. The three conservative parties in his cabinet swung from supporting him over the peace issue to withdrawing from his government. In a stormy session of the Knesset, Israel's unicameral legislature, Barak won a reprieve on July 10 when his opponents failed to muster enough votes to topple his government in a no-confidence vote. Barak flew to the United States immediately after the vote, but his foreign minister refused to accompany him to Camp David and several other ministers handed Barak their letters of resignation as he boarded the plane.

After two weeks of negotiations, the Camp David summit broke up without a substantive agreement. Upon returning to Israel, Barak clung to power when the Knesset again failed to pass no-confidence measures against him. But half his cabinet had deserted him, while his foes claimed that the concessions he had offered at Camp David went far beyond what he—or any previous Israeli leader—had ever suggested. As the Knesset adjourned for the rest of the summer, Israelis braced themselves for uncertain changes in the months ahead.

Dramatic political swings have become common in Israel since the 1980. A few decades before, such changes would have been unthinkable. Israeli public debates have often been bitter, but a strong consensus guided the state in its first three decades. That consensus has broken apart, partly because Israel has matured and partly because of deeper changes in Israeli society.

The Jewish state of Israel was born in warfare in 1948. For Israel's first three decades, most of the critical decisions were made by leaders who felt they had no choice: right or wrong, most Israelis agreed that they lived in a hostile region in which policies were dictated by a difficult security environment. All surrounding states maintained a formal state of war with Israel as well as an economic boycott. The first generation of Israeli leaders ensured the country's survival in this perilous situation, but in doing so they paved the way for a very different kind of politics. For the past twenty years Israelis have bitterly debated not *how* to maintain the state but *what sort* of state it should be. In the process, Israel has had to confront a host of problems arising from the five sources of conflict we enumerated in chapter 2:

- *Power:* Which political parties and personalities should govern Israel? What should be the respective powers of the prime minister, the cabinet, and the legislature? Are some social groups in Israel more powerful than others? To what extent should coercive power be used on Arab citizens of Israel or other Palestinians?

- *Resources:* Recognizing that land itself is a nation's most vital natural resource, what should the territorial boundaries of the land of Israel be? Is it necessary to control all the territory ruled by ancient Jewish kingdoms, or is it more important that Israel compromise with its neighbors to guarantee peace? In the domestic economy, what should be the proper balance between the public sector and private enterprise? Should state-owned enterprises be privatized?

- *Social identity:* If Israel is to be a Jewish state, what is its proper relationship with Jews outside of Israel? How should Jews from very different origins (especially from Eastern Europe and from the Middle East) live together? What is the place of non-Jews who live in Israel? And who has the authority to define who is a Jew? Israelis have also debated what it means to be Jewish: should the state of Israel be defined in strictly nationalist terms, making Israel a Jewish state in the same way that France is a French state? Or should it be defined in religious terms, making some attempt to govern in accordance with Jewish laws and values?

- *Ideas:* What is Zionism? Have Israelis always been committed to democracy? What do such terms as "socialism" and "capitalism" mean in the Israeli context?

- *Values:* What is the place of modern, liberal values, including such things as freedom of speech, freedom from arbitrary arrest, and the right to a fair trial, in a society threatened from the outside as well as from the inside by people who have yet to fully accept the idea of a Jewish state?

In its own way, Israel has had to deal with these and other problems arising from its own unique historical and geographical circumstances. It provides a graphic example of a *democracy under siege,* and offers important lessons about the ability of democratic institutions and practices to survive in conditions of prolonged internal and external strife. In this chapter we shall survey some of the main players and issues in Israeli politics and conclude by testing a hypothesis and making some generalizations about the character of Israeli democracy today.

HISTORICAL BACKGROUND: THE EVOLUTION OF ISRAELI DEMOCRACY

The Creation of Israel

In the late nineteenth century, rising anti-Semitism in Central and Eastern Europe led many Jews to seek new places to live. While quite a few went to the United States, smaller numbers decided to rebuild a Jewish homeland in Palestine. This Jewish nationalist movement was termed **Zionism.** While Jews had lived in Palestine in biblical times and a small number always remained in the area after the exodus of most Jews to other lands, no Jewish state had existed for two thousand years. At the time of the emergence of Zionism, the land that the Jews wanted for their home, Palestine, was ruled by the Turks. Centered in Istanbul, the Ottoman Empire was a Muslim state that controlled much of the Middle East. Palestine's population was largely Arabic-speaking. Most people who lived there were Muslims, though there was a sizable Christian minority. The Zionist movement drew some very dedicated adherents, but prior to the outbreak of the First World War in 1914, only a small number of Jews actually moved to Palestine. At the time fewer than ninety thousand Jews lived there, compared with about one-half million non-Jews.

During World War I, the Zionist movement secured a major diplomatic breakthrough when the British government—then fighting the Ottoman Empire—endorsed the effort to construct a Jewish national home in Palestine. The British policy statement came in 1917 in a letter that came to be known as the **Balfour Declaration.** British troops took control of Palestine during the war, and shortly afterward the League of Nations (the forerunner to today's United Nations) assigned a "mandate" for Palestine to Britain. Under the mandate, Britain was to rule the country temporarily while preparing it for independence. Significantly, however, the League of Nations also incorporated the Balfour Declaration's call for a Jewish national homeland into the text of the mandate.

Britain was therefore charged with two tasks: readying Palestine, with its Arab majority, for independence, while simultaneously allowing Jews to construct a national home for themselves. It proved difficult to do both at the same time, because the Arab majority feared that a Jewish national home would become an independent state with no place for the Arab population. The slow rate of Jewish immigration to Palestine during the 1920s allowed the British to postpone resolving the contradictions of their situation. Nevertheless, the Zionist movement achieved rapid successes in building up a network of Jewish businesses, banks, labor unions, factories, and farms. By 1933, Jews formed about one-fifth of Palestine's population.

In 1933, the viciously anti-Semitic Nazi party came to power in Germany and anti-Semitism grew elsewhere in Europe as well. The United States and some other countries had moved to restrict immigration, meaning that Jews wishing to flee Europe had few places to go. They began to move to Palestine in much larger numbers. By 1939, the Jewish population in Palestine had grown close to one-half million, one-third of its total population. Jewish organizations and institutions also grew, making the Jewish settlement partly self-governing even as the British mandate continued. The growth in the Jewish population led the Arabs to demand that the British take countermeasures. Already in 1936, some Arabs had moved to resist Zionism and the British mandate directly, launching violent attacks on Jewish and British targets.

At the onset of World War II, the British faced an unattractive choice. Reasoning that the Zionists would have to back the British in a contest with the Nazis but that the Arabs might not, the British issued a new policy in 1939 that greatly restricted Jewish immigration to Palestine while promising an independent state in ten years. This new state was to have an Arab majority and a Jewish minority. Zionists angrily rejected this policy as a violation of the mandate and the Balfour Declaration. Most Zionist leaders concluded that they could no longer rely on Britain and therefore began to work openly for the creation of an independent Jewish state. A minority launched violent attacks on British targets. Although the mainstream Zionist leadership disavowed extreme tactics as long as Britain was fighting Nazi Germany, the end of the war in 1945 brought the prospect of much more widespread disturbances. It also brought additional pressure on Britain, because many of those Jews who were not among the 6 million exterminated by the Nazis wished to emigrate to Palestine.

In 1947, Britain finally concluded that it could not solve the mounting crisis on its own and referred the issue to the newly created United Nations. The UN established a special commission to consult with the parties and make a recommendation. The Arabs of Palestine and surrounding countries hoped that the commission would urge the establishment of a single state with a permanent Arab majority; the Zionists hoped for a Jewish state. A majority of the commission suggested partitioning Palestine into two states, one Arab and the other Jewish. The Zionists reluctantly accepted this recommendation, but it was rejected by the Palestinians and their Arab neighbors. Meanwhile, a minority of the UN commission members proposed creating separate Arab and Jewish states on a somewhat different basis: while each of the two states would be responsible for its own internal affairs, they would be locked together in a federation

with joint responsibility for foreign affairs and defense. The UN General Assembly endorsed the majority plan in November 1947.

Britain criticized the UN plan as unworkable and refused to implement it. At the same time, the British announced that they would leave the country because they could neither impose their own solution nor get the Jews and Arabs to agree on a different one. Fighting broke out between Jews and Arabs as the end of the mandate approached. The Zionist effort to build up Jewish organizations and institutions in Palestine paid off during this fighting. Jewish forces were far better organized than the local Arab population, and by the time the British withdrew in May 1948, Jewish forces had achieved the upper hand. On May 14, 1948, the Zionist movement declared an independent state of Israel. The declaration of independence proclaimed that Israel was to be a Jewish state but also a democratic one.

The surrounding Arab countries now directly entered the fighting but could not agree on a coordinated attack. Israel succeeded in defeating each of the Arab armies sent against it. Armistices were finally declared, leaving the new state with more territory than the UN plan had originally allowed it. But parts of the country were still controlled by Arab armies. Egypt controlled a narrow strip of land along the Mediterranean coast (the **Gaza Strip**), while a large section of the middle of the country was held by Jordan, which annexed it. This area consisted of the West Bank of the Jordan River and included parts of the city of Jerusalem.

Many of the Arab inhabitants of the new Israeli territory had fled the fighting; Jewish forces evicted others. Consequently, the new state of Israel had an overwhelming Jewish majority. Many Jews who had lived in the Arab world (in places like Iraq, Yemen, Morocco, and Egypt) moved to the new Jewish state, sometimes fearful that the Arab societies that had served as their home for generations would no longer be friendly to them.[2] (See figure 20.1.)

What Kind of Jewish State?

The new state of Israel thus confronted some daunting tasks. On the one hand, the state was created as a *Jewish* state. Hence there was a strong commitment to integrate any Jew who came to the country. In July 1950 Israel proclaimed the **Law of the Return,**

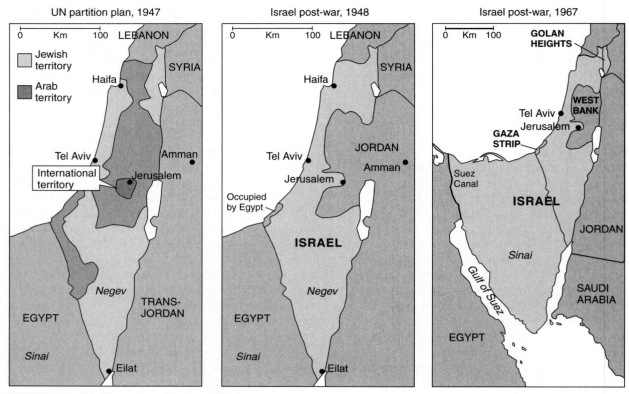

FIGURE 20.1　The Expansion of the Israeli State
Source: New York Times, February 28, 1988. Copyright © 1988 by The New York Times Company.

guaranteeing Israeli citizenship to any Jew who came and claimed it. But this policy, rooted in Zionist ideology, resulted in some difficult problems. First, the large influx of Jewish immigration from the Arab world had to be accommodated, even though many of these new Israelis came with no possessions and no knowledge of modern Hebrew, the language of the new state. Many of these new arrivals had little or no education. The Israeli government worked hard to integrate the new population, but it did so in a manner that was often callous and patronizing. Those who did have some useful education were deemed fit only for farming or manual labor; the customs of the new immigrants were often denigrated. A generation later, some of the resentments created in the process of assimilating the new immigrants came back to haunt Israel's early leaders.

A related problem was that there was no real consensus on what it meant to be Jewish. The main-

stream Zionist leadership conceived of Jewish identity primarily in national rather than religious terms; some were simply not interested in Judaism as a religion while others were downright hostile to it. Yet a sizable religious component of the population regarded religious identity as central and rejected any attempt to set up a non-religious Jewish national identity. In addition to these religious disputes, ideological issues also arose. Many Zionists viewed socialism as an essential part of the attempt to build a Jewish state. But not all Zionists accepted socialism: the *Revisionist movement,* which later evolved into Israel's main right-wing party, was very opposed to socialism. Nevertheless, most of the prominent Zionist leaders came from socialist backgrounds. Yet there was no real consensus on what socialism meant. Some Zionists came close to the Soviet definition of socialism, strongly identifying with the working class and attacking private ownership. This wing stopped short of full Marxist socialism only because Marxism rejected all forms of nationalism, including Zionism. Others focused not on revolutionizing society as a whole but on building socialism from the ground up. Many of Zionism's early leaders came from *kibbutzim*, collective and egalitarian communities in which differences in wealth were not tolerated. Still others subscribed to a socialism more akin to the social democracy that emerged in Western Europe: they focused on welfare benefits and public enterprise while allowing for some private enterprise and avoiding central planning. All strains of socialism agreed that the mission of Zionism was to build a Jewish society with Jewish labor, free from the sharp class divisions that existed in Europe at the time.

From the outset, the Zionists who founded Israel were nearly unanimous in their commitment to liberal democracy. Indeed, the idea of allowing the Jews to live as a free people in their own land naturally inclined Zionists to democratic ideals. Thus the decision to build a British-style, parliamentary system of government attracted wide support. Despite agreement on this general principle, however, serious problems arose when it came to realizing it in practice. First, a liberal democratic state is supposed to belong to all its citizens. Fully 20 percent of Israel's population in 1948 was not Jewish (the proportion is roughly the same today). Most non-Jewish Israelis are Arab. Could Israel's Arab population really be incorporated with full citizenship in a state that identified itself as Jewish? While Arabs were granted full citizenship in the legal sense, Arab areas were kept under military rule for quite some time. Even after this military rule ended in 1966, Arabs complained that their legal status as citizens did not prevent widespread discrimination against them. Today, Israeli Arabs are more likely to be searched when entering sensitive areas (such as airports) and are barred from certain occupations; they find Israel's government much less responsive to their needs.

A further problem was how to build a democracy in a state whose security was precarious. Liberal democracies often forget some of their ideals in wartime as political leaders come to feel that the risk of allowing full democratic freedoms is too great. It is not unusual for freedoms to be suspended in war, even in a robust democracy like the United States. In the American Civil War, Pres-

ident Lincoln allowed citizens to be detained without charges; in World War II, American citizens of Japanese descent were forcibly relocated into detention camps. With Israel constantly on guard against possible attack, how could fully democratic institutions be created and maintained?

The Basic Laws

Most newly independent states face very difficult questions about what sort of political system and society they wish to build. Many of them attempt to address these problems by writing constitutions that establish basic principles and structures. By contrast, the early leadership of Israel decided to postpone dealing with some of its most controversial problems. Elections were held in 1949 for an assembly that was supposed to write a constitution, but the new body decided to set itself up as a parliament instead (the Knesset) and opted to stretch out the writing of the constitution over many years. As the new millennium begins, this task has yet to be completed. To this day Israel has a set of **"Basic Laws"** that establish its main institutional structures, but there is still no constitution. Quite a few fundamental issues remain unresolved.

For example, rather than settling the issue of the role of religion in the Jewish state, the early leadership simply decided to keep many of the arrangements that were in effect before the creation of the state of Israel. Thus no public transportation is available on the Jewish sabbath except in the city of Haifa, because that was the situation prevailing before 1948. No unified school system was established; instead, a secular system operates alongside a set of religious schools, all obtaining government support. All Jewish citizens are required to serve in the army, but religious Jews can easily get exemptions for religious study. Arabs are considered full citizens but they are not called upon to serve in the army, nor are their neighborhoods and villages given the same level of social services that Jewish areas receive. While debate on most political issues is open, the security situation has limited public debate on foreign and defense policy, reflecting a widespread consensus that Israel's perilous predicament leaves little room for revealing sensitive information about these issues. In sum, Israel has established a working democracy in the context of a Jewish state *not* by solving all its difficult problems but by avoiding them for many years.[3]

Another difficulty Israel faced in making the transition to statehood centered on the organizations of civil society created by the pre-state Jewish settlers in Palestine. Initially it was not clear whether these well-organized institutions—labor unions, schools, parties, militias, and the like—would easily mesh with the new Israeli state. Israeli political parties, focused on building a Jewish homeland, did not restrict themselves to electoral competition, but often built their own youth clubs, economic enterprises, and even militias. To this day, for instance, many Israeli sports teams identify themselves not simply by city but also by political party. As a result, a red flag with a hammer and sickle represents not the Soviet Union but the "Tel Aviv Worker" soccer team (or, as it is now known, "Tel Aviv—Keter—Worker," with the name of the team's sponsor, a large manufacturer of household plastics, inserted).

David Ben-Gurion, Israel's first prime minister, concentrated on constructing strong state institutions, but he often did so at the expense of the pre-existing organizations. This approach led many of his colleagues to see him as dictatorial, because he tended to ignore the wishes of some of the political parties then so strong in all aspects of Israeli life. Ultimately he proved successful, however, and political parties became less important; they focused more narrowly on politics and elections rather than on building a new society themselves. Not until the 1970s and 1980s were some of the strong state institutions that he built questioned or dismantled.

PROFILE: David Ben-Gurion

David Ben-Gurion was born in 1886 in a part of Poland then ruled by the Russian Empire. In 1906 he made *aliya* (literally "ascending," the Hebrew term used to indicate moving to the land of Israel). He was expelled by the Ottoman Empire during the First World War, but returned when the British gained control of Palestine. He emerged as a labor leader and as a leader of one of the chief socialist parties of the Zionist movement. During the 1930s and 1940s he became the preeminent Zionist figure actually living in Palestine. It fell to Ben-Gurion to announce Israel's declaration of independence in 1948, and he served as prime minister until retiring for the first time in 1953.

David Ben-Gurion (right) with Albert Einstein. Einstein declined an invitation to serve as Israel's first president.

During his first five years as head of government, Ben-Gurion led the transformation of Zionism from a collection of ideological movements and parties to a state. A dominant, even domineering leader, he was unable to stay aloof from politics and returned in 1955, replacing the man who had previously succeeded him. Ben-Gurion served as prime minister for another eight years, leading Israel to military victory in a war with Egypt in 1956. His relations with many of his colleagues were often strained, and he therefore cultivated a new generation of leaders within his party. In 1963 a bitter split within the party occasioned Ben-Gurion's resignation. He gathered some of his younger followers in his own political party in 1965 and ran separately. When most of this group decided to return to join the Labor Alignment in 1968, he decided to form another new party for the 1969 elections. Far less successful this time, Ben-Gurion finally retired and died in 1973.[4]

The Six-Day War of June 1967

In June 1967, Israel's situation changed dramatically when it defeated three neighboring Arab states—Egypt, Syria, and Jordan. In the **Six Day War** Israel took possession of the Gaza Strip from Egypt and the Jordan River's West Bank from Jordan, leaving it in control of all of the British mandate territory of Palestine. It also occupied Egypt's Sinai peninsula and Syria's Golan Heights. Israel's fractious politics had always made it difficult to resolve longstanding political debates about the nature of the society that should be built, but the aftermath of the 1967 war made these debates much more acute.[5] (See figure 20.2.)

The defeat of the three Arab neighbors implied that Israel's security situation was less precarious than it was before the war. Israel did not take its continued existence for granted, but its political leadership finally seemed to have some room for maneuver. Indeed, Israel now possessed territory that the three defeated Arab states wished to reclaim and thus seemed to have a basis for negotiating peace with its neighbors. Israel's leaders debated about how best to combine military and diplomatic strategies for ensuring the country's security. Then in 1973, Egypt and Syria launched an attack on Israel. While Israel avoided defeat (and even gained some additional territory), this war was longer and more costly than the 1967 war. The result led some people within the Arab world— most notably Egypt's president, Anwar Sadat—to feel that the time had come to negotiate a settlement with Israel. No longer confronted with an Arab world uniformly unwilling to entertain peace, Israel was increasingly called upon to do what it had never been able to do: define the precise nature of the peace agreement it was willing to sign.[6]

Israel now controlled the entire territory of Palestine, which raised the possibility of modifying the country's borders. There were several reasons why such a change seemed attractive. Some argued that the borders acquired in the 1948 war were too long and not easily defended; modifying them would make them easier to defend. Others argued on nationalist grounds that Zionism should strive to build a Jewish society in all of Palestine. They therefore thought that the newly conquered territories—the West Bank and Gaza— should be settled by Jews and possibly even annexed to Israel. Other Israelis took a similar view for religious rather than simply nationalist reasons: they saw the construction of the state of Israel and the victory in 1967 as signs of the fulfillment of divine promises to Jews to settle the land and make it their own. These various reasons for maintaining some control over the West Bank and Gaza—security, national, and religious—were sometimes blended together. But others argued that annexation would raise real problems. In their

view it would probably make a negotiated peace with the Arabs impossible, because no Arab government would wish to endorse such a move. Annexation would also leave a large number of Arab inhabitants under direct Israeli rule. To offer them citizenship might endanger the Jewish nature of the state. To refuse them citizenship would contradict Israel's democratic nature. Faced with these contending arguments for and against annexation, Israel's leaders refrained from making any irrevocable decisions. They allowed (and even encouraged) Jews to settle in the West Bank and Gaza, but they refused to annex the territories. Instead they insisted that Israel draw its borders only after negotiating them with its neighbors.

THE PALESTINIANS

The Palestinians are an excellent example of a nation without a state (see chapter 7), though they have taken firm steps toward some form of statehood over the past decade. Palestinians are an Arabic-speaking people who inhabited the area designated as the Palestine mandate after World War I.

Palestinian national identity remains very controversial even among Palestinians themselves. Prior to the twentieth century, political boundaries in the Middle East (and most of the world outside Europe) bore little correspondence to national boundaries, and few questioned this situation. National identities became politicized only in the nineteenth and twentieth centuries, and Palestinians were no exception. When national identities emerged, the situation of the Palestinians was ambiguous. Many Palestinians argued that they are a branch of the Arab nation and are not distinct from it. Some Palestinian Muslims continue to this day to claim that their primary political identity should be religious rather than national. For many years, Israeli leaders argued that there was no such thing as a Palestinian nation; those who called themselves Palestinians were simply Arabs.

The political controversy made it very difficult for many years to define Palestinian identity in widely accepted terms. There can be no doubt, however, that most Palestinians opposed the Zionist movement and that this opposition cemented their already forming national identity. Under the British mandate, Palestinian political leaders constantly pressured the British to stop Jewish immigration to Palestine and demanded that the country become independent while it still had a substantial Arab majority. In 1936 a full-scale revolt broke out, but the British were able to suppress it after several years.

When Britain announced in 1947 that it was withdrawing from Palestine (and the UN General Assembly voted to partition the country), Palestinians found themselves in a potentially violent confrontation with the Zionist movement. While Palestinian Arabs outnumbered Jews, the Zionist movement was very well organized. The Palestinian leadership, on the other hand, was decimated by the 1936 revolt. Feeling that they had right on their side (and hoping for support from the surrounding Arab states), Palestinians rejected the partition plan. In the resulting conflict, however, the Palestinians proved militarily unequal to the Zionists, even after the Arab states entered the conflict. Not only was a Jewish state declared, but at the close of fighting Israel controlled more territory than even the UN partition plan had allocated to it. Still more troubling for Palestinians was the creation of an enormous refugee problem: a mixture of flight and expulsion had left 700,000 to 800,000 Palestinians displaced. Of the original British mandatory territory, only the West Bank of the Jordan River (including the eastern part of Jerusalem) and a narrow strip of land around the Mediterranean city of Gaza lay under Arab control. The Arab country of Transjordan controlled the West Bank; the Egyptian army was in control of Gaza at the end of the fighting.

Some prominent Palestinian leaders held a meeting they called a "Palestinian National Congress" in Gaza to set up a Palestinian state. But Egypt worried that the new state would cause trouble for it and brought Gaza under Egyptian control. Transjordan—which consisted of the East Bank of the Jordan River—annexed the Palestinian West Bank with the support of some, but not all, of the Palestinian population. (The newly merged country was called Jordan.) Talks between Israel and the Arab governments about borders and the return of refugees stalled, and what seemed like a temporary setback became far more permanent. Jordan did grant Palestinians citizenship, but most other Arab countries allowed Palestinians to stay as guests only; most Palestinians themselves hoped to return to their homes rather than to settle permanently in other countries.

In 1964, the Arab League helped establish an organization to represent Palestinians. Another Palestine National Congress was held in the part of Jerusalem controlled by Jordan; it set up a new organization, the **Palestine Liberation Organization** (**PLO**), to speak for Palestinians everywhere. At first, the PLO seemed designed more to serve intra-Arab rivalries than to liberate any territory. Since Jordan had annexed some Palestinian land, it viewed the PLO with great suspicion. In the same period, some Palestinians began to despair that

Yasser Arafat addresses the United Nations.

other Arab countries would ever come to their aid. They established their own small groups to pursue Palestinian aims. Some of these groups hoped to unify the Arab world (even if it meant overthrowing existing regimes) as a prelude to regaining Palestine. The largest groups, however, attracted support by attacking Israel directly, often through small-scale terrorist operations. The most influential group, led by **Yasser Arafat,** was named Fatah (Movement of Palestinian Liberation).

After the Arab defeat of 1967, it seemed unlikely that any existing Arab state would be able to confront Israel on the battlefield. Fatah and other groups used the opportunity to assume control of the PLO in 1969. Launching direct attacks on Israeli targets (both civilian and military), the groups of the PLO provoked international condemnation. For many Palestinians, however, these attacks represented the only concrete action being taken in their behalf. The Arab world was badly divided about the activity of the PLO groups. Some supported them, contrasting Palestinian activism with their own governments' inability to confront Israel. Others feared that they might be dragging the Arab world into a conflict that they could not win. In 1970, the more radical Palestinian groups engaged in a brief and disastrous war with the Jordanian government that had tried to suppress them. Even Fatah, which tried to avoid a battle with Jordan, found itself pulled in, and the PLO and its member groups were forced to relocate to Lebanon. In 1975, fighting broke out in Lebanon, and once again PLO groups found themselves engaged in a bloody conflict. This time they managed to maintain their presence. In 1982, however, the Israeli government invaded Lebanon to evict the PLO from that country. The PLO was now forced to relocate to Tunisia.

By the middle of the 1980s, the outlook for many Palestinians seemed very bleak. Some Palestinians (approximately 900,000) lived as citizens of Israel. While this population complained of discrimination, it did not seem to want to take part in the Palestinian battle against the Jewish state. Israel controlled the West Bank and Gaza (home to 1.8 million and 1 million Palestinians respectively), and the Israeli government was engaged in an ambitious effort to settle Jews in these predominantly Palestinian territories. Palestinians who lived elsewhere—perhaps as many as 4 million—found that the organization that represented them, the PLO, kept moving farther away from Israel.

In 1987, Palestinians in the West Bank and Gaza reacted to the situation by launching a popular rebellion against Israeli rule. The effort seems to have been spontaneous at first, but the PLO and its member groups quickly stepped in to try to organize the efforts. The uprising (*intifada* in Arabic) was certainly in no position to defeat Israel militarily, but it was able to impose costs on Israel for occupying the West Bank and Gaza through small-scale attacks and non-cooperation.

In light of the intifada, a window seemed to open for a negotiated solution for the conflict. In 1988, a Palestine National Conference meeting was held in Algiers. The meeting declared Palestine to be an independent state (albeit without any territory); it also indirectly but clearly recognized Israel's right to exist. The Israeli leadership was split on how to respond. The right-wing Likud party saw the PLO as an implacable enemy and opposed Israeli withdrawal from the West Bank and Gaza. Labor was more willing to compromise, though years of PLO attacks on Israeli targets made it difficult for any Israeli leader to deal directly with the PLO. In 1992, a Labor government came into office and began secret negotiations directly with the PLO leadership. By September 1993, the two sides had come to a very limited agreement. For the first time, the PLO and Israel directly recognized each other and began to negotiate a settlement.

Because the issues involved in a final settlement are so difficult, the two sides agreed on some interim arrangements involving the establishment of an autonomous **Palestinian Authority** in parts of the West Bank and Gaza. In 1994, Yasser Arafat moved to Gaza to establish the new Authority. He was very clear as to his goal: an independent Palestinian state in the West Bank and Gaza, with Jerusalem as its capital. Even the Labor party had objections to this goal, however, saying that it would not withdraw from all the West Bank and Gaza and could not give up any control of Jerusalem.

While the two sides tried to reach agreement, a new Palestinian government was set up. With the construction of the Palestinian Authority, Palestinians seemed to be a nation with a government, but they still lacked a full state. Elections were held for a legislative council; presidential elections resulted in a landslide victory for Arafat. The new Palestinian Authority worked to build courts, a police force, and a legislature; it issued postage stamps and passports and drafted a temporary constitution. But it lacked an army, clear borders, and international recognition as a state.

The Palestinian Authority quickly came under tremendous pressure from all directions. Palestinians living on the West Bank and Gaza placed tremendous hopes in the new entity. Many were disappointed when they saw that its authority was limited. Years of living under occupation and uprising had accustomed these Palestinians to running their own affairs, and some regarded the Palestinian Authority as heavy-handed and dictatorial in its methods. Palestinians living outside the West Bank and Gaza called for a final settlement that acknowledged their rights. While much international aid poured in, some donor states were critical of Arafat and his authoritarian style. Palestinians and international donors united in criticizing Arafat for tolerating corruption. Israel demanded that the Palestinian Authority fight terrorism, leading Arafat to take harsh measures that opened him up to criticism on human rights grounds. A series of terrorist attacks by Palestinian Islamic groups opposed to the Israeli-Palestinian agreements led to harsh Israeli countermeasures (such as prohibiting Palestinians from traveling between the pockets of Palestinian-ruled areas). Palestinian complaints that these actions violated the agreements were met by impatient Israeli demands that the Palestinian Authority move against groups operating out of Palestinian-ruled areas.

The Palestinian Authority soon discovered that it could not please everyone at the same time. The assassination of Rabin and the 1996 Israeli elections dealt the Palestinians another blow: they brought into office a government highly critical of the Israeli-Palestinian agreements. Peace negotiations collapsed, and the two sides traded accusations about violations of past agreements. The peace process broke down completely, and in the fall of 1996 violent confrontations took place between Palestinians and Israeli forces. A return to the intifada was averted by intensive international diplomacy, but Israel and the Palestinian Authority remained too suspicious of each other to negotiate seriously.

The 1999 Israeli elections brought the Labor party back into power, but this time under Ehud Barak, a military hero who had taken part in raids against PLO targets and who had no history of cooperation with Palestinian leaders. The peace process slowly revived, but the distance between the Israeli and Palestinian positions remained very great. Barak agreed to proceed with the transfer of additional parts of the West Bank to the Palestinian Authority in March 2000, but domestic resistance posed real problems. Prior to the July 2000 Camp David summit, Israel had already shifted 40 percent of the West Bank and two-thirds of Gaza to the Palestinian Authority. But these transfers sparked controversy inside Israel, especially on the part of some 180,000 Jewish settlers who lived in communities scattered across the West Bank, an area about the size of Delaware. Barak wanted an agreement that would permit a number of Jewish communities to remain, but the Palestinians objected that the West Bank would then be a "Swiss cheese" of isolated enclaves. They made it clear that any final settlement had to include total Israeli withdrawal from all of the West Bank and Gaza and the conversion of the Palestinian Authority into a full-fledged Palestinian state. They also renewed their insistence that the capital of their new state would have to be East Jerusalem, traditionally the Arab part of the ancient city. Israel claimed the entire city as its own capital, however, and disagreement over this difficult issue was especially intense at the Camp David summit.

While it was difficult for most Palestinians to avoid feeling apprehensive about the future, many could also take pride in the fact that Palestine—for a long time an abstract dream—was emerging as a recognized international entity and by mid-2000 stood on the brink of statehood.[7]

Changes in Israeli Society and Politics After 1967

The period after 1967 also witnessed a generational shift in Israeli society. All of Israel's pre-1967 leaders were dedicated Zionists who had taken part in the effort to build a Jewish homeland under difficult circumstances. Many of their differences were related to ideological debates over the nature of Zionism that lost their edge after a Jewish state was founded. Younger leaders now rose to the fore whose political careers had been built after statehood. For example, in 1974 Yitzhak Rabin became the first Israeli prime minister to be born in Palestine. More noticeable than the change in leadership was the change in the population: the Israeli electorate was increasingly made up of people who had not participated in the effort to build a Jewish state. As a consequence, political leaders could no longer expect that the earlier rhetoric of self-sacrifice and abstract ideologies could appeal to them.

Israeli politics after 1967 had to confront some additional demographic changes as well. Jews from the Middle East (or their children) now formed a majority, outnumbering Jews from Europe (see figure 20.2). This non-European Jewish population was increasingly resentful at being shut out of elite institutions in business, education, and politics that had been built by European Jews. The distinction between European and Middle Eastern Jews has begun to decline quite gradually (since the late 1970s, the majority of Israelis have been born in Israel), but it still is important both culturally and politically. The political influence of Israelis with a religious orientation grew as well. While the number of Jews who identified themselves as Orthodox or observant of Jewish law has remained around a quarter of the population, religious parties became both more popular and more ambitious after 1967. As we noted, most early Zionist leaders had little interest in religion. But some of the newer Israelis were either religious themselves or respectful of religious traditions even if they did not observe all Jewish rituals and practices to the letter of Jewish law. Religious Jews tended to have larger families as well. Since the state supported religious education and allowed religious students exemptions from military service, resentments between the religious and non-religious parts of the population began to intensify.

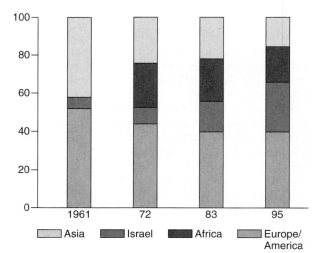

FIGURE 20.2   Place of Origin of Israel's Jewish Population. (% of Israeli Jews)
Source: The Economist, April 25, 1998.

Israeli political culture also began to evolve during the period after 1967. In the first two decades of statehood, the security situation and the political domination of the founding generation kept political debate within a fairly narrow spectrum. While there were sharp and sometimes angry divisions, the issues dividing the country's population were far less significant than those that later emerged. After 1967, the cleavages within Israeli society—between European and Middle Eastern Jews, between religious and secular Jews, and between those who favored territorial compromise and those who opposed it—gradually broke out into the open, leading to a more conflictual political atmosphere.

After the 1973 war, in which Israel's military and political elite seemed to falter, Israelis seemed far more willing to question their leaders. Indeed in 1977, the rightist opposition came to power for the first time. In 1982, the consensus regarding security issues seemed to break down completely, as the country fought a war in Lebanon that a significant proportion of the population questioned. The self-sacrificing ethos that characterized Israeli society before 1967 began to erode. By the 1980s, some postmaterialist values had begun to arise. (On postmaterialist values, see chapter 11.) A "post-Zionist" intellectual movement arose. Some people referred to as post-Zionists questioned the entire enterprise of building a Jewish state. Much more common was the argument that, because Zionism had succeeded in building a Jewish national home, it had completed its task and could no longer serve as a guide for Israel's development. Post-Zionism had many more critics than adherents, however, as the bulk of Israel's popula-

tion remained committed to Zionism even as it was split on what Zionism meant.

These changes in Israeli society and security had a substantial impact on the country's politics. During the country's first two decades, a single party predominated. Known as **Mapai** (the Hebrew acronym for the Party of the Workers of the Land of Israel), it represented the mainstream of the Zionist socialist movement. Although it was the largest party, other parties sprang up in the 1950s and 1960s, most of them representing pre-state movements from the left, the right, or the religious part of Israeli society. Even at its zenith, Mapai could not obtain a majority in Knesset elections, a predicament that forced it to rule with a series of coalition partners in Israel's emerging parliamentary system. After 1967 Mapai's influence declined. Though it reached out to form a slightly broader political grouping known as the **Labor Alignment** or **Labor** for short, Jews from the Middle East turned away from the party because of historical and economic grievances against the European founders of the Israeli state. Mapai's long period in office led many to see it as a machine dedicated simply to holding power rather than leading the country. Finally, in 1977, Mapai was ousted from government by the **Likud** bloc.

Likud in Power

Likud's nucleus lay in the rightist opposition to the pre-state Zionist socialist mainstream. The Revisionist movement of Zionism, Likud's pre-1948 predecessor, found the mainstream of the Zionist movement too willing to compromise, too inclined

TABLE 20.1

Knesset Election Results, 1949–99
(120 Seats)

	1949	1951	1955	1959	1961	1965	1969	1973	1977	1981	1984	1988	1992	1996	1999
Arab parties	2	5	5	5	4	4	4	3	1	0	0	1	2	4	7
Leftist parties	23	20	25	19	22	23	6	5	7	4	6	8	15	14	15
Mapai/Labor	46	45	40	47	42	45	56	51	32	47	44	39	44	34	26
Centrist parties	13	24	18	14	17	5	10	7	18	5	10	7	0	4	12
Ethnic parties	5	3	0	0	0	0	0	0	0	3	1	0	0	7	10
Religious parties	16	15	17	18	18	17	18	15	17	10	12	18	16	23	27
Herut/Likud	14	8	15	17	17	26	26	39	43	48	41	40	32	32	19
Rightist parties	1	0	0	0	0	0	0	0	2	3	6	7	11	2	4

to diplomacy, and excessively socialist. After 1948, the Revisionist movement turned itself into a political party; it formed a coalition with some small parties to form the Likud bloc. Likud's leader, **Menachem Begin,** had led operations against the British during the mandate; he also opposed any hint of compromise over territorial issues. Likud's victory in 1977 was assisted by the formation of the Democratic Movement for Change, a short-lived reform-oriented group that appealed to many Labor voters. In coalition with religious and centrist parties, Likud dominated Israeli politics until 1984.

PROFILE: Menachem Begin

Menachem Begin's victory in the 1977 elections came after a long career in which he was considered outside the mainstream of Israeli politics. Born in Poland in 1913, he became involved in the Revisionist movement, sharing the dissident Zionist group's opposition to territorial compromise in Palestine and its suspicion of socialism. Begin emerged as an important youth leader among Revisionists in Europe, but he was deported to Siberia by the Soviet Union at the beginning of the Second World War. While many of his family members were killed by the Nazis, Begin himself was allowed to leave Siberia and join the Polish army. In 1942 he finally made his way to Palestine, where he helped establish the military wing of the Revisionist movement. His

group began attacking British targets while other Zionist movements were still hoping for British support; the British offered a large reward for his capture. Shortly after the establishment of the state of Israel, Begin was involved in an effort to bring arms into the country. Ben-Gurion regarded the attempt as a challenge to the state, charging Begin with violating the law and attempting to arm his own group rather than the nascent Israeli army; he ordered the ship carrying the arms sunk. The enmity between Ben-Gurion and Begin never abated, and Ben-Gurion avoided referring to Begin by name.

Begin turned the Revisionist movement into the core of the Herut party for Israel's first elections. Until 1967, Herut remained outside the government, and Begin was often viewed as an ineffectual opposition leader. Begin finally entered the government as a minister without portfolio (that is, with a vote in cabinet meetings but without a ministry to head) when a national unity government was formed shortly before the 1967 war. He resigned in protest over the government's refusal to reject an American peace plan and led his party back into opposition. This time the environment was more favorable: the Labor party was increasingly seen as a directionless political machine, and the country's uncertain performance in the 1973 war dismayed many Israelis. Begin's political fortunes began to rise. He led his Herut party into an alliance with several small parties under his leadership; this combination became the Likud bloc. Begin's clear status as an outsider induced many voters, especially Middle Eastern Jews, to support him. In the 1977 elections, Likud emerged under Begin's leadership as Israel's largest party and Begin himself became prime minister. He remained in that post until 1983.[8]

U.S. President Jimmy Carter joins hands with Egypt's President Anwar Sadat (left) and Israeli Prime Minister Menachem Begin after signing the Egyptian-Israeli peace treaty negotiated at Camp David, 1979.

Under Likud-led governments, Israel underwent the beginnings of economic liberalization. It became easier to import foreign goods; restrictions on Israeli currency were also gradually removed. But the most dramatic moves came in foreign and security policy.

Shortly after Likud's triumph, Egypt's President Anwar Sadat decided to break the logjam in Arab-Israeli relations by traveling to Jerusalem and addressing Israeli leaders directly. By assuring the Israelis that Egypt would accept full peace with Israel, he hoped to budge the Israeli government from its opposition to territorial compromise. While Israelis greeted Sadat enthusiastically, an actual peace agreement proved elusive. Finally President Jimmy Carter of the United States called the

Egyptian and Israeli leaders to Camp David, where they negotiated two agreements. The first called for the elaboration of an Egyptian-Israeli peace treaty. Under its provisions, Israel would be obligated to withdraw from all Egyptian territory it occupied in 1967, and Egypt would formally end its state of war with Israel and establish peaceful relations on the basis of full diplomatic recognition. The second agreement called for granting autonomy to the Arab inhabitants of the West Bank and Gaza for a transition period, during which a final settlement over those territories would be negotiated. The first Camp David agreement resulted in the signing of an Egyptian-Israeli peace treaty in 1979. The second agreement was far less successful. Palestinians rejected its terms as insufficient, and negotiations between Egypt and Israel regarding its implementation achieved little progress.

Despite the Likud's successes in foreign policy, 1981 saw the first in a series of extremely close elections. In that year Begin was able to put together another coalition of Knesset members to support his government, but the following year the country was badly divided over the government's decision to invade neighboring Lebanon. Palestinian forces had established themselves there several years earlier, and frequent clashes with Israelis, including terrorist attacks launched by Palestinian fighters from their Lebanese bases, prompted Begin's government to send Israeli army units across the border. Fighting terrorism had broad support in Israel, and years of intermittent bombings, raids, and other attacks had led to public support for very tough measures. Rather than confining the operation to defeating the Palestinians, however, the Likud-led government occupied a large part of Lebanon and besieged Beirut, the capital city. After weeks of bombardment and negotiation, the Palestinian forces agreed to leave.

Unlike Israel's previous military conflicts, this one seemed to be pursued not simply for survival but for strategic objectives. Its broader aim was to evict the Palestinian movements from Lebanon, isolate the Palestinian population of the West Bank and Gaza, and remold Lebanon. By the time of the Israeli invasion of 1982, Lebanon had been involved in a civil war for seven years, pitting a coalition of several largely Christian groups against a coalition of various Muslims, leftists, and Palestini-ans. After the departure of Palestinian forces, Israel seized the opportunity to support the election of a Lebanese Christian leader it regarded as friendly. When he was assassinated, Israel allowed his supporters to enter the Palestinian camps of Sabra and Shatilla, where they massacred the inhabitants.

Even before the massacres, many Israelis had questioned the desirability of an invasion that aimed not to remove an immediate threat but to redraw the political map of the region. The internal Israel debate turned bitter after Sabra and Shatilla. Israel's ambitious hopes of making Lebanon into an ally collapsed, and any possibility of a national consensus on security issues seemed to evaporate. Israelis had always tried to forget their differences in wartime. Now, a war itself was the subject of vigorous debate, testing the ability of Israeli democracy to function in such trying circumstances.

In the midst of the furor unleashed by these events in 1983, Begin abruptly resigned as prime minister following the death of his wife. Leaving no explanation, he completely withdrew from active political life. He was succeeded by Yitzhak Shamir, whose pre-1948 politics had been more extreme than Begin's. But Shamir launched no major policy initiatives during his tenure as premier.[9]

Likud and Labor

In the parliamentary elections of 1984 and 1988, Likud and Labor were in rough balance. After both elections, the two parties each tried to assemble a Knesset majority by enticing smaller parties to join it. These efforts failed, and Labor and Likud were forced to join in "National Unity" governments that split the top cabinet posts between them. Smaller parties also joined. The first National Unity government produced some dramatic policy accomplishments. In the international arena, Israel withdrew its troops from most of Lebanon, maintaining a narrow band along the border as a "security zone." In domestic politics, a program of economic liberalization was approved, although it caused significant labor unrest. With strong support from the United States, Israel committed itself to a painful program of fighting inflation and reducing government expenditures. Democratic governments often have trouble implementing controversial economic polices, but the National Unity government in Israel managed to find the political will to make tough decisions. Since both major parties were in power, they were willing to bear the anger the plan caused in the short term.

Yet the two leading blocs could not come to agreement on many other issues, and an attempt by **Shimon Peres** (who alternated with Yitzhak Shamir as prime minister) to negotiate with Jordan was blocked by Likud. In 1990, Labor finally pulled out of the National Unity government, frustrated that Likud was obstructing progress in peace negotiations with Israel's Arab neighbors.

By the 1990s Israel's two major parties were no longer divided by sharp ideological issues. Their economic policies had become fairly similar. Both parties favored some privatization, support for Israel's growing high-tech economy, and cuts in government expenditures. In election campaigns they tended to move toward the center on security issues. Likud claimed it could negotiate with Israel's Arab adversaries despite its hawkish reputation, and Labor claimed that it would safeguard Israel's security despite its dovish reputation. Nevertheless, the two parties remained rivals and retained clear differences on certain issues, above all with respect to negotiating peace. Labor, for example, was far more willing than Likud to engage in territorial withdrawal in return for peaceful relations with its Arab neighbors. Likud was reluctant to consider any kind of territorial compromise. As each party struggled to gain the upper hand over the other (even when they were joined in a National Unity government), the smaller parties were in a position to extract significant concessions from them.

Proportional Representation and Coalition Politics

Israel's proportional representation voting system allows parties with little more than 1 percent of the vote to win seats in the Knesset, a phenomenon that often prevents the largest parties like Likud and Labor from winning an absolute majority (see table 20.1). Because it is often necessary to form multiparty coalition governments in order to cobble together a voting majority in the Knesset (sixty-one votes out of 120), the smaller parties at times enjoy extraordinary bargaining leverage over the larger ones, imposing demands for cabinet posts, policy changes, or other benefits in exchange for

their support in parliament. (Israel's electoral system is discussed in greater detail later in the chapter.) In 1992, an odd coalition managed to pass a constitutional reform providing for the direct popular election of the prime minister; the measure took effect in 1996. Backers of popular political leaders in both parties were attracted to the measure because they were convinced that their favorite candidate was more likely to win than their party was. And many thought that the reform would break the hold of the smaller parties.

In 1992, in the last election held under the old system, Labor eked out a narrow victory. It was able to form a Knesset majority with the support of a leftist party and one of the religious parties. The religious party later withdrew, however, leaving Labor without a Knesset majority. Only because the far left and Arab parties were willing to support the government (because they feared that Likud would be worse) was this government able to survive. In Israel, coalitions involving only a few parties rather than a large number of them have often proven to be more stable and decisive. As a consequence, the new government under Labor leader **Yitzhak Rabin** succeeded in September 1993 in reaching an agreement with the Palestine Liberation Organization for the formation of an autonomous Palestinian Authority in parts of the West Bank and Gaza as an interim measure. The two sides agreed to have an autonomous Palestinian entity arise and develop, while they negotiated a permanent settlement between them. A series of agreements was signed between 1993 and 1995. They are known collectively as the **"Oslo Accords"** because the original agreement had been brokered under the auspices of the Norwegian government in Oslo before being signed in Washington on September 13, 1993.

Following the signing of the first set of the Oslo Accords, Rabin concluded a peace treaty with Jordan. Negotiations with Israel's other two neighbors, Syria and Lebanon, continued but did not realize the same progress. The Oslo agreements with the Palestinians provoked bitter opposition among some Israelis, leading to Rabin's assassination in 1995.

PROFILE: Yitzhak Rabin

Yitzhak Rabin was Israel's first native-born prime minister. He was born in Jerusalem in 1922 to parents who

An Israeli citizen salutes a memorial to former Prime Minister Yitzhak Rabin at Kings Square, the site of his assassination on November 7, 1995.

had made *aliya* from Eastern Europe. He joined the Labor-oriented Jewish militia, and when the militia formed the nucleus of the new Israeli officer corps in 1948, Rabin became an officer. He rose to the rank of general in his early thirties and became chief of staff during the mid-1960s. Rabin headed the Israeli military during its stunning triumph in 1967. While he emerged as a war hero, rumors circulated that he had suffered a nervous breakdown under the strain of the prolonged showdown that preceded the outbreak of fighting. Upon stepping down from the army he was appointed ambassador to the United States. Despite his blunt style and strained relations with his boss, Israel's foreign minister, Rabin emerged as a highly successful ambassador. The U.S.-Israeli relationship grew closer during his tenure. After the 1973 war, the Labor government was besieged with criticism of the country's performance and brought Rabin home to serve as a minister. In 1974 Rabin narrowly defeated Shimon Peres in a bid for the Labor Party leadership and became prime minister. As a career officer, Rabin lacked political skills and could not keep his government united. On the eve of the 1977 elections, he stepped down as head of the party when it was revealed that his wife had maintained a bank account in U.S. dollars while they lived in Washington. At the time it was illegal for Israelis to hold such accounts, though the scandal would probably not have damaged a more experienced figure with stronger support in his party.

For the following two decades, Rabin and Peres were engaged in a sharp rivalry within the Labor Party. In three internal Labor elections in the 1980s Rabin finished in second place behind Peres, serving as minister of defense when Labor and Likud joined in National Unity govern-

ments. Rabin finally replaced Peres as head of Labor in 1992 because party activists were convinced that his military background might appeal to security-conscious voters. Labor's strong showing in the 1992 elections allowed Rabin to return to the premiership after fifteen years. This time he was far more successful in pursuing his political agenda, negotiating the Oslo interim agreement with the Palestinians and the peace treaty with Jordan. The agreement brought Rabin the 1993 Nobel Peace Prize, which he shared with Peres (Israel's foreign minister) and Palestinian leader Yasser Arafat. Israel prospered under Rabin's government and became a leader in high-technology industries.

But Rabin's agreements with the Palestinians deeply split Israeli society. His opponents grew increasingly bold, engaging in demonstrations and civil disobedience. This opposition culminated in Rabin's assassination in November 1995 at the hands of a law student who objected on nationalist and religious grounds to the Labor government's peace policies.

Rabin's personal style was often gruff and impatient, and he seemed ill at ease in the public spotlight. Yet he left a very strong legacy. His successor, Binyamin Netanyahu, strongly criticized Rabin's policies but could not bring himself to repudiate the agreement with the Palestinians. And when the Labor Party picked a new leader after the 1996 defeat, they turned to a follower of Rabin with a similar military background: Ehud Barak.[10]

Netanyahu in Power

In 1996, the first elections were held under the new system that provided for the direct election of the prime minister by the voters. Likud's **Binyamin Netanyahu** defeated Shimon Peres, Rabin's successor, by an extremely narrow margin.

PROFILE: Binyamin Netanyahu

Binyamin (Bibi) Netanyahu embodied a series of anomalies. The first prime minister to be born after the creation of the Israeli state, he spent a considerable portion of his life outside the country. The first prime minister to be directly elected by the people rather than by the Knesset, he nevertheless proved to be unpopular throughout most of his tenure. The son of a close aide to the founder of the Revisionist movement of Zionism, he drove many fellow second-generation party leaders out of the Revisionists' successor, Likud.

Born in 1949 in Tel Aviv, Netanyahu lived in the United States for five years while growing up. He returned to Israel in 1967 for his military service, distinguishing himself

Binyamin Netanyahu

as a member of an elite commando unit. (Ironically, his commander in that unit was his successor, Ehud Barak.) Upon his discharge from the army, Netanyahu returned to the United States to study at the Massachusetts Institute of Technology. After completing his degree, he remained in the United States to work, while at the same time actively supporting various Israeli political causes. In 1976 his older brother, Yonatan, was killed when leading a daring rescue mission in Uganda, where the passengers of a hijacked Israeli plane were held captive. The attention cast on the family following Yonatan's heroic death brought Netanyahu temporarily into the public spotlight. Netanyahu then returned to the United States, where the Israeli ambassador noticed his ability to present controversial Israeli policies in an aggressive and articulate manner. After working in the Israeli embassy, he was appointed Israel's ambassador to the United Nations. He quickly attracted the admiration of many in the American Jewish community for his telegenic presence and strident criticisms of terrorism and of the Middle Eastern states he accused of supporting it.

In 1988, Netanyahu returned to Israel to join Likud's election list and won a position not only in the Knesset but as a deputy minister. A rising star within the party, he was seen as a potential future leader. When Likud fared poorly in the 1992 elections, the party cast about for a forceful new chief. Since the subsequent elections would be carried out according to the new system, giving voters the opportunity to elect the prime minister directly, many members of Likud accepted the idea that they should designate a powerful spokesman rather than a party insider. Netanyahu won the leadership contest and became opposition leader. He bitterly criticized the Labor government's peace policies, leading

some Israelis to regard him as partly responsible for creating the highly charged political atmosphere that had led to Rabin's assassination. Netanyahu thus entered the 1996 elections at a distinct disadvantage, appearing to be a villain in the minds of many Israelis.

Yet in a closely fought campaign, Netanyahu triumphed. A series of terrorist bombings in Israel led some voters to question the benefits of the peace process. Netanyahu himself worked hard to appeal to centrist Israelis, attacking the Oslo agreements while not explicitly repudiating them. Promising Israelis "peace with security," Netanyahu portrayed his opponent, Shimon Peres, as unwilling to stand up to the Palestinians in negotiations. The campaign was very divisive but Netanyahu's strategy proved effective.

Having been directly elected by the people, Netanyahu initially attempted to govern with all the authority of an American president. But his efforts to centralize power in his own hands proved fruitless, and he found that he had to rely on the support of a shifting coalition of leaders both inside and outside his own party. Indeed, Netanyahu's coalition was even more fractious than preceding ones. Although he pledged to stimulate economic growth and the privatization of state-owned enterprises, his economic proposals encountered opposition among his supporters and proved difficult to implement. Whereas some favored rapid economic liberalization and privatization, others argued that such policies might hurt the country's poor.

Netanyahu also promised peace with security, but his position on negotiations with the Palestinians remained vague, in large measure because of divisions within his coalition government. Some opposed any continuation of the peace process, while others saw it as the only viable option facing the country. After two and a half years in office, he finally reached an agreement with the Palestinian leadership to continue implementing the interim accord that Rabin had signed in Oslo. The "Wye Accords" (so called because they were negotiated at the Wye Plantation in Maryland) were passed narrowly by the Knesset. Yet the opposition to their implementation was so strong within Netanyahu's own cabinet that he immediately claimed that the Palestinians had violated the agreement and froze Israel's compliance. Unable to pursue either a confrontational or a conciliatory policy, Netanyahu allowed the Knesset to move up the date of elections by one year to April 1999.

At times, Netanyahu seemed to bridge the gaps in his governing coalition effectively, but at other times he seemed far too combative. He quarreled with his foreign, defense, and finance ministers, driving them not only out of the cabinet but completely out of the party. His science minister, the son of Likud party founder Menachem

Begin, resigned in protest at Netanyahu's policies and eventually left the party. Even those Likud leaders who remained within the party seemed to keep their distance from him. When Netanyahu's coalition finally fell apart, he found himself without strong supporters. In the 1999 election, Netanyahu was soundly defeated by his Labor party rival, Ehud Barak. Likud's share of the parliamentary vote was the lowest since 1961. In light of this electoral failure, Netanyahu resigned as the party's leader.[11]

Barak Takes Office

During the 1999 election campaign, Ehud Barak pledged to resume the peace process, but he showed that he had learned the lessons of Netanyahu's 1996 triumph by minimizing the differences between the Likud bloc and his own Labor Party and appealing to centrist voters. Rather than campaigning enthusiastically for the peace process, Barak told Israeli voters the concessions he would *not* make. After bringing in American advisors who had helped elect Bill Clinton twice, Barak ran an American-style campaign. He focused his attention on Netanyahu as a leader. By winning 56 percent of the vote, he saw his strategy vindicated.

PROFILE: Ehud Barak

Ehud Barak, Israel's tenth prime minister, had a career that seemed to blend elements of his mentor, Yitzhak Rabin, and his rival and predecessor, Binyamin Netanyahu. Like Rabin, Barak was born in mandatory Palestine and had a brilliant military career. Like Netanyahu, Barak was educated partly in the United States and was chosen for his party's leadership despite his political inexperience because it was felt he would be popular with voters.

Barak was born on a kibbutz in 1942. Raised in the principles of socialist Zionism, Barak entered the army in 1959. He rose through the ranks and became the leader of the same elite commando unit that included Binyamin Netanyahu. He took part in several daring operations, including rescue missions and assassinations of Palestinian leaders. While in the army he pursued university studies, first in Israel and then in the United States completing his master's degree at Stanford University. He rose to the position of army chief of staff in 1991. When the Labor government began negotiations with the PLO, Barak seemed to distance himself from the process. This was partly because of the desire

Prime Minister Ehud Barak (second from left) with members of his six-party coalition government formed in 1999.

to keep the army out of politics, but it also seemed to reflect deeper concerns about the peace process. Barak participated in negotiations with the Syrian government, an action the opposition denounced as inappropriate for someone still in uniform. When he retired from the army in 1995, Rabin quickly brought him into politics, appointing him interior minister. A few months later, after Rabin was assassinated, Barak became foreign minister and assumed responsibility for a peace process about which he remained ambivalent. When Peres was defeated in the 1996 elections, Labor Party members elected Barak to succeed him, hoping that his military record and association with Rabin would win the party votes. Barak's decisive victory in May 1999 proved them right.[12]

While Barak's victory was decisive, the Israeli electorate also set him a difficult task by distributing its vote more evenly than in the past. The two largest parties shared only two-fifths of the seats in the Knesset; the remainder were scattered among a multitude of ethnic, religious, and ideological parties. Barak surprised many observers by managing to put together a diverse coalition, including a left-wing party, a Russian party, a nationalist religious party that supported Jewish settlements in the West Bank, and a religious party appealing primarily to Jews from Middle Eastern countries. Many predicted that such a coalition could never be assembled, much less hold together. But Barak managed to guide his fragile coalition into taking tentative steps toward reviving the moribund peace process, only to see it disintegrate just hours before he enplaned for the crucial Camp David Summit in the summer of 2000.

Israel and the Ten Conditions for Democracy

Over the course of slightly more than fifty years of existence as an independent state, Israel has managed to fulfill most of the ten conditions for democracy outlined in chapter 10. Its *state institutions,* resting on parliamentary democracy, were democratic from the outset. Israeli political *elites* have been overwhelmingly committed to ballot-box democracy, even those with a socialist orientation in economic matters. The country's *national wealth* has expanded considerably. Per capita GDP on average rose more than 5 percent per year in the 1950s and 1960s, and it climbed about 2 percent annually in subsequent decades. In 1998 Israel's per capita GDP was nearly $16,000, far surpassing its Arab neighbors in this and other economic categories. *Private enterprise* has flourished, especially since the 1980s. The *middle class* is sizable and relatively prosperous. A vibrant *civil society* promotes a vigorously participant *political culture.* As we shall observe later in this chapter, a first-rate *education* system is open to the population at all levels, and freedom of *information*—except in sensitive security matters—has expanded in recent years as state controls over the media have weakened.

Nevertheless, it is quite evident that several fundamental aspects of Israeli politics and society have placed enormous strains on the country's democratic system. Although they have not been strong enough to threaten the collapse of democracy itself, they have raised questions about the quality of Israeli's democracy and the extent to which it applies to all its citizens equally. For example, Israel since its inception has suffered from a *stateness* problem: exactly what are Israel's borders, and should the Israeli state be defined in religious or secular terms? These and related questions, as we have seen, have prevented Israel from adopting a constitution. Israel's mosaic-like *heterogeneity* adds enormous challenges to the quality of the country's democratic life. Not only have Jews from the Middle East and the former Soviet Union had reason to complain about discrimination at the hands of Jews of European background, but the country's large Arab minority have been subject to discriminatory treatment of various kinds in their dealings with Israeli authorities and elements of the Jewish population. Pockets of poverty remain for *disadvantaged* segments of the population, especially among the country's Arab citizens. Finally, Israel's parlous *international environment* surrounds the country with neighbors that for decades opposed its very existence. Following several wars and countless other military encounters, most of the states bordering Israel are at best only willing to tolerate it today. The Palestinians continue to demand a state of their own on territory Israel has long occupied, while anti-Israeli guerilla organizations pose a constant threat of terrorism. As a general rule, the impact of a near-permanent state of insecurity cannot be expected to have a salutary effect on democracy. We'll examine how Israel's democracy has dealt with this threatening environment in a hypothesis-testing exercise at the end of this chapter.

Despite the enormous challenges Israel has faced, it has nonetheless succeeded in building a stable, if still imperfect, democratic system. To have a better idea of how Israeli democracy works in practice, let's turn next to its state institutions.

ISRAEL'S STATE INSTITUTIONS

Although Israel can be described as a freewheeling democracy, its political institutions operate in the context of a difficult security situation and a socialist legacy that have produced a very strong and pervasive state. The mixture of a chaotic political arena with strong state institutions has marked Israeli politics in recent years.

The Knesset

As we mentioned at the start of this chapter, Israel has no written constitution, but it does have a series of Basic Laws that establish it as a parliamentary democracy. The British parliamentary system has served as the basic model for Israel's form of government, but the two systems are not exactly alike. Israel's version of parliamentarism has always had several features that differ from the British paradigm.

Israel's unicameral parliament, the **Knesset,** contains 120 seats and is directly elected by the people through a **proportional representation (PR)** electoral system. (The United Kingdom's House of Commons, by contrast, is elected under a single member district/plurality voting system. See chapter 9 for a fuller discussion of these electoral systems.) Israel uses one of the simplest forms of PR in the world. The entire country constitutes a single electoral district; there are no local districts. Israelis cast their vote for a political party rather than for an individual candidate. Hence the ballot lists the names of the parties rather than individuals. Each competing party wins a share of seats in approximate proportion to its share of the popular vote. Perhaps for this reason, voter turnout in Israel elections has always been high, never dipping below three-quarters of eligible voters. In the 1980s and 1990s, turnout was consistently between 77 percent and 80 percent. Until the 1992 elections, parties needed to capture at least 1 percent of the total popular vote to be represented at all in the legislature; since then, this hurdle has been raised to 1.5 percent. In this "party list" PR system, the parties themselves draw up lists of candidates and rank them in order of priority to determine which ones will be assigned Knesset seats, depending on how many seats the voters grant them. Thus if a party is entitled to ten seats, its top ten leaders will get them.[13]

For most of its history, Israel has followed a strictly parliamentary system. The central feature of this system is that the prime minister and cabinet, who possess most of the executive authority, are responsible to the legislature. That is, they can continue in office only as long as there is no majority of Knesset members opposed to them or their policies. Members of the Knesset can ask for a vote on withdrawing confidence from the government. Usually this tactic is employed to force a debate on a government policy, as opponents of the government rarely expect to win. On occasion, the Knesset has been so closely balanced that the outcome of a vote of confidence is uncertain, but generally a government that expects to lose will attempt to appear decisive by moving first and calling for new elections. Only twice (in 1951 and 1990) did a government lose a vote of confidence. On the first occasion, the party of the outgoing prime minister

did well in new elections; on the second occasion the prime minister at the time managed to avoid new elections by forming a new coalition.

These processes do not mean that Knesset debates are a mere formality. The prime minister and most members of the government are members of the Knesset. While there is no British-style question time, the presence of ministers leads to lively—and sometimes very bitter—debates. Heckling and name-calling are not uncommon. In recent years, even members of the governing coalition have felt free to criticize policies of their own government, though they generally either vote with the government or abstain. (In principle, voting against one's own government constitutes grounds for dismissal, but sometimes a coalition partner can get away with it. Six members of Barak's cabinet voted against his policy of land transfers to the Palestinians in March 2000, for example, but he kept them on board.) Because the government can survive only with the confidence of a parliamentary majority, Knesset committees tend to be weak. The Foreign Affairs and Defense Committee plays a notable role in reviewing policies, but most real decisions are made by the government.

While these and other aspects of Israel's parliamentary system of government are largely similar to what one finds in other parliamentary democracies, in the 1990s Israel introduced a major innovation by instituting the direct election of the prime minister by the voting population.

Selecting the Prime Minister and the Government

Until 1996, Israel's prime ministers were chosen through procedures commonly used in other parliamentary systems. The **president** of Israel, who is the country's **head of state,** used to play a critical role in this process. The president is elected by the Knesset rather than by the people, and his duties have always been mostly ceremonial. Generally, the president is a popular national figure enjoying widespread support. A majority of Israel's presidents have left office only because of death or ill health. President Ezer Weizman resigned in the summer of 2000, however, after Israel's attorney general issued a report criticizing him for financial improprieties. In a politically charged election that

TABLE 20.2

Israel's Presidents

Name	Years in Office
Chaim Weizman	1948–52
Yitzhak Ben-Tsvi	1952–63
Zalman Shazar	1963–73
Ephraim Katsir	1973–78
Yitzhak Navon	1978–83
Chaim Herzog	1983–93
Ezer Weizman	1993–2000
Moshe Katzav	2000–present

took place just after the Camp David summit, the Knesset elected **Moshe Katzav** as his successor. One of the president's few important functions consisted in naming a potential prime minister under the old pre-1996 system. But since 1996, the direct election of the prime minister by the voters has eliminated this function, leaving the president with largely ceremonial duties.

Parties that are being courted to participate in a governing coalition bargain very hard in Israel. They might seek certain ministries (for example, the ministries of education and religious affairs have traditionally been very important for the religious parties because of their networks of schools and religious institutions). They might also wish to obtain concessions on policy issues through cabinet positions (for instance, the Ministry of Finance is important for guiding economic policy, and the Ministry of Interior controls whether citizens are registered as Jews). They may also simply demand that the written policy guidelines for the government reflect their favored policies.

As a consequence of the need for coalition governments and the intense bargaining process, small parties in Israel have wielded a degree of political influence and have gained political advantages that far exceed their minority status. On occasion, parties will wish to have the best of both worlds: they will refuse to join the government (and be held responsible for its policies), but they will offer to vote with the government in return for certain concessions. Religious parties critical of the government's stand on religious issues will sometimes follow this path. The strategy works best if the government does not have the support of the majority of the Knesset and therefore needs

the support of some Knesset members outside the official coalition.

For the first three decades of Israel's existence, there was no question as to who was going to form the government. The Israeli Labor Party or its predecessors were always the largest party. They had their pick of coalition partners and generally turned to religious parties to obtain majority support from the Knesset. With this majority, the Labor prime minister and the cabinet could pursue any policy or legislation they thought necessary.

In 1977 Likud replaced the Labor Party as the largest parliamentary bloc, and the process of putting together a parliamentary majority became more complicated. The smaller parties found Labor and Likud competing for their support. On two occasions, as noted earlier, the two big parties were so evenly balanced that they agreed to form an uneasy coalition and invited small parties to join in governments of National Unity. The processes of coalition bargaining became so intense that they seemed to some Israelis to amount to public auctions in which Labor and Likud would bid for small party support with offers of cabinet positions and support for single-interest agendas.

The resulting coalitions were often unstable because the smaller parties seemed to feel that they could maximize their influence by threatening to switch allegiance to a rival bloc. The National Unity governments between Labor and Likud did not stop this bargaining game. In fact, the large parties would sometimes surreptitiously continue to entice the smaller parties into smaller coalitions that would replace the government of National Unity. In 1990, the Labor leader, Shimon Peres, led his party out of the National Unity government because he thought he had the support of a narrow Knesset majority that could govern without Likud. His calculations proved wrong, and for only the second time in Israeli history, a government lost a vote of confidence. The president then asked Peres to try to form a new government. However, some dissident members of parties that were supposed to support the new government refused to vote for a Labor-led coalition. The maneuver backfired, and the president turned then to Likud, which formed a narrow government without Labor.

Many Israelis found these processes unseemly. Secular Israelis felt that the large parties were too quick to make concessions to religious parties, and the constant threat of government collapse seemed to make governing more difficult. While it may have been true that only two governments have actually lost a vote of confidence, many crises had erupted over issues that seemed minor to most Israelis. In 1977, for instance, the National Religious Party turned against the government after a ceremony had taken place that ended too late for all government members to get home before the beginning of the Jewish Sabbath.

Table 20.3 summarizes Israel's kaleidoscopic history of coalition governments.

Direct Election of the Prime Minister

Many suggestions for political reform were put forward, but the problem was that any reform would have to be legislated by a Knesset brought into being under the old system. One political party arose in the mid-1970s that made electoral reform a central element of its program, but it disintegrated when it proved unable to institute any change. The 1992 reform requiring a party to receive 1.5 percent of the vote to be represented in the Knesset had limited effect. More extensive reforms—such as significantly raising that threshold or requiring members to be elected in districts—were discussed but not acted upon.[13]

Finally the Knesset approved a unique system: the direct election of the prime minister. The reform was enacted shortly before the 1992 Knesset elections, but was not slated to take effect until the next elections, held in 1996. A diverse coalition pursued the reform. Many members of the Labor Party were convinced that they had a strong candidate for prime minister—Rabin—who was more popular than the party itself. A few members of Likud (including the telegenic Netanyahu) joined the effort. Members of the country's legal community tended to support the reform, though most political scientists supported different solutions.[14]

The purpose of the reform was to strengthen the **prime minister,** who is Israel's **head of government.** Prior to the reform, Israel's prime ministers were often the prisoners of their coalition partners. The concept of **cabinet government**

tended to prevail, frequently forcing the prime minister to pursue policies backed by a majority of the cabinet members even if he or she did not personally favor those policies. The reform aimed to make the prime minister's role something of a cross between an American president, who can take initiatives fairly independently of the full cabinet, and a traditional prime minister, who is attentive to the cabinet's wishes. A directly elected premier would likely come from a large party and would be able to bargain with the small coalition partners from a position of strength, rooted in convincing popular support.

Under the new system, each voter on election day gets two ballots: one for electing the prime minister, which lists the individual candidates by name; the other for electing the Knesset, which lists the competing parties. Knesset seats are still allocated on the basis of proportional representation. The prime minister must receive an absolute majority (more than 50 percent) of the populor vote to be elected; if no candidate receives a majority, a runoff election between the two top vote getters is mandated. The reformed election system still allows the Knesset to bring down the prime minister and cabinet in a vote of no-confidence. However, an absolute majority of the full house (sixty-one of the 120 members) is now needed to pass a vote of no-confidence rather than a simple majority (more than half of those voting), as in the previous system. But by withdrawing their confidence in the prime minister, Knesset members may be endangering their own jobs. If a no-confidence motion passes with fewer than eighty votes, new elections must be held not only for the prime minister but also for the Knesset. At least eighty votes are required to bring about an election for a new prime minister without forcing new Knesset elections as well.

To be sure, it often happens in politics that institutional reforms or government policies do not produce their intended results. Such has been the case with Israel's electoral reform. Although it was designed to strengthen the prime minister and weaken the smaller parties, the reform has had precisely the opposite effect. In the 1996 elections, the first held under the new system, almost half the voters split their two votes, selecting either the Labor or Likud candidate for prime minister but a smaller party for the Knesset. Only one-quarter of

TABLE 20.3

Coalition Governments in Israel, 1948–96

Years in Office	Prime Minister (party)	Nature of Coalition	Reason for Leaving Office
1948	David Ben-Gurion (Mapai)	Provisional government created to found the state	First elections
1949–50	David Ben-Gurion (Mapai)	Mapai, religious parties, and a center party	Dispute between religious parties and state over education system; some religious parties leave government
1950–51	David Ben-Gurion (Mapai)	Mapai, religious parties, and a center party	Dispute over education committees; religious parties move into opposition and government loses vote of confidence
1951–53	David Ben-Gurion (Mapai)	Mapai, religious parties, and center parties	Retirement of Ben-Gurion
1953–55	Moshe Sharett (Mapai)	Mapai, a religious party, and center parties	Regularly scheduled elections; return of Ben-Gurion
1955–57	David Ben-Gurion (Mapai)	Mapai, other leftist parties, a center party, and a religious party	Dispute among cabinet members concerning leaking of security cooperation between Israel and Germany
1957–59	David Ben-Gurion (Mapai)	Mapai, other leftist parties, a center party, and a religious party	Dispute over weapons deal with Germany; regularly scheduled elections held slightly early
1959–61	David Ben-Gurion (Mapai)	Mapai, other leftist parties, a center party, and a religious party	Resignation of Ben-Gurion in dispute among Mapai leaders; early elections
1961–63	David Ben-Gurion (Mapai)	Mapai, another leftist party, and religious parties	Retirement of Ben-Gurion
1963–65	Levi Eshkol (Mapai)	Mapai, another leftist party, and a religious party	Regularly scheduled elections
1965–67	Levi Eshkol (Labor Party, based on union between Mapai and another socialist Zionist Party)	Labor, another leftist party, a center party, and religious parties	Formation of National Unity government in crisis preceding 1967 war
1967–69	Levi Eshkol (Labor)	National Unity government (excluding only Arab and communist parties)	Death of Eshkol
1969	Golda Meir (Labor)	National Unity government (excluding only Arab and communist parties)	Regularly scheduled elections
1969–70	Golda Meir (Labor)	National Unity government (excluding only Arab and communist parties)	Dispute over American Middle East peace plan; rightist parties resign
1970–74	Golda Meir (Labor)	Labor, another leftist party, a center party, and a religious party	Regularly scheduled elections (postponed because of 1973 war)
1974	Golda Meir (Labor)	Labor, another leftist party, and a center party	Resignation of Meir after independent commission faults government for performance in 1973 war
1974–77	Yitzhak Rabin (Labor)	Labor, a center party, and a religious party	Religious party splits from government; regularly scheduled elections held slightly early
1977–81	Menachem Begin (Likud)	Likud, center parties, and religious parties	Regularly scheduled elections
1981–83	Menachem Begin (Likud)	Likud, other rightist parties, and religious parties	Retirement of Begin
1983–84	Yitzhak Shamir (Likud)	Likud, other rightist parties, and religious parties	Early elections called to prevent disintegration of coalition
1984–86	Shimon Peres (Labor)	National Unity	Peres resigns to hand premiership to Shamir, following agreement between Labor and Likud to rotate position after two years
1986–88	Yitzhak Shamir (Likud)	National Unity	Regularly scheduled elections
1988–90	Yitzhak Shamir (Likud)	National Unity	Labor withdraws and brings down government; Labor tries to form narrow government but fails
1990–92	Yitzhak Shamir (Likud)	Likud, other rightist parties, and religious parties	Regularly scheduled elections
1992–95	Yitzhak Rabin (Labor)	Labor and another leftist party, with support from a religious party and Arab parties outside government	Assassination of Rabin
1995–96	Shimon Peres (Labor)	Labor and another leftist party, with support from a religious party and Arab parties outside government	Regularly scheduled elections (held slightly early)
1996–99	Binyamin Netanyahu (Likud)	Likud, plus religious, center, and rightist parties	Netanyahu calls for early elections as his coalition begins to fall apart over disagreements on peace process
1999 to present	Ehud Barak (Labor/One Israel)	Labor (joined with allies as One Israel), another leftist party, a center party, a rightist party, and religious parties (until summer 2000)	

the Knesset came from Likud, the party of the victorious candidate for prime minister, Binyamin Netanyahu. Netanyahu was therefore forced to bargain with religious parties, ethnic parties, and rightist nationalists in order to form a Knesset majority. As time went on, even members of Netanyahu's own party realized that they could threaten the prime minister with the loss of his majority. Netanyahu's troubles were magnified by his tendency to quarrel even with close supporters and by the strong ideological tensions within his coalition. After two and a half years of lurching from crisis to crisis, Netanyahu's coalition fell apart over the peace process.

In the second set of elections held under this system in 1999, almost two-thirds of Israeli voters split their votes. Victorious Labor leader Ehud Barak entered the Knesset with only twenty-five other members of his own party. His position initially seemed much more favorable than Netanyahu's: his style was more inclusive and less divisive, and the array of possible coalition partners was larger. Yet the fact remained that the supposed "Americanization" of the Israeli premiership has led to greater party fragmentation, more instability, and increased bargaining between the prime minister and smaller parties rather than a U.S.-style two-party system.

The Israeli Knesset has therefore taken up the issue of reform once again. It even passed a bill on its first reading to restore the old system. (A bill must be passed on three readings to become law). Still, no reform can nullify the fact that Israel has one of the most fragmented societies in the world from an electoral perspective. It is not merely that each segment of society has its own party: in some cases each segment has several parties. In the summer of 2000 the Knesset had three religious parties; three parties for Russian immigrants (one of which is a splinter of the largest one); two secularist parties; one party referred to as "Labor" (though it calls itself "One Israel") and another presenting itself as the "real" workers' party; two rightist parties; and three parties appealing primarily to Arabs.

Other State Institutions

Despite a fragmented electoral system, Israel possesses additional state institutions that are very strong. As the society has become more diverse, some of these institutions have come under criticism, but most retain their ability to protect their independence from turbulent political debates.

The Military Israelis often point to the **Israel Defense Forces** (**IDF**) as a critical institution not only for maintaining the country's security but also for integrating a very diverse population into a cohesive society. Military service is mandatory for most Israelis; most serve after completing high school. Men generally serve for three years, women for two. There are some exemptions: Israeli Arabs are not required to serve, and religious students can also avoid the military. But using these exemptions has costs. Israelis often question the loyalty of those who do not serve, and exemptions for ultra-Orthodox Jewish religious students (many of whom do not even accept the idea of a secular Jewish state) have become an increasingly controversial issue in Israeli politics. Those who do serve often obtain training and forge personal bonds that aid them in their transition to civilian life.

In recent years, some Israelis have concluded that the country's defense needs might be better served by concentrating resources on a smaller, more professional fighting force. Israel shoulders one of the most onerous peacetime defense burdens in the democratic world. Defense expenditures currently amount to approximately one-tenth of GNP; the proportion has risen above one-quarter during security crises, and even higher during actual war. In the United States, defense spending during the Cold War decades usually ran about 6 percent of GNP.

The IDF itself has become more willing to grant exemptions from mandatory military service, and some senior officers have begun to say that the army should have some of its social functions removed (such as the integration of new immigrants into Israeli society through mandatory service). Yet the ethos of a citizen-soldier remains quite strong, and most Israelis expect to serve before beginning college or a career.

Institutionally, the IDF was supposed to lie outside of politics. Several pre-independence militias (generally organized by political parties) were given no choice but to be absorbed into the IDF. But the officer corps came from the socialist Zionist movement, meaning that there were often strong

TABLE 20.4

Elections for Prime Minister and Knesset, 1996 and 1999

Prime Ministerial Election, 1996

Candidate for Prime Minister	Party	Share of Vote (%)*
Binyamin Netanyahu	Likud	50.5
Shimon Peres	Labor	49.5

Knesset Election, 1996

Party	Share of Vote (%)	Share of Knesset Seats (no.)	Knesset Seats (%)
Likud-Gesher-Tsomet (coalition of rightist parties)	25.8	26.7	32
Labor	27.5	28.3	34
Shas (religious)	8.7	8.3	10
National Religious Party	8.1	7.5	9
Shinui (leftist)	7.5	7.5	9
Communist	4.4	4.2	5
Israel Ba'Aliya (Russian immigrants)	5.8	5.8	7
United Torah Judaism (religious)	3.3	3.3	4
Third Way (splinter from Labor)	3.2	3.3	4
United Arab List	3	3.3	4
Moledet (rightist)	2.4	1.7	2

Prime Ministerial Election, 1999

Candidate for Prime Minister	Party	Share of Vote (%)*
Ehud Barak	One Israel (coalition of Labor and two small parties)	56.1
Binyamin Netanyahu	Likud	43.9

Knesset Election, 1999

Party	Share of Vote (%)	Share of Knesset Seats (no.)	Knesset Seats (%)
One Israel	20.2	21.7	26
Likud	14.1	15.8	19
Shas (religious)	13.0	14.2	17
Meretz (leftist)	7.6	8.3	10
Arab parties	5.3	5.8	7
Israel Ba'Aliya (Russian immigrants)	5.1	5.0	6
Shinui (secularist center)	5.0	5.0	6
Center	5.0	5.0	6
National Religious Party	4.2	4.2	5
United Torah Judaism	3.7	4.2	5
National Union	3.0	3.3	4
Israel Beitenu (Russian immigrants)	2.6	3.3	4
Communist	2.6	2.5	3
One Nation (workers' party)	1.9	1.7	2

*Does not total 100 percent because parties receiving less than 1.5 percent of the vote received no seats and are not listed.

personal bonds between military and civilian political leaders. This allowed the IDF to retain a great deal of autonomy from government officials. Formally, the IDF is under the control of the minister of defense and the cabinet, but the prestige and influence of the military are sufficiently strong to make it a direct (often hidden) player in debates over policy. The boundary between giving expert advice on military matters (which the IDF is asked to do) and taking political positions (which the IDF is supposed to stay away from) is often very unclear. In the past couple of decades, the boundary between the senior officers of the IDF and the political leadership has become especially porous: top civilian leaders often have a military background. Two prime ministers have served as army chief of staff, and several ministers of defense have been former generals. Retiring officers are often recruited by political parties.[15]

Some Israelis are troubled by this phenomenon, but it is not clear whether the military is being politicized by civilian life or, conversely, civilian politics is being colonized by the IDF. It is clear that the effectiveness and prestige of the IDF are still strong. The IDF remains the best example of an Israeli institution able to maintain its influential role in Israeli life despite the vicissitudes of party politics. Senior officers remain members of the elite of Israeli society.

The Judiciary The Israeli judiciary remains a similarly prestigious institution that seems to stand above party life even though its decisions provoke increasing controversy. Like most liberal democracies, Israel is caught between two principles. On the one hand, the people are held to be sovereign. This principle implies that the people's elected representatives should not be obstructed in their effort to enforce the popular will by nonelected authorities such as judges. On the other hand, fairness and stability require that the judiciary be granted independence, even from democratically elected political leaders. Different countries resolve this tension in various ways. In the United States, for instance, federal judges are nominated by the president but approved by the Senate, meaning that a democratic consensus supports their appointment. Once in office, however, they serve until they die or choose to retire.

Israel follows a different system that actually gives the judiciary even more autonomy from elected officials. Judicial appointments are made by a committee composed not only of Knesset and cabinet members but also of representatives from the bar association and the judiciary itself. Once appointed, judges serve for life. While this procedure means that Israeli judges do not owe their appointments exclusively to elected political figures and are therefore less dependent on them, they are weaker than their American counterparts in the decision-making process. American judges have a written constitution to work with, and their authority to strike down legislation they view as unconstitutional is unquestioned. Israel has no written constitution. As a consequence, the authority of Israeli judges to exercise judicial review was more difficult to establish and remains fairly weak. In recent years, Israeli courts have issued decisions asserting a right to review Knesset legislation that contradicts the country's Basic Laws (which are themselves passed by the Knesset). They have also used the country's fairly liberal Declaration of Independence as a guide for interpreting other laws. While there has been much public discussion of the increasing willingness of Israeli courts to engage in judicial review, the actual record reveals that judges remain fairly hesitant about pursuing the issue.

Nevertheless, the courts are increasingly brought into many political disputes. Controversial political decisions are regularly challenged in the courts; security prisoners go to the courts to demand release or an end to torture; and human rights activists increasingly look to the courts for support. The courts remain an elite domain: judges are often secular and liberal, leading some religious Jews to view the judiciary as hostile terrain. Such attitudes are especially focused on the **High Court,** which not only serves as the highest court for appeals in most cases but also is the first court to hear some cases involving complaints against government actions. Even some secular Israelis have complained that the courts have grown too powerful; some sympathetic observers worry that activist judges have exposed the courts to political attack. By American standards, the Israeli courts remain very deferential to the country's political leaders. The courts are likely to force government officials to justify their actions more explicitly or delay them, but they are less likely to block government initiatives. Like the military, the courts remain caught between the demands of professionalism and autonomy and the very partisan world of Israeli politics.[16]

Education and Universities　Israel's educational system reflects the tensions inherent in attempting to build an educated and cohesive citizenry in a partisan political environment. At the time of the founding of the state, much education was carried out by schools associated with specific political parties. One of the most controversial issues after the declaration of the state of Israel was whether to build a single, unified, national system of primary and secondary education. After some debate, such a system was built, but some independent systems were allowed to continue with government financial support. The most successful of these was the network of religious schools, some for the Orthodox and another system for the ultra-Orthodox who had yet to accept Zionism because of its secular premises. This arrangement continues to the present, though secular Israelis increasingly complain about a system in which the government funds schools whose students do not enter the army and are not taught that they are citizens of a Jewish state. These complaints are generally ignored by Israel's political leaders because they are often dependent on the support of religious political parties.

Most Israeli universities are state funded. For many years students were charged only modest fees, but in recent years universities have been allowed to collect more substantial tuition from their students. Despite strong financial support, universities retain almost complete political independence from the government. Faculty members are generally tenured and play a very strong role in the governance of their universities. Universities thus remain prestigious and autonomous institutions, and faculty members often play prominent public roles in a society that values education and expertise. But to some, the universities have become bastions of privilege, dominated by members of the elite and unresponsive to student needs. Admission to universities has grown increasingly competitive, as Israel becomes a more

prosperous society and younger Israelis are more anxious to enter the professions and lucrative fields (such as high technology). With public universities unable to meet the demand, private universities have begun to emerge. It seems likely that in a decade or two, Israeli academia will resemble the American system, with a mixture of private and public institutions.

Commissions of Inquiry　In Israel's partisan political environment, governments have sometimes wished to remove an issue from the political arena or have a neutral party investigate it. Israel has therefore developed the "Commission of Inquiry," an institution well adapted to resolve extremely contentious issues. The government generally retains control over the decision to appoint such a commission, generally doing so when there is sufficient public outcry, a sense of scandal, or an unresolvable controversy. For instance, in 1973 many Israelis felt the government had handled the war with Egypt and Syria very badly and did not trust the political leaders to investigate their own activities. A commission of inquiry was appointed. Similarly, in 1982, when Israeli forces allowed Christian militia forces into the Palestinian refugee camps in Lebanon, some Israelis held their government responsible for the ensuing massacre. The government replied bitterly that it could not be blamed for an action undertaken by its allies, the Lebanese Christians. As international and domestic controversy mounted, the government announced that a commission of inquiry would investigate the extent of Israeli responsibility.

Once the decision is made to form a commission, the commission itself works independently. The president of the High Court appoints the members. The resulting report is generally accepted by the politicians, though sometimes arguments ensue concerning the interpretation of the recommendations. The 1982 commission on the massacres of Palestinians in Lebanon suggested that the defense minister, Ariel Sharon, and the army chief of staff bore some responsibility and "should draw the appropriate conclusions," the euphemism for resignation. Both stepped down, though Sharon remained in the cabinet, leading some critics to charge that he was not fully accepting the report's recommendations.

Broadcast Media Israel's broadcast media provide the best illustration of Israel's shift from a socialist system with strong state institutions to a more freewheeling liberal society. Israeli radio was completely state controlled for many years, with direct political control over radio broadcasts. Israel did not suffer from the bombastic political propaganda that often comes with such a system, however. Until the 1960s, the Israeli government would not allow television broadcasting, fearing that the mass purchase of television sets would divert resources from other needs. In the 1960s, two important steps were taken. First, the government established the Israel Broadcasting Authority (IBA), granting the broadcast media more autonomy while retaining state control. (The IBA was patterned after the European system in which broadcasting is a state monopoly but retains some political independence from the government. The American system leaves broadcasting to the private sector.) Second, the government permitted the IBA to begin television broadcasting. To maintain the austere socialist atmosphere, only black-and-white broadcasts were allowed until the Likud government replaced Labor in the late 1970s. Some Israelis found the system confining, and one leftist even began broadcasting privately from a ship offshore to escape broadcast regulations.

This system remained in place for many years, even though Likud leaders often complained that the IBA remained a bastion of leftist journalists and editors. Labor leaders had an alternative complaint: Likud was using its political control to rein in independent broadcasters it did not like. In the 1980s the introduction of cable television widened the options for Israeli viewers, and in 1990 a commercial channel was added. At this point, state control over broadcasting began to break down (a similar pattern to that occurring in most European countries). Private radio broadcasters began to spring up all over the country, often without official permission. The government sometimes tried to control private broadcasting, but some broadcasters had powerful backers. Religious leaders and institutions, for example, saw independent broadcasting as a way to reach the population directly, avoiding the filter of secular institutions. One rightist and religious radio station (*Arutz Sheva*) claimed to be working offshore, though it

sometimes broadcast on land. It adopted a strident anti-government tone against the Labor government of 1992–1996, leading some Israelis to accuse it of responsibility for the atmosphere in which Prime Minister Rabin was assassinated. Palestinian autonomy has brought increased cacophony in the broadcast media, and the once thinly populated Israeli airwaves became crowded with a mixture of television and radio broadcasters.

In 1999 the outgoing Likud government, currying favor with its supporters, rushed through legislation legalizing some of this broadcast activity. The new legislation was immediately challenged in the courts. While it seemed doubtful that the judiciary would block any attempt at media liberalization, in a sense it did not matter: the state monopoly of broadcasting was long abolished. What remained was an amalgam of an old, centralized system and a completely decentralized one. The old IBA-controlled broadcasters remained and attracted a considerable number of listeners and viewers; commercial and foreign broadcasters drew increasing audiences; and smaller groups in Israeli society had their own radio stations, skirting the law and government regulation.

ISRAEL'S POLITICAL PARTIES

Proportional representation allows a large number of parties to flourish, but it does not *create* a multiplicity of parties. Israel has a large number of parties because its population is divided into a large number of social identities and political attitudes. Over the half century that the Israeli state has been in existence, eight general political tendencies have emerged.[17]

Labor

On the left, a group of parties descends primarily from the mainstream of the Zionist movement. Most (though not all) Zionist political parties were socialist in orientation. Strong doctrinal differences did emerge among some of these movements, especially over the question of how much stress to place on socialist goals and how much on nationalism. Even before the establishment of the state of Israel, one party emerged as dominant within the left: Mapai, led by David Ben-Gurion.

Several movements emerged on Mapai's left, eventually coalescing into a single party, Mapam (United Workers Party). Mapam was less nationalist than Mapai and more inclined toward the Soviet Union. On the far left, an Israeli communist movement attracted a small number of voters.

While Mapai dominated the left, it was itself often fairly fractious. Splinter groups ran separately in elections in the 1950s and 1960s. In 1969, all the non-communist leftist parties finally agreed to run together in the Labor Alignment, but by that point the size of the leftist vote had begun to decline. In 1988, Mapam split off from the Labor Alignment and joined two other smaller, more centrist parties oriented toward civil rights and political reform to form a new party, **Meretz** (a Hebrew acronym for the name of the three member parties).

Despite their socialist origins, Mapai and the Labor Alignment rapidly came to be seen as the party of the establishment and the dominant elite. While ideologically committed to equality, Labor leaders were increasingly seen as arrogant and patronizing, especially by newer immigrants to Israel. The intellectual, military, and political elites were strongly oriented toward Labor. Labor leaders debated security policy among themselves but exhibited a strong consensus toward the outside world, supporting the idea that Israel had few alternatives but to secure its existence through a strong military. After 1967, some Labor leaders were more inclined toward compromise with the Arab countries, but most felt that they did not receive any indication that a softer position would be reciprocated by Israel's adversaries. When Labor was finally ousted from power in 1977 by a center-right coalition, Labor had hardly shown itself to be the party of compromise in foreign policy. As it moved into opposition, Labor therefore had little to distinguish itself from Likud, now the dominant party. In the 1980s, Labor began to hint at greater flexibility than Likud on the Palestinian territories. Still trying to attract a large number of voters, however, Labor's policy remained vague. Only in the 1990s did very strong differences emerge with Likud when Labor, after returning to power in 1992, signed the Oslo Accords.

Labor gradually decreased its emphasis on socialism. Its positions increasingly attracted the more educated and wealthier segments of Israeli society. In the 1980s, the Labor leadership began to favor free-market policies and a stronger orientation toward exports and privatization along with decreasing support for government regulation of the private sector. And in the 1999 elections, Labor and Ehud Barak ran under the banner of **One Israel,** partly to allow some small parties to join and partly to avoid any socialist label. (The party feared that voters who had fled Russia and other parts of the former Soviet Union would not vote for anything with "labor" or "socialist" in its name.) Yet the Labor Party has not completely abandoned all of its commitment to being a bonafide labor party. The Histadrut, the country's trade union federation, retains very strong links with Labor.

The Labor party has also attempted to reform by becoming more democratic. Through the 1970s, the party was dominated by a few leaders who negotiated among themselves. A contest between Yitzhak Rabin and Shimon Peres for the party leadership continued intermittently between 1974 and 1992; that contest was referred to broader party conventions. In the 1980s, Labor moved toward a system of party primaries to determine its electoral list. While that system has never worked completely smoothly, Labor now is more democratic in its internal structure than it was in earlier decades.

Other Leftist Parties

There has always been a shifting group of parties on the left side of the Israeli political spectrum running for the Knesset outside the coalition of parties represented by Labor. The more significant parties have been Zionist in their strong support for a Jewish state, but they have differed from the Labor Party (or its predecessors) on grounds of policy or personality. In Israel's first decade of the state, some saw Mapai (the core of today's Labor Party) as insufficiently socialist and too willing to be allied with the Western powers. In the 1960s, Mapai was deeply divided by leadership struggles, leading some groups to split from the party. (On two occasions, Israel's first prime minister, David Ben-Gurion, led these efforts.) By the end of the 1960s, the entire Zionist left united under the Labor banner. That unity continued until the 1980s, when the most left-wing of the Zionist parties, Mapam, withdrew, forming the Meretz party with two other small, reform-oriented parties.

In many ways, Meretz has been the most successful leftist party. It has achieved that status by dropping any emphasis on socialism and instead basing its appeal on secularism and the peace process. The leaders of Meretz regularly clash with the leaders of Israel's religious parties. While many Israelis respect religious traditions, some chafe under the restrictions placed on daily life (such as the absence of public transportation on the Jewish sabbath). Others object to the high level of state funding for religious institutions. Meretz appeals to these Israelis. It has also staked out a strong position on the peace process, arguing that Israel should recognize a Palestinian state. Actually, Meretz currently differs little with the Labor Party on most issues, though it is less ambiguous than Labor in its commitment to secularism and compromise with the Palestinians.

Not all the parties of the left accept Zionism. Israel had a communist movement even before the establishment of the state. After Israel was founded, some Jews argued that the pursuit of nationalism was simply a way of obscuring the real interests of the working and lower classes. Such arguments also appealed to some Arab citizens, who found that Israel's leadership regarded communism as less threatening than Arab nationalism. Communist and other non-Zionist left-wing parties have generally tried to combine appeals to radical Jews as well as to Arabs. While they have always been represented in the Knesset, such parties have remained very small and marginal in political life. Jewish interest in these leftist parties has declined, and the non-Zionist left now primarily appeals to Arab voters.

Arab Parties

Arab citizens of Israel have formed a significant minority throughout the state's history but have not generally been able to translate their numbers into political influence. The portion of the population that is ethnically Arab has fluctuated between one-fifth and one-tenth; it is currently one-fifth of Israel's population. (The effects of the high birth rate in the Arab population have been offset by waves of Jewish immigration.) Arab political ac-

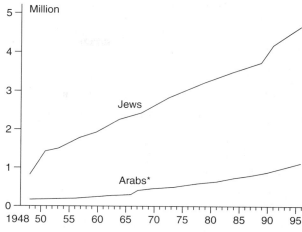

FIGURE 20.3 Jews and Arabs in Israel's Population (in millions)
Source: The Economist, April 25, 1998.

tivity was initially limited by the Israeli government. Arab areas were kept under military rule until the end of 1966. Arab residents did possess most rights of citizenship, however, including the right to vote. Zionist political parties established affiliated Arab parties to attract the Arab vote. Yet Zionism—or Jewish nationalism—had little ideological appeal to Israel's Arab citizens. In the early 1960s, an attempt to form a nationalist political party by members of Israel's Arab population was suppressed. Thus, for many years, only Israel's communist movement offered Arab citizens a viable alternative to Zionist parties. Most Arabs who voted opted for the Zionist parties, hoping to trade electoral support for the provision of government services. Arabs generally entered the Knesset as supporters of Jewish parties; a smaller number joined with communist Jews on the extreme left of Israel's political spectrum.

When political controls on the Arab population eased in the mid-1960s, Arab voters began to drift steadily away from the Zionist parties. The Arab parties that were aligned with the major Jewish parties gradually disappeared, and the Arab vote increasingly went to parties of the far left. Arabs were often attracted to such parties because they insisted that Arabs and Jews of the working and lower classes shared similar interests and they criticized Zionism for dividing the two populations.

In the 1980s and 1990s, independent Arab movements began to arise, and Israel's Arab population increasingly split its vote between far-left Arab-Jewish movements and exclusively Arab parties. In 1999, a prominent Arab political leader, Azmi Bishara, took the step of entering the race for prime minister. While he withdrew at the last moment (fearing that he was making it more difficult to defeat the incumbent prime minister, Netanyahu), his candidacy had attracted some support from Arabs and even some extremely secular Jewish intellectuals.

Israel's Arab parties have thus undergone a thorough transformation: those affiliated with the Zionist parties have been replaced by non-Zionist parties interested not only in obtaining government services but also in changing the nature of the Israeli state. No Arab party has called for Israel's destruction, but some Arab leaders have grown increasingly bold in supporting the PLO. Others have begun to call on Israel to become "a state of its citizens" (i.e., both Arabs and Jews) rather than a Jewish state. Even as they have shown greater willingness to challenge the ideological foundations of the state, these Arab parties have found themselves increasingly important. They are too radical to be invited to join the government coalition but they did provide important support for the Labor Party government between 1992 and 1996. In cases in which the two largest political parties, Labor and Likud, have been balanced, Arab parties have found in recent years that their votes in the Knesset, while few in number, can tip the balance in Labor's favor.

Parties of the Center

The sharply ideological nature of Israeli politics has left limited room for middle-of-the-road parties that try to avoid joining an ideological camp. Even before the founding of the state, however, some Zionist leaders who wished to avoid socialism or any other ideology began to label themselves simply "general Zionists." After the foundation of Israel, the general Zionists ran for the Knesset under the banner of the Liberal Party. The Liberals opposed some of the socialist measures of the early Mapai-led government but failed to develop a mass following. The party finally aligned

itself with the rightist Herut movement and was eventually absorbed into the Likud Party. While they played a subordinate role in Likud, the alliance greatly increased the credibility of the rightist camp, treated as a pariah throughout the 1950s and 1960s by the socialist mainstream. A section of the Liberals objected to the alignment with the right and managed to maintain its independence for many years until it finally merged with the Labor Party.

Since the decline of the Liberals and their absorption into other blocs, periodic movements have arisen that attempt to appeal to Israelis seeking alternatives to the major ideological tendencies. Most frequently, center parties have appealed to the voters primarily on domestic issues (such as an end to corruption). The Democratic Movement for Change (DMC) emerged in 1977 calling for constitutional reform and clean government, claiming that Labor's years in power had left its leaders more concerned with retaining their privileges than in reforming the country. The DMC received fifteen seats in 1977, making it the most successful reform party in Israel's history, but then disintegrated. A faction of the DMC survived as the **Shinui (Change)** Party. The Citizen's Rights Movement (CRM) emerged in the same period, pushing for women's rights, electoral reform, and greater respect for civil liberties. Shinui and the CRM aligned with Mapam to form Meretz in the 1990s (though Shinui withdrew in 1999).

In the 1990s a new group of center parties emerged, this time focusing not only on domestic reform but also on foreign and security policy. The Third Way, for example, claimed to support the peace process initiated by the Labor Party but opposed the party's perceived willingness to make concessions to Syria. A group of Labor and Likud dissidents joined independents in 1999 to form the **Center Party,** seeking to continue the peace process while appealing to voters who found Labor too inclined to compromise. And Shinui, having broken away from the leftist Meretz, ran on a strongly secular platform in 1999 with great success.

While some center parties have been successful in the short term, none has been able to sustain its success. Most have either evaporated or joined other groups. The rise and fall of the DMC was the most spectacular example of this. The DMC's main legacy seems to have been that it attracted voters away from the previously dominant Labor Party. The Center Party of 1999 followed a similar course, though less dramatically. The party attracted some prominent leaders, including members of both Likud and Labor. Initial opinion polls indicated that it was potentially very popular. Yet the party's support dissipated as voters opted for one of the traditional large parties or one of the smaller ideological ones. The Center Party's main effect seems to have been that it appealed to Likud voters discontented with the government.

Likud and the Nationalist Right

Before the establishment of the state of Israel, the Revisionist movement split off from the Zionist mainstream. As noted earlier, the Revisionists criticized the Zionist leadership for its socialism and its willingness to consider compromises over territorial issues. The Revisionists formed a military wing that began moving against the British mandate when the rest of the Zionist movement was still inclined toward lobbying and diplomacy. After the establishment of the state, the Revisionists established themselves as a political party under the leadership of the commander of its military wing, Menachem Begin. Begin's party, Herut (Freedom), was treated as a pariah by Israel's early leaders. The party's electoral support remained at relatively modest levels. In the 1960s, two steps turned the party toward greater acceptance. First, Herut formed an alliance with the Liberals, a well-established and respected, though fairly small party. Second, on the eve of the 1967 war, Israel's leaders decided to unify the country by inviting in all non-communist political parties to join the government. Menachem Begin became a cabinet minister.

When his party left this National Unity government in 1970, Begin became the leader of the most viable opposition to the Labor government. As a result, his party began to attract support from a variety of groups critical of the prevailing order in Israeli society. After widening its electoral appeal somewhat beyond the Herut-Liberal alliance, the party became known as the Likud bloc in the 1973 elections. At first, the parties in Likud kept their separate existence, but they later merged completely. Israel's performance in the 1973 war, pop-

ular perceptions of Labor Party arrogance and corruption, and growing feelings of exclusion on the part of Jews from Middle Eastern countries served to broaden Likud's electoral following. In 1977, Likud finally ousted Labor from power.

Between 1977 and 1999, the Likud Party was a member of every government except the Labor government of 1992–96. The party increasingly built its appeal on two sorts of issues. Domestically, Likud criticized the Labor Party as elitist and promised to be more responsive to Israel's poor. In foreign policy, Likud claimed to be a stern defender of Israel's security. Even Likud's leadership of Israel into a peace treaty with Egypt in 1979 did not diminish the party's image as uncompromising on security issues.

From 1984 until 1989, an even electoral balance forced Likud to share power with Labor in an uncomfortable arrangement. When Labor finally left the cabinet in 1989, Likud was able to govern with support only from religious and other rightist parties. Yet Likud's two issues proved to be a liability in the 1990s. Its claim to represent Israel's poor and middle classes was undermined by its uneven economic performance. And its uncompromising stance on security issues worried some Israelis who were convinced that compromise was the only path to peace. In 1992, Likud was ousted from power. A new generation of party leadership came to the fore, with Binyamin Netanyahu (who had never held the rank of minister) selected to head the party. The new party leadership was badly divided on a host of policy and personal issues. Though Netanyahu managed to defeat Shimon Peres in 1996 for the premiership, his party gained no additional seats in the Knesset. Netanyahu's rivals were hardly silenced by his victory, and his government was marked by acrimonious disputes and angry resignations. By the 1999 elections, most of the party's leaders had either publicly left the party or distanced themselves from Netanyahu's reelection effort.

Other Parties of the Nationalist Right

For many years, Herut (and later Likud) represented the right end of the political spectrum. When Likud finally came to power in 1977, however, it signed a peace treaty with Egypt that entailed withdrawal from the Sinai peninsula, Egyptian territory that Israel had occupied in the 1967 war. That withdrawal provoked some opposition from the right wing of Likud and led some of its members to split off from the party. Even more extreme groups emerged, calling for the expulsion of the Palestinian population from all territory occupied by Israel. One such party was banned from electoral competition for racism, but another (which argued that Palestinians should be peacefully "transferred" rather than forcefully expelled) managed not only to win Knesset representation but played an important role supporting Likud-led governments on occasion. The parties of the extreme right concentrate largely on a single issue: opposition to any territorial compromise with Arab states or the Palestinians. In 1999, Binyamin Begin, son of long-time Likud leader Menachem Begin, left Likud over the party's refusal to abandon the Oslo Agreements with the Palestinians. Begin united the far right parties under his leadership and ran directly for the prime ministership himself, withdrawing only at the last moment to avoid splitting the rightist vote.

Religious Parties

Before the establishment of the state of Israel, many Orthodox Jews were suspicious of much of the Zionist movement, viewing it as hostile to religion and fearing that it sought to substitute nationalism for religious observance. One group of Orthodox Jews organized a religious Zionist movement, eventually forming the **National Religious Party (NRP).** The NRP has participated in most Israeli governments throughout the country's history. Prior to the 1970s, the NRP allowed the other Zionist parties to dominate decision making in the critical areas of security and economic policy in return for concessions on their narrow political agenda. Generally, the NRP wanted the government to support religious institutions. Existing arrangements regarding religious practice (such as the absence of public transportation on the Jewish sabbath) and government respect for religious observances (such as the use of kosher food in official functions) were generally sufficient for the NRP. Alongside the NRP stood a non-Zionist Orthodox movement, which ran in Knesset elections but refused to participate in the cabinet.

In the 1970s, the role of the religious parties in Israeli politics began to increase for several rea-

sons. First, Labor and Likud were roughly even in parliamentary support, often leaving the religious parties holding the balance between them. Second, the religious parties evinced increasing interest in a broader political agenda. The leadership of the NRP, for instance, began to lean heavily toward the right on security issues. The non-Zionist religious parties finally showed a willingness to participate in the cabinet. Third, ethnic religious movements arose, particularly among Jews of Moroccan origin. A new political movement, **Shas** (Sephardic Torah Guardians) emerged to capture the support of many Moroccan Jews and other Sephardic Jews who felt excluded by the other political parties. (*Sephardic* Jews—or as they are known in Israel, Eastern Jews—tend to come from the Middle East. Jews from Europe and Russia are typically known as *Ashkenazy.*) Many Shas voters were not strongly religious, but they retained a strong respect for religious leaders. Shas is particularly interested in securing public funding for its religious schools, a position that brought it into a sharp confrontation with the outspokenly secular Meretz party, creating a source of instability in Barak's first cabinet. Finally, the religious parties found that their control of important ministries (such as interior and education) put them in a position to distribute benefits to their followers. Shas in particular was successful in building a patronage network that operated much like an American political machine.

While these trends led to an increase in the influence of the religious parties, they prompted a strong counterreaction among some secular Israelis. The two large parties, Labor and Likud, were generally careful to avoid alienating potential partners. But some smaller parties, all across the political spectrum, were not so shy. Meretz has been particularly strident on this issue, but other small center and right wing parties have sometimes joined in the criticisms. These parties denounce the religious parties as corrupt and undemocratic, seeking to impose religious practice on the secular majority. In addition, since many Orthodox Jews receive exemptions from mandatory military service so they can study religion, some secular politicians question the patriotism of the Orthodox parties (except the National Religious Party, which has always been Zionist) as well.

In the 1990s a new issue emerged: relations with Jews overseas. Orthodox rabbis, who control almost all religious functions in Israel, will not recognize non-Orthodox rabbis as legitimate. Moreover, the Orthodox parties prevent the Israeli state from recognizing any non-Orthodox form of Judaism. Since non-Orthodox rabbis form the decisive majority in the United States and some other countries, the attitudes of religious parties have begun to sour relations between Israeli and non-Israeli Jews. Very few Israelis have much interest in Reform and Conservative Judaism (the two most popular Jewish religious movements in the United States), but they criticize the Orthodox in Israel for needlessly antagonizing American Jews by refusing to accept people converted by non-orthodox rabbis as Jewish. This issue has become particularly prominent in the "Who is a Jew?" controversy: whether those who have converted to Judaism under the supervision of non-Orthodox rabbis are to be considered Jewish. Most secular Israelis show little concern for religious issues and do not feel personally affected by the controversy. But some feel that the religious parties have alienated the country's friends overseas. In recent years, therefore, the division between secular and religious Israelis has become increasingly contentious.

Jewish Ethnic Parties

Early Zionist leaders strove to downplay differences among Jews from different countries. To be sure, where Israelis came from and when they came did have some influence on their political loyalties: socialists were more likely to come from Eastern Europe; German Jews were more likely to hew to the liberal center. But most parties claimed to wish to represent all Jews, no matter where they came from. Although some parties based on ethnic appeals secured some Knesset seats in early elections, they soon faded. The Israeli government worked hard to build a common national identity.

Yet in the 1960s some Jews from Middle Eastern countries began to complain that they were victims of discrimination by the country's elite, almost all of whom were of European origin. Many felt that Israel's leaders were arrogant and patronizing and showed little understanding of the social and economic problems they were experiencing.

Middle Eastern Jews were more likely to be poor and less educated. Even those with a better education felt they were not granted the same opportunities as European Jews. Since they had mostly immigrated after the establishment of the state of Israel in 1948, they felt bereft of the personal connections necessary to gain entrance into elite institutions. Universities, elite army units, and leading political positions seemed closed to them. During the 1970s, many voters from such backgrounds turned increasingly to the Likud Party to express their discontent. Still, attempts to start explicitly ethnic parties generally foundered. Likud made room for some Middle Eastern Jews in top positions, but the party leader has always been of European background. Shas appeals primarily to Moroccan Jews, but it presents itself as a religious party first and an ethnic party second.

It was not until the 1996 elections that ethnic parties began to show their potential power. David Levy, the leading Middle Eastern Jew in Likud and a former foreign minister, bolted the party and formed an independent grouping, Gesher (Bridge). Although he was finally enticed to join the Likud electoral list in the 1996 elections, he quarreled with other members of the Likud government after their victory for spending too little on social programs for Israel's poor. He finally led his small party out of the alliance with Likud and into Barak's Labor-sponsored One Israel alliance in 1999, becoming foreign minister in Barak's cabinet. But Levy declined to accompany Barak to Camp David in 2000 because of reservations about

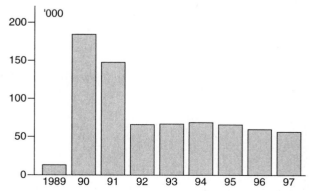

FIGURE 20.4   Russian Immigration in Israel (in thousands)
Source: The Economist, April 25, 1998.

Barak's readiness to make unprecedented compromises with the Palestinians, and he subsequently quit the cabinet.

Another Middle Eastern (Sephardic) Jew to achieve prominence was Moshe Katsav, Israel's new president. Prior to his election by the Knesset in July 2000, Katsav was a little-known Likud deputy. Born in Iran, he had come to Israel at the age of five and grew up in a working-class town. His election came as a shock to Israel's political establishment, which had assumed that Shimon Peres, the Polish-born Nobel laureate and veteran of numerous Labor cabinets, would handily win the ceremonial post with Prime Minister Barak's backing.

While the split between European and Middle Eastern Jews is of long standing, ultimately a different group showed the potential for ethnic parties in Israel. In the late 1980s and early 1990s, a wave of immigration from the former Soviet Union flooded Israel (see figure 20.4). At first, Soviet immigrants supported the existing parties. In 1996, however, a new party called **Israel Ba'Aliyah** emerged, claiming that the existing parties were doing little to address the problems of new immigrants. Natan Sharansky, the party's leader, had spent close to a decade in a Soviet prison before emigrating to Israel, making him a hero to many Russian Jews. The new party claimed that it would enter a coalition with either Likud or Labor, trying to make itself indispensable to a leader from either of the two largest parties. The strategy worked in 1996, leading Sharansky into a coalition with Likud. In 1999, the party found itself in a bitter dispute with Shas, whose leaders claimed that Russian Jews were insufficiently religious. The dispute drove many Russian voters to support the Labor Party, because they saw Shas as tilting toward Likud. Once again, the Russians found themselves in the position of kingmakers, making it possible for the Labor Party to obtain a majority of supporters in the Knesset. Yet success has had its costs: in 1999 a second Russian party—**Israel Beitenu**—emerged on the right. And shortly after the 1999 elections, a left-leaning group split off from Israel Ba'Aliyah. The formation of the new splinter party, known as **Democratic Choice,** meant that three Russian parties were now represented in the Knesset.

The rise of ethnic voting in Israel has helped ensure that previously excluded groups are brought into the political arena. But it has also led to increased tension among such groups, as the Moroccan-Russian rivalry during the 1999 elections showed.

ISRAEL'S TRADE UNIONS

The **Histadrut,** Israel's federation of trade unions, has undergone two transitions that have gradually reduced its role in Israeli life. Nevertheless, it remains a fairly powerful economic and political force and a very significant institution in the lives of ordinary Israelis. Founded before the state, the Histadrut initially seemed to embody the principles of socialist Zionism. It set its task as not simply bargaining for workers but building a new society on socialist principles. The Histadrut set up a bank and economic enterprises and established systems for medical care as well. In short, it combined many functions assigned to the state or to the private sector in many other societies. The Histadrut was forced to undergo its first transition in 1948, with the establishment of the state of Israel. While the organization maintained a number of its original functions, many of its members began to look to the Israeli state rather than the labor union for various forms of assistance. Since both the Histadrut and the government were dominated by socialist Zionists, the union seemed at times to be a part of the state itself.

The Histadrut underwent a second transformation in the 1980s and 1990s. With Likud in power much of the time, it no longer found itself closely connected to the country's leadership. Economic liberalization threatened many benefits that workers had come to expect; in 1985 Labor and Likud both cooperated on a liberalization plan that was enacted over strenuous Histadrut objections. The state began to privatize some economic enterprises, and the Histadrut soon had to follow suit. Many of its operations were not profitable, forcing the Histadrut to divest itself of some of its economic holdings. Even the health service operated by the Histadrut—a system that covered most Israelis—became difficult to operate. The Histadrut looked to the government for support but worried that it might be losing control over the health system. In 1995 a new system was finally approved that maintained the Histadrut system but introduced a far stronger measure of government control.[18]

These changes transformed the Histadrut from a quasi-governmental agency into a more narrowly focused trade union organization. The Histadrut had claimed to serve virtually all working Israelis (and in a sense it did so by providing health coverage to a substantial majority of the population until 1995), but its current membership now stands at about one-third of the labor force. It has increasingly focused on representing workers rather than attempting to operate its own separate economy. The Histadrut leadership remains associated with the Labor Party, but as both institutions have lost their socialist focus, the relationship has become quite strained. One Labor leader rebelled against his party and used the Histadrut as a power base under the Rabin government. In the 1999 elections, the Histadrut leader formed his own political party, winning two seats in the Knesset.[19]

POLITICAL ISSUES IN TODAY'S ISRAEL

Israeli politics in recent years has centered around three major issues: security and the peace process, religion and the state, and economic reform.

Security and the Peace Process

The strong national consensus on security issues has dissolved over the past two decades. For many years, Israelis were convinced that they had no alternative to a strong military and assertive security policy. Surrounding Arab states were unwilling to accept Israel's existence, giving the country's leaders few alternatives. The consensus began to break apart in the 1980s and 1990s, when many Israelis viewed their country as having a historic opportunity to build peaceful relations with neighboring Arab states and even settle the conflict with the Palestinians. The 1993 Oslo Agreement with the Palestinian Liberation Organization launched Israel into a new era in which formerly mortal enemies attempted to negotiate their differences. That process deeply divided the Israeli public.

Some wished to make no territorial concessions whatsoever, convinced that Israel had a strong nationalist or religious claim to the contested areas. Others doubted whether the prospect of peace with Arab neighbors was real or certain enough to justify any risks. At the other end of the spectrum, some Israelis were willing to withdraw from all of Gaza and the West Bank (but not Arab parts of Jerusalem) and allow a Palestinian state in return for a peace agreement. Between the two camps lay a large portion of the population, enticed by the possibility of peaceful relations but concerned that Israel might be making too many concessions too quickly. This middle camp provided the votes that led Netanyahu to defeat Peres in 1996; many such voters deserted Netanyahu in 1999 when he proved unable to pursue peace at any pace. Yet the three-year Netanyahu government did have a significant result: because he confirmed Israel's willingness to carry through past agreements, he cemented Israel's commitment to the Oslo Accords. Critics claimed that Netanyahu sought to undermine the peace process, but by the end of his government Israelis debated the pace and nature of the peace process more than they questioned its fundamental direction.

Ehud Barak promised fresh initiatives designed to achieve a breakthrough in Israel's relations with its neighbors. At the Camp David summit held in the summer of 2000, the prime minister engaged in intense negotiations with Arafat and President Clinton on several long unresolved issues in Israel's relations with the Palestinians:

The West Bank and Gaza—While Arafat and his team demanded full control of both areas, Barak and the Israeli negotiating team indicated their readiness to cede most of these territories to the Palestinian Authority as long as a certain number of Israeli settlers were allowed to remain in the West Bank (see figure 20.5).

Jerusalem and a Palestinian State—The Israeli government by 2000 appeared to accept the inevitability of a Palestinian state, and most Israelis are more concerned about a Palestinian army than a Palestinian government. But Barak maintained Israel's resistance to the Palestinian demand that its capital should be East Jerusalem, the Arab part of the city. Both sides have enormous historical and religious attachments to Jerusalem, which Israel has claimed as its own capital since the state was founded. (Israel annexed the eastern parts of the city after winning control of them in the 1967 war. The United States has maintained its embassy to Israel in Tel Aviv, however, pending a resolution of Jerusalem's status.) Jerusalem was perhaps the most intractable issue discussed at Camp David.

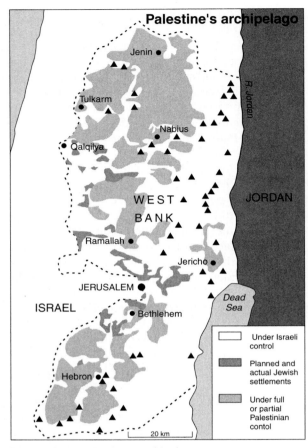

FIGURE 20.5   Palestine's Archipelago
Source: The Economist, February 19, 2000.

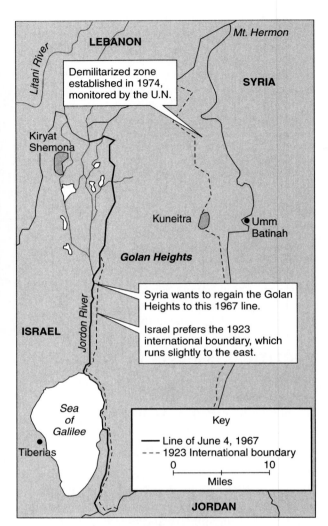

FIGURE 20.6   The Golan Heights in mid-2000

Palestinian Refugees—It is estimated that some 3.6 million Palestinian refugees are scattered across the West Bank, Gaza, Syria, Jordan and Lebanon, consisting primarily of people who took flight during the wars of 1948 and 1967 and their descendants. Many of them live in refugee camps under appalling conditions. The Palestinian authorities have long insisted that Israel allow the refugees to return to the homes they once had inside Israel, but in most instances those homes no longer exist. The Israelis have persistently refused to take formal responsibility for the refugees, arguing that they fled because war and other conflicts were imposed on Israel by hostile Arab countries. Though no resolution of the issue occurred at Camp David, Israel and the United States were reportedly prepared to provide financial compensation to displaced Palestinians in lieu of allowing them to move to Israel.

In addition to these issues at the heart of its relations with the Palestinians, Israel faced two additional unresolved security issues with its neighbors in the aftermath of Camp David:

The Golan Heights—In the months that preceded the Camp David summit, Prime Minister Barak expressed his willingness to return all but a small portion of the Golan Heights to Syria in exchange for security guarantees and the establishment of diplomatic relations between the two countries. Whereas Syria demanded the restoration of the entire area in its pre-1967 borders, giving it access to the Sea of Galilee, (an inland lake that forms an important water supply), the Barak government insisted on drawing the boundary in such a way that all of the shore line (and the lake itself) would remain in Israel (see figure 20.6.) For security reasons, Israel also wanted to maintain its electronic eavesdropping station on Mt. Hermon atop the Heights. Efforts to resolve the dispute foundered despite President Clinton's personal intervention with then-President Hafez Assad. Assad's death shortly before the Camp David talks awakened hopes for an eventual settlement.

Lebanon—Israel's troop pullout in the spring of 2000 from Lebanese territory it had occupied since 1982 may have created a security vacuum on its northern border. By mid-2000 it was not yet clear how stable the vacated areas would be, given the presence of anti-Israeli militias in the region. Israel wished to have the Lebanese government control the area it had vacated, but the Lebanese did not want to police the area on Israel's behalf.

Israelis are badly divided on these issues, and it was not clear after the Camp David summit whether Barak would be able to rally a stable government behind his policies.[20] The following account provides an indication of the problems he faced.

THE DOMESTIC POLITICS OF THE PEACE PROCESS

In an effort to unite as many parties as possible behind his peace initiatives, Ehud Barak assembled a broad-based coalition government on taking office in 1999. Consisting of twenty-three ministers and eight deputy ministers, the six-party government included twelve ministers from Barak's Labor-led One Israel; three from Labor's leftist partner, Meretz; two from the Center Party; four from Shas, the orthodox religious party backed mostly by Jews from the Middle East and North Africa; and one each from the orthodox National Religious Party and the conservative Russian immigrant party, Israel Ba'Aliyah. This volatile mixture of leftists, centrists, and conservatives together represented seventy of the Knesset's 120 deputies, a slim majority.

Squabbling among the coalition partners threatened to break up the government within less than a year after it came to office following the elections of May 1999. In March 2000, the cabinet agreed to proceed with a series of land transfers to the Palestinians, but its members were by no means unanimous. The deal was approved by a vote of sixteen to six. While ministers from Barak's One Israel Party, the Center Party, and the doveish Meretz voted for the transfer, cabinet members from Shas, the National Religious Party, and Israel Ba-Aliyah voted against it. (Barak himself did not vote.) Simultane-

ously, as President Clinton met with Syria's leader in hopes of breaking the logjam over the Golan Heights, Barak's government almost came apart over other issues, such as government support for religious education. The orthodox rabbi who headed Shas, which wants state funding for its schools, got into a war of words with leaders of the secular Meretz Party, which opposes such funding. Both parties threatened to quit the government but Barak persuaded them to stay on. Later, Barak was forced to make a choice between his two allies. Reasoning that Meretz would automatically support him on the peace process while Shas would not, Barak accepted the resignation of the Meretz ministers, keeping Shas in his cabinet a little longer. But Meretz decided to stick with him and Shas left the cabinet shortly before Camp David, complaining that Barak was not keeping his ministers informed of his negotiations with the Palestinians.

The prime minister was not so fortunate a few months later. In June, as Barak prepared for another round of negotiations with the Palestinians, the three conservative parties in his cabinet deserted him, voting in the Knesset to dissolve the government and call new elections. All three parties—Shas, the National Religious Party, and Israel Ba'Aliyah—had formerly participated in Prime Minister Netanyahu's government, and they voted with Netanyahu's Likud Party this time in calling for early elections. Things got even worse a month later. On the eve of his departure for the Camp David meetings, the same three parties pulled their ministers out of Barak's cabinet, paving the way for a vote of confidence that threatened to destroy his government. Barak had survived numerous confidence votes before, usually with a comfortable majority. Though he survived the vote taken the next day, July 10, the results were too close for comfort. Sixty-one Knesset votes are necessary to topple a government and force new elections. Fifty-four deputies voted against Barak, two more than the vote in his favor but not enough to unseat him. (Seven deputies abstained, and seven were absent.) Immediately after surviving the vote, Barak departed for Camp David.

When the summit was over, Barak survived two more no-confidence measures when the opposition—spurred on by Likud's combative leader, **Ariel Sharon**—failed to muster the requisite sixty-one votes. But in a subsequent vote held in early August, sixty-one deputies voted for snap elections for prime minister and the Knesset. The legislature thereupon adjourned for three months before voting on the snap election measure in two more readings, as required by law. Although Barak enjoyed favorable public opinion ratings and promised to submit any peace agreement to the people in a referendum, he entered the autumn of 2000 facing bleak uncertainty about his ability to carry on as prime minister at a critical juncture in the Middle East peace process. In Israel as in many countries, foreign policy is often a prisoner of domestic politics.

Religion and the State

The vast majority of Jewish Israelis support the idea that their state should be Jewish, but there has never been any consensus on what that means. For Orthodox Jews, a Jewish state must abide by Jewish law, so that public transportation on the sabbath would be unacceptable. Secular Israeli Jews regard their Jewish identity as national rather than religious in nature. While many respect Jewish law, few wish to be governed by it. No formal membership in the various camps exist, but perhaps one out of every five or six Israelis is Orthodox. A similar number might be referred to as "traditional" in that they respect Jewish traditions and follow some practices (such as eating only kosher foods) without observing all the dictates of Jewish law. Secular Jews probably are therefore the majority, though even among them there is a wide variation in attitudes toward religion.

The conflict between religious and secular Jews has always been latent in Israeli politics, but it has become more critical in the past few years. Many Israelis regard the division between secular and religious Jews as more troubling than the conflict between Arabs and Israelis. There are several reasons for the recent increase in tensions. For one thing, the religious parties have been growing in political influence. As we have noted, this influence has been particularly great when the Labor and Likud have had roughly even electoral support. For another, the ultra-orthodox part of the Israeli population has rapidly grown. Many ultra-Orthodox Jews have never fully accepted Zionism, leading secular Israelis to regard them with some misgivings. Most ultra-Orthodox men receive exemptions from mandatory army service even as separate ultra-Orthodox schools receive heavy government funding, increasing secular resentment. Because the Israeli state does not recognize any non-Orthodox form of Judaism, Israel allows only religious weddings. As a result, some Jewish Israelis complain that they cannot avoid Orthodox Jewish rabbis even if they wish to do so.

A final reason for the increase in tensions is connected with differences over the peace process. There are many secular hawks in Israel; there are also some religious doves. But after the Israeli capture of Arab parts of Jerusalem and the West Bank in 1967, a very influential movement of religious Zionism arose, dedicated to settling Jews in these new areas. In recent years, many of those most opposed to compromise with the Palestinians have been from this camp. Some extremist members of the group have launched terrorist attacks against Arab targets, claiming to be defending themselves against Arab terrorism. Israelis more inclined to compromise began to regard the religious nationalists as threatening Israeli security by drawing it into needless conflict. When a member of the nationalist religious camp assassinated Rabin in 1995, religious-secular tensions became especially acute.

In the 1999 elections, tensions became sufficiently severe that two Israeli political parties—Meretz and Shinui—ran very effective campaigns largely by appealing to secular resentments against the religious population. The Israeli Labor Party also made use of such themes, though its leadership did not want to alienate all religious voters and therefore moderated its tone somewhat. The share of votes going to religious parties also increased.

Tension between secular and religious Jews has now risen to the point that some Israelis wish to adopt a constitution in order to lay down definitive rules on the relationship between religion and politics. Many religious Jews oppose such a move, seeing it as a way to restrict religion and further increase the role for secular over religious law.

Economic Liberalization

Israel was founded as a socialist state, but it has been moving away from socialism since the 1970s. Economic liberalization has had many aspects: state-owned companies have been sold; the Histadrut labor union has sold off many of its holdings; government subsidies of some goods have been lifted; and restrictions on importing and foreign-currency holdings have been greatly reduced. The debate over this major shift in economic policy has not broken down on the left-right lines that have occurred in other countries. The right-leaning Likud Party began to shift Israel's economic orientation in the late 1970s. In 1985, a National Unity government approved further liberalization. While both Labor and Likud backed the plan in 1985, there was significant debate inside the parties. The Likud Party tends to appeal to poorer Israelis, some of whom felt the government was abandoning them. The Labor Party has strong ties to the Histadrut labor union, which has been very suspicious of liberalization.

In the 1990s, Israel began to emerge as a leading country in the export of high-technology goods and services. The associated economic boom supported those who argued that liberalization and openness were in Israel's long-term interest. When Binyamin Netanyahu was elected in 1996, he pledged further liberalization and privatization, but some leading members of his cabinet argued that the country's poor and working classes needed more government assistance and protection than liberalization would allow. When Labor returned to power in 1999, it again pledged similar policies. Yet important members of the new government retained a strong interest in the welfare of the poor; others were linked to the Histadrut and saw liberalization as a threat to workers.

Many issues in Israeli politics are characterized by an extreme ideological division. But in recent years the debate between economic liberalism and socialism has been characterized by less acrimony and extremism than in the past, largely because the largest parties themselves are divided internally on how to handle the issue. Instead of a debate between the left and right, or between doves and hawks, the argument over liberalization has taken place among political allies.

HYPOTHESIS-TESTING EXERCISE: Security and Democracy in Israel

Israelis often point with pride to their democratic system as the only one that functions in the entire Middle East. Historically, democracy is most common in political systems that are secure and at peace. Governments under severe threat often restrict freedoms. International threats often lead governments to emphasize the need for unity over democracy. Domestic threats lead governments to regard dissent as treason. Even in the United States, the oldest continuous democracy in the world,

wartime and security concerns have at times diminished democratic freedoms. These realities make Israeli democracy especially unusual, since the country has fought several wars and never escaped security concerns. Our hypothesis is that Israeli democracy will function best when security concerns are least prominent.

HYPOTHESIS
Israeli political structures are most democratic when external and internal security concerns are less severe.

VARIABLES
The **dependent variable**—that which we seek to explain—is *the democratic nature of Israeli political structures.* We seek to explain this by reference to the **independent variable,** *security concerns.*

EXPECTATIONS
If our hypothesis is correct, we would expect the evidence to show that (1) Israeli institutions become less democratic at times of major war or threat, and (2) Israeli institutions operate less democratically for those who question the fundamental nature of the state.

EVIDENCE
The first expectation does find some support from the evidence. Limitations on Israeli democracy were greater in its first two decades when the security risk was more acute. Arab citizens of Israel lived under martial law and military censorship was maintained over the press. Broadcasting was kept under fairly tight control. In the past decade, restrictions on democratic rights and freedoms have become far less noticeable. Arab citizens now complain of discrimination, but few formal restrictions remain on their political or other activities. The press is now very free and has found ways of evading most military restrictions. The Israeli triumph in 1967 and the peace treaty with Egypt, which together removed the threat of the immediate demise of the Jewish state, have led to a far broader range of political debate in Israel. Indeed, Israel now meets the most demanding requirements for electoral democracy: that the vote be open to all and that elections be free and meaningful. Not until 1977 was the ruling Labor Party thrown out of power; since that time, electoral competition has been free and fierce.

The second expectation also finds some support. The Arab population of the West Bank and Gaza, who are not Israeli citizens, are often seen as hostile to the Jewish state, and Israel grants them few of the customary rights that might be expected in a democracy. As non-citizens, they have no right to vote in Israeli elections (though some municipal elections have been allowed). Israeli courts generally shy away from questioning the actions of authorities. Indeed, the courts and Israeli law allow detention without charges. For many years, the courts also ignored evidence of widespread torture of Palestinians; they finally ordered an end to torture in 1999.[21] Israeli citizens who question the nature of the state are subject to real but less severe restrictions. One extremist Jewish political party was banned in the 1980s. Violent groups that do not threaten the existence of the state are sometimes treated surprisingly leniently. A Jewish terrorist group that attacked Arab targets in the 1980s was arrested, but most members received presidential pardons. When Rabin was assassinated in 1995, some Israelis felt that the time had come to move harshly against Jewish extremist groups, but little concrete action was taken.[22]

CONCLUSIONS

In fact, the security situation does account for some of the variation in Israeli democratic practices. Israeli behavior can be quite harsh when the nature of the state or the safety of its citizens might seem to be threatened. Until recently there was little public debate about such actions, and Israeli security institutions still escape most mechanisms by which authority is held accountable in democratic countries.

While the evidence is therefore largely *consistent* with the hypothesis, the fact that Israeli democracy has flourished in a difficult security setting is still surprising. In other words, the hypothesis explains much of the *variation* in Israeli democracy (that is, the specific ways in which it works). But its implication that democracy cannot exist at all, or only to a very limited extent, when the security environment is dangerous is contradicted by Israel's experience. Israel shows that democracy *can* exist—and even flourish—under such hostile conditions, albeit with some noteworthy limitations. This lesson is applicable to other countries that may face the challenge of building or maintaining democratic institutions under the perilous circumstances of external threats to their existence or of acute civil strife.

ISRAEL AND THE FOUR FACES OF DEMOCRACY

In sum, Israel has achieved considerable success in sustaining all four faces of democracy outlined in chapter 8 in spite of its difficult security environment, though its record is by no means entirely above criticism.

It has guaranteed Face I—popular sovereignty—through a parliamentary system of government, universal suffrage for all citizens (including Arabs), a proportional representation electoral system that allows numerous parties to be represented in the par-

liament, and an innovative variation on parliamentary government that allows the people to elect their prime minister directly. Israelis are more likely to complain about their political system today than they were a generation ago, but they have hardly abandoned it. Voter participation remains very high by international standards, as does interest in politics and participation in other ways (such as demonstrations).

Israel also grants the basic rights and liberties typically associated with Face II of democracy, including freedom of speech, freedom of religion, and freedom of political association. Not all of these freedoms have always applied to all Israeli citizens equally, however. Arabs and even Jewish citizens have had their freedom of speech or association curtailed at various times; press freedoms have been limited in certain circumstances; and citizens suspected rightly or wrongly of terrorist leanings have been subjected to rough treatment at the hands of Israeli security forces and the courts. The principle of religious equality is often infringed by the paramount influence of Orthodox parties. Nevertheless, Israel has provided basic rights and freedoms to most of its citizens most of the time, in spite of persisting tensions with its Arab citizens and neighbors and its identity as a Jewish state.

Israel has also been largely successful in realizing the values connected with Face III of democracy, though—like many democracies—it has serious shortcomings in this area. Significantly, Orthodox Jews, non-Orthodox religious Jews, non-religious Jews, and Jews from a number of different countries of origin have managed to live together and work out their differences peacefully in accordance with the rules of the game of representative democracy. While some have evinced intolerance of others, the level of tolerance and willingness to compromise has been sufficient to keep the Jewish majority from allowing its internal differences to erupt into civil war or otherwise destroy democracy. The relationship between Jewish and non-Jewish Israelis is similar: considerable discord has led to violence on only a very small number of occasions. Israel still exercises control over a large number of non-Israeli Palestinians in the West Bank and Gaza, however; tolerance for them varies considerably, and violence is more frequent. Israelis disagree over how far one should compromise with them. (Much the same can be said for Palestinian attitudes toward Jews.)

Israel has been quite successful in developing Face IV of democracy, namely, economic democracy. Many of the country's founders were democratic socialists who believed in social and economic equality as well as ballot-box democracy. The kibbutz movement and other aspects of Zionist socialism reflect these ideological commitments. Much has changed over the past several decades, however, and many of these socialist attitudes and institutions have not survived. A growing number of Israelis have come to favor a different concept of economic democracy, that of promoting the freedoms and opportunities of the marketplace. Since the 1980s there has been a widening consensus on the need to boost the private sector, a position many Israelis favor in the expectation that it will broaden economic opportunity and prosperity for greater numbers of people. At the same time, Israel has maintained a relatively generous welfare state in spite of the heavy burdens imposed by military expenditures. Though Israel has a socioeconomic pyramid like virtually all democracies, the gap between the richest and the poorest is not as great as in the United States or several other successful democracies.

Perhaps the most surprising thing about Israeli democracy is how normal it remains. Significant limits to Israeli democracy exist, but given the country's identity as a Jewish state and the very difficult security situation, it is remarkable that democracy exists at all.

KEY TERMS AND NAMES
(Underlined in the text)

Ehud Barak
West Bank
Golan Heights
Zionism
Balfour Declaration
Gaza Strip
Law of the Return
Basic Laws
David Ben-Gurion
Six Day War (1967)
Palestine Liberation Organization (PLO)
Yasser Arafat
Palestinian Authority
Labor
Likud

Menachem Begin
Oslo Accords
Yitzhak Rabin
Binyamin Netanyahu
Knesset
Prime minister
Israel Defense Forces (IDF)
Histadrut
Ariel Sharon

FOR DISCUSSION: WHAT WOULD YOU DO?

1. If you were an Israeli citizen, to which party (if any) would you belong? Why?
2. If you were Israeli, what would be your position on dealing with the Palestinians and the peace process with neighboring Arab states?
3. If you were Palestinian, what would be your position on dealing with Israel?

FOR FURTHER READING

In addition to the titles in the notes, consult the following:

Michael Barnett, ed., *Israel in Comparative Perspective* (New York: SUNY Press, 1996).

Martin Gilbert, *Israel: A History* (London: Doubleday, 1998). *Israel at 50* (Tel Aviv: Alfa Communications, 1997).

Fred Lazin, *Politics and Policy Implementation: Project Renewal in Israel* (Albany, N.Y.: SUNY Press, 1994).

Sam N. Lehman-Wilzig, *Wildfire: Grassroots Revolts in Israel in the Post-Socialist Era* (Albany, N.Y.: SUNY Press, 1992).

Amos Oz, *In the Land of Israel* (San Diego: Harcourt Brace Jovanovich, 1983).

Don Peretz and Gideon Doron, *Government and Politics of Israel* (Boulder, Colo.: Westview, 1997).

Bernard Reich and Gershon R. Kieval, *Israel: Land of Tradition and Conflict* (Boulder, Colo.: Westview, 1993).

Howard Sachar, *A History of Israel: From the Rise of Zionism to Our Time* (New York: Alfred A. Knopf, 1976).

———, *A History of Israel II: From the Aftermath of the Yom Kippur War* (Oxford: Oxford University Press, 1987).

Ehud Sprinzak and Larry Diamond, *Israeli Democracy Under Stress* (Boulder, Colo.: Lynne Rienner, 1993).

WEBSITES

Two daily English-language Israeli newspapers are available on line: the *Jerusalem Post* <www.jpost.com>

and *Ha'aretz* <www3. haaretz.co.il> offer high-quality coverage. The *Jerusalem Post* is originally in English; its editorial stance is center right, as are most of its columnists. *Ha'aretz* is Israel's most prestigious (but not most popular) Hebrew-language newspaper; it also publishes an edition in English. It leans toward the left. Many Israeli groups also have a web presence that they use for daily news; an example is the nationalist religious Arutz Sheva <www.a7.org> that has a news bulletin supportive of Jewish settlers in the West Bank.

Two official Israeli sites provide very full coverage of Israeli government and foreign policy. The government's general website, <www.index.gov.il>, gives a comprehensive list of all government websites. The Foreign Ministry offers a great deal of information on politics, foreign affairs, and the peace process at <www.israel-mfa.gov.il>. One other official site of interest belongs to the Israeli embassy in the United States at <www.israelemb.org>.

Israeli political groups are unevenly represented on the web. Two organizations from opposite sides of the spectrum are Peace Now (a nonpartisan group representing Israeli doves) at <www.peace-now.org> and Women in Green (an organization very opposed to the current peace process) at <www.womeningreen.org>.

The Tami Steinmatz Center at Tel Aviv University provides a monthly survey of Israeli public opinion on the peace process and related issues. Its site is found at <www.tau.ac.il/peace>. The Center for Palestine Research and Studies in Nablus on the West Bank carries out similar surveys of Palestinian public opinion. It can be found at <www.cprs-palestine.org>. The Israel Democracy Institute is a nonpartisan organization designed to study (and help strengthen) Israeli democracy. Its website is <www.idi.org.il>.

The major Israeli universities all have good websites. The address of Hebrew University in Jerusalem is <www.huji.ac.il>. Tel Aviv University's is <www.tau.ac.il>. Ben-Gurion University in Beersheva is found at <www.bgu.ac.il>. Haifa University is at <www.haifa.ac.il>.

NOTES

1. This figure refers to Israel's borders prior to 1967. In 1967, Israel annexed the eastern parts of Jerusalem and took control of the Sinai Peninsula, West Bank, Gaza Strip, and Golan Heights. Israel withdrew from the Sinai Peninsula as part of its peace agreement with Egypt, but retains some control over the other territories. The total area controlled by Israel at the start of 2000 is thus 10,290 square miles.

2. For writings on Zionism, see Walter Laqueur, *A History of Zionism* (London: Weidenfeld and Nicholson, 1972); Ben Halpern, *The Idea of a Jewish State* (Cambridge, Mass.: Harvard University Press, 1961); Arthur Herzberg, *The Zionist Idea* (New York: Meridian, 1960); and Zeev Sternhell, *The Founding Myths of Israel: Nationalism, Socialism, and the Making of the Jewish State* (Princeton, N.J.: Princeton University Press, 1998). *The Jewish State* by Theodore Herzl Zionism's founder has been translated into English (New York: Herzl Press, 1989).

For the conflict between Arabs and Jews prior to 1948, see J. C. Hurewitz, *The Struggle for Palestine* (New York: Schocken Books, 1976); Christopher Sykes, *Cross Roads to Israel* (London: New English Library, 1967).

For books on the entire history of the Arab-Israeli conflict, see Deborah Gerner, *One Land, Two Peoples: The Conflict over Palestine* (Boulder, Colo.: Westview Press, 1994); Charles D. Smith, *Palestine and the Arab-Israeli Conflict* (New York: St. Martin's Press 1996); and Ann M. Lesch and Dan Tschirgi, *Origins and Development of the Arab-Israeli Conflict* (Westport, Conn.: Greenwood, 1998). Important documents are collected in Walter Laqueur and Barry Rubin, eds., *The Israeli-Arab Reader* (New York: Penguin, 1984). Other documents can be found on the Israeli Foreign Ministry website at <www.israel.mfa.gov.il>.

3. For early Israeli history, see Nissim Rejwan, *Israel in Search of Identity: Reading the Formative Years* (Gainesville: University Press of Florida, 1999); Amos Elon, *The Israelis: Founders and Sons* (New York: Penguin, 1983); Simha Flapan, *The Birth of Israel: Myths and Realities* (New York: Pantheon Books, 1987); and Tom Segev, *1949, The First Israelis* (New York: Henry Holt, 1998).

4. For a biography of Ben-Gurion, see Michael Bar-Zohar, *Ben-Gurion: A Biography* (London: Weidenfeld and Nicholson, 1979). Also of interest is David Ben-Gurion, *Israel: A Personal History* (New York: Funk and Wagnalls, 1971).

5. See Nadav Safran, *From War to War: The Arab-Israeli Confrontation 1948–1967* (New York: Pegasus, 1969); Michael Brecher, *Decisions in Crisis: Israel, 1967 and 1973* (Berkeley: University of California Press, 1980); Randolph S. Churchill and Winston S. Churchill, *The Six Day War* (Boston: Houghton Mifflin, 1967); and Richard B. Parker, *The Politics of Miscalculation*

in the Middle East (Bloomington: Indiana University Press, 1993).

6. On the 1973 war, see Edgar O'Ballance, *No Victor, No Vanquished: The Yom Kippur War* (San Rafael, Calif.: Presidio, 1978); and Nadav Safran, *Israel: The Embattled Ally* (Cambridge, Mass.: Harvard University Press, 1978). Anwar al-Sadat's autobiography was published in English as *In Search of Identity* (New York: Harper and Row, 1978). Two excellent studies of the negotiations and agreements at Camp David are Shibley Telhami, *Power and Leadership in International Bargaining: The Path to the Camp David Accords* (New York: Columbia University Press, 1990); and William B. Quandt, *Camp David: Politics and Peacemaking* (Washington, D.C.: Brookings Institution, 1986). Kenneth W. Stein offers a study of Arab-Israeli diplomacy in the 1970s in *Heroic Diplomacy: Sadat, Kissinger, Carter, Begin, and the Quest for Arab-Israeli Peace* (New York: Routledge, 1999).

7. On Palestinian society and politics generally, see Samih K. Farsoun with Christina E. Zacharia, *Palestine and the Palestinians* (Boulder, Colo.: Westview, 1997); and Baruch Kimmerling and Joel S. Migdal, *Palestinians: The Making of a People* (Cambridge, Mass.: Harvard University Press, 1994). On Palestinian national identity, the best work is Rashid Khalidi, *Palestinian National Identity: The Construction of Modern National Consciousness* (New York: Columbia University Press, 1997). An excellent work on Palestinian history before the beginnings of the Arab-Israeli conflict is Beshara Doumani, *Rediscovering Palestine: Merchants and Peasants in Jabal Nablus, 1700–1900* (Berkeley: University of California Press, 1995). On the *intifada*, see Glenn E. Robinson, *Building a Palestinian State: The Incomplete Revolution* (Bloomington: Indiana University Press, 1997). On the PLO, the most comprehensive work is Yezid Sayigh, *Armed Struggle and the Search for a State: The Palestinian National Movement 1949–1993* (Oxford: Clarendon Press, 1997).

8. Menachem Begin wrote his autobiography before becoming prime minister; it was published as *The Revolt* (New York: Nash, 1981). Two biographies are Amos Perlmutter, *The Life and Times of Menachem Begin* (Garden City, Doubleday, 1979); and Sasson Sofer, *Begin: An Anatomy of Leadership* (Oxford: Basil Blackwell, 1988).

9. The war over Lebanon is covered in Itamar Rabinovich, *The War for Lebanon, 1970–1983* (Ithaca, N.Y.: Cornell University Press, 1984); Ze'ev Schiff and Ehud Ya'ari, *Israel's Lebanon War* (New York: Simon and Schuster, 1984); and Rashid Khalidi, *Under Siege: P.L.O. Decisionmaking during the 1982 War* (New York: Columbia University Press, 1986).

10. Yitzhak Rabin wrote his memoirs before his second term as prime minister. See *The Rabin Memoirs* (Boston: Little, Brown, 1979). For more recent analysis of Rabin's views, see Efraim Inbar, *Rabin and Israel's National Security* (Washington, D.C.: Woodrow Wilson Center, 1999).

11. Binyamin Netanyahu is the subject of a biography by Ben Caspit and Ilan Kfir, *Netanyahu: The Road to Power* (Secaucus, N.J.: Carol, 1998). Netanyahu himself has written extensively in English. His most recent book is *A Place Among Nations: Israel and the World* (New York: Warner, 1999).

12. There is no comprehensive biography of Barak yet available. A very brief official biography can be found on the prime minister's office website at <www.pmo.gov.il/english/pm/biography.html>.

13. The best overview of Israel's election system is contained in Asher Arian, *The Second Republic: Politics in Israel* (Chatham, U.K.: Chatham House, 1998); chapters 6–8.

14. Among the other proposals were (1) raising the threshold for representation to the Knesset far higher, (2) moving to some form of constituencies (districts), and (3) adopting the German system, which mixes single member district voting with proportional representation.

15. The impact of security concerns on Israeli democracy is analyzed by Menahem Hofnung in *Democracy, Law, and National Security in Israel* (Aldershot, U.K.: Dartmouth, 1996). Anthony Cordesman surveys the general security situation in *Perilous Prospects: The Peace Process and the Arab-Israeli Military Balance* (Boulder, Colo.: Westview, 1996). Ze'ev Schiff provides a history of the Israeli Defense Forces in *A History of the Israeli Army* (New York: Simon and Schuster, 1974).

16. For analysis of the Israeli legal and constitutional order, see Martin Edelman, *Courts, Politics, and Culture in Israel* (Charlottesville: University Press of Virginia, 1994); and Gary Jacobsohn, *Apple of Gold: Constitutionalism in Israel and the United States* (Princeton, N.J.: Princeton University Press, 1993).

17. General coverage of the party system is provided by Gershon Kieval, *Party Politics in Israel and the Occupied Territories* (Westport, Conn.: Greenwood, 1983); and by Nathan Yanai, "Israel," in *Political Parties of the Middle East and North Africa* ed. Frank Tachau (Westport, Conn.: Greenwood, 1994). The parties, election campaign, and election system in Israel are covered in Asher Arian and Michal Shamir, eds., *The Elections in Israel, 1996* (Albany, N.Y.: SUNY Press, 1999) and *The Elections in Israel, 1992* (Albany, N.Y.: SUNY Press, 1995). A similar series has been

edited by Daniel J. Elazar and Shmuel Sandler, *Israel at the Polls, 1996* (London: Frank Cass, 1998) and *Israel at the Polls, 1992* (Lanham, MD.: Rowman and Littlefield, 1995). Labor is studied in Myron J. Aronoff, *Power and Ritual in the Israeli Labor Party: A Study in Political Anthropology* (Armonk, N.Y.: M. E. Sharpe, 1993). Colin Schindler presents Likud in *Israel, Likud, and the Zionist Dream: Power, Politics, and Ideology from Begin to Netanyahu* (London: I. B. Tauris, 1995). The political identity of the Arab population is examined in Nadim Rouhana, *Palestinian Citizens in an Ethnic Jewish State: Identities in Conflict* (New Haven, Conn.: Yale University Press, 1997); and Ilana Kaufman, *Arab National Communism in a Jewish State* (Gainesville: University Press of Florida, 1997). The Israeli right wing is analyzed in Ehud Sprinzak, *The Ascendance of Israel's Radical Right* (New York: Oxford University Press, 1991).

18. In Israel, health care has generally been provided by the Histadrut and a few other insurers. The insurers received subsidies from the government. In 1995, the government began to regulate health care more directly, though it continued to work through the health insurers (with the Histadrut remaining the largest). While the system (especially before 1995) was criticized by many as excessively bureaucratic and biased in favor of the Labor party (which dominated the Histadrut), it was effective in covering almost all Israelis. Thus the health care crisis in the United States—in which tens of millions of citizens are uninsured—has no Israeli parallel. Israelis continue to complain about inefficiency, but not about lack of coverage.

19. General writings on labor and political economy issues in Israel include Michael Shalev, *Labor and the Political Economy in Israel* (Oxford: Oxford Univer-

sity Press, 1992); and Yakir Plessner, *The Political Economy of Israel: From Ideology to Stagnation* (Albany, N.Y.: SUNY Press, 1994).

20. Recent coverage of the Arab-Israeli peace process includes Laura Zittrain Eisenberg and Neil Caplan, *Negotiating Arab-Israeli Peace: Patterns, Problems, Possibilities* (Bloomington: Indiana University Press, 1998); and William Quandt, *Peace Process: American Diplomacy and the Arab-Israeli Conflict Since 1967* (Washington, D.C.: Brookings Institution, 1999). Israeli public opinion is analyzed in Asher Arian, *Security Threatened: Surveying Israeli Opinion on Peace and War* (New York: Cambridge University Press, 1995). Up-to-date polls are posted on the websites of the Tami Steinmatz Center of Tel Aviv University <www.tau.ac.il/peace> and the Center for Palestine Research and Studies <www.cprs-palestine.org>.

21. The Faculty of Law at Tel Aviv University publishes an annual volume, *Israel Yearbook on Human Rights,* that has extensive academic coverage of Israel. Two international human rights groups regularly report on Israel: Human Rights Watch <www.hrw.org>; and Amnesty International <www.amnesty.org>. The U.S. Congress requires the Department of State to report annually on the human rights situation in each country of the world. The reports may be found at <www.state.gov/www/global/human_rights/hrp_reports_mainhp.html>. One Palestinian group that covers both Israel and the Palestinian Authority is LAW/Al-Qanun <www.lawsociety.org>.

22. The assassin, Yigal Amir, was sentenced to life in prison. Israel has the death penalty in theory, but only once has it executed someone convicted of a crime—Adolf Eichmann, sentenced for his role in the Nazi Holocaust.

CHAPTER 21

RUSSIA

Population (1999): 146.4 million

Area: 6,592,745 square miles
(a little less than 1.8 times the area of the United States)

The map shows Russia and the other fourteen constituent republics of the former Soviet Union: Estonia, Latvia, Lithuania, Belarus (formerly Belorussia), Ukraine, Moldova (formerly Moldavia), Georgia, Armenia, Azerbaijan, Kazakhstan, Turkmenistan, Uzbekistan, Kyrgyzstan, and Tajikistan. All are now independent states, and all except Estonia, Latvia683, and Lithuania belong to the Commonwealth of Independent States.

Five scenes dramatically illustrate the extraordinary transformations that swept through Russia in the 1990s, capping a century of revolutionary change.

In scene one, **Boris Yeltsin,** the first person ever to be elected to Russia's presidency by popular mandate, stands atop a tank in the heart of Moscow, exhorting fellow citizens to resist a coup d'état aimed at toppling the government of the Soviet Union. It is August 19, 1991. The day before, a small group of Soviet officials, dismayed at the unraveling of the country's communist dictatorship at home and its hegemony over Central and Eastern Europe, placed Soviet leader **Mikhail Gorbachev** under house arrest and declared their takeover of the Soviet government. The conspirators blamed Gorbachev for leading the country to ruin by liberalizing its dictatorial political system, opening up its centrally planned economy to market forces, and ending its Cold War confrontation with the United States and its allies around the world. They were determined to halt the communist system's headlong disintegration and restore strong authoritarian rule to the Kremlin.

Gorbachev had been in power only since 1985. Although he was chief of the **Communist Party of the Soviet Union** (**CPSU),** he acknowledged severe problems in the ways the communists had governed the country for much of the twentieth century. While he did not wish to replace the Soviet system with a full-blown Western democracy, he believed that he could humanize communist rule and revive a stagnant economy through political and economic reforms. In place of an implacable dictatorship run by a handful of CPSU oligarchs, he called for "democratization" and greater "openness" in the party's dealings with the population. Without instituting a Western system of competing political parties, he permitted unprecedented elections to legislative and executive bodies. As events were to reveal, the most important of these votes was Yeltsin's election as president of Russia in June 1991, only two months before the coup attempt.

Russia was the most important of the fifteen "republics" constituting the **Union of Soviet Socialist Republics** (**USSR,** or **Soviet Union).** Sprawling across eleven time zones, it was the USSR's political heartland. Although Yeltsin was constitutionally subordinate to the Soviet state over which Gorbachev presided (he was president only of Russia while Gorbachev was president of the whole USSR). Yeltsin took charge of the situation as the coup plot unfolded. Emboldened by his defiance, tens of thousands of Russian citizens staged demonstrations against the coup, and key elements of the military high command refused to support it. Isolated, the plotters capitulated two days later and Gorbachev was released. The event proved to be a watershed in Russian history, undermining not only Gorbachev's power as president of the Soviet Union but the very existence of the Soviet Union itself.

The second scene marks a defining moment in the transfer of real political power from Gorbachev to Yeltsin. At a historic televised session of the Russian republic's legislature held only days after the coup plot fell apart, Gorbachev was in the process of acknowledging his mistakes when Yeltsin interrupted him with the disclosure that he had just signed a decree suspending all activities of the Soviet Communist Party within Russia. The stunning announcement effectively ended more than seventy years of the party's monopoly of power in Russia and the rest of the Soviet Union. Gorbachev quietly expressed his disapproval but his words no longer carried weight. Moments later, Yeltsin demonstratively approached Gorbachev at

Boris Yeltsin (holding papers), president of the Soviet Republic of Russia, reads a statement denouncing the coup against Soviet President Mikhail Gorbachev, August 1991.

the speaker's rostrum and handed him the minutes of a government meeting that had taken place the day the coup started. After wagging his finger contemptuously at Gorbachev, Yeltsin demanded, "Read it now!" The minutes revealed that key ministers of Gorbachev's government had supported the coup. Humiliated, Gorbachev meekly demanded their resignation. The next day he resigned as chief of the Communist Party and ordered the Soviet government to seize its assets.

The third scene took place three months later. In the interval the Soviet Union literally came apart. Only a few days after the coup was thwarted, Gorbachev declared that any Soviet republic wishing to declare its independence should be allowed to go free. One by one, the fifteen Soviet republics split off from the USSR and declared their independence. The first to go were the three states on the Baltic Sea that had been forcibly incorporated into the Soviet Union in World War II: Lithuania, Latvia, and Estonia. All three had already proclaimed their freedom in 1990. Though Gorbachev had sought to keep them in the Union, he was so weakened by the coup attempt that resistance to their demands was no longer possible. The Soviet government formally recognized the sovereignty of the Baltic states in September. Ukraine, the second-largest Soviet republic after Russia, also announced plans to secede, followed over the succeeding weeks by all the remaining republics.

On December 8, Russian President Yeltsin joined with the leaders of Ukraine and Belarus in forming a new grouping, the **Commonwealth of Independent States (CIS).** Two weeks later they were joined by eight more Soviet republics, an event that effectively sealed the fate of the Soviet Union. All eleven members of the new organization agreed to respect one another's sovereign independence while seeking ways to maintain economic cooperation. (The three Baltic states refused to join the CIS, and Georgia did not sign on until 1994.)[1]

On December 25, 1991, his state having cracked into its separate pieces, Gorbachev resigned as president of the Soviet Union, setting the stage for scene three: moments later, the Soviet flag was hauled down and the flag of independent Russia was hoisted in its place over the Kremlin, the historic seat of the nation's government. The USSR

was passing into history. It officially ceased to exist on December 31.

Scene four occurred in October 1993. After nearly two years as an independent country, Russia was in the grip of an acute political and economic crisis. Immediately after embarking upon independence, the Russian government under President Yeltsin launched a series of bold economic initiatives designed to transform the still largely state-run economy into a mixed economic system with considerably more private enterprise. Following the advice of liberal economists, the government removed price controls from consumer staples like milk and bread and accelerated the process of privatizing state-owned factories, retail outlets, restaurants, and other elements of the once centrally directed command economy.

While these and other measures produced rapid benefits for a few "new Russians" who understood the nature of the changes, most people saw their living standards deteriorate. Prices for a wide range of goods, long held in check by the stability-conscious Soviet regime, rose astronomically, far outpacing wages. Short of revenue, the Russian government lacked the means to pay millions of its employees. The privatization process raised fears of massive unemployment. Economic growth ground to a standstill. Hefty loans from the International Monetary Fund and other lenders were needed to keep the economy afloat. Organized crime reared its head as a Russian mafia expanded such illegal activities as gambling and extortion. And a small group of politically well-connected businessmen became instant billionaires, taking over the country's largest banks, newspapers, television stations, and other major assets.

Despite the dislocations caused by the economic transformation process, Yeltsin remained committed to it, buoyed by the expectation that it would eventually trigger sustained economic growth and consumer welfare. This commitment was not shared by the overwhelming majority of Russian legislators, however. Upon becoming independent, Russia inherited the bicameral parliament that had been elected in 1990, when the Soviet Union still existed. Both houses were elected at a time when the Communist Party of the Soviet Union was the only legally recognized party. Most of its members were avowed communists, openly disgruntled at the collapse of the Soviet system and hostile to the western-style political and economic changes Yeltsin's government was introducing.

For nearly two years, Yeltsin and the recalcitrant deputies sparred over Russia's political and economic direction. In an effort to discredit the legislature and set the stage for new elections, Yeltsin held a referendum in the spring of 1993 in which a majority of those who turned out to vote supported his call for early elections to a new parliament and expressed confidence in his economic policies. Bolstered by this support, he convened a special assembly to write a constitution for the new Russia and declared that the existing parliament was "illegitimate" because it had been elected under the Soviet Union's non-democratic electoral laws.

Over the summer the confrontation between the two warring sides intensified. And then in September, Yeltsin announced that he was dissolving the legislature and setting new elections for December. While admitting that he had no authority under the current constitution to take this action (the constitution, like the legislature, was inherited from the USSR), Yeltsin based his decision on the spring referendum, which he called the "supreme juridical power" in the land. Infuriated at this announcement, oppositionist legislators defied Yeltsin and named one of their own members as the new president of Russia. A group of diehards then barricaded themselves into the parliament building, known as the White House. Scarcely two years after the plot against Gorbachev, Russia was once again in the throes of an armed struggle for power.

The first shots were fired by opposition forces in early October. Armed with assault weapons, crowds of Communist Party sympathizers and rabid Russian nationalists stormed the headquarters of the state-run television station and attacked the Moscow mayor's office. The next day, Yeltsin ordered a military assault on the White House. The fourth scene in our newsreel of turning points in the 1990s is the Russian parliament building on fire, its top floors blackened by smoke following a heavy artillery barrage. Paratroopers and elite commando units moved in to arrest the barricaded legislators. By evening the standoff was over.

Two months later, Russian voters approved the new constitution that Yeltsin wanted. Modeled on the French constitution, it gives the Russian president a powerful arsenal of legal prerogatives while leaving the national legislature in a relatively weaker position. The people also elected a new parliament, but not the one that Yeltsin had hoped for. Most of the newly elected deputies were just as leery of the market-oriented reforms as the previous legislature was, and many were particularly opposed to Yeltsin and his newly acquired presidential powers. The Communist Party—legally reconstituted as the Communist Party of the Russian Federation—was the largest party, with others still struggling to get started.

A continuing tug-of-war between Yeltsin and the parliament characterized the remainder of the decade. Though Yeltsin managed to get reelected to a four-year term in 1996, beating the communist candidate in a runoff, his public approval ratings remained abysmal, hovering around 10 percent or less. The economy provided the main source of disaffection, as the long-awaited spurt in growth and production consistently failed to meet optimistic projections. By the end of the decade roughly 38 percent of the population lived below the official poverty line of $37 a month. Though private businesses increasingly sprouted up and a new middle class was emerging, the penury of the masses glaringly clashed with the accumulating riches of the new capitalist elite. Russia was forced to borrow tens of billions of dollars from the International Monetary Fund and other sources to meet its obligations, sums that became increasingly difficult to obtain as evidence of official theft became impossible to conceal.

Meanwhile, post-communist Russia was just as fractionated as the former Soviet Union in its last stages. Constituted as a federal system with 89 constituent units, the Russian Federation engaged in a constant struggle to make sure that the authority of the central government in Moscow was universally accepted. Its most violent challenge was in Chechnya, a largely Muslim region where a separatist movement launched a guerilla war for independence. Yeltsin sent Russian troops to the breakaway province in December 1994, resulting in a bloody confrontation that ended with a truce in 1996. The conflict flared up again in 1999, with troops once again dispatched to the troubled region.

Yeltsin himself got through the decade in a state of near-permanent illness. A serious heart problem, respiratory illnesses, and other infirmities required him to spend long weeks and months in sanatoria or at home, away from the center of political life in the Kremlin. In 1996 he underwent quintuple coronary bypass surgery. Rumors of alcoholism abounded, and his occasionally slurred speech and unsteady bearing gave the world the impression of a leader on the brink of complete incapacitation. In addition to his persisting health problems, Yeltsin ended the decade with a cloud of suspicion hanging over his head following allegations that he and members of his family had pocketed illegal benefits from a company doing business with the Russian government.

These personal problems culminated in scene five: on December 31, 1999, as the world prepared to greet the new century, Boris Yeltsin went on television and, in a surprise announcement, informed the Russian people of his immediate resignation from the presidency. "Russia must enter the new millennium with new politicians, new faces," he said, asserting that he had already completed his main task, which was to ensure that "Russia will never return to the past." Wiping away tears, the departing president also asked the Russian people for forgiveness. Acknowledging that "many of the dreams we shared did not come true," Yeltsin confessed to being naive in thinking, like many fellow citizens, "that at one stroke, in one spurt, we could leap from the gray, stagnant, totalitarian past into the light, rich, civilized future." Admitting that the challenge had proved "tormentingly difficult," Yeltsin concluded, "I did all I could."

With Yeltsin's unexpected departure only six months before the completion of his term, the presidency automatically passed to the prime minister, **Vladimir Putin.** Following the terms of the 1993 constitution, new presidential elections were held within three months of the transfer of power. On March 26, 2000, Putin bested ten rival candidates, winning the election with an absolute majority of 52.8 percent of the vote.

POLITICAL CONFLICT IN RUSSIA

The critical events of the twentieth century's last decade were not only the culminating developments of a century of revolution in Russia; they also encapsulated some of the central themes of several

hundred years of Russian history. The quest for a viable and legitimate system of government; the tortured relationship between state and society, exacerbated by excessive state authority and the "tormenting difficulty" of including the people in a democracy; the pursuit of prosperity and an economic system that permits the population to share in the country's wealth fairly and consistently; the relationship between Russia and the outside world, centered above all in the way Russians define themselves vis-à-vis the Western democracies—these and other persistent aspects of the Russian political tradition have much in common with the five sources of political conflict outlined in chapter 2:

- *Power:* How has Russia been governed? How powerful have the ruling authorities been? Have the people ever enjoyed any power? Who has power today?
- *Resources:* How successfully has Russia developed its economy? How have national resources—such as the land, oil, money, and other assets—been distributed? How is Russia managing the process of moving from a centrally planned to a market-based economy?
- *Social identity:* What have been the roles of class, ethnic, and religious identity in Russian politics? How have Russians defined themselves vis-à-vis the outside world?
- *Ideas:* What have such terms as "communism," "democracy," and "nationalism" meant in the Russian context?
- *Values:* How have Russians felt about such values as individualism and collectivism? Equality and liberty? Do Russians prefer authoritarian governments to democracy?

In a country whose current turmoil has deep roots in its past, it is vitally important to preface our examination of Russian politics today with an overview of its historical evolution.

RUSSIA'S HISTORICAL TRADITIONS: WHY NO DEMOCRACY?

Tsarism

The difficulties Russia has experienced since the 1990s in its attempts to establish democratic governance ultimately reflect the fact that, throughout its history, Russia was never able to sustain real democratic institutions and practices. Similarly, the difficulties currently encountered in building a successful market economy derive from the fact that, throughout its long history, private enterprise was either not allowed at all or, when allowed, was subjected to thorough regulation and direction by the state. The problems of the present are mired in the past. Under the tsars (or czars) and their predecessors, Russia deviated substantially from the historical paths to democracy taken by Britain and France. Subsequently, under the communists, national wealth improved but most of the other conditions remained far short of fulfillment. We'll look at the pre-communist heritage first, testing Russia's experience against the ten conditions for democracy hypothesized in chapter 10.[2]

HYPOTHESIS-TESTING EXERCISE: Tsarist Russia and the Conditions for Democracy

VARIABLES

Our **dependent variable** is *democracy*; our **independent variables** are the *ten conditions* listed in chapter 10.

EXPECTATIONS

We would expect the presence of each independent variable to enhance the prospects for democracy in Russia, and the absence of these variables to diminish democracy's prospects.

EVIDENCE

To begin with, Russia's *state institutions* were entirely or mostly undemocratic from their earliest appearance to the final decade of the twentieth century.

Prior to the establishment of a distinctly Russian government under a single political authority, the territories constituting the geographic heartland of Russia—the ancient forests surrounding Moscow—were increasingly populated by eastern Slavic tribes from the seventh to the ninth centuries. The political organization of these communities was fragmentary, but the formation of more solid centers of power began in earnest following the invasion of Norman warriors who stormed into continental Europe from Scandinavia in the ninth century. One of the Norman princes, Rurik, established himself in Novgorod ("New Town") around 860, giving rise to a tradition that regards him as the founder of the Russian state. In fact he never presided over a central Russian

government worthy of the name, but his successors created a more enduring basis of power farther south, in Kiev, the capital of modern Ukraine. The period known as "Kievan Rus" extended from around 882, when a Norman prince took over the town in the name of Rurik's son, to sometime in the twelfth century.

A seminal event in Russian history occurred when Grand Prince Vladimir and much of the population were converted to Christianity around 988. Because Kiev occupied a strategic position in the Norman trade routes running from northern Russia to Byzantium, Russia embraced the Byzantine variant of Christianity, whose Greek-influenced rituals and doctrines differed from the Western church centered in Rome. In 1054, what became known as the Eastern Orthodox church split off from Roman Catholicism, its adherents refusing to recognize the pope as Christianity's supreme authority. The embrace of Orthodoxy was to have fateful political and cultural repercussions: it effectively cut Russia off from developments in Western Europe, not only in the religious sphere but in the cultural and political realms as well. An attendant event was the adoption of the Cyrillic as opposed to the Roman alphabet at about the same time. Based on Greek letters, the new alphabet was initially designed by a monk, St. Cyril, who joined with his brother Methodius in converting the Slavs of Russia and neighboring areas to Christianity.

Russia during the Kievan period was no more centralized than it had been prior to the Norse invasions. A multiplicity of Norman-Slavic princes held sway over the territories that became collectively known as *Rus*; the Grand Prince of Kiev was only the most prestigious of many rulers. Most of these leaders based their authority on brute force, but democratic influences were also in evidence. Kiev, Novgorod, and other cities established local assemblies, called *veche*, that allowed heads of households to meet on a periodic basis and make effective decisions, a form of direct democracy. These assemblies never governed Russia as a whole, however, and as time went on they fell victim to the superior force of authoritarian rulers.

By the twelfth century, Kiev began to decline as a center of political predominance, ceding its place to more aggressive princes located in the north of Russia. The final deathblow came in 1236–37, when the first in a series of invasions by Mongols from Asia put an end to the suzerainty of the Russian princes over their scattered populations. Establishing a regime known as the Golden Horde, the Mongols required the Russian authorities to pay tribute. In 1241 they pillaged Kiev. But they also lent their support to Russian princes willing to acknowledge their preeminence.

By carefully cultivating the Golden Horde's favor, along with that of the Orthodox church, descendents of

Rurik gradually consolidated their hold over northern Russia starting around 1300. The ensuing century marked the rise of Moscow as the dominant center of political and military power in the region, a status it solidified following the collapse of Mongol hegemony in the fifteenth century. A burst of territorial expansion accompanied Moscow's ascendancy. The Muscovite leaders captured Novgorod and abolished its democratic assembly, eventually razing the city to the ground and massacring its population. Other historic towns and ever greater expanses of land progressively came under their sway. By 1600 Russia—or "Muscovy"—was as large as the rest of Europe; sixty years later, having absorbed Ukraine, it was the largest country in the world.

Along with relentless aggrandizement came imperial nomenclature. Grand Prince Ivan III (1462–1505) began referring to himself as "tsar," a term derived from Caesar and formerly used by the Byzantine emperors as well as by the leaders of the Golden Horde. His grandson, Ivan IV, formalized the title by proclaiming himself "Tsar of All Russia" in 1547. He later assumed the appellation of Lord of All the Orthodox, a position that reflected the symbiotic connection between the Eastern Orthodox hierarchy and the Muscovite crown and that confirmed the tsars' claims to legitimacy on the basis of divine right. Known as Ivan the Terrible, Russia's first titled tsar was a madman whose ferocity was legendary throughout Europe. He murdered his son in a fit of rage and boasted that his powers as "autocrat" of Russia—another of his official titles—far surpassed the authority of European monarchs. Two assemblies that were convened under his rule met briefly and were dissolved; under no circumstances was Ivan willing to countenance the development of an English-style parliament.

Following a violent period known as "the Time of Troubles" that ensued when Ivan IV's line died out, a special assembly was convened to elect a new tsar. Consisting mainly of Orthodox prelates and nobles, it also included ordinary townsfolk and peasants. In 1613 this assembly elected Michael Romanov, the sixteen-year-old son of the patriarch of the Orthodox church, as the new tsar. The **Romanovs** were destined to rule Russia for more than three hundred years, up to the abdication of Tsar Nicholas II in 1917 only months before the communist revolution. Never again would ordinary Russians be invited to elect their leader until Boris Yeltsin's election in 1991.

The autocratic nature of tsarist power expanded even more pronouncedly under Peter I, better known as **Peter the Great.** Born in 1672, he ascended the throne in 1685. A commanding figure at seven feet tall, Peter saw to it that even the most distinguished nobles were compelled to address him as "your majesty's lowliest slave." Russia's commoners, comprising 99.7 percent of the population, remained in a state of abject servitude, completely deprived of rights and subjected to onerous new taxes. Compulsory military service and slave labor were integral elements of Petrine Russia.

Peter's most lasting contribution was his determination to open up the country to European influences. Having lived in Holland in his youth, he clearly recognized Russia's economic inferiority to the West and was resolved to overcome it. He therefore extended an open hand to scientists and technicians from Germany and other countries and opened a "window on the West" by building the city of St. Petersburg on the Gulf of Finland. These efforts to introduce Western methods, however, stopped well short of political and social adaptations. Like his predecessors, Peter had no tolerance of parliamentary bodies or civil liberties; his borrowings were mainly technological in nature, with a pronounced military bent. Peter had every intention of building on Russia's past territorial acquisitions and shaping its army and navy into a force to be reckoned with. "We need Europe for a few decades," he said, "and then we must turn our back on it."[3]

Peter's approach created an ambivalence in Russian attitudes toward the West that endured throughout the entire tsarist epoch. That ambivalence subsequently stamped the communist regime and, at least to some degree, persists to this very day. From Peter's time onward, the defining hallmark of Russian nationalism became its double-edged orientation to Western Europe (and, later, to the United States). On the one hand, Russian leaders and intellectuals have both recognized and resented their country's economic backwardness, as well as its social and political inflexibility, vis-à-vis the West. But until quite recently they resisted copying the political freedoms and social structures that underlay Western economic dynamism, preferring instead to pursue their own models (whether tsarist or communist) while demonstratively asserting their country's spiritual or moral superiority to "decadent" Western norms and practices. The "Slavophile" strain in Russian culture, which crystallized as a body of thought in the nineteenth century, explicitly articulated these notions of spiritual supremacy.

As Liah Greenfeld has argued, however, Slavophilism and "Westernism" were simply two sides of the same coin: both were rooted in Russian resentment at the West's achievements and in a gnawing sense of humiliation. Neither concept of nationalism favored the development of democracy.[4]

Several of Peter's successors, keenly sensitive to Western perceptions of Russian backwardness, initiated reforms aimed at loosening up some of the more extreme aspects of the country's political and social rigidity. None, however, permitted real democratization.

Empress Catherine II (**Catherine the Great),** who ruled from 1762 to 1796, was a German princess fascinated with Voltaire and other luminaries of the Western philosophical Enlightenment. But though she initiated some administrative reforms, she had no intention of sharing power with a parliament modeled on Britain's constitutional monarchy. Like her predecessors, she regarded the vast majority of the populace as mere subjects, unworthy of guaranteed rights.[5]

Her great-grandson Alexander II took the giant step of abolishing serfdom in 1861, freeing tens of millions of peasants from bonded servitude to their landlords. He also allowed the creation of local organs of self-government in villages and cities. Neither of these great reforms extended real civil liberties or electoral power to the people, however. Demands for more revolutionary change proliferated, and in 1881 Alexander II was assassinated by a terrorist.

The growth of revolutionary unrest and terrorism that shook Russia in the second half of the nineteenth century, far from leading to democracy, only provoked the next tsar, Alexander III, to tighten the regime's grip on power more assertively. As historian Richard Pipes has observed, over the course of the 1880s and 1890s a series of new laws on crimes against the state gave Russia the institutional foundations of a modern police state. With wide discretionary powers to surveil and arrest people on the merest suspicion of anti-regime sentiments, and with no judicial system setting limits to its practices, the secret police became the principal effective authority in Russia when it came to day-to-day governance. Local government bodies were restricted in their activities and thousands of people were exiled to Siberia.[6] In the following century, the communists would take these repressive practices to ferocious extremes.

As revolutionary violence traumatized the regime into imposing preventive countermeasures, the reprisals only incited more popular indignation. In January 1905, military units brutally dispersed a crowd of peaceful petitioners in front of the tsar's palace, an event that set off revolutionary and anarchistic outbursts throughout the country. Faced with the most severe crisis in the history of tsardom, Tsar Nicholas II agreed to the creation of a parliamentary body, the Duma. The first Duma was elected in 1906 under fairly democratic conditions of universal male suffrage. But the tsar issued Fundamental Laws severely circumscribing the Duma's powers and reasserting his own status as "Autocrat of All the Russias." He also instituted a conservative upper chamber of notables to counterbalance the Duma's populist inclinations. The tsar's basic aversion to parliamentarism soon became evident when he dissolved the first Duma in less than three months. The next one did not last much longer. Then in 1907 he unilaterally changed the electoral laws, violating his own constitution. The change resulted in more docile Dumas and no advance toward real democracy; the tsar continued to rely on the old aristocratic elite to govern Russia and opposed a genuine constitutional monarchy.[7] Then in 1917, in the midst of World War I and mounting domestic unrest, Nicholas was forced to abdicate, bringing to an end more than four hundred years of tsarist autocracy.

Reinforcing the tsars' success in maintaining authoritarian state institutions over the centuries was widespread indifference to democracy on the part of Russia's *elites.* Whereas England's parliamentary traditions had originated in the landed nobility, as aristocrats sought property rights for their estates as well as a say in the government's tax policies, most Russian nobles did not own large estates. Peter the Great took especially forceful measures to keep the nobility subservient, forbidding them to own private property and compelling them to change their residences so as not to develop an attachment to landholdings that might serve as a base of local power, as it had in England. He also compelled them to render lifelong service to the state and diluted

TABLE 21.1

Selected Pre-Communist Russian Rulers			
Ninth century	Norman invasions	1682–1725	Peter I (the Great)
Late ninth century	Rurik (Novgorod)	1741–1762	Elizabeth I
Late ninth to twelfth centuries	Kievan Rus	1762–1796	Catherine II (the Great)
1236–late fifteenth century	Mongol Golden Horde	1796–1801	Paul I
1294–1263	Alexander Nevsky (Novgorod)	1801–1825	Alexander I
1328–1341	Ivan I (Moscow)	1825–1855	Nicholas I
1462–1505	Ivan III	1855–1881	Alexander II
1505–1533	Vasilii (Basil) III	1881–1894	Alexander III
1533–1584	Ivan IV (the Terrible)	1894–1917	Nicholas II
1598–1613	Time of Troubles	Mar.–Nov. 1917	Provisional Government
1613–1645	Michael Romanov	Nov. 1917	Communist takeover

their ranks by ennobling commoners and foreigners. When Catherine II allowed the nobility to own land and released them from their service obligations, they gladly accepted these concessions and raised no serious demands for a parliamentary share of power, taking little interest in the consultative assemblies she established. Most Russian nobles, moreover, were far from being rich; the vast majority were destitute and more concerned with eking out a living than with politics.

The first organized challenge to tsarist authority from noble ranks in the nineteenth century was a coup attempt staged in December 1825 by a small group of officers and fellow conspirators who were inspired by the French Revolution to seek a more liberal regime. The "Decembrist" uprising was quickly quashed and its initiators arrested, with scarcely a whimper of protest from the noble class.[8] Later, in the 1860s and 1870s, radical university students, largely from noble families, organized a far more serious threat to tsarism. Convinced that the political system was a disgrace and that Russia's peasant masses needed to be liberated from political and economic oppression, hundreds of young idealists fanned out into the countryside in the summer of 1874 in a concerted effort to stir up revolution. Animated by the slogan "go to the people," the so-called *populist movement* quickly fizzled, the victim of peasant apathy and the regime's harsh response.

Thereafter the populist movement split into two directions: one group embarked on terrorism, the other gravitated to the various socialist movements that proliferated as the century came to a close. Neither of them looked to Western democracy as a source of inspiration, and both groups were relatively small.[9] On the whole, the overwhelming majority of the Russian noble elite provided either firm support or docile acquiescence to the tsarist autocracy right up to the very end in 1917.

Russia's religious elites, consisting of the Orthodox church hierarchy, provided consistent support for tsarism, as did the military elites. Both were props of the tsarist ruling structure and ill-disposed to democracy.

The country's intellectual elites were more variegated. From the mid-eighteenth century onward a certain element of the Russian nobility possessed sufficient means to devote themselves to intellectual and cultural pursuits, a group that in the following century became known as the *intelligentsia*. Over the course of the nineteenth century, scientists, writers, patrons of the arts, and people with a passion for improving social conditions expanded the ranks of this social stratum. Some were genuinely interested in democracy and formed the basis of the Constitutional Democratic party, which emerged as the largest party in the first two Dumas. Others tended toward the populists or socialists, and

some actively supported tsarism. But a sizable portion of the Russian intelligentsia, perhaps the majority, remained politically inert, exhibiting a greater interest in literature and the arts than in politics.

A relatively low level of **national wealth** constituted another barrier to democracy in pre-communist Russia. Until the communist era, Russia was an agricultural country, with far lower levels of industrialization than in Britain, France, Germany, or the United States. Its agricultural system, moreover, was grossly inefficient: most landowners were either uninterested in commercial farming or unable to afford it, producing lttle in the way of a food surplus for sale. Russia was not significantly engaged in international trade, and even its domestic trade was subject to a panoply of government restrictions and disincentives. The mining of precious metals did not begin in earnest until the eighteenth century. It was not until the 1860s that a private banking system developed, hundreds of years behind the commercial nations of Europe. Relatively paltry amounts of money circulated among the population, far too little to stimulate economic growth.

A major cause of both the lethargy of Russia's economy and the authoritarianism of its political institutions was the lowly status of **private enterprise.** Until the reign of Catherine the Great in the eighteenth century, the tsars refused to allow the private ownership of land. The tsars themselves literally owned Russia, holding title to all its territory, natural resources, cities, and towns along with virtually all its manufacturing enterprises. As Pipes has emphasized, Russia was historically a **patrimonial state:** the princes and autocrats who ruled it, from Kievan Rus down to the late eighteenth century, made no distinction between public and private property, regarding Russia as their own personal estate. The people, from the most dignified nobles to the humblest peasants, were essentially slaves or, at best, tenants of the royal domains. In this respect Russia was vastly different from Western Europe, where private property was enshrined in the canons of ancient Roman law and respected by monarchs in legal theory and actual practice from the middle ages onward. It was largely to defend their property that European (and subsequently American) farmers and businesspeople demanded a say in how they were governed, advancing the cause of representative democracy and political rights through the assertion of their economic rights.

In 1785, Catherine II finally permitted members of the nobility to own property and abolished the state's centuries-old monopolistic control over domestic trade and industry. But more than 90 percent of the population, consisting mostly of peasants, did not acquire property rights until the nineteenth century. The tsars who followed her retained a "patrimonial mentality" that regarded the Russian state as their own exclusive preserve.

On the eve of the twentieth century, at a time when countries like Britain, the United States, France, and Germany were well advanced along the road to building powerful industrial economies with the help of private corporations, Russia continued to lag far behind in both the level of its industrial development and the scope of its private enterprise. When private industrial capitalism finally emerged in Russia, it did so under the guiding influence of the state. Count Sergei Witte, Russia's finance minister from 1892 to 1903, spearheaded this program, generously dipping into the state treasury to provide loans to Russian businesses and to purchase large amounts of what they produced, at the same time expanding the country's rail lines and other sinews of its economic infrastructure. Stimulated by these infusions of state investment and direction from above, the economy surged forward at a rate of 8 percent a year in the 1890s.[10] But a depression set in as the twentieth century began, and great segments of Russia's natural wealth and industrial production came under the control of foreign investors, mostly French, British, and German. Though Russia had become the fifth-largest industrial economy in the world by World War I, one-third of its industrial investment and half of its bank capital was in foreign hands, providing the communists and other revolutionaries with grounds for claiming that Russia's government and private capitalists had sold out the country to Western imperialists.

Tightly linked to the weakness of private enterprise in Russia was the accompanying social and political weakness of the *middle class.* As we have noted in previous chapters, a large and prosperous middle class, especially when it constitutes a "bourgeoisie" rooted in the private sector, has often been a standard-bearer of democratic values and popular demands for participation in the political process. The veritable absence of private property in Russia until late in the eighteenth century, and its narrow diffusion and weak development in subsequent phases of tsarist rule, provided slim grounds for the efflorescence of a Russian middle class that might have militated for democratic reform. The very concept of a bourgeoisie as an urban phenomenon (*bourg* meant "city") was largely absent from Russia through most of the tsarist epoch because the country's economy was predominantly agricultural and the bulk of its population was scattered across its immense rural expanse. Unlike pre-revolutionary France, there was no Russian Third Estate.

The closest Russia came to a middle class in the first half of the nineteenth century was the middle level of the nobility, comprising perhaps some 18,500 families. Unlike their contemporaries in Britain, France, and the United States, most of these people shunned political activity in the face of overweening tsarist opposition to democratic rights, turning instead to the less provocative pursuits of a cultural intelligentsia. Later, as private enterprise expanded at the turn of the twentieth century, Russia's entrepreneurial bourgeoisie remained small by Western standards, and only a portion of its members entered the political lists. Fewer than 6 percent of the deputies elected to the first Duma in 1906 were merchants or industrialists. With the fortunes of their businesses heavily dependent on state favors, a large number of Russia's businesspeople lent their support to tsarist authoritarianism rather than threatening it with demands for democracy.

In addition to lacking support from society's elites and middle class, democracy in Russia also failed to capture the allegiance of its *disadvantaged* masses. From the earliest inception of the Russian state to the ultimate demise of tsarism, the vast majority of the country's population consisted of impoverished peasants. Prior to the sixteenth century, most of them were tenants on the tsar's lands, and many were simply slaves. Between 1550 and 1650, virtually the entire peasant population became serfs under the dictates of an increasingly centralized Russian autocracy.

Russian serfdom was a form of servitude that differed in legal theory, and to some extent in practice, from feudalism as it was practiced in medieval Europe as well as from slavery as it was practiced in the United States. Unlike European feudalism, there were no legal precepts or customs obligating the Russian landlords to provide any forms of protection to their serfs. Moreover, serfdom took hold in Russia *after* the dissolution of the feudal order in most of Europe. Unlike American-style slavery, the landlords did not legally own the serfs, but they controlled them.

In actual practice, the serfs were not much better off than slaves. Although there were no statutes explicitly establishing or defining serfdom, it was understood that the serfs were legally bound to the land where they lived and were subject to the landlords' authority. Until the late eighteenth century, as we've seen, the tsars formally owned title to all the land; whenever they granted the use of land as farms and estates to favored nobles, they also handed over the serfs attached to it. Once the nobility acquired private property rights, the landowners retained their authority over the serfs. Like slaves, Russian serfs had no rights of any kind. Tsarist law forbade them from moving without specific permission. Runaways, if apprehended, were to be returned to their landlords. Despite the fact that they were not legally owned by their landlords, they were nevertheless bought and sold as chattel (though Russian landlords tended to refrain from breaking up their families). In effect, the Russian serfs—men, women, and children—were thoroughly subservient to the whims of the landholders, obligated to work at their command, and subjected to all sorts of punishments, including lashings and canings, for violating their wishes. They were also obliged to pay taxes.

And yet, in spite of their subjugation, most serfs supported tsarism and displayed little inclination to demand a more democratic regime. Displays of mass rebellion were rare and tended to be anarchistic eruptions directed at the local landlords rather than organized political movements aimed at overthrowing the government. In the 1870s, when the idealistic young populists took to the countryside to spark a revolution, they were shocked to find that the serfs revered their tsar and dismissed talk of an uprising with contempt. The notion that the tsar was a benevolent father, ordained by God to care for his people, was a common assumption in peasant lore. "Without the tsar, the people are an orphan" was one of many proverbs indicative of the serfs' political culture. Along with these deferential attitudes went the widely shared belief that, if the tsar had his way, he would give the land over to the serfs; only evil advisors prevented him from doing so. The populists were also disheartened at the crass materialism of the serfs, who seemed to want nothing more than the same property rights as the landlords, exhibiting little interest in the students' socialistic concerns for the welfare of society as a whole.

In February 1861, embarrassed at Russia's image as a backward society, Tsar Alexander II signed an Emancipation decree abolishing serfdom in Russia. (President Lincoln's Emancipation Proclamation was issued in January 1862.) The decree freed more than 22 million peasants, roughly 38 percent of Russia's population at the time, from their obligation to serve the landlords. (The serf-owning nobility comprised about 100,000 people.) The newly liberated serfs now became legal persons for the first time, endowed with the right to own property and to vote for newly created local councils.

But just as emancipation in the United States abolished servitude in legal terms without providing the former slaves with an accompanying measure of economic self-sufficiency, so the terms of emancipation in Russia imposed new shackles of economic dependency on the former serfs. One-third of the landlords' property was made available to the liberated peasants, but they had to buy it. Unable to meet the demanding schedule of payments to the state and the landlords, many sank hopelessly into debt. Emancipation also failed to provide the

full range of civil rights. The "liberated" serfs were obliged to remain in their communities; only by special permission were they allowed to leave for long periods. Their communes were given financial powers that stifled the development of viable, family-owned commercial farms.

Widespread dissatisfaction with these conditions ignited a series of peasant revolts that intensified between 1905 and 1907. Though things settled down after the government canceled the debts and instituted reforms promoting private land ownership, a smoldering discontent pervaded the Russian countryside. By 1917, self-employed peasants owned two-thirds of the country's farmland, but most were impoverished. Family farms tended to be small and land hunger was rampant, a predicament that induced many peasants to heed the siren call of revolution rather than seek an orderly passage to democracy.

Meanwhile, as Russia's industrial development quickened, a new class of disadvantaged people voiced their indignation. The industrial working class, toiling in the factories that proliferated in the late nineteenth and early twentieth centuries, grew from slightly more than half a million in 1860 to about 3 million by 1914. Although they still constituted only a small portion of the population (estimated at 170 million in 1914), their concentration in and around the country's main urban centers allowed them to join forces more easily than the widely dispersed peasant population and to make an immediate impression on the ruling elites. Though trade unions and strikes were not allowed, strikes began taking place in the 1870s and 1880s. In the revolutionary explosion of 1905, workers in St. Petersburg (the capital) and Moscow closed down factories and spontaneously formed workers' councils that were poised to replace government authority until the regime suppressed them. In 1912, 725,000 workers went on strike illegally, followed by more than a million and a quarter in the first half of 1914.

As World War I imposed new hardships on the working population—an increasing number of whom were women—labor agitation intensified. Strikes and mass demonstrations for "bread and peace" convulsed the cities and other areas where workers clustered, such as mines and oil fields.[11] By 1917, with much of Russia crying out for new leadership, its exploited working class was ready for radical solutions. It was the communists who spoke to their grievances more successfully than did the advocates of liberal democracy.

As the preceding account suggests, democracy in pre-communist Russia was also hampered by the absence of a *civil society* and a *democratic political culture.* One of the defining features of the tsarist era was the gaping chasm that separated the state from society. Until the mid-seventeenth century, the very idea of the state as an entity separate from the personage of the tsar did not even exist; nor was there any concept that the people constituted a "society" with its own needs and wishes, since virtually the entire population was regarded as the tsar's slaves. Even after the nobility won new privileges under Catherine the Great and after the serfs were emancipated in the following century, the heavy hand of tsarist rule remained so oppressive that the people had little latitude to develop viable associations of their own. Virtually all organizations independent of the state—civic associations, trade unions, political parties—were deemed seditious by the ruling authorities.

A pervasive sense of resignation and alienation from the government thus settled over the bulk of the population in the nineteenth century, including the intelligentsia. The intelligentsia's passivity was punctuated only by quixotic revolutionary movements like the populists or diffuse calls for spiritual salvation by writers or philosophers, at least until the creation of the Duma sparked an increase in associative activity. Thereafter, the tsar's determination to keep the emerging forces for change reined in had a radicalizing effect on civil society, intensifying political alienation and ultimately playing into the hands of those advocating a thoroughgoing political and social revolution.

Predictably, the attitudes and behaviors associated with a democratic political culture—participation, cooperation, consensus building, trust, and the like—also failed to blossom in Russia's rocky political soil. By the time the tsarist regime was ready to grant room to political and social forces outside its narrow orbit, in a country wracked by war and domestic turmoil, it was too late to develop the attitudinal bases for a measured, negotiated transition to democracy before the tide of revolution engulfed the country.

Prior to the nineteenth century, *education* was reserved to the upper nobility and clergy. The expansion of secondary and higher educational opportunities in the second half of the nineteenth century increased the size of the intelligentsia but the regime sought to restrict university access to the upper echelons of society. Besides, as we've seen, the tsarist regime permitted no real outlets for mass participation in the country's political life on the part of its educated strata. The political orientations of high school and university graduates therefore got diverted into a quiescent resignation or a desperate revolutionary radicalism, with only a relative few seeking a moderate democratic constitution. Starting in the 1860s, primary schools in the rural hinterlands multiplied, but the bulk of the population continued to consist of illiterate peasants, scarcely a promising basis for mass democracy.

The *flow of information* was seriously restricted by the regime. Official activities were tightly guarded state secrets, and the public was fed official versions of the truth as deemed appropriate by the authorities. A censorship system monitored non-official publications, though it was not as ruthlessly efficient under the tsars as it would become under communism.

Imperial Russia's appetite for territory remained undiminished in the eighteenth and nineteenth centuries, bringing an agglomeration of non-Russian peoples under tsarist rule. From Poles, Lithuanians, and Finns in the west to Georgians and Armenians in the Caucasus and an array of Turkic people across Central Asia, the Russian empire displayed a striking ethnic, linguistic, and religious *heterogeneity.* These subjugated peoples had just as few rights as the Russians themselves and were subjected to military reprisals for acts of insubordination. Any steps in the direction of democracy for these diverse populations could only spell suicide for a polyglot empire.

Ethnic Russians also exhibited a noticeable social heterogeneity, rooted mainly in class and status distinctions. Nineteenth-century Russian society consisted of the nobility, which was itself divided into a small minority of rich people, a somewhat larger mid-level gentry, and a large majority living at the margins of subsistence; the Orthodox clergy; the peasantry (mostly serfs until emancipation); a small merchant class; a small core of professionals, such as doctors, scientists, and teachers; and an industrial working class that was to triple in size by the eve of the Great War. The weakness of civil society and the absence of a universal educational system provided few opportunities for cross-class interaction, and the tsarist regime played one group off another while striving to keep them all down. Most Russians therefore developed a closer attachment to their own social class than to Russia as a whole, with few espousing a democratic conception of the common good.

Finally, Russia's *international environment* proved just as obstructive to democracy as its domestic characteristics. Russia was geographically and culturally removed from the seminal developments in European society that promoted the rule of law and the evolution of democratic attitudes and institutions, such as the traditions of Roman jurisprudence, the social obligations of feudalism, the Protestant Reformation, the Enlightenment, the advancement of bourgeois liberalism. Although the development of democracy proceeded in Britain in spite of its aggressive pursuit of imperial expansion and its intimate involvement in the "great game" of power politics in Europe, until World War I

Britain did not use conscripted armies. From the time of Peter the Great, however, Russians were impressed against their will into military service to fight for the emperor's personal ambitions rather than for their "country" in any democratic or patriotic sense of the term. (France did not have conscription until the Revolution, when it emerged as a democratic national duty. Its manipulation at the hands of Napoleon, however, was scarcely conducive to democracy.) Moreover, the empires established by democracies (or partial democracies) like Britain, France, and the United States were overseas empires. Russia's empire involved contiguous territory that encompassed a diversity of actively or potentially rebellious peoples living close to home, providing a pretext for stern authoritarian government in St. Petersburg.

When World War I broke out, Britain and France fought not only to defend their home territory and overseas colonies but also to protect their democracies; for the United States the war was supposed to "make the world safe for democracy." In the United Kingdom and the United States, the conflict resulted in an expansion of voting rights, particularly for women, who made major contributions to the war effort. But in Russia, the Great War only exacerbated the social and political conflicts that had been building up to a revolutionary explosion for decades. Far from promoting democracy, the First World War led Russia to communism.

CONCLUSIONS

With respect to all ten conditions for democracy, then, events consistently conspired to inhibit democratic development in Russia over the course of a thousand years. The barriers to democracy would be even more imposing under communist rule.

Communism

Marx and the Russian Revolution   If Karl Marx's predictions had been right, Russia would not have experienced a socialist revolution in 1917. As noted in chapter 13, Marx believed that socialism had to be built on the foundations of an industrialized capitalist economy in an advanced state of development. Only a highly industrialized economy could provide a working class large enough to wrest economic and political power from the capitalist bourgeoisie. But seventy years after Marx and Friedrich Engels authored the Communist *Manifesto*, Russia was still a predominantly agricultural nation. Industrial workers and their families barely amounted to 5 percent of the popu-

lace in 1917, a far cry from the majority Marx required for a successful proletarian revolution.

Peasants, in his view, were ill-suited to revolutionary activity. When he and Friedrich Engels were asked by Russian revolutionaries if it might be possible to create a socialist society in Russia on the basis of the peasantry, they replied that a rural revolution could indeed occur in Russia, but it would succeed over the long run only if it were followed by working-class revolutions in the industrialized countries of Europe, such as England, France, and Germany.[12]

Not only did the Russian Revolution deviate from the preconditions set by Marx, it also departed substantially from Marx's expectations about how a revolution would take place. For most of his life, the founder of modern socialism assumed that socialist revolutions, which would explode in different countries at different times, would be largely spontaneous working-class upheavals. He did not expect them to be highly organized operations managed by a political party or a charismatic personality. Nor did he expect them to lead to anything but the ultimate elimination of governmental power (the "withering away of the state," in Engels's terms). Only a slight exception to this rule might delay—but not prevent—the state's eventual disappearance. In various writings Marx indicated that, in some cases, the workers might first take over the reins of political power, located in government institutions, before moving on to expropriate economic power from the capitalist bourgeoisie. In these two-step revolutions, the workers would institute a "dictatorship of the proletariat" before liquidating private enterprise and the institutional structures of the state itself. But the proletarian dictatorship, in Marx's view, would be temporary, merely a short-lived transition to a stateless—and classless—society.

Contrary to Marx's expectations, the Russian Revolution was a carefully orchestrated coup d'état, skillfully managed by a revolutionary party that was in turn led by a charismatic personality, **Vladimir Ilich Lenin.** Although it was accompanied by working-class agitation in Russia's largest cities, its timing was due more to the decades-long dissolution of tsarism, the land hunger of the peasantry, and the general turbulence fostered by World War I than to a spontaneous uprising of the industrial working class. Political power in Russia was seized by a Communist Party elite acting in the name of the workers, not by the workers themselves.

The Russian "dictatorship of the proletariat," far from being a temporary affair under the direction of the workers, turned out to be a dictatorship of the *Communist Party* that endured until the final collapse of party rule in the early 1990s. Rather than wither away, the state in the Soviet Union burgeoned into one of the most oppressive totalitarian regimes ever seen, bolstered by a giant bureaucracy that imposed itself on just about every facet of the country's economic and social life. And instead of becoming a classless society, the USSR developed stark divisions between the mass of society (itself divided into several layers) and a select Communist Party elite, comprising at most 2 percent of the population, who arrogated to themselves a cornucopia of privileges and material goods not available to the wider population.

Lenin and Leninism   Lenin, the person most responsible for Russia's deviation from the Marxist paradigm, was not a proletarian but a product of the Russian intelligentsia. His father was a high school principal who was granted noble status at the end of his career. Born in 1870 as V. I. Ulyanov (Lenin was a pseudonym), he was introduced to revolution at an early age: his older brother was involved in a terrorist circle plotting to assassinate

Vladimir Ilich Lenin

Tsar Alexander III. Caught before the plan materialized, Alexander Ulyanov was executed by hanging. The future Lenin familiarized himself with his brother's populist literature, but he was influenced more compellingly by Marx's writings. By age eighteen he was a convinced Marxist. After completing his university education, Lenin left home in 1895 and moved to St. Petersburg, where he joined a small group of Marxist intellectuals. He was soon arrested by the political police and exiled to Siberia. Following his release in 1900, Lenin fled the country, joining a growing exodus of Russian socialists to Europe, where they formed the nucleus of the newly established Russian Social Democratic Labor Party.

In 1902, Lenin made his first major mark on the socialist movement with the publication of *What Is To Be Done?* The tract boldly staked out several positions that diverged from the tenets of classic Marxism. Whereas Marx regarded the industrial proletariat as the standard-bearers of revolution, Lenin insisted that the workers, if left to themselves, would never mount a revolution; at best they would form trade unions and come to terms with the captains of industry who controlled their lives. And whereas Marx foresaw spontaneous proletarian outbursts, Lenin declared that the revolution would have to be organized by a political party.

More specifically, Lenin called for the creation of a "party of a new type": not a mass party concerned with winning votes, like the German Social Democrats or the British Labour Party, but a smaller party consisting of professional revolutionaries who would act as the "vanguard of the proletariat," seizing power whenever the right opportunity presented itself. Lenin's strategy implied that the revolutionaries might not have to wait for industrial capitalism to reach an advanced stage in Russia, a process that would take decades. Armed with its "organizational weapon," a conspiratorial party might be able to topple the state, along with its economic base, long before capitalism had created a sizable working-class population.

These ideas split the Russian socialists into two groups. Lenin's followers called themselves **Bolsheviks,** meaning "the majority." In fact, they constituted a minority of Russian Social Democrats at the start of the century, but the name stuck. Most of the remaining party members, labeled Mensheviks (the minority), regarded Lenin's theses as heresy and remained faithful to Marx's teachings. In their view, Russian revolutionaries were compelled by the laws of history to wait until the advancement of industrial capitalism created an auspicious moment for a spontaneous working-class revolution.

The tumultuous events of 1905 seemed to validate Lenin's propositions. As Russia seethed with revolutionary ferment, Lenin returned home, remaining underground for two years. But the situation proved premature: the tsarist regime recovered its nerve and crushed the revolutionary outbreaks that flared up spontaneously in Russia's cities and countryside. Lenin returned to Europe, but when he went back to Russia the next time, in April 1917, the situation would be fully primed for revolution.

As Lenin's train arrived in Russia's capital city, renamed Petrograd during the war, the Bolsheviks could count on no more than 23,000 adherents. Between April and July, their ranks swelled to nearly a quarter million. The war's widespread unpopularity played directly into their hands, sapping the Russian government of what little support it may have possessed. In March, Tsar Nicholas II was persuaded to step down, leaving power in the hands of a Provisional Government consisting of politicians from the conservative right to the moderate left. (Because Russia was still using the Julian calendar, which lagged two weeks behind the more widely used Gregorian calendar, the transfer of power is known in Russian history as the "February Revolution.") Though the new government immediately conferred on Russia's citizens a wide range of democratic rights and freedoms they had never before enjoyed, its decision to prosecute the war hastened its undoing.

One-fourth of Russia's troops deserted the army over the ensuing months. Life on the home front was continuing turmoil: shortages of food and heating fuel intensified public outrage, resulting in strikes, work stoppages, and demonstrations in the cities. Out in the countryside, peasants intensified their demands for more land. In Petrograd and Moscow, workers set up councils to take over the management of their factories and, in a bold challenge to the governing authorities, acted as though they constituted the only legitimate political authority. The Russian word for council is *soviet*. As the crisis deepened, soldiers and peasants formed soviets of their own, electing deputies to join with representatives of the workers' soviets to coordinate their activities.

Bolshevik propaganda deftly exploited these discontents. Lenin and his followers called for an immediate end to the war, land for the peasants, and "all power to the soviets!" By early fall the Provisional Government was virtually powerless. In a methodical coup d'état, Bolshevik militia units moved into the main government buildings in Petrograd, most of which had already been vacated by Russian officialdom. The tsarist regime and the short-lived Provisional Government had collapsed like houses of cards, quietly falling into Bolshevik hands on November 7, 1917. (The date was October 25 on the Julian calendar; hence the Bolshevik takeover of power is known as the **October Revolution.**)

The Bolsheviks—also known as communists—promptly pulled Russia out of the Great War, moved the capital to Moscow, and turned their attention to consolidating power at home. Their first moves were calculated to court popularity. During their first months at the helm, the communists granted independence to nationality groups like the Poles, the Finns, and the Ukrainians, who had been incorporated into the Russian Empire under the tsars. They granted power to the workers' soviets, encouraged peasants to take over land, and allowed previously scheduled elections to a constitutional assembly to go forward. (The Bolsheviks won nearly 25 percent of the vote in these elections, capturing a majority in Petrograd and Moscow.)[13] Then, one by one, the new rulers proceeded to take back most of their concessions: Ukraine was reincorporated into Russia, the soviets came under communist control, farmland and produce were confiscated by the state, and the Constituent Assembly was liquidated the day after its first meeting, consigned to the "dustbin of history."

Private businesses were expropriated by the government in the name of socialism. Nicholas II and his family were executed so as to preclude any return to tsarism. Over the next several years the Bolsheviks (the reds) fought a bitter civil war against a variety of enemies, known collectively as the whites. As fighting and famine claimed millions of lives, the Red Army under Bolshevik command finally vanquished its remaining foes in 1921. In 1922 the Union of Soviet Socialist Republics (USSR) was formally proclaimed, uniting under communism the remnants of the Russian empire. The country lay in ruins.

Lenin assumed leadership of the fledgling communist government, acknowledged by the overwhelming majority of communists as their supreme leader. From the outset, Lenin was determined to impose Communist Party authority over all other political and social forces in the country. Driven by a keen sense of power, he believed that the most important question in politics was "Who—whom?" (in Russian, "*Kto-kovo?*"). "Who," in other words, "controls whom?" *The primacy of the Communist Party's power* was the single most characteristic feature of what came to be known as **Leninism.** It was the party, after all, that had made the Revolution on behalf of the working class. By Lenin's own candid admission, the dictatorship of the proletariat in Russia effectively meant the dictatorship of the Communist Party.

A second defining aspect of Leninism was what he called *"democratic centralism."* While discussion and debate among party members were supposed to be permitted until a final decision was reached, all were required to follow the policies eventually decided by the top party leaders. In actual practice, internal party democracy quickly dissipated in favor of a top-down structure of command not unlike a military hierarchy.

Violence and a highly centralized state were ruthlessly employed to secure party rule. Accordingly, Lenin set up a powerful secret police—the forerunner of the KGB—and presided over the creation of a large state bureaucracy dominated by Communist Party adherents. Though he recognized that bureaucratic routine threatened to smother revolutionary elan, Lenin was in practice a Jacobin: a devotee of strong, centralized state power.

The Soviet system of government that took shape under Lenin's aegis thus revolved around two institutions: the Communist Party of the Soviet Union (CPSU) and the state. The two were so closely intertwined as to be virtually indistinguishable. Both the party and the state had large bureaucracies with overlapping responsibilities for governing the country, and both were topped by small, powerful committees that constituted the highest decision-making bodies in Russia. The highest party committees were the Political Bureau, or *Politburo,* and the *Secretariat.* The highest state committee eventually became known as the *Council of Ministers,* the country's formal executive branch of government. The links connecting the parallel party and state institutions were strengthened by the simultaneous presence of several key individuals in the Politburo, the Secretariat, and the Council of Ministers. In the Soviet system, the Communist Party and the state were fused. Over time, as we shall see, the *party* institutions emerged as more powerful than the state institutions when it came to making the key decisions. Until Mikhail Gorbachev began restructuring this fused party-state institutional system in the late 1980s, its basic structure remained largely intact. Even today, Communist China retains a very similar fusion of party and state institutions modeled on the old Soviet system.

Another feature of Leninism was *tactical flexibility.* After the Civil War, Lenin recognized that the Bolsheviks needed to buy time and rebuild the economy in order to stabilize their authority. In 1921 Lenin initiated a reform known as the *New Economic Policy (NEP),* which reversed the state's efforts to take over the economy, putting socialism on hold. Peasants were allowed to buy and sell land; industrialists and merchants were invited to lease property from the state and run their own businesses, with strong encouragement to turn a profit. The Russian state retained control of what Lenin called "the commanding heights" of the economy: energy and steel production, the communication and transportation systems, and the like. The partial reintroduction of private enterprise was only supposed to be temporary, however. Once economic activity revived, Lenin had every intention of reimposing socialist controls over the economy under the communist-run central government. But he was sufficiently flexible to set no time limit to the New Economic Policy, allowing Russia to have a respite from rigid state controls in hopes of building popularity for the communist regime over time.

The founder of Bolshevism never lived to see the reimposition of socialism in Russia. In 1922 he suffered a debilitating stroke, and in January 1924 he died. He can be rightfully credited with leading the Russian Revolution and creating the bases of Communist Party rule. Although he reinterpreted a number of the central axioms of Marxism to fit Russia's peculiar conditions, Lenin always considered himself a good Marxist. Following his death, Soviet ideology officially became known as **Marxism-Leninism,** a concept that combined Marx's revolutionary anti-capitalism with Lenin's reliance on the communist party-state.

One of his most enduring legacies was to haunt all the Soviet governments that followed him: his failure to establish an orderly procedure for succession to power. Lenin ruled through his charismatic hold over the communists and unrelenting coercion against his party's opponents. He had no taste for the regularized procedures for transferring power spelled out in written constitutions, especially those in the hated "bourgeois democracies" of the West. Moreover, he designated no successor. As a consequence, a struggle for power within the highest reaches of the Communist Party leadership commenced as soon as Lenin was incapacitated. Through a combination of manipulativeness, guile, and bureaucratic intrigue, the winner of the struggle was **Joseph Stalin,** a man who developed Lenin's legacy of centralization and coercion to unimaginable excesses.

Stalin   Born in 1879 to an impoverished Georgian family, Stalin studied at a seminary but turned to revolutionary Marxism while still in school. As a young man he sided with Lenin and the Bolsheviks when the Russian socialists split into opposing camps, rising to prominence as one of the party's top leaders by the time of the Revolution. After the Bolshevik seizure of power, Lenin entrusted him with a number of sensitive party and government posts, including that of General Secretary of the Communist Party. Initially, that position was nothing more than a routine bureaucratic office charged with managing the party's records. But Stalin transformed it into a sinecure of personal power, building a loyal following by promoting people to both party and government jobs. Through the calculated use of political patronage, Stalin created a large party bureaucracy, or "apparatus" *(apparat),* dependent on his favors. Toward

Joseph Stalin

the end of his life, Lenin criticized Stalin as "too rude" for the post and called for his removal, but the incapacitated Bolshevik was in no physical condition to press his views. Stalin stayed on as General Secretary until he died some thirty years later.

During the 1920s, in the years that followed Lenin's untimely illness and death, Stalin masterfully exploited the rivalries and disagreements among the party's top leaders, playing one faction against another while quietly cultivating his own coterie of loyalists. By the end of the decade he could count on a voting majority in the party Politburo. Utilizing this support, in 1928 and 1929 he engineered the wholesale reversal of the Soviet Union's economic course. The broadly popular New Economic Policy was summarily abandoned, probably much earlier than Lenin would have liked, and the first in a series of five-year plans established the bases of a **centrally planned economy (CPE)** in the Soviet Union. These measures constituted the building blocks of the Soviet model of socialism, which represented another deviation from classical Marxism. Marx, whose descriptions of socialism were inscrutably vague, had left no clear blueprint for building a socialist economy other than to imply that it would *not* be run by a powerful state. The brand of socialism that Stalin and the Communist Party now forced upon the population was defined in Soviet terms as a command economy controlled by the leadership of an all-intrusive party-state dictatorship.

Stalin applied his policy with a vengeance. The first five-year plan, introduced in 1928, had set a series of ambitious growth targets to be achieved in various sectors of the economy. In 1929, Stalin suddenly raised these targets astronomically, especially in such critical industrial areas as coal, iron, steel, and electricity production. Factories and dams sprang up at a dizzying pace, with gangs of workers toiling around the clock in twelve-hour shifts for meager wages. Although Stalin's plan targets were too unrealistic to be achieved, by the end of the first five-year period the Soviets had nevertheless accomplished one of the most rapid spurts of industrial development in human history.

From its inception, this forced-pace industrialization policy was guided by transparently political motivations, both external and internal in nature. Externally, Stalin was acutely aware of the capitalist countries' hostility to the USSR and feared the possibility of a new world war. "We lag behind the advanced countries by 50 to 100 years," he acknowledged. "We must make up this distance in ten years. Either we do this," he said, "or they will crush us." Internally, Stalin recognized that the New Economic Policy had created a new generation of capitalists, both in the cities and on the farms. If continued, NEP risked undermining the population's tolerance of the communist dictatorship. Despite the fact that industry was growing at 20 percent to 30 percent a year and agricultural production was beginning to flourish, Stalin felt compelled to impose stringent controls over the economy for the purpose of retaining the Communist Party's control over Russia's political and social life.

An even more severe policy accompanied the accelerated industrialization drive: the **collectivization** of agriculture. By 1929, thanks largely to NEP, there were 25 million private farm households in Russia. Most farmers were sufficiently productive to feed their families, while perhaps as many as 2 million became quite successful, selling their surpluses at a profit and earning enough money to buy more land. Stalin had no intention of tolerating commercial agriculture, with its dangerous political implications. He

also needed to squeeze more food out of the countryside to feed the throngs of workers dragooned into the heroic industrialization effort.

In an operation conducted with unparalleled brutality, the Stalinist regime liquidated all privately owned farms and corraled the rural population into newly created *collective farms*. Farm produce was confiscated by government agents, often at gunpoint, for distribution to the cities; animals were also taken from their owners and attached to the collectives. Anyone resisting these measures, or even suspected of potential resistance, might be executed on the spot or rounded up for deportation to the work camps *(gulagi)* that now proliferated in the empty vastness of Russia, forming a great chain that later became known as the "gulag archipelago." Violence in Ukraine was especially widespread. Lacking the means to resist, many peasants killed their horses, cows, and other livestock rather than surrender them. Starvation stalked the countryside as food production plummeted. Stalin's own wife killed herself after speaking out against the terror gripping the nation. Stalin himself justified his actions with cynical distortions of Marxist ideology.[14]

By 1934, when the job was done, perhaps as many as 14.5 million Russian peasants had perished in the collectivization campaign, though estimates vary and no precise figure can be authenticated. (Stalin himself told Winston Churchill that collectivization had cost 10 million lives and was more arduous than confronting the German invasion of World War II.) In contrast to the relative success of Stalin's industrialization campaign, however, it took several decades for Soviet agriculture to recover from the catastrophe of the collectivization process. As late as 1953, the USSR possessed 23 million fewer horses and 2 million fewer heads of cattle than in 1916.[15]

Having imposed his will on the population and the economy, Stalin next turned his attention to the Communist Party itself. Between 1934 and 1939, he cleansed the party's ranks from top to bottom, dismissing undesirable members and in many cases consigning them to labor camps or firing squads. Known as the **Great Purge,** the process took on the macabre pathology of a witch hunt. An atmosphere of paranoia gripped the party as accusations and denunciations, most of them fabricated, struck terror into the membership from the highest to the lowest echelons. More than 1.6 million members were expelled from the CPSU.

Not even the most powerful Soviet leaders were spared Stalin's wrath. A series of "show trials" subjected dozens of the most senior party officials to public vilification. Many of them had been Lenin's trusted comrades-in-arms during the early days of Bolshevism. Under the relentless questioning of Stalin's prosecutors, the defendants made humiliating confessions to such crimes as plotting Lenin's assassination or spying for the West. In virtually all instances, the charges were false. The defendants went along with the charade either because they knew that resistance was futile or because their families had been threatened with retaliation, or perhaps because they did not wish to weaken the Soviet regime in the eyes of the hated West by openly challenging its all-powerful leader. Invariably, the show trials ended in a string of death sentences, often carried out immediately.[16]

Stalin's terror fanned out from the Communist Party to the general population. According to one estimate, between 1936 and 1938 alone there were 7 million arrests and at least a million executions; in 1939 the camps contained as many as 8 million prisoners. Stalin's deadly reach even extended to the military high command, decimating about a fourth of the officer corps by the eve of World War II. We shall probably never really know whether Stalin's gruesome bloodletting reflected the paranoid visions of a psychotic or the rational calculations of a tyrant bent on securing his power in a cutthroat system. Perhaps it involved an eery combination of sociopathic irrationality and cold-blooded rationality. Whatever the case, by the end of the 1930s there was little question that Stalin was the unchallenged autocrat of the USSR and that the Soviet system was a paradigm of totalitarianism.[17]

The sufferings of the Soviet masses did not end with the attenuation of the **Great Terror,** however. World War II exacted an even heavier price. Though Stalin managed to delay a German invasion by cutting a deal with Hitler in 1939, the Nazi regime broke the agreement and invaded the USSR with full force in June 1941.[18] By the time the war ended in 1945, more than 22 million Soviet people had died and some 1,700 Soviet cities were destroyed.

Stalin emerged from the war with his powers intact. Victory even brought him a measure of re-

spect and popularity among a portion of the masses, though the magnitude of this support is hard to estimate. Anyone expecting a postwar diminution of autocratic rule was in for a disappointment, however. The concentration camps remained crowded and the Kremlin voiced suspicions of dark plots. The Cold War added fears of impending nuclear annihilation. Stalin was said by his successors to be planning a new party purge when he died in 1953.

Khrushchev Although the Great Purge inflicted a painful toll on nearly 2 million party members, it also opened up new opportunities for eager young recruits as well as for more senior party members who were fortunate enough to survive the onslaught. Most of the men who were to run the Soviet Union from Stalin's death until the mid-1980s rose up the ladder of the party apparatus during the purges and World War II. Stalin's party enticed this generation to its ranks by offering careers, social status, and for the politically ambitious, the prospect of power.

One of the most ambitious was **<u>Nikita Khrushchev.</u>** Born to poverty in 1894, Khrushchev joined the party in 1925 as a full-time *apparatchik*— a member of the party apparatus—just as Stalin was gathering effective control over it. His enthusiastic embrace of communism caught the eye of one of Stalin's top lieutenants, who rapidly pulled him up the rungs of the party leadership. In the

Nikita S. Khrushcher meets U.S. President John F. Kennedy, 1961

early 1930s Khrushchev won swift promotions within the party's Moscow branch and supervised the construction of the city's subway system, a task accomplished by conscripted laborers forced to work in forty-eight-hour shifts. As the Great Purge got under way, Khrushchev wholeheartedly supported Stalin, lauding him as "our leader and teacher" while reviling the show-trial defendents as "fascist dogs" and "degenerates" deserving execution.[19] His loyalty was rewarded with a seat in the powerful CPSU Politburo, where he replaced one of Stalin's purge victims, and an even more spectacular appointment as the party's top leader in Ukraine. In assuming control of the most important Soviet republic after Russia in 1939, Khrushchev stepped into another post freshly vacated by a hapless casualty of the purges.

Khrushchev's notoriety among the Soviet people escalated during World War II, when he assumed responsibility for organizing the Ukrainian government's war effort. His main task was to ensure that Stalin's military orders were faithfully carried out by local commanders. A garrulous barnstormer who enjoyed mixing with ordinary people, Khrushchev fraternized with troops along the front and exhorted workers to carry on in the face of adversity. One of his sons perished in the battle of Stalingrad.

After the war, Khrushchev was well placed to jockey for power in the Soviet hierarchy. When Stalin died in 1953 without leaving a designated successor, the struggle for his mantle intensified among his closest associates. Over the next two years, Khrushchev outmaneuvered his chief rivals and emerged as the Soviet Union's top leader by 1955. His behind-the-scenes machinations bore a distinct resemblance to Stalin's rise to power in the 1920s. Moreover, as we've seen, he owed his career to Stalin's blessings. It is thus ironic that Khrushchev's main claim to fame in Russian history derives from his sweeping denunciation of Stalin and his effort to rid the Soviet system of Stalinism's horrors.

In a speech delivered in February 1956 at the Twentieth Congress of the Communist Party of the Soviet Union, a gathering of several thousand top party bureaucrats, Khrushchev excoriated Stalin as a madman whose actions had repeatedly brought the Soviet Union to the brink of disaster.

Denouncing the "cruel repression" and "mass terror" of the Great Purge as an utterly unjustified breech of legality and berating Stalin for military blunders that had cost hundreds of thousands of lives, Khrushchev disclosed that, after the war, Stalin's "persecution mania reached unbelievable dimensions." He lambasted the former Soviet dictator's megalomaniacal "cult of personality" and his callous disregard of the people's welfare.

Khrushchev's broadside became known as the **secret speech** because it was delivered behind closed doors. Although it was not published in the Soviet Union until the Gorbachev era, it was read out to CPSU members at local party meetings. Not long after Khrushchev made the speech, foreign intelligence services obtained copies and the U.S. State Department published the text. When the secret speech appeared in the *New York Times* and other newspapers, it hit the world like a bombshell. Soviet officials declined to verify the text but did not deny its authenticity.[20]

Shortly after Khrushchev's speech, the Soviet Communist Party embarked on a campaign of *de-Stalinization.* Everywhere throughout the USSR, anything bearing Stalin's name was renamed, from streets and schools to the city of Stalingrad itself (it became Volgagrad). Statues and paintings of Stalin, once ubiquitous, were pulled down. Stalin's body was removed from the Red Square mausoleum it shared with Lenin's and reburied in a nondescript grave beside a Kremlin wall. The authorities even tried to expunge the very memory of Stalin: old photographs were doctored to remove his image. Owners of the *Great Soviet Encyclopedia* were instructed to return volume "S"; the volumes were later sent back to their owners with the pages devoted to Stalin excised. Khrushchev even allowed writers like Alexander Solzhenitsyn to publish works denouncing Stalin's deeds.[21]

One of Khrushchev's motives in initiating the de-Stalinization program was to buttress his own authority by cultivating support from Communist Party leaders and bureaucrats. In effect, Khrushchev was signaling his assurance that he would never inflict a Stalinist purge on them and that they were safe as long as they supported him in power. But de-Stalinization provoked serious misgivings on the part of a number of high-level Soviet officials. They knew that by linking his personal enemies in the leadership with Stalin's deeds (but never, of course, himself), Khrushchev had a pretext for dismissing them. They also feared that, by attacking Stalin, Khrushchev had demeaned the party itself in the eyes of the Soviet people and the rest of the world. Actually, Khrushchev never blamed the party or communist ideology for the terrors of the Stalin years. He attached primary responsibility for the USSR's afflictions to one man, not to the political system that had produced and sustained him. Even so, several senior party leaders were sufficiently troubled by the anti-Stalin campaign, along with other Khrushchev policies, that they tried to unseat him in 1957. But Khrushchev rallied his supporters within the party and turned the tables on his opponents, reasserting his grip on power.

Over the next several years, Khrushchev strove to make sure that his position as chief of the Communist Party was the single most powerful position in the USSR. As the generally acknowledged leader of the Soviet Union, he took the initiative in promoting a number of reforms, including adjustments to the central planning system and the shifting of military spending from the army and navy to the newly created missile forces. He proposed changes in the educational system that would have required high school graduates to enter the work force for a couple of years before starting college. Like de-Stalinization, these and other reforms had their critics: admirals and army generals grumbled, and the educational establishment managed to block Khrushchev's work-for-students scheme. Even so, most of Khrushchev's reform proposals were halfhearted at best and did nothing to undermine central planning or diminish the Communist Party's monopoly of power in the Soviet Union. Khrushchev wanted a "thaw" in the system Stalin had created, not its wholesale transformation.

Throughout his life, Khrushchev remained a devout Soviet communist, utterly committed to the authoritarian system he served. He asserted Soviet controls over Central and Eastern Europe and vigorously pursued the Cold War rivalry with the United States. While acknowledging the necessity of avoiding nuclear war, he deployed troops to crush the Hungarian uprising against communism in 1956, approved the Berlin wall in 1961, and put missiles in Cuba in 1962. (On the Cuban missile crisis, see chapter 5.) He was also con-

vinced of the inherent economic superiority of communism over capitalism, vowing that the Soviet Union would overtake the U.S. economy by 1970 and would build the most productive and egalitarian welfare state in the world by 1980.

In the end, however, he proved that he was no Stalin. Having antagonized a number of key party officials and bureaucratic agencies with his unsettling reforms, arrogant manner, and occasionally erratic behavior, Khrushchev proved far less adept than his predecessor in maintaining his authority. In October 1964, upon returning to the Kremlin from a trip, he was informed by his Politburo colleagues that he was no longer in power. Chastised by his successors for "hare-brained scheming," Khrushchev became a "non-person" and was never seen in public again. In 1970, the party newspaper *Pravda* carried a brief notice in its back pages that "pensioner N.S. Khrushchev" had died.[22]

Many of the events of the next twenty-five years in Soviet politics were reactions to Khrushchev's reformist impulses. His immediate successor, **Leonid Brezhnev,** was opposed to any rash tampering with the basic Stalinist model of firm party rule and central planning. Under his guidance, the Soviet leadership undertook virtually no reforms. When reform finally came, in the second half of the 1980s, it was initiated by a man who had drawn considerable hope and inspiration from Khrushchev's anti-Stalinism during his younger years: Mikhail Gorbachev.

The Brezhnev Years Just as Nikita Khrushchev had turned on Stalin, so Leonid Brezhnev turned on the man who had been his chief benefactor during his own climb up the apparatus of the Soviet Communist Party. Thanks to Khrushchev's patronage, Brezhnev had risen from obscurity to the most powerful leadership committees in the USSR. An ethnic Russian, Brezhnev was born in an industrial town in Ukraine in 1906. He joined the party in 1931, at the height of Stalin's industrialization and collectivization campaigns, both of which were especially savage in the Ukrainian republic. After taking a degree in metallurgy, he began his political career in 1935 as deputy mayor of his native city. As the Great Purge combed the ranks of the party, with chilling consequences for many, Brezhnev prospered: he won successive

Leonid Brezhnev

promotions during the purge years and became the party's top man in the city of his birth in 1939, stepping into the shoes of a purge victim. During World War II Brezhnev served under Khrushchev as a political officer in Ukraine.

After the war, Brezhnev's fortunes rose with Khrushchev's. As Khrushchev quietly enhanced his influence in Stalin's last years and came away with the leadership after Stalin's death, he entrusted Brezhnev with a succession of important positions. Following the secret speech, Khrushchev brought Brezhnev into the party's all-important Secretariat. When he triumphed over his adversaries in 1957, Khrushchev rewarded Brezhnev for his support by promoting him to full membership in the powerful Politburo. Between 1960 and 1964, Brezhnev also served as president of the Soviet legislature, a largely ceremonial position that carried with it the formal designation as the USSR's head of state. In the eyes of Western "Kremlinologists" peering into the secretive black box of Soviet politics, Brezhnev stood out as a solid Khrushchev loyalist.

Gratitude is a rare virtue in politics, alas, and its absence was especially conspicuous in the conspiratorial world of the Kremlin. As dissatisfaction with Khrushchev reached a critical mass within the Soviet elite, Brezhnev joined the cabal that unseated his benefactor in October 1964. From then until his death in 1982, Brezhnev was the official leader of the Communist Party of the Soviet

Union, and thus the single most powerful figure in the USSR.

It was not long before the transfer of power brought noticeable changes in style and substance. In contrast to Khrushchev's mixture of folksy charm and brash invective, Brezhnev spoke in the measured tones of a stolid bureaucrat. Whereas Khrushchev was prone to impromptu declarations and unilateral initiatives, Brezhnev governed as part of a team. Though he shrewdly demoted his principal opponents, he presented himself as the chief spokesman of an oligarchy acting on the basis of consensus. In the policy realm, one of Brezhnev's first departures from his predecessor was his termination of public attacks on Stalin. Khrushchev himself had begun toning down his shrill blasts against Stalin once it became evident that powerful party chieftains opposed to de-Stalinization might oust him. Brezhnev halted virtually all further criticisms and even allowed positive accounts of Stalin to appear sporadically in the heavily controlled press.

Perhaps the most telling evidence of the leadership change was the Brezhnev team's manifest aversion to experimentation. Khrushchev's attempts to update Marxist-Leninist ideology to take account of modern science and technology and his efforts to shake up the party's ossified institutional structures were stopped in their tracks. Brezhnev and company were not interested in ideological creativity, and they made sure that the party's bureaucrats could count on retaining their jobs in a stable institutional environment. Nor were they prepared to tolerate Khrushchev's efforts to open up the censorship system a crack so as to permit a bit more literary and artistic diversity. A grim pall of uniformity descended on the country's cultural life, with strict censorship rigidly enforced.

Political repression as a whole grew even tighter than under Khrushchev, who was himself no advocate of democratic freedoms. The Brezhnev regime was determined to keep the USSR's small collection of dissidents—mostly writers, artists, and academics—under close surveillance. The dreaded KGB (the Committee on State Security) had carte blanche to investigate, harass, and arrest anyone suspected of engaging in dissident activities, such as the writing or dissemination of anti-communist literature. (Known as *samizdat*—or "self-published"—material, these writings were laboriously copied by carbon paper or mimeographed and passed hand to hand among trusted fellow dissidents. (The Brezhnev regime did not have to contend with the Internet or e-mail.) Internationally renowned figures like the physicist Andrei Sakharov and the writer Alexander Solzhenitsyn were subject to continuing repression. Sakharov was exiled to a city closed off to foreigners and Solzhenitsyn was denied permission to return home from a trip abroad. While the Stalin-era prison camps for the most part had been closed down under Khrushchev, a few still survived under Brezhnev. They were augmented by psychiatric prisons where political dissidents could be subjected to debilitating drug regimens on fabricated diagnoses of lunacy.[23]

The Brezhnevites were also resolved to crack down on any signs of ethnic unrest. Soviet Jews who sought to emigrate to Israel, Europe, or the United States had to contend with endless red tape and prolonged delays, often losing their jobs upon applying for a passport. Many were granted permission to leave only after deals were struck between the Soviet and U.S. governments. One reason for the Kremlin's reluctance to allow Jews to leave was its fear that other ethnic minorities would demand the same privilege. The USSR's population of 260 million at the time consisted of sixteen major nationality groups, each with at least a million people, plus more than eighty smaller nationality groups that together comprised 6 percent of the population. Because the Brezhnev leadership left little doubt that even the slightest signs of ethnic nationalism would be met with swift retribution, there were few outward displays of such dissent. The Russians, who constituted slightly more than half the Soviet population, remained in firm control of the country's levers of power.

Lest there be any uncertainty about the government's readiness to use force against challenges to its authority, the Brezhnev regime intervened vigorously on two occasions when communist rule was threatened in its hegemonic preserve of East-Central Europe. In 1968, when a reform movement initiated by the Communist Party of Czechoslovakia unleashed broad popular demands for democracy and closer ties to the West, the Soviets led a massive invasion force to restore hard-line communists to power. In 1981, when Poland's Solidarity movement backed the communist regime against the wall with a massive show of public support, the Soviets stiffened the resolve of Polish authorities to impose martial law and outlaw Solidarity. The Brezhnev government had no intention of losing its controls over Stalin's postwar empire in the region.

This dedication to projecting Soviet power abroad was another defining element of the Brezhnev regime. The Brezhnevites were no different than Khrushchev or Stalin in affirming their hostility to the "bourgeois democracies" and "Western imperialism"; like their predecessors, they were ardent cold warriors. But whereas Khrushchev had sought to redistribute the military budget in favor of modern nuclear missile technology, Brezhnev presided over an across-the-board expansion of Soviet military might that boosted spending in all branches of the armed forces. Over the course of the 1970s the USSR outproduced the entire NATO alliance in tanks and various forms of artillery, overtook the United States in the deployment of long-range guided missiles, and installed a new generation of intermediate-range missiles capable of striking Western Europe and Japan within minutes. This unrelenting military buildup occurred in spite of arms control agreements with the United States and talk of "détente," which was supposed to bring about a relaxation in East-West tensions. East-West relations suffered another rude jolt when the Soviet Union invaded Afghanistan in late 1979 to shore up a friendly leadership faction in a country teetering on the brink of civil war. The United States and other NATO countries responded by boycotting the 1980 Olympic Games held in Moscow.

It was Moscow's escalating military expenditures, however, that exacerbated the Brezhnev regime's most pressing problem, the economy. Khrushchev's attempts to tinker with the central planning system were little more than cosmetic in nature; he had no taste for free enterprise. Brezhnev retreated from even these modest changes and shelved plans for future experiments proposed by members of his leadership team. Aside from small private plots that collective farmers were allowed to maintain in order to grow food for their own consumption, the USSR had no private property.

Everything from paper clips to space rockets were planned, produced, priced, and distributed by the government under the direction of the State Planning Commission (*Gosplan*). Basic consumer goods and services were heavily subsidized so as to curry favor with the population. Prices for bread, milk, potatoes, and other staples of the Russian diet were kept artificially low; so were prices for beef and pork, which were in shorter supply and quickly sold out. Transportation fares were minimal; rents were cheap; education was free from the lowest to the highest levels. Conversely, many goods were relatively more expensive than in the West. An ordinary pair of shoes could cost a third of an average monthly wage; new cars were inordinately expensive and potential owners had to wait years before taking delivery.

Although in material terms most Soviet citizens lived better in the Brezhnev years than ever before in Russian history, by the 1970s the economy was stagnating. Between 1978 and 1985, the Soviet Union experienced zero economic growth. Military spending took a growing slice out of a diminishing budgetary pie, with annual increases. According to estimates by the U.S. Central Intelligence Agency, during the Brezhnev years the USSR was probably spending about 12 percent of its GNP on the military, roughly double the U.S. rate. After Gorbachev came to power and decided to cut military expenses drastically, the Soviets disclosed that their actual military spending was between one-fourth and one-third of GNP, far higher than CIA assessments.

Meanwhile, the Soviets were falling far behind the West and Japan in high-technology development. The Information Age left the USSR trailing its adversaries by a wide margin, particularly in such sectors as computers, software, and telecommunications. Communication, after all, is not something a dictatorship likes to encourage among its citizens. The Soviet Union's cumbrous planning system moved with bureaucratic lethargy and lacked the financial incentives that lure capitalist entrepreneurs and stimulate innovation. It proved poorly equipped to make the rapid improvements that market-oriented companies must constantly make in order to stay competitive.

Despite these problems, Brezhnev and his colleagues were even less inclined than Khrushchev to change the system they had known all their lives. Triumphalist slogans substituted for realistic self-criticism ("We are steadfastly fulfilling the plans of the 26th Party Congress!"). Rather than institute reforms, they purchased industrial goods from the West, such as pipelines and turbines. Even here, their resistance to capitalism was barely surmountable: Soviet trade with the outside world lagged far behind the averages for most other advanced economies and was conducted mainly with the communist-ruled states of East-Central Europe.

When Brezhnev died in 1982, after nearly eighteen years in office, the ruling elite that clung to power for a few last years was a veritable gerontocracy: most members of the Politburo and other key committees were in their late sixties or seventies. Brezhnev's immediate successor as party General Secretary was former KGB chief **Yuri Andropov,** who was sixty-eight when he took over. He was soon overcome by a debilitating illness and died in 1984. The next party chief, **Konstantin Chernenko,** was an old Brezhnev crony who assumed power at eighty-three. He died the following year. An entire generation of Soviet leaders was receding into history, a generation whose political careers and policy outlooks rightfully label them as Stalin's successors.[24]

THE COLLAPSE OF SOVIET COMMUNISM

With the accession of Mikhail Gorbachev to power, not only a new generation rose to the fore, but a radically new political orientation as well.

PROFILE: Mikhail Gorbachev

"We can't go on living like this." Mikhail Gorbachev's words to his wife, Raisa, spoken in March 1985 on the eve of his assumption of power in the Soviet Union, reflected his conviction that the USSR was on the brink of disaster. "By the mid-1980s," he later recalled, "our society resembled a steam boiler." Major changes were absolutely necessary; otherwise, he feared, "an explosion of colossal force would be inevitable."

The inertial forces that had led the USSR to such a catastrophic turning point were plainly visible to anyone willing to see. Growth rates had fallen by more than half since the early 1970s, leading Gorbachev to characterize the late Brezhnev years as an "era of stagnation." The

Soviet leader Mikhail Gorbachev and U.S. President Ronald Reagan sign the treaty providing for the destruction of Soviet and NATO intermediate range nuclear missles, 1987.

country's industrial infrastructure, much of it built in the Stalinist epoch, was woefully outdated, and its high-technology lag behind the West and Japan was widening to unbridgeable lengths. Consumer goods were shoddy and scarce, environmental hazards widespread. Public health and even mortality rates were deteriorating, and the population lived in a state of political powerlessness and cultural isolation, demoralized by the regime's routine indifference to its everyday problems. Military expenditures gobbled up 40 percent of the national budget.

The USSR's foreign policy had built a trenchline of confrontation around the world. Soviet troops, many of them conscripts, were still bogged down in Afghanistan more than five years after an invasion that was supposed to have completed its aims within a few months. Government authorities refused to disclose casualties, but the steady stream of coffins returning from the battle areas touched off angry murmuring beneath the outwardly serene surface of Soviet society. A major crisis with NATO over guided missiles was in progress: in 1983, several years after the Soviets began installing new missiles on their territory within range of Western Europe and much of Asia, NATO responded by deploying newly designed U.S. missiles in Western Europe, countering Moscow's move. In Asia, people were still incensed at the 1983 shoot-down by nervous Soviet defense forces of a Korean Airlines flight that had accidentally strayed into the USSR's airspace; all 269 passengers were killed. And in Africa and the Middle East, governments and political movements friendly to the USSR received weaponry and other assistance from Moscow, enabling them to pursue their opposition to pro-Western interests and partners. On the whole, world politics was still dominated by Cold War hostilities and fears that a nuclear holocaust might yet be unleashed by the two superpowers.

YOUTH AND EARLY CAREER

As the man inheriting these problems, Gorbachev seemed far more capable of tackling them than were any of his immediate predecessors. At age fifty-four, he was the youngest of the twenty-one men who occupied the highest rungs of power in the Communist Party of the Soviet Union. Born in 1931 to a peasant family in southern Russia, Gorbachev grew up in a poverty-stricken collective farm region. Like millions of Russians, his family was not spared the horrors of Stalinism. His maternal grandfather, an ardent communist and collective farm manager, was taken away in the middle of the night by Soviet police and wrongfully charged with belonging to an anti-Stalin conspiratorial movement. He denied the charges despite repeated torture; miraculously, he was set free and allowed to return home a year later. Gorbachev's other grandfather opposed collectivization and retained his small private farm, but was arrested for failing to fulfill the government's crop quotas and sent to a labor camp in Siberia. Upon his return two years later, he joined the collective farm. Young Mikhail retained lifelong impressions of these tragedies, along with the terrors of World War II. His village was occupied by German troops for several months, and his father fought in a number of major battles, returning home with a leg injury at the end of the conflict. Gorbachev spent the remaining years of his youth attending school and taking part in the collective farm's fieldwork.

In 1950 Gorbachev was admitted as a young man of "worker-peasant" background to Moscow State University, the most prestigious university in the country. He pursued his studies in the law faculty at a time when conformity to the Stalinist variant of Marxism-Leninism was rigidly enforced and independent thinking forbidden. On a few occasions Gorbachev had the gumption to question the prevailing ideology with his professors, a risky exercise, but he also joined with millions of saddened Muscovites in filing reverentially past Stalin's bier when the all-powerful leader died in 1953. Later that year he married Raisa, a philosophy student, and following graduation in 1955 returned to his native region, taking a job in the prosecutor's office in the city of Stavropol. Finding legal work uninteresting, Gorbachev quickly changed professions and became a full-time Communist Party employee. Over the course of the next twenty-three years he remained in Stavropol as a CPSU functionary, rising to the top of the local political heap in 1970 with his appointment as chief of the district's party organization.

Khrushchev's secret speech in 1956 was an event of profound importance in Gorbachev's life. As an official in Stavropol's Communist Party youth organization, it was his job to explain Khrushchev's condemnation of Stalin to young people. In later years Gorbachev stated that he approved of the anti-Stalin campaign as a thoroughly justified attack on the oppressiveness of the Soviet system. "The criticism morally discredited totalitarianism," Gorbachev wrote in his memoirs, exposing the regime's lack of legitimacy and giving rise to hopes for change. But Khrushchev had not gone far enough, Gorbachev believed, in analyzing the roots of communist totalitarianism; he had simplistically blamed one man for the faults of an entire political system. In 1961 Gorbachev was invited to attend the Twenty-Second Party Congress, where he heard Khrushchev renew his attacks on Stalin. Thereafter he remained one of the Soviet Union's so-called "sixties people," a designation shared by those who hoped Khrushchev's initiatives would open the door to real political reform. With Khrushchev's ouster in 1964, those hopes were rudely dashed and the sixties people had to accommodate themselves to Brezhnev's torpid neo-Stalinism.

Though Stavropol is located in the Caucasus region at considerable distance from Moscow, Gorbachev took advantage of its attractiveness as a vacation resort for Soviet leaders to ingratiate himself with leading members of Brezhnev's ruling clique. Several powerful party chieftains came away from their visits with a favorable impression of the intelligent and articulate apparatchik who governed his region with enthusiastic dedication. Gorbachev's success in cultivating these ties paid off in 1978, when he was appointed to the party's powerful Secretariat in Moscow and assigned responsibility for overseeing the Soviet agricultural system. Ever since Stalin, agriculture had been a thorn in the side of the Soviet economy. In addition to the obstacles imposed by mother nature on the USSR's fertile black earth regions, with their short growing season and variable weather patterns, problems rooted in the collective farm system and a backward economic infrastructure created human-made impediments to efficient and productive farming. Crop yields would fluctuate unpredictably from year to year, requiring grain imports from abroad in lean periods. Gorbachev had no magic formula for alleviating the situation, but his ability to point out shortcomings in the party's agricultural policies without calling the system itself into question won him quick promotions in Brezhnev's oligarchy. Within a year he was appointed candidate member of the party Politburo, and the following year he became a full (voting) member.

After Brezhnev's death in 1982, his successor Yuri Andropov, who understood the urgent need for economic reorganization, took Gorbachev under his wing and gave every indication that he was grooming the younger man as his eventual replacement. But it was the aged Chernenko who stepped into Andropov's shoes in early 1984; Gorbachev and others impatient for reform would have to cool their heels a while longer as the Brezhnevites held on to power for one last gasp. As Chernenko's decrepitude proved an embarrassment to the mighty Soviet Union, Gorbachev increasingly stepped forward as the country's most dynamic spokesman. In 1984 he was chosen to lead a Soviet delegation to Italy and Britain; it was only his second trip outside the Soviet bloc. Prime Minister Margaret Thatcher was instantly impressed with Gorbachev's straightforwardness, assuring the world he was "a man I could do business with."

Gorbachev's crowning moment finally came on March 11, 1985. On the day after Chernenko's death, the party hierarchy elected him General Secretary. Andrei Gromyko, who had served as Moscow's foreign minister since the 1950s, assured his fellow comrades of Gorbachev's readiness for the job by observing that "this man has a nice smile, but he's got iron teeth."

STARTING THE REFORM PROCESS

Gorbachev ascended the throne of Soviet power with a sure conviction that change was imperative, but with little clear idea of what to do. During his first year in power he adopted the term "restructuring" (**perestroika**) as the masthead of the reform process. But for nearly two years he provided no clear blueprint for a comprehensive economic or political transformation. Right from the start, however, Gorbachev recognized that no perestroika of any kind would be possible without broad public support. Shortly after assuming office he embarked on a series of trips around the country, employing his natural charm and communicative talents to full advantage in exchanging views with crowds assembled on the streets and in factories. These spontaneous dialogues with the population stood in marked contrast to Gorbachev's distant and incommunicative predecessors and stimulated a groundswell of popular support for the new leader.

Gorbachev's avowed purpose was to galvanize public opinion in favor of a reform process that would surely meet with resistance on the part of Soviet officialdom, the party apparatchiks and state bureaucrats who had run the political and economic system for decades. These officials were collectively known as the **nomenklatura.** Since Stalin's time, the nomenklatura referred to the occupiers of party and state jobs who were selected from lists of people approved by the Communist Party. This vast group, numbering 18 million by Gorbachev's account, included everyone from the most prominent members of the party leadership in

Moscow to local party bosses and their staffs throughout the USSR; from the ministers and agency heads directing the country's central government to the mayors and village council members in the state's institutional structure; from the economists and bureaucrats in the massive State Planning Agency to the factory managers, collective farm functionaries, and other people taking part in the operation of the gargantuan centrally planned economy. The nomenklatura had prospered under Brezhnev, constituting the Soviet Union's power elite. Gorbachev had no illusions about the fact that any serious reorganization of the economy and political institutions would have to upset the nomenklatura's customary ways of doing things, directly assaulting its power, privileges, and arrogant disdain for the people's needs and wishes.

Not long after taking office, Gorbachev therefore began combining his call for restructuring with equally persistent appeals for "democratization" and "openness" *(glasnost)*. These two words would have been regarded as heresies by his predecessors, and even some of his contemporaries in the party elite shared similar fears that they might be misinterpreted by the masses. At least during his initial years in power, Gorbachev did not intend democratization to mean the replacement of Communist Party rule by a Western-style electoral democracy with competing political parties. Rather, he meant that the people should be granted greater latitude than in the past to articulate their demands for more effective government and for better treatment at the hands of party and government bureaucrats. Gorbachev's object was to give voice to public discontent as a means of exerting pressure on Soviet officials to support his reform plans. He fully intended to lead and guide the democratization process, channeling public frustration in the directions he desired rather than giving the population complete freedom to replace the communist system.

Gorbachev's concept of openness was similarly limited in its aims. It meant that the party and government elites who controlled the Soviet system should be more forthcoming with information about the true state of the Soviet Union's economic and social problems. Gorbachev's predecessors had been notoriously mum when it came to informing the public about the sorry plight of the economy, the environment, public health, and other aspects of Soviet reality. Rather than treating the populace like children, Gorbachev wished to share essential information with the public with a view to stimulating open discussion of the country's problems. The party and government, for their part, would have to be willing to engage in more realistic self-criticism, accepting blame for their failures as a precondition of reasserting

their leadership. As with democratization, the aim of glasnost was to exert public pressure for change on the lethargic bureaucratic elite. At least in its initial stages, it was not designed to introduce full-scale freedom of speech of the kind guaranteed by the world's democracies. The explosion of a nuclear reactor in Chernobyl in April 1986 provided Gorbachev with a powerful pretext for promoting his openness campaign, as his government, after some hesitation, informed the public about the gravity of the situation and opened up the damaged site to foreign technicians (see chapter 2).

Both democratization and openness contained tremendous risks for Gorbachev. What if the public wouldn't settle for a limited and controlled democratization process but instead insisted on a real multiparty electoral democracy that might topple the Communist Party from power? What if they interpreted openness just as broadly and demanded the complete removal of the party-controlled censorship system and called for guaranteed rights of free speech, including freedom to condemn the entire communist system? From the outset, Gorbachev's dilemma was how to release the forces of democratization and openness *without losing control over them.* "What we had in mind," Gorbachev later wrote of his first years in power, "was not a revolution but a specific improvement of the situation."

Improvements were painfully slow in coming. So, too, were practical ideas for bringing them about without jeopardizing the structures of communist power and central planning. A precise definition of perestroika and such accompanying notions as "radical reforms" remained elusive as long as the Gorbachev team continued to act within the inherited framework of "the leading role of the party" and a state-dominated economy. Gorbachev's thoughts on perestroika remained vague, as a book he published on the subject testified.[25] His speeches denouncing Stalinism and its lingering effects on the mindset of Soviet officials were mixed with praise for Lenin and socialism. Halfhearted, piecemeal reshufflings of the planning bureaucracy and shifts in its accounting procedures only seemed to generate confusion and opposition among the bureaucrats charged with implementing them, at times provoking outright sabotage. The introduction of market forces, such as privately owned restaurants and other services, remained strictly limited.[26]

As industrial production fell through 1987 and 1988, popular demands for real change intensified. Boris Yeltsin, Gorbachev's appointee as the Communist Party boss of the city of Moscow, emerged as an outspoken critic of the slow pace of the reform process. But as the radical reformers pressed their attacks on Gorbachev, so did the entrenched party elite and their supporters, now openly in revolt at the changes being forced on them and, above all, at their diminishing status in Soviet society. Articles attacking Gorbachev and his reforms by neo-Stalinist hardliners grew increasingly shrill, and it was widely assumed that they reflected the attitudes of high-level officials in the Politburo and Secretariat. By the end of 1988, Gorbachev found himself squeezed between proponents of more radical economic and political reforms on one side and, on the other, hardline conservatives fighting a rearguard action to conserve as much of the old Brezhnevite communist system as they could. As events were to show, the center could not hold.

1989

In an effort to undercut the power of the conservative party apparatchiks and encourage their replacement by reform-minded communists more attuned to his own thinking, Gorbachev called for the creation of a new legislative body, the Congress of People's Deputies, to act as the country's supreme law-making organ. Daringly, he insisted that a portion of the new legislature be elected by the people rather than handpicked by the party. Once again, Gorbachev's hope was to energize his reform process through limited democratization without fully relinquishing control over it. Of the 2,250 Congress deputies, 750 were to be elected; the rest (including Gorbachev himself) were to be appointed by the party hierarchy. Candidates for the electoral contests were to be nominated by organizations traditionally dominated by the Communist Party, such as the Communist Youth League and the official trade union organization. Gorbachev thus had good reason to believe that friendly communists would thoroughly dominate the new legislature. To his surprise, the nomination process sparked considerable participation by people eager for far more radical reform than Gorbachev was offering. The country became politically energized as 170 million people were given the right to vote in the first contested elections since 1917. Gorbachev's efforts to effect change from above had awakened long-dormant demands for change from below.

The results of the 1989 elections to the Congress were a shock to the Communist Party elite. Although approved party stalwarts, as anticipated, won the majority of contests, dozens of fairly prominent officials were humiliatingly beaten. In a number of races where an unpopular official ran unopposed, the candidates lost when a majority of voters took advantage of their right to vote against them. The winners included reform-minded party candidates as well as academics and others calling for more radical reforms. The most prominent winner of all was Yeltsin, who scored a resounding triumph in Moscow after being disgraced by Gorbachev for criticizing the government's feeble reform policies

(see later in this chapter). Another winner was Andrei Sakharov, the country's most famous physicist. Though credited with developing the Soviet hydrogen bomb in the Stalin years, Sakharov by the 1960s had stepped forward as a courageous proponent of Western-style democracy and human rights. The Brezhnev regime responded by exiling him to Gorky, a city off limits to foreign visitors. Gorbachev released him in 1986 in a bid to gain the support of Russia's intelligentsia. Soon after his release, Sakharov joined the chorus of those demanding more thoroughgoing democratic transformations, to Gorbachev's consternation. Though the leadership managed to keep his name off the ballot in the first round of the elections, he won a seat in the second round.

Gorbachev sought to put a positive spin on the results, but as subsequent events were to prove, the 1989 elections marked a major turning point in his administration. From this moment on, Gorbachev increasingly lost control over the reform process. Much of the party leadership and its bureaucratic apparatus, he admitted in retrospect, "did not immediately recognize that we would be operating under completely different conditions, that we had to learn to play by the new rules." With the possibilities of electoral choice and the freedoms of democratic expression now available to the population, denunciations of the communist system of one-party rule and central planning could only multiply and grow bolder. Demands for complete independence from the USSR would escalate in the Baltic states. Far more alarmingly, the winds of democratic change swirling in the Soviet Union could not help but have a devastating effect on the communist-run governments of Central and Eastern Europe. Within only a few hectic months, the emergence of democracy in the USSR would sweep away communist rule in the Soviet Union's hard-won postwar empire.

GORBACHEV'S FOREIGN POLICY

From its very beginnings, Gorbachev's policy of domestic reform had an important foreign policy component. One of the principal obstacles to economic growth and modernization in the Soviet economy was the stultifying effect of military spending, a burden whose true dimensions Gorbachev himself would learn only after becoming General Secretary. Under Brezhnev the military devoured a share of the budget and the country's national income far in excess of what military spending consumed in the United States and its NATO allies. The military got the lion's share of the country's high technology and operated its own industrial production facilities. Gorbachev knew that if the economy was to be rescued, he had to start by removing the dead weight of the Soviet military-industrial complex on the budgetary process and the powerful political influence of the high command. Changes of this sort inevitably required a radical reorientation in the Kremlin's policies toward the West.

One of Gorbachev's first decisions upon taking office was to remove Gromyko as foreign minister, the man whose incessant opposition to Western proposals had earned him the moniker "Mr. Nyet." Instead of reaching for an experienced diplomat, Gorbachev chose Eduard Shevardnadze, the Communist Party chief of the Soviet republic of Georgia, as his foreign minister. The two men had developed a close friendship in the years when Gorbachev governed in Stavropol, not far from the Georgian border. Their common aversion to the corruption and decay of the Brezhnev period drew them together. In 1984 they held a conversation in which Gorbachev agreed with Shevardnadze's remark, "Everything's rotten. It has to be changed."[27] In joining forces the following year they also reached quick agreement on the need to end the expensive arms race with the United States, replace Cold War hostilities with greater East-West cooperation, and bring the troops home from Afghanistan. Moscow's confrontationist foreign policy would now give way to "new thinking."

Considering that the Cold War had dominated international politics for forty years, it was extraordinary how rapidly the two contending superpowers resolved so many differences and transformed their relationship from nuclear-armed antagonism to negotiated cooperation and a growing measure of trust. A quick meeting between Gorbachev and President Ronald Reagan in 1985 broke the ice and established a personal rapport between the two leaders. Reagan had built his presidency around tough anti-Soviet rhetoric and a major arms buildup in response to Soviet military deployments in the Brezhnev years. His immediate affinity for Gorbachev as a potentially trustworthy negotiating partner created a breakthrough in East-West ties of historic proportions. When they met again a year later in Iceland, their negotiating teams discussed potential disarmament measures that would have been unthinkable in the pre-Gorbachev era.

The first major result of the heady new atmosphere came in December 1987, when the two sides agreed on the elimination of all the intermediate range missiles they had installed in the European theater in recent years (along with Soviet missiles facing Asia). Thus ended one of the most rancorous disputes of the Cold War. For the first time, the superpowers agreed to destroy hundreds of existing missiles, with each side permitting on-site inspection teams from the other side to verify compliance. In 1988, Gorbachev declared his intention of withdrawing all Soviet troops from Afghanistan in the following year (a goal achieved in February 1989) and announced plans to reduce the Soviet military by 500,000 troops within two years.

But it was in East-Central Europe that the Gorbachev phenomenon had its most unexpected consequences. After imposing communist party rule throughout the region following World War II, Moscow had reasserted its hegemony with armed force several times in the ensuing decades, intervening against popular manifestations of opposition to communism in East Germany in 1953, Hungary in 1956, and Czechoslovakia in 1968. The Soviets also stood solidly behind the Polish government when it imposed martial law in 1981. Though few people ever expected the Kremlin to surrender its hold over its European empire, Gorbachev hoped that the ruling communist parties in the area would replace their repressive, Brezhnev-style regimes with more pliable reform-oriented communists like himself. He also gave hints that the USSR would no longer intervene with troops to rescue communist regimes encountering opposition from their populations. He understood that military intervention in Central and Eastern Europe would abruptly snap his cooperative ties with the United States and its allies, cutting off the Soviet Union from potential economic cooperation and resuscitating the military's influence in Soviet politics.

The tumultuous East-Central European revolutions of 1989 began quietly enough. As the year got under way, Hungary's ruling communist party, whose reformist wing was even more radical than Gorbachev's, announced it would hold democratic, multi-party elections the following year. In April, shortly after the first elections to the Congress of People's Deputies in the Soviet Union, the Polish government completed eight weeks of intensive bargaining with representatives of the once-outlawed Solidarity organization. The "round-table agreement" committed the Polish communists to holding elections to a new parliament, with Solidarity permitted to compete for a minority of the lower house seats and all the upper house seats. When the elections were held in June, Solidarity swept into parliament, setting the stage for the complete replacement of communist rule in 1990 with the election of Lech Walesa, Solidarity's leader, as Poland's president.

By far the most dramatic transformation occurred in East Germany, where a hardline communist elite incensed at Gorbachev's reformism clung to power. As thousands of East Germans managed to flee to Western Europe in the summer and spontaneous demonstrations took place in East German cities in the following months, Moscow showed no readiness to support a military crackdown on a society in open revolt against communist power. In November, the East German authorities decided to open the Berlin wall, the fortress-like barrier that had prevented East Germans from traveling freely to West Germany for nearly thirty years. The opening released a surge of pent-up opposition to communism and a desire on the part of most East Germans to be united with West Germany. The communist state, once the most heavily guarded outpost of the Soviet Union's East-Central European empire, swiftly disintegrated, permitting the incorporation of eastern Germany into the Federal Republic of Germany in 1990.[28]

The East German example immediately inspired millions of Czechoslovaks to take to the streets of Prague to vent their anger against an equally anti-reformist communist dictatorship. With no signs of imminent assistance from Gorbachev, the Czechoslovak authorities quietly yielded power to democratic forces led by Vaclav Havel, the playwright who epitomized the country's courageous dissident movement. In December, scarcely a month after Czechoslovakia's "velvet revolution," demonstrators in Bucharest shouted down the country's tyrannical dictator, Nicolae Ceausescu, in the middle of a speech. He was immediately arrested by rivals within Romania's communist elite and executed. Meanwhile, the Soviet Union engineered a behind-the-scenes transfer of power in Bulgaria, replacing an aging communist autocrat with a more flexible party leadership.[29]

To the world's astonishment, the Soviet Union's reformist government had let East-Central Europe and the Warsaw Pact military alliance slip through its fingers, standing on the sidelines as a half-dozen countries went through one of the most sudden and widespread revolutions the world had ever seen. In the West, Gorbachev won universal acclaim and was awarded the Nobel Peace Prize. But at home, hardline critics of his reformist policies were mortified, while proponents of an even more radical reform course set the stage for the USSR's eventual disintegration.

THE USSR FALLS APART

As resistance to Gorbachev stiffened at all levels of the CPSU, Gorbachev sought to shift the locus of decision-making power in the Soviet Union from the party organs, over which he presided as General Secretary, to newly created state institutions like the Congress of People's Deputies. In March 1990 the Congress elected him to a new post as president of the Soviet Union. At no time, however, was Gorbachev ever elected to any of his positions by popular vote. His failure to obtain a mandate from the people was a significant factor in accelerating the collapse of his authority. Meanwhile, Gorbachev made no effort to establish a new party that might compete with the communists. Acting under the pressure of reformers calling for a real multiparty system in the Soviet Union, Gorbachev got the party hierarchy to adopt a commitment to "humane, democratic socialism." He also encouraged the Congress to amend the Soviet constitution by eliminating the provision guaranteeing the CPSU its monopoly of political power. But he remained reluctant to institute a multiparty system immediately, preferring instead to maintain the CPSU's dominance—and thus his own power—for an unspecified period of time.

Time, however, was running out on Gorbachev's efforts to reform a one-party system that was proving highly resistant to change. The public's patience was also wearing thin. In the summer of 1989, Soviet coal miners staged a wave of strikes that threatened the regime with the specter of working-class uprisings. In a chilling display of animosity the following year, tens of thousands of protesters marched behind the official May Day parade, bearing anti-Communist placards and loudly reviling Gorbachev and the Soviet leadership assembled atop the Kremlin wall. Utterly humiliated, the stunned party oligarchs quietly withdrew as the crowd chanted, "Shame! Shame!"

The economy continued to deteriorate. Lacking a clear policy vision, Gorbachev was caught in a tug-of-war between traditionalists who hoped to preserve the central planning system with as few alterations as possible, and an increasingly vocal chorus of radicals who believed that the system was incapable of being reformed and needed to be replaced by a market economy. In the summer of 1990 the pro-market camp published a detailed blueprint for a rapid transition to capitalism. Known as the "500 days" program, it called for the liberalization of prices for goods and services and the privatization of Soviet state-owned factories, farms, retail outlets, and other parts of the economy as swiftly as possible. The authors of the plan, acting on the advice of Western economists and government officials, argued that massive Western assistance could be obtained so as to ease the economic transition process. Gorbachev accepted the notion of introducing more market mechanisms into the Soviet economy, calling for a "regulated market economy," but he opposed adopting the 500-day plan's insistence on the wholesale replacement of the command economy and its argument that it had to be done in less than two years. The proposal was never adopted, but Gorbachev offered no concrete alternative. Attempts to forge a compromise between a market economy and central planning proved futile. His refusal to permit the privatization of Russia's collective farms was another major disappointment for the market-oriented reformers.[30]

An equally serious problem was the growth of independence movements in key Soviet republics. Gorbachev's democratization policies had mobilized the populations of Lithuania, Latvia, and Estonia to militate for independence, some fifty years after they were annexed by Stalin. Even Communist Party leaders in the Baltic states joined in the liberation movements. After elections held in 1990 brought pro-independence forces to power, Lithuania declared its independence and the other two states announced their intention to secede from the Soviet Union in the near future. Separatist movements also sprang up in Georgia, Armenia, and other Soviet republics. Far more ominously for Gorbachev, the Russian Republic, the largest and most populous part of the USSR, was also moving toward greater independence from the central government. In March 1990 Russia elected its own parliament. Two months later, Russian legislators elected Boris Yeltsin as the Russian Republic's top official in spite of Gorbachev's explicit opposition to the move. The Russian legislature then took the bold step of declaring that its laws superseded the laws of the Soviet Union within its territory, a flagrant repudiation of Gorbachev's central Soviet government.

Over the summer months of 1990, Ukraine and several other Soviet republics declared their sovereignty within the USSR. Gorbachev's efforts to halt the Soviet Union's progressive dismemberment proved futile. When Soviet military forces launched attacks in Latvia and Lithuania in early 1991, Gorbachev was roundly criticized in the west and the troops had to be withdrawn. As the Soviet president and CPSU chief gamely struggled to acquire new powers, prompting fears that he was planning a more assertive dictatorship, the USSR was crumbling beneath his feet.

In June 1991, the first popular elections ever held for president of Russia gave Boris Yeltsin a strong popular mandate to lead the Russian Republic. Yeltsin's victory added a powerful impetus to the fissiparous tendencies eating away at the USSR. It also gave him a popular legitimacy that Gorbachev, who never faced the voters, could not claim. Gorbachev worked assiduously to negotiate an agreement with most of the constituent republics of the USSR to establish a new set of ground rules for the Soviet Union. With the final draft completed, he set off on a fateful vacation in the Crimea in early August.

THE 1991 COUP AND ITS AFTERMATH

Gorbachev and his family knew that something was amiss when they were informed that a group of uninvited senior officials had arrived at the Soviet president's lavish vacation retreat. Before receiving the visitors, Gorbachev picked up the phone to call the head of the KGB in Moscow, Vladimr Kryuchkov, only to find the telephone lines cut off. Kryuchkov was in fact the ringleader

of a plot to remove Gorbachev from power and reimpose a stern Communist Party dictatorship. The delegation sent to the Crimea by the conspirators instructed Gorbachev to sign a decree declaring a state of emergency throughout the USSR and urged him to resign. According to his own account, Gorbachev refused both ultimata.

From August 18 to 21, the Gorbachevs were prisoners in their official *dacha* (country house); armed guards patrolled the grounds, Soviet warships cruised into the neighboring bay, all communication links were broken. In addition to Kryushkov, the small band of conspirators included some of the most powerful officials in the Soviet government: the vice president, prime minister, defense minister, interior minister, the head of Soviet ground forces, the head of the military-industrial complex, Gorbachev's chief of staff, the chief of his personal security detail, and a few others. But right from the outset, the coup attempt went awry.

On the morning of August 19, a statement issued by the plotters was read over the radio, informing the population that Gorbachev's reforms had led them into a blind alley and that the country was sinking into a quagmire of lawlessness and immorality. On hearing the news, Russia's President Yeltsin rushed to the White House, the home of the Russian parliament. Mounting one of the tanks the plotters had ordered into downtown Moscow, Yeltsin denounced the coup as illegal and called on the citizens of Russia to oppose it. Together with a group of Russian officials, he then ensconced himself in the White House while barricades went up outside its doors. At noon he went on radio and appealed to Soviet military forces to refrain from shedding blood. Within a few hours some 25,000 people were forming a protective phalanx outside the parliament. Yeltsin called for a general strike of the whole population.

The coup then unraveled like a bizarre comedy. One of the plotters called a televised press conference only to be bombarded with embarrassing questions. Clearly rattled, his hands shook visibly as his answers were greeted with derision. Another plotter, the prime minister, was completely drunk. The next day, Yeltsin addressed 100,000 people from the White House balcony, and the crowds surrounding the barricades grew larger. Soviet generals and KGB leaders met to discuss how to disperse the throng, but the high command was divided: a number of commanders and other officers were clearly reluctant to attack the civilians in front of the White House. Later that evening, the plotters made the crucial decision to back away from the use of force. At 3 A.M. the KGB chief called the White House to inform Yeltsin that the coup was over.

On August 21, a Russian government delegation went to the Crimea to escort Gorbachev and his weary family home. Both his wife and his daughter suffered nervous disorders as a result of their ordeal. The plotters were arrested, with the exception of two who committed suicide. (All were eventually released without being convicted in court.) On arriving in Moscow, Gorbachev found himself in "a new country": for the first time in their history, Russian citizens had openly defied the coercive power of the state and won a victory for democracy.[31]

For Gorbachev himself, the end of his extraordinary run in office was at hand. Over the next several months, Yeltsin took full advantage of his enormous popularity and orchestrated the final disintegration of the Union of Soviet Socialist Republics. On December 25, Gorbachev resigned the presidency of a country that was about to expire. As the bells tolled midnight on December 31, the USSR formally ceased to exist. Looking back on his experience several years later, Gorbachev wrote, "I never for a moment thought that the transformations I had initiated, no matter how far-reaching, would result in the replacement of the rule of the 'reds' by that of the 'whites'." With the failure of his attempt to reform Soviet communism, the fate of Russia now passed into non-communist hands for the first time since the October Revolution seventy-four years earlier.[32]

Gorbachev's Legacy Unquestionably, Gorbachev left office having granted the Russian people far more freedom than they had ever before enjoyed. Greater freedom of speech and the ability to criticize the ruling authorities without fear of violent retribution; growing freedom of political association and opportunities to vote in competitive elections; freedom of religious worship; freedom to leave the country; freedom to own private property and start a business—these and other liberties that emerged in the course of Gorbachev's tenure, however limited in scope, would have been unimaginable under previous Communist leaders. Most of the *political* liberties Gorbachev permitted (as opposed to the economic liberties) were in fact unprecedented in Russian history, if one regards the few brief months of constitutional democracy under the Provisional Government in 1917 as but a momentary aberration. Gorbachev's efforts to create the bases of a "law-bound state" represented an attempt to hold state officials to the rule of law, another concept virtually without precedent in Russia's long, tortured history. His decision to end the Cold War,

resulting in the extraordinary collapse of Soviet-imposed communist rule in East-Central Europe and the sudden retrenchment of Soviet military power, was quite probably the single most important development in international politics in the second half of the twentieth century.

And yet, while Gorbachev's place in history as one of the greatest political reformers of the modern world is secure, no account of his leadership would be accurate without a reminder of the limitations of his initiatives. To the very end of his incumbency, Gorbachev bore indelible markings of the authoritarian Communist Party system that had nurtured his political career. While trying to remold the CPSU apparatus, he never broke entirely free of it. The country's main political and economic decisions were still made by a handful of unelected officials and implemented by the vast party-controlled administrative machinery. Gorbachev made no serious attempt to subject himself or the nomenklatura to precisely defined laws guaranteeing their public accountability, not even when it was clear that the apparatus was blocking his reforms.

Competitive elections were tightly restricted, and the party leadership worked hard to discourage the nomination or election of undesirable candidates, employing techniques that would have to be condemned as improper in any true democracy. Gorbachev himself never submitted his own candidacy to the voters' judgment. Although he spoke of instituting a multiparty system in the "next phase" of the reform process, he did not commit himself to a specified timetable but insisted that party pluralism should not come "all at once."[33] He vigorously opposed new parties established to challenge the CPSU's monopoly of power. Though he treated Soviet citizens to the unheard-of spectacle of televised debates between party officials and their challengers, Gorbachev presided magisterially over party meetings and the newly created parliamentary bodies, at times subjecting critical speakers to strict time limitations and sharp retorts. The principle of freedom of speech was never fully codified into law. Gorbachev's economic reforms were just as restricted as his political reforms, carefully calibrated to retain the party's ultimate control over the country and, not incidentally, his own primacy within the party.

In sum, Gorbachev's policies triggered a real revolution in Russian politics, but it was an unintended revolution. It was a revolution pushed forward by the forces of mass democracy and elite disarray that he had unleashed but could not rein in. Gorbachev's abiding aims were to humanize the tyrannical neo-Stalinist political system he inherited, not destroy Communist Party dominance; to revitalize the creaky central planning system, not replace it with capitalism; to restore the USSR's power in the world, not lose it. In his heart of hearts, Gorbachev was a *reformer,* not a revolutionary. Perhaps no one better understood the limitations of Gorbachev's approach more deeply, or suffered from them more painfully, than the man who would rise as his most vocal challenger and ultimate successor: Boris Yeltsin.

PROFILE: Boris Yeltsin

"A sickening deathly silence fell on the entire assembly," Yeltsin recalled. "In that silence . . . I walked straight forward, looking Gorbachev right in the eye. Every step reverberated within my soul. I could feel the breathing of more than five thousand people, every one of them staring at me. Reaching the presidium, I climbed three steps, approached Gorbachev . . . and, staring at him, said in a firm voice, 'I demand to be allowed to speak.' "

The shocking scene, broadcast live on Soviet television, took place at a special Communist Party conference summoned by Gorbachev in early summer 1988. Ostensibly, Gorbachev had called the conference "to make perestroika irreversible," a euphemism for his attempt to compel obstructionists within the party to submit to his political and economic reforms. Little did he know that his main antagonist would be none other than Yeltsin, who would berate him for not pushing reform fast enough. Only a few weeks earlier, Yeltsin appeared to be politically dead, his attempts to criticize Gorbachev decisively silenced. His appearance at the 1988 party conference was something Gorbachev and his chief lieutenants had labored strenuously to prevent. Their inability to do so was another sign that the reform process was spinning out of control. As events were to demonstrate, Yeltsin would use his unanticipated conference appearance as a springboard to political power, stepping forward as the main focal point for all those dissatisfied with the slow pace of reform.

Like Gorbachev, Yeltsin was born in 1931 into a peasant family. The Yeltsins came from a village near Ekatar-

inburg, the Ural mountain city where Tsar Nicholas II and his family were assassinated by the Bolsheviks. The Soviets renamed the city after Yacob Sverdlov, a Bolshevik, and it was in Sverdlovsk province that Yeltsin was to spend the first fifty-five years of his life. He passed his childhood in grueling poverty. His family shared a barrackslike hut with several other families, sleeping on the floor curled up against a goat for warmth. Yeltsin's father was a construction worker with a temper—and a strap—that were easily provoked by young Boris's pranks. At the height of Stalin's terror in 1937, the elder Yeltsin was arrested and detained for several months, an event that six-year-old Boris never forgot. Despite the frigid winters and fierce living conditions, Boris excelled at school and was voted class leader. In a characteristically bold move he lambasted an unpopular teacher in an impromptu graduation day speech, earning immediate expulsion without a diploma and another severe lashing from his father. But he doggedly talked the local authorities into investigating the situation, getting his diploma restored and the teacher fired.

Whereas Gorbachev got an early introduction to life in Moscow as a law student, Yeltsin remained in the provinces and obtained a civil engineering degree at the Urals Polytechnic Institute. He saw a good bit of the Soviet Union on a makeshift summer vacation trip, riding atop railway cars and scrounging enough food to keep him going. After graduating in 1955 with straight As and a reputation as a fierce volleyball competitor, Yeltsin took a year to learn carpentry and other construction trades, then worked his way up to the post of chief engineer at local state-run construction enterprises. His garrulous nature and political instincts induced him to get involved in the local Communist Party leadership, and in 1976 he was invited to Moscow to take a course for party functionaries. While the course was in progress he was unexpectedly summoned to meet with high-ranking party leaders, including Brezhnev. The CPSU brass had decided to appoint Yeltsin party chief of Sverdlovsk, in effect making him the most powerful political official in the region.

Yeltsin plunged into the job with intense energy, working long hours and assuming chief responsibility for the regional economy. Sverdlovsk was the USSR's third largest industrial center, and Yeltsin quietly built up a reputation as one of the Communist Party's most successful local leaders. It was during his ten-year stint in this post that he met Gorbachev, who held a similar leadership position in Stavropol. He also acquired a firsthand view of the Brezhnev regime's inattention to the population's needs and the corruption that poisoned the closed world of the privileged party elite.

Despite his success, Yeltsin was surprised in the spring of 1985 when the newly ensconced Gorbachev team called him to Moscow and named him chief of the CPSU Central Committee's section overseeing the Soviet construction industry. Though the post was an important one, Yeltsin initially declined, preferring instead to remain in his native Sverdlovsk rather than uproot his family. But he was given no choice in the matter, and his fateful involvement in the highest reaches of the Soviet political establishment now began. At the end of the year, Gorbachev and his top aides handed him a considerably more important assignment, naming him chief of the party's Moscow city organization. In effect, Yeltsin was given authority to govern the country's capital city, a position of considerable political responsibility. With more than a million party members, many of them bureaucrats, Moscow was the showpiece of Soviet communism and the hub of its highly centralized political system. Inevitably, it was tasked to play a critical role in promoting Gorbachev's reform policies, showing the Soviet population and the outside world that real change was at last taking place in the USSR.

Once again, Yeltsin vigorously charged into his assignment, working eighteen-hour days and immersing himself in the daily life of the city. He rode subways with ordinary citizens and poked into stores to check on supplies. He railed against the privileges of the party elite, who had their pick of special shops, hospitals, cars, tailors, trips abroad, and other perquisites of power that the mass of Soviet citizens could only dream about. He exposed the theft of food supplies and other corrupt practices perpetrated by officials and their friends in the city's mafia-like criminal underground. He encouraged muckraking journalistic exposes and met with newly formed political opposition groups. He even took Diane Sawyer of the American television news show *60 Minutes* on a tour of Moscow stores, enabling millions of television viewers in the West to share his outrage at empty shelves and long lines of frustrated shoppers. Convinced that the local party apparatus was riddled with inefficiency and corruption, he fired half its members.

In the process, he became increasingly critical of Gorbachev, viewing him as vague and indecisive. In Yeltsin's opinion, Gorbachev had failed to elaborate a clear long-term strategy for perestroika and was too reticent to take on the party and state bureaucrats who had dug in their heels in bitter resistance to any kind of reform. Gorbachev and his closest adjutants, in turn, came to view Yeltsin as too independent and outspoken to be tolerated much longer. After a sharp clash at a Politburo meeting in 1987, Yeltsin submitted his resignation. Gorbachev did not act on it until the next meeting of the party Central Committee, where another angry exchange of views appeared to seal Yeltsin's fate. In a sharp break with precedent, which dictated the Com-

mittee's rubber-stamp approval of the leadership's policies, Yeltsin delivered a stinging critique of the party's failure to implement a concrete reform program. Even more provocatively, he accused Gorbachev of indulging in his own "personality cult" and vehemently attacked the party's number two leader, Yegor Ligachev, for obstructing the reform process. Yeltsin's attack, which sprang from his admittedly "difficult" nature and his determination to speak his mind, was immediately repudiated by a succession of Central Committee members, including Gorbachev and Ligachev.

Though transcripts of the meeting remained secret for more than a year, rumors of what had transpired soon circulated in the world press. Battered by exhaustion and stress, Yeltsin was hospitalized with chest pains. Gorbachev summoned him from his sick bed to a meeting of the Moscow party organization, where Yeltsin had to endure another stream of vitriolic denunciations by party officials. Gorbachev thereupon dismissed Yeltsin from his Moscow post and demoted him to deputy chairman of the construction ministry, a humiliatingly subordinate position. At this juncture, Yeltsin considered himself a political corpse.

Seven months were to elapse before Yeltsin got a chance to express himself at the 1988 Party Conference described at the start of this biographical profile. Gorbachev's lieutenants had worked diligently behind the scenes to prevent Yeltsin's selection as a conference delegate, but his supporters in the party managed to win him a seat. When his requests to address the assembly were ignored, Yeltsin then decided to "take the rostrum by storm," marching straight up to the dais demanding to be heard. After Gorbachev finally relented, Yeltsin resumed his earlier attacks on the party apparatus as a nest of corruption and a bastion of opposition to real reform, fully realizing that most of his listeners in the hall were the very people he was attacking. "The rottenness has surely gone deeper than many people suppose," he asserted, taking the Gorbachev leadership to task for preventing critical voices within the party from being heard. For millions of Soviet citizens glued to their television screens, the image of a party leader openly vilifying the most powerful official in the country—and the Communist Party itself—was truly astonishing. Though Gorbachev and other speakers followed Yeltsin with stern criticisms of his views, Yeltsin emerged from the meeting with an international reputation as the most vocal advocate of radical reform in the USSR. He would have to spend almost another year in political limbo, however, before being heard once again.

His next chance came in February 1989 as the process of nominating candidates for elections to the Congress of People's Deputies got under way. Though 750 out of the 2,250 Congress representatives were to be elected in open contests, the Communist Party did everything in its power to prevent radicals like Yeltsin from getting nominated. Yeltsin himself was subjected to constant obloquy in the party press and at public meetings. In a thirteen-hour candidates' meeting at which he was harangued by party loyalists, Yeltsin bluntly answered every question put to him and secured his nomination for the seat representing Moscow by a substantial majority. In the election campaign that followed, Yeltsin won the lion's share of coverage by the international media but had to fend off a smear campaign orchestrated by party authorities. His populist message calling for an end to the elite's privileges, a faster pace of reform, and the possibility of a multiparty system struck a responsive chord in the Moscow electorate, however. Thousands of people staged demonstrations in his behalf, another novelty in Russia. On election day he captured more than 5.1 million votes, 89.6 percent of the total, soundly thrashing his Gorbachev-backed opponent. The party hierarchy displayed its pique by refraining from reporting Yeltsin's victory in its main newspaper, *Pravda*.

The Congress completed its first ten-day session with Gorbachev and the party elite in control, but Yeltsin's improbable political comeback and his prominence as a lightning rod for more radical reform caused the CPSU leadership worsening headaches. Their next attempt to block his progress backfired when they endeavored to prevent him from being elected to the Supreme Soviet, a smaller parliamentary body chosen by Congress deputies to legislate when the Congress was not in session. A pro-Yeltsin deputy yielded his place in the Supreme Soviet, and Yeltsin remained in the legislative limelight. Yeltsin was also instrumental in forming the Inter-Regional Group of Deputies, the first serious organized challenge to the Communist Party.[34]

It was in the USSR's Russian republic that Yeltsin made his next, most decisive, moves. One year after the elections to the USSR Congress of People's Deputies, the various constituent republics of the Soviet Union elected their own parliaments. Official Communist Party candidates fared badly; radical reformers won half the seats in Russia's Congress, an ominous sign for Gorbachev. The new Russian Supreme Soviet was also evenly balanced. When Yeltsin ran for the Supreme Soviet's presidency in the spring of 1990, Gorbachev once again pulled out all the stops to halt his rival's advance, intervening personally with a speech urging the delegates to vote against him. Two ballots were held with no clear victor, while thousands of pro-Yeltsin demonstrators chanted their support outside. On the third ballot Yeltsin defeated his main opponent, in effect becoming

Russia's president. A week later, the Russian parliament declared that its laws would henceforward take precedence over Soviet laws throughout the Russian republic. This historic decision laid down a direct challenge to the authority of the Soviet government and to Gorbachev personally. Yeltsin followed up this maneuver by dramatically announcing his resignation from the Communist Party at its Twenty-Eighth Congress. From this point on, Yeltsin and Gorbachev were on a collision course that threatened the very survival of the centralized Soviet state.

Yeltsin's ascendancy won another boost in June 1991 when he went before the people in the first-ever popular election to Russia's presidency. Not content with his election by a small group of legislators the previous year, Yeltsin wanted validation by as many Russian citizens as possible. Deftly playing upon mounting dissatisfaction with Gorbachev's ineffectiveness, he won a convincing 57.3 percent of the vote, besting five rivals. (Turnout was 75 percent.) Yeltsin's inauguration ceremonies highlighted his newfound attachment to the Russian Orthodox church, with the patriarch bestowing a special blessing on the newly elected president.

The sudden reversal in Yeltsin's political fortunes took another upward swerve only a few months later, when he boldly defied the plot to unseat Gorbachev in a coup d'état. Curiously, in a book published before that pivotal event, Yeltsin reported that rumors were already circulating about a possible coup to be staged by hardliners eager to remove Gorbachev from the CPSU leadership. Prophesying that Gorbachev's indecisiveness would eventually be his downfall, Yeltsin asserted that he would nevertheless support Gorbachev if a coup were attempted. "Yes, I shall fight for him," he wrote, "my perpetual opponent, the lover of half-measures and half-steps." Gorbachev, for all his faults, was infinitely preferable to the Brezhnevite old guard. Once the actual coup took place, Yeltsin resisted the plotters in Gorbachev's behalf, but moved quickly to press his advantage over Gorbachev as the plotters' most visible opponent. When Gorbachev sought to explain himself before the Russian parliament several days after the coup collapsed, Yeltsin demonstratively rebuked him.

Over the next several months, as Gorbachev's personal authority drained away, Yeltsin worked frenetically to dismantle the last vestiges of the Soviet leader's power by dismantling the Soviet Union itself. In December, Russia signed an accord with Ukraine and Belarus establishing a new association outside the framework of the Union of Soviet Socialist Republics. Eight other Soviet republics soon joined them in the Commonwealth of Independent States. Each member of the CIS agreed to respect the sovereign independence of all the others.

With the Soviet state over which he presided now a legal fiction, Gorbachev resigned as president of the USSR on December 25. A few days later, when he returned to his Kremlin office to remove his effects, he found Yeltsin already in his place.[35]

On January 1, 1992, the Russian Federation formally entered the world as an independent country under President Boris Yeltsin.

BORIS YELTSIN'S RUSSIA

Transforming the Economy   Yeltsin and his advisors wasted no time in their attempts to transform Russia's economy from a largely state-run operation to a mixed economy with market mechanisms. To some extent they were guided by prescriptions offered by Western economists calling for a rapid "shock therapy" approach to restructuring the economy. Advocates of shock therapy—or the "big bang," as some called it—argued that it would be better to change the economic system all at once rather than in a piecemeal process stretched out over a long period of time. They advised the Russian government to free prices from state controls immediately, allowing the market forces of supply and demand, rather than bureaucrats, to determine the prices and allocation of goods and services. They also called for the elimination of wasteful government subsidies to unprofitable state-owned companies, letting them go bankrupt so that more successful, privately funded companies could take their place. They insisted that the national budget be brought closer into balance, a move that would require sharp cuts in government spending. And they advised the Kremlin to permit the ruble to be traded freely in world currency markets so as to facilitate foreign investment. Proponents of shock therapy readily acknowledged that these and other recommended changes were bound to cause severe hardships, such as inflation and massive unemployment. But they argued that the sooner the Russian economy accepted these short-term pains, the sooner it would reap long-term gains. To help Russia cope with the anticipated difficulties, they appealed to the International Monetary Fund, the World Bank, the United States, Western Europe, and Japan to provide generous financial assistance so that the Russian government would be in a position to compensate pensioners, the unemployed, and other people likely to be devastated by the convulsive transformation process in the short and medium terms. Variants of shock therapy were already under way in Poland and the Czech Republic.

While several of Yeltsin's key advisors saw merit in the shock therapy blueprint, quite a few economists and political leaders feared that an excessively rapid and all-encompassing transformation program might trigger social disruptions and political instability. After all, the task of switching from a state-controlled planning system to a more variegated economy with substantial private enterprise was historically unprecedented. Neither Russia nor the former communist states of East-Central Europe engaged in such a switch could accurately predict its outcome. Moreover, the political forces arrayed against the rapid demolition of the communist state planning system were still quite powerful. Yeltsin's government therefore began with a partial approach to shock therapy, adopting bits and pieces of the shock therapists' guidelines rather than their entire program. Even so, Yeltsin's initial measures went considerably farther than Gorbachev's, and their effects were shocking enough for many Russians.[36]

On January 2, 1992, the day after Russia formally became an independent state, the government removed price controls on a host of products and lifted wage controls on various job categories. The new administration also announced substantial cuts for military spending and other items in an effort to reduce the government's budget deficit. Several months later it declared the convertibility of the ruble, permitting it to be exchanged into other denominations in world currency markets. Most important, over the course of its first year in power the new Russian government unveiled an ambitious privatization timetable. Half the state's large and medium-sized companies were expected to be privatized by 1995, and all state-owned small industries and consumer services and a considerable portion of the nation's housing were to be in private hands by 1994.

In the fall of 1992, the government began distributing vouchers to every man, woman, and child in Russia—some 148 million people. The vouchers, which Yeltsin touted as the "ticket for each of us to a free economy," were investment securities designed to give ordinary Russians a stake in the newly emerging private sector. Initially valued at about $66 each, the equivalent of several months' average pay, they could be swapped for stock in private firms, bought and sold at market prices, or invested in special funds set up to finance private enterprises. The government hoped that people would understand the vouchers' investment value and expected their market price to rise over time, providing growing amounts of money for the creation and development of private companies while bringing real financial returns to investors. (The Czech Republic adopted its own voucher scheme with some success.) A related decision permitted workers in state-owned firms to buy a controlling 51 percent share in the companies where they worked. Together these policies were intended to lay the foundations for a "people's capitalism" in the new Russia. "We need millions of owners," Yeltsin said, "rather than a handful of millionaires."

From the outset, the Yeltsin government's economic initiatives failed to meet the expectations of the optimists in the president's entourage. With the removal of price controls and with the government's failure to rein in the printing of rubles by Russia's central bank, inflation soared soared 20 to 30 percent per month, finishing out 1992 at 2,500 percent for the year. Though more food and other goods began appearing on store shelves, prices were too high for many Russians, long habituated under the old central planning system to cheap government-subsidized prices for milk, bread, and other staples. The disjointed nature of the transition process, with a large number of nearly bankrupt state-owned firms continuing to dominate the economy while private companies were still in the process of getting organized, created severe dislocations in the production process. Gross domestic product in 1992 was 18.5 percent lower than in the previous year and plummeted another 12 percent in 1993.

The Russian government's budget deficits bulged to as much as 20 percent of GDP, a figure more than double the IMF's recommended target. An early political compromise with the managers who directed the public sector of the economy resulted in a greater effusion of money for insolvent state-owned companies than the government could afford. The government lacked the funds to pay millions of people employed in the state sector, while pensions fell far behind the galloping price increases. Unemployment grew to more than 150,000 in 1992, a far cry from the zero unemployment the old communist regime used to boast. Russian economists voiced fears that the expected wave of bankruptcies of state-owned companies might boost unemployment to more than 4 million within a year or two.

Although 144 million Russians claimed their vouchers, many failed to understand what they were all about or simply did not believe they were worth very much. Some sold them cheaply or simply gave them away, with shrewd investors and insiders acquiring a disproportionately large share. Even though more than 60 million Russians invested their vouchers in the privatization process, very few made any money from their investment and the value of the vouchers actually fell as the inflation rate soared. Meanwhile, a growing number of unsuspecting people were lured without adequate government warnings or safeguards into pyramid schemes or other financial frauds promising instant riches, only to lose their meager fortunes to crooks. On the international scene, the ruble quickly sank relative to stronger currencies, while the IMF imposed stringent conditions on the Russian government's budgetary spending and money-printing policies, insisting on stern anti-inflationary measures and a rapid privatization process.

The dislocations engendered by the economic transformation only worsened living standards for most Russians, already reeling from years of decline under Brezhnev and the economic crisis produced by Gorbachev's halfhearted reforms. By the fall of 1993, Russians had experienced an 86 percent drop in household wealth over the previous three years. In a poll taken in early 1994, 33 percent said they were "bad off" and 28 percent claimed they were living in "intolerable poverty"; only 8 percent said they were well off. Statistics released by the Labor Ministry later in the year revealed that 24 million people—more than 16 percent of the population—lived below the government's official poverty line, a subsistence level of $1 to $2 a day. In stark contrast, a small minority of ambitious capitalists, some of them with exceptional political connections or ties to criminal elements, reaped overnight fortunes, resulting in a widening gap between rich and poor. By the summer of 1994, the richest 10 percent of the population earned 23 percent of incomes, while the poorest 10 percent earned only 3 percent of incomes.

The stresses of economic change and uncertainty took a visible toll on public health. Life expectancy for males fell from 65 years in 1987 to 62 in 1992 and 59 in 1994. For women it fell from 74 in 1985 to 73 in 1994. Alcoholism and smoking were commonplace. Deaths due to heart attacks or strokes were double the rate prevailing in the United States, while the death rate for infants and children in Russia was two to three times the rates applying in the West. Strikingly, suicides rose 50 percent between 1990 and 1993, while the number of births in 1992 was only a third of the 1988 level. The incidence of cancer, tuberculosis, typhus, and other debilitating diseases multiplied considerably in the first half of the 1990s as government spending on health care was down to only 4 percent of GNP (compared with 8 percent to 12 percent in the West). Harmful levels of air, water, and soil pollution—another legacy of Soviet communism—added to Russia's health hazards.[37]

On top of all this, the Yeltsin administration did not do an effective job communicating with the public about what to expect from the reform process. Its optimistic predictions were often hammered by harsh realities. It was not surprising that support for market reforms and even for democracy itself began to dissipate during Yeltsin's first years as president of independent Russia. By August 1992, only 42 percent of Muscovites identified themselves as part of the "democratic camp," down from 62 percent following the previous year's coup attempt against Gorbachev. Less than two years later, only 25 percent of Russians said they favored market reforms, compared with 40 percent in 1989; a majority described privatization as "legalized theft."

Nevertheless, the Yeltsin government persevered in its reform course. By the end of its first year, some 20 percent of the population lived off the private sector. Less than two years later, half the work force was employed by private enterprise, while 70 percent of Russian industry was privatized and over a million small businesses were in operation. It was the *political* aspect of economic reform that was to cause Yeltsin more headaches than the privatization process per se.

The Politics of Reform   On assuming control of the newly independent Russian state, Yeltsin inherited the legislature that had been elected in the Russian part of the Soviet Union in March 1990, a time when the Communist Party of the Soviet Union still dominated the Soviet political system. Of 1,046 deputies elected to Russia's Congress of People's Deputies that year, only about a hundred were strongly committed to Yeltsin's vision of radical economic transformation, with perhaps another 150 willing to support Yeltsin fairly consistently. Divided into as many as seventeen factions, the Congress included more than 350 hardliners opposed to the wholesale dismantling of the state-controlled economic system. Another 350 deputies were centrists who were prepared to go along with a modicum of privatization, as long as the state retained an important role in economic decision making and as long as Soviet-era managers and bureaucrats acquired a large share of the ownership and direction of privatized firms. Somewhat more than 200 delegates were not entirely sure of their position and were prone to shift back and forth between pro-market and pro-state orientations. Yeltsin's powers as Russia's president, moreover, were rather limited compared to those of the Congress under the constitutional provisions prevailing at the time of the Soviet Union's dissolution at the end of 1992.

Starting in the very first year of Russia's independence, Yeltsin was forced to temper his reformist zeal in order to placate the opponents of a far-reaching market-oriented economic transformation. In June 1992, he appointed **Yegor Gaidar,** a thirty-five-year-old market economist, as acting prime minister. (Until then, President Yeltsin had served as his own prime minister, with Gaidar serving as deputy prime minister.) Gaidar advocated a radical restructuring of the economy, adopting a modified version of shock therapy. Though he was willing to make concessions to state bureaucrats anxious to preserve their jobs and power, his determination to make the privatization process irreversible as quickly as possible antagonized more conservative forces. In December 1992 the anti-reform majority in the Congress pressured Yeltsin to jettison his young prime minister.[38]

In Gaidar's place Yeltsin appointed **Victor Chernomyrdin,** a figure from the Soviet period who had served as the USSR's minister for the natural gas industry since 1982. Chernomyrdin at first attempted to assuage the conservatives by reimposing price controls, but he subsequently withdrew them. On the whole he favored market reforms and the privatization process, much to the conservatives' dismay. But he preferred a slower pace than Gaidar's and retained a certain nostalgia for a strong role for the state in the national economy and continuing subsidies for key industries, especially his own bailiwick, the powerful energy sector. To counterbalance Chernomyrdin's moderation and to retain the favor of more radical reformers, Yeltsin appointed Boris Fedorov, an economist even more devoted to market reforms and tight monetary policy than Gaidar, as finance minister and deputy prime minister. He also retained Anatoly Chubais, another young reformer, as privatization minister, a post he had occupied since the start of Yeltsin's transformation process.

The clash between President Yeltsin and his anti-reform opponents escalated throughout 1992 and 1993. Restive legislators sought to impeach Yeltsin, while the president threatened to rule by decree and demanded the adoption of a new constitution giving him stronger governing powers. In April 1992 a referendum gave Yeltsin a boost of popular approval. Some 58 percent of those who turned out to vote expressed their confidence in him, while 53 percent approved of his government's policies. Two-thirds of those voting approved of early parliamentary elections, while less than half wanted early presidential elections. Armed with these results and infuriated at the conservatives' obstructive tactics, Yeltsin dissolved the legislature in September and ordered new parliamentary elections to be held three months later. Yeltsin admitted that his action violated the existing constitution, but he insisted that the April referendum gave him the right to take extraordinary measures to break the country's political gridlock. Incensed at Yeltsin's breach of constitutional authority, conservative politicians declared that Yeltsin was no longer the legitimate

president of Russia and barricaded themselves in the White House, the legislature's home. They named one of their leaders, Vice President Alexander Rutskoi, as Russia's new president.

With no signs of compromise, the crisis threatened to crack the fragile foundations of Russian democracy. After eleven days of confrontation, Rutskoi ordered thousands of anti-Yeltsin demonstrators to storm the state-owned television station, a beacon of pro-Yeltsin propaganda. Fortified with assault weapons and waving Communist Party flags, the crowd next marched on the Moscow mayor's office.

Yeltsin responded to the violent provocation the next day, October 4, by ordering a military attack on the White House. Members of the military high command debated what to do upon receiving their orders, and leading generals decided to support Yeltsin as the only duly elected president of the country. The operation was quick and effective: Rutskoi and others ensconced in the White House were arrested and parts of the building were set ablaze. More than 100 people were killed in the fracas, with hundreds more wounded.

Yeltsin declared a state of emergency, imposed censorship, and reaffirmed his plan to set new legislative elections for December. The Russian people would also be asked to vote on a new constitution prepared under his direction. In a marked display of anger at Russia's Constitutional Court, which had declared his dissolution of the legislature illegal, Yeltsin pressured the chief justice to resign and summarily fired the court. These actions added fuel to the fire of those who regarded Yeltsin as a power-hungry authoritarian. Not only antagonists like Gorbachev and other communists held this view, but proponents of democracy both in Russia and around the world increasingly wondered if Yeltsin perhaps remained a communist-style dictator at heart.

The 1993 Elections and Constitutional Referendum The parliamentary elections and constitutional referendum held on December 12, 1993, brought 55 percent of Russia's 106 million eligible voters to the polls. They returned a mixed result for President Yeltsin. On the positive side, they overwhelmingly approved Yeltsin's proposed constitution, with 58.4 percent of the turnout voting in its favor. The new charter created a dual executive modeled on the French constitution, with a politically active president sharing power with a prime minister. The bicameral legislature, as in France, was kept relatively weak. (We'll discuss the constitution's provisions later in the chapter.)

The vote for the new lower house, the State Duma, was considerably less satisfactory from Yeltsin's point of view. The electoral system involved a combination of proportional representation (with a 5 percent hurdle) and single-member districts: half the Duma's 450 seats were elected under PR and the other half under the SMD/plurality system. (See chapter 9 for a description of these electoral systems.) Thirteen parties fielded candidates, most of them fairly new.

Shockingly, the party to emerge with the largest share of the popular vote was the **Liberal Democratic Party (LDP)**, an arch-nationalist grouping under the leadership of **Vladimir Zhirinovsky**, a flamboyant right-winger with outrageously chauvinistic views. Denouncing the West for "bringing Russia to its knees," Zhirinovsky spurned the advice of Western economists and issued crude threats that left observers wondering whether he was a warmonger or a buffoon. He threatened, if elected, to reestablish the Russian empire throughout the former USSR and Eastern Europe, establish colonies on the Indian Ocean, use nuclear weapons against Germany, blow radiation into the Baltic states with giant fans, shoot down U.S. weapons in space, invade Turkey, and reclaim Alaska. Zhirinovsky also defamed Jews while praising Hitler and Saddam Hussein, though it was later revealed that he had Jewish roots. The LDP ended up with 23 percent of the PR vote and sixty-four seats.

Another determined foe of Yeltsin's economic policies was the **Communist Party of the Russian Federation (CPRF**; also known as the **Russian Communist Party**, or **RCP).** Led by **Gennady Zyuganov**, a party apparatchik since the 1960s, the Communists opposed the rapid economic transformation process but offered no clear alternative program. Professing their acceptance of democracy, they blasted Yeltsin for abusing his authority. Although they had the largest party organization in the country, they captured a modest 12.4 percent of the PR vote and won only forty-one seats, a con-

vincing sign that most Russians wanted nothing more to do with communism.

A close ally of the Communists was the **Agrarian Party,** a new party organized to represent the interests of Russia's collective farmers, many of whom were worried about their future in a country headed toward private agriculture. Only 4 percent of Russia's arable land was privatized at the time, but Yeltsin had issued a decree just before the elections allowing a general privatization of farmland. The Agrarians won sixteen Duma seats.

The most outspokenly pro-reform party was **Russia's Choice**, led by a number of prominent figures connected with Yeltsin's reform government, including Gaidar, Fedorov, and Chubais. Though it entered the elections with high hopes, Russia's Choice garnered a disappointing 15.5 percent of the PR vote and only sixty-five seats in the Duma.[39]

Quite a few voters gravitated instead to moderate parties that were favorable to economic reform in principle but opposed to the accelerated tempo of Gaider's variant of shock therapy. The most successful was **Yabloko,** a party whose name derived from **Grigory Yavlinsky** and two other cofounders. (*Yabloko* is the Russian word for apple.) Yavlinsky, a Western-oriented economist who was the principal author of the "500 days" plan in the Gorbachev years, advocated a more socially harmonious path to reform than Gaidar's and opposed Yeltsin's constitution, with its highly centralized presidential power. Yabloko won 7.9 percent of the PR vote and twenty-seven seats. Two other moderate reform parties together won twenty-six seats.

A half dozen centrist parties, located at various points between the reformers and the anti-reform LDP-Communist-Agrarian grouping, together won 18 percent of the vote and forty-eight Duma seats. The divisions in the Duma among all these contending parties was further complicated by the election of some 136 independent candidates with no party affiliation at all. In the end, about 220 of the Duma's 450 members were opposed to serious economic reform, while even many reformers had reservations about Yeltsin's economic policies and political style.[40] (See table 21.2.)

The Duma's checkered political composition was to create insurmountable problems for Yeltsin. The lack of a clear popular mandate for radical reform

TABLE 21.2

State Duma Elections, 1993 and 1995

Party	Seats Won in PR Party Llist		Seats Won in Districts		Total Seats		% of Seats	
	1993	1995	1993	1995	1993	1995	1993	1995
Left (socialist) wing								
Communists (CPRF)	32	99	9	50	41	149	9.1	33.1
Agrarian Party	21	0	16	35	37	35	8.2	7.7
People's Power	-	0	-	37	-	37	-	8.2
Centrists (moderate reformers)								
Yabloko	20	31	7	15	27	46	6.0	10.2
Our Home Is Russia	-	45	-	20	-	65	-	14.4
Unity and Accord	18	-	3	-	21	-	4.7	-
Russian Regions	-	0	-	41	-	41	-	9.1
Women of Russia	21	0	2	3	23	3	5.1	0.7
Others	14	-	16	-	29	-	6.4	-
Radical Reformers								
Russia's Choice	40	-	25	-	65	-	14.4	-
Russia's Democratic Choice	-	0	-	9	-	9	-	2.0
Nationalists								
Liberal Democratic Party	59	50	5	1	64	51	14.2	11.3
Independents and small parties	0	0	136	14	136	14	30.2	3.1

Sources: Timothy J. Colton and Jerry F. Hough, eds., *Growing Pains: Russian Democracy and the Election of 1993* (Washington, D.C.: Brookings Institution, 1998); and Jerry F. Hough, Evelyn Davidheiser, and Susan Goodrich Lehmann, *The 1996 Russian Presidential Election* (Washington, D.C.: Brookings Institution, 1996). Six seats went unfilled in 1993.

and the absence of a reliable majority of Duma deputies in Yeltsin's favor resulted in a series of policy flip-flops and political maneuvers that were to plague Yeltsin's presidency until his resignation on New Year's Eve, 1999.

Chechnya   On December 11, 1994, one year after Russia's first post-communist parliamentary elections, an invasion force of forty thousand Russian troops stormed into **Chechnya**. The operation sought to put a quick end to a secessionist movement that threatened to unravel Russia's structure as a federated state. Based largely on the territorial subdivisions of the former USSR, the Russian Federation consisted of eighty-nine administrative units. While most had an ethnic Russian majority, twenty-one of these subdivisions, designated as *republics*, had a non-Russian majority, having mostly been incorporated into Russia's expanding empire in the tsarist era. Chechnya was acquired by conquest in 1859. Though the Chechens' origins are obscure, they are a distinct ethnic group practicing Islam. Resistance to tsarist rule earned the

Russian troops stand guard amid devastation in Chechnya.

Chechens a reputation as the most rebellious people in the empire. The region suffered heavily under Stalin, who deported a half million Chechens and Ingush from their homelands during and after World War II, allegedly because of complicity with the German army.

Administrative Divisions in Russia

1	Krasnodar	7	Ingushetiya
2	Stavropol'	8	Chechnya
3	Adygeya	9	Mordoviya
4	Karachayevo-Cherkesiya	10	Chuvashiya
5	Kabardino-Balkariya	11	Mariy-El
6	Severnaya Osetiya-	12	Udmurtiya
	Alaniya (North Ossetia)		

Legend:
— Administrative boundary
Kray
Republic
Autonomous okrug
Oblast
Autonomous oblast

*An oblast is named only when its name differs from that of its administrative center.
The cities of Moscow and St. Petersburg are federal cities having oblast-level status.*

FIGURE 21.1   Russia's subdivisions
Source: U.S. Central Intelligence Agency

Right from the first months of Russia's existence as an independent state in 1991, the leadership of the Chechen Republic, an area smaller than Massachusetts nestled in the Caucasus Mountains, began militating for complete independence. Chechnya had a population of about 1.2 million in that year, of whom only about 250,000 were Russians. Any attempt to break out of the freshly established Russian Federation constituted a serious provocation to the central government in Moscow, which had reason to fear that other regions might insist on independence as well if the Chechens succeeded. Moreover, an underground oil pipeline ran through Chechnya, giving it enhanced economic importance.

Under the leadership of Dzhokar Dudayev, a general initially regarded by Yeltsin's staff as loyal to the Russian Government, Chechens boycotted the 1993 elections and appeared to be on the verge of splitting off from Russia in the following year. Preoccupied with the struggle for political survival and economic change, Yeltsin's administration paid little attention to Chechnya until the summer of 1994, when it hatched a plan to oust Dudayev using troops from the Federal Counterintelligence Service, a successor to the Soviet-era KGB. The Chechens quickly repulsed the small force in November, and television images of Russian troops in captivity may have induced Yeltsin to take immediate military action rather than seek a negotiated settlement. On December 2, Soviet planes began bombing Grozny, Chechnya's capital city. With the invasion nine days later, the war was on.

Yeltsin's defense minister, General Pavel Grachev, assured the civilian leadership that the operation would be "a piece of cake," lasting anywhere from a few hours to a week. It quickly became apparent that the Chechens were dug in for a protracted conflict. Russian army troops, already demoralized following the collapse of the Soviet Union, were poorly led. Within a month the government decided to replace them with better trained troops from Russia's Interior Ministry, traditionally an agency charged with maintaining domestic security. Fighting was ferocious on both sides, with the Russians bombing and shelling indiscriminately and the Chechens showing no signs of surrendering despite overpowering odds. Casualties mounted heavily, with estimates running between forty thousand and sixty thousand civilians killed in the cross fires by the end of 1995. Several hundred thousand Chechens became refugees; reports of rape and looting by Russian troops were widespread.[41]

In addition to claiming battle victims, the Chechen conflict inflicted severe political damage on Yeltsin and his supporters. Opposition to the war flared up across the political spectrum. Reformers like Gaidar and Fedorov, anti-reformers led by the Russian Communist Party, and even members of the military high command immediately denounced the invasion. (The nationalist Zhirinovsky voiced support for it.) Only a few weeks after Russian troops entered Chechnya, public opposition to the war ran as high as 75 percent, while Yeltsin's personal popularity plunged to single digits. Meanwhile, as the economy continued to sputter, the war was costing $300 million a day. The United States and the European Union expressed their concern about the escalating human devastation, prompting Russia's foreign minister, an erstwhile supporter of friendly ties with the West, to proclaim that the "honeymoon" in Russian-Western relations was "at an end." Stung by these criticisms, Yeltsin moved closer to his more conservative advisors in the intelligence and military wings of his government and appeared to turn his back on the reformers.

The strains generated by the Chechen hostilities, occurring in the midst of continuing economic decline and political turmoil, finally caught up with Yeltsin's health. In the summer of 1995, Yeltsin was hospitalized with cardiac ischemia, a painful condition brought on by stress and alcohol. In the fall he was hospitalized again for the same problem. It was in a state of acute political and physical weakness that Yeltsin had to prepare

for the legislative elections of December 1995 and the presidential contest of the following year.

The Legislative Elections of December 1995 The first Duma was elected to serve only a two-year term. If Yeltsin had hoped to widen his popularity during those two years, he was bound to be disappointed. By the first months of 1995, 75 percent of Russian survey respondents were opposed to the market economy as it was currently operating. (By contrast, two-thirds were in favor of it in Poland and other parts of East-Central Europe.) Another poll revealed that 23 percent of Russians were against the market economy per se, while only 7 percent favored a rapid transition to a market economy (down from 13 percent in 1993) and 44 percent favored a more gradual transition (up from 42 percent two years earlier). There was also a rise in the percentage of Russians who believed that the collapse of the Soviet Union was either a "harmful" event or "more harmful than useful" (76 percent in 1995, 69 percent in 1993).

Between 20 percent and 40 percent of the population lived below the poverty line in 1995. The richest 10 percent earned fourteen times the income of the poorest 10 percent—a gap that had widened appreciably since 1993, when the former earned 5.4 times the latter's income. Meat and milk consumption were 12 percent to 15 percent below 1991 levels. Though inflation declined to 250 percent for the year, nominal prices had risen 280,000 times since the end of 1990 while the population's real income (adjusted for inflation) had fallen 39 percent. The official unemployment figure was 7.7 percent just before the elections, though it was assumed that hidden unemployment accounted for at least another 6 percent. In many outlying regions unemployment topped 30 percent. Some 40 percent of state employees had not been paid in full or on time. Out on the land, the 1995 grain harvest was the worst in thirty years.

Meanwhile, the privatization process was slowing down. With some of the largest state-owned companies still in government hands, including the giant oil and natural gas firms that accounted for 17 percent of Russia's GDP, managers, banks, and political insiders worked quietly behind the scenes to acquire large stakes in their privatization. Gazprom, the largest gas company in the world and Chernomyrdin's former preserve, shifted more than 60 percent of its assets to politically connected insiders, with the state retaining the rest. "People's capitalism" was giving way to "nomenklatura capitalism" and "bandit capitalism." A new breed of powerful tycoons, some with ties to the old Soviet regime and all with carefully cultivated connections with the current political elite, was taking over the "commanding heights" of the Russian economy, including banks, energy firms, mines, television stations, publishing houses, holding companies, and other lucrative assets. In addition, the criminal networks that made up the Russian mafia cast an ominous shadow over the entire economy, extorting protection money from businesspeople, bribing public officials, and extending their criminal operations across Russia and around the world. Crime in general was also on the rise, especially violent crime.[42]

A poll taken in the summer revealed that 78 percent were dissatisfied with their economic status and 62 percent were worse off than in 1990. Although only a third favored the restoration of communist rule (mostly elderly), two-thirds said they preferred the old central planning system. Fully a third had sold their vouchers, while more than three-fourths voiced dissatisfaction with their investments. Ominously for Yeltsin, only 10 percent viewed him favorably, while 10 percent said they wanted a tsar and 12 percent favored military rule.[43]

Not surprisingly, the elections held in December 1995 were a sharp rebuke to Yeltsin. The Communists staged a comeback, earning 22 percent of the proportional representation vote and 157 seats. With slightly more than a third of the Duma, the Communists emerged as Russia's largest party. The Liberal Democrats slipped to 11 percent of the PR vote and won fifty-one seats, a sign that many voters had tired of Zhirinovsky's bizarre rhetoric. The Agrarians won twenty seats. These three parties, the most obstinately opposed to radical economic reform, controlled nearly 47 percent of the votes in the Duma. Together with like-minded deputies to be found among more than 100 independents and small party representatives, the opponents of Yeltsin's reform policies held the majority.[44]

The radical reformers, now regrouped in the Democratic Choice of Russia party, fared badly. Their share of the PR vote fell below the 5 percent hurdle, and they managed to win only nine single member-district seats. The somewhat more moderate reform party, Yabloko, did slightly better, gathering 7 percent of the PR vote and forty-five seats. **Our Home Is Russia,** a new government-backed party organized by Prime Minister Chernomyrdin with President Yeltsin's blessing, won 10 percent of the PR vote and fifty-five seats, a disappointing showing. A moderately pro-reform party called **Russian Regions** won forty-one seats.

On balance, the left-wing and nationalist parties opposed to Yeltsin had upped their share of the proportional representation vote from 43 percent in 1993 to 54 percent; the reform parties fell from 34 percent to 24.5 percent. (See table 21.2 on page 673.) Perhaps the only positive result from the government's vantage point was that the anti-reform parties had failed to acquire the two-thirds supermajority needed to veto most presidential decrees. Since the constitution confers considerable decree-making authority and policy initiative on the president, Yeltsin could at least hope to circumvent the legislature in the struggles that loomed inevitably before him. First, however, he would have to win reelection in a troubled electoral environment.

The 1996 Presidential Election   Yeltsin instantly reacted to the Duma elections by reshuffling the cabinet. The biggest change was the appointment of **Grigory Primakov** as foreign minister. Primakov was another holdover from the Soviet era, an international affairs specialist with expertise in the Middle East. (He had served as Gorbachev's special envoy to Saddam Hussein during the Persian Gulf crisis of 1990–91.) Although he advocated cooperative ties with the West now that the Cold War was over, his presence in the cabinet signaled a more assertive articulation of Russian national interests in its dealings with the West, as advocated by Communists and nationalists in the Duma.

At age sixty-five and in poor health, Yeltsin entered the presidential fray against ten other contenders with surprising vigor. He categorically dismissed talk of postponing the vote, a suggestion bruited by hardliners who may have wanted to cancel the elections entirely. The first polls showed him trailing his chief rival, Gennady Zyuganov of the Russian Communist Party. Zyuganov appealed to Russian voters nostalgic for "the good old days" of economic stability and international respect in the former USSR. He called for the "voluntary" reestablishment of the Soviet Union by its former constituent elements—an unlikely occurrence—and advocated a vaguely defined "mixed economy" with a stronger role for the state than Yeltsin's reformers wished to retain. Yeltsin combated his challengers with all the powers of his office. At the risk of running up Russia's already bloated budget deficit, he promised higher pensions and student aid and vowed to pay some $2.8 billion in wages still owed to government employees. (In a display of mass pressure on Yeltsin, upward of a million coal miners throughout Russia went on strike.) He also compensated bank depositors for losses due to inflation at a cost of $21 billion.

Recognizing that his chances were slim as long as the bloody Chechen war dragged on, Yeltsin arranged a hasty meeting with a separatist leader and signed a cease-fire, promising Chechnya maximum autonomy within the Russian Federation. Some sixty thousand to eighty thousand people had perished in the conflict, most of them civilians. Declaring "the war's over," he went to Chechnya on the eve of the election to demonstrate his political agility and physical stamina. With the state-owned television station at his disposal, Yeltsin dominated the airwaves as the campaign intensified, aided by Western political advertising specialists. He dipped deeply into a lavish war chest of nearly $1 billion in campaign funds, provided largely by a group of tycoons who were determined to stop Zyuganov and the Communists at all costs.

In the election round held on June 16, 1996, Yeltsin topped the list with 35.3 percent of the vote. Zyuganov finished second, with 32 percent. Third place went to a late entrant in Russian politics, Alexander Lebed, an outspoken former general whose opposition to the Chechen war and sharp denunciations of official corruption won him a startling 14.5 percent of the vote. Yavlinsky was next with 7 percent, while the shrill Zhirinovsky won only 5.7 percent. Mikhail Gorbachev, relentless in his opposition to Yeltsin, cut a forlorn figure with 0.5 percent of the vote. Four other candidates won less than 1 percent each, and 1.5 percent of the voters marked their ballots against all the candidates (see table 9.4 on page 204).

Because Yeltsin had not won an absolute majority of the votes cast, he was obliged to run head-to-head against Zyuganov in a second round. Politically reinvigorated by his first-round comeback, Yeltsin promptly fired several hardliners connected with the Chechen invasion and appointed Lebed as his top assistant for national security, charging him with pursuing a settlement in Chechnya. But his triumph brought no physical reinvigoration. Several days later Yeltsin collapsed and dropped out of sight. Panic gripped his entourage as rumors circulated about a heart attack or stroke. Yeltsin finally emerged on election day, looking haggard and expressionless as he cast his ballot. But the returns were positive: on July 3, the president edged out Zyuganov by 53.8 percent to 40.3 percent. Nearly 5 percent voted against both contestants. Yeltsin's margin of victory was surprisingly high in some regions, the result of pressures exerted on local officials to report an exaggerated result in the president's favor. Kremlin officials had apparently threatened them with a cutoff of energy and electricity. Zyuganov graciously accepted the final result, perhaps because he did not really want the responsibilities of the presidency after all.[45]

Yeltsin's Ills Yeltsin's 1996 electoral victory marked the high point of his presidency. From then until his resignation at the end of 1999, his declining health required him to spend long periods away from his desk at the Kremlin. Yeltsin's prolonged absences created a void at the highest levels of Russia's political system, stimulating intense rivalries for power among a handful of well-placed oligarchs in the executive branch as well as fierce attacks on the Yeltsin administration by his opponents in the legislature. As Yeltsin struggled gamely to retain control of the situation and convince a skeptical public that he was still the country's chief decision maker, he progresssively lost his grip on governmental operations. His actions and statements appeared erratic, while his efforts to occupy the center ground between radical reformers and more conservative forces in his administration became increasingly reminiscent of Gorbachev's futile attempt to play a similar balancing act between advocates and foes of perestroika. The absence of a legislative majority in the

Duma in favor of radical market reforms and amicable relations with the West further constricted Yeltsin's ability to pursue a consistent reform course and a more cooperative pro-Western foreign policy.

Meanwhile, the Russian economy veered from one obstacle to the next. Despite impressive gains in the fight against inflation, it floundered dismally in the critical tasks of stimulating production and overall growth. Privatization came to a near stop, tax revenues withered, and the budget shrank. Capital flight—the transfer of money to safe havens outside Russia—was estimated at more than $100 billion. Corruption festered, with possibly more than 40 percent of the Russian economy controlled by organized crime. Cronyism remained pervasive, resulting in what the head of the International Monetary Fund described as "incestuous relationships between governments, banks and enterprises."[46] Political and economic power was concentrated in the hands of rival "clans." As a consequence, the IMF and other vitally important sources of external economic assistance slowed down their disbursements of financial aid. Only their fear of a total breakdown of Russia's economy prevented them from turning off the taps of assistance completely. The Asian financial crisis of 1997–98 dealt Russia an even more telling blow (see chapter 1). As Yeltsin declined, the country's political and economic status declined with him.

Immediately after winning reelection, Yeltsin reappointed his chief cabinet officers, retaining Chernomyrdin as prime minister and Primakov as foreign minister. The reinstated leadership team held steady to a course of moderate economic reform, keeping the budget deficit and money supply within manageable limits so as to lower inflation. (The inflation rate for 1996 was 22 percent, a marked improvement over the previous year's rate of 250 percent.) Lebed secured an agreement with the Chechens in August 1996 that required Russia to withdraw all its troops while deferring a final agreement on Chechnya's juridical status until 2001.

But Yeltsin's infirmities quickly overshadowed these successes. The president was barely able to speak at his inauguration, and several weeks later he announced that he needed heart surgery. The quintuple bypass operation took place in early November and kept Yeltsin away from the Kremlin until late the following month. Within weeks of his return he was hospitalized again for viral pneumonia. Another viral infection sidelined him at the end of 1997, followed by severe colds and other medical problems. In October 1998 Yeltsin formally removed himself from day-to-day responsibilities and entered a sanitarium, returning briefly only to be hospitalized in January 1999 with a bleeding ulcer. His health continued to fluctuate until his retirement at the end of the year.

The Contest for Power   In the power vacuum opened up by Yeltsin's afflictions, several ambitious figures jockeyed for influence behind the scenes. One of the key players was Anatoly Chubais, the energetic proponent of market reforms who had served Yeltsin as minister of privatization from late 1991 until 1994, and then as first deputy prime minister in charge of the privatization process. After becoming Yeltsin's chief of staff following the 1996 elections, Chubais moved quickly to get the outspoken Lebed removed from his post as national security advisor after the ex-general declared that Russia was standing on "the edge of the abyss."

Before too long Chubais crossed swords with another influential, Boris Berezovsky. A former car dealer, Berezovsky was the most visible of the tycoons who had amassed spectacular wealth since the collapse of the USSR by acquiring some of Russia's most lucrative businesses. His empire included a 49 percent share of Russia's state-dominated television station, a large bank, publications, a chain of auto dealerships, and other holdings. Both men enjoyed Yeltsin's trust, Chubais as the prime mover of the privatization process and Berezovsky as the principal organizer of the president's reelection campaign. But Chubais favored expanding the web of ownership in privatized companies to a wider constituency, advocating a more open bidding process for large state companies as they were sold off to private buyers. He also wanted Russia's largest companies to pay their fair share of taxes. Berezovsky and other tycoons wanted to confine the sale of large state enterprises to a privileged inner circle and sought tax breaks and other favors as well. Yeltsin played a game of musical chairs with Chubais and Berezovsky, hoping to retain the loyalties of both without becoming too dependent on either.[47]

The leading business magnates also had competitive rivalries among themselves. At times their conflicts spilled over into the political arena, as well-connected tycoons sought allies in the cabinet or Yeltsin's entourage. On several occasions Yeltsin intervened personally in these disputes, assembling six to ten of the country's most powerful business leaders—the so-called financial oligarchy—in an effort to smooth over their rivalries and maintain their support. In a candid acknowledgment of the oligarchy's enormous political influence, one tycoon declared, "We understand that we are part of the state. We depend on the state and the state depends on us."[48]

Secondary figures in the secretive world of Kremlin intrigues were not the only ones to get caught up in Yeltsin's dizzying leadership reshufflings during his final years in power. Prime ministers also came and went at an accelerating pace.

In March 1998, Yeltsin summarily fired Chernomyrdin, describing him as "lacking in dynamism and initiative." In his place Yeltsin nominated **Sergei Kiriyenko,** a little-known thirty-six-year-old reform-oriented technocrat with no parliamentary experience. Kiriyenko was Russia's first deputy minister for fuel and energy when Yeltsin tapped him to head the government. His appointment to such an important post caused head-shaking in Russian political quarters and world capitals, providing Yeltsin's opponents in the Duma with a new opportunity to embarrass him.

Russia's constitution gives the Duma the right to vote down the president's nominee for prime minister. The president retains the upper hand, enjoying the option of dissolving the Duma and calling snap elections in the event the Duma rejects his nominee three times. Kiriyenko failed to get the necessary majority in the first two ballots, with the Communists, Liberal Democrats, and Yabloko deputies voting against him. But with the threat of dissolution hanging over their heads, a number of opposition deputies swung to Kiriyenko's support in the third ballot, including Zhirinovsky's Liberal Democrats and a rump group of Communists led by Gennady Seleznyov, the speaker of the house. Kiriyenko was confirmed in office in April 1998 by a vote of 251 to 25, with 174 abstentions.

The timing of the newcomer's arrival in office could hardly have been less propitious. Kiriyenko immediately found himself caught in the crosswinds of the global financial crisis buffeting developing economies from Asia to Latin America. Only weeks after he assumed the premiership, Russia's stock market lost half its value and interest rates jumped to 50 percent. The new government's hopes of stimulating market reforms had to take a back seat to tax increases and budget cuts. President Yeltsin named Boris Fedorov to take charge of the country's laggard tax collection system. (Corporations and individuals owed an estimated $100 billion in back taxes.) The IMF, the World Bank, and the Japanese government put together a $22.6 billion loan package to prop up the ruble and ward off economic collapse, but it was too late. On August 18, Kiriyenko's government announced a 34 percent devaluation of the ruble and a moratorium on Russia's payments on its international commercial debts. (At the time, Russia's total foreign debt was $200 billion.) For Kiriyenko, the die was cast. Yeltsin fired him less than a week later and called on Victor Chernomyrdin to replace him.

By designating as his next head of government the man he had recently dismissed for his putative lack of "dynamism and initiative," Yeltsin invited another barrage of parliamentary vitriol. The Communists once again led the charge. They rejected Chernomyrdin and demanded Yeltsin's resignation along with a new constitution more favorable to the legislature. They also called for a reversal of the austere budgetary and monetary policies Yeltsin had followed in conformity with the IMF's anti-inflationary guidelines. Berezovsky and most of the financial oligarchy backed Chernomyrdin, while reformers like Chubais retained their support for Kiriyenko.

After Chernomyrdin failed to secure the Duma's support in two ballots, a weary Yeltsin bowed to the forces arrayed against him and named Foreign Minister Yevgeny Primakov as the new prime minister. Primakov's appointment was an olive branch extended to the Communists, who quickly nodded their assent. He was duly confirmed by the Duma on September 11, 1998 by a vote of 317 to 63.

As a Russian nationalist and former communist, Primakov had no difficulty giving cabinet posts to representatives of the Communist Party and the

Liberal Democrats. He also brought in members of Chernomyrdin's Our Home Is Russia party and the Yabloko group. His choices for the top economics posts were proponents of a much slower reform process and a stronger role for the state in the economic system. They also advocated the printing of more rubles to subsidize faltering state-owned companies. Primakov himself brushed off the IMF's advice as the work of "young kids who've seen almost nothing in life but have read a lot of books." It took the new leadership several months to devise a coherent economic strategy, however; in the meantime, growth had dipped 5.7 percent in 1998. Primakov's misgivings notwithstanding, Russia remained heavily dependent on loans and other forms of financial assistance from the international community. The entire Russian state budget for 1999 was set at $23 billion, while the U.S. federal budget was set to top $1.7 trillion.

Although Primakov's government offered virtually no new initiatives to extract the country from its economic impasse, his personal popularity rose. With Yeltsin's absences from the Kremlin growing more protracted, Primakov acquired broader decision-making powers and enhanced his prospects as a possible presidential candidate in 2000. Yeltsin's own popularity continued to nosedive, and in the spring of 1999 the Communists launched an impeachment process against him for presiding over the Soviet Union's demise and other alleged political offenses. Summoning his waning strength for the next battle, Yeltsin fired Primakov in May and designated another political novice, **Sergei Stepashin,** to replace him.

Stepashin was a Yeltsin loyalist who had served as chief of the Federal Counterintelligence Service during the Chechen conflict. He subsequently resigned the post, expressing regret for his role in the Chechnya operations. A proponent of market reforms, he was Russia's interior minister when Yeltsin elevated him to the the premiership. Several days after the Communists failed to secure enough votes to impeach Yeltsin on five counts of misconduct, the Duma accepted Stepashin by a wide margin.

His term in office was the shortest yet. In another unexpected move, Yeltsin dismissed Stepashin without explanation after only three months. His new choice, Vladimir Putin, was just as much a political unknown as his predecessor. Even more surprising, Yeltsin declared his support for Putin in the presidential race set for 2000, a proposal Putin immediately accepted.

At forty-six years old, Putin was a graduate of the Leningrad University law school. He spent his early career from 1975 to 1990 in the KGB, mostly as an agent in communist East Germany. One of his law professors had been Anatoly Sobchak, a liberal reformer who became mayor of Leningrad (later renamed St. Petersburg) and a staunch opponent of the anti-Gorbachev coup in 1991. Sobchak offered his former student a position as the city's unelected deputy mayor, a slot Putin held from 1990 to 1994, the formative years of post-communist Russia. In 1994 the privatization chief Chubais brought Putin to Moscow, where he initially headed the bureau responsible for Kremlin property and subsequently the office overseeing Russia's eighty-nine regional governors. In the

TABLE 21.3
Yeltsin's Prime Ministers	
Boris Yeltsin	1991–June 1992
Yegor Gaidar	June 1992–December 1993
Viktor Chernomyrdin	December 1993–March 1998
Sergei Kiriyenko	March 1998–August 1998
Yevgeny Primakov	September 1998–May 1999
Sergei Stepashin	May 1999–September 1999
Vladimir Putin	September 1999–Spring 2000

Vladimir Putin

summer of 1998, Yeltsin named him director of the Federal Security Service (FSB), a powerful intelligence agency that succeeded the KGB, and later appointed him to the National Security Council. During the intense negotiations between Russia and NATO on the Kosovo situation in 1999, Putin met with the U.S. State Department's specialist for Russian affairs, Strobe Talbott.

Despite the votes of Communists and some radical reformers against him, Putin was confirmed on August 16, only a week after his nomination. He retained his predecessor's cabinet and announced no new policy initiatives, but his government was quickly thrown into a severe crisis. A week earlier, Chechen separatists had invaded the neighboring Russian province of Dagestan and declared their intention of creating an independent state. As soon as Putin took office, he transferred control of military operations in the troubled region from the Interior Ministry to the army and gave the military one week to oust the rebels. Russian forces accomplished their task within the deadline, driving the rebels back into Chechnya. But the skirmishes proved to be the opening salvo in a new round of intense confrontation between the Russian government and the Chechen independence movement. Within weeks a large-scale invasion force was in place, with aerial and artillery bombardments pounding Grozny and rebel strongholds. More than 100,000 civilians streamed out of the battle areas and casualties on both sides mounted rapidly. Putin received strong public endorsement from most Russians for his determination to crush the rebels once and for all, especially after a series of random bombings of apartment buildings and other civilian centers rattled Moscow and other urban areas. The government attributed the attacks to Chechen terrorists. As in the previous round of fighting, hopes for a quick victory proved illusory: Russian troops were still mired in the conflict in the summer of 2000.

December 1999 Legislative Elections Another immediate challenge confronting the new prime minister was the upcoming parliamentary election set for December. In the months preceding the vote, Russia's fledgling party system underwent a number of changes. Five reform-oriented parties consolidated their forces in a new grouping, the **Union of Rightwing Forces.** Prominent reformers like Gaidar, Kiriyenko, and Boris Nemtsov, a former deputy prime minister, spearheaded the movement. Efforts to forge a single party committed to the market reform process fell through because the Union of Rightwing Forces failed in its attempt to link up with Chernomyrdin's Our Home Is Russia and because leading reform politicians kept their distance from the new party. (Stepashin joined Yabloko, and Fedorov gravitated to Our Home Is Russia.) On the more traditionalist end of the spectrum, Primakov joined forces with Moscow mayor Yuri Luzhkov in forming a new party, **Fatherland,** dedicated to a "strong state" within the framework of democratic freedoms and a mixed economy. Support for the new party widened when another new grouping, a collection of regional leaders calling themselves the **All Russia Movement,** linked up with Fatherland. The

TABLE 21.4

1999 Elections to State Duma

Party	% of PR Vote	PR Seats	SMD Seats	Total Seats	% of Seats
Communists	24.8	67	46	113	25.1
Unity	23.8	64	9	73	16.2
Fatherland-All Russia	13.6	37	31	68	15.1
Union of Rightwing Forces	8.7	24	5	29	6.4
Yabloko	6.0	16	4	20	4.4
Zhirinovsky bloc	6.1	17	0	17	3.7
Our Home Is Russia	1.2	0	7	7	1.5
Independents and small parties	<2% each; 12.37 total	0	115	115	25.5
Against all candidates	3.4				

Source: International Foundation for Election Systems, *Elections Today,* May 2000; Russian Federal Election Commission <www.fci.ru>. As of March 2000, eight SMD seats were still unfilled.

chief leader of the All Russia Movement was the governor of oil-rich Tatarstan, a republic that had already secured considerable autonomy in negotiations with Yeltsin.

Prime Minister Putin's followers took urgent steps to create a new pro-government party called **Unity.** (It was also known by its symbol, a bear, or *Medved* in Russian.) Led by Sergei Shoigu, the minister for disaster relief, it was a curious mix of liberals, Christian Democrats, communists, nationalists, and pure opportunists.

To the surprise of many observers, Unity did quite well, garnering seventy-two seats. The pro-reform parties all lost seats, with the Union of Rightwing Forces capturing only twenty-nine; Yabloko fell from forty-five to twenty-two seats, and Our Home Is Russia declined from fifty-nine seats in 1995 to a mere seven. All of these parties could be counted on to support economic reform as a general rule. The Communists won the largest share of popular votes in the party list vote (25 percent) and remained the largest party with 113 seats. The traditionalist Fatherland-All Russia bloc came close to matching Unity's performance (sixty-six seats). Zhirinovsky's party, the Liberal Democrats, was disqualified before the election for failing to meet election law requirements, but he quickly assembled a new bloc of candidates (the Zhirinovsky bloc). His supporters lost seats, falling from forty-nine in 1995 to seventeen. The real political coloration of the new Duma ultimately depended on more than 100 deputies elected as independents or as representatives of small parties. (See table 21.4.)

Unexpectedly, a scant two weeks after the Duma elections, President Boris Yeltsin stepped down from the presidency. By the terms of the constitution, Prime Minister Putin immediately assumed the role of acting president while preparations began for a rescheduled presidential election to be held within three months. In the interval, Putin enlarged his own share of popular support, winning plaudits for his success in providing full financing for Russia's social welfare programs for the first time since independence while simultaneously raising pensions and paying a substantial portion of back wages. His government also achieved a measure of economic stability, aided by a global rise in prices for oil, Russia's most valuable export commodity. Despite more than a thou-

TABLE 21.5

Presidential Elections, 2000	
Candidate	% of Vote
Putin (No party affiliation)	53.4
Zyuganov (Communist)	29.5
Yavlinsky (Yabloko)	5.9
Tuteev (No party affiliation)	3.0
Zhirinovsky (Liberal Democratic Party)	2.7
Six others	3.6
Against all candidates	1.9

Source: Russian Federal Election Commission <www.fci.ru>.

sand Russian army casualties in Chechnya and international criticism for harsh battle tactics, Putin's prosecution of the war against the secessionists remained acceptable to many Russians.

Once his potentially most serious challenger, former Prime Minister Primakov, dropped out of the race, Putin was able to secure a convincing first-round victory, garnering nearly 53.4 percent of the vote. Because of his absolute majority, a second round of voting was not necessary. More than 39.9 million citizens had voted for Putin, compared with 22 million for his nearest competitor, the Communist Gennady Zyuganov. The liberal economist Grigory Yavlinsky finished third with 4.35 million votes, while slightly more than 2 million voted for the arch-nationalist, Vladimir Zhirinovsky.

Putin was inaugurated president on May 7. With his ascendancy, a new stage in Russia's quest for a democratic political order had begun. How can we assess its chances for success?

CONTEMPORARY RUSSIA AND THE TEN CONDITIONS FOR DEMOCRACY

State Institutions: "Stateness"

What is Russia? With the dismemberment of the Soviet Union at the end of 1991, large portions of what had once been part of the Russian empire became formally independent. Some of these areas—especially Ukraine, Belarus, and Kazakhstan—were integral parts of pre-twentieth-century Russia and retain large concentrations of ethnic Russians (or, in the case of Belarus, White Russians). In all, some 25 million Russians reside in former Soviet republics along Russia's periphery, areas known in Russia as "the near abroad." Russian nationalists ranging from extremists like Zhirinovsky to moderates like Yeltsin and Primakov have asserted Russia's national interest in speaking up for these Russian populations whenever they are subjected to discrimination. At the same time, Russian political elites largely accept the fact that USSR is not likely to be reconstituted on a voluntary basis and that, for all intents and purposes, Russia is now confined to the Russian Federation.[49]

But even the integrity of the Federation is open to challenge, as the Chechen conflict has amply demonstrated. However that issue is resolved, Russia will quite probably have to deal with continuing efforts on the part of various subdivisions to maintain or even widen their autonomous rights within the Federation, especially in those republics and regions whose populations are mostly non-Russian and non-Christian. Russia's ethnic and religious *heterogeneity,* one of the factors that may undermine the prospects for democracy, combines with its federal structure to pose serious problems. Approximately 82 percent of the country's population consists of ethnic Russians, but many of the remaining 18 percent are concentrated in administrative subdivisions that provide a territorial basis for wide autonomy or outright independence. If Chechnya succeeds in winning its freedom from Moscow, pressures for outright secession may rise in some of these areas. At the very least, republics that can count on indigenous sources of wealth, like Tatarstan or mineral-rich Yakutia in the far east, may continue to insist on a large sphere of independent initiative in matters of economic strategy, taxation, and economic relations with foreign countries. Even regions with a predominantly Russian population may also demand the right to organize their political or economic affairs with maximum freedom from Kremlin interference.[50]

In short, the new Russia is saddled with what Juan Linz and Alfred Stepan call a *stateness* problem: the problem of defining the territorial boundaries of the nation-state and the distribution of decision-making power among its constituent units.[51] The nature of Russia's federal system has yet to be fully worked out, leaving open a wide range of unresolved questions. How much self-determination and local decision-making power will the people of Russia's regions be allowed to have, or to what extent will they have to follow Moscow's will? Will local leaders be fully accountable to their citizens, or will they succeed in establishing local dictatorships? In an effort to bring assertive regions to heel, President Putin soon after taking office decreed the creation of seven administrative districts to supervise Russia's eighty-nine regions and he hand-picked seven super-governors to take charge of the new districts. He also secured parliamentary legislation allowing the president, with court approval, to dismiss elected regional governors and legislatures and to remove on his own authority elected mayors and other lower-level officials. How the government in Moscow deals with these "center-periphery" problems in the years ahead, whether through negotiated compromises or strong-armed dictates, will surely affect the quality of democracy both regionally and in Russia as a whole.[52]

State Institutions: The Institutional Structure

The constitution approved by Russia's voters in the December 1993 referendum took effect on January 1, 1994. Written to Boris Yeltsin's specifications, it establishes a mixed **presidential-parliamentary** institutional structure modeled to a considerable extent on the constitution of contemporary France (the Vth Republic). At the national level it consists of the following:

- a dual executive, with a powerful decision-making **president,** who is head of state, and a responsible **prime minister,** who is head of government
- a bicameral legislature, the **Federal Assembly,** consisting of the **State Duma** (the lower house) and the **Federation Council** (the upper house)
- an independent judiciary, consisting at the national level of the **Constitutional Court,** empowered to rule on the constitutionality of laws and treaties and to settle disputes concerning the competence of state institutions; the **Supreme Court,** the highest court with jurisdiction over civil and criminal law and other cases arising from courts of common pleas; and the **Supreme Arbitration Court,** the highest court authorized to settle economic disputes arising from lower economic arbitration courts.

The President   Russia's **president,** elected directly by the people to a four-year term (with a limit of two consecutive terms), is the country's single most important decision maker. In addition to being the "guarantor" of the population's civil rights and freedoms and commander-in-chief of the armed forces, the president enjoys the right to "determine the guidelines of the domestic and foreign policy of the state," thus possessing considerable authority to initiate and conduct policy. Like France's president, the president of Russia has real political power, in contrast to ceremonial heads of state like the presidents of Germany and Israel. The most important presidential prerogatives include the authority to

- nominate the prime minister for approval by the Duma
- appoint and remove deputy prime ministers, upon the prime minister's proposals
- preside over government (cabinet) meetings
- submit bills directly to the Duma
- veto federal laws passed by the Federal Assembly, subject to an overriding vote by two-thirds of the membership of each house
- dissolve the Duma in the event that it rejects three presidential nominations for prime minister or passes a vote of no-confidence in the government
- issue decrees and directives binding throughout the country
- nominate the chairman of Russia's State Bank for approval by the Duma and nominate the justices of the three high courts for approval by the Federation Council
- place referendums before the voters
- announce a state of emergency in all or part of Russia, informing the Federal Assembly of this decision
- take charge of Russia's foreign policy and sign international treaties

The president may be removed from office only for high treason or some other "grave crime." The procedure requires the Duma to pass formal accusations by two-thirds majority, followed by validation of the charges by the Supreme Court and the Constitutional Court. The Federation Council may then remove the president by two-thirds vote.

In some respects the Russian president's powers are even greater than those of France's president, especially the right to issue decrees, a prerogative Yeltsin utilized enthusiastically. The French president also lacks the right to veto bills passed by the legislature.

The Prime Minister and Government   The **prime minister**—more formally, the chairman of the government—also has significant constitutional powers, though they are less sweeping than the president's. Most important, the premier is authorized to "determine guidelines" for the government's activities and to "organize its work," a somewhat vaguely worded provision that grants the head of government a certain amount of latitude to initiate and conduct domestic and foreign policy without trespassing on the president's primacy in these domains. The question is, how much latitude?

As France's experiences since 1959 have shown, the formal language of the constitution cannot specify whether the president will always be able (or willing) to impose his will on the prime minister. The relationship between the two executives can vary with their leadership styles and political circumstances. Because the French prime minister (like the Russian) must be approved by the legislature, the president may be forced to choose a premier he does not want if his opponents control the lower house. French experiences with "cohabitation," which occurs when the president and prime minister belong to opposing parties, clearly demonstrate that the president, despite his enormous constitutional authority, may at times be compelled to let the prime minister take the lead in formulating national policies. Because Russia's constitutional and party structures are still in their embryonic stages, it is still too early to tell if the country's presidency may turn out to be weaker in actual practice than it appears on paper. Yeltsin's reluctant appointment of Primakov as prime minister following the Duma's rejection of Chernomyrdin on two votes may be an early portent of a far more complicated pattern of relations between the two executives than proponents of presidential primacy may expect.

The government's most important responsibilities center on the federal budget, which it prepares, submits to the Duma, and subsequently implements. The government is also tasked with ensuring a "uniform state policy" in education, health care, social welfare, the environment, science, and culture. It may also issue "resolutions and directives" within the limits of the law. Other clauses of the constitution more explicitly confine the government's authority to "carrying out" measures concerning defense and foreign policy and the protection of civil liberties, property rights, and public order. Whether "carrying out" precludes the government from "initiating" actions in these fields is still an open question.

The Russian prime minister and the government are responsible to both the president and the Duma. The president nominates the premier and may dismiss him, along with the rest of the government. The Duma has the right to vote the government out of office in a no-confidence vote passed by the majority of its 450 members. If the president opts to reject this vote, the Duma may override his decision by passing another vote of no-confidence within three months. If it succeeds, the president must then either nominate a new prime minister or dissolve the Duma and call snap elections. Snap elections called under these circumstances may not be called again for at least a year.

The Duma   The **State Duma** consists of 450 legislators elected to a four-year term. As noted earlier, the electoral law combines proportional representation and the single member district/plurality system, with half the delegates elected under each system. (Germany has a roughly similar process for elections to the Bundestag.) The Duma's chief functions are to hold the government accountable and enact legislation. Accordingly, it may accept or reject the president's nominee for prime minister, and it may unseat the government in a vote of confidence initiated either by the Duma itself or by the government. It is to the Duma that the president or the government submits bills for adoption into law. In addition, the Duma has the right to lodge accusations against the president for possible impeachment by the Federation Council. (The Duma may not be dissolved once the impeachment process begins, nor may it be dissolved during an emergency period.) And the Duma may approve or reject the president's nominee for State Bank chairman and dismiss the incumbent. In short, the Duma has ample authority to check certain presidential powers and to hold the prime minister and cabinet accountable.

Among its limitations, the Duma, as we've indicated, can be dissolved by the president under specified conditions. Moreover, its members may not propose any financial legislation, such as tax bills or proposals to increase or reduce budgetary spending, without the government's approval. (The lower houses of Britain and France face similar restrictions on finance matters.)

Federation Council   The **Federation Council** consists of two members from each of Russia's eighty-nine republics and regions. One is appointed by the local governor, the other by the local legislature. The Council's principal function is to vote on legislation already adopted by the Duma. (Members of the Federation Council who wish to initiate legislative proposals must submit their bills to the Duma.) However, the Council's assent is not always required for a bill to be enacted into law. If the Council rejects a law passed by the Duma and the disagreement cannot be settled by a reconciliation committee of the two houses, the Duma may pass the bill on its own by two-thirds majority. Certain particularly important areas of legislation require the Federation Council's consideration, including the federal budget, tax laws, the ratification of international treaties, and declarations of war. In addition, the upper house has the sole authority to approve or reject presidential decrees declaring a state of emergency or imposing martial law in case of war. The Federation Council also has the exclusive right to remove the president from office once the Duma passes articles of impeachment. Both houses have the right to establish investigative committees.[53] As part of his attempt to rein in the autonomy of the regions from the central government's authority, President Putin in 2000 sought parliamentary approval of a proposal granting the president the right to dismiss individual regional leaders from the Federation Council.

Democracy and the State   Although Russia's institutional framework is heavily weighted in favor of expansive presidential powers, and their abuse by a power-hungry president is an ever-present danger, the legislature nevertheless possesses important countervailing powers. Most significant is that it can play a decisive role in selecting the prime minister and holding the government accountable for its decisions. With a roughly similar institutional structure, France managed to stabilize a highly unstable democratic system and warded off severe challenges to democracy in the 1960s (see chapter 17).

In sum, Russia is undergoing the difficult process of *redefining the role of the state.* A country whose historic traditions made for an inordinately powerful central state must now build a governmental structure that is strong enough to make and execute effective decisions, yet sufficiently restricted in the scope of its authority to submit to the rule of law, popular accountability, and the operation of market forces. At various times since 1992, Russia's nascent state has been alternately too strong and too weak, with the president occasionally taking heavy-handed actions and at other times leaving a gaping vacuum of power at the apex of the political system. Striking the proper balance between effective power and democratic limitations will be the Russian state's central challenge in the years ahead. President Putin appeared to be cognizant of this dilemma right from the start of his administration. In a hard-hitting state-of-the-nation address delivered only a few months after he took office, Putin insisted that democracy and a strong central state in Russia were inseparable. "It is only a strong, an effective state," he affirmed, "that is capable of protecting civil, political, and economic freedoms."[54]

Elites Committed to Democracy

If Russia's emerging state institutions are to promote democracy, it will take more than just a democratic constitution to make them succeed. Ultimately, everything depends on how the responsible political officials *behave* when it comes to implementing the constitution and establishing precedents for future conduct. If they deliberately seek to thwart the constitution's democratic purposes, no statutes on paper, no matter how well-intentioned or explicit, will save democracy. But if they act cooperatively and in strict accordance with the rule of law, Russia's constitution, for all its problems, may well succeed in anchoring an enduring democracy. Russia's political elites, in other words, must be thoroughly committed to democracy for democracy to work. Not only must professional politicians and bureaucratic officials throw their weight behind the procedures and spirit of democracy; so too must the country's military elites, business elites, religious elites, and other influential leaders and opinion shapers.[55]

At the very least, Russian elites must commit themselves to observing the rights and liberties spelled out in the constitution. Recognizing that Russia has endured centuries of tsarist autocracy and more than seventy years of communist dictatorship, the framers of the new constitution made special efforts to enumerate the civil and political rights of the population with greater detail than one finds in most other constitutions, including the U.S. French, and Japanese constitutions. (Britain had no written bill of rights until 2000, while Germany and Israel specify a somewhat shorter list of rights in their "basic laws.") Article 1 of the Russian constitution starts out by describing Russia as a "democratic state," while article 2 declares, "Human beings and human rights and freedoms shall be of the highest value," their protection constituting the state's highest duty. Other articles prohibit the appropriation of power by any individual and ban associations advocating the use of force for political purposes. Among a wide array of civil and political rights, the constitution formally guarantees such things as citizenship, ideological pluralism, and a multiparty system along with the right to vote and participate in government, to form associations and assemble for political purposes, to own property (including land) and engage in free economic activity, and to move freely inside and outside Russia. It also guarantees the dignity of the individual, personal inviolability, a variety of legal protections, and the freedoms typically associated with democracy, including freedom of conscience and religion, thought and speech. All these and other rights and freedoms are to be enjoyed equally by all citizens, without regard to gender, race, nationality, religion, or other defining social characteristics.

If the country's elites follow the letter of the constitution by protecting these rights, they will make a major contribution to the cause of democracy. On the whole, Russia's post-communist officials and the leaders of the main parties, including the Communists, have voiced their support in principle for democracy's fundamental rights and procedural rules of the game. As the new millennium begins, the Russian political system appears to be settling down after the shocks of the 1991 coup attempt, communism's collapse, and the 1993 confrontation between Yeltsin and his legislative opponents. It is significant that key elements of the military have backed democracy's advocates at crucial moments (while largely combating separatist tendencies in Chechnya).

Nevertheless, encroachments on democratic freedoms and values on the part of Russia's elites have by no means ceased. Yeltsin and Putin have both restricted or manipulated the media, and Putin has widened the intelligence service's surveillance operations. Official corruption, from high-level officials down to the police, is rampant. Some business leaders are more interested in profits than in democracy per se.[56] Should they choose to do so, Russia's elites still have ample power to strangle democracy in its infancy.

Socioeconomic Conditions: National Wealth, Private Enterprise, the Middle Class, and the Disadvantaged

Inevitably, economic conditions play a critical role in democracy's success. As we've repeatedly seen in this chapter, the Russian economy has suffered a prolonged depression since the stagnation of the late Brezhnev era, punctuated by the jolts of Gorbachev's helter-skelter reforms, Yeltsin's rapid liberalization measures starting in 1992, and the ruble devaluation of 1998. By the late 1990s, Russia's per capita GNP hovered around $2,700, less than Thailand, Turkey, or Mexico. President Putin inherited an economy marked by high levels of foreign indebtedness, laggard tax collections, inflation, unemployment, and a host of other problems. But Russia's economy grew about 3 percent in 1999 and began 2000 on a positive note as rising prices for Russia's oil exports fueled a modest growth spurt. Evidence of higher industrial production and a balanced budget as Putin assumed the presidency raised hopes that the Russian economy's long overdue turnaround was at least in view. Similar hopes had been frustrated before, however.

The privatization of large segments of the economy has taken place in spite of the previous ab-

sence of an entrepreneurial culture. Though the privatization of state-owned companies slowed down in the late 1990s, dipping from forty thousand a year in 1992 and 1993 to fewer than five thousand annually by the end of the decade, the Russian government acted in Yeltsin's final years to widen the bidding for large state companies in an attempt to break the hold of well-placed political insiders and giant banks on the last phases of privatization. Yeltsin bequeathed the Putin administration a complicated mixture of private enterprise and a still significant state-owned sector. For its part, the private sector displayed a variegated collection of hundreds of thousands of small and medium-scale enterprises—some successful, some struggling—coexisting with vast new conglomerates and criminal elements. (Farmland was still predominantly non-privatized.) On taking office, Putin installed a team of advisors who appeared committed to intensifying liberal reforms. His first prime minister, **Mikhail Kasyanoy**, quickly produced a 10-year strategic plan and short-term policies to bolster the private sector, including a new tax code. It remains to be seen whether the benefits of privatization and other facets of a market economy will spread wide enough across the population to create a real "people's capitalism" and deepen popular support for democratic property rights. Polls in the late 1990s indicated that more than 60 percent of Russians favored private enterprise in principle, though only a third approved of the government's approach to carrying out the privatization process.

As we noted earlier in this chapter, the development of democracy in Russia was hampered in earlier eras by the absence of a large, dynamic middle class. In the Soviet period, when there was no private sector, a "middle stratum" of sorts existed in between the exceptionally privileged upper ranks of the Communist Party elite and the mass of manual laborers and farm workers. For the most part this middle grouping consisted of state bureaucrats, military officers, and the intelligentsia—teachers, scientists, journalists, and the like, most of them living in urban areas. Very few of them exerted pressures for democracy until Gorbachev's democratization policies of the late 1980s opened the door to greater freedom to criticize the ruling authorities.

Since 1992, a more Western-style middle class has come into view, though sociologists have differed in their attempts to define who these people are. Definitions based on income range suggest that the middle class in the late 1990s earned between $100 and $1,000 a month (about 20 percent of the population in 1997), with those earning up to $3,000 comprising an upper middle class (another 15 percent). Occupational definitions focused on middle-level managers and employees of the state, independent professionals, and small and medium-level businesspeople, together comprising about 27 percent of the population. People in these groups enjoyed a large enough income to buy cars and other consumer goods, though many of them were devastated by the 1998 ruble crisis. If they find a way to prosper in the coming years, they may grow into a reliable bulwark of democracy, but a great deal depends on how they fare in an unpredictable economic environment.[57]

The disposition of vast numbers of Russians left destitute by the political and economic shocks of the post-Brezhnev decades remains a major question mark. As noted earlier, by mid-1999 nearly 38 percent of the population lived below the official poverty line of $37 a month. Many scrape by on an extra job without reporting the income to tax authorities. Though Yeltsin's constitution commits the state to a raft of welfare supports, such as free medical care, family allowances, unemployment compensation, disability payments, pensions, and other benefits, the money to finance them has been scarce. The government's wage and pension arrears have been substantial.

Will Russia's underprivileged actively support democracy in spite of their distress? Will they retreat into quiet apathy, or swing to demagogues who promise to end their misery through stern authoritarian measures? Perhaps the most we can say for now is that, thus far, the vast majority of Russia's poor have not shown any organized opposition to democracy as such. Strikes by miners, teachers, and others left uncompensated by the state were mainly aimed at getting their money, not overthrowing democracy. For most, the exigencies of day-to-day survival take precedence over political activity. The lingering question is whether a demagogic personality or party may find a way to mobilize the simmering discontent of the impoverished in an all-out bid for power.

Civil Society and a Democratic Political Culture

Another important task confronting democratizers in Russia is the development of an active civil society. For a country with virtually no tradition of independent citizen associations, the challenge is to create grassroots organizations from scratch. Political parties are the most important organizations of this kind, since they serve as a conduit between the country's eligible voters at the bottom and the elites who occupy the top rungs of the party leadership and aspire to political office. In between are the party activists who help organize meetings and get-out-the-vote activities, often on a voluntary basis. The parties that have fielded candidates since 1993 have all been recent creations, with the exception of the Russian Communist Party, which branched off from the Communist Party of the Soviet Union in 1990. Not surprisingly, the formative stages of Russia's party system have been characterized by kaleidoscopic change, as parties have merged with other parties, regrouped, or simply dissolved. In the span of less than a decade it has been difficult for individual parties to find a large core of voters who consistently identify themselves with its programs and ideas. One survey showed that in 1994, no single party reflected the interests of more than 10 percent of the people. Trade unions, representative business groups, and other associations have also had little time to get organized well enough to make a great impact on the policy-making process. The next decade or two should be critical in the formation and consolidation of parties and interest groups in Russia's emerging associational life.

President Putin acknowledged the importance of these issues in his July 2000 state-of-the-nation speech. Admitting that Russia had managed to create only "the carcass of a civil society," in its first decade as an independent state, the president voiced emphatic support for a competitive Western-style multiparty system. "A strong government has an interest in having strong opponents," he declared.

Attitudes toward politics will also need time to change, though there is evidence that Russia's political culture underwent very rapid changes once greater freedom of expression was permitted under Gorbachev. Russians increasingly broke out of their "subject" political culture around 1989, and many began taking an avid interest in the country's awakening political life. But interest in politics quickly subsided once the economic shocks of the early 1990s set in. Only about 10 percent said they took a "great" interest in politics in 1993, as opposed to 22 percent in 1990. The percentage of people taking little or no interest in politics rose from 32 percent in 1990 to 60 percent in 1993. Political participation also fell off after 1992 compared with 1989–90. Even so, these percentages were not significantly different from what one finds in more mature democracies. Turnout in the 1996 presidential election was 69 percent of registered voters, 60.5 percent in the 1999 legislative elections, and 68.6 percent in the 2000 presidential contest.

Sizable segments of the population continued to hold non-democratic attitudes in the 1990s. Support for a strong leader, for example, remained an enduring legacy of Russia's pre-democratic political culture. Between 1991 and 1994, 55 percent said they preferred a leader with an "iron hand," while only 30 percent favored democracy. By 1998, only a third said that they would favor a dictator in order to restore order, but half said that they would *not* fight a dictatorship to preserve their freedoms. Surveys also revealed widespread intolerance among Russians for non-Russian ethnic groups; large minorities in favor of suspending civil rights to maintain order; and low levels of interpersonal trust. These and related attitudes will have to shift over time if Russia is to achieve a stable democracy based on widely shared democratic values. On the whole, the younger and more educated tend to favor democracy and privatization at higher rates than do older and less educated segments of the population. Still, support for democratic processes and values sprouted visible roots in Russian public opinion in the 1990s, providing grounds for hope that they will take hold and blossom in the years to come.[58]

RUSSIAN ATTITUDES TOWARD DEMOCRACY, 1996–99

As one might expect from Russia's rapid and bumpy road to democracy, popular attitudes reflect a mixture of assertiveness and confusion, hope and disappointment.

WHAT IS DEMOCRACY?

In 1999, slightly more than half (52 percent) of Russians claimed they did not know how democracy is supposed to work in Russia. The other half said they didn't know what democracy is at all or how it is supposed to work. Nevertheless, almost half of Russia's young people (44 percent) said that Russia had a democratic form of government, more than double the number of older Russians (21 percent). When asked to be specific about protecting civil liberties, sizable majorities of all Russians firmly opposed restricting their new freedoms for the sake of restoring order in the country. By large margins they opposed limiting habeas corpus rights (73 percent), banning demonstrations and meetings (68 percent), canceling elections (63 percent), restricting the right to travel abroad (62 percent), and censoring the media (60 percent).

HOW WELL IS RUSSIA DOING?

Attitudes are also mixed when it comes to assessing the Russian government's performance in living up to the ideals and goals of democracy. In late 1996, almost all Russians (96 percent) believed that democracy requires the judicial system to treat everyone equally and punish the guilty, no matter who they are; but only 15 percent said that justice of this sort actually existed in their country. Similarly, nearly all Russians believed that it is important in a democracy that everyone receive free education and health care (again, 96 percent). But only 21 percent said that this social aspect of democracy was being fulfilled. Though similar numbers (88 percent) held that democracy must permit the media to report the news without censorship, only 37 percent felt that Russia actually had free media. And only 36 percent believed that Russian elections were honest. Only 9 percent felt that Russia was making progress toward the rule of law, with 22 percent saying there was very little progress in this direction and fully 61 percent seeing no progress at all.

In 1999, large majorities rated the Russian government's performance as "bad" or "very bad" when it came to paying wages and pensions on time (94 percent), providing social protection for the needy (93 percent), fighting organized crime (92 percent), maintaining law and order (87 percent), cutting inflation (83 percent), and cleaning up the environment (62 percent). Majorities gave similarly low ratings for protecting citizens' rights (62 percent) and developing free enterprise (61 percent).

Two out of three Russians in 1999 expressed their lack of confidence in the national legislature and judicial system. By similar or even wider margins they perceived corruption in the federal government, the police, large corporations, and banks. The only institutions in which a majority had any confidence were the Orthodox church (63 percent), the military (53 percent), and the broadcast media (54 percent).

Amid these negative evaluations there stood out a few signs that Russian democracy was not entirely lost. Large majorities in 1996 agreed that everybody is now free to practice their religion (89 percent), that one can choose from several parties and candidates in elections (88 percent), and that there is freedom to criticize the government openly (61 percent). Large majorities also agree that these things are important in a democracy. At least to some extent, therefore, the vast majority of Russians acknowledge that they now have certain rights and opportunities that they did not possess through most or all of communist rule. In sum, the vast majority of Russians seem to want democracy; they just want it to work much better.

Sources: U.S. Information Agency, *The People Have Spoken: Global Views of Democracy*, vol 1 (January 1998) and vol. 2 (September 1999).

Education and Freedom of Information

Russia's new constitution guarantees tuition-free higher education on a competitive basis, and since the fall of communism the country's educational system has freed itself from the shackles of communist ideology and the censorship of politically unacceptable ideas. Russians are now free to pursue artistic creativity and scientific research without government interference. Press freedom has ushered in the most open period of political expression in Russian history, with the fleeting exception of the Provisional Government in 1917. A selection of six thousand newspapers and four thousand magazines is now available, providing a lively contrast to the dull uniformity of Soviet-era propaganda. A number of private radio stations also fill the airwaves.

Nevertheless, problems remain. Although 80 percent of newspapers and magazines are privately owned, most are subsidized by the government to some degree. Large segments of the print and broadcast media are controlled by a handful of tycoons with close connections to state authorities. Editorial pressure from national and local government officials continues to be exerted on politically oriented journalists and broadcasters. Although the constitution guarantees the secrecy of private communications, e-mail transmissions

are monitored by the federal intelligence service. Russia must therefore take remedial measures to ensure that press freedoms and the privacy of individuals are fully observed in practice, a task the courts are gradually assuming.

Control of the three largest television networks appeared to be up for grabs in 2000. When President Putin took office the Russian government owned one of the networks outright (RTR) and held 51% of a second one (ORT), with a group of tycoons led by Boris Berezovsky controlling the remaining 49%. The third station (NTV) was owned by another tycoon, Vladimir Gusinsky. Berezovsky, as we have seen, had close ties to Yeltsin, but Putin showed signs of pressuring Berezovsky to hand over full control of ORT to the state. Gusinsky, whose network was critical of Putin's government, was arrested on charges of fraud. The charges were soon dropped and Gusinsky was released, but he was under intense pressure to give up his ownership of NTV. Despite these signs of wanting to bring Russian television under government supervision, President Putin declared in his state-of-the-nation speech that "without really free mass media, Russian democracy simply will not survive." Precisely how Putin intended to reconcile a powerfully intrusive state with press freedom was not clear.

A Favorable International Environment

From its inception in the Gorbachev period, Russia's democratization process has been intimately connected with the international environment. For Gorbachev, the liberalization of the communist system required an end to Cold War hostilities. This symbiotic relationship between Russia's internal developments and its ties to the outside world has continued since independence in 1992 with mixed results. On the positive side, Russia's relations with the United States, Western Europe, Japan, and other democracies remain largely amicable: there has been no return to the confrontation and military posturing of the Cold War era. Russia's democratization has been greeted with warm enthusiasm by the USSR's former enemies, resulting in considerable amounts of assistance in the form of loans, technical advice, food, and other forms of aid. By the end of 1999, Russia owed the International Monetary Fund nearly $12 billion, with a total liability to foreign creditors amounting to $195 billion. Foreign governments and banks have forgiven large sums of prior debt. The U.S. Congress authorized a $3 billion program to help Russia dismantle nuclear and biological weapons, keep its nuclear fuels safeguarded, and provide employment for Russian scientists and technicians who might otherwise sell their services to countries trying to build nuclear weapons. These and other endeavors have been motivated by the assumption that a democratic Russia will be a peaceful and cooperative Russia.

At the same time, Russia remains a country with its own national interests, like all countries. The catastrophic disappearance of the Soviet Union, once respected as the only superpower in the world next to the United States, has been a shock to many Russians, deeply wounding their national pride and at times evoking bitter feelings of humiliation and resentment. A number of issues have created frictions with the United States and its allies in recent years, especially NATO's enlargement to include Poland, the Czech Republic, and Hungary and its military involvement in Bosnia and Kosovo against the Serbs, Russia's historic allies.[59]

For its part, the West has complained of the Russian parliament's failure by mid-2000 to ratify the START II nuclear disarmament agreement signed by Presidents Yeltsin and Bush in January 1993.[60] It has also criticized Russia's efforts to sell nuclear reactor equipment to Iran, its use of force in Chechnya, and its failure to prevent the government's central bank and criminal elements from illegally secreting large sums of hard currency abroad, much of it Western assistance money intended for the improvement of Russia's economy. The Russian elite and its politically attentive population, meanwhile, are still gripped by the identity crisis that has perplexed their country for centuries: is Russia basically a European country, an Asiatic country, or some amalgam of both? Today's Russia has a formal consultative arrangement with NATO as well as trade agreements with the European Union; but in 1998, Prime Minister Primakov proposed the creation of a "strategic triangle" with India and China to counterbalance the Western alliance. And in 2000 the Putin administration made it clear that cooperation with the West did not mean that there would be agreement on all issues. Contemporary Russia in some respects still resembles the double-headed eagle that symbolized tsarist Russia: one head facing west, the other east.

CONCLUSION

It would be foolhardy to predict what the coming years will bring for Russia. Nevertheless, our survey of its performance thus far encourages guarded optimism. Without minimizing the magnitude of the challenges Russia faces, we cannot deny that the final decade of the twentieth century saw a phenomenally rapid—and largely unpredicted—advance toward democracy. For a country whose history marched steadfastly against the democratic idea for a thousand years, the revolutionary transformations of little more than a decade offer fragile but palpable grounds for believing that democracy in Russia can survive and flourish in the decades ahead. Of course, history is littered with failed democracies. How the freshly installed Putin administration will fulfill its declared aim of strengthening both the Russian state and democratic freedoms simultaneously is the critical question, and its outcome is by no means self-evident. The uncertainty of the country's future aptly reminds us of Winston Churchill's famous characterization of Russia as "a riddle wrapped in a mystery inside an enigma."

KEY TERMS AND NAMES
(Underlined in the text)

Boris Yeltsin
Mikhail Gorbachev
Communist Party of the Soviet Union (CPSU)
USSR/Soviet Union
Commonwealth of Independent States (CIS)
Vladimir Putin
Romanovs
Peter the Great
Catherine the Great
V.I. Lenin
Bolsheviks
October Revolution
Marxism-Leninism
Joseph Stalin
Centrally planned economy (CPE)
Collectivization

Great Purge
Nikita Khrushchev
Leonid Brezhnev
Perestroika
Nomenklatura
Communist Party of the Russian Federation
   (Russian Communist Party, RCP)
Chechnya
President
Prime minister
State Duma
Federation Council

FOR DISCUSSION: WHAT WOULD YOU DO?

1. If you were a Russian citizen, to which party (if any) would you belong? Why?

2. If you were a Russian citizen, how optimistic would you be about the fate of democracy?

3. What is your view on the Chechen conflict?

4. Should the outside world continue to provide financial and other forms of assistance to Russia? Should it impose conditions?

FOR FURTHER READING

In addition to the titles in the notes, consult the following:

Joseph R. Blasi, Maya Kroumova, and Douglas Kruse, *Kremlin Capitalism* (Ithaca, N.Y.: ILR, 1997).

Maxim Boycko, Andrei Schleifer, and Robert Vishny, *Privatizing Russia* (Cambridge, Mass.: MIT Press, 1995).

Karin Dawisha and Bruce Parrott, eds., *Democratic Changes and Authoritarian Reactions in Russia, Ukraine, Belarus, and Moldova.* (Cambridge: Cambridge University Press, 1997).

Louis Fischer, *The Life of Lenin* (New York: Harper and Row, 1964).

W. Bruce Lincoln, *The Romanovs* (New York: Dial, 1981).

Lynn D. Nelson and Irina Y. Kuzos, *Radical Reform in Yeltsin's Russia* (Armonk, N.Y.: M. E. Sharpe, 1995).

David Remnick, *Lenin's Tomb: The Last Days of the Soviet Empire* (New York: Random House, 1993).

———. *Resurrection: The Struggle for a New Russia* (New York: Vintage, 1998).

Richard Sakwa. *Russian Politics and Society* (London: Routledge, 1993).

Leonard Schapiro, *The Communist Party of the Soviet Union,* rev. ed. (New York: Vintage, 1971).

Donald W. Treadgold and Herbert J. Ellison, *Twentieth Century Russia,* 9th ed. (Boulder, Colo.: Westview, 2000).

Bertram D. Wolfe, *Three Who Made a Revolution* (New York: Delta, 1954).

Boris Yeltsin, *The Struggle for Russia,* trans. Catherine A. Fitzpatrick (New York: Belka, 1994).

Daniel Yergin and Thane Gustafson, *Russia 2010* (New York: Random House, 1993).

NOTES

1. The CIS now consists of Russia, Ukraine, Belarus, Moldova, Georgia, Armenia, Azerbaijan, Kazakhstan, Uzbekistan, Kyrgyzstan, Turkmenistan, and Tajikistan.

2. A classic survey of Russian history is Nicholas V. Riasanovsky, *A History of Russia,* 5th ed. (New York: Oxford University Press, 1993).

3. Robert K. Massie, *Peter the Great* (New York: Knopf, 1980).

4. Liah Greenfeld, *Nationalism: Five Roads to Modernity* (Cambridge, Mass.: Harvard University Press, 1992), ch. 3 (especially p. 265). She argues that whereas the Slavophiles abandoned the attempt to catch up with the West on the economic and political planes, exalting instead the pristine Russian "soul," the Westernizers favored borrowing technology from the West with the ultimate aim of demonstrating Russia's economic or military capabilities (like Peter the Great) or of eventually overtaking the West (like the communists).

5. Isabel de Madariaga, *Russia in the Age of Catherine the Great* (New Haven, Conn: Yale University Press, 1981).

6. Richard Pipes, *Russia Under the Old Regime* (New York: Scribner's, 1974), 281–318.

7. Dominic Lieven, *Russia's Rulers Under the Old Regime* (New Haven, Conn.: Yale University Press, 1989).

8. Marc Raeff, ed., *The Decembrist Movement* (Englewood Cliffs, N.J.: Prentice Hall, 1966).

9. Franco Venturi, *Roots of Revolution,* trans. M. Haskell (New York: Grosset and Dunlap, 1960).

10. Alexander Gerschenkron, *Economic Backwardness in Historical Perspective* (Cambridge, Mass.: Harvard University Press, 1962).

11. Victoria E. Bonnell, *Roots of Rebellion* (Berkeley: University of California Press, 1983).

12. See, for example, Engels's letter to the Russian revolutionary Peter Tkachov in Robert C. Tucker, ed., *The Marx-Engels Reader* (New York: W. W. Norton, 1972), 589–99.

13. The big winners were the Socialist Revolutionaries, with 40 percent of the vote. The Socialist Revolutionaries were the heirs of the populists and had a

large rural following. Though their left wing was quite radical, their large right-wing faction favored Western-style democracy. The Western-oriented liberals, the Constitutional Democrats, won 5 percent.

14. In 1930, Stalin said, "We are for the withering away of the state. But at the same time we stand for the strengthening of the proletarian dictatorship. . . . Is this 'contradictory'? Yes, it is 'contradictory.' But this contradiction is life, and it reflects completely the Marxian dialectic." In justifying the terror, Stalin said that the closer one gets to socialism, the more intense the class struggle becomes. Biographies include Adam B. Ulam, *Stalin* (New York: Viking, 1973); Robert B. Tucker, *Stalin as Revolutionary, 1879–1929* (New York: W.W. Norton, 1973) and *Stalin in Power* (New York: W.W. Norton, 1990); Isaac Deutscher, *Stalin* (New York: Vintage, 1960).

15. Robert Conquest, *The Harvest of Sorrow* (New York: Oxford University Press, 1986).

16. One of the most famous defendants was Nikolai Bukharin. See Stephen F. Cohen, *Bukharin and the Bolshevik Revolution* (New York: Vintage, 1975). His trial formed the basis of the novel by Arthur Koestler titled *Darkness at Noon.*

17. Robert Conquest, *The Great Terror* (Harmondsworth, U.K.: Penguin, 1971); J. Arch Getty, *Origins of the Great Purges* (Cambridge: Cambridge University Press, 1985).

18. On August 23, 1939, the Soviet Union and Germany signed an agreement to partition Poland. Several weeks after the German army invaded that country on September 1, 1939, Soviet forces moved into eastern Poland and annexed it. (The annexed territory today is part of Ukraine.) The Germans also handed over Lithuania, Latvia, and Estonia to the USSR.

19. Lazar Pistrak, *The Grand Tactician* (New York: Praeger, 1961).

20. The full text is in *The Anti-Stalin Campaign and International Communism* (New York: Columbia University Press, 1956).

21. Solzhenitsyn's *One Day in the Life of Ivan Denisovich,* published in a Soviet literary journal, was based on his own incarceration in a Stalinist labor camp.

22. Carl A. Linden, *Khrushchev and the Soviet Leadership, 1957–1964* (Baltimore, Md.: Johns Hopkins University Press, 1966). See also Khrushchev's memoirs, *Khrushchev Remembers,* trans. and ed. Strobe Talbott, vol. 1 (Boston: Little, Brown, 1970) and vol. 2 (Boston: Little, Brown, 1974), and *Khrushchev Remembers: The Glasnost Tapes,* trans. and ed. by Jerrold L. Schechter and V. V. Luchkov (Boston: Little, Brown, 1990). Khrushchev's son, Sergei, became a U.S. citizen in 1999.

23. Sidney Bloch and Peter Reddaway, *Soviet Psychiatric Abuse* (London: V. Gollancz, 1984).

24. Seweryn Bialer, *Stalin's Successors* (Cambridge: Cambridge University Press, 1980).

25. Mikhail Gorbachev, *Perestroika* (New York: Harper and Row, 1987 and 1988).

26. Anders Åslund, *Gorbachev's Struggle for Economic Reform* (Ithaca, N.Y.: Cornell University Press, 1989); Marshall I. Goldman, *Gorbachev's Challenge* (New York: W. W. Norton, 1987).

27. Eduard Shevardnadze, *The Future Belongs to Freedom,* trans. Catherine A. Fitzpatrick (New York: Free Press, 1991), 37; Carolyn McGiffert Ekedahl and Melvin A. Goodman, *The Wars of Eduard Shevardnadze* (University Park: Pennsylvania State University Press, 1997), 31.

28. Michael J. Sodaro, *Moscow, Germany, and the West from Khrushchev to Gorbachev* (Ithaca, N.Y.: Cornell University Press, 1990). See chapter 18 for additional sources.

29. Gale Stokes, *The Walls Came Tumbling Down* (New York: Oxford University Press, 1993); David Pryce-Jones, *The Strange Death of the Soviet Empire* (New York: Henry Holt, 1995).

30. Grigory Yavlinsky, Boris Fedorov, Stanislav Shatalin, et al., *500 Days,* trans. David Kushner (New York: St. Martin's Press, 1991). See also Marshall I. Goldman, *What Went Wrong with Perestroika?* (New York: W. W. Norton, 1991).

31. On the coup, see Victoria E. Bonnell, Ann Cooper, and Gregory Freidin, eds., *Russia at the Barricades* (Armonk, N.Y.: M. E. Sharpe, 1994).

32. Mikhail Gorbachev, *Memoirs,* trans. Wolf Jobst Siedler (New York: Doubleday, 1995). The most substantial monographs are Archie Brown, *The Gorbachev Factor* (Oxford: Oxford University Press, 1996); and Jerry F. Hough, *Democratization and Revolution in the USSR, 1985–1991* (Washington, D.C.: Brookings Institution, 1997). For surveys of the Gorbachev period, see also Anne de Tinguy, ed., *The Fall of the Soviet Empire* (Boulder, Colo.: East European Monographs, 1997); Dusko Doder and Louise Branson, *Gorbachev: Heretic in the Kremlin* (New York: Penguin, 1991); John B. Dunlop, *The Rise and Fall of the Soviet Empire* (Princeton, Princeton University Press, 1993); and John Miller, *Mikhail Gorbachev and the End of Soviet Power* (New York: St. Martin's Press, 1993). For an insider's account, see Yegor Ligachev, *Inside Gorbachev's Kremlin,* trans. Catherine A. Fitzpatrick, Michele A. Berdy, and Dobrochna Dyrcz-Freedman (New York: Pantheon, 1993). See also Carl Linden, "Gorbachev and the Fall of the Marxian Prince in Europe and Russia," in *Russia and China on the Eve of a New Millennium,* ed. Carl Linden and Jan A. Prybyla (New Brunswick, N.J.: Transaction, 1997), 59–87.

33. Gorbachev, *Memoirs,* 315–16.

34. On the formation of opposition movements in this period, see Judith Devlin, *The Rise of the Russian Democrats* (Aldershot, U.K.: Edward Elgar, 1995); and Michael Urban, Vyacheslav Igrunov, and Sergei Mitrokhin, *The Rebirth of Politics in Russia* (Cambridge: Cambridge University Press, 1997).

35. Boris Yeltsin, *Against the Grain: An Autobiography*, trans. Michael Glenny (New York: Summit, 1990). See also Andrei S. Grachev, *Final Days*, trans. Margo Milne (Boulder, Colo.: Westview, 1995).

36. Martin J. Peck and Thomas J. Richardson, *What Is to Be Done? Proposals for the Soviet Transition to Market* (New Haven, Conn.: Yale University Press, 1991); Anders Åslund, *How Russia Became a Market Economy* (Washington, D.C.: Brookings Institution, 1995).

37. Olga Bridges and Jim Bridges, *Losing Hope: The Environment and Health in Russia* (Aldershot, U.K.: Avebury, 1996).

38. Yegor Gaidar, *Days of Defeat and Victory*, trans. Jane Ann Miller (Seattle: University of Washington Press, 1999).

39. Several factors accounted for the party's uninspired showing. To begin with, Russia's Choice was formed only two months before the election and involved the merger of several pro-reform movements; it lacked a stable organizational base. The fact that several of its most well-known leaders were associated with the first months of Yeltsin's administration only seemed to turn away many reform-oriented voters who were materially affected by the sudden downturn in the economy. A large number of them voted instead for more moderate reform parties espousing a less frenetic pace of change. President Yeltsin's refusal to join the party or to campaign vigorously for its candidates was another detriment. Yeltsin considered it best to remain above the fray of inter-party conflict so as to maintain his freedom of political maneuver, a strategic choice that may have cost his supporters votes. Finally, Russia's Choice conducted a lackluster, poorly organized campaign. See Michael McFaul, "Russia's Choice: The Perils of Revolutionary Democracy," in *Growing Pains: Russian Democracy and the Election of 1993*, ed. Timothy J. Colton and Jerry F. Hough (Washington, D.C.: Brookings Institution, 1998), 115–39.

40. Elections to the upper chamber of the legislature, the Federation Council, took place in Russia's regions and were less affected by party affiliations than the Duma vote was. The result was a somewhat larger percentage of pro-reform winners than in the Duma. In subsequent years, the Federation Council was appointed by local authorities. For a thorough analysis of the elections, see Colton and Hough's book, ibid.; and Peter Lentini, ed., *Elections and the Political Order in Russia* (Budapest: Central European University Press, 1995).

41. Carlotta Gall and Thomas de Waal, *Chechnya* (New York: New York University Press, 1998), and Anatol Lieven, *Chechnya* (New Haven, Conn.: Yale University Press, 1998).

42. Phil Williams, ed., *Russian Organized Crime: The New Threat?* (London: Frank Cass, 1997); Stephen Handelman, *Comrade Criminal: Russia's New Mafiya* (New Haven, Conn.: Yale University Press, 1995).

43. Jerry F. Hough, Evelyn Davidheiser, and Susan Goodrich Lehmann, *The 1996 Russian Presidential Election* (Washington, D.C.: Brookings Institution, 1996), 40.

44. Smaller left-wing parties opposed to radical economic reform included three new ones, the *Power to the People* party headed by Nikolai Ryzhkov, a former prime minister under Gorbachev; the *Great Power (Derzhava)* party, headed by Alexander Rutskoi, the leader of the 1993 legislative opposition to Yeltsin; and the *Working Russia* party, organized by Viktor Anpilov, another 1993 opposition leader. All three parties won less than 5 percent of the PR vote each, but picked up district seats.

45. Lilia Shevtsova, *Yeltsin's Russia* (Washington, D.C.: Carnegie Endowment for International Peace, 1999), 180–93. On Zyuganov and his party, see Joan Barth Urban and Valerii D. Solovei, *Russia's Communists at the Crossroads* (Boulder, Colo.: Westview, 1997).

46. According to the Institute of International Finance, a Western organization, Russia by the spring of 1998 had borrowed $99 billion from abroad, but $103 billion had left the country (*Washington Post*, May 30, 1998). Another Western estimate reported $136 billion in capital outflows between 1993 and 1998 (*Financial Times*, August 21/22, 1999). The organized crime figure was estimated by American scholar Louise Shelley, *Financial Times*, March 20, 1997. See also *The Economist*, August 28, 1999. The quote by IMF Managing Director Michel Camdessus is in the *Washington Post*, June 17, 1999.

47. In 1996 Yeltsin named Berezovsky deputy secretary of the National Security Council, the powerful committee charged with coordinating military and police activities. The following year he elevated Chubais to first deputy prime minister and finance minister while simultaneously naming one of Chubais's proteges, Boris Nemtsov, as another first deputy premier. But controversies surrounding the two archrivals, who had no lack of additional enemies, later induced Yeltsin to remove Chubais from the finance

ministry and Berezovsky from his national security post. In 1998, Yeltsin removed Chubais from his deputy premiership but compensated him with an appointment as chief of the company that monopolizes Russia's electricity production. At the same time he named Berezovsky executive secretary of the Commonwealth of Independent States, then had him removed from that position in 1999.

48. The remark by Mikhail Khodorkovsky, a prominent banker, is quoted in the *Washington Post*, September 16, 1997. On the financial oligarchy and Russia's economic development, see Rose Brady, *Kapitalizm* (New Haven, Conn.: Yale University Press, 1999); and Bertram Silverman and Murray Yanowitch, *New Rich, New Poor, New Russia* (Armonk, N.Y.: M. E. Sharpe, 1997).

49. Belarus, the former Soviet republic of Belorussia, sought to form a close political union with Russia under Belarusan president Alexander Lukashenka, a Soviet-style communist who abolished democratic reforms in his country. Though the two states signed a union agreement, Yeltsin and other Russian leaders appeared reluctant to assume responsibility for Belarus's faltering economy.

50. The Russian Federation's eighty-nine constituent parts, based on the USSR's territorial subdivisions, consist of twenty-one republics; six territories; forty-nine regions; ten autonomous areas; the Jewish autonomous region (created in the Stalinist era); and the cities of Moscow and St. Petersburg.

51. Juan J. Linz and Alfred Stepan, *Problems of Democratic Transition and Consolidation* (Baltimore, Md.: Johns Hopkins University Press, 1996), 28.

52. On regionalism, see Mary McAuley, *Russia's Politics of Uncertainty* (Cambridge: Cambridge University Press, 1997); Vladimir Shlapentokh, Roman Levita, and Mikhail Loiberg, *From Submission to Rebellion: The Provinces Versus the Center in Russia* (Boulder, Colo.: Westview, 1997); and Kathryn Stoner-Weiss, *Local Heroes: The Political Economy of Russian Regional Governance* (Princeton, N.J.: Princeton University Press, 1997).

53. Jeffrey W. Hahn, ed., *Democratization in Russia: The Development of Legislative Institutions* (Armonk, N.Y.: M. E. Sharpe, 1996).

54. *New York Times*, July 9, 2000.

55. On these points, see Robert B. Ahdieh, *Russia's Constitutional Revolution* (University Park: Pennsylvania State University Press, 1997).

56. In 1995, a group of businessmen tried to postpone the impending December legislative elections out of fear that the Communists and Zhirinovsky's nationalists might win and reverse the privatization program. Voicing a typical attitude, one said, "If people tell me that for the sake of symbolic democracy I must give up my property—well democracy is not worth that much to me"(*Financial Times*, November 7, 1995).

57. Thane Gustafson, *Capitalism, Russian-Style* (Cambridge: Cambridge University Press, 1999), 43–44, 176–79.

58. Matthew Wyman, *Public Opinion in Postcommunist Russia* (New York: St. Martin's Press, 1997); Vladimir Tismaneanu, ed., *Political Culture and Civil Society in Russia and the New States of Eurasia* (Armonk, N.Y.: M. E. Sharpe, 1995); U.S. Information Agency, *The People Have Spoken: Global Views of Democracy*, vol. 1 (January 1998), 14–19, and vol. 2 (September 1999), 24–25.

59. James Goldgeier, *Not Whether, But When* (Washington, D.C.: Brookings Institution, 2000).

60. START II (for Strategic Arms Reduction Treaty) commits the two sides to reduce their strategic nuclear warheads (i.e., nuclear bombs capable of being delivered at long range) from about 6,000 on each side to between 3,000 and 3,500 each within ten years. It was ratified by the U.S. Senate in January 1996. The United States and Russia subsequently discussed a potential START III agreement mandating further cutbacks. Russia's budgetary constraints will probably require even deeper nuclear reductions in the coming years.

CHAPTER 22

CHINA

Bruce J. Dickson

Population (1999, estimated): 1.25 billion

Area: 3.7 million square miles
(between the size of the United States and Canada)

On the morning of June 5, 1989, a young man blocked a line of tanks moving through downtown Beijing. Holding nothing but a paper shopping bag, he faced off against the first tank in the line. As it tried to maneuver to one side or the other, he would also move to remain in its way. This bizarre little drama lasted for a few minutes until several of the man's friends ran out into the street and removed him from harm's way. The tanks continued on their path.

This vignette—as short as it was, and in the end as fruitless as it was—had a lasting impression on people in China and especially on observers overseas who had been captivated by the pro-democracy movement that gripped China in the spring of 1989. The picture of the man before the tanks became a symbol of individual bravery in the face of tyranny, of the power of nonviolent political protest against the overwhelming military power of the state. But it also reminds us of the futility of such efforts. Although the pro-democracy movement lasted weeks and spread from Beijing to dozens of other cities, it was crushed overnight once the government decided to enforce the martial law it had announced several weeks before.

A perhaps apocryphal exchange between **Deng Xiaoping** (Dung Shyaow-ping*) and Zhao Ziyang revealed the underlying truth of China's political system. Deng was China's preeminent leader at the time and wanted to crush the pro-democracy movement at any cost. Zhao was the formal chief of the **Chinese Communist Party (CCP),** the man Deng had tapped as his successor before losing faith in him, and he advocated a more conciliatory response. In debating whose view should prevail, Deng reportedly said, "I have 3 million soldiers behind me." Zhao claimed he had the support of 1 billion Chinese, to which Deng replied, "You have nothing." In the end, Deng was right. The millions of people who had left their classrooms, jobs, homes, and offices to support and participate in the spontaneous, unorganized movement were no match for the monopoly on political organization and weaponry enjoyed by the state.

Young man defies tanks as Chinese authorities crack down on the pro-democracy demonstrations in Tiananmen Square, 1989.

This episode reveals the central fact of China's political system: it is governed by a communist party. Virtually every other aspect of Chinese politics—including the policy-making process, relations between state and society, and opportunities for political participation—are derived from that one fact. The top government officials, at the central level and at the local level, are party members. As in the former USSR, the party and the state are *fused* in Communist China. Policies are normally debated, decided, and implemented by party members (often in their additional capacity as government officials) with little consultation with nonparty people or organizations. Most large organizations, including universities, factories, and government offices, have party organizations within them to monitor compliance with party policies. The party has a monopoly on political organization and zealously enforces it. Whether organized to represent labor or business, to pursue sports or other hobbies, or to enhance any common interest, every organization must be authorized by the party or else it runs the risk of being disbanded and having its leaders face arrest. The goal of these organizations is not to be independent of the state, which is often the case in a pluralist democracy. Instead, the goal is to be connected to the state, to be "within the system," because everyone knows that to be outside the system means you are powerless.

These realities do not mean that the CCP is monolithic or omnipotent. The history of the CCP's rule in China after coming to power in 1949 and establishing the **People's Republic of China (PRC)** has been marked by occasionally intense

---

*In Pinyin, China's official system of transliteration into the Roman alphabet, "x" is pronounced like "sh" and "q" like "ch." Also, "en" is pronounced like "un." Some names, however, are still widely transliterated in the more traditional Wade-Giles system (e.g., Chiang Ching-kuo).

conflict over issues of power and policy. Party leaders do not always agree on the proper course of policy or even on the question of who should be in a position of power to make those decisions. The central state often cannot get lower levels of government, from the provincial level to the grass roots, to comply with its current policies. Moreover, the economic and political reforms of the past twenty years have reduced the state's control over the daily lives of most Chinese people, giving them greater independence to switch jobs, change their place of residence, travel, and have access to ideas and sources of information not controlled by the state. These changes have complicated the policy process and relaxed the state's dominance over society, but they have not challenged the CCP's preeminent position in China's political system. In a word, China's party leaders and state officials enjoy a considerable degree of latitude, or *autonomy,* when it comes to making decisions that affect the population, but the population does not have much autonomy from the party and state authorities to act in its own behalf.

The "**Democracy Spring**" of 1989 demonstrated that there are few legitimate and effective means of political participation for aggrieved individuals and groups in Chinese society. Even though the basic demands of the movement—a crackdown on corruption and inflation, enforcement of the rule of law—were consistent with the government's own policies, the state felt threatened by the spontaneous nature of the movement and the growing popular support it elicited from all walks of life. Moreover, the communist party-state saw the formation of autonomous (but short-lived) student groups and labor unions as a direct challenge to its authority and an unacceptable change in China's political system. Without these types of autonomous groups, there is little accountability for government officials and very limited access to decision-making arenas by people affected by policy decisions. On an every day basis, **clientelism**—that is, one-to-one relations based on the personal exchange of favors—is very common, and collective action by interest groups and other organizations is extremely rare. (On clientelism, see chapter 1.) Episodes of mass participation tend to be sporadic and unpredictable, prone to rapid escalation and extreme demands that result in a government crackdown rather than a negotiated compromise. The government protects its monopoly

on political organization vigorously, without hesitation and without exception. It is motivated by reinforcing sentiments: a deep-rooted cultural fear of instability and the self-interested desire to preserve the Communist Party's power.

These issues reflect the five sources of conflict enumerated in chapter 2 and raise a number of related questions about China's past, present, and future:

- *Power:* How is political power organized in China? Who should lead China, and on what basis should they govern? What is the proper relationship between state and society?
- *Resources:* How should China's resources be utilized? Should some regions and individuals be allowed to prosper while others lag behind, or is a more equitable distribution of wealth desirable? What is the proper balance between state regulation and market forces in shaping economic development?
- *Social identity:* How many of China's traditions can be carried forward into the modern world? How much can be borrowed from the West without losing a sense of national identity? How is economic development changing the shared identities of regions and professions?
- *Ideas:* How did communism develop in China? Is an authoritarian state necessary to hold the country together during a time of rapid development? Is democracy suitable or viable in China?
- *Values:* Is China's traditional emphasis on the collective needs of the group (family, community, workplace, nation) compatible with individual freedoms? Is rapid economic growth weakening the fabric of Chinese society?

Each of these sources of conflict has generated considerable debate in China, debates that continue to this day. The outcome of these debates will tell us much about where China is heading. To understand the nature of the debates, it is necessary to know where China has been.

CHINA'S HISTORICAL LEGACIES: WHY NO DEMOCRACY?

A fascination with democracy began in China early in the twentieth century, but the Chinese have never had a democratic government on any meaningful scale for any length of time. Instead, twentieth-century China was governed by a succession of authoritarian governments of the right (mostly nationalists and military leaders) and the left (the communists). These regimes were more concerned with maintaining order and national unity and fostering economic development than with promoting liberty or government accountability.

The first major turning point in the direction of fundamental political change in China came in 1911, when a revolution put an end to the long succession of imperial dynasties that had ruled China almost continually for nearly four thousand years. As one of the world's oldest civilizations, China is believed to have established its first dynasty sometime around 1875 B.C. With the establishment of the Qin (or Ch'in) dynasty in 221 B.C., followed by the Han dynasty (206 B.C. to A.D. 200), the rulers of China embarked on a period of territorial expansion and laid the groundwork for the institutional structures whose basic pattern would endure for much of the ensuing millennia.

Despite long periods of disunity and the breakdown of centralized authority, until the twentieth century China would be governed for most of its history by an imperial bureaucracy emanating from the personal authority of the emperor. The emperor, in turn, typically based his legitimacy on the "mandate of heaven," a Chinese variant of what would later be known in Europe as the divine right of kings. The teachings of **Confucius** (Kung Fu-tzu, approximately 551–479 B.C.) provided ethical guidance to imperial rule, emphasizing the hierarchical principles of moral leadership from above and the importance of authority in political and social relationships.

As the centuries unfolded, the most successful dynasties reinforced the system of government they inherited. They appointed scholar-bureaucrats to manage the government's affairs, and they established the central authority of the state over all of China. They acquired new territory and contributed to such major undertakings as the building of the Great Wall along the border with Manchuria (a project begun under the Qin dynasty and reconstructed around 1600) and the construction of large irrigation and river management projects. Nothing in the way of democracy ever emerged from dynastic rule, however: no parlia-

ments or social movements that might pry open the closed world of imperial administration. If we measure imperial China against the ten conditions for democracy specified in chapter 10, it would come up short in virtually every respect.

State institutions were authoritarian from the beginning and remained so until the collapse of the dynastic system. The governing *elites* were wholly committed to the imperial system, with its claims to divine legitimation and its Confucian ethos. The nation's *wealth* was based on an agricultural economy, with the imperial tax collection system assuring the state a large share of the national product. Commerce and *private enterprise* were frowned upon until late in the dynastic era, leaving little room for the emergence of a European-style entrepreneurial bourgeoisie or a *middle class*. China's masses, mostly destitute, illiterate peasants, were too dispersed, disorganized, and subjugated by the power of local landlords and ruling authorities to provide a groundswell of support for democracy on the part of the *disadvantaged*.

Civil society was dormant, and China's *political culture* was thoroughly imbued with Confucianism's reverence for authority and social harmony. The *educational system* was tightly connected to the state power structure, as the ruling dynasties created a system of rigorous examinations for entry into the prestigious state bureaucracy. The Ming Dynasty (1368–1644) reinforced this system, making sure that faithful adherence to the Confucian classics, rather than innovation or independence of thought, was the ultimate litmus test for a qualified Chinese official.

Ethnic *heterogeneity* also played a major role in strengthening the power of the imperial state. In the seventeenth century, invaders from Manchuria swooped down into China and took over the government, capturing Peking (Beijing) in 1644. China's new rulers, who established the Qing (or Manchu) dynasty, were not ethnic Chinese; they constituted only about 2 percent of the country's population, whose dominant ethnic group was the Han. To impose their authority on a foreign people, they had to fortify the strong arm of the imperial state. The Manchu rulers adopted the system of bureaucratic authoritarianism already in place and ruled through a judicious combination of military power and the cultivation of the leading elements of Chinese society, who in turn obligingly supported imperial rule. The Manchus compelled the Chinese to wear the queue (pigtail) as a sign of submission and never integrated themselves into the population. But they also allowed about a million Han Chinese to earn prestigious degrees and to occupy the vast majority of some forty thousand administrative posts.

The Qing emperors presided over a country with perhaps 300 million inhabitants by 1800, reaching the apogee of their power in the eighteenth century as the arts and invention flourished. The local *international environment* provided another girder of support for the imperial government, as the rulers of China—the "Middle Kingdom"—dominated the East Asian mainland. But a portent of trouble ahead arrived in 1793, when Britain's Lord Macartney called on the imperial court to discuss trade. Shockingly, the visitor refused to kowtow (bow) before the emperor, an affront to the Son of Heaven that signaled far ruder treatment at the hands of foreign intruders in the coming century.

The nineteenth century was a period of catastrophic decline for imperial China. A series of humiliating defeats at the hands of "barbarians" from abroad and organized challenges to imperial rule at home, coupled with the long-term consequences of several centuries of rapid population growth without any increase in the number of officials to govern the now much larger country, resulted in a spiraling process of political disintegration. By the start of the century, Britain was already in command of the tea trade in the southern coastal region of Guangdong (Canton). To finance their purchases, the British imported opium from India and sold it in China for substantial profits, spreading drug addiction among a growing segment of the Chinese population in the process. When the Chinese authorities tried to halt the drug traffic and suspended all trading, the British refused to back down. The "Opium War" began with a naval skirmish in 1839; it ended in 1842 with a British victory as the Chinese government was forced to cede Hong Kong and grant extraterritorial rights to foreigners in China. Another defeat in 1860 compelled the Chinese to open their doors even wider to foreign businesses and diplomatic representatives. These and other "unequal treaties" intensified the

government's xenophobia, an attitude shared by many Chinese. Meanwhile, a series of rebellions broke out in China's provinces, further sapping the central government's authority.

In 1894–95, Japan defeated China and took over the Chinese island of Taiwan. A last-ditch effort by China's dowager empress in 1900 to expel the foreigners with the aid of a superstitious peasants' movement known as the Boxers ended in dismal failure as foreign troops fought back, preserving their presence in Beijing. Meanwhile, the Russians gained a foothold in Manchuria, the home base of the Qing dynasty, eventually ceding much of their influence to the Japanese.

With China reduced to a shadow of its former glory, a debate broke out over how to rescue the country. Some blamed China itself for its predicament. The more iconoclastic thinkers argued that Confucianism was such an obstacle to China's progress that it had to be entirely abandoned, rooted out of both government and society, and replaced with an alternative system of beliefs. Confucianism valued orthodoxy over competition, stability over change, and deference to authority over individual freedoms. In the eyes of its critics, it was unsuitable to handle the challenges of the modern world, brought on by rapid population growth, urbanization, and the mounting demands from Western powers to open up China to foreign goods, technology, and ideas. They believed there was nothing to be salvaged from China's past; the only way forward was the wholesale replacement of China's tradition with the values and technology imported from the West.

Others did not want to go quite that far and advocated balancing a reliance on Chinese ways as the nation's ethical foundation and Western ways for practical purposes. In the late nineteenth century, conservative writers argued that the solution to China's problems was not the adoption of Western ways, but the exact opposite: they believed that foreign pressures were the cause of China's problems, not their solution, and those pressures needed to be countered with a determined return to orthodox traditions.

Thus began an intense debate in China that has endured to the present: how should China become modern, what parts of its past are compatible with modernity, and what are the reasons for China's current backwardness? Ultimately, the debate concerns what it means to be Chinese at a time when there is little consensus on which elements of the country's traditions should be preserved and which ones should be abandoned.

After nearly a century of humiliation, reformers in the imperial entourage won the upper hand, vowing to adapt the country's Confucian traditions to the imperatives of the modern world. Their aim was to import Western technological and administrative ideas in an effort to save the monarchy. But their ambitious reform efforts ended when conservative elements in the court, led by the empress dowager (who ruled on behalf of the last emperor of China, then still a young boy), regained control and imprisoned or exiled the erstwhile reformers, returning China to the traditions that were no match for the modern world. In October 1911, a Chinese army garrison staged a revolt, triggering a stampede of independence movements in China's provinces. The revolutionaries named **Sun Yat-sen,** a reformist intellectual trained in Western schools, as China's president. With their backs to the wall, the imperial officials ruling in the child-emperor's behalf reached an agreement with Sun Yat-sen on the dissolution of the monarchy. In February 1912, the last dynasty gave up its authority and the **Republic of China** stepped into its place.

Following the collapse of the imperial system, China was governed by a succession of authoritarian governments. The empress dowager wanted Yuan Shikai, a former general in the imperial army, to be the first president of the Republic of China, and Sun Yat-sen agreed, relinquishing the post in a spirit of compromise. But Yuan Shikai later attempted to restore the empire with himself as emperor rather than pursue real political reform. The new republican government was weak from the start. It never established its full authority over China's disparate provinces, some of which fell under the sway of local warlords.[1] Rival governments were established in Beijing under the influence of northern warlords, and in Guangzhou under the influence of Sun Yat-sen and his successor, **Chiang Kai-shek.**

Meanwhile, the debate over how far China should go in adapting Western methods gained intensity. The **May 4th Movement** epitomized the critique of Confucianism.[2] It began around 1915,

reaching full flower in 1919 after the conclusion of World War I. The hallmark of the May 4th Movement was its critical evaluation of China's condition: too weak to fend off foreign pressures, too restricted by Confucian traditions to adopt more effective policies, and too conservative to consider more innovative ideas in politics, the arts, and basic social values. During the May 4th Movement, Chinese intellectuals advocated the adoption of Western-style liberalism in China. They exalted the superiority of democracy and science over China's Confucian traditions: democracy because it entails a plurality of voices debating the common good rather than the obedience to orthodoxy required by Confucianism; science because it entails empirical investigation of nature and society in the pursuit of truth rather than the sterile application of an outmoded philosophy to rapidly changing times. Their slogan, "Let a hundred flowers bloom, let a hundred schools of thought contend" (a slogan that would be reprised in the 1950s), was itself based on Confucian traditions, but after centuries as the guiding influence over China's imperial government, Confucianism—or at least its practitioners—had become a conservative force, resistant to reform at a time of tremendous change. China's reform-minded intellectuals saw the solution to China's problems in the political traditions and systems of government in the West.

That attitude abruptly changed with the end of World War I in 1918. As the allies were deciding what to do with the territories controlled by defeated Germany, China expected that the German concessions in China—territories that had been granted to Germans by a weakened dynastic government—would be returned to Chinese control. Instead, they were given to Japan, a rising Asian power. Chinese who were inspired by the enlightened beliefs that seemed to be the foundation of Western governments were disillusioned by this turn of events. Once it became known that the Beijing government's representatives at the Versailles conference at which these decisions were made had acquiesced in this action, anti-Western protests turned into anti-government protests. This turn of events illustrates another common theme of modern Chinese politics: when Chinese society blames foreign countries for damaging or insulting China, it often also blames its own government for not being strong enough to defend China's interests against foreign threats.

For their part, the leaders of the republican government were in no hurry to embrace Western liberal democracy. Some introduced the trappings of democratic institutions or procedures, but none had the intention of actually implementing democracy in China. Although they abandoned Confucianism, the preference for a single orthodoxy prevailed over the uncertainties inherent in liberalism. Sun Yat-sen, the Republic's leading ideologist, expounded an odd mixture of Western scientific and educational theories, Christianity, Chinese nationalism, and a residual adherence to certain Chinese traditions. His lasting contribution was the establishment of a political party, the **Chinese Nationalist Party,** or **Kuomintang (KMT).** Sun devised the influential "Three Principles of the People" (nationalism, democracy, and social well-being) as the KMT's guiding political doctrine. But despite his concern for the people's welfare, Sun also believed that China was not ready for democracy and advocated a prolonged period of political tutelage to educate and prepare the Chinese people for participation in a future democratic government. Subsequently this notion was used as a rationale to maintain authoritarian controls over the country after the KMT became the ruling party of China in the late 1920s and even after it fled to Taiwan upon its defeat by the CCP in 1949.

This paternalistic belief that the Chinese people are not ready for democracy and unable to govern their own affairs remains influential in China, affecting elites and masses alike. One of the main challenges facing democratic reformers in China today is to convince not only their colleagues in government but also in society at large that democracy is valuable and will not generate chaos, a fundamental concern in Chinese political culture.

The Chinese Communist Party and China's Civil War

After a brief flirtation with liberalism, socialism grew in popularity in China for two reasons. First, it had the ironic appeal of being a Western theory that criticized the West. The writings of Marx and Lenin were used to criticize capitalist and Western imperialist influences in China. Second, the new

communist government of the Soviet Union, which took power in 1917, renounced the "unequal treaties" that the previous tsarist government had used, much like the Western countries, to gain trade and other concessions from China in the past. The new Soviet government returned the territories it controlled in China, a gesture that cost very little but that gained the Soviet communist regime tremendous popular appeal within China, especially among urban intellectuals. These events culminated in the formation of the Chinese Communist Party (CCP) in 1921. One of its first adherents was **Mao Zedong,** who would eventually rise to prominence as the party's supreme leader. The son of peasants from Hunan province, Mao developed the unconventional strategy of relying on the potential of the rural peasants, as opposed to urban workers, to lead the revolution in China. His ideas were a leading cause of both the communist victory and enormous political and human tragedies after the CCP became the ruling party in 1949.[3]

PROFILE: Mao Zedong

Born in 1893 in Hunan province, Mao Zedong was the son of successful small farmers. Ironically, his social origins placed him in the landowning class of rural China, the very class he would systematically destroy after the communists came to power. An avid reader, Mao began acquainting himself with Chinese history at an early

Mao Zedong

age. At the age of eighteen he sought out tutors in Hunan's provincial capital, and was soon caught up in the excitement emanating from Beijing as word spread about the monarchy's collapse in 1911. Young Mao followed events in radical newspapers and cut off his queue to mark his personal break with the old regime. After spending six months as a volunteer in the new Chinese Republic's army, he returned to the local libraries, immersing himself in the works of Jean-Jacques Rousseau, Adam Smith, Charles Darwin, and other Western thinkers. Between 1913 and 1918 he was a full-time student, a rarity in China for a youth of his modest background. After graduating, he followed his favorite teacher to Beijing University, where he got a job as a library clerk. The library's director at the time was Li Dazhao, a Marxist who would be a formative intellectual figure in the establishment of the Chinese Communist Party. Mao attended Li's Marxist discussion group, but he did not immediately embrace Marx's revolutionary theories.

After less than a year in the capital city, Mao returned home, where he started his own newspaper and organized a student strike against the local military figure who had taken control of Hunan's provincial government. He subsequently became a grade school teacher and established a small chain of bookstores in the region, an enterprise that made him a successful businessman. (His main store was located in a building owned by Yale University, which had a medical education program in Hunan.) He also kept up his political contacts, and in 1921 was invited to attend the founding congress of the Chinese Communist Party in Shanghai. The new party was put together largely by agents of the Soviet-sponsored Communist International organization, the Comintern. Mao was one of only fifteen people in attendance. Armed with a strong independent streak, Mao spent the next two years pursuing his own revolutionary activities, organizing strikes and workers' organizations, and he did not formally accept the party's iron rules of discipline until 1923.

Even then, Mao did not go along with all the party leadership's positions. He particularly objected to the policy imposed on the Chinese communists by Joseph Stalin, the up-and-coming Soviet leader who increasingly masterminded the USSR's international strategy. Stalin was not disposed to favor a communist revolution in China at this time. On the contrary, he was primarily concerned about Japanese expansionism, a phenomenon Russia had experienced all too acutely when the tsarist navy suffered a crushing defeat at the hands of the Japanese in the war of 1904–5. Rather than encourage the Chinese communists to launch an all-out assault on the Republican government, an action that

could only weaken China further and perhaps invite a Japanese invasion, Stalin instead instructed the CCP to come to terms with the Republic's government under the Nationalist party and offer its support. In his view, a united China might provide a more reliable buffer against potential Japanese aggression than a China embroiled in civil strife. Though a number of Chinese communists disagreed with this strategy, they complied with Stalin's wishes.

China was already very weak, its vast territory carved up into separate territories under the influence of warlords and other figures. The Nationalists (the KMT) had assumed formal control of the central government of the Republic of China, but the government's authority was limited. In 1925, Sun Yat-sen died, leaving the KMT in the hands of his son-in-law, Chiang Kai-shek, an officer who had studied military tactics in Bolshevik Russia. (Chiang's wife had attended college in the United States.) After defeating rival forces in northern China, the KMT set up the Republic's capital in the central city of Nanjing (also known as Nanking). Needing a respite from civil conflict so as to consolidate his government's authority, Chiang Kai-shek initially accepted the Chinese Communist Party's offer of collaboration. The relationship was short-lived. In 1927, Chiang turned on the CCP, attacking its stronghold in Shanghai. From this point on, the communists and the Nationalists were locked in a fierce struggle for control of China. As the years unfolded, Chiang set up a fascist form of government heavily influenced by Nazi Germany in order to consolidate his own power and defeat his enemies inside his own party and elsewhere in China.[4] Mao Zedong was soon to be his most implacable opponent.

Incensed at the party leadership's decision to collaborate with the Nationalists, Mao dropped out of the CCP's upper ranks and went back to rural Human in the mid-1920s to organize local peasants. He was convinced that the key to a socialist revolution in China lay with the peasant masses, not with the minuscule Chinese industrial proletariat extolled in Marxist-Leninist doctrine. After Chiang Kai-shek turned on the communists in 1927, Mao led a force of 10,000 peasants in search of a secure base of operations where they could evade—and eventually attack—the Nationalist army. "We must know," Mao wrote at the time, "that all power is obtained from the barrel of a gun."

Between 1930 and 1934, Mao hunkered down with his troops and closest lieutenants in Jiangxi province in southern China. It was there that they established the "Jiangxi Soviet," a model peasant communist society. After Japan attacked Shanghai, a number of the the Communist Party's principal leaders joined Mao in Jiangxi. But as Chiang Kai-shek's Nationalist forces closed in on the communist stronghold, the CCP leadership decided to move their forces out. With no clear destination in mind, they embarked on what became known in Chinese communist lore as the **Long March,** an arduous year-long journey that ended in the fall of 1935 in Shaanxi province in north China, more than a thousand miles away from where they had started. Though tens of thousands of communist troops had begun the trek, only about seven to eight thousand made it to the end. While some of these forces were deliberately left behind along the way so as to establish pockets of resistance, many were killed by Nationalist soldiers or died of illness. (Mao's second wife had already been killed in an earlier encounter with the KMT army; his third wife was hit by shrapnel on the Long March.) Installing themselves in caves near the town of Yanan in 1936, Mao and other party leaders remained in the region for the next eleven years. These leaders included people who were to become China's ruling elite until well into the 1970s and, for some, the 1980s and 1990s.[5]

Over time they were joined by tens of thousands of fresh recruits, mostly peasants who managed to elude Chiang-Kai-shek's Nationalist army. The communists' success in winning large numbers of people to their cause was aided by Japan's invasion of Manchuria in 1931, followed by its all-out attack on China in 1937. Despite American assistance in the war effort, Chiang Kai-shek's government proved largely ineffective against the Japanese, whose occupation was marked by such atrocities as the "rape of Nanking," the wholesale slaughter of hundreds of thousands of civilians.[6] Chiang himself was more interested in defeating the communists, hoping that the United States would eventually take care of the Japanese.

In their propaganda messages aimed at the population, the communists deftly combined nationalist themes, which focused on the need to fight the Japanese, with ideological themes that stressed the need for a socialist revolution that would liberate the downtrodden peasant masses from exploitation by their capitalist landlords, who tended to support the KMT government. Though China was still a predominantly peasant country, a far cry from the advanced industrialized society Karl Marx required for a true socialist revolution, Mao believed that a peasant socialist revolution was possible. The revolutionary potential of the peasantry was one of Mao's seminal contributions to the Marxist tradition, a creative adaptation of Marxism to Chinese conditions. (Even today, roughly 80 percent of China's population lives in rural areas, though half are now engaged in non-agricultural jobs.) These two themes struck a responsive chord among millions of people, and the communists gradually attracted vast numbers of adherents to their fighting force, the **People's Liberation Army.** (China's army retains this name today.) But the combination of the civil war against the Nationalist Chinese government and the war against the Japanese occupation took a heavy toll on communist forces; it is probable that hundreds of thousands of communist supporters died at the hands of one or the other of their two foes.

As the casualties mounted with no victory in sight, factional struggles among the Communist Party's leaders intensified, with rivals pointing fingers at one another in ascribing blame for the party's plight. It was in these years that Mao Zedong responded to his critics by affirming his preeminence as a military strategist and revolutionary theorist. As his "personality cult" emerged, Mao adopted a harsh stance against party intellectuals, enjoining them to learn from peasants and workers instead of imposing their own doctrines on them. This notion of learning from the masses so as to more effectively lead them became known as the "mass line." In some cases Mao and his followers brought force to bear on opponents within the party. Mao's assertion of political and ideological authority proved increasingly successful. Between 1943 and 1945 he became chairman of the party's Central Committee and Politburo, its leading decision-making bodies. Lauded as "the helmsman of the revolution" as his rivals retreated, Mao saw to it that his thought was adopted as "the guide for all the party's work."

After Japan's surrender in 1945, the civil war between the Nationalists and the communists resumed in full force. It was not much of a contest. The KMT army was demoralized, its government corrupt, and its popular base eroded by its military and economic failures.[7] The United States tried to broker a collaborative agreement between the Nationalists and the communists in an effort to forestall a conflict that might prompt the Soviet Union to exert its influence in China. But both sides broke the agreement, and Mao elaborated a military strategy that kept the weary Nationalist forces on the defensive over the next four years and repeatedly encircled. Communist troops entered Beijing in January 1949 and Shanghai in April. Chiang Kai-shek retreated from mainland China and headed for the offshore island of Taiwan, taking 500,000 Nationalist troops with him. On October 1, Mao Zedong proclaimed the People's Republic in Beijing, and over the next few months his government pursued the "liberation" of areas formerly controlled by the Nationalists in the southern provinces.

For Mao, the long quest for power was at an end; but his historic impact on China's people and institutions was only just beginning.

The Nationalists' defeat in the Chinese civil war led not only to a change of government in China but also to a fierce debate in the United States over "who lost China?" in the 1950s. Meanwhile, as the Nationalists repaired to **Taiwan** to relocate their government of the Republic of China, Chiang Kai-shek and his followers hoped one day to retake the mainland. The KMT remained the Republic's ruling party in Taiwan until it finally lost the presidency when its candidate finished a distant third in the 2000 elections. Ever since 1949, Taiwan has been a source of tension in Communist China's foreign policies, especially in its relations with the United States. The United States retained diplomatic relations and a mutual defense treaty with the Republic of China on Taiwan until 1979, when it switched its China policy by recognizing the People's Republic as the sole legitimate government of all China. Although the United States recognizes Communist China's claim that there is but one China and that Taiwan is part of it, it continues to sell defensive arms to Taiwan and has an implicit commitment to defend Taiwan against an attack from mainland China. In recent years, the KMT has become a model of democratic government, in stark contrast to the continued authoritarian politics exercised on the Chinese mainland.

China's post–1949 split into "two Chinas" (in fact if not in international law) has severely complicated the meaning of Chinese nationalism. What, in fact, is the "Chinese nation"? Nationalism has been an influential force at various times in twentieth-century China, but it has also been a very ambiguous one. There is still little consensus on the values and symbols that define the Chinese nation.

THE REPUBLIC OF CHINA ON TAIWAN

After its defeat by the communists in the Chinese civil war in 1949, the Kuomintang (KMT) leaders retreated to Taiwan, an island off the coast of the Chinese mainland. Also known in the West by its Portuguese name of Formosa, the island had been a Japanese colony from 1895 to 1945. After Japan's defeat in World War II, Taiwan was returned to Chinese sovereignty. From this outpost, the KMT hoped to regroup its forces and once again retake the mainland. It installed its government in the city of Taipei.

Most non-communist countries maintained formal diplomatic ties with the government on Taiwan, still officially called the Republic of China. Both the KMT and the CCP claimed they were the sole legitimate government of all China, and countries had to choose whether they would have diplomatic ties with the one or the other. Neither Beijing nor Taipei would accept dual recognition, that is, allowing foreign countries to have diplomatic relations with both Beijing and Taipei. (Dual recognition was similarly rejected by the two states of divided Germany until unification in 1990, and is still rejected by the states of North and South Korea.) The KMT government even held China's permanent seat on the United Nations Security Council until it was expelled in 1971 to make room for the People's Republic of China to assume this seat. As the United States, Japan, and most other countries began establishing diplomatic ties with the People's Republic in the 1970s, Taiwan's diplomatic standing steadily declined. Today, it has formal diplomatic ties with only around thirty countries, mostly small countries in Africa, Latin America, and the Pacific Islands.

The KMT established a harsh authoritarian government under Chiang Kai-shek upon its arrival on Taiwan and suppressed the desire of the Taiwanese people for self-determination and greater democracy. The native Taiwanese are themselves émigrés from mainland China, but they arrived several centuries earlier and developed a subculture of their own. Most Taiwanese resented the heavy-handed rule of the mainlanders who arrived after World War II and who took over the positions of authority and even the property previously held by the Japanese. (The mainland émigrés and their descendants now comprise about 15 percent of Taiwan's population.) Tensions between the native Taiwanese and the mainlanders remained high and often took a violent turn. With the gradual democratization of Taiwan in recent years, those tensions have largely dissipated, but not entirely.

The KMT reorganized itself as a Leninist-style party on Taiwan, maintaining control over the government and the military and maintaining party organizations in most communities and workplaces. It allowed no other political parties to organize and imprisoned or forced into exile those who sought democratizing reforms. Most positions were held by mainlanders, even at the very local level. Only in the 1970s were indigenous Taiwanese gradually appointed to influential positions, a process known as "Taiwanization."

While retaining tight political controls, the KMT simultaneously promoted Taiwan's economic development. Using a combination of state leadership and market incentives, the government adopted an outward-oriented trade strategy that produced rapid economic growth and the creation of globally competitive industrial and high-technology firms. Based on this model of development, Taiwan became one of the most successful newly industrializing countries in the world and a dynamic leader of the "Asian tigers" that included South Korea and Singapore. Today it enjoys a very high standard of living, with a per capita GDP of roughly $13,000. It is the seventh-largest trading nation in the world.

President Chiang Kai-shek died in 1975, and the mantle of leadership fell to his son, Chiang Ching-kuo. Beginning in the 1970s, the KMT gradually loosened its political grip, making a transition from "hard" to "soft" authoritarianism. In the 1980s, the KMT initiated the gradual democratization of Taiwan's political system under pressure from a loosely organized group of opposition politicians, which later evolved into the Democratic Progressive Party, Taiwan's main opposition party. The growing middle class has played a significant role in exerting pressures for democracy. Taiwan now has elections for all leadership posts, including the presidency. During this democratization process, the KMT transformed itself from a party that was dominated by mainlanders—and widely regarded as out of touch with the wants and needs of Taiwan's society—into a mainstream conservative party whose top leaders are now primarily Taiwanese.

Upon Chiang Ching-kuo's death in 1988, Lee Teng-hui, the KMT's new chief, became Taiwan's next president. In 1990 he was confirmed in that post by a vote of the National Assembly, the first presidential election in Taiwan. In 1996, Lee was reelected, this time in a direct vote by the people. In March 2000, Taiwanese voters removed the KMT from power, electing **Chen Shui-bian** of the Democratic Progressive Party as their new president. Chen's outspoken support for Taiwan's

independence evoked harsh criticism in the People's Republic, which sought to prevent his election by issuing intimidating threats during the election campaign. A former mayor of Taipei whose anti-KMT views once landed him in prison, Chen vowed to clean up corruption and expressed admiration for British Prime Minister Tony Blair's "third way," which seeks to combine a globally competitive capitalism with compassionate social welfare.

Taiwan's international status still has not been finally resolved. It is a de facto independent country; that is, it is independent *in fact* but not in international law. The Nationalist government's initial official position was that it hoped for eventual reunification in a democratic and capitalist China. But in 1991, the KMT renounced its claim of sovereignty over the mainland. The PRC and most foreign countries still maintain a "one China" policy that asserts that there is only one China and that it includes Taiwan. Taiwan is allowed to participate in some international organizations, such as the Asian Development Bank and sports competitions such as the Olympics, but only under an unofficial name, such as "Chinese-Taipei." Because of the PRC's insistence, Taiwan does not belong to the most important organizations, such as the UN, the World Bank, the IMF, or the World Health Organization. Taiwan's efforts to play a more active and visible role in international affairs frequently creates tensions with China and other countries, which are concerned that such efforts may lead to a declaration of independence by Taiwan.

In 1996, for example, the People's Republic conducted naval maneuvers off Taiwan's coast in an effort to influence the presidential elections, manifesting its displeasure at candidates calling for independence. The United States responded by sending aircraft carriers to the region. In 1999, when President Lee declared that Taiwan would henceforth conduct its relations with the People's Republic on a "state-to-state" basis, the communist government in Beijing immediately denounced the statement as a provocation. And in early 2000, in a transparent attempt to affect the outcome of the presidential elections, the PRC issued an ominous warning that any delay on Taiwan's part in commencing negotiations on reunification would compel Beijing "to adopt all drastic measures possible, including the use of force." Unfazed by these threats, a plurality of Taiwanese voters (about 39 percent) gave their votes to the pro-independence candidate, Chen Shui-bian, who outpolled two competitors. Chen subsequently toned down his rhetoric, calling for negotiations with Beijing and asserting that Taiwan would declare its independence only if attacked by Communist China. The PRC also backed off from its bellicose threats several months later.

President Chen Shui-bian

In sum, despite its remarkable record of economic and political progress, Taiwan still does not enjoy the international recognition that its government and people feel it deserves.[8]

The Communists Take Over

After the CCP became the ruling party in 1949, it promised a "new democracy" with the active involvement of non-CCP elites and organizations. Two key institutions begun during the civil war years were intended to be the basis of this new democracy. The *mass line* was a process by which concerns and suggestions would come *from the masses* and the policy decisions would be communicated by officials *to the masses*. This cycle of deliberation envisioned a closed relationship between the state and society in which society would better understand policy decisions and thereby support them, and the state would better understand the concerns of society and the impact of its policies and thereby devise more effective policies.

The second political institution that was central to China's "new democracy" was the *united front*. The CCP promised to consult and cooperate with non-CCP elites, such as businesspeople, scholars, and even religious leaders, in order to promote China's modernization. The united front promised a consensual policy process rather than a conflictual one. Today, united front policies are again being publicized to promote cooperation between government and business in China's economic modernization.

Although the mass line and united front policies had some democratic aspirations, in practice they provided at best consultation without accountability. The communist party-state could listen to a variety of viewpoints, but it selected which views would be heard and which would be suppressed. If the state chose to ignore the concerns of society or the suggestions of non-CCP elites, there was little these groups could do to seek redress. If state policies failed, there was no way for the public to replace the policy makers. In fact, the mass line and the united front more often than not have been means of enforcing dictatorship and state domination at the expense of democratic principles and procedures.

Let us now turn to a more detailed discussion of China's political institutions and their performance during the post-1949 communist era.

CHINA'S POLITICAL INSTITUTIONS

As noted at the beginning of this chapter, the most basic fact of China's political system is that it is ruled by a communist party. The party is organized along Leninist lines: like V. I. Lenin's Bolshevik Party, the CCP resembles a military hierarchy, with the chain of command going from the top down. Though lower-level party officials may have a chance to have their views communicated to the party's upper echelons, once a final decision has been taken by the top leaders, all party members are obliged to fall into line behind it. The party elite rules. Virtually every other aspect of China's politics and government, including the policy process and relations between state and society, are derived from that fundamental truth.

The Chinese Communist Party

At the top of China's political system, and integrated throughout it at all levels, is the Chinese Communist Party. Although it came to power relying on the support of peasants, workers, and soldiers, the CCP today is a broad-based party, drawing its members from all walks of life, including bureaucrats, teachers, and other people in white-collar jobs. It has over 60 million members, a group which is roughly 5 percent of China's population but larger than the population of many countries in the world.

The most important organization within the CCP is the **Politburo.** This body consists of the top two dozen or so leaders in China. Members of the Politburo often hold other important positions in the central government and the military simultaneously. Some local governments, especially Beijing and Shanghai, are also represented on the Politburo. It approves all major policies and personnel changes. Its actual deliberations are clouded in secrecy, but it is believed to make its decisions by consensus rather than majority rule. Within the Politburo there is a subgroup of China's five to seven most powerful leaders, known as the **Standing Committee** of the Politburo.

The top party official is the **General Secretary,** currently **Jiang Zemin.** Mao Zedong had the title of "Chairman" of the party, but that post was eliminated after his death in 1976 to prevent any leader from accumulating the degree of uncontrolled power that Mao had. The General Secretary is formally in charge of the **Secretariat,** a small organization connected to the Politburo that handles the daily affairs of the party leadership, such as the flow of reports and memos among party leaders and the organization of important meetings.

According to party statutes, the Politburo and Secretariat are supposed to be elected in a sequential process by two larger bodies: the **Central Committee** and the **Party Congress.** The Central Committee is a group of 150 to 200 people that meets once or twice a year to formally endorse important policies and leadership changes that have been approved by the Politburo beforehand. The members of the Central Committee represent a broader range of the party's top elites, mostly senior party and government officials from around the country. Some discussion takes place, but the Central Committee rarely, if ever, initiates policy or forces the senior leaders to change course. The Central Committee formally elects the Politburo and its Standing Committee, the Secretariat, and the General Secretary. These votes, too, are usually pro forma, as the top leaders invariably decide among themselves how the senior decision-making positions will be distributed.

The Central Committee is formally elected by the National Party Congress, a meeting of more than a thousand party leaders. Although it is supposed to meet every five years, in the past it met on an irregular basis. The Seventh Party Congress met in 1945, and the next ones did not meet until 1956 and 1969. Since then the body has met more regularly: in 1973, 1977, 1982, 1987, 1992, and most recently, 1997 (the Fifteenth Party Congress). Very little actual debate goes at these week-long sessions; the Congress typically provides the party leadership with an opportunity to review past achievements and outline the main lines of policy to be pursued in the coming years. Though the Congress takes a formal vote in electing the Central Committee, in fact the Central Committee's membership has already been decided by higher party authorities, leaving the Congress only mar-

FIGURE 22.1 Organization of the Chinese Communist Party

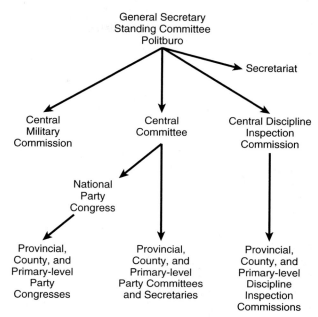

The Central Military Commission is the CCP's organization for overseeing the military. The Central Discipline Inspection Commission, and lower-level discipline inspection commissions, are responsible for monitoring the behavior of party members, especially party and government officials. They have the authority to charge and punish those guilty of corruption, malfeasance, and other violations of party policy. Primary-level party bodies are organized at workplaces, schools, neighborhoods, military companies, and small towns.

ginal influence. (For instance, the Politburo may present the Congress a list of 170 names, of which 165 will be elected to the Central Committee.)

Party supremacy over the government, the military, and other institutions is achieved through a combination of oversight and personnel appointments. Within all government ministries, factories, schools, and other work units is a party committee that monitors compliance with party directives. The party also nominates or approves all key personnel, from cabinet ministers and department heads to even such relatively low-level positions as heads of university departments and bank officials.

The State

China's government is organized like many parliamentary governments. The executive branch is headed by a **prime minister,** currently **Zhu**

FIGURE 22.2   Structure of State Institutions

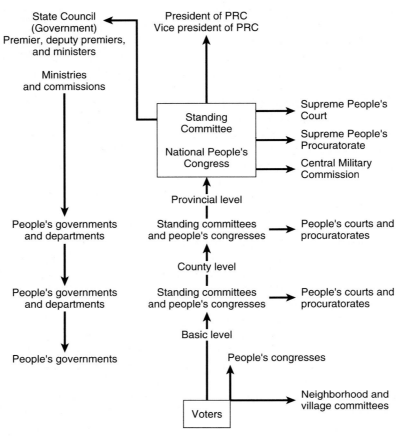

The provincial level includes 22 provinces, 5 autonomous regions, and 3 large cities (Beijing, Shanghai, and Tianjin). At the county level there are approximately 1,700 counties, 400 cities, and 700 urban districts. The basic level consists of towns and villages. The people elect basic and county-level people's congresses as well as neighborhood and village committees, but their choices are usually limited to candidates picked by the party.

Rongji, who also appoints officials to head the other ministries and commissions of the government. This group of people comprises the State Council, the equivalent of a cabinet. Almost all top officials in the government are also CCP members, with a few symbolic exceptions to show the party's continued adherence to a "united front" approach to governing. Even non-party officials, however, are approved and appointed by the CCP. *Although the CCP approves the broad principles of policy, it is the government that has the main responsibility for actually implementing policy and monitoring results.*

China's legislative branch is called the **National People's Congress.** It is the weakest of the three

main political institutions (the other two being the party and government), although it has been getting more assertive and more influential in recent years. Formerly derided as a rubber-stamp legislature because it unanimously approved all motions proposed by the CCP without dissent or discussion, it now takes an active role in drafting legislation, approving annual budgets, and monitoring the results of reforms. In the past, it met irregularly to ratify party policy; it now has permanent committees with full-time staffs that work year-round. Despite these changes, the National People's Congress is not a democratic or deliberative body. Though its three thousand members are elected by lower-level "People's Congresses," the

Communist Party hierarchy carefully supervises their selection. Even those who advocate a more active role for it do not see it as a vehicle for democratization. Instead they want to make it an institution capable of overseeing the work of the party and government, perhaps delaying or reversing policy decisions made by higher authorities when necessary. They seek to make it a stronger institution, but not necessarily a more liberal or democratic one.[9]

One of the duties of the National People's Congress is to elect the **president** of the People's Republic as China's formal head of state. Jiang Zemin has held this post since 1993, but it is largely a ceremonial one that gives him formal standing as a government official, a useful status when engaging in international diplomacy with other heads of state or heads of government. Within China, however, the presidency is nowhere nearly as important a position as Jiang's other positions, that of General Secretary of the Chinese Communist Party and chairman of the party's Central Military Commission. Unlike Deng Xiaoping, who selected people other than himself to fill these top posts in order to prevent a power struggle from taking place when he died (like the one that occurred after Mao's death), Jiang has accumulated three of the most important posts for himself. This concentration of so many offices in one person is reminiscent of Mao's concentration of power. However, Jiang is not the powerful leader Mao was, nor is he even as powerful as Deng, for that matter. He holds the formal positions, but he lacks the informal characteristics of personal authority associated with Mao and Deng: a clear vision, the respect of colleagues and society, and a reputation for past accomplishments.

These three main institutions—the party, the executive branch of government, and the legislature—are present at all levels of the political system, from the center in Beijing to the local levels around the country, including provinces, cities, counties, and townships. At each level, *the party is the most important body,* and the *party secretary* is the most important leader. Higher-level party officials appoint or approve lower-level officials to maintain some degree of oversight over local affairs. Nevertheless, making sure that local governments faithfully and efficiently carry out the policies decided by higher levels has been an ongoing challenge in China, as it is in many countries. Very few officials are directly elected by the people.

Over the past decade, China has been experimenting with direct village elections for the positions of village chief and villagers' representative assemblies, but even where these elections have been successful, the people elected have authority over only a small range of issues. (These elections will be described later in this chapter.) Delegates to county-level People's Congresses are directly elected, but then these delegates elect delegates to the next level people's congress, a process that is repeated up to the National People's Congress. In practice, all people's congress delegates are screened and approved by the *party* before assuming their posts.

POLITICS IN MAO'S CHINA

The leader of China's communist revolution, Mao Zedong, once said, "A revolution is not a dinner party, or writing an essay, or painting a picture, or doing embroidery; it cannot be so refined, so leisurely and gentle, so temperate, kind, courteous, restrained and magnanimous. A revolution is an insurrection, an act of violence by which one class overthrows another."[10] By the time the civil war was over in 1949, China had suffered more than a century of decline, due to both internal problems and foreign encroachment. As Chairman Mao declared in Beijing in the fall of 1949, after the revolution was won, China had finally stood up for itself. But the problems faced by China after decades of war were numerous and severe. Mao and the CCP had three main goals.[11]

The first goal was *national unification.* After a period of national disunion, China needed to reintegrate its fractured society. China had long been a unified country, but after being carved into sections formerly occupied by the Japanese, the KMT, and communist armies, plus areas controlled by warlords, the first task was to create a unified country and system of government. Although the civil war was essentially over in 1949, mopping up operations in the south and western border areas lasted into the early 1950s.

The second goal was *transformation.* Mao and the CCP leadership were determined to carry out a revolution of the political and social system, which they viewed as the ultimate cause of

China's backwardness. In some ways, the revolution truly *began* in 1949; only the civil war had ended. During the early 1950s, the CCP implemented land reform on a nationwide basis. It overthrew the traditional hold of landlords—who comprised a class of about 15 million people—over the rest of rural society and gave their land to the peasants. It is estimated that tens of thousands—and perhaps hundreds of thousands—of landlords were killed in the process. The party also implemented a new marriage law that outlawed the traditional arranged marriages. The marriage law was designed not only to enhance the rights of women, but also to break down the traditional power of clans and heads of families. They also banned opium and prostitution, putting addicts and prostitutes into rehabilitation centers where their medical problems were addressed and they were taught new skills. On the basis of the political and social revolution, China's new leaders believed that economic modernization would then be possible.

Their third task was *modernization:* this entailed both economic recovery (especially ending inflation and restoring agricultural and industrial production to their levels before the Japanese invasion) and economic development, using the Soviet model of rapid industrialization and a centrally planned economy. Mao wanted China to be recognized as a great power among nations. But this goal could be accomplished only if the other two goals were accomplished first.

How successful were Mao and the CCP in carrying out their goals? There is an old saying in China, "You can conquer a country on horseback, but you cannot govern it on horseback." After winning the civil war, the CCP had to make the transition from being a military organization fighting a hit-and-run guerilla campaign to being a ruling party responsible for a national government. Whereas they used to control only remote rural areas, the communists now had to govern the entire nation, a task that required them to move into the cities, where they did not have a great deal of popular support.

In the early 1950s, they took a moderate approach to governing. They did not immediately expel all the officials from the old government or confiscate all private property, but instead set up a kind of coalition government under their direction in order to elicit popular support from diverse groups in China. Most officials from the old regime were retained out of necessity: the CCP simply did not have enough members with the skills necessary to take over a nationwide bureaucracy. These old officials had the requisite experience and were therefore relied on, at least in the early 1950s. This practice caused resentment among the CCP's veterans, who felt they had devoted themselves to the revolution and deserved to be given these important positions as a reward. They also resented the party's efforts to recruit better-qualified members and to upgrade the qualifications of existing members. The revolutionaries felt insulted by this emphasis on skills over experience and political reliability.[12]

These conflicts gave rise to one of the most divisive issues in Communist China, the **red versus expert debate.** While we can assume that most, if not all, Chinese leaders share the same ultimate goals, they disagree on the proper methods and the pace of change. During the Maoist period (1949–76), many policy debates and power struggles were linked to the issue of whether to emphasize "redness" or expertise. "Reds" were the most ideologically oriented revolutionaries, characterized by their political reliability and ability to mobilize the masses rather than by their technical, administrative, or scientific skills. They believed that economic questions could not be solved until political obstacles (namely anything resembling Western or capitalist values) were eliminated. Consequently, they believed that political factors should determine all policies, whether economic, social, or cultural.

"Experts," by contrast, were more interested in creating a sound, growing economy that would provide the basis for achieving the communists' ultimate goals. They typically had better educational backgrounds than most reds and had not served in the guerilla armies. But the reds questioned the experts' commitment to the CCP and resented their arrogance. Experts in turn resented the intrusion of poorly trained zealots into their complicated work.

The red versus expert debate was closely related to the question of the party's primary goal: whether to promote the country's *economic development* or to be more concerned with **utopianism**.[13] During the Maoist era, China had the political goal of creating a Marxian communist utopia in which there would be no exploitation and in which an abundance of goods and services would be available for distribution to the population on a relatively equitable basis. In the end, the state would wither away, as Marx and Engels had predicted, and its former tasks would be carried out on a voluntary basis by individuals sharing communist values. But China's existing political and economic conditions prevented this utopia from coming about naturally. Therefore, in the eyes of the CCP leadership, a strong party was necessary for two reasons.

One was to lead the "class struggle" against so-called class enemies who resisted the policies advocated by the Communist Party. These were the former landlords, businesspeople, government officials, and others who benefited from the old system or who were believed to have capitalist attitudes inconsistent with communism. The second reason was to *prevent the backsliding of society*, which was likely to occur as the economy developed. As class enemies were eliminated and standards of living improved, people could be expected to lose their enthusiasm for revolutionary goals and might favor a return to more normal, less disruptive lives. Economic interests tend to be more important than political ones for most people most of the time, especially for individuals living in underdeveloped areas like China during the Maoist period. Consequently, the party had to carry out periodic propaganda campaigns to remind people of the communist ideology's ultimate goals and prevent them from being corrupted by less pure thoughts.

Party policy in the Maoist period therefore oscillated between economic development and ideological utopianism. When economic development was the primary goal, party and state policies emphasized production goals and allowed a limited amount of private enterprise and market activity, permitting people to make a little money on the side (thereby creating incentives for more production). They emphasized technical skills in personnel matters and minimized the intrusiveness of political campaigns. In contrast, when utopian goals were paramount, party-state policies prohibited or greatly constrained markets, political campaigns became more coercive and dangerous, and economic growth suffered.

Mao was the champion of both sets of policies, and he often shifted between the two as he felt na-

tional conditions mandated. Policy did not change without Mao's consent: his support was necessary for policy decisions, and in fact his change of heart was often sufficient to bring about a change of goals or a change of policies. As a result, during Mao's lifetime China lurched back and forth between these divergent goals of development and utopia. As time went on, Mao seemed to favor utopian goals above all else. Mao wanted to modernize China, but for him, the means were as important as the ends. He was more concerned with questions of equity than he was with growth per se. His supporters often said it was better to be poor and communist than rich and capitalist.

Key episodes in the post-1949 history of China are impossible to understand without appreciating Mao's central role in the political system. In fact, in 1953 the Central Committee passed a resolution that authorized Mao to personally approve all decisions made by the Politburo and Central Committee or else they would be invalid. In 1988, a dozen years after Mao's death, the Central Committee passed a similar secret resolution, this time allowing Deng Xiaoping, Mao's successor as supreme leader, to approve all decisions. Both resolutions violated not only democratic procedures but also the party's traditional norms of consensual decision making. Nevertheless, they reflected the preeminent authority these two men held within China's political system.

During the Maoist period there were three main episodes in which policy shifted from development to utopia. The first came with the **collectivization** of industry and agriculture in 1955–56. By the mid-1950s, the CCP had consolidated its power, eliminated its rivals, and restored the economy to pre-war production levels. It then decided to eliminate all remaining private ownership of land and capital. On the land, some 110 million farm households were converted into about 300,000 communist "cooperatives" under the party's direction. In cities and towns, privately owned factories and other businesses were completely taken over by the party-state authorities. Capitalism in China was virtually extinguished by 1956 (although the former owners were often retained as managers). This turning point was of major significance in party policy: the CCP's basis for popular support had been its land reform policies, and now the land that had just recently been given to the poorest peasants was being taken away. The new policies toward industry and agriculture required a greater role for the party. It had to coordinate production and make sure that its policies were followed. Resistance to the collectivization policies, especially in the countryside, caused the party to pull back a little, but only temporarily. However, there was none of the violence that accompanied the land reform of the early 1950s, which in turn was much milder than the Soviet experience under Stalin in the 1920s.

The collectivization of agriculture and industry was followed by the **Hundred Flowers Movement** in 1957.[14] As noted earlier, the slogan came from a saying of Confucius, "Let a hundred flowers bloom, let a hundred schools of thought contend." It implied that the give and take of ideas was not only healthy but beneficial to the state. Mao invited criticisms of the party's performance from experts and intellectuals, confident that his policy successes so far had created considerable enthusiasm and support for the regime. He expected mild criticism of the bureaucratic work style of some party and government officials, in line with his own view that the conservative nature of bureaucracies would inevitably slow progress toward the nation's development. Mao felt that the government was comprised of bureaucrats who, as he put it, behaved like women with bound feet, tottering along taking small steps, afraid to take bold strides.

When Mao began encouraging people to voice their criticisms—an opening seized by intellectuals— what he got instead was a stream of complaints about the fundamental nature of the political system. There were complaints about the absence of democracy, the rule of law, free expression, and free scientific inquiry; complaints about party interference in all walks of life; and above all, complaints about the intrusion of incompetent and illiterate reds in the work of the experts. These were precisely the kinds of criticisms Mao's colleagues feared when they opposed the Hundred Flowers policy.

Mao seems to have been genuinely taken aback by the vehemence of the intellectuals' complaints. Rather than address their concerns, he labeled them "rightists" (akin to being a counterrevolutionary, a very serious crime). He then launched an *Anti-Rightist campaign* to persecute them, replacing many of them with his own political supporters. The sense of betrayal was deep and long-

lasting on the part of China's intellectuals. After responding to Mao's personal request to air their views freely, they were ridiculed, persecuted, and in many instances, imprisoned. Zhu Rongji, China's current prime minister, was imprisoned during this time. The Anti-Rightist campaign alienated most of China's intellectuals and made them wary of voicing their political views again.[15] Their wariness was not just due to the political culture's emphasis on respecting authority; more important, they had learned from their own experience the high cost of dissent.

Following the Anti-Rightist campaign, the second episode of promoting utopian goals took shape. After disregarding the concerns of China's experts, Mao decided to tap into the latent energy of the masses to create economic growth. The party would encourage people to work harder, not with higher wages, but with propaganda and persuasion. This campaign became known as the **Great Leap Forward** (1958–59), the period when the communes were created.[16] Communes were large-scale economic and administrative units, each combining ten or more villages. Work teams were sent out to mobilize the efforts of peasants and organize their work. Sometimes they would work twenty-four-hour shifts of intensive labor. At first, it seemed that the Great Leap policies were working: most communes reported a bumper harvest, and the counties and provinces began competing with one another to claim the highest production achievements (thus proving that they were the most loyal to Mao). Nightly dinners became banquets at the commune's mess halls as people tried to eat up the excess food, thinking that there was too much to actually harvest and transport to urban areas. But in fact, the harvest was far below the forecast. Much of the grain that would normally have been stored for the winter and for spring planting was eaten in the summer and fall. By 1959, it became clear that the country was in deep trouble. Economic forecasts were drastically cut back. Reports of unrest in the countryside and general unhappiness with the mass mobilization tactics of the Great Leap Forward circulated among the party leadership. The policy excesses of the Great Leap combined with unusually bad weather to create a crisis of huge proportions. During the "three bad years" of 1960–62, close to 30 million people starved to death.

This calamity resulted in a full-scale retreat from the policies of the Great Leap Forward and a period of recovery that lasted for several years.[17] Once again, restoring order and increasing production through proper planning and the use of economic incentives became official policy. Private plots, banned with the creation of the communes, once again were approved. These plots allowed farmers to grow a little extra fruit and vegetables for themselves and to sell some for extra cash. Mao grudgingly tolerated these recovery policies, recognizing that they were necessary to solve the severe crisis facing his country. But he was unwilling to accept them as long-term policies for fear that they would restore capitalism to China and because the reliance on regularized procedures—those favored by experts—minimized the role of his supporters and, not incidentally, his own influence.

By 1965, Mao had several main grievances against his colleagues. For one thing, he felt their policies were leading the country in the wrong direction. The recovery policies sponsored and implemented by such party leaders as Liu Shaoqi and Deng Xiaoping were successful in creating growth and restoring order, but they were leading the country away from the communist utopia Mao envisioned. In 1962, Mao reminded his colleagues, and China more generally, "Never forget class struggle." In other words, the work of economic recovery should not distract people from the true goal of achieving communism.

Another grievance was that Mao was being marginalized. He was no longer consulted in the policy-making process. He complained that Deng had stopped giving him policy briefings and at meetings sat with his bad ear toward Mao. The party chairman referred to himself as a living Buddha: revered but generally ignored.

Indeed, Mao was not happy with his potential successors. With his life running out, Mao wanted to be sure that loyal successors were in place at the top of the party and that a new generation of party members filled with his revolutionary zeal and preference for redness over expertise would be ready to fill posts at all levels of the political system. By the mid-1960s, however, Mao felt betrayed by his heirs apparent, Liu and Deng, and felt that the next generation of leaders lacked the experience of forging a revolution necessary to instill the correct virtues.

Political victims of the Cultural Revolution, wearing dunce caps, are denounced by angry mobs.

These frustrations led him to launch the **Great Proletarian Cultural Revolution,** the third episode of utopianism.[18] Mao became convinced that his own party had lost its revolutionary fervor and had become hostile to himself personally as well as to his policies. He felt that many party members were too concerned with economics, including recovery from the Great Leap, and had forgotten the goals and methods of revolution. Moreover, he felt that the younger generation of China, which had not been tempered in the furnace of the revolution, would benefit from the struggle and the chaos that revolution entails. He therefore encouraged young people, especially students, to form groups of **Red Guards** to attack, verbally and physically, the representatives of the party and state: local leaders, teachers, factory managers, and even high-ranking party leaders and cabinet ministers.

This campaign blurred the distinction between mobilization and participation: people were mobilized by the top leader, but the target was the state itself. The Red Guards succeeded in attacking people who exercised or symbolized power, along with anyone else suspected of not being loyal to Mao. They fanned throughout China bearing copies of the "little red book" of Mao's choice quotations, haranguing people in lengthy propaganda sessions in factories, on farms, and out in the streets. They broke into party and government offices and released information that supposedly revealed the anti-Maoist activities of the officeholders. They held public "struggle" sessions, in which selected targets were harshly criticized and assaulted. Those being attacked were subjected to beatings, imprisonment, and killings, and some committed suicide. They included many who had fought in the civil war alongside Mao and whose involvement in the CCP went back to the 1930s. Deng Xiaoping, Mao's ultimate successor, was publicly humiliated, removed from his high-ranking party posts, and sent to work as a common laborer for several years. Most schools and government offices closed down, and most regular activities ceased; all but one of China's ambassadors was called home. Economic production ground to a halt.

This convulsive part of the Cultural Revolution came to a close in 1968 after armed clashes between Red Guard groups, each proclaiming to be more loyal to Mao, broke out all over China. The Red Guards were often given weapons by local troops who supported one side against the other. The result was not so much civil war as complete anarchy: the party and government had collapsed under Red Guard pressure. But though the Red Guards knew they had Mao's backing, they were too divided to offer an alternative form of authority. The Cultural Revolution was not a military coup, but in its aftermath the nation came under effective martial law for several years because the military was the only nationwide organization still intact and able to carry out government responsibilities.

After being nearly destroyed during 1966–69, the party now had to be rebuilt. Although it was weakened by intense factional conflict at all levels, from society's point of view the party was stronger than ever. Virtually every aspect of life had political implications, from opinions about Mao and the party to the clothing one wore, hairstyles, and taste in books and music. (The plain blue or green "Mao jacket" and short hair were in, Beethoven and Western writers were out.) Even owning a pet was considered a "bourgeois" affectation. It was a period of political correctness run rampant, with decisions about jobs, housing, access to food, and opportunities to travel or see a play determined by the local party committee.

Just as the Great Leap Forward was an economic disaster, the Cultural Revolution was a political disaster. Many of China's best qualified and most experienced leaders were falsely accused of various crimes, removed from their posts, put in prison, or sent to remote areas of China to perform menial tasks. Eventually many of these people were brought back to their old posts but they were forced to work alongside the very people who had accused them and caused their suffering.

The Cultural Revolution was a turning point for many of China's citizens. By the time Mao died in 1976, there was a crisis of confidence, a feeling that the party and government were no longer legitimate. Many came to believe that the Cultural Revolution was not about revolutionary goals at all, but just a cynical struggle for power among party leaders. Ironically, the Cultural Revolution also taught people that they should question the authority of their leaders; after all, Mao had told them to do so, and their own experience verified that many officials were indeed worthy of criticism. But the result was not what Mao intended. Contrary to his assumptions, many Chinese came to believe it was not necessary to assume that the leaders always knew what was best or that they had the best interests of society at heart. For a country ruled by a Leninist party, these ideas could only undermine the party's ability to rule.

Each swing toward utopianism enhanced the power of the party and widened the scope of its jurisdiction. By the end of the Cultural Revolution, the CCP had usurped almost all the government's responsibilities and there were no social organizations capable of challenging it. But at the same time, society had grown weary of the incessant political campaigns and frequent policy shifts. People had become disillusioned by a political system that seemed intrusive, arbitrary, inconsistent, and unresponsive to society's desire for higher standards of living. With Mao's death in 1976, an opportunity arose to fundamentally change the style and direction of policy.

LEGACIES OF THE CULTURAL REVOLUTION

The Cultural Revolution left several different legacies for China's leaders and members of society. The CCP's elites recognized the danger of charismatic authority, as epitomized by Mao, and acknowledged the need for regular institutions to debate and implement policies. Mao had resisted this institutionalization because he felt it would diminish revolutionary zeal, the creative spontaneity of the masses, and his own discretion, but most other leaders felt the costs of Mao's preferred methods were too high. China's leaders were also aware of the CCP's failure to improve the lives of most Chinese. Party and government leaders who became victims of the Cultural Revolution and were sent to live and work in the countryside learned firsthand that the political system they had created could be completely arbitrary. They realized it had failed to bring China out of its extreme poverty and that it had thereby lost the legitimacy with which it came to power in 1949.

The Cultural Revolution left lasting marks on Chinese society. People learned that it was acceptable to challenge authority and that it was necessary to think for themselves. Mao's assault on his colleagues and the party as a whole taught Chinese society that it need not, indeed should not, accept the prevailing political orthodoxy as the truth. This critical attitude marked a break from traditional Confucian views as well as a break from post-1949 China. How could the CCP be infallible if it was filled with capitalist "roaders" (a commonly used epithet for those who emphasized economic development over Mao's brand of politics) and counterrevolutionaries? For the same reason, many people experienced a loss of idealism. They learned too late that the Cultural Revolution ultimately was not about revolutionary goals but about petty power politics. Even Mao's reputation was tarnished. The result was considerable soul-searching about how Chinese culture could have produced such a strange phenomenon as the Cultural Revolution. Many of those who had administered beatings or engaged in the public humiliation of authority figures—such as officials, teachers, and even parents—or who had taken part in armed violence that almost led to civil war now began to experience guilt over their actions.

By the time of Mao's death in 1976, the party was in crisis. Society had grown weary of the continual political witch-hunts and had lost confidence in the party's wisdom. The party itself was divided between the reds, who believed the goals of the Cultural Revolution had to be continued,

even intensified, and the experts, who believed the Cultural Revolution had done more harm than good and needed to be abandoned. The economy was shrinking, political instability was rising, and factions within the party prevented any single policy line from being agreed upon and pursued. The end result was a state so weakened by internal divisions that it was unable to adopt and implement a coherent and consistent set of policies, and a society that was unable to influence the policy-making process in any institutionalized way.

This conflict between continuing and ending the Cultural Revolution was resolved a month after Mao's death when the main reds, the so-called Gang of Four (one of whom was Mao's widow)[19] were arrested. After a brief succession struggle, a new consensus emerged: the utopian goals of the Maoist era had to be abandoned for the sake of economic development. This decision was solidified at a historic Central Committee meeting in December 1978. Henceforth, the party would abandon class struggle as its main task (a main rationale for needing a strong party), and the victims of past political campaigns would be rehabilitated. More important, the party would concentrate its energies on the economic modernization of the country and shift its policy choices and selection of personnel with this goal in mind. Throughout the post-Mao period, the party's ability to foster economic growth, rather than its ideology or the charisma of its leader, has been the basis of its legitimacy. While several of the party's leading figures wanted these policy shifts, the man most responsible for initiating them was Deng Xiaoping.

PROFILE: Deng Xiaoping

At five feet tall, Deng Xiaoping was not a physically imposing figure. But his political stature was large enough to fix his reputation as one of twentieth-century China's most influential leaders. Born in 1904 in Sichuan (Szechuan) province in southwest China, Deng—like Mao Zedong—was raised by modestly successful landowning farmers. Deng's father, though not a well-educated man, wanted his son to go abroad so as to acquire industrial skils and a first-hand knowledge of the outside world. He arranged for Deng to take part in a work-study program in France that had been organized by a Chinese businessman who was eager to

Deng Xiaoping

develop China's contacts with the French. In 1920, at the age of sixteen, Deng set sail for Europe, only to embark soon after his arrival there on his career as a Chinese revolutionary.

The work-study program that brought Deng to France went broke within a year, but the young man from rural China found a succession of factory jobs and other forms of employment that enabled him to live in different parts of the country for five years. Though he never acquired the industrial training his father intended for him, Deng quickly attached himself to a group of young Chinese workers and students who used their stay in France to debate China's future and form political organizations. One of Deng's first contacts was **Zhou Enlai,** another worker-student in the same program that Deng had initially joined. With a powerful, rationally oriented mind, Zhou soon became Deng's "elder brother"; the two men were destined to remain close allies at the pinnacle of power in Communist China. In 1922, under Zhou's influence, Deng joined the Communist Party of Chinese Youth in Europe. The following year, Deng was elected to the executive committee of another radical organization, the European branch of the Chinese Socialist Youth League. From the League's main office in Zhou Enlai's bedroom in Paris, Deng wrote for its newspaper while subsisting on milk and croissants. Then in 1924 Deng joined the European branch of the Chinese Communist Party. (By the time he died in 1997, Deng was probably the longest-serving member of any communist party in the world.) As his activities in communist organizations increasingly came

to the attention of French authorities, Deng was subjected to official surveillance. But a police raid on his apartment outside Paris in 1926 was too late: Deng had already left for his next destination, Moscow.

Deng spent eleven months in the Soviet Union, attending special schools the Soviet Communist Party had established for revolutionaries from around the world. At Sun Yat-sen University, the Soviet institute for Asian workers and political organizers, Deng met Chiang Ching-kuo, the son of the Nationalist leader Chiang Kai-shek and himself a future president of the Republic of China on Taiwan. It was during this period that Stalin compelled the Chinese communists to cooperate with the Nationalists. But by the time Deng returned to China in early 1927, the country was already tilting toward civil war. Once Chiang Kai-shek attacked the communists in Shanghai, killing hundreds, the war began in earnest. Deng himself went to Shanghai that year, the newly appointed chief secretary of the Communist Party's Central Committee. In 1929 he moved to southwest China to begin what turned out to be a long career as one of the party's top military leaders.

After two years of desultory fighting against Nationalist forces, in 1931 Deng moved to Jiangxi, the base area established by Mao Zedong. Although he was not in the party's top leadership, Deng got caught up in the personal rivalries and doctrinal feuds that divided the Communist Party hierarchy but managed to retain his role as editor-in-chief of the party's military newspaper. In 1934 and 1935 he participated in the Long March, contracting typhoid along the way. He then settled into Shaanxi province, where Mao was trying to impose his will on the party from his redoubt in the caves of Yanan. Promoted to deputy director of the political department of the Communist Party's first army, Deng was now a seasoned political soldier. He was appointed to higher military positions over the next several years as the communist army grew to more than 2 million. From 1938 to 1945, Deng led troops in northern China's mountainous regions, launching periodic attacks on KMT and Japanese forces. In the spring of 1945 he was rewarded for these bold efforts with membership in the party's Central Committee. He was now formally ranked twenty-eighth in the party hierarchy.

When the war against Japan ended and the clash between the communists and Nationalists resumed its earlier intensity, Deng swung into action as one of the party's most successful commanders. In a series of major battles in 1948 and 1949 he inflicted heavy losses on the Nationalists, putting more than a half million KMT troops out of action and playing a leading role in the communist takeover of Manchuria. As the war neared its conclusion, Deng was given charge of China's vast southwest region, including his native Sichuan and three other provinces containing 150 million people. Deng took control of the new communist regime's land reforms in the area between 1950 and 1952, methodically dispossessing the landlord class that had dominated the area—and indeed China itself—for nearly two thousand years. (He saw to it that members of his own family were spared their lives, however.) Then in 1952 he was summoned to Beijing to serve as vice-premier of the Chinese government and in various economic positions under the supervision of his old comrade, Zhou Enlai. In 1954 he won an even more important promotion, gaining the newly created post of secretary general of the Central Committee. Deng was now the chief organizational link between the party leadership in Beijing and its large bureaucracy throughout China. He also entered the party Politburo. Two years later he was a member of the Politburo's Standing Committee, taking his place among the six most powerful people who ruled China.

The next two decades were shaken by the frenetic oscillations of Chairman Mao's policies. As Mao plunged China headlong into the whirlwinds of the Hundred Flowers campaign, the Great Leap Forward, and the Cultural Revolution, only to recoil from their disastrous consequences, Deng loyally followed the prevailing line but occasionally intimated his lack of enthusiasm for Mao's excesses. At one point during the Great Leap he publicly stated that Mao was not above the party's collective leadership. He was more enthusiastic about reversing the Great Leap's catastrophic effects on China's economy, joining with Zhou Enlai, one of the country's top leaders, in reviving economic growth in the first half of the 1960s. Deng risked Mao's indignation when he opined that some of Mao's programs "clearly didn't work." Mao fired back that Deng was establishing an "independent kingdom" in his post as general secretary, implying insubordination.

It was during the Cultural Revolution, however, that an open breach developed between the two men that almost proved fatal for Deng. As Mao turned to the Red Guards in 1966 to spearhead his attack on intellectuals and bureaucrats for their alleged rejection of socialist ideals, Deng sought to hold them in check. Mao's allies responded with a vicious verbal attack, forcing Deng to make a humiliating public disavowal of his "grave errors." Mao himself openly accused Deng of refusing to consult with him on major policy matters. In December 1966, Deng was placed under virtual house arrest inside the compound where he and other party leaders lived. He then disappeared from public view for six years.

In 1967, Red Guards broke into the compound and forced Deng and Liu Shaoqi, another prominent party leader subjected to Mao's wrath, to endure bitter denunciations at "struggle meetings." At one such meeting Deng was forced to kneel down with his arms extended backwards in an "airplane position"; he was then marched through the streets in a dunce cap, a traditional symbol of humiliation in China. Luckily, however, Chairman Mao still had grudging respect for Deng, who was allowed to remain under house arrest with his family. Less fortunate was Liu Shaoqi, whom Mao regarded as a potential rival. Liu was arrested, tortured, and later died of pneumonia on a prison floor. In the fall of 1968 Deng's eldest son, a physics student, fell from a rooftop at Beijing University. Apparently he was hounded by Red Guards, who then refused to allow his rescuers to take him to a clinic. The young man was permanently paralyzed from the waste down and was forced to spend the next several years away from his family in a home for the handicapped. In 1969, Deng and his wife were moved from Beijing to a remote corner of Jiangxi province. They remained there for three years, working at a tractor repair plant and raising their own food.

In 1969, Mao began applying the brakes to the Cultural Revolution and headed in a new political direction, criticizing some of the very people who were conducting his radical policies. The most prominent of these was Lin Biao, who tried to have Mao assassinated in 1971. The plot was foiled, and Lin died in a plane crash while trying to escape to Russia. Lin had been one of Deng's chief enemies. In 1973, after receiving two letters from Deng, Mao allowed him to return to Beijing, appointing him vice-premier of the government, the same rank as Zhou Enlai, another quiet opponent of the Cultural Revolution. After Zhou and Mao engineered a diplomatic opening to the United States, Zhou gave Deng practical control of China's foreign policy in 1974. Both men also began pursuing an economic reform policy aimed at modernizing China's industrial, agricultural, and technological base after the long years of economic paralysis during the Cultural Revolution. Mao personally expressed approval of Deng's work, and in 1975 Deng was back in charge of the Communist Party's headquarters.

Although Mao was increasingly frail and removed himself from day-to-day political activity, he remained attuned to party and state affairs. His weakness, however, permitted palace intrigues to continue. High-ranking radicals, led by Mao's fourth wife, Jiang Qing, were still powerful in the party hierarchy and were determined to halt the more pragmatic course now being set in place by Deng and Zhou Enlai. Jiang Qing, in particular, hated Deng Xiaoping. In January 1976, Zhou Enlai died, and large crowds gathered in his honor at a commemorative event several months later. (Zhou had been widely regarded as a cool-headed rationalist who secretly disapproved of Mao's radicalism.) Police moved in to disperse the throng, some of whom openly expressed their approval of Deng Xiaoping. From his sickbed Mao reversed course again and turned against Deng, stripping him of his positions. Jiang Qing and three other radicals—later known as the "Gang of Four"—were back in favor. Fearing for his life, Deng slipped out of Beijing and went into hiding in south China.

On September 9, 1976, Mao Zedong died. A fierce struggle for power now threatened to tear the Chinese Communist party apart. But opponents of the radicals, including members of the military command, acted quickly: a month later, the Gang of Four were arrested. Deng offered his services in a letter to the new head of the party, Hua Guofeng, who had taken over Deng's duties after his purge and exile in 1976. In the summer of 1977, Deng was reinstated to all his former positions in the party and government and later became chairman of the party's powerful Central Military Commission. For the next twenty years, Deng Xiaoping would be the principal figure in Chinese politics.

POLITICS IN THE REFORM ERA

During the 1980s, party leaders identified a series of problems inherited from the Maoist period and attempted reforms to remedy them, but with mixed results.[20]

Overconcentration of Power

Most Chinese leaders agreed that Mao had too much power. So the solution was to create a collective leadership and prevent any one individual from dominating the political system. Although Deng Xiaoping was the paramount leader from 1978 until his death in 1997, he had to work to forge and maintain a consensus behind his policy preferences and was forced to abandon some policies when faced with opposition among his colleagues. He retired from his posts as party vice chairman and vice prime minister in the mid-1980s and from the chairmanship of the CCP's Central Military Commission in 1989. Although he never held the top post in either the party or the

government, symbolizing his commitment to collective leadership, he was nevertheless recognized as China's preeminent leader. His successor, Jiang Zemin, has even less authority over his colleagues and has to work hard to build support among party, government, and military leaders. The title of party chairman was abolished because it was so closely identified with Mao and because there were no suitable checks on the power of the office. Instead, the post of General Secretary was created as the party's top leadership position: the party needed an individual leader, but not one with unchecked authority.

At lower levels, efforts were made to distinguish the party from the government more clearly. The party was to limit itself to making decisions, allowing the government to implement the policies. To this end it was decided to limit the number of concurrent posts held by top party leaders. For instance, during the Maoist period, the top party leader in a province was also its governor, and the top party leader in a city was also its mayor. Beginning in the 1980s, these posts were separated and held by different people.

These efforts had mixed results. For one thing, all key positions were still held by party members (with rare and usually symbolic exceptions), and party committees remained more powerful than their government counterparts. In fact, after the 1989 student demonstrations, the efforts to separate the party and the government were rolled back because party leaders believed the party had become too weak as a consequence.

Lack of Formal Institutions

Because Mao preferred to rule by virtue of his charismatic authority, formal bodies became virtually meaningless. In the post-Mao period, reforms were implemented that emphasized collective decision making and restored the regular operations of formal bodies. For instance, the Politburo, which had fallen into disuse under Mao, again began to meet regularly, and the National People's Congress, China's nominal legislature, became rejuvenated, passing a variety of laws and overseeing government operations. In addition, the decision-making process has been opened up to a wider variety of people in the post-Mao period. The most important decisions are still made by a handful of people at the top, but now they consult with government officials, experts, local leaders, and others whose opinions are valued or who will be affected by the decision. Instead of decisions being made in secret, regular conferences are held to share ideas, and drafts of major policies are circulated several times before a final decision is made.[21]

However, Deng and other top leaders continued to intervene in the policy-making process. The personal attributes of individual leaders, their connections with other leaders, and their reputations as revolutionaries were still more important than their formal posts. In fact, during the 1980s and 1990s, a group of "elders" constituted the true center of political power in China even though they had formally retired from their party and government positions. They continued to shape policy and personnel decisions from behind the scenes and through their younger protégés. The clearest example of this was the 1988 decision giving Deng authority over all major decisions. Moreover, there was no legal system to impose limits on the abuse of power by institutions or individuals. It is often said that whereas the United States has the rule *of* law, because even the top leaders are accountable to the legal limits of their power, in China there is only rule *by* law. The party creates laws to help govern the country, but it is above the law. In this type of system, the law is a tool of governance, not a means for protecting the rights and liberties of the citizens.

Rejuvenation of the Party

At the end of the Maoist era, the party had about 35 million members, up from fewer than 5 million in 1949. From the perspective of Deng and his allies, the composition of the party's membership had several danger signs. Many members were too old. Less than 5 percent of the members were under twenty-five years old, compared to about 25 percent in 1949. The majority were still poorly educated: 45 percent had only a primary education, and 11 percent were illiterate. This educational profile was an improvement over 1949, when 95 percent were illiterate or had only a primary education, but it was hardly exemplary. More important, party members were not educated enough to handle the technical matters required by the new tasks of economic modernization.

And most party members had been recruited during periods of utopianism and therefore had dubious political and professional qualifications. In short, by the time Deng Xiaoping took control, party members on the whole were too old, too uneducated, and too radical. This state of affairs led to a change in recruitment policies. The CCP began to target the young and educated, the new elites of the reform era. By 2000, the party had grown to over 63 million members. Almost half had a high school or college education (up from 27 percent in 1978), and 22 percent were under thirty-five years old. Women constituted approximately 20 percent of CCP members, about the same as in the Maoist years.

These changes led to inevitable conflicts. Veteran cadres resisted the reforms, recognizing that their political skills were being denigrated for the sake of professionalization. There was strong ideological opposition to letting people formerly designated as "rightists" into the party, especially the newly emerging class of private entrepreneurs. In 1989, after the imposition of martial law, the party imposed a ban on the admission of private entrepreneurs into the party and the appointment of entrepreneurs already in the party to official positions. This ban was widely ignored at the local level, however. Also after 1989, the party once again began to emphasize political reliability, not simply expertise, as a criterion for recruitment and promotion.

Another challenge to the rejuvenation of the party was that there was less enthusiasm within society to join the party. It was no longer necessary to become a party member to have a successful career. People could now concentrate on acquiring technical skills in school, especially in foreign universities, or open their own business. Party membership was still beneficial, but it was not a prerequisite for prestigious and high-paying jobs. Throughout the reform era, the CCP has continued to lose prestige, and many of its own members do not support it. Society as a whole has lost faith in socialist ideals and no longer responds to ideological appeals. Nevertheless, the party remains an effective distributor of jobs, education, and travel opportunities and provides special access to loans, technology, and markets, along with other valuable goods and services. Party membership is still a valuable asset, even to those who do not believe in communist ideology.

Weak Bureaucracy

China's officials suffered from the same problems as the party membership as a whole: they were too old, poorly skilled, and more supportive of Maoism than modernization. To address these problems, the party undertook two somewhat contradictory policies: it rehabilitated victims of the Cultural Revolution, and it recruited skilled expertise. The rehabilitation of veteran officials denigrated in the Cultural Revolution was designed to build support for reform policies and to push the reds out of their posts. Once the goal of replacing the reds was accomplished, the party introduced a retirement program for veteran officials that would entice them to leave their posts and allow younger and better-educated people to be appointed.[22]

One of the most important transitions has been the recruitment of large numbers of young, highly educated officials to staff the bureaucracy. China is often described as a government of "technocrats," a term referring to bureaucrats with high levels of technical training.[23] This transition was necessary to fulfill the party's main task of the post-Mao era: economic modernization. With the period of class struggle over and the party concentrating on economic modernization, it needed new people with new skills to staff the bureaucracy. The party recruited young, better-educated and better-skilled people to replace the aged veterans, many of whom had first been appointed in the 1950s. It weeded out those who were too old or who lacked the skills necessary to carry out the economic reforms. It established minimum requirements for certain positions, such as a college degree or a specialized degree in engineering or management. In the past, no such requirements existed, and people were appointed not on the basis of their professional merit but on their political virtue. In the post-Mao period, the emphasis has been on upgrading the quality of party and government officials.

Reconciliation of Party and Society

Party leaders recognized they had lost much of their prestige and public support during the Cultural Revolution by trying to micromanage all aspects of daily life. In the post-Mao period, they have tried to limit the scope of politics. For instance, the party now allows a greater array of plays and music to be performed and literature to be published. Traditional festivals and customs have reappeared, especially in the countryside. New social organizations are allowed to form as long as they are not politically oriented. In recent years, China has witnessed an explosion of chambers of commerce, sports leagues, hobby groups, professional associations for writers, teachers, and businesspeople, and other types of civic and professional groups. It is now possible for citizens to read traditional novels or listen to Western music without accusations of being a counterrevolutionary. The foundations of a civil society are increasingly emerging, albeit under the ever-watchful eye of the communist authorities.[24]

Above all, the party declared that the period of class struggle was over, replaced by a commitment to economic modernization. Those who had been falsely accused and punished during the Maoist period had their records cleared and their derogatory labels of "landlord," "capitalist," "rightist," and so on removed. Unfortunately, many of the victims of past class struggle campaigns had already died, but even they had their good names restored. In some cases, their families received property or personal belongings back or received a cash settlement.

But not everything has changed. The party still remains the most important institution in the political system. All decisions are made by the party, and there is little opportunity for non-party people to be involved in the decision-making process. While the party now tolerates a wider assortment of nonpolitical activities, the definition of what is nonpolitical has varied considerably. For instance, religious activities have increased dramatically with official approval, but the state still arrests those religious practitioners whom it sees as stepping over the line between religion and politics. The boundaries are not always clear, but the punishments can be severe for those who cross over. And anything clearly political is strictly prohibited and immediately repressed. Citizens who have tried to create new political parties and autonomous labor unions have been severely punished, losing their jobs and housing, and in some cases, receiving long jail sentences. The CCP, like all Leninist parties, insists on protecting its monopoly on political organization. It does not allow the existence of any organization that it does not approve of or that it perceives as any kind of threat to its power.

CHINA'S ECONOMIC DEVELOPMENT STRATEGIES

During the more than fifty years of the People's Republic, China's government has pursued three separate strategies of economic development: the Soviet model, self-reliance, and the post-Mao emphasis on markets and "openness."

The Soviet Model (1953–57)

Following the communist victory in 1949, China was first concerned with economic reconstruction: controlling hyperinflation and restoring industrial production to its prewar levels (in 1949, industrial production was only 56 percent of prewar levels). After restoring stability, it adopted the Soviet model of development. The model's main characteristic was a commitment to growth that emphasized heavy industry at the expense of agriculture, light industry, and commerce and trade. In order to achieve this commitment and to promote heavy industry, new central planning institutions were created.

New central ministries were needed to create and implement the plans governing the economy. All key decisions were made at the top in Beijing. Central planning, which did not rely on market mechanisms, required a bureaucracy to run the economy, and the bureaucracy needed experts to do the planning. Production targets were set for each province, which then set targets for lower administrative levels, which then set targets for individual enterprises. Prices were set by the bureaucracy, not by the market forces of supply and demand. Supplies of raw materials, energy, and other inputs to the production process were also determined by planning agencies. Manufactured goods were also distributed according to the plan.

The state took over ownership of the means of production. Private ownership was abolished with the collectivization of industry and agriculture beginning in 1955, giving the state great control over the economy and allowing the party to strengthen its control over all organized activities. The party

directly managed production: party committees were created in all workplaces, and most managers eventually became party members.

In addition, the state enforced high savings and low consumption rates. Because heavy industry was emphasized over other economic sectors, there were few consumer goods for people to buy. Because decisions regarding production and investment were made by planning agencies rather than enterprises, all profits were handed over to the state. Agricultural production was diverted to industry in two ways. First, the state paid a lower price to farmers for grain and other crops than urban residents paid to the state for their food. The profits were then reinvested in industry. Second, agricultural production was geared toward serving industrial needs. Beyond meeting basic nutritional requirements, agriculture provided raw materials for factories instead of promoting a diversified diet.

Why did China adopt the Soviet model? The Cold War that began after World War II precluded any other choice. Moreover, the Soviet Union in the 1950s was an example of successful and rapid industrialization. CCP leaders were communist, but they were also nationalistic. They sought rapid development in order to catch up to the West. The Soviet model therefore offered the promise of success plus ideological justification. The private sector was associated with the bourgeoisie, the class enemy of communism in orthodox Marxist thinking; in contrast, state ownership was associated with the elimination of the bourgeoisie and capitalism in China. The Soviet Union was the "elder brother," and China followed its example.

Initially, the Soviet model was largely successful. During the period of the First Five-Year Plan (1953–57), the economy grew by almost 9 percent per year (industrial output grew by 128 percent between 1952 and 1957, agriculture by 25 percent). This was accomplished not only with the Soviet model, but also with direct Soviet assistance. Soviet aid to China during this period has been described as the largest transfer of technology in history. The Soviet Union sent over ten thousand advisors, blueprints for factories, the machinery and technology for running them, and plans for over 150 major projects in addition to training almost forty thousand Chinese engineers in the Soviet Union. This aid made the Soviet model successful in China.

Not all Chinese leaders were satisfied with adoption of the Soviet model, especially its emphasis on expertise for planners in the bureaucracy and managers in factories. One reason was practical: the CCP simply did not have enough members with the necessary skills or education. In 1949, 69 percent of CCP members were illiterate, and less than 1 percent had more than a high school education. Out of 4.5 million members, only 720,000 had even the minimal qualifications for being a party or government official. In the meantime, the CCP had to rely upon holdovers from the old government.

The second reason some of China's leaders were unhappy with the Soviet model's emphasis on expertise was political: the Soviet model got caught up in the red versus expert debate. In addition, Mao resented the way the Soviet Union treated China as a nation and himself in particular. He and others in China were not satisfied with their reliance on Soviet advice and assistance; they preferred to develop their economy in their own way. Mao grew angry at the Soviets' patronizing attitudes and at their refusal to share nuclear technology with China. Tensions between China and the Soviet Union grew as Mao veered from the path of the Soviet model, leading ultimately to the withdrawal of Soviet advisors from China in 1960. This development created a bitter rift between the two largest communist states in the world that lasted for more than two decades. Above all, Mao was a revolutionary, and he was not satisfied with planned, incremental progress. He preferred struggle, transformation, turmoil, even violence as a learning experience. Mao wanted to keep the revolution going, to face new challenges with the tactics that had worked in the past. He also did not trust intellectuals, who were necessary for the Soviet model to work. The result was a change in economic planning strategy that had major implications for China's development and for its relationship with the Soviet Union.

Self-Reliance (1957–76)

By the end of the First Five-Year Plan, Mao and other CCP leaders designed a new strategy of "self-reliance," initiated by the policies of the Great Leap Forward and continuing until Mao's death in 1976. Rather than rely on markets or central planning, the Maoist strategy of self-reliance used mass mobilization to tap into China's most abundant resource: its people, not money or machines. The CCP used propaganda and mobilization to create a spirit of team work, emphasizing collective well-being at the expense of personal self-interest. The reward for hard work and successful accomplishments was praise, not money.

The careful planning and setting of feasible targets that characterized the Soviet model were replaced with political enthusiasm. During the Great Leap Forward, local and provincial officials competed with one another in reporting grossly inflated production estimates, which contributed to the subsequent famine that claimed tens of millions of lives. The most enduring feature of the Great Leap Forward era was the commune. China's countryside was reorganized to fit the new economic strategy. There were roughly eighty thousand communes altogether, with each commune divided into brigades, and each brigade into teams. (Communes, brigades, and teams corresponded to the traditional townships, villages, and neighborhoods, respectively.) Farming was not done by individuals or families but by teams. Wages were set according to a person's work as well as his or her political attitudes, a very subjective evaluation. There was little financial incentive to work harder, and little available to buy even if money had been plentiful. The self-reliance strategy preserved the low emphasis on consumption that was a key feature of the Soviet model.

Just as China itself was to become self-reliant, each region was supposed to be self-reliant as well. Instead of producing according to its comparative advantage, concentrating on those items in which it excelled, and instead of trading with other areas of the country for other types of food, each area had to provide its own grain, meat, fruit, and vegetables even if the climate was not appropriate. China also invested in new industrial plants throughout the country, not just in the industrial centers along the eastern coast. Factories were built throughout the inland areas, often far from transportation lines and sources of energy and other raw materials. This effort was also part of Mao's preference for regional balance and self-reliance, but it led to wasteful duplication and inefficient farming.

Although the self-reliant approach that began with the Great Leap Forward turned out to be catastrophic, there was a rationale for this policy: China faced serious national security threats from the Soviet Union and the United States during the 1960s, and its economic strategy was designed in part to prepare the country for the likelihood of war. Throughout the decade, China and the Soviet Union were embroiled in a worsening dispute fueled by ideological and national rivalries. China's insistence on a status of equality with the USSR as co-leader of the world communist movement was brusquely rebuffed by the Kremlin, while unresolved Sino-Soviet border disputes eventually erupted into a series of military clashes in 1969. Tensions with the United States, still roiling from the Korean War of 1950–53, intensified over Vietnam in the following decade. In Mao's strategy, if one area of China were to be devastated or lost to the enemy, the rest of the country should still be able to provide for its own needs.

Chinese leaders who promoted self-reliance preferred autarky (economic self-sufficiency) in the extreme. They wanted to cut China off from all economic ties to foreign countries, who were suspected of wanting to undermine the integrity of the communist revolution in China. But the war scenario never materialized, and the cost of preparing for it was tremendous.[25]

Self-reliance was an unmitigated disaster. It was extremely wasteful for several reasons. Factories and communes were not required to operate at a profit, and their losses were compensated by the state. As a result, there was no incentive for efficient production. Projects were started in the wrong areas of the country, often without adequate resources, inputs, or skilled labor. These policies cut China off from the outside world, with little trade or other interactions. At a time when other Asian countries were experiencing rapid growth, industrialization, and modernization, China was out of touch with the technological advances of other countries and fell increasingly behind. Self-reliance also had a personal price for most Chinese: wages were frozen after the early 1960s. By 1976, those with fifteen years of experience were earning the same amount as those with much less seniority. However, the older workers had higher costs of living because they had

spouses, children, and elderly parents to support. A greater share of the older workers' wages went to housing, food, education, medical care, and so on, whereas younger workers often only had to support themselves, and in many cases lived with their parents if they were not married. Wages were equally distributed to all workers, but this egalitarianism did not seem fair to most workers, who resented policies that did not recognize their seniority or personal needs.[26] For all these reasons, self-reliance led to stagnant growth. The Maoist approach ignored the principles of comparative advantage and material incentives that would have provided more efficient and rapid growth.

During the Maoist era, economic strategy was an outgrowth of the red versus expert debate. The CCP had groups of leaders with different goals; in fact, the methods used were debated more intensely than the goals themselves. Most leaders were in favor of rapid growth; the question was how best to achieve it. During the early 1960s, as China was attempting to recover from the Great Leap Forward, Deng Xiaoping voiced the idea that the means of achieving growth were less important than the results: "It doesn't matter if the cat is black or white, as long as it catches mice it is a good cat." Such a view was heresy for orthodox Maoists, for whom the *method* of development mattered as much, if not more, than the outcome. But Maoist self-reliance was unable to produce growth, so China's leaders in the post-Mao era abandoned it in favor of the economic policies of reform and an opening to the outside world.

The Reform Era (1978–Present)

By 1978, Deng Xiaoping and his allies were able to consolidate their position and adopt new policies that called an end to the political campaigns and ideologically oriented policies of the past in favor of economic modernization. They embarked on the pursuit of the "Four Modernizations": the modernization of agriculture, industry, science and technology, and the military. In the early reform era, this goal was pursued by a variety of experiments, such as promoting private—as opposed to communal—farming, attracting foreign trade and investment through the creation of "Special Economic Zones" along the eastern coast of China, and allowing small-scale enterprises and street vendors to operate. Many of these experiments later became national policy.

Although China's post-Mao leaders agreed that the Maoist policies had to be abandoned, they disagreed about the proper set of policies that should be adopted and the pace at which they should be introduced. Above all, they debated the proper balance between central planning and market mechanisms for regulating the economy. Some saw the early 1950s, when China followed the Soviet model, as a golden era during which the economy achieved high growth rates without having to rely on the market. Others preferred to push ahead to a fully market-oriented economy, believing that a planned economy is too inefficient. Ultimately, this market-oriented group prevailed. Although there has been occasional backtracking from economic reform and international trade since their victory, the reformers have repeatedly regained the initiative and pushed ahead. These policies have transformed China's economy, creating prosperity and dynamism that were unimaginable in the Maoist era. Although rapid economic growth has created a number of problems, such as regional inequalities, corruption, environmental damage, and occasionally dangerously high inflation rates, support for economic reform remains strong.[27]

The post-Mao economic reforms have had several main goals. First, China's leaders wanted to achieve technological dynamism. They believed that mass mobilization was not sufficient to achieve modernization: the enthusiasm of workers and peasants could not compensate for technological backwardness. Instead, they have sought access to Western technology, capital, and management practices essential for modernization.

The reformers wanted to limit bureaucratic controls. A centrally planned economy needs bureaucratic controls to establish production goals, disseminate materials, monitor results, and redistribute industrial and agricultural goods to consumers and other end users. But these controls also stifle technological dynamism. Markets are needed to enliven the economy via competition and material incentives. Related to limits on bureaucratic controls was decentralization: the devolution of decision making to local governments and firms. Deng wanted to make local governments and individual firms responsible for their

own profits and losses and reduce subsidies paid by the central government to compensate for their losses. But he also believed that, if they were to be given responsibility, they also had to be given the authority to make decisions they thought best and the right to keep a larger share of the profits. These benefits provided incentives for experimentation and new investments that created the explosive growth seen in China during the past generation.

Another goal of the reforms was to raise living standards. Mao made a virtue out of poverty, but most people want higher living standards and a more comfortable life and are not very enthusiastic about ideological purity. Self-reliance and the resulting poverty and stagnation damaged the prestige of the party and undermined the legitimacy of the government. In the post-Mao period, China's leaders have based their legitimacy on their ability to create economic growth and better living standards rather than on political correctness.

Along with the goals of creating a more vibrant and prosperous economy came a political goal: that of maintaining stability in general and the unquestioned leadership of the CCP in particular. Although most of China's leaders are willing to accept competition within the economy, they do not want a similar logic to seep into the political system. They believe that China must still be ruled by a unified, authoritarian political system in order to provide overall coordination and to keep the country unified. They believe that economic growth cannot be allowed to create political disorder, including demands for democracy. Although some within China (and most foreign analysts) believe that the resulting imbalance between economic openness and political controls cannot be sustained indefinitely, most of China's leaders are worried that introducing more ambitious political reforms would threaten the party's hold on power, creating great uncertainty and potential chaos and undermining the economic gains of the reform era. They view the collapse of the Soviet Union and communist governments in Central and Eastern Europe as a warning of the dangers of initiating reform before achieving a stable and prosperous economy.

Finally, China's reformers wanted to maintain a peaceful environment in which development could occur. Prior to 1989, when anti-government demonstrations took place throughout China,

Deng and other reformers thought they could enjoy prolonged peace via astute diplomacy, allowing them to divert resources away from military spending toward the civilian economy. Since 1989, military spending has risen sharply, as the party leaders seek to guarantee the support of the military. Moreover, many of China's leaders, especially conservative elites, believe that the power of the United States has risen dramatically since the collapse of the Soviet Union and the end of the Cold War, and they wonder if China should not perhaps give greater priority to security issues, even as it continues its economic modernization. One of the major questions facing the United States and other countries today is whether China still puts a priority on maintaining peace and stability or is preparing to have a more disruptive influence on its neighbors and the international system more generally. The evidence remains ambiguous on this important question, but it has generated an ongoing debate among American policy makers and analysts about the international implications of China's rapid modernization.[28]

If these have been the goals of the economic reforms, what have been the means for achieving them?

Increasing Market Forces   China dismantled the communes, perhaps the most prominent symbol of the Maoist approach to economic development. In their place, new policies have encouraged individual and family farming and allowed farmers to sell their produce on the open market after they sold their quota to the state.[29] China gradually eliminated price controls on most industrial and consumer goods, allowing prices to better reflect supply and demand. State controls over the economy were reduced, including production targets and monopolies on the distribution of supplies and finished goods.[30] In contrast to the Maoist era, economic policies also encouraged consumption instead of enforced savings (although China's savings rate is still much higher than that of most countries) and the production of consumer goods. Finally, comparative advantage was made a priority, allowing regional variation and specialization.

Increasing Foreign Trade and Investment   China created the Special Economic Zones along its coast and "open cities" to encourage greater foreign

China old and new: the sign advertises an Internet company.

trade and investment. This approach was part of its comparative advantage strategy: the cities with already developed industrial bases and access to external markets were allowed to exploit their advantages. As a result, coastal areas have developed much more rapidly than inland China, creating much resentment from officials and residents in the disadvantaged areas.[31] Whereas China closed itself off during its self-reliance phase, it now encourages joint ventures and other types of foreign investment. The state no longer has a monopoly on foreign trade: individual enterprises are allowed to make deals on their own.

Reliance on the Private Sector   China's private sector was virtually eliminated during the 1950s, but beginning in the mid-1980s it gradually reemerged. The private sector now accounts for almost all economic growth, having gradually caught and surpassed the state sector in terms of total production. The state sector, in contrast, has been stagnant during the reform era. In the late 1990s, China's leaders began making plans to sell off some of the debt-ridden state-owned enterprises. The private sector also accounts for most new jobs. Township and village enterprises are creating industrial jobs in rural areas to minimize the amount of rural-urban migration. Less than half the work force in the countryside is actually engaged in agriculture. But this process has had a limited impact: China's "floating population" of workers who migrate from rural areas to the cities in search of higher-paying jobs is estimated to be roughly 100 million, almost 10 percent of the total population.[32]

The results of reform have been both positive and negative. On the positive side, China has experienced extraordinarily rapid growth. Per capita GNP doubled between 1978 and 1988, and China averaged growth rates of almost 10 percent per year between 1978 and 1998. The fastest growing sectors have been agriculture and light industry, the reverse of the Maoist years. There has been tremendous growth in the volume of China's foreign trade and the foreign capital invested in China: the total volume of trade increased by 15.6 percent per year between 1978 and 1997, from $20.7 billion to $325.1 billion, and the volume of direct foreign investment increased from a negligible amount in 1978 to $45.3 billion in 1997 (most of this growth occurred after 1992). As a result of increased trade and foreign investment, technological standards have increased. Factories have been upgraded technologically, allowing them to be more innovative and better able to respond quickly to market demands. For example, China quickly became a major supplier of satellite launches despite several costly accidents. Higher incomes created new markets for a wide variety of consumer goods, better-quality and more fashionable clothing, fresh and processed foods, better entertainment, and tourism within China and abroad. In sum, the living standards for most Chinese are higher now than ever before.

At the same time, a variety of negative consequences also emerged. Most important, the problem of corruption exploded as party and government officials at all levels took advantage of rapid growth, the desire of Chinese and foreign entrepreneurs to develop new projects, and weak laws and regulations to line their own pockets. China now ranks among the most corrupt countries in which to do business, according to surveys of foreign businesspeople (see table 5.1 on page 111). Corruption was the primary cause of the 1989 student demonstrations, and it continues to provoke local disturbances. In 1995, dissidents presented a petition to the National People's Congress warning that corruption "pervades the entire society." A month later, the Communist Party boss of Beijing was forced to resign amid charges that city administrators had accepted illegal payments in exchange for construction permits. He was later convicted of those charges and received a long jail sentence.

Inflation has also been a recurring problem and was another contributor to the 1989 demonstrations. Inflation ate up most of the gains of rapid growth during the 1980s. Ironically, by the late 1990s, the problem had become *deflation*: prices for many goods were falling, leading many people to postpone purchases to see if they would drop even farther. This reduced consumer spending and as a result contributed to a general economic slowdown that China's leaders have not been able to reverse.

The push for rapid growth also created tremendous environmental pollution. China's water, air, and land are being damaged by companies that find it cheaper to pollute than to be energy efficient or to dispose of waste properly. The growing numbers of cars and trucks contribute to this increasingly serious problem. Rising inequality is another result of economic reform. Although incomes have generally risen, they have not risen evenly. There is a growing gap between urban and rural areas and between coastal and inland areas. The conspicuous consumption of China's nouveaux riches has created resentment among the less fortunate. Rising income levels have also let crime flourish. Social ills such as gambling, drug use, pornography, and prostitution have reemerged after being eliminated in the early 1950s. Reports of violent crime, kidnappings, and blackmail have become common. Women in particular have encountered problems during the reform era. They receive lower wages than men for the same work and are often the first to be laid off from state-owned enterprises. They also face physical and sexual harassment in the workplace. Women who migrate to urban areas for factory work are occasionally kidnapped and sold as wives to men in other rural areas.

In addition, another unexpected consequence of economic development has been a spiritual crisis. The emphasis on making money and material interests has taken a toll on Chinese society. Many feel there has been a loss of a commitment to group welfare and collective well-being. China no longer has a shared set of values that binds the country together. First, the communists denigrated the Confucian traditions and promoted the revolutionary virtues associated with Mao; then the post-Mao leaders rejected the values promoted by Mao without offering an alternative ideology or belief system. Deng's emphasis on pragmatism, symbolized by the slogan "seek truth from facts" (as opposed to ideology), and his advice that to "get rich is glorious" may have been the basis for policy making, but it did not give people much to believe in.[33]

This nearly exclusive interest on materialism has led to the revival of traditional religious practices and a growing interest in Christianity. Local temples have been rebuilt, usually with public funds, and individual families have rebuilt ancestor shrines. Some Protestant and Catholic churches are officially recognized by the state, but others are "underground churches" that meet in private homes without official approval. Some of these churches are persecuted by local officials, their leaders and parishioners arrested and often mistreated. But in other areas, the churches operate with the tacit approval and even the encouragement of the local leaders. Some churches have rented space from government offices to hold their worship services, while others have borrowed money from the local government to construct their own building. Despite foreign criticisms of widespread and systematic persecution of religious practices in China, the number of religious believers has never been higher than it is today. There is no question that religious freedoms still do not enjoy full protection, but at least in some communities the growth in religious faith has come with the knowledge and often the support of local officials. More important, it reflects the search for a meaning to life that goes deeper than just rising living standards.

The most visible manifestation of this longing for a spiritual meaning to life is the rapid rise of **Falun Gong.** This spiritual movement combines meditation and exercises similar to traditional Buddhist and Taoist practices with claims of miraculous healings through the cultivation of a person's inner energy. In addition, it warns of a coming apocalypse and urges its followers to adopt simpler and purer lives in preparation for the end of the world. It was banned in 1999 after some ten thousand of its members staged a silent protest, surrounding the party and government leadership compound in Beijing in an effort to seek official recognition. Estimates on its size range from 10 million to 100 million members, which would make it larger than even the CCP,

but there is no way to confirm the number of its adherents. Its members include not only retirees and housewives, but also leading party, government, and even military officials. The size of the group and its diverse membership reflect the widespread longing for a deeper meaning in life and a return to a society less dominated by corruption and commercialism. The government's repression of Falun Gong, in contrast, reflects its continued insistence that all organizations be formally approved. The CCP may no longer represent a coherent ideology, but it still insists on preserving its monopoly on organized power.

Economic Reform: A Balance Sheet   In the post-Mao era, economic growth has been the primary goal, and equity has been deemphasized. Deng in particular was a fan of rapid growth at any cost. But he was forced to compromise with those who were more concerned about order and stability and believed that the negative consequences of reform required a slower pace of reforms and even a periodic rollback. Advocates of continued reform among China's current leaders, in particular Jiang Zemin and Zhu Rongji, still face these same challenges. The more orthodox or conservative leaders feel that economic equity should not be totally abandoned, because rising resentment against the regions and individuals who are getting rich faster than others may also threaten political stability and ultimately the legitimacy of the CCP. Despite these negative and generally unintended consequences, the benefits of reform—a more dynamic economy, rising standards of living, a flourishing cultural life, greater access to an increasing variety of goods and services, opportunities for entrepreneurship and innovation, improvements in transportation and housing, and so on—have created tremendous popular support for further economic reform.

STATE-SOCIETY RELATIONS IN CHINA

Fundamental Features of State-Society Relations

One-Party Rule Means No Organized Opposition
The CCP guards its political monopoly quite zealously. One of its primary goals has been to prevent the organization of any group outside its control. To

this end the CCP operates a network of party cells throughout the government, the military, and society to monitor compliance with party policies. All labor unions, student organizations, professional associations, and even religious groups must be sanctioned by the government, and their leaders are subject to official approval. Even China's so-called democratic parties have communist party cells. Any attempt to form independent organizations is immediately squashed, and those leaders are punished. The party proscribes trade unions, student groups, political parties, and religious organizations like the Roman Catholic Church, which is banned in China because its priests are loyal to the Pope in Rome, not to the leaders in Beijing.

Communication Between State and Society
China developed the "mass line" concept during the revolutionary period when it was competing with landlords and the Nationalist government for popular support. The ideal of the mass line was that the state would get information from the masses in order to create correct policies and then communicate those policies to the masses. But after 1949, there was no competition for popular support, and the need to solicit public opinion as a guide to policy became less important. The mass line remained, but it became ritualized. Citizens learned the high price of offering contrary opinions and instead learned to recite current slogans.

As in pluralist societies, individuals in China can write letters or visit newspapers or government offices to complain. Most papers have investigative departments to look into reports of official corruption, workplace problems, housing complaints, and so on. So long as people only complain about how they have been adversely affected by the improper implementation of policy, their complaints are likely to be resolved. However, they cannot complain about the merits of the policy itself or its general impact.

Moreover, the newspapers and other forms of media are themselves owned by the state, which obviously limits their effectiveness as a form of feedback on the state's performance. Reading the newspaper is a form of political participation in China, as it is in other countries, but after the revolution, reading the paper was frequently a matter of self-preservation. The state often required participation in political study groups after work as a form of thought control. It did not provide objective information but only the party's current propaganda line, thereby imparting important clues about how to think and behave. Even today, media reports rarely break news of scandal, the abuse of power, poor governmental performance, or other exposés that people living in democracies come to expect of the media.

There is no possibility for organized political action except by officially recognized groups. As part of the economic reform process, the state has created a variety of corporatist-style organizations, especially for businesspeople and enterprise managers, to serve as bridges between state and society. These groups tend to be cooperative with the state and do not seek autonomy or an adversarial role, contrary to the ways we expect such groups to operate in a democracy. However, these groups do seem to communicate the perspective of their members to the state and are no longer confined to simply transmitting the state's position downward to the population, as in the Maoist era.[34] It has been difficult to organize other types of interest groups, such as those concerned with the environment, women's issues, labor, or minority groups. The policy-making process has gradually become more inclusive, allowing a wider range of people and perspectives to be involved, but many voices are still excluded from the process.

State Autonomy Because the Chinese party-state allows no organized opposition and imposes limits on the flow of information, it is largely free to decide for itself what policy should be. Decisions are made in secret, and officials are not subject to voter approval; nor are they held accountable to the population through such democratic mechanisms as citizen initiatives, referendums, and the recall of unacceptable officeholders. The results of policy cannot be assessed through citizen feedback because of the lack of information on public opinion and the danger of punishment for excessive criticism of Chinese officialdom. But the state does not always get what it wants: bureaucratic inertia, lower-level resistance, or outright evasion are quite common in China and prevent new policies from being implemented in a timely and proper fashion.[35]

The CCP justifies its autonomy from the population on the ideological grounds that it is a vanguard party with special insights into the laws of history. Therefore, it is uniquely qualified to decide what is best for the nation. Individuals and interest groups are not allowed into the decision-making process—except at the invitation of the party—because they only represent their narrow special interests. Only the CCP, in its own estimation, is concerned with collective well-being and the national interest. On a more basic level, the CCP recognizes that its own rise to power was based on its ability to organize society against the former government, which was unaware of what was going on. The CCP is determined not to be the victim of the same methods that brought it to power. Hence it does not allow alternative voices to be a part of the political process; it has no intention of competing with others for popular support.

Role of Law Democracies are based on the rule *of* law: both state and society are bound by the same laws. Many of our laws are designed to restrict the ability of the state to interfere in our private lives. The courts (in theory) enforce these laws, preventing the state from infringing on individual rights and civil liberties. This concept is very foreign in China, whose system is more aptly described as rule *by* law: laws are tools of governance but they do not restrict the scope of the state's actions. A legal code was not adopted until the late 1970s, thirty years after the founding of the People's Republic of China, and many laws and regulations remain secret or are revised at the discretion of China's leaders to meet current needs. Moreover, there is no independent judiciary to mediate public and private disputes; the courts are an arm of the state, not part of a checks and balance system. For major cases, such as for student demonstrators in 1989 or organizers of opposition parties and independent labor unions, verdicts and sentences are determined by the party in advance.

In short, individual citizens have little recourse if they are the target of state actions. And they have often been innocent victims of the state. For instance, during the Great Leap Forward, as many as 30 million people died of starvation as a result of mistaken policies decided without consultation with society, but the recovery policies were similarly undertaken without consultation. There were no demonstrations against the government, no newspapers calling for the resignation of the country's leaders, no calls for nationwide elections. Passive resistance, however, did occur, at times conducted by local officials who did not support the central government's policies or who felt that conditions in their area were so bad that they could not force their people to obey. This was a risky strategy, but local-level resistance was one of the things that led to the outbreak of the Cultural Revolution in 1966.

Post-Mao Changes in State-Society Relations

After painting such an ugly picture, we must also recognize how state-society relations improved during the post-Mao period. First, most victims of past political campaigns had their verdicts overturned; they were rehabilitated and assigned new jobs, and the old political labels used to stigmatize them in the past ("rightist," capitalist, landlord, and the like) were removed. People were no longer punished for actions that used to be considered political crimes, and they regained their lost reputations and status. The use of mass campaigns as a way of implementing new policies was drastically reduced in number and intensity. Daily life was "depoliticized," and a range of activities that were once prohibited or proscribed were now possible once again. However, the boundary between the permissible and the prohibited was often unclear and subject to change. Finally, there were more opportunities for a lively cultural and social life without political overtones, stimulating an outpouring of new literature, the resurgence of traditional culture, and the importation of Western goods and values (in part as an incentive to make money and to provide a model for China's future). The result was more color and variety, but also fears that China was losing its traditional identity and straying too far from communist ideals.[36]

In addition, Deng Xiaoping's economic reforms undermined the state's control over society. This effect was largely intentional. As noted earlier, Deng Xiaoping and other leaders learned firsthand during the Cultural Revolution about the irrationality and arbitrariness of the political system they helped create. They recognized that the state was too intrusive and only inhibited development rather than fostering it. With more goods and services available on the free market thanks to the reforms, with jobs being created in a small but growing private sector, and with expanding opportunities and even encouragement to make money, citizens became less dependent upon the approval of local officials. During the Maoist period, housing, education, medicine, and welfare were all tied to the workplace; if you were fired, you would no longer have access to any of these things. You would therefore have to cultivate good relations with your superiors, especially the party boss, to make sure you got your share of these scarce goods and services.[37] But the market now gives people more options. The state cannot threaten to withhold things it does not control, and individuals have become less dependent upon the state.

In fact, many local officials are somewhat dependent on local businesspeople. Rewards and promotions are increasingly based on local economic performance, and the fastest growing sectors are not the state-owned enterprises but private and collectively owned enterprises. Local officials now cooperate with businesspeople to help them succeed—they procure loans, find inputs and markets for goods, give tax breaks, protect local firms from outside competition, and do other similar things to promote economic growth in their communities.

Moreover, the CCP has sponsored the creation of numerous civic and professional associations to both liberalize social life and promote economic development. As the state pulled back from micromanaging society and operating a centrally planned economy, it created new organizations to link the state with key sectors of society. China allowed some organizations even during the Maoist era for officially recognized groups, such as workers, women, and youth, but they were generally seen as "transmission belts" that monitored and enforced state policy toward these groups but had little ability to represent the interests of their nominal members or to influence policy. In the post-Mao era, the state has allowed new organizations to form and has even allowed the older organizations to be more active in representing their members, not simply conveying the official line.[38] China now has a dense variety of associations for businesspeople, for specific professions (e.g., soft-

ware writers, factory managers, lawyers, etc.), for various religions and traditional practices, and for many others. However, there are still no independent trade unions.

These organizations and the state's relationship with them follow an authoritarian variant of **corporatism** (see chapter 11) as well as the logic of Leninism. Most organizations are created, or at least approved, by the state, and many have government officials as their leaders. For instance, local branches of the Industrial and Commercial Federation, whose members include the largest of China's manufacturing and commercial enterprises, are normally headed by the party official in charge of united front work (which handles relations between the CCP and non-party individuals and groups), and their offices are often in the government compound. In addition, there is only one organization for any given profession or activity. In cases where two groups with similar interests exist in a community, local officials will force them to merge or will disband one in favor of the other. This practice prevents competition between the associations and limits how many associations are allowed to exist, making it easier for the state to monitor and control them.

Are these new associations like the transmission belts of old, or are they able to truly represent the interests of their own members vis-à-vis the state? The state's strategy in allowing them to exist is to provide an indirect means to maintain its leadership over the economy and society, in contrast to the more direct Maoist approach to state penetration into all aspects of economic and social life. The goal is not to relinquish the state's power but instead to "give up control to gain power."[39] Nevertheless, the associations are not simply loyal agents of the state. Business associations try to balance their mission of representing the state's interests with the desire of their members to have an organized voice to solve business-related problems and even to try to influence the local implementation of policy. The leaders of these associations, even though they are also government officials, often begin to identify with the interests of their members and use the associations as a vehicle to increase their own authority relative to other officials.

This growth of civic and professional organizations in China has created a great deal of excitement among outside observers. Many see these organizations as forming the foundation of a **civil society,** a key component of liberal democratic government.[40] The emergence and spread of such organizations in China may facilitate a transition from authoritarian rule to democracy. But democratization is not the only possible outcome. A key component of civil society is autonomy from the state, and that element is missing in China. In fact, members of these associations do not seek autonomy, because they recognize that, in China's political system, being autonomous means you are powerless and inconsequential. Instead, they want to be embedded in the state in order to increase their influence. The non-governmental associations serve as links between the state and society: the state is unwilling to allow them autonomy, and the associations do not seek it. China may be undergoing a transition from a corporatism dominated by the state to a corporatism that gives greater leeway to the associations and the economic and social interests they represent. Can such a shift in the balance of power between the state and society occur without a more fundamental change in China's political system? That is the question that China's leaders, its citizens, and even foreign observers cannot definitively answer.

But there have been no dramatic *political* changes comparable to the economic and social changes of the post-Mao period. The opportunities for political participation are still limited and the risks remain high. One reason is the legacy of the Cultural Revolution: every episode of mass political participation, whether the goals are greater government responsiveness or more citizen representation, have been categorized by party leaders as similar to the Red Guard activities during the Cultural Revolution and are therefore quickly repressed. This was the case during several episodes we shall consider later in this chapter: the 1978–79 Democracy Wall movement, the student demonstrations in the winter of 1986–87, and the crackdown against the democracy movement of 1989.[41] Unlike South Korea and Taiwan, where demands for political change were gradually accepted and the opportunities for participation within the system gradually enlarged, in China all demands from society have been met with a tightening of party controls and a retreat from political reform.

Although there are supporters of political reform within the CCP, they have been on the defensive since 1989. Indeed, there is a fear (among party leaders and society as well) that the post-Mao reforms have created economic and social freedoms that will lead to political instability, and chaos is perhaps the greatest fear of China's traditional political culture.

Consequently, during the mid-1980s, a new concept called the "New Authoritarianism" sprang up, based on the experience of the East Asian newly industrializing countries (NICs), like Singapore and South Korea.[42] (On the NICs, see chapter 15.) The "New Authoritarians" suggested that China needed to concentrate its energies on economic development and needed a strong leader and a strong party not only to drive the country forward but also to repress other types of demands, such as greater democracy. Opponents of this view said that China had suffered too long from too much authoritarianism; their answer was more freedom, not less. Once dictatorship is in place, they argued, it is hard to oust. This school argued for more controls on the state's authority and more protection of civil liberties, in short, more democracy. Here was a classic debate between the goals of economic development and political liberty, both of which are worthwhile.[43] So far, the supporters of economic development have been able to prevail, although the debate remains ongoing.

POLITICAL PARTICIPATION IN CHINA

In the United States and most democracies, political participation is primarily voluntary and spontaneous. People may join interest groups, donate time or money to a cause they support, sign petitions on various policy issues, write letters to their elected representatives or a newspaper, or take a variety of other actions to make their views known to policy makers and other influential observers. In non-democratic countries, taking part in these kinds of political participation is often risky or even illegal. Rather than allow spontaneous participation, authoritarian states often mobilize participation to support their policies and strictly limit society's opportunities to influence policy making.

During the Maoist era, most participation was mobilized by the state. China underwent periodic mass political campaigns to both educate society on current policy and promote proper implementation. Often a campaign occurred when policy changed suddenly, as when the Anti-Rightist Movement followed the Hundred Flowers Campaign or when the Cultural Revolution got underway. People were expected to study the new policies and the propaganda that accompanied them, learn the new slogans, internalize the new party line, and change their behavior accordingly. People were not allowed to be passive: it was not enough to be quiet or to avoid politics. The regime engaged in **mass mobilization,** requiring everyone to actively support the new policy in word and deed. However, people were *not* expected to question the new policy or its goals, to compare the results of the new policies with the past, or to criticize their leaders for changing policy. The purpose of the mobilization style of political participation was to have the people publicly affirm their support of the new policy, even if inwardly they did not.

In the post-Mao period, the campaign style of policy implementation has generally been abandoned and the state has tried to be less intrusive in most aspects of social life. There are exceptions, of course: the state resorted to these old tactics after the violent end of the 1989 demonstrations and again beginning in the summer of 1999 against the Falun Gong spiritual movement. The general theme of the reform era has been to have the state pull back from its direct involvement in most areas, including the economy, social life, and even politics. People are no longer required to voice their approval of all policies, to denounce the old policies and the leaders who promoted them, or to refer to the ideology as the measure of correct policies. Instead, they have been encouraged to experiment to find the set of policies best suited to promoting economic development and improved standards of living.

In addition, there are now more opportunities for people to spontaneously participate in political issues. Writing letters to national newspapers to report on local problems, such as corruption or the abuse of authority by local officials, is common. In the post-Mao period the state seems to have taken a greater interest in investigating these allegations than in the past. More recent forms of political

participation include lodging complaints, relying on the courts, and voting for local leaders. Chinese citizens are now more able to complain about local conditions to higher levels of government. A village may send a team to the county government to report on excessive taxation or misuse of government funds. What is distinctive about this trend is that the people lodging complaints are becoming better versed in official policy and are using that knowledge to further their cause. For instance, they do not complain that taxes are simply too high: they complain that local officials are demanding taxes higher than what is allowed by the central government. In other words, they do not seek a change in policy, they seek to make local officials actually comply with the existing policies.[44] Once deviations from policies are brought to the attention of higher-level officials, they are very difficult to ignore.

China is trying to strengthen its legal system, in part to support the push for economic modernization (enforcement of contracts, protection of property including copyrights, etc.) and in part to create more predictability by clearly spelling out which types of conduct are appropriate and which are not. This strengthening of the legal system also gives people the power to defend their interests and protect themselves from capricious actions by their neighbors, other businesses, and even government officials. Private entrepreneurs have turned to the courts to force the government to honor its contracts or to compensate them for confiscating their property. Artists have been known to sue government-owned media for printing libelous accusations against them or for criticizing their works on political grounds. These types of suits are not always successful; China's courts are still not independent of the state nor are they neutral interpreters of the law. But they are successful often enough to encourage others to follow their precedent. As businesspeople, artists, and other groups in society are becoming better educated about the state's own laws and regulations, they are increasingly using them to their advantage.

China's villagers are now able to elect their own leaders. In the past, all local officials were appointed by higher levels of government, which made officials accountable to their superiors but not to the people they actually governed. This system meant, not surprisingly, that many local officials became petty tyrants toward local society. Now, villagers can use the opportunity of village elections to replace unpopular or abusive officials.

Village elections have been a controversial experiment, with a range of supporters and opponents. Many of the leaders in Beijing who promoted village elections saw them as a chance to remedy the deteriorating relations between state and society at the local level. Ironically, most of the supporters of village elections belonged to the conservative wing of the CCP and had little interest in promoting democracy. Instead, they sought political stability and saw village elections as a way to address the shortcomings of local leadership.[45] Local officials, particularly in counties and townships with authority over the village leaders, were opposed to implementing elections because they feared that they would not be able to control leaders they did not appoint but who were instead chosen by the people. They worried that it would be even harder to implement unpopular policies, such as tax collection and family planning policies, which limit the number of children per family. (Urban couples are limited to one child. Couples in rural areas can have more than one child under several circumstances: for instance, if the first child is a girl or has severe handicaps, if one of the parents is an orphan or an only child, or if they belong to one of China's minorities.) Much to their inhabitants' surprise, villages that held successful elections where there was real competition between candidates, where the candidates were not simply chosen by higher-level officials, and where voting procedures were fair have done a much better job at policy implementation than elsewhere.[46] Villagers recognize that they cannot change the policies, but they are willing to support their fairer implementation. This development has encouraged other areas also to allow more competitive elections with less intrusion by higher officials. It is still common to hear of incidents in which higher authorities refuse to let a person be a candidate, or throw out the results of elections they do not like, or even refuse to hold elections in the first place. However, national law now requires periodic elections for village chief and village councils, and the Ministry of Civil Affairs is in charge of publicizing and monitoring compliance with the law.[47]

These conventional forms of participation are not always effective and are often risky. In a political system with only one political party and limited citizen's rights, the state does not have to be responsive to the wants and needs of society. Most party and government officials are not accountable to the people and are more used to protecting other officials against what are often seen as troublemakers and whistle-blowers. Those making complaints are often subjected to intimidation, arrest, the loss of their job, and occasionally beatings and even death. Nevertheless, some people are willing to appeal to higher and higher levels and even to travel to Beijing, if necessary, in order to seek justice. Politics can be a high-stakes game in China with tremendous costs and benefits for all involved.

Not all types of political participation are so conventional. Rural protest has become increasingly common. Incidents of protest are usually provoked by the government's payments for grain with IOUs instead of cash, by its confiscation of farmland for other uses, by excessive taxation, or by corruption. Even when policies are properly carried out, those unhappy with the consequences have been known to sprinkle broken glass in the officials' rice paddies (which are farmed in bare feet), set fire to the officials' houses, or physically assault them.

Labor unrest is also growing. More than 120,000 contractual disagreements, work stoppages, strikes, and other forms of protest were recorded in 1999, up from only about 8,000 in 1992. Most of these actions were undertaken by individuals or small groups at local levels; only about 6,500 were organized attempts to initiate broad-based collective action. Still, the communist authorities apppear to be taking the protests seriously, often giving in to worker grievances over unpaid wages, medical insurance, timely pension payments, and other demands while continuing to outlaw strikes and independent labor unions. But a ninefold increase in collective bargaining disputes in the 1990s and a violent miners' strike in 2000 may portend more troublesome developments in the years ahead.[48]

Meanwhile, modern technology is providing new opportunities for people to express their views. Internet chat rooms and radio call-in shows in China are full of criticisms of official corruption. Groups such as Falun Gong use the

Internet and e-mail to communicate with their followers. In early 2000 the Chinese government issued new regulations aimed at bringing electronic communications by individuals and private companies under tighter control, a challenge in a country where the number of Internet users had risen to 8.9 million by the end of 1999.

While noting the changes in political participation that have occurred in the reform era, it is also important to note what has not changed. Although the party is willing to allow experimentation with economic policies, complaints about improper policy implementation, and village elections, it is not willing to allow direct challenges to its authority or demands for changes in the basic political system. During the reform era, three episodes of demands for political reform and even democracy occurred in China, always with the same result: the movements were suppressed, their leaders arrested, and their demands ignored.

The Democracy Wall Movement, 1978–79

In the immediate aftermath of the Cultural Revolution, a group of intellectuals began putting up posters in an area of downtown Beijing that became known as **"Democracy Wall."**[49] Initially, the protesters were supportive of Deng's efforts to replace the remaining Maoists in the party and government. They wanted to hear official criticism of the Cultural Revolution, of Mao, and of those leaders pledged to remain loyal to his policies. The protesters also called for the rehabilitation of the Cultural Revolution's victims and for political reforms to loosen state controls over society. The movement led to the formation of politically oriented journals and inspired similar developments in other cities. Most of the writers of the posters and the new journals that arose at this time portrayed themselves as loyal citizens who were seeking to reform and improve the political system but not to challenge or replace it. But some advocated positions more radical than even Deng and his allies were willing to permit.

The best known dissident to emerge in China at the time was **Wei Jingsheng,** who bemoaned the absence of democracy and rule of law in China. He characterized Deng Xiaoping as just another authoritarian ruler who was not chosen by Chinese society and who would not be bound by the

public's interest. As the demands of the Democracy Wall protesters moved in this direction, the state initiated a crackdown, arresting leading figures (including Wei) and sentencing some to long prison sentences. It also moved the authorized site of Democracy Wall from a downtown street to a remote park. In 1980, the party removed from the constitution the right to put up wall posters, eliminating one of the few avenues for public criticism of the government. China's leaders were still not willing to be accountable to public opinion.

PROFILE: Wei Jingsheng

Before rising to prominence in the 1978–79 Democracy Wall movement in Beijing, Wei Jingsheng, China's most famous political dissident was a Red Guard during the Cultural Revolution and worked as an electrician at the Beijing Zoo. An unyielding proponent of democracy and law in the post-Mao period, he was the founder and editor of a short-lived journal entitled *Explorations* in 1979, in which he published his best-known political writings. His criticism of Deng Xiaoping as a potential dictator who was not elected by the Chinese people boldly suggested that Deng was not deserving of their support. He was sentenced to fifteen years in prison in 1979, but was briefly released in 1993 when China was trying to improve its image in order to be selected as the host of the 2000 Olympics, an ultimately unsuccessful bid.

After meeting with foreign journalists and the U.S. State Department's top official for human rights, to whom he gave a letter addressed to President Bill Clinton in March 1994, Wei was arrested and eventually

Wei Jingsheng

sentenced to another fourteen years in jail for plotting to overthrow the government. Under pressure from the United States to improve its human rights record, China released Wei from prison in 1997 and immediately put him on a plane to the United States, where he remains in exile. He is still an active supporter of democracy in China and a critic of China's current leaders. He also challenges foreign governments that seek to improve relations with the People's Republic. Wei has been nominated for the Nobel Peace Prize and travels frequently throughout the United States, Europe, and Asia, speaking to audiences and publishing articles and editorials.[50]

Student Demonstrations, 1986–87

During the early 1980s, while dramatic economic reforms were taking place, political reforms were more limited. The political system was not opened to new voices and groups; instead, political reform was primarily administrative and bureaucratic in nature. The number of government ministries, commissions, and offices was reduced (although the number of officials continued to grow), new criteria for appointing and promoting officials were put in place, and mandatory retirement rules were established for officials. Officials debated policy matters more extensively and drew upon feasibility studies and other technical considerations, rather than ideological rhetoric, in making their decisions. These measures had important implications for how well the party and government did their work, but they did not make the state more responsive to popular opinion. The state may have been more efficient, but it was not more democratic.

By the mid-1980s, many in China, especially in academic and intellectual circles, grew frustrated at the slow pace of political change. In December 1986, college students in Shanghai began public demonstrations about poor living conditions on their campuses, but these demonstrations soon included calls for more extensive political reform.[51] Reports on these demonstrations spread to other campuses, and other areas of China reported similar outbreaks. Although the official media initially described the demonstrators as patriotic, the leadership soon changed its viewpoint and chose to crack down on the demonstrations without offering political concessions. Moreover, the general secretary of the CCP, Hu Yaobang, was forced to resign his post and to accept responsibility for the outbreak and spread of demonstrations, which other leaders feared might lead to increased instability if not handled forcefully.

The Tiananmen Crisis, Spring 1989

Hu Yaobang's death in April 1989 sparked the largest popular demonstrations in post-1949 China. From the point of view of China's leaders, these demonstrations—ostensibly about issues such as inflation and corruption—were aimed at overthrowing the government and were seen as a serious threat to their hold on power. The students, workers, professionals, and others who joined in the growing demonstrations in the following weeks were motivated by a variety of concerns. Some were concerned that double-digit inflation was undermining their standard of living, wiping away the gains of a decade of reform.[52] Others were alarmed at the rise of rampant corruption accompanying economic reforms. Both these issues in fact mirrored the government's own position. But others used the opportunity of these demonstrations to demand more fundamental changes in China's political system, calling for labor unions and student organizations free of government and party controls and even for the removal of Deng Xiaoping and Li Peng, the unpopular prime minister who was widely viewed as an opponent of reform. In the end, it was the form of these demands—popular demonstrations without government approval—more than their content that frightened China's leaders and led to the tragic outcome of June 4, when martial law was imposed with deadly force and thousands of people were killed or wounded.[53]

This outcome was not predetermined. It was the result of a long and divisive debate among China's top leaders about how to respond to these demonstrations. In fact, it was the perceived divisions among the elite that fueled the demonstrations, creating expectations that the state might actually give in. The longer the state delayed its response, the more these expectations grew. Some of China's leaders were sympathetic to the demands of the protesters and sought a compromise to bring the demonstrations to a close. Others saw the dramatic surge of protest as a repetition of Red

Guard activism, from which they had suffered earlier in their careers, and wanted to nip the movement in the bud. Others were embarrassed by the swelling numbers of protesters and the diversity of people who joined in, including government officials and journalists connected with the official media, people who were responsible for conveying the official line to the public.

The open display of discontent indicated a severe loss of legitimacy for the leadership in Beijing, which appeared incapable of controlling events in Tiananmen Square, the political and symbolic center of China. For more than a month, demonstrators occupied the square and began a hunger strike to dramatize their cause. The willingness of these young idealists to march in defiance of the state's orders, to remain in the square after the declaration of martial law, and to persist in their food strike created sympathy and support among other Chinese citizens and foreign audiences, who watched the drama unfold live on their television sets at home. Foreign television crews had arrived in China to cover the visit of Soviet leader Mikhail Gorbachev, but his visit was quickly overwhelmed by the growing popular protests. The television crews stayed in China even after Gorbachev departed, providing almost continuous coverage of the protests.

The failure of these demonstrations in Beijing and elsewhere in China to bring about lasting change was due to several factors. First and most important, the party refuses to recognize the legitimacy of any group of which it does not approve and refuses to accept demands for change from outside the limited channels of communications. The political system was created to change society, not to be changed by it, and the party defends its monopoly on political organization quite vigorously. One consequence of this monopoly is that there are no organizations in China with which the state can negotiate a peaceful settlement. There is no equivalent of Poland's Solidarity or the church, which in various ways contributed to political change in Central and Eastern Europe, Latin America, and elsewhere. Also, the students, workers, and others who participated in the demonstrations had no durable organization to plan their protests and shape their demands. Organizations formed spontaneously during the demonstrations, but they had little interaction with each other or with the state. The protesters themselves

were divided over their agenda: some were seeking the reform of existing policies and institutions, others had more revolutionary ambitions, feeling the system was incapable of reform. Ultimately, it was the CCP's past success in preventing autonomous organizations and its refusal to negotiate even with those making demands that echoed the state's own policies that led to the tragic outcome of these demonstrations.

The Tiananmen legacy was devastating and long-lasting. Hard-liners in the party ousted many of the most prominent reformers, including Zhao Ziyang, who had been prime minister and later head of the party and who was widely seen as Deng's heir apparent. Diplomatic and foreign economic relations were frozen and are still haunted by the image of tanks and soldiers firing on civilians. For those who participated in the protests, the crackdown led to months and years of anxiety. Some fled the country rather than risk arrest and jail. Some, like student leader Wang Dan, were jailed for years. Some had career prospects dimmed because of their involvement. Nearly all were disillusioned by the outcome, convinced more than ever that the party was beyond hope. If it refused to accommodate even the moderate demands of the protesters, it would never sponsor more far-reaching political reforms. Its willingness to use overwhelming force against unarmed demonstrators suggested that it was foolish to try to bring about change through popular appeals. This was a depressing revelation, but one deeply learned.[54] Today, it is difficult to find people willing to talk about the prospects for political reform. To people now focused on business opportunities made possible by the ongoing economic reforms, engaging in idealistic talk about democracy is a waste of time that is better spent on making money. This is, of course, exactly how the CCP wants it. The new social contract in China is built on this trade-off: people who are prospering are unlikely to be rebels.

PROFILES: China's Current Leadership

JIANG ZEMIN

The "core" of China's current generation of leaders, Jiang is China's president, the general secretary of the CCP, and the chairman of the Central Military Commission, making

Jiang Zemin

him head of state, head of the party, and head of the military. He was promoted to these posts after the 1989 Tiananmen demonstrations; during the 1990s he gradually built his networks of supporters in the central government and military. He is seen as an affable leader, but not a visionary in the likes of Mao Zedong and Deng Xiaoping.

LI PENG

Formerly prime minister, Li is now head of the National People's Congress and the number two leader in the CCP. He is seen as an opponent of reform and an advocate of continued state controls over the economy and society. He is reviled at home and abroad for his role in the 1989 Tiananmen demonstrations, during which he advocated a crackdown against the student protesters and publicly announced the declaration of martial law.

ZHU RONGJI

Zhu is China's prime minister and an outspoken advocate of economic reform and bureaucratic streamlining. His blunt style has made him popular with the Chinese people and foreign leaders, but it has also created deep resentment among China's national and local leaders. He was given credit for achieving a "soft landing" for China's overheated economy in the mid-1990s, bringing inflation down without creating a recession. By 1999, however, he was blamed for China's sluggish economy and for not taking a stronger stand against the United States in foreign affairs.

HU JINTAO

Widely seen as Jiang Zemin's successor, Hu is currently China's vice president and a member of the CCP's Politburo, the inner circle of political power in China. He has been groomed for success since the early 1980s, holding a variety of positions in Beijing and elsewhere in China, including party secretary of Tibet. Like many of China's leaders, his personal policy views are not well known.

ZHAO ZIYANG

Zhao was prime minister from 1980–87 and head of the CCP from 1987–89, when he was removed from all posts after supporting the Tiananmen demonstrators. He was responsible for many of the economic reforms of the 1980s and also sponsored some ambitious political reforms, such as the creation of a professionalized civil service and a clearer separation of party and government. Most of these reforms were abandoned before his ouster. He was never formally charged with any crime for his actions in 1989, but he remains under a loose form of house arrest. Periodically he releases a letter to the press recommending that the official verdict on the Tiananmen demonstrations as a counterrevolutionary rebellion be rescinded and that his removal from office be declared a mistake. Now in his 70s, he is too old for a return to political office, but he remains a symbol of political reform, even though he was not a supporter of elections or other democratizing reforms while he was in office.

HYPOTHESIS-TESTING EXERCISE: Prospects for China's Democratization

HYPOTHESIS, VARIABLES, AND EXPECTATIONS

What are the chances that China will undergo democratization in the future? Chapter 10 outlined a series of ten **independent variables** that influence the establishment and survival of democracies and that provide us with a framework for answering this question. *China's democratization*, therefore, is our **dependent variable.** The hypothesized conditions for democracy create a series of **expectations** about their probable effects. As chapter 10 indicates, we can fairly confidently expect most of these variables to promote democracy, while a few others are likely to produce mixed results, depending on local circumstances. Analyzing China's situation against these ten variables provides a useful hypothesis-testing exercise for theories of democratization.[55]

EVIDENCE

China has strong *state institutions* that exercise sovereignty over Chinese territories (with the important exception of Taiwan, as noted earlier). But these institutions are, in general, not compatible with democracy. The rule of law, as described earlier, is not protected; the courts and even the constitution are political tools of the state and are strongly influenced by the changing preferences of the leaders rather than by constraints on the state's own actions. The leaders themselves are not accountable to the people, except at the grassroots level. China also lacks *elites committed to democracy* in numbers large enough to influence decision making. China certainly does have leaders who favor political reform, even including democratization, but they are wary of being too open in their beliefs for fear of losing their jobs. Ironically, the leaders who were instrumental in promoting village elections were not supporters of democratization: instead, they were concerned with maintaining political order over the restive countryside. Supporters for reform had a potential window of opportunity in 1989, but were outmaneuvered by hard-liners. Obviously, the state itself is the main obstacle to democratization in China.

Economic reform, however, is bringing about changes that may increase pressures from below for democratic change. For more than two decades, China has experienced rapid growth in its *national wealth.* Its GNP topped $1 trillion by the late 1990s, though its per capita income remained quite low (around $750). This new wealth has been accompanied by other changes that are more intriguing. The growth of *private enterprise* in China has created less state control over the economy and society, and most people are less dependent on the state than at any time since before the communist revolution. The number of private enterprises continues to grow, and most new jobs and economic growth are created by the private sector. However, private entrepreneurs themselves do not seem interested in promoting democracy, at least not now. As in some other authoritarian countries, especially in East Asia, private entrepreneurs in China are partners of the state and benefit from many of its policies. They are indifferent, or even opposed, to calls for political change, a reality strikingly inconsistent with our supposition that private enterprise generally fosters democracy.[56]

But the growth of China's private sector may have indirect effects on potential democratization. It may, for example, give rise to a *middle class* and a *civil society* that will be more supportive of democracy. Here, too, however, the evidence thus far is limited. China's growing middle class is closely tied to the state and remains generally passive in its political behavior, another reality at variance with our expectations. Its civil society is still undeveloped, largely because the state represses efforts to organize groups independent of its control. The state has pursued an authoritarian neo-corporatist strategy of setting up business and trade groups to link economic and political elites. Some have hoped that these business associations will develop their own identity and stake out a more independent position and influence policy, but so far their efforts have been focused on narrow business and commercial interests, not on more fundamental political issues.[57] Meanwhile, there are no independent trade unions that might represent the labor force in tripartite neo-corporatist negotiations.

How China's large numbers of economically *disadvantaged* workers and peasants will affect the prospects for democracy is an intriguing question. It seems clear that no mass movement from below is likely to remove the communist authorities at the top. It is nonetheless possible that people favorable to democratic change in the business elite or the middle class may find support from those who have been left out of the private sector's phenomenal growth, or who have been harmed by such things as inflation or the exploitation of low-wage labor.

Attitudinal issues are also important. Many people—including Chinese intellectuals—have argued that Chinese *political culture,* with its emphasis on hierarchy and order and its lack of emphasis on individual rights and interests, is not compatible with democracy. According to this perspective, only after an extensive period of economic growth, rising levels of *education, increased freedom of information,* and greater interaction with the outside world, will China's political culture be suitable for democracy. Literacy levels have been rising, allowing people to absorb more information, and the state is no longer able to control the flow of information as thoroughly as in the past (especially in an age of Internet access and fax machines). Ironically, not only do the new communications technologies allow for more diverse sources of information, but the commercialization of information also allows people to avoid politics more than ever, diverting their attention to other areas of interest.

Not all aspects of this argument stand up to scrutiny, however. The success of village-level elections suggests that people can participate in government even before a democratic culture is created. The gradual democratization of Taiwan—where traditional Chinese values were even more important than on the mainland—shows that democratization creates democratic values.[58] So even though democratic values may be necessary for democracy to survive, they may not be necessary to get the process started.

Roughly 92 percent of China's population belongs to the Han nationality. However, minority groups, though few in number, occupy strategically important areas of the country. The largest such areas are Tibet, the Buddhist nation that was forcibly annexed in 1949–51; the western province of Xinjiang, which is predominantly Muslim; and inner Mongolia. The periodic activity of independence movements in these areas has provided the Chinese government with a rationale to keep them under control. It denies them autonomy and cracks down on political restiveness, at times quite severely. Thus China's ethnic and religious *heterogeneity* works against democratization.

The *international environment* is an ambiguous factor. Clearly, many countries, including the United States, would like to encourage China's democratization. But this very willingness to promote political change makes the international environment seem threatening to China's leaders. They recognize that foreign governments would prefer that China not remain communist, a direct threat to their hold on power. They see the foreign promotion of "peaceful evolution" toward liberal democracy and a market-based economy as an attempt to undermine their political system.

These attitudes cannot help but create difficult dilemmas for the world's democracies in their policies toward China. The debate in the United States on approving China's admission into the World Trade Organization (WTO) is a case in point. The Clinton administration, following a policy of "engagement" with China, approved its entry into the WTO in 1999 in hopes that integrating China more fully into the global trading order will promote its democratization over the coming years. Critics of this strategy opposed bringing China into the WTO or granting it other benefits until it democratized or, at the very least, ceased flagrant human rights abuses such as the exploitation of labor. This debate intensified in 2000 as the Clinton administration sought Congressional approval of "permanent normal trade relations" with China to set the stage for its future admission into the WTO. The measure provided for the removal of Congress's right to vote every year on whether to renew China's trade privileges, in exchange for Chinese pledges to gradually ease restrictions on U.S. companies wishing to do business in China. The debate cut across party lines. Organized labor and many Democrats opposed Clinton's bill, along with various human rights activists like Wei Jingsheng. Business groups and a large number of Republican legislators supported the bill, as did pro-democracy activists who believed that expanded trade would promote the cause of human rights in China over the long term. After intense debate and lobbying, the bill facilitating trade passed in the House of Representatives in May and cleared the Senate in September. China was now expected to lower tariffs on a wide assortment of American-made goods and to widen direct investments by U.S. firms in selected industries. The Chinese had already come to terms with the European Union on expanded trade relations.

Though the opposing positions in the U.S. debate may differ as to the *means* of promoting democracy in China, both favor democracy as the ultimate goal. Not only are both sides motivated by concerns about the civil rights of China's vast population, but many advocates of democratization also believe that a democratic China will be a peaceful China. The communist government's current efforts to strengthen its nuclear arsenal and its occasionally bellicose statements regarding Taiwan provide continuing cause for concern about its military intentions in the Pacific region. In addition, the large imbalance in U.S.-PRC trade in China's favor ($68 billion in 1999 alone), and the prospect that China's low-wage economy may attract American firms to relocate there, thus reducing job opportunities in the United States, are concerns that trouble many Americans, regardless of party affiliation.

For their part, the PRC's leaders are suspicious of foreign motives and critical of efforts to meddle in their internal affairs. As we've seen, mistrust of foreigners has deep historical roots in China, and any attempt by outside powers to manipulate the Chinese people or its government invariably strikes a raw nerve, evoking bitter memories of past exploitation. China's pride was fully evident during the celebrations in July 1997 that greeted its assumption of sovereignty over Hong Kong, which reverted to the People's Republic upon the expiration of Britain's ninety-nine-year "lease."[59] Chinese sensitivities were also on view during the Kosovo conflict in 1999 when U.S. warplanes hit the People's Republic's embassy during a bombing run over Belgrade. Washington quickly apologized for the incident, insisting it was an accident. In Beijing, thousands of angry protesters surrounded the U.S. embassy for weeks, chanting anti-NATO slogans; relations between the two governments remained chilly for months afterward.

As a general rule, the communist authorities have tried as much as possible to suppress foreign influences. Thus far, efforts to promote democratization from the outside have in fact had the opposite of their intended effect.

CONCLUSIONS

On the whole, some of the conditions for democracy are weak in China, while others are getting stronger. Perhaps the most striking phenomenon is the failure thus far of economic growth and the emergence of a large private sector to stimulate more intense pressures for democratization, a development largely inconsistent with our expectations. Nevertheless, as the spontaneous student demonstrations of 1989's Democracy Spring showed, events can take a sudden turn. Hopes for democracy may still lie just beneath the currently placid surface of Chinese society. The events of 1989 also showed, however, that if democracy is to take hold, it must have the support of key elites, both in the government and in society, who are committed to a democratic transition. So far, China lacks sufficient numbers of those kinds of elites.

CONCLUSION

As China enters the twenty-first century, many of the most important issues it faced at the beginning of the twentieth century are still unresolved. Is the West the cause of China's problems or part of their solution? Which Chinese traditions and values are appropriate for the modern world? Is democracy suitable to China, given its traditions, distinctive characteristics, and current level of economic and social development? These questions are fundamental ones, and no definitive answer may be possible any time soon. Nor are these questions unique to China: many developing countries face the same dilemmas. Given China's size and potential for future development, however, how China answers these questions is likely to affect not only its future, but the future of its neighbors and perhaps even the international community of nations as a whole. For that reason, China's future is worth watching.

How China develops will also have important implications for the study of comparative politics as well. As the hypothesis-testing exercise on democratization showed, China will be an important test case for many theories in comparative politics. At first glance, China often seems exotic, difficult to understand, an exception to many theories developed on the basis of the experience of Western countries. Indeed, China prefers to portray itself as exceptional and argues that conventional theories cannot capture the country's complexities. But it is only by comparing and contrasting contemporary China with its own past and with other countries that we can gain a clearer understanding of what is truly distinctive and what fits more general patterns of behavior. All countries are unique to some extent, and China no more so than many others. Its ultimate fate will surely tell us a great deal about democracy's potential as a universally applicable system of government and about the capacity of societies to change their political order. For centuries, China has captured the imagination of scholars and policy makers, and it still does today.

KEY TERMS AND NAMES
(Underlined in the text)

Deng Xiaoping
Chinese Communist Party (CCP)
People's Republic of China (PRC)
Democracy Spring (1989)
Confucius
Sun Yat-sen
Republic of China
Chiang Kai-shek
May 4th Movement
Chinese Nationalist Party (Kuomintang, KMT)
Mao Zedong
Long March
People's Liberation Army
Taiwan
Chen Shui-bian
Politburo
General Secretary
Jiang Zemin
Prime minister
National People's Congress
Red versus expert debate
Utopianism
Collectivization
Hundred Flowers Movement
Great Leap Forward
Great Proletarian Cultural Revolution
Democracy Wall

FOR DISCUSSION: WHAT WOULD YOU DO?

1. If you were a Chinese student and your friends asked you to sign a petition in favor of democracy or to join in an illegal demonstration, would you do it?
2. If you were a Chinese citizen, what would be your attitude toward foreign governments or organizations seeking to promote democracy in your country?
3. As a citizen of another country, what should be the policy of your government toward China?

FOR FURTHER READING

In addition to the titles in the notes, consult the following:

General History
John King Fairbank and Merle Goldman, *China: A New History* (Cambridge, Mass.: Harvard University Press, 1998).
Jonathan Spence, *The Search for Modern China* (New York: W. W. Norton, 1990).

Mary C. Wright, *The Last Stand of Chinese Conservatism: The Tung-chih Restoration, 1862–1874* (Stanford, Calif.: Stanford University Press, 1957).

The Communist Revolution and Mao Era

Lucien Bianco, *Origins of the Chinese Revolution, 1915–1949* (Stanford, Calif.: Stanford University Press, 1971).

Anita Chan, Richard Madsen, and Jonathan Unger, *Chen Village Under Mao and Deng*, 2d ed. (Berkeley: University of California Press, 1992).

Hong Yung Lee, *The Politics of the Chinese Cultural Revolution: A Case Study* (Berkeley: University of California Press, 1978).

Li Zhisui, *The Private Life of Chairman Mao: The Memoirs of Mao's Personal Physician* (New York: Random House, 1994).

Andrew Nathan, *Chinese Democracy* (Berkeley: University of California Press, 1985).

The Reform Era

Richard Evans, *Deng Xiaoping and the Making of Modern China*, rev. ed. (London: Penguin, 1995).

Bruce Gilley, *Tiger on the Brink: Jiang Zemin and China's New Elite* (Berkeley: University of California Press, 1998).

Kenneth Lieberthal, *Governing China: From Revolution Through Reform* (New York: W. W. Norton, 1995).

James A. R. Miles, *Legacy of Tiananmen: China in Disarray* (Ann Arbor: University of Michigan Press, 1996).

Orville Schell and David Shambaugh, eds., *The China Reader: The Reform Era* (New York: Vintage Books, 1999).

Vaclav Smil, *China's Environmental Crisis: An Inquiry into the Limits of National Development* (Armonk, N.Y.: M. E. Sharpe, 1993).

Yanqi Tong, *Transitions from State Socialism: Economic and Political Change in Hungary and China* (Lanham, Md.: Rowman and Littlefield, 1997).

Jeffrey N. Wasserstrom and Elizabeth J. Perry, eds., *Popular Protest and Political Culture in Modern China: Learning from 1989,* 2d ed. (Boulder, Colo.: Westview, 1994).

Benjamin Yang, *Deng: A Political Biography* (Armonk, N.Y.: M. E. Sharpe, 1998).

WEBSITES

<www.chinaonline.com> is a good source for business-related news and information.

<www.insidechina.com.> is the site for Inside China Today. It offers up-to-date information on political, social, and economic affairs in China, Taiwan, and Hong Kong.

<www.taiwansecurity.org.> provides a good collection of current articles and commentary on U.S.-China relations and related issues.

NOTES

1. Edward A. McCord, *The Power of the Gun : The Emergence of Modern Chinese Warlordism* (Berkeley: University of California Press, 1993).

2. Chow Tse-tsung, *The May 4th Movement* (Cambridge, Mass.: Harvard University Press, 1960).

3. Stuart Schram, *Mao Tse-tung* (New York: Simon and Schuster, 1967); Benjamin I. Schwartz, *Chinese Communism and the Rise of Mao* (Cambridge, Mass.: Harvard University Press, 1951); Jonathan D. Spence, *Mao Zedong* (New York: Lipper/Viking, 1999).

4. Lloyd E. Eastman, *The Abortive Revolution: China Under Nationalist Rule, 1927–1937* (Cambridge, Mass.: Harvard East Asian Monographs 153, 1990).

5. Edgar Snow, *Red Star over China* (New York: Grove Press, 1968); Harrison E. Salisbury, *The Long March: The Untold Story* (New York: Harper and Row, 1985).

6. Iris Chang, *The Rape of Nanking: The Forgotten Holocaust of World War II* (New York: Basic Books, 1997); Joshua A. Fogel, ed., *The Nanjing Massacre in History and Historiography* (Berkeley: University of California Press, 2000).

7. Barbara W. Tuchman, *Stilwell and the American Experience in China, 1911–1945* (New York: Macmillan, 1971); Suzanne Pepper, *Civil War in China* (Berkeley: University of California Press, 1978).

8. Hung-mao Tien, *The Great Transition: Political and Social Change in the Republic of China* (Stanford, Calif.: Hoover Institution Press, 1989); Thomas Gold, *State and Society in the Taiwan Miracle* (Armonk, N.Y.: M. E. Sharpe, 1986); Bruce J. Dickson, *Democratization in China and Taiwan: The Adaptability of Leninist Parties* (London and New York: Oxford University Press, 1997); Ralph N. Clough, *Cooperation or Conflict in the Taiwan Strait?* (Lanham, Md.: Rowman and Littlefield, 1999); Shelley Rigger, *Politics in Taiwan: Voting for Democracy* (New York: Routledge, 1999).

9. Kevin J. O'Brien, *Reform Without Liberalization: China's National People's Congress and the Politics of Institutional Change* (New York: Cambridge University Press, 1990); Murray Scot Tanner, *The Politics of Lawmaking in Post-Mao China: Institutions, Processes, and Democratic Prospects* (New York: Oxford University Press, 1999).

10. *Selected Works of Mao Tse-tung*, vol. 1 (Beijing: Foreign Languages Press, 1965), 28.

11. Frederick C. Teiwes, "Establishment and Consolidation of the New Regime," in *The Politics of China*, 2d ed., ed. Roderick MacFarquhar (Cambridge: Cambridge University Press, 1997), 5–86.

12. Harry Harding, *Organizing China: The Problem of Bureaucracy, 1949–1976* (Stanford, Calif.: Stanford University Press, 1980).

13. Richard Lowenthal, "Development Versus Utopia in Communist Policy," in *Change in Communist Systems,* ed. Chalmers Johnson (Stanford, Calif.: Stanford University Press, 1970).

14. Roderick MacFarquhar, *Origins of the Cultural Revolution,* vol. 1, *Contradictions Among the People 1956–1957* (New York: Columbia University Press, 1974).

15. Deng Xiaoping was in charge of running the Anti-Rightist campaign. As far back as 1957, Deng was associated with strictly enforcing the limits on free speech and dissent. Despite his emphasis on science and technology in later years and his support for rehabilitating many of the victims of Mao's campaigns (including the Anti-Rightist campaign), he was also opposed to letting the experts turn their expertise into political influence.

16. Roderick MacFarquhar, *Origins of the Cultural Revolution,* vol. 2, *The Great Leap Forward, 1958–62* (New York: Columbia University Press, 1983); David M. Bachman, *Bureaucracy, Economy, and Leadership in China: The Institutional Origins of the Great Leap Forward* (New York: Cambridge University Press, 1991).

17. Kenneth Lieberthal, "The Great Leap Forward and the Split in the Yanan Leadership," in MacFarquhar, *Politics of China,* 87–147.

18. Harry Harding, "The Chinese State in Crisis," in MacFarquhar, *Politics of China,* 148–247.

19. Roxane Witke, *Comrade Chiang Ching* (Boston: Little, Brown, 1977); Ross Terrill, *The White Boned Demon: A Biography of Madame Mao Zedong* (New York: Morrow, 1984).

20. Richard Baum, *Burying Mao: Chinese Politics in the Age of Deng Xiaoping* (Princeton, N.J.: Princeton University Press, 1994).

21. Kenneth Lieberthal and Michel Oksenberg, *Policy Making in China: Leaders, Structures, and Processes* (Princeton, N.J.: Princeton University Press, 1988).

22. Melanie Manion, *Retirement of Revolutionaries in China: Public Policies, Social Norms, Private Interests* (Princeton, N.J.: Princeton University Press, 1993).

23. Hong Yung Lee, *From Revolutionary Cadres to Party Technocrats in Socialist China* (Berkeley: University of California Press, 1991).

24. Timothy Brook and B. Michael Frolic, eds., *Civil Society in China* (Armonk, N.Y.: M. E. Sharpe, 1997).

25. Barry Naughton, "The Third Front: Defence Industrialization in the Chinese Interior," *China Quarterly,* no. 115 (September 1988): 351–86.

26. Martin King Whyte, "State and Society Under Mao," in *Perspectives on Modern China: Four Anniversaries,* ed. Kenneth Lieberthal et al. (Armonk, N.Y.: M. E. Sharpe, 1991), 255–74.

27. Joseph Fewsmith, *Dilemmas of Reform in China* (Armonk, N.Y.: M. E. Sharpe, 1994).

28. The "China threat" perspective is best represented by Richard Bernstein and Ross Munro, *The Coming Conflict with China* (New York: Knopf, 1991); the alternative viewpoint is presented in Andrew J. Nathan and Robert S. Ross, *The Great Wall and The Empty Fortress: China's Search for Security* (New York: W. W. Norton, 1997). An interesting contribution to this debate comes from a collection of essays by young Chinese scholars now teaching in American colleges and universities: Yong Deng and Fei-Ling Wang, eds., *In the Eyes of the Dragon: China Views the World* (Lanham, Md.: Rowman and Littlefield, 1999).

29. Jean C. Oi, *Rural China Takes Off: Institutional Foundations of Economic Reform* (Berkeley: University of California Press, 1999).

30. Barry Naughton, *Growing Out of the Plan: Chinese Economic Reform, 1978–1993* (New York: Cambridge University Press, 1996).

31. Dali L. Yang, *Beyond Beijing: Liberalization and the Regions in China* (New York: Routledge, 1997).

32. Dorothy Solinger, "China's Floating Population," in *The Paradox of China's Post-Mao Reforms,* ed. Merle Goldman and Roderick MacFarquhar (Cambridge, Mass.: Harvard University Press, 1999), 220–40.

33. Jianying Zha, *China Pop: How Soap Operas, Tabloids, and Bestsellers Are Transforming a Culture* (New York: New Press, 1995).

34. Jonathan Unger and Anita Chan, "Corporatism in China: A Developmental State in an East Asian Context," in *China After Socialism: In the Footsteps of Eastern Europe or East Asia?* ed. Barrett L. McCormick and Jonathan Unger (Armonk, N.Y.: M. E. Sharpe, 1995), 95–129; Christopher Earle Nevitt, "Private Business Associations in China: Evidence of Civil Society or Local State Power?" *China Journal,* no. 38 (July 1996): 25–43; Jonathan Unger " 'Bridges': Private Business, the Chinese Government, and the Rise of New Associations," *China Quarterly,* no. 1996 (September 1997): 795–819.

35. Kenneth Lieberthal and David Lampton, eds., *Bureaucracy, Politics, and Decision Making in Post-Mao China* (Berkeley: University of California Press, 1992); Susan Shirk, *The Political Logic of Economic Reform in China* (Berkeley: University of California Press, 1993).

36. Harry Harding, *China's Second Revolution: Reform After Mao* (Washington, D.C.: Brookings, 1987).

37. Andrew Walder, *Communist Neo-Traditionalism: Work and Authority in Chinese Industry* (Berkeley: University of California Press, 1986).

38. Gordon White, Jude Howell, and Shang Xiaoyuan, *In Search of Civil Society: Market Reform and Social*

Change in Contemporary China (Oxford: Oxford University Press, 1996).

39. This is not a new strategy: it was used in the early twentieth century to give chambers of commerce some autonomy but to also have them serve state goals; see David Strand, *Rickshaw Beijing: City People and Politics in the 1920s* (Berkeley: University of California Press, 1989).

40. Martin K. Whyte, "Urban China: A Civil Society in the Making?" and Dorothy Solinger, "Urban Entrepreneurs and the State: The Merger of State and Society," both in *State and Society in China: The Consequences of Reform*, ed. Arthur Lewis Rosenbaum (Boulder, Colo.: Westview, 1992); Timothy Brook and B. Michael Frolic, eds., *Civil Society in China* (Armonk, N.Y.: M. E. Sharpe, 1997).

41. Bruce J. Dickson, *Democratization in China and Taiwan: The Adaptability of Leninist Parties* (London and New York: Oxford University Press, 1997).

42. Barry Sautman, "Sirens of the Strongman: Neo-Authoritarianism in Recent Chinese Political Theory," *China Quarterly*, no. 129 (March 1992): 72–103.

43. Samuel Huntington, "The Goals of Political Development," in *Understanding Political Development*, ed. Myron Weiner and Samuel P. Huntington (Boston: Little, Brown, 1987), 3–32.

44. Lianjiang Li and Kevin J. O'Brien, "Villagers and Popular Resistance in Contemporary China," *Modern China* 22, no. 1 (January 1996): 28–61.

45. Daniel Kelliher, "The Chinese Debate over Village Self-Government," *China Journal*, no. 37 (January 1997): 63–86; Lianjiang Li and Kevin J. O'Brien, "The Struggle over Village Elections," in Goldman and MacFarquhar, *Paradox of China's Post-Mao Reforms*, 129–44.

46. Kevin J. O'Brien, "Implementing Political Reform in China's Villages," *Australian Journal of Chinese Affairs*, no. 32 (July 1994): 33–59.

47. Tyrene White, "Village Elections: Democracy from the Bottom Up?" *Current History* (September 1998): 263–67.

48. Thomas P. Bernstein, "Farmer Discontent and Regime Responses," in Goldman and MacFarquhar, *Paradox of China's Post-Mao Reforms*, 197–219, and his "Instability in Rural China," in *Is China Unstable? Assessing the Factors*, ed. David Shambaugh (Armonk, N.Y.: M. E. Sharpe, 1999). On labor unrest, see the *Washington Post*, 23 April 2000.

49. Roger Garside, *Coming Alive: China After Mao* (New York: McGraw-Hill, 1981); Andrew J. Nathan, *Chinese Democracy* (Berkeley: University of California Press, 1985).

50. Wei Jingsheng, *The Courage to Stand Alone: Letters from Prison and Other Writings* (New York: Viking, 1997).

51. Orville Schell, *Discos and Democracy: China in the Throes of Reform* (New York: Anchor Books, 1989).

52. Andrew G. Walder, "Urban Industrial Workers: Some Observations on the 1980s," in Rosenbaum, *State and Society in China*, 103–20.

53. See Michel Oksenberg, Marc Lambert, and Lawrence Sullivan, eds., *Beijing Spring 1989: Confrontation and Conflict* (Armonk, N.Y.: M. E. Sharpe, 1990); Orville Schell, *Mandate of Heaven: A New Generation of Entrepreneurs, Dissidents, Bohemians, and Technocrats Lays Claim to China's Future* (New York: Simon and Schuster, 1989).

54. James Miles, *The Legacy of Tiananmen: China in Disarray* (Ann Arbor: University of Michigan Press, 1996).

55. Martin King Whyte, "Prospects for Democratization in China," *Problems of Communism* 41, no. 3 (May–June 1992): 58–70.

56. Margaret M. Pearson, *China's New Business Elite: The Political Consequences of Economic Reform* (Berkeley: University of California Press, 1997), and her "China's Emerging Business Class: Democracy's Harbinger?" *Current History* 97, no. 620 (September 1998): 268–72.

57. David S. G. Goodman, "The New Middle Class," in Goldman and MacFarquhar, *Paradox of China's Post-Mao Reforms*, 241–61.

58. Hung-mao Tien, ed., *Taiwan's Electoral Politics and Democratic Transition: Riding the Third Wave* (Armonk, N.Y.: M. E. Sharpe, 1996).

59. Britain forced China to hand over Hong Kong (more specifically, the New Territories) in 1898. In a joint declaration signed with Britain in 1984, China agreed to respect Hong Kong's legal, political, and economic autonomy for fifty years after taking control. Though Hong Kong has an elected legislature, its chief executive, Tung Chee-hwa, was essentially handpicked by the People's Republic. Since assuming his functions he has sought to limit the scope of Hong Kong's democratic institutions.

CHAPTER 23

MEXICO AND BRAZIL
Joseph L. Klesner

Millions of Mexicans hope to remember July 2, 2000 as the day they brought democracy to their nation. On that election day, almost 2.5 million more Mexicans voted for **Vicente Fox** of the **National Action Party** (known as the **PAN**) than for Francisco Labastida of the ruling **Institutional Revolutionary Party** (known as the **PRI**). The PRI's control of the Mexican presidency thereby ended after seventy-one years in which it had never relinquished power. After the polls closed and television networks broadcast the results of exit polls that indicated that— unexpectedly—Fox had won, Mexicans streamed into the streets to celebrate what they regarded as a vote for change. They agreed with Vicente Fox's campaign slogan: *!Ya!* (Enough Already!)

To be sure, the 2000 electoral contest was strikingly different from the previous presidential election, held in 1994, in more ways than one. Not only did the PRI lose in 2000, but the entire campaign took place in a considerably less chaotic atmosphere. As 1994 began, outgoing President Carlos Salinas de Gortari learned that a rebellion had broken out in Chiapas, the nation's southernmost state. Rebels, almost all of whom were Mayan Indians, had seized six town halls. In March, Salinas's hand-picked successor as the PRI's presidential candidate, Luis Donaldo Colosio, was assassinated during a campaign event. In September, the PRI's

Vicente Fox hails supporters after winning the presidency.

secretary general was gunned down. Shortly after Salinas's second choice for PRI candidate, Ernesto Zedillo, won the presidency at the end of the year, the Mexican peso tumbled precipitously, taking the economy down with it. Carlos Salinas ended up leaving Mexico in disgrace, badgered by corruption charges. His brother Raúl went to prison for arranging the murder of the PRI secretary general and was suspected of having embezzled tens of millions of dollars during Carlos Salinas's presidential term. Mexico's giant step in the direction of democracy in 2000 in large measure reflected the intention of many Mexicans to put this legacy of corruption and turmoil behind them.[1]

TABLE 23.1

Mexican Presidential Elections, 2000		
Candidate	Party or Coalition	% of Valid Votes
Vicente Fox	Alliance for Change*	43.4
Francisco Labastida	Institutional Revolutionary Party (PRI)	36.9
Cuauhtémoc Cardenas	Alliance for Mexico**	17.0
Others		2.7

*Alliance for Change was composed of the National Action Party (PAN) and the Mexican Green Party (PVEM).
**Alliance for Mexico was composed of the Democratic Revolutionary Party (PRD) and four smaller parties of the left.
Source: Instituto Federal Electoral.

Mexico's transition to a fully democratic regime has come slowly, the result of many efforts by opposition politicians and democracy advocates to pressure the PRI to yield power. It may seem paradoxical that one of the developing world's most economically advanced countries—a nation that shares a 2000-mile border with the world's oldest democracy—would have embraced democracy so recently. However, formally democratic institutions can sometimes be used to perpetuate undemocratic rule, as you will learn in this chapter. The Peruvian novelist Mario Vargas Llosa, himself a failed presidential candidate in his home country, once called Mexico the world's "most perfect dictatorship." The PRI's adept use and abuse of democratic institutions to prolong its rule forced the opposition to struggle within those democratic arenas—the electoral system, the Congress, and state and local government—to remove the PRI from power. Thus Mexico offers an intriguing example of a country in which *a democratic transition has taken place within the existing constitutional framework.*

However, even while an enthusiastic public buoys his chances for success, Fox will face several major challenges as he seeks to restructure the Mexican political institutions that we shall describe below. He must convince Congress to pass his legislative initiatives, even though his party lacks a majority in that body. He must deal with the revolt in the Chiapas region, where many Mexicans have chosen a violent path as they have confronted what they regard as an unjust political and economic system. He must confront the reality of Mexico's highly unequal income distribution, which leaves almost half the population in poverty. And he must conduct Mexico's relations with the United States, the often meddlesome

neighbor to the north, which worries about such interests as its $170 billion in trade with Mexico,[2] the nearly 3 million Mexicans living in the United States,[3] and an often violent trade in cocaine and heroin that passes through Mexico on its way to the American market.

PROFILE: Vicente Fox

Born in Mexico City in 1942, the son of a wealthy farmer of Irish descent and a Spanish-born mother, Vicente Fox was educated at Jesuit schools in Mexico and Wisconsin; he later studied business at Harvard. Before entering politics he rose up the ranks of Coca-Cola's Mexican and Central American division, eventually becoming its president, but he declined an offer to take charge of the company's entire Latin American operation. In 1988 Fox was elected to Mexico's Congress along with a number of other entrepreneurs in the National Action Party. He lost a bid for governor of Guanajuato province in 1991, apparently because of fraud perpetrated by the well-entrenched Institutional Revolutionary Party. In his second attempt four years later, however, he won a landslide victory. A successful cattle rancher and avid horseman, Fox also raises vegetables for export around the world. He is a strong supporter of the North American Free Trade Agreement, Mexico's trading arrangement with the United States and Canada.

Meanwhile, half a continent away, Brazil is struggling to maintain its fragile democratic institutions and stabilize its economy under President **Fernando Henrique Cardoso,** a former leftist intellectual who once wrote a famous book in which he described how global capitalism constrained Latin American countries' economic development.[4] But Cardoso now favors democratic rule, a market economy, and a major role for Brazil in the global economy. While he was writing about economic dependency in exile in Santiago, Chile, during the late 1960s, the military was governing Brazil with a firm hand and promoting a model of state-supported capitalism that led to phenomenal economic growth before the oil crises of the 1970s undermined their effort. President João Figueredo, the last military president, turned power over to a civilian in 1985, but democratically elected Brazilian presidents since then have had to contend with widespread poverty, one of the most unequal distributions of income in the world, a tradition of political corruption, rampant crime, and environmental degradation. Like Mexico, Brazil is tied to the world economy and subject to financial instability because of high levels of foreign debt and the fickleness of foreign investors.

The challenges confronting Mexico and Brazil are typical of the problems besetting many countries in Latin America. Since becoming independent from Spain or Portugal in the first quarter of the nineteenth century, most countries in Latin America have experienced political instability, often expressed as periodic alternation between democratic structures and authoritarianism, usually in the form of military rule. For example, Brazil had a limited, oligarchical democracy until 1930, when a military coup led to an authoritarian regime that lasted until 1946. From 1946 until 1964, Brazil enjoyed democracy, although the military meddled in politics several times. A military coup ousted Brazil's president in 1964, and the military as an institution ruled until 1985, when democracy returned. Argentina, Peru, and Bolivia have experienced similar cycles of democracy and military rule.

Like Brazil and Mexico, many Latin American nations have joined in the "third wave" of democracy that has swept the world since 1975.[5] However, endemic poverty, corruption, and difficulties in bringing to justice the military officers who committed gross violations of human rights have complicated these democratization processes, along with many other problems. Here are some examples:

- When Raúl Alfonsín became the democratically elected president of **Argentina** in 1983, he assumed direction of an economy that had been wrecked by the military's failed economic policies.

- In 1999, while visiting Britain, Augusto Pinochet, the former dictator of **Chile,** was indicted for human rights violations. Tellingly, he was indicted by Spain, not by his own country, where democratic leaders are loathe to upset the former president's admirers and thereby risk undermining the remarkable economic development that they have enjoyed in the past fifteen years. (The British government allowed him to return home on medical grounds.)

- In **Colombia,** where democratically elected presidents have governed since 1958, a prolonged civil war threatens to carve up the country and render democracy meaningless. The war is caused to some extent from the inequitable distribution of land and economic opportunities, but it is also driven by drug trafficking, which threatens to draw the United States into that nation's troubles.

- **Guatemala** recently ended a thirty-six-year civil war that cost as many as 150,000 lives.

- **Nicaragua** suffered considerable poverty in the 1990s as the result of the economic damage incurred in the 1980s under the revolutionary rule of the Marxist Sandinistas and the civil war waged against them by the U.S.-backed *contras.* Nicaraguan voters ousted the Sandinistas in 1989 and embarked on democracy, but economic conditions remain difficult.

- **Peru** saw its democracy buffeted in the 1980s by a vicious revolutionary organization, the Shining Path; in the 1990s, Peruvians applauded President Alberto Fujimori's defeat of the Shining Path, but their democracy has been compromised by Fujimori's *caudillo* (strongman) rule. Fujimori won a third term in a May 2000 presidential election that Organization of American States observers called unfair.

- Mirroring Fujimori, President Hugo Chavez of **Venezuela,** once the leader of a failed military coup, succeeded in throwing that nation's democratically elected congress out of office so that he could rewrite the constitution to a form more compatible with his *caudillo* rule.

Latin America's new democracies remain in place, but a "third reverse-wave," in which some of them succumb to dictatorship, has become a distinct possibility.

In this chapter we shall undertake a focused comparison of Mexico and Brazil, Latin America's most populous and richest countries. Along the way we'll indicate how they have dealt with the five sources of political conflict outlined in chapter 2:

- *Power:* Which groups have exercised predominant power in these countries? Is power being distributed more broadly among elites and organizations in civil society now that democratization is more widespread than it was fifteen to twenty years ago?
- *Resources:* How have Mexico and Brazil dealt with the challenges of economic growth, inflation, poverty, and globalization? How wisely have they used their natural resources? How have the fruits of their economic development been distributed to groups in their societies?
- *Social identity:* How are problems of ethnic diversity being addressed in Mexico, with its large Indian population, and in Brazil, perhaps the most racially mixed society in the world?
- *Ideas:* How has democracy been conceived in these countries? Is it understood in U.S. or European terms, or is there a specific Latin American model of democracy?
- *Values:* Which values and attitudes have shaped the political cultures of Mexico and Brazil? Are those values compatible with democracy and economic development?

In addition to looking at these conflicts, we'll assess these two countries' prospects for building and sustaining democracy by relating their experiences to the conditions for democracy and democratization discussed in chapter 10. Central to democracy's viability in Mexico and Brazil are the political institutions that each of these societies has inherited from previous political regimes. Thus we shall pay close attention to the democratic institutions of Mexico and Brazil, institutional forms discussed in chapter 9. Does it matter how the electoral systems of Brazil and Mexico are arranged? What are the power relationships between the Congress and the president in each case? Does federalism function as outlined in the constitutions of Mexico and Brazil?

These and related issues are especially important in Mexico and Brazil. The size and economic potential of these nations are so immense that their fate cannot help but influence future developments throughout Latin America. Brazil and Mexico are the largest Portuguese- and Spanish-speaking countries in the world, respectively. Nearly 165 million people live in Brazil, while the population of Mexico tops 100 million. Together, their 265 million form almost 65 percent of the population of Latin America.[6] The actions of the governments of these two nations thus have a direct impact on nearly two-thirds of the population of this hemisphere south of U.S. borders. Further, their economies rank eighth (Brazil) and thirteenth (Mexico) in size in the world.[7] To foreign policy makers and to the leaders of banks and other transnational corporations in the United States, what happens in Mexico and Brazil can have major repercussions for U.S. political and economic interests in the hemisphere, as financial crises in Mexico in 1995 and in Brazil in 1998 proved.

MEXICO

Population (1999, estimates): 100.3 million
Area: 761,602 square miles
(roughly the size of Texas, California,
New Mexico, Arizona, and Nevada combined)

For students of comparative politics, Mexico has proven to be an endlessly fascinating but difficult-to-describe country. On the one hand, in a continent beset by political crises and upheavals, twentieth-century Mexico has demonstrated remarkable political stability. The constitution promulgated at the end of the Mexican revolution has been in place since 1917, amended but not changed in its fundamentals. The PRI, whose leaders sat in the president's chair for over seventy years since the party was founded in 1929, was the longest-ruling party in the world until Vicente Fox took over on December 1, 2000. Mexicans elect a new president every six years; none has refused to hand over power to his successor. Moreover, the PRI oversaw seventy years of economic development—not without setbacks, of course—but the Mexico entering the twenty-first century is profoundly different from the nation that came out of the revolution around 1920. It is now predominantly urban, not rural; it has industrialized; most of its people can read and write; and modern health facilities, sanitation, communications systems, and electricity are available almost every-

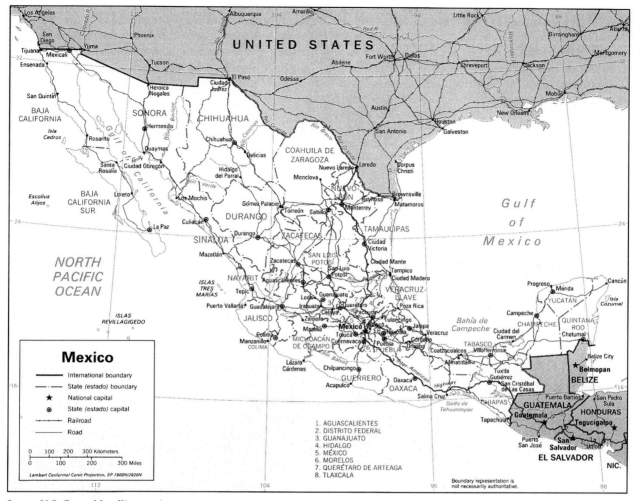

Source: U.S. Central Intelligence Agency

where in Mexico today. In many ways, Mexican politics since the revolution can be considered a success story in the turbulent twentieth century.

On the other hand, for thirty years or more, analysts of Mexican politics have said that Mexico is in crisis. The end of Mexican stability seems always just around the corner. The same party has ruled for seventy years, making it seem as though no real alternative existed (or was allowed to exist). Formally democratic institutions hid an authoritarian political regime, but only to those who did not look closely. The PRI's challengers only recently defeated the ruling party in the electoral arena, leading many opponents of the regime to

consider guerrilla insurrection or other unorthodox challenges to its supremacy. Economic modernization has failed to reach many of Mexico's millions of poor peasants and urban dwellers because of severely inequitable distributions of income and wealth. Apparently often at the edge of breaking into the First World, Mexico's great economic promise repeatedly goes unfulfilled.

The Setting

Mexico's 100 million people occupy a country that is about a quarter the size of the forty-eight contiguous states of the United States, meaning that the population density is nearly twice that of the U.S.[8] Mexico's vastness makes for considerable regional diversity, from the deserts of the north to the semi-tropical regions of the south. The greatest concentration of Mexicans lives in the center of the country. Mexico City is one of the world's largest cities, with over 16 million inhabitants. Its growth has been phenomenal: in 1950, Mexico City had fewer than 4 million people.[9] Also in the central region are the states of Puebla, Guanajuato, and Jalisco, and with them several large cities, including Puebla, León, and Guadalajara. While the center of the nation has experienced rapid urbanization, the cities have grown even faster in the north, where the industrial center of Monterrey has been joined by Ciudad Juárez, Tijuana, and other border cities.

With such rapid urbanization has come a wholesale uprooting of much of Mexico's population. The cities have grown because many citizens living in the countryside have seen no prospect for employment and prosperity in their families' villages. As they have moved to the cities, neighborhoods have mushroomed in rings around the old central cities, posing enormous challenges to city planners and to those local politicians and administrators charged with providing services and amenities.

At the same time, nearly 25 million Mexicans still live in rural areas, a number larger than the populations of many Latin American countries.[10] Mexico's south has been slower to urbanize than other parts of the country. For all the challenges facing country people moving to large cities like Mexico City, rural conditions are more rigorous yet: imagine life without running water, sewage systems or even a septic tank, sometimes even electricity. Millions of Mexicans likewise send their children to rudimentary schools and get along without doctors or emergency room personnel who are on call at all hours.

Regionalism   Mexico's regions differ in their economic pursuits, too. The northern states, for example, have concentrations of export-oriented industries, such as the assembly plants that have sprung up in the border cities, industries that have benefited from NAFTA. Central Mexico, especially the greater Mexico City area, is the site of heavy industry—automobiles and steel, among others—and has not prospered so much with hemispheric economic integration. The south remains more agricultural than the rest of the country and has been especially threatened by the prospect of cheap grain imports from the grain belt of the United States.

One other important regional difference is culture. Like the western states of the United States, Mexico's north has been a frontier region since colonization. Northern Mexicans thus share some characteristics Americans associate with their own west, especially an emphasis on rugged individualism. The much greater influence of the United States on northern Mexico has probably reinforced the individualism of northerners. Northerners have often complained about what they have seen as excessive intervention in their affairs by the Mexican state (located in Mexico City), and they have preferred private enterprise to state ownership of industry. Mexico City residents, in contrast, see themselves as urbane and even cosmopolitan and sometimes view the northerners as too rough around the edges—barbarians of the north. They have been much more inclined to support a large state presence in the economy and other aspects of social life, perhaps because so many of them work for the state. In many parts of Mexico's south, indigenous peoples remain concentrated in their traditional villages, practicing communal landholding and rejecting private ownership of the land. In states like Oaxaca, Chiapas, and Guerrero, indigenous groups have sought to retain whatever control of their communities' political arrangements they can, arrangements that are sometimes based on long-standing community traditions.

Associated with these different regional economic and political cultures are perceptions of racial differences. Northerners, for example, are more likely to be Caucasians or of mixed European and indigenous heritage (**mestizos**). Southerners are more likely to be of indigenous heritage or mestizos. A latent racism can often be witnessed in statements by northerners of their perceptions of the other regions of the country. For example, a newly elected governor of the state of Aguascalientes couldn't contain himself after his victory, describing the regional differences this way: "The north works, the center thinks, and the south rests."[11]

It is almost impossible to understate the importance of Mexico's proximity to the United States. The countries share a two-thousand-mile border. The bulk of Mexico's trade is with the United

States—as much as 70 percent annually. Millions of Mexicans have traveled to the United States to work, visit family members, shop, or just vacation. United States cultural influences have become very powerful in Mexico—many Mexicans look to the United States for their popular culture and for cues about their own futures.

Moreover, the border serves as Mexico's social safety valve: when Mexicans can't find satisfactory employment in their country, they often go to the United States, legally or illegally. Often Mexicans come to the United States to work several times in their lives; sometimes they come only once to earn money for an important purchase, like a car or improvements to their home; sometimes they come to the United States and don't return. Because everyone involved in the U.S.-Mexican relationship knows about this phenomenon, everyone also worries about the consequences of political instability in Mexico, since that would likely increase the flow of Mexicans northward. The willingness of the United States to support Mexico economically has much to do with American worries that immigration would greatly increase if the U.S. government did not help Mexico out. The Clinton administration orchestrated a $49 billion bailout in collaboration with international financial institutions in 1995. But that economic support usually has a price: the United States has put restrictions on Mexico's economic policy options.

The Evolution of Mexican Politics

Prominent Features of Mexican Politics When students of comparative politics looked at Mexico in the 1970s, they noted that, although Mexicans elected their president, a Congress, state governors, and state assemblies, the political regime had more in common with the military-ruled political systems of South America than it did with the democracies of North America or Europe.[12] As stated in chapter 2, *authoritarianism is the opposite of democracy. Whereas democracy places the people above the government, authoritarianism (or dictatorship) places the governing authorities above the people.* Mexican authoritarianism had several features. Perhaps the easiest feature to notice was *the long rule of the PRI:* until the 1980s, it had lost no significant election since it was founded in 1929. Democracy without alternation in power—or the serious prospect

of it—could hardly be called true democracy, and no opposition party posed any real challenge to the PRI even as late as the 1970s. Some scholars will argue that the PRI itself should be understood not as a ruling party, but as the electoral organ of a ruling elite that has used its control of state institutions to practice authoritarian rule.[13] For our purposes, the lack of alternation in power remains the paramount issue, however we understand the relationship of the PRI and the ruling elite.

Another feature of Mexican politics that everyone recognized was **presidentialism.** Mexican presidents have been in some ways akin to limited-term dictators. During his six years in office, the president dominated Congress, the judiciary, the military, the states and their governors, the party that elected him, and the media that reported his every move. Observers also agreed that the Mexican political system was highly centralized, despite a constitution that was formally federalist. Mexican **centralism** meant that Mexico City dominated the nation and that the federal government dictated to the states in ways that other federalist societies like the United States or Canada would find unacceptable. Another aspect of the central role of the government in Mexican life was the heavy *state intervention in Mexico's market economy.* The Mexican government held many state-owned enterprises and the economy was highly regulated. Associated with the government's close regulation of the economy was its control of the interest groups spawned from that economy, for Mexico was a clear example of **state corporatism.** The labor movement, peasant associations, state employees, small business owners, all were captured in a system of interest representation that channeled their demands through the PRI. (On corporatism, see chapter 11.)

Two other features of Mexican politics also caught the attention of political analysts: *clientelism* and *corruption.* The Mexican political elite has been recruited through a system of patron-client relationships "in which the 'patrons'—persons having higher political status—provide benefits such as protection, support in political struggles with rivals and chances for upward political or economic mobility to their 'clients'—persons with a lower political status."[14] (On patron-client relationships, see chapter 11.) **Clientelism** has extended beyond the political class, however, so that many organizations and individuals have found themselves regularly approaching powerful individuals in politics and government agencies to petition for assistance, usually with the expectation that those being helped by powerful patrons will reciprocate by supporting those politicians as they seek to climb the political ladder.[15] It is not surprising that corruption becomes bound up with clientelism, since the favors asked by clients of patrons often involve gaining access to public resources for those clients' private gain. At the same time, the asymmetrical power relationships fostered by clientelism encourage the powerful to demand a great deal of their clients or would-be clients.

How did Mexico come to exhibit these features of political life? As the next sections explain, each feature has some antecedent in Mexican political history.

Conquest and Colonialism The makings of the modern Mexican nation came together in the **Spanish Conquest,** when Hernán Cortés led his band of 550 Spaniards against the mighty Aztec empire in 1519.[16] One member of the Spanish band was La Malinche, an indigenous woman who served as translator for Cortés. She also bore him a son, a child who symbolically represents the first Mexican, the first mestizo. Further examples of miscegenation (racial interbreeding) between Europeans and indigenous people, mostly between Spanish men and indigenous women, created a nation whose majority is now mestizo. For those who lament the conquest, this miscegenation represents a gigantic violation of the indigenous peoples. Some intellectuals have argued that it produced a tendency to violence in Mexican political culture as well as a national inferiority complex (because Mexico is the product of a vast rape).[17] For other observers with a more optimistic perspective on the conquest, this miscegenation produced a new race in Mexico and Latin America, the "cosmic race," people who have the best qualities of both Europeans and indigenous peoples.[18]

The conquest of the Aztec empire and then of other indigenous peoples—such as the Mayans—was facilitated by a catastrophic decline of the native population that resulted when Old World diseases spread throughout the Americas. During the following three hundred years of colonial rule, Eu-

ropeans and those of European heritage held complete political control, gaining the fruits of the indigenous people's labors in Mexico's mines and on its landed estates, known as *haciendas*. The idea that Indians were meant to work for white people became firmly embedded in the minds of Mexico's elites. At the same time, indigenous communities were allowed to hold their lands communally and to decide how to farm them through community institutions, an arrangement known as the *ejido*.

Independence and the Creation of a Mexican Nation The Spanish royal government may have ruled on behalf of people of European descent, but it distrusted whites who were born in the Americas (creoles). The crown appointed only those born in Spain, known as *peninsulares* (referring to the Iberian peninsula, where Spain is located), to its highest-level colonial offices, considering them more loyal. Independence came to Mexico and other Spanish colonies not as a consequence of an uprising of the exploited indigenous peoples and mestizos, but rather because of a conflict between creoles and *peninsulares*. However, in the course of Mexico's struggle for independence, the poor and non-white became mobilized in a rebellion against the Spanish, a rebellion that began in 1810 but was subsequently put down by troops loyal to the crown. The rebellion created great fear among the country's rich and powerful whites.

Political instability characterized the first half-century after Mexico became independent in 1822. Conservatives and Liberals struggled over the definition of the new nation and its political institutions. Conservatives favored a restoration of some form of monarchy, centralized power, and a privileged political position for the Catholic church. Liberals, in contrast, sought a federal republic without an established church, much along the model earlier created in the United States. Battles between Liberals and Conservatives contributed to much political instability, with coups d'état and civil wars leading to very short terms of office for Mexico's presidents. In the thirty-two years from 1823 until 1855, twenty-four men served as president of Mexico, some of them multiple times. General Antonio López de Santa Anna, whom Americans know best as the Mexican commander at the Alamo, was president no fewer than eleven times.

Meanwhile, Mexico's restive neighbor to the north had outlined the doctrine of *manifest destiny*, the notion that the United States should stretch from the Atlantic to the Pacific. Mexico's weakness—a product of its domestic political turbulence—contributed in no small part to the success of the Texas independence movement (Remember the Alamo!) and to Mexico's defeat in the Mexican-American War, known in Mexico as the War of North American Aggression. In addition, Mexico was invaded by French forces in 1861 while the United States was preoccupied with its own Civil War. Conservatives abetted the French invasion and were rewarded with their long-sought-after monarch, an Austrian archduke named Maximilian who became emperor and, ironically enough, an advocate of liberal policies. After a six-year struggle for independence, liberal forces led by Benito Juárez defeated the French and executed the hapless Maximilian in 1867.

Mexico's unfortunate history of foreign invasion during the nineteenth century played an important role in the formation of Mexican *national identity*. Mexico's colonial heritage had provided little to unite its people: indeed, colonial institutions and practices tended to divide Mexicans into rather rigid social categories based on race. But the struggle against foreign intervention could unite Mexicans of all classes by casting them as victims of foreign aggression. And while Mexico's experiences with the United States reinforced Mexican perceptions of weakness, its successful ouster of the French produced a great national hero—Juárez, who was a Zapotec Indian from Oaxaca—and solidified the conception of Mexico as a republic.

Mexican nationalism became further defined by the nation's experiences in the remainder of the nineteenth and the first decade of the twentieth centuries. After Juárez and his successor, Sebastian Lerdo, each served one term as liberal presidents, Lerdo stood for a second term in 1876. Another hero of the war against the French, General **Porfirio Díaz,** led a successful military rebellion against Lerdo under the slogan "Effective Suffrage and No Reelection." After ousting Lerdo, Díaz was duly elected by Mexico's very restricted electorate. He served one term, then stood aside so that one of his political allies could be elected in 1880. But he returned to the presidency in 1884, not to step down until the revolution of 1910. During his long rule, he

Porfirio Díaz

relied on a small coterie of political followers known as *científicos*.[19] Many of them espoused social Darwinism, the notion that only the fittest would survive in social life. In the Mexican context, social Darwinists suggested that Europeans or their descendants would be most likely to survive the social struggle, while the indigenous would not. In their view, it would be better for Mexico if the indigenous population remained marginalized.

During Díaz's thirty-five-year rule, known as the *porfiriato* (after his first name), Mexico experienced unprecedented economic growth, spurred by major investments in mining and in the railroads. These investments came disproportionately from the United States, and they gave Mexicans of all classes a feeling that they were being cheated out of the fruits of the new economic advances. Americans, in contrast, had been favored in order to attract their investment dollars. In addition, many investors from the United States became large landowners in Mexico and United States banks became major lenders to Mexico's economic elites.[20] In reaction, a strong sense of economic nationalism emerged by the turn of the century.

The *porfiriato* led to the beginnings of industrialization and the incorporation of Mexico's commercial agriculture and mining sectors into the world economy, but the poor were further marginalized. In a development parallel to the enclosure movement in England, poor peasants were effectively denied access to their lands. The Liberal Constitution of 1857 had outlawed land ownership by corporate groups. By this provision, the church lost its lands to large landholders, mostly to people associated with the Liberals. But this provision also barred communal property holding in *ejidos,* so individual families in rural villages were given properties previously owned by the entire village. Many such villagers subsequently lost their lands because of economic failures (caused by poor harvests) or were cheated out of them by rich landowners intent on consolidating large estates that increasingly produced commercial crops for the national and international markets. Thus, Mexico's peasantry became more and more proletarianized, forced to become wage laborers on land they formerly owned or to seek employment on the railroads or in the new factories, where wages were low because so many people sought work.

The Revolution   Mexico's 1910 revolution brought together several different social groups who found themselves dissatisfied by Díaz's regime. The man who initiated the revolution, Francisco Madero, came from a wealthy landowning family in the north. Madero and many like him were angry that Díaz had excluded them from political power and they were frustrated because U.S. investors seemed to get most of the best investment opportunities. Madero remembered Díaz's slogan, "Effective Suffrage and No Reelection," and raised it as his own revolutionary battle cry. Madero's followers were political liberals and economic nationalists, but were not very interested in serious social reforms.[21]

Other Mexicans sought more revolutionary changes. Among them was **<u>Emiliano Zapata,</u>** a villager from Morelos who led an army of peasants demanding land reform. They wanted to reclaim the land they had lost to investors in sugar plantations and they sought a return of the *ejido,* the system of communal land ownership. **Pancho Villa,** once a bandit in the northern state of Chihuahua, led an army of cowboys, miners, and railroad workers in a rather unfocused struggle for power.

Díaz abdicated the presidency in 1911 and Madero became president later that year. But he was overthrown and assassinated by a counterrevolutionary coup d'état in 1913 that had been orchestrated by the U.S. ambassador, Henry Lane

Emiliano Zapata

Wilson, who thought Madero was incapable of securing foreign investors' interests. After Madero's assassination, chaos reigned as revolutionaries of all stripes united to defeat the counterrevolutionary leader, General Victoriano Huerta. After ousting Huerta in 1914, however, the revolutionaries fell to fighting among themselves for direction of the new regime.

The revolution became a conflagration, and as many as a million Mexicans lost their lives and much property was destroyed. Millions more were mobilized into revolutionary armies that marched or rode (on horses and the railroads) the length and breadth of Mexico, learning thereby what the rest of their country and their countrymen looked like. Although Mexicans were divided during their revolution, a sense of *national identity* and unity emerged from the struggle, breaking down some of the provincialism that had to that point characterized Mexican society. Those revolutionary soldiers, the majority of them peasants and workers, were now mobilized by their involvement in the revolution and became experienced in using violence against their adversaries. They would not be easily demobilized and excluded from having a political voice after the revolution.

In the end, the revolutionary faction that most closely followed Madero's political philosophy, the Constitutionalists (led by Venustiano Carranza, also a large landowner from the north), emerged as the dominant force. The Constitutionalists defeated the armies of Zapata and Villa and wrote a new constitution at a constitutional assembly in Querétaro in 1917. Although the Constitutionalists did not favor changes as radical as those proposed by the forces of Zapata and Villa at an earlier convention in Aguascalientes in 1914, they did include clauses that reserved subsoil rights to the nation, facilitated agrarian reform, permitted labor to organize and to strike, and placed heavy restrictions on the activities of the Catholic church. However, few of these progressive clauses could be implemented immediately because Mexico had to rebuild after the destruction of the revolution and to reestablish political stability, a task that took up the entire decade of the 1920s.

Mexico Under the PRI

In 1928, former president Alvaro Obregón (1920–24) had the 1917 constitution amended so that he could run for another presidential term.[22] Shortly after winning the presidential race, Obregón was assassinated. A political crisis immediately ensued because Mexico has no vice presidency. With Obregón now dead, the most powerful politician in Mexico was the sitting president, Plutarco Elias Calles (1924–28). But Calles could hardly run for reelection, especially given that a reelected president had just been killed. To resolve the crisis and to confront the problem of political instability that had plagued Mexico in the 1920s, Calles proposed the creation of a national political party that would unite all "revolutionaries" in one

TABLE 23.2

Mexican Postrevolutionary Presidential Administrations

President	Years	Vote(%)
Venustiano Carranza	1917–20	98.1
Alvaro Obregón	1920–24	95.8
Plutarco Elías Calles	1924–28	84.1
Emilio Portes Gil	1928–29	appointed
Pascual Ortiz Rubio	1929–32	93.6
Abelardo Rodríguez	1932–34	appointed
Lázaro Cárdenas	1934–40	98.2
Manuel Avila Camacho	1940–46	93.9
Miguel Alemán	1946–52	77.9
Adolfo Ruiz Cortines	1952–58	74.3
Adolfo López Mateos	1958–64	90.4
Gustavo Díaz Ordaz	1964–70	88.6
Luis Echeverría	1970–76	85.5
José López Portillo	1976–82	98.7
Miguel de la Madrid	1982–88	74.3
Carlos Salinas de Gortari	1988–94	50.7
Ernesto Zedillo	1994–2000	50.1
Vicente Fox	2000–present	43.4

Source: Mario Ramírez Rancaño, "Estadísticas electorales: presidenciales," *Revista Mexicana de Sociología* 39, no. 1 (1977): 271–99; Instituto Federal Electoral.

political organization that would resolve the problems of political succession within its own organizational structures. Thus was born the National Revolutionary Party (or PNR), the predecessor to today's PRI. With all revolutionaries united in a single party and agreeing to join forces to support its candidates, a PNR nomination became tantamount to an electoral victory. This scheme proved itself when the PNR candidate, an unknown named Pascual Ortiz Rubio, defeated the well-known philosopher and former secretary of education José Vasconcelos by a 1,948,848 to 110,979 margin.[23]

Because Calles stacked the PNR's national executive committee with politicians loyal to him, he was able to continue to control Mexican politics without sitting in the presidential chair, at least until 1935. In 1934, Calles approved the PNR's nomination of General **Lázaro Cárdenas** as the party's presidential candidate. Cárdenas embarked on a program of extensive land reforms, finally fulfilling the revolutionary goals of Zapata and other agrarian leaders. When Calles objected to this and other progressive reforms, Cárdenas used his authority as president to exile the former leader. *Presidentialism*, a pattern of executive dominance in the political system that had been firmly established under Porfirio Díaz and practiced by Obregón and Calles, was thus reestablished in Mexican politics. It has not been superseded since then.

Cárdenas Fulfills Revolutionary Promises   Cárdenas (1934–40) did more than any other man to build the political regime we have come to describe as uniquely Mexican. In policy terms, Cárdenas engaged in an energetic program of land reform, redistributing more land to Mexican peasants than any other president before or since his term. Unlike Obregón and Calles, Cárdenas had not been born in the north and thus he did not share the northerners' barely veiled scorn for the indigenous peasants felt by his predecessors. He had governed the southern state of Michoacán and understood the desire of indigenous communities

Gen. Lázaro Cárdenas

to have their land returned to them and to be able to return to a communal ownership of that land. As Cárdenas undertook land reform, he thus preferred to distribute land not to individuals, but to villages set up as *ejidos.* To represent the new beneficiaries of land reform, Cárdenas created the **National Peasant Confederation (CNC),** a peak association of peasant groups.

He also promoted labor organization and militance. During his presidency, the **Mexican Workers' Federation (CTM),** a peak association of labor unions, was formed and won substantial wage increases for industrial workers. Here Cárdenas was not necessarily creating labor militance where it did not exist; rather, he sympathized with worker demands for shorter workdays and better wages. In 1938, taking advantage of a labor confrontation between petroleum workers and U.S.- and British-owned oil companies, Cárdenas nationalized the oil industry, thereby creating the giant state-owned enterprise Petroleos Mexicanos (PEMEX). The oil expropriation was the defining moment of Mexican economic nationalism, the ultimate example of Mexico standing up against powerful foreign firms and the nations from which they came, especially the United States. The United States, sensing the coming war in Europe, chose not to get into a confrontation with Mexico about the expropriations. Under Cárdenas, then, the PRI became known as the party that struggled for justice for workers and peasants and that protected the national interest by building state-owned enterprises in crucial economic sectors.

Political Institutions   In political terms, Cárdenas's legacy has had a lasting impact. In 1938, the PNR became the Party of the Mexican Revolution (PRM). More important than the name change, however, was an organizational innovation. Cárdenas organized the PRM into four sectors, one for peasants (organized into the CNC), another for the workers (represented by the CTM), a third for state bureaucrats (organized into the **Federation of Unions of Workers in Service to the State, or FSTSE**), and a fourth for the military. This organizational structure made the PRM a *corporatist* institution. By incorporating these organizations of peasants, workers, bureaucrats, and the military into the PRM, Cárdenas gave them privileged access to decision makers. At the same time, however, the incorporation of these groups within the party, and especially of their leaders within the PRM hierarchy, made them vulnerable to co-optation and control. In particular, labor and peasant leaders were co-opted (incorporated or taken over) by the PRM's national leadership (and later by the PRI). They were offered personal political opportunities in return for exercising restraint in their demands on behalf of their constituents.

The PRM's corporatist organization also had the advantage of providing the party with an unparalleled capacity to turn out voters on election day. Local representatives of the CNC served as political bosses in their villages and municipalities, providing the party with unusual abilities to get rural voters to the polls and to ensure that they would vote for the ruling party. Labor union leaders were similarly able to convince their membership to vote for the PRM. With so much of Mexico still rural in the 1930s and 1940s (65 percent of the labor force was involved in agriculture in 1940)[24] and with a considerable number of additional Mexicans incorporated into the official labor movement, the PRM (and then the PRI) could easily overcome any challengers. It demonstrated this capacity in the elections of 1940, 1946, and 1952, when mavericks within the party did not accept the presidential nominations put forward by the sitting presidents. Those mavericks ran for president at the head of hastily arranged parties. Although the 1940 and 1952 challengers put up strong challenges to the ruling party, official electoral statistics reported that they lost by considerable margins.

Under Cárdenas, the powerful position of the presidency within the political regime became cemented too. At times in the 1920s and early 1930s, presidents faced hostile Congresses. President Ortiz Rubio resigned in 1932 in part because of inability to work with the Congress.[25] However, Cárdenas built a presidency that could dominate Congress effectively.

The Mexican presidency has held a formidable set of powers, which the Mexican scholar Luis Javier Garrido has characterized as constitutional, metaconstitutional, and anticonstitutional.[26] Garrido argues that the Mexican presidency was granted greater powers by the 1917 constitution than those that had existed under the earlier 1857 constitution. However, these constitutional powers were not more extensive than those held by most presidents in other Latin American political systems.[27] Beyond the constitutionally designated powers, Mexican presidents have enjoyed "metaconstitutional powers," a "series of prerogatives [that] corresponds to the 'unwritten norms' of the Mexican system. They allow the president to centralize his power progressively through a distortion of constitutional mechanisms."[28] Garrido identifies ten such metaconstitutional powers, the most important of them being the effective capacity to amend the constitution, the role of "chief legislator," the capacity to designate one's successor to the presidency, and the domination of lower levels of government in the Mexican federal system. The president's anticonstitutional powers, in Garrido's view, are a capacity to violate the legal code and the right to immunity from prosecution.

Such powers set up a characteristic of Mexican politics that scholars have labeled *presidencialismo*, or presidentialism. *Presidencialismo*, as defined by Roderic Ai Camp, is "the concept that most political power lies in the hands of the president and all that is good or bad in government policy stems personally from the president."[29] The president of the United States, of course, has also had great political power, especially since the time of Franklin Delano Roosevelt, and Americans mark political time by presidential administrations in much the same way as Mexicans do. But in the United States, presidents often find themselves unable to be the "chief legislators" because Congress often refuses to pass the bills sent to it by the White House. U.S. congressional committees often write their own legislation without presidential prompting, sometimes openly defying presidential wishes on important policy issues.

The Mexican Congress is charged with the responsibilities of auditing the public accounts of the previous year, approving the budget of the coming fiscal year, and voting on all bills introduced to it by the president or by members of the **Chamber of Deputies** or the **Senate,** the two houses of the bicameral legislature. In the formal rules about making laws established in the Mexican constitution, a bill becomes a law in ways that are similar to the process in the United States. Bills must pass both houses of the Congress; they can be approved or vetoed by the president; and if they are vetoed, the veto can be overridden by a two-thirds vote of both houses. However, until the 1990s, the Mexican Congress had not rejected a presidential bill since the 1930s. U.S. presidents must envy their Mexican colleagues.

How can we explain *presidencialismo*, this seemly unprecedented domination of the legislature and other national institutions by the president? When we take into account the incredible advantages accruing to the PRI because of its having been the incumbent party between 1929 and 2000 (it could take credit for all the benefits of economic development that came to Mexico in those years) and the mobilizational capacity it enjoyed because of its corporatist incorporation of peasants, workers, and urban popular groups, we should not be surprised that a PRI nomination was equivalent to an appointment to that "elected" position. This quasi-automatic election ensured by the PRI's endorsement applied not just to presidential candidates but also to candidates for Congress, governor, state assembly, mayor, or membership on municipal councils. If we then remember that postrevolutionary Mexico has forbidden reelection to the many positions just mentioned, it becomes easier for us to understand why the president has been so powerful.[30]

Politicians cannot develop support bases in constituencies that will return them to office in the way that U.S. politicians can. Each "elected" PRI politician had to thus expect to be looking for a new position, either elected or appointed, within three years (for municipal officers, state assembly members, or federal deputies) or six years (for governors or federal senators). Likewise, because each new president brought a new administration, those appointed to political positions in the bureaucracy knew that they had to plan to be appointed to some new position—probably in another area of the bureaucracy—or nominated for an elected post within six years. Who controlled these appointments and nominations? Ultimately, the president. However, for younger politicians to gain presidential approval, patrons in their *camarrillas*, or political groups, could provide essential support to indicate that an aspiring politician was worthy of appointment to a lesser elected or ap-

pointed position. Hence, clientelism became an essential means of ascent in a system in which political recruitment was dominated at the top by the president.

In this situation, the reasons for congressional subordination to the president become clear. Even though the PRI typically had ample majorities in the Congress, which PRI deputy or senator would want to demonstrate opposition to a presidentially initiated bill? What would a vote against a bill proposed by the president accomplish? Since a member of the Congress could not be reelected, why would he care about his constituents' reactions to a bill that might not be favorable to their district? Since his career required getting another position within three or six years, why would he risk antagonizing the president by voting against a presidential initiative?

This logic produced an incredible record of legislative accomplishment for Mexican presidents. As mentioned earlier, between the 1930s and the late 1990s, no presidential bill was turned down by the Mexican Congress. This is not to say that the Congress did not occasionally amend legislation sent to it by the office of the president, but usually these amendments were intended to fix sloppy language that the president's office had not written carefully. Opposition members of the Congress usually spoke against bills emanating from the presidency, but to little practical effect, especially if the national media paid little attention to their speeches, which was generally true before the 1970s.

Mexico's 1917 constitution also enshrined the concept of the "free municipality": in principle, local governments have the autonomy to make local laws and policies. But in actual practice, municipalities (equivalent to U.S. counties, the lowest level of government in Mexico) have been subordinate to the federal government in the same way that the Congress has been dominated by the president. This local political subordination to the center developed despite the strong regionalism we described at the outset of this chapter.

Central government domination of the states can be attributed to three factors. First, the federal government raises by far the greatest proportion of tax revenues which it then "shares" with states and localities. State and local governments thus have had to be careful about their relationship with the federal government, especially with the all-powerful executive, for fear of getting relatively small shares of federal revenues.[31] Second, once the PRI was formed and came to control political recruitment throughout the nation, further political advances for state governors and other aspiring politicians in a state depended on staying in the good political graces of the president. Third, like other elected officials in Mexico, governors cannot be reelected; thus they have been constrained in the degree to which they could build local political machines that would be support bases for resisting central government demands. In effect, because most or all state governors have had further political ambitions in the PRI, the president has had the *de facto* power to appoint and remove them. Thus the power of the Mexican presidency has extended beyond the federal government to the states and the municipalities.

HYPOTHESIS-TESTING EXERCISE: Explaining Mexican Authoritarianism

HYPOTHESES, VARIABLES, EXPECTATIONS, AND EVIDENCE

Until the 1990s, Mexicans were governed by an authoritarian regime, despite living with a constitution that provided for democratic institutions. Let us briefly review some of the factors discussed in chapter 10 that can best explain Mexican authoritarianism. What follows is a hypothesis-testing exercise in which our **dependent variable** is *authoritarianism in Mexico* (i.e., the absence of democracy) and our **independent variables** are the *ten conditions*. In each case, our **expectation** is that Mexico's failure to meet each condition enhances the likelihood of authoritarianism. Our **evidence** is presented in the following sections.

State Institutions

Although Mexico's constitution prescribes a set of democratic institutions that would ensure popular sovereignty, the no reelection clause has effectively removed the capacity of the electorate to hold elected officials accountable for their actions. Because the PRI has so monopolized the electoral process until 2000 and the president has so dominated the PRI, Mexico would be better described as having had *presidential sovereignty* instead of popular sovereignty. *Presidencialismo*, which has been encouraged by the no reelection principle and by the

PRI's control of the electoral process, explains the absence of democracy in Mexico for most of the past century better than any other factor.

Elites Committed to Democracy

When Mexico was debating an electoral reform initiative in 1977, the PRI representative to the Federal Electoral Commission, in an indiscreet statement that cost him his position, said that he and his party could not support a reform that undermined the two central institutions of postrevolutionary Mexico: the presidency and the "party of the majority," meaning the PRI.[32] This assertion captured the view that was held by most of the political elites during the long rule of the PRI: the continued rule of their party was more important than democracy. The willingness of PRI militants and PRI party leaders to engage in electoral fraud to ensure their party's victories provided further testament to their lack of commitment to democracy.

It is interesting that the electoral reform bill about which the PRI representative spoke in 1977 had been initiated by the secretary of government (or interior), Jesús Reyes Heroles, himself a former party president of the PRI. Reyes Heroles said that his fear was that his country would become a *"México bronco,"* a rough or rude society, if electoral rules were not adhered to more closely and if Mexico's own political elites ceased to respect the rule of law. So, within the PRI political elite there have been proponents of democratizing reforms and rule of law, often motivated by a sense that the PRI's long-term rule would be threatened if the Mexican people came to believe that the PRI governed solely for its own interests, and especially for the interests of its party leaders and higher government officials. In short, many PRI members and leaders have wanted to ensure that the party continued to win and thereby to rule Mexico, but they believed it essential that the party win fair and square for its continued rule to be legitimate. The relative moderation of Mexican authoritarianism owed much to this commitment on the part of liberals within the PRI elite.

National Wealth

In Mexico as in other Latin American countries, the growth of national wealth has not brought democracy in the sure and direct way that many political scientists predicted that it would in the 1950s and 1960s. Although Latin America as a region and Mexico as a country have been near the top of rankings of developing countries in terms of income per capita and other measures of wealth since the Second World War, that wealth has been inequitably distributed. Some political scientists have argued that the maldistribution of income in Latin America has deterred the easy spread of democracy because rich elites have too much to lose if the poor use democratic institutions to take power and redistribute that wealth. Certainly many of the richest Mexicans have been PRI supporters over the decades and have encouraged the government to control the political activities of the poor.

Private Enterprise

As we noted earlier, Mexico was a market economy throughout the twentieth century, but one in which the state has played a large part, as "banker and entrepreneur of last resort."[33] What this means is that in earlier postrevolutionary decades the Mexican state played a crucial role in promoting the development of Mexican business by providing subsidized loans, building the infrastructure needed by industry, selling critical manufacturing inputs like energy at subsidized prices, offering critical government contracts to preferred businesspeople, and protecting the economy from foreign competition. Important segments of Mexican private enterprise became highly dependent for their business success on good relationships with government officials and the continued rule of the PRI. Until the mid-1970s, at least, the business sector did not serve as a counterweight to the authoritarian tendencies of the state. Furthermore, as Mexican development proceeded through the postwar decades, the Mexican state came to directly control larger and larger portions of Mexican enterprise. By the 1970s, the Mexican state owned 42 percent of the assets of the fifty largest firms in the country; the fifty largest **parastatal enterprises**—companies that are owned jointly by the state and private interests—contributed about a quarter of the overall production in the Mexican economy.[34] Many Mexicans owed their very livelihood to the PRI-controlled state, not a situation likely to lead them to support opposition to the PRI.

A Middle Class

Given the development of the Mexican economy mentioned in the previous section, the middle class hardly has been a homogeneous class. Because Mexico's population is now 100 million with several large cities, the Mexican middle class has been large enough to have a distinct political impact for many decades. That middle class incorporates people from many different occupations, however: people from the liberal professions (doctors and lawyers), intellectuals, the white-collar salaried employees of large firms and the state, teachers, and small business owners, among others. For some members of the middle class, advancement has depended upon the success of the PRI-controlled system, especially those employed by the state. Teachers, for instance, have been one of the bulwarks of the PRI's efforts to get out the vote. Others have been more critical

of the PRI's domination of Mexican politics and, most important, more able to criticize the existing political arrangements because of their independence from the state. The middle class has been the support base of the longest-lived of the opposition parties, the National Action Party (PAN), the party of Vicente Fox. Thus, in Mexico, the standard hypothesis that the middle class has been in favor of democracy is supported.

Support of the Disadvantaged for Democracy

Whether the members of the Mexican working class or peasantry have been in favor of democracy or not for most of the postwar years matters less than whether they have been *able* to support democracy. There exists strong evidence that at times large sectors of the working class have sought to break free of the official labor movement. A railroad workers strike in 1958–59 and the growth of an independent union movement in the early 1970s are examples. At other times there have been many efforts to create peasant associations independent of the official peasant sector of the PRI. However, the PRI's corporatist organizations for peasants and workers proved very durable. The party was able to co-opt (buy off) the leaders of independent worker and peasant associations, and the government demonstrated a willingness to repress those insurgencies within unions or peasant associations that threatened union leaders who had cozy relationships with the state.[35]

An Active Civil Society and a Democratic Political Culture

Studies of Mexican political attitudes during the years of the PRI's unquestioned hegemony tended to argue that Mexico had an authoritarian political culture. Early psychoanalytically oriented studies by Mexican intellectuals Samuel Ramos and Octavio Paz (who was later awarded the Nobel Prize for literature) tended to emphasize the *machismo* of Mexican men and to see a collective sense of national inferiority as a national characteristic. These traits, Ramos and Paz argued, promoted political violence and a desire to dominate others, both inhibiting democratic practice.

In the late 1950s, Mexico became a case study in Gabriel Almond's and Sidney Verba's famous *Civic Culture* study (see chapter 12). Among other dimensions of their analysis, Almond and Verba categorized the respondents to their surveys into holders of differing types of political attitudes, including "parochials," those who expect nothing from the political system; "subjects," those who look to government for the outputs they can get from it; and "participants," those more inclined to be actively involved on the input side of government.[36] "Participants" would be expected to form the basis of an active civil society and hence to lay the foundations of democracy. However, few participants could be found in Mexico, where about one-quarter of respondents were "parochials" and two-thirds were "subjects." Without citizens with democratic attitudes who really embraced citizen roles, authoritarian practices naturally would be easily implemented by the ruling party. Since few independent organizations could be found in Mexican civil society, one might chalk up that absence to the lack of participant citizens to lead and to join them.

However, the situation may have been more complex than these early studies suggested. For example, observers frequently cited the tendency to petition government officials for favors as a manifestation of Mexicans' "subject" political culture. So long as people saw the government as a dispenser of individualized benefits via the clientelist networks promoted by the PRI and government agencies, they would not likely organize viable civic organizations or opposition parties to oppose the PRI and the captive organizations it had created (like the official labor and peasant movements). However, perhaps a more fruitful way of explaining Mexicans' "subject" political attitudes is to argue that the structures of government and the official party had been created precisely to encourage individuals to contact elected officials and bureaucratic agencies. The PRI understood that it was cheaper and less politically threatening to provide benefits to individuals (such as the extension of a water line to a petitioner's house or help in obtaining a government job) than to favor large groups of mobilized people who might challenge the PRI's rule. Mexicans who tended to see themselves as "subjects" instead of "participants" were simply reacting rationally to the clientelist institutions that had been created in the 1930s and 1940s. Indeed, other studies conducted in the 1970s concluded that Mexicans held democratic attitudes; if Mexico remained authoritarian, that authoritarianism had to be attributed to factors other than the political culture, such as institutions like the PRI and the presidency.[37]

Education and Freedom of Information

Studies of Mexican voting behavior have consistently reported a close correlation between education levels and voting for the PRI.[38] In parts of the country where illiteracy is high, the PRI does much better than in areas populated by more educated people. Why? The simple answer is that less educated people can be persuaded or coerced to vote *against* their interests more easily than is true of more educated people. Less educated people tend to have more tenuous job situations, they are more often financially dependent on powerful individuals in their localities, and of course, they follow politics less closely in the media. Perhaps more important, they have been less able to read between the lines for the truth in the esoteric prose that has characterized political reporting in the Mexican press. Thus, they can be strongly urged—or coerced—to vote for PRI candidates by local power holders. Illiterates (who made up 38 percent of the population as late as 1960, and over half the rural population then)[39] have received another voting cue: ballots have included both the name of the candidates' party and the parties' symbols in full color. The PRI's symbol—despite a legal restriction against it—has the same colors as the Mexican flag. So when voting, illiterates have been reminded to do their "patriotic" duty by putting their X over the colors of the flag.

Even the well educated have had to struggle to obtain independent political information and analyses, however, because until the 1970s, the Mexican press censored itself. Until the mid-1990s, television and radio were strongly in the PRI's camp. For years, many articles in newspapers were simply government-written stories placed in the papers in the guise of independent reports. Newspaper reporters often took payoffs from government agencies to place these reports or to write their own favorable articles about those agencies. Newspapers depended on government-placed advertisements to meet their costs and thus they declined to threaten those advertising revenues by writing critically about the government. For many years, newsprint was controlled by a government agency, and thus the government could punish a critical newspaper by delaying its newsprint deliveries or cutting its allocation of newsprint.

Broadcast media have been even less critical of the government than the print media has. Like the U.S. government, the Mexican government controls broadcast licenses. This situation alone can explain why Mexican television and radio were very favorable to the PRI in its reporting and unwilling to grant much paid advertising time to the opposition parties. On top of that, Mexican television is dominated by Televisa, a broadcast conglomerate that accounts for as much as 85 percent of the Mexican viewing audience. Over the years Televisa, in essence, exchanged a strongly pro-PRI, pro-government television news orientation for access to new broadcast licenses in Mexico's growing media market. In short, even in the absence of formal censorship, with a comparatively undereducated population and government-manipulated press and mass media, we should not be surprised that competitive democracy has been hindered in its development in Mexico.

A Homogeneous Society

Far from being homogeneous, Mexico remains a heterogeneous society even five centuries after the conquest. Indeed, one key element of the official postrevolutionary national identity celebrates the heterogeneity of Mexican society: a trip to the Museum of Anthropology in Mexico City (the largest in the world), where each surviving indigenous group has its own celebratory exhibit and where the heritage of pre-Hispanic civilizations receives unparalleled attention, will reinforce the view that Mexico is a multicultural society and that multiculturalism is good for the nation. However, closer analysis reveals a bitter truth: Mexico's indigenous communities have been marginalized by the dominant mestizo culture and exploited both politically and economically. The areas of the country with high densities of people who speak indigenous languages have tended to produce the highest rates of voting for the PRI, at least until recently. Indigenous peoples, who have been poorer and less educated than other Mexicans, have been prime candidates for the kind of coercion that we have just described as being used against illiterates and other less educated people. Although the Mexican state under the PRI voiced a respect for the nation's multicultural heritage, its policies have encouraged the assimilation of Indians into mainstream mestizo culture. Those who have chosen not to be assimilated have been left to the poverty and violence of rural life.

A Favorable International Environment

Porfirio Díaz reputedly said of Mexico's international situation, "Poor Mexico! So far from God and so close to the United States!" For much of Mexico's postrevolutionary era the Mexican government has sought to keep the United States at arm's length, but the overpowering influence of the United States has proven impossible to avoid. While the United States government has often made the promotion of democracy a key plank in its foreign policy platforms, that commitment to democracy has often been left aside when other national interests come under consideration. Particularly in view of the already large flows of migration back and forth across the two-thousand-mile U.S.-Mexican border, U.S. foreign policy makers have tended to define the chief U.S. national interest in terms of promoting political stability in Mexico rather than democracy, because instability—which could very well result from a democratic revolution—would surely lead to massive refugee flows into the United States. The United States has also benefited from the business opportunities created by a succession of Mexican presidents. In short, official United States foreign policy did not emphasize promoting democracy in Mexico until quite recently.

At the same time, the huge volume of immigration between the two neighbors, most of which is temporary in nature, has meant that millions of Mexicans have been exposed directly to United States culture and the United States political system. Other United States cultural impacts include Hollywood movies, television, and popular music, among other things. Many members of the Mexican political and economic elite have been educated in United States universities. In this interchange, the example of the world's oldest democracy has been conveyed to Mexicans of all social classes. Of course that message has not always been uniformly positive. Many Mexicans who come to the United States as undocumented workers learn about racial discrimination and the circumvention of the law rather than about equality before the law. Yet, on balance, the impact of social interactions between the two nations has promoted democracy in Mexico.

Conclusions

While there is *mixed* evidence that both supports and undermines the prospects for democracy in Mexico, the country's failure to meet many of the main conditions for democracy is consistent with the notion that, under these circumstances, democracy was not likely to succeed (or come about in the first place), and that some form of authoritarianism was likely to prevail. At the same time, several factors (such as the middle class) hold out the possibility that democracy may take hold in the aftermath of the 2000 elections. We'll take another look at these ten conditions later in this chapter and see what they tell us about the prospects for democracy in contemporary Mexico.

Economic Development

The political system that Lázaro Cárdenas built survived long after the policy direction he represented no longer held sway. Presidents coming to power after 1940 were much friendlier to business interests than Cárdenas was. During the Second World War, Mexico was not able to import manufactured goods from abroad to the same degree as before. Consequently, after the war Mexico began to implement an economic development strategy centered on **import-substituting industrialization (ISI).** The country's relatively large and growing population permitted Mexican manufacturers of formerly imported products to have privileged access to a large market of consumers, especially among the middle and working classes of the rapidly growing cities, as long as foreign suppliers were prohibited from selling their goods to Mexico. High tariffs on imported finished goods as well as import licensing and nontariff barriers to trade effectively promoted Mexico's "infant industries" in the postwar decades, and the economy and industrial employment took off. A class of Mexican industrialists who had close links to the political elite grew out of the ISI policy. To promote industrial development, the state made large investments in infrastructure, especially around Mexico City, where ISI-oriented industries tended to locate. In addition, the official labor movement, which was tightly associated with the PRI, practiced wage restraint. It advocated a philosophy of economic nationalism, promoting the national interest of industrialization in lieu of Marxist-style class conflict.

The result came to be known as the "Mexican miracle." From the mid-1950s until the mid-1970s, Mexico's economy grew at rates of 6 to 7 percent per year, while inflation remained below 5 percent. Once a largely rural, agricultural nation, Mexico urbanized extremely rapidly in the fifty years between 1940 and 1990. Whereas the country was 22 percent urban in 1940, 72 percent of the population lived in cities by 1990. Government investments modernized the nation's transportation system. Illiteracy, once characteristic of half the population, was nearly eliminated.

Yet the Mexican miracle did not spread its benefits equitably across the population. Because of the emphasis on ISI and the growing urban population, Mexican governments after Cárdenas tended to grant government credit to larger, commercial farmers at the expense of the *ejidatorios* who had been granted land for the community in the agrarian reforms of the 1930s. Continuing poverty among rural villagers co-existed with the income gains of industrialists, the middle classes, and to a lesser extent, organized labor. Meanwhile, new generations of villagers fled their poverty, moving to the cities where they lived in the impoverished neighborhoods that mushroomed around Mexico City, Monterrey, Puebla, and other cities.[40] Few of these new urban poor have been able to land the jobs protected by the labor movement, so their wages have remained low. Many others have been unable to land wage-paying jobs at all, becoming itinerant salespeople or domestic workers. Mexico's distribution of income has been among the most inequitable in the world, rivaling that of Brazil, with the richest 20 percent of the population sharing at least 55 percent of the income, while the poorest half of the society has had to make do with 15 percent to 20 percent of the nation's income (see table 2.2 on page 37). For the poorer half of Mexican society, the years since 1940 have hardly been miraculous.

Another outlet for the rural poor has been emigration to the United States. Emigration has often been called Mexico's "safety valve," a means for venting the pressures associated with a rate of population growth that has outpaced the growth of jobs. Millions of Mexicans have made the trek to the north over the past half century. Most go with the intention of staying only temporarily, just long enough to earn sufficient money to support a growing family, generate the capital to improve the family's housing back home, or invest in a small business or truck or taxi. Most who work temporarily in agriculture, construction, or (increasingly) manufacturing jobs in the United States return home. For some the trip north becomes regularized: they go annually, or at least more than once during their working lives. Because of its largely temporary nature, Mexican emigration hardly threatens to change the ethnic composition of the U.S. population, despite suggestions to the contrary by some American politicians.

For Mexico, the earnings of migrants to the United States have served as an important source of foreign exchange. It is not surprisingly that the Mexican government would therefore prefer to see the border remain relatively open. (After his election in 2000, President-elect Fox proposed completely open U.S.-Mexican borders in the future.) Of course, it prefers not to admit that Mexico needs this safety valve, since to do so would suggest that the Mexican economy cannot create enough jobs for its own people.

The Mexican experience with ISI thus brought mixed results, just as it did for most nations that chose to follow an industrialization strategy largely focused on producing manufactured products for the domestic market. The state, as the "rector" of the economy, promoted industrial development that certainly benefited millions of Mexicans, but there were many unexpected consequences of that industrialization. The cities exploded, the rural poor could not be adequately absorbed into the labor force, income remained maldistributed, and eventually, the state developed a large presence in the economy that threatened the private sector. In the mid-1970s, an activist president, **Luis Echeverría** (1970–76), came into conflict with the business community over his attempts to reinvigorate the populist policies of Cárdenas, which included new land reforms, greater government spending on social programs, and a larger role for the state in the economy. The standoff between Echeverría and the private sector ended when his term expired in 1976, but not before capital flight—the transfer of large sums of money from Mexico to banks and investment opportunities abroad—weakened the peso's declining value even further, necessitating its devaluation.

Echeverría's successor, his boyhood friend **José López Portillo** (1976–82), mended relations with the business community. In doing so he was much aided by discoveries of large oil reserves off Mexico's Gulf coast. With an oil boom coming, López Portillo thought he would be able to please nearly all constituencies: businesspeople, the poor, oil and construction workers, and the middle class. All these groups could benefit from a state flush with petrodollars. Since the state-owned PEMEX controlled all petroleum production in Mexico, the profits from oil sales would go to the state's coffers, eliminating the need to pay for the López Portillo government's programs with tax increases. To finance petroleum exploration and development, López Portillo's government borrowed from international banks, which were only too happy to be able to lend to a stable government that had oil reserves to offer as collateral. Mexico quickly became indebted to international banks to the sum of over $80 billion.

Had oil prices remained at the high levels of the late 1970s for a few more years, perhaps Mexico's new petroleum-financed development strategy would have succeeded (although the failures of that model in Venezuela would suggest otherwise). But when oil prices fell in 1981, Mexico was faced with a cash flow problem of global proportions. It did not have the hard currency to make payments on loans coming due at U.S. and other banks. A global debt crisis was set off by the threat of a Mexican default of 1982. Capital flight and another devaluation of the peso accompanied the economic crisis of 1982, to which López Portillo responded by nationalizing privately owned banks in Mexico in a last-gasp populist measure to try to rescue his presidency.

Eventually, with the help of the U.S. government, Mexico's foreign debt was restructured.

López Portillo's successors, **Miguel de la Madrid** (1982–88) and **Carlos Salinas** (1988–94), finally abandoned the ISI strategy of development, opting instead for incorporation into the rapidly globalizing world economy and an attempt to position Mexico as an exporter of manufactured goods, especially to the United States. Mexico's decisions to join the General Agreement on Tariffs and Trade (GATT) and to become a part of NAFTA cemented the redirection of the nation's economic strategy. (In 1995 the GATT was succeeded by the World Trade Organization.) That new strategy, called **neoliberalism,** has involved the lowering of the nation's barriers to imports, a reduction in state subsidies for staples like cooking oil and tortillas and in expenditures on social welfare, and the privatization of most of the state-owned enterprises accumulated since the 1930s. Foreign investment in Mexico, once discouraged by laws that limited foreign ownership of enterprises to 49 percent of a company's stocks, has been encouraged to come into the country with fewer encumbrances.

Neoliberalism has led to a dramatic restructuring of Mexican industry. Much new investment has improved the competitiveness of Mexican exporters. Many entrepreneurs have made billions of pesos as new opportunities have come their way, not least by being able to acquire equity stakes (stocks) in newly privatized firms. After nearly a decade of economic depression (and that's not too harsh a label to apply to the 1980s), Mexico's economy began to grow again under Salinas. However, the adjustments associated with the "lost decade" of the 1980s and the economic restructuring of the 1990s have been borne disproportionately by the poor. The end of subsidies for consumer staples hurt the poor much more than it did the middle classes. Bankruptcies by (mostly smaller) firms unable to compete with foreign imports led to layoffs of workers. State employees saw their salary increases lag behind inflation, making their real incomes decline. Overall, real wages may have dropped as much as 41.5 percent between 1983 and 1988.[41] To make up for lost income, families had to send a second or third wage earner out into the work force, or the principal breadwinner had to take on additional income-earning tasks. The size of the "informal sector" of the economy—jobs where income is not reported, such as itinerant sales (street vendors), housekeeping, and repair work—grew in the 1980s. (Of course, the informal economy is, by its nature, nearly impossible to measure.)

The financial crisis at the beginning of **Ernesto Zedillo's** presidency in 1994–95, described in chapter 14, demonstrates that the restructured Mexican economy remains vulnerable to sudden international capital flows associated with the loss of investor confidence, perhaps even more so than in the 1970s and early 1980s. In the year following that downturn, Mexicans suffered yet one more sustained period of unemployment and job changes. The accumulated economic crises of the past quarter century, coming after the apparent successes of the Mexican miracle, have played an enormous role in undermining the legitimacy of the PRI's rule, as we will describe in the next section. For the future, Mexicans certainly will be less confident of the state's ability to guarantee economic progress, a confidence they enjoyed during the heyday of the revolutionary regime's rule.

Is Democratization Under Way?

Although many scholars were impressed with the stability imposed on Mexico by the postrevolutionary PRI elite, the party's rule has now ended. The Mexico that enters the twenty-first century differs substantially from the Mexico of the third quarter of the twentieth century. A president from a party other than the PRI now sits in the President's Chair and no party commands a majority in either house of Congress. In 2000, governors from the largest opposition party, the PAN, headed the state governments of the large and important states of Baja California, Nuevo León, Jalisco, and Guanajuato as well as Aguascalientes, Morelos, and Querétaro, and the PAN governed Chihuahua until 1998. Almost all of Mexico's largest cities and many state capitals were headed by opposition mayors, including Mexico City, Monterrey, Guadalajara, and Ciudad Juárez. These opposition governments have challenged centralism.[42] Mexicans of all social backgrounds have joined popular organizations and social movements in the past thirty years, attempting to circumvent the clientelist linkages preferred by the PRI and created by organizations associated with it. The top electoral agency in the country, the Federal Electoral Institute (IFE), has gained autonomy from the PRI and the government. Maybe the most spectacular develop-

ment of all was that the rebellion of indigenous (Indian) people in Chiapas was able to stand up to the regime for over six years. The Zapatistas in Chiapas were not able to get the PRI government to concede to their demands for local autonomy and a new development strategy, but neither was the PRI government willing to destroy them militarily in the way that it would likely have done a generation ago.

What factors account for these changes in the political system? The main sources of change can be summarized in two categories: the *modernization of Mexican society* and major *political failures by the ruling elite* and its party, the PRI.

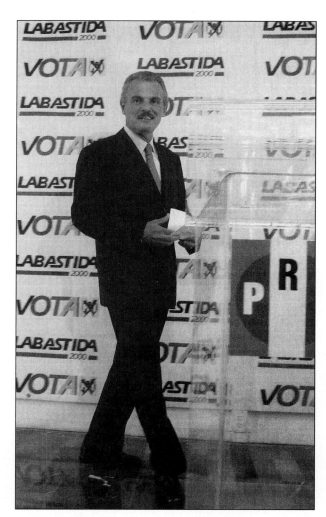

Francisco Labastida, candidate of the Institutional Revolutionary Party (PRI), stumps for votes in the 2000 presidential election.

Modernization First, Mexico's economic modernization, a process at work since the 1940s, has altered the social structure upon which the PRI's hegemony was based. The Mexico of the 1980s, when political change began to accelerate, had become more urban, more educated, and more influenced by the outside world than had the Mexico of the 1930s when Lázaro Cárdenas built the PRI-dominated regime. Consequently, Mexicans in the 1980s were less subject to the control of the PRI's corporatist organizations, more informed about alternatives to the PRI, and more attracted to the democratic practices observed outside Mexico, especially in the United States. A more complex social structure meant that public policy could not please all Mexicans all the time. As economic development proceeded, suppport for the opposition grew. In more modern parts of the country, especially in cities, the opposition performed much better than in the past. However, economic modernization cannot by itself explain the sudden fall in the PRI's electoral fortunes in 1988 and thereafter.

Policy and Political Failures Equally important in the erosion of the PRI's dominance was a series of policy and political failures that delegitimated the PRI's rule. The first came in 1968 when a large student movement that began as an objection to government interference in the National Autonomous University (UNAM) grew to become a protest against the regime's development strategy. Students and others questioned the government's priorities when it spent millions of dollars hosting the 1968 Summer Olympics in Mexico City while poverty remained widespread throughout the country. A political standoff between students and the government ended tragically when troops fired on a large assembly, killing an unknown number of protesters. In that event the regime lost the support of the intelligentsia and found its democratic facade torn away.

A second blow to the regime's image came with the debt crisis of the 1980s. The debt crisis revealed that the government had squandered the opportunities presented by the oil boom of the late 1970s. When López Portillo nationalized the banks in order to halt capital flight, he angered much of the private sector and the middle class, leading them into more vigorous electoral activity in support of the PAN. Miguel de la Madrid's administration chose to respond to the debt crisis with an austerity program that became a liberalization project that promoted the business sector. Salinas accelerated the liberalization program. The pain resulting from austerity and liberalization severely afflicted peasants and workers, the very sectors whose support played such a key role in PRI electoral victories. The sudden change in the development strategy also produced severe divisions within the PRI. In 1987, **Cuauhtémoc** (kwow-TAY-mock) **Cárdenas,** the son of the man who had shaped the PRI, defected from the party and declared his candidacy at the head of a union of left-wing parties and groups known as the **National Democratic Front (FDN).** Mexico's "lost decade of the 1980s," during which economic growth stagnated, contributed significantly to the growing dissatisfaction of many sectors of the society with the government.

Moreover, de la Madrid's administration responded poorly to a devastating earthquake that hit Mexico City in 1985, providing too little assistance too late in the view of the millions of capital city residents made homeless by the tremor. Many Mexicans questioned the government's capacity to perform its most important tasks in the aftermath of its tardy response to the earthquake. Those made homeless by the tremor eventually formed their own organizations to help them deal with their predicaments, organizations that pointedly refused to be incorporated into the PRI's organizational structure and that questioned the lack of democratic representation in Mexico City (which was still governed by a presidential appointee).

Cárdenas's presidential candidacy, the first by a PRI maverick since 1952, ruptured the stability of the hegemonic party system. His success at drawing millions to his campaign rallies and then to vote for him indicated significant disaffection from the ruling elite. To defeat Cárdenas, the PRI and the government had to take extraordinary measures, even by their own standards. The electoral authorities' computer allegedly "crashed" on the night of the election, the vote tallies of nearly half of the polling places were never reported, and those ballots were subsequently destroyed. Even then, Carlos Salinas received only half the votes. Consequently, he entered office with the legitimacy of his presidency questioned by substantial portions of the Mexican population, the effective leader of a party whose capacity to carry elections had come under question.

PROFILE: Carlos Salinas de Gortari

The mention of no other name produces stronger reactions in Mexico today than that of **Carlos Salinas de Gortari,** president from December 1988 until December 1994. (In Spanish nomenclature, one's second last name is one's mother's family name.) The changes Salinas made to Mexico's development strategy would have greater lasting impact than the actions of any president since Lázaro Cárdenas in the 1930s. Indeed, Salinas undid many of the reforms Cárdenas introduced. He ended land reform, invited foreign capital into Mexico, privatized much of the public sector of the economy, undertook political moves that helped undermine the PRI's corporatist structure, and entered into the North American Free Trade Agreement with the United States and Canada. The breadth and depth of Salinas's political initiatives demonstrated the powers the Mexican presidency has held. The reluctance of his successor, Ernesto Zedillo, to wield the full powers of the presidency reflected both his personal disinclination to subject Mexican society to the degree of change introduced by Salinas as well as the society's rejection of the use of such great powers by a single leader once it witnessed what a Mexican president could do, for good and for ill.

Born into a political family in Mexico City in 1948, Salinas was the most prominent among many recent Mexican leaders who took Ph.D.s in economics or political science in the United States or Europe before rising

Carlos Salinas de Gortari

to political power back in their home country. Salinas attended Harvard's Kennedy School of Government and received a Ph.D. in political economy. Often these technically trained leaders are called **technocrats** (*técnicos* in Spanish), implying that they rise to power because of their technical expertise in managing the economy or some other nonpolitical realm of state responsibility. Salinas's predecessor, Miguel de la Madrid, and his successor, Zedillo, also held advanced degrees from U.S. institutions, as did most of the closest advisors and cabinet ministers under Salinas. (Similarly, a growing number of government officials and their advisors who have come to the fore throughout Latin America since the 1980s were educated in the United States.) The three presidents who preceded Salinas, as well as Salinas and Zedillo, had never held elective office before running for the presidency. The term "technocrats" often invites derision from more politically experienced leaders. Those who worked their way up through the PRI's party organization and legislative posts often suggest that technocrats may think they know how to plan and run an economy, but they don't understand the game of politics. Salinas proved many *politicos* wrong.

Salinas rose to prominence as the minister of planning and budget under de la Madrid during the worst of the 1980s economic crisis. As de la Madrid struggled to correct the economy and figure out how to deal with the massive foreign debt that had triggered the crisis, Salinas and other technocrats associated with him began to advocate a set of reforms to the economy that have come to be called "neoliberalism." As the most powerful economics minister under de la Madrid, Salinas began to push the administration toward market-oriented reforms similar to those undertaken in Chile under the dictatorship of General Augusto Pinochet and inspired by Margaret Thatcher in Britain (see chapter 16) and Ronald Reagan in the United States. The reforms had several key elements. One was the opening up of Mexico's highly protected economy to international trade, a change symbolized by Mexico's decision to join the General Agreement on Tariffs and Trade in 1986. Another was deregulation, with the government loosening its regulatory controls over the private sector. And a third was the decision to sell off some of Mexico's many state-owned enterprises, beginning with several acquired as part of the nationalization of the banks decreed by José López Portillo in the last great act of Mexican populism in 1982.

Salinas was never just a market-oriented ideologue, however. One of the most important components of the economic program he helped put together was a wage-and-price freeze agreed to by organized labor, business, and the state. That agreement, whose purpose was to halt hyperinflation, represented a vivid example of how

Mexican corporatism could intervene in the economy, imposing limits on the free play of market forces. While Salinas was a liberal at heart, he was not beyond using the powers of the state—in conjunction with business and labor—to rein in some of the market's undesirable effects.

Mexican presidential hopefuls would usually begin jockeying for the PRI incumbent's favor early in a presidential term. Salinas was no different from others eyeing the ultimate prize in Mexico. His unofficial candidacy was identified from the beginning as one that would continue or perhaps intensify the nation's movement toward a neoliberal development strategy. When Salinas got the nod from de la Madrid in 1987, those who advocated adherence to Mexico's legacy of revolutionary nationalism, especially Cuauhtémoc Cárdenas, left the party to form a coalition that would eventually become the Democratic Revolutionary Party (PRD). Cárdenas ran against Salinas in the 1988 presidential race, losing by what he claimed was blatant fraud. Salinas thus entered the presidency with his right to rule in question.

Demonstrating his political acumen, Salinas went right to work to restore his lost legitimacy. He jailed corrupt union bosses who had unofficially supported Cárdenas's candidacy, including leaders of the powerful petroleum workers organization. He accelerated the privatization of state-owned firms and the reduction of Mexico's high barriers to trade. He made it clear that he would not compromise in his effort to restructure Mexico's economy and redefine its development model. Quickly Salinas became admired at home and abroad for his forceful leadership. His approval levels in public opinion polls shot up, and amazingly enough, many former leftists came to take on roles in Salinas's administration or to offer supportive analyses of the new direction of the Mexican economy in their newspaper and magazine columns.

One of Salinas's most creative initiatives was called the National Solidarity Program. With Solidarity, Salinas updated (but did not eliminate) Mexican clientelism. Worried about the defection of many PRI supporters to Cárdenas and the PRD, especially after six years of economic dislocation associated with the debt crisis, Salinas introduced a new program by which government funds would be distributed to community organizations that proposed specific projects to improve their localities. Mostly these projects involved building new infrastructure—roads, sewage systems, schools, and so forth; hardly a novel way to spend public funds. However, the political design of the program, which grew out of Salinas's dissertation at Harvard, was a stroke of political genius. Those who petitioned for Solidarity funds to create organizations were required to

commit themselves to providing labor inputs and supervising the projects; as a result, Salinas and the Solidarity bureaucracy (which remained under his control, not the PRI's) could identify natural leaders in localities and target them for co-optation. By making them petition for resources, Salinas reinforced the image of the state as the provider of particularistic benefits and of himself as its ultimate patron, the one to be politically rewarded by the recipient community's gratitude. By doling out Solidarity funds only to those community orgainzations able to organize and petition for them, Salinas created a relatively cheap way of responding to those who could otherwise become alienated oppositionists. Indeed, several studies indicated that Solidarity spent disproportionate amounts of money in those states and municipalities in which Cárdenas did especially well in 1988, essentially to buy back the support of those places.

Salinas's two most controversial acts were to create NAFTA and to reform article 27 of the constitution. We'll discuss NAFTA later in this chapter. The reform of article 27 essentially put an end to land reform in Mexico. Land reform had been moribund for many years; only spectacular actions of populist presidents like Luis Echeverría had produced more land redistribution in the late twentieth century. Reforming article 27 required Salinas to win over his main opponents, the PAN, to his cause, since he needed that party's votes to pass the reform bill in the Chamber of Deputies. With this success, Salinas made it possible for the *ejido* land, which was owned in common by local communes, to pass to private investors.

To many, the Salinas presidency had uncomfortable similarities to the reign of Porfirio Díaz. Ignoring the needs of peasants was one of those parallels to the *porfiriato*. Another was a pattern of decisions that seemed to benefit the president's friends. Several Mexicans became billionaires (in dollars, not inflated pesos) when they were able to get in on the ground floor of the privatization of state-owned firms like the telephone company. Mexico's stock market boomed as private investors—including many foreigners, like U.S. pension fund managers—bought shares of newly privatized firms and other companies invigorated by the new direction of the Mexican economy. Among those benefiting financially during the Salinas term was the Salinas family itself. Raúl Salinas, the president's brother, stashed away tens of millions of dollars in Swiss bank accounts; whether Carlos Salinas made financial gains by having insider information about privatization of publicly owned firms is not known.

Salinas was only forty years old when he became president. A man of incredible ambitions, he aspired to be a world leader after leaving office. Even after the

Chiapas uprising at the beginning of 1994 and the assassination of his chosen successor, Luis Donaldo Colosio, several months later, Salinas chose not to undertake overdue exchange rate adjustments while he was still in office for fear of ruining his reputation. When Zedillo came to power, a financial crisis that was long in the making awaited him and his advisors. When the peso collapsed at the end of 1994, sending the economy into a tailspin, Salinas criticized Zedillo for mismanaging the currency's devaluation, perhaps seeking to deflect criticism from his own decisions. (Salinas's three predecessors had devalued the currency before leaving office, thus sparing their successors the humiliation of having to start their presidency with an unpopular devaluation decision.) After his brother Raúl was arrested and charged with arranging the murder of José Francisco Ruiz Massieu, the PRI's secretary general, former president Carlos Salinas left Mexico for Ireland. He is now widely reviled for the corruption whose shocking dimensions became known during the Raúl Salinas investigation. When he occasionally returns to Mexico, his visits attract great attention by the press and new condemnations by oppositionists and political columnists, powerful evidence of the impact Carlos Salinas has had upon Mexican society.

Manifestations of Political Change

How do we know that Mexican politics has entered a new era? There are several manifestations of political change, the most important being the rise of more vigorous opposition parties that have more effectively competed against the PRI in recent elections, the development of a freer press, and the emergence of many popular organizations and social movements. These forces together have propelled Mexico into a democratic era where the PRI's regular victories and its control of governments at all levels have come to an end.

Opposition Parties and Electoral Reform The most significant electoral reform came in 1977. It relaxed the rules that had previously restricted the registration of opposition parties. It also reserved one quarter of the seats (100 of 400) in the Chamber of Deputies for opposition parties, selected on the basis of proportional representation, and instituted a mixed system for elections to the legislature roughly similar to that in place in Germany, Japan, and Russia. The remaining 300 seats are chosen on the basis of single member districts. (See chapter 9 for a discussion of these electoral systems.) Opposition parties were stimulated by this reform and by new rules that lowered the requirements for registration as parties. However, since the barriers to entry for new parties were set quite low, the opposition parties of the left remained divided and small. In 1986, the de la Madrid government doubled the number of deputies chosen by proportional representation to 200 (increasing the Chamber of Deputies to 500 seats at the same time). But the PRI became eligible for some of those seats, so that if it lost significant numbers of the 300 single member district seats it would still receive seats in proportion to its national vote share. Since then, the PRI and the opposition parties have negotiated back and forth about how the 200 proportional representation seats should be allotted among the parties. The current formula limits the extent to which a party can be overrepresented in the Chamber of Deputies to 8 percent. In other words, a party must receive at least 42 percent of the national vote in order to obtain an absolute majority of seats in the lower house of Congress.

Other electoral reforms in the 1990s leveled the playing field for the parties, reducing the advantages held by the PRI as an incumbent party. These included making the agency that oversees elections (the IFE) autonomous from the government and reforming campaign financing so that the opposition parties were not at a severe disadvantage compared to the PRI. These reforms were promulgated largely to bolster the legitimacy of the political regime in the aftermath of the crises described earlier. But electoral reform contributed to the effective emergence of opposition parties, especially the Democratic Revolutionary Party (PRD) and the National Action Party (PAN).

The Democratic Revolutionary Party (PRD)
Cuauhtémoc Cárdenas's presidential campaign in 1988 enjoyed the support of a wide range of left-wing parties, some independent and some that had collaborated with the PRI. These parties initially banded together under the umbrella of the National Democratic Front (FDN), with each maintaining its separate legal identity while advancing Cárdenas

Cuauhtémoc Cárdenas

as its presidential candidate. When Cárdenas subsequently proposed forming a single, united party of the left to consolidate and channel the gains of 1988, three collaborationist parties left the FDN. The remaining parties eventually took over the old Mexican Socialist Party and changed its name to the **Democratic Revolutionary Party (PRD).** Although former socialists composed an important contingent of the original PRD, they were gradually overwhelmed by ex-PRI members who defected to the PRD. The PRD has had to deal with a number of internal struggles over ideological and strategic issues as well as personal differences among leaders.

Revolutionary nationalism motivates most followers of the PRD, but most also recognize that the former policies of economic nationalism and ISI will not lead Mexico to economic prosperity. The PRD has been unable to define a distinct development strategy, making it seem more a party of emotion than of reason on this critical issue. PRD militants hold very bad feelings toward the PRI because of the 1988 elections and the repression of many party militants in the years that followed, especially in southern states like Michoacán and Guerrero. The party therefore rejected compromise with the PRI and its governments over electoral results and legislative proposals for electoral reform.

As a party that came together out of other organizations of the left and from the defection of a substantial portion of the left wing of the PRI, the PRD remains faction-ridden. PRD leaders must trade off the need to reward those PRD members who have supported them for many years with the desire to attract new PRD members who come from other organizations—both popular organizations and the PRI itself. Squabbles among leaders have been widely reported in the press, contributing little to the party's public image. Recently, one of the PRD's founders, Porfirio Muñoz Ledo (who had been head of the PRI in the mid-1970s), left the party as the result of differences with Cárdenas. These internal weaknesses have made the consolidation of the PRD as the party of the left somewhat disappointing to those who saw bright opportunity in the 1988 *cardenista* campaign.

The PRD faced an equally difficult external challenge: the unwillingness of the PRI and its governments to recognize its successes. Because of Cárdenas's strong performance in 1988 and the PRD's ardent opposition to neoliberalism, the Salinas government felt more threatened by the PRD than by the PAN. Many *priístas* (PRI adherents) detested Cárdenas and other PRD leaders for betraying the PRI. While the PAN's triumphs in gubernatorial races were recognized by Salinas in Baja California (1989) and Chihuahua (1992), the PRD's claims to victory were often invalidated by the electoral authorities, who usually declared the PRI the winner. In the states of Michoacán and México in 1989 and 1990, state and local elections produced intense conflicts between the PRD and the PRI, and the government sided with the PRI. The PRD may have exaggerated its actual vote count, but it seems clear that the government permitted extensive fraud by the PRI.

In federal elections in both 1991 and 1994, the PRD finished third. It performed much better in the 1997 federal elections and in the first election for the head of government of the Federal District (Mexico City), won by Cárdenas. Compared with the historical performance of the independent left, the PRD's 1994 and 1997 finishes were a significant advance. However, Fox's performance in the 2000 federal elections dealt a setback to the PRD, which lost more than half of its seats in the Chamber of Deputies (see table 23.3). For all intents and

TABLE 23.3

	Recent Elections to the Chamber of Deputies							
	PAN		PRI		PRD		Others	
Year	% of Vote	No. of Seats	% of Vote	No. of Seats	% of Vote	No. of Seats	% of Votes	No. of Seats
1991	18	89	61	320	8	41	13	50
1994	27	119	50	301	17	70	6	10
1997	27	121	39	239	26	125	9	15
2000	41	223	39	209	20	68	0	0

The percentages of the vote reported in table 23.3 are the percentages of the total votes received by parties eligible for seats (that is, those receiving more than 2.0 percent of the vote in 1997 and 2000, or 1.5 percent in earlier elections).

In 2000, PAN ran with the Mexican Green Party (PVEM) in the Alliance for Change, with the PAN receiving 208 seats and the PVEM 15. The PRD joined with four smaller parties in the Alliance for Mexico, from which the PRD received 40 seats and the other parties 28.

Source: Instituto Federal Electoral.

purposes, the PRD is now the electoral left in Mexico. PRD members who defected from the PRI now govern Zacatecas, Baja California Sur, and Nayarit in addition to Mexico City. Furthermore, the PRD has consolidated the second position electorally in many states in the south, especially Chiapas, Guerrero, Michoacán, Oaxaca, Tabasco, and Veracruz. In those states of the south where the effects of economic liberalization have been harsh for many peasants, the PRD offers a voice of opposition.

In his presidential campaigns of 1988 and 1994, Cárdenas did not rely on pollsters and media consultants. But he ran a modern campaign in the 1997 Mexico City contest.[43] His campaign, conducted in the city that was the home of the national broadcast media, could be watched by most of the nation. As a result, Cárdenas's candidacy had long coattails that pulled other PRD candidates to victory in various parts of the country. The new smiling Cárdenas, a sharp contrast to the dour man who contested the presidency in 1988 and 1994, led a PRD surge that brought the party back to the second position in the Chamber of Deputies. It took 125 (25 percent) of the seats, just barely eclipsing the PAN's 121 seats (24.2 percent). Governing Mexico City has proven more difficult than winning its top post, however. Cárdenas ran a distant third in the 2000 presidential race. His unwillingness to ally with Fox early in the campaign and the decline of the PRD's electoral fortunes suggest that his influence in the party may be superceded by younger

leaders, especially Andres Manuel López Obrador, who won the election for mayor of Mexico City.

The National Action Party (PAN). Many analysts relegated the **National Action Party (PAN)** to a permanent third position in light of the *cardenista* surge in 1988. However, since then the PAN has won several governorships and the city halls of most of the nation's largest cities; in 2000, most spectacularly, its candidate, Vicente Fox, won the presidency. The PAN's congressional delegation was instrumental in the passage of electoral reform legislation and laws altering the church-state relationship and the status of the *ejido* under Salinas. The PAN's acceptance of Ernesto Zedillo's presidential victory in August 1994 made an attempt by Cárdenas to organize protest across the country ring hollow.

In 1985 and 1986, the PAN was subjected to PRI-engineered electoral fraud, prompting its leaders to organize massive demonstrations and hunger strikes in defense of the party's vote. Despite these open displays of discontent, the PAN since its founding has been the main party of legal and gradual reform. The influx of middle-class and business militants like Vicente Fox into the party in the early 1980s (in reaction to López Portillo's nationalization of the banks) may have made the party seem more stridently opposed to state intervention in the economy than ever before, but the PAN has always stood for constraints on state power. Salinas's accession to the presidency and the

Vicente Fox on the campaign trail in 2000.

León after holding on to the Baja California governorship in 1996. The PAN also took many city halls in important provincial cities in 1995–96.

Did this accommodation with the PRI compromised the PAN's capacity to serve as a party of opposition? Some former PAN leaders argued it did when they left the party in the early 1990s. But the 1994 presidential campaign of Diego Fernández de Cevallos did not seem accommodationist in tone, nor did the 2000 campaign of Vicente Fox. Overall, the PAN has advanced electorally, and the experience of governing large states and municipalities has produced leaders capable of presenting themselves as realistic presidential candidates in the future, perhaps no one more so than former Governor Fox of Guanajuato, Mexico's new president. Although it has lacked the resources available to the PRI as the party of the state, the PAN runs far more professional campaigns than it could a decade or two ago. Still primarily a party of the middle class, the PAN could not win the gubernatorial races it has won without attracting working-class voters. Hence, the PAN has converted itself into a catch-all party with a somewhat right-of-center ideology. But this conversion is less the result of changes in ideology than changes in circumstance, principally the rise of the rival PRD.

Cárdenas surge presented both the president and the PAN leadership with good reasons to seek accommodation in the 1990s. Salinas needed the PAN to help pass his legislation curtailing state power and initiating economic policy changes that the PAN had favored for decades, while the PAN needed Salinas's acknowledgment of its electoral victories to help meet the growing challenge of Cárdenas and the left.

The accommodation between Salinas and the PAN proved highly successful for both sides. The PAN won the gubernatorial races in Baja California and Chihuahua in 1989 and 1992, respectively, and saw Salinas force the resignation of PRI candidates for governor after blatantly fraudulent elections in Guanajuato and San Luis Potosí in 1991. Salinas even appointed a *panista* (a PAN member) as governor of Guanajuato. (Fox had been the PAN candidate in Guanajuato, but Salinas did not appoint him as interim governor.) Salinas was able to point to PAN victories as evidence of a political opening to the opposition. The PAN also achieved some electoral reforms, while the PRD was left looking intransigent on this issue. Shortly after Zedillo took office and the financial crisis hit, the PAN won the governorships of Jalisco and Guanajuato. In 1997, it also won Querétaro and Nuevo

Other Parties   In the past twenty-five years there have been several other opposition parties, and several contested the 2000 elections either as members of political alliances with the PAN or the PRD, or separately. Mexican electoral rules since 1977 have generally favored the development of small parties. A cynical way to look at this phenomenon (but probably the correct way) is to say that the PRI encouraged the fragmentation of the independent parties of opposition by keeping the barriers to creation of new parties low.[44] Those low barriers tended to encourage the fragmentation of the left in the late 1970s and 1980s, until the emergence of the PRD. Recently, several mavericks from the PRI have created new parties, parties that they probably hope will be courted by one of the three large parties as allies. Only one party that can be said to have a distinctly different ideology has emerged in the past decade, the **Mexican Green Party (PVEM),** an environmentally oriented party that has proven capable of attracting voters and of acting independently in Congress and the electoral arena.

The Media and Politics The broadcast media's traditional prejudice in favor of the PRI at election time once paralleled its overall uncritical attitude toward the Mexican state and toward closeness in U.S.-Mexican relations. The major private television network, Televisa, which owns major radio stations as well, started out with close ties to former president Miguel Alemán (1946–52). The state owns one of the other major television stations. The uncritical attitude of television news toward the government inhibited public debate about major issues essential to democracy, especially because the majority of Mexicans rely on television and radio for their news. However, campaign finance reforms and new laws mandating that broadcasters provide equal time to all major parties, which took effect before the 1997 midterm elections, weakened some of the excessively pro-government, pro-PRI orientation of the broadcast media. In the 2000 elections the broadcast media finally broke its longstanding practice of favoring the PRI in news coverage. The decision of Televisa and its rival, TV Azteca, to be neutral in their coverage contributed significantly to Fox's successful campaign.

In contrast to the relatively pro-regime attitudes of broadcasters, the print media became much more critical of the political system and of specific public policies over the past twenty years. Mexico City and the cities of the north have been especially well served by newspapers that have shown a willingness to criticize the government and in which opposition politicians and intellectuals could add their perspectives to the debate about public policy. Newspapers such as *Unomásuno* and *La Jornada* and magazines such as *Proceso* and *Nexos* have both given a voice to the left and permitted investigative journalists to publish articles that reveal government corruption and describe the way some critical public decisions have been made. In the mid-1990s, the Mexico City daily *Reforma* was launched by a media enterprise that published Monterrey's *El Norte*. *Reforma* created a sensation by refusing to distribute its papers through the newsstands controlled by a pro-PRI union, and it set a new standard for investigative reporting in Mexico. Several critical intellectuals have written regular columns for *Reforma, La Jornada,* and *Pro-*

ceso, meaning that anti-PRI perspectives got circulated before 2000. However, these newspapers are not the most widely read periodicals in Mexico. The degree of independence of these new press outlets will only grow as the liberalization of the economy diminishes the importance of advertising by the state and parastatal firms (advertising sometimes has been withheld from overly critical periodicals) and as sources of newsprint other than the state-owned monopoly become available.

Popular Organizations and Civil Society Mexico, like several other Latin American countries, has experienced a surge in popular organizations and social movements, especially in the aftermath of the 1968 student movement. These organizations vary widely in their size, the issues they address, and the extent to which they try to maintain a distance from the government. In the 1980s, popular movements, most of which had sprung up at the grass roots in poor urban neighborhoods as well as among peasant communities, began to make connections among themselves, thus forming networks of popular movements, sharing ideas and seeking collective responses to the government. Many of those who have studied such popular movements argue that they hold more promise for a democratization of Mexican life than the political parties and that the flowering of popular organizations witnessed in the past two decades indicates that many Mexicans increasingly wish to create a more participatory society.[45]

Popular organizations typically begin with very local objectives that are closely related to the material needs of their members, such as clean water or other city services, the regularization of land titles, or the government's response to the 1985 Mexican earthquake. Veterans of the 1968 student movement organized many such organizations, but others have sprung up as the result of local leaders' initiatives. Popular movements often have an explicit commitment to internal democracy. Moreover, in both membership and leadership, popular movements tend to redress the gender imbalance otherwise evident in Mexican public life.

These local organizations have slowly established links with one another, thereby creating more broadly oriented social movements. Movements have tended to focus on either socioeconomic or political issues, but seldom both. In the 1970s and 1980s, popular movements more heavily emphasized socioeconomic issues, and they have sought to avoid being captured by the PRI's corporatist structures. Until the 1988 presidential candidacy of Cárdenas, most of these organizations were explicitly abstentionist in electoral politics, seeing electoral politics as an arena of corruption and a distraction from more important local concerns that would never be affected by electoral politics anyway. In 1988, though, after six years of economic austerity under de la Madrid, a time marked by the Mexican government's unusually low responsiveness to the needs of the poor, some popular organizations and their members supported the Cárdenas candidacy, since Cárdenas promised to reject the neoliberal development model and return Mexico to a concern about social justice.

In addition to the growth of popular movements concerned primarily with the socioeconomic needs of localities, Mexico has witnessed the emergence of movements more focused on human rights and dedicated to fairer elections and a more democratic regime. These organizations have broader membership and a more national scope than the popular movements just described. Middle-class professionals constitute a far larger share of their membership than in urban popular movements.

Human rights associations began to form in the late 1970s and early 1980s and proliferated in number. A relatively freer print media that was willing to report instances of political corruption, police abuse, and political violence; support from international human rights organizations; and a record of assassinations of Mexican journalists all helped to motivate this movement. The Catholic church and church-based groups have also contributed to the development of human rights associations. The Salinas government responded to the growth of attention to human rights by creating a National Human Rights Commission, staffed by highly respected persons committed to human rights who were permitted to investigate reported instances of human rights abuses.

During the 1994 election campaign, civic associations came into prominence because of their role (largely self-appointed) in watching over the electoral process. The best known of these was the **Civic Alliance,** a self-described nonpartisan network of organizations dedicated to protecting the right of Mexicans to have a free and fair electoral process. While some have questioned the nonpartisan nature of the Civic Alliance because many of its most prominent members sympathized with or belonged to the PRD, certainly the development of such associations dedicated to promoting more democratic practices in Mexican politics have contributed to a less authoritarian political system. In addition, the open sympathy of many such organizations and human rights groups toward the rebels in Chiapas has served to constrain government abuses in putting down that rebellion and has kept the pressure on the government to find a political solution to the armed resistance there.

Value Change?   Gauging changes in Mexican political attitudes proves somewhat difficult because we lack public opinion polls from before the late 1980s. Earlier studies based on samples of local populations or of specific occupational groups found that Mexicans held democratic values but that they were unable to act upon them, given the structure of the PRI-dominated political system.[46] A recent survey intended to explore the extent to which Latin Americans support democracy found that 50 percent of Mexicans say democracy is preferable to other regime types, but 20 percent were willing to state that authoritarianism could be preferable, and 26 percent did not think the difference between democracy and authoritarianism mattered to them.[47] Of course, many respondents to a question offering this choice of answers may not have the same clear definition of democracy and authoritarianism in their minds as we offer in this book. Mexicans, after all, have been told by their leaders since 1917 that they live in a democracy, so for many Mexicans, "democracy" simply means the regime under which they live, whatever its flaws. In contrast, fully 80 percent of Costa Ricans surveyed in the same poll responded that they preferred democracy to other alternatives. Costa Rica has been an electoral democracy since 1949.

What do Mexicans mean by "democracy?" Again, a comparative perspective may help us discover Mexican meanings of the word (see table 23.4). Costa Ricans overwhelmingly choose "liberty" as their one-word definition of democracy, a choice political scientists would consider vital for supporting the institutions and processes of liberal democracy. In surveys conducted in the 1990s, Mexicans tended to

TABLE 23.4
The Meaning of Democracy

In one word, could you tell me what democracy means to you?	Mexico	Costa Rica	Chile
Liberty	21	54	25
Equality	21	6	18
Voting/elections	12	3	10
Form of government	14	6	12
Progress	14	7	8
Respect/lawfulness	13	3	10
Other	2	7	8
No answer	3	13	8

Source: MORI Internacional, *Visión Latinoamericana de la democracía: encuestas de opinión pública en México, Chile, y Costa Rica,* Final Report, October 20, 1998.

be split on how they defined democracy, with some seeing democracy in terms of processes and political *institutions* (liberty, elections, legality, the form of government), but almost as many defining democracy in terms of political and social *outcomes* (equality, welfare, and progress). Chileans also tended to define democracy in terms of outcomes, although perhaps somewhat less so than Mexicans. We should also note that most Mexicans did not perceive their country as being democratic: only 11% said that there was much democracy in their country, while fully half said that Mexico had little or no democracy. Perhaps most indicative of the people's perspective on their government were the very low levels of trust in governmental and political institutions. While Mexicans said they had confidence in the church, schools, and the family, about two-thirds reported they had little or no confidence in such national institutions as the police, the government, the Congress, the press, and political parties.[48] A picture emerged of a society just prior to the 2000 elections that was somewhat divided about what it hoped democracy would bring it, but that believed it did not enjoy true democracy at that time, in no small part due to the failure of its national political institutions.

NAFTA

On January 1, 1994, the **North American Free Trade Agreement (NAFTA)** came into effect, marking the culmination of President Salinas's efforts to reorient the Mexican economy away from ISI toward a more outward orientation. With NAFTA, Mexico is bound by a treaty with the United States and Canada to retain its outward orientation. Treaties can be broken, of course, but by joining NAFTA, Mexico's political elite made any attempt to reverse the neoliberal economic model much more difficult.

Salinas provided the chief impetus behind NAFTA. The reorientation of the Mexican economy toward a more open embrace of free trade and foreign investment had begun in the 1980s with the onset of the foreign debt crisis. When Miguel de la Madrid's government decided to join the General Agreement on Tariffs and Trade in 1986, Mexico made a commitment to open its economy to free trade. Earlier in Salinas's own term, he moved vigorously to reduce trade barriers unilaterally and to be more welcoming of foreign investment. However, when Salinas sought to diversify sources of foreign investment in Mexico during a 1990 trip to Europe, he returned disappointed. Germans were financing their nation's reunification, and they and other Europeans were excited about opportunities in the new market economies of the former Soviet bloc. Salinas and his advisors worried that the fall of the Berlin wall would so refocus the attentions of the world's investors that Mexico would be left without the new capital it needed to make its economy competitive in world trade. The United States and Canada had recently signed their own bilateral free trade treaty. At that point, Salinas reluctantly decided that Mexico's economic future lay in the Western Hemisphere. Mexico would commit itself to a future linked to the United States, the overbearing neighbor whose economy had dominated the country for over a century. But decades of experience had shown that economic nationalism had been able to free Mexico from U.S. control only temporarily.

Convincing both Mexicans and U.S. politicians that the free trade agreement should be adopted would prove a formidable challenge. Of course, presidential domination of the Congress meant that the Mexican government would quickly approve the concept of a trade agreement, but many sectors of what Mexicans euphemistically call "public opinion"—the views of intellectuals and columnists and the privately stated views of politicians—saw the agreement as including far too many unwise concessions to the United States. On the U.S. side, first George Bush and then Bill Clinton trumpeted the many new advantages that NAFTA would bring U.S. industry, thereby unintentionally supporting the case of NAFTA's Mexican critics. U.S. critics have been especially concerned about the likelihood that American firms will relocate south of the border, where they believe labor laws and environmental regulations are much less rigorously enforced.

Eventually, to ensure the passage of the 1,100-page NAFTA treaty, the United Sates and Mexico had to negotiate a set of side agreements that allow for tri-national panels of experts to be called to hear complaints about the non-enforcement of any member nation's labor or environmental laws, with the power to issue sanctions against the offending nation.

What does NAFTA mean for the Mexican economy? What does it portend for Mexican politics, especially for the promotion of Mexican democracy?

The different sides in the debate about economic policy argue about the impact—both actual and expected—of NAFTA as much as any other topic. Trade volumes have increased dramatically among the NAFTA countries, more rapidly than their trade with the rest of the world, which itself is growing rapidly. Direct investment by U.S. firms in Mexico has contributed to trade growth because those firms have located in Mexico specifically to produce goods for export to the United States. However, while investment by North American firms has grown rapidly in Mexico, it has not increased as rapidly as investment from other parts of the world. Businesses from Europe and Asia are seeking to get into the Mexican and the NAFTA market by investing there.

Because of the asymmetry in the sizes of the Mexican and the United States economies, we should not be surprised that the impact of NAFTA on Mexico has been considerably greater than on the United States. There is little conclusive evidence about employment creation or job losses in the United States due to NAFTA. Some U.S. firms have relocated to Mexico, but they would likely have relocated somewhere else in the world to find lower labor costs, with or without NAFTA. Many Mexicans have suffered job dislocations since NAFTA came into effect; those working in small and medium-sized firms have been especially vulnerable to bankruptcies, as have employees of privatized former state-owned firms. Many of these job losses or changes came about in the 1995 economic crisis associated with the peso devaluation of December 1994. Those involved in agriculture, especially peasant producers of corn (maize) and beans, have found it difficult to compete against cheap grain imports from the U.S. midwest. Again, to what extent NAFTA has been responsible for causing Mexicans to need to change jobs, as opposed to the overall changes in the economy brought about by Salinas and Zedillo, is not so clear. Those who would prefer to return to an inwardly oriented economic model put the blame for the burdens of adjustment on neoliberalism in general and on NAFTA in particular. Subcomandante Marcos of the Zapatista National Liberation Army in Chiapas has been especially eloquent in condemning the current economic development strategy, NAFTA included.

The renewed ties to Mexico created by NAFTA have engendered a sense of obligation on the part of the United States to promote its neighbor's economic development. A vivid example came during the 1994–95 peso crisis when the Clinton administration put together a nearly $50 billion package of loans and loan guarantees from U.S. government funds and international financial institutions to help Mexico stop the fall of the peso. This loan package forced the Zedillo administration to undertake a painful recovery program that kept the Mexican economy on the neoliberal development path. Since 1996, the Mexican economy has grown rapidly.

Some proponents of NAFTA have argued that it would speed Mexico's transition to democracy. Their argument followed the standard account offered by modernization theory: NAFTA would promote a market economy and economic growth in Mexico. As a result, a middle class and economic pluralism would grow there. With a larger middle class and economic pluralism would come more demands for liberalization of Mexico's political regime. In addition, with the interaction of the cultures in North America, more Mexicans would be exposed to democratic values and adopt them as their own. Salinas himself said, "as we move along the path toward consolidating our economic reforms, political reform will continue to evolve in Mexico."

Opponents of NAFTA have expressed a less sanguine view. They have generally argued that the economic dislocations associated with economic integration, especially in the countryside, will lead to political conflicts that the government will choose to repress. Furthermore, the Mexican beneficiaries of economic integration will likely be a small group of very wealthy businesspeople who become the owners of privatized firms or the Mexican partners of U.S. multinationals. These oligarchs will not want the Mexican masses to have even greater power as the result of democratization.

NAFTA does seem to have put Mexico higher on the agenda of U.S. politicians and political activists. Consequently, Mexican politics have come under greater scrutiny from abroad in the past ten years. Changes in communications technologies—satellite television broadcasts and the Internet—have played a significant role in keeping U.S. political figures attentive to Mexico, mostly for the good of democracy. During the course of NAFTA negotiations and the debate about its passage by the U.S. Senate, many linkages were developed between U.S. political activists and Mexican organizations and between U.S. and Mexican business groups. These binational links probably helped promote the liberalization of the PRI regime.

At the same time, conflict has escalated in the Mexican countryside, best illustrated by the rebellion in Chiapas but by no means limited to it. A Mexican student strike in 1999–2000 ended up with a focus on the Mexican development model. In these conflicts, some activists and some representatives of Mexican police forces resorted to violence, and many political observers worried that the government would cover up examples of repression. A balanced assessment, however, ought to note that despite increased political conflict, the federal government generally exercised restraint, although some state and local authorities have been more willing to put down protesters.

Rebellion in Chiapas   To respond to their dissatisfaction with political institutions, some Mexicans joined opposition parties to try to overturn the PRI electorally. Others sought to create new popular organizations that would function democratically and attempt to accomplish some of their objectives at which the national institutions have failed. We see a more extreme reaction with the rebellion in **Chiapas.**

The Chiapas uprising reveals the cross-cutting pressures on the Mexican elite and its difficult path to democracy. Many of the social reforms of the Mexican revolution had never reached Chiapas, an economically backward state where political violence and *caciquismo*—the rule of local despots *(caciques)*—reached notorious levels. Economic liberalization in the 1980s and 1990s meant that economic elites in Chiapas, such as ranchers and those engaged in lumbering in the rain forest, could benefit greatly by foreign trade. But most Chiapas residents, primarily of Indian heritage,

Zapatista rebels on the march in Chiapas, 1999

found themselves increasingly marginalized economically, unable to survive on the small plots of land to which they had access and forced to search farther and farther afield for agricultural jobs that paid little. The Mexico City elite was content to allow regional strongmen to govern as they always had, so long as the economic liberalization project was unhindered. Human rights promoters, including Bishop Samuel Ruiz, however, had encouraged the organizing of popular organizations among the long-exploited indigenous communities of Chiapas.

Despite their political oppression, the people of Chiapas had a high capacity to express their democratic orientation and their real economic and political needs. When the Zapatista National Liberation Army (which took its name from Emiliano Zapata) rose up against the government on January 1, 1994, it effectively articulated its differences with the Salinas government and its development project. (It chose the day that NAFTA became effective to indicate its objection to economic liberalization.) The rebels found sympathy for their cause in both Chiapas and around the nation and the world. Indeed, many other popular organizations took up the cause of the Zapatistas in public demonstrations. The national and international press willingly published the communiques of Subcomandante Marcos, much to the government's embarrassment.

The Salinas government quickly recognized that in the age of satellite and other international electronic communication, it could not simply crush the Zapatistas militarily. Such a reaction would look too much like the act of a scared authoritarian regime, even though it was by no means clear that anything approaching a majority of Mexicans agreed with the Zapatistas' goals or their methods. The Salinas government designated a negotiator to find a solution. Negotiating with the rebels damaged the reputation of the presidency and made the 1994 elections much more difficult for the PRI than had been expected. Moreover, it threatened to create the dangerous precedent that rebellions of sufficient scale would be met by compromises, thereby encouraging revolution as a path of resistance to PRI rule. Crushing the rebellion would have satisfied the president's neoliberal allies, but it likely would have greatly damaged the regime's reputation on human rights, even more than the rebellion had already done.

Curiously, the electoral opposition could not effectively exploit the Chiapas situation for its advantage. Initially, the conservative PAN did not sympathize with the rebels. It rejected both their methods and their ideology. For its part, the PRD clearly sympathized with the Zapatista cause. Advocating violent revolution is difficult for an electorally oriented opposition to do in Mexico, however, because its status as a legally registered party could be threatened by it. The Zapatistas were not won over by the PRD because the electoral path did not seem particularly promising to them. Indeed, when they met, Subcomandante Marcos strongly criticized the PRD presidential candidate, Cuauhtémoc Cárdenas. Meanwhile, the local PRI arranged to steal the Chiapas governor's race when it was held in August 1994, and local landowners and ranchers organized militias against the Zapatistas. Electoral violence has characterized Chiapas in each election held since 1994. In 2000, the PAN's Vicente Fox advocated a negotiated settlement with the rebels as soon as possible.

Hypotheses on Democratization

Does Mexico have a democratic future? With Vicente Fox's election, most Mexicans had good reasons to think that democracy would be their future. However, rather than simply gazing into a crystal ball or asking pundits to prognosticate for us, let's briefly review our hypotheses on democratization from chapter 10, summarizing as we do the evidence we have just covered.

State Institutions   The PRI's loss of the Chamber of Deputies majority in the 1997 elections helped to considerably reduce presidential domination of the Congress. The PRI's loss of the presidency in 2000, along with the failure of Fox's PAN to gain congressional majorities, means that presidentialism is essentially dead. The opposition parties have attempted to build democratic processes within the Congress, but they will need more time to accomplish that task. So long as reelection is constitutionally proscribed, legislators cannot

build legislative careers and serve as powerful committee chairs, who can block presidential initiatives in the way that a senator such as Jesse Helms can in the United States. However, Mexican federalism has been bolstered by efforts at administrative decentralization and an increase in the revenue sharing that the federal government grants to the states. Similarly, with opposition parties governing many states and municipalities, a majority of Mexicans can now imagine alternation in power: they can throw the rascals out if they are angry about public services, which they did by electing Fox in July 2000.

Elites Committed to Democracy   President Zedillo demonstrated a commitment to democracy unparalleled among postrevolutionary presidents. He forced the PRI to accept the opposition victory in the 1997 midterm legislative elections, and he made the party introduce primaries for the selection of gubernatorial and presidential candidates, essentially voluntarily, giving away some of the metaconstitutional powers of the presidency. He also recognized Vicente Fox's presidential victory in 2000. Some leaders of the PRI clearly see that their party must accept these democratic advances and indeed that it may well win future elections by adopting primaries as its means of choosing candidates. However, there remain high-level members of the PRI who would prefer to return to the practices of the 1960s. Zedillo's disinclination to impose his will on the PRI has meant that in many states and localities, his adversaries in the party are engaging in the old-time practices of intimidation and repression. The Fox presidency will prove an enormous challenge to the PRI: it must either learn to act like an ordinary political party or it will come into open conflict with the government if it tries to continue behaving as if there are no constraints on its exercise of power.

National Wealth   Problems of maldistribution of income continue to cast a shadow over Mexico's path toward democratization. The violent uprisings in Chiapas, Guerrero, and other southern states have their origins in the poverty suffered by millions of Mexicans and in their perception that the neoliberal policies advocated by Salinas and

Zedillo are intended to make them bear the burden of Mexico's adjustment to globalization, a process they would just as soon not embark upon.

Private Enterprise   In the past two decades many entrepreneurs have come over to the opposition parties, especially to the PAN. The presidential campaign of Vicente Fox, for instance, was funded in part by an organization called Amigos de Fox, in which businesspeople have played a key role. These business connections with the PAN should enrich Mexican political pluralism. At the same time, the very wealthy members of the private sector who gained most under Salinas's privatization of the economy have demonstrated little concern for political pluralism; rather, when asked by Salinas to make large contributions to the PRI's campaign war chest for the 1994 race, they willingly offered to ante up the funds.[49]

The Middle Class   More than any other group, the Mexican middle class has supported political pluralism with its votes. The PAN is a thoroughly middle-class party, and the left-wing PRD draws many of its supporters from the middle class too. To the extent that the middle class continues to grow, democracy in Mexico should benefit.

Support of the Disadvantaged for Democracy Although the disadvantaged—the urban poor, the working class, and the peasantry—were controlled by the PRI and its corporatist organizations a generation ago, the socioeconomic changes of the last twenty years have ruptured the PRI's strong control over these social groups. The poor are now able to vote for the opposition parties and to join popular organizations, and they do.

Civil Society and Political Culture   Mexico now has a much more vibrant civil society, with neighborhood associations, women's groups, and organizations devoted to the promotion of human rights. Mexicans by and large prefer democracy, although there are people who have withdrawn from politics or who have never taken an interest in politics, and these politically alienated Mexicans may support an authoritarian regime as quickly as a democratic polity. Overall, however, in the past

three decades the forces for democracy at the grass roots have been bolstered.

Education and Freedom of Information   Fewer and fewer Mexicans cannot read, so the capacity of democracy's foes to dupe the people is declining from year to year. Information is so much more available and of such high quality today that anyone in Mexico seeking political information would have no difficulty in obtaining it. Of course, Mexicans remain television watchers instead of quality newspaper readers. Even here, however, the last five years have brought major improvements in the degree of journalistic integrity and the extent to which critical questions are being posed.

Homogeneous Society   If anything, Mexico's indigenous people have become more demanding of their rights. They have found more and more members of the intelligentsia and the political elite willing to espouse their causes too. The Chiapas rebellion has played a critical role in bringing these issues to the attention of the wider world, so that indigenous people have international allies to help support their efforts to gain greater autonomy from the state and the PRI.

Favorable International Environment   Again, the Chiapas rebellion has brought much world attention to the progress of democracy in Mexico. The globalization of communications now constrains the Mexican government in its actions toward dissident groups. At election time, the world's television cameras were pointed on ballot boxes throughout Mexico, limiting the PRI's ability to undertake electoral shannanigans. The U.S. government is more involved than ever in providing advice to its Mexican counterpart about how to treat its own citizens. However, many human rights activists have suggested that the U.S. government remains too uncritical of the political elite ruling Mexico.

Conclusions   Although Mexico faces many significant political and social problems, the past two decades have enabled it to confront them directly. Most important, the forces favoring democracy have grown greatly, having seized on the opportunities granted them by government failures to question the merits of continued rule by the PRI. In view of the factors we have just reviewed, we can regard Mexico's potential for consolidating a successful democracy as reasonably high. In 2000, Mexico elected a president from a party other than the long-ruling PRI. President Fox will face many challenges as he seeks to reform Mexico's political system so that it can never be governed by a single party again. However, millions of Mexicans themselves took the most important step in consolidating democracy by voting the PRI out of the presidency; they recognized the historic character of their collective act. As he entered into his critical six-year term of office, Fox had every reason to count on the continued support of the many voters who had cast their ballots for him.

BRAZIL

Population (1999, estimated): 171.9 million
Area: 3.29 million square miles
(a little smaller than the United States)

In contrast to the political stability enjoyed until recently by Mexico under the PRI's one-party-dominant rule, Brazil's political history in the twentieth century was marked by political instability. Brazil now is governed under the fifth (or perhaps sixth) distinctly different political regime since the Brazilian imperial monarchy fell in 1889. A nation of great promise, whose leaders have aspired to *grandeza,* or greatness, Brazil enters the twenty-first century having failed to deliver on that promise. A nation vast in population, territory, and resources, it has become in some ways nearly ungovernable. Brazil is by far the most industrialized of the South American countries and has the highest per capita income in the region; but no other major country has an income distribution so unequal, and its politics has been characterized by paradoxes and frustrations.

The Setting

Brazil occupies over half the land mass of South America. As the largest Portuguese-speaking country in the world, Brazil has about 170 million peo-

Source: U.S. Central Intelligence Agency

ple, making it the fifth most populous nation-state. As in Mexico, Brazil's struggle to industrialize has led to rapid urbanization in the twentieth century. São Paulo, with over 16 million inhabitants, rivals Mexico City's size. Its growth has been phenomenal: in 1950, São Paulo did not have as many as 4 million people and was not even Brazil's largest city. (Rio de Janeiro was; its population currently tops 10 million.)[50] The Amazon basin, the largest tropical rain forest in the world, remains one of the world's last frontiers. Brazilians and many foreigners have scrambled to exploit its richness—lumber, iron ore, hydroelectric power, and an extraordinary diversity of flora and fauna. In short, Brazil clearly has great potential, and it should be easily understandable that Brazilian leaders would seek to realize that potential by making the country a *grande potência,* a great power.

Regionalism   Even more than Mexico, Brazil has distinct regions with different political and economic histories. One challenge of any national government is to accommodate these regional differences. Four regions can be identified: the northeast, the southeast, the south, and the Amazon and west. Let's briefly explore their distinct characters.

Sugar production made the northeast Brazil's most prosperous region in its eighteenth century heyday.[51] Sugar production also brought millions of Africans to Brazil in the Atlantic slave trade, creating the multiethnic society Brazil has become. But centuries of sugar cultivation exhausted the soil of the northeast. Combined with cycles of droughts, the decline of the sugar industry has made this region Brazil's poorest one, with per capita incomes at the lowest levels in the country.[52] Yet the northeast remains home to 28 percent of Brazil's population.

In the past two centuries, the southeast has emerged as Brazil's most prosperous region. Brazil's major urban centers, including São Paulo, Rio de Janeiro, and Belo Horizante, are located in the southeast states of São Paulo, Rio de Janeiro, and Minas Gerais,[53] respectively. The foundation for São Paulo's prosperity came from its world-renowned coffee industry, which has produced much wealth in the past two centuries. Coffee profits provided the basis for industrial investments in the southeast region, where 39 percent of Brazil's population now lives on 11 percent of the nation's territory.[54] Most of Brazil's industry is located in the southeast, including its large automobile industry. The state of São Paulo is home to about half the nation's industries, where per capita income is about twice the national average.

Brazil's southern states border Uruguay and Argentina,[55] and like those Spanish-speaking nations, Brazil's south is largely agrarian. The climate here is temperate, and in the far south, the topography resembles the pampas of the two neighboring countries. The 14 percent of Brazilians who live in the south enjoy a relatively high standard of living.

The part of Brazil that the rest of the world most readily identifies as a distinct region is the **Amazon** (Amazonas) and the west.[56] The interest of outsiders has been drawn to the Amazon by concerns about the implications of its development for the world's environment, especially by fears that the greenhouse effect will be exacerbated by excessive clearing of the Amazon rain forest (see chapter 1). Many Brazilians have come to share the sense that the Amazon should be saved from the clear-cutting of the forest and from development that would

threaten the Amazon's biodiversity and the lives of its indigenous inhabitants. However, in the not-too-distant past the Amazon represented opportunity to Brazilians bent upon economic development and national grandeur. It has been a magnet for northeast peasants and southeast slum dwellers heading for the frontier to break out of their poverty as well as for generals and presidents seeking the resources that could feed Brazil's growing industrial sector with abundant raw materials and cheap sources of energy. This vast region, where only 13 percent of Brazilians live, covers 64 percent of the nation's territory.

A nation of such size and regional variety can be difficult to govern from a central capital, as the experiences of other large nations (Russia, Canada, India, and even the United States) can attest. Yet, without a strong centralized government, such nations tend to fragment when regional political forces strive for autonomy. Brazil's history has reflected the tension between centralism and regional desires to avoid domination by the center. Federalism, or more precisely, the character that federalism will take (the balance between federal power and local prerogatives), thus has been a major theme in Brazilian political development.

Socioeconomic Development   Brazil, like Mexico, is usually considered a middle-income country. Its economy has grown rapidly in the twentieth century, with industry leading the way. Although Brazil retains a substantial agricultural sector—best known for its coffee, but successful in producing other items as well—industrial growth has made Brazil one of the most attractive places for foreign investors to locate. Starting in the 1930s, the Brazilian state followed an **import-substituting industrialization (ISI) strategy** of development. It pursued expansionist fiscal (i.e., tax and spending) policies, protected Brazil's nascent industries against foreign competition (through tariffs and other trade barriers), and made considerable investments in the country's infrastructure (roads, bridges, and the like) and state-owned enterprises. The result was one of the most rapid spurts of economic development in the Third World. In terms of industrial development, Brazil clearly surpasses all its South American neighbors. However, as we shall learn, industrialization may have brought a relatively high per capita income to Brazil, but it has not guaranteed that the proceeds of that development have been fairly distributed.

Associated with rapid industrialization in the twentieth century has been rapid population growth and urbanization. Brazil's population was about 17 million in 1900, but it grew nearly ten times in the twentieth century, now reaching more than 170 million. As we mentioned, Brazil includes two of the world's largest metropolises, São Paulo and Rio de Janeiro, plus several other cities whose populations exceed one million. At the same time, Brazil retains a large rural society: almost 50 million people live in towns and the countryside. Thus we must recognize that Brazil presents one of the developing world's most complex societies, a society that no political regime can easily govern.

Brazil's Political Development

Prominent Features of Brazilian Politics As in Mexico, we can identify in Brazil a number of distinguishing features of politics that need explaining. In the twentieth century, Brazil was subjected to several instances of *military intervention in politics*. Usually they were of short duration, intended to force the resignation or ouster of an unacceptable president with a view to scheduling new elections. However, the nation was governed for over two decades (1964–85) by the military as an institution, a period that saw the repression of the regime's opponents and an effort to realize Brazil's great power potential.

Brazil, like Mexico, has a history of *state intervention in the economy*. State ownership of industry, state financing of huge infrastructure and development projects, state subsidized financing of private industry, and state attempts to regulate the market economy have characterized the Brazilian political economy in the last half of the twentieth century. Much of the attention of the current president, **Fernando Henrique Cardoso,** is given to reducing this large state role. *State corporatism* has characterized the government's relationship with economic actors, especially labor and business. Although corporatism is breaking down today—more so for business groups than for labor—past corporatist practices reflect the desire of the Brazilian state to control its economy, especially its labor force.

The centrality of the state in politics is manifested in two other political features that Brazil shares with Mexico: *clientelism* and *corruption.* Brazil's state bureaucracy has been the preserve of clientelism. Political patrons place their clients in positions in the bureaucracy not because of their merits but to reward them for their political loyalty. These patrons also use their connections in the bureaucracy to reward private sector supporters with state contracts. The many huge construction projects undertaken by the government have provided especially lucrative bonanzas for well-connected "clients" of the political leadership. Clientelism almost naturally leads to corruption scandals when it becomes known how individuals who have benefited from these patron-client relationships have distorted the public interest, using the public purse to finance their private projects. In the most celebrated recent corruption case, President Fernando Collor de Mello (1989–92) was impeached in 1992 for the embezzlement of public funds—after running for president on a campaign to clean up corruption.

In contrast to the centralism evident in much of Brazil's political life, there are other forces in the society antithetical to centralism. For our purposes, the two most important are *federalism* and the *fragmentation of the party system.*

Many of Brazil's states have often sought autonomy from a federal government that they worry will govern with the interests of other regions in mind. But central government officials concerned about national security worry that granting too much power to the states may threaten national unity and invite a fragmentation of the federal union. Brazil's more authoritarian regimes have strived to promote unity by establishing central controls over the states. Brazil's more democratic regimes, in contrast, have allowed the states to gather more power to themselves at the expense of the central government.

Related to the dispersion of power associated with federalism is the weakness of the party system, even its fragmentation. Brazilian parties, reflecting the personal aspirations of politicians and regional interests, have proven unusually weak. Politicians have demonstrated little party discipline, displaying instead a marked unwillingness to sacrifice their personal interests for their party's

TABLE 23.5

Brazilian Political Regimes

Date	Regime	Regime Type
1822–89	Empire	Constitutional monarchy
1889–1930	Old Republic	Oligarchical democratic republic
1930–37	Provisional Government (Vargas)	Dictatorship
1937–45	Estado Nôvo	Corporatist state
1946–64	Second Republic	Democratic republic
1964–85	Military Regime	Military dictatorship
1985–present	New Republic	Democratic republic

national purposes. Quite a few have proven unusually fickle, defecting from the parties that supported them for election and switching to other parties after taking their congressional seats.

In this section we'll explore the historical antecedents of these prominent features of Brazilian politics, highlighting how they emerged and how political reformers have sought to address them.

Independence and the Empire   In contrast to the wars of independence that rocked Spanish America and contributed to nearly a half century of political instability in Mexico, Central America, and most of South America in the first half of the nineteenth century, Brazil's independence from Portugal came peacefully and paved the way for a century of political stability and order. Portugal's royal family fled Lisbon before Napoleon's invasion in 1808, moving to Brazil for the duration of the occupation. When the king, Dom João VI, returned after Napoleon's defeat, his son, Dom Pedro I, remained in Brazil. In 1822, Dom Pedro I declared Brazil to be an independent empire. He and his son, Dom Pedro II, ruled the **Brazilian Empire** for sixty-seven years (1822–89).[57]

Brazil's imperial constitution of 1824 created the foundations of a centralized state. Whereas many former Spanish colonies witnessed effective resistance to central state authority on the part of regions, under the Brazilian Empire the central state established centralized authority. This constitutional monarchy created executive, legislative, and judicial branches of government. But it also introduced a "moderating power" (*poder moderador*), reserved to the monarchy, which allowed the monarchy to step in and resolve disputes among the branches of government and the politi-

cal parties. A centralized bureaucracy also emerged during the Empire, but this bureaucracy quickly came to be "colonized" (taken over) by provincial elites seeking to promote their interests. Although the emperor retained unusual powers, the political system also had some liberal features, including a constitution that was promulgated and carefully observed, regular elections to the legislature, and parties that alternated in power.

The monarchy came to an end in 1889 in a military coup backed by coffee planters from São Paulo. Although several issues precipitated the military's actions, the most significant was a conflict between the government and the planters over the abolition of slavery. With the end of the Empire, Brazil became a republic with a presidentialist constitution.

The Old Republic (1889–1930)   The **Old Republic,** as it is now known, was given its birth with the constitution of 1891, when the military chose to limit its role in the political process to that of the "moderating power" formerly held by the emperor. Formally democratic, the constitution became subverted by the oligarchy, the small clique of people who actually wielded real power. Thus the Old Republic can at best be considered a limited democracy. Power was divided between the coffee-rich state of São Paulo and the cattle-raising state of Minas Gerais, hence the pejorative term given to the politics of the Old Republic: *café com leite* (coffee with milk). The dominance of these two states in national politics and their rotation in the office of the presidency was reinforced by another practice called "the politics of the governors."

That procedure allowed the incumbent president to choose his successor and then enforce his decision on the electorate through a vertically downward chain of pressure. The president's choice was imposed on the state governors and *coroneis,* or local political bosses (the Brazilian equivalents of the Mexican *caciques*). The local bosses' task was to turn out the votes on election day, making sure that the president's designated candidate won. *Coronelismo* is a Brazilian variant of clientelism, with local notables (usually landlords) serving as patrons to the less advantaged people in patron-client relationships.[58] Through this process, the southeast region controlled national politics, excluding the south and the northeast from political power. The Old Republic thereby introduced a strong element of federalism into Brazilian politics.

As the success of *coronelismo* implies, the rural underclass could not act independently in politics. Moreover, neither a strong business class nor a large industrial proletariat existed in Brazil at this time. Brazilian politics in the Old Republic was controlled by landowners, its economic development driven by the coffee growers' link to the international economy. These rural oligarchs preferred a weak central state. Federalism flourished, with regional governors rather than the central government holding the greater power.

In 1930, the Old Republic faced a crisis in its "coffee with milk" system. Opposition to the hegemony of the São Paulo–Minas Gerais alliance had been mounting in the states of the northeast and south, particularly in Rio Grande do Sul. A group of young army officers also opposed the southeast's hegemony. These two groups were supported by the small but growing urban business class and by the coffee growers, who were hurt by President Washington Luis's policies. When the president violated the established system of rotation in office by choosing someone from his home state as his successor, the main opposition party led a revolt that threatened to overthrow both the president and his designated successor. Alarmed at the increasing polarization of the political elites, the military chose to invoke its "moderating power" and moved in. The officers were convinced that political reforms were necessary, however, and they did not wish to replace a civilian government. Within a few days the junta stepped down in favor of **Getulio Vargas,** the leader of the opposition party, the Liberal Alliance.

President Getulio Vargas (center, in civilian dress), flanked by officers. Military support was a vital element of Vargas's *Estado Nôvo.*

Vargas and the Estado Nôvo (1930–45)   The Liberal Alliance favored an early return to constitutional rule, though segments of the military opposed it on the grounds that elections would only return the old elite to power. In 1934, Vargas approved a new constitution that included elements of both political liberalism and social reformism. But as the global depression jolted Brazil, sending coffee prices tumbling and derailing the first stages of the country's industrialization, the ruling elites had to face a new constellation of opposing forces.[59]

Vargas's Liberal Alliance and the radical junior officers were quickly superseded by two mass-oriented movements, the neo-fascist *integralista* movement and the communist-supported National Liberation Alliance (ANL). The *integralista* movement received most of its support from economic nationalists who opposed international capitalism and the coffee growers who were linked to it. Because they were Catholic or had other traditional ties, these people opposed the communists and found their political home in a Brazilian brand of fascism. As the name implies, the *integralistas* had a nationalist project for integrating all aspects of Brazilian life. The communist-oriented ANL, for its part, attracted Brazil's small but growing working class along with segments of its discontented middle class.

As in many other parts of the world, communism and fascism in Brazil were now set against each other. National politics became polarized precisely at the time when the liberal reformist constitution of 1934 was being put into effect. In addition, Vargas manipulated these two oppositions to make the situation appear to be even more polarized. Since the Brazilian military feared communism every bit as much as it disliked "irresponsible" politicians, the officers invoked their "moderating power" once again, vesting exclusive civilian authority in Vargas. Armed with military backing, Vargas established a dictatorship and began constructing his corporatist *Estado Nôvo* (**New State**).

The period of the *Estado Nôvo* is important for the subsequent development of Brazilian politics because it concentrated power in the central government. In doing so it created three long-lasting effects. First, the corporatist labor legislation of the *Estado Nôvo* gave control of the labor movement to the state, particularly to the minister of labor.[60] This approach provided the government with a means of mobilizing the working class and keeping its demands under control. It deprived Brazilian workers of the right to organize their own unions, and cut off the outlawed communists from their natural working-class base. Second, the state began to take a strong, relatively interventionist role in the direction of the economy and economic development.[61] And third, the New State's centralization of power marked a major political dividing line for many years to come. From here on, Brazilians would be divided between those who favored an interventionist state with a strong executive and those who wished a return to the politics of the Old Republic, with its weaker executive and its diffusion of power to the states and *coroneis*.

Brazil's involvement in the Second World War on the side of the Western Allies undermined any legitimacy that the dictatorial *Estado Nôvo* might have created for itself by stabilizing social conflict. As the military fought alongside the United States and Britain to preserve the world for democracy, the lack of democracy at home became a source of incongruity. Vargas himself recognized the dilemma and therefore planned for the return of democracy by developing a strong following among the corporatized labor movement. Under his leadership, liberal democracy returned to Brazil with the end of the war. But the real key to the return of democracy lay in the perspectives of the military, who held the ultimate source of coercive power.

The Second Republic (1946–64)   Brazilian populism emerged with the return of democratic rule.[62] While the first administration following the end of the *Estado Nôvo* was the conservative administration of General Eurico Dutra, in 1951 Vargas was swept back into power by a populist coalition of urban workers in the Brazilian Workers' Party (PTB) and old-time clientelistic politicians in the Social Democratic Party (PSD). His opposition was primarily composed of conservatives who favored laissez-faire policies and a weak central state. Vargas initially steered a delicate path between market-oriented orthodoxy and state-centered economic nationalism, but by 1953 had chosen the latter path, a choice revealed in his support for the creation of the state-owned oil company, Petrobras. Vargas also came to depend more and more on his working-class following. However, when Vargas made **João Goulart** his minister of labor in 1953 to strengthen his support on the left, opposition to his government grew. His chief adversaries were the middle class, which was threatened by inflation, and the thoroughly anti-leftist military, for whom Goulart's pro-worker orientation was an internal security threat.

When the military invoked its moderating power and moved to overthrow Vargas in 1954, he committed suicide. The 1955 elections returned the Workers Party–Social Democratic choice of **Juscelino Kubitschek,** with Goulart as vice president. When business-oriented conservatives and the more rabid ultra-right attempted to prevent Kubitschek's assumption of power, the military staged another coup, this time to ensure Kubitschek's inauguration. Democratic constitutional rule was upheld, although it was becoming obvious that its continuation depended upon military support.

Kubitschek continued the populist developmental policies of Vargas, perhaps with even more support from national industrialists than Vargas had received. Brazil's economic development proceeded apace, with economic growth rates reaching 8 to 9 percent annually as foreign investment and foreign loans streamed into Brazil. However, this development exacerbated both inflation and trade balance problems, leading the International Monetary Fund (IMF) to propose a stabilization plan in 1958. This stabilization plan threatened Kubitschek's ability to reach his economic development targets and to preserve his reputation and political future. Kubitschek rejected the IMF plan in 1959, to the acclaim of Brazilian nationalists.

The 1961 presidential election was a victory for democratic constitutionalism as the left-wing alliance was defeated by **Jânio Quadros,** the popular governor of São Paulo. Goulart was again elected vice president. However, the apparent gain for democratic legitimacy quickly became a loss when Quadros resigned less than a year after being inaugurated. He knew that the conservatives and the military could not abide Goulart, his vice president and constitutional successor, because of the latter's suspected far-left sympathies. Goulart was forced to wait fourteen months before taking full power, ruling as a parliamentary president.

By the time Goulart assumed the full powers of the presidency, he was faced with a full-blown economic crisis. Inflation was mounting, mobilizing opposition from the working class on the left to the capitalists and upper classes on the right. Balance of payments pressures, reflecting an excess of imports over exports, were inhibiting Brazil's ability to import badly needed industrial goods, thus threatening future economic growth. Furthermore, the working class had gained more autonomy from political control since it was not incorporated into any of the parties.[63] The right favored stabilizing the business climate while the left favored the nationalization of privately owned companies. In this polarized climate, the presence in the presidency of a man who was suspected by the right of leftist sympathies created an unworkable situation. The right would not cooperate with Goulart, so he turned to the left for support.

In fact, Goulart turned so far to the left as to become a serious advocate of land reform. His left turn, however, only confirmed the right's view of him and gave the military a justification to move against him, ostensibly to protect Brazil from communism. In April 1964 the military removed Goulart from power. But rather than arranging new elections as it had when exercising its "moderating power" in the past, the military settled in to rule as an institution.[64]

Military Rule (1964–85)   The two decades of **military rule** in Brazil proved less politically disruptive than did other Latin American military dictatorships, especially when compared with the events that followed Argentina's 1976 coup or the 1973 overthrow of Salvador Allende's socialist regime in Chile by a junta led by General Augusto Pinochet. In those nations the military clamped down severely on the left, "disappearing" thousands of progressive activists or suspected activists, effectively banning civilian politics and the public activities of politicians altogether. In contrast, Brazil's military allowed some democratic institutions to survive the fall of Goulart, although the activities of the Congress were greatly restricted and the former political parties were disbanded. Elections continued to be held. It is interesting that the military regime made electoral performance an indicator of its legitimacy. However, the military manipulated the electoral rules so as to ensure a government majority in the Congress, thereby undermining the legislature's legitimacy.

Although government candidates won congressional majorities in 1966 and 1968, high percentages of blank ballots cast doubt on the popularity of the generals in power. After pro-Kubitschek figures won governorships in Minas Gerais and Guanabara in 1966, the military issued Institutional Act No. 2, a government decree that abolished the existing parties. Urban guerrilla violence and agitation in the legislature followed the military's failure to carry out a promised liberalization in 1968. These events strengthened the hand of hardliners in the military and helped to touch off the most repressive stage of the regime (1968–74), marked by the issuance of Institutional Act No. 5, which gave unlimited powers to the president to protect national security.[65] Generally, the military regime strengthened the executive and the central government to the detriment of legislative bodies and the states.

The repression unleashed by Institutional Act No. 5 proved mild by comparison to what the

Chilean military did after the 1973 coup and the crimes that the Argentine military perpetrated in its "Dirty War" against "subversion" in the late 1970s. Still, the Brazilian military regime inflicted arbitrary detentions, exile, and torture on its victims. Hundreds disappeared or were killed for their "subversive" politics. It is significant that the Brazilian military entrusted its anti-communist crusade to an intelligence agency, the National Intelligence Service (SNI). However, in the campaign against subversion, the SNI and other intelligence agencies proved too autonomous for the comfort of many military leaders who worried that they could no longer control them.[66]

Throughout the military's rule, factional infighting between hard-liners and those military leaders more disposed to an early return to democracy gave the regime's opponents opportunities to push for a liberalization of the political system. By 1974, a major division had appeared between those who wanted to loosen the grips of the state's repression and those who wanted to maintain complete control over society. The more moderate faction prevailed, buoyed in part by fears that the repressive apparatus (the SNI and other internal security agencies) was developing an independence that could eventually allow it to be used against other elements within the military. A "decompression" process began.

One of the military regime's greatest challenges was legitimating its rule. Because it was not born of a true revolution (though the military called its seizure of power in 1964 by that term) and because it was not disposed to the populist, redistributive politics of social welfare for the poor, the Brazilian military could not generate the popular support that Mexico's postrevolutionary rulers enjoyed. In an effort to simulate legitimacy, the military tried to create a two-party electoral competition that would in some ways mirror Mexico's one-party-dominant regime. A pro-regime party was founded called the National Renovating Alliance, or ARENA. A smaller, weaker opposition party, the Brazilian Democratic Movement (MDB), was also encouraged to form. The idea was that, like Mexico's PRI, ARENA would always win. And like the weak opposition parties in Mexico, the MDB would contest elections but lose.

However, when the regime held very strictly controlled elections in 1974 that severely constrained the opposition, the oppositionist Democratic Movement still won. Various efforts to stack the electoral deck in the military's favor after 1974 kept ARENA and its successors in control of Congress, but no one was fooled by the blatant rigging of the contest between regime and opposition. For example, in 1978 the military banned the existing parties (both ARENA and the MDB) in an effort to destroy the MDB before it became too popular. ARENA reformed as the Democratic Social Party (PDS) while many members of the MDB created the Party of the Brazilian Democratic Movement (PMDB) and returned to their struggle to oust the pro-military party.

In the end, the military's rule created a larger central state presence in Brazilian society, especially in its economy. However, after the spectacular rise in oil prices in the mid-1970s, the pro-growth policies pursued by the military government led it to take on large volumes of foreign debt, which came due in the early 1980s at a time when Brazil could not repay its obligations (just like Mexico). Brazil put off a severe restructuring of its economy for longer than any other major Latin American country, waiting until the mid-1990s, a decade after the military left power, to adopt neoliberal restructuring policies. In the meantime, Brazilian society suffered a decade of hyperinflation.

The military's quest for Brazilian greatness also encouraged it to undertake massive development projects in the Amazon and other parts of Brazil, projects that have proven environmentally disastrous. These projects generally benefited society's "haves" to the detriment of its "have-nots." While the nation's gross domestic product (GDP) grew immensely during the military's two decades (an average of about 7.5 percent annually),[67] the poor gained little. The military saddled its civilian successors with a development model that had exhausted its potential, enormous foreign debts, a bloated central bureaucracy, environmental crises, and the most unequal income distribution of any large country in the world. One had to ask, as civilians returned to power in the mid-1980s without the coercive force of the military behind them, "Would this society be governable?"

Explaining Brazilian Authoritarianism

Why did democracy fail in Brazil? How could the military manage to rule for two decades? These questions have haunted Brazilians and the social scientists who have studied their society. Let's look at the conditions for democracy laid out in chapter 10 and see if they help us understand Brazil's experience with authoritarianism.

State Institutions Brazil's two previous democratic regimes came to their ends in 1930 and 1964 as the result of impasses that emerged among the civilian politicians running those regimes. In the Second Republic, state institutions—the constitutional order—contributed to the political crisis that ended with the military's seizure of power. The Second Republic had a presidential system. Popular candidates could win the presidency even without strong party backing. Unfortunately, Brazil's party system failed to produce reliable majority coalitions for any president. With three major national parties and other regional parties, no single party gained a majority in either house of the bicameral Congress. Federalism encouraged politicians to pay close attention to the needs of local constituencies, often leading them to vote against their national parties on important bills. Without majorities to back their reform measures, presidents were tempted to bypass Congress by issuing decrees or to engage in popular mobilization to gather support. Goulart's use of popular mobilization to push an intransigent Congress into accepting agrarian reform and other populist policies provoked the military to stage its coup in 1964.[68]

Elites Committed to Democracy Various groups with elite status held at best a lukewarm commitment to democracy from the time of the fall of the Old Republic until late into the military regime. Traditional political elites—local elites (the *coroenis*), governors, and political bosses—were willing to work through formally democratic institutions, but they engaged in practices inimical to democracy. Even when operating through political parties and contesting elections, these traditional elites practiced clientelism, regionalism, and personal power.[69] Traditional elites might figure out how to manipulate democratic institutions to promote their interests, but democracy was not their primary goal. In 1964, traditional elites conspired to help bring off the military coup that ousted Goulart.[70]

Military elites have also shown at best conditional support for democracy, at worst outright hostility to it. On the one hand, liberals within the military managed to retain constitutional forms during the military dictatorship, including elections and political parties. (Of course, they permitted only the parties they created rather than the pre-existing parties). These *blandos*, as they were called (the softliners), also pushed to liberalize the regime after 1974. However, the *blandos* were offset by the *duros* (or hardliners), those opposed to democracy. In addition, from the late 1950s onward, the Brazilian military adopted a doctrine of national security and development alleging that threats to the nation's security came from insurgencies and other revolutionary challenges to the state. The military regarded civilian politicians as incapable of confronting these internal security threats.[71] This internal security doctrine, we should note, went beyond the military's earlier notion that it held the "moderating power" in the Brazilian constitutional structure, for although the moderating power might provide a justification for the removal of a chief executive, it did not justify long-term rule by the military as an institution. In either event, however, we can see that military elites could be indifferent to democracy or hostile to it.

One final elite group whose commitment to democracy has been in question are the technocrats who came to staff the large state bureaucracy, especially in those ministries, agencies, and state-owned enterprises charged with promoting national economic development. Many of these technocrats have been trained in engineering programs or in neoclassical economics, disciplines that have emphasized the efficacy of rational planning processes. Guillermo O'Donnell has argued that technocrats tended to consider the messy politics of populism, in which politicians like Goulart or Vargas mobilized the urban masses by promising inflationary spending programs (subsidies for staple goods, cheap public transportation, higher minimum wages, among others), to be threatening to their capacity to plan and administer the economy. Hence, civilian technocrats—many of whose services were indeed retained by the military after they came to power—and military technocrats preferred to see the masses demobilized so that they could more "rationally" operate the economy.[72]

The foregoing suggests that elites in Brazil have been lukewarm toward democracy, if not hostile to it. Although many have found themselves able to prosper under democratic institutions, they have also been able to get along well under authoritarianism. Moreover, some elites have considered democracy to be inimical to their interests.

National Wealth and Its Distribution If the hypothesis that higher levels of national wealth tend to promote democracy were to hold true in its simplest form, we would expect Brazil to be democratic before many of its South American neighbors because its national wealth is the greatest on the continent. However, in addition to a high per capita income, Brazil has a highly unequal distribution of income and wealth, the worst of the world's largest nations. Income inequality is manifested in several ways that have implications for democracy.

In the countryside, where as many as a quarter of Brazilians still live, rural poverty and landlessness permits the local bosses, the *coroneis*, to use their economic power and their connections with the state to dominate the lives of peasants and rural workers. Their domination has kept the rural masses from effectively articulating a preference for democracy, perhaps even from realizing that democracy could be an alternative to authoritarian rule. Nor can the rural poor, often in debt to the *coroneis* and fearful of their willingness to use violence against their opponents, create a real alternative to the control of local government by the political machines of the rural bosses.

The millions of urban poor in the mushrooming *favelas* (slums) surrounding Brazil's cities serve to remind the rich, who live as well as or better than people do in the world's richest nations, of what could become of their privileged status and their material well-being. Associated with inequality are high levels of crime in Brazil's major cities. Consequently, there has been considerable support from the well-to-do for hardline policies that would clamp down on antisocial behaviors resulting from inequality, even if at the expense of civil liberties.

Even when democratic institutions have been in place, those opposed to redistributive policies have found ways to defeat legislative or presidential efforts to address inequality. In the early 1960s, frustration at the Congress's unwillingness to pass land reform legislation led President Goulart to undertake the populist mobilization of the poor that prompted the military coup. Maldistribution of income often leads to the rise of populist leaders; those leaders threaten the middle and upper classes and encourage them to side with military officers against democracy.

Private Enterprise Brazil has had a sizable private sector even while the state has owned many large firms in important industries. The private sector worried both about the growth of inflation in the years leading up to 1964 and about the populist mobilization of workers and peasants in which Goulart was engaged at the time of the coup.[73] However, Brazilian entrepreneurs came to join the opponents of the military regime in the 1970s after the economic successes of the early years of the military's rule began to wane. Furthermore, the private sector became frustrated with the growth of the state-owned sector of the economy, as businesspeople thought they were being denied opportunities to make investments in profitable industries because of the state's presence.[74] Thus Brazil's business sector has alternately opposed and supported democracy.

The Middle Class Brazil's large middle class consists mainly of the many white-collar employees, self-employed professionals, and small business owners necessary in an industrial economy. While the middle class might desire the political and personal freedoms associated with democracy, there are other political goals that its members seek as well. Among them are price stability and prosperity. The inflation that came to characterize Brazil in the early 1960s brought the middle class into the coalition supporting the coup. During the later 1960s, especially during the years of the economic miracle (1968–74), support for the military regime by the middle class was high because of the prosperity it enjoyed in those years.[75] However, middle-class support for authoritarianism has been as conditional as its support for democracy. When their interests have been adversely affected by authoritarian rule, as for example when the military's crackdowns on dissidents put their children in prison, members of the middle class have advocated democracy. Brazil's economic difficulties in the later 1970s and 1980s also led the middle class to oppose the continuation of military rule.

Support of the Disadvantaged for Democracy

The most important point about the support or nonsupport of the disadvantaged for democracy is that, until recently, neither the rural poor nor the urban poor were in a position to act upon a preference for democracy even if they had one. In the later 1950s and early 1960s, the working class had become increasingly politically active under the Workers Party of Brazil and President Goulart. But the political mobilization of labor became one of the reasons other groups in society supported the 1964 coup. During much of the military regime, the government sought to use the corporatist labor laws originally written during the *Estado Nôvo* to keep organized labor under control. From 1977 onward, however, a "new unionism" within Brazilian labor played an essential role in opposing the military's continued rule, using strikes to put pressure on the military to leave power.[76]

Others among Brazil's poor, especially those organized in grassroots popular movements, also opposed military rule. Like the unions, however, these grassroots movements were weak or nonexistent in the early years of the military's rule. When in the later 1970s they were able to act, they came to promote democratization of the regime and an expansion of the definition of who ought to be allowed to participate politically. The nonexistence of such organizations in the 1960s, however, made it difficult for the poor to articulate their needs to the state.[77]

An Active Civil Society and a Democratic Political Culture

As the previous comments should suggest, during the years of the Second Republic, many elements of Brazilian society were what could be described as semi-loyal to the society's democratic institutions.[78] They found themselves willing to desert the nation's democratic institutions when their interests were not served by democracy. Moreover, a major aspect of Brazilian political culture until recently could be labeled **patrimonialism:** the sense that much of society needs political patrons—local bosses, people with connections to state agencies that can provide material resources, even a state that can dole out projects that benefit specific groups or localities. Patrimonialism is necessary, in this view, because people are themselves unable to participate independently in the political system or are unable to accomplish collective projects on their own. Of course, this patrimonial political culture was much cultivated by the *coroneis,* the state governors, and other traditional political elites who came to power with its backing. The military, in contrast, simply sought a nonpoliticized society in which people did not turn to politics to address their needs. They preferred that people focus their attention on the exploits of the Brazilian national soccer team—the world's best in the early 1970s—than on national political affairs. Given these attitudes held by elite groups and the pervasiveness of low levels of education among the masses, it should come as no surprise that Brazil had little in the way of an active civil society until well into the 1970s, after the military had been in power for over a decade.

Education and Freedom of Information

In contrast to the mass media in some of its South American neighbors—for example, Argentina and Chile—but like Mexico, Brazil's mass media have been dominated by television. Television has reached even the many illiterates or semi-literates who populate Brazil's *favelas.* Brazil's inequalities have historically extended to severe inequalities in education, and the lack of education has led many Brazilians to become trapped in the system of *coronelismo* described earlier in this chapter. Even as late as 1997, 16 percent of Brazilian adults were illiterate and 29 percent of students did not reach the fifth grade. (Mexico had 10 percent illiterate and 14 percent not reaching the fifth grade; Chile had 5 percent illiterate and less than 1 percent failing to reach the fifth grade.)[79] These low levels of educational attainment created a society vulnerable to control by political bosses and easily manipulated by the mass media. Those not subject to the control of political bosses may nevertheless be constrained in their political choices because the media, especially television, were controlled under military rule and thus disinclined to broadcast the opposition's messages. In short, continuing low levels of education among the poor and the dominance of television among the mass media limited the capacity of Brazilians to formulate and advocate democratic alternatives during the military dictatorship.

A Homogeneous Society Brazil's society is far from ethnically homogeneous. As many as 40 percent of Brazilians can claim some descent from African slaves, and others are descended from native Americans. On the other hand, in contrast to societies in Eastern Europe and even to some extent the United States, these ethnic or racial differences have had little salience in Brazilian political conflict. Certainly those Brazilians of African heritage are more likely to be among the poor and thus subject to clientelistic control. Myths about "racial democracy" in Brazil have hidden the reality of prejudice and discrimination. However, ethnic differences have not led to political conflict in Brazil and have not therefore promoted dictatorship.

A Favorable International Environment The United States has had much less influence on South American nations than on Mexico or the small countries of the Caribbean and Central America. However, the United States can influence politics even in more distant nations like Brazil through its diplomacy and its foreign economic assistance programs. During Goulart's presidency, the U.S. embassy conspired with anti-Goulart politicians and provided some intelligence assistance to those conspirators as they aided the military in bringing off its coup. The United States then quickly recognized the new military government. U.S. assistance may not have been critical in bringing authoritarianism to Brazil, but the U.S. did nothing to stop it.

Brazilian Economic Development

One of the central tenets of the military's internal security doctrine was the notion that subversion prospered in circumstances in which economic stagnation prevented people from achieving their goals in life. The military thus made the promotion of economic development a high priority in the struggle against communism. Once the military regime had eliminated any evidence of insurrectionary violence in the early 1970s, maintaining healthy economic growth rates became its most important source of legitimacy.

To promote economic development, the Brazilian military embarked on a **state-led growth strategy.** The state took on large roles both in the overall direction of the economy and in investing public capital in specific industries. The military's ambitions for Brazilian grandeur led it to lean toward large projects and those that emphasized high technology. As Peter Evans has argued, this approach meant that Brazilian businesspeople often were unable to make the new investments sought by the military government because they lacked sufficient capital (money)—the projects were too big for them—or they lacked access to technology. Hence the Brazilian state encouraged foreign investors to enter some of the higher technology industries such as automobiles and petrochemicals. Today several of the world's largest automobile firms have sizable operations in Brazil, including Volkswagen, Ford, and General Motors. At the same time, the state's national development bank channeled investment capital to private firms to encourage them to develop other sectors of the economy. Domestic entrepreneurs came to be involved in important joint ventures with foreign firms so as to facilitate the transfer of technology in pharmaceuticals and computers in the 1970s and 1980s.[80] As Evans argues, in some state agencies, very able administrators learned the skills necessary to encourage development in specific sectors of the economy.[81]

In other areas of the economy, especially where the state considered investment to be of strategic importance, the state itself became the investor, creating state-owned companies (public enterprises) designed to operate under capitalist logic. Though they were owned by the state, they had to observe the market forces of supply and demand in setting prices, and they were expected to earn profits. The state became a large investor in the steel, petroleum, aluminum, mining, and shipbuilding industries, among others. In essence, the Brazilian military propelled the economy further in the direction of import substitution as opposed to free international trade. It sought to produce not only finished light consumer goods in Brazil but also consumer durables (autos, refrigerators, televisions) as well as intermediate goods (steel, petrochemicals) and capital goods (factory equipment). The essence of this strategy was to make Brazil as economically self-sufficient as possible, reducing its dependence on imports to the lowest feasible levels.

However, the large state investments had their costs. The military's economic strategy encouraged the intensive use of energy, especially oil. But Brazil has few deposits of petroleum, making imports mandatory. The oil crises of the 1970s, which provided a great opportunity for oil-rich Mexico, threatened to wreck the Brazilian economic miracle. When world oil prices shot up in 1974, so did Brazil's oil bill. Rather than discourage consumption and slow the economy, the generals borrowed from international banks. Large infrastructure projects and borrowing to provide finance capital for the national development bank also contributed to the nation's foreign debt, which reached about $85 billion at the beginning of the 1980s.

Thus the Brazilian miracle emphasized an import substitution model that was capital intensive, technology intensive, and energy intensive. Although this model produced high economic growth rates, the nation's dependence on international sources of capital grew. This pattern of development did not begin to meet Brazilian society's needs in terms of jobs, however, a flaw in the development strategy that had unfortunate consequences for income distribution. While Brazilian incomes may have grown significantly *on average* during the military regime, income distribution became so unequal that Brazil now has one of worst structures of income distribution in the world (see table 2.2 on page 37).

Brazil's New Democracy

In January 1985, Tancredo Neves, a leader of the opposition to the military regime, was elected Brazil's first civilian president in over two decades. His election came as a surprise to the military leadership, which had stacked the electoral college with its own supporters. Neves's vice presidential running mate was **José Sarney,** recently the leader of the pro-government party, the PDS. On the eve of his inauguration, Neves, a seventy-four-year-old survivor of the Second Republic (1946–64), was hospitalized with an intestinal ailment from which he did not recover. So, on March 15, 1985, José Sarney entered the presidency. Although Neves and Sarney had been elected indirectly, their successors would be directly elected by the Brazilian people. Brazil's new constitution, approved in 1988, inaugurated the **New Republic,** a presidentialist, federal republic.

TABLE 23.6

Brazilian Presidents Since 1930		
Name	**Term of Office**	**Mode of Succession**
Getulio Vargas	1930–45	Populist dictator
Eurico Dutra	1946–50	Elected
Getulio Vargas	1951–54	Elected
João Café Filho	1954–55	Assumed office as vice president
Juscelino Kubitschek	1956–61	Elected
Jânio Quadros	1961	Elected
João Goulart	1961–64	Assumed office as vice president
Humberto Castelo Branco	1964–67	Military dictator
Artur Costa e Silva	1967–69	Military dictator
Emilio Garrastazú Médici	1969–74	Military dictator
Ernesto Geisel	1974–79	Military dictator
João Figueiredo	1979–85	Military dictator
José Sarney	1985–90	Indirectly elected while vice president
Fernando Collor de Mello	1990–92	Elected
Itamar Franco	1992–95	Assumed office as vice president
Fernando Henrique Cardoso	1995–present	Elected

Although a democratic regime, the New Republic has not spared Brazil from political strife. Sarney and the new Congress were immediately deadlocked over economic stabilization plans during his four-year presidential term. Unable to count on any party to support him in the Congress, Sarney engaged in the widespread use of patronage in exchange for support for his economic policies. But patronage politics ended up undermining the policy coherence of his economic stabilization efforts; distributing patronage required federal expenditures at a time when economic stabilization dictated that expenditures be curtailed. Hyperinflation resulted, nearing 2,000 percent before Sarney left office.[82]

When direct presidential elections were held in 1989, **Fernando Collor de Mello,** a former governor of the northeast state of Alagoas with unprecedented skills as a television campaigner, took office on a populist platform of cleaning up corruption in government. Within three years, Collor would be impeached on charges of corruption. A prime example of personalism in politics, Collor had created his own party to campaign for the presidency, but he brought few of his fellow party members into the Congress and commanded very little loyalty there. Amid charges of misappropriating $20 million, he resigned in 1992. His successor was the vice president, **Itamar Franco,** an impulsive politician with little interest in the presidency. Only with the election to the presidency of Fernando Henrique Cardoso in 1994 has Brazil found solid leadership.

What were the forces that brought democracy's return to Brazil? Do the institutions put in place in the New Republic promote political stability and a capacity to confront the daunting social and economic problems facing the nation? What are the greatest challenges facing Brazil as it enters the twenty-first century?

Democratization   Democracy came to Brazil only after a long process of political liberalization in which the military regime sought to use democratic institutions to place its allies in positions of power. The opposition fought for democracy on two fronts. The first was the electoral arena, in which an opposition party sought to deny victory to the government's allies. Initially, that party was

the Brazilian Democracy Movement (MDB), which later changed its name to the **Party of the Brazilian Democracy Movement (PMDB).** The second front consisted of non-electoral arenas, where grassroots organizations and the organized labor movement fought for the democratization of local government and labor relations. Progress in all arenas came slowly, as the military managed to control the transition to civilian role and to limit progress in the democratization of society. The government of President Ernesto Geisel (1974–79) began a process of "decompression" in 1974. A civilian became president in 1985, and the first direct elections for the presidency did not take place until 1989.

The most severe repression by the military regime coincided with the period known as the **economic miracle** (1968–74). By 1974, after a successful campaign against armed opponents of its rule, the military could not easily claim that repression was necessary to counter subversion, since the subversives had been killed or imprisoned. Moreover, the campaign against urban and rural guerrillas had already begun to have an impact on those members of the middle class whose family members were accused of subversion. As mentioned earlier, liberal members of the military also had become worried about the growing autonomy of the state intelligence agency in charge of countering subversion.[83]

Seeking to capitalize on the good feelings associated with the economic miracle and to rein in the hardliners, moderates in the military supported the decompression policy, one element of which involved allowing more open elections for the Congress and governorships in 1974. To the military's chagrin, the opposition Brazilian Democratic Movement defeated the pro-government ARENA. Having opened the electoral process, the moderates in the military could not easily close it down, but they feared losing the Congress to the opposition if ARENA did not have some guarantees that would ensure its victories. Thus began a long series of electoral "reforms" intended to forestall a genuine opposition win. Perhaps the most dramatic of these reforms came in 1979 when the ARENA-dominated Congress voted to dissolve the existing political parties (ARENA included) and to create new rules for party registration designed to fragment the opposition by making the rules for registration easier than they had been in the past. Civilian supporters of the military formed a new party, the PDS, which continued to hold a majority in the Congress, but it became increasingly obvious that it lacked genuine popular support. To retain a government majority in the electoral colleges that chose state governors and the president, the government appointed one member of the senate from each state, so-called "bionic senators."[84]

As economic problems such as the foreign debt crisis and increasing restiveness of industrial workers mounted in the late 1970s and early 1980s, the government's efforts to stack the deck electorally proved inadequate. The truth was that the military's social support bases had begun to abandon the regime. The military could forestall the advent of a civilian regime, but it could not legitimize its own rule.

Perhaps the most notable allies to abandon the military's coalition in the mid-1970s were businesspeople in Brazil's private sector. Businesspeople had become dissatisfied by the growth of state-owned enterprises during the miracle, an expansion of the public sector that they saw as coming at the expense of investment opportunities that they would be denied. In 1974–76, entrepreneurs led a campaign against the expansion of the state-owned sector. Businesspeople also had become frustrated by what they saw as excessive bureaucratic autonomy under the military; they preferred the more regular access to decision makers promised by democratic institutions.[85] In addition, business leaders found themselves somewhat embarrassed when dealing with business partners or customers in other parts of the world to have to admit that they lived and did business in a military regime. By the late 1970s, business leaders also felt that the military had mismanaged the economy, undermining one of the military's major justifications for being in power.[86]

Other social groups withdrew their support in much the same way that business became disenchanted with the military. Some elements of the middle class such as lawyers and journalists advocated democracy so that their civil liberties would be protected. Given that members of some middle- and upper-class families had been treated as "ordinary" subversives—and thus tortured and held without trial—during the 1968–74 period, the withdrawal of support for the military by many members of the middle class comes as no surprise.[87] The middle class may seek the economic security that dictatorships sometimes provide, but many elements of the middle class value their civil liberties, which dictatorships often trample. Traditional political elites prospered under military rule, but many abandoned the military when it seemed prudent for their political futures.[88]

Meanwhile, the difficulty of producing progressive change through the channels of representation available during the military's rule led many groups among Brazil's poor to create new organizations independent of the political parties or officially sanctioned labor unions. Although grassroots organizations and the "new labor" movement cannot be credited as the only source of democratization in the 1970s and 1980s, they did pose challenges to the military regime. Grassroots organizations ran the gamut of issue areas, from women's organizations to environmental movements to neighborhood associations. Many became active during the military government because no other political organizations—parties or government agencies—gave adequate attention to their members' needs.

Neighborhood associations, for instance, formed to make demands on state and local governments for the extension of public services: utilities, law and order, roads, and schools. These associations perceived that a transition to democracy would be necessary to get the representation that could bring responses to their demands. Popular organizations did not succeed in creating a national movement that shaped the transition process, but they did succeed in raising people's consciousness of the importance of democracy for meeting the needs of ordinary Brazilians.[89] The Catholic church, a progressive force in Brazil, supported grassroots groups and provided a critical voice when few others could be found. Popular movements undoubtedly contributed to the willingness of politicians and representatives of interest groups representing better-off elements of Brazilian society to push for regime liberalization.

The "new union" movement reflected a desire of some segments of the industrial labor force to escape the corporatist organizations of the state-run labor movement. In a wave of strikes begun in 1978–79 by metalworkers and eventually extending to many other industries, the new union movement focused attention on the capacity of ordinary people to organize themselves and make demands on the government. The strikes produced only modest gains for workers, and they also demonstrated to the movement's leaders that they needed to create a political organization to focus their efforts at the national level. The **Workers' Party (PT)** was formed after the new law regulating party formation was passed in 1979.[90]

The pressure for democratization increased dramatically in the early 1980s. The most dramatic example of that pressure came in the *Diretas Já* (Direct Elections Now) campaign of 1984. Many opposition politicians, social movements, and labor unions participated in this mass movement, which swept the country. The military resisted the demand for direct elections in 1984, but only after alienating many of its civilian allies, several of whom left the pro-government party to form a party of their own. That new party supported Tancredo Neves, the Brazilian Democracy Movement's candidate in the 1985 indirect elections; together they defeated the military's candidate, thereby ushering out the military regime.

The New Republic and Its Institutions

Brazil's transition to democracy included the writing of a new constitution, completed in 1988. In many of its fundamental elements, the lengthy new constitution drafted by the Constituent Assembly (245 articles) looks much like the constitution of the Second Republic. The military and President Sarney significantly defeated an effort by reformers to introduce a parliamentary regime in Brazil that would have increased the powers of the legislature by giving it an opportunity to vote no-confidence in the executive (including the cabinet officers in charge of the military branches).[91]

The Institutional Structure   Roughly patterned on the U.S. Constitution's principle of separation of powers, the New Republic provides for a **president** who is both head of state and head of government (like the U.S. president). The president is now elected directly by the people.

The bicameral **Congress** consists of the **Chamber of Deputies,** the lower house with 513 members drawn from the country's twenty-six states and the Federal District of Brasilia, the national capital; and the **Senate,** the upper house, which has three representatives from each state and the Federal District (eighty-one total). Members of the Chamber of Deputies serve four-year terms; senators serve eight years. The powers of the two houses are evenly balanced, with both possessing the right to initiate legislation and review the federal budget. Congress may also override presidential vetoes. The **Supreme Court** has the power of judicial review.

Brazil's federal structure gives ample powers to the governors of the twenty-six states and the Federal District. Each state and the Federal District also has a unicameral state legislature. County-level governments called *municipios* are the main institutions of local government.

The Electoral System and Its Consequences   To most observers, the most notable aspect of relations between the executive and legislative branches is the difficulty that presidents have in putting together majority coalitions for their legislative initiatives. Consequently, Brazilian presidents have found it difficult to accomplish major policy objectives. Weak parties (and the large number of them) play the most important role in producing a governability crisis.

Many of the ills of Brazil's new democracy can be traced to the electoral system put in place with the new constitution. In elections to the Chamber of Deputies, the representatives are chosen in a **proportional representation** system. The twenty-six states plus the Federal District serve as the electoral districts. Because the states vary in size, so do state deputations; some have as few as six seats and others as many as seventy. Voters can either vote for a party's label or *write in* the names of individual candidates, whose names do not appear on the ballot itself. (Japan had a similar system before its 1994 electoral reforms.) The total votes received by the party label or by individuals belonging to a party are then added up. Each party receives a number of seats from that state roughly equivalent to the percentage of the total votes its label and its candidates have garnered. So if the Party of the

Brazilian Democracy Movement and its candidates get 35 percent of the vote in São Paulo state, they get roughly 35 percent of that state's total delegation to the Chamber of Deputies.

The actual composition of each party's congressional delegation depends on how many *individual write-in* votes each candidate receives. The candidates with the greatest number of write-in votes are the ones who tend to get elected. In order to stand a good chance of winning, therefore, candidates must have name recognition; membership in a particular party might help them, but only marginally. Furthermore, in many states there may be several candidates running under a party's name, thus crowding the field.

How does one gain name recognition? A politician seeking office for the first time would benefit from the help of political patrons who might urge their followers to vote for an individual—for example, a governor or senator might tell his followers to vote for a particular deputy candidate. Once a politician has gained a congressional seat, she must figure out how to reward those who have voted for her; she may, for example, direct public spending toward the localities where her votes have been concentrated or intervene to ask for public jobs for constituents. This system strongly encourages pork-barrel politics and clientelism (as in Japan before the reforms). Politicians even attempt to focus the government's spending on those specific localities within their states in which they expect to get the most votes, so they can return from Brasilia (the capital) to those localities and claim credit for the spending. Because pork-barrel politics discourages politicians from developing strong ideological identities and because personal name recognition matters more than a party label does at reelection time, politicians have little incentive to be loyal to their parties and the programs they might put forward. Weak parties result from this electoral system.

Weak Parties and an Underdeveloped Party System Given the incentive structure created by the electoral system, we would expect that political parties have a hard time retaining the loyalty of their elected representatives. As table 23.7 shows, Brazilian politicians have been notorious for switching parties after they are elected. Politicians have jumped from party to party as they have bargained for political benefits that they can distribute to their supporters. Parties' fortunes have thus risen and fallen even between elections, without the voters having rejected a party at the ballot box. If a politician is willing to abandon the party that elected him, would we expect him to vote with the party when crucial issues come before the Congress? Surely not, if it threatens his reelection chances.

Weak parties cannot be counted on by party leaders or the president to support major policy initiatives. As a consequence, presidents have a daunting task before them when they seek to pass legislative bills they consider important: they must constantly cobble together a congressional major-

TABLE 23.7

Composition of the Brazilian Chamber of Deputies by Party, 1987–90 Term				
Party	Feb. 1987	Sept. 1988	Jan. 1990	Oct. 1990
Party of the Brazilian Democracy Movement (PMDB)	305	235	200	153
Party of the Liberal Front (PFL)	134	125	108	103
Democratic Socialist Party (PDS)	37	34	32	35
Brazilian Social Democratic Party (PSDB)	0	48	61	72
Democratic Labor Party (PDT)	26	28	35	43
Brazilian Labor Party (PTB)	19	29	26	32
Workers' Party (PT)	16	16	16	17
Liberal Party (PL)	7	7	19	13
Christian Democratic Party (PDC)	6	13	17	22
Party of National Reconstruction (PRN)	0	0	24	34
Others	9	24	32	43

Source: Adapted from Scott Mainwaring, "Brazil: Weak Parties, Feckless Democracy," in *Building Democratic Institutions: Party Systems in Latin America*, ed. Scott Mainwaring and Timothy R. Scully (Stanford: Stanford University Press, 1995), p. 377.

ity by making deals with groups of legislators or individuals whose votes are essential. Controlling public spending in this context has proven very difficult; legislators expect favors for their votes, usually in the form of budgetary allocations for their home states. That is one reason why inflation has plagued Brazil. Significantly, public spending has not been directed toward major efforts to confront poverty or lessen inequality, for the weakness of the party system has ensured that programs threatening the privileges of the better-off segment of Brazilian society simply don't pass the Congress.[92]

Despite incentives against the formation of strong parties, several parties have emerged that have some durability. Not all of Brazil's parties have clear ideologies, but most have something akin to a policy stance on the important issues facing their society. The largest party on the conservative side of the political spectrum is the **Party of the Liberal Front (PFL).** The PFL can trace its ancestry to the military-backed parties, ARENA and the PDS; it was put together during the 1984–85 transition by PDS members seeking to erase their association with the former military regime. In the 1998 congressional elections, the PFL polled the highest percentage of votes for the Chamber of Deputies, 20 percent. As a party of the right it generally favors reducing the size of the public sector, hence it favors pro-business neoliberal policies. Other parties on the right include the **Brazilian Labor Party (PTB),** founded by Getulio Vargas's grandniece in the early 1980s, but much more conservative than its namesake during the Second Republic; the **Progressive Party (PPB),** formed in a merger of the Labor Renewal and Social Labor parties; and several smaller parties. Together these parties of the right or center-right took about 40 percent of the vote in 1998's Chamber of Deputies race.

On the other end of the political spectrum, the **Workers' Party (PT)** has sought to avoid practicing clientelism as it attempts to represent Brazilian workers and the poor. Its popular leader is Luis Inácio "Lula" da Silva, a metallurgical worker who has now run unsuccessfully for president three times, each time polling tens of millions of votes for a leftist party or coalition. A party that strives to promote internal democracy, the PT has not suffered defections to the same extent as other Brazil-

ian parties. Other parties on the left have found breaking into the already crowded party system difficult because of the PT's successes. However, a **Green Party (PV),** a **Brazilian Socialist Party (PSB),** and two communist parties—the **Communist Party of Brazil (PC do B)** and the **Popular Socialist Party (PPS),** formerly the Brazilian Communist Party—contend for votes. The **Democratic Labor Party (PDT),** a populist party led by Goulart's brother-in-law, Leonel Brizola, himself a former governor of Rio de Janeiro before the military regime, gains about 5 percent of the vote.

In the center and center-left of the party system sit the **Party of the Brazilian Democratic Movement (PMDB)** and Cardoso's **Brazilian Social Democracy Party (PSDB).** These parties rival the PFL in their quest to be the largest party in the nation; the three draw about 20 percent of the vote each. While they can be placed in the middle of the ideological spectrum, the PMDB and the PSDB include members on both the right and the left. The PSDB itself was founded by dissidents from the PMDB in 1988 who desired a social democratic alternative in Brazil. However, the PSDB has followed centrist policies since Cardoso assumed the presidency in 1994. The PMDB, meanwhile, has attracted conservative politicians to its ranks in the 1990s.

Table 23.8 indicates the strength of the most important parties in different electoral settings in the 1990s. Note that the three largest parties (PMDB, PFL, and PSDB) do especially well in elections where only one candidate stands, namely, gubernatorial and senatorial races. Other parties that cannot swing a whole state or that can only rarely do so can nevertheless win several federal deputy races. Thereby they gain congressional representation, but with that representation they can make coalition formation all the more difficult in the lower house.

The Presidency and the Congress The new constitution gives the president a formidable set of constitutional powers, making the Brazilian presidency on paper among the most powerful in Latin America,[93] with much more sweeping powers than the Mexican presidency. Presidents can veto legislative acts, wholly or partially, and they have exclusive rights to initiate legislation in several important policy areas, including most that deal with

TABLE 23.8

Governors, Senators, and Deputies Elected in 1994 and 1998

Party	Governors 1994	Governors 1998	Senate 1994	Senate 1998	Chamber of Deputies 1994	Chamber of Deputies 1998
Party of the Brazilian Democratic Movement (PMDB)	9	6	22	27	107	82
Party of the Liberal Front (PFL)	2	5	18	20	89	106
Brazilian Social Democratic Party (PSDB)	6	7	11	16	62	99
Brazilian Progressive Party (formerly the PDS) (PPB)	3	2	6	5	52	60
Workers' Party (PT)	2	3	5	7	49	58
Progressive Party (PP)	—	—	5	—	36	—
Democratic Labor Party (PDT)	2	1	6	2	34	25
Brazilian Labor Party (PTB)	1	—	5	—	31	31
Liberal Party (PL)	—	—	1	—	13	12
Others	—	1	1	1	25	21
Total	27	27	81	81	513	513

Source: Maria D'Alva G. Kinzo and Simone Rodrigues da Silva, "Politics in Brazil: Cardoso's Government and the 1998 Re-election," *Government and Opposition* 34, no. 2 (spring 1999), p. 259.

public spending. (The Congress can override a presidential veto.) The president can also insist that the Congress take up legislation that he deems urgent within a forty-five-day period. However, to rate the Brazilian presidency's powers on the basis of formal constitutional powers alone would be to ignore other key aspects of presidential power. As we learned by considering the Mexican presidency, if the president has sufficient partisan support in the Congress, he can accomplish feats not envisioned by the constitution. In the Brazilian case, in contrast, insufficient partisan support in the Congress can make it very difficult for the president to accomplish major policy objectives, much as divided government can frustrate U.S. presidents.

To get legislation passed, Brazilian presidents must attempt to hold coalitions together. Since the legislators don't always show party discipline and sometimes even defect from their parties, presidents cannot count on party leaders whipping their members to vote for a presidential initiative. Instead, presidents contribute to the clientelist politics described earlier. They control federal funds and federal jobs, both of which are coveted by members of Congress seeking to satisfy their constituents. Old-fashioned horse trading may be essential to pass laws considered key to a president's agenda. It bears repeating that pork-barrel politics contributes to Brazil's out-of-control federal spending.

Even then, presidents have found it difficult to accomplish major objectives. Scott Mainwaring demonstrated that in nine policy areas critical to economic stabilization and state reform in the 1985 to 1994 period (including the privatization of state monopolies, cutting public sector employment, passing new tax bills, even collecting debts owed to the federal government by private business), Presidents Sarney, Collor, and Franco ran into the opposition of members of Congress who were protecting constituents or supporters and made no progress in those pressing policy areas.[94] Brazil's underdeveloped party system contributes to a legislature more inclined to protect the status quo and vested interests than to promote change or to address major social problems. Presidents are often forced to rule as much as possible by "emergency measures," which allow the president to make laws for thirty days, after which the Congress can either pass or reject the new legislation. Without those measures, presidents would find governing nearly impossible.

PROFILE: Fernando Henrique Cardoso

Now in his second term as Brazil's president and often lauded as the country's greatest president of the twentieth century, Fernando Henrique Cardoso did not become

President Fernando Henrique Cardoso

a politician until he was in his late forties. Born in 1931 in Rio de Janeiro to an upper-middle-class military family, Cardoso had an earlier career as a world-famous sociologist. His best known academic publication, *Dependency and Development in Latin America,* written with Enzo Faletto while the two worked in Santiago, Chile, in the 1960s, explored the ways in which an economy's relationship with the larger world economy could create ties of dependency that effectively limited a country's prospects for economic development. Much of the literature on economic dependency forecast nothing but continued poverty and underdevelopment for the dependent nations of the Third World (see chapter 15). Cardoso and Faletto, on the other hand, suggested that development could take place within the context of dependency provided that the government followed policies carefully chosen to enhance the nation's industrialization.

Cardoso's earlier career as a sociologist who trained under the Marxist Florestán Fernandes at the University of São Paulo led to his expulsion from his faculty position at the university by the military in 1964. After a period of exile in Santiago, Cardoso returned to São Paulo and founded a research center where academic opponents of the military regime wrote analyses of contemporary Brazil and Latin America and formulated alternatives to military rule. He and his fellow researchers were harassed by the military, often being detained or imprisoned. From this research center, Cardoso and his

colleagues advised the Brazilian Democracy Movement (MDB) in its 1974 electoral upset of ARENA. Cardoso's international fame as a scholar grew until he was elected president of the International Sociological Association in 1982.

Cardoso became an MDB member and ran as an alternative senator (one who would replace an elected senator if the latter resigned) from São Paulo in 1978; when the elected senator resigned in 1983, Cardoso joined the Senate. He was chosen senate leader in the first civilian government in 1985, a year in which he lost the São Paulo mayoral race to former president Quadros. In 1988, Cardoso split from the Democracy Movement to form the Brazilian Social Democratic Party (PSDB), which he served as senate leader until he left the Senate in 1992.

Obviously very able and politically influential, Cardoso was sought for important cabinet posts by President Collor, but he declined them. After Collor's resignation, Cardoso did accept an offer from President Franco to become foreign minister in 1992. A year later, in the midst of a desperate economic crisis, Cardoso became minister of finance.

As minister of finance, Cardoso truly established the authority that has permitted his success in the presidency. He was given much autonomy in the Finance Ministry because of the weakness of President Franco and the disarray then prevailing in the Congress. Cardoso fashioned the Real Plan, an anti-inflation program that pegged the new currency, the *real,* to the dollar and undertook serious fiscal reforms that involved reforming social security, the civil service, and the tax system. Following neoliberal principles, he also embarked on the privatization of state-owned enterprises and cut deficit spending. The plan, coming after six failed stabilization plans in the late 1980s and early 1990s, proved remarkably successful. Inflation plummeted and foreign investors showed their confidence in Brazil by maintaining their levels of investment.

The success of the Real Plan made Cardoso a powerful contender for the presidency in 1994. He ran against the PT's Lula, who led in the polls until the Real Plan's success became apparent. Cardoso defeated Lula by a resounding 54 percent to 27 percent margin, a ringing vote of confidence. His electoral coalition included his own Social Democratic Party along with the main conservative parties, the Liberal Front (PFL) and the Labor Party (PTB), a rather broad alliance. The new president parlayed the momentum from the presidential race into legislative successes in the first eighteen months of his presidency, gaining congressional support for constitutional amendments eliminating provisions that discriminated against foreign investors and permitting the sale of state-owned monopolies in several key sectors of the economy. As Cardoso pressed for a reduction in social security and civil service entitlements, however, he ran into congressional opposition that forced him to get involved in horse-trading with members of the Congress who were not enthusiastic about his reform measures. Only when the Asian economic crisis of 1997–98 and a domestic budget crunch made the Brazilian economy vulnerable to skittish foreign investors was Cardoso able to force through his civil service reform bill. In the meantime, the real underwent a sudden devaluation, prompting the International Monetary Fund to provide Brazil with a $41.5 billion rescue package.

How does Cardoso, as a social democrat who once wrote the most sophisticated dependency analysis about Latin America's vulnerability in the international capitalist order, square his social democratic preferences with his policy initiatives, which many take to be an embrace of market principles? First, Cardoso has never denied the difficulties of economic dependency, and indeed he has often argued that one can make the most of a dependent situation by implementing the appropriate policies. The import-substitution strategy may have been suitable in an earlier era, but an opening to globalization is more relevant today. Second, Cardoso's major efforts have been directed against the bloated, inefficient, and frequently ineffective state and against the efforts of state governors and other clientelist politicians to build rather than dismantle such bureaucracies. Given the difficulty of Brazil's predicament and the unpredictability of international financial crises, Cardoso has managed remarkably well to begin to dismantle the state's excessive role in the economy, as Brazilian voters recognized when they returned him for a second term as president in October 1998.

A Robust Federalism[95]

That Brazil's Congress overrepresents small states, most of which are rural states from the northeast and the Amazon, exacer-

TABLE 23.9

Brazilian Presidential Elections in the 1990s		
Candidate	1994	1998
Fernando Henrique Cardoso	54.3	53.1
Luis Inácio "Lula" da Silva	27.0	31.7
Others	18.7	25.2

Source: Maria D'Alva G. Kinzo and Simone Rodrigues da Silva, "Politics in Brazil: Cardoso's Government and the 1998 Re-election," *Government and Opposition* 34, no. 2 (spring 1999), p. 258.

bates a set of structural problems in the Brazilian political system. Those northeastern and Amazonian states depend more on distributions from the federal government than do the southeastern and southern states. Their representatives have parlayed presidential need for their votes in Congress into continuing public spending in their states and localities. Such processes reinforce the sense held by other Brazilians that corruption and backwardness characterize the politics of the north and the northeast.

The 1988 constitution grants significant public funds to state and local governments, but it does not impose greater expectations on those subnational governments for spending on education, health, or infrastructure, the typical responsibilities of subnational authorities. Indeed, about half the nation's tax revenues collected by the federal government is returned to states and municipalities with no mandates about how that money will be spent. Governors and mayors thus have resources they can distribute to help their political clients, including members of the Congress elected from their states. Consequently, governors (who can now be reelected) and mayors can use their influence over members of the Congress to see that their states are favored by federal laws or that their states are recipients of federal spending in infrastructure projects and the like. Development projects in the northeast and infrastructure projects in the Amazon have thus been well supported in the Congress.

The enormous influence of the states was vividly evident in 1998, when the governor of Minas Gerais—Brazil's former president, Itamar Franco—declared a moratorium on his state's $15.3 billion debt to the federal treasury. The unilateral announcement provoked a budgetary crisis that frightened foreign investors and threatened to derail Cardoso's austerity policies, which were central to retaining the confidence of the IMF. It took all of Cardoso's political skills to resolve the issue.

Hypotheses on Democracy and Democratization

Can Brazil's New Republic survive the challenges it faces? Does democracy have a future in South America's giant? Again, let's review our hypotheses on democratization to see if they suggest a bright or a bleak future for Brazil.

State Institutions The institutions of the New Republic provide powerful groups many points of access to defeat measures that threaten their interests. This means that measures designed to reform the economy so as to address the needs of the poor and redistribute income prove nearly impossible to legislate. A legislature composed of weak and undisciplined parties whose members seek all the patronage they can acquire, and a federal system in which states and governors can use their power to defeat measures in the national Congress or resist implementing them at the state and local levels have made socioeconomic reform difficult to accomplish. A democratic process may be in place in Brazil, but it fails to produce policies that reflect the interests of the majority of society.

Elites Committed to Democracy Most important, Brazil's military has apparently withdrawn from politics. If the New Republic has had a notable success, it has been in returning the military to the barracks.[96] Since the transition to democracy, most elite groups seem to support the New Republic, perhaps because the military's rule has been discredited in Brazil as in most of the hemisphere. But the depth of elite commitment to democracy has yet to be tested.

National Wealth and Its Distribution Income distribution remains severely unequal in Brazil. However, the opponents of income redistribution seem to have learned how to defeat redistributive measures through the institutions of democracy. For those proponents of redistribution, few alternatives to democracy recommend themselves, however, other than "deepening" democracy, a process not very likely to come to Brazil soon.[97]

Private Enterprise The Brazilian state has divested itself of considerable portions of the public sector over the past five years. (The 1999 sale of Telebras, the telecommunications giant, is a recent example.) In part because of the neoliberal policies followed by the government, business owners do not feel threatened by democratic institutions at this time. Having lived through a military regime that enhanced the public sector of the economy, perhaps at their expense, business has little desire to return to military rule.

Middle Class Brazil's middle class seems solidly supportive of democracy.

Support of the Disadvantaged Brazil's working class has become the voter base of one of its most important, pro-democratic parties, the Workers Party (PT). The PT has expanded its voter base to others among the urban poor. But poverty is a festering wound in Brazilian cities, where millions live in overcrowded shanty towns. Many of Brazil's poor are prey to criminal gangs, drugs, and flagrant police brutality. (A recent poll indicated that 70 percent of the residents of São Paulo are terrified of the police.) Brazilian court officials estimate that three homeless street children are killed every day in Rio de Janeiro, usually by police acting at the behest of local merchants. A UNICEF report said that more than half of the 17.5 million minors forced to work in Latin America are in Brazil, about a million of them under the age of ten. Childhood prostitution is common.

Rural poverty and political marginalization are also endemic. Land remains heavily overconcentrated in the hands of wealthy farmers; the poorest 30 percent of Brazilians share just 2 percent of the country's arable land, and nearly 5 million people have no land at all. Though the constitution reserves 11 percent of Brazil's land for indigenous Indians, numbering about a

Children gather next to a campaign poster of President Cardoso in one of Brazil's squalid shanty towns.

quarter million, recent laws have facilitated encroachment on Indian territory for lumbering and mining purposes. Illegal encroachments spark periodic violence with native populations.[98] The rural poor have few allies in the Congress, while many remain controlled in clientelist networks run by local political bosses. In spite of these enormous problems, however, a non-democratic revolutionary movement representing the poor is not in evidence in contemporary Brazil.

Civil Society and Political Culture   Like Mexicans, many Brazilians remain skeptical about whether democracy can make a difference in their lives. Many doubt that it solves society's problems.[99] However, Brazilian civil society has much more vibrancy than it did a quarter century ago. Many social movements have organized the poor and the middle classes to promote the interests of women, indigenous peoples, and local communities and to save the environment. This more active civil society would not as easily succumb to military rule as Brazil did in 1964.

Education and Freedom of Information   While educational levels have improved in the last quarter century and while there exist many more sources of information in today's Brazil, in these dimensions of Brazilian society all is not strongly supportive of democracy. On the one hand, the news media have played an important role in investigating allegations of political corruption, thereby demonstrating a degree of journalistic independence critical for keeping politicians somewhat honest. On the other hand, however, the Brazilian reliance on television for news and the popularity of *telenovelas* (soap operas) among the viewing public does not promise to promote political sophistication in the mass public.

Homogeneous Society   Brazil's society is not homogeneous, but as we noted earlier, as yet the racial diversity of the nation has not promoted political conflict on racial lines.

Favorable International Environment   Since 1964, and especially with the end of the Cold War, the likelihood that the United States and other major powers would support a military coup in Brazil has declined drastically.

CONCLUSION

In this chapter we have suggested that significant forces are at work in Brazil and Mexico to promote democratization. Certainly each nation continues to confront serious social problems and an increasingly challenging international economic environment. However, these societies' relatively recent experiences with less than democratic regimes—a civilian authoritarian regime in Mexico, military rule in Brazil—have led both elites and mass publics to prefer democratic politics. In some other Latin American nations—Argentina and Chile, for instance—democracy seems even more firmly consolidated than in Mexico and Brazil. In the views of many scholars, the most recent wave of democratization in Latin America will likely be more permanent than earlier waves.

Of course, Mexico and Brazil do not reflect all of Latin American political experience. The rise of strongmen like Alberto Fujimori in Peru and Hugo Chavez in Venezuela does not bode well for democracy in their nations. Democracy does not necessarily solve all problems, as Latin Americans learned in the 1990s. The important but yet-to-be-answered question is, do Latin Americans value democracy for its own sake?

KEY TERMS AND NAMES
(Underlined in the text)

Mexico

Vicente Fox
National Action Party (PAN)
Institutional Revolutionary Party (PRI)
Mestizos
Presidentialism
Centralism
Gen. Porfirio Díaz
Emiliano Zapata
Gen. Lázaro Cárdenas
Parastatal enterprise
Import-substituting industrialization (ISI)
Neoliberalism
Cuauhtémoc Cárdenas

Carlos Salinas de Gortari
Democratic Revolutionary Party (PRD)
NAFTA
Chiapas

Brazil

Fernando Henrique Cardoso
Amazon
Brazilian Empire
Old Republic
Getulio Vargas
New State
João Goulart
Military rule (1964–85)
Patrimonialism
New Republic

FOR DISCUSSION: WHAT WOULD YOU DO?

1. If you were a citizen of Mexico or Brazil, to which party (if any) would you belong?
2. Which economic strategy or priorities would you favor with respect to developing the economy, dealing with the private sector, and addressing poverty?
3. What should be the role of the United States in dealing with these countries?

FOR FURTHER READING

In addition to the titles in the notes, consult the following:

Mexico:

Jorge G. Castañeda, *The Mexican Shock: Its Meaning for the United States.* New York: New Press, 1995.

Neil Harvey and Mónica Serrano (eds.), *Party Politics in an Uncommon Democracy: Political Parties and Elections in Mexico.* London: Institute of Latin American Studies, 1994.

Roberto Newell and Luis Rubio, *Mexico's Dilemma: The Political Origins of Economic Crisis.* Boulder: Westview Press, 1984.

Riordan Roett (ed.), *The Challenge of Institutional Reform in Mexico.* Boulder: Lynne Rienner, 1995.

Mónica Serrano (ed.), *Governing Mexico: Political Parties and Elections.* London: Institute of Latin American Studies, 1998.

Brazil:

Sonia E. Alvarez, *Engendering Democracy in Brazil: Women's Movements in Transition Politics.* Princeton: Princeton University Press, 1990.

Ted G. Goertzel, *Fernando Henrique Cardoso: Reinventing Democracy in Brazil.* Boulder: Lynne Rienner, 1999.

Peter R. Kingstone and Timothy J. Power (eds.), *Democratic Brazil: Actors, Institutions, and Processes.* Pittsburgh: University of Pittsburgh Press, 1999.

Scott P. Mainwaring, *Rethinking Party Systems in the Third Wave of Democratization: The Case of Brazil.* Stanford: Stanford University Press, 1999.

Kurt von Mettenheim. *The Brazilian Voter: Mass Politics in Democratic Transition, 1974–1986.* Pittsburgh: University of Pittsburgh Press, 1995.

WEBSITES

Latin American Network Information Center, <http://lanic.utexas.edu/>, the best-organized and most extensive collection of links to websites on Latin America. Links are organized by country (for Mexico, see <http://lanic.utexas.edu/la/mexico/>; for Brazil, <http://lanic.utexas.edu/la/brazil/>) and by theme.

Political Database of the Americas, <http://www.georgetown.edu/pdba/>, a source for information about political parties, elections, constitutions, and other political institutions in Latin America. Information is available for both Mexico and Brazil.

MEXICO - A Country Study, from the Federal Research Division of the Library of Congress, <http://lcweb2.loc.gov/frd/cs/mxtoc.html>, a searchable source for basic information on Mexico.

BRAZIL - A Country Study, from the Federal Research Division of the Library of Congress, <http://lcweb2.loc.gov/frd/cs/brtoc.html>, a searchable source for basic information on Brazil.

NOTES

1. For an account of the tumultuous year of 1994, see Andres Oppenheimer, *Bordering on Chaos: Mexico's Roller-Coaster Journey Toward Prosperity* (Boston: Little, Brown, 1996).
2. U.S. Department of Commerce statistics, available at <http://www.census.gov/foreigntrade/top/dst/1998/12/balance.html>.

3. Immigration and Naturalization Service, "INS Releases Updated Estimates of U.S. Illegal Population," news release, February 7, 1997.

4. Fernando Henrique Cardoso and Enzo Faletto, *Dependency and Development in Latin America,* trans. Marjory Mattingly Urquidi (Berkeley: University of California Press, 1979).

5. Samuel P. Huntington, *The Third Wave: Democratization in the Late Twentieth Century* (Norman: University of Oklahoma Press, 1991).

6. United Nations Development Program, *Human Development Report 1999* (New York: Oxford University Press, 1999), 199–200.

7. Ibid., 184–86.

8. The U.S. population density was 70.3 persons per square mile in 1990; Mexico's was 124 persons per square mile. See *The World Almanac and Book of Facts 1996* (Mahwah, N.J.: Funk and Wagnalls, 1995).

9. See the United Nations Development Program, Department of Economic and Social Affairs, Population Division, "Urban Agglomerations 1996," at <http://www.undp.org/popin/wdtrends/urb/turb.htm>.

10. United Nations Development Program, Department of Economic and Social Affairs, Population Division, "Urban and Rural Areas 1996," at <http://www.undp/popin/wdrends/-20ura/ura.htm>.

11. Carlos Antonio Gutiérrez, "Extienden su constancia de mayoria a candidatos ganadores en Aguascalientes," *Excelsior* (Mexico City), August 7, 1998.

12. José Luis Reyna and Richard S. Weinert, eds., *Authoritarianism in Mexico* (Philadelphia, Pa.: Institute for the Study of Human Issues, 1977).

13. Victoria E. Rodríguez and Peter M. Ward, "Disentangling the PRI from the Government in Mexico," *Mexican Studies/Estudios Mexicanos* 10, no. 1 (1994): 163–86.

14. Wayne A. Cornelius, *Mexican Politics in Transition: The Breakdown of a One-Party-Dominant Regime* (La Jolla: Center for U.S.-Mexican Studies, University of California at San Diego, 1996), 39.

15. Jonathan Fox, "The Difficult Transition from Clientelism to Citizenship: Lessons from Mexico," *World Politics* 46, no. 2 (January 1994).

16. For a comprehensive historical overview, see Michael C. Meyer and William L. Sherman, *The Course of Mexican History,* 5th ed. (New York: Oxford University Press, 1995).

17. Octavio Paz, *The Labyrinth of Solitude: Life and Thought in Mexico,* trans. Lysander Kemp (New York: Grove Press, 1961).

18. José Vasconcelos, *La raza cosmica: misión de la raza iberoamericana, Argentina y Brasil* (Mexico City: Espasa, 1977).

19. They were called *cientificos* because they adopted the positivist political philosophies then current in Europe that suggested that pursuing scientific progress would lead to economic and social development, just as it had (according to the positivists) in Europe.

20. John M. Hart, *Revolutionary Mexico: The Coming and Process of the Mexican Revolution* (Berkeley: University of California Press, 1987).

21. Charles C. Cumberland, *Mexican Revolution: Genesis under Madero* (Austin: University of Texas Press, 1952).

22. The 1917 Constitution had forbidden reelection for the presidency and other federal offices. Because "no reelection" had been such an important slogan of Madero, dispensing with the no reelection clause seemed unwise. Thus Obregón, who had held the presidency from 1920 until 1924, had the constitution amended to forbid only "immediate reelection."

23. Meyer and Sherman, *Course of Mexican History,* 591.

24. Pablo González Casanova, *Democracy in Mexico,* trans. Danielle Salti (New York: Oxford University Press, 1970), 226.

25. Jeffrey Weldon, "Political Sources of *Presidencialismo* in Mexico," in *Presidentialism and Democracy in Latin America,* ed. Scott Mainwaring and Matthew Sobert Shugart (New York: Cambridge University Press, 1997).

26. Luis Javier Garrido, "The Crisis of *Presidencialismo,*" in *Mexico's Alternative Political Futures,* ed. Wayne A. Cornelius, Judith Gentleman, and Peter H. Smith (La Jolla: Center for U.S.-Mexican Studies, University of California at San Diego, 1989), 417–34.

27. Mainwaring and Shugart, *Presidentialism and Democracy in Latin America.*

28. Garrido, "The Crisis of *Presidencialismo,*" 422.

29. Roderic Ai Camp, *Politics in Mexico,* 3d ed. (New York: Oxford University Press, 1999), 11.

30. Daniel Cosío Villegas, *El sistema político mexicano* (Mexico City: Joaquín Mortiz, 1978).

31. Victoria E. Rodríguez, *Decentralization in Mexico: From Reforma Municipal to Solidaridad to Nuevo Federalismo* (Boulder, Colo.: Westview, 1997).

32. Joseph L. Klesner, "Electoral Reform in an Authoritarian Regime: The Case of Mexico," Ph.D. dis., Massachusetts Institute of Technology, 1988, 312–13.

33. Douglas C. Bennett and Kenneth E. Sharpe, "The State as Banker and Entrepreneur: The Last Resort Character of the Mexican State's Economic Interventions," *Comparative Politics* 12, no. 2 (January 1980): 165–89.

34. Richard S. Weinert, "The State and Foreign Capital," in Reyna and Weinert, *Authoritarianism in Mexico.*

35. For example, the leaders of the 1958–59 railroad workers' movement ended up spending many years

in prison, and their followers were told to return to work or lose their jobs. Fidel Velázquez, leader of the CTM from 1941 until his death in 1997, played the leading role in keeping Mexican labor in the PRI's camp and discouraging developments within the labor movement that would have given a greater voice about workers' interests or about the nature of the political regime to rank-and-file workers.

36. Gabriel A. Almond and Sidney Verba, *The Civic Culture: Political Attitudes and Democracy in Five Nations* (Princeton, N.J., Princeton University Press, 1963), 17–19.

37. John A. Booth and Mitchell A. Seligson, "The Political Culture of Authoritarianism in Mexico: A Reexamination," *Latin American Research Review* 19, no. 1 (1983), 106–24.

38. Joseph L. Klesner, "Modernization, Economic Crisis, and Electoral Alignment in Mexico," *Mexican Studies/Estudios Mexicanos* 9, no. 2 (summer 1993): 187–224.

39. González Casanova, *Democracy in Mexico,* 217.

40. Howard Handelman, *Mexican Politics: The Dynamics of Change* (New York: St. Martin's Press, 1997), 122.

41. Ibid., 135.

42. Victoria Rodríguez and Peter Ward, eds., *Opposition Government in Mexico* (Albuquerque: University of New Mexico Press, 1995).

43. The position of *jefe de gobierno* is sometimes referred to as the governor of the Federal District, sometimes as the mayor of Mexico City. In fact, it lies somewhere between a gubernatorial and a mayoral post, lacking some of the powers of a governor, but essentially it is the second most important office in Mexico because it governs the largest city (by far) in the nation.

44. Klesner, "Electoral Reform in an Authoritarian Regime."

45. Joe Foweraker and Ann L. Craig, eds., *Popular Movements and Political Change in Mexico* (Boulder, Colo.: Lynne Rienner, 1990).

46. Booth and Seligson, "The Political Culture of Authoritarianism in Mexico."

47. MORI Internacional, *Visión Latinoamericana de la democracia: encuestas de opinión púplica en México, Chile, y Costa Rica,* final report, October 20, 1998.

48. Ibid.

49. See the account in Oppenheimer, *Bordering on Chaos.*

50. See the United Nations Development Program, Department of Economic and Social Affairs, Population Division, "Urban Agglomerations 1996," at <http://www.undp.org/popin/wdtrends/urb/turb.htm>.

51. The northeast is made up of the states of Alagoas, Bahia, Ceará, Maranhão, Paraíba, Pernambuco, Piauí, Rio Grande do Norte, and Sergipe.

52. Rex A. Hudson, ed., *Brazil: A Country Study* (Washington, D.C.: Federal Research Division, Library of Congress, 1997), at <http://lcweb2.loc.gov/frd/cs/brtoc.html>.

53. Espírito Santo joins São Paulo, Rio de Janeiro, and Minas Gerais as the four southeastern states.

54. Hudson, *Brazil: A Country Study.*

55. The states of Paraná, Rio Grande do Sul, and Santa Catarina form the southern region.

56. The Amazonian states are Rondônia, Acre, Amazonas, Roraima, Pará, Amapá, and Tocantins, while the western states are Goiás, Mato Grosso, and Mato Grosso do Sul.

57. A comprehensive political history of Brazil can be found in Peter Flynn, *Brazil: A Political Analysis* (Boulder, Colo.: Westview, 1978).

58. Eul-Soo Pang, "Coronelismo in Northeast Brazil," in *The Caciques: Oligarchical Politics and the System of Caciquismo in the Luso-Hispanic World,* ed. Robert Kern (Albuquerque: University of New Mexico Press, 1973).

59. Thomas E. Skidmore, *Politics in Brazil, 1930–1964: An Experiment in Democracy* (New York: Oxford University Press, 1967).

60. Kenneth P. Erickson, *The Brazilian Corporative State and Working Class Politics* (Berkeley: University of California Press, 1977).

61. Peter B. Evans, *Dependent Development: The Alliance of Multinational, State, and Local Capital in Brazil* (Princeton, N.J.: Princeton University Press, 1978).

62. Skidmore, *Politics in Brazil, 1930–1964.*

63. Ruth Berins Collier, "Popular Sector Incorporation and Political Supremacy: Regime Evolution in Brazil and Mexico," in *Brazil and Mexico: Patterns in Late Development,* ed. Sylvia A. Hewlett and Richard S. Weinert (Philadelphia, Pa.: Institute for the Study of Human Issues, 1982).

64. Alfred C. Stepan, "Political Leadership and Regime Breakdown: Brazil," in *The Breakdown of Democratic Regimes,* ed. Juan J. Linz and Alfred C. Stepan (Baltimore, Md.: Johns Hopkins University Press, 1978); Michael Wallerstein, "The Collapse of Democracy in Brazil: Its Economic Determinants," *Latin American Research Review* 15, no. 3 (1980): 3–40.

65. Maria Helena Moreira Alves, *State and Opposition in Military Brazil* (Austin: University of Texas Press, 1985).

66. Alfred Stepan, *Rethinking Military Politics: Brazil and the Southern Cone* (Princeton, N.J.: Princeton University Press, 1988).

67. Thomas E. Skidmore and Peter H. Smith, *Modern Latin America,* 3d ed. (New York: Oxford University Press, 1992), 408.

68. Scott Mainwaring, "Multipartism, Robust Federalism, and Presidentialism in Brazil," in Mainwaring

and Shugart, *Presidentialism and Democracy in Latin America;* Stepan, "Political Leadership and Regime Breakdown: Brazil."

69. Frances Hagopian describes their rule: "In thousands of municipalities across Brazil, local bosses exploit the economic dependence of their clients on resources they own or control to boost their position and power." See her *Traditional Politics and Regime Change in Brazil* (New York: Cambridge University Press, 1996), 16–17.

70. Ibid., 69.

71. This particular doctrine of national security, taught at the military's Superior War College from the late 1950s onward, justified in their own eyes the military's seizure of power. See Alfred Stepan, *The Military in Politics: Changing Patterns in Brazil* (Princeton, N.J.: Princeton University Press, 1971); Alves, *State and Opposition in Military Brazil.*

72. Guillermo A. O'Donnell, *Modernization and Bureaucratic-Authoritarianism: Studies in South American Politics* (Berkeley: Institute of International Studies, University of California, 1973).

73. Skidmore, *Politics in Brazil, 1930–1964.*

74. On business and democratization, see Leigh A. Payne, *Brazilian Industrialists and Democratic Change* (Baltimore, Md.: Johns Hopkins University Press, 1994).

75. Thomas E. Skidmore, *The Politics of Military Rule in Brazil, 1964–85* (New York: Oxford University Press, 1988), 142–43.

76. Margaret Keck, "The New Unionism in the Brazilian Transition," in *Democratizing Brazil: Problems of Transition and Consolidation,* ed. Alfred Stepan (New York: Oxford University Press, 1989).

77. Scott Mainwaring, "Grassroots Popular Movements and the Struggle for Democracy: Nova Iguaçu," in Stepan, *Democratizing Brazil.*

78. This concept is from Juan Linz, *Crisis, Breakdown, and Reequilibrium,* vol. 1 of *The Breakdown of Democratic Regimes,* ed. Juan J. Linz and Alfred Stepan (Baltimore, Md.: Johns Hopkins University Press; 1978).

79. United Nations Development Program, *Human Development Report 1999,* 176–77.

80. Evans, *Dependent Development.*

81. Peter Evans, *Embedded Autonomy: States and Industrial Transformation* (Princeton, N.J.: Princeton University Press, 1995).

82. Mainwaring, "Multipartism, Robust Federalism, and Presidentialism in Brazil."

83. Stepan, *Rethinking Military Politics.*

84. David V. Fleischer, "Constitutional and Electoral Engineering in Brazil: A Double-Edged Sword, 1964–1982," *Inter-American Economic Affairs* 37, no. 1 (spring 1984).

85. Stepan, *Rethinking Military Politics,* 56.

86. Leigh A. Payne, "Brazilian Business and the Democratic Transition: New Attitudes and Influence," in *Business and Democracy in Latin America,* ed. Ernest Bartell and Leigh A. Payne (Pittsburgh, Pa.: University of Pittsburgh Press, 1995).

87. Skidmore, *Politics of Military Rule,* 126–27.

88. Hagopian, *Traditional Politics and Regime Change in Brazil.*

89. Mainwaring, "Grassroots Popular Movements and the Struggle for Democracy."

90. Keck, "The New Unionism in the Brazilian Transition."

91. Juan J. Linz and Alfred Stepan, *Problems of Democratic Transition and Consolidation: Southern Europe, South America, and Post-Communist Europe* (Baltimore Md.: Johns Hopkins University Press, 1996), 169.

92. Kurt Weyland, *Democracy Without Equity: Failures of Reform in Brazil* (Pittsburgh, Pa.: University of Pittsburgh Press, 1996).

93. Mainwaring, "Multipartism, Robust Federalism, and Presidentialism in Brazil," 65–66.

94. Ibid., 99–100.

95. The term comes from Scott Mainwaring, ibid.

96. Wendy Hunter, *Eroding Military Influence in Brazil: Politicians Against Soldiers* (Chapel Hill: University of North Carolina Press, 1997).

97. Weyland, *Democracy Without Equity.*

98. *Freedom in the World 1998–1999* (New York: Freedom House, 1999), 104–7.

99. Linz and Stepan, *Problems of Democratic Transition and Consolidation.*

CHAPTER 24

NIGERIA AND SOUTH AFRICA

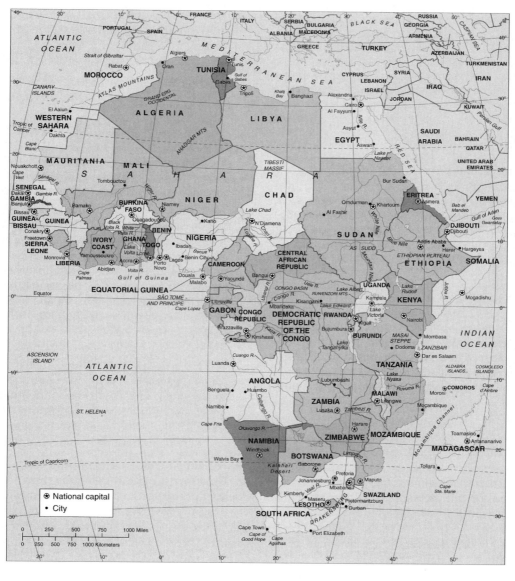

In recent years, some African leaders have called for a "renaissance." This appeal for a rebirth is a response to disillusioned pessimists who decry the persistence of war, authoritarian rule, and poverty in Africa and its marginalization in the international economy. Led by South Africa's new president, Thabo Mbeki, advocates of a renaissance point to the need for African leaders to take responsibility for the continent's security and economic well-being. As Mbeki put it:

> Renaissance has to be about democracy, peace and stability throughout our continent. It has to be about economic regeneration so that we pull ourselves out of the category "the underdeveloped" permanently. It has to be about vastly improving the quality of life of all our citizens.[1]

If the hoped-for African renaissance is to occur, there is widespread agreement that the further broadening and deepening of democracy in Africa's fifty-four countries will be necessary. This chapter reviews recent gains, and setbacks, in African democracy. In particular it evaluates progress toward the consolidation of democracy in the continent's two most important countries: Nigeria, Africa's most populous state, and South Africa, its wealthiest and most developed. Both these countries have undergone profound transitions to a more democratic political life in recent years. The future of these countries will determine the fate of much of the rest of Africa.

Africa—a continent whose countries share some similarities while exhibiting many differences—is a vast and varied geographic entity. Although many headline-grabbing calamities have befallen it in recent years—drought and famine in Ethiopia, faction fighting in Somalia, genocide in Rwanda, a tragic AIDS epidemic, and enduring poverty throughout the region—the continent has also witnessed a number of remarkable success stories in peacemaking and democratization. Civil wars in countries such as Mozambique and Liberia have come to an end. Multiparty democracy has been introduced in many countries after years of single-party rule, as in Ghana, Zambia, and Senegal. This wide range of experience, from the "implosion" of national governments and economic collapse in some countries to the dawning of a democratic age in others, offers many insights for students of comparative politics.

Comparing politics in Africa's states reveals a very complex picture. In Africa today there are established democracies, partial democracies in which there is some freedom and inter-party competition while life continues to be an economic struggle for most people, authoritarian regimes ruled by corrupt military leaders, and countries wracked by regional and civil war. We shall explore the complexities of politics on the continent and relate these varied experiences to the core issues of democracy that have been highlighted in the previous chapters. We'll point out some hypotheses about the viability of democracy in this, the world's most impoverished region, and apply them to our two primary case studies.

Nigeria and South Africa deserve special attention as pivotal states for the entire continent.

> In **Nigeria,** a country of more than 120 million, military coups have repeatedly ended experiments in democracy, some with popular backing and some with fierce opposition. Yet in 1999, the military stepped aside and elections in May inaugurated a new period of civilian rule—the Third Republic—with Olusegun Obasanjo (o-BAH-san-jo), as the country's first popularly elected president in fifteen years.
>
> **South Africa,** with about 45 million citizens, is a very special case. For centuries, a European white minority dominated the African majority, exercising a democracy for themselves while brutally exploiting and oppressing the black majority through the policies of apartheid (*separateness*; pronounced "apart-hide"). Yet voting rights and democracy for all came to that country in April 1994 after negotiations that averted a race war, an achievement seen as a miracle by some and by others as an inevitable consequence of the world's condemnation of racial discrimination. In 1999 South Africa successfully held a second election and its democratic system now seems durable.

No single chapter can capture the range of experience with politics generally, and with democracy in particular, in a region as wide and complex as Africa.[2] However, by focusing on common challenges to democracy and the continent's most important and powerful states, we can gain useful insights into modern African political development and the challenges democracy faces as we enter the twenty-first century. Along the way, we'll investigate how African states—Nigeria and South Africa in particular—have dealt with the five sources of political conflict identified in chapter 2:

- *Power:* How did the military usurp power in Nigeria? How did South Africa's white minority, comprising only 18 percent of the population, exercise its dominance over the non-white majority for so many years? How have turbulent transitions to democracy affected these power relationships in recent years?
- *Resources:* How have chronic poverty and high levels of inequality affected the prospects for democracy in these and other African countries? How is national wealth distributed?
- *Social identity:* How did national identities develop in countries with so many disparate social groups? How have ethnic and religious conflicts played out in Nigeria? How has racial diversity affected political life in South Africa?
- *Ideas:* How have African countries like Nigeria and South Africa understood the concept of democracy? Have other ideologies been developed to justify non-democratic rule?
- *Values:* To what extent are traditional African values compatible with modern practices of democracy, such as elections? How widespread are such core democratic values as tolerance, compromise, and freedom?

We take a special look at democracy in this chapter because the conventional wisdom in the first three decades of independent African political development (roughly 1960–90) held that democracy is impossible in relatively poor, multiethnic societies. The prevailing view during that period was that Africa's societies would be best served by domineering one-party states. Few were convinced that Africa's multiethnic societies could withstand the inherent strains of multiparty politics. Many argued that authoritarian rule is required to guide economic development, a notion known as **"developmental dictatorship."** These views no longer hold. As noted in chapter 4, democracy has flourished in some countries (like India) despite widespread poverty and diversity, resulting in a need to assess the conventional wisdom anew.[3] We therefore hypothesize that *more*

democracy—not less—is needed for Africa's states to meet their challenges in the twenty-first century and to realize the dream of a renaissance. Today, democracy is viewed as a prerequisite to economic growth and social harmony; one-party "developmental dictatorship" clearly did not yield a better quality of life.

THE POLITICAL DEVELOPMENT OF MODERN AFRICA

Africa is more than just a continent that is distinguished by its natural boundaries of the Atlantic and Indian oceans and the Mediterranean Sea. It is a large political unit that shares such things as a history of colonial oppression; a new, but still evolving, state system; a subordinate place in the international political economy; and a widespread desire for political and economic change.[4] To understand where Africa's countries are headed today, we must understand their common past.

Current anthropological theories suggest that Africa is the cradle of all humankind. The "African genesis" theory holds that the earliest hominids—the primordial ancestors of the human race—lived in the Great Rift Valley of central Africa and the Ethiopian highlands. Thus the beginning of African history is the beginning of human history. Africa's history, and its present, are marked by extensive migration, changing structures of authority and governance, evolving boundaries, and changing notions of ethnic and national identity. Great ancient kingdoms developed in Africa, including the Gao in present-day Senegal, the Mali dynasties of the twelfth and thirteenth centuries, and the regal traditions of the Ashanti in present-day Ghana. During these times, Africans interacted with Islamic traders such as the Berbers, and a vibrant system of exchange developed across the sands of the Sahara.

Early in the fifteenth century, Portuguese invaders crossed the straits of Gibraltar and began the European colonization of Africa, a system of domination that lasted until the early 1990s, when independence for Namibia put a final end to **colonialism.** Prior to European rule, traditional authority in the persons of African monarchs and chiefs, rooted in agrarian systems of livelihood, was the dominant mode of governance. These societies led a fairly isolated existence. Colonial rule changed Africa significantly, and its long-term effects down to the present day cannot be overstated.

Over the course of the next several centuries, additional imperial powers invaded Africa. They carved up the continent along artificial and illogical boundaries, manipulated social systems, and created economic legacies that continue to bedevil African countries today. An initial impetus for the colonial exploitation of Africa was the slave trade, in which at least 12 million unfortunate souls were enslaved and sent to the United States alone. Many more never survived the arduous "middle passage" across the seas. Along the coast of Senegal lies Goree Island, once a prison where slaves were auctioned to slave traders in passing ships; today it houses an institute for democracy, development, and human rights.[5]

With the British decision to abolish slavery in 1833 and with the abolition of slavery in the Americas following the U.S. Civil War, the nature of European subjugation changed. Colonial powers annexed large swaths of Africa in an effort to fuel their industrial revolution with raw materials extracted from the rich natural resources found on the continent. Principally, these resources included cotton, peanuts, cocoa, palm oil, coffee, sisal, and minerals such as copper. Colonization accelerated in the final three decades of the nineteenth century. In 1870 only 10 percent of Africa was colonized; by 1900 only 10 percent was not. At the infamous Berlin Conference of 1884, the major European colonial powers—Britain, France, Belgium, Germany, Italy, Portugal, and Spain—divvied up Africa's territory among themselves. Their basis for determining the boundaries of these colonies was rather arbitrary in terms of existing African social patterns. For the most part, the new entities simply reflected the patterns of military control exercised by the colonial armies of the European imperialist powers: whoever controlled an area took it as a colony. *The borders of most African states today are the legacy of the ill-considered partition of Africa in the mid-nineteenth century,* based on the "principle of effective occupation" of territory. These boundaries did not correspond to any geographic, national, or ethnic logic. Ultimately they created many of the problems of ethnic tension that challenge the majority of African countries today.

Patterns of Colonialism

The discovery of rich diamond and gold deposits in South Africa in the 1860s heightened what became known as the "scramble for Africa." To fully exploit Africa's wealth, colonialism required more effective occupation and social control. Although different in their approaches—the British used "indirect rule" whereas the French, Belgians, and Germans preferred more direct control of territory—the colonial powers engaged in the widespread political manipulation of African societies.

- The **British** relied on agreements with traditional rulers to impose their policies, usually backed up with superior military might. Consequently, we find today that in erstwhile British colonies such as Kenya or Ghana, traditional rulers remain very powerful and territorial control by ethnic groups remains critically important.
- In **French** and **Belgian** colonies, centralized power was more important and it eroded traditional power structures. The French sought to exert cultural influence through their language policy, and they ruled their colonies as an extension of France itself. Colonial subjects were to become *évolués,* or "people evolving" into Frenchmen. Belgian colonies such as the vast Congo were ruled as the personal property of the eccentric King Leopold II.
- In **Portuguese** colonies, such as Angola, Mozambique, and Cape Verde, assimilation was encouraged and many interracial marriages occurred. As a result, *assimilados* (or mulattos, the products of mixed marriages) became important social groups that blurred the lines between colonial and indigenous rule.[6] Lusophone (Portugese-speaking) countries in Africa today thus have social structures that are remarkably different from those of former British or French colonies, and *assimilados* are still influential leaders in these countries.

Yet another legacy of the colonial period was the stark division of a large part of Africa into Anglophone (English-speaking) and Francophone (French-speaking) colonies. These language differences affect the way today's African countries relate to one another and stymie the development of a common approach to contemporary problems.

Former British colonies tend to have special ties with one another, as do former French colonies. For example, former English colonies are active members of the Commonwealth,[7] while French West African countries have adopted a common currency.

The reliance on African land and labor to grow crops and extract mineral wealth in service to the colonial powers resulted in severe distortions in traditional African societies. The intruders introduced alien concepts and social "fictions" with no indigenous roots in Africa: Christianity, monogamy, formal education, and wage labor, among others. New stratifications based on socioeconomic class came into being, ethnic identities were transformed, and basic economic infrastructures and modes of production were created to serve the single-commodity economies needed by the colonial powers. In southern Africa, European immigrants set up white minority "settler states" that systematically displaced Africans from the land and created a new form of modern feudalism. In many colonies, the imperial powers imposed a "head tax," in which an African peasant had to work for a European plantation owner or an enterprise to pay off debt to the metropolitan state (the colonial power).

After the creation of the Union of South Africa following the British defeat of the Dutch colonists (known as the Boers) in 1902 and after Germany's defeat in World War I, the shape of colonialism in Africa was nearly complete. European plenipotentiaries and bureaucrats ruled the vast continent, and their oppression of the indigenous population was universal. Once Germany lost its colonies after 1918, most decisions affecting the masses of the continent were made in Paris or London, with little regard for their implications for the millions of people whom colonial policy affected.

Legacies of Colonialism

Colonialism's legacies are thus pervasive throughout Africa some fifty years after the system of domination began to crumble. These legacies are political, economic, and cultural.[8]

- *Politically,* as noted before, the territorial boundaries of today's countries are the result of the greedy competition among the European powers over arable land, water, blue water harbors, transportation arteries such as rivers, and precious mineral resources.

- *Economically,* the African colonies were reliant on single-commodity, resource-extraction economies. Urbanization was inhibited, subsistence agriculture encouraged, and the development of diversified industrial production was stultified.

- The *cultural* units that had existed prior to colonialism were also affected, and in many regions ethnic and linguistic groups are now divided by artificial lines on a map. As a result, most African countries today are a mosaic of ethnic, linguistic, racial, and religious diversity. One of the consequences is a pattern of distorted social relations. Some say that the differences, for example, between the higher-class Tutsi and the peasant Hutu in Rwanda are the creations of the Belgian colonists. In 1994, 800,000 people died in 100 days in the worst genocide since World War II as Hutus lashed out against their Tutsi foes. A common Catholicism, which ostensibly united the population, could not prevent the division of the country along these ethnic lines.

African Nationalism

World War II had significant material and psychological effects on the continent and its people. As a consequence of the war, the colonial powers were weakened and the legitimacy of occupation began to erode; at the same time, the message of the struggle for civil rights in countries such as the United States spread abroad. U.S. presidents such as Eisenhower pressed for decolonization to open Africa's markets to free trade. Encouraged by civil rights activism in the United States, African nationalist movements emerged to resist colonial rule and exploitation. Under the leadership of these movements, demands for independence from the colonial powers grew rapidly in the late 1940s and 1950s. Although there had been prior resistance to colonial rule—notably by the Ashanti Kingdom in the late nineteenth century, the Ndebele-Shona uprisings in current-day Zimbabwe in 1896–97, and the Maji-Maji rebellion in 1905–7—real resistance to European rule spread with the winds of change that swept rapidly over

TABLE 24.1

The Decolonization of Africa

Colonizer (as of 1914)	Country Colonized (Modern Name)	Independence
France	Algeria	3 July 1962
	Benin	1 August 1960
	Burkina Faso	5 August 1960
	Central African Republic	13 August 1960
	Chad	11 August 1960
	Congo (Brazzaville)	15 August 1960
	Côte d'Ivoire	7 August 1960
	Djibouti	27 June 1977
	Equatorial Guinea	12 October 1968
	Gabon	17 August 1960
	Guinea	6 March 1957
	Madagascar	26 June 1960
	Mali	22 September 1960
	Mauritania	28 November 1960
	Niger	8 August 1960
	Senegal	20 August 1960
	Tunisia	20 March 1956
United Kingdom	Botswana	30 September 1966
	Gambia	18 February 1965
	Ghana	6 March 1957
	Kenya	12 December 1963
	Lesotho	4 October 1966
	Malawi	6 July 1964
	Nigeria	1 October 1960
	Sierra Leone	27 April 1961
	South Africa	31 May 1961
	Sudan	1 January 1956
	Swaziland	6 September 1968
	Uganda	9 October 1962
	Zambia	24 October 1964
	Zimbabwe	18 April 1980
Portugal	Angola	11 November 1975
	Cape Verde	1 July 1975
	Guinea-Bissau	10 September 1974
	Mozambique	25 June 1975
	Sao Tome and Principe	12 July 1975
Belgium	Burundi	1 July 1962
	Congo (Kinshasa, formerly Zaire)	30 June 1960
	Rwanda	1 July 1962
Italy	Eritrea	Seceded from Ethiopia 1991
	Libya	24 December 1951
	Somalia	1 July 1960
	Western Sahara	Disputed territory
Germany	Cameroon	1 January 1960
	Namibia	21 March 1990
	Tanzania	9 December 1961
	Togo	12 April 1960
Independent	Liberia, Ethiopia	

the continent after World War II. Among the most significant of these new awakenings was the Mau Mau rebellion in Kenya in 1950, in which Kikuyu tribespeople articulated the legitimacy of African aspirations to be free of the colonial yolk.

African nationalism arose from the frustrations of a small but growing *middle class* that deeply resented the fact that the highest positions in commerce, finance, government administration, and even religious organizations were controlled by foreigners, as were the rewards of economic success. African nationalists who emanated from this middle class sought independence from the colonial powers, a goal that would bring them complete control over the state apparatus and territory of their respective countries. Buoyed by the promise of the Charter of the United Nations to promote the "self-determination of peoples," and imbued with the postwar optimism reflected in the 1948 Universal Declaration of Human Rights, African leaders began to agitate for decolonization. Western-educated, skilled professional leaders organized independence movements and petitioned for independence. Tanzania's **Julius Nyerere, Jomo Kenyatta** of Kenya, **Leopold Senghor** of Senegal, **Kwame Nkrumah** of Ghana, and **Kenneth Kaunda** of Zambia, to name a few, articulated philosophies of independence, self-reliance, and economic development for African colonies.

These men were the founding fathers of today's African states, much like Mahatma Gandhi and Jawaharal Nehru, who led India to independence in 1947. Senghor, for example, argued for a rekindling of traditional African values. He coined the term *Négritude* to encompass "the whole complex of civilized values (cultural, economic, social, and political) which characterize the black people." Senghor and other nationalists believed that cultural nationalism could unify countries whose people had little in common other than their suffering to bind them in their postcolonial political units. To achieve this unity, African anti-colonial nationalists sought the reins of state power. This drive for power, waged in revolutionary struggles of armed resistance and guerilla warfare in many colonies, was heralded by Nkrumah's dictum, "Seek ye first the political kingdom." At the same time, the United States, in conformity with its own anti-colonial past, pressured the European powers to loosen their control of markets and commerce with Africa.[9]

Independence came rapidly for many countries in the 1960s. Fueled by United Nations General Assembly Resolution 1514 (1960), which called for decolonization and the sanctity of existing borders, the claims of African nationalists could not be denied. By 1957, Ghana's Nkrumah had succeeded in his effort to seize the political kingdom. His Convention People's Party won a pivotal election, assumed power, and forced the British to relinquish control. In 1960 alone, twenty-six African colonies became independent, and by 1969 some forty-two countries emerged as sovereign states, becoming full-fledged members of the United Nations. In subsequent years, after bitter struggles for independence, Portuguese colonies such as Mozambique and Angola were finally freed in the mid-1970s. The settler societies of southern Africa, such as Rhodesia (now Zimbabwe), Namibia, and South Africa, also came to be ruled by African nationalist movements. Across the continent, in the short historical span of some thirty years, colonial-era flags went down and the flags of newly independent African countries were raised.

As it happened, however, African nationalism in these formative decades of decolonization was not tightly linked to democracy. Unlike leaders in Britain and the United States, where nationalism and democratic tendencies were virtually inseparable from the beginning, most African independence leaders defined their nationalism in pronouncedly anti-Western terms. Upon taking power, most of them quickly abandoned any pretense to Western liberal democratic ideas and practices, establishing authoritarian or quasi-authoritarian regimes based on the military or one-party dominance. African democracy was set back for decades as a result.

DEMOCRACY IN AFRICA

Initially, the constitutions of the newly liberated states tended to establish the minimal framework of democracy: constitutionalism, the rule of law, and elections. In countries throughout Africa, the anti-colonial nationalist movements—such as TANU in Tanzania, KANU in Kenya, and UNIP in Zambia—won elections. With charismatic leaders such as Nyerere, Kenyatta, and Kaunda, these movements inherited a highly centralized state and highly diverse populations. But contrary to the democratic tenets of political pluralism, which rest on free and open competition among political parties and freedom of expression, some of the most prominent leaders of African independence quickly uprooted the newly sprouting shoots of democracy. Each of them argued that African states needed one-party rule in order to unify their populations and "build nations." Creating new countries required emphasizing common struggles and sufferings; competitive, parliamentary elections, in their view, would tear the nascent nations apart.

This hypothesis—that multiparty competition is ill suited to African's multiethnic, impoverished societies because it divides rather than unifies—is a common and recurrent theme in Africa's political development.[10] It reverberates throughout the region today. For example, Uganda's President Yoweri Museveni has introduced a system of "no-party" politics, in which candidates for office stand as individuals and are not allowed to assume a party identification. The National Resistance Movement, which he leads, is the guiding force in the country. Although it espouses such democratic notions as market-oriented economics, freedom of expression, and free primary education (a rarity in Africa), it resolutely monopolizes political power. In 2000, 70 percent of Ugandans who turned out to vote in a referendum approved the continuation of the "no party" system. But less than half the electorate voted, and advocates of a competitive, multiparty democracy feared violence if parties are not permitted to exist.

While rejecting British-style parliamentarism and other Western models of democracy, most African states in the postcolonial period turned to one form or another of authoritarian or semi-authoritarian rule. In virtually every newly independent African country, the formal institutions of democracy that may have been in place when self-rule began were systematically undermined. Democratic practices and human rights fell prey to political and military elites who sought the reins of office for their own personal power and enrichment. These elites relied on the centralized, bureaucratic structures of the states that they inher-

ited from the colonial powers to become Africa's new dominant class.[11]

Regimes in Africa:
Non-Democratic and Democratic

Among the several forms of authoritarianism that emerged in Africa between the early 1960s and the late 1980s, one variant is **semi-authoritarian one-party rule.** Examples include TANU in Tanzania and Guinea's Parti Démocratique de Guinée. In these and similar manifestations of this political system, political power is monopolized and guided by famous and generally popular political leaders. The government and party structures operate in parallel, with some similarities to the relationship between party and state in communist Russia and China. These parties have generally voiced socialist rhetoric and have sought to achieve economic development by breaking the bonds of dependency that tied the prosperity of their country to uneven and disadvantageous trade relations with Europe. These parties still exist in most countries. Some of them, such as the Kenyan African National Union, are still in power despite the introduction of multiparty politics. Elsewhere, as in Zambia, one-party governments were defeated in elections when political liberalization began in the early 1990s. Zimbabwe experienced a fundamental transformation of its one-party system in 2000 as a relatively new party—the Movement for Democratic Change—won nearly half the parliamentary seats up for election, delivering a stunning blow to the Zimbabwe African National Union (ZANU), the party that had dominated the country for twenty years under President Robert Mugabe.

Other countries have featured **patrimonial rule,** which is rule by a domineering and personalistic elite.[12] In the former Belgian Congo (later known as Zaire and more recently as the Congo), a troubled decolonization process in the 1960s was marked by civil war, UN military intervention, superpower rivalry, and assassinations. Eventually, Mobutu Seso Seko seized power and ruled as a veritable monarch until his despotic regime was toppled by rebels in May 1997. Mobutu's assets at the time of his death were estimated at $8 billion in property and money, while his country had sunk to the bottom of the global list in virtually every conceivable development indicator. A prolonged civil war for control of the country was still raging in 2000.

In other countries, the **military** stepped in and took over power. Military coups were rampant in Africa from the 1960s through the 1980s: in seventy-four instances between 1952 and 1990, military officers gained power through violence or the threat of it and ruled the country as dictators. In Ethiopia, military officers with pro-Soviet leanings and a Marxist ideology seized power in 1975, replacing the aging emperor, Haile Selassie. Under Mengistu Haile Meriam, the Derg—as the junta was known—unleashed a reign of terror and embroiled the country in devastating civil wars and wars with its neighbors (notably the war with Somalia over the Ogaden desert in 1975). It used its radical Marxist-Leninist ideology to justify dictatorial rule at home and to establish international alliances with the Soviet Union, Cuba, and other communist states. After inflicting untold suffering on the Ethiopian people, Mengistu fled the country in 1991 as rebel forces closed in on the capital, Addis Ababa. Today Ethiopia is edging closer to democracy, though it has engaged in border skirmishes with Eritrea, an independent state that was once a part of Ethiopia.

Some countries, notably Angola and Mozambique, suffered from **protracted civil wars** in which independence movements fought against the Portuguese and among themselves over who would wield power in the independence era. In both instances, the hasty retreat of Portuguese colonizers in 1974–75 left a power vacuum in which the competing local factions vied for dominance. These factions obtained arms and ideological support (and sometimes troops) from their respective benefactors—especially the United States, the Soviets, and the Cubans—who were locked in their global Cold War confrontation. Despite several efforts and peace agreements and UN peacekeeping efforts in the 1990s, Angola's civil war continues today after twenty-five years of fighting. Tragically, Angola has the highest proportion of victims of landmines of any country in the world, including some 100,000 amputees. In 1999, an estimated two hundred people died per day in Angola's tragic war. The Congo, Liberia, and Sierra Leone were also embroiled in civil wars in the 1990s and early 2000.

Several countries in Africa—such as Botswana, Mauritius, Gambia, and Senegal—have managed to remain **partial democracies** with constitutional systems, regular elections, and relatively good human rights records.[13] But only in a few instances have elections ever led to the ouster of the ruling party and the assumption of power by an opposition party. For example, in Botswana, Africa's oldest surviving democracy, elections held in 1999 returned to power the only party that has governed the country since independence in 1966. Alternation in power—the periodic transfer of state power from one party to another over a succession of elections—is a key indicator of the vibrancy of democracy as traditionally defined. Unfortunately, it has been largely absent from Africa. The relative success of some of these countries in avoiding the complete collapse of democracy has tended to stem from the responsiveness of the dominant party to ethnic and religious groups. This type of political system has been labeled a **"hegemonic exchange"** regime: in exchange for the right to exercise its hegemony over the state and the population, the dominant party provides benefits to the country's main ethnic or religious groups.[14]

In the 1980s and 1990s, global factors like the collapse of communism in the Soviet Union and Central and Eastern Europe and the new assertiveness of multilateral financial institutions converged with domestic pressures to undermine the alternatives to democracy in Africa. International lending organizations like the World Bank and the International Monetary Fund, along with aid providers like the United States and Western Europe, increasingly insisted on "good governance," private enterprise, and trade liberalization as conditions for future economic assistance. They called on the states of Africa to root out official corruption, reduce state controls over economic activity, and remove tariffs and other barriers to trade with the outside world. They also enjoined them to take more responsibility for their governance, economic development, and human rights records.[15] A worldwide embargo on South Africa in the 1980s placed special external pressures on that country's white minority government to open negotiations with African nationalists with the aim of democratizing the entire country. Under these mounting outside pressures, political practices within individual African countries gave way to new continental and global realities.

In many countries, popular movements arose that demanded space for the development of an autonomous civil society outside the single-party framework. They called for multiparty competitive elections, new constitutional frameworks, an end to corruption, and a more equitable distribution of wealth. In Ghana, Kenya, Malawi, and Zambia, new coalitions of organizations in civil society came together and pressured the incumbent governments to open up the political system to multiparty competition. Africa was clearly caught up in the "third wave" of democratization that spilled across the world in the early 1990s.

Over the course of the decade, nearly all of Africa's fifty-four states underwent dramatic political changes. As we've seen, the pressures for democratization were both external, a condition of further loans and foreign aid, and internal, the result of widespread public disaffection with the status quo.[16] Whether through negotiated agreements ("pacts"), the victory of rebel movements on the battlefield, or the passing of long-time patriarchs, the stereotypical African one-party state became a relic of the past in the early 1990s. Africa has witnessed scores of governments that have come to power seeking to inaugurate a new era. Some have dubbed the period of the 1990s "Africa's second independence." More than anything, the process of democratization in Africa was characterized by the rush to multiparty elections. Between 1992 and 1994, twenty countries held national-level elections. These elections swept away one-party regimes in the Cote d'Ivoire, Gabon, Mali, and Zambia. In some instances, as in Angola, Eritrea, Ethiopia, Liberia, Namibia, Mozambique, Sierra Leone, South Africa, and Uganda, votes were held to restore and legitimate a new political order after years of civil war and violence. Many Francophone countries held "national conferences" to arrive at new constitutional rules of the game for democratic politics.

The track record of the remarkable attemts at democratization in much of Africa is demonstrably mixed. Some experiments of the 1990s were relatively successful, in that legitimate government was reconstituted and the stage was set for a longer-term evolution to more mature democracy and its consolidation (e.g., frequent or occasional alternation in power by governing coalitions). In Benin, Eritrea, Madagascar, Malawi, Mali, Mozambique, Namibia, South Africa, Uganda, and Zambia, elections have been more or less successful vehicles for ushering in fledgling democracies. But there have been failures, as well. Elections went awry in Angola, Burundi, and Sierra Leone, leading to renewed civil violence, the suspension of human rights, and sharp declines in the standard of living as well as in the prospects for future prosperity. Observers have differed over whether the electoral contests of the 1990s produced greater accommodation among conflicting groups within these countries—especially along ethnic lines—or whether they exacerbated tensions and undermined national cohesiveness.[17]

Among the alternatives to elections as a route to democracy is the promotion of viable *civil societies* in Africa. Some have suggested that popular participation and consensus-building decision-making processes are more suited to Africa's divided societies than are the rough-and-tumble of Western-style competitive elections.[18] John Harbeson suggests that democratization efforts in Africa have relied too much on elections, arguing that "this overemphasis derives from an inaccurate reading of the most widely accepted definition of 'democracy,' upon which much of the contemporary democratic transitions theory appears to rest." He suggests as an alternative that "a broadened conception of democratization will result in a significantly improved understanding of the status and quality of democracy [in Africa] and the prospects for it." African countries should engage in more constitution-making exercises that establish a consensus on the rules of the democratic game before rushing into elections in the absence of that consensus, Harbeson maintains.[19]

Two countries that in recent years have undergone dramatic transitions to democracy will be bellwethers of the ability of the continent to further democratize and competitively enter the globalizing world economy. Nigeria is a pivotal state. As we've noted, it is Africa's most populous country and, with its vast oil and natural gas deposits,

TABLE 24.2

Political Status of Selected African States (January 2000)

Country	Political System	Freedom Rating
Angola	Civil war	Not free
Benin	Democratic	Free
Botswana	One-party dominant	Free
Burkina Faso	Partial democracy	Partly free
Burundi	Civil war	Not free
Cameroon	Autocratic rule	Not free
Cape Verde	Democratic	Free
Central African Rep.	Partial democracy	Partly free
Chad	Partial democracy	Partly free
Congo-Brazzaville	Autocratic rule	Not free
Congo-Kinshasa	Civil war	Not free
Côte d'Ivoire	Military rule	Not free
Djibouti	Autocratic rule	Not free
Equatorial Guinea	Military rule	Not free
Eritrea	Partial democracy	Partly free
Ethiopia	Partial democracy	Partly free
Gabon	Partial democracy	Partly free
Gambia	Autocratic rule	Not free
Ghana	Democracy	Partly free
Guinea	Autocratic rule	Not free
Guinea-Bissau	Partial democracy	Partly free
Kenya	Partial democracy	Not free
Lesotho	Military rule	Not free
Liberia	Partial democracy	Not free
Madagascar	Partial democracy	Partly free
Malawi	Partial democracy	Free
Mali	Democracy	Free
Mauritania	Autocratic rule	Not free
Mozambique	Partial democracy	Partly free
Namibia	Democracy	Free
Niger	Autocratic rule	Not free
Nigeria	Partial democracy	Partly free
Rwanda	Autocratic rule	Not free
Sao Tome	Democracy	Free
Senegal	Democracy	Partly free
Sierra Leone	Civil war	Not free
Somalia	No functioning government	Not free
South Africa	Democracy	Free
Sudan	Civil war	Not free
Swaziland	Autocratic rule/monarchy	Not free
Tanzania	Democracy	Partly free
Togo	Partial democracy	Not free
Uganda	Partial democracy	Partly free
Zambia	Democracy	Partly free
Zimbabwe	Democracy	Partly free

Source: Freedom rating from *Freedom in the World, 1998–1999.* New York: Freedom House, 1999. In chapter 4, we substitute the term "democratic" for "free."

potentially one of its most prosperous. Despite its democratic elections of 1999, few believe that democracy and national unity in Nigeria are a foregone conclusion. Nigeria in the future can be a force for either stabilization or destabilization in all of West Africa. South Africa is another harbinger of the direction that many southern African countries may take. These two countries are amenable to comparison because they share common challenges in managing ethnic and religious diversity. Moreover, both must provide for expanding populations in difficult environments, both possess vibrant civil societies, and both must directly face the challenges of consolidating democratic gains under very difficult and trying conditions.

After first looking at the troubled transitions to democracy that these countries have experienced and the elections that ushered in a fresh start, we'll next examine their prospects for consolidating a pluralist, competitive system that protects human rights, manages diversity, and fosters economic development into the twenty-first century.

NIGERIA

Population (1999, estimated): 114 million
Area: 356,668 square miles
(more than double the size of California)

Nigeria is an enigmatic case in sub-Saharan Africa. In many ways, this important country of more than 120 million people—20 percent of Africa's population—has long possessed a high potential for developing into a regional and global superpower with national wealth and a strong and vibrant democracy. Nigeria boasts abundant natural resources (especially light sweet crude oil, exports of which account for 30 percent of GDP), a vigorous civil society, highly educated elites, and an enduring commitment to freedom, pluralism, and enterprise among its people. At the same time, the country has been plagued since independence from Britain on October 1, 1960, by poor leadership and a social structure that does not support unity of purpose. Since independence, Nigeria has suffered six successful military coups d'état and many other unsuccessful ones, a brutal civil war, costly military engagements in the region, endemic kleptocracy (rule by theft) and corruption, and deeply ingrained religious and ethnic ten-

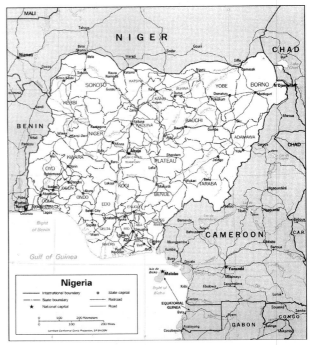

Source: U.S. Central Intelligence Agency

sions. That the promise of Nigeria has not been realized remains one of the most important facts of postindependence Africa. The stark reality is that this vast country has been ruled by military leaders longer than by civilian politicians.

Ethnic, Regional, and Religious Divisions

Nigeria is not only Africa's most heavily populated country; it is also one of its most diverse. There are some 250 ethnic groups in Nigeria. The principal division centers on three major ethnic groups that account for some two-thirds of the population: the **Igbo** (or **Ibo**) in the southeast, accounting for about 18 percent of the population; the **Yoruba** in the southwest (21 percent); and the **Hausa-Fulani** group in the northern third of the country (the Hausa comprise about 21 percent of the population, and the Fulani, 11 percent). These divisions reflect linguistic and historical divisions from the precolonial period. Hausa, for example, is a language spoken by several groupings with a history as distinct ethnic groups, including the Fulani, the Tiv, the Kanuri, the Nupé, and others. The Igbo, who initially lived in autonomous villages and spoke their own language and dialects, proved especially receptive to Western religious, cultural, and commercial influences. The Yoruba, also with their own language, were divided prior to British rule into several kingdoms that occasionally clashed in bloody rivalries. Eventually they joined together under a common identity. They, too, were highly receptive to Western influences, both religious and commercial.

In addition to having these ethnolinguistic divisions, Nigeria is deeply divided along religious lines. In general, the Igbo are mostly Christian and the Yoruba and Hausa-Fulani mostly Islamic. In all, Muslims comprise about half of Nigeria's population, and Christians about 40 percent. A large number of Igbos are Roman Catholics, but other Christian denominations, such as Baptists and West African Evangelicals, also attract Nigerian adherents. Traditional animism remains widely practiced as well.

While the three largest ethnic groups tend to dominate Nigerian politics, it is important not to overlook Nigeria's numerous smaller minority groups, which often play an important role in regional and national politics. As we shall see, Nigeria's extraordinary ethnolinguistic and religious *heterogeneity* has proven a serious barrier to democracy.

Although current patterns of ethnic awareness had antecedents in the precolonial period, the effects of colonialism in molding today's social divisions cannot be overlooked. The British, who colonized Nigeria from the mid-eighteenth century to 1960, fostered regional devolution (indirect rule, as described earlier). They promoted the development of regional and ethnic identities in Nigerian political consciousness on the one hand and superimposed a highly centralized administrative system on the other. In many ways, this colonial system set up a tug-of-war among various regional forces in a fight over the central reins of power, creating precedents for postindependence political conflicts.

Like many phenomena in Africa, today's problems have deep roots in colonial misrule. During the British colonial period, the regions of Northern and Southern Nigeria, fused in 1914, were only loosely integrated. Using indirect rule, the British fostered local autonomy in the more Islamic North but offered less autonomy and self-rule to those in the mostly coastal South, where colonial "penetration"—the existence of civil and military administrators—was more extensive than in the hinterlands. But the British also systematically disadvantaged the northern Muslims in terms of education, access to political influence, and economic development, setting up a paradoxical problem that continues to influence Nigerian politics today. Side by side, a relatively politically powerful but economically weak Muslim North competes with a more wealthy but historically less powerful South.

Regionalism fostered by the British has left a poor legacy for nation building in Nigeria. In 1939, the British divided its Nigerian territories into three regions (along with the then-capital Lagos, which was administratively separate): the Western (predominantly Yoruba) region, the Eastern (mostly Igbo), and the Northern (generally Hausa-Fulani). After World War II, this regional division evolved into a federal structure. Federalism and related policies in the colonial period set up the basic dynamics that continue to threaten Nigeria's territorial integrity today. It also strongly influenced political organization, such that during the first elections in the early 1950s in the run-up to independence, ethnic parties quickly emerged and gained control of their respective territories.

An important hypothesis worth considering—for then and now—is that ethnically based parties produce such intense competition for power that they consistently undermine opportunities to consolidate democracy. The test for this hypothesis in Nigeria doesn't yield a definitive conclusion. While ethnic politics has plagued every attempt at democratic politics, other factors—namely, corruption stemming from the irresistible temptation to skim national oil export earnings—also account for the recurring breakdown of Nigeria's experiments at civilian rule.

As in much of Africa, rising nationalism in Nigeria in the 1950s forced the British colonizers to expand Nigerian participation in the country's administration, create elected representation, and ultimately move toward independence. The constitution of 1954 reinforced the colonial legacy by formalizing the regions and fostering the hegemony of a dominant ethnic group within each region. If it were simply a matter of constitutional structure, Nigeria might have overcome its ill-considered regional structure that reinforced social tensions.

Throughout the years, through legal reforms, the number of states in Nigeria has ballooned—from four in the early 1960s to some thirty-six states today—in efforts to change the regional basis of Nigerian politics. Other administrative and technical solutions to resolving ethnic tensions have been tried. Nigeria has witnessed innovative constitutional devices that, on paper at least, try to foster ethnic tolerance and the creation of political alliances across the regional divides. But constitutional "engineering" has not been enough. Nigeria's periods of incipient democracy have been consistently undermined by anti-democratic tendencies and military misrule, much of it driven by avarice and greed.

The First Republic (1960–66)

Nigeria's first start at democracy after independence led to the creation of two broad political orientations: the National Republican Convention (NPC) and the Social Democratic Party (SDP). The former had its base in the northern part of the country among the largely Muslim Yoruba and Hausa, while the latter had a more southern base, rooted in the mostly Catholic Igbos. Generally, the NPC was slightly to the right of the center of the political spectrum and the SDP slightly to the left. A high degree of unity marked the time of independence and the First Republic's initial years. The country's first president was an Igbo (Nnamdi Azikiwe), and its prime minister came from the Hausa-Fulani group (Tafawa Balewa). But corruption and ethnic tensions quickly undermined the civilian regime. In particular, a major dispute over the national census of 1964 (which was to determine the allocation of state spending) heightened antagonisms along ethnic lines. A devastating national strike also undermined the authority and capacity of the government.

Another factor that served to undermine the **First Republic**—and many Nigerian governments since then—is what Richard Joseph terms **prebendalism,** or the use of state offices as "prebends" (instruments) for wealth and gain for individuals and their ethnic brethren.[20] This use of the government for wealth-gathering (sometimes known as "rent-seeking") behavior has systematically undermined constitutionalism, which places an emphasis on the statutory functions of an office (that is, its legal competence as set forth in the constitution and other laws). Because prebendilism has become so prevalent, democratic competition in Nigeria, and elections in particular, have been fought with unusual vigor and often violence. Political party organization has often broken down along ethnic lines, threatening to lead the country into disintegration. These problems stalked the First Republic from its inception.

By the time the first independently administered national elections came around in 1964, politics had deteriorated into a sharp struggle along North-South, Muslim-Christian, and conservative-reform lines. The election itself was hotly contested, but eventually the northern-based NPC emerged as the strongest party. Tensions mounted particularly in the Western region, where the Yoruba felt repressed, and these tensions were exacerbated by regional elections. Rising violence further undermined the legitimacy of the country's first experience with democracy. Corruption, too, became endemic, and support for President Azikiwe quickly eroded.

Military Intervention and Civil War

In an abrupt move, the military intervened in early 1966, murdering the prime minister, the governors of the West and North, and some military officers. Most of the coup-makers were Igbo, including the first head of the military government, Gen. Johnson Aguiyi-Ironsi. His efforts to establish an Igbo-dominated central government and his suppression of the North provoked anti-Ibo reprisals against their ethnic kin in the northern part of the country. In July 1966 Aguiyi-Ironsi was assassinated by rival northern officers, and Lt. Col. **Yakuba Gowon,** a Tiv, emerged as the new military head of state. Fleeing the massacres in the north, more than a million Igbos migrated eastward, and calls for secession—independence—for the East (known as **Biafra**) grew substantially.

In July 1967, civil war broke out after a unilateral declaration of independence by the Eastern region's military commander proclaimed the creation of the Republic of Biafra. In the ensuing violence, federal forces battled the mostly Igbo secessionists for three years, but by January 1970 the

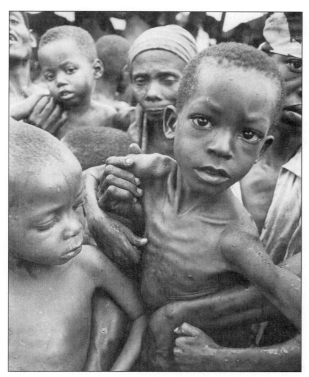

Starvation was widespread during the war precipitated by the Eastern Region's attempt to establish an independent state of Biafra, 1967–1970.

East had been defeated. At least 600,000 people perished in the bitter struggle and perhaps as many as a million. Most died of starvation, as government forces cut off Biafra from the outside world. Several countries recognized the breakaway republic, but many others sided with the Nigerian central government. After the Biafran secessionists were defeated, Gowon's policy of forgiveness and national reconciliation managed to keep the country together. He worked hard to foster a new national identity based on ethnic accommodation and tolerance, buttressed by a renewed commitment to federalism and equitable sharing of resources.

As it happened, however, Gowon's military rule ushered in a long succession of military governments in Nigeria. Sometimes the military takeover of power has been popular, as civilian administrators squandered their opportunity to govern and lost public support. Often, civilian leaders have brought the country to ruin as a re-

sult of factionalism, personal power struggles, corruption, and ethnic favoritism. The military has thus stepped in as the guardian of order, only to rule repressively and in the interests of individual leaders. Almost always, the military in Nigeria has justified its intervention and the suspension of the constitution by promising to lead a transition to restore clean governance and democracy. But more often than not they retracted these pledges and retained their grip on power, burying hopes for democracy under a heap of broken promises.

Gowon headed the Federal Military Government from 1966 to 1975 with continuing social and economic problems; he was then removed in a bloodless coup and succeeded by Brig. Gen. Murtala Muhammed (1975–76), a Hausa-Fulani from the North. The new military leader purged the government of thousands of corrupt officials. Soon thereafter Lt. Gen. **Olusegun Obasanjo,** Muhammed's chief of staff, was appointed president by the military leadership after Mohammed was assassinated in a failed coup attempt by disgruntled elements of the military who opposed his corruption-busting campaign. Obasanjo, a Yoruba from the southwest region, was genuinely interested in reestablishing democracy. Governing from early 1976 to the restoration of constitutional government in 1979, he restored order in the military and combated corruption. The Obasanjo-led regime led many Nigerians to believe that the military rulers were genuinely committed to the restoration of democracy and would respond to popular pressure for it.

Nigeria's fortunes were also buoyed by a rapid expansion of oil production, along with the bounty provided by the escalation in global oil prices during the mid-1970s. Up to 90 percent of Nigeria's foreign exchange earnings were from oil during this highly volatile period. Obasanjo's commitment to the restoration of civilian rule at a time of economic expansion set the stage for a carefully managed, protracted transition to democracy, giving birth to the Second Republic.

The Second Republic (1979–83)

One of the most important developments in Nigeria's political history was the 1979 constitution, which established several important precedents. One such precedent was the creation of new federal states in an effort to break up the troubled regionalism. Gradually the number of states was increased, under Gowon to twelve, and by the time of the Second Republic to nineteen states. Also important to Nigeria's political evolution was the introduction of the "federal character" clause of the 1979 constitution that required equitable representation among ethnic groups in state institutions (especially the military) and an equitable allocation of Nigeria's oil bounty. This federal character principle retains its importance in today's Third Republic.

The constitution featured the creation of a directly elected president with substantial independent powers, a popularly elected National Assembly (lower house), and a Senate with representatives drawn from the states. Many considered the constitution to have been modeled on the U.S. system, although there is no evidence of a direct influence in the constitution-drafting process. The judiciary was fairly independent.

Nigeria's new constitution also featured innovative devices designed to curb the influence of ethnic identity in political organization and leadership. To win the all-important presidential election, a candidate was required to garner an absolute majority of the electorate nationwide and at least 25 percent of the vote in each region of the country. This mechanism provided an incentive for political leaders to eschew narrow appeals to ethnicity and encouraged them to broaden the base of their political organizations to all parts of the country.[21] Political parties were to meet specific and detailed criteria to ensure they did not simply reflect regional or ethnic constituencies. The constitution also provided for compromise on the divisive issue of when Islamic law, the *Sharia*, could be used to adjudicate domestic disputes. The careful compromise allowed it to be used in the Muslim northern areas but did not provide for its imposition on non-Muslims elsewhere or in instances where a party to a dispute preferred modern, constitutional legal procedures.

The **Second Republic** was widely seen as a reasonably good start for Nigeria's second attempt at democracy. The election results were disputed; the victor, Alhaji Shehu Shagari, won a nationwide majority, though he may not have garnered sufficient support in all the states. The election commission declared him the winner however, and

this outcome was eventually accepted by most Nigerians. But Shagari was a Hausa-Fulani, a northerner whose assumption of the leadership was resented by those who chafed under the North's domination of the central government. Thus the troubles of the Second Republic began right from its inception.

On the positive side of the ledger, political coalitions crystallized into two blocs, one predominantly right of center, or conservative on domestic social and foreign policy (now organized under the National Party of Nigeria), the other predominantly left-leaning, or more socialist in orientation (the Unity Party of Nigeria). Yet mounting ethnic violence, especially in Kaduna and Kano states where Muslim-Christian tensions flared, undermined the fragile regime. Once again, impending elections heightened tensions and popular support for democracy quickly waned. Factionalism and political infighting grew rife and increasingly violent. The prebendal inclinations of politicians were revealed in a number of scandals, often reported by Nigeria's vibrant and independent press. Ever since the advent of Nigeria's oil wealth in the mid–1970s, for example, control over the central administration had been a point of deep contention and unceasing power struggles. The central government was seen as a funnel through which the nation's oil wealth flowed. Control over the narrow end of the funnel allowed predatory politicians to siphon off the nation's wealth for their own personal enrichment. Corruption, malfeasance, manipulation, neglect and political thuggery undermined the legitimacy of the government and civilian politicians in general. Ultimately it eroded popular support for democracy itself.

When the next presidential elections occurred in mid–1983, they were widely perceived as fraudulent; few believed the Shagari government had been returned to power by the will of the people. Violence ensued among the major political factions, and disillusionment with democracy was pervasive.

Babangida's Dictatorship

Poor leadership and prebendal politics set the stage for the next military coup. Launched by Maj. Gen. Mohammed Buhari in December 1983, it was led by officers who, like some of their predecessors, pledged to restore order, civility, and good governance to Nigeria. They promised a new election to overturn the theft of democracy in the failed elections earlier that year, but it was not to be. Although the military moved quickly to arrest hundreds of corrupt political leaders and made some headway on economic reform, they mishandled the treatment of many individuals in unfair trials, meting out especially harsh punishment to southern politicians. "Ethno-military rule"—the junta was dominated by northerners—also limited the credibility of the government's promises to restore democracy. (Buhari came from the Hausa-Fulani group.) Malfeasance and popular unrest produced a popularly supported usurpation of power by other generals.

This time the coup was led by Maj. Gen. **Ibrahim Babangida,** who would become one of Nigeria's most dictatorial and despised military leaders. Under Babangida, authoritarian repression grew widespread despite initial expectations that he would lead the country back to democracy.

Indeed, there was a brief period in which the dictator opened up Nigeria's political space, allowing party politics to resume and initiating a halting process of constitution making. From his seizure of power in 1985 to his ultimate political demise in 1993, a process of transition to democracy seemed to be underway. First, Babangida announced a drawn-out transition that was supposed to culminate in the creation of a **Third Republic** in 1990. A new constitution was drafted

Major-General Ibrahim Babangida (center) shortly after assuming Nigeria's presidency in a military coup, 1985.

that made modest improvements on the 1979 charter. The reforms included clarifying the electoral law while retaining the feature that requires the president to have broad support drawn from a wide variety of ethnic, regional, and religious groups. The new constitution also expanded the number of states to thirty to further encourage the development of more fluid, multiethnic coalitions. (Babangida himself was a northerner, but he came from a small ethnic group, the Gwari.) Some political prisoners from the Second Republic were released. Yet the dictatorial and kleptocratic nature of his government could not be denied. Despite all the trappings of a transition to democracy, at the end of the day the military regime was ruling for its own immediate benefit and wealth. A bloody but failed coup attempt occurred in 1990, which nearly provoked a new civil war. During his rule, Babangida earned a reputation as the most corrupt ruler in Africa, vying for this dubious distinction with the Zairian strongman Mobutu Seso Seko. One of Babangida's most lavish projects was the creation of a new national capital in Abuja, where billions were spent on official buildings, luxury hotels, and hundreds of bridges in a city with no major river. Compared to the former capital of Lagos, Abuja was a gleaming showplace, but its amenities have been enjoyed mainly by visiting foreign dignitaries. The new capital is too expensive for ordinary Nigerians and remains virtually deserted. Under his rule, Nigeria became a pariah state subject to international sanctions. Its external reputation was in shambles, its vast oil wealth was squandered, drug trafficking flourished, and ethnic and religious tensions rose dramatically.

The Aborted Transition (1993)

Babangida's so-called transition to democracy was consistently manipulated and often deferred. Presidential elections were first slated for 1990, but they were shunted aside until June 1993. From the very beginning, the military's pledge to restore democracy lacked credibility. The ruling junta used the protracted and tightly controlled "democratization" process to enhance its power, with a view to remaining the arbiter of national politics even after its military dictatorship came to an end and a democracy governed by civilians took its place.

Among the many ways the military leaders governed Nigeria was their tight control over the registration of political parties. It was the ruling officers who required, through decrees, the creation of two centrist political parties. The military created a left-leaning Social Democratic Party and the more conservative National Republican Convention as a means to control the process of selecting candidates for office as well as the ways the parties would position themselves in the ethnically and regionally divided electorate. These parties were to be loosely based on the party structure of the First Republic, but in reality they were entirely new constructs. In 1992, the government allowed elections to the National Assembly. The voting revealed ethno-regional divisions between the northern groups backing the NRC and the southern and western groups backing the Social Democrats. The Social Democrats won a majority of seats in both the newly reconstituted Senate (earning 55 percent of the seats) and in the lower chamber, the House of Representatives (with 65 percent of the seats). The elections were flawed, however, because of the use of non-secret voting measures and a very low turnout rate. Subsequent primary elections for presidential candidates were also troubled, with widespread vote buying and rigging. At the end of the troubled process, both presidential candidates turned out to be businessmen with close ties to the Babangida regime, although the SDP candidate, Chief **Moshood Abiola,** stood out for his cross-communal profile and broad appeal. The NRC nominated a little-known candidate, Bashir Tofa.

A genuine democratic fervor accompanied the presidential elections when they were finally held in 1993, and Babangida pledged to leave power in August. But the elections of June 12 were fraught with turmoil. At the end of the balloting, ten days after the election, Babangida reneged on his pledge to restore civilian power. He annulled the results of the election when it became apparent that the southern traditional leader, Chief Abiola, had been elected by an estimated 58 percent of the vote. The international community was outraged, Abiola was subject to house arrest, and the country was further driven into isolation and condemnation. Within a few weeks Babangida was forced to leave under pressure, but an "interim" civilian government under Ernest Shonekan fell within

months to another military coup, this one led by an especially inept and corrupt military dictator, **Sani Abacha.**

Abacha's Dictatorship

Abacha, a northerner from the Kanuri group, ruled with an iron fist. Despite modest efforts to recruit credible civilians to his cabinet, he and his subordinates engaged in the systematic theft of the nation's wealth. Like other military leaders before him, he too announced a new draft constitution and pledged to lead the country back to civilian rule. But the military government's deeds spoke louder than its words. Corruption and arbitrary rule reached new depths. Abacha himself is thought to have embezzled billions of dollars from the national treasury, perhaps tens of billions. His cronies also profited handsomely from stolen wealth. A pivotal event in the deepening crisis in Nigeria was the execution on November 10, 1995, of **Ken Saro-Wiwa** and eight other activists who had sought to raise international attention to the plight of an ethnic group in the southeast, the Ogoni, whose area had been desecrated by pollution from the extraction of oil and gas. The executions led to the application of economic and political sanctions against the Abacha regime by the world community and reinforced Nigeria's status as a pariah state. In 1996, the British Commonwealth suspended Nigeria's membership and the United States imposed sanctions on the regime.

Only a bizarre twist of fate allowed Nigeria to find its way out of the abyss. Dramatically, Abacha succumbed to a heart attack on June 8, 1998. Hopes rose that Abiola would now lead a transition to democracy. But exactly one month later, on July 8, Abiola died suddenly in the middle of a meeting with U.S. and Nigerian officials. Abiola's death set off riots by his supporters, many of whom suspected foul play because he was still in detention when he died. (An international investigatory team found no evidence of it.) General Abacha's demise set the stage for a new military government under General Abdulsalami Abubaker, a member of the Housa-speaking Nupé group. Abubaker realized that the military's ability to retain power was at an end. Popular discontent was at the boiling point. He organized a rapid transition to democracy that featured local elections in December 1998 and presidential elections on February 27, 1999. Abiola's passing set aside the lingering controversy over the aborted elections of 1993. Nigeria now seemed poised for a fresh start.

Obsanjo Returns

With the establishment of an independent election commission and heavy involvement by the international community, the 1999 elections were a major turning point for Nigeria. The presidential vote—widely seen as the most important in the transition—featured Gen. Olusegun Obasanjo, the man who had tried to restore democracy in the late 1970s, running for the People's Democratic Party. Until the transition of 1999, Obasanjo was the only Nigerian head of government who had gained power as a military leader (in 1976, when Muhammed was assassinated), only to hand over the reins of government to a civilian leader. Subsequently, in 1995, he was arrested by the military for advocating a return to civilian rule and democracy during the brutal and incompetent rule of Sani Abacha. In a secret trial, Obasanjo was convicted of plotting a coup and remained imprisoned for several years. His main opponent in the February 1999 elections, Olu Falae, was the joint candidate of the Alliance for Democracy and the All People's Party and was alleged to be a favorite candidate of the outgoing military regime.

In a vote deemed somewhat less than free and fair by independent Nigerian and international ob-

servers—including Falae, who claimed they were fraudulent—Gen. Obasanjo won a lopsided victory. With the support of a large majority (62.8 percent), mostly in the Southeast and North, Obasanjo enjoyed the backing of some 18.7 million voters from all major ethnic and religious groups. Although Obasanjo is Yoruba from the Southwest (and a Christian), most Yorubas disliked him because of his past support for the Hausa-led military and his close associations with Hausa leaders during the presidential campaign. The majority of Yorubas voted for Falae, who also comes from their group, and many voiced displeasure with the election results. Nevertheless, Obasanjo's victory represented the first time someone from his region and ethnicity had been elected president with an ethnically mixed base of support. Falae garnered about 11 million votes. Despite the apparent irregularities, the victory of Obasanjo and his party was undeniable. On May 29, 1999, the military formally stepped aside and civilian rule at long last returned to Nigeria. The country's **Third Republic** was at last a reality.

Obasanjo is widely believed to be the one leader who can lead Nigeria out of its deep crisis. The country now has the opportunity to restore some legitimacy to its government, to begin developing anew, and to realize its long-lost potential. The obstacles are enormous. Nigeria's tradition of democratic pluralism and constitutionalism has been undermined systematically for years by military officers and inept civilian leaders. Larry Diamond, a renowned scholar of the struggle for democracy in that country, uses the term **praetorianism** to characterize Nigeria's postindependence political system: a system in which raw power occupies the pursuits of political leaders and factions, and constitutional rules are manipulated for individual gain. Diamond perceptively argues that the "the modern state was a resource, devoid of moral content or attachment, to be pursued, occupied, milked—and later plundered—for the individual politician and his support group."[22] Against this inherited weight of the past, the Obasanjo regime has little time to restore the country's vitality. The future of democracy in Nigeria is by no means assured. But what strikes observers of Nigerian politics as particularly impressive is the dogged commitment of democratic activists to embark on yet another transition from

President Olusegun Obasanjo with U.S. Secretary of State Madeleine K. Albright.

TABLE 24.3
Rulers of Post-independence Nigeria

Ruler	Dates of Rule	Ethnic Group	How Power Attained
The First Republic, 1960–66			
Tafawa Balewa (Prime minister)	1960–66	Hausa-Fulani	Elected
Nnamdi Azikiwe (President)	1963–66	Igbo	Appointed
Gen. Johnson Aguiyi-Ironsi	1966	Igbo	Military coup
Lt. Col. Yakabu Gowon	1966–75	Tiv	Military coup
Brig. Gen. Murtala Muhammed	1975	Hausa-Fulani	Military coup
Lt. Gen. Olusegun Obasanjo	1976–79	Yoruba	Appointed by military
The Second Republic, 1979–83			
Alhaji Shehu Shagari	1979–83	Hausa-Fulani	Elected
Maj. Gen. Mohammed Buhari	1983–85	Hausa-Fulani	Military coup
Maj. Gen. Ibrahim Babangida	1985–93	Gwari	Appointed by military
Chief Ernest Adegunle Shonekon	1993	Yoruba	Appointed by military
Gen. Sani Abacha	1993–98	Kanuri	Military coup
Gen. Abdulsalami Abubaker	1998–99	Nupé	Appointed by military
The Third Republic, 1999–			
Olusegun Obasanjo	1999–	Yoruba	Elected

military dictatorship in spite of the poor record of democratic governments in Nigeria.

HYPOTHESIS-TESTING EXERCISE: Democracy in Nigeria

The new civilian rulers of Nigeria's Third Republic, which finally got off the ground with the 1999 elections, must deal with a daunting array of challenges. We can usefully assess where Nigeria stands at the start of the new millennium and speculate about its possible future course by measuring it against the ten criteria for democratization discussed in chapter 10.

HYPOTHESES AND VARIABLES
We hypothesized that democracy's prospects depend to a considerable extent on meeting these criteria. Each *condition* constitutes an **independent variable** that has a presumed impact on whether democracy comes about at all and, if it does, how likely it is to survive the initial democratization process and become consolidated into a stable democracy over the long term. *Democracy, the democratization process,* and *the gradual consolidation of democracy* are thus the **dependent variables** in our hypotheses; that is, they are *dependent* on the independent variables on our list.

EXPECTATIONS
If our hypotheses are correct, we would expect that if a country succeeds in meeting most of the conditions we've set forth, then its prospects for developing a

democracy in the first place and sustaining it through the consolidation process rise appreciably. Conversely, failure to meet even a few of these criteria should tend to diminish democracy's chances. How has Nigeria done thus far in fulfilling these conditions, and what are its likely prospects in the future?

EVIDENCE
State Institutions
State institutions in Nigeria have been well conceived in theory, but in practice historically frail and unable to withstand the pressures of ethnic and regional divisions and the temptations presented for officeholders to skim from the national coffers. The strict observance of the rule of law—and the elimination of corruption in particular—will be crucial in the coming years if democracy is to succeed in Nigeria. Similarly, a fair application of federalist principles to the country's diverse regional, ethnic, and religious groupings will also be essential. Institutions alone, however, are not enough to consolidate democracy.

Elites Committed to Democracy
In the past, Nigerian political leaders often substituted military dictatorship for civilian democracy and used state offices to enhance their own personal wealth. The new ruling elite under President Obasanjo seems genuinely committed to democracy, though corruption remains rife in many institutions. In view of the importance of Nigeria's central government in holding the reins of power and national wealth, the commitment of its political elites to democratic rule—above all the military elites—will be vital to the survivability of democracy in Nigeria.

National Wealth

Nigeria's national wealth is highly dependent on a single commodity, oil. Oil accounts for 95 percent of the government's revenues and has reaped about $280 billion in total revenues since the 1970s. Unfortunately, just about all of that money was squandered by corrupt leaders. In early 2000, buoyant world oil prices helped improve economic performance and increase export earnings. But the volatility of the oil market suggests that Nigeria needs to deal with endemic poverty and structural inequality before its economic bounty can truly contribute to the consolidation of democracy. Nigeria remains one of the poorest countries in the world, with a per capita GNP in the late 1990s of about $300 a year. Oil revenues alone are insufficient to provide a suitable economic base for the consolidation of democracy. The country will need a painful and disruptive structural adjustment in the economy, a process that is just as likely to destabilize the democratization process as lead to the consolidation of democracy.

Private Enterprise

The entrepreneurial spirit of many Nigerians is legendary, and the informal economy contributes significantly to the welfare of many citizens. At the same time, rampant corruption limits the ability of private enterprise to grow and prosper. (Nigeria is rated as one of the most corrupt countries on the globe; see table 5.1 on page 111.) State ownership of the country's oil reserves and nearly all its farmland has facilitated government corruption in the past. Private enterprise will contribute to the consolidation of democracy only if the Obasanjo government can effectively root out the deep-seated corruption that limits a flourishing private sector.[23]

Middle Class

The development of a vibrant middle class in Nigeria has been stunted by the poor economic performance engendered by decades of misgovernment by the military. The country's oil wealth, in particular, has not trickled down to support the development of a strong and consolidated middle class. The absence of a secure middle class will quite probably continue to limit the consolidation of Nigeria's democracy.

Support of the Disadvantaged

Endemic poverty characterizes the lives of most Nigerians today. According to World Bank estimates, nearly 60 percent of the population lived on less than $2 a day in the early 1990s, and half of them survived on less than $1 a day. Some 35 percent of children under the age of five were malnourished in the first half of the decade and about 20 percent died before their fifth birthday. Nearly 40 percent of city dwellers lacked access to sanitation. (Nigeria's urban population exploded from 27 percent in 1980 to 41 percent by 1997.)[24] Life ex-

pectancy is fifty years. In addition, Nigeria has one of the worst maldistribution of wealth patterns in the world (see table 2.2 on page 37). AIDS is taking a rising toll—though not as severely as in other parts of Africa. About 5.4 percent of Nigerians were HIV-infected by the end of 1999, with as many as five million AIDS deaths to be expected in the next ten years. AIDS research and medical facilities have received scant funding in Nigeria thus far, however. Agricultural production has fallen far below the country's potential as a producer of cocoa, rubber, cotton, and other valuable commodities, thanks in large measure to inept government policies under the military. While there is support among the disadvantaged for clean democratic governance, this support will likely dissipate if economic growth and a fairer distribution of wealth is not achieved by the Obasanjo regime. Widespread poverty and high levels of inequality will quite probably limit Nigeria's ability to consolidate democratic institutions.

Civil Society and Political Culture

Nigeria boasts a vibrant civil society with a plethora of associations and trade unions. The vigor of Nigeria's civil society has been one reason why military regimes have experienced strong pressures for a return to civilian rule. We believe that Nigeria's civil society will contribute to the likelihood that democratic institutions will continue to be perceived as the only truly legitimate form of government, bolstering the chances that democracy can be consolidated over time.

Education and Freedom of Information

Illiteracy in Nigeria exceeds 35 percent of the population in some areas. Without a greater emphasis on education and the extension of literacy to a great proportion of the population, Nigeria's chances for long-term consolidation of democracy are slim. Though the country boasts a vigorous free press, the newly elected government will have to take action to lift prior decrees restricting press freedoms and refrain from exercising excessive government controls over the media if democratic liberties are to be fully guaranteed.

Homogeneous Society

As we've abundantly observed, Nigeria's ethnic divisions have been a constant strain on its attempts at democracy, even though the immediate causes of the downfall of the First and Second Republics were other factors such as corruption and malfeasance. Ominous signs of religious and ethnic strife confronted the new Third Republic in its first year. In March 2000, some 800 people were killed in separate clashes between Christians and Muslims as the leaders of Muslim-dominated parts of the North sought to impose Islamic law in their localities and Christians in both the North and South vented their anger. Fortunately,

Nigeria's political institutions—while not fully consociational as described in chapter 8—have been carefully crafted to help manage ethnic differences. Nigeria's diversity is thus a possible, but not inevitable, barrier to the consolidation of its democracy, depending upon how fairly the central authorities apply the constitution's federalist principles. Multiethnicity in and of itself need not undermine democracy in Nigeria, however.

Favorable International Environment

Nigeria's external environment has not been especially conducive to supporting democratic institutions; civil wars in Liberia and Sierra Leone, for example, have drawn Nigeria into costly engagements abroad. Yet the broader international community has been very supportive of democracy in Nigeria, and pressure from overseas has been one of the reasons why military regimes have been compelled to return to civilian rule. (President Clinton visited the country in August 2000.) Considerable international assistance—in the form of political party training, election monitoring, and development aid—will be critical to the long-term viability of democracy in Nigeria.

CONCLUSIONS

The evidence from Nigeria's checkered experience with democracy since independence, and from its current situation, is quite *mixed*. Positive tendencies coexist with less favorable ones. Political science predictions can by no means plot Nigeria's trajectory with any degree of certainty. Much depends on the ability of the government to manage ethnic tensions, contain political infighting, revive its flagging economy, and especially, root out deep-seated corruption. As a purely speculative prognosis, we can regard Nigeria's chances as doubtful, given the strains to which it will be put.

The consolidation of democracy in Nigeria will no doubt be a lengthy process; there seems to be widespread popular support for the notion of democracy, but not a great deal of satisfaction with the institutions and practices of successive civilian and military governments. It is by no means clear that the rules of the democratic game in this most populous African country are entrenched and that its national unity will be restored and maintained. Clearly the first step in the consolidation process will be to ensure that democratic governance pays direct dividends to a people who have long suffered under corruption, mismanagement, and staggering poverty. Only one thing is for sure: as Nigeria goes, so goes much of West Africa.

SOUTH AFRICA

Population (1999 estimated): 43.4 million
Area: 471,444 square miles
(about twice the size of Texas)

Democratization in South Africa, Africa's other most important state, has taken a path markedly different from Nigeria. The dramatic transition from white minority rule and apartheid—the enforced separation of people on the basis of race and ethnicity—to democracy in 1994 reveals a remarkable story of a country that was on the brink of civil war, yet managed to avoid the abyss. In doing so, it embraced a multiracial democracy in which all citizens are entitled to vote and enjoy equal human rights regardless of race or ethnic origin. South Africa's success at democratization is a consequence of an unusual confluence of historical events, such as the end of the Cold War, and the equally unique quality of its leadership, particularly the Nobel Prize–winning Nelson Mandela, the legendary freedom fighter who became the country's first black president.

South Africa's path of transition was the result of extensive negotiation and compromise among its competing political forces.[25] A white minority settler society ruled over the majority black population of South Africa for some 350 years, from the day the first settlers set foot on the Cape Peninsula in 1648. After mounting pressures in the 1980s and 1990s, the ruling regime—led by the **National Party (NP),** which gained power in 1948 and implemented the policies of apartheid—agreed to a series of extensive negotiations on a new constitution with the leading force in the liberation movement, Mandela's African National Congress. These negotiations were highly turbulent: indeed, some fourteen thousand people died in political violence during this widely heralded "peaceful" transition. But in the end they yielded one of the most progressive democratic constitutions on the globe. Today, South Africa is a highly regarded developing state. Although it faces tremendous challenges in confronting the legacy of apartheid, the country's prospects for the consolidation of democracy are widely considered good. How did a country headed for a brutal war manage to transform itself into a model multiethnic democracy?

The Roots of Apartheid

Apartheid means "separateness" in Afrikaans, the language of the descendants of Dutch and French settlers of southern Africa known as **Afrikaners.** The policy of apartheid has its antecedents in the

South Africa

domination of the white settlers over the indigenous African peoples that begin with the arrival of the first colonists in the late seventeenth century. Yet apartheid was more than just colonial domination; rather, it was a systematic division of the country's peoples based on race and ethnic origin. The policies of apartheid were intensified by the National Party, led by Afrikaners, after it took power in whites-only elections in 1948; but its roots lay deep in South African history. Indeed, some suggest that the more pernicious effects of apartheid were as much a legacy of British rule in South Africa (extending roughly from 1800 to 1910) as they were the result of the Afrikaners and the National Party. Even so, the post-1948 white-majority regimes in South Africa perfected laws of racial domination—especially the exclusion of the country's majority black population from the voting franchise—and it was these measures particularly that led to a black uprising that eventually brought apartheid to an end.

South Africa's historical trajectory is rich and complicated.[26] Originally, it was a colony of the Dutch East India Company, which needed this southern crossroads of the world as a way station for ships rounding the Cape of Good Hope en route to and from the colonies of the West Indies.

Shortly after the founding of the Cape Colony in 1648, settlers arrived and the dynamics of a highly diverse society began to emerge. Upon their arrival, the Dutch settlers found indigenous Khoikhoi and San peoples, whom they quickly subjugated using their superior technology, firearms. The settlers imported slaves and indentured labor from Dutch colonies in East Asia and began to implement strict policies of racial segregation. Imperial contests ended Dutch rule by the turn of the nineteenth century, and the British took over the southern African colonies. British suzerainty and policies banning slave ownership led to an uprising by the Dutch-speaking settlers (the Boers), and by 1838 all slaves in the colony had been emancipated. Consequently, the Boers migrated into the vast interior of the subcontinent, in a pioneer march known as the Great Trek. At the same time, however, African tribes such as the Zulu and Xhosa had settled into the east and south, and black-white conflicts and wars erupted on the frontier. In 1838, for example, the well-known battle of Blood River occurred in which Afrikaner commandos (known as Voortrekkers) defeated the army of **King Shaka** of the Zulus.

By the mid-nineteenth century, the British controlled the Cape Colony as well as the eastern coastal zone of Natal. The Voortrekkers set up independent republics known as the Transvaal and the Orange Free State. In perhaps the most pivotal historical event in South African history, in 1867 diamonds and later huge gold deposits were discovered in the deep interior of the country; a rush for wealth began. Hundreds of thousands of new European settlers migrated into the Boer republics as tremendous mineral deposits were discovered. Conflict among the whites soon grew over the newfound treasure. The British governor, Sir Cecil Rhodes, sought to undermine the Boer republics and the result was the **Boer War** of 1899–1902, in which British control of the entire territory of southern Africa was secured. The struggle embittered many Afrikaners: British troops committed untold atrocities, including the incarceration of Boer women and children in concentration camps. Although South Africa became independent in 1910, conflict among the whites and domination over blacks became the hallmarks of South African society.

Steadily throughout the early half of the twentieth century, South Africa's economy boomed from mineral wealth. Meanwhile the Afrikaners, many of whom were farmers or laborers, became increasingly nationalistic. They mobilized against black migrants to the cities who threatened their meager wages and also against English-speaking whites who controlled South Africa's capital, its mines, and the means of industrial production. Blacks were relegated to 13 percent of the land, encompassing the least agriculturally productive parcels. The Afrikaner nationalists, stirring up so-called poor white resentments, won progressively larger support among the Afrikaners, who themselves constituted a majority of the whites. They argued for stricter policies of racial segregation and discrimination against the burgeoning black population. They also claimed a Christian basis for their policies, locating its origins in a highly puritan form of Calvinism that they claimed ordained white domination over blacks in South Africa.

White Domination and Black Protest

By 1948, the Afrikaner-led National Party managed to gain power in an all-white election by employing the political and religious myths that demanded Afrikaner control of southern Africa as a matter of destiny. The policies of apartheid began to be systematically implemented. The entire population was registered by race: African (70 percent in 1960), Colored (mixed ancestry, 10 percent), Indian/Asian (10 percent), and white (20 percent). Mixed marriages and romance across the race bar were forbidden. Racially exclusive areas were demarcated, and blacks were forbidden in cities unless they had a pass that certified their employment. Blacks were assigned separate services such as water fountains, public transportation, and bathrooms, and they were denied education, health services, and other opportunities despite the fact that it was on their backs that a prosperous, modern industrial country was being built.

In the vision of the architect of "grand apartheid," President **Henrik Verwoerd,** South Africa was to be partitioned. The "homelands," or reservations, were created for the ten major black linguistic groups; gradually they became independent black islands in a broader white South African sea. The South African government regarded the homelands as independent states, and their residents were not regarded as South African citizens. Hence they could be classified as migrant workers and were denied unemployment compensation and other benefits. No foreign country ever recognized the homelands' independent status, however. Apartheid was created to systematically exclude the majority black population from citizenship and economic opportunity in its own country.

At the same time that the pernicious policies of apartheid were being implemented, blacks began to develop their own competing national identity, arguing for an end to apartheid policies in their petty form (such as separate amenities) as well as in their more extensive form of "grand apartheid," which set up the system of homelands. On March 21, 1960, in the township of Sharpeville. the first black riots erupted. Blacks burned the passes that they were required to carry; sixty died as the result of police brutality. Today that date is celebrated as Human Rights Day. In a spiral of revolt and repression, black anger grew and the state responded with brutal force. The **African National Congress (ANC)**—the organizational arm of the

A sign reflects the realities of apartheid in South Africa.

anti-apartheid movement—was banned, along with other black organizations. **Nelson Mandela,** a young ANC activist, was arrested and convicted of treason in the landmark Rivonia trial; he entered prison in 1962. As the protests grew, so did the repression and the whites' commitment to the systematic exclusion of blacks. Although some whites argued for progressive change, most supported the National Party's program of separation and domination. From 1948 to 1984, National Party governments were returned to power with enlarged electoral majorities among whites.

Black protest grew more fervent in the 1970s. By June 1976, widespread riots erupted throughout the sprawling townships that lay astride South African's major cities. Beginning in **Soweto** near Johannesburg, youths set the country aflame, and widespread unrest drew more outside attention to the tragic oppression of the country's majority black population. In 1977 the United Nations imposed an arms embargo on South Africa and the litany of denunciation by the international community against apartheid began. Subsequent sports and cultural boycotts heightened pressure on the white government to reform. Just as the rest of the world was moving away from colonialism, racial segregation, and denial of human rights in the 1960s and 1970s, South Africa was moving in the opposite direction.

Apartheid could not hold back the economic forces that led desperately poor black laborers to flock to the cities. The country's cities and their environs witnessed a growing influx of blacks—despite brutal government policies of influx control—

pushed by the country's tremendous industrial development after World War II and by the diamond and gold wealth extracted from the earth. The government tried various measures to stem the tide of urbanization, such as forced removals and the deeply hated "pass" system, which required blacks to carry cards certifying their employment eligibility. Despite ever-increasing repressive measures, domestic discontent and international condemnation continued to ratchet up the pressure on a recalcitrant and entrenched white minority government.

By the mid-1980s, more comprehensive economic sanctions dried up new foreign investment, technology transfers, and trade opportunities. The once-roaring economy floundered and a recession set in during the early 1980s. About the same time, the first fissures emerged in what had been a brick wall of resistance put up by white South Africans. Under the reformist president **P. W. Botha,** the South African government began to ease some of the more discriminatory laws of apartheid while reinforcing its commitment to maintaining white dominance in general.

The halfhearted reforms of the 1980s eliminated some of the more overtly discriminatory laws—such as separate public amenities like drinking fountains—but not the foundation of the system, the race-based categories of citizenship. Far from diffusing black anger and international disapproval, the reforms led instead to a renewed protest movement and a significant energizing of the international anti-apartheid movement.[27] Widespread protests erupted again in September 1984 in a popular upsurge of demands for democracy, human rights, and full enfranchisement of the black majority. In 1986, the U.S. Congress passed the Comprehensive Anti-Apartheid Act, which included a ban on new investment and promised new sanctions if further reforms weren't enacted. (President Ronald Reagan had opposed the measure on the grounds that it would limit the administration's ability to persuade the white minority government to peacefully cede power.)

Many other countries imposed stiff economic sanctions. With internal and external pressures mounting, the white minority reached a turning point by 1989, the same year that the Berlin Wall opened. White leaders could try to defend their indefensible polices of racial domination and face an all-out race war with the majority blacks in their country, or they could seek to reach an accommodation with black leaders such as Mandela before it was too late. Wisely, they chose the latter. Political violence was already high between 1984 and 1989, and without further reforms the black townships would once again explode in protest.

A series of unpredictable events unleashed the process of transition in South Africa. In early 1989, the recalcitrant President Botha suffered a debilitating heart attack. Though he had initiated contacts with Mandela, who was still in jail, Botha was a reluctant reformer who would not take the steps necessary to end the unrest. Later that year, the fall of communism created a situation in which the white minority—which had long claimed that the ANC was controlled by the Soviets in Moscow—could feel comfortable that black rule would not result in the widespread expropriation of property and industry. Botha was succeeded by a man with a reputation as a hard-liner, **F. W. de Klerk,** in August 1989.

The stage was now set for a dramatic change of fortune for South Africa. On February 2, 1990, de Klerk shocked white South Africans and the world. He announced the release of Mandela and scores of other political prisoners, lifted the bans on the ANC and other anti-apartheid organizations, invited exiles to return home, and promised to negotiate in good faith the end of apartheid and the dawn of a fully inclusive democracy for all South Africans. Addressing the white minority government's longstanding enemies, de Klerk invited them to "walk through the open door, take your place at the negotiating table together with the government and other leaders who have important power bases inside and outside of parliament. . . . The time for negotiation has arrived." The transition had begun in earnest. Two weeks later Mandela appeared on the steps of City Hall in Cape Town before a joyous crowd after twenty-seven years in prison.

PROFILE: Nelson Mandela

Nelson Rolihlahla Mandela is the father of post-apartheid South Africa. He led the independence struggle from his jail cell on Robben Island off Cape Town for nearly three decades, finally emerging from prison to ne-

gotiate with the white regime a new constitution that would guarantee voting rights to the majority black population. He served as the country's first president under the new political order from 1994 to 1999. He is extremely popular among all segments of the population—including the white minority—and is hailed as the one individual most responsible for South Africa's dramatic transition to democracy. In 1993, he and F. W. de Klerk were awarded the Nobel Peace Prize for their dedication to a negotiated settlement.

Born July 18, 1918, in a small village in the former Transkei homeland (in today's Eastern Cape province, near Umtata), Mandela was the son of the principal councillor to the Acting Paramount Chief of Thembuland. After his father passed away, he emerged as the Paramount Chief's principal aide, a position that was certain to lead to high office in the traditional tribal hierarchy. At an early age, he dedicated himself to the study of law. To prepare for that path, he was educated in a local mission school. Upon graduation from high school, Mandela entered the University of Fort Hare, where he was for a time suspended for protesting discriminatory racial policies in the country. He eventually migrated to Johannesburg, where he studied law and began his political career by joining the African National Congress in 1942.

In the booming Johannesburg metropolis, Mandela forged ties with other young, intelligent black activists, such as Oliver Tambo and Walter Sisulu, and they banded together to found the ANC Youth League. The League and these fraternal ties became extremely important to South Africa's trajectory; Mandela and his companions espoused an ideology of African nationalism and began to organize and mobilize the ANC to challenge the powerful white minority establishment. The youth organizers eventually were elected to the National Executive Committee of the ANC.

After the end of World War II, when the extreme Afrikaner National Party won elections and began to implement policies of apartheid, Mandela and the ANC became more militant, organizing boycotts, strikes, civil disobedience campaigns, and other acts of non-cooperation with the authoritarian regime. Among their demands were full citizenship and direct parliamentary representation for all South Africans regardless of color. In the early 1950s, Mandela helped organize the Defiance Campaign, traveling about the country organizing passive resistance to apartheid. Mandela and the law firm he established with Oliver Tambo were the targets of the government's security forces. In 1952, Mandela created a plan of further nonviolent resistance, particularly against the system of inferior education for blacks (known as Bantu education). In 1955, he was instrumental in the drafting of the Freedom Charter, which committed the ANC to a tolerant, multiracial South Africa with freedom and equality for all. During this time, Mandela was at times banned, arrested, and briefly imprisoned. He was accused of treason in the so-called Treason Trial of 1961, a charge that was eventually dropped.

In the early 1960s, as it became clear that the apartheid government's policies were becoming ever more cruel and discriminatory, Mandela went underground to form the armed wing of the ANC and to launch a struggle for liberation. He later wrote that only the intransigence of the apartheid government—which refused many petitions for reform—led him and his ANC colleagues turn to violent armed struggle. Mandela became commander-in-chief of Umkhonto we Sizwe, "the spear of the nation." During this time, he constantly evaded the net of the white police who sought to arrest him. Eventually they managed to apprehend him, and he was charged with treason. At the Rivonia trial, as it became known, he conducted his own defense, uttering words that continue to ring in the South African national psyche:

> I have fought against white domination, and I have fought against black domination. I have cherished the ideal of a democratic and free society in which all persons live together in harmony and with equal opportunities. It is an ideal which I hope to live for and to achieve. But if needs be, it is an ideal for which I am prepared to die.

He was convicted, sentenced to life in prison, and he spent the next twenty-seven years quietly and clandestinely directing the liberation movement from prison. By the late 1980s, white political leaders were visiting him in prison seeking a negotiated settlement. Finally, in February 1990, he was released. Remarkably, Mandela demonstrated tremendous courage and called for national reconciliation. He embraced white leaders with no sign of bitterness and steadfastly led the ANC through the difficult negotiations that produced a new constitution. With the far-reaching victory of the ANC in the first full-franchise elections in 1994, Mandela was elected president. From 1994 to 1999, he served not only as the country's chief executive, but as its moral force, firmly launching the new republic on a path of tolerance, moderate policies, and national reconciliation. After stepping down at the age of 81 in 1999, he now travels the world advocating international assistance to help poor children and mediating disputes in other countries. Mandela lives near his birthplace in a quiet rural area, tending his garden and providing moral guidance to his country.

The Turbulent Transition

The historic events of February 1990 set in motion a transition from apartheid to democracy that was full of hope for a brighter future for all South Africans but that simultaneously unleashed tremendous uncertainty. Initially, the negotiations went well, and an early accord was reached by May of that year that pledged the ANC and the government to a negotiation process that would culminate in the advent of a new, multiracial democracy in which no racial, religious, or ethnic group would dominate another. Individual human rights would prevail over structured domination by a group. All political prisoners would be released, free political activity would be allowed, and negotiations would proceed on convening a constitutional convention to draft a charter that would guide the new democracy into a more peaceful future.

Yet there were significant forces that were either opposed to the end of apartheid altogether or that were afraid that the ANC would emerge as a domineering political force despite the promises of toleration and reconciliation contained in the early agreements. In particular, the Zulu-based **Inkatha Freedom Party (IFP),** led by **Mangosutho Buthelezi,** felt excluded from the negotiations. With the help of clandestine forces in the white-led police and military, IFP cadres instigated violence, especially in the urban areas outside Johannesburg

Mangosutho Buthelezi

and in the already simmering province of KwaZulu-Natal, which included the traditional Zulu homelands. Although some analysts saw the emerging violence as ethnic—alleging that the ANC was primarily Xhosa—in reality it was a political struggle over power and turf. In the uncertainty of the transition, when apartheid was dead but the new order had not yet been created, when the rules of the political game were in flux, violence among various factions soared. Thousands died in factional fighting and fingers were pointed in all directions.

Political violence soured the initial goodwill that had been generated by Mandela's release. In 1991 and 1992, mass killings, assassinations, clashes among armed militia, and continuing police brutality undermined the incipient talks on democracy. For a while in 1992 it appeared that the talks would fail and a civil war would ensue. Clashes between ANC and IFP supporters left more than two thousand people dead in 1992 alone. Despite a major agreement in December 1991 to curb the violence—the National Peace Accord—the deaths continued to mount and several major incidents scuttled the talks. One particularly traumatic event was the June 1992 Boipatong incident, which left scores of innocent civilians dead after an attack by Zulu migrant laborers on a nearby township. Only after the intervention of the United Nations, which dispatched senior mediator Cyrus Vance, a former U.S. Secretary of State, to investigate the violence, did the country's transition get back on track. As the killing escalated, the realization set in that the country faced a truly stark choice between anarchy and war, on the one hand, and compromise and power sharing on the other.

By late 1992, the violence had shocked the political leaders—especially Mandela and de Klerk—into reaching a series of agreements that formed the essential bargain of the negotiated transition from apartheid to democracy in South Africa. Black South Africans would gain voting rights and other human rights in exchange for assurances to white South Africans that their property rights would be protected, Security force members would receive amnesty for any human rights abuses they may have committed, provided that they supplied all the details on any incidents of abuse. The African National Congress and the Na-

Uniformed members of a white supremacist Afrikaner group display their flag.

tional Party would share power after an initial election, and a government of national unity would be installed until a final constitution could be drafted that would guarantee both majority prerogatives and minority rights. South Africa would have a period of democratic power sharing in which decisions were to be taken by consensus among all the major political parties. This pact was sealed in multiparty talks that concluded in June 1993 with an agreement on a new interim constitution and a specific plan for managing the transfer of power at the end of white-minority rule.

The IFP and conservative Afrikaner parties, however, balked at the deal. They demanded greater autonomy for their respective ethnic groups—the Zulus and the Afrikaners—and vowed a campaign of violent resistance unless their demands were met. On the left, opponents of the ANC, organized in the **Pan-Africanist Congress (PAC),** also objected to the agreement, arguing that it granted too many concessions to the whites. The PAC demanded unfettered majority rule by the blacks. These disaffected parties boycotted the signing of the new interim constitution and pledged to boycott—and possibly disrupt—the momentous elections slated for April 27, 1994, the elections that would end apartheid. Preparations for the culmination of the transition and the hotly contested electoral campaigns generated tremendous tension in late 1993 and early 1994. The far-right whites and the IFP as well as the PAC were poised to spoil the vote.

Mandela's renowned qualities as a conciliator, however, produced a breakthrough in early 1994 that brought the far-right **Afrikaner Volksfront** into the election. Significantly, the Inkatha Freedom Party remained outside the agreement. Preparations for the elections went ahead and a potential showdown loomed. After a bloody confrontation in downtown Johannesburg between the IFP and the African National Congress in which scores died, cooler heads once again prevailed. Deft politicking and international mediation produced a last-minute agreement among Mandela's African National Congress, the National Party government, and the Imicatha Freedom Party, leading to an end to the latter's election boycott.[28] Stickers were placed on the already-printed ballots to include the IFP. South Africa's elections would proceed, and they would be broadly representative of all the country's major political forces.

Remarkably, the elections held on April 26 and 27, 1994, brought South Africa some of the most peaceful days in the troubled country's history. Very little political violence was reported, the vote was relatively free and fair (despite widespread administrative irregularities), and the mood in the country was joyous. The results of the election were as expected: the ANC won a handsome majority of 63 percent of the vote, the NP garnered 20 percent, and the IFP 10.5 percent. All three parties would be in the government of national unity. Nelson Mandela, the great conciliator and guardian of national reconciliation, would be president. De Klerk, along with the number-two leader in the ANC, Thabo Mbeki, would be vice presidents. Buthelezi was offered a cabinet post as home affairs minister, which he readily accepted.

THE NEW SOUTH AFRICA

The new South Africa was imbued with tremendous hope for reconciliation, economic revival, and newfound legitimacy in the world. Mandela's famous acts of magnanimity toward white South Africans and his Imkatha foes—such as meeting with the

South Africans line up to vote in the country's first multiracial national elections, April 1994.

widow of the former pro-apartheid president Henrik Verwoerd, donning the cap of the national (and historically all-white) rugby team, appointing Buthelezi acting president while he traveled abroad—did much to consolidate legitimacy for the new government. A new flag and anthem seemed to symbolically unify the nation, and many blacks and whites alike seemed relieved that the tensions generated by the enforcement of apartheid were lifted from the nation's collective shoulders.

The elections of 1994 not only produced a new power-sharing government, they also produced a constitutional assembly that would create a new national charter to permanently guide South Africa's newfound democracy. In a process known for its thoughtful deliberations, its progressive embrace of human rights, and its delicate balance between majority demands and minority fears, the Constitutional Assembly produced a new constitution in 1996. It is in many ways the greatest achievement of the democratization process that today all the major political actors in South Africa see the constitution as a legitimate set of rules for ordering the country's political life.

Yet South Africa faces tremendous economic, social, and political problems. Some are new, but others are a direct consequence of the perverse nature of apartheid. Among the critical challenges the country faces are very high levels of violent crime, economic stagnation, uneven performance in delivering key services (housing, health care, education, water, environmental quality), corruption, tensions over employment and affirmative action, a highly unequal distribution of wealth and income, and a deadly AIDS epidemic. Another significant problem is the lack of a viable opposition. Divisive struggles between labor and industry have also limited the country's "peace dividend," that is, the improvement in economic efficiency resulting from reductions in spending on military and security forces. Power sharing withered away in South Africa in 1996 as opposition parties (except, interestingly, the Inkatha Freedom Party) found their role in government too uncomfortable and chose instead to work from a position of opposition. This situation leaves the ANC in control of the government for the foreseeable future, as the party's electoral majority is secure. Some argue that it may lead to a dominant one-party state. Fortunately, the country enjoys a highly developed civil society that helps mediate social tensions. It includes a well-developed and assertive media, vigorous civic and trade associations, an active multiracial women's advocacy network, and a strong business community.

Challenges Facing the New South Africa

• **Reconciling justice and forgiveness for apartheid crimes.** The country created a **Truth and Reconciliation Commission** to review past crimes, hear testimonies, grant pardons for atrocities, and offer recommendations for social healing. Bishop **Desmond Tutu,** the Nobel Peace Prize laureate, chaired the Commission. But few were satisfied with the Commission's final report, issued in early 1999, because it not only condemned the former white minority regime for human rights abuses but also criticized the African National Congress for abuses committed during its liberation war. It also criticized Nelson Mandela's former wife, Winnie Madzhikela Mandela, for her involvement in several killings in Soweto. A lingering question for South Africa is, how can the demands of justice be reconciled with the need for forgiveness?

• **Unemployment and poverty.** South Africa's unemployment level hovers around 30 percent of the working population; half of all black youth are unemployed. About half the population lives on less than $2 a day, with about a quarter subsisting on less than $1 a day. The

maldistribution of wealth is the worst in the world with the exception of Brazil: the wealthiest fifth of the population enjoys 65 percent of the national income, while the bottom 40 percent share only about 8 percent of the country's income. Some fear that with such widespread poverty, South African society is a cauldron that will eventually boil over.

• **HIV/AIDS and other infectious diseases.** Since 1990, South Africa has witnessed a terrible epidemic of HIV/AIDS. By 2000 it had more HIV-infected people than any other country in the world: approximately 4.2 million, or one-fifth of its adult population.[29] In many hospitals, half the emergency room patients test HIV positive. Government efforts to combat the disease, as well as other threats to public health such as tuberculosis, have been riddled with corruption. Alcoholism is also rampant, posing additional health hazards.

• **Crime.** Johannesburg is the most dangerous city in the world, with a staggering number of murders and other criminal activities. Throughout the country, carjackings, rape, violence against children, robbery, killings of farmers, extortion, and other crimes make South Africa's crime situation one of the worst in the world. In 1998 there were 59 murders per 100,000 people, ten times the U.S. rate. (In 1994 the murder rate was even higher, at 69.5 per 100,000.) Some 6,000 white farmers have been killed by blacks since 1994. The police system is crippled with the legacies of apartheid, which have left it wholly illegitimate in many communities. Many South Africans are uncertain if their country can prosper as a democracy with such high crime levels. (See table 12.1 on page 272.)

• **South Africa's role in Africa and the world.** Now that South Africa is a model of interracial reconciliation and a powerhouse in sub-Saharan Africa, with the largest economy and military force, it is increasingly being called upon to assume a leadership role in world affairs. Already, South African troops have intervened in neighboring states to promote stability, and the country has contributed to regional and international peacemaking and peacekeeping efforts. For example, it has played an important role in efforts to settle the war in the Congo (formerly Zaire), but risks a possible quagmire if its troops

TABLE 24.4

National Assembly, Elected 1999 (400 Seats)	
Party	Seats
African National Congress	266
*Democratic Party	38
Inkatha Freedom Party	34
*New National Party	28
Nine others	34

*The Democratic Party has been an anti-apartheid white party, but now attracts conservative white voters; the New National Party is the descendant of the formerly pro-apartheid National Party.

President Thabo Mbeki

are sent there to keep the peace. South Africa has also adopted an open international trade and finance regime, though it remains vulnerable in a globalized international economy. Foreign investment shot up after the 1994 elections, but investors remain fickle and especially wary of the country's comparatively high labor costs (propelled upward by aggressive trade unions), its crime wave, and creeping corruption.

Some expected that the 1999 elections would generate tensions and potentially undermine social consensus in the new South Africa. Fears were raised that if the ANC garnered more than 66 percent of the vote, it could vitiate aspects of the constitution that limited its rule and protected minorities. But the elections revealed that even though the ANC does command a large majority of support in the country—it won handily with just under 66 percent of the popular support and 266 seats in the 400-member National Assembly—opposition parties are vigorous and the country's system of constitutional checks and balances remains vibrant. The country's judiciary, which has undergone major reforms, has won high praise for integrity, fairness, and a well-earned reputation for safeguarding human rights.

Many analysts around the world were concerned that, without Mandela, South Africa's fledgling democracy would begin to unravel. So far, however, his successor, **Thabo Mbeki,** a long-time ANC activist who was for many years its representative to the international community has been able to reassure the outside world and South Africans alike that he can successfully lead the country and carefully balance the need for change

with the imperative of stability. Mbeki is a technocratic leader who has taken bold steps to revise the economy and work with business. He has also sought to assuage minority concerns and to carry on Mandela's legacy of balancing social reconciliation with the long-term transformation of South Africa's highly unequal distribution of income. In some ways, Mbeki and South Africa are struggling with the reality that the enormous challenges they now face are similar to those of many other "ordinary" developing countries. These problems are enormous, to be sure, but compared with the difficulties of the past, South Africa is well along the way toward its own renaissance.

HYPOTHESIS-TESTING EXERCISE: Hypotheses About Democracy in South Africa

HYPOTHESES, VARIABLES, AND EXPECTATIONS
We conclude our analysis of South Africa in the same way we concluded our exploration of Nigeria: with a brief overview of its prospects for democracy in light of the ten conditions for democracy and democratization we developed in chapter 10. Each of these *conditions* constitutes an **independent variable** that, according to our hypotheses, has an impact on the *emergence of democracy and its consolidation* (the **dependent variables**). Our **expectation** is that the more of these conditions South Africa manages to fulfill successfully, the greater its chances are of sustaining democratic institutions and practices over the long run.

How has South Africa done thus far in fulfilling these conditions, and what are its likely prospects of the future?

EVIDENCE

State Institutions

South Africa's new democratic constitution, finalized in 1996, enjoys broad support and is widely respected within the country and abroad. It puts human rights at the forefront of state policy, strikes an admirable balance between majority prerogatives and minority protections, and shows appreciation for the principle of proportionality in representation and in the allocation of state resources. It also recognizes that South Africa must move beyond widespread economic inequality for the long-term survival of democracy. The constitution was broadly debated and is accepted by virtually all segments in South Africa's diverse social mosaic. The government's Commission on Gender Equality enforces the constitution's guarantee of equal rights for women. (About one-third of the National Assembly deputies are female, one of the highest such percentages in the world. See table 2.4 on page 42.) With such a widely accepted and progressive constitution, South Africa's state institutions are aptly designed and should help meet the society's needs for balancing stability and change.

SOUTH AFRICA'S GOVERNMENT

South Africa has a variant of what may be called a **presidential-legislative** governmental system.

- The **Parliament** is bicameral, consisting of the **National Assembly,** its lower house, and a **National Council of Provinces,** which represents the country's nine provinces as well as local governments. The National Assembly consists of between 350 and 400 deputies, elected to five-year terms on the basis of proportional representation. The National Council has ninety members selected by provincial legislatures and local governments.

- The **president** is the country's head of government and, as a member of the National Assembly, is elected by that body (not by the people). The president presides over the cabinet and appoints the **Deputy President** and other cabinet ministers, and may dismiss them. The National Assembly may remove the president only for malfeasance in office or disability.

- One of the top judicial organs is the **Constitutional Court,** which hears cases on constitutional matters and has powers of judicial review. Its eleven members are appointed by the president upon the advice of the Judicial Service Commission. The **Supreme Court of Appeal** is the highest court in civil and criminal matters.

At the same time, some government bodies—such as some regional governments—suffer from ineptitude and corruption. On balance, however, South Africa's institutions will probably contribute to the consolidation of democracy because of the broad public support for them and for the principles on which they are based.

Elites Committed to Democracy

South Africa's governing elite, especially high-level leaders of the ruling ANC, fought for decades against a strong and bitter foe to gain their right to vote and exercise basic human rights. Their commitment to democracy is thus deep and strong. At the same time, civic elites such as white business leaders have dedicated themselves to working with the new black-majority government. Similarly, opposition political party leaders have learned to work very effectively within the new institutions, and they too are committed to democratic processes. It appears that elite attitudes in South Africa are conducive to long-term democratic consolidation.

National Wealth

South Africa is the strongest regional economy in southern Africa and a significant "newly emerging market" for international investors. Its per capita GNP in the late 1990s was in the middle-income range at about $3,500. Much of the country's current infrastructure and economic development was built on mining as the critical sector—especially gold and diamonds. But mining revenues alone are insufficient to carry today's South Africa into the twenty-first century as a competitive country in the bustling international marketplace. Although natural endowments such as minerals still contribute to economic growth, South Africa will need to develop a more diverse economic base in high-technology industries. At present, its growth rate is only 2 percent to 3 percent per year, not enough to keep up with population pressures that add another 10 percent of job seekers into the employment market virtually every year. We hypothesize that national wealth will contribute to democracy's success in South Africa, but that a prolonged recession could cool public attitudes toward democracy.

Private Enterprise

The private sector remains strong in South Africa, and the ANC's moderate economic policies have begun to woo more international investors. Although domestic and international investors are still nervous about South

Africa's long-term economic prospects—especially about the power of the trade unions—the country fosters private industry and, increasingly, a burgeoning tourist economy. South Africa's strong private enterprise sectors should thus contribute to democracy's consolidation.

The Middle Class

Class distinctions in South Africa are very pronounced, and a solid, multiethnic middle class is just beginning to form. Considerable emphasis has been placed on the development of a black middle class (to include other minority groups disadvantaged by apartheid as well), and signs that such a development is occurring are encouraging. The evidence to date suggests that, over the long term, South Africa will likely develop a fairly broad middle class that will contribute to democracy's consolidation.

Support of the Disadvantaged

Endemic poverty still grips many South Africans; some 20 percent of the population live below the poverty line. The country has alarmingly high rates of rural and urban poverty, unemployment, and health issues such as pandemics of AIDS and tuberculosis. The ANC government is committed to building a more viable social safety net even as resource scarcity limits initiatives such as those to build more houses for people who still live in informal settlements (shantytowns). The likely continued commitment to poverty eradication should increase the probability of democratic consolidation in South Africa.

Civil Society and Political Culture

One of the consequences of the anti-apartheid struggle has been the strengthening of civic institutions, from neighborhood committees to professional associations, trade unions, women and youth groups, and numerous others. The political culture remains one that emphasizes consensus building and compromise. South Africa's diverse and sophisticated civil society and its newfound tolerant political culture are making major contributions to the survivability of democratic decision making.

Education and Freedom of Information

Transforming the education system in South Africa in recent years has been one of the most difficult challenges for the ANC government. Eighteen percent of the population is illiterate, according to the Development Program.[30] Years of inferior "Bantu education" for blacks, as it was known, has left a system of schools for the majority black population that are riddled with problems. Teachers and resources are extremely scarce and the administrative aspects of education have been dismal. At the same time, the country has a world-class system of higher education and a strong potential in developing new models of community college development. While education policies are improving, the travails of South Africa's education system are a serious impediment to the long-term survivability of democracy. A poor education system will limit the opportunities for democratic consolidation in South Africa. Meanwhile, the country also enjoys a vigorous, capable, and independent media sector.

Homogeneous Society

Ethnic, racial, and religious diversity has been a challenge for South Africa since the very first days of European settlement. Nevertheless, it has emerged from apartheid as one of the most progressive, multicultural countries on the globe, with a widespread commitment to unity in diversity—the "rainbow nation," as some have termed it. Blacks now comprise about 75 percent of the population, whites about 14 percent; about 9 percent are of mixed race and 2 percent are East Indian. Two out of three South Africans are Christian (including 60 percent of blacks), while about 30 percent have traditional animist beliefs. There are also small communities of Muslims (2 percent) and Hindus (1.5 percent). If present trends continue, ethnic and racial diversity will not seriously impede progress toward the consolidation of democracy in South Africa.

International Environment

South Africa's regional environment remains perilous. Civil wars and instability in neighboring states such as Angola and the Congo seriously threaten regional stability and could draw South Africa into costly military engagements—as combatants or peacekeepers—in the years to come. These wars and regional economic stagnation also limit South Africa's ability to be the economic engine of southern Africa, as it purports to be. At the same time, the broader support among the international community for democracy and development in South Africa remains high. International support for South Africa's mascent democracy will, on balance, help bolster the likelihood that it will continue to develop as a democracy.

CONCLUSIONS

South Africa remains a society deeply divided by race, wealth, and ethnicity. Will South Africa's "miracle" transition succumb to the pressures of ethnic and racial extremism, as some competent and highly regarded analysts of politics in deeply divided societies have predicted?[31] Although there are incipient stresses in the newfound social cohesion that was the immediate outcome of the South African transition,[32] the patterns of intergroup bargaining that arose during the 1990–94 transition from apartheid to nonracial democracy are deeply embedded in many sectors of South African society, including its new political institutions. Remarkably, this political culture of bargaining, steeped in the necessity of pragmatic moderation that propelled the transition, has been sustained in the post-apartheid era despite the overwhelming electoral predominance of the African National Congress government. Ethnic conflict—which characterizes the vast majority of contemporary civil wars and political violence—still remains a long-term threat to this newborn democracy, if conclusions from the comparative studies of deeply divided societies are any guide.[33] Moreover, there is a growing sense that the multiracial "rainbow-nation" ethos is fading as clouds of ethnic and racial assertiveness appear on the horizon. For example, tensions have flared in the Western Cape province, especially near Cape Town, between blacks and coloreds (those of mixed ancestry). A persistent problem remains that of "white flight," in which skilled whites are emigrating overseas in search of better employment and more security; some estimates are that ten thousand skilled white professionals leave the country every year.

Moreover, South Africa's new constitution, approved in May 1996 (and subsequently amended in response to the Constitutional Court), establishes a system of rules that provide incentives for moderation on divisive ethnic and racial themes. Even though it is essentially a majoritarian constitution, conferring primary governmental responsibility on the majority party or parties, the institutions it has created contain myriad features that may check majority powers and mediate current and potential intergroup conflicts. The judiciary and an independent human rights commission, for example, have helped mediate disputes relating to own-language education and to women's rights, both in the workplace and on reproductive issues. The new political system, over time, will likely encourage the continued integration of South African society, providing institutional remedies and protections to its various minority ethnic and religious groups. For democracy to succeed, a strong civil society and a reinvigorated state (one that has earned legitimacy from its people) will be required, and South Africa appears to be well on the way to securing them.[34]

As long as South Africa's homegrown culture of bargaining, consultation, and intergroup consensus seeking is maintained—however inefficient and laborious such decision making may be—the country's transformation from being the locus of one of the most intractable ethnic conflicts on the globe to one of the world's most promising multiethnic democracies is likely to continue its present, relatively successful, course. This transformation has much to do with the high quality of its leadership, particularly the exceptional efforts of former president Nel-

son Mandela to keep nation building and reconciliation on the front burner of the country's political life.

In sum, we can conclude that the evidence available thus far is mostly *consistent* with the notion that democracy is gaining a firm foothold in South Africa. These grounds for optimism do not mean that South Africa won't remain deeply divided along ethnic and racial lines. Indeed, as South African political analyst Steven Friedman writes, "The post-1948 legacy of violence and racial polarization seems likely to ensure that a South African democracy will be partial, at least for the next decade. South Africa remains a divided society in which pluralism and compromise presented themselves to political leaders as an unavoidable necessity, not a preferred option."[35] The cleavages of conflict exacerbated by apartheid endure, to be sure. Although the negotiated transition to democracy buried apartheid laws, black-white tensions continue and new, unforeseen social tensions have emerged that deserve careful analysis and preventive, meliorative policies. Racial violence among youth in the mega-cities of Johannesburg and Cape Town have set off alarm bells that the new generation is not fully committed to interracial harmony and ethnic diversity.

The critical question for South Africa is whether its political leaders will succumb to the lure of "playing the ethnic card." To what extent, for example, will they try to outbid one another in making extravagant or inflammatory promises to their constituents on sensitive ethnic and racial themes in forthcoming national, local, and provincial electoral contests? And how will the public respond to such overtures?[36]

CONCLUSION

United Nations Secretary General Kofi Annan, who hails from Ghana, has echoed South African President Thabo Mbeki's call for an African renaissance. After witnessing great suffering as a result of the brutal civil war in Sierra Leone, he saw, in the midst of the atrocities of this war, a sense of optimism about Africa emanating from "the resilience and hope that form the reality of Africa today. . . . Never has Africa been more in need of political and financial help," he said. "But never, perhaps, has it been better placed to benefit from it."[37] Africa's fifty-four countries are potentially on the cusp of a new era in which these societies will learn from past mistakes and embrace a course of development and prosperity. Virtually all observers agree that if such a rebirth is to occur, democratic governance will need to be fostered.

Today, Africa's two most important countries—Nigeria, its most populated, and South Africa, its most economically developed—have seen dramatic transitions to democratic rule. The conclusion of this chapter is that consolidating democratic governance in these two countries, which are pivotal players in their regions and throughout the continent, will be a principal prerequisite to realizing the dream of renaissance and renewal for Africa.

KEY TERMS AND NAMES
(Underlined in the text.)

Africa

Developmental dictatorship
Colonialism
Julius Nyerere
Jomo Kenyatta
Leopold Senghor
Kwame Nkrumah
Kemmeth Kaunda
Patrimonial rule
Hegemonic exchange

Nigeria

Igbo (Ibo)
Yoruba
Hausa-Fulami
First Republic (1960–66)
Prebendalism
Biafra
Olusegum Obasanjo
Second Republic (1979–83)
Ibrahimm Babangida
Third Republic (1999–present)
Praetorianism

South Africa

National Party
Apartheid
Afrikaners
King Shaka
Boer War
Verwoerd
African National Congress
Nelson Mandela
Soweto

P.W. Botha
F.W. De Klerk
Inkatha Freedom Party
Pan-Africanist Congress
Desmond Tutu
Thabo Mbeki

FOR DISCUSSION: WHAT WOULD YOU DO?

1. If you were a member of a particular ethnic group in Nigeria, what would be your attitudes toward democracy?
2. If you were a black South African, what would be your attitudes toward white South Africans guilty of persecuting blacks in the apartheid period?

FOR FURTHER READING

Naomi Chazan, Robert Mortimer, John Ravenhill, and Donald Rothchild, *Politics and Society in Contemporary Africa,* 2d ed. (Boulder, Colo.: Lynne Rienner, 1992).

Pierre Du Toit, *State Building and Democracy in Southern Africa: Botswana, Zimbabwe, and South Africa* (Washington, D.C.: United States Institute of Peace Press, 1995).

Donald Horowitz, *A Democratic South Africa? Constitutional Engineering in a Divided Society* (Berkeley: University of California Press, 1991).

Robert H. Jackson and Carl G. Rosberg, *Personal Rule in Black Africa* (Los Angeles and Berkeley: University of California Press, 1982).

R. W. Johnson and Lawrence Sclemmer, eds., *Launching Democracy in South Africa: The First Open Election, April 1994* (New Haven, Conn.: Yale University Press, 1996).

Richard Joseph, ed., *State, Conflict, and Democracy in Africa* (Boulder, Colo.: Lynne Rienner, 1999).

Robert Kaplan, *The Ends of the Earth* (New York: Random House, 1996).

Andrew Reynolds, ed., *Election '94 South Africa: An Analysis of the Campaigns, Results, and Future Prospects* (New York: St. Martin's Press, 1994).

Donald Rothchild, *Managing Ethnic Conflict in Africa: Pressures and Incentives for Cooperation* (Washington, D.C.: Brookings Institution, 1997).

——— and Victor O. Olorunsola, eds., *State Versus Ethnic Claims: African Policy Dilemmas* (Boulder, Colo.: Westview, 1983).

Peter J. Schraeder, *African Politics and Society: A Mosaic in Transformation* (New York: St. Martin's Press, 1999).

Timothy Sisk, *Democratization in South Africa: The Elusive Social Contract* (Princeton, N.J.: Princeton University Press, 1995).

————and Andrew Reynolds, eds., *Elections and Conflict Management in Africa* (Washington, D.C.: United States Institute of Peace Press, 1998).

Leonard Thompson, *A History of South Africa* (New Haven, Conn.: Yale University Press, 1990).

————, *The Political Mythology of Apartheid* (New Haven, Conn.: Yale University Press, 1985).

John A. Wiseman, *Democracy in Black Africa: Survival and Renewal* (New York: Paragon House, 1990).

Crawford M. Young, *The Politics of Cultural Pluralism* (Madison: University of Wisconsin Press, 1976).

WEBSITES

African Studies WWW, University of Pennsylvania: www.sas.upenn.edu/African_Studies/AS.html

African Studies Internet Resources, Columbia University: www.columbia.edu/cu/libraries/indiv/area/Africa/

Northwestern University: www.nwu.edu./african-studies/

Africa News Online: www.africanews.org

Nordic Africa Institute: www.nai.uu.se

U.S. Institute of Peace: www.usip.org

Nigeria: Brown University: www.stg.brown.edu/projects/hypertext/landow/post/nigeria/

Electoral Institute of South Africa: www.eisa.org.za

African National Congress of South Africa: www.anc.org.za

NOTES

1. Statement at the Africa Telecom Forum, Johannesburg, May 4, 1998.
2. For a more thorough treatment, see Peter J. Schraeder, *African Politics and Society: A Mosaic in Transformation* (New York: St. Martin's Press, 1999) and Naomi Chazan et al., *Politics and Society in Contemporary Africa*, 2d ed. (Boulder, Colo.: Lynne Rienner, 1992).
3. For the rankings of African states on the United Nations Development Program's Human Development Index (a combination of a number of development indicators), see <http://www.undp.org/hdro/98hdi3.htm>.
4. We will concentrate on the states of sub-Saharan Africa in this chapter. Although part of the African land mass and active players in African politics, the Arab states of the Maghreb region—Morocco, Algeria, Tunisia, Libya, and Egypt—are more closely associated with the Mediterranean and Middle East regions.
5. See <http://www.refer.sn/sngal_ct/cop/goree/fgoree.htm>.
6. See Gerald Bender, *Angola Under the Portuguese: The Myth and Reality* (Berkeley and Los Angeles: University of California Press, 1978).
7. The Commonwealth consists of former British colonies or dependencies that are now independent countries. Membership is voluntary, and the organization's main function is consultation on such matters as economic cooperation, technical assistance, terrorism, and drug trafficking. At the end of 1999 there were fifty-two member states.
8. See Gus Liebenow, "The Impact of Colonialism," in *African Politics: Crises and Challenges* (Bloomington; Indiana University Press, 1986).
9. See Zaki Laidi, *The Superpowers and Africa: The Constraints of Rivalry, 1960–1990* (Chicago: University of Chicago Press, 1990).
10. This argument was first articulated by Sir Arthur Lewis in his classic book, *Politics in West Africa* (London: Allen and Unwin, 1965).
11. See Richard Sklar, "The Nature of Class Domination in Africa," *The Journal of Modern African Studies* 17, 4 (1978): 531–52.
12. See Robert Jackson and Carl Rosberg, *Personal Rule in Black Africa* (Los Angeles and Berkeley: University of California Press, 1982).
13. See John Wiseman, *Democracy in Black Africa: Survival and Revival* (New York: Paragon House, 1990).
14. See Donald Rothchild and Victor Oloronsula, eds., *State Versus Ethnic Claims: African Policy Dilemmas* (Boulder, Colo.: Westview Press 1983).
15. See Francis Deng et al., *Sovereignty as Responsibility: Conflict Management in Africa* (Washington, D.C.: Brookings Institution Press, 1996).
16. See Michael Bratton and Nicolas van de Walle, "Popular Protest and Political Reform in Africa," *Comparative Politics* 24 (1992): 419–42.
17. See Harvey Glickman, ed., *Ethnic Conflict and Democratization in Africa* (Atlanta, Ga.: African Studies Association Press, 1995).
18. See Timothy Sisk and Andrew Reynolds, eds., *Elections and Conflict Management in Africa* (Washington, D.C.: United States Institute of Peace Press, 1998).
19. John W. Harbeson, "Rethinking Democratic Transitions: Lessons from Eastern and Southern Africa," in Richard Joseph, ed., *State, Conflict, and Democracy in Africa* (Boulder, Colo.: Lynne Rienner Press, 1999).
20. Richard Joseph, "Autocracy, Violence, and Ethnomilitary Rule in Nigeria," in Joseph, *State, Conflict and Democracy in Africa*.
21. Donald Horowitz, *Ethnic Groups in Conflict* (Berkeley and Los Angeles: University of California Press, 1985).
22. Larry Diamond, "Nigeria: The Uncivil Society and the Desent into Praetorianism," in *Politics in the Developing Countries: Comparing Experiences with*

Democracy, ed. Larry Diamond, Juan J. Linz and Seymour Martin Lipset, 2nd ed. (Boulder, Colo: Lynne Rienner, 1995), 419.

23. See the special section on Nigeria in *The Economist*, January 15, 2000.

24. *World Development Report 1998/1999* (New York: Oxford University Press, 1999).

25. See Timothy Sisk, *Democratization in South Africa: The Elusive Social Contract* (Princeton, Princeton University Press, 1995).

26. See Leonard Thompson, *A History of South Africa* (New Haven, Conn.: Yale University Press, 1990).

27. See Robert Price, *The Apartheid State in Crisis: Political Transformation in South Africa, 1975–1990* (New York: Oxford University Press, 1991).

28 Donald Rothchild notes that international mediation was critical to the success of the South African transition despite the reluctance of the parties to external influence. See his *Managing Ethnic Conflict in Africa* (Washington, D.C.: Brookings Institution Press, 1997), 191–211.

29. *Washington Post*, June 28, 2000. In seven South African countries, at least 20 percent of the adult population are HIV-infected, with as many as 36 percent in Botswana.

30. <http://:undp.org/hdro>.

31. Comparativist scholars such as Arend Lijphart in *Power Sharing in South Africa*, (Berkeley, California: Institute of International Studies, 1985) and Donald Horowitz in *A Democratic South Africa? Constitutional Engineering in a Divided Society* (Berkeley and Los Angeles: University of California Press, 1991) predicted severe ethnic strife if the cluster of political institutions they advocated for South Africa (consociational versus integrative institutions, respectively) were not adopted. Horowitz went so far as to predict "Zulu-Xhosa" polarity as the greatest threat to post-apartheid South Africa. Marina Ottaway in *South Africa: The Struggle for a New Order* (Washington, D.C.: Brookings Institution Press, 1993) referred to the transition from apartheid as a process of conflict generation as much as conflict management and saw ethnic nationalism increasing and threatening any political settlement that might emerge.

32. Sisk, *Democratization in South Africa*.

33. See Donald Horowitz, "Democracy in Divided Societies," *Journal of Democracy*, 4, no. 4, (1993): 18–38.

34. See Pierre du Toit, *State Building and Democracy in Southern Africa: Botswana, Zimbabwe, and South Africa* (Washington, D.C.: United States Institute of Peace Press, 1995).

35. Steven Friedman, "South Africa," in Seymour Martin Lipset, ed., *Encyclopedia of Democracy* (Washington, D.C.: Congressional Quarterly, 1996), 1167.

36. Alvin Rabushka and Kenneth A. Shepsle, *Politics in Plural Societies* (Columbus, Ohio: Charles E. Merrill, 1972).

37. Kofi Annan, "Window of African Promise amid Great Suffering," *International Herald Tribune*, 31 July 31–August 1, 1999.

PHOTO CREDITS

CHAPTER 1

Page 12: © 1997, The Washington Post. Reprinted with permission; p. 15: Associated Press/Volodymyr Repik (Stringer); p. 21: CORBIS-Bettmann

CHAPTER 2

Page 30: Reuters/CORBIS-Bettmann; p. 40: AP Wirephoto/Val Rodriguez; p. 41: UN/DPI/AP Photo

CHAPTER 5

Page 95, 103: Reuters/CORBIS-Bettmann; p. 106: AP Photo/Mohammad Sayad; p. 109: Library of Congress

CHAPTER 6

Page 123: © Archivo Iconografico, S.A./CORBIS; p. 124, 126: © Bettmann/CORBIS; p. 133: Associated Press, AP; p. 139: © CORBIS

CHAPTER 7

Page 154: Associated Press, AP; p. 158: © Reuters New Media Inc./CORBIS

CHAPTER 8

Page 183: © Bettmann/CORBIS

CHAPTER 9

Page 196: PA; p. 198 Associated Press, AP

CHAPTER 10

Page 218: Reuters/Juda Ngwenya/Archive Photos; p. 231: Reuters/Joseph Czarnecki/Archive Photos; p. 233: ©AFP/CORBIS

CHAPTER 11

Page 264: © Liba Taylor/CORBIS; Associated Press, AP

CHAPTER 13

Page 289: © CORBIS; p. 291: © Hulton-Deutsch Collection/CORBIS; p. 292: © Bettmann/CORBIS; p. 303 © Hulton-Deutsch Collection/CORBIS; p. 308: © CORBIS

CHAPTER 14

Page 319: © Hulton-Deutsch Collection/CORBIS; p. 322: © Bettmann/CORBIS

CHAPTER 15

Page 347: Courtesy, Embassy of the Republic of Korea; p. 357: © Bettmann/CORBIS

CHAPTER 16

Page 372: Associated Press, PA; p. 387; © Bettmann/CORBIS; p.391: © Sean Aiden; Eye Ubiquitous/CORBIS; p. 407: © AFP/CORBIS; p. 417: Reuters/Jim Bourg/Archive Photos;

CHAPTER 17

Page 435: Archive Photos; p. 442: Associated Press Photo; p. 452: Associated Press AFP; p. 469, 475: © AFP/CORBIS

CHAPTER 18

Page 486: Reuters/CORBIS; p. 521: © Hulton-Deutsch Collection/CORBIS; p. 523: © Bettmann/CORBIS; p. 524: Owen Franken/CORBIS; p. 525, 528: © Reuters New Media Inc./CORBIS; p. 530: © AFP/CORBIS

CHAPTER 19

Page 545: Associated Press, AP; p. 549: Reuters/CORBIS-Bettmann; p. 555: © Bettmann/CORBIS; p. 559: © Hulton-Deutsch Collection/CORBIS; p. 573: Reuters/Pool/Archive Photos

CHAPTER 20

Page 594: © Bettmann/CORBIS; p. 596: © AFP/CORBIS; p. 600, 603, 604: Associated Press, AP; p. 605: © AFP/CORBIS

CHAPTER 21

Page 634: Associated Press, AP; p. 646: Archive Photos; p. 649: © Bettmann/CORBIS; p. 651: AP/Wide World Photos; p. 654: © Hulton-Deutsch Collection/CORBIS; p. 657: © CORBIS; p. 673: © AFP/CORBIS; p. 680: © Reuters New Media Inc./CORBIS

CHAPTER 22

Page 698, 703, 707: Associated Press, AP; p. 715: © Bettmann/CORBIS; p. 718, 727: Associated Press, AP; p. 736, 738: © Reuters New Media Inc./CORBIS

CHAPTER 23

Page 747: Associated Press, AP; p. 755: Archive Photos; p. 756: Associated Press, AP; p. 758: Archive Photos; p. 767, 769, 772, 774, 779: Associated Press, AP; p. 786: © Bettmann/CORBIS; p. 801: © AFP/CORBIS; p. 803: Associated Press, AP

CHAPTER 24

Page 823: © Bettmann/CORBIS; p. 825: Reuters/Stringer/Archive Photos; p. 827: © AFP/CORBIS; p. 833: UN/DPI; p. 835: Reuters/Juda Ngwenya/Archive Photos; p. 836: © David Turnley/CORBIS; p. 837, 839 Associated Press, AP

TEXT AND LINE ART PERMISSIONS

Figure 2.1
From *Freedom in the World 1998-1999*. Copyright © 1999 Freedom House. Reprinted with permission.

Table 5.1
Reprinted by permission of Transparency International.

Table 6.2
Table 18.1
From Jan-Erik Lane, et al., *Political Data Handbook OECD Countries, 1997*. Reprinted with permission of Oxford University Press UK.

Figure 10.2
From *The Third Wave: Democratization in the Late 20th Century* by Samuel P. Huntington. Copyright © 1991 by Samuel P. Huntington. Reprinted by permission of the University of Oklahoma Press.

Figure 12.5
From *The Economist*, July 17, 1999. Copyright © 1999 The Economist Newspaper Group, Inc. Reprinted with permission. Further reproduction prohibited. www.economist.com

Figure 14.1
Reprinted with permission of OECD.

Table 14.2
Table 14.4
Table 15.2
From *World Development Report 1999/2000*. Reprinted by permission of World Bank.

Figure 14.2
From *The Washington Post*, July 22, 1994, by Laura Stanton. Reprinted with permission.

Table 14.3
From *Social Expenditure Database 1980-1996*.Copyright © 1996 OECD. Reprinted with permission.

Table 14.5
Table 14.6
From *OECD Economic Outlook*, June 1999. Copyright © 1999 OECD. Reprinted with permission.

Table 16.3
From David Butler & Dennis Kavanagh, The British General election of 1997, p. 319. Copyright © 1997 David Butler and Dennis Kavanagh. Reprinted with permission of St. Martin's Press, LLC and Macmillan Ltd.

Table 16.4
From *Chronicle of Parliamentary Elections*, vol. 31, p. 211 and vol. 32. P. 226. Reprinted

by permission of Inter-Parliamentary Union, Geneva, Switzerland.

Table 17.6
From *Chronicle of Parliamentary Elections,* vol. 31 (1997). Reprinted by permission of Inter-Parliamentary Union, Geneva, Switzerland.

Table 19.3
Revenue Statistics of OECD Member Countries 1965-1993. Copyright © 1994 OECD. Reprinted with permission.

Figure 20.2
From *The New York Times,* February 29, 1988, p. E3. Copyright © 1988 The New York Times. Reprinted with permission.

Figure 20.3
From *The Economist,* February 19, 2000. Copyright © 2000 The Economist Newspaper Group, Inc. Reprinted with permission. Further reproduction prohibited. www.economist.com

Figure 20.3
Figure 20.4
Figure 20.5
From *The Economist,* April 25, 1998, © 1988 The Economist Newspaper Group, Inc. Reprinted with permission. Further reproduction prohibited. www.economist.com

Table 24.2
From *Freedom in the World 1998-1999.* Copyright © 1999 Freedom House. Reprinted with permission.

INDEX